PENGUIN BOOKS

THE PENGUIN GUIDE TO OPERA ON COMPACT DISC

EDWARD GREENFIELD has been Record Critic of the *Guardian* since 1954, and from 1964 its Music Critic too. At the end of 1960 he joined the reviewing panel of *Gramophone*, specializing in operatic and orchestral issues. He is a regular broadcaster on music and records for the BBC not just on Radios 3 and 4 but also on the BBC World Service. In 1958 he published a monograph on the operas of Puccini. More recently he has written studies on the recorded work of Joan Sutherland and André Previn. He has been a regular juror on International Record awards and has appeared with such artists as Dame Elisabeth Schwarzkopf, Dame Joan Sutherland and Sir Georg Solti in public interviews.

ROBERT LAYTON studied at Oxford with Edmund Rubbra for composition and with Egon Wellesz for the history of music. He spent two years in Sweden at the universities of Uppsala and Stockholm. He joined the BBC Music Division in 1959 and was responsible for such programmes as *Interpretations on Record*. He has contributed a "Quarterly Retrospect" to *Gramophone* for a number of years, and he has written books on Berwald and Sibelius and has specialized in Scandinavian music. He has written a monograph on the Dvořák symphonies and concertos for the BBC Music Guides, of which he was General Editor for many years. His translation of the first two volumes of Erik Tawaststjerna's definitive study of Sibelius was awarded the 1984 Finnish State Literary Prize. In 1987 he was awarded the Sibelius Medal and in the following year was made a Knight of the Order of the White Rose of Finland for his services to Finnish music. His recent publications have included *A Companion to the Concerto* and *A Companion to the Symphony*, which appeared earlier this year.

IVAN MARCH is a former professional musician. He studied at Trinity College of Music, London, and at the Royal Manchester College. After service in the RAF Central Band, he played the horn professionally for the BBC and travelled with the Carl Rosa and D'Oyly Carte opera companies. Now director of the Long Playing Record Library, the largest commercial lending library for classical music on compact discs in the British Isles, he is a well-known lecturer, journalist and personality in the world of recorded music. As a journalist, he contributes to a number of record-reviewing magazines including *Gramophone*.

The Penguin Guide to
Opera on Compact Disc

Edward Greenfield, Robert Layton and Ivan March

Edited by Ivan March

Plots researched and realized by Kathleen March

PENGUIN BOOKS

PENGUIN BOOKS

Published by the Penguin Group
Penguin Books Ltd, 27 Wrights Lane, London W8 5TZ, England
Penguin Books USA Inc., 375 Hudson Street, New York, New York 10014, USA
Penguin Books Australia Ltd, Ringwood, Victoria, Australia
Penguin Books Canada Ltd, 10 Alcorn Avenue, Toronto, Ontario, Canada M4V 3B2
Penguin Books (NZ) Ltd, 182–190 Wairau Road, Auckland 10, New Zealand

Penguin Books Ltd, Registered Offices: Harmondsworth, Middlesex, England

First published 1993
10 9 8 7 6 5 4 3 2 1

Set in 8/9.5pt Times
Typeset by Barbers Ltd, Wrotham, Kent
Made and printed in Great Britain by Clays Ltd, St Ives plc

Contents

Preface vii

The Plots ix

Introduction xi

Price Ranges – UK and USA xvii

An International Mail-Order Source for Recordings xix

Abbreviations xx

Composer Index 1

Vocal Recitals and Choral Collections 575

And Finally . . . 625

Index of Singers 627

Preface

Opera is suddenly in the news, apparently no longer an art form reserved for the wealthy minority. Undoubtedly the recent projection of Luciano Pavarotti and Plácido Domingo on to the world stage as superstars has brought a remarkable general public awareness of the electrifying potential of an aria sung by a vibrant tenor voice. But opera is a great deal more than a series of vocal purple-patches, delivered in the rain or at a sporting event, and its popularity is not new. In Italy, famous singers of Verdi and Puccini have long been among the public's favourite heroes and heroines, while Germany has always taken it for granted that any major city should have an opera house. The most reliable sign that opera is currently burgeoning is its spread away from the capital cities of the world, creating new sources of excellence based in the provinces. France is looking away from Paris towards Lyon, and in America opera is flourishing in unexpected places.

In Britain, until quite recently, opera outside London was kept alive only by a rather patronizing annual visit from the London-based organizations while, before the war, opera's provincial survival was left to touring companies like the good old Carl Rosa. Performances, sung in the vernacular, were rough-and-ready but reliably red-blooded; production values were dictated by scenery and sets which could be quickly assembled and taken down and, above all, were portable for ready transfer by lorry to the next town. Today we expect more than that, although small touring opera groups have taken over where the Carl Rosa left off, but with the flexibility to mount productions in a village hall, if necessary.

We also expect more from recorded opera. No longer are recordings limited by the 4-minute time-span of a 78-r.p.m. record. In those heady pre-war days, the patience needed to wade through the first complete recordings of a Puccini or Verdi opera, spread over a couple of dozen discs, was likely to daunt all but the most dedicated enthusiast. Popular recorded opera was then by necessity devoted to individual arias and excerpts of a suitable length to fit a ten- or twelve-inch shellac disc. Indeed Puccini was accused by jealous detractors of tailoring his big set-piece arias to fit conveniently on to a 78 record-side.

All this was revolutionized by the coming of the long-playing record, coincident with the emergence of a post-World War Two generation of singers who were able to take full advantage of the new medium. Decca showed the way with an outstanding two-LP recording of Johann Strauss's *Die Fledermaus*, conducted by Clemens Krauss. Artistically that has never been surpassed, and Decca followed it with an almost equally famous *La Bohème*, starring Renata Tebaldi. Walter Legge, at EMI, went to Vienna to assemble an armful of distinguished singers and began his outstanding Mozart series, besides recording works by Johann and Richard Strauss, plus equally famous sets of *The Merry Widow* and Humperdinck's *Hänsel und Gretel*.

Suddenly listening to opera at home became a new and pleasurable experience. It is an experience that can be enjoyed in solitary splendour or shared with family and friends; in either case the listener has to use his or her imagination. In the opera house the intercommunication between audience and performers can be electrifying, but it can also bring disappointments, especially when a jet-hopping superstar has not found time in a busy commercial schedule for adequate rehearsal with fellow artists.

Over the years, and in their turn, famous singers, and conductors who are a law unto themselves (like Toscanini), have each had an autocratic influence on performance style. Today it is the turn of the producer and designer. On occasion the results can be so distracting that, apart from being visually unsatisfactory, there is a conflict with the music rather than illumination, and the plot can be perverted or rendered barely intelligible.

These problems disappear when one listens to a really distinguished opera recording. Armed with a pocket translation and synopsis, the listener can make his or her own mind up about 'sur-titles', and there is a choice between sitting back and wallowing in the musical inspiration or following the dramatic action in every detail. The listener can happily paint his or her own mental images of characters and backcloth without a suspicion of creaking stage machinery or an inept visual realization of the instructions left by the composer and librettist. As one gently depresses the control button to set the CD in motion, the end of the room turns into the listener's very own sound-stage, and the greatest singers in the world step forward to provide a truly engulfing musical experience.

The Plots

When this book was in the planning stage, we decided it would be useful to incorporate the basic storyline into our review of each opera. The original plan was to condense such synopsis into the space of a single paragraph but it soon became obvious that this was entirely impractical. Few opera plots are so conveniently compact and, if our storylines were to be really useful, the various twists and turns of events that serve to motivate the characters could not properly be omitted.

We also discovered that – outside the obvious major repertory – many plot synopses were not readily available, and in most cases it was necessary to return to the libretto in order to discover all the implications of the vocal exchanges. So, apart from being a unique appraisal of the major operas available on record, *The Penguin Guide to Opera on Compact Discs* includes a uniquely comprehensive survey of opera plots. There are a few omissions, but not too many. We have tried to condense the essence of each story into readable prose, and they often make fascinating reading. We are now far more aware of the intricacies of Greek mythology than we were when we began. In *King Priam* Sir Michael Tippett makes his characters ask a very pertinent question: Do the humans, as portrayed in these sagas, have any control whatever over their destinies, or are their (usually disastrous or tragic) nemeses irrevocably ordained from the moment they are born?

The other fascination is to discover how closely the various vocal ranges are linked to the roles they are given to sing. It is an operatic cliché that the hero and heroine frequently fall in love the moment they set eyes on each other. So tenor arias are usually short bursts of passion. But baritones usually have a much wider range of emotions to convey. They seldom end up married to the heroine; if they live in Spain, they spend their operatic lives in endless jealousy, bitterness and frustration. Moreover they are usually dedicated above all to honour (and this sometimes rubs off on the tenors too). The women are altogether more thoughtful and emotionally perceptive than their male counterparts, but they receive short shrift for it, frequently tormented by guilt or doubt, and usually ending up committing suicide or taking the veil. Wagner's heroines seldom stay alive long enough to enjoy themselves (the exception being *Die Meistersinger*) and they are expected to sacrifice themselves without question in order to save their men from eternal damnation. After spending years on her rock surrounded by a protective ring of fire and waiting for Siegfried to find her, Brünnhilde is almost immediately betrayed; even Isolde, though she experiences profound human passion, is allowed only a 'love-death' as her apotheosis.

When one turns to Italian *opera buffa*, the baritones have a less painful but still frustrating time. Often they covet the charms of a younger woman, who is inevitably intended for the tenor, and they are hardly pictured as having much common sense, let alone any intellectual capacity. Here the women have a much better time and are allowed to enjoy themselves manipulating the men; they may even enjoy a happy ending. But after the precocious Rosina has successfully married her lover in Rossini's *Barber of Seville*, her later destiny, when she becomes the Countess in Mozart's *Marriage of Figaro*, is to suffer disillusionment as her husband neglects her and tries to seduce her maid, Susanna.

Romantic love does, however, blossom gloriously in Puccini's *La Bohème*, and it also redeems the icy Princess in *Turandot*. But after listening to Iago's frighteningly evil machinations against Desdemona in Verdi's *Otello* and being horrified by the dénouement of Halévy's *La Juive*, wherein the villainous Cardinal unwittingly consigns his own daughter to immersion in a cauldron of boiling oil, one needs to turn to French opera for genial cynicism, redeemed by a winning charm.

In Offenbach's *Orpheus in the Underworld* the bored hero is only too delighted when his wife is taken away from him, and only the pressure of Public Opinion forces him to go to her rescue down below; while in the delicious closing scene of Messager's *Fortunio* the old husband and elderly ex-lover unintentionally leave the hero and heroine joyously embracing in her bedroom, even locking the door behind them as they leave!

The Russians are altogether more serious, and in Mussorgsky's *Boris Godunov* and Prokoviev's *War and Peace* the epic scale of Russian history is overwhelmingly conveyed.

What emerges throughout our survey is that, while the importance of the music is pre-eminent (and memorable tunes most important of all), the construction of the plot remains a vital factor in the success of any great opera. Mozart's *Nozze di Figaro*, Richard Strauss's *Der Rosenkavalier* and Verdi's *Don Carlos* are all wonderful examples in which the characters and what happens to them vividly mirror human experience, while Wagner compellingly created his own mythological world of gods, heroes and ever-vulnerable heroines.

There are failures, too. Weber, who has given us the epitome of German romantic opera in *Der Freischütz*, must surely win the prize for trying to set fine music to the most banal of storylines. It is difficult to decide whether the trophy for the most unconvincing plot should be awarded to *Euryanthe* or to *Oberon*. Yet on record these operas are easy to enjoy: one simply ignores the absurdities and relishes the music.

Introduction

The object of *The Penguin Guide to Opera on Compact Discs* is to give the opera-lover a comprehensive survey of the finest recordings of opera available on CD. Certain oratorios are also included. With Handel the dividing line between the two media is almost impossible to draw, save that – following the convention of the day – his operas were written to be sung in Italian and the equally dramatic oratorios were performed in the vernacular. Having crossed that threshold, we have also covered certain dramatic oratorios by other composers, not least Elgar's *Caractacus* and *The Dream of Gerontius*, both very operatic in feeling, even if greatly contrasted in content.

Very few complete operas are now available on cassette; on the other hand, a great many of the recitals of favourite arias and choruses, and certain highlights collections, do have a tape equivalent. Where they exist, these are indicated, as many will be found attractive for in-car use. We have also included key operetta recordings and a selective representation of musicals. In the late twentieth century any survey of opera would be incomplete without Lehár's *Merry Widow* or Gershwin's *Porgy and Bess*, and it could be argued that Stephen Sondheim's *A Little Night Music*, Frank Loesser's *Guys and Dolls* and *Most Happy Fellah*, Meredith Willson's *Music Man*, Cy Coleman's *On the Twentieth Century*, Cole Porter's *Kiss Me Kate*, Irving Berlin's *Annie get your gun*, the Rodgers and Hammerstein *Oklahoma!* and certainly Jerome Kern's *Show Boat* offer music and lyrics of comparable quality. Bernstein's *Candide* and *West Side Story* are in many ways the modern equivalent of the German Singspiel, and both contain inspired music of universal appeal. So, inevitably, our survey does not have clearly defined boundaries.

As most records are issued almost simultaneously on both sides of the Atlantic and use identical international catalogue numbers, this *Guide* should be found to be equally useful in Great Britain and the USA. The internationalization of repertoire and numbers is increasingly applying to CDs issued by the major international companies and by many smaller ones too, while most of the smaller European labels are imported in their original formats into both Britain and the USA.

EVALUATION

Most recordings issued today by the major companies are of a high technical standard and offer performances of a quality at least as high as is experienced in the opera house – and usually higher. In adopting a starring system for the evaluation of records, we have decided to make use of from one to three stars. Brackets round one or more of the stars indicate some reservations about its inclusion, and readers are advised to refer to the text. Brackets round all the stars usually indicate a basic qualification: for instance, a mono recording of a performance of artistic interest, by great singers from an earlier era where sometimes considerable allowances have to be made for the sound-quality, even though the recording may have been digitally remastered.

Our evaluation system may be summarized as follows:

*** An outstanding performance and recording in every way, with fine singing and musical direction of a similar calibre.

** A good performance and recording, offering singing of an acceptably high standard.

* A fair performance, sometimes combining a cast of good and less impressive artists, reasonably well or well recorded.

ROSETTES

To a very few recordings we have awarded a Rosette: ❀.

Unlike our general evaluations, in which we have tried to be consistent, a Rosette is a quite arbitrary compliment by a member of the reviewing team to a recorded performance which, he finds, shows special illumination, magic, or a spiritual quality, or even outstanding production values, that places it in a very special class. The choice is essentially a personal one (although often it represents a shared view), and in some cases it is applied to an issue where certain reservations must also be mentioned in the text of the review. The Rosette symbol is placed before the usual evaluation and the record number. It is quite small – we do not mean to imply an 'Academy Award' but a personal token of appreciation for something uniquely valuable. We hope that, once the reader has discovered and perhaps acquired a 'Rosetted' opera or recital, its special qualities will soon become apparent.

DIGITAL RECORDINGS

Virtually all new compact discs are recorded digitally, but an even greater number of opera recordings date from the analogue LP era, and even before that. They are, of course, digitally remastered, and this process usually (though not always) brings an improvement in sound-quality, plus a reduction of background noise. We think it important to include a clear indication of the difference:

Dig. This indicates that the master recording was digitally encoded.

MONO AND STEREO RECORDINGS

From the earliest days of sound recording, the primitive equipment used for picking up the sound through a 'tin' horn (or horns), transducing it in the form of physical vibrations, and thence cutting the wax masters was comparatively faithful in its reproduction of the human voice. Soon after the turn of the present century, vocal records were being made by this acoustic-recording process which still sound remarkably realistic, even by today's more exacting standards. One thinks, for instance, of the début of Caruso (1902–5), or the slightly later records of Frieda Hempel (1910–14). However, allowances have to be made for the often crude quality of the orchestral (or, initially, piano) accompaniments, which were much less realistically conveyed before the coming of electrical recording in 1925. But the 78-r.p.m. era readily established the gramophone as equipped to celebrate the so-called 'Golden Age' of singing.

Long-playing records were first introduced in America in July 1948 by the American Columbia Company (which was to become the CBS label – more recently taken over by Sony). The English Decca Company (known as 'London' in North America), now part of the Polygram group, followed on in the USA in 1949, and then pioneered the LP in Britain in 1950. High technical standards were achieved on this label from the word go. Mono vinyl long-playing records brought an immediate reduction in steady background noise, although they introduced sporadic clicks and pops, which were in some ways worse than the old 78 scratch, and this fault was emphasized with the coming of high-fidelity reproducing equipment, with pick-ups becoming lighter in order to avoid record wear. However, from 1950 onwards there was undoubtedly a noticeable and a steady improvement in sound-quality on LP and, as it became possible to put up to 30 minutes' playing time on to an LP side, the blessings of continuity were added to the relatively quiet background.

But it was the coming of stereo which finally achieved a recording system which, in its spatial realism and naturalness of balance and tone, at last made it possible to produce complete operas on record which gave the listener the illusion that a normal-sized domestic living room could be sonically 'converted' to convey the ambience of an idealized opera house. Stereo experiments were being conducted by the major companies from around 1954 onwards, and a universal system for making stereo LPs was agreed at an international technical conference of audio engineers in New York in March 1958. Stereo records became generally available in the autumn of that year, and within a short time recordings of astonishing realism were appearing. One of the huge advantages of stereo – which was to be mirrored by the coming of the CD a quarter of a century later – was that the startling improvements in realism afforded by the new techniques were noticeable on quite modest reproducing equipment.

Two great recording producers were involved in this sonic revolution, Walter Legge at EMI/Angel and John Culshaw at Decca/London, and it can be said that, in the field of opera recording, Decca and EMI led the world through most of the analogue LP era. Walter Legge was content to refine, and to carry through to stereo, the natural balances he had already achieved on mono LPs. John Culshaw, however, saw recorded opera as a challenge – something entirely new. He sought to aid the listener's imagination with specially conceived production effects, and his vision is readily demonstrated by his greatest project, pioneering the first complete stereo version of Wagner's *Ring*, conducted by Sir Georg Solti, surely one of the outstanding recording achievements of all time.

The great majority of recordings discussed in our survey are in stereo, but those deriving from mono masters are clearly indicated by the use of the word 'mono' before the manufacturer's catalogue number.

BARGAIN AND MEDIUM-PRICED ISSUES

Many – though by no means all – the key opera recordings are on full-priced labels and are therefore not inexpensive, unless one makes a comparison between them and the price of an average seat at Covent Garden or the Met. However, a large number of outstanding older sets – by no means inferior in technical quality – are now in the mid-price range, and some of these would be a first choice, quite irrespective of their cost. One thinks immediately of Karl Boehm's glorious EMI/Angel recording of Mozart's *Così fan tutte* with Schwarzkopf and Christa Ludwig, or Dame Janet Baker's unforgettable portrayal of Dido in the Anthony Lewis *Dido and Aeneas* on Decca/London. In other cases, such as the Karajan set of *Tosca* with Leontyne Price, Di Stefano and Taddei, if that Decca/London version is not at the very top of the list, it nevertheless remains uniquely desirable in its own right. Then there are the many highly collectable unfamiliar operas costing less than full price, often superbly sung, of which Messager's *Fortunio* on Erato is a sparkling (and Rosette-worthy) example. A smaller number of operas are available at bargain price, notably those from Naxos, which are well sung and have the advantage of modern digital recording. There are no starry names on the Naxos roster (which generally uses East European vocal talent); even so, the Naxos set of Puccini's *Manon Lescaut*, for example, is more than worth its modest cost. Among the recitals there are plenty of splendid bargains and even one or two at super-bargain price (again Naxos).

Our listing of each recording first indicates if it is *not* in fact in the premium-price category, as follows:

(M) Medium-priced label

(B) Bargain-priced label

(BB) Super-bargain label

See below for price structures for CDs and cassettes in the UK and the USA.

LAYOUT OF TEXT

We have aimed to make our style as simple as possible, even though the catalogue numbers of recordings are no longer as straightforward as they once were. So, immediately after the evaluation and before the catalogue number, the record make is given, often in abbreviated form (a key to the abbreviations is provided on pages xx–xxi). In the case of a set of two or more CDs, the number of units involved is given in brackets after the catalogue number.

AMERICAN CATALOGUE NUMBERS

The numbers which follow in square brackets are US catalogue numbers, while the abbreviation [id.] indicates that the American number is identical to the European, which is increasingly the case.

There are certain small differences to be remembered by American readers. For instance, a CBS/Sony number could have a completely different catalogue number on either side of the Atlantic, or it could use the same digits with different alphabetical prefixes. Both will be clearly indicated. EMI/Angel use extra digits for their British compact discs; thus the US number [CDMC 69330-2] becomes CMS7 69330-2 in Britain (the -2 is the European indication that this is a compact disc). We have taken care to check catalogue information as far as is possible, but as all the editorial work has been done in England there is always the possibility of error; American readers are therefore advised, when ordering records locally, to take the precaution of giving their dealer the fullest information about the music and recordings they want.

The indications (M), (B) and (BB) immediately before the starring of a disc refer primarily to the British record, as pricing systems are not always identical on both sides of the Atlantic. However, records are seldom more expensive in the USA and usually are cheaper, whichever category they fall into.

Where no American catalogue number is given, this does not necessarily mean that a record is not available in the USA; the transatlantic issue may not have been made at the time of the publication of this *Guide*. Readers are advised to check the current *Schwann* catalogue and to consult their local record store.

ABBREVIATIONS

To save space we have adopted a number of standard abbreviations in naming orchestras and performing groups (a list is provided below). Also we have not usually detailed the contents of operatic highlights and collections; this information can often be found in *The Classical Catalogue*, published twice-yearly by *Gramophone* magazine (177–179, Kenton Road, Kenton, Harrow, Middlesex, England, HA3 0HA).

We have followed common practice in the use of the original language for titles. Where arias are sung in an alternative language (usually that of the singer), this is normally indicated, in either the listings or the text.

RECITALS

Most operatic recitals involve many composers, and it is quite impractical to deal with them within the alphabetical composer index. In any case, it is the interest of the singer or singers that is paramount. Such miscellaneous collections are grouped separately towards the end of the book. Recordings are usually arranged in alphabetical order of the performers' names. In certain cases, where the compilation features many different performers, it is listed alphabetically under its collective title, or under the key word in that title (thus *Favourite operatic duets* is listed under 'Operatic duets'). For such compilations of favourite operatic excerpts (which often repeat the same popular repertoire again and again, but with different singers in the limelight) we have not always felt it necessary to list individually every item included; only brief details of contents and performers are usually given; fuller information can often be found in *The Classical Catalogue*.

CATALOGUE NUMBERS

Enormous care has gone into the checking of catalogue numbers and the contents of CDs to ensure that all details are correct, but the editor and publishers cannot be held responsible for any mistakes that may have crept in despite all our zealous checking. When ordering CDs, readers are urged to provide their record-dealer with full details of the music and performers, as well as the catalogue number.

DELETIONS

We have tried to ensure that, at the time of going to press, all the listed recordings are still available, unless the word '**Withdrawn**' appears immediately before the listing. This indicates what it says: that the recording has recently been deleted by its manufacturer. It has been left in our book because of the interest of the repertoire and the artists concerned, and also because it is likely that the recording may appear again sooner or later, perhaps on a cheaper label. Sometimes copies may still be found in specialist shops, and there remains the compensatory fact that most really important and desirable recordings are eventually reissued, usually costing less!

COVERAGE

We believe the present coverage is reasonably comprehensive. However, we do welcome suggestions from readers about any obvious omissions if they seem to be of special interest, and particularly if they are inexpensive. But borderline music on specialist labels that are not readily and reliably obtainable on both sides of the Atlantic cannot be given any kind of priority.

ACKNOWLEDGEMENTS

Our thanks, as ever, are due to Roger Wells, our Copy Editor, who has worked closely alongside us throughout the preparation of this book and who, as a keen CD collector himself, also frequently made valuable creative suggestions. Besides formulating most of the plot outlines, Kathleen March once again checked the proofs for errors and reminded us when the text proved ambiguous, clumsily repetitive in its descriptive terminology, or just plain contradictory. Our thanks go also to Adrian Edwards who read the Musicals entries and made several helpful suggestions. Winifred Greenwood zealously checked the catalogue numbers. Barbara Menard contributed to the titling, never an easy task – and especially complicated in the many anthologies involving a bouquet of different singers. She also helped at the last minute with operas for which we had no synopses. Our team of Penguin proof readers are also indispensable. Grateful thanks go to all those readers who write to us to point out factual errors and remind us of important recordings which have escaped our notice.

Price Ranges – UK and USA

Compact discs and cassettes in all price-ranges are more expensive in Britain and Europe than they are in the USA but, fortunately, in nearly all cases the various premium-price, mid-price, bargain and super-bargain categories are fairly consistent on both sides of the Atlantic. However, where records are imported in either direction, this can affect their domestic cost. For instance, (British) EMI's Classics for Pleasure and Eminence labels are both in the mid-price range in the USA, whereas CfP is a bargain series in the UK. Of course retail prices are not fixed in either country, and various stores may offer even better deals from time to time, so our price structure must be taken as a guideline only. One major difference in the USA is that almost all companies make a dollar surcharge (per disc) for mid-priced opera sets (to cover the cost of librettos) and Angel applies this levy to all their boxed sets. The Vanguard CD label (except for the 8000 Series, which retails at around $15) is upper-mid-price in the USA but lower-mid-price in the UK. In *listing* records we have not used the major record companies' additional label subdivisions (like Decca/London's Opera Gala, DG's Privilege, EMI's Référence, and so on) in order to avoid further confusion, although these designations are sometimes referred to in the text of reviews.

(M) MID-PRICED SERIES (sets are multiples of these prices)

Includes: BMG/RCA; Decca/London; DG; EMI/Angel (Studio and Références; Eminence); Erato/Warner (Libretto) (UK), Erato/WEA (Libretto) (USA); HM/BMG (UK), DHM/BMG (USA); Mercury; Philips; Saga; Sony; Teldec/Warner (UK), Teldec/WEA (USA)

CDs: under £10; more usually £8–£9
Cassettes: under £5

USA

CDs: under $11
Cassettes: $5–$6.50

(B) BARGAIN-PRICED SERIES (sets are multiples of these prices)

Includes: BMG/RCA; Decca/London; CfP (UK only); DG; EMI Laser; Hungaroton White Label; Naxos; Philips; Pickwick; Sony

UK

CDs: £5–6
Cassettes: under £4

USA

CDs: under $7
Cassettes: under $4

(BB) SUPER-BARGAIN SERIES – CDs

Naxos (Recitals only)

UK

CDs: under £5

USA

CDs: under $7

(In a few cases equivalent cassettes are available, usually costing slightly less than bargain cassettes.)

An International Mail-Order Source for Recordings

Readers are urged to support a local dealer if he is prepared and able to give a proper service, and to remember that obtaining many CDs involves perseverance. If, however, difficulty is experienced locally, we suggest the following mail-order alternative, which operates world-wide:

PG Dept
Squires Gate Music Centre
Squires Gate Station Approach
Blackpool
Lancashire FY8 2SP
England
Tel: 0253 44360
Fax: 0253 406686

This organization (which is operated under the direction of the Editor of *The Penguin Guide to Opera on Compact Discs*) patiently extends compact disc orders until they finally come to hand. A full guarantee of safe delivery is made on any order undertaken. Please write for further details, enclosing a stamped and self-addressed envelope if within the UK.

American readers seeking a domestic mail-order source may write to the following address where a comparable supply service is in operation (for both American and imported European labels). Please write for further details (enclosing a stamped, self-addressed envelope if within the USA) or send your order to:

PG Dept
Serenade Records
1713 G St, N.W.
Washington DC 20006
USA
Tel: (202) 638-6648
Fax: (202) 783-0372
Tel: (for US orders only) 1-800-237-2930

Abbreviations

Ac.	Academy, Academic
AAM	Academy of Ancient Music
Amb. S.	Ambrosian Singers
Ang.	Angel
Ara.	Arabesque
arr.	arranged
ASMF	Academy of St Martin-in-the-Fields
Bar.	Baroque
Bav.	Bavarian
BMG	Bertelsmann Music Group (distributor)
BPO	Berlin Philharmonic Orchestra
Cal.	Calliope
Cap.	Caprice
CBSO	City of Birmingham Symphony Orchestra
CfP	Classics for Pleasure
Ch.	Choir; Chorale; Chorus
Chan.	Chandos
CO	Chamber Orchestra
COE	Chamber Orchestra of Europe
Col. Mus. Ant.	Musica Antiqua, Cologne
Coll.	Collegium
Coll. Aur.	Collegium Aureum
Coll. Mus.	Collegium Musicum
Concg. O	Royal Concertgebouw Orchestra of Amsterdam
cond.	conductor, conducted
Cons.	Consort
DG	Deutsche Grammophon
Dig.	digital recording
E.	England, English
ECCO	European Community Chamber Orchestra
ECO	English Chamber Orchestra
ENO	English National Opera Company
Ens.	Ensemble
Fr.	French
GO	Gewandhaus Orchestra
HM	Harmonia Mundi France
HM/RCA	Deutsche Harmonia Mundi
Hung.	Hungaroton
L.	London
LAPO	Los Angeles Philharmonic Orchestra

LCO	London Chamber Orchestra
LMP	London Mozart Players
LOP	Lamoureux Orchestra of Paris
LPO	London Philharmonic Orchestra
LSO	London Symphony Orchestra
Mer.	Meridian
Met.	Metropolitan Opera House, New York
N.	North
nar.	narrated
Nat.	National
NY	New York
O	Orchestra, Orchestre
OAE	Orchestra of the Age of Enlightenment
O-L	Oiseau-Lyre
Op.	Opera (in performance listings); opus (in music titles)
orch.	orchestrated
ORTF	L'Orchestre de la radio et télévision française
Ph.	Philips
Phd.	Philadelphia
Philh.	Philharmonia
PO	Philharmonic Orchestra
Qt	Quartet
R.	Radio
RLPO	Royal Liverpool Philharmonic Orchestra
ROHCG	Royal Opera House, Covent Garden
RPO	Royal Philharmonic Orchestra
RSO	Radio Symphony Orchestra
S.	South
SCO	Scottish Chamber Orchestra
Sinf.	Sinfonietta
SNO	Royal Scottish Orchestra
SO	Symphony Orchestra
Soc.	Society
Sol. Ven.	I Solisti Veneti
SRO	Suisse Romande Orchestra
Sup.	Supraphon
trans.	transcription, transcribed
V.	Vienna
Van.	Vanguard
VCM	Vienna Concentus Musicus
VPO	Vienna Philharmonic Orchestra
VSO	Vienna Symphony Orchestra
W.	West
WNO	Welsh National Opera Company

Adams, John (born 1947)

The Death of Klinghoffer (complete).

*** Nonesuch/Warner Dig. 7559 79281-2 (2) [id.]. Sanford Sylvan, Sheila Nadler, James Maddalena, Thomas Hammons, Janice Felty, English Op. Ch., Op. de Lyon, Nagano.

Of all minimalist composers, the one who most strikingly rises above the obvious limitations is John Adams, showing an emotional depth rare in music that relies on the basic minimalist technique of the 'eternal um-chum' or endless ostinato. The key to that emotional impact lies in Adams's melodic gift. Far more than his minimalist colleagues he regularly has a free-flowing, beautifully shaped line soaring above the minimalist texture. That love of melody also points to his potential as an opera-composer. As in his first opera, the headline-catching *Nixon in China*, so too in *The Death of Klinghoffer*, Adams has moved away from subjective expression, traditional in opera, to a stylized setting of a modern myth.

To take the painful 1985 news-story of the hijacking of the cruise-liner, *Achille Lauro*, and the gratuitous murder by Palestinian terrorists of a helpless old man in a wheelchair, Leon Klinghoffer, was certainly bold. Dramatic treatment of an incident inspiring such natural revulsion could easily have spilled over into embarrassment. In his stylization Adams with his librettist, Alice Goodman, has worked towards countering that. He even dares to relate his opera to the Bach *Passions*, and the gravity and intensity of what he is saying is never in doubt. That brings *The Death of Klinghoffer* far closer to a dramatic oratorio than to an opera, with its lack of incident and its sequence of meditative solos and choruses of comment. A recording loses very little, and that is particularly true in as strong a performance as this one, in which Kent Nagano conducts Lyon Opera forces with the original singers who directly inspired the composer.

The treatment of the story, based on the age-old conflict between Palestinians and Jews, is conscientiously dispassionate. Even the murder of Klinghoffer and the casting of his body into the sea are merely described, not shown, yet Adams at structured points in his broadly contemplative score cleverly screws up tension with faster ostinatos and long-sustained crescendos. That leads finally at the climax of Act II to an emotional resolution on a poignant posthumous solo for Klinghoffer, set in the form of a *Gymnopédie*, with Adams echoing Satie but finding a depth far beyond his model.

The closing scene brings the one solo of fully operatic intensity, the bitter concluding lament of Klinghoffer's wife, Marilyn. It is as though after all the detachment Adams is bringing us back finally to emotional reality, and the result is the more moving. The mezzo, Sheila Nadler, rises to the challenge superbly, and the baritone Sanford Sylvan is comparably sensitive as Klinghoffer himself, well matched by James Maddalena as the Captain, an Evangelist-like commentator, and Thomas Hammons and Janice Felty in multiple roles. The recorded sound is excellent, but the booklet reproduces an unrevised version of the libretto.

D'Albert, Eugen (1864–1932)

Tiefland (complete).

(M) (***) Ph. mono 434 781-2 (2) [id.]. V. State Op. Ch., VSO, Moralt.

Marta (Gré Brouwenstijn), Pedro (Hans Hopf), Sebastiano (Paul Schoeffler), Moruccio (Eberhard Waechter), Tommaso (Oskar Czerwenka), Nando (Waldemar Kmentt).

Tiefland has been described as the principal German example of opera in the Italian *verismo* style. Taken from a Spanish play, *Terra baixa* by Ángel Guimerá, it has a strong, earthy story-line based on the conflict between the unscrupulous Sebastiano and the innocent shepherd, Pedro (his employee), who lives alone in the Pyrenees and to whom Sebastiano wants to marry off his mistress, Marta. At the same time Sebastiano intends to marry an heiress, for he is badly in debt.

The offer of marriage comes at the very opening of the opera. Marta is not a party to the arrangement, but she has to do what she is told, and neither she nor Pedro knows that Sebastiano intends to retain access to her bedroom even after she is married! But this comes out when Pedro arrives in the village, to be treated with contempt by the villagers, while Sebastiano tells Marta that he intends to visit her on her wedding night. Nevertheless the marriage goes ahead, and Pedro is now shocked by his wife's reserve and coolness towards him, since she believes he is party to the arrangement. But in the event, Sebastiano does not gain access to her bridal bedroom and in the morning Marta finds herself in love with her new husband.

She confides in Tommaso, the village elder, who advises her to tell Pedro the truth about her previous relationship with Sebastiano. Meanwhile Pedro discovers this for himself from village gossip. Disillusioned, he wants to leave Marta and return to his mountain hut. She begs him to stay, and in the angry altercation that follows he stabs her in the arm. Sebastiano now enters and and suggests that Marta dance for him, and at this point Marta confesses to her previous relationship with Sebastiano and refuses to continue with the marriage. The two men fight, Sebastiano is strangled, and the opera ends with Pedro taking his bride back with him to the Pyrenees.

The story is set with a powerfully melodramatic score which reaches a climax in the bedroom scene between husband and wife at the end of Act 1. She has refused to share his bed; he relates how in the mountains he was nearly killed by a wolf, and she finds tender feelings towards him emerging. Then at the story's dénouement there is no shortage of melodrama when Marta tells Sebastiano she loves her husband, he is reluctant to relinquish her, and Pedro arrives in the nick of time.

All three protagonists are strongly portrayed in this 1957 mono recording. Gré Brouwenstijn makes a convincing Marta, singing powerfully but with tender moments. Hans Hopf is an ardent Pedro and Paul Schoeffler a thoroughly believable villain. The music itself has fine lyrical moments but no really memorable tunes, in the way of Mascagni or Puccini. The recording, with the singers well forward and the orchestra clear but not sumptuous, projects the action vividly, though there is a touch of hardness on the voices. Excellent documentation and a full translation, and plenty of access points.

Alwyn, William (1905–85)

Miss Julie (complete).
*** Lyrita SRCD 2218 (2) [id.]. Philh. O, Tausky.
   Miss Julie (Jill Gomez), Jean (Benjamin Luxon), Kristin (Della Jones), Ulrik (John Mitchinson).

As a highly successful film composer William Alwyn is a master of atmosphere and dramatic timing. Strindberg's chilling study of Miss Julie's sudden infatuation for her father's manservant, Jean, adapted by the composer himself, is given the punch and power of verismo opera, with much learnt from Puccini above all. Alwyn centres the entire action of the opera on the kitchen, but he introduces an extra character, the gamekeeper, Ulrik, and instead of having a pet bird killed by Jean, the manservant, Alwyn – much less chillingly – has the heroine's pet dog killed by the gamekeeper.

But the basic plot remains and Miss Julie is seduced into spending the night with her lover, desperately believing his promise that in the morning they will escape together to Lugano in Switzerland and start a hotel where 'it's always summer, orange trees and a deep blue lake'. However, the next morning, the count returns, the dream evaporates, and Miss Julie – who has already stolen her father's money for the venture – leaves the kitchen alone, to take her own life with a razor.

Alwyn's operatic gestures are big, and though the melodies hardly match Puccini's, the score is rich ands confident, passionately performed by the Philharmonia under Tausky's direction. Jill Gomez sings ravishingly as Miss Julie and Benjamin Luxon gives a most convincing characterization of the manservant lover, with roughness a part of the mixture. Della Jones's mezzo is not contrasted enough with the heroine's soprano, but she sings warmly, and it is good to have as powerful a tenor as John Mitchinson in the incidental role of Ulrik. The 1983 Lyrita recording is well up to standard, beautifully clear as well as full, and it projects the narrative evocatively and involvingly.

Auber, Daniel (1782–1871)

Manon Lescaut (complete).
(M) **(*) EMI CMS7 63252-2 (2). Ch. & O Lyrique of R. France, Marty.
  Manon Lescaut (Mady Mesplé), Des Grieux (Jean-Claude Orliac), Lescaut (Yves Bisson).

Ending, like Puccini's setting of the same story, in 'a desert in Louisiana', Auber's opera, written in the 1850s when he was already seventy-four, bears little resemblance to that example of high romanticism. But the music demonstrates that the liveliness we know from his overtures persisted to the end of his career. Scribe's libretto is a free and often clumsy adaptation of the Prévost novel.

The Marquis d'Hérigny has fallen in love with the pleasure-loving Manon and enlists the good offices of her cousin Lescaut to further his suit. Manon's lover, Des Grieux, has borrowed money to dine with her; Lescaut joins them and, while they are dining, he slips away with the money, which he loses at the gambling tables. Being unable to pay the bill, Lescaut suggests that Des Grieux enlist in d'Hérigny's regiment to pay off the debt. Manon performs as a singer and earns enough to buy him his freedom, but too late.

Act II finds Manon living with d'Hérigny; Des Grieux, having struck an officer, then deserts but returns and tries to elope with Manon. D'Hérigny challenges him and in the ensuing duel is badly wounded. Des Grieux is sentenced to death but flees.

In Act III Manon is deported with a group of other prisoners to America and Des Grieux follows her. They succeed in escaping and in the desert of Louisiana Manon, suffering from exhaustion, dies in Des Grieux's arms.

The sequence of arias and ensembles, conventional in their way, restores some of the original poëtry. Manon herself is a coloratura soprano (here the tweety but agile Mady Mesplé) and Des Grieux a lyric tenor (here the lightweight Jean-Claude Orliac). A recording as lively as this, with excellent sound in a vivid CD transfer, is very welcome.

La muette de Portici.
Withdrawn: *** EMI CDS7 49284-2 (2). Ch. & Monte Carlo PO, Fulton.
  Masaniello (Alfredo Kraus), Elvira (June Anderson), Alphonse (John Aler).

Auber's overture to this opera– generally called by the work's subtitle, *Masaniello* – was long a favourite of brass bands, but the rest of the work is also well worth investigating. Among the lively ensembles there is even one chorus that anticipates Gilbert and Sullivan in *Mikado*, a cross between *Three little maids* and Pish-Tush's song. Historically based, the opera is set in Italy in 1647 when the population of Naples rose up against Spanish oppression.

Masaniello, a fisherman but also a hero of the people, is defiant against privileged nobility, a popular theme when Auber wrote the piece in 1829. Wagner praised it both for its heroic plot (the first really romantic French opera, he said) and for Auber's trend towards ridding the opera of set numbers. The writing may not, as a rule, be very distinguished, but it has striking melodic ideas, and there is a magnificent aria for the hero. In that role, the Spanish tenor Alfredo Kraus sings as stylishly as ever, even if the heroic voice shows signs of age.

There is another important tenor role, that of Alphonse, the thoughtless duke's son who seduces then leaves Masaniello's sister Fenella, the dumb girl of the title. The American tenor, John Aler, provides an ideal contrast to Kraus, singing most beautifully; and June Anderson in the principal soprano role of Elvira, Alphonse's bride-to-be, sounds sweeter than often heretofore on record.

The peasants also feature strongly in the narrative, at one point declaring that the eruption of Vesuvius must be the wrath of Heaven descending upon them all! Masaniello is finally slain and Fenella commits suicide. Strongly cast and vigorously conducted by Thomas Fulton, this makes an attractive two-disc set, warmly recorded.

Barber, Samuel (1910–81)

Vanessa: complete.
(M) *** BMG/RCA GD 87899 (2) [7899-2-RG]. Met. Op. Ch. & O, Mitropoulos.
  Vanessa (Eleanor Steber), Erika (Rosalind Elias), The Old Baroness (Regina Resnik), Anatol (Nicolai Gedda), The Old Doctor (Giorgio Tozzi).

Barber's *Vanessa* dates from 1958. The original conception was in four Acts, subsequently (in

1965) compressed into three, but the Mitropoulos recording is of the four-Act version. Gian-Francesco Menotti's libretto is based on Isak Dinesen's *Seven Gothic Tales*.

The setting is northern Europe in the first decade of the present century. Vanessa has waited for twenty years for her lover to return. His son, Anatol, who bears a strong resemblance to him, arrives to tell her that his father is dead. Anatol sweeps Vanessa off her feet, but he is something of an adventurer and opportunist, and soon seduces Vanessa's niece, Erika, who bears him a child. He eventually marries Vanessa, however, and they settle in Paris. The opera ends with Erika realizing that she must now assume Vanessa's role and wait.

For long *Vanessa* was underprized as being old-fashioned, but time undermines any objections, for it is a work of some charm and warmth. It inhabits much the same civilized world as Strauss or Henry James. Although it has not held the stage, its melodic freshness will ensure a reversal of its fortunes some day. This, its only recording so far, was made at the time of its first performance in 1958, but no apologies are needed for its quality; it stands the test of time as well as does the opera itself. Eleanor Steber, an outstanding soprano too little heard on disc, is full-toned in the title-role, as are Gedda as Anatol and Resnik as the old Baroness. In fact the first-production cast has no real weakness, and the orchestral playing under Mitropoulos is wholly committed; it is good to have this lovely opera back, sounding better than ever.

Bart, Lionel (born 1930)

Oliver!
*** That's Entertainment Dig. CDTER 1184 [id.]. King's College School, Wimbledon Boys' Ch., Nat. SO, John Owen Edwards.
  Oliver (Richard South), Fagin (Julian Forsyth), Nancy (Josephine Barstow), Bill Sykes (Richard Van Allan), Artful Dodger (Irfan Ahmad), Mr Bumble (Stuart Kale), Mr Sowerby (Nickolas Grace), Mrs Sowerby (Rosemary Ashe), Bet (Megan Kelly).

It is extraordinary that this is the one Dickens musical that can be regarded as a classic, and it is a pity that Decca have not yet seen fit to reissue the excellent record by the original (1960) London cast, with Ron Moody an unforgettable Fagin, Martin Horsey splendid as the Artful Dodger and Georgia Brown and Danny Sewell well cast respectively as Nancy and Bill Sykes. The new record is generous (63 minutes) and very well recorded and the performance has plenty of vitality.

The singing of the members of the Wimbledon Boys' Choir gets the show off to a rousingly heartfelt start with *Food, glorious food*. Its star performance is Josephine Barstow's appealing Nancy; though Julian Forsyth is a convincing Fagin (and his *Pick a pocket or two* and *Reviewing the situation* have plenty of individuality), he does not erase memories of Ron Moody. Richard South as Oliver sings his *Where is love?* in the same rather watery style affected by Keith Hampshire in the original cast. This is taking musical characterization too far – there is no reason why Oliver himself should not be able to sing his little song with a bit more presence.

For the new record John Owen Edwards has used the original orchestrations by Eric Rogers to good effect, judiciously expanded – without any sense of inflation – for the larger orchestra he has at his command. An enjoyable reminder of a fine score, strong in cockney flavour – witness Nancy's exuberant *Oom-pah-pah* – while Irfan Ahmad as the Artful Dodger manages *I'd do anything* very adeptly.

Bartók, Béla (1881 – 1945)

Bluebeard's Castle (sung in Hungarian).
(M) *** Sony Dig. MK 44523 [id.]. Hungarian State O, Adám Fischer.
  Bluebeard (Samuel Ramey), Judith (Eva Marton).
(M) *** Decca 433 082-2 [id.]. LPO, Solti.
  Bluebeard (Kolos Kováts), Judith (Sylvia Sass).
(M) **(*) DG 423 236-2 [id.]. Bav. State O, Sawallisch.
  Bluebeard (Dietrich Fischer-Dieskau), Judith (Julia Varady).
**(*) Decca 414 167-2 [id.]. LSO, Kertész.
  Bluebeard (Walter Berry), Judith (Christa Ludwig).
**(*) Hung. Dig. MCD 12254 [id.]. Hungarian State Op. O, Ferencsik.
  Bluebeard (Evgeny Nesterenko), Judith (Elena Obraztsova).

(M) **(*) Mercury Dig. 434 325-2 [id.]. LSO, Dorati – BERG: *Wozzeck* (excerpts). **(*)
Bluebeard (Mihály Székely), Judith (Olga Szönyi).

Bartók's idea of portraying marital conflict in an opera was as unpromising as could be, but in
the event *Bluebeard's Castle* is an enthralling work with its concentration on mood, atmosphere
and slow development as Bluebeard's wife, Judith, finds the key to each new door, which all
open out of the central ill-lit chamber.

As she nervously opens each, she expects light, but discovers blood, first within a torture
chamber, then an armoury, on jewels, on flowers, and on a great cloud covering the castle. The
sixth door brings the water of tears, and the seventh reveals finally three gorgeous women,
Bluebeard's previous wives. The doors slowly close, one after the other, then Judith, leaving
Bluebeard alone, passes through the seventh door. The opera's comparative lack of action makes
it an ideal work for the gramophone, and there have been a surprising number of attempts to
record it.

The glory of the Sony/CBS version is the magnificent singing of Samuel Ramey in the title-
role. With his dark bass, firm and true, beautiful up to a high F, he carries the necessary threat
but equally brings nobility to the part. With him, Bluebeard is virile and even heroic, the master
of his fate; and that goes with a tellingly rugged account of the score from Hungarian forces,
under a Hungarian conductor, who understand this music from the inside. At well over an hour,
this is a noticeably more measured reading than most on record; far from hanging fire, that
spaciousness, in its totally idiomatic, four-square, relentless way, adds to the keenly dramatic
tension. Eva Marton, also Hungarian-born, may lack the vulnerability as well as the darker tone-
colours of the ideal Judith, but, with more than a touch of abrasiveness in the voice, she still
gives a powerful reading. The recording, a joint production with Hungaroton, matches the finest
achievements of that company, with full and brilliant sound, well balanced and clear. The single
CD comes with its libretto in a separate box.

Solti directs a richly atmospheric reading of Bartók's ritualistic opera, not as searingly
dramatic as one might have expected but with analogue recording of spectacular range. The
performance is introduced by the Hungarian verses which are printed in the score. The
Hungarian soloists are tangibly authentic, though their voices are not always perfectly steady, but
Sylvia Sass with her exquisite pianissimo singing is more appealing than Eva Marton on CBS.
The Kingsway Hall recording, produced by Christopher Raeburn and engineered by Kenneth
Wilkinson – less analytical than is normal from Decca – produces a rich carpet of sound to
which the CD transfer adds an extra degree of brilliance. The resulting effect is more romantic
than usual, even revealing an affinity with Richard Strauss. With full libretto included, this
makes a fine mid-priced alternative to the Sony/CBS version, which is dominated by Samuel
Ramey.

The reissue of the Sawallisch version at mid-price on DG's 20th-Century Classics series makes
an excellent bargain, particularly when libretto and notes are included in a slip-case with the
disc. The performance is warmly expressive rather than biting, as you might expect from
Sawallisch and the Bavarian State Orchestra. Varady and Fischer-Dieskau – husband and wife
in real life – give a Lieder-like intensity to the exchanges, full of refined detail. The voices are
more forward than on some versions; but on CD, with the digital transfer adding brightness to
the 1979 analogue recording, the separation from the orchestra is far cleaner than it was on LP.
The orchestral sound of the Bavarian State Orchestra has satisfying weight.

When it was first issued on LP in 1966, Kertész set new standards in his version with Christa
Ludwig and Walter Berry, not only in the playing of the LSO at its peak and in the firm
sensitivity of the soloists and the brilliance of the recording, but also in the natural Hungarian
inflexions inspired by the conductor. The remastering for CD is admirably vivid and present,
with voices and orchestra beautifully balanced. The serious snag – astonishing in a reissue at full
price – is that, unlike the rival versions, it provides no libretto, very important in a work that
consists entirely of spoken exchanges and with the sparest of plots.

With two distinguished Soviet singers taking the roles of Bluebeard and Judith, Ferencsik's
Hungaroton version (his fourth recording of the work) is vocally resonant and delicately
atmospheric, with the hushed pianissimo of the opening tellingly caught. Yet in musical weight
and intensity, not to mention dramatic detail and technical virtuosity, this inevitably must yield
before the finest versions using Western orchestras. The digital recording is full and faithful.

Antal Dorati, drawing brilliant playing from the LSO, recorded in vivid, immediate, Mercury
sound, finds power rather than mystery in Bartók's unique one-Acter. It is a positive, often
urgent reading of a work which, with its absence of action, in the wrong hands can seem to

meander. The abrasiveness of the vision is enhanced by having two Hungarian soloists. Székely as Bluebeard is taut and intense, using his characterful bass imaginatively; Olga Szönyi is more uneven, strong and incisive but with squally moments. Though rival versions are more atmospheric than this, Dorati relates the work more clearly to later Bartók. The CD transfer is very vivid, though tape-hiss is quite high. As a practical advantage the disc not only comes at mid-price but uniquely offers a generous coupling, an equally positive account of the three concert-excerpts from Berg's *Wozzeck*. There are adequate notes, but no libretto.

Beethoven, Ludwig van (1770– 1827)

Fidelio (complete).

⊛ (M) *** EMI CMS7 69324-2 (2) [Ang. CDMB 69324]. Philh. Ch. & O, Klemperer.

Leonore (Christa Ludwig), Florestan (Jon Vickers), Pizarro (Walter Berry), Rocco (Gottlob Frick), Marzelline (Ingeborg Hallstein), Jaquino (Gerhard Unger), Don Fernando (Franz Crass).

(M) *** EMI CMS7 69290-2 (2) [Ang. CDMB 69290]. German Op. Ch., BPO, Karajan.

Leonore (Helga Dernesch), Florestan (Jon Vickers), Pizarro (Zoltan Kélémen), Rocco (Karl Ridderbusch), Marzelline (Helen Donath), Jaquino (Horst Laubenthal), Don Fernando (José Van Dam).

*** DG 419 436-2 (2) [id.]. V. State Op. Ch., VPO, Bernstein.

Leonore (Gundula Janowitz), Florestan (René Kollo), Pizarro (Hans Sotin), Rocco (Manfred Jungwirth), Marzelline (Lucia Popp), Jaquino (Adolf Dallapozza), Don Fernando (Dietrich Fischer-Dieskau).

(M) (***) EMI mono CHS7 64496-2 (2). V. State Op. Ch. & O, Furtwängler.

Leonore (Martha Mödl), Florestan (Wolfgang Windgassen), Pizarro (Otto Edelmann), Rocco (Gottlob Frick), Marzelline (Sena Jurinac), Jaquino (Rudolf Schock), Don Fernando (Alfred Poell).

*** Ph. Dig. 426 308-2 (2) [id.]. Dresden State Op. Ch. & O, Haitink.

Leonore (Jessye Norman), Florestan (Reiner Goldberg), Pizarro (Ekkehard Wlaschiha), Rocco (Kurt Moll), Marzelline (Pamela Coburn), Jaquino (Hans-Peter Blochwitz), Don Fernando (Andreas Schmidt).

(M) *** DG 437 345-2 (2) [id.]. Bav. State Op. Ch. & O, Fricsay.

Leonore (Leonie Rysanek), Florestan (Ernst Haefliger), Pizarro (Dietrich Fischer-Dieskau), Rocco (Gottlob Frick), Marzelline (Irmgard Seefried), Jaquino (Friedrich Lenz), Don Fernando (Kieth Engen).

(M) (**(*)) BMG/RCA mono GD 60273 (2) [60273-2-RG]. NBC SO, Toscanini.

Leonore (Rose Bampton), Florestan (Jan Peerce), Pizarro (Herbert Janssen), Rocco (Sidor Belarsky), Marzelline (Eleanor Steber), Jaquino (Joseph Laderoute), Don Fernando (Nicola Moscona).

** Decca 410 227-2 (2) [id.]. Chicago Ch. & SO, Solti.

Leonore (Hildegard Behrens), Florestan (Peter Hofmann), Pizarro (Theo Adam), Rocco (Hans Sotin), Marzelline (Sona Ghazarian), Jaquino (David Kuebler), Don Fernando (Gwynne Howell).

(M) *(*) BMG/Eurodisc GD 69030; *GK 69030* (2). Leipzig R. Ch. & GO, Masur.

Leonore (Jeannine Altmeyer), Florestan (Siegfried Jerusalem), Pizarro (Siegmund Nimsgern), Rocco (Peter Meven), Marzelline (Carola Nossek), Jaquino (Rüdiger Wohlers), Don Fernando (Theo Adam).

* Decca Dig. 436 627-2 (2). V. State Op. Ch., VPO, Christoph von Dohnányi.

Leonore (Gabriele Schnaut), Florestan (Josef Protschka), Pizarro (Hartmut Welker), Rocco (Kurt Rydl), Marzelline (Ruth Ziesak), Jaquino (Uwe Heilmann), Don Fernando (Tom Krause).

Beethoven's great humanist opera, with its celebration of marital love and a wife's bravery, is set in eighteenth-century Seville. Leonore, its heroine, resolves to free her husband, Florestan, from unjust imprisonment and certain death at the hands of his enemy, Pizarro, the prison governor. Resourcefully disguised as a man, she adopts the name Fidelio and penetrates the prison, where she befriends the jailer, Rocco. The latter's daughter, Marzelline, becomes enamoured of this very personable new assistant, who seems more attractive than Jaquino, the janitor who is already courting her.

Pizarro learns that the Minister of State is to make an unannounced inspection of the prison and resolves to kill Florestan forthwith. Anguished by the foreboding that she may not be able to prevent her husband's death, Leonore is forced to help dig the grave for the prisoner who is hidden in the prison's deepest dungeon. At last Rocco takes her to see Florestan; on the arrival of Pizarro, she prevents the murder by throwing herself in front of her husband and drawing her gun to hold back the governor.

Fortunately (heralded by a famous trumpet-call) the Minister of State arrives at the prison in the nick of time, recognizes Florestan as an old friend and declares him guiltless of any charges against him. He insists that Leonore be the one to release her husband from his chains; Pizarro is himself taken prisoner, and a final chorus of rejoicing celebrates the opera's theme: *Wer ein holdes Weib errungen* ('He who such a wife has adored').

Klemperer's magisterial set of the opera has dominated the catalogue since it first appeared in 1962, and it sounds admirably full and fresh on CD, making a clear first choice. Its incandescence and spiritual strength are unique, with splendid performances from the whole cast, with Christa Ludwig as Leonore magnificent in the *Abscheulicher* and Jon Vickers at his finest as Florestan. The confrontation between Leonore and Pizarro in the Quartet of Act II has never been more thrillingly dramatic, and the final scene, more than in any other recording, underlines the parallel with the finale of the *Choral Symphony*.

Comparison between Karajan's strong and heroic reading and Klemperer's version is fascinating. Both have very similar merits, underlining the symphonic character of the work with their weight of utterance. Both may miss some of the sparkle of the opening scene, but it is better that seriousness should enter too early than too late. Since seriousness is the keynote, it is rather surprising to find Karajan using bass and baritone soloists lighter than usual.

Both the Rocco (Ridderbusch) and the Don Fernando (Van Dam) lack something in resonance in their lower range. Yet they sing dramatically and intelligently, and there is the advantage that the Pizarro of Zoltan Kélémen sounds the more biting and powerful as a result – a fine performance. Jon Vickers as Florestan is, if anything, even finer than he was for Klemperer; and although Helga Dernesch as Leonore does not have quite the clear-focused mastery of Christa Ludwig in the Klemperer set, this is still a glorious, thrilling performance, outshining lesser rivals than Ludwig. The orchestral playing is superb.

Bernstein, as one would expect, directs a reading of *Fidelio* full of dramatic flair. The recording was made in conjunction with live performances by the same cast at the Vienna State Opera, and the atmosphere in the domestic scenes at the start might almost come from a predecessor of the stage musical (compliment intended), with Lucia Popp as Marzelline particularly enchanting. The spoken dialogue is splendidly produced too. The Canon Quartet in Act I has warmth and humanity rather than monumental qualities; although Bernstein later rises splendidly to the high drama of Act II (the confrontation with Pizarro in the Quartet can compare with Klemperer's classic reading), it remains a drama on a human scale.

Gundula Janowitz sings most beautifully as Leonore, shading her phrases in the long opening section of the *Abscheulicher*, coping superbly with the intricacies of the *Allegro* and falling short only at the very end, in a less than triumphant pay-off. Kollo as Florestan is intelligent and musicianly but indulges in too many intrusive aitches, and there is some coarseness of tone. Hans Sotin as Pizarro sings with superb projection, and the size of voice makes up for its not sounding villainous. Manfred Jungwirth makes an engaging Rocco, though his singing is not always perfectly steady. Fischer-Dieskau – once an incomparable Pizarro – here makes a noble Don Fernando in the final scene. On CD the quality of the solo singing and the imagination of Bernstein's interpretation make it a strong contender, except for the cost – it remains at full price. The digital transfer of an analogue recording is very vivid, even if slight discrepancies of balance emerge the more sharply.

Though Furtwängler's classic reading of 1953 comes in mono sound only, there is an amazing sense of atmosphere and presence, particularly with the voices. As these same singers had been performing the opera live with Furtwängler, the sense of drama is thrilling, particularly from Martha Mödl, a weightily Wagnerian Leonore, and from Wolfgang Windgassen, a Wagnerian Heldentenor with an exceptionally sweet and focused tone. Sena Jurinac's voice has rarely sounded more sweetly tender than here as Marzelline, Otto Edelmann is a magnificent Pizarro and Gottlob Frick dark and firm as Rocco. As for Furtwängler, his direction is as incandescent as in his other great studio recording of an opera, Wagner's *Tristan und Isolde*, made the previous year. It is astonishing that so commanding a performance could have remained unavailable through most of the LP era. As in Toscanini's historic recording, there is no spoken dialogue.

The unsurpassed nobility of Jessye Norman's voice is perfectly matched to this noblest of operas. In detail of characterization she may not always match Christa Ludwig, Klemperer's firm and incisive Leonore, or Helga Dernesch, Karajan's warmly emotional heroine, but her reading is consistently rich and beautiful. She brings a new revelation most strikingly in her speaking of the dialogue, with the personality beaming out in individuality even before she starts singing. The Canon Quartet of Act I is then taken dangerously slowly, but it is superbly sustained by Haitink at a steady tempo, with Pamela Coburn and Hans-Peter Blochwitz well matched as Marzelline and Jaquino, and the resonant Kurt Moll as the jailer, Rocco.

The great test of the *Abscheulicher* then finds Norman at her peak, not as animated as Dernesch but rich and varied. Reiner Goldberg, strained at times and no match for Jon Vickers on both the Klemperer and Karajan sets, still makes an impressive Florestan by latterday standards, and Ekkehard Wlaschiha, best known for his portrayal of Alberich in various *Ring* cycles, is a superb Pizarro, strong and sinister. With excellent digital sound and strong, forthright conducting from Haitink, this is the finest of modern versions, even if it does not replace Klemperer or Karajan.

Though the Fricsay set dates from 1957, the recording has responded well to CD remastering, with clean and well-focused sound that lacks a little in body. This was the first recording of this opera to offer not just Beethoven's score but a sprinkling of dialogue between numbers, which in DG's CD transfer are separately banded. As for Fricsay's direction, from the *Overture* onwards it matches the excitement and keen tension of a Toscanini performance, though the very clarity makes it more lightweight than many rivals. The principals sing with exceptional clarity and point. Ernst Haefliger is a fine, clear-cut Florestan, lyric in timbre rather than fully heroic, and Frick and Fischer-Dieskau offer strong, intense characterizations, with Pizarro's aria chilling in its villainy. Rysanek's Leonore is also impressive and her *Abscheulicher* is both dramatic and beautifully shaded, one of her finest performances on record. As for Irmgard Seefried, she makes an enchanting Marzelline. Full libretto and translation with this mid-priced Dokumente set. The *Leonore No. 3 Overture* is included as a supplement after the opera, not before the final scene as used to be the custom; with CD, however, listeners can re-programme it if they wish.

Recorded in December 1944, when victory was in sight at the end of the Second World War, this was the first of the concert performances of complete operas that Toscanini conducted in New York. Though the sound is even drier and less helpful to voices than in his latest NBC opera-recordings, the performance is characteristically incandescent. There is no attempt at a dramatic presentation. This is just Beethoven's score with no dialogue whatever, not even in the great confrontation of the Act II quartet, but that makes one concentrate the more on the music, which is plainly what Toscanini wants. Typically his choice of soloists favours voices that are clean-cut and accurate rather than conventionally beautiful, and it is good to have Rose Bampton as a powerful Leonore, an American singer too little appreciated in Europe and too little recorded. Eleanor Steber is a weightier Marzelline than usual, but the clarity and precision are impressive, well matched by the Jaquino of Joseph Laderoute. Sidor Belarsky as Rocco is similarly clean of attack, and though Herbert Janssen is not as fresh-toned as he was earlier, this is a strong and characterful performance. As Florestan, Jan Peerce, Toscanini's favourite American tenor of the time, sings cleanly too if not with great imagination. The transfer follows the honest if unflattering pattern favoured in RCA's Toscanini Edition. The *Leonore No. 3 Overture* is included before the final scene.

Solti's set was the first-ever digital recording of an opera. The sound is full, clean and vividly atmospheric, matched by the conductor's urgent and intense direction. With fine choral singing the ensembles are excellent, but the solo singing is too flawed for comfort. Hildegard Behrens seems ungainly in the great *Abscheulicher*, and both Peter Hofmann as Florestan and Theo Adam as Pizarro too often produce harsh, unattractive tone.

Masur's version is offered in well-balanced, modern, analogue sound. It is played very well by the Leipzig orchestra, but this is a surprisingly small-scale view, lacking the full dramatic bite needed in this towering masterpiece. Neither Jeannine Altmeyer nor Siegfried Jerusalem had achieved their peak when they made the recording in 1982 and, though there is fine singing from the male members of the cast, the Marzelline of Carola Nossek is thin and unsteady. The whole performance has the feeling of a well-behaved run-through.

The great merit of the latest Decca version, using its magnificent studio in the Konzerthaus in Vienna, is the spectacular sound. Never has Beethoven's score glowed so richly on disc as in this opulent and beautifully balanced recording, with the Vienna Philharmonic under Christoph von Dohnányi sounding sumptuous, with incandescent singing from the Vienna State Opera Choir and vividly convincing production of the spoken dialogue. The irony is that the effort achieves so little, when this is the worst-sung *Fidelio* in years, one that does not begin to match the classic sets of the past under such conductors as Klemperer, Karajan, Furtwängler or Fricsay. The main problem is that almost all the principals are wobblers. By far the worst culprit is the Leonore of Gabriele Schnaut, alone making the set unrecommendable. Quite apart from her ill-focused wobbling, she regularly lets out painful yowls of indeterminate pitch. The great *Abscheulicher*, so far from being a vocal climax, comes to sound like a Disney farmyard, with her piercing top notes the steadiest she manages. Ruth Ziesak as Marzelline is the one principal who, with a warm, sweet tone, focuses well, singing with animation to create a rounded character. Both Hartmut Welker's Don Pizarro and Kurt Rydl's Rocco are distractingly unsteady on sustained notes, and Uwe Heilmann as Jaquino whines disagreeably, while Josef Protschka as Florestan, after starting well, also finds it hard to sing sustained notes without at least a judder. Ironically the best-sung solo passage comes in the glorious, hushed ensemble in the Act II finale, beginning with Leonore's *O Gott, welch'ein Augenblick*.

Fidelio: highlights.
(M) *** EMI CDM7 63077-2; *EG 763077-4* (from above recording with Dernesch, Vickers; cond. Karajan).

Those who acquire Klemperer's classic set will welcome just under an hour of well-chosen highlights from the fine alternative Karajan recording, made in 1970. It opens with the *Overture* and includes key items like Pizarro's Act I aria, the *Abscheulicher*, the *Prisoners' chorus* and the closing scene, all vividly presented in bright, clear sound. There is a brief synopsis but no libretto.

Bellini, Vincenzo (1801–35)

Beatrice di Tenda (complete); Arias: *Norma: Casta diva. I Puritani: Son vergin vezzosa; Oh rendetemi la speme. La Sonnambula: Ah, non credea mirarti.*
(M) *** Decca 433 706-2 (3) [id.]. Amb. Op. Ch., LSO, Bonynge.
   Beatrice di Tenda (Joan Sutherland), Orombello (Luciano Pavarotti), Filippo Maria Visconti (Cornelius Opthof), Agnese del Maino (Josephine Veasey), Rizzardo del Maino (Joseph Ward).

Beatrice di Tenda was Bellini's last opera but one, coming after *Sonnambula* and *Norma* and before *I Puritani*. It had an unfortunate birth, for the composer had to go to the law courts to wring the libretto from his collaborator, Romani, and the result is not exactly compelling dramatically.

The story involves a whole string of unrequited loves. Filippo, Duke of Milan, is in love with Agnes, who is in love with Orombello, the Duke of Ventimiglia, who loves Beatrice, wife of Filippo, and the culminating point comes when the heroine, Beatrice, is denounced falsely for alleged infidelity. There is torture, followed by an impressive trial scene – closely based on the trial scene of Donizetti's *Anna Bolena* – and the unfortunate Beatrice is condemned to death and executed despite the recantation of false witnesses.

Bellini always intended to revise the score but failed to do so before his death. As it is, the piece remains essentially a vehicle for an exceptional prima donna with a big enough voice and brilliant enough coloratura. Joan Sutherland has made it her own in recent years – this recording was made in 1966 – and although here she indulges in some of the 'mooning' one hoped she had left behind, there are many dazzling examples of her art.

The other star of the set is Richard Bonynge, whose powers as a Bellini conductor are most impressive. The supporting cast could hardly be better, with Pavarotti highly responsive. The recording, made in Walthamstow Assembly Hall, is of Decca's best vintage and has transferred splendidly to CD, with vivid atmosphere and colour. Four famous arias are provided as a filler, one from Sutherland's 1964 *Norma*, two from her 1963 *I Puritani* and one from the 1962 *La Sonnambula*.

I Capuleti ed i Montecchi (complete).
Withdrawn: **(*) EMI CDS7 47388-8 (2) [Ang. CDCB 47387]. ROHCG Ch. and O, Muti.
   Giulietta (Edita Gruberová), Romeo (Agnes Baltsa), Tebaldo (Dano Raffanti), Capellio (Gwynne Howell), Lorenzo (John Tomlinson).

Bellini's adaptation of the famous Shakespearean story of the star-crossed lovers has its own variations on the original, with Tybalt still Romeo's rival, but with Lorenzo, physician to the Capulets, persuading Juliet to take the sleeping draught. After that, the nemesis of the plot continues. Romeo, finding Juliet, thinks she is dead and takes poison. Juliet awakens, only to suffer Romeo dying in her arms. She then dies from grief.

Muti's set was recorded live at a series of performances at Covent Garden when the production was new, in March 1984. With the Royal Opera House a difficult venue for recording, the sound is hard and close, far less agreeable and well balanced than in the previous EMI version of this opera, recorded in the studio with Beverley Sills and Dame Janet Baker and now deleted. On the later version, Agnes Baltsa makes a passionately expressive Romeo and Edita Gruberová a Juliet who is not just brilliant in coloratura but also sweet and tender. It is an unlikely but successful matching of a Carmen with a Zerbinetta; but it is the masterful conducting of Muti that, more than anything, makes one tolerant of the indifferent sound. If (for good reasons) he has often been considered something of a sprinter in opera, here he is superb with the pacing, balancing fast and incisive choruses against passages of warmth, relaxation and repose. That mastery is especially striking at the end of Act I, when the five principals sing a hushed quintet in which Romeo and Juliet musically reveal their understanding, singing sweetly in thirds. With excellent contributions from the refined tenor Dano Raffanti (as Tebaldo), Gwynne Howell and John Tomlinson, it is a performance to blow the cobwebs off an opera that – even in the earlier recording – seemed one of Bellini's less compelling pieces.

Norma (complete).

(M) *** Decca 425 488-2 (3) [id.]. London Symphony Ch., LSO, Bonynge.
> Norma (Joan Sutherland), Adalgisa (Marilyn Horne), Polione (John Alexander), Oroveso (Richard Cross), Flavio (Joseph Ward), Clotilde (Yvonne Minton).

**(*) Decca Dig. 414 476-2 (3) [id.]. WNO Ch. & O, Bonynge.
> Norma (Joan Sutherland), Adalgisa (Montserrat Caballé), Polione (Luciano Pavarotti), Oroveso (Samuel Ramey), Flavio (Kim Begley), Clotilde (Diana Montague).

(***) EMI mono CDS7 47304-8 (3) [Ang. CDCB 47303]. La Scala, Milan, Ch. and O, Serafin.
> Norma (Maria Callas), Adalgisa (Ebe Stignani), Polione (Mario Filippeschi), Oroveso (Nicola Rossi-Lemeni), Flavio (Paolo Caroli), Clotilde (Rina Cavallari).

(M) **(*) EMI CMS7 63000-2 (3) [Ang. CDMC 63000]. Ch. & O of La Scala, Milan, Serafin.
> Norma (Maria Callas), Adalgisa (Christa Ludwig), Polione (Franco Corelli), Oroveso (Nicola Zaccaria), Flavio (Piero De Palma), Clotilde (Edda Vincenzi).

(M) ** BMG/RCA GD 86502 (3) [RCA 6502-2-RG]. Amb. Op. Ch., LPO, Cillario.
> Norma (Montserrat Caballé), Adalgisa (Fiorenza Cossotto), Polione (Plácido Domingo), Oroveso (Ruggero Raimondi), Flavio (Kenneth Collins), Clotilde (Elizabeth Bainbridge).

* Olympia OCD 160 A-B-C [id.]. USSR Ministry of Culture State Chamber Ch., Bolshoi Theatre O, Ermler.
> Norma (M. Bieshu), Adalgisa (L. Nam), Polione (G. Grigoryan), Oroveso (G. Seleznev), Flavio (N. Vasiliev), Clotilde (L. Yurchenko).

The plot of Bellini's *Norma* is the very stuff of which operatic melodrama is made. Druids and soldiers of ancient Gaul, led by the High Priest, Grovesco, call on the gods to inspire the people to fight the invading Romans. However, Grovesco's daughter, the High Priestess Norma, states that war without holy sanction is unacceptable and, rebuking the Druids for their aggressive response, instead intercedes for peace.

She has her own reasons for such a course of action, for she has already broken her vows of chastity and has had a clandestine affair with Polione, the Roman Pro-Consul, and borne him two children. Alas, he no longer loves her, preferring instead Adalgisa, a virgin of the temple, who returns his feelings, though with considerable misgivings.

Norma guesses that Polione will desert her and, when she hears from Adalgisa that she too is in love, she sympathetically gives permisssion for Adalgisa to renounce her temple vows for her lover. At the entry of Polione the truth becomes apparent, Norma confronts him with his infidelity, and Adalgisa loyally refuses to betray Norma and flee with her lover. Yet on reflection Norma remains willing to let Adelgisa become Polione's wife, provided that she takes Polione's two children with her to safety in the Roman camp.

Adalgisa again refuses to betray Norma and instead vows to try to persuade Polione to reconsider his actions. But she fails and Norma's anger knows no bounds. She strikes the brazen temple shield/gong to summon everyone to her presence, and declares war. Then Polione is captured and, to save his life, Norma, having entrusted her children to her father's care, sacrifices herself instead, moving towards the sacrificial pyre to the god of war. Here she is joined by the finally repentant Polione – stirred by her passion – and they go to their deaths together.

In her first (mid-1960s) recording as Norma, Sutherland was joined by an Adalgisa in Marilyn Horne whose control of florid singing is just as remarkable as Sutherland's own and who sometimes even outshines the heroine in musical imagination. The other soloists are very good indeed, John Alexander and Richard Cross both young, clear-voiced singers. Sutherland's own contribution is dramatically very much after the school of Callas, while at the same time ensuring that something as near as possible to musical perfection is achieved, even if occasionally at the expense of masked diction. That the performance is so compelling owes much to the conducting of Richard Bonynge, who keeps musical interest alive in the many conventional accompaniment figures with sprung rhythm and with the most subtle attention to the vocal line. The Walthamstow recording is vivid but also atmospheric in its new format.

It was an amazing achievement for Dame Joan Sutherland, fifty-eight when her second *Norma* recording was made, to give so commanding a performance of this most taxing of Bellini roles at so late a stage in her career. Few other sopranos could even have attempted it, but, with signs of age undisguisable, it is an amazing achievement considering, not absolute. There are some advantages in the extra weight of voice, and the beat which latterly developed is at its minimum. The coloratura is still remarkably flexible, but the ornamentation in the great melody of *Casta diva* is flicked off a little too lightly to sound completely secure, and in the cabaletta the tone is masked, not as sparklingly fresh as it used to be. The remarkable conjunction of Sutherland with Pavarotti and Caballé does not always work easily.

Though Pavarotti is in some ways the set's greatest strength, easily expressive yet powerful as Polione, Caballé as Adalgisa seems determined to outdo Sutherland in mooning manner, cooing self-indulgently. The advantage in relation to Sutherland is that, with a lighter voice, she is more convincingly a younger sister, and the extra challenge of the duet, *Mira o Norma*, makes for thrilling results. Equally, in the big Act II Trio the three principals effectively and excitingly sink their stylistic differences. Bonynge, as in the earlier Sutherland recording, paces Bellini well, and the Welsh National Opera Orchestra and Chorus respond most sympathetically. Full, brilliant, well-balanced recording. Unlike the Callas set, which makes the traditional cuts, this is complete.

In Callas's earlier, mono set, though the flatness of the 1954 recording is emphasized by the precision of CD, the sense of presence gives wonderful intensity to one of the diva's most powerful performances, recorded at the very peak of her powers, before the upper register acquired its distracting wobble. Balance of soloists is close, and the chorus could hardly be dimmer, but, as a perfect re-creation of a classic, irreplaceable recording, this is one of the jewels of the CD catalogue. With Callas in much fresher, firmer voice with electric intensity in every phrase, the casting of the veteran, Ebe Stignani, as Adalgisa gives Callas a worthily characterful partner in the sisters' duets. Filippeschi is disappointing by comparison, thin-toned and at times strained, and Rossi-Lemeni is not well treated by the microphone either.

By the time Callas came to record her 1960 stereo version, the tendency to hardness and unsteadiness in the voice above the stave, always apparent, had grown more serious, but the interpretation was as sharply illuminating as ever, a unique assumption, helped – as the earlier mono performance was not – by a strong cast. Christa Ludwig as Adalgisa brings not just rich, firm tone but also a real feeling for Italian style and, despite moments of coarseness, Corelli sings heroically. Serafin as ever is the most persuasive of Bellini conductors, and the recording, very good for its period, is the more vivid on CD while still retaining its atmosphere – not surprisingly, as Walter Legge masterminded the original production.

Montserrat Caballé's recording of *Norma*, made in 1972, on paper has an exceptionally strong cast, and there are many vocal delights; but it fails to add up to the sum of its parts. Reissued in RCA's mid-price CD opera series, it makes a fair enough bargain, particularly for devotees of Caballé. She characteristically exploits a wide range of dynamic, so that the opening of *Casta diva* is very gentle, sweet and reflective, with delicate ornamentation, later expanding strongly and easily – maybe too easily when, even at this key point, the singing does not sound deeply involved, though the cabaletta to the aria is fierily positive.

The extremes in the Norma – Adalgisa duet, *Mira o Norma*, bring exaggeratedly drawn-out phrasing in the main part and no delicacy at all in the cabaletta. Cossotto sings strongly at all points but, with diction poor, it is a generalized performance. Plácido Domingo makes a fine, heroic Polione, but the voice is really too robust for Bellini. The diction is excellent, with intelligent illumination of words, but the duet with Adalgisa finds him growing coarser by association. Cillario's conducting is intelligent but a little underpowered. With recording that still sounds well, this might be worth considering at the price, but hardly matches the finest versions.

In a full-bodied digital recording from Soviet Melodiya, with voices and orchestra closely balanced, it is the dramatic impact rather than any musical subtlety in Bellini that comes out of the Olympia performance. The power of Mark Ermler's conducting makes its mark at the very start, which is made to sound like early Verdi. That is fair enough and good, strong, Slavonic singers follow that line further, though increasingly the lack of Bellinian finesse is a serious drawback. The Polione of G. Grigoryan in particular is strenuous to the point of sounding strangulated in his passionate expression of the hero's emotions. The second tenor, N. Vasiliev, as Flavio is far preferable. M. Bieshu as Norma has a rich, warm soprano but is balanced so close that *Casta diva* loses all poise when sung so lustily, almost like a Russian folksong. G. Seleznev as Oroveso is a comparably rugged bass.

Norma: highlights.
(M) *** Decca 421 886-2; *421 886-4* [id.] (from above recording with Sutherland, Horne; cond. Pritchard).
(M) **(*) EMI CDM7 63091-2; *EG 763091-4* (from above recording with Callas, Corelli; cond. Serafin).

Those who have opted for Sutherland's later set of *Norma* will find in this highlights disc a valuable supplement from the earlier set featuring her unsurpassed partnership with Marilyn Horne. This highlights CD (65 minutes) includes their classic collaboration in the famous duets from both Acts. *Mira o Norma* is taken rather slowly, with a degree more mannerism than the singers might later have allowed themselves. An excellent, vivid transfer of the full-blooded 1964 Walthamstow recording.

Those who already have Callas's mono set should investigate the generous (63 minutes) highlights disc of her later stereo version, including *Casta diva* and the three principal Norma–Adalgisa duets.

Norma: Scenes and duets: Act I: *Oh! rimembranza!; Ah! sì fa core, abbracciami . . . Ma di', l'amato giovane quale fra noi si noma? . . . Oh! non tremare; Oh! di qual sei tu vittima; Oh! qual traspare orribile; Norma! de 'tuoi rimproveri.* Act II: *Introduction; Dormono entrambi; Mi chiami, o Norma!; Deh! con te, con te li prendi . . . Mira o Norma . . . Sì, fino all'ore estreme.*
(M) **(*) 436 303-2 [id.]. Norma (Joan Sutherland), Adalgisa (Marilyn Horne), Polione (John Alexander), LSO, Bonynge – ROSSINI: *Semiramide: Scenes & duets.* ***

The 1964 collaboration of Joan Sutherland and Marilyn Horne is a classic one, and it was a good idea to collect the great duets from Rossini's *Semiramide* as well as from *Norma*, a feast for vocal collectors. Those who have the old LP will notice that the CD selection is extended. *Mira o Norma* is taken rather slowly, with a degree more of mannerism than is absolutely ideal. The Decca recording is characteristically vivid and present.

Il pirata (complete).
(M) ** EMI CMS7 64169-2 (2). Rome R. & TV Ch. & O, Gavazzeni.
    Ernesto (Piero Cappuccilli), Imogene (Montserrat Caballé), Gualtiero (Bernabé Marti), Goffredo (Ruggero Raimondi).

This is the first complete recording of *Il pirata*, the composer's third opera, written for La Scala and first produced in 1827. Imogen's lover, Gualtiero, in fact the Count of Montalto, has been forced to take to the seas as a pirate, while Imogen has been given in a loveless marriage to Ernesto. Gualtiero is conveniently shipwrecked in Caldora, near the home of his beloved, and hopes to win her back after being given accommodation by Goffredo (his former tutor).

Even though Imogen refuses Gualtiero's advances (she already has a son by Ernesto and her father is imprisoned and in her husband's power), Ernesto soon discovers the presence of Il Pirata and finally husband and lover fight a duel. In the best traditions of Italian opera, Ernesto is killed, Gualtiero is condemned to death, and Imogen loses her mind.

It is not a very promising scenario, and the opera itself is too long for its material. Caballé is well suited to the role of the heroine, though by her finest standards there is some carelessness in her singing – clumsy changes of register and less than the expected beauty of tonal contrast. Nor are the conducting and presentation sparkling enough to mask the comparative poverty of Bellini's invention at this early stage of his career. Bernabé Marti, Caballé's husband, makes a fair stab at the difficult part of the pirate himself. The 1970 recording flatters the voices and has plenty of atmosphere but is not as vividly projected as the best Decca offerings from this period.

I Puritani (complete).
*** Decca 417 588-2 (3). ROHCG Ch. & O, Bonynge.
    Elvira (Joan Sutherland), Arturo (Luciano Pavarotti), Riccardo (Piero Cappuccilli), Giorgio

(Nicolai Ghiaurov), Enrichetta (Anita Caminada), Gualtiero (Giancarlo Luccardi), Bruno (Renato Cazzaniga).
(M) **(*) EMI CMS7 69663-2 (2) [Ang. CDMC 69663]. Amb. Op. Ch., Philh. O, Muti.
   Elvira (Montserrat Caballé), Arturo (Alfredo Kraus), Riccardo (Matteo Manuguerra), Giorgio (Agostino Ferrin), Enrichetta (Júlia Hamari), Gualtiero (Stefan Elenkov), Bruno (Dennis O'Neill).
(***) EMI mono CDS7 47308-8 (2) [Ang. CDCB 47308]. La Scala, Milan, Ch. & O, Serafin.
   Elvira (Maria Callas), Arturo (Giuseppe Di Stefano), Riccardo (Rolando Panerai), Giorgio (Nicola Rossi-Lemeni), Enrichetta (Aurora Catellani), Gualtiero (Carlo Forti), Bruno (Angelo Mercuriali).

'Opera must make people weep, shudder, die through the singing,' Bellini wrote to his librettist; and Bonynge's sharply committed performance of *I Puritani* on Decca breathes life into what can seem a rather limp story about Cavaliers and Roundheads. It takes place in Plymouth, during the English Civil War, where a fortress of soldiers are preparing to defend themselves against the Stuarts. Simultaneously Elvira, the heroine, is getting ready to marry Sir Richard Forth, a Puritan general, although she loves Lord Arthur Talbot, a Stuart sympathizer.

She is delighted when she learns that she may marry the man of her choice after all; however, politics intervene and Lord Arthur is forced to act as chaperon to Queen Henrietta, who escapes to London disguised as Elvira. Elvira is devastated at this turn of events, even temporarily losing her reason. Months pass by but finally the lovers are re-united, the Stuarts suffer defeat, and Cromwell pardons all prisoners.

Ten years after her first recording of *I Puritani*, made in Florence, Dame Joan Sutherland returned to this limpidly lyrical music, with ensemble much crisper than in the earlier version and with Bonynge this time adopting a more urgently expressive style. Where the earlier set was recorded when Sutherland had adopted a soft-grained style, with consonants largely eliminated and a tendency to lag behind the beat, this time her singing is fresher and brighter. The lovely aria *Qui la voce* is no longer a wordless melisma and, though the great showpiece *Son vergin vezzosa* is taken dangerously fast, the extra bite and tautness are exhilarating. Pavarotti, with his most radiantly beautiful of tenor voices, shows himself a remarkable Bellini stylist, rarely if ever coarsening a legato line, unlike so many of his Italian colleagues. Ghiaurov and Cappuccilli make up an impressive cast, and the only disappointing contributor is Anita Caminada in the small role of Enrichetta – Queen Henrietta Maria in disguise. Vivid, atmospheric recording enhanced and given added presence by the digital remastering.

In the EMI version of *I Puritani* Riccardo Muti's contribution is most distinguished. As the very opening demonstrates, his attention to detail and pointing of rhythm make for refreshing results, and the warm but luminous recording is excellent. But both the principal soloists – Bellini stylists on their day, but here below form – indulge in distracting mannerisms, hardly allowing even a single bar to be presented straight in the big numbers, pulling and tugging in each direction, rarely sounding spontaneous. The big ensemble *A te, o cara*, in its fussiness at slow speed, loses the surge of exhilaration which the earlier Decca set with Sutherland and Pavarotti shows so strongly.

Those who complain that this opera represents Bellini at his dramatically least compelling should certainly hear Callas. In 1953, when she made the recording, her voice was already afflicted by hardness on top with some unsteadiness, and for sheer beauty of sound Sutherland is consistently preferable. But Callas, once heard, is unforgettable, uniquely compelling. None of the other soloists is ideally stylish, though most of the singing is acceptable. As can be heard at the very opening, the upper range of the sound is restricted, though later the recording opens up and the solo voices project vividly. In this two-disc set, Act I is complete on the first disc, with Acts II and III on the second.

La Sonnambula (complete).
*** Decca Dig. 417 424-2 (2) [id.]. L. Op. Ch., Nat. PO, Bonynge.
   Amina (Joan Sutherland), Elvino (Luciano Pavarotti), Rodolfo (Nicolai Ghiaurov), Lisa (Isobel Buchanan), Teresa (Della Jones), Alessio (John Tomlinson), Notary (Piero De Palma).
(***) EMI mono CDS7 47378-8 (2) [Ang. CDCB 47377]. La Scala, Milan, Ch. and O, Votto.
   Amina (Maria Callas), Elvino (Nicola Monti), Rodolfo (Nicola Zaccaria), Lisa (Eugenia Ratti), Teresa (Fiorenza Cossotto), Alessio (Giuseppe Morresi), Notary (Franco Ricciardi).

La Sonnambula, written in 1831, is considered by many to be Bellini's masterpiece. The simple story of the village girl compromised when sleep-walking produced some of the composer's most engaging music. Elvino, a young farmer, loves the heroine, Amina, who returns his feelings, but she has a rival in Lisa, proprietress of the village inn, who wants Elvino for herself. Nevertheless a marriage contract is signed between Amina and Elvino. Count Rodolfo is staying at the inn, and consternation reigns when Amina is found lying on the Count's bed. Elvino rejects his betrothed in jealous rage while Lisa, happily making the most of this situation, persuades Elvino to marry her instead. Count Rodolfo realizes that Amina is an unwitting somnambulist, but Elvino cannot comprehend that such a thing could happen. Finally the entire village sees Amina walking in her sleep, and without waking she appals the watchers by crossing a bridge. Elvino at last understands and begs her forgiveness for his lack of trust in her fidelity.

As Joan Sutherland said, when she decided to record *La Sonnambula* again in her fifties, there was no question of her trying to be kittenish. As Richard Bonynge has pointed out, the original Amina was also the original Norma, and the extra weight of the voice – still not sounding at all old – suits the music, if not the character. The result is a performance even more affecting and more stylish than her earlier version, generally purer and more forthright, if with diction still clouded at times.

The challenge of singing opposite Pavarotti adds to the bite of the performance, crisply and resiliently controlled by Bonynge. The star tenor may be stylistically coarser than Nicola Monti on Sutherland's earlier set, but the beauty and size of the voice help to focus the whole performance more positively, not least in such ensembles as the finale of Act I. The rest of the cast is vocally strong too, and the early digital recording comes up very vividly on CD, with excellent separation of voices and orchestra. Like the earlier LPs, the CD set has on its box a delightful, not-quite-serious portrait by Michael Stennett of Sutherland as the Sonnambula.

Substantially cut, the Callas version was recorded in mono in 1957, yet it gives a vivid picture of the diva at the peak of her powers. By temperament she may not have related closely to Bellini's heroine, but the village girl's simple devotion through all trials is caught touchingly, most of all in the recitatives. The recording has transferred remarkably well to CD. There is a fair amount of atmosphere, and both orchestra and chorus are well caught. Nicola Monti makes a strong rather than a subtle contribution but blends well with Callas in the duets; and Fiorenza Cossotto is a good Teresa. Strongly recommended to Callas admirers.

Arias and duets: *Norma: Casta diva;* (i) *Mira o Norma. Il Pirata: Cor sorriso d'innocenza.*
(M) **(*) BMG/RCA 09026 61458-2. Montserrat Caballé, LPO & Ch., Cillario, (i) with Fiorenza Cossotto – DONIZETTI: *Arias.* **(*)

Montserrat Caballé's début recital for RCA was made in 1965 and was devoted to Bellini and Donizetti. It reveals something of the quality which brought her such spectacular succcess in New York, above all the ravishing, creamy beauty of the voice. What it also reveals is the artistic limitation at that time in her career. The two main arias are tenderly and sensitively done, but even in the cabalettas one cannot help sensing a lack of vibrant energy, of undercharacterization. The orchestra and chorus are conducted expertly by Carlo Felice Cillario. The duet, *Mira o Norma*, comes from the complete set, made in 1972 under the same conductor, and features an uncredited Fiorenza Cossotto. The phrasing is expansive to an extreme, though the two voices blend richly.

Berg, Alban (1885–1935)

Lulu (with orchestration of Act III completed by Friedrich Cerha).
*** DG 415 489-2 (3) [id.]. Paris Op. O, Boulez.
    Lulu (Teresa Stratas), Doctor Schön (Franz Mazura), Alwa (Kenneth Riegel), Countess Geschwitz (Yvonne Minton), Painter / Negro (Robert Tear), Schigolch / Professor of Medicine / Police Officer (Toni Blankenheim), Dresser / High Schoolboy / Groom (Hanna Schwarz).
*** EMI Dig. CDC7 54622-2 (3) [Ang. CDCC 54622]. O Nat. de France, Tate.   Lulu (Patricia Wise), Dr Schön / Jack the Ripper (Wolfgang Schöne), Alwa (Peter Straka), Countess Geschwitz (Brigitte Fassbaender).

The full three-Act structure of Berg's *Lulu*, first unveiled by Boulez in his Paris Opéra production and treated by DG to studio recording, was a revelation with few parallels. The third Act, musically even stronger than the first two and dramatically essential in making sense of the stylized plan based on a palindrome, transforms the opera. Although it ends with a lurid portrayal of Jack the Ripper's murder of Lulu – in Boulez's version recorded with hair-raising vividness – the nastiness of the subject is put into context, made artistically more acceptable. Lulu as the plot's central figure is its catalyst, but she has no apparent control over her destiny, except in the sexual magnetism she exerts over her many lovers.

Her story begins as a pierrot in a circus and it is in a pierrot's costume that she is painted, at the instigation of her patron, Dr Schön. He soon leaves with his son, Alwa, and the painter promptly tries to seduce her but is interrupted by the arrival of Lulu's husband who, finding his wife compromised, collapses and dies of shock. Lulu now marries the painter, but when Dr Schön tells him the wild details of Lulu's love-life he commits suicide.

Lulu now has her eye on Dr Schön, and eventually persuades him to marry her. But there are many others of both sexes in her life, including Alwa, an athlete, the pimp Schigolch and the Countess Geschwitz. In an altercation with Schön, she shoots him dead and is taken to prison where she catches cholera. Her lovers plan her escape and she goes to Paris and then on to London. Alwa, Schigolch and Countess Geschwitz are still around, living on her earnings as a prostitute.

Finally Lulu falls victim to Jack the Ripper. The last scene of the opera, with Yvonne Minton singing the Countess Geschwitz's lament, is most moving, though Lulu remains to the end a repulsive heroine. Teresa Stratas's bright, clear soprano is well recorded, and there is hardly a weak link in the cast. Altogether this is a historic issue, presenting an intensely involving performance of a work which in some ways is lyrically more approachable than *Wozzeck*. The CD version brings a layout on three discs, one per Act, and immediacy of sound. A note by Boulez and Friedrich Cerha's commentary on his completion are both included, as well as the libretto.

Jeffrey Tate conducts the Orchestre National and an excellent non-French cast in a live recording of the full three-Act version. It provides a welcome alternative to the pioneering DG recording from Pierre Boulez with the original Paris Opéra cast. Tate's reading is more flexible, more volatile, more emotional than Boulez's. There are stage noises, some minor flaws of ensemble, and the recording is at a relatively low level, not as satisfying as the firmer, clearer, better-balanced DG sound for Boulez, who as a Berg interpreter is forceful, direct and rugged rather than affectionate. On casting Tate's set is marginally preferable, with Patricia Wise in the title-role more sensuous than Teresa Stratas for Boulez, and with Brigitte Fassbaender incomparable as the predatory Countess Geschwitz, spontaneously expressive for Tate. Otherwise Graham Clark is a fine match for Robert Tear in various tenor roles, and Peter Straka is a more idiomatic Alwa than the clear-toned Kenneth Riegel for Boulez.

(i) Lulu; (ii) Wozzeck.
(M) ** DG 435 705-2 (3) [id.]. (i) Schönberger Sängerknaben German Op. Ch.; German Opera O, Berlin, Boehm.
(i) Lulu (Evelyn Lear), Doctor Schön (Dietrich Fischer-Dieskau), Alwa (Donald Grobe), Countess Geschwitz (Patricia Johnson).
(ii) Wozzeck (Dietrich Fischer-Dieskau), Marie (Evelyn Lear), Drum Major (Helmut Melchert), Andres (Fritz Wunderlich), Captain (Gerhard Stolze), Doctor (Karl Christian Kohn), Margret (Alice Oelke).

With Evelyn Lear and Fischer-Dieskau common to both operas, it was a good idea to pair Boehm's recordings of *Lulu* and *Wozzeck* for CD reissue. In both scores Boehm reveals more beauties in the writing than one would have thought possible. Berg himself is quoted as saying that Lulu must be regarded as a female counterpart of Don Juan; if that is so, Boehm's leaning away from harshness is justified. Evelyn Lear – not a singer one would have expected to be cast in the role – matches Boehm in his approach, and the keen intelligence of Fischer-Dieskau as Dr Schön confirms this as a performance without hysteria. If it fails to convey Berg's full message, it is in every way a worthy counterpart to Boehm's companion reading of *Wozzeck*.

Thanks largely to the timbre of Fischer-Dieskau's voice and to the intensity of projection in his words, one can hardly picture Wozzeck here as in any way moronic. His situation is much closer to conventional tragedy than one imagines Berg (or, for that matter, Büchner, original creator of the character) ever conceived. The result may be unconventional, inauthentic even, but it certainly makes one listen to the opera afresh, and on record there is a case for a performance which brings out clarity, precision and beauty, even in a work like this. Evelyn Lear makes a fairly convincing, though hardly ideal, Marie, and generally the supporting cast is vocally assured. But the lack of any feeling of vibrant drama means that a dimension is missing, in spite of the atmospheric DG sound.

Wozzeck (complete).

*** Decca Dig. 417 348-2 (2) [id.]. VPO, Dohnányi – SCHOENBERG: *Erwartung.* *******
  Wozzeck (Eberhard Waechter), Marie (Anja Silja), Drum Major (Hermann Winkler), Andres (Horst Laubenthal), Captain (Heinz Zednik), Doctor (Alexander Malta), Margret (Gertrud Jahn).

**(*) DG 423 587-2 (2) [id.]. V. State Op. Ch., VPO, Abbado.
  Wozzeck (Franz Grundheber), Marie (Hildegard Behrens), Drum Major (Walter Raffeiner), Andres (Philip Langridge), Captain (Heinz Zednik), Doctor (Aage Haugland), Margret (Anna Gonda).

(M) ****(*)** Sony M2K 79251 (2) [M2K 30852]. Paris Op. Ch. & O, Boulez.
  Wozzeck (Walter Berry), Marie (Isabel Strauss), Drum Major (Fritz Uhl), Andres (Richard Van Vrooman), Captain (Albert Weikenmeier), Doctor (Karl Dönch), Margret (Ingeborg Lasser).

Dohnányi, with refined textures and superb playing from the Vienna Philharmonic, presents an account of *Wozzeck* that not only is more accurate than any other on record but also is more beautiful, even though the opera's narrative line is far from beautiful. Wozzeck is a soldier. Marie, who has borne his child, is unfaithful to him with the regiment's drum-major and, although she is remorseful, Wozzeck's jealousy engulfs him, his vivid imagination running riot so that his thoughts become obsessed with blood – drawing a parallel with Lady Macbeth.

He unsuccessfully attacks the drum-major, who has been boasting about the seduction of Marie. Finally Wozzeck cuts Marie's throat, then throws the knife away, and his mental world disintegrates as he tries to escape from his constant visions of blood and dives into the water, which closes over his head. His orphaned child is playing in the street, unaware of the tragedy and the passions which have tortured the lives of his parents.

Dohnányi's overall direction of the opera may lack some of the bite of Pierre Boulez's CBS version, but with superb digital sound the Decca set stands as first choice. Unfortunately, the beauty of the performance does not extend to Eberhard Waechter's vocal quality in the name-part, but he gives a thoughtful and sensitive performance. The edge of Anja Silja's voice and her natural vibrancy of character make her a memorable Marie, first cousin to Lulu. An excellent supporting cast too. The sense of presence and clarity of the spectacular digital sound is all the more apparent in the excellent CD transfer. It is worth noting that, unlike its CD rivals, it comes with a substantial coupling in Schoenberg's monodrama, *Erwartung*, also with Silja.

The Abbado version, recorded live in the opera house, is very compelling in its presentation of the drama, given extra thrust through the tensions of live performance. However, there are drawbacks, too. Not only do you get all the bangs, shuffling and clonkings inevitable on stage; the voices are also put at a serious disadvantage, consistently set behind the orchestra, with the instrumental sound putting a gauze between listener and singers. The ensemble is amazingly precise for a live performance, and the cast is a good one, headed by a clear-toned if lightweight Wozzeck in Franz Grundheber. Hildegard Behrens sings affectingly as Marie, but the microphones exaggerate the flutter in her voice and she produces unpleasantly curdled tones, even in the scene where she sings a lullaby to her child. There is a lack of simplicity too: this Marie is sophisticated rather than elemental. For some this will be the best choice, but the extra vividness and clarity of sound, as well as the extra bite and precision of the performance in the Decca Dohnányi set, make it preferable.

Walter Berry's view of the hero's character includes a strong element of brutishness, and Boulez's uncompromising, thrustful view of the whole score matches this conception; he is less concerned with pure atmosphere than with emotional drive, and undoubtedly he provides a powerful experience. One is made to suffer. The forward recording gives strong projection on CD, but the sound is brightly lit to the point of harshness.

Wozzeck (excerpts).

(M) ****(*)** Mercury Dig. 434 325-2 [id.]. Marie (Helga Pilarczyk), LSO, Dorati – BARTÓK: *Bluebeard's Castle* (complete). ****(*)**

These three concert-excerpts from *Wozzeck* come as a very generous fill-up to Dorati's 1962 recording of Bartók's *Bluebeard's Castle*. The LSO play brilliantly, with the highly analytical Mercury recording bringing out both the power and the delicate poetry, even though pianissimos tend to be overamplified. The snag is the abrasive, at times under-the-note singing of Helga Pilarczyk in the brief vocal passages.

Bergman, Erik (born 1911)

The Singing Tree.
*** Ondine Dig. ODE 794-2D (2) [id.]. Dominante Ch., Tapiola Chamber Ch., Finnish Nat. Op.
O, Ulf Söderblom.
  King (Peter Lindroos), Witch (Charlotte Hellekant), Princess (Kaisa Hannula), Prince Hatt
  (Petteri Salomaa), Fool (Sauli Tiilikainen), Fruit Seller (Martti Wallén), Princess I (Anna-
  Lisa Jakobsson), Princess II (Marianne Harju).

Erik Bergman is one of Finland's most respected composers. He first came to wider notice
with his *Aubade* for orchestra (1958) with its images of dawn mists over the Bosphorus. His
incursions into exotic music and dodecaphony have enriched his vocabulary; and his music
always seems to conjure up mysterious sound worlds. *The Singing Tree* (*Det sjungande trädet*),
which occupied him from 1986 to 1988, is a setting of a libretto by Bo Carpelan, the leading
Swedish-speaking Finnish poet. The opera comprises 22 different scenes, spread over two Acts
with prologue, an intermezzo and an epilogue.
  It is a fairy-tale which explores the familiar theme of the princess who may not look at her
husband's face, albeit in an unfamiliar way. As the fable unfolds, we hear of Prince Hatt's
attempts to free himself from the power of his mother, a witch. The King of Light asks his three
daughters what he should bring them as gifts on his return; the youngest asks for the branch of a
singing tree which she has heard in a dream. As the king returns through the forest, he passes the
singing tree and is made to promise that the prince shall marry the first maiden he meets on his
return to the castle.
  The world of sorcery is vividly evoked and the witch almost bears a resemblance to a Disney
character. The music encompasses the usual range of musical resource and technical devices that
Bergman has made so much his own. There is a strong sense of atmosphere, though musically
the work is inclined to be static. For all the sophistication of Bergman's aural imagination, one
misses a certain dramatic cut-and-thrust and sense of momentum. The performance under Ulf
Söderblom is in every respect authoritative and compelling, and the recording is marvellously
detailed and vivid.

Berlin, Irving (1888–1989)

Annie get your gun (musical).
⊛ *** EMI Dig. CDC7 54206-2 [id.]; *EL 754206-4.* Amb. Ch., L. Sinf., McGlinn.
  Annie (Kim Criswell), Frank Butler (Thomas Hampson), Tommy Keeler (Jason Graae),
  Winnie Tate (Rebecca Luker), Charlie Davenport (David Garrison), Buffalo Bill (David
  Healy), Chief Sitting Bull (Alfred Marks).
(M) *** EMI ZDM7 64765-2 [id.]. Ch. & O, Louis Adrian.
  Annie Oakley (Mary Martin), Frank Butler (John Raitt).

This is one of the most delectable of all show records. John McGlinn follows up the pattern of
his best-selling set of Jerome Kern's *Show Boat* with another performance that is at once
scholarly and pulsating with life. Not only is the singing strong, characterful and idiomatic, the
whole performance – not least from the players of the London Sinfonietta – is full of fun,
conveying the exuberance of a score that contains more 'standards' among its numbers than
almost any other Broadway show. *Doin' what comes natur'lly, The girl that I marry, You can't
get a man with a gun, There's no business like show business* and *They say it's wonderful* are five
that appear consecutively early in Act I, with such unforgettable numbers as *Anything you can do*
– hilariously done by Kim Criswell and Thomas Hampson – still to come.
  Though the full complement of numbers is included on the single disc, McGlinn also manages
to include in an appendix the brilliant duet – added to the score at the 1966 production, twenty
years after the original show – *An old-fashioned wedding*, with its G & S-style superimposition of
lyrical ballad and point number (though *You're just in love* from *Call Me Madam* was the model
for this song).
  Kim Criswell as Annie with her electric personality and bitingly bright voice here confirms
herself as the natural successor to Ethel Merman, the original Annie Oakley, characterizing
strongly while pitching precisely. Equally remarkably, Thomas Hampson makes an ideal hero,
an opera-singer with an exceptionally rich and firm baritone who gets inside the idiom naturally.

First-rate, full-bodied sound. The disc comes with a booklet containing copious documentation and the full lyrics.

Even with the outstanding new EMI digital version around, the combination of Mary Martin and John Raitt is not upstaged. The reissue – which includes the wonderful string of hits characteristic of Irving Berlin's finest score – comes from a record made in conjunction with an NBC TV production of 1957. There is only one Mary Martin, and she was at her peak when this show was recorded. No one sings numbers like *Doin' what comes natur'lly, You can't get a man with a gun* and *I got the sun in the morning* quite as she does, while the duets with John Raitt, *They says it's wonderful* and *Anything you can do*, are just as memorable. *There's no business like show business* rounds off the selection exuberantly. This amazingly well-recorded CD concentrates entirely on the Martin/Raitt partnership, and it becomes an essential supplement to John McGlinn's remarkably successful re-creation of the whole score. There are only 38½ minutes here – but what minutes!

Berlioz, Hector (1803–69)

Béatrice et Bénédict (complete).
*** Ph. 416 952-2 (2). Alldis Ch., LSO, C. Davis.
  Béatrice (Janet Baker), Bénédict (Robert Tear), Héro (Christiane Eda-Pierre), Ursule (Helen Watts), Claudio (Thomas Allen), Somarone (Jules Bastin), Don Pedro (Robert Lloyd), Léonato (Richard Van Allan).
*** Erato/Warner Dig. 2292 45773-2 (2) [id.]. Lyon Opera Ch. & O, John Nelson.
  Béatrice (Susan Graham), Bénédict (Jean-Luc Viala), Héro (Sylvia McNair), Ursule (Catherine Robbin), Claudio (Gilles Cachemaille), Somarone (Gabriel Bacquier), Don Pedro (Vincent Le Texier), Léonato (Philippe Magnant).

Well produced for records, with a smattering of French dialogue between numbers, *Béatrice et Bénédict* in Davis's Philips version reveals itself as less an opera than a dramatic symphony, one of the important Berlioz works (like *Romeo and Juliet*) which refuse to fit into a conventional category. The plot is loosely based on Shakespeare's *Much Ado About Nothing* but omits the intrigue of some of the subsidiary characters and comedy triumphs, with the action moving forward in spoken dialogue.

The army of Moors have been driven from Messina and the people rejoice in their brave army and its general. The capricious and spirited heroine first feigns indifference to the heroic Bénédict, who in turn is taunted by his companions – he is, after all, a confirmed bachelor. Tempestuous argument between the couple takes place but gradually it becomes evident that they love each other truly, and the opera concludes as the marriage contract is signed.

The score presents not just witty and brilliant music for the hero and heroine (Robert Tear and Dame Janet Baker at their most pointed) but sensuously beautiful passages such as the duet for Héro and Ursule at the end of Act I and the trio they later share with Béatrice, both incidental to the drama but very important for the musical structure. First-rate solo and choral singing, brilliant playing, while the CD transfer – like the others in Davis's Berlioz series – brings out the exceptionally high quality of the Philips engineering, with sound refined and clear in texture, bright and fresh, even if minimal hiss betrays an analogue source.

The Lyon Opera version conducted by John Nelson makes an excellent alternative to the vintage Colin Davis recording. In spacious, modern, digital sound it offers substantially more of the French dialogue, well spoken by actors but more drily recorded than the musical numbers. Nelson's reading is light and crisp but, at generally faster speeds, sparkles rather less than Davis's. The radiant ensembles for women's voices – the *Duo Nocturne* for Héro and Ursule which ends Act I and the Act II Trio with Béatrice in addition – are taken more flowingly here but, with well-matched voices, are comparably beautiful. Susan Graham is a characterful Béatrice, lighter in the big aria than Janet Baker for Davis but aptly younger-sounding. Jean-Luc Viala is a comparably light Bénédict, pointing the fun in his big aria, and Sylvia McNair and Catherine Robbin are superb as Héro and Ursule.

La damnation de Faust, Op. 24.
*** Ph. 416 395-2 (2) [id.]. Josephine Veasey, Nicolai Gedda, Jules Bastin, Amb. S., Wandsworth School Boys' Ch., London Symphony Ch., LSO, C. Davis.
*** Decca Dig. 414 680-2 (2) [id.]. Kenneth Riegel, Frederica Von Stade, José Van Dam, Malcolm King, Chicago Ch. & SO, Solti.

**(*) Ph. Dig. 416 199-2 (2) [id.]. Michael Myers, Jean-Philippe Lafont, Anne Sofie Von Otter, René Schirrer, Edinburgh Festival Ch., Lyon Opera O, Gardiner.

(M) **(*) DG 423 907-2 (2) [id.]. Edith Mathis, Stuart Burrows, Donald McIntyre, Thomas Paul, Tanglewood Festival Ch., Boston Boys' Ch. & Boston SO, Ozawa.

(M) (***) BMG/RCA mono GD 87940 (2) [7940-2-RG]. (i) David Poleri, Suzanne Danco, Martial Singher, Donald Gramm, Harvard Glee Club, SO, Munch (with DEBUSSY: *La damoiselle élue* with Victoria De los Angeles, Carol Smith, Radcliffe Choral Soc. (**)).

La damnation de Faust: highlights.
**(*) Decca Dig. 410 181-2 [id.] (from above recording; cond. Solti).

Berlioz's setting of the Faust legend is certainly not an opera, but it is as worthy of inclusion in an operatic survey as are Handel's biblical oratorios. Stage action would add little to either, but the music carries and illustrates the narrative with the same dramatic force as in a piece intended for the theatre. The storyline, not surprisingly, is similar to that for Gounod's opera; taking place in sixteenth-century Hungary, however, it opens with a pastoral scene with peasants and soldiers which gives Berlioz the opportunity for introducing the *Rákóczy march*.

Then we move to Germany where Faust, with nothing left to live for, sits in his study and attempts to swallow poison. Mephistopheles appears; he offers great worldly enticements and the two set off to participate in these earthly pleasures, beginning in a beer cellar in Leipzig. Faust is treated to a vision of Marguerite in a dream; they meet and share a mutual declaration of love, but Mephistopheles joins them and after a trio insists that Faust depart.

Marguerite's feelings are ecstatic, and she is devastated when Faust deserts her and she faints, overcome by her despair. Faust then enters a mountain glen, to be overwhelmed by the elements and a vision of Hell, while Marguerite, abandoned and alone, is forgiven her sin and is welcomed by angels into Heaven.

Both Gedda as Faust and Bastin as Mephistopheles are impressive in the 1974 Philips set. The fresh, clear response of the chorus and orchestra, tenderly expressive in the quieter passages, goes with a recording perspective that is outstandingly natural and realistic. The subtlety and fantasy of Davis's reading are finely matched. The only snag is the tape-hiss, but that is easily ignored.

Solti's performance, searingly dramatic, is given stunning digital sound to make the *Ride to Hell* supremely exciting. But with Von Stade singing tenderly, this is a warmly expressive performance too; and the *Hungarian march* has rarely had such sparkle and swagger. The extra brightness matches the extrovert quality of the performance, less subtle than Davis's.

Gardiner's version was recorded live by Radio France at the Berlioz Festival in Lyon in September 1987; though this means that sound-balances are not always ideal, there is a natural sense of presence to bring out the vitality and dramatic thrust of the performance. Gardiner persuasively draws on the spark of humour in this work, lifting rhythms, finding the sparkle in Berlioz's inspiration more readily than his current rivals. His solo team is a strong one: Michael Myers as Faust gives a warm, relaxed performance, producing beautiful tenor tone, a believable, vulnerable hero; Anne Sofie Von Otter makes an appealingly tender Marguerite, but Jean-Philippe Lafont is a lightweight – if lively – Mephistopheles, not firm or dark enough. The singing of the Edinburgh Festival Chorus adds to the bite of the drama, even though they are balanced a little too distantly.

Ozawa's performance provides an admirable mid-priced alternative, in a much more moulded style. The relative softness of focus is underlined by the reverberant Boston acoustics; with superb playing and generally fine singing, however, the results are seductively enjoyable. The digital remastering has improved definition without losing the effect of the hall ambience.

In the mid-1950s Charles Munch made a series of Berlioz recordings which at the time were revelatory and readily stand revival today. His version of the *Damnation of Faust* is a fine example, taken faster and more vigorously than has since become the custom, with lusty singing from the chorus of Harvard alumni. Suzanne Danco is outstanding among the soloists, sounding warmly sympathetic – even though Munch presses her with his fast speeds, and the recording allows no pianissimo. The others have fine voices but rarely sound idiomatic. The mono recording is dry and boxy but, with sharp focus, fully conveys the dramatic punch of Munch in Berlioz. At mid-price the two discs bring a generous coupling in the rare recording of Debussy's *La demoiselle élue* with Victoria de los Angeles, made at the same period.

Roméo et Juliette, Op. 17.
(M) *** DG 437 244-2 (2) [id.]. Yvonne Minton, Francisco Araiza, Jules Bastin, Ch. & O de Paris, Barenboim – FRANCK: *Chasseur maudit* etc. ***
Withdrawn: *** DG 423 068-2 (2) [id.]. Júlia Hamari, Jean Dupouy, José Van Dam, New England Conservatory Ch., Boston SO, Ozawa (with TCHAIKOVSKY: *Romeo and Juliet* ***).
**(*) Ph. 416 962-2 (2) [id.]. Patricia Kern, Robert Tear, John Shirley-Quirk, Alldis Ch., London Symphony Ch., LSO, C. Davis.
Withdrawn: ** EMI Dig. CDC7 47437-8 (2) [Ang. CDCB 47437]. Jessye Norman, John Aler, Simon Estes, Westminster Ch., Phd. O, Muti.

(i) *Roméo et Juliette, Op. 17. Symphonie funèbre et triomphale, Op. 15.*
*** Decca 417 302-2 (2) [id.]. (i) Florence Quivar, Alberto Cupido, Tom Krause, Tudor Singers, Montreal Ch. & SO, Dutoit.

Roméo et Juliette, Op. 17; Les nuits d'été.
**(*) DG Dig. 427 665-2 (2) [id.]. Anne Sofie Von Otter, Philip Langridge, James Morris, Berlin RIAS Chamber Ch., Ernest Senff Ch., BPO, Levine.

Dutoit's is a masterly, heart-warming reading of Berlioz's curious mixture of symphony, cantata and opera, to follow the narrative line of Shakespeare's tragedy. It is superbly recorded in richly atmospheric sound. Dutoit consistently brings out the romantic, lyrical warmth of the work – not least in the great orchestral love-scene – while giving Berlioz's instrumentation all the refinement and subtlety it needs. When that is coupled with brilliant choral singing, incisive and atmospheric, it is an unassailable mixture. Though the mezzo, Florence Quivar, is less steady than she should be, the other soloists are first rate, Alberto Cupido witty in his scherzetto, Tom Krause aptly firm and resonant. A triumphantly successful account of the epic ceremonial, *Symphonie funèbre et triomphale*, makes a generous coupling. Here Dutoit is at his most uninhibited, brilliantly skirting the very edge of vulgarity in this outgoing ceremonial piece.

Barenboim's 1980 DG set of *Roméo et Juliette* is a clear first recommendation in the budget range, particularly in view of its generous and attractive Franck couplings. Moreover it compares quite favourably with Dutoit's masterly, heart-warming Decca digital set. Barenboim directs a warmly romantic reading of Berlioz's great dramatic symphony. Adopting his Furtwänglerian mantle, he takes a very flexible view of the great set-pieces such as the Love scene, which here sounds very Wagnerian in a *Tristan*-like way. Barenboim's magnetic purposefulness hold the work together impressively so that any minor lapses in the playing of the Paris orchestra (as, for instance, in the *Queen Mab Scherzo*, which misses something in mercurial lightness) are not too important when the soloists are first rate and the choral singing is also impressive. The analogue sound is full and atmospheric and very well transferred to CD.

If not as strongly characterized as Dutoit's Decca performance, Ozawa's reading is convincingly dramatic. His spontaneity helps to unify the early fragmentary passages; the party music has swagger and the great love-scene – source of inspiration for Wagner in *Tristan* – is concentratedly built over the longest span, with a tempo not too expansive. With a fine team of soloists, this is a warmer, less severe reading than Davis's. The 1976 recording has been remastered successfully for CD; the sound is more refined in detail, yet the ambient atmosphere remains and, though the chorus is not sharply focused, the Boston acoustics are pleasingly warm. The coupling of Tchaikovsky's *Romeo and Juliet* is appropriate enough: a first-class performance, even if it will involve most collectors in duplication.

Levine gives a powerful performance of Berlioz's great dramatic setting, marked by playing of exceptional polish and precision from the Berlin Philharmonic, and with Anne Sofie von Otter outstanding alongside two other very positive soloists. Von Otter adds to the attractions of the set in the generous fill-up, *Les nuits d'été*, again fresh and radiant, underlining the dramatic contrasts between the songs. Levine is nevertheless rather heavy-handed in his treatment of Berlioz. Compare him in the music for the Capulets' party with such an outstanding rival as Dutoit on Decca and, for all the precision and power, he has less feeling of jollity.

There is also less sparkle in the *Queen Mab Scherzo*, for all the high brilliance of the playing, while the night music of the love scene emerges in the full brightness of day. Yet the very weight of Levine's reading, his electricity, still puts this verion high on the list. The recording, made in the Jesus-Christus Kirche in Berlin, is very full and weighty, while catching pianissimo strings most delicately, even if it falls short of the Decca in transparency.

Sir Colin Davis – it hardly needs saying – has a rare sympathy with this score and secures playing of great vitality and atmosphere from the LSO. His soloists are first rate too, and so is the chorus. The 1968 recording still sounds excellent: it is natural in tone and balance, and the CDs bring added presence. But with no coupling this is less competitive, especially compared with Dutoit.

Despite the starry line-up of soloists, Muti's version is disappointing. This is partly a question of recording, relatively thick and ill-focused, but also of interpretation, less idiomatic and fanciful than Dutoit's, no matter how brilliant the Philadelphia playing. It is good to hear Jessye Norman in the lovely *Strophes*, even if the weight of voice and personality are not quite apt for that sequence.

Les Troyens, Parts 1 & 2 (complete).
Ⓢ *** Ph. 416 432-2 (4) [id.]. Wandsworth School Boys' Ch., ROHCG Ch. & O, C. Davis.
    Dido (Josephine Veasey), Aeneas (Jon Vickers), Cassandra (Berit Lindholm), Choroebus / Ghost (Peter Glossop), Anna (Heather Begg), Narbal (Roger Soyer), Pantheus (Anthony Raffell), Ascanius (Anne Howells), Iopas (Ian Partridge).

The complete recording of Berlioz's great epic opera was an achievement to outshine all other centenary offerings by this composer, indeed to outshine almost all other recording projects whatever. Davis had long preparation for the task, both in his concert performances and in his direction of the Covent Garden production on which this recording is firmly based. The result is that, even more than in most of his other Berlioz recordings, he conveys the high dramatic tension of the music.

The opening scene of *Les Troyens* depicts the abandoned Greek camp in front of Troy, and a great curiosity, a huge wooden horse that intrigues the population. Only Cassandra predicts the fall of Troy, but Choroebus, her lover, thinks her deranged and cannot believe her premonition which will bring his death. Finally, after much speculation, the great horse is dragged inside the city walls. Cassandra begs that it be destroyed, but no one heeds her warnings. In the middle of the night the horse opens, to disgorge the well-armed Greek soldiers, and Troy falls.

Meanwhile Aeneas in his camp has heard about the destruction of Troy and the death of Priam, and he escapes. Back in Troy, her lover dead, Cassandra fears slavery. She urges the women to follow her example and commit suicide; she dies and all the women stab themselves.

The story moves to Carthage. The Trojan war is over. There, Queen Dido urges the people to build a magnificent city. Their loyalty towards her is affirmed. But the city is threatened by a barbarian troop of Numidians whose king seeks to marry her against her will. Dido accepts the help of Aeneas, whose ships have sought shelter in the port, to defend Carthage. She falls in love with him and he with her, but she is heartbroken when, sensing his destiny, he finally departs for Italy. She dies by the sword, mounting a funeral pyre but with a vision that Rome would finally triumph.

Throughout this long and apparently disjointed score Davis compels the listener to concentrate, to appreciate its epic logic. His tempi are generally faster than in the theatre, and the result is exhilarating with no hint of rush. Only in the great love scene of *O nuit d'ivresse* does one miss the more passionate hand of a Beecham. It is interesting too to find Davis pursuing his direct, dramatic line even in Dido's death scene at the end. Veasey on any count, even next to Dame Janet Baker, makes a splendid Dido, single-minded rather than seductive, singing always with fine heroic strength.

Of the rest, Berit Lindholm as Cassandra, in the first half of the opera, is the only soloist who falls short – the voice is not quite steady – but otherwise one cannot imagine a more effective cast, with Vickers as a ringing Aeneas. The Covent Garden Chorus and Orchestra excel themselves in virtuoso singing and playing, while CD brings out the superb quality of sound all the more vividly, and the new format brings even more advantages than usual. Quite apart from the ease with which one can index any section of this epic structure, the Acts are arranged on the four discs with no break within any Act. Acts II and III come together on the second disc, with the other Acts on a disc apiece.

Bernstein, Leonard (1918–90)

THEATRE MUSIC

Candide (musical: original Broadway production): *Overture and excerpts.*
*** Sony SK 48017 [id.]. Candide (Robert Rounseville) Cunegonde (Barbara Cook), Pangloss (Max Adrian) and original New York cast, Krachmalnick.

Bernstein's *Candide* was a Broadway flop on its first appearance in 1956: in spite of an outstanding cast and a highly praised production by Tyrone Guthrie, it ran for only 73 performances. This exhilarating record encapsulates the original production and it has all the freshness of discovery inherent in a first recording, plus all the zing of the American musical theatre. The Rossini-styled *Glitter and be gay* is given a scintillating coloratura performance here by Barbara Cook, while Max Adrian is hardly less memorable, with the Gilbert and Sullivan influences delightfully pointed. Brilliantly lively, forward sound.

Candide (revised 1982 version).
*** New World Dig. NWCD 340/1 [id.]. NY City Op. Ch. & O, Mauceri.
   Candide (David Eisler), Cunegonde (Erie Mills), Pangloss etc. (John Langston), Maximilian (Scott Reeve), Paquette (Maris Clement), Old Lady (Joyce Castle).

John Mauceri in this issue from New World Records conducts what is described as the 'Opera House Version 1982' of Bernstein's musical based on Voltaire. For that, Mauceri himself edited together a text incorporating as much as possible of the material that had been written for the piece at its various revivals from the first production in 1956 onwards. Though this set has been superseded by Bernstein's own recording, based on Mauceri's own later version with Scottish Opera, the result on record makes a splendid, fizzing entertainment, held together by the electricity of the conductor's direction and the singing of a cast that nicely bridges the demands of opera and musical. Some of the numbers quoted in the brilliant overture, like *The best of all possible worlds* and *Oh, happy we*, are a particular delight. The recording is aptly bright and clear, with voices placed in firm focus well in front of the orchestra.

Candide (Scottish Opera production): highlights.
** That's Entertainment Dig. CDTER 1156; *ZCTER 1156* [id.]. Nickolas Grace, Mark Beudert, Marilyn Hill Smith, Bonaventura Bottone, Ann Howard, Mark Tinkler, Scottish Op. Ch. & O, Justin Brown.

Based on the imaginative Scottish Opera production, the TER disc of highlights from *Candide* was recorded well before the stage performances – not with John Mauceri conducting (the prime mover in the whole project, who had already done the 'opera-house' version on the New World label) but with his assistant, Justin Brown. Almost inevitably that made for less electric results, though it is a strong and characterful cast. Rather disappointingly, the selection of items is relatively conventional, not drawing on the extra material revived in this production. The recording, set in a rather dry acoustic, is apt for most of the music, if a little constricting in the ensembles.

Candide (final, revised version).
❀ *** DG Dig. 429 734-2; *429 734-4* (2) [id.]. London Symphony Ch., LSO, composer.
   Candide (Jerry Hadley), Cunegonde (June Anderson), Pangloss / Martin (Adolph Green), Old Lady (Christa Ludwig), Governor / Vanderdendur / Ragotski (Nicolai Gedda), Paquette (Della Jones), Maximilian / Captain / Jesuit Father (Kurt Ollmann).

John Mauceri, dissatisfied with the results of his 1982 score of *Candide*, undertook yet a further revision in the mid-1980s, this time with Bernstein's collaboration. The original order of the music was restored, as were several musical numbers not heard since the original production. Perhaps most importantly, the spirit of the original was recaptured, with the survival of hero and heroine and their feelings towards each other through all the incredible vicissitudes of Dr Pangloss's 'best of all possible worlds'.

Two of the finest songs are placed where the composer wanted them and *Candide's lament* (so movingly sung by Jerry Hadley) is again heard near the beginning of the show. This version was first performed by Scottish Opera in 1988, and it forms the basis for the new recording. Bernstein saw his work – written in the wake of McCarthyism during the chilliest days of the Cold War when the American government even withdrew the composer's own passport – as essentially serious. Its humour, satirically reflecting Voltaire's rubbishing of enforced establishment values, at one point draws a ready parallel between the Spanish Inquisition and Bernstein's own experience during America's darkest political era.

The result is a triumph, both in the studio recording which Bernstein made immediately after the concert performances and in the video recording of the actual concert at the Barbican. It confirms *Candide* as a classic, bringing out not just the vigour, the wit and the tunefulness of the piece more than ever before, but an extra emotional intensity, something beyond the cynical Voltaire original.

Bernstein was a great devotee of Gilbert and Sullivan, and here he not only revels in a comparable topsy-turvy world, as in such hilarious ensembles as *What a day, what a day for an auto da fé!* but also draws out an underlying depth of feeling, just as Sullivan did. So the expansion of the title-role gives Candide himself a series of meditations that strike a deeper note, matching the tender fulfilment of the final ensemble when Candide and Cunegonde are united, *Make our garden grow*. There Bernstein grabs our hearts as he always loved to do, but with a finesse he did not always achieve.

There is no weak link in the cast. Jerry Hadley is touchingly characterful as Candide, producing heady tone, and June Anderson as Cunegonde is not only brilliant in coloratura but warmly dramatic too, making *Glitter and be gay* into much more than a tinkly showpiece. The character roles are also brilliantly cast. It was an inspired choice to have Christa Ludwig as the Old Woman, stopping the show with *I am easily assimilated*, and equally original to choose Adolph Green, lyric writer for Broadway musicals as well as cabaret performer, for the dual role of Dr Pangloss and Martin, the equivalent of the Grossmith roles in G & S. Green is helped out on his falsetto top notes for the very Sullivan-like *Dear boy*, first by his baritone colleague, Kurt Ollman, singing Maximilian, and finally by the chorus, a delicious *tour de force*. Nicolai Gedda also proves a winner in his series of cameo roles, and the full, incisive singing of the London Symphony Chorus adds to the weight of the performance without inflation.

What is missing in the CD set is the witty narration prepared by John Wells and spoken by Adolph Green and Kurt Ollman in the Barbican performance. As included on the video of the live concert (VHS DG 072 423-3; Laser disc DG 072 423-1), those links leaven the entertainment delightfully, where reading them from the booklet is not the same, particularly when the plot lurches so improbably from one situation to the next, with characters dying and then often getting resurrected. Even those with the CD should investigate the video version, which also includes Bernstein's own moving speeches of introduction before each Act. And seeing Christa Ludwig as the Old Lady provocatively clicking her castanets as she sings *I am easily assimilated* adds further delight.

Candide (opera/musical): highlights.
*** DG Dig. 435 487-2; *435 487-4* [id.] (from above set; cond. composer).

Those who don't wish to purchase the complete set (perhaps because they already have the video of the Barbican live performance) may be glad to have this 64-minute CD of highlights offering most of the key numbers, including the *Overture*, *Candide's Meditation* and *Lament*, *Auto-da-fé*, *Glitter and be gay*, *I am easily assimilated* and the finale, *Make our garden grow*.

A Quiet Place (complete).
*** DG Dig. 419 761-2 (2) [id.]. Vocal Ens., Austrian RSO, composer.
  Dinah (Wendy White), Old Sam (Chester Ludgin), Dede (Beverly Morgan), Junior (John Brandstetter), François (Peter Kazaras).

Soon after writing his one-Act opera, *Trouble in Tahiti*, in 1951, Leonard Bernstein started thinking about the characters involved – a suburban American couple – and wondering how they might have developed. Thirty years later he finally got around to following up their story in a full-scale opera. That is the concept behind *A Quiet Place*, which in flashbacks in Act II incorporates the 1951 score, with its popular style set in relief against the more serious idiom adopted for the main body of the opera. The opening Act is sharply conceived, set in a funeral parlour. The wife from *Trouble in Tahiti* (its exotic title taken from a film) has just died in a car crash, and for the first time in years the family is reunited, along with an assortment of relatives and friends, all sharply characterized.

Sadly, those characters never reappear; the central figures of the family (father, daughter, gay son and lover who has been passed on to the daughter in a *ménage à trois*) quickly seem to have come not from a grand opera but from a soap opera. Bernstein's score is full of thoughtful and warmly expressive music, but nothing quite matches the sharp, tongue-in-cheek, jazz-influenced invention of *Trouble in Tahiti*. It does not help that all three Acts end reflectively on a dying fall. Admirers of Bernstein will find much to interest them in the recording, which was made at the time of the first performance of the definitive version in Vienna, with an excellent cast of American singers, and with the Austrian Radio Orchestra responding splendidly on its first visit to the Vienna State Opera. With each CD containing over 74 minutes of music, a long work is neatly contained on two discs merely. Considering the problems of live recording of opera, the sound is excellent, remarkably well balanced.

West Side Story: complete recording; *On the Waterfront* (Symphonic suite).
ⓑ *** DG Dig. 415 253-2 (2) [id.]. Ch. and O, composer.

Maria (Kiri Te Kanawa), Tony (José Carreras), Anita (Tatiana Troyanos), Riff (Kurt Ollmann), Off-stage voice (Marilyn Horne).

Bernstein's recording of the complete score of his most popular work – the first time he had ever conducted the complete musical himself – takes a frankly operatic approach in its casting, but the result is highly successful, for the great vocal melodies are worthy of voices of the highest calibre. Dame Kiri Te Kanawa may not be a soprano who would ever be cast as Maria on stage, but even in the kittenish number, *I feel pretty*, the magnificence of the voice adds a dimension, when the girlishly coy lines of each stanza, sparklingly done, explode with vitality for the pay-off phrase.

José Carreras, the only Spanish-speaking member of the cast, but ironically the one in the story who has to be a real American guy, may apparently be miscast, but the beauty of such songs as *Maria* or *Tonight*, or even a sharp number like *Something's coming*, with floated pianissimos and subtly graded crescendos, has one admiring the score the more. Tatiana Troyanos, herself brought up on the West Side, spans the stylistic dichotomy to perfection in a superb portrayal of Anita, switching readily from full operatic beauty to a New York snarl and back, and Kurt Ollman as Riff equally finds a nice balance between the styles of opera and the musical.

The clever production makes the best of both musical worlds, with Bernstein's son and daughter speaking the dialogue most affectingly. If patently more mature voices take over when the music begins, one readily adjusts when the singing itself so gloriously captures the spirit of the piece. Bernstein conducts a superb instrumental group of musicians 'from on and off Broadway', and they are recorded with a bite and immediacy that is captivating, whether in the warm, sentimental songs or, above all, in the fizzing syncopated numbers, sounding even more original when played and balanced as precisely as here.

On CD, the power of the music is greatly enhanced by the spectacularly wide dynamic range of the recording. With a relatively dry acoustic keeping the sound-picture within an apt scale but without losing bloom, the two humorous ensembles (*America* for the girls and *Gee, Officer Krupke* for the boys) are given tremendous vitality and projection, with the chorus (and the exuberant orchestral percussion) adding colour most winningly. The two-disc set includes, besides the musical, the vivid *Symphonic suite*, which was arranged from Bernstein's film music for the Marlon Brando film, *On the Waterfront*, written about the same period.

West Side Story (film soundtrack recording).
**(*) Sony SK 48211 [id.]. Ch. & O, Johnny Green.

Maria (Natalie Wood – sung by Marni Nixon), Tony (Richard Beymer – sung by Jim Bryant), Riff (Russ Tamblyn), Anita (Rita Moreno – sung by Betty Wand), Bernardo (George Chakaris).

Few musicals have been transferred to the screen with more success than *West Side Story* and there are some who feel that, even though the principals' voices are ghosted, the soundtrack recording is preferable to Bernstein's own version using opera stars. The film was splendidly cast and the 'ghosts' were admirably chosen. In the romantic scenes, *Tonight* and *One hand, one heart*, the changes from sung to spoken words are completely convincing and the tragic (mostly spoken) final scene – here included on record for the first time – is very moving. Russ Tamblyn, who sings his own songs, is first class and Marni Nixon and Jim Bryant as the pair of lovers sing touchingly and with youthful freshness. The performance is vibrantly conducted by Johnny Green, and it is a pity that the CD transfer is so 'toppy' and brings a degree of edge both to voices and to the brilliant orchestral playing. Even so, the performance is very involving, and it is good that the *Overture* and end-titles sequence are included here, like the finale, for the first time on disc. The result is an essential supplement to the composer's own later version.

West Side Story: excerpts.
* Pickwick Dig. IMGDC 1801 [id.]. Ch., RPO, Barry Wordsworth.

Maria (Barbara Bonney), Tony (Michael Ball), Anita (La Verne Williams), Riff (Christopher Howard).

This new recording from Pickwick is a non-starter. The opening music is surprisingly slack, and not everyone will respond to Michael Ball's pop-style delivery in the famous *Maria*. The Balcony scene between the two lovers fails to project. There is nothing to detain anyone here.

West Side Story: highlights.
(M) *** DG Dig. 431 027-2; *431 027-4* (from above recording, with Te Kanawa, Carreras; cond. composer).

By cutting the dialogue, all the main numbers are included here, presented as vividly as on the complete set, and, with just over 53 minutes of music included, this is very good value. But the moving *Tonight* loses much without the spoken interchanges between the lovers, although the 'mock marriage' sequence is included in *One hand, one heart*, as is the introductory interchange which sets the scene for *Gee, Officer Krupke.*

Bizet, Georges (1838-75)

Carmen (complete).
*** DG Dig. 410 088-2 (3) [id.]. Paris Op. Ch., Schoenberg Boys' Ch., BPO, Karajan.
Carmen (Agnes Baltsa), Don José (José Carreras), Micaëla (Katia Ricciarelli), Escamillo (José Van Dam), Frasquita (Christine Barbaux).
(B) *** DG 427 440-2 (3) [id.]. Manhattan Op. Ch., Met. Op. O, Bernstein.
Carmen (Marilyn Horne), Don José (James McCracken), Micaëla (Adriana Maliponte), Escamillo (Tom Krause), Frasquita (Colette Boky).
(M) *** BMG/RCA GD 86199 (3) [6199-2-RG]. V. State Op. Ch., VPO, Karajan.
Carmen (Leontyne Price), Don José (Franco Corelli), Micaëla (Mirella Freni), Escamillo (Robert Merrill), Frasquita (Monique Linval).
**(*) Decca 414 489-2 (2) [id.]. John Alldis Ch., LPO, Solti.
Carmen (Tatiana Troyanos), Don José (Plácido Domingo), Micaëla (Kiri Te Kanawa), Escamillo (José Van Dam), Frasquita (Norma Burrowes).
**(*) DG 419 636-2 (3) [id.]. Amb. S., LSO, Abbado.
Carmen (Teresa Berganza), Don José (Plácido Domingo), Micaëla (Ileana Cotrubas), Escamillo (Sherrill Milnes), Frasquita (Yvonne Kenny).
Withdrawn: **(*) EMI CDC7 49240-2 (3) [Ang. CDCB 49240]. Fr. R. Ch. and O, Petits Chanteurs de Versailles, Beecham.
Carmen (Victoria De los Angeles), Don José (Nicolai Gedda), Micaëla (Janine Micheau), Escamillo (Ernest Blanc), Frasquita (Denise Monteil).
** Erato/Warner Dig. 2292 45209 (3) [id.]. French R. Ch. & Children's Ch., O Nat. de France, Maazel.
Carmen (Julia Migenes), Don José (Plácido Domingo), Micaëla (Faith Esham), Escamillo (Ruggero Raimondi), Frasquita (Lilian Watson).
Withdrawn: ** EMI CDS7 54368-8 (3) [Ang. CDC 47312]. René Duclos Ch., Children's Ch., Paris Nat. Op. O, Prêtre.
Carmen (Maria Callas), Don José (Nicolai Gedda), Micaëla (Andréa Guiot), Escamillo (Robert Massard), Frasquita (Nadine Sautereau).
Withdrawn: (M) **(*) EMI CMS7 63643-2 (2) [CDMB 63643]. Les Petits Chanteurs à la Croix de Bois, Paris Op. Ch. & O, Frühbeck de Burgos.
Carmen (Grace Bumbry), Don José (Jon Vickers), Micaëla (Mirella Freni), Escamillo (Kostas Paskalis), Frasquita (Eliane Lublin).
* Ph. Dig. 422 366-2 (3) [id.]. O Nat. de France, Ozawa.
Carmen (Jessye Norman), Don José (Neil Shicoff), Micaëla (Mirella Freni), Escamillo (Simon Estes), Frasquita (Ghyslaine Raphanel).
(M) *(*) BMG/Eurodisc GD 69147 (2). Schönberg Boys' Ch., German Op. Ch. & O, Berlin, Maazel.
Carmen (Anna Moffo), Don José (Franco Corelli), Micaëla (Helen Donath), Escamillo (Piero Cappuccilli), Frasquita (Arleen Augér).
(M) * Decca 411 630-2 (2) [id.]. Geneva Grand Theatre Ch., SRO, Schippers.
Carmen (Regina Resnik), Don José (Mario Del Monaco), Micaëla (Joan Sutherland), Escamillo (Tom Krause), Frasquita (Georgette Spanellys).
(B) * Naxos Dig. 8.660005/7 [id.]. Slovak Philharmonic Ch., Bratislava Children's Ch., Slovak RSO (Bratislava), Alexander Rahbari.
Carmen (Graciela Alperyn), Don José (Giorgio Lamberti), Micaëla (Doina Palade), Escamillo (Alan Titus), Frasquita (Ann Liebeck).

In a square in Seville the timid Micaëla approaches the guardhouse of the barracks, seeking her brother, Don José. Among the working girls streaming out through the nearby gates of the cigarette factory is the flirtatious Carmen who, fancying Don José, throws him a flower provocatively. In a quarrel she knifes a fellow worker and is arrested but, when Don José is put in charge of her, persuades him to set her free. She then enters the local tavern where she entertains seductively.

Escamillo the toreador enters and is captivated by her fiery performance but Carmen spurns his advances, favouring instead Don José when he arrives. Carmen now dances for José alone and he produces the dead flower to show his deep love for her. When she invites him to join her in the mountains, he at first refuses, but after an altercation with his superior officer, who also has designs on Carmen, Don José flees with her and they find a temporary haven in a gypsy encampment, where a game of cards ominously brings portents of death. Micaëla now arrives and begs Don José to pay a visit to his sick mother. He agrees, reassuring Carmen that he will return. The bold Escamillo now reappears and sings confidently of his prowess. Back in the city, Carmen, ever fickle and now infatuated with her new toreador lover, joins the triumphant bullfighter.

Don José appears and pleads for her love, but she turns scornfully from him and tries to rejoin Escamillo in the arena where the crowd is rapturously praising his professional victory. Don José stabs her wildly then desolately acknowledges his crime as the curtain falls.

The opera's dramatic Spanish scenario, with its involving interplay of human love and jealousy, brought from Bizet vivid musical characterization, marvellous orchestral colouring and a whole string of unforgettable vocal hits. Not surprisingly, few operas have been more successful on record and any of the first half-dozen listed versions will afford much satisfaction in their different ways. Karajan's later, DG set offers a performance combining affection with high tension and high polish. Where in his earlier, RCA version he used the old text with added recitatives, here he uses the Oeser edition with its extra passages and spoken dialogue; this may account in part for the differences of approach, more intimate in the presentation of the drama, less extreme over certain controversial tempi. In Carreras he has a Don José, lyrical and generally sweet-toned, who is far from the conventional hero-figure – more the anti-hero, an ordinary man caught up in tragic love. The *Flower song* is exquisitely beautiful in its half-tones.

The Micaëla of Katia Ricciarelli is similarly scaled down, with the big dramatic voice kept in check. José van Dam – also the Escamillo for Solti – is incisive and virile, the public hero-figure, which leaves Agnes Baltsa as a vividly compelling Carmen, tough and vibrant yet musically precise and commanding. Where on stage (as at Covent Garden) Baltsa tends to exaggerate the characterization, here Karajan encourages her to be positively larger than life but remain a believable figure, with tenderness under the surface. In her brief exchanges with Escamillo before the final scene, you are made to believe in her love for the bullfighter, though her portrait is more provocative than alluring.

As for Karajan, he draws richly resonant playing from the Berlin Philharmonic, sparkling and swaggering in the bullfight music but delicate and poetic too. The digital recording is bright and atmospheric, if not always ideally balanced. The spoken dialogue distractingly sounds like the soundtrack of a French film. The CDs bring benefit in extra clarity but they also bring out more noticeably the degree of close-up aggressiveness in the recording, with a tendency to bass-lightness.

Bernstein's 1973 *Carmen* was recorded at the New York Metropolitan Opera, the first recording undertaken there for many years. It was based on the Met.'s spectacular production with the same cast and conductor as on record, and the sessions clearly gained from being interleaved with live performances: Bernstein adopted the original version of 1875, with spoken dialogue but with variations designed to suit a stage production. Some of his slow tempi are extreme; but what really matters is the authentic tingle of dramatic tension. Marilyn Horne – occasionally coarse in expression – gives a red-blooded reading of the heroine's role, a vivid characterization, warts and all. The rest of the cast similarly works to Bernstein's consistent overall plan. The singing is not all perfect, but it is always vigorous and colourful, and so (despite often questionable French accents) is the spoken dialogue. It is very well transferred and comes on three bargain CDs.

Karajan's earlier, RCA version was made in Vienna in 1964 and, like all recordings up to that date, uses the traditional text with Guiraud's sung recitatives in place of dialogue. For those who are prepared to accept Karajan's sometimes unconventional speeds, often slow, this is perhaps the most seductive reading of all, with Leontyne Price at her peak a smoky-toned heroine who is a sexual threat as well as a charmer. Corelli has moments of coarseness, but his is still a heroic performance. Robert Merrill sings with gloriously firm tone, while Mirella Freni is enchanting as

Micaëla. With more spectacular recording than is given to Beecham, this set, now offered at mid-price, remains a keen competitor, with Karajan always inspired and with the CDs giving added presence and immediacy.

By the side of the digital Karajan recording, the Solti discs sound less strikingly brilliant than they seemed on first appearance. But this Decca performance, apart from offering a satisfactory solution to the vexed question of text, is remarkable for its new illumination of characters. Tatiana Troyanos might be counted the subtlest Carmen on record. The blatant sexuality which is so often accepted as the essential ingredient in the heroine's character is here modified to reveal a degree of vulnerability. You can understand why she falls in love and then out again. Escamillo too is more readily sympathetic, not just the flashy matador who steals the hero's girl, in some ways the custodian of rationality, whereas Don José is revealed as weak rather than just as a victim.

Troyanos's singing is delicately seductive too, with no hint of vulgarity, while the others make up an exceptionally consistent cast. Solti, like Karajan on DG, uses spoken dialogue and a modification of the Oeser edition, deciding in each individual instance whether to accept amendments to Bizet's first thoughts. Fine though other versions of a much-recorded opera may be, this dramatic and sensitive account from Solti comes high on the list. Though the CD transfer brings out the generally excellent balances of the original analogue recording, it exaggerates the bass to make the sound boomy. The voices retain their fine realism and bloom, but orchestral textures are heavier and less clear than they should be, unless controls are adjusted.

Superbly disciplined, Abbado's performance nails its colours to the mast at the very start in a breathtakingly fast account of the opening prelude. Through the four Acts there are other examples of idiosyncratic tempi, but the whole entertainment hangs together with keen compulsion, reflecting the fact that these same performers – Sherrill Milnes as Escamillo excepted – took part in the Edinburgh Festival production directly associated with this recording project. Conductor and orchestra can take a large share of credit for the performance's success, for though the singing is never less than enjoyable, it is on the whole less characterful than on some rival sets. Teresa Berganza is a seductive if somewhat unsmiling Carmen – not without sensuality, and producing consistently beautiful tone, but lacking some of the flair which makes for a three-dimensional portrait. If you want a restrained and thoughtful view, then Tatiana Troyanos in Solti's set, also opposite the admirably consistent Plácido Domingo, is preferable. Ileana Cotrubas as Micaëla is not always as sweetly steady as she can be; Milnes makes a heroic matador. The spoken dialogue is excellently produced, and the sound is vivid and immediate, with the CDs hardly betraying the fact that the sessions took place in different studios (in London as well as Edinburgh).

Beecham's approach to Bizet's well-worn score is no less fresh and revealing. His speeds are not always conventional but they always *sound* right. And unlike so many strong-willed conductors in opera, Beecham allows his singers room to breathe and to expand their characterizations. It seems that he specially chose De los Angeles to be his Carmen although she had never sung the part on the stage before making the recording. He conceived the *femme fatale* not as the usual brazen character but as someone far more subtly seductive, winning her admirers not so much by direct assault and high voltage as by charm and femininity.

De los Angeles suits this conception perfectly: her characterization of Carmen is bewitching, and when in the Quintet scene she says *Je suis amoureuse* one believes her absolutely. The other singers are not nearly so dominant as this, but they make admirable foils; Gedda is pleasantly clear-toned, Janine Micheau is a sweet Micaëla, and Ernest Blanc makes an attractive Escamillo. The stereo recording is undistracting, for there seems to have been little attempt at stage production, but in the CD transfer the sound is brilliant enough, and the recording does not show its age too greatly.

The glory of Maazel's Erato version is the Don José of Plácido Domingo, freer and more spontaneously expressive than in his two previous recordings, not least in the lovely account of the *Flower song*. Julia Migenes (Johnson) is a fresh-toned Carmen, often exaggerating detail but presenting a vibrant, sexy character as she does in Francesco Rosi's brilliantly atmospheric film. Ruggero Raimondi sings cleanly and strongly as Escamillo, but Faith Esham is a shrill, thin-toned Micaëla, vocally quite out of character. Maazel's conducting is bright and dramatic, if not always tender enough. The recording is clean, well balanced and natural, and very well reproduced on CD, less brilliant than Karajan's DG version but arguably the best yet in the new medium. A recommendable set for those who enjoyed the film.

Though in so many ways the vibrant, flashing-eyed personality of Maria Callas was ideally suited to the role of Carmen, her complete recording – unlike two separate aria recordings she made earlier – is disappointing. One principal trouble is that the performance, apart from her, lacks a taut dramatic rein, with slack ensemble from singers and orchestra alike. The moment the heroine enters, the tension rises; but by Callas standards this is a performance rough-hewn, strong and characterful but lacking the full imaginative detail of her finest work. 'Callas is Carmen', said EMI's original advertisements, but in fact very clearly Callas remains Callas. The CD transfer clarifies textures but brings out the limitations of the Paris recording.

Frühbeck's version of 1970, made before the Oeser edition appeared, was the first to use the original 1875 version of Bizet's score without the cuts that were made after experience in the theatre, and with spoken dialogue instead of the recitatives which Guiraud composed after Bizet's early death. Well-recorded on two mid-priced discs, it makes a fair bargain, though Grace Bumbry gives a generalized portrait of the heroine, singing with firm tone but too rarely with musical or dramatic individuality. Vickers makes a strong, heroic Don José; and though, surprisingly, Frühbeck's conducting lacks sparkle, it is very well-paced. Paskalis makes a gloriously rich-toned Escamillo and Freni an exquisite Micaëla.

It was a bold idea to cast Jessye Norman as Carmen, and it says much for her artistry that hers is the most compelling performance in a disappointing set. The sound she produces is glorious and the command of detail formidable, with the voice as rounded in speaking as in singing – but this is a monumental rather than a vivacious Carmen. She scales her voice down beautifully where necessary, but it is not unlike watching a great and beautiful ocean-liner threading its way through the Panama Canal. The set is well worth hearing for Norman alone; but, with slow speeds for the key solos and with a large-sounding chorus set too distantly, well behind any action, in a church-like acoustic, you might even describe this as 'Carmen the oratorio'.

One's disappointment is sealed by the contributions of the other soloists, not to mention that of the conductor, Ozawa. Freni, many years ago a superb Micaëla for Karajan, is here shrill and grainy, Shicoff makes a coarse Don José, belting out the Flower song, and Simon Estes is surprisingly rough both in his singing and in his speaking of the French dialogue (which at times is unintentionally comic). It is sad that such a set should have achieved such wide circulation thanks to hype from the publicity machine.

At mid-price on only two discs, Maazel's 1979 Eurodisc version of Carmen, using the expanded Oeser edition, makes a doubtful bargain. The casting is starry – with such celebrated singers as Arleen Augér and Jane Berbié in the small roles of Frasquita and Mercedes – but almost totally non-French and not always apt. Anna Moffo, lacking mezzo weight, is hardly an ideal Carmen, and she makes up for that by underlining her characterization too heavily. Franco Corelli too is heavy-handed as Don José, not as effective as he was for Karajan in his earlier recording. Helen Donath makes a charming Micaëla, light and sweet, while Piero Cappuccilli as Escamillo produces a stream of strong, firm tone, even if – like others in the cast – his French is not his strong point.

As in his later, Erato version (the one used in Franco Rosi's film), Maazel directs a bright and forceful performance, dramatically tense, exaggerated by the fierceness of the recorded sound in tuttis. Otherwise the recording (not digital) is reasonably atmospheric.

Despite brilliant engineering, Decca's early stereo set is very variable. Resnik has a big, fruity tone, but her aim is wild. Del Monaco sings coarsely, and vocally the main joy is having Sutherland as Micaëla, even if it sounds as though Lucia had strayed into the wrong opera. Schippers drives very hard indeed.

The Naxos Carmen is reasonably priced and very naturally recorded, if with no striking brilliance. But with so many distinctive versions of this opera available, one wonders if this will prove a good investment for repeated listening. Graciela Alperyn is not a Carmen one would turn away from on a warm Spanish evening, but neither her Don José (Giorgio Lamberti, singing in a very Italianate style) nor her Escamillo (Alan Titus) offers the kind of vocal personality to make the opera tingle with seductive tension, nor is the somewhat fluttery Micaëla of Doina Palade distinctive.

Rahbari directs the proceedings theatrically enough, although Les tringles des sistres tintaient which begins the second disc (after the Entr'acte) starts rather limply. By the end, however, the action generates real impetus, and the final confrontation between Carmen and her lover is telling enough. The chorus contributes enthusiastically but without disciplined finesse and, although the orchestral playing is generally very good (especially the Entr'actes), overall this is not a Carmen to write home about. The libretto is given in French, without a translation, although there is an adequate synopsis.

Carmen: highlights.
*** DG Dig. 413 322-2 [id.] (from above recording with Baltsa, Carreras; cond. Karajan).
(M) *** Decca 421 300-2 (from above recording with Troyanos, Domingo; cond. Solti).
(M) *** DG 435 401-2; *435 401-4* [id.] (from above recording with Berganza, Domingo; cond. Abbado).
(M) ** EMI CDM7 63075-2 (from above recording with Callas, Gedda; cond. Prêtre).
(B) *(*) Decca 433 626-2; *433 626-4* [id.] (from above recording with Resnik, Del Monaco; cond. Schippers).
* Ph. Dig. 426 040-2 [id.] (from above recording with Norman, Shicoff; cond. Ozawa).

A good representative selection from the Karajan DG set, with recording to match, while the reissued compilation of 'scenes and arias' from Solti's sharply characterful version is generous, and the remastered recording sounds very well indeed.

Although issued as part of the 'Domingo Edition', the 69-minute selection from the Abbado recording is well balanced and does not just concentrate on Domingo's contribution. It is vividly and atmospherically transferred and thus fairly reflects the qualities of the complete set. There is no libretto, but the cued synopsis is perfectly adequate with this opera.

Perhaps wisely, the selection from the Callas set, which is very generous with a playing time of 71 minutes 35 seconds, is not designed so much to highlight the heroine as to provide as many 'pops' as possible from the opera. In isolation, Callas's shortcomings – dramatic as well as vocal – are just as clear as in the complete set, and Prêtre on this occasion is hardly a sensitive or understanding Bizet conductor. Gedda's *Flower song* is the outstanding number here: but Callas devotees will no doubt take comfort from the comparatively effortful examples of Callas's individual artistry. The 1964 recording has no lack of vividness. As usual with EMI's mid-priced CDs, a synopsis is included but no translation of the contents.

Sutherland's Micaëla was the only memorable contribution to the Schippers recording, and it is disappointing that Decca included only her Act III aria in a 56-minute selection which matches the old LP without any additional material. Del Monaco's Don José is predictably coarse.

The single disc of highlights from the Philips set with Jessye Norman was for many weeks at the top of the classical charts in Britain, but few issues have deserved such an accolade less.

Carmen: highlights (sung in English).
(B) **(*) CfP CD-CFP 4596; *TC-CFP 4596.* Patricia Johnson, Donald Smith, Raimund Herincx, Elizabeth Robson, Rita Hunter, Leon Greene, John Stoddart, Julian Moyle, Sadler's Wells Ch. & O, Sir Colin Davis.

Those who enjoy opera in English will find this a highly successful example, thanks both to the strongly animated conducting of Sir Colin Davis and to the rich-voiced, reliable singing of Patricia Johnson as Carmen, with phrasing often most imaginative. The voice is well caught, and Donald Smith, the Don José, also sings with attractive, ringing tone. The selection is well made, if not especially generous (52 minutes) and the ensemble has the authentic enthusiasm of a live performance. The CD transfer is extremely natural.

La jolie fille de Perth (complete).
Withdrawn: *** EMI Dig. CDS7 47559-8 (2). Ch. and New PO of R. France, Prêtre.
Catherine (June Anderson), Henry Smith (Alfredo Kraus), Duke of Rothsay (Gino Quilico), Ralph (José Van Dam), Simon (Gabriel Bacquier), Mab (Margarita Zimmermann).

Based on Scott's *Fair Maid of Perth*, the plot of Bizet's opera is as unlikely as many others of the Romantic period. Henry Smith in his workshop is persuaded by the gypsy, Mab, to give her shelter. However, on the arrival of Smith's beloved, Catherine, with her father and Ralph, his apprentice, Mab makes herself scarce. Ralph, too, is attracted to Catherine and he is openly jealous of the obvious warmth between Catherine and Smith.

The Duke of Rothsay now appears and he also shows an interest in Catherine which culminates in an invitation to his castle at night, which Mab (who has previously been his mistress) overhears in her hiding place. Smith is jealous; Catherine is independent of spirit and, although she still loves him, they quarrel and she throws down the golden flower he has given her as token of his feelings. Mab now emerges and steals the golden flower.

The Duke enlists Mab's help in the seduction of Catherine, but she has her own ideas about that and, cleverly disguised and masked and in possession of the flower, she substitutes herself to accept his advances. When Smith later sees the flower pinned to the Duke's tunic he promptly accuses Catherine of infidelity; he and the jealous Ralph also quarrel to the point of fighting a duel in which Ralph has the advantage of youth. Thankfully, after the heroine almost loses her reason and Henry Smith his life, a last-minute dénouement brings the two lovers back together.

Remarkably, this absurd series of improbable events inspired Bizet to write one delectable number after another, not just the famous *Serenade* for the tenor hero, Henry Smith. Even that *Serenade* has generally been done in a corrupt version with two parallel verses; in the original score, faithfully reproduced on this fine first recording, the restatement of the melody in the second verse is developed dramatically. Some of the other numbers – not just arias but choruses too, including some of the finest – were either modified or cut entirely. One of the many delights of the piece lies in relating it to Bizet's supreme masterpiece of eight years later. Here, as in *Carmen*, you have a principal gypsy role for mezzo soprano contrasted against a purer-toned soprano heroine; but this time it is the soprano who is the deliberately provocative one, leaving Henry Smith almost as wounded as Don José in *Carmen*.

Unlike *Carmen*, however, this piece ends happily, with the crazed heroine delivering a Lucia-like mad song (coloratura delightfully done by June Anderson) before being shocked into sanity for the final curtain. Alfredo Kraus as the hero sings stylishly – even if at times the voice shows its age. Gino Quilico is superb as the predatory Duke of Rothsay; José van Dam as the apprentice Ralph is aptly lugubrious in his drunken song, and the veteran Gabriel Bacquier makes a delightfully bluff figure of the heroine's father. Margarita Zimmermann (not always well treated by the microphone) as Mab, queen of the gypsies, makes an equivocal role convincing. Georges Prêtre's conducting is warm and understanding, even if ensemble is not always ideally crisp. Full, warm recording to match, which sounds most attractive in its CD format.

Les pêcheurs de perles.
(M)(***) Ph. mono 434 782-2 (2) [id.]. Brasseur Ch., LOP, Fournet.
　　Leila (Pierrette Alarie), Nadir (Léopold Simoneau), Zurga (René Bianco).
** EMI Dig. CDS7 49837-2 (2) [Ang. CDCB 49837]. Capitole, Toulouse, Ch. & O, Plasson.
　　Leila (Barbara Hendricks), Nadir (John Aler), Zurga (Gino Quilico).
(B) ** CfP CD-CFPD 4721 (2). Paris Op. Ch. & O, Prêtre.
　　Leila (Ileana Cotrubas), Nadir (Alain Vanzo), Zurga (Guillermo Sarabia).

(i) *Les pêcheurs de perles* (complete). (ii) *Ivan IV: highlights.*
Withdrawn: (M) ** EMI CMS7 69704-2 (2) [Ang. CDMB 69704]. (i) Paris Opéra-Comique O, Dervaux; (ii) Michel Roux, Janine Micheau, Henri Legay, Michel Sénéchal, Louis Noguera, Pierre Savignol, French R. Ch. & O, Tzipine.
　　(i) Leila (Janine Micheau), Nadir (Nicolai Gedda), Zurga (Ernest Blanc).

Just as Sir Walter Scott's ripe but unlikely romanticism could elicit from Bizet a remarkable musical response, so did this exotic tale of passion at a Brahmin temple. An oath of friendship exists between the fishermen Nadir and Zurga (the leader), even though both had at one time been rivals in love for the priestess, Leila.

A boat arrives carrying an unknown virgin, whose duty it is to pray for the fishermen while they are at sea. The effectiveness of her intercession is believed to be dependent on her solitude at the temple; she must not be seen by anybody during her solemn, lonely vigil. Zurga threatens her with death should her oath be broken. Needless to say, it is Leila; she and Nadir recognize each other and his love for her is undimmed.

The High Priest, Nourabad, sees them together and accuses them of sacrilege. They call on their god, Brahma, for help, the crowd demand revenge and they are condemned. Zurga laments both for Leila, because long ago she saved his life, and also over his broken friendship with Nadir. When a funeral pyre is built at the place of execution Zurga diverts attention with a fire of his own and thus allows Leila and Nadir to escape. They are seen far away, safely on a rock, but Zurga remains to face the wrath of the community and is denounced by Nourabad.

The Philips version of 1953, recorded in mono only, offers a far more warmly idiomatic reading of Bizet's evocative opera under Jean Fournet than the many disappointing stereo versions since. The performance is dominated by the headily beautiful, totally unstrained singing of the tenor, Léopold Simoneau, as the hero, Nadir, with his wife, Pierrette Alarie, light and clear as the priestess, Leila. René Bianco as Zurga and Xavier Depraz are less distinguished but cleanly characterful, and the chorus sings sympathetically too. The clean, bright transfer of a carefully balanced recording quickly makes one forget the absence of stereo atmosphere and the famous male duet projects vibrantly. In the Philips Opera Collector series, this is a limited edition.

EMI's newest, digital version of *Pearlfishers* from Toulouse, well recorded, should have provided an ideal recommendation for this lovely opera but, for all its qualities, sadly this is not so. Michel Plasson with the choir and orchestra of the Capitole, though sympathetic, fails to draw out as warmly committed a performance as he usually does in his French opera recordings. John Aler and Gino Quilico as the two fishermen sing cleanly and with lyrical freshness, but often their phrasing could be more affectionate. Barbara Hendricks is aptly alluring as Leila, beloved of both of them, but too often she attacks notes from below, coming near to crooning her lovely Act II solo, *Comme autrefois*, as well as the following love-duet. The original text has been used but, rightly, this new set (unlike the earlier one with Prêtre, now on CfP) gives the listener the choice of versions of the great *Pearlfishers' duet*. The original version, given as an appendix, is maddening when it fails to bring a reprise for the big tune and instead launches into a trivial *Polonaise-cabaletta*.

At CfP's bargain price the Prêtre set of 1978, well recorded, has much in its favour, yet there are serious snags. Ileana Cotrubas is superb as the high priestess, Leila, projecting character as well as singing beautifully. The tenor, Alain Vanzo, is also most stylish, but after that the problems begin, not only with the singing (Sarabia a variably focused baritone) but with the conducting (Prêtre is generally fast, unlilting and unfeeling) but also with the recording (not sufficiently atmospheric). In principle it may seem a positive gain to have the original (1863) score reinstated, but it is hard not to feel disappointed when the great duet for the pearlfishers culminates so weakly.

Paul Dervaux is no more than an efficient conductor, failing to draw out the relaxed charm of this exotic score with its soaringly lyrical set numbers. The lack of affection infects the principals, who are all stylish artists but who here sing below their best, even the dependable Nicolai Gedda. On two mid-price CDs the set might still be worth considering, however, when it also includes selections from the opera which Bizet wrote immediately after *Pearlfishers*, *Ivan IV*. There is a fine scene for the heroine, beautifully sung by Janine Micheau; and the heady-toned tenor, Henri Legay, an outstanding artist, sings superbly in his vengeance aria. It is also good to hear the fine bass, Pierre Savignol. In EMI's Studio series, the package includes the libretto of *Pearlfishers* but, as yet, no translation, and only garbled notes and a synopsis for *Ivan IV*, a work which on this showing deserves to be better known. The CD transfers hardly betray the age of the recordings.

ARRANGEMENTS

Carmen Jones (with lyrics by Oscar Hammerstein II).
(M) **(*) BMG/RCA GD 81881 [81881-2-RG]. Film soundtrack recording. Ch. & O, Herschel Burke Gilbert.
    Carmen Jones (Marilyn Horne), Joe (LeVern Hutcherson), Cindy Lou (Olga James), Husky (Marvin Hayes), Frankie (Pearl Bailey).

The great librettist Oscar Hammerstein II was fascinated by *Carmen* with its string of popular hits, and he determined to place it before the widest possible audience in the 1940s when, partly because of wartime restrictions, opera was going through an elitist period. In the event, Bizet's *Carmen* (with the surname Jones) emerged unscathed from her facial, for it was only skin-deep, with the orchestral colours remaining much as the composer intended. Opera is often updated today, but in the 1940s performances were usually traditional, and the idea of transporting its Spanish heroine to an American parachute factory was distinctly innovative. In an ingenious reworking of the plot, her lover becomes Corporal Joe, and she seduces him away from his childhood sweetheart (Cindy Lou) who in turn becomes besotted with a prize-fighter, Husky Miller.

As in the opera, Joe is a natural loser and ends the story by stabbing Carmen to death. But it is the imaginative new lyrics that capture the attention in *Carmen Jones*. The *Habañera* becomes *Dat's love*, the *Toreador song*, relocated in the boxing ring, emerges as *Stan' up and fight*, the *Seguidilla* is *Dere's a café on de corner*. The two most striking transformations are *Beat out dat rhythm on a drum*, which fits Bizet's melody and rhythm so perfectly, and the wonderful railroad evocation of the Quintet, *Whizzin' away along de track*. In spite of the characteristically dead acoustic of the soundtrack, the music is well projected, the performances animated and communicative and, if some will not like LeVern Hutcherson's crooning of the *Flower song*, he presents it very affectingly. The young Marilyn Horne ghosted Dorothy Dandridge's voice to make her a most believable *Carmen Jones*. Bizet is certainly not upstaged here, but Oscar Hammerstein's new version comes off in its own terms.

Blitzstein, Marc (1905–64)

Regina (opera, after the play by Lillian Hellman).
**(*) Decca Dig. 433 812-2 (2) [id.]. Scottish Op. Ch. & O, John Mauceri.
   Regina Giddens (Katherine Ciesinski), Horace Giddens (Samuel Ramey), Alexandra Giddens (Angelina Réaux), Birdie Hubbard (Sheri Greenawald).

Poised on the cusp between opera and musical is this equivocal piece, *Regina* by Marc Blitzstein. It is an adaptation of Lillian Hellman's memorable play, *The Little Foxes*. The composer, at the time he was murdered, had left the score in disorder, but the conductor of Scottish Opera, John Mauceri, and Tommy Krasker have painstakingly deduced and reconstructed what the composer ideally wanted.

This vivid Decca recording yet leaves one with serious questions. Like Porgy, and equally like Jerome Kern's *Show Boat*, *Regina* is set in the American Deep South, if against a strikingly different atmosphere of family and business deals. Yet, far more than those similarly cross-border works, *Regina* offers a musical cop-out. Blitzstein is in no way a melodist of the calibre of Gershwin or Kern, even though his invention is always lively. He resorts far too readily to the spoken word for the big dramatic confrontations, with music merely as a background. Nor does the score reflect in its moods and atmosphere the full biting acidity of Hellman's dramatic situations.

Yet this is a beautifully made recording of a lively performance, invaluable for giving permanent accessibility to an opera unlikely to be staged regularly. The Scottish Opera Orchestra plays brilliantly for Mauceri, and the cast includes such fine singers as Samuel Ramey, James Maddalena and the late Bruce Hubbard, all of them strong in both voice and character. The microphone is far less kind to the more uneven, less steady voices of the women principals, Katherine Ciesinski in the title-role, Sheri Greenawald and Angelina Réaux. The full text, lasting over 2½ hours, including a sharply conceived prologue for the black principals, is fitted on to just two CDs.

Blomdahl, Karl-Birger (1916–68)

Aniara (complete).
*** Cap. CAP 22016:1/2 [id.]. Swedish R. Ch. and SO, Westerberg.
   Blind Poetess (Lena Hoel), Daisi Doody / La Garçonne (Viveka Anderberg), The Mimarobe (Erik Saedén), Chefone (Jerker Arvidson), Blind Man / Chief Technician (Björn Haugan).

The action of the opera *Aniara* is placed in the remote future when interplanetary travel is almost commonplace. *Aniara* is a spaceship bound for Mars with some 8,000 people on board who are escaping from the poisoned, radio-active atmosphere of the Earth. Soon the *Aniara* is thrown off course by a shower of meteorites, and her passengers are panic-stricken to learn that they are doomed to travel for ever in intergalactic space. The years of travel and the immensities of space take their toll and various sects emerge; the ship's evil master, Chefone, establishes a tyranny over the passengers. Ultimately, one by one they perish, until the only survivor, the woman pilot, remains to dance her sad and lonely swan song.

There is no doubt that Blomdahl possessed a sophisticated aural imagination and a vital sensibility. What he does lack is real thematic vitality: it is not just a matter of good tunes – most contemporary operas suffer a similar handicap – but the fact that the lines lack both real direction and interest and the stamp of a commanding personal idiom. *Aniara* adds up to a good deal less than the sum of its parts: there is good craftsmanship rather than white-hot inspiration, and expertise rather than mastery. This persuasive and totally committed account by this wonderful cast certainly shows it to best advantage. The recording is in the demonstration class, with remarkable range and altogether superb definition.

Blow, John (1649–1708)

Venus and Adonis.
(M) *** HM/BMG GD 77117 (2). Consort of Musicke, Rooley – GIBBONS: *Cupid and Death.* ***
  Cupid (Evelyn Tubb), Venus (Emma Kirkby), Adonis (Richard Wistreich), Shepherdesses
  (Tessa Bonner, Poppy Holden, Cathy Cass), Shepherds (Joseph Cornwell, Andrew King,
  Rufus Müller, Jeremy White).
(B) *** HM Dig. HMA 90 1276 [id.]. L. Bar. & Ch., Medlam.
  Cupid (Nancy Argenta), Venus (Lynne Dawson), Adonis (Stephen Varcoe), Shepherdess
  (Emily Van Evera), 1st Shepherd (John Mark Ainsley), 2nd Shepherd (Charles Daniels), 3rd
  Shepherd (Gordon Jones), Huntsman (Rogers Covey-Crump).

Venus and Adonis, 'a masque for the entertainment of the king' dating from around 1682, was
the first through-composed opera in English with no spoken dialogue. The librettist is unknown.
Dido and Aeneas by Blow's pupil, Purcell, followed it before the end of the decade, and it is sad
that so promising a start never led to the development of a school of English opera. In form, this
is like a Lully opera in miniature. Its length makes it more likely to suit twentieth-century taste,
with the Prologue and three brief Acts presenting a fast-moving sequence of choruses, dances
and 'act-tunes' as well as arias, often with chorus.

The curtain rises on a room in Venus's Palace and finds her and Adonis embracing on a
couch; she is about to succumb to him when the sound of hunting horns is heard. Adonis is
reluctant to leave but Venus sends him off ('Absence kindles new desires') to show his skill in the
chase. In Act II, Cupid is taking lessons from his mother (Venus) in the Art of Love, and he in
turn teaches the cherubs to spell, tossing letters of the alphabet around the stage. Cupid urges
Venus to treat Adonis badly in order to ensure his fidelity and the Act concludes with a chorus
for the Graces ('Mortals below, Cupids above'), a series of dances and a chaconne. In the last Act
Adonis, fatally gored by the wild boar, begs to die in Venus's arms and she and her courtiers
mourn the dying youth and sing in praise of his virtues. Rooley directs an elegant, lightly sprung
performance, very well sung, recorded in good analogue sound (1984) in a warm acoustic. It
takes up only part of the first disc of the two-disc set, now reissued by BMG at mid-price.

Charles Medlam with London Baroque also gives a sprightly account of John Blow's delightful
masque, one of the few that has survived today as a living entertainment. Though this is a period
performance, the ensemble is full and substantial, and Medlam takes care that the early
instruments are well blended rather than edgy. The choral sound is full, bright and clean, with a
rather larger choir used than in the direct rival performance. The *Huntsmen's chorus* in Act I has
splendid bite and panache. The soloists too are all remarkable for sweetness and freshness of
tone, with the bright, clear tones of Nancy Argenta as Cupid and Lynne Dawson as Venus nicely
counterpointed, and with Stephen Varcoe a clear, youthful-sounding Adonis. This record is now
offered at bargain price in the Musique d'Abord series.

Boito, Arrigo (1842–1918)

Mefistofele (complete).
**(*) Decca Dig. 410 175-2 [id.]. L. Op. Ch., Trinity Boys' Ch., Nat. PO, Fabritiis.
  Mefistofele (Nicolai Ghiaurov), Faust (Luciano Pavarotti), Margherita (Mirella Freni), Elena
  (Montserrat Caballé).
** Sony Dig. S2K 44983 (2) [id.]. Hungarian State Op. Ch. & O, Patanè.
  Mefistofele (Samuel Ramey), Faust (Plácido Domingo), Margherita / Elena (Eva Marton).
Withdrawn: ** EMI CDS7 49522-2 (3) [CDCB 49522]. Amb. Op. Ch., Wandsworth School
  Boys' Ch., LSO, Rudel.
  Mefistofele (Norman Treigle), Faust (Plácido Domingo), Margherita (Montserrat Caballé).

Boito's *Mefistofele* is a strange, episodic work to come from the hand of the master-librettist of
Verdi's *Otello* and *Falstaff*, but it has many fine moments. Boito's version of the Faust legend is
highly individual and imaginative. Mefistofele, disguised as a friar, shadows the ageing and
disillusioned Faust but is forced to reveal his true identity. He tells Faust his all-pervading desire
is to witness the complete ruination of the world and a return to chaos and the night. He suggests
a wager to Faust, offering him one hour of true peace in which to rest his soul. They will travel
together and, if he is successful, Faust will pay with his soul for ever in Mefistofele's power.

Faust, rejuvenated, witnesses the orgies of the Witches' Sabbath and then he sees Margherita lying in prison, having drowned her child and been accused of murdering her mother. Faust begs her to fly away with him but the voice of Mefistofele brings her to full realization of her plight and of her real choice. Instead, she prays to heaven then dies. There follows an interlude with Helen of Troy (Elena) and Faust pledges his love to her.

But the time is up and at last Faust returns to his laboratory an old man. In desperation he turns at last to Heaven to aid him and dies as a celestial choir sings triumphantly that Mefistofele has lost his wager and that holy influences prevail.

Boito's setting is nothing if not spectacularly worthy of his scenario and the modern digital recording given to the Fabritiis Decca set brings obvious benefits in the extra weight of brass and percussion – most importantly in the heavenly prologue. With the principal soloists all at their best – Pavarotti most seductive in *Dai campi, dai prati*, Freni finely imaginative on detail, Caballé consistently sweet and mellifluous as Elena, Ghiaurov strongly characterful if showing some signs of strain – this is a highly recommendable set, though Fabritiis in his last recording lacks a little in energy, and the chorus is placed rather distantly.

Just as Oliviero de Fabritiis died soon after making his Decca recording of this opera about heaven and hell, so ominously did Giuseppe Patanè soon after this Sony recording. Sadly, unlike the Decca recording, it does not do the conductor justice, for this is a stiff, rather perfunctory reading. It is not helped by a studio acoustic which, with the chorus cleanly but unatmospherically placed, makes it sound more like an oratorio than an opera. Plácido Domingo sings well but there is little bloom on the voice, and, noble and commanding as Samuel Ramey's performance is, he does not sound sinister. The biggest snag is the singing of Eva Marton, far too heavyweight and unsteady a soprano for Margherita and hardly better suited to the role of Elena (Helen of Troy) which she doubles – another drawback to the set. Its only advantage over the Decca is that it comes on two discs instead of three.

On the mid-1970s EMI set, Caballé assumed the principal role of Margherita; though her performance lacks detail and she misses some of the dark intensity that makes Freni's Decca account so moving, particularly in *L'altra notte*, she is in very good voice. Norman Treigle, renowned in the role of Mefistofele at the New York City Opera, sings strongly. Though he is not as characterful as Ghiaurov, the Faust/Margherita duet is beautifully done. Plácido Domingo as Faust is stylish and confident, and Rudel conducts with warmth. The sound, however, even in its remastered form, cannot compare with the spectacular Decca set, particularly in the Prologue.

Mefistofele: Prologue.
(m) (***) BMG/RCA mono GD 60276; *GK 60276* [60276-2-RG; *60276-4-RG*]. Nicola Moscona, Robert Shaw Ch., Columbus Boychoir, NBC SO, Toscanini – VERDI: *I Lombardi; Rigoletto*: excerpts. (**)
(m) **(*) DG 431 171-2 [id.]. Nicolai Ghiaurov, V. State Op. Ch., VPO, Bernstein – R. STRAUSS: *Salome* etc. **(*)

Whatever the limitations of the sound, the hair-raising intensity of Toscanini's performance gives Boito's multi-layered *Prologue* a cogency never matched since on record. The dryness of sound even seems to help, when offstage choruses are accurately focused, and the singing of the Robert Shaw Chorale has thrillingly dramatic bite. This was taken from one of the very last broadcasts Toscanini ever made and, with the Verdi items, it makes a magnetically involving historic document.

The DG recording was made in Vienna in 1977 and finds Ghiaurov in excellent form. Bernstein, too, conducts this highly imaginative piece vividly and atmospherically. The CD transfer has greatly improved the focus and now the offstage choruses register impressively. This does not have quite the electricity of Toscanini but, for those wanting a modern version, it will serve admirably.

Nerone (complete).
*** Hung. Dig. HCD 12487/9-2 [id.]. Hungarian R. and TV Ch., Hungarian State Op. O, Queler. Nerone (János Nagy), Simon Mago (Jószef Dene), Fanuèl (Lajos Miller), Asteria (Ilona Tokody), Rubria (Klára Takács), Tigellino (József Gregor).

Eve Queler conducts a powerful and atmospheric performance of Boito's massive incomplete opera which dramatized the conflict between Christianity and the dying world of paganism. The work opens dramatically as Nero, Emperor of Rome, buries the ashes of his mother, Agrippina, whom he has murdered. The plot then hinges on sorcery and the power of faith, the Christians reliant on Fanuèl, their spiritual leader, the pagans placing their allegiance with Simon Mago, a sorcerer. Rubria, a vestal virgin, loves Fanuèl, and he returns her love and calls her his bride.

When the Christians go to their deaths, she dies with an image of Christ in her mind. The sorcerer, Simon, does not survive either.

It is a sombre, powerful work and it occupied the composer for the last fifty years of his life, and though (not surprisingly) it hardly matches his earlier *Mefistofele* in freshness and variety and presents an unsatisfyingly episodic plot, there are dozens of marvellous ideas. The very opening is strikingly original, sliding in like *Aida* updated. Later, too, the piece is full of prayers and ceremonial music, all of it richly colourful and superbly performed by the company of the Hungarian State Opera, whose soloists are far less afflicted with Slavonic wobbles than is common in Eastern Europe. Notable in the cast are Ilona Tokody as the heroine, Klára Takács, Lajos Miller as the Christian leader, and János Nagy as a disconcertingly engaging Nero, a tenor role. The recording is of outstanding quality, with the atmospheric perspectives demanded by the score conveyed most realistically.

Borodin, Alexander (1833–87)

Prince Igor: complete.
*** Sony Dig. S3K 44878 (3) [id.]. Sofia Nat. Op. Ch. & Festival O, Tchakarov.
　　Igor (Boris Martinovich), Yaroslavna (Stefka Evstatieva), Vladimir (Kaludi Kaludov), Prince Galitzky (Nikola Ghiuselev), Khan Kontchak (Nicolai Ghiaurov), Kontchakovna (Alexandrina Milcheva).
(M) **(*) EMI CMS7 63386-2 (3) [Ang. CDMC 63386]. Sofia Nat. Theatre Op. Ch. & O, Jerzy Semkow (with BORODIN: *Songs* ***).
　　Igor (Constantin Chekerliski), Yaroslavna (Julia Wiener), Vladimir (Todor Todorov), Prince Galitzky / Khan Kontchak (Boris Christoff), Kontchakovna (Reni Penkova).

Borodin's great opera takes place in medieval Russia towards the end of the twelfth century. An eclipse of the sun which has just occurred is regarded as a bad omen. Nevertheless Prince Igor ignores the warnings of his advisers and departs with his son Vladimir from Putivl to pursue the Tartar tribe, the Polovtsi, enemies of his father. Igor's wife, Yaroslava, is left behind and her brother, the none too reliable Prince Vladimir Galitzky, is appointed as regent in the Prince's absence.

News soon arrives that Igor and his followers have been defeated and that both he and his son have been taken prisoner. Yaroslava is comforted when the loyal boyars swear to defend her. However, in the Polovtsi camp Khan Kontchak, surprisingly, proves generous to Igor and his fellow prisoners and entertains them with the famous *Polovtsian dances.* Igor's son falls in love with the Khan's daughter, Kontchakovna, and she returns his passion.

The Khan welcomes the match but, hearing that the victorious Polovtsians are about to attack Putivl, Prince Igor escapes, leaving his son behind to marry Kontchakovna, and returns home to his welcoming wife who is still alive in the ruined city.

Tchakarov's complete recording of *Prince Igor* fills one of the most important gaps in the catalogue. It may give an idea of the quality of the singing that the soloist over whom there are most reservations, Nicola Ghiuselev as Galitzky, powerful but rather unsteady, is one of the two most celebrated international stars in the Sofia cast. The other, Nicolai Ghiaurov, makes a splendid Kontchak, if not quite as characterful as Christoff on the EMI set. Boris Martinovich makes a firm, very virile Igor, and both the principal women have vibrantly Slavonic voices which still never distract in wobbling: Stefka Evstatieva very moving and young-sounding as Igor's wife, Yaroslavna, and Alexandrina Milcheva as Kontchak's daughter. Kaludi Kaludov sings with Slavonic tightness at times, but that too is apt. Tchakarov takes a generally brisk view of the score. The dramatic tension in this long work is held very well and its richness of invention over its episodic span comes across vividly, notably in all its memorable melody and high colour. The performance is particularly moving in Act III, where – thanks to the 'creative editing' of Rimsky-Korsakov and Glazunov – the score is enhanced by the ideas they also used in the *Overture,* culminating in the glorious final trio between Igor, his son and Kontchak's daughter. Full, brilliant recording to match the orchestration.

Recorded in Paris in 1966, the colourful EMI version of *Prince Igor* was never given international circulation – except briefly in a highlights disc – until this mid-price CD transfer appeared in 1990. Its great flaw is that Act III is completely omitted on the grounds that it was almost entirely the work of Rimsky-Korsakov and Glazunov. The great glory of the performance is the singing of Boris Christoff as both Galitzky and Kontchak, easily outshining all rivals. Jerzy Semkow with his Sofia Opera forces is most sympathetic, but the other soloists are almost all disappointing, with the women sour-toned and the men often strained and unsteady. There is no libretto; but EMI is very generous with cueing points, and you can follow the story easily by checking them against the very detailed synopsis. The sound is limited but agreeably atmospheric. As makeweight, EMI include 16 songs by Borodin, rare items given glorious performances by Boris Christoff, recorded in the 1960s when his voice was at its richest and most expressive.

Boughton, Rutland (1878-1960)

The Immortal Hour: complete.
*** Hyp. Dig. CDA 66101/2 [id.]. Geoffrey Mitchell Ch., ECO, Melville.
   Dalua (Roderick Kennedy), Etain (Anne Dawson), Eochaidh (David Wilson-Johnson), Midir (Maldwyn Davies).

This gently lyrical evocation of Celtic twilight took London by storm in the 1920s and early 1930s, with four extended runs. There is far more to it than the still-celebrated *Faery song*, which first is heard hauntingly at the end of Act I, from a chorus in the distance, singing the praises of 'the lordly ones who dwell in the hollow hills'.

The heroine, Etain, who comes from the Land of the Young but who has lost her memory and cannot recall her fairy past, is discovered wandering in the forest by the King of the Druids. He has begged the gods to send him a lady fairer than any mortal. It is, of course, Etain, and the Druid King tells her that he loves her and together, spellbound, they listen to the magical voices.

The Druids welcome Etain and celebrate the nuptials of the happy couple; but they are both uneasy after hearing faraway laughter, and sense the presence of ghostly shapes. Their forebodings are realized when a stranger, Midir, appears, clad in pure gold. Etain is mystically drawn towards him and the haunting melody of the fairies is heard again. He kisses Etain's hand and, entranced, she follows Midir as he sings of the Land of Youth where there is no death. She does not heed her new husband's voice imploring her to stay. Darkness suddenly surrounds them and the desolate Druid King falls to the ground.

Analysed closely, much of the opera may seem like Vaughan Williams and water, but this fine performance, conducted by a lifelong Boughton devotee, brings out the hypnotic quality which had 1920s music-lovers attending performances many times over. The simple tunefulness goes with a fine feeling for atmosphere. The excellent cast of young singers includes Anne Dawson, as the heroine, Princess Etain, and Maldwyn Davies headily beautiful in the main tenor rendering of the *Faery song*. Warm, reverberant recording, undoubtedly enhanced in its CD format.

Britten, Benjamin (1913-76)

Albert Herring (complete).
**(*) Decca 421 849-2 (2) [id.]. ECO, Ward, composer.
   Albert Herring (Peter Pears), Lady Billows (Sylvia Fisher), Mr Gedge (John Noble), Mr Budd (Owen Brannigan), Miss Wordsworth (April Cantelo).

The CD transfer of Britten's own 1964 recording of the comic opera, *Albert Herring*, is a delight. On two CDs instead of six LP sides, the comedy comes over with an immediacy and sense of presence which have you involved straight away in the improbable tale of the May King, chosen when no local girl is counted suitable, for none has a sufficiently unstained character. Lady Billows hosts the committee which makes the choice and it includes her housekeeper, the local head teacher, the vicar, the mayor and Superintendent Budd. Albert Herring, it is decided, is sufficiently virtuous, if possibly backward.

Meanwhile Albert in the grocer's shop owned by his mother decides that something is missing from his life and reflects that his mother is very strict. She nevertheless encourages him to become May King; delighted children, peering through the windows, discover that his mother has taken a stick to Albert to help persuade him.

The May Festival takes place. Lady Billows presents Albert with twenty-five sovereigns as his prize. But the lemonade he has been given at the ceremony is laced with rum and, with money in his pocket, he sets out to have a good time, changing from a docile mother's boy into an exuberant male. His disappearance first causes consternation then brings a catalogue of debauchery (albeit not too serious) and, unrepentant, he throws his orange-blossom wreath out to the audience.

With only a single break, the opera flows easily on record, and the casting is exceptionally strong. Peter Pears's portrait of the innocent Albert was caught only just before he got too old for the role, but it is full of unique touches. Sylvia Fisher is a magnificent Lady Billows, and it is good to have so wide a range of British singers of the 1960s so characterfully presented – as, for example, Sheila Rex, whose tiny portrait of Albert's mother is a gem. The recording, made in Jubilee Hall, remains astonishingly vivid.

The Beggar's Opera – see below under John Gay

Billy Budd (complete).
*** Decca 417 428-2 (3) [id.]. Wandsworth School Boys' Ch., Amb. Op. Ch., LSO, composer
(with *Holy sonnets of John Donne; Songs and proverbs of William Blake* ***).
Billy Budd (Peter Glossop), Captain Vere (Peter Pears), Claggart (Michael Langdon), Mr
Redburn (John Shirley-Quirk).

This was the last opera recording supervised for Decca by John Culshaw; by then he had already taken up his new role at the BBC, but he returned with the keenest enjoyment for this long-cherished project and successfully capped his earlier outstanding achievements in Wagner as well as Britten. The opera itself, daring in its use of an all-male cast without however lacking variety of texture, emerges magnificently. The libretto, by E. M. Forster and Eric Crozier, is more skilled than those Britten usually set, and the range of characterization – so apparently limited in a tale of good and evil directly confronting one another – is masterly, with Peter Pears's role of Captain Vere presenting the moral issue at its most moving.

The French Revolution provides the historical background to the opera. At that time the Admiralty feared that the new spirit of freedom might undermine discipline and even encourage mutiny in the Royal Navy. When the opera opens, Captain Vere as an old man is musing on the mystery of good and evil, then he recalls the events of 1797 when he was in command of HMS *Indomitable*. The young Billy Budd is recruited from a merchant ship, the *Rights-o'-Man*, and Billy sings out exuberantly, and with unknowing irony, 'Farewell to old comrades, farewell to the *Rights-o'-Man*'. The fear of mutiny haunts the ship and a novice is mercilessly flogged.

As action against the French draws near, Captain Vere pledges to support his men to the utmost. The crew respond and show every faith in their captain. Throughout the voyage Vere retains his good opinion of Billy; but other officers taunt the lad when he stammers, and Claggart, full of evil and loathing innocence, sings, 'I, John Claggart, Master-at-Arms upon the *Indomitable*, have you in my power and I will destroy you.' And so he does, accusing him of mutiny in a confrontation before the captain. Billy stutters his innocence and then lashes out in despair at Claggart, hitting him on the forehead. Claggart falls dead.

Although Vere still believes that Billy is essentially blameless in the affair, he is powerless to prevent Billy's execution. However, Billy does not lose faith in his captain and, as he is sentenced, shouts, 'Starry Vere, God bless you!' finally ascending the mast to his death.

Britten's master-stroke, representing the confrontation of Vere and the condemned Billy in a sequence of 34 bare common chords, is irresistible, and the many richly imaginative strokes – atmospheric as well as dramatic – are superbly managed. An almost ideal cast, with Glossop a bluff, heroic Billy and Langdon a sharply dark-toned Claggart, make these symbol-figures believable. Magnificent sound. The layout on three CDs begins with the *John Donne Holy Sonnets* and *Songs and Proverbs of William Blake* (admirably sung by Peter Pears and Dietrich Fischer-Dieskau respectively, with the composer at the piano). This is followed by the Prologue and Act I of the opera, which continues on the second disc; Act III is on the third disc.

The Burning fiery furnace (2nd parable for church performance), Op. 77.
(M) *** Decca 414 663-2. Ch. & O of E. Opera Group, composer and Viola Tunnard.
Nebuchadnezzar (Peter Pears), Astrologer (Bryan Drake), Ananias (John Shirley-Quirk),
Misael (Robert Tear), Azarias (Stafford Dean), Herald (Peter Leeming).

Britten's conception of the church parable, so highly individual with its ritual elements (the audience turned into a medieval congregation), yet allows the widest variety of construction and expression. The story of *Burning fiery furnace* is obviously dramatic in the operatic sense, with vivid scenes like the *Entrance of Nebuchadnezzar*, the *Raising of the idol* and the putting of the three Israelites into the furnace. Britten is as imaginative as ever in his settings, and one must mention also the marvellous central interlude where the instrumentalists process round the church, which is stunningly well conveyed by the recording. The performers, both singers and players, are the same hand-picked cast that participated in the first performance at Orford

Parish Church, where this record was made. This is another example of the way Decca served Britten in providing definitive versions of his major scores for the guidance of all future performers, as well as for our enjoyment at home. The recording on CD possesses great vividness and presence.

Curlew River (1st parable for church performance).
(M) *** Decca 421 858-2 [id.]. Instrumental Ens., composer and Viola Tunnard.
    Madwoman (Peter Pears), Ferryman (John Shirley-Quirk), Abbot (Harold Blackburn), Traveller (Bryan Drake), Voice of the Spirit (Barbara Webb).

Few dramatic works have been based on a more unlikely idea than *Curlew River*. Whether you call it an opera or, as the composer himself did, a parable for church performance, the result is a dramatic entertainment that defies all convention, anticipating later developments and in many ways undercutting the avant-garde.

The work was initially inspired by Britten's recollection of a Noh-play which he saw in Japan, and in *Curlew River* he not only transferred the setting to a medieval monastery by the Curlew River in East Anglia but also deliberately adopted the slowest possible pace for the bald, uncomplicated drama. There are overtones too of Eastern music (Balinese rather than Japanese) in the highly original instrumentation and often free approach to rhythm, but the work's ultimate success stems mainly from the vividness of the atmosphere within a monastery setting.

Actively helped by Britten, John Culshaw, the recording manager, succeeded wonderfully well in conveying the church atmosphere by stereo sound alone, and in some ways this presents a more intimate and vivid experience than even a live performance. Harold Blackburn plays the Abbot of the monastery who introduces the drama, while John Shirley-Quirk plays the ferryman who takes people across the Curlew River, and Peter Pears sings the part of the woman who, distracted, has searched fruitlessly for her abducted child. Now she is to find out what happened to him.

Her coming is foretold by a traveller who, together with a group of pilgrims, accompanies her across in the boat, where the ferryman recalls a little boy whom he ferried across exactly a year before; the boy had been kidnapped from his home in the Black Mountains and, after escaping from the kidnapper who had ill-treated him, the boy died of his injuries on reaching the far shore. The ghost of the murdered boy appears and commiserates with his mother.

Following monastic as well as oriental practice, the role of the madwoman goes to a male singer, but one accepts the convention amazingly quickly, for the stylization involved somehow adds to the impact of the emotions underlying the story. The recording is outstanding, even by Decca standards, as the vivid CD transfer readily demonstrates.

Death in Venice (complete).
*** Decca 425 669-2 (2) [id.]. E. Op. Group Ch., ECO, Bedford.
    Gustav von Aschenbach (Peter Pears), Voice of Dionysus, etc. (John Shirley-Quirk), Voice of Apollo (James Bowman), Hotel Porter (Kenneth Bowen), English Clerk (Peter Leeming).

Thomas Mann's novella, which made an expansively atmospheric film far removed from the world of Mann, here makes a surprisingly successful opera, totally original in its alternation of monologue for the central character (on two levels, inner and external) and colourful set-pieces showing off the world of Venice and the arrival of the plague. Aschenbach's tortured aspirations and inner turmoil are at the core of everything that happens. Yet he is not entirely in control of his own destiny, being urged along what appears to be a predestined route by a strange group of characters, a fop, a gondolier, a barber and the hotel manager.

In Munich he dwells upon his inability to write – he cannot find the words. Without truly understanding his own motives, he embarks for Venice. The Elderly Fop taunts him, and again Aschenbach wishes himself elsewhere. In a black gondola (to suggest death) he is taken against his inner will to the Lido. Here he meets the Lady with the pearls and her son Tadzio, the key figures in the story's nemesis. The sirocco, the street vendors and the beggars all cause Aschenbach discomfort. He wishes to move on but he cannot.

He sits alone in his chair and dreams of Apollo of ancient Greece, perhaps a mirror-image of Tadzio whom Aschenbach now believes he loves. He feels that the boy could again inspire him to write. Now Aschenbach craves youth: he dyes his hair and applies rouge to his cheeks. Then he is told that cholera has been diagnosed in Venice; the hotel guests leave. But Tadzio is playing with his friends on the beach and roughly they push his face into the sand. Aschenbach cries out his name and falls back in his chair, dead.

Britten's inspiration, drawing together threads from all his earlier operas from *Peter Grimes* to the *Church parables*, is nothing less than exuberant, with the chamber orchestra producing the richest possible sounds. Pears's searching performance in the central role of Aschenbach is set against the darkly sardonic singing of John Shirley-Quirk in a sequence of roles as the Dionysiac figure who draws Aschenbach to his destruction. The recording is extremely vivid in its CD format and, though Steuart Bedford's assured conducting lacks some of the punch that Britten would have brought, the whole presentation makes this a set to establish the work outside the opera house as the culminating masterpiece of Britten's cycle of operas.

Gloriana (complete).
*** Decca Dig. 440 213-2 (2) [id.]. WNO Ch. & O, Mackerras.
    Queen Elizabeth I (Josephine Barstow), Earl of Essex (Philip Langridge), Lady Essex (Della Jones), Lord Mountjoy (Jonathan Summers).

It took exactly 40 years for Britten's coronation opera, *Gloriana*, to appear in a recording, reflecting the deep disappointment, even derision, that greeted its first staging at Covent Garden in 1953 as a tribute to Queen Elizabeth II on her coronation. It was not just that the first-night audience was largely made up of notables with little musical knowledge or taste, but that its searching portrait of Queen Elizabeth I had more than its measure of darkness. If Britten, mindful of the need to celebrate a new Elizabethan Age, included pageants, processions, balls and masques, by the final Act they had faded away in favour of painful tragedy. Instead of a celebration, *Gloriana* represents a dying fall, with no happy ending, only the portrait of a lonely monarch forced to do her duty and condemn to the scaffold a man, the Earl of Essex, whom she loved more than anyone, but who had rebelled against her.

As the opera opens, a tournament is being held. The Earl of Essex jealously watches its outcome, since Lord Mountjoy is the victor. They quarrel and in their fight Essex receives a minor wound. The queen commands a reconciliation. Later she discusses the rivalry between Essex and Mountjoy with Sir Robert Cecil at Nonesuch Palace, and Cecil warns her of Essex's impulsiveness. She admires that very feature of his character but she reassures Cecil that, though she loves him, she is not looking for a marriage – England is her prime interest.

Cecil leaves as Essex enters, and it is obvious that the queen is very fond of her earl, whom she calls her Robin. He accompanies on his lute as they sing nostalgically of a life without the responsibilities of court and throne. But the queen is on her guard against his feelings getting out of hand. He urges her to dispatch him to deal with the rebel, Tyrone, in Ireland but she is noncommittal.

The queen, on her progress to Norwich, watches a masque in which Time and Concord pay her homage. Essex feels isolated when he cannot be close to her. Meanwhile Mountjoy and Lady Penelope Rich are meeting secretly in the garden of Essex's house and, when they come upon Essex and his wife, Essex's frustration leads to what amounts to treasonable disrespect for the queen's authority, in which Lady Essex does not participate.

In the Great Room of Whitehall Palace, Essex and his wife make a grand entrance. Lady Essex's dress (chosen by her husband) is spectacularly opulent and obviously is designed to upstage the queen. The latter eyes the costume critically then orders a vigorous dance, and subsequently suggests that the ladies might like to change their clothes. Lady Essex reappears, altogether more soberly garbed and obviously distressed, for her elaborate costume has disappeared. But now the queen re-enters wearing that same dress, which is too small for her and makes her look very undignified. She goes off in a display of chagrin, leaving Lady Essex in tears and Mountjoy and Essex furious. Returning as soon as she has changed back into her own regal costume, she announces the appointment of Essex as Lord Deputy in Ireland, to his evident gratification.

Now Essex unceremoniously bursts in on the queen in her dressing room. She is still in her night attire and without her wig, but he cannot wait. He has been unable to defeat Tyrone in Ireland and is frightened that in consequence he may be out of favour. She coolly rebukes him and sends him off, and Cecil warns her later that Essex may be a danger to her. In the streets of London we hear the news that Essex has escaped from house arrest and is now leading an untrained army. Cuffe, Essex's confidant, tries to stir up the crowd to support the renegade earl but he is unsuccessful and Essex is found guilty of treason and condemned to death.

The queen has not yet signed the warrant for his execution, and Lady Essex, Lady Rich and Mountjoy beg for leniency. Though she feels sympathy for Essex's wife, the queen feels insulted by the boldly aggressive pleas of Lady Rich. She signs the execution order.

We last see Queen Elizabeth, old, frail and alone, but still dedicated to England and loved by her people.

Britten wrote that central role of the Virgin Queen for his friend and collaborator, Joan Cross, and one would have thought that many more sopranos or mezzos towards the end of their careers would have jumped at such a rich acting role. There were earlier plans for recording *Gloriana* with Dame Janet Baker, first with Britten himself conducting and later with Simon Rattle, but they fell through. Without effacing memories of earlier interpreters, Josephine Barstow gives a splendid reading, tough and incisive, with the slight unevenness in the voice adding to the abrasiveness. No easy option, this one.

Only in the final scene when, after the execution of Essex, the queen muses to herself in fragments of spoken monologue does the reading lack weight. A chestier speaking voice would have helped, but just before that the final confrontation between Elizabeth and Essex brings a thrilling climax in what amounts to an 'out-of-love' duet. Elizabeth attacks her lover not for infidelity but for treason. This astonishingly original sequence, full of anger, finally resolves itself in a tender reminiscence of one of Essex's lute-songs, movingly indicating the queen's continuing love.

Philip Langridge's portrait of Essex is, if anything, even more striking. More than the original interpreter, Peter Pears, he consistently brings out the character's arrogant bravado, the quality which first attracted the queen but then finally destroyed the man. Though Langridge's voice is mellifluous and flexible in the lute songs, its bright, cutting quality helps to enhance that characterization.

The rest of the cast is equally starry, with Alan Opie as the queen's principal adviser, Sir Robert Cecil, balefully dark rather than sinister, while the warm-toned Della Jones as Essex's wife and the abrasive Yvonne Kenny as his sister, Lady Penelope Rich, both well cast, sharply draw out the opposing sides of the queen's character, when in turn they make their final pleas for Essex's life, the latter with disastrous results.

In addition, it is generous casting to have such outstanding and characterful singers as Bryn Terfel, Willard White, John Shirley-Quirk and John Mark Ainsley in tiny roles, all very well suited. Sir Charles Mackerras directs his Welsh National Opera forces in a performance that brings out the full splendour of this rich score, characteristically full of original effects, as well as boasting the colourful genre pieces that have become known separately. The Decca recording, made in Brangwyn Hall, Swansea, is comparably splendid, a crowning achievement in the complete cycle of Britten operas begun by the composer himself.

Gloriana: Choral dances.
*** Hyp. CDA 66175 [id.]. Martyn Hill, Thelma Owen, Holst Singers & O, Hilary Davan Wetton (with BLISS: *Lie strewn the white flocks;* HOLST: *Choral hymns from the Rig Veda* ***).

It is little short of a scandal that it took so long for so great an opera as *Gloriana* to be recorded in its entirety. The composer's own choral suite, made up of unaccompanied choral dances linked by passages for solo tenor and harp, makes a valuable supplement, an excellent coupling for the equally attractive Bliss and Holst items. Excellent, atmospheric recording.

(i) *The Little Sweep* (children's opera); (ii) *Children's Crusade*; (iii) *Gemini variations.*
(M) (***) Decca mono/stereo 436 393-2 [id.]. (i) Jennifer Vyvyan, April Cantelo, Marilyn Baker, Gabrielle Soskin, David Hemmings, Michael Ingram, Robin Fairhurst, Vyn Vaughan, Nancy Thomas, Peter Pears, Trevor Anthony, E. Op. Group O; (ii) Wandsworth School Boys' Ch. & O; composer; (iii) Gabriel & Zoltán Jeney.

The Little Sweep is the one-Act opera taking place in a country house in 1810, rehearsed and finally performed in the entertainment, *Let's make an opera*. The opera is set in the nursery of Iken Hall, in January 1810. Black Bob, the sweep-master, enters with Clem, his son and assistant. Black Bob is an oafish character who cares little for the feelings of his young apprentice, Sam, who has the task of actually going up the chimneys, which nearly asphyxiates him.

He enters, looking wretched and miserable, but Miss Baggott, the housekeeper, is impatient for the chimneys to be swept. Rowan, the nursery-maid, sees the boy weeping for fear and takes pity on him; Black Bob tries to convince her that Sam enjoys going up, and the boy is forced to agree, or be 'roasted'. Sam duly goes up the chimney and gets stuck.

The children of the house now come in and, hearing his cries for help, pull hard on his rope and down he comes in a shower of soot. He is not hurt and they hide him, then bathe him, and he stands before them, squeaky clean, until they can find him clothes, at the same time discovering he is only nine years old. Hidden in the toy cupboard, he is about to be discovered by Miss Baggott, when Juliet, the daughter of the house, collapses and distracts her attention. Sam is fed and Juliet gives him some money, then, hidden in a trunk, off he goes on the coach to make his escape.

The joy of the piece in performance is that the members of the audience not only see the work developing but are themselves rehearsed and finally perform in the four choruses which punctuate the scenes. Here, understandably, the recording is limited to the completed opera, with the choruses sounding slightly under-sung. With dated language, it has become a period piece, but in this original mono recording, conducted by Britten himself, the fizzing vitality comes over very vividly. The spatial effects involving offstage voices – as in the search for the little sweep, Sammy – are so well focused that they almost give the impression of stereo. The transfer is very clean, bringing out the bite of the composer's own direction of a strong cast drawn from singers he had worked with at the Aldeburgh Festival, notably April Cantelo as Juliet, the eldest child, Jennifer Vyvyan as Rowan, the nursery-maid, and the boy treble, David Hemmings, later an adult film-star, as the sweep-boy, Sammy.

The two works provided as a very generous coupling are the ingenious 'Quartet for two players', written for the Jeney twins, who play it here, and the dark and rather sour cantata that Britten wrote to words by Berthold Brecht for the fiftieth anniversary of the Save the Children Fund. Both have good 1960s stereo recording.

A Midsummer Night's Dream (complete).
*** Decca 425 663-2 (2) [id.]. Downside and Emanuel Schools Ch., LSO, composer.
   Oberon (Alfred Deller), Tytania (Elizabeth Harwood), Lysander (Peter Pears), Demetrius (Thomas Hemsley), Hermia (Josephine Veasey), Helena (Heather Harper), Theseus (John Shirley-Quirk), Hippolyta (Helen Watts), Bottom (Owen Brannigan).
*** Virgin/EMI Dig. VCDC7 59305-2 (2). Trinity Boys' Ch., City of L. Sinfonia, Hickox.
   Oberon (James Bowman), Tytania (Lilian Watson), Lysander (John Graham Hall), Demetrius (Henry Herford), Hermia (Della Jones), Helena (Jill Gomez), Theseus (Norman Bailey), Hippolyta (Penelope Walker), Bottom (Donald Maxwell).

Britten and Pears together prepared the libretto for this opera by careful compression of the Shakespeare words. What this recording confirms – with the aid of the score – more than any live performance is how compressed the music is, as well as the words. The opera places greater emphasis than the original play on the somewhat sinister powers of Oberon. Tytania, his queen, has stolen a changeling boy and Oberon craves him, so they quarrel and Oberon plots revenge.

Puck, Oberon's lively agent, is sent to find a herb whose juice will cause any man or woman on waking to fall in love with the nearest mortal. Oberon sprays the juice on Tytania's eyes. She wakens and falls in love with Bottom, the weaver, who is wearing an ass's head. The other mortal characters in the opera have similar problems, Lysander, Hermia, Demetrius and Helena each in love with the wrong person.

The climax comes with a performance of a play by the rustics to celebrate the nuptials of the Duke of Athens, and then in lordly fashion Oberon releases Tytania from the spell and the mortals too are able to realign their affections.

One may regret the absence of rich and memorable tunes at first, but there is no thinness of argument and the atmosphere of every scene is brilliantly re-created in the most evocative orchestral sounds. The beauty of instrumental writing comes out in this recording even more than in the opera house, for John Culshaw, the recording manager, put an extra halo round the fairy music to act as a substitute for visual atmosphere. The problem of conveying the humour of the play-scene at the end with the 'rude mechanicals' cavorting about the stage proved more intractable. Humour is there all right, but the laughter of the stage audience is too ready for comfort.

Britten again proves himself an ideal interpreter of his own music and draws virtuoso playing from the LSO (marvellous trumpet sounds for Puck's music). Among the singers Peter Pears has shifted from his original role as Flute (the one who has the Donizetti mad-scene parody to sing) to the straight role of Lysander. The mechanicals are admirably led by Owen Brannigan as Bottom and, among the lovers, Josephine Veasey (Hermia) is outstanding. Deller, with his magical male alto singing, is the eerily effective Oberon.

Britten's own version sets standards all round almost impossible for any rival to outshine, yet Richard Hickox in his recording with the City of London Sinfonia provides an alternative which in significant ways is preferable. With a chamber orchestra rather than the LSO, the scale is more intimate, and the full, immediate, digital recording captures the sound just as vividly as John Culshaw's vintage Decca. The chorus of boy-treble fairies is smaller and more believable in the new performance, bright and vigorous with an attractively raw timbre of which Britten himself would have approved.

Hickox, too, with his smaller band points jazzy syncopations more infectiously, yet only in the final Pyramus and Thisby play with its operatic parodies from Donizetti to Berg does the comedy of the rude mechanicals come over as it did under Britten. Donald Maxwell sings the role of Bottom with a clear, virile directness, but he does not have the sense of fun of Owen Brannigan on the earlier set.

Conversely, the two pairs of lovers on the new set capture more pointedly than their predecessors the element of melodramatic parody in the mismatching of partners caused by Puck's machinations, and the quarrel between Hermia (Della Jones) and Helena (Jill Gomez) is both vivid and amusing. John Graham Hall as Lysander and Henry Herford as Demetrius are both aptly fresh and young-sounding. Among the others, Lilian Watson makes a bright Tytania, less beautiful in tone than Elizabeth Harwood on Britten's set but more clearly an other-worldly spirit; while central to the success of Hickox's performance is the masterly characterization of Oberon by James Bowman, far more telling and mysterious than Alfred Deller's original.

What makes the set indispensable is that it includes a brief 90-second sequence, intensely poetic, in the scene of the lovers' awakening in Act III, where Britten's own recording observes a cut as made in the original Aldeburgh staging. The exchanges among the four, asking if they are still dreaming, provide a tenderly charming preparation for their final reconciliation, a moment it is surprising that Britten ever agreed to cut.

(i) *Noye's Fludde;* (ii) *The Golden Vanity.*
(M) *** Decca 436 397-2. (i) East Suffolk Children's Ch. & O, E. Op. Group O, Del Mar; (ii) Wandsworth School Boys' Ch., Burgess, composer (piano).
Noye (Owen Brannigan), Mrs Noye (Sheila Rex), Voice of God (Trevor Anthony).

(i) *Noye's fludde;* (ii) *Serenade for tenor, horn & strings, Op. 31.*
**(*) Virgin/EMI Dig. VC7 91129-2; *VC7 91129-4* [id.]. (i) Salisbury & Chester Schools Ch. & O, Coull Qt, Alley, Watson, A. Harwood, Endymion Ens. (members); (ii) Martyn Hill, Frank Lloyd, City of L. Sinf., Hickox.
Noye (Donald Maxwell), Mrs Noye (Linda Ormiston), Voice of God (Richard Pasco).

The Golden Vanity is a 'vaudeville' written for the Vienna Boys' Choir. The tale of the cabin boy who sinks the threatening pirate ship and is then drowned by his wicked captain is simply and vividly told, with the help of the well-known folksong, and the recording does wonders in recapturing the fun of performance, with its play ritual round the stage. The Wandsworth Boys are completely at home in the music and sing with pleasing freshness. The coupling, Britten's infectious children's oratorio, was recorded during the 1961 Aldeburgh Festival, and not only the professional choristers but the children too have the time of their lives to the greater glory of God. All the effects have been captured miraculously here, most strikingly the entry into the Ark, while a bugle band blares out fanfares which finally turn into a rollicking march. Altogether this coupling makes a wonderful record, with the stereo readily catching the sense of occasion and particularly the sound of *Eternal father* rising above the storm at the climax of *Noye's Fludde.*

A modern digital recording of Britten's vividly atmospheric setting of the Chester Miracle Play based on the biblical Noah's Ark story is also welcome. The sound for this fine Hickox performance is clearer, fuller and richer than Del Mar's Decca version, and the performance generally has cleaner attack and discipline, yet in one important way it does not match its predecessor. On the Virgin disc the instrumental forces, including a schools' orchestra as well as professional soloists, are relatively recessed. Compare the storm sequence here with the Decca account, and the distancing undermines any feeling of threat so that the entry of the hymn, *Eternal father,* instantly submerges the orchestral sound instead of battling against it. There the Del Mar performance remains far more exciting, and not even Donald Maxwell as Noah, strong and virile, can efface memories of the incomparable Owen Brannigan. The entry of the animals and birds is also caught less dramatically here, though it is much more precise on detail. Taken on its own, this is a splendid issue, made the more attractive by the inclusion of Martyn Hill's account of the *Serenade.*

(i) *Owen Wingrave* (complete). (ii) *6 Hölderlin fragments;* (iii) *The Poet's Echo.*
*** Decca 433 200-2 (2) [id.]. ECO, composer; (ii) Pears, composer (piano); (iii) Galina Vishnevskaya, Mstislav Rostropovich (piano).
(i) Owen Wingrave (Benjamin Luxon), Spencer Coyle (John Shirley-Quirk), Lechmere (Nigel

Douglas), Miss Wingrave (Sylvia Fisher), Mrs Coyle (Heather Harper), Mrs Julian (Jennifer Vyvyan), Kate Julian (Janet Baker), Sir Philip Wingrave / Narrator (Peter Pears).

Britten's television opera had a bigger audience for its world-wide first performance than most composers receive for all the performances of all their operas put together. It marked a return after the church parables to the mainstream Britten pattern of opera with a central character isolated from society.

Owen Wingrave is the son of a military family that is obsessed with the codes and traditions of the service. The women of the household are, if anything, more intimidating than the men, notably Miss Jane Wingrave who has already been responsible for her betrothed going off to meet his death in the Indian Mutiny. His sister, Mrs Julian, is now housekeeper, and her young daughter, Kate, is attracted to Owen. She, unfortunately, is infected with the need to find valour in the man with whom she chooses to mate, and she is quite unrelenting.

Owen's father died in the field; his mother met her match in childbirth. His older brother is confined to an asylum. The other male member of the household is a relic of the past, the grandfather, Sir Philip. The great-grandfather (a colonel) has created the family legend. In a fit of anger he had struck one of his children a mortal blow; next morning he was found dead in the room where the boy's body had been lying. Kate demands that Owen prove his courage by spending the night in the 'haunted' room, and he, too, is found dead in the morning, looking like 'a soldier on the battlefield'.

Each of the seven characters is strongly conceived, with the composer writing especially for the individual singers chosen for the television and gramophone presentations. The recording was made immediately after the trials of the television recording, and the result is even more concentrated and compelling. Strangely enough, the drama, based on a short story by Henry James, seems less contrived when one has to imagine the setting instead of having it presented on the screen, particularly as the recording is so atmospheric and the production so sensitive. The recording of the orchestra is particularly vivid in the admirable CD transfer and the additional items to fill up the second CD are most welcome.

The *Six Hölderlin fragments* stand rather apart from Britten's other songs, reflecting a highly individual response to the German language and the sensitive word-painting of Hölderlin. They may not be as striking as Britten's English songs, but, with Pears and the composer to interpret them, they make a highly original impression.

The Poet's Echo – Britten's setting of Pushkin poems in the original Russian – was written as a personal tribute to Vishnevskaya and her versatile cellist/pianist husband, and these miniatures have all the composer's characteristic crispness of image. Vishnevskaya's voice with its Slavonic unevenness is not the most suited in controlling the subtle line of such delicate songs, but with the help of Rostropovich the (1969) performance is committed and atmospheric.

Paul Bunyan (complete).
⊛ *** Virgin/EMI Dig. VCD 790710-2 (2) [id.]. Soloists, Ch. & O of Plymouth Music Series, Minnesota, Philip Brunelle.

Paul Bunyan (James Lawless), Johnny Inkslinger (Dan Dressen), Tiny (Elisabeth Comeaux Nelson).

Aptly, this first recording of Britten's choral operetta comes from the state, Minnesota, where the story of this legendary giant is set. Though written by an Englishman, it has been described as 'the most American opera yet'. The atmospheric opening Prologue brings a forest chorus of trees, rivers and wild birds. The name of Paul Bunyan is heard, due to be born at the next blue moon. The moon then turns blue and Paul, too large to be seen, sings that America is on its way. Lumberjacks appear and need a foreman. The King of Sweden sends a Western Union telegram recommending his finest lumberjack, Hel Helson, and the choice is clear.

Meanwhile Bunyan seeks and finds a wife, comparably large in build, and a daughter, Tiny, is born. Among the lumberjacks is Johnny Inkslinger, a pseudo-intellectual. He philosophizes about life and grumbles about the food, while the rest combine an interest in the food with the attractions of Tiny. Inkslinger finally admits that 'a guy's gotta eat'. However, Hel Helson decides to take over and incites rebellion against Bunyan's authority; Bunyan and he fight (offstage) to settle the matter in a traditional American manner. The engagement is announced of Tiny to Hot Biscuit Slim, while Inkslinger becomes a hotel manager in Manhattan. Bunyan's prolific ideas about the new world become practicalities, and a telegram from Hollywood promises Inkslinger fame. Bunyan reminds them all that 'America is what you do, what you choose to make it.'

The Plymouth Music Series under Philip Brunelle fields a team not of international singers but of enthusiasts. That they are American brings an immediate advantage not just in the spoken and sung accents but in the idiomatic feeling for the syncopated rhythms in this bold but initially unsuccessful attempt of the poet, W. H. Auden, and Britten to invade Broadway. It took many years before Britten would even look at this early score and agree to revise it. What now emerges is that the libretto, for all its point and wit, is largely to blame for any failure. When the principal character is a giant who can appear only as a disembodied voice, the piece works rather better on record or radio than on stage.

Musically, Britten's conscious assumption of popular American mannerisms does not prevent his invention from showing characteristic originality. Rightly, Michael Kennedy in his 'Master Musicians' book on Britten has argued that this is a key work in the composer's development, clearly anticipating later operas, notably *Peter Grimes* which was also spawned in Britten's American period. It is not just the jazzy, ballad-like songs and ensembles that stick in the memory but such charming numbers as *Tiny's song* (sung very freshly and sweetly by Elisabeth Comeaux Nelson). Also most memorable is the choral section of the *Prologue*, with its memorable Auden lines which specially moved Britten: 'But once in a while the odd thing happens, / Once in a while the dream comes true.' (He confessed many years later that he was thinking of how he met Peter Pears.) Recorded in clean, vivid sound, with Philip Brunelle a vigorous conductor, this excellent first recording richly deserves the prizes it won for the Virgin Classics label, now part of EMI. The cassettes are first class, too.

Peter Grimes (complete).
ⓢ *** Decca 414 577-2 (3) [id.]. Ch. and O of ROHCG, composer.
   Grimes (Peter Pears), Ellen Orford (Claire Watson), Balstrode (James Pease), Auntie (Jean Watson), Bob Bowles (Raymond Nilsson), Swallow (Owen Brannigan), Ned Keene (Geraint Evans), 1st Niece (Marion Studholme).
*** EMI Dig. CDC7 54832-2 (2) [id.]. Ch. & O of ROHCG, Bernard Haitink.
   Peter Grimes (Anthony Rolfe Johnson), Ellen (Felicity Lott), Balstrode (Thomas Allen).
(M) *** Ph. 432 578-2 (2) [id.]. ROHCG Ch. & O, C. Davis.
   Grimes (Jon Vickers), Ellen Orford (Heather Harper), Balstrode (Jonathan Summers), Auntie (Elizabeth Bainbridge), Bob Bowles (John Dobson), Swallow (Faye Robinson), Ned Keene (Thomas Allen), 1st Niece (Teresa Cahill).

The Decca recording of *Peter Grimes* was one of the first great achievements of the stereo era. Few opera recordings can claim to be so definitive, with Peter Pears, for whom it was written, in the name-part, Owen Brannigan (another member of the original team) and a first-rate cast. Claire Watson as Ellen Orford is not nearly as characterful as Joan Cross, for whom the part was written, but she gives a most sympathetic performance, and her voice records smoothly. Another member of the cast from across the Atlantic, James Pease, as the understanding Captain Balstrode, is brilliantly incisive musically and dramatically; but beyond that it becomes increasingly unfair to single out individual performances.

In the opera's Prologue an inquest is being held in the Moot Hall inquiring into the death of Peter Grimes's apprentice. Grimes tells of a change of wind driving his boat off course and of three desperate days without water, and he avers that the boy died of exposure. Feelings run high but a verdict of accidental death is recorded. Ellen Orford, the schoolmistress, tries to comfort Peter and a friendship is established.

Ned Keene the apothecary tells Grimes that he has located another apprentice; reluctantly the villagers agree to bring the boy from the workhouse. A storm rages and they are suspicious of the taciturn Grimes, an obvious misfit, who refuses to take shelter in the local inn. Captain Balstrode, however, lends a sympathetic ear when Grimes recounts his dreadful period in the boat with the dead boy's corpse. Grimes takes the orphan apprentice, John, home with him.

On Sunday morning Ellen talks to John and, while the church service is being held, she notices that he has a bruised neck and a torn coat. She begs Grimes to take heed of the boy's youth but Peter strikes Ellen and drives the boy off in front of him. The villagers abjure Ellen and set off to investigate Grimes's hut. In a violent reaction Grimes rushes the boy down the cliff-face towards the beach and, turning back to face the crowd, hears the shrill cry from the apprentice as he falls to his death.

Grimes disappears, but the boy's jersey is washed up on the shore, recognized by Ellen. Finally Grimes reappears, half crazed, dwelling on memories of his tragic existence. In a quiet, merciful tone Captain Balstrode tells Peter Grimes to take his boat out to sea and to scuttle her there.

Presently a coastguard reports that a boat has been seen sinking. The villagers, uninterested, go about their workaday lives.

Britten as conductor secures splendidly incisive playing, with the whole orchestra on its toes throughout. The recording, superbly atmospheric, even enhances what is possible in the theatre, for example making the distancing of the procession in Act II very vivid indeed. The digital remastering for CD miraculously has improved the sound still further. The striking overall bloom remains, yet solo voices and chorus are vividly clear and fully projected. Owen Brannigan sounds wonderfully ripe and present in the Prologue, while the orchestral sound is glorious. Some background noise remains, but it is not intrusive and, apart from that, one might think this a modern digital set. The 44 cues bring access to every item in the score. A marvellous sampler is provided by trying band 5 on the first disc; this brings the evocative *First Sea Interlude*, glowing with atmosphere, the very slight edge on the upper strings adding to the sense of bleakness. One hopes that before long Decca will transfer the set to two CDs instead of three.

Bernard Haitink's reading of *Grimes*, after Britten's own recording of 1959 and Sir Colin Davis's of 1978, represents a third generation of interpretation which, while learning from the composer's own example, brings new vitality and renewed freshness. That is in great measure due to Haitink's inspired conducting which, with heightened contrasts – helped by one of EMI's most spectacular recordings yet – finds more light and shade in this extraordinarily atmospheric score. Haitink is not the only one who has learnt from the composer's own recording. Far more than the Philips team, the EMI engineers have followed the vivid example of the 1959 Decca recording, as when the procession marches off to Grimes's hut in Act II. The distancing on EMI, as on Decca, reflects Britten's imaginative lowering of pitch – the Doppler effect in musical terms – as the voices get further away. By comparison the Philips reminds one more clearly of the studio.

Anthony Rolfe Johnson too comes far closer to Peter Pears in the Britten recording than Jon Vickers does for Davis, with his rugged, bull-like portrait. Vickers' speeds are almost all slower, not least in the two key monologues – when in Act II Grimes sees the sea 'boiling' with fish, and when, crazed in the fog at the end of Act III, he eludes the searchers. Rolfe Johnson is the most inward of the three, singing the most beautifully, less troubled than Pears by the high tessitura. He presents Grimes as suffering from hysteria rather than outright madness, and the result is at least as touching. Felicity Lott makes a tenderly sympathetic Ellen Orford, less mature than Heather Harper for Davis, more characterful than Claire Watson for Britten.

The sharply drawn characters of the Borough are all cast from strength with portraits, where necessary, larger than life. Sarah Walker, for example, is unforgettable as Mrs Sedley, the laudanum-taking gossip, and Thomas Allen is a wise and powerful Balstrode, making the Act III duel with Ellen an emotional resolution, preparing for the final tragedy. The Covent Garden Chorus and Orchestra are used in all three recordings, outstanding in all three but with the extra range and vividness of EMI's latest digital recording adding to the impact, not least of the chorus, whether singing on stage or in evocative off-stage effects. The set has the advantage over Britten's own of coming (like the Davis) on two instead of three discs, though the three-disc format allows each Act to be offered complete on a single disc.

Sir Colin Davis takes a fundamentally darker, tougher view of *Peter Grimes* than the composer himself. In some ways the result on his Philips set is even more powerful, if less varied and atmospheric, with the Borough turned into a place full of Strindbergian tensions and Grimes himself, powerful physically (not a misplaced intellectual), turned into a Hardy-like figure. It was Jon Vickers' heroic interpretation in the Met. production in New York which first prompted Davis to press for this recording, and the result sheds keen new illumination on what arguably remains the greatest of Britten's operas, even if it cannot be said to supplant the composer's own version. Plainly close in frame and spirit to Crabbe's rough fisherman, Vickers, slow-spoken and weighty, is frighteningly intense. Heather Harper as Ellen Orford is very moving, and there are fine contributions from Jonathan Summers as Captain Balstrode and Thomas Allen as Ned Keene. The lack of atmospheric effects in this set reinforces Davis's contention that the actual notes need no outside aid. The recording is full and vivid, with fine balancing.

The Prodigal Son (3rd parable for church performance), Op. 81.
(M) *** Decca 425 713-2. E. Op. Group Ch. & O, composer and Viola Tunnard.
     Tempter / Abbot (Peter Pears), Father (John Shirley-Quirk), Elder son (Bryan Drake), Younger son (Robert Tear).

The last of the parables is the sunniest and most heart-warming. Britten cleverly avoids the charge of oversweetness by introducing the Abbot, even before the play starts, in the role of Tempter, confessing that he represents evil and aims to destroy contentment in the family he describes: 'See how I break it up' – a marvellous line for Peter Pears.

Alas, the younger son of the famous biblical story is only too willing to respond to temptation and seek unknown delights in the city. He takes his inheritance along, and the Parasites spend it for him and leave him to join the beggars and share the food of the pigs. Utterly repentant, he returns home to be welcomed with the 'fatted calf' and the generous forgiveness not only of his father but also of his elder brother.

Britten's setting brings the story to vivid life and the piece, so suitable for recording, receives an ideal performance here, with characteristically real and atmospheric Decca recording.

(i) *The Rape of Lucretia* (complete); (ii) *Phaedra, Op. 93.*
*** Decca 425 666-2 (2) [id.]. (i) ECO, composer; (ii) J. Baker, ECO, Bedford.
  (i) Lucretia (Janet Baker), Male Chorus (Peter Pears), Female Chorus (Heather Harper), Tarquinius (Benjamin Luxon), Collatinus (John Shirley-Quirk).

In combining *The Rape of Lucretia* with *Phaedra* on CD, Decca celebrates two outstanding performances by Dame Janet Baker, recorded at the peak of her career. In particular her performance as Lucretia underlines the depth of feeling behind a work which, in its formal classical frame, may superficially appear to hide emotion. The logical problems of the story remain: why *should* Lucretia feel so guilty? The opera is framed by the comments of a male and female chorus who, at the close, hint at this enigma. They sit on thrones throughout the action and are almost static. As the story begins, Collatinus, Lucretia's husband, reasons with the Roman general, Junius, to control his angry jealousy of his wife's behaviour. But apparently he has good reason for his suspicions, as she was not at home on his return to their quarters. The virtue of Lucretia, however, is without question, and the smarting Junius taunts Tarquinius, Prince of Rome, suggesting that her chastity is unassailable. The ladies find tranquillity in their day-to-day lives and the female chorus upholds that view.

Prince Tarquinius owns a palace nearby but he amazes Lucretia and her companions by asking for her hospitality. She cannot refuse. The male chorus quietly describes Tarquinius's progress that night towards Lucretia's bedroom, where he takes his opportunity and awakens her with a kiss. Lucretia pleads for mercy and her honour, and both choruses take her part, exhorting him to leave the chamber. But Tarquinius extinguishes the candle with his sword, his mind made up.

Collatinus returns; Lucretia confesses all to him and he declares his forgiveness; totally distraught, she stabs herself and dies in his arms. The opera ends with the disbelief of the female chorus, while the words 'Christ is all' pervade the scene.

With Dame Janet Baker as Lucretia the heart-rending tragedy of the heroine is conveyed with passionate conviction. Her range of tone-colours, her natural feeling for words and musical phrasing are all used with supreme artistry. Among other distinguished vocal contributions to the opera, Peter Pears and Heather Harper stand out, while Benjamin Luxon makes the selfish Tarquinius into a living character. The stylization of the drama with its frame of Christian comment comes over even more effectively when imagined rather than seen. The seductive beauty of the writing – Britten then at his early peak – is splendidly caught, the melodies and tone-colours as ravishing as any that he ever conceived.

Similarly *Phaedra* – written at the very end of Britten's life – provides vocal writing which brings out every glorious facet of Dame Janet's voice. Setting words from Robert Lowell's fine translation of Racine's play, the composer encapsulates the character of the tragic heroine. The use of harpsichord in the recitatives linking the sections of this scena is no mere neo-classical device but a sharply dramatic and atmospheric stroke.

The Turn of the Screw.
(***) Decca mono 425 672-2 (2) [id.]. E. Op. Group O, composer.
  Prologue / Quint (Peter Pears), Governess (Jennifer Vyvyan), Miles (David Hemmings), Flora (Olive Dyer), Mrs Grose (Joan Cross), Miss Jessel (Arda Mandikian).

Britten's *Turn of the Screw* is a faithful adaptation of a story by Henry James, with the music, written in the form of variations, adding greatly to the malevolent atmosphere, to produce a growing sense of evil beneath the surface of everyday events.

A governess arrives at a lovely turreted house called Bly. Her duties have been made clear to her by the children's guardian: she is to be solely responsible for their welfare, with full jurisdiction over their actions. She must not at any time trouble the guardian with problems. But as the story proceeds, the menacing screw of nemesis is steadily turning so that the final tragedy seems inevitable.

At first the governess suffers misgivings at the strictures placed on her, but she finds the children, Flora and Miles, physically beautiful and the housekeeper, Mrs Grose, a chatty soul. Nevertheless foreboding creeps in when Miles is expelled from school, accused of injuring a friend. Mrs Grose defends him, saying he is not bad, only wilful, and the governess is somewhat reassured when the children sing nursery rhymes. However, her equanimity is further disturbed when she sees an unknown figure high up in the turret. She informs Mrs Grose, who is appalled, and it is evident that the figure is the ghost of Peter Quint, who had once dominated the household but who died.

It soon becomes evident that Peter Quint has a malignant influence over Miles while, hardly less alarmingly, Flora is beset by the equally sinister apparition of Miss Jessel, a former governess. The sayings and doings of the children become increasingly disconcerting and during a lesson Miles recites gender rhymes from his Latin grammar, and when the governess asks him what other tags he knows he sings and repeats a curiously enigmatic example: 'Malo: I would rather be / Malo: in an apple-tree, / Malo: Than a naughty boy, / Malo: in adversity.'

The horrified governess soon realizes that the two ghosts are holding sway over the children, no matter what she may do or say. In the churchyard they parody sacred words and, reaching breaking point, she is greatly tempted to leave. But instead, realizing that she cannot abandon her charges, she writes a letter to the children's guardian. Miles, urged on by the malevolent Quint, steals the letter. Then the sinister Miss Jessel tempts Flora to cross the lake and the child turns viciously against the governess. Mrs Grose tries to help, revealing that Miles has stolen the letter, but it is too late, Quint has won the struggle for the boy's soul and Miles dies screaming, 'Peter Quint – you devil!' The opera ends with haunting repetitions of Miles's 'Malo' song.

Though the recording is in mono only, the very dryness and sharpness of focus give an extra intensity to the composer's own incomparable reading of his most compressed opera. With such sound, the claustrophobic quality of this weird ghost story is intensified, along with the musical cogency of this sequence of 15 closely knit scenes. Peter Pears as Peter Quint is superbly matched by Jennifer Vyvyan as the governess and by Joan Cross as the housekeeper, Mrs Grose. It is fascinating too to hear the film-star-to-be, David Hemmings, as a boy treble, already a confident actor. Excellent CD transfer.

Busoni, Ferruccio (1866–1924)

Doktor Faust: complete.
(M) *** DG 427 413-2 (3) [id.]. Bav. Op. Ch. & R. O, Leitner.
  Doktor Faust (Dietrich Fischer-Dieskau), Mephistopheles (William Cochran), Duchess of Parma (Hildegard Hillebrecht), Wagner (Karl Christian Kohn).

That Busoni's epic *Doktor Faust*, left incomplete at the composer's death, is far more than just a cult opera or one to appeal only to German audiences was triumphantly proved when the English National Opera staged it at the Coliseum in London in 1986. Unlike that production – which used a more complete text than had ever been assembled before – this recording is full of small but tiresome cuts; however, with a magnificent performance from Fischer-Dieskau in the name-part and superb, fierily intense conducting from Leitner, it fully conveys the work's wayward mastery, the magnetic quality which establishes it as Busoni's supreme masterpiece, even though it was finished by another hand. The parallel with Puccini's *Turandot* (similarly left unfinished when its composer died in the same year, 1924) becomes closer than ever.

The narrative line takes a course utterly different from the works of Berlioz and Gounod. As the opera opens, Doktor Faust, working in his study, is informed by his companion, Wagner, that three students from Cracow are outside and wish to see him. They are apparently carrying a remarkable book, *Clavis Astartis Magica*, which Faust is aware contains magical powers. The students enter, dressed in black, and present him with the book plus its key and deeds of ownership. They refuse his offer of refreshment and leave. Wagner then returns to the study and declares that he has seen no one pass him.

Immediately aware that Mephistopheles has visited in one of his many disguises, Faust then uses the powers of the magic book to summon him back, calling on Lucifer to send down his servant. Flames blaze up and Mephistopheles, in his commoner human form, rises up from the sixth flame. Faust demands of him unconditional fulfilment of every wish of his life. Mephistopheles accedes, but his price is high: Faust must agree to serve Mephistopheles for eternity. Faust demurs, but Mephistopheles points out to him that his life is in ruins, with pressing debts and other problems.

Faust agrees reluctantly to the contract and is presented with a series of experiences, both strange and pleasurable, but always with a hint of evil subtly underlying them. He is given the dead body of a newborn babe, the outcome of an amorous adventure with the Duchess of Parma. Mephistopheles sets fire to the corpse, and Helen of Troy appears in the smoke and flames. The vision vanishes and the three students reappear to demand the return of the magic book, which Faust refuses.

The *Dies irae* is heard and again a dead child is thrust into the arms of Faust. Drawing a magic circle round the child, he wills his spirit to enter its body so that, reborn, he can atone for his past grievous behaviour. Faust dies and midnight strikes. A naked youth with arms held aloft rises from Faust's body and walks across the snow, while a night watchman bends over the corpse which remains on the ground and wonders how death occurred.

This performance, recorded in conjunction with a broadcast mounted by the European Broadcasting Union in 1969, fully substantiates the vision and originality of the opera. Being offbeat in its layout, the piece works more predictably on record than on stage. The cast is dominated by Fischer-Dieskau, here at his very finest; and the only weak link among the others is Hildegard Hillebrecht as the Duchess of Parma. In the CD transfer the vividness of the sound is intensified, with voices – rather forward of the orchestra – cleanly focused. Though this is a mid-price set in DG's 20th-Century Classics series, the documentation is generous, with essays and synopsis in four languages, and the complete libretto in English translation as well as the original German.

Campra, André (1660–1744)

L'Europe galante (opéra-ballet).
(M) *** HM/BMG GD 77059 (2) [77059-2-RG]. Rachel Yakar, Marjanne Kweksilber, René Jacobs, La Petite Bande, Leonhardt – LULLY: *Bourgeois gentilhomme.* ***

The sheer tunefulness of *L'Europe galante* has ensured its appeal over the years. This record, the first with period instruments, dates from 1973 and gives us the complete entertainment – and very delightful it is. Like Couperin's *Les Nations*, though in a very different fashion, this enchanting divertissement attempts to portray various national characteristics: French, Spanish, Italian and Turkish. The three soloists all shine and the instrumentalists, directed by Leonhardt, are both expert and spirited. The recording, too, is well balanced and sounds very fresh on CD. The only snag is that this now comes in harness with Lully's *Le bourgeois gentilhomme*, which is musically much thinner. Full translations are provided.

Idoménée (tragédie lyrique).
**(*) HM HMC 901396/8 (id.]. Les Arts Florissants, Christie.
Idoménée (Bernard Delétré), Electre (Sandrine Piau), Ilione (Monique Zanetti), Idamante (Jean-Paul Fouchécourt), Venus (Marie Boyer).

Representing a generation of French opera-composers between Lully and Rameau, André Campra was equally successful writing church music as in writing for the stage. One incidental distinction of this opera, *Idoménée*, the fifth of Campra's tragédies lyriques, first given in 1712, is that the libretto by Antoine Danchet was later used as a basis of the libretto for Mozart's great *opera seria* of 70 years later. The plot follows much the same course as that familiar from Mozart's opera. The big difference is that, where Mozart's opera is made to end happily, Danchet had fate triumphing at the end, when Idoménée in a fit of madness slays Idamante, his son. Ilione, the equivalent of Mozart's Ilia, then concludes that the king's punishment will be to go on living.

In this first complete recording of any opera by Campra, Christie opts for the later revision of the piece which the composer made for the revival in 1731, eliminating two incidental characters and reworking several scenes. It is a fluent opera in five Acts, preceded by an allegorical prologue. In the manner of the time, it relies on free cantilena rather than formal numbers, with set-pieces kept short and with the chorus often contributing to such brief arias as there are. There are fine processional marches and choruses with a Purcellian flavour, and Christie with his talented Les Arts Florissants team presents the whole work with a taut feeling for its dramatic qualities, though there is nothing here to compare with the big moments in Mozart's opera.

The matching of voices to character is closer here than what we would conventionally expect in Mozart. The title-role is given to a wide-ranging bass, the clear-toned if not always steady Bernard Delétré, while Idamante is a high tenor, the expressive Jean-Paul Fouchécourt, on balance the most successful of the soloists. The bright tones of Monique Zanetti as Ilione verge too often on shrillness, and there is also an edge on the warmer soprano voice of Sandrine Piau as Electre. Nevertheless, in the breadth of its span and its frequent hints as to what Purcell might have achieved had he tackled a full-length opera, this is a fascinating work, vividly recorded.

Tancrède: complete.
** Erato/Warner Dig. 2292 45001-2 (2). The Sixteen, La Grande Écurie et la Chambre du Roy, Malgoire.
　　Tancred (François LeRoux), Clorinda (Daphne Evangelatos), Herminie (Catherine Dubosc), Argant (Pierre-Yves Le Maigat), Ismenor (Gregory Reinhart), Peace / Female Warrior / Dryad (Colette Alliot-Lugaz), Wood-nymph (Dominique Visse).

André Campra had an extraordinary melodic facility (on which Milhaud drew in his *Suite provençale*) and collectors who do not have it should seek out the Harmonia Mundi/BMG reissue of his delightful opéra-ballet, *L'Europe galante*, written at the end of the seventeenth century (see above). *Tancrède*, the first of his tragédies-lyriques, comes at the beginning of the eighteenth: it is very much in the tradition of Lully but is stronger in its blend of lyricism and dance than in dramatic coherence. The libretto is by Antoine Danchet, based on Tasso's *Gerusalemme liberata*.

The action is set at the time of the First Crusade. Argant, the Saracen chief, is in love with Clorinda, a Saracen princess who has been made captive by Tancred, whom she secretly loves. Herminie, daughter of the King of Antioch, is also in love with him, though she is herself the object of the Saracen magician Ismenor's affections. After declaring his feelings for Clorinda, Tancred frees all his Saracen prisoners.

At Argant's instigation the sorcerer creates a magic forest in which Tancred can himself be captured. Herminie and then Clorinda successively foil attempts on his life. There follows a battle in which Tancred believes he has slain Argant. However, Argant appears, mortally wounded, and announces that it is Clorinda, attired in his armour, whom he has killed. Tancred leaves the stage in suicidal despair. (The 1737 ending has Clorinda appearing before Tancred, begging him to forget the wounds he has inflicted on her but not her love for him.)

This recording was made at a performance in Aix-en-Provence in 1986 and, though there are stage noises and at times some less than polished playing, it is well worth investigating.

Casken, John (born 1949)

Golem (chamber opera in 2 parts).
*** Virgin/EMI Dig. VC7 91204-2 [id.]. Music Projects London, Richard Bernas.
　　Maharal (Adrian Clarke), Golem (John Hall), Miriam (Patricia Rozario), Ometh (Christopher Robson).

Golem is based on the well-known Jewish legend of the rabbi, the Maharal, who creates a saviour figure, a Golem, from lifeless clay. The Maharal's altruistic aims are thwarted when the Golem, developing human feelings, refuses to be controlled. It was this score which in 1990 won for Casken the first Britten Award for Composition, with this recording as part of the prize. It is a curious piece but a memorable and atmospheric one, with this splendid performance taken from a brilliantly re-edited version of BBC tapes.

The piece is the more involving for the often sinister atmospheric writing, as when at the start of the story, after the flashback opening scene, the orchestra simulates the beating of the wings of a great bird, a frightening sound. Although through the Prelude and five continuous scenes the Maharal's monologues take up a disproportionate share of the whole, that matters little in a recording, particularly when the role is so confidently taken by Adrian Clarke.

John Hall as the Golem is equally convincing, and most striking of all is Christopher Robson in the counter-tenor role of Ometh, 'a Promethean figure of hope and conscience'. The meeting between the Golem and Ometh in the final scene brings a tender resolution, when in their halting way they realize that, but for the Maharal's obstruction, their partnership could have brought success, not tragedy.

Catalani, Alfredo (1854–93)

La Wally: complete.
(M) *** Decca 425 417-2 (2) [id.]. Turin Lyric Ch., Monte Carlo Op. O, Fausto Cleva.
Wally (Renata Tebaldi), Giuseppe Hagenbach (Mario Del Monaco), Vincenzo Gellner (Piero Cappuccilli), Stromminger (Justino Diaz), Walter (Lydia Marimpietri).
** BMG/Eurodisc Dig. RD 69073 (2) [69073-2-RC]. Bav. R. Ch., Munich R. O, Pinchas Steinberg.
Wally (Eva Marton), Giuseppe Hagenbach (Francisco Araiza), Vincenzo Gellner (Alan Titus), Stromminger (Francesco Ellero D'Artegna), Walter (Julie Kaufmann).

This unashamed piece of hokum was much loved by Toscanini, who named his children after characters in it. The title-role prompts Renata Tebaldi to give one of her most tenderly affecting performances on record, a glorious example of her singing late in her career. Her poise and control of line in the celebrated aria, *Ebben? Ne andro lontana*, provide a model for any generation. The work's mixture of sweetness and melodrama has its attractions despite the absurdity of the story.

Stromminger, father of the heroine, is celebrating his seventieth birthday with friends. Hagenbach, the hero, enters, boastfully carrying the skin of a bear he has shot. Stromminger belittles Hagenbach and insults his father. Hagenbach throws the aged Stromminger to the ground. Dashing to her father's aid, Wally recognizes Hagenbach as a secret love of her youth, but he does not recollect her. Gellner of Hochstoff warns the old man about his daughter's love for Hagenbach and her father promptly orders Wally to marry Gellner, which she vehemently refuses to do.

When her father dies, Wally inherits his fortune, and by this time Hagenbach is engaged to the landlady, Afra. For a bet he kisses Wally, however, and immediately realizes that it is she whom he really loves. In an angry response Wally demands that Gellner punish Hagenbach for his impertinence – and too late she repents her hasty action after finding that Gellner has done her bidding and in the darkness has pushed Hagenbach down into a snowy abyss.

The last Act is set in the Swiss mountains. Resourcefully the heroine sets out to find her lover, descending on a rope to rescue the unconscious youth. Eventually recovered, he declares his love for her. She in return acknowledges her responsibility for what happened, and is duly forgiven. Hagenbach then sets off to find a pathway to safety. This leads to a concluding love-duet, when the warbling of hero and heroine sets off an avalanche. The hero is swept away, and the heroine distractedly throws herself after him.

Tebaldi is well matched by a strong cast. Mario del Monaco begins coarsely, but the heroic power and intensity of his singing are formidable, and it is good to have the young Cappuccilli in the baritone role of Gellner. The sound in this late-1960s recording is superbly focused and vividly real, a fine example of Decca recording at a vintage period, with only a touch of over-brightness in the CD transfer. At mid-price on two discs only (two Acts per disc) with libretto and translation, it will not easily be displaced.

The Eurodisc version fails to match its Decca predecessor, even in recorded sound. The voices are set a little fuzzily at a slight distance, with the recording tending to exaggerate the vocal unevennesses of all three principals. Eva Marton makes a powerful but erratic heroine and, though Francisco Araiza is more subtle than most Italian tenors would be, the heroic Italianate timbre is missing. Alan Titus in the principal baritone role is disappointing too. The orchestral playing under Pinchas Steinberg is a degree more polished than on the Decca version, but the performance is nowhere near so warmly expressive.

Cavalli, Francesco (1602–76)

La Calisto (complete version – freely arranged by Raymond Leppard).
(M) *** Decca 436 216-2 (2) [id.]. Glyndebourne Festival Op. Ch., LPO, Leppard.
Calisto (Ileana Cotrubas), Giove (Ugo Trama), Diana (Janet Baker), Endimione (James Bowman), Mercutio (Peter Gottlieb), Linfea (Hugues Cuénod), Satirino (Janet Hughes).

No more perfect Glyndebourne entertainment has been devised than this freely adapted version of an opera written for Venice in the 1650s but never heard since. It exactly relates that permissive society of the seventeenth century to our own. It is the more delectable because of the brilliant part given to the goddess Diana, taken by Dame Janet Baker. In Leppard's version she has a dual task: portraying the chaste goddess herself but then in the same costume switching immediately to the randy Jupiter disguised as Diana, quite a different character.

In the Arcadian Prologue, Destiny proposes to Nature and Eternity that Calisto should be added to those whose illustrious names are written in the stars. The opera then shows why. When it opens, the earth has been ruined and laid bare by wars; Mercury has come down to see what can be done to put the matter right. He meets Calisto, closely followed by Jove, who proposes earth's restoration in return for certain favours. Calisto denounces Jove's amatory intentions so Jove transforms himself into an exact resemblance of Diana whom Calisto then welcomes warmly.

Endimione and the real Diana now arrive on the scene, and Calisto causes confusion by expressing her ardour for the goddess. Diana is outraged. In fact she is in turn attracted to Endimione and they fantasize about their feelings. Physical temptation is strong but must not be allowed to go too far, for Diana is a virgin goddess. Juno, thoroughly suspicious, now descends from the heavens looking for Jove and, meeting Calisto who tells her about 'Diana's' ardour, soon guesses about Jove's substitution and is convinced that he is unfaithful to her.

Jove and Mercury now re-enter and, after an encounter with Juno, lament interfering wives. Further complications follow when Endimione tries to embrace Jove (mistaking him/her for Diana). Pan then abducts Endimione. But Calisto is also waiting for the goddess, so Juno and the Furies defuse the situation by transforming her into a little bear. The real Diana rescues Endimione and they vow a chaste relationship, and Jove (now returned to his own form) discovers the little bear that was Calisto and takes her up to the heavens to shine as the stellar constellation, Ursa Minor.

The opera is splendidly cast. Parts for such singers as James Bowman draw out their finest qualities, and the result is magic. No one should miss Dame Janet's heartbreakingly intense singing of her tender aria, *Amara servitù*, while a subsidiary character, Linfea, a bad-tempered, lecherous, ageing nymph, is hilariously portrayed by Hugues Cuénod. The opera has transferred admirably to a pair of CDs with each of the two Acts offered without a break, and the recording, made at Glyndebourne, is gloriously rich and atmospheric, with the Prologue in a different, more ethereal acoustic from the rest of the opera. A full libretto is provided.

Giasone (complete).
*** HM Dig. HMC 901282/4 [id.]. Concerto Vocale, Jacobs.
 Giasone (Michael Chance), Ercole / Giove (Harry Van der Kamp), Besso / Volano (Michael Schopper), Hypsipyle (Catherine Dubosc), Oreste (Bernard Delétré), Alinde / Amore (Agnès Mellon), Medea (Gloria Banditelli), Delfa / Eolo (Dominique Visse), Egeo / Sole (Guy De Mey), Demo (Gianpaolo Fagotto).

Giasone, with a libretto by Giacinto Andra Cicognini, first heard in 1648, was the most frequently performed opera of its period. Hercules and Besso (the Captain of the Guard) fear that Jason's nocturnal exploits may prevent his capturing the golden fleece. However, Jason enlists the support of Medea, by whom he has fathered twins and whom he agrees to marry. Hypsipyle, the Queen of Lemnos, is also in love with Jason and has also borne him twins; Orestes, her confidant, reveals that Jason is now betrothed to Medea and she vows to take vengeance.

In the next Act Jove, Aeolus and Cupid, furious at Jason's success in carrying off the golden fleece, sabotage his flight to Corinth by raising a storm. Jason and Medea reach port and set up camp, but on Hypsipyle's arrival Jason pretends she is a madwoman he had met in Lemnos. In the last Act Hypsipyle surprises the lovers and Jason promises to return to her if she leaves without waking Medea. Medea overhears this and eventually persuades Jason to have Hypsipyle murdered.

There is much subsequent confusion of identities; Medea herself is mistakenly thrown into the sea instead of Hypsipyle, and is saved by Aegeus. Medea now proclaims that her allegiance must be to him and persuades Jason to return to Hypsipyle.

With the brilliant and sensitive counter-tenor, Michael Chance, in the title-role of an opera that roams so far away from the authentic tale of Jason and the Argonauts, René Jacobs's recording of Cavalli's opera is a remarkable achievement. Based on a stage production given in Innsbrück, it brings fine, stylish singing and playing which uses period performance positively to communicate with a modern audience.

Drawing on no fewer than twelve sources, Jacobs prepared a text which necessarily omits much material but still runs for almost four hours of music. In the instrumentation Jacobs adds recorders in particular to the strings, to give greater variety.

The admixture of comedy that can be embarrassing in operas of this period is here handled splendidly. The vividly characterful Dominique Visse in particular scores a huge success in the drag-role of the nurse, Delfa, very much in the tradition of Hugues Cuénod's performances for Raymond Leppard in Cavalli at Glyndebourne. It is a pity that none of the others characterize like Visse, beautifully as they sing. Clean, well-balanced sound.

Xerse (complete).
*** HM HMC 901175/8; *HMC 401175/8* [id.]. Instrumental Ens., Jacobs.
  Serse (René Jacobs), Amastre (Judith Nelson), Arsamene (Jeffrey Gall), Romilda (Isabelle Poulenard), Adelanta / Curiosity (Jill Feldman), Ariodante / Sesotre (John Elwes), Eumene / Architecture (Guy De Mey), Aristone / Scitalce (Richard Wistreich), Periarco / Painting (Jean Nirouët), Elviro / Poetry (Dominique Visse), Clito / Music (Agnès Mellon), Captain (François Fauché).

Ombra mai fù, sings King Xerxes in the opening scene, addressing a plane tree, and most listeners will have a double-take, remembering first Handel's *Largo*, and then that Cavalli set the same libretto 84 years earlier than Handel, in 1654. Handel's *Serse* (note the difference in the spelling) is a perky comedy, full of sparkling ideas, as the inspired English National Opera production made clear on stage; but Cavalli's opera, even longer but equally brisk in its action, can be presented just as winningly, as here in the first ever recording.

Xerse is based on Herodotus (Book 7). While waiting for his army to cross the Hellespont, Xerxes, the King of Persia, and his brother, Arsamene, are both courting Romilda, the daughter of Ariodate, Prince of Abydos. Although Romilda prefers Arsamene, Xerxes determines to marry her himself despite the fact that he is betrothed to Amastre, Princess of Susa. The latter, disguised as a soldier, arrives in search of Xerxes, and further complications arise when Romilda's sister also falls in love with Arsamene.

Acts II and III concern a letter from Arsamene that is read by everyone except Romilda, for whom it is intended. Amastre herself composes a touching letter to the king, who in remorse pledges himself to her while Romilda and Arsamene consecrate their own nuptials.

Authentic performances of Cavalli have often sounded bald after Raymond Leppard's ripe renderings for Glyndebourne, but Jacobs's presentation is piquant to match the plot, often genuinely funny, sustaining the enormous length very well. As well as directing his talented team, Jacobs sings the title-role. He is only one of the four counter-tenors, nicely contrasted, who take the castrato roles. The fruity male alto of Dominique Visse in the role of a comic servant is particularly striking, and among the women – some of them shrill at times – the outstanding singer, Agnès Mellon, takes the other servant role, singing delightfully in a tiny laughing song.

Most of the text is set to fast-moving recitative, but Cavalli flexibly introduces charming and concise songs and the occasional duet. The three Acts of the opera are preceded by an allegorical prologue taken from *Il Ciro*, an opera Cavalli wrote at about the same time. Excellent sound which consistently allows the fresh, young voices of the principals to make every word plain. Notes and libretto are first rate.

Cesti, Antonio (1623–69)

Orontea: complete.
⊛ *** HM HMC 90 1100/2 [id.]. Giacinta Instrumental Ens., Jacobs.
  Philosophy (Andrea Bierbaum), Love (Cettina Cadelo), Orontea (Helga Müller-Molinari), Ceronte (Gregory Reinhart), Aristea (Guy De Mey), Alidoro (René Jacobs), Gelone (Gastone Sarti), Corindo (David James), Silandra (Isabelle Poulenard), Giacinta (Jill Feldman).

As performed here under the singer and musicologist, René Jacobs, this early Italian opera – written in various versions from 1656 onwards – emerges as far more than an interesting historical curiosity. Its vigour and colour and (perhaps most important of all) its infectious sense of humour in treating a conventional classical subject make it a delight even today. It was – after the operas of Monteverdi and Cavalli – the most popular Venetian opera of its day, and those who know Cavalli will recognize similar fingerprints.

In the prologue Philosophy and Cupid argue the merits of the intellect over the senses, and Cupid promises to make Orontea Queen of Egypt and, although she has so far proved impervious to love, succumb to his arrows. Her court philosopher, Ceronte, reproaches her for rejecting all suitors but the arrival of Alidoro, a young painter, excites her emotions.

In Act II she confides her feelings, which are further inflamed by the claim that Giacinta, a former lady of the court disguised as a boy, has wounded Alidoro. The Act ends with her leaving the sleeping Alidoro her crown and sceptre, and a declaration of her love. Ceronte tries to persuade the Queen to dismiss Alidoro on account of his low birth.

There are various confusions and misunderstandings among the secondary characters before a resolution satisfactory to all concerned is reached: Alidoro is discovered to be of noble ancestry, and he and Orontea are united.

This performance using singers who both sing authentically and characterize strongly presents the piece very much as a dramatic entertainment, and the vividly immediate recording gives an excellent sense of presence in a small-scale domestic performance. Outstanding among the singers are Helga Müller-Molinari, David James, Gastone Sarti and Jacobs himself. The sound is first class.

Chabrier, Emmanuel (1841–94)

L'Étoile (complete).
⊛ *** EMI Dig. CDS7 47889-8 (2) [Pathé id.]. Lyon Opéra Ch. and O, Gardiner.
  Lazuli (Colette Alliot-Lugaz), King Ouf I (Georges Gautier), Siroco (Gabriel Bacquier), Princess Laoula (Ghyslaine Raphanel), Aloès (Magali Damonte), Hérisson de Porc Epic (François LeRoux), Tapioca (Antoine David).

This fizzing operetta is a winner. Musically a cross between *Carmen* and Gilbert and Sullivan, with plenty of Offenbach thrown in, the subtlety and refinement of Chabrier's score go well beyond the usual realm of operetta, and Gardiner directs a performance that from first to last makes the piece sparkle bewitchingly.

Improbably, it was the poet Paul Verlaine who suggested the original idea to his friend Chabrier, when he wrote some naughtily sado-masochistic Impalement Verses. As they emerge in the finished operetta, they are no more improper than the Mikado's song in G & S, and the exotic plot about King Ouf I who enjoys the spectacle of a little capital punishment has plenty of Gilbertian twists.

Central to the story, the star of *L'Étoile* is the pedlar, Lazuli, a breeches role; and Gardiner has been lucky to include in his company at the Lyon Opéra a soprano with just the personality, presence and voice to carry it off, Colette Alliot-Lugaz.

As the opera opens King Ouf I, inordinately influenced by astrology, is prowling around the town incognito. He desires to provoke subversion against the monarchy because he has decreed that – for his own pleasure and that of the citizens – a public execution must take place each year on his birthday. Not surprisingly, none of his subjects will oblige with comments critical of him. The king angrily vents his frustration on the court astrologer, Sirico, and tells him that by the edict of a clause in his will, Sirico must die fifteen minutes after the king's own death. He then orders Sirico to seek out omens regarding a forthcoming proposed marriage to Princess Laoula.

For diplomatic reasons a courtier, Hérisson, passes the princess off as own wife, Aloès. Unfortunately a pedlar, Lazuli, falls in love at first sight with the princess and gives his last golden coin to Siroco in return for his horoscope. After singing a tender romance to the star on which his future depends, Lazuli falls asleep. He is thus discovered by the Princess Laoula and Aloès (pretending to be shop assistants) who tickle him awake. Lazuli tells Laoula that he loves her and kisses her to prove it, but Hérisson and his private secretary, Tapioca, now appear to interrupt this romantic interlude.

Lazuli is led to believe that Laoula is Hérisson's wife and, now in a thoroughly bad temper, frustratedly rails against the government and, when the eager King Ouf approaches him, boxes his ears. Joyful that he has discovered his victim for the execution, the king consults Siroco but is thwarted when the astrologer's predictions reveal that Lazuli's future is closely connected with the king personally and that in the event of Lazuli's death the king's own demise will follow. Lazuli, hastily pardoned, is installed in the royal palace.

The situation is further complicated by the king's belief that Aloès is the princess whom he himself would like to marry. Meanwhile Siroco has Hérisson temporarily removed in order to leave the way clear for Lazuli to elope with Laoula (which the king is willing to finance), as Siroco obviously has a vested interest in keeping Lazuli alive and well! Hérisson, finding that his secretary has escorted Aloès to her room and suspecting that the king has designs on her, sends his guards to bring back the eloping couple. The princess returns alone and proclaims that Lazuli lies dead in a lake.

This bad news convinces King Ouf and Siroco that they have only an hour to live and they comfort themselves by drinking Chartreuse together and altering the clock. Laoula is aware that Lazuli, whom she loves, is alive still and in hiding. The observatory clock chimes and the king and Siroco regain their spirits and good humour when they discover that they are still alive. Lazuli is found by the police, and the king finally gives his blessing to the marriage of Lazuli and Laoula.

The EMI recording is splendidly cast. Except for Alliot-Lugaz and Gabriel Bacquier as the astrologer Siroco, none of the others are well known, but all are first rate. The helpful French dialogue adds to the sparkle (just long enough to give the right flavour), and numbers such as the drunken duet between king and astrologer are hilarious. Outstandingly good recording, especially tangible and vivid on CD, with excellent access.

Le roi malgré lui (complete).
(M) *** Erato/Warner 2292 45792-2 (2) [id.]. French R. Ch. & New PO, Dutoit.
  Minka (Barbara Hendricks), Alexina (Isabel Garcisanz), Henri de Valois (Gino Quilico), Comte de Nangis (Peter Jeffes), Duc de Fritelli (Jean-Philippe Lafont).

This long-neglected opera is a Chabrier masterpiece, and Erato (in collaboration with French Radio) is to be congratulated on putting it on record, albeit in flawed form. Ravel said that he would rather have written this opera than Wagner's *Ring* cycle and, though the plot is an impossible muddle, the music makes one understand that extravagant remark. The reluctant king of the title is Henri de Valois, elected to the throne of Poland, who rather sympathizes with those who are plotting against him and adds to the muddle by changing places with his friend, Nangis. The result is a modified Cinderella story, ending happily.

As the opera opens, bored French nobles are playing cards, chess and similar games to pass the time, and the king, equally bored, longs for a diversion. He is also sure that, while his French courtiers support him, their Polish colleagues (led by Count Laski) do not. The Comte de Nangis, a member of his entourage, feels that an amorous diversion for the king would not come amiss and one of Henri's supporters, the unattractive Italian Duc de Fritelli, has a beautiful Polish wife, Alexina, who might be a possible mistress.

The king recalls a previous enjoyable masked interlude in Venice with an Italian beauty when neither discovered the other's identity. But Alexina confides in her husband about her amorous liaison in her native Venice and the duke fully understands the significance of her story and immediately withdraws his allegiance to the king. Meanwhile the latter, sensing that rebellion is in the air, decides to find out how serious the situation really is by travelling around incognito, accompanied by Nangis.

Fortunately for the king, Nangis in turn loves Minka, a serf in Count Laski's household, and she is a ready informer, telling her lover of Laski's plotting against the king. When the king, disguised as Nangis, approaches her, she confides in him the news that the Duc de Fritelli has also turned traitor. Alexina and the king now meet and recall their previous Venetian meeting, and the king realizes that he is in love with a Pole!

With everyone gathered under his roof, Count Laski orders all doors to be closed. He orders 'Nangis' to sign the king's death warrant, and the king is forced to reveal his true identity. His conduct at the ball which follows finally impresses the Polish nobility and with his popularity comes a relief from boredom; moreover he is also able to retain his throne.

This rather convoluted plot prompts a series of superb numbers, some *España*-like in brilliance (the well-known Waltz of Act II transformed in its choral form) and some hauntingly romantic, with even one sextet suggesting a translation of Wagner's Rhinemaiden music into waltz-time. The pity is that the linking recitatives have been completely omitted from this recording, and in addition the score has been seriously cut. But Charles Dutoit is a most persuasive advocate.

Star among the singers is Barbara Hendricks as the slave-girl Cinderella figure, Minka, who is finally united with Nangis (well sung by the light tenor, Peter Jeffes). Gino Quilico is the king, Isabel Garcisanz (rather shrill-toned) is Alexina, the ambitious wife of the *buffo* character, Fritelli, who is sung by Jean-Philippe Lafont. The recording is naturally balanced and has plenty of atmosphere. The choral focus is not absolutely sharp, but the soloists are vividly projected, the orchestra has plenty of colour and the CD transfer has not brightened the sound-picture artificially. There is excellent documentation and a clearly printed libretto, to make this a highlight among Erato's reissued operas at mid-price.

Charpentier, Gustave (1860–1956)

Louise: complete.
*** Sony S3K 46429 (3) [id.]. Amb. Op. Ch., New Philh. O, Prêtre.
  Louise (Ileana Cotrubas), Julien (Plácido Domingo), Father (Gabriel Bacquier), Mother (Jane Berbié), Noctambulist / King of Fools (Michel Sénéchal).

Even more than Mascagni and Leoncavallo, Gustave Charpentier is a one-work composer, and one might be forgiven for thinking that that work, the opera *Louise*, is a one-aria opera. No other melody in the piece may quite match the soaring lyricism of the heroine's *Depuis le jour*, but this fine, atmospheric recording, the first in stereo, certainly explains why *Louise* has long been a favourite opera in Paris.

It cocoons the listener in the atmosphere of Montmartre in the 1890s, with Bohemians more obviously proletarian than Puccini's, a whole factory of seamstresses and an assorted range of ragmen, junkmen, pea-sellers and the like making up a highly individual cast-list. Only four characters actually matter in a plot that remains essentially simple, even though the music (not counting intervals) lasts close on three hours.

Louise is torn between loyalty to her parents and her love for the Bohemian, Julien. The opera starts with a love-duet and is then concerned with the heroine's mother eavesdropping and being thoroughly unpleasant to Julien. Julien writes a letter to her father asking for his support and his daughter's hand, which further enrages Louise's mother. From there the plot meanders along happily, enlivened mainly by the superb crowd scenes. One of them, normally omitted but included here, proves as fine as any, with Louise's fellow seamstresses in their workhouse (cue for sewing-machines in the percussion department) teasing her for being in love, much as Carmen is teased in Bizet's quintet.

Mother now reveals that Louise's father is very ill and, with a promise that she is free to return to Julien, Louise goes back home. But her father is at first morose and dwells on the ingratitude of children. Mother joins his diatribe and both state that they cannot think of her returning to her lover. But the outside Parisian world calls to Louise (in waltz-time) and her father, finally losing his temper, chases his daughter from the house.

It is not a very promising narrative, but the love-duets are enchanting and, although the confrontations with the boring parents are far less appealing, the atmosphere carries one over. Ileana Cotrubas makes a delightful heroine, not always flawless technically but charmingly girlish. Plácido Domingo is a relatively heavyweight Julien and Jane Berbié and Gabriel Bacquier are excellent as the parents. Under Georges Prêtre, far warmer than usual on record, the ensemble is rich and clear, with refined recording every bit as atmospheric as one could want. A set which splendidly fills an obvious gap in the catalogue.

Louise (gramophone version conceived and realized by the composer).
(M) (***) Nimbus mono NI 7829 [id.]. Les Choeur Raugel & O, Eugène Bigot.
  Louise (Ninon Vallin), Julien (Georges Thill), Father (André Pernet), Mother (Aimée Lecouvreur), Irma (Christiane Gaudel).

These substantial excerpts from *Louise* were recorded in 1935 under the 75-year-old composer's supervision, and feature two ideally cast French singers as the two principals, Ninon Vallin enchanting in the title-role and the tenor Georges Thill heady-toned as the hero, Julien. France has produced few singers to rival them since. The original eight 78 records are neatly fitted on a single CD, and – in the selection of items made by the composer himself – just the delights and none of the longueurs of this nostalgically atmospheric opera are included.

The voices are superbly caught in the Nimbus transfers, but their system of playing the original 78s on an acoustic horn gramophone works far less well over the orchestral sound, which with an early electrical recording like this becomes muddled. Yet even Nimbus has rarely presented voices as vividly as here.

Charpentier, Marc-Antoine (1634–1704)

Actéon (complete).
(B) *** HM HMA 901095 [id.]. Les Arts Florissants Vocal & Instrumental Ens., Christie.
  Actéon (Dominique Visse), Diane (Agnès Mellon), Junon (Guillemette Laurens), Arthébuze (Jill Feldman), Hyale (Françoise Paut).

Actéon is a short work in six scenes; the exact date of its composition remains unknown.

Actéon is hunting but leaves his companions to rest in a nearby glade. Here he finds Diane and her nymphs bathing. To forestall his gloating and lasciviously telling his friends what he has seen, Diane turns him into a stag. When his fellow hunters return, Juno announces that Actéon has been torn to pieces by his hounds.

As in so many other works which Harmonia Mundi and Erato are now investigating, the sheer fecundity and, above all, quality of invention take one by surprise – though, by this time, one should take for granted Charpentier's extraordinarily rich imagination. Actéon is particularly well portrayed by Dominique Visse; his transformation in the fourth tableau and his feelings of horror are almost as effective as anything in nineteenth-century opera.

William Christie has devoted such energy and scholarship to this composer that the authority of his direction ensures the success of this venture. Although scholarship is an important ingredient in this undertaking, musicianship and flair such as Christie shows are even more important. The other singers are first rate, in particular the Diane of Agnès Mellon. Alert playing and an altogether natural recording which is truthfully balanced and sounds splendidly fresh, as well as excellent presentation, make this a most desirable issue.

Les Arts Florissants (opéra et idylle en musique).
(B) *** HM HMA 901083 [id.]. Les Arts Florissants Vocal & Instrumental Ens., William Christie.
    La Paix (Jill Feldman), La Musique (Agnès Mellon), La Discorde (Gregory Reinhart), La Poésie (Catherine Dussaut), L'Architecture (Guillemette Laurens), La Peinture (Dominique Visse), Un Guerrier (Philippe Cantor).

Charpentier was kept away from the principal Parisian stage as a result of Lully's monopoly; *Les Arts Florissants*, which he called variously an opera and an 'idyll in music', was composed for Marie of Lorraine, Duchesse de Guise, who maintained a small group of musicians and mounted little chamber operas. *Les Arts Florissants* is a short entertainment in five scenes; the libretto tells of a conflict between the Arts who flourish under the rule of Peace, and the forces of War, personified by Discord and the Furies. (In the first performance Charpentier himself sang one of the roles, representing the art of Painting.)

This and the little Interlude that completes the music include some invigorating and fresh invention, performed very pleasingly indeed by this eponymous group under the expert direction of William Christie. Period instruments are used, but intonation is always good and the sounds often charm the ear. The recording is excellent as regards both timbre and balance, and the CD transfer is totally natural. A bargain.

David et Jonathas (complete).
*** HM Dig. HMC 90 1289/90 [id.]. Les Arts Florissants, Christie.
    David (Gérard Lesne), Jonathas (Monique Zanetti), Saül (Jean-François Gardeil), Achis / Ghost of Samuel (Bernard Delétré), Joabel (Jean-Paul Fouchécourt), La Phythonisse (Dominique Visse).
(M) *** Erato/Warner 2292 45162-2 [id.]. Lyon Opera Ch., E. Bar. Festival O, Corbóz.
    David (Paul Esswood), Jonathas (Colette Alliot-Lugaz), Saül (Philippe Huttenlocher), Achis (Roger Soyer), Joabel (Antoine David), La Phythonisse (René Jacobs).

David et Jonathas comes from 1688, the year after Lully's death had brought to an end his monopoly of the musical stage, and precedes Charpentier's only real opera, *Médée* (1693). Although the formula and the instrumental layout are thoroughly Lullian, Charpentier's music has greater imagination and musical substance than Lully's. The action follows the biblical narrative, after the Book of Samuel, in broad outline.

On the eve of battle Saul consults a witch; she summons the spirit of Samuel, who predicts defeat. David, who has been banished by Saul, has joined the Philistines and is forced to fight against the Israelites and his beloved Jonathan, son of Saul. Seeing the coming defeat and the approaching death of his sons, Saul falls on his sword; Jonathan dies in David's arms. The Israelites proclaim David Saul's successor. The music, fresh and inventive, is remarkably free from period cliché. It confirms the impression, made by many other Charpentier records during the last few years, that in him France has one of her most inspired Baroque masters.

Christie's version on Harmonia Mundi may not always be as dramatic as Corbóz's, but it has a far surer sense of baroque style and scale, with finer choral singing. Christie adopts generally brisk speeds, yet he paces the closing death scenes of Jonathan and of Saul to make them most tenderly affecting. In keeping with period performance, Christie's soloists are generally lighter-toned than their rivals on the Erato set, including two outstanding counter-tenors, Gérard Lesne clear-toned as David and the characterfully distinctive Dominique Visse, who gives a vivid, highly theatrical performance in the role of La Pythonisse (as the Witch of Endor becomes in this telling of the Bible story).

Jean-François Gardeil with his light baritone lacks the menace needed for the role of Saul, but as Jonathan the soprano Monique Zanetti with her bright soprano contrasts well with Lesne's David, and Jean-Paul Fouchécourt's tenor is ideally fresh for the role of Joabel, the Philistine leader. Christie's imaginative way with period performance will make this a clear first choice for many. The French libretto is presented in facsimile style but with English and German translations conventionally printed. However, index points are hard to identify. Very well recorded.

The Erato set offers a stylish performance from a slightly earlier generation of period performers. The first-rate team of soloists is headed by two of the most noted counter-tenors of the time, Paul Esswood and René Jacobs. The other principals too are often firmer-toned and more characterful than Christie's, as for example Colette Alliot-Lugaz as Jonathan. Though not always ideally polished, the performance under Michel Corbóz is strongly paced and very well recorded. This reissue in Erato's mid-priced series makes an excellent bargain, complete with excellent libretto, translation and comprehensive notes.

Le malade imaginaire (incidental music).
*** Erato/Warner Dig. 2292 45002-2. Isabelle Poulenard, Jill Feldman, Guillemette Laurens, Gilles Ragon, Michel Verschaeve, Jean-Louis Bindi, Jean-Paul Fouchécourt, Les Musiciens du Louvre, Marc Minkowski.
*** HM Dig. HMC 90-1336 [id.]. Monique Zanetti, Noémi Rime, Claire Brua, Dominique Visse, Howard Crook, Jean-François Gardeil, Les Arts Florissants, Christie.

Molière, having fallen out with Lully, dictator of French music in Louis XIV's time and not an agreeable man, turned instead to Charpentier for the music he needed for his last comedy, *Le malade imaginaire*. This sequence of extended prologue and three *intermèdes* tingles with energy, and is superbly realized on this first recording of the complete incidental music, much of which was lost for three centuries. The extended allegorical prologue works like a miniature comic opera, fresh and speedy, amply confirming that the long-underappreciated Charpentier was a master at least equal to Lully. Eight first-rate soloists and a lively period orchestra are spurred by the consistently animated direction of Marc Minkowski, and the vivid recording adds to the illusion of live performance.

Even next to the outstanding first recording made a little earlier for Erato by Marc Minkowski, the Harmonia Mundi issue brings important advantages, not least the practical ones of a rather more extended treatment and more cueing points. It was recorded after a live stage production, and the acting is more uninhibited than on the Erato issue, perhaps too much so. With rather less forward and more refined sound, Christie – though he uses percussion just as dramatically as his rival – is lighter in his textures and rhythms, often opting for faster speeds. Whichever version is preferred, this is a masterly example of writing for the stage and, in the vigour and speed of its comic-opera interludes, it makes one wish Charpentier had had more chance to rival Lully. The format is cumbersome, with a single disc contained in a double jewel-case, but the libretto is far more readable.

Médée (complete).
⊛ *** HM HMC 90 1139/41; *HMC 40 1139/41* [id.]. Les Arts Florissants Ch. & O, Christie. Médée (Jill Feldman), Créon (Jacques Bona), Créuse (Agnès Mellon), Jason (Gilles Ragon), Oronte (Philippe Cantor), Nérine (Sophie Boulin).

Few records of early Baroque opera communicate as vividly as this, winner in 1985 of the International Record Critics' Award and the Early Music prize in the *Gramophone* record awards.

In Charpentier's setting of the famous story, using a libretto by Thomas Corbeille, Medea has helped Jason obtain the golden fleece. Together they plot the murder of the King of Thessaly but are discovered and flee to Corinth. Jason falls in love with the Princess Creusa and assures Medea that their children are safe in her hands.

Oronte, Prince of Argos, to whom Creusa is betrothed, offers asylum to Medea and Jason but Creon, King of Corinth, decrees Jason's marriage to Creusa. Medea and Oronte both vow that they will be revenged. She uses sorcery to inflict madness on Creon, and at the beginning of Act V the Corinthians announce that Creon has killed first Oronte then himself. Creusa swears vengeance but is herself poisoned by Medea's magic robe and dies in Jason's arms. Medea completes her vengeance by murdering their children.

Despite the classical convention of the dramatization and a strictly authentic approach to the performance, Christie's account has a vitality and a sense of involvement which bring out the keen originality of Charpentier's writing, his implied emotional glosses on a formal subject. This was Charpentier's only tragédie-lyrique, and richly extends our knowledge of a long-neglected composer. Les Arts Florissants, in the stylishness of their playing on period instruments, match any such group in the world, and the soloists are all first rate. Excellent recording.

Chausson, Ernest (1855–99)

Le roi Arthus (complete).
(M) *** Erato/Warner Dig. 2292 45407 (3) [id.]. Fr. R. Ch. & New PO, Jordan.
   Arthus (Gino Quilico), Guenièvre (Teresa Zylis-Gara), Lancelot (Gösta Winbergh), Mordred (René Massis).

Chausson, like many of his French colleagues in the 1890s, was a dedicated Wagnerian, and in *Le roi Arthus*, based on the legend of King Arthur, he boldly produced a French Wagnerian epic to his own libretto, answering Bayreuth in its own language. Though completed ten years before the composer's tragic death – he was knocked off his bicycle and killed – it was never performed in his lifetime, and has long been dismissed as inflated and unoperatic.

As the work opens, Arthus is celebrating his conquest of the Saxons and he pays tribute to Lancelot. Mordred surprises Lancelot at a tryst with Arthus' queen, Guenièvre. Lancelot challenges and wounds Mordred then flees. Reluctant to believe in their guilt, Arthus summons Lancelot who refuses to obey the summons and elopes with Guenièvre.

The king consults the wizard Merlin, who predicts that the kingdom will fall. Arthus pursues the couple but Lancelot flees from his sword, Excalibur. Guenièvre upbraids Lancelot for not fighting then, in shame, strangles herself with her own hair. Arthus forgives the dying Lancelot, and the opera ends with the descent of a heavenly chariot to spirit the king to a better world.

This first ever recording helps to restore the work's reputation, revealing *Le roi Arthus* as a powerful piece, full of overt Wagnerian echoes, which puts Arthus, Lancelot and Guenièvre in a sequence of situations closely parallel to those of King Mark, Tristan and Isolde. The musical parallels are often bare-faced, and the result could easily have emerged as just a big Wagnerian pastiche, but the energy and exuberant lyricism of the piece give it a positive life of its own.

The vigour and panache of the opening suggest *Tannhäuser* and *Valkyrie* rather than *Tristan*, while the forthright side of *Parsifal* lies behind the noble music for Arthus himself, a more virile figure than King Mark. The love-duets in Tristan-style, of which there are several, have a way of growing ever more lusciously lyrical to bring them close to Massenet and Puccini.

In this joint production from Radio France and Erato, Armin Jordan directs a warmly committed performance which brings out the full stature of the work, far more than just a radio recording translated. Gino Quilico in the name-part sings magnificently, and the freshness and freedom of Gösta Winbergh's tone is very apt for Lancelot's music. Teresa Zylis-Gara, though not always ideally sweet-toned, is an appealing Guenièvre, and the recorded sound is generally full and well balanced, a valuable addition to the catalogue, guaranteed to delight many more than specialists in French opera.

Cherubini, Luigi (1760–1842)

Lodoiska (complete).
**(*) Sony Dig. S2K 47290 (2) [id.]. La Scala, Milan, Ch. & O, Muti.
   Lodoïska (Mariella Devia), Lysinka (Francesca Pedaci), Floreski (Bernard Lombardo), Titzikan (Thomas Moser), Varbel (Alessandro Corbelli), Dourlinski (William Shimell), Altamoras (Mario Luperi).

Muti, a lifelong devotee of Cherubini's music, resurrected this opera in a production at La Scala, Milan, to celebrate the work's 200th anniversary in 1991, with the Sony engineers recording a series of live performances. Set in Poland, it tells how Count Floreski meets Titzikan, a Tartar warrior, outside Baron Dourlinski's castle. Floreski tells of his love for Lodoïska, whom Dourlinski has imprisoned and wishes to marry. Floreski attempts to rescue her but is himself imprisoned. However, the Tartar forces lay siege to the castle, enabling Floreski to rescue the eponymous heroine.

The plot and its setting are a prime example of an 'interesting historical curiosity' when, with its story of false imprisonment and rescue, it profoundly influenced the composer's great admirer, Beethoven. Whereas in *Fidelio* the heroine rescues her husband, Cherubini's scheme of hero rescuing heroine is far more conventional. The layout of narrative is also most ungainly, so that the heroine arrives only at the very end of the extremely long Act I and the villain, Dourlinski, by far the most interesting character, is not heard at all until well into Act II.

Cherubini's score, often urgently dramatic, lacks memorable tunes, as so much of his music does. He also has a disconcerting way at moments of high drama of switching into a major key with crashing banality. Yet Muti's conviction in this live recording brings much to enjoy, suggesting that the piece is more effective on disc when the staging is left to one's imagination.

The British baritone, William Shimell, is a splendid Dourlinski, almost making one forget how much more colourful Beethoven's Pizarro is. As Lodoïska herself, the soprano Mariella Devia sounds sweeter and purer than when heard live, and so does Thomas Moser in the heavyweight tenor role of the Tartar chief, Titzikan. In the high tenor role of the hero, Floreski, Bernard Lombardi copes well with the high tessitura, but the voice bleats disagreeably. In the dry acoustic of La Scala the voices have been recorded close, so that there is a lack of atmosphere, and stage noises keep intruding, though the Sony engineers have done well to get such body in the sound. Squeezed on to two well-filled discs, Act I on the first, Acts II and III on the second, the set makes a colourful rarity.

Medea (complete).
*** Hung. HCD 11904/5 [id.]. Hungarian Radio and TV Ch., Budapest SO, Gardelli.
  Medea (Sylvia Sass), Jason (Veriano Luchetti), Creon (Kolos Kováts), Neris (Klára Takács), Glauce (Magda Kalmár), Captain of the Guard (József Gregor).
(M) ** EMI CMS7 63625-2 (2) [Ang. CDMB 63625]. La Scala Ch. & O, Serafin – BEETHOVEN: *Ah! perfido.* **
  Medea (Maria Callas), Jason (Mirto Picchi), Creon (Giuseppe Modesti), Neris (Miriam Pirazzini), Glauce (Renata Scotto), Captain of the Guard (Alfredo Giacomotti).

Gardelli conducts a powerful performance of Cherubini's formidable opera, illustrating very clearly why Beethoven so admired this composer. Written originally before *Fidelio*, it anticipates much that was to follow in the world of opera, not just with Beethoven or Weber, but even Berlioz. In our times, Maria Callas brought the piece back to life, but the recording she made at La Scala with limited sound gave only a partial idea of her dramatic dynamism, and her supporting cast was seriously flawed.

Jason, rightful heir to the throne of Thessaly, comes of age and his uncle, Pelias, usurper of Jason's throne, commands him to recover the golden fleece. So Jason sets off in the *Argo* and, reaching Colchis, is aided by Medea, the king's daughter. They find the golden fleece then elope together. But her father, King Aeetes, has followed. To delay him, Medea has her younger brother murdered and his body chopped into pieces, knowing that her father would be forced to stop to reassemble his son's torso and bury him.

Jason, not surprisingly, eventually abandons Medea and flees with their two sons to Corinth. There he meets Glauce, King Creon's daughter, who prepares for their marriage. With well-justified foreboding, she implores the God of Love to aid her against Medea. The king gives his support to Jason, while the populace, hating and fearing Medea, demand the lives of her two children if she is not killed.

The sailors of the *Argo* now offer the golden fleece as homage to Glauce, but Medea appears on the scene and intimidates everyone by her presence. King Creon threatens her with imprisonment if she remains longer than twenty-four hours, then leaves her with Jason. Remembering both the strength of Jason's love and his gratitude for her help in recovering the golden fleece, Medea reminds him of his previous feelings for her, and begs for his pity. Jason's reason is swayed and together they curse the golden fleece. Then he rejects her and tells her to depart.

Neris, Medea's trusted servant, arrives to warn that the mob is approaching, seeking her death. She remains nevertheless and begs Creon for an extension of her stay for a further day. This is granted, as is her request to Jason to see her children. Medea then orders that Neris procure, as a wedding gift for Glauce, a robe and a poisoned diadem. Jason and Glauce walk in procession to their temple for their marriage to be solemnized.

As they leave, Medea snatches up a burning torch from the altar and disappears, re-emerging at the temple to evoke the aid of the infernal gods. Neris begs her to be merciful to the children and to be content with her wedding 'gift' as Glauce's dying screams emerge from within the temple. Neris then tries to warn Jason – too late, for Medea emerges holding the dagger with which she has killed her children and completed her revenge. Then the temple bursts into flames.

This Hungarian set, originally made in 1978 but sounding very fresh and vivid on CD, shows off the formidable strengths of the Hungarian State Opera, and in particular the artistry of Sylvia Sass, who has rarely if ever sounded so impressive on disc as here, full and firm, the tone creamier than it has latterly become, unexaggerated in expression yet intensely dramatic. One hardly misses the extra individuality of a Callas in a consistently gripping performance, helped by fine support from the other principals, not to mention Gardelli and the orchestra. Kolos Kováts as Creon and Klára Takács as Neris are particularly fine, and Veriano Luchetti is stronger and more individual than he has generally been on disc. Well-balanced sound, cleanly transferred. The two CDs give exceptionally generous measure with 137 minutes of music.

Callas's 1957 studio recording of *Medea* may not bring out the full expressiveness of her historic reading of a long-neglected opera (live recordings reveal it better), but it is still a magnificent example of the fire-eating Callas. She completely outshines any rival. A cut text is used and Italian instead of the original French, with Serafin less imaginative than he usually was, but with a cast more than competent – including the young Renata Scotto – it is an enjoyable set. Callas's recording of the Beethoven scena, *Ah perfido*, makes a powerful fill-up, even though in this late recording (1963/4) vocal flaws emerge the more.

Cilea, Francesco (1866–1950)

Adriana Lecouvreur (complete).
*** Decca Dig. 425 815-2; *425 815-4* (2) [id.]. WNO Ch. & O, Bonynge.
   Adriana (Joan Sutherland), Maurizio (Carlo Bergonzi), Michonnet (Leo Nucci), Princess de Bouillon (Cleopatra Ciurca).
(M) **(*) Sony M2K 79310 (2) [M2K 34588]. Amb. Op. Ch., Philh. O, Levine.
   Adriana (Renata Scotto), Maurizio (Plácido Domingo), Michonnet (Sherrill Milnes), Princess de Bouillon (Elena Obraztsova).
(M) **(*) Decca 430 256-2 (2) [id.]. St Cecilia, Rome, Ac. Ch. & O, Capuana.
   Adriana (Renata Tebaldi), Maurizio (Mario Del Monaco), Michonnet (Giulio Fioravanti), Princess de Bouillon (Giulietta Simionato).
** BMG/RCA Dig. RD 71206 (2). Bulgarian Ch., TV & RSO, Arena.
   Adriana (Raina Kabaivanska), Maurizio (Alberto Cupido), Michonnet (Attilio D'Orazi), Princess de Bouillon (Alexandrina Milcheva).

In the foyer of the Comédie-Française the cast gather and Prince de Bouillon enters with the Abbé de Chazeuil. The house is full: Adriana Lecouvreur and Duclos are playing that night. Adriana acknowledges her popularity and practises her words: '*Io son l'umile ancella*' ('I am but the humble handmaid'). Adriana regards the stage-director Michonnet as a friend, and when he starts to confess his love for her, she interrupts with the admission that she already loves an unknown admirer, connected with the Count of Saxony. The admirer arrives, addresses her passionately, and she says she will play only for him that night, giving him violets for his buttonhole.

Prince de Bouillon and the abbé have intercepted a letter purporting to come from the prince's mistress, the actress Duclos, regarding an assignation arranged for eleven o'clock in her villa; but in fact it is a trap set by the Princess de Bouillon, who has written it herself. We now meet the princess, musing on the torments of love. Maurizio, the Count of Saxony, arrives wearing violets in his buttonhole and allays the suspicions of the princess by saying he bought the flowers for her. Hearing the sound of her husband, she hides; finding only Count Maurizio, the prince and the abbé taunt him about his presence. He angrily suggests a duel, but the prince wearily suggests Maurizio takes Duclos as a lover as he himself is tired of her.

Adriana arrives and recognizes her admirer as none other than the Count of Saxony himself. They confess their love for each other. The stage director, Michonnet, now comes in seeking Duclos; he needs a decision about a new role. The abbé (remembering the letter) informs him that she is at hand; Maurizio tells Adriana that she is not, and that his appointment with her is political. Adriana believes him and prevents the abbé from discovering the identity of the lady hidden within. She discovers the princess, who admits that she too loves Maurizio, but Adriana claims the count for herself. The princess manages to elude the prince when he returns and jealously convinces Adriana that Maurizio has been gravely injured in a duel.

Adriana is desolate, even more so when she receives a casket containing violets, withered and dead. Suddenly Maurizio's voice is heard and he enters, proposes marriage to Adriana, and declares that all his political troubles are now over and he can claim his full and rightful titles. The couple embrace happily; then Adriana turns suddenly pale and is convinced that the flowers are affecting her. Maurizio strongly denies that this could be possible and sends for Michonnet, who suggests that the flowers could have been poisoned by a rival. How right he was! The princess has taken her full revenge and Adriana dies in the arms of the count.

Sutherland's performance in the role of a great tragic actress could not be warmer-hearted. The generosity of Sutherland as an artist, her ability to magnetize as well as to thrill the ear with her distinctive timbre, still full and rich, make this an essential set for all devotees, a recording made right at the end of her career. There are others on record with a more natural feeling for the role – Renata Scotto for one on the rival Sony/CBS set, much happier as an Italian in the passages of spoken dialogue – but, despite the beat in her voice, Sutherland outshines Scotto in richness and opulence in the biggest test, the aria, *Io son l'umile ancella*, an actress's credo.

Sutherland's formidable performance is well backed up by the other principals, and equally by Richard Bonynge's conducting, not just warmly expressive amid the wealth of rich tunes, but light and sparkling where needed, easily idiomatic. Carlo Bergonzi, like Sutherland, is a veteran acting a young character, but his feeling for words and his legato line never fail him. Among the others, Cleopatra Ciurca makes a sympathetic, warm-toned Princess. Full, warm recording. A clear first choice.

Renata Scotto gives a vibrant, volatile, dramatically strong account of the title-role, not as electrifying as Callas would have been (to judge by her recordings of the two big arias) but vividly convincing as a great actress. The tendency for her voice to spread on top is exaggerated by the closeness of the balance of the voices on CD, but her control of legato and a beautiful line amply compensate. Domingo, Milnes and Obraztsova make a strong supporting team, not always idiomatic but always relishing the melodrama, while Levine draws committed playing from the Philharmonia.

Tebaldi's noble characterization misses some of the flamboyance of Adriana's personality, but she sings with consistently rich and creamy tone, and both *Io son l'umile ancella* and *Poveri fiori* bring lyrical high-points. One wishes that Del Monaco had been as reliable as Tebaldi but there are too many coarse moments among the fine, plangent top notes. Simionato, though a little more variable than usual, gives a characteristically strong performance. The recording is outstanding for its time (early 1960s), brilliant and atmospheric.

Just as Hungaroton has produced some very enjoyable, well-recorded sets of Italian opera in Budapest, so Bulgarian Balkanton shows what Sofia can produce, with a cast assembled by Bulgarian Radio and Television. The digital sound is bright and clean, the direction by Maurizio Arena is brisk and lively, and most of the singing is very enjoyable. Rival recordings may be subtler and more refined, but this melodrama about a great actress caught up in an international intrigue survives bold treatment. Raina Kabaivanska, Bulgarian born but long domiciled in Italy, makes a characterful, vibrant heroine.

The recording exaggerates her vibrato only a little, and her performance is strongly presented from the first aria onwards, *Io son l'umile ancella*, the grand tune of which then pervades the whole opera. Alberto Cupido sings capably as Maurizio, even if his rather unrounded tenor shows signs of strain under pressure. In some ways the most memorable singing comes from Alexandrina Milcheva as the Princess de Bouillon, rival to Adriana for the love of Maurizio. She is a trumpet-toned Slavonic mezzo whose fire-eating style and keen projection strike home powerfully.

Cimarosa, Domenico (1749–1801)

Il maestro di cappella (complete).
(M) *** Decca 433 036-2 (2) [id.]. Fernando Corena, ROHCG O, Argeo Quadri – DONIZETTI: *Don Pasquale.* **(*)
*** Hung. Dig. HCD 12573 [id.]. József Gregor, Boys of Schola Hungarica, Corelli CO, Pál (with TELEMANN: *Der Schulmeister ***).

Corena's classic assumption of the role of incompetent Kapellmeister makes a most welcome return to the catalogue after being unavailable for far too long. The Decca stereo allows his orchestral rehearsal to come over most vividly, with the poor man dashing first to the left then to the right, to one instrument after another, trying to keep each in order. Corena shows complete mastery of the *buffo* bass style, and he is so little troubled by the florid passages that he can relax and bring out the fun. The vintage 1960 recording is clear and atmospheric, with the directional effects naturally conveyed, and the CD transfer is outstanding. It makes a valuable and generous fill-up for Kertész's recording of *Don Pasquale*.

Gregor's firm rich bass goes with a comparably strong personality and a striking ability to act the buffoon in this romp of an intermezzo, with its comic conflict between the maestro di cappella and the orchestra. Plainly, Gregor's performance has benefited from stage experience. Though his comic style is on the broad side, his magnetism pulls the piece together very effectively, with Tamás Pál a responsive conductor. It is aptly if ungenerously coupled with the more heavily Germanic Telemann cantata featuring a stupid schoolmaster. Here too Gregor is partnered by the boys of the Schola Hungarica (a rowdy bunch, to judge by the decibel level), and their enthusiastic contribution helps to make the simple humour of the piece endearing. First-rate recording.

Il matrimonio segreto (complete).
⊛ (M) *** DG 437 696-2 (3) [id.]. ECO, Daniel Barenboim.
   Geronimo (Dietrich Fischer-Dieskau), Elisetta (Arleen Augér),Carolina (Julia Varady), Fidelma (Júlia Hamari), Count Robinson (Alberto Rinaldi), Paolino (Ryland Davies).

Barenboim directs a fizzing performance of Cimarosa's comic masterpiece. This operatic comedy of manners involves a rich old merchant, Geronimo, who wants to find aristocratic husbands for his two daughters, but Carolina is already in love with his clerk, Paolino. The latter introduces Count Robinson to seek the hand of Elisetta, but the count spoils everyone's plans by preferring Carolina.

Elisetta is angry and complains to her Aunt Fidelma, who fancies Paolino for herself, and both take their cause to Geronimo, who unjustly orders Carolina to be sent to a convent in order to cure her flirtatious behaviour.

Not to be outdone, Paolino arrives in the dead of night to 'elope' with Carolina. But Elisetta betrays their escape and the lovers now have to confess that they are already married. Geronimo takes the news philosophically, and the count readily turns to Elisetta instead.

Cimarosa's setting may not have the finesse of the greatest Mozart, and in duller hands it can seem conventional, but not here when the singing is as sparkling as the playing. The joys are similar to those of Mozart, and some of the ensembles in particular, not least the Act I finale, relate directly to *Figaro*. Fischer-Dieskau relishes the chance to characterize the old man, Geronimo, but the three principal women singers are even more compelling, with Arleen Augér and Julia Varady singing superbly; their sisterly duets (especially in the lively Act I example with its crisp triplets) are among the most captivating items in the whole work. Alberto Rinaldi as Count Robinson, promised to the elder daughter, Ryland Davies as Paolino, secretly married to the younger, along with Júlia Hamari as Geronimo's sister, make up an outstanding cast and the recording, warmly atmospheric, has transferred vividly to CD.

Il pittor parigino (complete).
**(*) Hung. Dig. HCD 12972/3-2 [id.]. Salieri CO, Pál.
   Eurilla (Márta Szücs), Cintia (Veronika Kincses), M. de Crotignac (Gérard Garino), Baron Cricca (József Gregor), Broccardo (Martin Klietmann).

The Parisian painter of the title is the beloved of the heroine, who will lose her inheritance if she marries anyone but a baron she detests. With plenty of misunderstandings and disguises and with some nice touches of parody of operatic tradition in Cimarosa's frothy score, it makes a delightful entertainment in a performance recorded – rather drily in the studio – after a stage production given in both Budapest and Monte Carlo. Tamás Pál is an efficient conductor, himself playing harpsichord recitatives, and he draws a lively performance – using modern instruments – from the Salieri Chamber Orchestra. The cast is a strong one, using a number of soloists from the Budapest Opera who are becoming increasingly well-known on record, though Márta Szücs as the heroine, Eurilla, is less sweet on the ear than Veronika Kincses as her scheming cousin, Cintia. The outstanding performance comes from the veteran *buffo* bass, József Gregor, brilliant as the Baron.

Coleman, Cy (born 1929)

On the Twentieth Century.
⊛ *** Sony SK 35330 [id.]. Ch. & O, Paul Gemignani.
> Oscar Jaffee (John Cullum), Lily Garland / Mildred Plotka (Madeline Kahn), Letitia Primrose (Imogene Coca), Owen O'Malley (George Coe), Oliver Webb (Dean Dittman), Bishop (Charles Rule), Conductor Flanagan (Tom Batten), Bruce Granit (Kevin Kline).

Cy Coleman's score for *On the Twentieth Century* is a winner all the way. This immensely enjoyable show was a modest success on Broadway but failed to sustain its London run, possibly because the very idea of a musical celebrating a train journey seems strange in a country that has all but abandoned railways as a normal means of public transportation.

The Twentieth Century was a crack express in the heyday of the New York Central Railroad that travelled between Chicago and New York in sixteen hours. During the 1930s it was considered the epitome of luxury and elegant travel.

The musical is based on a Hecht–MacArthur play which in turn became a classic 1934 film, directed by Howard Hawkes, with John Barrymore and Carole Lombard perfectly cast as producer, Oscar Jaffee, and Lily Garland (once plain Mildred Plotka), who is his mistress and also his great star vehicle. Betty Comden and Adolph Green have skilfully adapted the book for the musical theatre, shortening it so that (apart from the introductory scene, and a flashback audition) the entire action takes place on the train. They refined the dialogue, making it more waspish, and changed the sex of the religious nut (who puts up 'Repent' stickers everywhere).

So the male Mr Clark of the movie becomes a deliciously eccentric female 'millionairess', Miss Primrose, who writes bouncing cheques. It is she who offers to put up the money for Oscar's new play about Mary Magdalene in which Lily will star. Oscar and Lily (who owes him her stardom) have fallen out; she has since made a success in Hollywood but his last play has failed. Meanwhile Lily has taken a new lover, a dashing but boring matinee idol who – to her great dismay – also boards the train. So Oscar and Lily badly need each other to resolve their problems, but their egoistical temperaments make compatibility more than a little bit difficult.

Throughout this entertaining if ridiculous farrago, the expert lyrics help to make the songs sparkle. Above all, neither the authors nor Cy Coleman, the composer, forget that this is primarily a musical about a train. The result is a series of numbers which contain some of the most exhilarating of all train music, certainly worthy to be ranked alongside Johann Strauss, Villa-Lobos and Lumbye's *Copenhagen Steam Railway galop*, which is whimsically evoked in the *Overture*, as the Twentieth Century sets off from Chicago.

The title-song rattles along at an exhilarating pace and seems to get better every time it is reprised, and many of the other numbers have underlying train rhythms, notably Madeline Kahn's vibrant *Veronique*, the fizzing ensemble *Together*, the enticing opening number of Act II, *Life is like a train*, and even the endearingly infectious description of Miss Primrose, *She's a nut, she's a nut.* The joyous highlight of Act II is the Sextet, when Lily has to be persuaded to sign her new contract, with the train rhythm interrupting every now and then; at the climax, the engine pistons somehow seem to add to the pressure on Lily to sign. There is a strong element of ham in the character of Oscar (displayed with flair by the resonant-voiced John Cullum) and Lily has plenty of fake temperament, and this all comes out in the romantic numbers. But it is for celebration of a railway journey that this piece is to be remembered.

It is difficult to imagine the performances being bettered. The whole cast work as a team, yet the personalities of Oscar and Lily dominate the action. Paul Gemignani keeps the train on the tracks with consistent energy and momentum, and the recording is first rate, with the one proviso that the important bass-line which adds weight and provides a springboard for the title-theme needs to have more resonant impact – as it did, live in the theatre.

Coleridge-Taylor, Samuel (1875–1912)

Scenes from The Song of Hiawatha (complete).
*** Argo Dig. 430 356-2 (2) [id.]. Helen Field, Arthur Davies, Bryn Terfel, WNO Ch. & O, Kenneth Alwyn.

Coleridge-Taylor's choral trilogy based on Longfellow's epic poem had its first performance under the composer in the Royal Albert Hall in 1900. It took a while to catch on, but every year from 1924 until the outbreak of war in 1939 it was given a staged presentation at the same venue. Often nearly a thousand costumed 'Red Indian' performers came to enjoy themselves hugely, singing under the baton of their tribal chief, Sir Malcolm Sargent. His splendid record of Part One, *Hiawatha's Wedding Feast* (currently withdrawn), remains unsurpassed by the present, complete version, and its ambience is more convincing too.

Part One is still regularly performed by choral societies in the north of England, though not usually with Indian costumes! The reasons for the neglect of Parts Two and Three, *The Death of Minnehaha* and *Hiawatha's Departure*, are made only too clear by this complete recording: there is a distinct falling-off in the composer's inspiration, so fresh and spontaneously tuneful in Part One. Indeed, when the main theme of *Hiawatha's Wedding Feast* returns in Part Three (band 12), with the words 'From his place rose Hiawatha', one realizes how memorable it is, compared with what surrounds it. Of course the choral writing is always pleasingly lyrical and makes enjoyable listening.

Part Two has plenty of drama, and towards the end Helen Field has a memorably beautiful solo passage, which she sings radiantly, echoed by the chorus, 'Wahonomin! Wahonomin! Would that I had perished for you.' There is also an almost Wagnerian apotheosis at the actual moment of the Farewell (band 14), which is sung and played here with compelling grandiloquence.

Kenneth Alwyn is completely at home in this music. (By coincidence, he attended the same school in Croydon as the composer – although not, of course, at the same time!) He directs a freshly spontaneous account and has the advantage of excellent soloists, though the Welsh Opera Choir seem less naturally at home in the idiom than Sargent's own Royal Choral Society. The recording was made in the rather intractable Brangwyn Hall, Swansea, and the engineers have put their microphones fairly close to the performers. The result, while vivid, lacks the glowing ambient effect of the Royal Albert Hall, which would have been a much better venue.

Copland, Aaron (1900–90)

The Tender Land: complete.
*** Virgin/EMI Dig. VCD7 91113-2 (2) [id.]. Soloists, Ch. and O of Plymouth Music Series, Philip Brunelle.
Laurie (Elizabeth Comeaux), Martin (Dan Dressen).

Commissioned by Rodgers and Hammerstein to write a piece to celebrate the thirtieth anniversary of the American League of Composers, Copland wrote as guileless an opera as could be, to a libretto by Horace Everett after James Agee's *Let Us Now Praise Famous Men*. Innocent-seeming in its diatonic harmony, it is sparing of dissonance, to match the rustic simplicity of the story of a farming family. Set in the mid-West in the 1930s, the plot concerns the Moss family, who engage two drifters (Martin and Top).

Thought to be child-molesters – though innocent of the charge – they are asked to leave. Laurie, the eldest daughter who is about to graduate, has however succumbed to Martin's attractions and decides to leave with him. Top persuades him that theirs is no life for Laurie, and they depart without taking her along. Nevertheless, she decides to leave home, and her mother is forced to look to the younger child for the family future. So this is not just a story of love's young dream with a happy ending.

Copland himself likened *The Tender Land* to the ballet *Appalachian Spring*, but the opera is gentler. The key passage is the big quintet at the end of Act I, *The promise of living*; it brings a simple tune that builds up to a memorable, moving climax and, though not quoted, fragments of the melody then seem to underpin the rest of the score, with its set-numbers including a square-dance ensemble and a big love-duet. Nothing has quite the sharpness of *Appalachian Spring*, but it is an amiable piece, beautifully performed here in a rather lighter style than Copland himself adopted on a much earlier recording of excerpts. Elizabeth Comeaux and Dan Dressen make an affecting pair of lovers, and the recording is open and atmospheric, conveying the stage picture very effectively.

Coward, Noël (1899–1973)

Bitter sweet.
*** That's Entertainment Dig. CDTER2 1160 (2) [id.]. New Sadler's Wells Opera Ch. & O, Michael Reed.

Lady Shayne / Sarah ('Sari') Linden (Valerie Masterson), Carl Linden (Martin Smith), Manon (Rosemary Ashe), Captain Little (Donald Maxwell).

The idea of writing his enchanting pastiche Viennese operetta came to Noël Coward in 1928, after hearing an orchestral selection from *Die Fledermaus* on a gramophone record. Hours later, in his car parked on Wimbledon Common under the shade of a huge horse-chestnut tree, the story of its heroine, Sari Linden, was planned and some of the principal melodies began to form in Coward's subconscious. The opera was finished a year later, and the composer relates how its great hit-tune (perhaps the finest operetta melody written after Lehár's *Merry Widow waltz*, with which it has much in common) came to him 'whole and complete', while waiting in a twenty-minute traffic-jam in a London taxi.

The finished show gave its composer enormous satisfaction – as well it might for, apart from the inspiration of its stream of hit songs and the charm of the story, it is cunningly constructed, moving back from its opening scene in the (then) present to centre on the tragic romance of its heroine – which takes place in the Vienna of the 1880s – and then forward again to give the piece an upbeat ending.

Bitter sweet was an enormous success in its time and then disappeared from the repertoire until several quite recent revivals (in Plymouth and then, appropriately, Wimbledon – a marvellous semi-amateur production of fully professional standard by the London Transport Operatic Players). The present re-creation at the New Sadler's Wells Opera, so vividly caught in this recording, could hardly be better cast. Valerie Masterson is a wholly engaging Sari. *What is love?* and the delicious *Zigeuner* are enchantingly sung, and Martin Smith as Carl makes a fine partner in *Dear little café* and the famous *I'll see you again*. There are lots of fizzing ensembles, not least *Ladies of the town*, *Tokay* (well led by Donald Maxwell) and, of course, the bouncy *Ta-ra-ra-boom-de-ay*, which few realize derives from this source. But the other great number of the show comes from a subsidiary character (the appropriately named) Manon's sad little soliloquy, *If love were all*, sung with just the right mixture of tenderness and philosophical resignation by Rosemary Ashe. Michael Read directs the show with fine spirit and much affection (the orchestral *Bitter sweet waltz* has a nice Viennese lilt), and the recording is brightly atmospheric.

Debussy, Claude (1862–1918)

Le Martyre de Saint Sébastien (incidental music) complete – see also under RAVEL: *L'enfant et les sortilèges*.
*** Sony Dig. SK 48240 [id.]. Leslie Caron; Sylvia McNair, Nathalie Stutzmann, Ann Murray, London Symphony Ch., LSO, Tilson Thomas.

It was in 1910 that Debussy was asked to provide music for the decadent drama, *Le Martyre de Saint-Sébastien*, by Gabriele d'Annunzio. He did it unashamedly as a rush job for money. He had to bring in as helper his friend, André Caplet, so as to meet the deadline of two months for the hour of music required – a task, he said, that would normally have taken a year. The result is a problem work, for the original entertainment lasted no less than five hours, much of it distasteful. It crudely distorts the saint's Christian message to fit the author's fascist philosophy of 'strength through joy', a key phrase in the full text which raises uncomfortable memories of the Nazi period.

Working against the clock, Debussy produced music far less concentrated than in his major masterpieces, but its sweetness and simplicity often point forward to his late works. Michael Tilson Thomas here records the complete incidental music in a form that the composer approved, using a narrator, Leslie Caron, to provide the spoken links between sections. What it shows is how much richer and more varied the complete score is than the usual symphonic fragments. This is as near an ideal performance as could be imagined, with Sylvia McNair singing radiantly in the principal soprano roles, with brilliant playing from the LSO, and glorious recording which brings out the full atmospheric beauty of the choral singing, often off-stage.

Pelléas et Mélisande (complete).
*** DG Dig. 435 344-2 (2) [id.]. Vienna Konzertvereingung, VPO, Abbado.
Pelléas (François LeRoux), Mélisande (Maria Ewing), Golaud (José Van Dam).
*** Decca Dig. 430 502-2 (2) [id.]. Montreal Ch. & SO, Dutoit.
Pelléas (Didier Henry), Mélisande (Colette Alliot-Lugaz), Golaud (Gilles Cachemaille).
*** EMI CDS7 49350-2 (3) [Ang. CDCC 49350]. Ch. of German Op., Berlin, BPO, Karajan.

Pelléas (Richard Stilwell), Mélisande (Frederica Von Stade), Golaud (José Van Dam).
(M) *** Erato/Warner 2292 45684-2 (3) [id.]. Monte Carlo Op. Ch. & O, Jordan.

Pelléas (Eric Tappy), Mélisande (Rachel Yakar), Golaud (Philippe Huttenlocher).
(M) **(*) Sony M3K 47265 (3) [id.]. ROHCG Ch. & O, Boulez.

Pelléas (George Shirley), Mélisande (Elisabeth Söderström), Golaud (Donald McIntyre).
(M) (***) EMI mono CHS7 61038-2 (3) [id.]. Paris CO, Désormière (with DEBUSSY: *Mélodies*).

Pelléas (Jacques Jansen), Mélisande (Irène Joachim), Golaud (Henri-Bertrand Etcheverry).
(M) (***) Decca mono 425 965-2 (2). SRO, Ansermet.

Pelléas (Pierre Mollet), Mélisande (Suzanne Danco), Golaud (Heinz Rehfuss).
(M) (***) Ph. mono 434 783-2 (2). LOP, Jean Fournet.

Pelléas (Camille Maurane), Mélisande (Janine Micheau), Golaud (Michel Roux).

Abbado's outstanding version broadly resolves the problem of a first recommendation in this opera, which has always been lucky on record. If among modern versions the choice has been hard to make between Karajan's sumptuously romantic account, almost Wagnerian, and Dutoit's clean-cut, direct one, Abbado satisfyingly presents a performance more sharply focused than the one and more freely flexible than the other, altogether more urgently dramatic. Hearing Abbado, one registers the developments in the dream-like story more involvingly, and the beauty of the playing of the Vienna Philharmonic outshines even that of Karajan's Berlin Philharmonic, making it one of the most seductive of all Debussy recordings.

As the opera begins, Golaud, son of King Arkel and Queen Geneviève, has lost his way in the forest, and discovers a delicate, nymph-like girl sitting by a stream, quite alone. Her name is Mélisande, and he coaxes her to leave the dark woods and follow him. He takes her back to the castle, where she is accepted by his family and they are married.

Mélisande is distressed by the gloomy surroundings of the castle. Golaud loves her, but she remains to him remote and mysterious. She finds his younger brother, Pelléas, much more sympathetic. Golaud has given Mélisande a ring, which slips from her finger while she is with Pelléas by a spring in the garden, and it falls into the water. Strangely, at that moment Golaud suffers a hunting accident. Mélisande sits by his bed and comforts him, but tells Golaud of her oppressed spirit in the confines of the castle. Taking her hand to comfort her in return, Golaud realizes that the ring is missing. Angrily he sends her out into the darkness to find it and Pelléas must help her.

The ring seems to be more precious to Golaud than everything else that he owns. Mélisande lies to Golaud, saying that the ring was lost in the sea. In a tower in the castle Mélisande sings and combs out her long tresses. Pelléas comes to bid her farewell and her hair falls over him as she leans from the window and there is obvious warmth between them. Golaud arrives and, taking Pelléas to an underground cavern tainted with the atmosphere of death, warns his brother to keep away from his young wife, who is now with child. The young pair are unhappy but plan to meet for the last time at the fountain before Pelléas leaves; Mélisande does not comprehend why he is leaving.

Yniold, Golaud's young son by his first marriage, is encouraged to eavesdrop on the young pair and in consequence Golaud feels old, angry and impotent. Goaded with jealousy at the sight of his innocent-seeming wife, he drags her across the room by her hair, to the distress of the little boy.

In the twilight Mélisande goes to meet Pelléas. The awareness of their shared emotions steals over them and death together seems bliss. Golaud follows them, and Pelléas dies by his sword while Mélisande rushes away, wounded. Golaud, remorse-stricken at Mélisande's bedside, longs for her to live, yet at the same time ponders whether or not she has been unfaithful to him. Agonized, he presses her for an answer, but she drifts away into death. Arkel brings to her the child she has borne her husband, as she painlessly escapes from life.

The casting of the DG set is excellent, with no weak link. François LeRoux as Pelléas sounds younger and more ardent than his rivals, and Maria Ewing makes a fresh, bright-eyed Mélisande, responding girlishly, far more than a wilting medieval heroine. José van Dam – Golaud also for Karajan – repeats his biting yet beautifully sung portrait of this far-from-villainous character. Philippe Courtis is a firm, dark Arkel, and Christa Ludwig a strongly characterful Geneviève, with Patricia Pace convincingly childlike as Yniold. Like the Dutoit version, the DG one comes on two discs instead of three, with a better break-point in Act III between the discs, when Pelléas and Golaud emerge from the cavern into the open air.

In the first complete opera recording made in the warm ambience of St Eustache, Charles Dutoit brings out the magic of Debussy's score with an involving richness typical of that venue which has played so important a part in the emergence of the Montreal orchestra into the world of international recording. This is not the dreamy reading which some Debussians might prefer, but one which sets the characters very specifically before us as creatures of flesh and blood, not mistily at one remove.

The first inspiration was to choose Colette Alliot-Lugaz as Mélisande, already well known from her commanding performances in Lyon Opera recordings, notably under John Eliot Gardiner. She presents, not the fey, elfin figure often portrayed, but a bright, characterful heroine, full of girlish fun.

With Dutoit choosing his singers most carefully, much is gained from having an entirely French-speaking cast, with Alliot-Lugaz well matched by Didier Henry as Pelléas, light and young-sounding. Gilles Cachemaille, strong and incisive, is also young-sounding as Golaud, not as sinister or sumptuous-toned as some but much more a potential lover, no mere villain. Apart from Pierre Thau, wobbly at times as the aged Arkel, the rest are first rate, and the aural staging adds realism discreetly without being intrusive. As with Abbado's DG set, all five Acts are squeezed on to only two CDs instead of three.

Karajan's is a performance that sets Debussy's masterpiece as a natural successor to Wagner's *Tristan* rather than its antithesis. To that extent the interpretation is controversial, for this is essentially a rich and passionate performance with the orchestral tapestry at the centre and the singers providing a verbal obbligato. Debussy after all rests a high proportion of his argument on the many interludes between scenes; paradoxically, the result of this approach is more – not less – dramatic, for Karajan's concentration carries one in total involvement through a story that can seem inconsequential.

The playing of the Berlin Philharmonic is both polished and deeply committed, and the cast comes near the ideal, with Frederica von Stade a tenderly affecting heroine and Richard Stilwell a youthful, upstanding hero set against the dark, incisive Golaud of Van Dam. Few operas gain so much from CD as *Pelléas*, whether in absence of background noise, extra vividness of atmosphere or sense of presence. In the three-disc format the first and third discs contain two Acts, with Act III contained on the much shorter middle disc. Voices are particularly vivid, with the orchestra, pleasantly mellow, set rather behind. Presumably in due course EMI will reissue this set on a pair of CDs.

For those looking for a modern, mid-priced version, Armin Jordan's sensitive and idiomatic version of Debussy's masterpiece can be recommended on almost all counts. At its centre is the finely focused Golaud of Huttenlocher, fresh and expressive, well contrasted with the tenor of Eric Tappy, a brighter-toned singer than is usual for Pelléas, a role generally taken by a *bariton marin*. Rachel Yakar's vocal acting as Mélisande is first rate and, if neither the playing nor the recording quite matches that on the full-priced sets, the whole performance is most convincing. The documentation includes a libretto and translation.

Boulez's sharply dramatic view of Debussy's atmospheric score made a strong impact at Covent Garden at the end of the 1960s, and this admirable complete recording vividly recaptures the intense excitement of that experience. This is a performance which will probably not please the dedicated Francophile – for one thing there is not a single French-born singer in the cast – but it rescues Debussy from the languid half-tone approach which for too long was regarded as authentic. Boulez's attitude may initially stem from a searching analysis of the musical structure – Debussy anticipating today's avant garde in so many ways – but the dramatic element has been focused more sharply too, for he sees the characters as flesh and blood, no mere wayward shadows.

He is supported by a strong cast; the singing is not always very idiomatic but it has the musical and dramatic momentum which stems from sustained experience on the stage. In almost every way this has the tension of a live performance. The recording, made at EMI's Abbey Road Studios in December 1969 and January 1970, does not allow a true pianissimo, but it is still both vivid and atmospheric; indeed the balance is theatrically more convincing on CD than it was on LP. There is a well-produced booklet with full translation.

Roger Désormière's wartime recording with Irène Joachim as Mélisande, Jacques Jansen as Pelléas and Henri-Bertrand Etcheverry's powerful Golaud is still in circulation. Made in 1942, it still has a special claim on the collector's attention in spite of its sonic limitations. Etcheverry is arguably the most strongly characterized Golaud committed to disc, and neither Joachim's Mélisande nor Jansen's Pelléas has been readily surpassed. A *Pelléas* without atmosphere is no *Pelléas*, and this classic reading puts you under its spell immediately. Perhaps wartime conditions served to heighten the special Gallic qualities one feels on encountering this.

Like so many pre-war performances (Massenet's *Werther* with Ninon Vallin and Georges Thill is another instance), it is distinguished not only by wonderful singing but also by marvellous articulation: every syllable is beautifully articulated and there is a sense that every detail is in the right perspective and every nuance perfectly inflected. A further inducement for collectors is a generous selection of Debussy songs from Maggie Teyte and the celebrated recording of *Mes longs cheveux* by the original Mélisande, Mary Garden, accompanied on the piano by Debussy himself in 1904. A very special – indeed indispensable – set.

Ansermet's 1952 recording of *Pelléas* first appeared on four Decca LPs and caused something of a stir at the time; silent surfaces – essential in this of all operas – were something of a novelty at the period. Ansermet's 1964 recording with Erna Spoorenberg, Camille Maurane and with George London as Golaud never succeeded in dimming the impression made by his earlier version. Of course the stereo recording was both richer and more present, but the achievements of the 1952 Decca engineers were amazing for the period.

Ansermet puts us immediately under his spell and, although there are weaknesses in the Suisse Romande Orchestra (a vinegary oboe and wiry upper strings), these can easily be corrected on high-grade equipment – and in any event they are of little significance. Vocally the set is not as striking as the Désormière, but the Mélisande of Suzanne Danco has a radiance and purity that are unforgettable. Heinz Rehfuss is a Golaud of appropriate menace and there are few real weaknesses, even if Pierre Mollet's Pelléas is not always at ease. However, this remains one of the best recordings of the opera and one of the finest performances from Ansermet's baton. The transfer comes up very well indeed.

The success of the Ansermet rather overshadowed Jean Fournet's recording, made in Paris only a year later and issued on three Philips LPs. It had Camille Maurane at the height of his powers and a memorable Mélisande in Janine Micheau, who was a brilliant coloratura singer (she was a marvellous Rossignol in André Cluytens's LP of Stravinsky's opera of that name) and is not quite as other-worldly as Danco. However, Fournet is absolutely steeped in Debussy's world and yields nothing in terms of magic or atmosphere to his rivals; and the Golaud of Michel Roux is powerful. This was as underrated in its day as the Boulez was overrated, and it brings one much closer to the score than Boulez's clean and clinical account. The sound is less finely detailed than the Decca but the orchestra is better than Ansermet's Suisse Romande.

Delibes, Léo (1836–91)

Lakmé: complete.
(M) *** Decca 425 485-2 (2). Monte Carlo Op. Ch. and O, Bonynge.
    Lakmé (Joan Sutherland), Gérald (Alain Vanzo), Nilakantha (Gabriel Bacquier), Malika (Jane Berbié).
** EMI CDS7 49430-2 (2). Paris Opéra-Comique Ch. & O, Lombard.
    Lakmé (Mady Mesplé), Gérald (Charles Burles), Nilakantha (Roger Soyer), Malika (Danielle Millet).

Lakmé is a strange work, not at all the piece one would expect knowing simply the famous *Bell song*. Predictably enough, at the beginning it has its measure of orientalism, but quickly comedy is introduced in the shape of Britons abroad, and Delibes presents it with wit and charm.

Lakmé is the daughter of Nilakantha, a Brahmin priest. He harbours a fanatical hatred of the British who have invaded his land and forbidden his religious practices. While he pours out invective against them, his daughter, her companions and cult followers sing an invocation to the gods, Durga, Siva and Ganesha. When Nilakantha departs, Lakmé and her slave, Malika, sing together in their famous *Flower duet* about the beauty surrounding them and they prepare to bathe in the stream. Lakmé then places her jewels on a bench and they set off in a boat.

A pair of British army officers, Gérald and Frédéric, two girls and a governess, Miss Bentson, now arrive and break down the bamboo fence surrounding the temple in order to view the scene more fully. They see the jewels, and the flowers delight them, but Frédéric warns that they are poisonous. He goes on to relate that a dangerous Brahmin lives in the hut, together with his beautiful daughter. Fascinated, the girls ask for a sketch of the jewels and Gérald agrees to draw one. The party leaves, except for Gérald who sings rapturously of the jewels and of the possible allure of their owner. He hides as Lakmé reappears.

Though at first alarmed, when his presence is discovered she dismisses Malika and tells Gérald that one call for help from her would also bring his death-knell. Disregarding her warning, he stays on the sacred land and, as his infatuation grows, they sing together. Hearing her father returning, common sense prevails and Gérald is persuaded to return through the damaged bamboo fence. Nilakantha then reappears, crying vengeance against whomever has sullied his temple grounds.

At a bazaar, Miss Bentson is robbed and Frédéric comes to her aid. Gérald's fiancée, Ellen, is with them and Frédéric warns Gérald quietly that the regiment must leave before dawn to deal with a native rebellion. Meanwhile, Lakmé tries unsuccessfully to reconcile her father to the sacrilegious behaviour of the British and, after rejecting her pleas, he introduces her to the crowd as a Hindu singer, hoping that whoever entered the temple grounds will make himself known to her and betray his identity. Lakmé sings her famous *Bell song*, but fortunately Gérald does not appear and Lakmé faints.

Nilakantha's servant, Hadji, then promises Lakmé his help. Gérald at last reappears and the pair of prospective lovers plan to elope and live together in a hut in the forest. Frédéric is philosophical about this turn of events, as he knows the regiment is leaving that very night. But Nilakantha takes his revenge and Gérald is stabbed. Yet he lives, and Hadji carries him to the forest hut and the lovers meet and dream of a life together.

However, Frédéric joins them and points out to Gérald his duty to Ellen and his regiment. Gérald visualizes in his mind an army of marching soldiers and Frédéric knows he has won. Lakmé, sensing Gerald's change of heart, swallows a poisoned leaf. Together the pair drink a cup of water from a sacred spring which promises eternal love and Lakmé dies. Gérald is in anguish, but Nilakantha believes that his daughter has achieved eternal life and is content.

The Decca performance (with Monica Sinclair a gloriously outrageous Governess) seizes every opportunity, while the more serious passages are sung with a very persuasive regard for the finely moulded vocal line. Sutherland swallows her consonants, but the beauty of her singing, with its ravishing ease and purity up to the highest register, is what matters; and she has opposite her one of the most pleasing and intelligent of French tenors, Alain Vanzo. Excellent contributions from the others too, spirited conducting and brilliant, atmospheric recording. Highly recommended in this mid-price reissue which costs little more than the original LPs.

The EMI version with Alain Lombard conducting Opéra-Comique forces dates from the beginning of the 1970s, just after the Decca, but it was relatively recently that a British Airways TV commercial made the *Flower duet* a top classical pop. This is delicately sung by Mady Mesplé and Danielle Millet and those who want that duet on CD or tape would do better with the highlights issue than with the complete set, for otherwise the singing of Mesplé in the title-role is thin and wobbly. Charles Burles sings with some charm as Gérald and Roger Soyer offers strong support as Nilakantha. Lombard conducts with understanding, and the recording is agreeable if rather reverberant.

Lakmé: highlights.
(M) *** Decca 436 305-2 [id.] (from above recording with Sutherland, Vanzo, Bacquier, Berbié; cond. Bonynge).
(M) ** EMI CDM7 63447-2; *EG 763447-4* (from above recording with Mesplé, Burles; cond. Lombard).

Those wanting a shorter selection will find that the highlights CD reflects the qualities of the Decca complete set admirably and is quite generously filled (68 minutes). It opens with the delightful *Flower duet*, never more engagingly sung than by Joan Sutherland and Jane Berbié.

The *Flower duet*, attractively sung by Mady Mesplé and Danielle Millet, also provides the main interest for the EMI highlights issue. Otherwise the performance is marred by the thin-toned – if idiomatic – singing of Mesplé in the title-role. The rest of the cast give adequate support.

Delius, Frederick (1862–1934)

Irmelin (complete).
Withdrawn: **(*) BBC Dig. CD 3002 (2). BBC Singers & Concert O, Del Mar.
Irmelin (Eilene Hannan), Nils (John Mitchinson), Rolf (Brian Rayner Cook), Voice in the Air (Sally Bradshaw).

'The best first opera by any composer,' said Sir Thomas Beecham of *Irmelin*, and this recording, conducted by one of Beecham's most individual and inspired pupils, goes a long way towards confirming that. The piece – a strange amalgam of *Parsifal*, *Turandot* and *Pelléas et Mélisande* (those last two operas postdating this) – is dramatically flawed, with Rolf the Robber hardly a convincing figure, but the love music here for Irmelin and Nils is among the most sensuously beautiful that Delius ever wrote. Though the plot disconcertingly prevents the two meeting until Act III, each continually dreams of an ideal of love, finally found. That draws from Delius his warmest writing, as is well known from the so-called *Prelude* which the composer confected, with the help of Eric Fenby, from salient motifs in the then unperformed opera.

The soaring arc of the main love-motif hauntingly recurs in every conceivable transformation. It finally returns as the lovers depart, unconcerned, into the sunset, fast and rhythmic with orchestral jingles adding a trimming of silver. Outstanding in the cast is Eilene Hannan in the name-part, singing radiantly. Sally Bradshaw sings sweetly as the heavenly Voice in the Air, the messenger to Irmelin that her ideal of a prince is on his way. It is a pity that, for all the power of his singing, John Mitchinson does not sound younger as the hero, Nils, and a darker voice is needed for Rolf than Brian Rayner Cook's light baritone; but with Del Mar drawing warmly committed playing from the BBC Concert Orchestra (not quite sumptuous enough in the string section) this is a richly enjoyable set, beautifully balanced and recorded. The set was issued by the BBC on a pair of CDs, and the libretto had no cue indications, which made it awkward for finding a particular point in the story. We hope that this will be corrected when the recording reappears.

A Village Romeo and Juliet (complete).
*** Argo Dig. 430 275-2 (2) [id.]. Schoenberg Ch., Austrian RSO, Mackerras.
   Manz (Barry Mora), Marti (Stafford Dean), Sali (Arthur Davies), Vreli (Helen Field), Dark Fiddler (Thomas Hampson).

A Village Romeo and Juliet (opera; complete); (i) *Sea drift*.
(M) (***) EMI mono CMS7 64386-2 (2). (i) Gordon Clinton; Ch. & RPO, Beecham.
   Manz (Denis Dowling), Marti (Frederick Sharp), Sali (René Soames), Vreli (Lorely Dyer), Dark Fiddler (Gordon Clinton).

There are some wonderfully sensuous moments in this highly characteristic opera of Delius, written at the turn of the century, one of his most beautiful and heart-warming scores. The famous *Walk to the Paradise Garden* with its passionate orchestral climax (superbly performed on Argo) is the most memorable passage, but the music of the Dark Fiddler and much of the music for the two ill-starred lovers is intensely expressive. Sir Charles Mackerras brings all that out lovingly. His approach is broad and affectionate, with each scene timed to press home the full emotional thrust, however flimsy the story-line.

Two farmers quarrel over a fertile strip of land which lies directly between their respective farms. From time to time each steals a furrow of the land if sure that the action will be unseen and remain undiscovered. Manz has a son, Sali, and Marti a daughter, Vreli. The children regularly play together in the woods and they are often aware of the sound of the Dark Fiddler in the distance. Sali and Marti bring food for their respective fathers, and all of them are uneasy about the Dark Fiddler's presence. The strip of land is sold and Manz and Marti quarrel violently, each accusing the other of the theft of some furrows. The children are forbidden to see each other again.

Six years pass. Vreli, now grown up, watches expectantly at the window of her father's house, now uncared-for and forlorn. Sali approaches and they decide to meet in the fields later that evening. In the poppy-covered woodland, wild and overgrown, they relish their rediscovered friendship. But the sound of the Dark Fiddler returns to remind them of past times together and of their enforced separation.

Marti comes to find his daughter and drags her away. Sali strikes him. In Marti's bare house Vreli sits alone, her father's mind apparently deranged after Sali's attack. The house is sold and she must leave, but Sali returns and their meeting is ecstatic and they pledge never again to part. They sit by the fire and dream that they are married in the old church at Seldwyla. The organ is playing and the choir is singing a hymn; the church bells ring merrily. But it was just a dream, and they go out again into the woods.

Hearing yodelling, they are drawn to a village fair, sharing in the jollity. The peasants stare at them and they feel constrained to move on. So they begin their 'Walk to the Paradise Garden'. Presently they arrive at a run-down country house, now an inn. The Dark Fiddler and his vagabond friends are there and he is recounting the quarrel between their fathers. He plays his fiddle while the young lovers dance.

He invites them to take to the road with him, but Sali and Vreli understand that this is not their destiny. Rather they must drift down the river on a barge, never to return. Watched by the

Dark Fiddler, Vreli throws her nosegay into the water and Sali begins the scuttling of the barge by pulling out the plug and throwing that too into the river. The bargemen sing in the distance as the boat drifts, unguided, into the middle of the stream.

The Argo recording captures the opera's elusive spirit admirably and the cast is even finer than the previous EMI one for Meredith Davies (now withdrawn) with Helen Field and Arthur Davies very sympathetic as the lovers and with the rich-toned Thomas Hampson adding international glamour. Drawing sensuous, refined playing from the Austrian Radio Orchestra, Mackerras consistently brings out the ecstasy of the piece. The spacious, atmospheric recording has the voices cleanly focused, with offstage effects beautifully caught.

Beecham made his complete recording of Delius's evocative opera in the days of 78s in 1948 and, though the mono sound is limited in range, it is well focused, and Beecham's ability to mould Delius's melodic lines gives it an extra warmth and magic, even compared with later, stereo recordings. The cast is drawn from a representative group of singers of the immediate post-war period, most of whom were too little heard on record, for example René Soames (who sings Sali as a man) and Margaret Ritchie (who sings Sali as a child).

Even less appreciated has been the baritone, Gordon Clinton, who not only sings the role of the Dark Fiddler with clean attack, but is even more impressive in the big baritone solo of *Sea drift*, the generous coupling. It is worth any Delian getting this set for that magnificent performance of *Sea drift*, even warmer than the two other Beecham recordings, early and late, of this evocative setting of Walt Whitman, expansive but tautly held together. For some reason this 1951 version was never issued and appears for the very first time in this CD Beecham edition, a superb, unexpected memorial not only to the conductor but to a fine, long-unappreciated singer.

Dibdin, Charles (1745–1814)

(i) *The Brickdust Man* (A musical dialogue); (ii) *The Ephesian Matron* (A comic serenata); (iii) *The Grenadier* (A musical dialogue).
*** Hyp. Dig. CDA 66608 [id.]. Opera Restor'd, Parley of Instruments, Holman.
    (i) Molly (Yvonne Barclay), John (Kevin West).
    (ii) Matron (Bronwen Mills), Maid (Jane Streeton), Centurion (Mark Padmore), Father (Andrew Knight).
    (iii) Jenny (Susan Bisatt), Ralph (Kevin West), Tom (Andrew Mayor).

Dibdin, best known as the composer of the song, *Tom Bowling*, heard every year at the Last Night of the Proms, here provides three delightful pocket-operas, the shorter ones officially described as musical dialogues and *The Ephesian Matron* as a comic serenata. *The Grenadier* – dating from 1773 – lasts well under a quarter of an hour, using a text that is possibly by David Garrick. The love-affair of Ralph and the flighty Jenny is disrupted by the arrival of the dashing Grenadier, Tom. The brief numbers – duets and solos – are linked by equally brief recitatives, then rounded off with a final trio. Jenny and Tom end up in each other's arms, and Ralph is perfectly reconciled to playing gooseberry, in fact rather glad. The other two pieces are just as delightful in these performances by a group specializing in presenting just such dramatic works of this period in public. Excellent Hyperion sound.

Donizetti, Gaetano (1797–1848)

Alina (complete).
(*) Nuova Era Dig. 033.6701 [id.]. Ch. of Regional Theatre of Parma, Arturo Toscanini SO, Antonello Allemandi.
    Alina (Daniella Dessì), Fiorina (Adelisa Tabiadon), Seide (Rockwell Blake), Volmar (Paolo Coni), Belfiore (Andrea Martin), Assan (Sergio Bertocchi).

Alina, Regina di Golconda, was given its first performance this century at the Ravenna Festival in July 1987, and this recording was made live on that occasion. Set in India, in the imaginary realm of Golconda, it is an early piece, dating from 1828, which distinctively mixes comic opera, fable and serious opera. It proves an attractive piece of hokum which held its place in the Italian repertory for most of the last century.

Alina, a French girl captured by pirates, has married the aged King of Golconda, but is then left a widow. By happy coincidence the love of her girlhood, Volmar, a French naval officer, arrives as an emissary and, after many hitches – not least that she disguises herself from him – they are united in love.

Following an old operatic convention, there is a second couple of confidant characters to mirror Alina and her beloved. The principal tenor is Seide, the prince who expects to marry Alina, and to that degree is an anti-hero, giving the piece an unconventional twist.

Though the cast includes a first-rate tenor in Rockwell Blake as Seide, the performance is very rough. The most successful numbers are ensembles such as the big quartet in Act I. Despite the attractiveness of the score, it is a set to recommend with caution. The two CDs are generously filled, but it is a pity that the break had to come – unnecessarily – before the Act I finale instead of after it.

Anna Bolena (complete).
*** Decca Dig. 421 096-2 (3) [id.]. WNO Ch. & O, Bonynge.
   Anna Bolena (Joan Sutherland), Enrico VIII (Samuel Ramey), Giovanna Seymour (Susanne Mentzer), Riccardo Percy (Jerry Hadley).

Donizetti's *Anna Bolena* may not be authentic in its historical detail, but it dramatizes the queen's plight very effectively and even manages to interpolate a mad scene as the heroine awaits her execution in the Tower of London. As the story begins, King Henry VIII's love for Jane Seymour, lady-in-waiting to Anne Boleyn, is increasingly apparent. The courtiers gossip and the queen is obviously disturbed as her page, Smeaton, tries to beguile and cheer her.

Jane Seymour has been enjoying Anne's favour and kindness and feels guilty about her situation, with the queen unsuspecting of her rival. The king enters and states that he is determined to marry Jane and expose his wife's supposed unfaithfulness. Lord Richard Percy is recalled to the court.

The king seeks evidence from him of a previous love affair with his wife. Percy admits that his love for Anne as a girl still remains with him. Rochefort, Anne's brother, views Percy's imprudent outpourings with alarm. Smeaton also loves the queen and wears her miniature, but he hides when Rochefort and Lord Percy appear. The queen tells Percy that she will not see him again. Percy draws his sword to kill himself, but Smeaton rushes out to prevent his death. The king arrives and observes the implications of the scene, and the queen faints.

The miniature makes the most damning evidence and all are imprisoned in separate cells, while Anne is to be summoned before her judges to state her defence. She faces the prospect of the scaffold – yet Jane Seymour advises her to plead guilty, then reveals that she is the usurper; the queen forgives her.

In the Council Chamber the queen refutes all the allegations made against her, but Smeaton confesses under pressure and implicates her, while Percy acknowledges his love. Anne admits that before becoming queen she had indeed loved Percy. No hope remains; even though Jane Seymour pleads for her, she is sentenced to death along with her 'accomplices'. She is taken to the Tower where, losing her reason, the queen chides her ladies for weeping, as the king is waiting to marry her.

Smeaton confesses his falsehoods to her, but the three condemned with her are ordered to proceed to the scaffold. Anne orders Smeaton to sing to her and all the accused share a prayer together. A cannon shot heralds the new queen and the opera ends with an outburst of denunciation from Anne.

In this 1987 recording of *Anna Bolena*, Sutherland crowns her long recording career with a commanding performance. Dazzling as ever in coloratura, above all exuberant in the defiant final cabaletta, she poignantly conveys the tragedy of the wronged queen's fate with rare weight and gravity. Ramey as the king is outstanding in a fine, consistent cast. Excellent recording.

L'Assedio di Calais (complete).
*** Opera Rara OR 9 (2) [id.]. Geoffrey Mitchell Ch., Philh. O, David Parry.
   Eustachio (Christian Du Plessis), Aurelio (Della Jones), Eleonora (Nuccia Focile), Giovanni d'Aire (Rico Serbo), Giacomo de Wisants (Paul Nilon), Pietro de Wisants (Ian Platt), Armando (Mark Glanville), Edoardo III (Russell Smythe), Edmondo (John Treleaven), Isabella (Eiddwen Harrhy), L'Incognito (Norman Bailey).

Donizetti's invention was at its peak in this unjustly neglected opera, written in 1839, the year following *Lucia di Lammermoor*. In *L'Assedio di Calais* ('The siege of Calais'), based freely on the story of the burghers of Calais, he branched out from the Italian tradition towards French fashion, including a ballet in Act III. What above all must strike us today is the weight and intensity he gave to the big ensembles, bringing them very close not just to early but to mature Verdi.

The Opera Rara set is one of the most invigorating of all the complete opera recordings made over the years by that enterprising organization. With such outstanding Opera Rara stalwarts as Della Jones and Christian du Plessis in the cast, as well as a newcomer, Nuccia Focile, as Queen Eleanor, David Parry conducts the Philharmonia in a fresh, well-sprung performance which gives a satisfying thrust to the big ensembles. The one which ends Act II, including a magnificent sextet and a patriotic prayer for the chorus, brings the opera's emotional high-point. When in Act III Edward III's big aria turns into a sort of jolly waltz song, the music seems less apt.

Il Campanello (complete).
(M) *** Sony Dig. MK 38450 [id.]. V. State Op. Ch., VSO, Bertini.
   Serafina (Agnes Baltsa), Don Annibale Pistacchio (Enzo Dara), Spiridione (Carlo Gaifa), Madame Rosa (Biancamaria Casoni), Enrico (Angelo Romero).

A modern recording of this sparkling one-Act opera is very welcome, a piece based on a similar story to the one which Donizetti developed later at greater length in *Don Pasquale*. Don Annibale Pistacchio is holding a party to celebrate his marriage to Serafina. Enrico, who has also been infatuated with Serafina, is also present at the festivities and he plots to disrupt the proceedings.

Relying on the law that requires the pharmacist to answer the bell at any time of the night, Enrico assumes several disguises to keep Don Annibale busy, as a dandified Frenchman, an out-of-voice opera singer and a quarrelsome old man with lots of prescriptions. On returning upstairs, he sets off fireworks that Enrico had planted. Annibale then sets off for Rome to see about an inheritance, while Enrico wishes him a lifetime of nights as happy as the last.

In this Vienna performance the principals all catch a nice balance between musical precision and playing for laughs, generally preferring to rely on vocal acting. Enzo Dara as the apothecary, Don Annibale, and Angelo Romero as the wag, Enrico, are delightful in their patter duet, and Agnes Baltsa is a formidable but sparkling Serafina. Gary Bertini is a sympathetic conductor who paces things well, and the secco recitatives – taking up rather a large proportion of the disc – are well accompanied on the fortepiano. Generally well-balanced recording, given even great immediacy in its CD format.

Don Pasquale (complete).
*** EMI Dig. CDS7 47068-2 (2) [Ang. CDCB 47068]. Amb. Op. Ch., Philh. O, Muti.
   Don Pasquale (Sesto Bruscantini), Norina (Mirella Freni), Ernesto (Gösta Winbergh), Malatesta (Leo Nucci).
(M) *** Decca 433 036-2 (2) [id.]. V. State Op. Ch. & O, Kertész – CIMAROSA: *Il maestro di cappella.* ***
   Don Pasquale (Fernando Corena), Norina (Graziella Sciutti), Ernesto (Juan Oncina), Malatesta (Tom Krause).

Muti's is an outstanding set of Donizetti's most brilliant comic opera. With sparkle and spring on the one hand and easily flexible lyricism on the other, this is a delectably idiomatic-sounding reading, one which consistently captures the fun of the piece.

The miserly Don Pasquale is determined to marry, but he is anxious that his nephew, Ernesto, shall not marry too and threatens to disinherit him if he carries out such a plan. Ernesto and his betrothed, Norina, a young widow, are both understandably upset. Dr Malatesta (Pasquale's confidant, but also in league with Ernesto) is unable to dissuade Pasquale from his embargo on Ernesto's nuptials, and artfully proposes his 'sister' Sofronia as Pasquale's bride.

He describes her as shy and retiring, a simple girl, convent bred. In fact the designated bride-to-be is not related to him in any way: it is Norina. Malatesta now arrives, having come to explain to Norina that Ernesto's uncle has fallen for his deception and that he will soon acquiesce to Ernesto's marriage, if she will go along with his plan. Norina has had an angry letter from Ernesto, who is not aware of Malatesta's scheming.

Ernesto is now banished from the house by Pasquale and is desolate at losing both home and prospective bride. Meanwhile Don Pasquale waits to see his future bride. Malatesta ushers her in (veiled) and, acting her part, Norina speaks modestly and only of homely things; Don Pasquale listens, enraptured. A witness must be found to the marriage terms, dictated to the supposed notary. Ernesto (now in the know) obliges and the contract is signed.

Norina immediately becomes a spiritedly animated virago. Don Pasquale is appalled at the change in her character. Ernesto must take her walking, as Norina asserts that Pasquale is too old and too stout for such exercise. She doubles both the number of servants and their wages; Don Pasquale, beside himself, sings 'I'm the victim of collusion'.

So he is, and Norina and Ernesto exchange sweet words behind his back. Soon the house is alive with servants, new possessions are arriving, and Norina, dressed up, states that she is off to the theatre with Ernesto. When Pasquale objects, she boxes his ears.

As she leaves she drops a note which Pasquale picks up. It purports to be from Ernesto, an assignation to meet her in the garden. Don Pasquale reads it and sees a way out of his problems, and he confers with Malatesta. Ernesto is serenading Norina in the garden when Pasquale and Malatesta appear unexpectedly. Ernesto makes himself scarce and Norina remains to face them. Pasquale learns the truth and forgives the young lovers, finally consenting to their marriage.

It helps that three of the four principals in the EMI set are Italians. Freni is a natural in the role of Norina, both sweet and bright-eyed in characterization, excellent in coloratura. The *buffo* baritones, the veteran Bruscantini as Pasquale and the darker-toned Leo Nucci as Dr Malatesta, steer a nice course between vocal comedy and purely musical values. They sound exhilarated, not stressed, by Muti's challenging speeds for the patter numbers. On the lyrical side, Muti is helped by the beautifully poised and shaded singing of Gösta Winbergh, honey-toned and stylish as Ernesto. Responsive and polished playing from the Philharmonia and excellent studio sound.

Kertész's performance with the Vienna State Opera Chorus and Orchestra brings moments that suggest operetta rather than Italian opera, but it is full of high spirits, with much laughter and jollity expressed along with the singing. The effects may seem coarse out of context but, heard as a whole, the performance works well. Corena is an attractive *buffo*, even if his voice is not always focused well enough to sing semiquavers accurately. Juan Oncina sounds rather strained, not least in his serenade, but he captures the spirit of the piece; and Krause makes an incisive Malatesta. Graziella Sciutti is charming from beginning to end, bright-toned and vivacious, and remarkably agile in the most difficult passages. The 1964 Decca recording is excellent, with plenty of atmosphere as well as sparkle. A good recommendation at mid-price.

L'elisir d'amore (complete).
*** Decca 414 461-2 (2) [id.]. Amb. S., ECO, Bonynge.
Adina (Joan Sutherland), Nemorino (Luciano Pavarotti), Belcore (Dominic Cossa), Dulcamara (Spiro Malas).
*** Erato/Warner Dig. 4509 91701-2 (2) [id.]. Tallis Chamber Ch., ECO, Viotti.
Adina (Mariella Devia), Nemorino (Roberto Alagna), Belcore (Pietro Spagnoli), Dulcamara (Bruno Praticò).
Withdrawn: (M) *** Sony M2K 79210 (2) [M2K 34585]. ROHCG Ch. & O, Pritchard.
Adina (Ileana Cotrubas), Nemorino (Plácido Domingo), Belcore (Ingvar Wixell), Dulcamara (Geraint Evans).
Withdrawn: **(*) Eurodisc 601 097 (3). Munich R. Ch. & O, Wallberg.
Adina (Lucia Popp), Nemorino (Peter Dvorský), Belcore (Bernd Weikl), Dulcamara (Evgeny Nesterenko).
Withdrawn: (M) **(*) Decca 411 699-2 (2). Maggio Musicale Fiorentino Ch. & O, Molinari-Pradelli.
Adina (Hilde Gueden), Nemorino (Giuseppe Di Stefano), Belcore (Renato Capecchi), Dulcamara (Fernando Corena).
** DG Dig. 429 744-2; *429 744-4* (2) [id.]. Metropolitan Op. Ch. & O, James Levine.
Adina (Kathleen Battle), Nemorino (Luciano Pavarotti), Belcore (Leo Nucci), Dulcamara (Enzo Dara).
*(*) Ph. Dig. 412 714-2 (2) [id.]. Turin R. Ch. & O, Scimone.
Adina (Katia Ricciarelli), Nemorino (José Carreras), Belcore (Leo Nucci), Dulcamara (Domenico Trimarchi).
(M) *(*) EMI CMS7 69897-2 (2) [Ang. CDMB 69897]. Rome Op. Ch. & O, Molinari-Pradelli.
Adina (Mirella Freni), Nemorino (Nicolai Gedda), Belcore (Renato Capecchi), Dulcamara (Mario Sereni).
* DG Dig. 423 076-2(2) [id.]. Maggio Musicale Fiorentino Ch. & O, Ferro.
Adina (Barbara Bonney), Nemorino (Gösta Winbergh), Belcore (Bernd Weikl), Dulcamara (Rolando Panerai).

Joan Sutherland's comic talents in a Donizetti role came out delectably in her performances (on stage and on record) of *La fille du régiment* – see below. Here she repeats that success, making Adina a more substantial figure than usual, full-throatedly serious at times, at others jolly like the rumbustious Marie, regimental *vivandière*.

Adina, spoilt by wealth, is courted by Nemorino, a shy peasant. She deplores his reticence; she lives in a world of fantasy, derived from her reading, and she recounts the legend of Tristan and Isolde and the love-potion which fired the lovers. Sergeant Belcore, her other suitor, is not shy, he seeks to capture Adina by bravado; and Nemorino despairs of his chances. Dr Dulcamara, making the most of Nemorino's innocence, sells him a flask of cheap wine, assuring him that it is an elixir with magic powers which will quickly win the heart of Adina. Nemorino swallows the elixir in one gulp, believing implicitly in the quack doctor's promises.

The wine has an immediate effect so that Nemorino dances and sings, ignoring Adina. She responds to this by promptly favouring Sergeant Belcore. As the sergeant is under orders to depart with his troops, he persuades Adina to marry him forthwith, but Adina is slow to sign the marriage contract and, in order to make sure that the elixir will work, Nemorino imbibes a second bottle and pays for it by promising to sign up as a new recruit with Belcore.

Nemorino's personality now begins to fizz and the village girls admire his bravery for enlisting. Adina, piqued at being ignored, now turns back to him. Fortuitously, Nemorino's rich uncle chooses this moment to die and leave Nemorino his fortune, which makes him even more popular with the ladies. Not yet aware of his wealth, he attributes his new-found success to the potion.

Meanwhile Adina, realizing that she prefers Nemorino after all (she is a wealthy owner of a farm, so it can't be the money), postpones signing the marriage contract with Belcore to enable her to purchase Nemorino's papers of enlistment. Having set him free, at first she is coy but then falls into his arms. The sergeant is reconciled and Dulcamara, his reputation enhanced, sells his whole stock of Bordeaux to the villagers.

Malibran, the first interpreter of the role of Adina, was furious that the part was not bigger and got her husband to write an extra aria. Richard Bonynge found a copy of the piano score, had it orchestrated, and includes it here, a jolly and brilliant waltz song. Though that involves missing out the cabaletta, *Il mio fugor dimentica*, the text of this frothy piece is otherwise unusually complete, and in the key role of Nemorino Luciano Pavarotti proves ideal, vividly portraying the wounded innocent. Spiro Malas is a superb Dulcamara, while Dominic Cossa is a younger-sounding Belcore, more of a genuine lover than usual. Bonynge points the skipping rhythms delectably, and the recording is sparkling to match. The CD transfer brings out the fullness, brilliance and clean focus of the 1971 sound, which has more presence than many modern digital recordings.

The Erato version may offer no star names but it presents an exceptionally winning performance, in many ways the finest of all on record, with no weak link. Marcello Viotti proves an inspired Donizetti conductor, drawing playing from the ECO that sparkles consistently, with witty pointing of phrase and rhythm, subtle in rubato and finely polished. Consistently too, his timing helps the singers. This is a light, generally brisk account of the score that provides an ideal modern alternative to Richard Bonynge's version with Joan Sutherland as Adina and with the young Pavarotti. On Erato, Mariella Devia cannot match Sutherland for beauty of tone in the warmly lyrical solos, but she sparkles more, bringing out what a minx of a heroine this is.

Roberto Alagna's tenor timbre is not unlike Pavarotti's, lighter if not quite so firm, and, like Devia, he delectably brings out the lightness of the writing. His performance culminates in a winningly hushed and inner account of the soaring aria, *Una furtiva lagrima*. Rounding off an excellent cast, Pietro Spagnoli is a fresh, virile Belcore, and Bruno Pratico a clear, characterful Dr Dulcamara, an excellent *buffo* baritone, making the very most of a voice on the light side. The sound is first rate, if not as forwardly focused as the analogue Decca.

Originating from a successful Covent Garden production, the CBS reissue presents a strong and enjoyable performance, well sung and well characterized. Delight centres very much on the delectable Adina of Ileana Cotrubas. Quite apart from the delicacy of her singing, she presents a sparkling, flirtatious character to underline the point of the whole story. Plácido Domingo by contrast is a more conventional hero and less the world's fool that Nemorino should be. It is a large voice for the role and *Una furtiva lagrima* is not pure enough in its legato, but otherwise his singing is stylish and vigorous. Sir Geraint Evans gives a vivid characterization of Dr Dulcamara, though the microphone sometimes brings out roughness of tone, and this is all the more noticeable with the added projection of CD. Ingvar Wixell is an upstanding Belcore. The stereo staging is effective and the remastered recording bright and immediate.

Wallberg conducts a lightly sprung performance of Donizetti's sparkling comic opera, well recorded and marked by a charming performance of the role of Adina from Lucia Popp, comparably bright-eyed, with delicious detail both verbal and musical. Nesterenko makes a splendidly resonant Dr Dulcamara with more comic sparkle than you would expect from a great

Russian bass. Dvorský and Weikl, both sensitive artists, sound much less idiomatic, with Dvorský's tight tenor growing harsh under pressure, not at all Italianate, and Weikl failing similarly to give necessary roundness to the role of Belcore. Like other sets recorded in association with Bavarian Radio, the sound is excellent, naturally balanced and with voices never spotlit. Though this does not displace the Sutherland/Pavarotti/Bonynge set on Decca, it makes a viable alternative, especially for admirers of Lucia Popp.

Decca's first stereo set of this opera dates from the mid-1950s but still sounds fresh. Giuseppe di Stefano was at his most headily sweet-toned and Hilde Gueden at her most seductive. Capecchi as Belcore and Corena as Dulcamara are both splendidly comic, and the performance overall admirably conveys the sparkle and charm of Donizetti's inspiration. Though without the sophistication of the later Decca version with Sutherland and Pavarotti, this makes a fine alternative, mid-priced recommendation.

It is a welcome development that opera recordings are again being made with the company of the Met. in New York, but Levine's conducting proves too heavy-handed for this frothy, comic piece. Speeds tend to be on the slow side, and with Pavarotti – who can be incomparable in the role of Nemorino – that brings an element of coarseness. He sang much better when he took this role in the Decca recording opposite Joan Sutherland. Kathleen Battle makes a delightfully minx-like Adina, and Leo Nucci as Belcore and Enzo Dara as Dulcamara are both characterful, but necessary lightness is missing.

Scimone's set is disappointing. In a gentle way he is an understanding interpreter of Donizetti; but with recording that lacks presence, the chorus and orchestra's sound is slack next to rivals on record, and none of the soloists is on top form, with even Carreras in rougher voice than usual, trying to compensate by overpointing. Leo Nucci too as Belcore produces less smooth tone than normal, and Domenico Trimarchi as Dulcamara, fine *buffo* that he is, sounds too wobbly for comfort on record. Katia Ricciarelli gives a sensitive performance, but this is not a natural role for her and, unlike Sutherland, she does not translate it to her own needs.

The EMI version, now issued on two mid-price CDs, dates from 1966. Though each element in the performance is acceptable, the whole fails to take wing. Even Mirella Freni as Adina and Nicolai Gedda as Nemorino are far less characterful than they were in these roles on stage, while Sereni and Capecchi in the *buffo* roles are colourless, not helped by Molinari-Pradelli's conducting. Even as a bargain, the set is a doubtful recommendation.

It is surprising to find such a scholar of the period as Gabriele Ferro conducting so charmlessly in the DG set. It is a coarse reading from conductor, orchestra and soloists alike, with pianissimos very few and far between. Gösta Winbergh sets the pattern with an unrelievedly loud and unsympathetic account of Nemorino's first aria, *Quanto e bella* – nothing shy or tentative about this. As for *Una furtiva lagrima* in Act II, at an unrelieved forte, it has no charm or tenderness at all, and one is amazed that this is the singer who made an appealing Ernesto in the Muti set of *Don Pasquale* for EMI. Barbara Bonney has her moments of sweetness as Adina but, with a hint of flutter in the voice, the sound does not record well and she shows little charm or delicacy. Bernd Weikl's un-Italianate voice makes his portrait of Sergeant Belcore unconvincing, and among the principals it is the veteran Rolando Panerai as the quack, Dulcamara, who is by far the most stylish. When on his entry he cries out *Udite, udite, o rustici*, the simple phrase at once establishes a different degree of communication, though even he rarely sings softer than forte, perhaps a reflection of the recording as well as of the unsympathetic conducting. Voices in a relatively dry theatre acoustic (the Teatro Verdi in Florence) are balanced well forward. It is odd that a recording of this of all Donizetti operas should convey so little sparkle or sense of comedy.

L'elisir d'amore: highlights.
** DG Dig. 435 880-2 (from above recording with Battle, Pavarotti; cond. Levine).

A good 68-minute sampler of DG's 1989 set, made at the Met., which shows neither Pavarotti nor James Levine at their best and is most notable for Kathleen Battle's engaging Adina. Her contribution is well represented in the chosen selection; however, at premium price the disc can hardly have any kind of priority.

Emilia di Liverpool (complete). *L'eremitaggio di Liwerpool* (complete).
*** Opera Rara OR 8 (3) [id.]. George Mitchell Ch., Philh. O, Parry.
   Emilia (Yvonne Kenny), Candida (Anne Mason), Luigia (Bronwen Mills), Don Romualdo (Sesto Bruscantini), Claudio di Liverpool (Geoffrey Dolton), Federico (Chris Merritt).

The very name, 'Emilia di Liverpool', makes it hard to take this early opera of Donizetti seriously, described in the score as a '*dramma semi-serio per musica*', which means it ends happily. Yet, as Dame Joan Sutherland showed as long ago as 1957 in concert and broadcast performances, it contains much splendid material.

The action is set in the mountains close to Liverpool. Emilia does good work in a hospice to expiate her past: she has been seduced by Federico. Her father, Claudio di Liverpool, arrives just as Federico has been overturned in a carriage. The opera ends happily when, seeing that there is to be a duel between Claudio and Federico and believing that Federico is a reformed character, Emilia agrees to marry him.

Here in this set, sponsored by the Peter Moores Foundation, we have not only the original version of 1824 but also the complete reworking of four years later, which was given the revised title noted above. Having both versions side by side, very different if comparable, gives searching insights into the composer's methods. Neither version won success, but these discs amply confirm the good impressions from 1957, particularly in the duets and ensembles. Such a veteran as Sesto Bruscantini makes an enormous difference in the *buffo* role of Don Romualdo in *Emilia*, a character who speaks in Neapolitan dialect. His fizzing duet with Federico (the principal tenor role, superbly sung by Chris Merritt) sets the pattern for much vigorous invention.

The baritone, Geoffrey Dolton, sings stylishly, but the microphone catches a pronounced flutter, and even the brilliant Yvonne Kenny's singing is disturbed by occasional unevenness. But with fresh, direct conducting from David Parry this is a highly enjoyable set for all who respond to this composer. The booklet contains the libretti of both versions as well as the spoken dialogue not included on the discs. Good, clear recording.

La Favorita (complete).
(M) **(*) Decca 430 038-2 (3). Teatro Comunale Bologna Ch. & O, Bonynge.
  Leonora (Fiorenza Cossotto), Fernando (Luciano Pavarotti), Alfonso (Gabriel Bacquier), Baldassarre (Nicolai Ghiaurov), Ines (Ileana Cotrubas).

No opera of Donizetti shows more clearly than *La Favorita* just how deeply he influenced the development of Verdi. Almost every scene brings anticipations, not just of early Verdi but of the middle operas and even of such mature masterpieces as *Don Carlos* and *La forza del destino*. *La Favorita* may not have as many memorable tunes as the finest Donizetti operas, but red-blooded drama provides ample compensation.

Set in Spain in the early fourteenth century, the story revolves around the predicament of Fernando – strongly and imaginatively sung here by Pavarotti – torn between religious devotion and love for the beautiful Leonora, who (unknown to him) is the mistress of the King of Castile.

At the opening, Fernando renounces his monastic vows to Baldassarre, his Superior at the Monastery of St James, because he has fallen in love with a lady whose name and rank are unknown to him. The lady in question is Leonora and she returns Fernando's feelings.

Travelling to a beautiful island, Leonora's home, Fernando unsuccessfully questions Ines, Leonora's companion, as to her identity. When he meets Leonora, she tells him they must part, that nothing can come of their love. She gives Fernando a scroll, an army commission; and he now believes she must be high-born and willing to help him in his aspiration to an honourable career.

Meanwhile the king, alone, sings passionately of his love for Leonora. He confers with his minister and finds that Fernando has led the Spanish army to victory against the Moors. Baldassarre enters, bearing a Papal edict. The king must renounce Leonora and reinstate his wife. The king agrees reluctantly and sends for Leonora. Fernando arrives and asks to be rewarded for his military prowess, requesting the hand of Leonora in marriage. Reluctantly the king concurs and, quite ignorant of Leonora's past, Fernando marries her; her letter revealing everything has never reached him.

Horrified when he discovers the truth, he tears off the chain of honour received from the king and returns to the sanctuary of the monastery, as Baldassarre had anticipated when Fernando asked for his freedom at the beginning of the story. Leonora later appears, begs for his forgiveness and dies in his arms.

The Decca set, made in Bologna, is not ideal – showing signs that the sessions were not easy – but the colour and vigour of the writing are never in doubt. The mezzo role of the heroine is taken by Fiorenza Cossotto, formidably powerful if not quite at her finest, while Ileana Cotrubas is comparably imaginative as her confidante, Ines, though also not at her peak. Bacquier and

Ghiaurov make up an agreeable team which should have been even better. Bright recording, well transferred, though not one of Decca's most vivid.

La fille du régiment (complete).
⊛ *** Decca 414 520-2 (2) [id.]. ROHCG Ch. & O, Bonynge.
  Marie (Joan Sutherland), Tonio (Luciano Pavarotti), Sulpice (Spiro Malas), Marquise (Monica Sinclair), Duchess (Edith Coates).

Recorded at a vintage period in Decca history, Joan Sutherland's set of *La fille du régiment* – she dominates it from first to last, even in competition with the young Pavarotti – comes out with tingling freshness and immediacy in the CD transfer. It was with this cast that the piece returned to Covent Garden in the 1960s, and Sutherland immediately showed how naturally she takes to the role of tomboy. Marie is a *vivandière* in the 21st Regiment of Grenadiers in the army of Napoleon, and the jolly, almost Gilbertian plot involves her translation back to a noble background from which as an infant she had been abducted.

As the opera opens, Marie and the Regimental Sergeant, Sulpice, perform a drill and Marie demonstrates her skill with drumsticks. Together they sing a '*Rataplan*' duet and she confides in Sulpice that her life was saved by a young man when she almost fell down a rocky mountain face. Tonio, the young man in question, is caught prowling in the camp but, in telling of her rescue, Marie saves his life. The two are now in love and he decides to enlist.

But at that moment the Marquise de Berkenfield sees some papers which had been secreted on the young Marie's person when she was discovered on the battlefield as a child. She declares that Marie is her long-lost niece. Marie is forced to leave the regiment and live at the castle, where she is expected to wed a nobleman. Marie rebels.

Tonio is now a captain and, encouraged by the sergeant, decides to elope with Marie. But to ensure that Marie weds the nobleman of her choice, the marquise tells Sulpice that she is Marie's mother. This information is conveyed to Marie and dutifully she prepares to renounce Tonio and marry her aunt's choice.

At the wedding she sings to the guests who are there to witness the signing of the marriage contract. She tells them of her happiness with the Grenadiers as a child and as a *vivandière*. The marquise is overcome with great emotion and, relenting, draws Marie and Tonio together. All sing 'Salute to France' and the opera ends happily.

The original French version, favoured here by Richard Bonynge, is fuller than the Italian revision and, with a cast that at the time of the recording sessions was also appearing in the theatre, the performance could hardly convey higher spirits with keener intensity. Sutherland is in turn brilliantly comic and pathetically affecting, nowhere more tellingly than in the last scene, where Marie is reunited with her army friends (including the hero).

Pavarotti makes an engaging Tonio, Monica Sinclair a formidable Marquise, and even if the French accents are often suspect it is a small price to pay for such a brilliant, happy opera set, a fizzing performance of a delightful Donizetti romp that can be confidently recommended for both its comedy and its fine singing. Recorded in Kingsway Hall, the sound has wonderful presence and clarity of focus. The CD format is all the more convenient but, irritatingly, Tonio's celebrated 'High-C's' solo in the finale of Act I is not banded separately, or even indicated in the libretto. (It comes half-way through band 13 of the first disc.)

Lucia di Lammermoor (complete).
*** Decca 410 193-2 (2) [id.]. ROHCG Ch. & O, Bonynge.
  Lucia (Joan Sutherland), Edgardo (Luciano Pavarotti), Enrico (Sherrill Milnes), Raimondo (Nicolai Ghiaurov), Alisa (Huguette Tourangeau), Arturo (Ryland Davies).
(M) *** Decca 411 622-2 (2) [id.]. St Cecilia Academy, Rome, Ch. & O, Pritchard.
  Lucia (Joan Sutherland), Edgardo (Renato Cioni), Enrico (Robert Merrill), Raimondo (Cesare Siepi), Alisa (Ana Raquel Satre), Arturo (Kenneth Macdonald).
*** DG Dig. 435 309-2 (2) [id.]. Amb. Op. Ch., LSO, Marin.
  Lucia (Cheryl Studer), Edgardo (Plácido Domingo), Enrico (Juan Pons), Raimondo (Samuel Ramey), Alisa (Jennifer Larmore), Arturo (Fernando De la Mora).
(M) (***) EMI mono CMS7 63631-2 (2) [Ang. CDMB 63631]. La Scala Ch. & O, Karajan.
  Lucia (Maria Callas), Edgardo (Giuseppe Di Stefano), Enrico (Rolando Panerai), Raimondo (Nicola Zaccaria), Alisa (Luisa Villa), Arturo (Giuseppe Zampieri).
**(*) EMI CDS7 47440-8 (2) [id.]. Philh. Ch. & O, Serafin.
  Lucia (Maria Callas), Edgardo (Ferruccio Tagliavini), Enrico (Piero Cappuccilli), Raimondo (Bernard Ladysz), Alisa (Margreta Elkins), Arturo (Leonardo Del Ferro).

(M) (***) EMI mono CMS7 69980-2 (2) [Ang. CDMB 69980]. Ch. & O of Maggio Musicale
Fiorentino, Serafin.
Lucia (Maria Callas), Edgardo (Giuseppe Di Stefano), Enrico (Tito Gobbi), Raimondo
(Raffaele Arié), Alisa (Anna Maria Canali), Arturo (Valiano Natali).

(M) **(*) Ph. 426 563-2 (2) [id.]. Amb. S., New Philh. O, Lopez-Cobos.
Lucia (Montserrat Caballé), Edgardo (José Carreras), Enrico (Vicente Sardinero), Raimondo
(Samuel Ramey), Alisa (Ann Murray), Arturo (Claes Hakon Ahnsjö).

(M) ** EMI Dig. CMS7 64622-2 (2) Amb. Op. Ch., RPO, Rescigno.
Lucia (Edita Gruberová), Edgardo (Alfredo Kraus), Enrico (Renato Bruson), Raimondo
(Robert Lloyd).

(M) ** BMG/RCA CD 86504 (2) [6504-2-RG]. RCA Italiana Op. Ch. & O, Prêtre.
Lucia (Anna Moffo), Edgardo (Carlo Bergonzi), Enrico (Mario Sereni), Raimondo (Ezio
Flagello), Alisa (Corinna Vozza), Arturo (Pierre Duval).

** Teldec/Warner Dig. 9031 72306-2 (2) [id.]. Amb. S., LSO, Bonynge.
Lucia (Edita Gruberová), Edgardo (Neil Shicoff), Enrico (Alexandru Agache), Raimondo
(Alistair Miles), Alisa (Diana Montague), Arturo (Bernard Lombardo).

Donizetti's ripely romantic Scottish opera has long been a favourite vehicle for divas, and the
music triumphs over the melodramatic storyline.

Lord Henry Ashton, who has usurped control of the estates of Edgar, Master of Ravenswood,
hears that his sister Lucy is meeting Edgar clandestinely and is enraged, determined to prevent
any possible match between the lovers. He also has political problems and is hoping to solve
them by marrying off Lucy to Arthur Bucklaw.

Accompanied by Alice, her confidante, Lucy meets Edgar in the moonlit park and they plight
their troth; Edgar then bids her a tender farewell – he is off to France. He hopes he may be
reconciled with the family, but Lucy knows that the feud is too strong for Edgar to be accepted
by Henry. She then discovers the proposed arranged marriage and Henry shows her a forged
letter suggesting that Edgar is unfaithful. Henry also tells her that the marriage may well save his
life. She is dismayed and consults the chaplain, Raymond, who persuades her to obey Henry,
otherwise he may be executed as a traitor to the king. Lucy reluctantly accedes and signs the
marriage contract in front of the assembled guests.

Edgar makes his dramatic entry at the key moment and the principals in the affair participate
in the famous *Sextet*, each expressing his or her own conflicting interest. Edgar angrily returns
Lucy's ring and she his, and he storms out, cursing the Lammermoors.

The wedding celebrations continue, then Raymond enters and tells the guests that Lucy has
lost her reason and slain her husband. She enters and sings the Mad scene, fantasizing a wedding
with Edgar. Edgar, unaware of Lucy's predicament, is mournfully considering suicide in the
Tomb of the Ravenswoods. Finally discovering what has happened he stabs himself.

It is hardly surprising that Decca re-recorded Sutherland twice in the role with which she is
inseparably associated. Though some of the girlish freshness of voice which marked the 1961
recording disappeared in the 1971 set, the detailed understanding was intensified, and the
mooning manner, which in 1961 was just emerging, was counteracted. No one outshines
Sutherland in this opera; rightly for this recording she insisted on doing the whole of the Mad
scene in a single session, making sure it was consistent from beginning to end. Power is there as
well as delicacy, and the rest of the cast is first rate. Pavarotti, through much of the opera not as
sensitive as he can be, proves magnificent in his final scene with the hero's big aria. The sound-
quality is superb, though choral interjections are not always forward enough. In this set, unlike
the earlier one, the text is absolutely complete. The analogue recording is greatly enhanced by
the remastering for CD, with balance and focus outstandingly firm and real. The silent
background is particularly valuable in the pauses and silences of the Mad scene, the opera's
powerful climax.

The earlier Sutherland version remains an attractive proposition at mid-price. Though in
1961 Sutherland was smoothing over her consonants, the voice is obviously that of a younger
singer, and dramatically the performance is closer to Sutherland's famous stage appearances of
that time, full of fresh innocence. Though the text is not quite as full as the later version, a
fascinating supplement is provided in an aria (from *Rosamonda d'Inghilterra*) which for many
years was used as a replacement for the big Act I aria, *Regnava nel silenzio*). The recording
remains very fresh and vivid, though not everyone will like the prominent crowd noises.
Sutherland's coloratura virtuosity remains breathtaking, and the cast is a strong one, with
Pritchard a most understanding conductor.

On DG Cheryl Studer is an affecting heroine, singing both brilliantly and richly, and with Plácido Domingo rebutting any idea that his tenor is too cumbersome for Donizetti. This is the finest version yet in digital sound, with the young Romanian, Ion Marin, drawing fresh, urgent playing from the LSO. The rest of the cast is outstandingly strong too, with Juan Pons as Lucia's brother, Enrico, and Samuel Ramey as the teacher and confidant, Raimondo, Bide-the-Bent.

It was Callas who, some years before Sutherland, emerged as the Lucia of her time and established this as a vividly dramatic role, not just an excuse for pretty coloratura. The La Scala set was recorded live in 1955, when Karajan took the company of La Scala to Berlin, but for years this finest of Callas's recordings of *Lucia* was available only on pirate issues. Callas was an artist who responded vividly to an audience and an occasion, particularly with a great conductor in charge. Karajan's insight gives a new dimension to the work, even though the usual, much-cut text is used. Despite the limited sound, Callas's voice is caught with fine immediacy. Her singing is less steely than in the 1953 studio recording, and far firmer than in the later stereo set.

The Callas stereo version was recorded in Kingsway Hall in 1959, at the very same time that Serafin was conducting this opera at Covent Garden for the newly emergent Joan Sutherland. The sound is very good for its period and comes over the more freshly on CD, with Callas's edgy top notes cleanly caught. Her flashing-eyed interpretation of the role of Lucia remains unique, though the voice has its unsteady moments. One instance is at the end of the Act I duet with Edgardo, where Callas on the final phrase moves sharpwards and Tagliavini – here past his best – flatwards. Serafin's conducting is ideal, though the score, as in Callas's other recordings, still has the cuts which used to be conventional in the theatre.

Callas's earliest mono set, which dates from 1954, is given an effective remastering which brings out the solo voices well, although the acoustic is confined and the choral sound less well focused. Here, needless to say, is not the portrait of a sweet girl, wronged and wilting, but a formidably tragic characterization. The diva is vocally better controlled than in her later stereo set, with excitingly brilliant coloratura; and there are memorable if not always perfectly stylish contributions from Di Stefano and Gobbi. As in the later sets, the text has the usual stage cuts, but Callas's irresistible musical imagination, her ability to turn a well-known phrase with unforgettable inflexions, makes this indispensable as a historic recording.

The idea behind the set with Caballé is fascinating, a return to what the conductor Jésus Lopez-Cobos believes is Donizetti's original concept, an opera for a dramatic soprano, not a light coloratura. Compared with the text we know, transpositions paradoxically are for the most part upwards (made possible when no stratospheric coloratura additions are needed); but Cobos's direction hardly compensates for the lack of brilliance and, José Carreras apart, the singing, even that of Caballé, is not very persuasive. Good, refined recording.

Edita Gruberová brings dramatic power as well as brilliance and flexibility to the role of Lucia and rises well to the challenge of the Mad scene, the opera's powerful climax, where her rather over-emphatic manner suits both the music and the drama best. Elsewhere a degree of gustiness in the vocal delivery – the microphones are not kind to her – and the occasional squeezed note, together with noisy breathing, detract from the purity needed. Legato lines, too, tend to be overpointed. Kraus conceals his age astonishingly well, with finely controlled singing (no problems over legato) but with an occasional over-emphasis to match his heroine. Bruson and Lloyd are both first rate, but Rescigno's conducting lacks point, rather matching the plainness of the recorded production. Full and natural if unremarkable 1983 digital sound – the recording was made at Abbey Road.

Prêtre's version, recorded in 1965 with Anna Moffo as the heroine, has been reissued in RCA's series of operas on mid-priced CDs. It makes a fair bargain. Though the male principals – notably Carlo Bergonzi – sing stylishly, Moffo, for all the sweetness of her voice, adopts a performing style more appropriate to Puccini than to Donizetti. The sound is good for its period.

Edita Gruberová on the Teldec set underlines expressive gestures far more obtrusively than in her earlier, EMI recording opposite Alfredo Kraus. The intention is to intensify the emotional weight of the performance but, with such exaggeration, she quickly comes to sound self-conscious. Neil Shicoff as Edgardo sings strongly but is relatively coarse in his style and though, as ever, Richard Bonynge demonstrates his mastery at springing Donizettian rhythms, this hardly matches the classic Decca set he recorded with his wife, Joan Sutherland.

Lucia di Lammermoor: highlights.
(M) *** Decca 421 885-2; *421 885-4* [id.] (from above recording with Sutherland, Pavarotti; cond. Bonynge).

(M) **(*) EMI CDM7 63934-2 [id.]; *EG 763934-4* (from above recording with Callas, Tagliavini, Cappuccilli; cond. Serafin).

For those who have chosen Callas or Sutherland's earlier, complete set, the 63-minute selection from her later (1971) version should be ideal. It includes the Fountain scene, the sextet, the Mad scene and the great tenor aria in the last scene. The splendid Kingsway Hall recording, produced by Christopher Raeburn and engineered by Kenneth Wilkinson and James Lock, has been transferred admirably to CD.

The hour-long selection from Callas's 1959 Kingsway Hall recording makes a useful supplement for those who have her earlier, mono set, where she is more completely in control vocally and the rest of the cast is preferable. The stereo sound is very good for its period.

Lucrezia Borgia (complete).
(M) *** Decca 421 497-2 (2) [id.]. London Op. Voices, Nat. PO, Bonynge.
  Lucrezia (Joan Sutherland), Gennaro (Giacomo Aragall), Alfonso (Ingvar Wixell), Orsini (Marilyn Horne).
(M) *(*) BMG/RCA GD 86642 (2) [6642-2-RG2]. RCA Italiana Op. Ch. & O, Perlea.
  Lucrezia (Montserrat Caballé), Gennaro (Alfredo Kraus), Alfonso (Ezio Flagello), Orsini (Shirley Verrett).

Lucrezia Borgia is set in Venice in the early sixteenth century. In the Prologue a young nobleman is found sleeping on a bench by the masked Lucrezia, who clearly regards him warmly. Gennaro wakes up and tells her about his background – that a poor fisherman looked after him as a child. Maffio Orsini arrives with friends and unmasks Lucrezia. Gennaro thinks her most beautiful. He does not know her identity, but his friends do: each has lost a relative, poisoned by her. Gennaro is horrified by the news and Lucrezia faints when he repulses her.

Outside a palace in Ferrara, Duke Alfonso reveals his jealousy of Gennaro who, he believes, is Lucrezia's lover. He is her fourth husband; all his predecessors have been poisoned. Gennaro desecrates lettering on the palace: with his sword he obliterates the 'B', leaving 'orgia'. He is arrested and is to be put to death. Lucrezia discovers who the perpetrator is. She pleads with the duke to spare him but is refused and is ordered to give Gennaro poisoned wine. The duke leaves and Lucrezia hands Gennaro an antidote and tells him to make his escape while he can.

Later, at a banquet nearby, the chanting of monks is heard. They sing a dirge, for Lucrezia has poisoned their wine. Lucrezia enters and discovers Gennaro is there too. Again she offers him an antidote but he refuses, for his friends are dying around him. Lucrezia tells him she is his mother. He still turns away from her in disgust and she drinks from the chalice and falls dead across his motionless body.

Sutherland is in her element here. In one or two places she falls into the old swooning style but, as in the theatre, her singing is masterly, not only in its technical assurance but in its power and conviction, making the impossible story of poisoner-heroine moving and even sympathetic. Aragall sings stylishly too, and though Wixell's timbre is hardly Italianate he is a commanding Alfonso. Marilyn Horne in the breeches role of Orsini is impressive in the brilliant *Brindisi* of the last Act, but earlier she has moments of unsteadiness. Thanks to researches by Richard Bonynge, the set also includes extra material for the tenor, including an aria newly discovered, *T'amo qual dama un angelo*. The recording is characteristically full and brilliant.

Lucrezia Borgia was the opera which brought Montserrat Caballé overnight fame when she stepped in at the last minute at a stage performance in New York. Even so, her performance in this recording is disappointing. In no way does she enter into the character of the wicked Lucrezia caught out by fate and, though there is much beautiful singing, the uninspired direction of Perlea does not help. When Caballé in the final Act enters the banquet where her enemies (and, unknown to her, her son) are being entertained to poisoned wine, she sounds like a hostess asking whether her guests would like more tea. Alfredo Kraus is the most successful soloist here, for even Shirley Verrett seems affected by the prevailing lassitude. However, the remastered recording is excellent.

Maria Padilla (complete).
**(*) Opera Rara ORC 6 (3) [id.]. Geoffrey Mitchell Ch., LSO, Francis.
  Maria Padilla (Lois McDonall), Ines Padilla (Della Jones), Don Ruiz di Padilla (Graham Clark), Don Pedro (Christian Du Plessis), Ramiro (Roderick Earle), Don Luigi (Ian Caley), Don Alfonso (Roderick Kennedy), Francisca (Joan Davies).

Described as a melodrama and written in 1841, *Maria Padilla* marks a return to Donizetti's Italian manner, a piece based on strong situations. It even matches *Lucia di Lammermoor* in places, with the heroine ill-used by the prince she loves, Pedro the Cruel. When the obligatory mad scene is given not to the heroine but to her father, even a tenor such as Graham Clark – future star in Bayreuth – can hardly compensate, however red-blooded the writing and strong the singing. In the title-role Lois McDonall is brightly agile, if at times a little raw. Alun Francis directs the LSO in a fresh, well-disciplined performance and, as ever with Opera Rara sets, the notes and commentary contained in the libretto are both readable and scholarly.

Maria Stuarda (complete).
(M) *** Decca 425 410-2 (2) [id.]. Ch. & O of Teatro Comunale, Bologna, Bonynge.
> Maria Stuarda (Joan Sutherland), Elisabetta (Huguette Tourangeau), Leicester (Luciano Pavarotti), Talbot (Roger Soyer), Cecil (James Morris), Anna (Margreta Elkins).

** Ph. Dig. 426 233-2 (2) [id.]. Bav. R. Ch., Munich RSO, Patanè.
> Maria Stuarda (Edita Gruberová), Elisabetta (Agnes Baltsa), Leicester (Francisco Araiza), Talbot (Francesco Ellero D'Artegna), Cecil (Simone Alaimo), Anna (Iris Vermillion).

In Donizetti's tellingly dramatic opera on the conflict of Elizabeth I and Mary Queen of Scots the confrontation between the two queens is so brilliantly effective that one regrets that history did not actually engineer such a meeting between the royal cousins.

As the opera opens, court rumours imply that Queen Elizabeth may unite England and France by marriage. The Earl of Shrewsbury (Talbot) begs her to be merciful to her cousin, Mary Queen of Scots, now imprisoned in Fotheringhay Castle. Lord Burleigh (Cecil) counters this by saying that Mary cannot be trusted. Robert Dudley, Earl of Leicester, whom Elizabeth clearly favours, is now appointed as her ambassador to France but seems unenthusiastic about the appointment.

Mary writes to Leicester, who has visited her at Fotheringhay and admired her beauty, and he is sympathetic to her cause. Elizabeth sees the letter and believes that Mary has designs both on Leicester and on her throne. But she agrees to visit Mary in prison. The queen and her hunting party now arrive in the park at Fotheringhay. Leicester goes ahead and tells Mary to be humble, vowing vengeance if the queen remains without pity, and he plans to ask Mary to marry him.

Cecil further encourages Elizabeth's mistrust of Mary, and she also worries about Leicester's relationship with her Scottish adversary. When the queens meet, Mary kneels in submission and pleads for mercy, but Elizabeth accuses her of complicity in the death of her husband, Darnley. Mary, stunned into revolt, cries out that Elizabeth is a bastard and is promptly sentenced to death, with Leicester ordered to attend the execution. Elizabeth grants Mary a final wish, that Hannah should walk with her to the scaffold. Watched by Leicester, she dies.

In the Decca set, the contrast between the full soprano Maria and the dark mezzo Elisabetta is underlined by some transpositions, with Tourangeau emerging as a powerful villainess in this slanted version of the story. Pavarotti turns Leicester into a passionate Italian lover, not at all an Elizabethan gentleman. As for Sutherland, she is at her most compellingly dramatic too, and the great moment when she flings the insult *Vil bastarda!* at her cousin brings a superb snarl. In the lovely prayer before Mary's execution with its glorious melody, Sutherland is richly forthright but does not quite efface memories of Dame Janet Baker in her recording with English National Opera – see below. Otherwise she remains the most commanding of Donizetti sopranos, and Richard Bonynge directs an urgent account of an unfailingly enjoyable opera. Unusually for Decca, the score is slightly cut. The recording is characteristically bright and full and the CD transfer first rate.

Giuseppe Patanè, in one of his last recordings, conducts a refined account of *Maria Stuarda*, very well sung and well recorded. The manner is lighter, the speeds often faster than in the immediate CD rivals, and that makes the result less sharply dramatic, a point reflected in the actual singing of Gruberová and Baltsa which, for all its beauty and fine detail, is less intense than that of Sutherland and Tourangeau (on Decca) or Baker and Plowright (on EMI – see below). Whether it is Mary singing nostalgically of home in her first cantilena or leading the surgingly memorable Scottish prayer in Act III, or even in the confrontation between the two queens, this account keeps a degree of restraint – even on the thrusting insult from Mary to Elizabeth, *Vil bastarda!*. Some may prefer this, particularly if they have not seen the opera on stage. Araiza sings well as Leicester, but again gives a less rounded performance than Pavarotti with Sutherland. Not that the rivalry is exact, when the EMI is a live performance in English, and the Decca uses a slightly different text. This is the only digital version. The Philips sound is well balanced, but there is less sense of presence than in the fine analogue Decca.

Mary Stuart (complete, in English).
(M) **(*) EMI Dig. CMS7 69372-2 (2). ENO Ch. and O, Mackerras.

Maria Stuarda (Janet Baker), Elisabetta (Rosalind Plowright), Leicester (David Rendall), Talbot (John Tomlinson), Cecil (Alan Opie), Anna (Angela Bostock).

Mary Stuart was one of the English National Opera Company's outstanding successes in 1973, when it was first presented with Dame Janet Baker in the name-part. It was also the opera chosen at the ENO when, nine years later, Dame Janet decided to retire from the opera stage; and happily EMI took the opportunity to make live recordings of a series of performances at the Coliseum. Though far from ideal, the result is strong and memorable, with Dame Janet herself rising nobly to the demands of the role, snorting fire superbly in her condemnation of Elizabeth as a royal bastard and, above all, making the closing scenes before Mary's execution deeply moving, with the canary-fancying associations of Donizetti totally forgotten. Her performance is splendidly matched by that of Rosalind Plowright, though the closeness of the recording of the singers makes the voice rather hard. The singing of the rest of the cast is less distinguished, with chorus ensemble often disappointingly ragged, a point shown up by the recording balance. The acoustic has the listener almost on stage, with the orchestra relatively distant. It is a valuable and historic set, but the Decca version with Sutherland – see above – gives a fuller idea of the work's power.

Mary Stuart: highlights (in English).
(M) **(*) EMI Dig. CDM7 63727-2 [id.] (from above recording; cond. Mackerras).

The highlight of Donizetti's dramatization of the conflict between Elizabeth I and Mary Queen of Scots reaches its climax at the confrontation between the two queens, historically incorrect but dramatically irresistible. The meeting is the more communicative when the interchange occurs in English, with Dame Janet (as Mary Stuart) and Rosalind Plowright rising to the challenge superbly. This scene is at the centre of the 61 minutes of highlights from the memorable if uneven ENO performance. Many will enjoy this while not requiring the complete set. The balance is very close to the singers, with some hardness on the voices.

Poliuto (complete).
(M) *** Sony Dig. M2K 44821 (2) [id.]. V. Singakademie Ch., VSO, Oleg Caetani.
Poliuto (José Carreras), Paolina (Katia Ricciarelli), Severo (Juan Pons), Callistene (László Polgár).

Set in Rome in the early Christian period, *Poliuto* is based on Corneille's tragedy, *Polyeucte*, a story of martyrdom. Written in 1838, it was originally banned by the censor and was first heard in a version that Donizetti arranged for Paris under the title *Les martyres*. The opera takes place in Melitene, the capital of Armenia, in AD 257.

Poliuto receives the rite of baptism and is converted to Christianity, then a proscribed faith. His wife, Paolina, attracted by the serene hymn, enters and learns that Severo, with whom she was once in love, is returning as the Roman pro-consul.

In Act II, the high priest, Calistene, whose advances Paolina has repulsed, brings Poliuto to eavesdrop on a conversation between Severo and Paolina in which she confesses that, although she once loved him, her allegiance is now to her husband. Poliuto is consumed with jealousy, but at the end of the Act he reveals his conversion to Christianity and is condemned to death.

In the last Act, Paolina visits her imprisoned husband and tells him that, if he renounces his new faith, he will be pardoned. He remains constant, and the opera ends with her deciding to share her husband's martyrdom. It is a piece that was revived at various periods, thanks to the advocacy of such tenors as Tamagno and Lauri-Volpi; Maria Callas, attracted to the dramatic role of the heroine, Paolina, appeared opposite Franco Corelli in a revival at La Scala, Milan, in 1960.

This version was recorded in the Vienna Konzerthaus in 1986. Carreras's voice is in splendid form. Ricciarelli as Paolina lacks something in dramatic bite, but she gives the heroine an inward warmth and tenderness. Pons and Polgár are also excellent and, though the piece is not remarkable for any depth of character-drawing, it is well worth investigating for the foretastes it brings of middle-period Verdi, and specifically for one of Donizetti's most inspired ensembles in the Act II finale. The recording is clear and vivid, hardly betraying the fact that it was made live at a concert performance.

Ugo, conte di Parigi (complete).
*** Opera Rara ORC 1 (3) [id.]. Geoffrey Mitchell Ch., New Philh. O, Francis.
Luigi (Della Jones), Emma (Eiddwen Harrhy), Bianca (Janet Price), Adelia (Yvonne Kenny), Ugo (Maurice Arthur), Folco di Angiò (Christian Du Plessis).

The 1977 recording of *Ugo, conte di Parigi* was the result of formidable detective work, revealing in this early opera of 1832 a strong plot and some fine numbers, including excellent duets. Matching such singers as Janet Price and Yvonne Kenny, Maurice Arthur sings stylishly in the title-role, with a clear-cut tenor that records well. Della Jones and Christian du Plessis, regular stalwarts of Opera Rara sets, complete a stylish cast. Reissued on CD thanks to the Peter Moores Foundation, it offers a fresh and intelligent performance under Alun Francis, and the scholarly, readable notes and commentary, as well as libretto and translation, are models of their kind.

Arias: (i) *Anna Bolena: Piagete voi? . . . Al dolce guidami.* (ii) *Lucrezia Borgia: Com' è bello! Maria di Rohan: Havvi un Dio. Roberto Devereux: Vivi, ingrato.*
(M) **(*) BMG/RCA 09026 62458-2. Montserrat Caballé, (i) Barcelona SO or (ii) Ch. & LPO, Cillario: BELLINI: *Arias.* **(*)

Montserrat Caballé came to sudden fame when she stepped in at the last minute to undertake a stage performance in New York of Donizetti's *Lucrezia Borgia.* The impact on the opera-going public of the time was so great that at once she was one of the most sought-after sopranos in America. This Donizetti/Bellini collection includes her follow-up recital for RCA in 1965 and the disc contains some really assured coloratura and much creamy-toned legato to delight any of this artist's admirers, if less strength in terms of characterization. The choice of items is interesting too, given in unusually complete form. The *Anna Bolena* aria was recorded later, in 1970, when she had gained greater histrionic confidence, the performance expressive and brilliant in equal measure. The excellent recording of the main recital was supervised by Decca engineers.

Arias from: *Don Pasquale; Don Sebastiano; Il Duca d'Alba; L'elisir d'amore; La Favorita; La fille du régiment; Lucia di Lammermoor; Maria Stuarda.*
**(*) Decca 417 638-2 [id.]. Luciano Pavarotti with various orchestras & conductors.

A cleverly chosen compilation of Pavarotti recordings of Donizetti from various sources – not just complete sets but previous recital discs. It is an asset that Pavarotti so readily encompasses both comic and tragic. It is good to have one or two rarities along with the favourite numbers, including Tonio's celebrated 'High-C's' solo from the Act I finale of *La fille du régiment.* Sound from different sources is well co-ordinated. This collection demonstrates clearly that Pavarotti is at his very finest in this repertoire.

Dukas, Paul (1865–1935)

Ariane et Barbe-bleue: complete.
(M) *** Erato/Warner Dig. 2292 45663-2 (2) [id.]. Fr. R. Ch. & O, Jordan.
Ariane (Katherine Ciesinski), Barbe-Bleue (Gabriel Bacquier), La Nourrice (Mariana Paunova), Sélysette (Hanna Schaer), Ygraine (Anne-Marie Blanzat), Mélisande (Jocelyne Chamonin), Bellangère (Michèle Command).

Ariane et Barbe-bleue is a welcome rarity, here making its first appearance on CD. It is rich in invention and atmosphere, as one would expect from the composer of *La Péri* and *L'Apprenti sorcier,* and its vivid colours should ensure its wide appeal. Dukas was enormously self-critical and consigned an earlier opera, *Horn and Rimenhild,* to oblivion, along with much other music. *Ariane* is, like Debussy's *Pelléas,* set to a Maeterlinck text, but there is none of the half-lights and the dream-like atmosphere of the latter.

As the opera begins, a crowd gathers outside Bluebeard's castle and a carriage arrives with the lovely Ariane and her nurse. Angry murmurs from the assembled villagers question the whereabouts of Bluebeard's former wives. Are they prisoners, or murdered? But Ariane innocently enters Bluebeard's domain. Once inside, the nurse dreads the worst but Ariane is sure that Bluebeard loves her too much to harm her.

He has given her six silver keys and one gold key which she is forbidden to use. Retaining the gold key, she throws the others away, but the nurse retrieves them and opens six doors. Jewels of every kind are displayed and, while diamonds delight her, Ariane heads for the seventh door. They hear strange sounds which she decides are coming from the wives. Bluebeard tries to stop her opening the door and a struggle ensues. A stone is thrown and the crowd pours in, but Ariane assures them that she is quite unharmed.

Exploring a dark underground hall, Ariane and the nurse trip over the five wives, lying in a heap on the floor. Ariane tells them not to be afraid; she is not a prisoner and has come to save them. In a dark corner is a securely bolted door, and the wives warn her that if she opens it the sea will flood in. Ignoring the warning, Ariane forces the door open and light streams from a window beyond. She leads her companions to freedom. But they are unable to escape as the drawbridge rises in front of them and water appears in the moat.

Trapped, they adorn themselves with the jewels to which they have been given access by the silver keys. Bluebeard approaches the castle and the waiting crowd seize and wound him. Ariane intercedes, cuts off his bonds which could have strangled him, then, although he pleads with her to stay, she leaves. The other wives refuse to accompany her and remain with Bluebeard in his castle.

The present performance derives from a French Radio production and is generally well cast, with Katherine Ciesinski splendid in the taxing part of Ariane opposite Gabriel Bacquier as a characterful Bluebeard and Mariana Paunova rich-toned as the nurse. Armin Jordan is a sensitive and often powerful conductor, and the digital recording is warmly atmospheric and well balanced. The complete libretto is included, and this most enterprising and valuable reissue is strongly recommended.

Dvořák, Antonín (1841–1904)

Rusalka (complete).
*** Sup. Dig. 10 3641-2 (3) [id.]. Prague Ch. & Czech PO, Neumann.
   Rusalka (Gabriela Beňačková), Watergnome (Richard Novák), Witch (Vera Soukupová), Prince (Wieslaw Ochman), Foreign Princess (Drahomira Drobková).

Dvořák's fairy-tale opera is given a magical performance by Neumann and his Czech forces, helped by full, brilliant and atmospheric recording which, while giving prominence to the voices, brings out the beauty and refinement of Dvořák's orchestration. Written right at the end of the composer's career in his ripest maturity but with Wagnerian influences at work, the piece has a unique flavour; where on stage it can seem too long for its material (though not in the highly imaginative version staged by the English National Opera at London's Coliseum), on record it works beautifully.

The evocative opening, with singing wood nymphs and the Spirit of the Lake (Rusalka's father) rising from the depths, immediately grips the listener. Rusalka enters and tells her father that she is in love with a mortal, a prince. If only she were human! She expresses her innermost feelings in an invocation to the moon. She then seeks help from Ježibaba, a witch, and is told that if she appears as a human she will be dumb, and if the prince were then to deceive her their joint fate would be eternal damnation. The Spirit of the Lake overhears and cries out in despair, but the spell is irrevocable.

The prince then arrives at the lake searching for a white doe and he is suddenly aware of a magical presence near at hand. Presently Rusalka appears and they embrace tenderly, though she cannot speak of her love. He departs and her sisters and the Spirit of the Lake mourn.

The scene now changes to the palace where guests are gathering for the prince's wedding. Gossip in the kitchen is rife: a kitchen boy is frightened by Rusalka, while a forester hints at witchcraft. Then, sadly, a foreign princess takes the prince's fancy and he begins to have misgivings about his forthcoming marriage.

Rusalka's father appears and becomes downcast when Rusalka is able to speak with him and tell him about the rival princess. When the prince embraces the princess, Rusalka flings her arms round him in despair. The prince begs for aid from her rival but she refuses and the Spirit of the Lake foretells that the prince will be in Rusalka's power for ever.

Rusalka is now an eternal wanderer as a will-o'-the-wisp. She longs to end her life, but the witch reminds her that the curse is on her for eternity, unless the prince ends his life. Desolately Rusalka sinks back into the lake. Finally the prince, seemingly drawn to the lake by the snow-white doe, remembers his romantic first meeting with Rusalka. She appears at his side and he begs forgiveness for his infidelity. He offers his life, asking for a kiss which will be fatal, and so he dies.

The title-role is superbly taken by Gabriela Beňačková-Čápová. The voice is creamy in tone, characterfully Slavonic without disagreeable hooting or wobbling, and the famous *Invocation to the moon* is enchanting. Vera Soukupová as the Witch is just as characterfully Slavonic in a lower register, though not so even; while Wieslaw Ochman sings with fine, clean, heroic tone as the Prince, with timbre made distinctive by tight vibrato. Richard Novák brings out some of the

Alberich-like overtones as the Watersprite, though the voice is not always steady. The banding on CD is both generous and helpful.

Rusalka: highlights.
(B) *** Sup. Dig. 110617-2 (from above recording; cond. Neumann).

This first-class selection from Neumann's fine set makes a welcome bargain-priced disc, offering an hour of music. Only a synopsis is provided, but no text.

Elgar, Edward (1857–1934)

(i) *Caractacus, Op. 35. Severn suite* (full orchestral version).
*** Chan. Dig. CHAN 9156/7 [id.]. (i) Judith Howarth, Arthur Davies, David Wilson-Johnson, Stephen Roberts, Alistair Miles, London Symphony Ch.; LSO, Hickox.

Elgar's *Caractacus* – the nearest the composer ever came to writing an opera – draws from Hickox and his splendid LSO forces a fresh, sympathetic reading of a disconcertingly episodic piece. Caractacus was truly an operatic personality, brave to the point of foolhardiness, so that his Roman conquerors took him back home with them as a hero rather than a captive! The oratorio is generally very well sung, with David Wilson-Johnson in the title-role, and recorded in opulent Chandos sound.

This is Elgar at his happiest, inspired by the countryside, and one of the high-spots is a glowing duet for Eigen, Caractacus's daughter, and her lover, Orbin, sung by Judith Howarth and Arthur Davies. Much the most memorable item is the well-known *Imperial march*, introducing the final scene in Rome, made the more exciting with chorus. One even forgives the embarrassment of the concluding chorus after that, which predicts that 'The nations all shall stand, and hymn the praise of Britain hand in hand'. The only reservation is that the earlier EMI recording, conducted by Sir Charles Groves, a sure candidate for CD, was crisper in ensemble and even better sung, with even more seductive pointing of rhythm. For coupling, Hickox has the full orchestral arrangement of Elgar's very last work, originally for brass band, the *Severn suite*.

The Dream of Gerontius, Op. 38.
*** EMI CDS7 47208-8 (2). Helen Watts, Nicolai Gedda, Robert Lloyd, John Alldis Ch., LPO, Boult (with *The Music Makers* **(*)).
*** Chan. Dig. CHAN 8641/2 (2) [id.]. Felicity Palmer, Arthur Davies, Gwynne Howell, London Symphony Ch., LSO, Hickox (with PARRY: *Anthems* ***).
**(*) EMI Dig. CDS7 49549-2 (2) [Ang. CDCB 49549]. Janet Baker, John Mitchinson, John Shirley-Quirk, CBSO Ch. & O, Rattle.
**(*) CRD CRD 3326/7 [id.]; *CRDC 4026/7*. Alfreda Hodgson, Robert Tear, Benjamin Luxon, SNO Ch. & O, Gibson.
(M) **(*) Decca 421 381-2 (2) [id.]. Yvonne Minton, Peter Pears, John Shirley-Quirk, King's College Ch., London Symphony Ch., LSO, Britten (with HOLST: *Hymn of Jesus* ***).
(M) (**(*)) EMI mono CHS7 63376-2 [Ang. CDHB 63376]. Marjorie Thomas, Richard Lewis, John Cameron, Huddersfield Ch. Soc., Royal Liverpool PO, Sargent (with WALTON: *Belshazzar's Feast* **(*)).

(i) *The Dream of Gerontius; Sea Pictures.*
(M) **(*) EMI CMS7 63185-2 (2). Janet Baker, Hallé O, Barbirolli; (i) with Richard Lewis, Kim Borg, Hallé & Sheffield Philharmonic Ch., Amb. S.

Cardinal Newman's poem on which *The Dream of Gerontius* is based may not be operatic in intention, but there are surely few more compelling moments in any opera than the great scene at the dying man's bedside when the priest's powerful send-off, '*Proficiscere, anima Christiana*' – 'Go forth upon thy journey, Christian soul', is taken up so movingly by the chorus. Later the dialogue between Gerontius and the angel as he questions his fate; his meetings with the demons of hell, and – that test safely past – the shattering orchestral climax when he confronts his maker, is matched in intensity by the glowing closing scene in heaven.

'This is the best of me,' wrote Elgar on the score, and the comment could be applied equally to Sir Adrian Boult's wonderfully glowing performance. Boult's total dedication is matched by a sense of both wonder and drama. The spiritual feeling is intense, but the human qualities of the narrative are fully realized and the glorious closing pages are so beautiful that Elgar's vision is made to become one of the most unforgettable moments in all musical literature. Boult's unexpected choice of Nicolai Gedda in the role of Gerontius brings an operatic dimension to this characterization, which is perfectly matched by Helen Watts as the Angel. The dialogues between the two have a natural spontaneity as Gerontius's questions and doubts find a response which is at once gently understanding and nobly authoritative. It is a fascinating vocal partnership, and it is matched by the commanding manner which Robert Lloyd finds for both his roles.

The orchestral playing is always responsive and often, like the choral singing, very beautiful. The lovely wind playing at the opening of Part II is matched by the luminosity of tone of the choral pianissimos, while the dramatic passages bring splendid incisiveness and bold assurance from the singers. The fine 1976 analogue recording is extremely well balanced and has responded admirably to its CD remastering. There is slight loss of ambience, but the added clarity adds impact to the big choral climaxes and the magical opening and closing pages of Part II are not robbed of their atmosphere and sense of mystery. There is one misjudgement and it is a serious one. In order to make room for *The Music Makers*, a welcome enough bonus, Part I of *Gerontius* is broken at the end of the first disc, immediately before the priest's dramatic *Proficiscere, anima Christiana*, a most unfortunate choice, robbing the listener of the surprise entry of the brass.

Hickox's version outshines all rivals in the range and quality of its sound. Quite apart from the fullness and fidelity of the recording, on tape as well as CD, Hickox's performance is deeply understanding, not always ideally powerful in the big climaxes but most sympathetically paced, with natural understanding of Elgarian rubato. The soloists make a characterful team. Arthur Davies is a strong and fresh-toned Gerontius who arouses the sort of echoes of Italian opera that Elgar himself – perhaps surprisingly – asked for. Gwynne Howell in the bass roles is powerful if not always ideally steady, and Felicity Palmer, though untraditionally bright of tone with her characterful vibrato, is strong and illuminating. Though on balance Boult's soloists are even finer, Hickox's reading in its expressive warmth conveys much love for this score, and the last pages with their finely sustained closing *Amen* are genuinely moving.

Barbirolli's red-blooded reading of *Gerontius* is the most heart-warmingly dramatic ever recorded; here it is offered, in a first-rate CD transfer, in coupling with one of the greatest Elgar recordings ever made: Dame Janet Baker's rapt and heartfelt account of *Sea Pictures*, originally the coupling for Jacqueline du Pré's first version of the *Cello concerto*. No one on record can match Dame Janet in this version of *Gerontius* for the fervent intensity and glorious tonal range of her singing as the Angel, one of her supreme recorded performances; and the clarity of CD intensifies the experience. In pure dedication the emotional thrust of Barbirolli's reading conveys the deepest spiritual intensity, making most other versions seem cool by comparison. Barbirolli also scores even over the finest modern rivals in the forward immediacy of the chorus.

The recording may have its hints of distortion but the sound is overwhelming, not least in the great outburst of *Praise to the Holiest*, and in the surge of emotion behind the radiant choruses ending each half. Richard Lewis gives one of his finest recorded performances, searching and intense, and, though Kim Borg is unidiomatic in the bass roles, his bass tones are rich in timbre, even if his projection lacks the dramatic edge of Robert Lloyd on the Boult set – however, that has the comparably unidiomatic Nicolai Gedda in the role of Gerontius. The Barbirolli reissue has rather a high tape-hiss, but in such a performance one quickly forgets it after the Prelude; and the layout is preferable to the Boult set, opening with the *Sea Pictures*, then offering Part 1 of the main work on the first CD, and Part 2 complete on the second.

Although undoubtedly it has moments of great imaginative force, Simon Rattle's digital recording is in the last resort a disappointment. The flamboyant operatic style of the performance is certainly not lacking in dynamism and there is much that is moving, but Rattle's control of the ebb and flow of tempo and tension is not always convincing. The most striking instance is in the famous *Praise to the Holiest in the height*, where the chorus, while producing gloriously rich and luminous sounds, is pressed into an impetuous accelerando at the close, so that the climax is approached at breakneck speed, in complete contrast to the broad and heavily accented opening section. Similarly, the brief but profound orchestral interlude where the soul of Gerontius goes forward to meet his Maker is robbed of dignity by a sudden quickening of pace, so that the apocalyptic fortissimo chord conveys the bizarre impression that the Lord has smitten him down for his eagerness. John Mitchinson sings powerfully and dramatically in Part 1 and Rattle's accompaniment throbs with fervour; but the voice soon develops an uncomfortably wide vibrato under pressure, which is less congenial in Part 2. Dame Janet Baker's assumption of the Angel's role is justly famous but the close microphones are not kind to her high fortissimos; she comes into her own, however, at the work's valedictory close, helped by the rapturously lovely sounds made by chorus and orchestra alike. Rattle's view of heaven is more romantic than Boult's, but the ravishing textures he creates are wonderfully supportive, both here and in the earlier dialogue between soul and angel. John Shirley-Quirk's contribution is authoritative, eloquent and commanding, no more so than in the histrionic *Proficiscere, anima Christiana* where Rattle (not robbed, like Boult, of the element of surprise, by a break in continuity) heightens the effect by a magnetic pause before the stabbing brass chord. The *Go forth* chorus expands magnificently, while later, in Part 2, the demons are given comparable bite and malignancy.

The recording has the widest possible dynamic range (this is not a record for a small flat) and, with the solo voices recessed and pianissimos having a tendency to recede, it is difficult, though not impossible, to achieve a setting which is comfortable in the work's lyrical sections and yet not overwhelming at climaxes. The use of the Great Hall of Birmingham University has brought a wide reverberation but this is cushioned by the microphone placing. The effect, though not wholly natural, is certainly evocative, and the amplitude and weight of the climaxes are arresting.

Gibson's performance cannot quite compete with Boult's version. It is impressively spontaneous and very dramatic, as is immediately apparent in the strong contrasts of dynamic in the *Prelude*. When in his opening section Gerontius (Robert Tear) describes 'this strange innermost abandonment, this emptying out of each constituent', the orchestral response sends a shiver down the spine. The same sense of drama attends the demons (who are forthright rather than sinister), although here the brightness of the CD transfer verges on fierceness. The male soloists match Gibson's urgency, although there is no lack of repose in the dialogue between the Angel (sensitively portrayed by Alfreda Hodgson) and Gerontius at the opening of Part 2. But Gibson does not manage to create the sense of unearthly stillness and quiet beauty that is so moving in Boult's marvellous performance.

Equally the accelerando to the close of the *Praise to the Holiest* section is not as intuitively calculated as in Britten's version (which uncannily matches the composer's own performance, which Britten could not have heard, as it was not published when he made his Decca recording). The closing pages with Gibson are sensitively done but are without the magical feeling of blissful infinity that Boult conjures up. The CRD recording is generally excellent. Like Rattle's EMI set, it has almost too wide a dynamic range: a volume setting where the gentler music is agreeably present is very loud indeed at fortissimo. The cueing is inadequate, with only two bands for Part 1 and three for Part 2. The tapes are first class.

Reissued on two mid-price CDs with a generous coupling, in Decca's British Collection series, the Britten version brings searching and inspired conducting from a fellow-composer not generally associated with Elgar. Britten was persuaded to conduct the piece as a result of hearing Peter Pears sing it under Sir Adrian Boult. His approach is red-blooded, passionate and urgent, and with speeds never languishing – as in this oratorio they can. Elgar himself wanted to get away from the Victorians' sanctimonious approach towards something essentially dramatic, even operatic; and Britten certainly does that. The London Symphony Chorus – supplemented by the King's Choir – is balanced backwardly in the warmly atmospheric recording, made at The Maltings, but the extra projection and precision of CD brings out, far more than the LP ever did, how bitingly dramatic the singing is, even if the actual choral sound is not sharply focused. The soloists are a fine, responsive team, with Peter Pears an involving if sometimes over-stressed Gerontius and Yvonne Minton and John Shirley-Quirk both excellent. On CD the layout, with the Holst work placed first, allows the break between discs to come in the ideal place, between the *Oratorio*'s two parts.

Sargent directs a thoughtful and moving account of *Gerontius*, with the 1950s sound coming up remarkably well, but it is sad that his earlier (1945) recording, the first complete one ever issued, was not chosen instead, more intense, more dedicated, more spontaneous-sounding. But with three excellent soloists and the Huddersfield Choral Society at its traditional peak, this is an excellent example of Sargent's work in his most successful area, conducting an amateur chorus. The coupling is both generous and apt and, with Walton coming before Part 1 of the Elgar, it means that the break between discs is ideally placed between the two Parts.

Enescu, Georges (1881–1955)

Oedipe: complete.
⊕ *** EMI Dig. CDS7 54011-2 (2) [Ang. CDCB 54011]. Orfeon Donostiarra, Monte Carlo PO, Lawrence Foster.

Oedipe (José Van Dam), Tirésias (Gabriel Bacquier), Créon (Marcel Vanaud), Shepherd (Nicolai Gedda), High Priest (Cornelius Hauptmann), Phorbas (Laurence Albert), Watchman (Jean-Philippe Courtis), Thésée (Gino Quilico), Jocaste (Brigitte Fassbaender), Sphinx (Marjana Lipovšek), Antigone (Barbara Hendricks), Mérope (Jocelyne Taillon), Laios (John Aler).

This is an almost ideal recording of a rare, long-neglected masterpiece, with a breathtaking cast of stars backing up a supremely fine performance by José van Dam in the central role of Oedipus. Unlike others who have adapted Sophocles for the opera stage, in his four compressed, vividly atmospheric Acts Enescu attempts to cover the whole story, from Oedipus's birth and the baleful prophecy of his tragic fate through to his exile in Attica. So Act III alone encapsulates the story as told by Stravinsky in *Oedipus Rex*.

The first Act (Prologue) takes place in Laius's palace where festivities are in progress celebrating the birth of a son to Laius and Jocasta. But as they are about to name the boy, the prophet Tiresias announces that the child is destined to kill his father and marry his mother. They order a shepherd to take the infant to the gorge of Cithaeron and kill him.

The shepherd disobeys Laius's orders and gives the child to Phorbas, who puts him in the place of the son of Polybus, the King of Corinth, who has died in his care. Oedipus grows up believing that Polybus and Merope are his parents and, when an oracle reveals his destiny, he flees from Corinth.

The familiar encounter with and killing of Laius takes place in the second Act, after which Oedipus learns that a sphinx is ravaging Thebes: she asks riddles of the passers-by and devours those who fail to answer. Whoever answers correctly will cause her death, which is what Oedipus does. The Thebans welcome him as their new king and offer him the hand of the newly widowed Jocasta.

The third Act takes place twenty years later when Thebes is stricken with plague. An oracle consulted by Creon tells that the city will be punished until the murderer of Laius, who lives within its walls, is found and punished. At first Oedipus perceives this as a plot of Creon to depose him, but gradually the truth emerges. The Act ends with Jocasta's death and Oedipus, having blinded himself, leaving Thebes accompanied by his favourite daughter, Antigone.

The fourth Act or Epilogue is derived from *Oedipus at Colonus*. After years of wandering, Oedipus comes to the grove in which the Furies, now acting as the protector of Athens and its king, Theseus, live. Creon tries to persuade him to return to Thebes, now plagued by new misfortunes. He refuses, whereupon Creon tries to abduct Antigone. On Theseus' entry he accuses Oedipus of patricide and incest, to which Oedipus replies that he is innocent since he committed these crimes unknowingly. His sight is restored as the Furies summon him to his resting place.

The idiom is tough and adventurous as well as warmly exotic, with vivid choral effects, a revelation to anyone who knows Enescu only from his *Romanian rhapsody*. The only reservation is that the pace tends to be on the slow side, but the incandescence of the playing of the Monte Carlo Philharmonic under Lawrence Foster and the richness of the singing and recorded sound amply compensate for that. The veteran, Gabriel Bacquier, is a moving Tiresias, Brigitte Fassbaender characterful as Jocasta, while Marjana Lipovšek's one scene as the Sphinx makes the spine tingle. With such stars as Barbara Hendricks, Nicolai Gedda, John Aler and Gino Quilico in incidental roles, this is a musical feast.

Erkel, Ferenc (1810–93)

Hunyadi László: complete.
*** Hung. HCD 12581/3 [id.]. Hungarian People's Army Male Ch., Hungarian State Op. Ch. and O, Kovács.
László V (András Molnár), Count Ulrik Cilley (Istvan Gáti), Erzsébet Szilágyi (Sylvia Sass), László (Dénes Gulyás), Mátyás (Zsuzsanna Dénes), Miklós Gara (Sándor Sólyom-Nagy).

Hunyadi László is a patriotic piece which, in 1844 at its first performance, aroused the sort of nationalistic fervour in Hungary that Verdi inspired in Italy with *Nabucco*. The end of Act I even brings a rousing chorus which, like *Va pensiero* in *Nabucco*, has all the qualities of a pop tune. Like the much later Erkel opera, *Bank ban*, *Hunyadi László* has never been out of the repertory in Hungary, and this live recording makes one understand why. Unlike its predecessor in the Hungaroton lists, it goes back to the original score instead of the corrupt reworking devised in the 1930s.

Erkel's use of national music may not be as strikingly colourful as Smetana's in Czechoslovakia or Glinka's in Russia – both comparable figures – but the flavour is both distinctive and attractive, strongly illustrating a red-blooded story. Janos Kovács conducts with a vigour suggestive of long experience of this work in the opera house. Dénes Gulyás is a heroic, heady-toned hero, while András Molnár is equally effective as the villainous king, surprisingly another tenor role. Sylvia Sass is excellent as the hero's mother, in this version allowed to sing the beautiful prayer just before Laszlo's execution, excised from the earlier recording. First-rate sound. An excellent, if unusual set, full of strong ideas, making easy listening.

Falla, Manuel de (1876 – 1946)

La vida breve (complete).
Withdrawn: (M) ***** EMI CDM7 69590-2 [id.]. Orfeon Donostiarra Ch., Nat. O of Spain, Frühbeck de Burgos.
Salud (Victoria De los Angeles), Carmela (Ana Maria Higueras), Grandmother (Ines Rivadeneyra), Paco (Carlo Cossutta), Uncle Salvador (Victor De Narké).
(M) ***(*)** DG 435 851-2 [id.]. Ambrosian Op. Ch., LSO, Navarro.
Salud (Teresa Berganza), Carmela / 1st and 3rd Street Vendor (Paloma Perez Iñigo), Grandmother / 2nd Street Vendor (Alicia Nafé), Paco (José Carreras), Uncle Salvador (Juan Pons).

La vida breve is a kind of Spanish *Cavalleria rusticana* without the melodrama. The setting is the courtyard of a gypsy house in the Albaicín district of Granada. Salud has been seduced by a local playboy, Paco, who has promised marriage. He is late and she is anxious; but eventually he comes in and swears his undying devotion. Act I ends, however, with the news that he is to marry Carmela, a rich girl of his own class, the very next day. Act II opens with a wedding party and Salud appears, voicing her grief and rage. In the last scene, the distraught Salud and her uncle, Salvador, offer to dance for the newly wed couple. Carmela cannot understand Paco's embarrassment. Salud denounces his treachery and falls dead at his feet.

Unquestionably the opera's story is weak; but if the music for the final scene is undermined by a fundamental lack of drama in the plot, Frühbeck de Burgos makes the most of the poignancy of the closing moments. Victoria de los Angeles deepened her interpretation over the years, and her imaginative colouring of the words gives a unique authority and evocation to her performance. *Vivan les que rían* is most expressively done, with Frühbeck following the soloist with great skill. The flamenco singer in Act II (Gabriel Moreno) also matches the realism of the idiom with an authentic 'folk' style. The other members of the cast are good without being memorable; but when this is primarily a solo vehicle for De los Angeles, and the orchestral interludes are managed so colloquially, this is readily recommendable. The recording remains atmospheric, as well as having increased vividness and presence. It now fits conveniently on a single CD. We hope it will soon be restored to the catalogue.

Teresa Berganza may not have the light-of-eye expressiveness of her compatriot, Victoria de los Angeles (whose version is currently withdrawn), but she gives a strong, earthy account which helps to compensate for Falla's dramatic weaknesses; and it is good to have so fine a singer as José Carreras in the relatively small tenor role of Paco. Reliant as the piece is on atmosphere above all, it makes an excellent subject for recording and with vivid performances from the Ambrosian Singers and LSO, idiomatically directed, the result here is convincing, even if the balance is not always ideal. However, while this 1978 recording comes in a box with libretto, it is ungenerously reissued at full price and so is rather uncompetitive.

Fauré, Gabriel (1845 – 1924)

Pénélope (opera; complete).
*** Erato/Warner 2292 45405-2 (2) [id.]. LaForge Vocal Ens., Monte Carlo PO, Dutoit.
Pénélope (Jessye Norman), Ulysse (Alain Vanzo), Eurymaque (Philippe Huttenlocher), Eumée (José Van Dam), Euryclée (Jocelyne Taillon).

Pénélope, Fauré's only opera, is a rarity in the theatre and seldom surfaces on the radio. A concert performance mounted by the French Radio in the mid-1950s, with Régine Crespin in good voice and no less a conductor than Inghelbrecht in charge, appeared in a mono recording, but this Erato issue is the first commercial stereo set. The work itself is often haunting, noble and compelling. Though it is overtly Wagnerian in its adoption of *leitmotiv*, it seldom sounds in the least Wagnerian and, as it was written in the years immediately before the First World War, it has all the harmonic subtlety and refinement of late Fauré.

Ulysses, King of Ithaca, is away at sea, and Penelope, his most virtuous wife, fends off all the amorous usurpers who pester her. With great dignity she tells them that Ulysses has commanded her to wait for his homecoming, which will be a true moment of glory. The suitors believe that he will never return. The queen weaves a shroud for her father-in-law, Laertes. Until this is complete, the suitors will keep their distance.

One of the most persistent, Eurimachus, organizes the flautists and the dancers to perform while Penelope, fearing the worst, cries out, 'Ulysses, powerful and gentle husband, help me!' She hears a voice answer, an old beggar enters and she grants him hospitality. It is Ulysses in disguise and no one recognizes him. Eurycleia, Ulysses' old nurse, cares for the beggar's needs. Meanwhile Penelope, to gain time, surreptitiously unpicks her day's work on the shroud; but the suitors discover her deception and demand that she choose a new partner immediately.

Penelope and Eurycleia take the old beggar with them as they go to the seashore each day to look out for her husband's returning ship, and Ulysses is impressed. Penelope confides in him, without knowing his real identity, and he tells her that in Crete he had been with Ulysses for twelve days. He comforts her by reassuring her as to Ulysses' safety and love. He proposes a trial of strength among her suitors: if any one of them can bend the bow Ulysses left in her care he shall win her hand. Reluctantly and miserably Penelope agrees.

Revealing his identity to the shepherds, Ulysses receives their promise of help, and he comforts Eurycleia in her despair, telling her that the bow belonged to Hercules. The suitors gather to try their strength. All fail until the beggar picks up the bow, bends it and aims first at the target, then at each traitorous suitor in turn. With the help of the shepherds, he completes his triumphant takeover and is reunited with Penelope, and there is general rejoicing. What a pleasant change to have a happy ending in a mythological tale!

The title-role is eloquently sung by Jessye Norman, a beautifully characterized performance, and the singing throughout is first class. Charles Dutoit secures good ensemble and committed playing from his orchestra, and the only possible criticism would be concerning one or two inconsistencies of balance. The work, which takes not much more than two hours, has been accommodated on two CDs, with the extra advantage of an admirable essay by the French Fauré expert, Jean-Michel Nectoux, as well as the usual libretto, to enable the listener fully to reap the musical rewards of this glorious work.

Fibich, Zdeněk (1850–1900)

Šárka (opera; complete).
*** Sup. CO 1746/8 [id.]. Brno Janáček Op. Ch. & State O, Štych.
    Prince Přemsyl (Václav Zítek), Ctirad (Vilém Přibyl), Vitoraz (Josef Klán), Šárka (Eva Děpoltová), Vlasta (Eva Randová).

Some of Fibich's invention is prosaic and predictable, but there is much that is both endearing and fresh. *Šárka* is his sixth opera and was composed in 1896–7, during the last years of his short life. In addition to the nationalist element, there is also a strong awareness of Wagner. Although it has never caught on outside Czechoslovakia, it has been recorded before (by the Prague National Opera under Chalabala), but this version has the advantage of far superior recording and an atmospheric and committed performance. There are colourful and melodically appealing episodes here, even if the quality of the inspiration is not consistent. Readers will still find it worth investigation, although copies are not easy to obtain as it is available only sporadically. The CD transfer has improved the sound in definition and depth; a complete English libretto is provided.

Flotow, Friedrich (1812–83)

Martha (complete).
(M) *** Eurodisc 352 878 (2) [7789-2-RG]. Bav. R. Ch. and O, Wallberg.

Harriet (Lucia Popp), Nancy (Doris Soffel), Lionel (Siegfried Jerusalem), Plunkett (Karl Ridderbusch), Tristram (Siegmund Nimsgern).
(M) **(*) EMI CMS7 69339-2 (2). Bav. State Op. Ch. & O, Heger.
Harriet (Anneliese Rothenberger), Nancy (Brigitte Fassbaender), Lionel (Nicolai Gedda), Plunkett (Hermann Prey), Tristram (Dieter Weller).

Martha is a captivating opera that should be much better known than it is. The delicacy of its story, set in England at the beginning of the eighteenth century, allows for moments of broader humour that are not far distant from the world of Gilbert and Sullivan, and there are always the established favourite numbers to look forward to, culminating in the often repeated but still exquisite *Letzte Rose* – 'The last rose of summer'.

We are in Richmond, in the reign of Queen Anne. Lady Harriet Durham, her maid Nancy and her elderly cousin and unwelcome suitor, Sir Tristram Mickleford, watch from the window as villagers pass by, all seeking work on neighbouring farms; they are hoping to find an employer at the forthcoming Richmond Fair, and they are certainly not suffering from boredom like Lady Harriet, spoilt by the ministrations of her servants.

A sudden idea enters Lady Harriet's mind as they are watching the procession: why should not she, Nancy and her cousin go to the fair, dressed simply – perhaps they might even be hired out for work. What fun that would be! She even chooses their names: Martha, Julia and Bob!

We now move on to the morning of the fair. Plunkett, a wealthy farmer, and his foster-brother Lionel are there to bid for able workers. We discover that Lionel had been left as a child in the care of Plunkett's mother; the dying man who had brought him instructed her to show the queen a ring if ever the boy found himself in any trouble. Thus the dénouement of the plot is nicely established.

Lady Harriet and Nancy are eventually hired as servants by Plunkett and Lionel. Their joke over, the ladies look around for Bob (Sir Tristram) to rescue them but are obviously unaware that their contracts, to work at menial duties, are for a year and are legally binding. Thus they find themselves in the Plunkett farmhouse working as kitchen maids. They are not at all competent and have to be shown how to use the spinning wheel. Nancy playfully runs off, chased by Plunkett. Martha starts to sing of 'The last rose of summer' and Lionel is so moved that he proposes, telling her that she need no longer be a servant. But she is aware that her noble position makes such a match impossible.

The next morning dawns and the pair of recalcitrant servants have flown. The trusty Sir Tristram had waited nearby in his carriage and at midnight they managed to escape through a window. Later Plunkett comes upon Nancy riding at the hunt. At first she denies knowing him, for she is worried as to her legal position: by law he is her master. She calls for aid, and Sir Tristram and Lionel join them; then the two farmers comprehend the situation. Fortunately the queen is present at the hunt and Lionel, in some distress, remembers the ring. It is duly produced to prove that Lionel is an heir to the considerable estates of Lord Derby, who had been unjustly accused of treason.

This does not alleviate Lionel's misery, for it does not occur to him that now he is a most eligible prospective husband. He refuses Lady Harriet's hand when she expresses her love and remorse. But this new situation is not lost on Nancy, who has her eye on Plunkett; she plans to bring Martha (Lady Harriet) and Lionel together. Lionel again hears the sweet strains of 'The last rose of summer', a hit tune if ever there was one, and the opera ends happily as he takes Martha in his arms, and Nancy and Plunkett are united, too. What more could anyone wish for!

The Eurodisc cast is as near perfect as could be imagined. Lucia Popp is a splendid Lady Harriet, the voice rich and full (her *Letzte Rose* is radiant), yet riding the ensembles with jewelled accuracy. Doris Soffel is no less characterful as Nancy, and Siegfried Jerusalem is in his element as the hero, Lionel, singing ardently throughout. Not only is his famous *Ach! so fromm* a superb highlight; the *Gute Nacht* sequence which becomes the *Mitternacht notturno* is glorious, a quartet to equal almost any rival in operatic magic. Siegmund Nimsgern is an excellent Lord Tristram, and Karl Ridderbusch matches his genial gusto, singing Plunkett's *Porter-Lied* with weight as well as brio. Wallberg's direction is marvellously spirited, and the opera gathers pace as it proceeds; the Act I finale is taken at a fizzing tempo, and the drama and passion of Acts III and IV bring genuine grandeur. The Bavarian Radio Chorus sings with joyous precision and the orchestral playing sparkles. With first-class recording, full and vivid, this is highly recommended, for the transfer to CD has been managed admirably.

The EMI (Electrola) recording is not ideal but captures the right atmosphere and still gives considerable pleasure. Curiously, the veteran conductor Robert Heger, for all the delicacy of his pointing, sometimes chooses slow tempi. Gedda sings agreeably, but his characterization of Lionel is a little stiff; otherwise there is stylishness and jollity all round, with Rothenberger in clear, fresh voice as the heroine and Fassbaender at her finest as Nancy. Prey, agreeably expressive in a light-toned way, makes a youthful-sounding Plunkett. Minimal cuts and bright, atmospheric recording, and a distinct price advantage; but the Eurodisc set remains first choice.

Frumerie, Gunnar de (1908–87)

Singoalla.
**(*) Cap. Dig. CAP 22023 (2) [id.]. Hägersten Motet Ch., Stockholm PO, Ahronovich.
  Riddar Bengt Månesköld / Assim (Per-Arne Wahlgren), Fru Elfrida / Helena Ulvsax (Catharina Olsson), Erland (Björn Haugan), Pater Henrik (Erik Saedén), Broder Johannes (Anders Andersson), Hövdingen (Stig Tysklind), Singoalla (Anne Sofie Von Otter), Assim's Mother (Inger Blom), Sorgbarn (Lasse Bergström).

Gunnar de Frumerie regarded his only opera, *Singoalla* (1940), with particular affection, and it is currently enjoying a revival of interest in Sweden and Finland. It is set in Sweden during the fourteenth century, just before the onset of the Black Death, and is a story of love and betrayal. It draws for its inspiration on a novella by Viktor Rydberg, whose verse features in Sibelius's song output.

Erland, the young son of a nobleman, Lord Bengt Månesköld, returns home through the forest, hoping to find Singoalla, daughter of the chief of a nomadic band of gypsies. When he does, they swear eternal devotion. Knowing that she will be expelled from the tribe if their love is discovered, she persuades him to come with her. Assim, a gypsy from a noble tribe to whom her father has promised her, takes them unawares and a scuffle ensues.

In Act II, Assim's mother prepares a sleeping potion for Erland whom they hold hostage; Lord Bengt and his soldiers arrive to retrieve the valuables the gypsies have stolen but are forced to allow them to keep their loot in exchange for Erland's freedom. Assim now rejects Singoalla, who is driven out into the wilderness.

A decade elapses and Erland has married the gentle Helena Ulvsax but is tormented by nightmares; he speaks of a plague boy who goes from house to house predicting the coming of the Black Death. A pale, dark-haired boy called Sorgbarn (literally Child of Sorrow) enters and Sir Erland takes him into his service but treats him harshly. One night the boy hypnotizes him and takes him to the forest where he meets Singoalla, and it is revealed that he is their son.

In the last Act the vision gradually fades but Erland asks Sorgbarn to take him to Singoalla every night. One night he resists Sorgbarn's spell and, in a fit of rage, kills the child. In the last scene, the plague has begun to ravage all, including the gypsies. Overcome with remorse, he offers to sacrifice himself, and the opera ends with the death first of Erland then of Singoalla.

De Frumerie's style is resolutely diatonic with a powerful modal flavouring: indeed the opening has strong overtones of Kodály or Vaughan Williams. While much of the opera strikes a responsive chord, it lacks dramatic sophistication, variety of invention or any real sense of scale; at the same time there is a certain freshness and atmosphere. The recording emanates from two concert performances in which some roles are doubled and in which the leading part was taken at short notice by the Norwegian, Björn Haugan. He gives a thoroughly committed account of the role, and Anne Sofie von Otter is a good Singoalla.

The rest of the cast is also excellent, though the boy soprano is often strained by the awkward writing in Act III; this must have been one of the factors that militated against wider acceptance of the opera. The recording itself is good and so, too, is the orchestral playing under Ahronovich. *Singoalla* is no masterpiece – and certainly not a major discovery – but parts of the score are imaginative and have a simple and unpretentious quality.

Gay, John (1685–1732)

The Beggar's Opera (realized Barlow).
**(*) Hyp. Dig. CDA 66591 (2) [id.]. Broadside band, Jeremy Barlow.
  Polly (Bronwen Mills), Macheath (Adrian Thompson), Lucy (Anne Dawson), Lockit (Richard Jackson), Peachum (Charles Daniels), Mrs Peachum (Sarah Walker), Beggar (Bob Hoskins), Player (Ian Caddy).

Jeremy Barlow in his realization has attempted to go back as nearly as possible to what might have been presented as *The Beggar's Opera* in the eighteenth century. He points out that it is in fact a play punctuated by 69 very brief songs, with melodies drawn from the widest range of sources, well known at the time – popular ballads, theatre songs (including three by Purcell) and country dances, as well as tunes from Scotland and France. Barlow's accompaniments are sensitive and discreet in an authentic, eighteenth-century style, and his own group, the Broadside band, play them with zest. Particularly next to the Britten, the results are anything but perverse, with 'O what pain it is to part' the more movingly tender for its total simplicity at a relaxed speed.

With Bob Hoskins characterizing well as the Beggar and Ian Caddy as the Player (also the stage director), the dialogue is brisk and charactcrful, though many will find there is too much of it for repeated listening, particularly when such favourite songs as 'How happy could I be with either', sung through once, last only a few seconds. Though Adrian Thompson's tenor is not quite steady enough in the role of Macheath, he makes an engagingly earthy hero, and the others sing and characterize very vividly, with fresh young voices predominating and with Sarah Walker a wonderfully fruity Mrs Peachum. The directness of the musical presentation is a major attraction next to rival versions, giving the freshest results. Each disc is most generously filled (roughly 75 minutes on each), with copious tracks. The well-balanced recording captures each scene immediately and vividly.

The Beggar's Opera (arr. Bonynge and Gamley).
*** Decca Dig. 430 066-2 (2) [id.]. London Voices, Nat. PO, Bonynge.
  Polly (Kiri Te Kanawa), Macheath (James Morris), Lucy (Joan Sutherland), Lockit (Stafford Dean), Peachum (Alfred Marks), Mrs Peachum (Angela Lansbury), Mrs Trapes (Regina Resnik), Filch (Anthony Rolfe Johnson), Jenny Driver (Ann Murray), Beggar (Warren Mitchell), Player (Michael Hordern).

In *The Beggar's Opera* John Gay parodies both the stylistic devices of baroque opera and the contemporary scene, social and political – the Prologue suggests that the opera had been written to celebrate the nuptials of two ballad-singers, James Chanter and Moll Lay, and thus immediately pokes fun at royal and aristocratic wedding celebrations. Johann Christian Pepusch chose and arranged the music, borrowing from various sources and including popular and traditional songs from England, Scotland and even France. The amalgam was an enormous success in its day.

After the Prologue we meet Mr Peachum, a fence, cynically studying his nefarious accounts and considering the dishonest talents of his colleagues in crime. Filch, his henchman, is given messages to deliver to those of Peachum's gang of rogues who are currently in prison. Mrs Peachum is no better than her husband and they wonder whether delivering other of their 'employees' to the courts may prove a more profitable course of action. Their daughter, Polly, is smitten by the charms of the highwayman Captain Macheath and has become his 'wife'; the lovers know full well that her father is not to be trusted.

Macheath and his gang meet near Newgate and sing the famous chorus, *Let us take the road* (derived from Handel's *Rinaldo*). But Macheath has other women in his life besides Polly, and two other of his doxies, dallying with him in the tavern, relieve him of his pistols so that Peachum and the police can take the opportunity to arrest him and haul him off to prison. Lockit is the jailer; his daughter, Lucy, is another of Macheath's mistresses and, as she is pregnant, they lose no time in seeking out the prison priest, Lucy interceding with her father that her prospective 'husband' be freed.

But then Polly arrives, claiming Macheath for herself. Peachum removes her, and Lucy is prevailed upon by Macheath to release him from his chains and abet his escape. Lockit is furious and turns on his daughter.

Later he and Peachum, drinking together, plan Macheath's downfall with the help of yet another jealous female (though Polly and Lucy are the main protagonists, there are four more claimants to his heart). Macheath, captured again, fortifies himself with drink against their combined demands. The plot is resolved with the sentiment that Macheath must be pardoned, for the opera will be deemed a tragedy if Macheath dies on the gallows. Instead he leads the finale 'with his doxies around'.

The entertaining Decca version of *The Beggar's Opera* creates the atmosphere of a stage musical. The spoken Prologue comes before the Overture (rather in the way some films complete their opening sequence before the main titles appear). With Warren Mitchell and Sir Michael Hordern immediately taking the stage, the listener's attention is caught before the music begins. The musical arrangements are free – including an unashamedly jazzy sequence in Act II, complete with saxophones – but the basic musical material is of vintage quality and responds readily to a modern treatment which is always sparkling and often imaginative.

The casting is imaginative too. With Alfred Marks and Angela Lansbury as Mr and Mrs Peachum a touch of humour is assured; if James Morris is not an entirely convincing Macheath, he sings well, and Joan Sutherland makes a spirited Lucy. The other principals are equally at home in their roles, both singing and speaking, an essential if the piece is to spring fully to life. Kiri Te Kanawa as Polly steals the show, as well she should in such a part, singing deliciously, with delivery of the dialogue hardly less striking. The whole entertainment is presented with gusto, and the digital recording is splendid, as spacious as it is clear.

The Beggar's Opera (complete) (arr. Britten).
*** Decca Dig. 436 850-2 (2) [id.]. Aldeburgh Festival Ch. & O, Bedford.
   Polly (Ann Murray), Macheath (Philip Langridge), Lucy (Yvonne Kenny), Lockit (John Rawnsley), Peachum (Robert Lloyd), Mrs Peachum (Anne Collins).

There is much more Benjamin Britten than John Gay in this version, making it an extra Britten opera in effect, neglected on disc until this 1993 recording. What Britten has done is to take the simple melodies assembled by Gay and treat them to elaborate, very Britten-ish accompaniments and development that go even further in individuality than his folksong settings. It becomes very much a twentieth-century piece, starting with an overture that is pure Britten, with Gay tunes woven in. 'Fill every glass' is then no longer a simple drinking-song but a slow contrapuntal movement, and 'The modes of the court', to the tune of 'Lillibullero', becomes another elaborate mosaic.

Conversely, some nostalgic airs like 'O what pain it is to part' are done briskly, even abrasively, almost as though Britten was determined to counter received ideas on any well-known number. Both traditionalists and authenticists may well find the result perverse, but Britten's genius and imagination are what matter, together with his brilliant sense of instrumental colouring.

Under Steuart Bedford this first recording is based on a staged presentation, given at The Maltings in the Aldeburgh Festival, with Declan Mulholland as an Irish beggar bluffly introducing the entertainment. Philip Langridge sings clearly and incisively as Macheath, portraying him very much as a gentleman, and Robert Lloyd is outstanding as Peachum, dark and resonant, a bluff Cockney. The team is a strong and characterful one, though neither Ann Murray as Polly Peachum nor Yvonne Kenny as Lucy Lockit is caught very sweetly. Britten's distinctive orchestration, one instrument per part, is well played by a distinguished group, including Jennifer Stinton on the flute, Nicholas Daniel on the oboe and Richard Watkins on the horn. Excellent sound, and good direction of the well-edited spoken dialogue by Michael Geliot.

German, Edward (1862–1936)

Merrie England: complete (without dialogue).
Withdrawn: (B) ** CfP CD-CFP 4710; *TC-CFPD 4710* (2). Williams Singers, O, Michael Collins.
   Sir Walter Raleigh (William McAlpine), Bessie Throckmorton (June Bronhill), Earl of Essex (Peter Glossop), Queen Elizabeth I (Monica Sinclair), Jill-All-Alone (Patricia Kern), Walter Wilkins (Howell Glynne).

We badly need a good modern recording of German's *Merrie England*, last heard in London in the Queen's coronation year. Like many older operettas, the book doesn't really stand up in a stage production to meet the tastes of modern audiences, yet much of the music is delightful (even if it sounds at times like diluted Gilbert and Sullivan). If the moments of coarseness in the libretto can be forgiven, there is much pleasing lyricism in German's settings and one or two really outstanding tunes which will ensure that the score survives: the frisson-creating melody of *With sword and buckler by my side* is surely worthy of Elgar.

The only available modern recording slips in and out of the catalogue at regular intervals and is currently withdrawn. Although all the singers here were in fact from the Sadler's Wells company, this is not the Sadler's Wells production but one conceived at EMI. The 1960 recording, which has a tendency to edginess, suggests a production team from the popular rather than the classical side of the company. However, the stereo has atmosphere, though the focus is not absolutely clean. Among the soloists Howell Glynne is splendid as King Neptune, and Monica Sinclair sings with her usual richness and makes *O peaceful England* more moving than usual. Patricia Kern's mezzo is firm and forward, while William McAlpine as Sir Walter Raleigh sings with fine ringing voice. The Rita Williams Singers are thoroughly professional even if just occasionally their style is suspect.

Gershwin, George (1898–1937)

Crazy for you.
**(*) EMI Dig. CDC7 54618-2 [id.]. Original Broadway cast. Ch. & O, Paul Gemignani.
  Bobby (Harold Groener), Polly (Jodi Benson), Bella (Bruce Adler), Irene (Michele Pawk), Lank Hawkins (John Hillner), Manhattan Rhythm Kings (Brian Nalepka, Tripp Hanson, Hal Shane).

Crazy for you is a re-working of the Gershwin original, *Girl crazy*. It includes six numbers from the original and adds many more, including *Someone to watch over me*, *Tonight's the night*, *I'll build a stairway to paradise* and a very early song, *Naughty baby*, taken from *Primrose*. The story, about the saving of the Gaiety Theatre in Deadrock, an old mining town, is the stuff of showbiz folklore, but the result is a string of (mostly) hits that are too obviously interpolated. Harold Groener as Bobby makes an effective hero (son of a banker, who helps to finance the show), and his numbers are lively and pleasing, but everything stands or falls by whether one takes to Jodi Benson's individual and rather abrasive Polly.

She gets many of the big numbers to sing, including *Someone to watch over me*, *Embraceable you* (with Bobby), *But not for me* and *They can't take that away from me*. She is at her best in *I got rhythm*. Michele Pawk and John Hillner in *Naughty baby* affect an even more exaggerated style, but this duet comes off with plenty of zip. Indeed there is no lack of spirit in this production, and Paul Gemignani keeps everybody on his or her toes. Bright, vivid recording, but one's reaction here will depend on one's response to the show's female lead.

Girl crazy (musical).
*** Elektra-Nonesuch/Warner Dig. 7559 79250-2; *7559 79250-4*. Judy Blazer, Lorna Luft, David Carroll, Eddie Korbich, Frank Gorshin, O, John Mauceri.

Girl crazy, despite its hit numbers – *Embraceable you*, *I got rhythm* and *Bidin' my time* – has always been counted a near miss, but this lively recording, with an ensemble of distinguished New York musicians conducted by John Mauceri, gives the lie to that. It is an escapist piece, typical of the early 1930s, about a New Yorker, exiled by his rich father to the Wild West, who sets up a dude ranch in an outpost previously bereft of women. The story of love and misunderstanding is largely irrelevant, but the score has point and imagination from beginning to end, all the brighter for having removed the sugar-coating which Hollywood introduced in the much-mangled film version of 1943.

The casting is excellent. Judy Blazer takes the Ginger Rogers role of Kate, the post-girl, while Judy Garland's less well-known daughter, Lorna Luft, is delightful in the Ethel Merman part of the gambler's wife hired to sing in the saloon. David Carroll is the New Yorker hero, and Frank Gorshin takes the comic role of the cab-driver, Gieber Goldfarb. The whole score, 73 minutes long, is squeezed on to a single disc, packaged with libretto and excellent notes, the first of a projected Gershwin series. The only serious reservation is that the recording is dry and brassy, aggressively so – but that could be counted typical of the period too.

Lady be good (musical).
*** Elektra Nonesuch/Warner Dig. 7559 79308-2; *7559 79308-4* [id.]. Lara Teeter, Ann Morrison, Jason Alexander, John Pizzarelli, Ch. & O, Eric Stern.

This Elektra-Nonesuch issue is the third in the series of authentic recordings of Gershwin musicals sponsored by the Library of Congress and the Gershwin estate. Happily, the pursuit of authenticity under such official guidance has not in any way undermined the spontaneous energy of the piece, far from it. This charming score, dating from 1924, just after *Rhapsody in blue*, emerges as one of the composer's freshest. Such numbers as the title-song, as well as *Fascinatin' rhythm* and the witty *Half of it, dearie, blues*, are set against such duets as *Hang on to me* and *So am I*, directly reflecting the 1920s world that Sandy Wilson so affectionately parodied in *The Boy Friend*.

Lady be good was the piece originally written for the brother-and-sister team of Fred and Adele Astaire, and the casting of the principals on the disc is first rate. These are not concert-singers but ones whose clearly projected voices are ideally suited to the repertory, including Lara

Teeter and Ann Morrison in the Astaire roles and Michael Maguire as the young millionaire whom the heroine finally marries. The score has been restored by Tommy Krasker, and an orchestra of first-rate session musicians is conducted by Eric Stern.

Let 'em eat cake; Of thee I sing (musicals).
(M) *** Sony Dig. M2K 42522 (2) [id.]. Jack Gilford, Larry Kert, Maureen McGovern, Paige O'Hara, David Garrison, NY Choral Artists, St Luke's O, Tilson Thomas.

Of thee I sing and *Let 'em eat cake* are the two operettas that George Gershwin wrote in the early 1930s on a political theme, the one a sequel to the other. Though the aim is satirical in both works, the musical tone of voice has the easy tunefulness of typical Gershwin shows, with only the occasional hint of Kurt Weill to suggest a more international source of inspiration. What the British listener will immediately register is the powerful underlying influence of Gilbert and Sullivan, not just in the plot – with Gilbertian situations exploited – but also in the music, with patter-songs and choral descants used in a very Sullivan-like manner.

In every way these two very well-filled discs are a delight, offering warm and energetic performances by excellent artists under Michael Tilson Thomas, not just a star conductor but a leading Gershwin scholar. Both Larry Kert and Maureen McGovern as his wife make a strong partnership, with Jack Gilford characterful as the Vice-Presidential candidate, Alexander Throttlebottom, and Paige O'Hara excellent as the interloping Diana in *Of Thee I Sing*. With the recording on the dry side and well forward – very apt for a musical – the words are crystal clear, not least from the splendidly disciplined chorus that, for much of the time, is protagonist. The well-produced booklets (one for each operetta) give full words – though, as with many CD sets, you need a magnifying glass to read them.

Strike up the Band (musical).
**(*) Nonesuch/Warner Dig. 7559 79273-2; *7559 79273-4* [id.]. Ch. & O, Mauceri.
JimTownshend (Brent Barrett), Horace J. Fletcher (Don Chastain), Joan Fletcher (Rebecca Luker), Timothy Harper (Jason Graae), Mrs Draper (Beth Fowler), Colonel Holmes (Charles Goff), Anne Draper (Juliet Lambert), Spelvin (Jeff Lyons), Soldier (Dale Sandish), Sloane (James Rocco).

Dating originally from 1927, *Strike up the Band* was the nearest that George and Ira Gershwin ever came to imitating Gilbert and Sullivan. The very subject is Gilbertian – a satirical story about the United States going to war with Switzerland over the price of cheese. In addition, Ira's ingenious lyrics sparked George to write with a rhythmic point that regularly suggests a syncopated Sullivan. Quite apart from the two undoubted hits from the show, *The man I love* and *Strike up the band*, there is a whole sequence of delightful numbers that it is good to have revived in this first really complete recording. Despite the ingenuity and musical imagination, in the end the piece fails to match Gershwin's later political satires, *Of Thee I Sing* and *Let 'Em Eat Cake*, which, at least until the CBS/Sony recordings conducted by Michael Tilson Thomas, were even more seriously underappreciated.

This Elektra-Nonesuch recording brings a fresh, crisp performance, rather drily recorded with little bloom on the singing voices and with the spoken dialogue sounding too close. For all its vigour, the performance lacks something of the exuberance which marks the recordings of musicals conducted by John McGlinn for EMI. The scholarly preparation of the score from original and newly rediscovered sources is admirable, but the results in performance too often sound a little too literal rather than spontaneous. It may be correct to observe the dotted rhythms of *The man I love* as precisely as this performance does, but something is lost in the flow of the music, and to latterday ears the result is less haunting than the customary reading. The singers are first rate, but they would have been helped by having at least one of their number with a more charismatic personality. The second disc includes an appendix containing seven numbers used in the abortive 1930 revival.

OPERA

Porgy and Bess (complete).
⊛ *** EMI Dig. CDS7 49568-2 (3) [Ang. CDCC 49568]. Glyndebourne Ch., LPO, Rattle.
Porgy (Willard White), Bess (Cynthia Haymon), Clara (Harolyn Blackwell), Serena (Cynthia Clarey), Sportin' Life (Damon Evans), Crown (Gregg Baker), Jake (Bruce Hubbard).
*** Decca 414 559-2 [id.]. Cleveland Ch., Children's Ch., Cleveland O, Maazel.
Porgy (Willard White), Bess (Leona Mitchell), Clara (Barbara Hendricks), Serena (Florence

Quivar), Sportin' Life (François Clemmons), Crown (McHenry Boatwright), Jake (Arthur Thompson).

*** BMG/RCA RD 82109 (3) [RCD3 2109]. Children's Ch., Houston Grand Op. Ch. and O, DeMain.

Porgy (Donnie Ray Albert), Bess (Clamma Dale), Clara (Betty Lane), Serena (Wilma Shakesnider), Sportin' Life (Larry Marshall), Crown (Andrew Smith), Jake (Alexander B. Smalls).

EMI's gloriously rich and colourful recording of Gershwin's masterpiece directly reflects the spectacular success enjoyed by the Glyndebourne production. Simon Rattle here conducts the same cast and orchestra as in the opera house, and the EMI engineers have done wonders in re-creating what was so powerful at Glyndebourne, establishing more clearly than ever the status of *Porgy* as grand opera, not a mere jumped-up musical or operetta.

As the story begins it is night-time and Catfish Row in the Charleston tenement district is alive with movement, singing and dancing. Clara is nursing her baby and, to soothe it to sleep, sings the famous *Summertime*. Jake, Clara's husband, contributes the thought that 'A woman is a sometime thing'. Porgy, a cripple, appears in his goatcart; he loves Bess, who is married to Crown, a stevedore.

Bess and Crown now enter, the latter the worse for drink. He is beaten at craps and, angry at losing his money, he knocks down his opponent, Robbins, and kills him with a cotton hook. To help her husband escape the police, Bess gives him money. As he leaves, Crown gives Bess permission to associate with other men, so long as no permanent relationship develops.

Seizing his opportunity, Sportin' Life (among other things a dope pedlar) invites Bess to go to New York with him, but she refuses and Porgy comes to her aid. A saucer is placed on Robbins's body so that the cost of his burial can be collected and Serena, his wife, sings 'My man's gone now'. A police detective arrives and soon discovers the identity of the murderer. The undertaker reassures Serena that he will bury her dead husband even though the collection has realized only $15. Sportin' Life continues to pester Bess with his attentions and Porgy warns him off.

Alone, Porgy and Bess discover their mutual love, then she and her friends go off for a picnic on Kittiwah Island, leaving Porgy to reflect *I got plenty o' nuttin'*. At the picnic, after a mock sermon from Sportin' Life (*It ain't necessarily so*), Crown suddenly reappears and the infatuated Bess stays behind with him on the island. Yet she is drawn back to Porgy as the fishermen prepare to go to sea, and he again offers his protection.

There is a great storm and Clara rushes out, leaving her baby with Bess, when she sees that her husband's fishing boat has capsized. Crown follows to give assistance, and it appears that Clara, Jake and Crown have been drowned, but Crown is not dead and he crawls to Porgy's door. Porgy murders him and is taken away by the police.

Sportin' Life once again offers Bess his protection in the form of 'happy dust', and this time she accepts, and Sportin' Life goes off singing of a 'boat dat's leaving soon for New York'. A week passes and normality has returned to Catfish Row. Porgy has been jailed, but only for contempt of court, and he now returns to find Bess gone and Serena looking after Clara's baby. Singing *Oh Lord, I'm on my way*, he sets off for New York in his goatcart to find her.

In the EMI production, the coloured singers – both the soloists and those in the chorus – responded to Glyndebourne and Glyndebourne to them in a way that generated a very special electricity. As Damon Evans, the superb Sportin' Life on stage and in the recording, put it, 'At Glyndebourne, *Porgy and Bess* came of age.' The recording was made, not at Glyndebourne during the opera's run, but in the studio some months later, after two preparatory concert performances. That care has paid off triumphantly when the impact of the performance is consistently heightened by the subtleties of timing that come from long experience of live performances.

By comparison, Lorin Maazel's Decca version sounds a degree too literal, and John DeMain's RCA set, also associated with a live stage production and dating from the mid-1970s, is less subtle. Both these versions need reissuing at mid-price. More than their rivals, Rattle and the LPO capture Gershwin's rhythmic exuberance with the degree of freedom essential if jazz-based inspirations are to sound idiomatic. He and his team are more daring, using rubato more freely, so that the chugging choo-choo rhythms of *Leavin' for the promis' lan'*, with sharper accelerations, convey a train image more infectiously and are the more effectively contrasted against the hushed middle section, sung very delicately at high speed. The chorus is the finest and most responsive of any on the three sets, and the bass line-up is the strongest.

Willard White, not as youthful-sounding as for Maazel, but warmer and weightier, is superbly matched by the magnificent Jake of Bruce Hubbard, singing as characterfully as in the role of Joe in the EMI *Show Boat* set, and by the dark and resonant Crown of Gregg Baker. As Sportin' Life, Damon Evans gets nearer than any of his rivals to the original scat-song inspiration without ever short-changing on musical values, heightening them with extra expressive intensity and characterization. The women principals too are first rate, if no more striking than their opposite numbers on Decca and RCA: Cynthia Haymon as Bess movingly convincing in conveying equivocal emotions, Harolyn Blackwell as Clara sensuously relishing Rattle's slow speed for *Summertime*, and Cynthia Clarey an intense and characterful Serena. EMI's digital sound is exceptionally full and spacious. Voices are naturally balanced, not spotlit, so that words are not always as crystal clear as on Decca and RCA; but the atmosphere and sense of presence are the more winning.

For those who doubted whether in *Porgy and Bess* Gershwin had really written an opera, Decca's 1975 recording with Cleveland forces conducted by Maazel established the work's formidable status beyond question. Creating a precedent, Maazel included the complete text, which had in fact been cut even before the first stage presentation. Some half-hour of virtually unknown music, including many highly evocative passages and some striking choruses, reinforces the consistency of Gershwin's inspiration. It is not just a question of the big numbers presenting some of the most memorable melodies of the twentieth century, but of a grand dramatic design which triumphs superbly over the almost impossible conjunction of conventions – of opera and the American musical.

With a cast that makes up an excellent team, there is no attempt to glamorize characters who are far from conventional, and the story is the more moving for that, with moments potentially embarrassing ('I's the only woman Porgy ever had,' says Bess to Crown in Act II) given genuine dramatic force *à la* Puccini. The vigour and colour are irresistible, and the analogue recording is one of the most vivid that even Decca has produced. Willard White is a magnificent Porgy, dark of tone, while Leona Mitchell's vibrant Bess has a moving streak of vulnerability, and François Clemmons as Sportin' Life achieves the near-impossible by actually singing the role and making one forget Cab Calloway. But above all this pioneering first recording was and is Maazel's triumph, with dazzling playing from the Cleveland Orchestra. The compact disc version is one of the most impressive transfers of an analogue original that Decca has yet issued, with the excellent balance and sense of presence intensified.

The distinction is readily drawn between Maazel's Cleveland performance and John DeMain's equally complete and authoritative account on RCA. Where Maazel easily and naturally demonstrates the operatic qualities of Gershwin's masterpiece, DeMain – with a cast which had a riotous success with the piece on Broadway and elsewhere in the United States – presents a performance clearly in the tradition of the Broadway musical. There is much to be said for both views, and it is worth noting that American listeners tend to prefer the less operatic manner of the RCA set. The casts are equally impressive vocally, with the RCA singers a degree more characterful. Donnie Ray Albert as Porgy uses his bass-like resonance impressively, though not everyone will like the suspicion of hamming, which works less well in a recording than on stage.

That underlining of expressiveness is a characteristic of the performance, so that the climax of the key duet, *Bess, you is my woman now*, has a less natural, more stagey manner, producing, for some ears, less of a frisson than the more delicate Cleveland version. For others, the more robust Houston approach has a degree of dramatic immediacy, associated with the tradition of the American popular theatre, which is irresistible. This basic contrast will decide most listeners' approach, and although the RCA recording has not quite the Decca richness it is strikingly vivid and alive. The RCA CD transfer is not quite as sophisticated as the Decca, but it readily creates a theatrical atmosphere. The sound has plenty of bloom and excellent presence, within a believable acoustic setting – it is as if one were sitting in the middle stalls.

Porgy and Bess: highlights.
*** EMI Dig. CDC7 54325-2 [id.] (from above recording with White, Haymon; cond. Rattle).
(M) ** BMG/RCA GD 85234 [5234-2-RG]. Leontyne Price, William Warfield, John Bubbles, McHenry Boatwright, RCA Victor Ch. & O, Skitch Henderson.
** BMG/RCA RD 84680 (from above recording; cond. DeMain).
** Ph. Dig. 412 720-2 [id.]. Simon Estes, Roberta Alexander, Diane Curry, Berlin R. Ch. and SO, Slatkin.

Rattle's highlights disc is most generous (74 minutes) and most comprehensive, with the selection evenly divided between the three Acts and with nearly all the key numbers included.

However, not all the tailoring is clean: *Summertime* ends rather abruptly and there is at least one fade.

The RCA studio compilation was recorded in 1963, a decade before the complete Decca and RCA versions appeared. Using a cast of the finest opera-house singers, rather than those trained in the American Musical tradition, it underlines the claims of *Porgy and Bess* to be regarded as a work in the mainstream of opera. Both Price and Warfield sing magnificently, and the supporting group is given lively direction by Skitch Henderson. One may miss favourite touches – the style is direct and full-blooded – but the impact of such committed singing is undeniable. The CD transfer tends to brilliance – the opening orchestral introduction is a little shrill – but the voices are well caught, including the chorus, and much use is made of stereo antiphony in the presentation.

The DeMain highlights disc is taken from the robust and colourful, highly idiomatic complete recording made by RCA in the late 1970s, with the natural feeling in this performance for the tradition of the American musical, as distinct from grand opera. The recording gives fine projection to the voices, particularly on CD. There is an element of shrillness in the orchestral sound.

Slatkin's collection of highlights, opulently recorded, is totally geared to the glorious voices of Simon Estes and Roberta Alexander, both of them richer-toned than their opposite numbers in the complete sets. Naturally, each soloist sings numbers from several characters, not just hero (anti-hero?) and heroine. The rich darkness of Estes' voice is clearly operatic in style, but tough and incisive too, not just as Porgy but equally impressively as Sportin' Life in *It ain't necessarily so*. Only the Berlin Chorus lacks sharpness. Slatkin draws understanding playing from the orchestra, and the sound on CD is particularly rich. The chrome tape, too, is strikingly vivid and wide-ranging.

Gibbons, Christopher (1615–76)

Cupid and Death (with Matthew Locke).
(M) *** HM/BMG GD 77117 (2). Consort of Musicke, Rooley – BLOW: *Venus and Adonis*. ***
   Chamberlain (Andrew King), Host / Mercury (David Thomas), Cupid (Poppy Holden), Death (Joseph Cornwell), Nature (Emma Kirkby), Despair (Cathy Cass); Evelyn Tubb, Mary Nichols, Richard Wistreich.

Cupid and Death, 'a masque in four entries', dates from 1653, or nearly 30 years before the better-known Blow work with which it is coupled. Gibbons, the son of Orlando Gibbons and the teacher of Blow, seems to have been the lesser partner in the project, with Matthew Locke providing the bulk of the music for this rustic fantasy on an ancient fable using a text by James Shirley after Aesop. The piece was revised in 1659. Each of the five 'entries' or Acts is formally laid out in a set sequence of items, a suite of dances, a dialogue, a song and a chorus.

Cupid and Death – for the most part speaking characters – are staying at the same inn. The chamberlain of the inn changes over their arrows while they are asleep. As a result, Cupid kills many young lovers, while Death's arrows make many old and infirm vibrant with passion as Mother Nature looks on with amazement. In revenge, Death strikes the chamberlain, who immediately makes love to his trained apes. Mercury then descends to impose order: Cupid is banished from the court; Death, while his power to kill is restored, must avoid those favoured by marks of art or honour.

The masque ends with a scene in Elysium for the unfortunate lovers! Rooley's team consistently brings out the fresh charm of the music. For repeated listening, the spoken sections, up to ten minutes long, can easily be programmed out on CD. This is especially welcome at mid-price.

Giordano, Umberto (1867–1948)

Andrea Chénier (complete).
(M) *** BMG/RCA GD 82046 (2) [RCD-2-2046]. Alldis Ch., Nat. PO, Levine.
   Andrea Chénier (Plácido Domingo), Maddalena (Renata Scotto), Carlo Gerard (Sherrill Milnes), Bersi (Maria Ewing).
Withdrawn: (M) (***) EMI mono CHS7 69996-2 (2) [Ang. CDHB 69996]. La Scala, Milan, Ch. & O, Fabritiis.

Andrea Chénier (Beniamino Gigli), Maddalena (Maria Caniglia), Carlo Gerard (Gino Bechi), Bersi (Giulietta Simionato).

**(*) Decca Dig. 410 117-2 (2) [id.]. WNO Ch., Nat. PO, Chailly.

Andrea Chénier (Luciano Pavarotti), Maddalena (Montserrat Caballé), Carlo Gerard (Leo Nucci), Bersi (Kathleen Kuhlmann)).

(M) **(*) Decca 425 407-2 (2) [id.]. Ch. & O of St Cecilia Ac., Rome, Gavazzeni.

Andrea Chénier (Mario Del Monaco), Maddalena (Renata Tebaldi), Carlo Gerard (Ettore Bastianini), Bersi (Fiorenza Cossotto).

(M) *(*) Sony Dig. M2K 42369 (2) [id.]. Hungarian State R. & TV Ch., Hungarian State O, Patanè.

Andrea Chénier (José Carreras), Maddalena (Eva Marton), Carlo Gerard (Giorgio Zancanaro), Bersi (Klára Takács).

Giordano always runs the risk – not least in this opera, with its obvious parallels with *Tosca* – of being considered only in the shadow of Puccini; but this red-blooded score can, as on the RCA recording, be searingly effective. As the opera opens the Countess of Coigny is hosting a large party in the ballroom of her château. Her daughter, Madeleine, with Bersi, Madeleine's mulatto maid, approves the preparations. In contrast Gérard, a servant in the household, who is secretly in love with Madeleine, gives vent to his loathing of all the trappings of aristocracy.

The abbé and Fléville arrive and bring with them a poet, Chénier, who sings controversially of those in authority. The countess organizes a gavotte, but this is interrupted by Gérard, who bursts in, leading a crowd of beggars. The major-domo dismisses the protest, and as he departs Gérard contemptuously flings his uniform coat to the floor – it is the epitome of slavery.

As Act II opens, the revolution has begun and Gérard is now discovered alone at a table in a Paris café. Bersi and Incredible, a spy, sit talking. As a servant, the former has nothing to fear. Chénier is advised by his friend Roucher to flee, and a passport is provided, but Chénier is indifferent to danger. Gérard ingenuously gives Incredible a glowing description of the beautiful Madeleine, who is sought by the authorities.

Madeleine and Chénier meet and Madeleine asks for his help: they plan to leave together. But Gérard appears with the spy, he and Chénier fight and Gérard is wounded. In a whisper he warns Chénier that he is listed as a counter-revolutionary. When the police arrive, Gérard refuses to identify Chénier as his assailant, but later Chénier is arrested and, although he suffers pangs of conscience, Gérard's desire for Madeleine triumphs over his misgivings and he signs the indictment.

Madeleine arrives and Gérard confesses his motives to her. After first spurning him, Madeleine agrees to give him her love if he will intercede with the Revolutionary Tribunal on Chénier's behalf. Despite his protestation that the indictment was false, the court sentences Chénier to death. Later, as Chénier awaits the tumbril, Gérard brings in Madeleine, who takes the place of another condemned woman in order to die alongside her lover, for in death they will be united.

Levine has rarely displayed his powers as an urgent and dramatic opera conductor more potently than on this splendid set, now reissued as a striking bargain in RCA's mid-priced opera series. In almost every way it is a reading that will be hard to better. Its defiant poet-hero provides a splendid role for Domingo at his most heroic, and the former servant, later revolutionary leader, Gérard, is a character who genuinely develops from Act to Act, a point well appreciated by Milnes. Scotto was here near the beginning of the intensive spell of recording which compensated for the record companies' earlier neglect of her, and though a few top notes spread uncomfortably, it is one of her most eloquent and beautiful performances on record. On CD the bright recording intensifies the dramatic thrust of playing and singing.

The title-role in this opera was always among Gigli's favourites; if he could, he would always choose it for his début in a house new to him. Here, in a recording made in 1941 in wartime Italy, he gives a glowing and characterful performance, full of totally distinctive touches. There is the occasional hint of the lachrymose Gigli, but it is of little importance next to the golden assurance of the singing, with the voice showing remarkably few signs of wear. And where most of Gigli's complete opera sets are simply star vehicles, this one brings some fine performances from the others too, including the young Giulietta Simionato, Giuseppe Taddei and Italo Tajo, all early in their careers, in small character-roles. Gino Bechi gives a thrillingly resonant performance as Gérard, and Maria Caniglia – who regularly recorded with Gigli – was never finer on record than here. The transfers from 78s are first rate.

The sound of the Decca set is so vivid and real, particularly on CD, that it often makes you start in surprise at the impact of fortissimos. Pavarotti may motor through the role of the poet-hero, singing with his usual fine diction but in a conventional, barnstorming way; nevertheless, the red-blooded melodrama of the piece comes over powerfully, thanks to Chailly's sympathetic conducting, incisive but never exaggerated. Caballé, like Pavarotti, is not strong on characterization but produces beautiful sounds, while Leo Nucci makes a superbly dark-toned Gérard. Perhaps to compensate for the lack of characterization among the principals, a number of veterans have been brought in to do party turns; Hugues Cuénod as Fléville delightfully apt, Piero de Palma as the informer, Incredible, Christa Ludwig superb as Madelon, and Astrid Varnay well over the top caricaturing the Contessa di Coigny. Though this cannot replace the RCA/Levine set with Domingo, Scotto and Milnes, it is a colourful substitute with its demonstration sound.

Apart perhaps from *La forza del destino*, the 1960 Decca set represents the most desirable of the Tebaldi / Del Monaco collaborations in Italian opera. The blood and thunder of the story suits both singers admirably and Gavazzeni is also at his best. Sample the final duet if you have any doubts concerning the power of this performance. Finer still than the soprano and tenor is Bastianini as Gérard. His finely focused voice is caught beautifully and he conveys vividly the conflicts in the man's character. Bold, vivid sound projects the drama splendidly.

The Sony/CBS set, featuring the same soprano, tenor and conductor as in its other Giordano set from Hungary, *Fedora*, is disappointing. Eva Marton is less well cast here, with the vibrato often obtrusive and the scale of the voice too heavy. José Carreras sings with passion and involvement, but there are many signs of strain, as in the climax of the poet's outburst in the *Improvviso* of Act I; the voice at such points grows disappointingly grainy. Giorgio Zancanaro as Gérard sings cleanly, but without sinister weight he sounds too noble for the revolutionary leader. With the orchestra set behind the voices, Patanè's direction sounds underpowered.

Fedora (complete).
(M) **(*) Decca 433 033-2 (2) [id.]. Monte Carlo Nat. Op. Ch. & O, Gardelli – ZANDONAI: *Francesca da Rimini.* **(*)
   Fedora (Magda Olivero), Loris (Mario Del Monaco), Siriex (Tito Gobbi).
Withdrawn: (M) ** Sony Dig. M2K 42181 (2). Hungarian R. & TV Ch. & O, Patanè.
   Fedora (Eva Marton), Loris (José Carreras).

Puccini was unique among his contemporaries in sustaining his operatic reputation over a long series of works. Giordano, like Leoncavallo, Mascagni and others, failed to live up to early success; with Giordano it is significant that this opera, like his most famous one, *Andrea Chénier*, dates from the earliest part of his career. He went on to marry the rich daughter of a hotelier, and prosperity was no doubt the bogey of invention.

Fedora is mostly remembered for one ripely expansive tune, the hero's solo, *Amor ti vieta*, which arrives in Act II as suddenly as love itself and then pervades the opera, one fine example of Giordano's stagecraft. There are other memorable ideas too, as well as many of the effects we associate with Puccini; but Giordano's piece, with its episodic libretto, is crude by comparison. Like *Tosca*, it was based on a Sardou play designed as a vehicle for Sarah Bernhardt; but in fact *Fedora* anticipated *Tosca* by two years, and the influence, if anything, is the other way around.

Count Andreievich is to marry Princess Fedora Romanov, a rich widow, but he will have to give up his feckless gambling and profligacy to do so. She arrives at his palace in St Petersburg and the count is carried in, dying of a gunshot wound. He was found on the terrace of a house belonging to an elderly lady who had brought him a letter earlier that day. A young man, Count Loris Ipanov, was another visitor that fateful morning and Fedora suspects he is guilty of the crime, thinking the motivation is political and anti-Tsarist. Grech, the police investigator, goes off to question Ipanov but cannot find him. Andreievich dies.

The action now moves to Fedora's house in Paris. De Siriex, a diplomat, is introduced to Count Ipanov who has been traced by Fedora. Ivanov is in love with her and she is attracted to him, but nevertheless she hopes he will confess to the murder of her intended husband. A Polish virtuoso pianist, Boleslao (in fact a Tsarist police spy incognito), is to give a recital and he begins to play, interrupting Ipanov's confession.

Loris admits to killing Andreievich but declares himself innocent of murder, giving no further explanation of the deed. Loris leaves and Fedora gives Grech a letter accusing Loris of political murder and suggesting that his brother, Valerian, is an accomplice.

The police go off to question them both. Loris returns and Fedora suggests he is plotting against the Tsar, but he explains that he killed Andreievich because the latter had seduced Wanda, Loris's wife. The lovers were caught with damning evidence and in the following altercation between lover and husband Andreievich fired the first shot; Loris had no choice but to return his fire. Fedora is horrified: she has falsely accused someone she now loves, and she realizes that he may be abducted back to Russia by the Tsar's political police.

The pair manage to escape to Switzerland where De Siriex arrives and tells Fedora that the investigation of Loris has been dropped, but that Valerian was captured and died in his cell and that his mother died of shock. Loris then discovers for himself that he has been pardoned, but also that Fedora was responsible for his betrayal and the death of his family. She begs his forgiveness in vain and takes poison then dies in his arms, as he finally accepts her plea of remorse.

As the highly enjoyable Decca recording of 1969 confirms, there is much that is memorable in the score, even though the absurd plot involves a passionate *volte face* when the heroine's suspicious disdain for the hero suddenly turns to love. Meaty stuff, which brings some splendid singing from Magda Olivero and (more intermittently) from Del Monaco, with Gobbi in a light comedy part. Fine, vintage, atmospheric recording. Well worth trying by anyone with a hankering after *verismo*, especially given its rare Zandonai coupling, added for the CD reissue.

On Sony, Eva Marton as Fedora, Romanov princess, is more aptly cast than in the companion set from the same source of *Andrea Chénier*, also conducted by Patanè with José Carreras taking the role of hero. In a work that should sound sumptuous it is not a help that the voices are placed forwardly, with the orchestra distanced well behind. That balance exaggerates the vibrato in Marton's voice, but it is a strong, sympathetic performance; Carreras, too, responds warmly to the lyricism of the role of the hero, Loris, giving a satisfyingly forthright account of *Amor ti vieta*. The rest of the cast is unremarkable, and Patanè's direction lacks bite, again partly a question of orchestral balance.

Glass, Philip (born 1937)

Akhnaten: complete.
(M) *** Sony M2K 42457 (2) [id.]. Stuttgart State Op. Ch., Russell Davies.
  Akhnaten (Paul Esswood), Nefertiti (Milagr Vargas), Queen Tye (Melinda Liebermann), Horemhab (Tero Hannula).

Akhnaten, Glass's powerful third opera, is set in the time of Ancient Egypt; here the composer's minimalist ostinatos, proceeding uninterrupted in the accompaniment, represent time itself. Against this is set a historical parade of events; the construction and style are remorselessly ritualistic, yet there are some powerful sounds to bring a sense of drama, and the opera's haunting closing scene with its wordless melismas is like nothing else in music.

The work was commissioned by the Stuttgart State Opera, and both orchestra and chorus make superb contributions. Among the soloists, Paul Esswood in the title-role is reserved, strong and statuesque; perhaps a more red-blooded approach would have been out of character – this is an opera of historical ghosts, and its life-flow lies in the hypnotic background provided by the orchestra. It offers a theatrical experience appealing to a far wider public than usual in the opera house, as the English National Opera production readily demonstrated.

Einstein on the Beach (complete).
(M) (***) Sony Dig. M4K 38875 (4) [id.]. Lucinda Childs, Samuel Johnson, Paul Mann, Sheryl Sutton, Ch., Zukofsky (violin), Philip Glass Ens., Riesman.

As the surreal title implies, *Einstein on the Beach* is more dream than drama. In this, his first opera, Glass, a leader in the minimalist movement, translated his use of slowly shifting ostinatos on to a near-epic scale. In the original stage production, the impact of the piece was as much due to the work of the avant-garde director, Robert Wilson, as to Glass's music.

The opera takes significant incidents in Einstein's life as the basis for the seven scenes in three Acts, framed by five 'Knee Plays'. Einstein's life – starting with the child watching the trains go by – is then linked with related visual images in a dream-like way, reflecting the second half of the title, *On the Beach*, a reference to Nevil Shute's novel with its theme of nuclear apocalypse.

The hallucinatory staging exactly reflected the music, which on its own conveys little. Other works of Glass, including the operas, are more communicative on record than this. Dedicated performances and first-rate recording. The booklet gives copious illustrations of the stage production.

Satyagraha.
(M) *** Sony Dig. M3K 39672 (3) [id.]. NY City Op. Ch. and O, Keene.
   Gandhi (Douglas Perry) with Claudia Cummings, Rhonda Liss, Robert McFarland, Scott
   Reeve, Sheryl Woods.

Like Glass's first opera, *Einstein on the Beach*, this one takes scenes from the life of a great
man as the basis for the 'plot' and sets them not in a narrative way but with hallucinatory music
in Glass's characteristic repetitive style. The libretto was developed by the composer in
collaboration with Constance DeJong and the work was first performed by the Netherlands
Opera at Rotterdam in 1980. The subject here is the early life of Mahatma Gandhi, pinpointing
various incidents; and the text is a selection of verses from the Bhagavadgita, sung in the original
Sanskrit and used as another strand in the complex repetitive web of sound.

The narrative describes Gandhi's struggles during the period 1893–1914 to achieve the repeal
of the so-called 'Black Act', a law restricting the movement of non-Europeans. Gandhi's ideas of
passive resistance and *satyagraha*, or 'truth force', eventually led to a partial (albeit temporary)
success. In each Act a historical figure is seen watching the developments on earth as a kind of
spiritual guardian.

In the first it is Tolstoy (with whom Gandhi corresponded in the first decade of the century);
in the second it is Tagore, and in the last Martin Luther King. The plot does not progress in
chronological order but finds the scenes set at various times between 1896 and 1913, though
each scene forms a self-sufficient dramatic entity.

The result is undeniably powerful. With overtones of India Raga at the very start, Glass builds
long crescendos with a relentlessness that may anaesthetize the mind but which have a
purposeful aesthetic aim. Where much minimalist music in its shimmering repetitiveness
becomes static, a good deal of this conveys energy as well as power, notably the moving scene at
the start of Act II in which Gandhi, attacked in the streets of Durban, is protected by Mrs
Alexander, wife of the superintendent of police.

The writing for chorus is often physically thrilling, and individual characters emerge in only a
shadowy way. The recording, using the device of overdubbing, is spectacular. Warning has to be
given of potential damage to loudspeakers from some of the sounds.

Glinka, Mikhail (1805–57)

A Life for the Tsar.
**(*) Sony Dig. S3K 46487 (3) [id.]. Sofia Nat. Op. Ch. & O, Tchakarov.
   Ivan Susanin (Boris Martinovich), Antonida (Alexandrina Pendachanska), Sobonin (Chris
   Merritt), Vanya (Stefania Toczyska).

When this opera was first given in St Petersburg in November 1836, it marked a breakthrough
in Russian music. Though Glinka broadly kept to a formalized layout in set numbers, as in
Italian opera, he introduced Russian themes far more than his predecessors, and the subject
itself reflected the nationalist fervour behind his inspiration. Even over the 70 years of the
Soviet period in Russia it was a revered masterpiece, though the text was amended (as in this
present Bulgarian recording) to tone down the praise for the tsar.

The opera opens at the beginning of the seventeenth century in Domnin, a Russian village.
Ivan Susanin announces that invading Polish troops are about to attack Moscow, but his
prospective son-in-law, Sobonin, declares that they have been firmly pushed back. Susanin
makes it plain that Sobonin's marriage to his daughter, Antonida, must be postponed until the
situation is stable. But when Sobonin tells him that a Romanov has been made tsar, consent is
given for the wedding to proceed.

When the Poles hear the news about the tsar, they decide to abduct him. At Ivan Susanin's
house there are rumours of the plot concerning the tsar, but Antonida and Sobonin are
congratulated on their marriage. Then Polish soldiers enter forcibly and demand that Susanin
shall lead them to the monastery where the new tsar is hiding. He pretends to accede and goes
along with them, but Vanja, his foster-son, is tipped off to ride ahead and warn the tsar.

Sobonin now follows with a group of peasant guerrillas to save Susanin. The journey is
difficult and we meet them camped in the forest, enduring the bitter Russian winter. (Another
scene, offered by Glinka as an alternative, and not included here, has Vanya – after his horse
has perished in the cold – arriving at the monastery, to warn the tsar.) The Poles are delayed, for

Susanin has made a detour. In the morning they awaken to discover that they have been wilfully led in the wrong direction, and Susanin is killed.

But the Epilogue, in Moscow, ends the opera optimistically. The crowd is welcoming the new tsar as he enters in procession. Antonida, Sobonin and Vanya are among the onlookers, also celebrating Ivan Susanin's heroism.

Even before the Epilogue, the opera is not as cheerless as it sounds. There are many delightful sequences, not least the many choruses and dances, which regularly inspire the late Emil Tchakarov to spring rhythms infectiously, bringing out the peasant flavour. Against the background of a good ensemble performance, the soloists are more than reliable, with Boris Martinovich as Ivan Susanin singing characterfully, if not always steadily.

Alexandrina Pendachanska is bright and fresh as his daughter, Antonida, only occasionally edgy in a Slavonic way, and Stefania Toczyska sings beautifully as the orphan, Vanya, Susanin's ward, performing this character's two arias delightfully. From outside the Slavonic area the American tenor, Chris Merritt, is well attuned, singing without strain. Though with its clear recording this gives little idea of a staged rather than a studio performance, it is more than a stopgap for an essential work in the repertory.

Gluck, Christophe (1714–87)

Alceste (complete).
** Orfeo Dig. C 02782 (3) [id.]. Bav. R. Ch. and SO, Baudo.
    Alceste (Jessye Norman), Admète (Nicolai Gedda), High Priest (Tom Krause), Hercule (Siegmund Nimsgern), Apollon (Bernd Weikl).
(M) ** Decca 436 234-2 (3) [id.]. Geraint Jones Singers & O, Geraint Jones (with HANDEL: Arias: *Radamistro: Gods all-powerful. Semele: O sleep! Why dost thou leave me? Messiah: He shall feed his flock; I know that my Redeemer liveth.* OCHS, attrib. Handel: *Praise ye the Lord.* Flagstad, LPO, Boult).
    Alceste (Kirsten Flagstad), Admeto (Raoul Jobin), Eumelo (Joan Clark), Aspasia (Rosemary Thayer), Evandro (Alexander Young), Ismene (Marion Lowe), Apollo (Thomas Hemsley).

The story of *Alceste* has much in common with the legend of *Orpheo and Euridice*. King Admetus is dying and Alcestis, his queen, asks the gathered crowd to accompany her into the temple of Apollo, to make sacrifices. Therein the Oracle's judgement is announced: if a substitute can be found to take his place, the king will live. Alcestis is willing to sacrifice herself and is without fear when she invokes the ruler of the Underworld as she sings '*Divinités du Styx*'.

Admetus recovers and holds court and is then appalled when he hears from Evander, a courtier, that Alcestis is to take his place. He refuses to permit his wife's sacrifice and follows her into the Underworld. Hercules appears and vows to restore Admetus and Alcestis to their subjects. At the gates to the Underworld Admetus defies the presiding Thanatos, but Thanatos announces that Alcestis must determine which of them shall enter.

As Alcestis refuses to retract her intended sacrifice, Hercules appears; together, he and Admetus confront the power of Thanatos. They are triumphant and Apollo rewards Hercules by making him a god, while Admetus and Alcestis return to rule on earth.

The French version of *Alceste*, quite different from the Italian, was for many years seriously in need of a complete recording; it was a great pity that the opportunity was not taken of recording Dame Janet Baker in the Covent Garden production conducted by Sir Charles Mackerras. However, this very well-cast set makes a valuable substitute, with Jessye Norman commanding in the title-role, producing gloriously varied tone in every register. What is rather lacking – even from her performance – is a fire-eating quality such as made Dame Janet's performance so memorable and which comes out to hair-raising effect in Callas's recording of *Divinités du Styx*. Here it is beautiful but relatively tame.

That is mainly the fault of the conductor, who makes Gluck's score sound comfortable rather than tense. The other protagonist is in effect the chorus, generally singing well but recorded rather distantly to reduce dramatic impact. The other principals sing stylishly; however, as a set, this does not quite rebut the idea that in Gluck 'beautiful' means 'boring'. Good, well-focused sound from Bavarian Radio engineers.

Although it uses the Italian edition of 1767, edited by Geraint Jones, and the result is hardly authentic by today's standards, the Decca recording, made in Walthamstow Assembly Hall in 1956 and supervised by John Culshaw, is notable for Kirsten Flagstad's noble queen. The stereo is genuine and, considering its age, remarkably good. Flagstad is not ideally cast, her voice too big for the part, and she is not always in perfect sympathy with the style. Moreover her intonation is a trifle suspect at times, but all this is of small account, given her star quality.

The rest of the cast is perfectly acceptable, even if Raoul Jobin's Admetus is not ideal. Geraint Jones directs the chorus and orchestra to good effect. Tempi are well judged in terms of the speeds considered correct at the time the recording was made. If the playing lacks the last ounce of polish and the performance fails to thrill, it remains a useful reminder of a great artist at the end of her career. The arias, recorded a few months later with Boult at the helm, are also worth having; although the voice is not always fully in control in *Gods all-powerful*, the other items show the voice more impressively.

Le Cinesi (The Chinese Woman).
(M) *** HM/BMG Dig. GD 77174 [77174-2-RG]. Schola Cantorum Basiliensis O, Jacobs.
Sivene (Isabelle Poulenard), Lisinga (Anne Sofie Von Otter), Tangia (Gloria Banditelli), Silango (Guy De Mey).

Gluck's hour-long opera-serenade was inspired by an earlier libretto by Metastasio (1735) and rewritten in 1754 for a palace entertainment given by Prince Joseph Friedrich of Saxe-Hildburghausen. A fashion for chinoiserie swept Europe at this time and *Le Cinesi* was Gluck's response. It takes place in China, where Lisinga and her two friends, Silvia and Tangia, are seeking ways of amusing themselves.

Lisinga's brother, Silango, who has just returned from Europe, enters. They decide to banish boredom by play-acting; each chooses a scene in a different style, one tragic (Andromache's aria after the death of Hector), another pastoral, and the third comic. Each must describe the action before embarking on their scene. Then follows a discussion as to which aria was acted best, but no agreement can be reached. Finally Silango suggests they dance together, as there would then be no crying, no yawning and no bad feelings. Thus the opera ends with a ballet.

The music provides a fascinating view of the composer's lighter side. In the comedy here, one can even detect anticipations of Mozart, though, with recitative taking up an undue proportion of the whole – including one solid span, near the beginning, of over ten minutes – Gluck's timing hardly compares. The chinoiserie of the story was reflected at that first performance in elaborate Chinese costumes, a novelty at the time; more importantly for us, Gluck, rather like Mozart in *Entführung*, uses jangling and tinkling percussion instruments in the *Overture* to indicate an exotic setting.

Otherwise the formal attitudes in Metastasio's libretto are pure eighteenth century. René Jacobs, a distinguished singer himself, directs a fresh, lively and understanding performance, marked by good singing from all four soloists, notably Anne Sofie von Otter and Guy de Mey. There is an aria for each of the soloists and, typical of the genre, they come together for a final quartet. First-rate playing and excellent sound. This is especially welcome in the mid-price range.

(i) *La Corona* (complete). (ii) *La Danza* (dramatic pastoral).
**(*) Orfeo Dig. C 135872H (2) [id.]. (i) Bav. R. Ch; Warsaw CO, Bugaj.
(i) Atalanta (Alicia Slowakiewicz), Meleagro (Halina Gorzyńska), Climene (Lidia Juranek), Asteria (Barbara Nowicka).
(ii) Nice (Ewa Ignatowicz), Tirsi (Kazimierz Myrlak).

La Corona was an opera never performed in Gluck's lifetime; it had to wait till 1937 to be heard, for the original production was frustrated when the Emperor, Franz I, for whose birthday the piece had been written, suddenly died. To a libretto by Calzabigi, it tells of Atalanta and a sequence of hunting exploits.

Apollo transforms himself into the huntsman Meleager, while the trio of Muses turn into Atalanta and two other hunting nymphs; the wreath, contested between those who aim at slaying the wild Calydonian boar, is awarded to neither but, needless to say, is offered to the emperor.

Hunting-calls set the scene evocatively in the three-movement sinfonia, which is followed by six arias (including a particularly brilliant one for Atalanta), a delightful duet and a final quartet.

This performance, originally recorded for Bavarian Radio, is fresh and direct, with first-rate singing from the three sopranos. The much shorter fill-up, described as a dramatic pastoral but involving no plot or development whatever, is less interesting and is less reliably done. It is none the less welcome as an extension of the Gluck repertory.

Echo et Narcisse.
(**(*)) HM HMC 90 5201/2 [id.]. Hamburg Op. Ch., Cologne Concerto, Jacobs.

Echo (Sophie Boulin), Narcisse (Kurt Streit), Amour (Deborah Massell), Cynire (Peter Galliard), Egle (Gertrud Hoffstedt), Aglae (Christina Högman).

Though Gluck wrote *Echo et Narcisse* at the end of his operatic career – in 1779, four months after *Iphigénie en Tauride* – he was rather turning his back on the dramatic reforms central to his greatest masterpieces. He here reverted to the stylized traditions of the classical pastoral, even though there are moving moments which (in a not dissimilar story) bring reminders of *Orfeo ed Euridice*. The fable of Echo and Narcissus is related in the third book of Ovid's *Metamorphoses*.

Echo loves the beautiful shepherd, Narcissus, but he is enamoured only of his own beauty. Her love unrequited, she turns herself into nothing more than a voice; this is heard only when called on by human sounds, when Echo answers the call from the depths of the mountains and the caverns. Narcissus becomes aware of his selfishness by her death and, in token of his remorse and despair, is turned into a flower.

Tschoudi's version goes as far as Echo's death and Narcissus' attempted suicide. He introduces Cupid in the Prologue and at the end of the opera and implies that Apollo had at one time pursued Echo and visits this fate upon her in retribution for her rejection of him.

In the climate of the Parisian theatre of 1779, with talk of revolution in the air, *Echo et Narcisse* was a failure and it was so again the following year. It did score a success two years later, but in a private amateur presentation. In this delightful performance, directed by René Jacobs, one can understand why that failure occurred: with its gently swinging triple-time rhythms, much of this is very different from the solid Gluck we encounter in the big operas. Jacobs' direction in this live Schwetzingen Festival performance carries you winningly from one number to the next, right up to the jolly final chorus, a *Hymn to Love*.

Though one or two of the singers are disappointing, notably the tremulous Sophie Boulin as Echo, the singing is generally good, with excellent choral support from the Hamburg Opera Chorus. The big snag – which may well make enjoyment impossible for many – is that the live recording captures all too faithfully the incessant background noises of the stage production. At times the bangs, shufflings and clonks, directionally reproduced, are so loud, improbable and unfortunately timed that one might be listening to a *Goon Show*. Those who can ignore that background will find great pleasure here, as they would have done in the intimate Schwetzingen theatre.

Iphigénie en Aulide (complete).
*** Erato/Warner Dig. 2292 45003-2 (2). Monteverdi Ch., Lyon Op. O, Gardiner.

Iphigénie (Lynne Dawson), Agamemnon (José Van Dam), Clytemnestra (Anne Sofie Von Otter), Achilles (John Aler).

Following up the success of his recording of the more celebrated *Iphigénie en Tauride*, John Eliot Gardiner here tackles the earlier of the two *Iphigénie* operas, much more neglected. *Iphigénie en Aulide* was written in 1774 – Gluck's first piece in French – and anticipated the *Tauride* opera in its speed and directness of treatment, so different from the leisurely and expansive traditions of *opera seria*. Based on Euripides by way of Racine, this does not have quite the emotional variety of the later opera but it is just as moving. Gardiner here eliminates the distortions of the piece which the long-established Wagner edition created and reconstructs the score as presented in the first revival of 1775.

As the opera opens, the Greeks are welcoming Clytemnestra and her daughter, Iphigénie, as they arrive on the island of Aulis. Iphigénie is to marry Achilles. Her father, King Agamemnon, and Calchas the high priest confer about their presence, for the king, desiring a safe passage for himself and his army to Troy, has implored the Oracle for help and has agreed that in return he must sacrifice his daughter Iphigénie to Diana.

While the Greeks insist on the sacrifice to placate the gods, Calchas prays that they will allow a different victim. Meanwhile Agamemnon tells his wife that she must leave at once with their daughter since Achilles is not worthy of her.

Clytemnestra passes her father's feelings on to Iphigénie, who at first responds coolly to Achilles but is won over. As Achilles leads his prospective bride to the altar a messenger arrives to announce that Agamemnon is waiting to sacrifice her; Achilles swears to defend her life even though Iphigénie reaffirms her love and loyalty to her father.

When Agamemnon and Achilles meet, Achilles warns him that anyone daring to harm Iphigénie will have him to reckon with first. The king finally gives in and elects to send his wife and daughter at once to Mycenae and perhaps avert the wrath of the gods. Achilles begs

Clytemnestra to escape; instead, in pent-up frustration, she calls upon Jove to release his fury on them.

Achilles now arrives leading an army of Thessalonians ready for battle, but Calchas defuses the situation by reporting that after all the gods will grant Agamemnon a fair passage to Troy, even though he has not kept his sacrificial agreement. With the situation now satisfactorily resolved the Greeks depart for Troy.

Though the original final chorus was omitted in the revival, Gardiner rightly includes it here, amazingly original, with the bass drum prefacing a number which is less a celebration than a dramatic call to war, very different from the conventional happy ending. The darkness of the piece is established at the very start, with men's voices eliminated, and a moving portrait built up of Agamemnon, here superbly sung by José van Dam, with his extended solo at the end of Act II tellingly contrasted with the brevity and economy of the rest.

In the title-role Lynne Dawson builds up a touching portrait of the heroine from the contrasted sequence of brief arias, a character developing in adversity, always vulnerable. Her sweet, pure singing is well contrasted with the positive strength of Anne Sofie von Otter as Clytemnestra, and John Aler brings clear, heroic attack to the tenor role of Achilles.

The performance is crowned by the superb ensemble-singing of the Monteverdi Choir in the many choruses. Based on a production at the Aix-en-Provence Festival, the recording conveys the tensions of a live performance without the distractions of intrusive stage noise. Gardiner persuades the Lyon Opera Orchestra, using modern instruments, to adopt some of the manners of period players, minimizing any disappointment that – like Gardiner's recording of *Iphigénie en Tauride* – this is not a true period performance.

Iphigénie en Tauride (complete).
⊛ *** Ph. Dig. 416 148-2 (2) [id.]. Monteverdi Ch., Lyon Op. O, Gardiner.
    Iphigénie (Diana Montague), Pylade (John Aler), Oreste (Thomas Allen), 1st Priestess
    (Nancy Argenta), Thoas (René Massis).
* Orfeo CO 52832H (2). Bav. R. Ch. & SO, Gardelli.
    Iphigénie (Pilar Lorengar), Pylade (Franco Bonisolli), Oreste (Walton Groenroos), 1st
    Priestess (Alma Jean Smith), Thoas (Dietrich Fischer-Dieskau).

Gardiner's electrifying reading of *Iphigénie en Tauride*, based on the team he built up at the Lyon Opera House, is a revelation. Anyone who has found Gluck operas boring should hear this dramatically paced performance of an opera that is compact and concentrated in its telling of a classical story, departing strongly from the *opera seria* tradition which Gluck inherited, even while it contains some of the composer's loveliest melodies.

Iphigenia, the daughter of Agamemnon, is now a Priestess of Diana on the island of Tauris and, as the opera opens, in dreams she has had premonitions of misfortune to her family far away. Her father has in fact been slain by his wife, Clytemnestra, and in consequence Clytemnestra has been killed by Iphigenia's brother, Orestes. However, Iphigenia knows nothing of this and she and Orestes have not seen one another for many years.

We now meet Thoas, King of Scythia, who, warned of approaching danger, demands a human sacrifice. At that moment two shipwrecked Greek captives are brought in, Orestes and his friend Pylades. It appears that Orestes is haunted by the crime he has committed and by the Furies, who pursue him.

Once inside Diana's temple, Pylades is separated from Orestes, whose mind is temporarily unhinged. Iphigénie questions Orestes and, becoming calmer, he tells her of the events in Mycenae, about the murder of Agamemnon and the subsequent revenge. He does not reveal his identity but instead tells her that only one member of the family remains alive, a daughter, Electra.

Perceiving a likeness to her brother and to save him from Thoas, Iphigenia instructs him to take a letter to Electra, but Orestes refuses to leave Pylades to his fate, and Pylades agrees to deliver the letter instead. Thoas insists on the sacrifice of Orestes, but at the very moment of carrying out his slaughter Iphigenia recognizes him as her brother. This makes no difference to Thoas and Iphigenia says she will die alongside her brother.

Pylades returns with a rescue party just in time, and Thoas is killed. The goddess Diana now appears and pardons Orestes. The Scythians, it appears, had stolen her likeness: she now wishes the statue to be returned to Mycenae, and so it is that the opera can end with a chorus of joyful celebration.

Far more than usual, one can here understand how advocates of romantic opera such as Berlioz and Wagner were excited by this culminating example of Gluck's reformism, with its speed and fluidity and the breaking down of formal structures. Gardiner, who made his Covent Garden début in 1973 conducting this opera, is an urgent advocate, bringing out the full range of expression from first to last. He leads from the Overture into the storm music with *Otello*-like intensity and, though his Lyon orchestra does not use period instruments, its clarity and resilience and, where necessary, grace and delicacy are admirable.

The cast is first rate. Though Diana Montague in the name-part does not attempt a grand romantic characterization such as a conventional prima donna might have given, she sings with admirable bite and freshness, making the lovely solo *O malheureuse Iphigénie* pure and tender. Thomas Allen is an outstanding Orestes, characterizing strongly – as in his fury aria – but singing with classical precision. John Aler is a similarly strong and stylish singer, taking the tenor role of Pylades, with some fine singers from Gardiner's regular team impressive in other roles. The recording is bright and full, with the balance favouring voices but not inappropriately so.

The brief contribution of Fischer-Dieskau in the unsympathetic role of Thoas underlines by contrast the serious disappointment of the alternative, Orfeo set as a whole. His imagination and life provide quite a different perspective on the music from the rest, and Pilar Lorengar as recorded sounds so tremulous and uneven as the heroine that it is wearing to listen to. Bonisolli produces fine heroic tone but sings unimaginatively, and Walton Groenroos is gritty-toned as Orestes. This is a total disappointment, despite the good recorded sound.

Orfeo ed Euridice (complete).
*** EMI Dig. CDS7 49834-2 (2) [Ang. CDCB 49834]. Monteverdi Ch., Lyon Opera O, Gardiner.
   Orphée (Anne Sofie Von Otter), Eurydice (Barbara Hendricks), Amour (Brigitte Fournier).
(M) *** Erato/Warner Dig. 2292 45864-2 (2). Glyndebourne Ch., LPO, Raymond Leppard.
   Orfeo (Janet Baker), Euridice (Elisabeth Speiser), Amor (Elizabeth Gale).
**(*) Decca 417 410-2 (2) [id.]. ROHCG Ch. & O, Solti.
   Orfeo (Marilyn Horne), Euridice (Pilar Lorengar), Amor (Helen Donath).
**(*) Capriccio Dig. 60 008-2 (2) [id.]. Berlin R. Ch., C. P. E. Bach CO, Hartmut Haenchen.
   Orfeo (Jochen Kowalski), Euridice (Dagmar Schellenberger-Ernst), Amor (Christian Fliegner).
**(*) Sony Dig. SX2K 48040 (2) [id.]. Stuttgart Chamber Ch., Tafelmusik, Bernius.
   Orfeo (Michael Chance), Euridice (Nancy Argenta), Amor (Stefan Beckerbauer).
(M) **(*) BMG/RCA GD 87896 (2) [7896-2-RG]. Rome Polyphonic Ch., Virtuosi di Roma, Fasano.
   Orfeo (Shirley Verrett), Euridice (Anna Moffo), Amor (Judith Raskin).
**(*) Ariola 302588. Munich R. O, Hager.
   Orfeo (Marjana Lipovšek), Euridice (Lucia Popp), Amor (Julie Kaufmann).
** Accent ACC 48223/4D (2). Ghent Coll. Vocale, La Petite Bande, Kuijken.
   Orfeo (René Jacobs), Euridice (Marjanne Kweksilber), Amor (Magdalena Falewicz).
Withdrawn: (M) ** EMI Dig. CMS7 63637-2 (2) [Ang. CDMB 63637]. Amb. Op. Ch., Philh. O, Muti.
   Orfeo (Agnes Baltsa), Euridice (Margaret Marshall), Amor (Edita Gruberová).

The most famous of early classical operas has a story with which everyone can readily identify. At the opening Eurydice lies in her tomb. Orpheus and his friends mourn her and Eros, the God of Love, heeds their tears. Orpheus is told that Zeus has given permission for him to descend into Hades to enchant its guardians with his music and return with Eurydice, but he must not look back at her on their return journey. At the entrance to the Underworld the Furies and Demons repel him vehemently, but soon Orpheus is placating them with his music and gradually they disappear.

The gates of the Elysian Fields open before him and he sees (and hears) the *Dance of the blessed spirits*. Eurydice comes towards him with the Spirits. He leads her away and, obeying the command, makes no attempt to look at her. She cannot understand his behaviour and thinks he no longer loves her. He tries to soothe her apprehension; then at last his willpower fails him. He cannot resist her pleas and turns and embraces her. She dies.

Frantic with grief, Orpheus sings the famous *Che farò, senza Eurydice?* and determines to die with her. But Eros reappears: Orpheus has proved his constancy and Eurydice is restored to him. The chorus rejoice and praise the power of love.

Gardiner here cuts through the problem of which text to use in this opera – the original Vienna version with alto in the title-role or the Paris version with tenor – by opting broadly for the Berlioz edition, which aimed at combining the best of both, very similar to the solution adopted by Raymond Leppard in his performances and Erato recording at Glyndebourne. For Gardiner, Anne Sofie von Otter is a superb Orfeo, tougher than Dame Janet Baker on Leppard's set, less vulnerable but less feminine too, and dramatically most convincing. The masculine forthrightness of her singing matches the extra urgency of Gardiner's direction; and both Barbara Hendricks as Eurydice and Brigitte Fournier as Amor are also excellent. The chorus is Gardiner's own Monteverdi Choir, superbly clean and stylish. Unlike the Leppard/Glyndebourne production, Gardiner's omits the celebratory ballet at the end of the opera. The recording is full and well balanced.

The Erato version, directly based on the Glydebourne production in which Dame Janet Baker made her very last stage appearance in opera, was recorded in 1982, immediately after the run of live performances. That brought the advantage of the sort of dramatic commitment and spontaneity of a live performance allied to studio precision. Leppard, abetted by the producer, Sir Peter Hall, aimed in the theatre to contrast the bitingly passionate quality in the score against the severely classical frame. Often credited with being a romanticizer of the eighteenth century, Leppard in fact presents the score with freshness and power, indeed with toughness. Nowhere is that clearer than in the great scene leading up to the aria, *Che farò*, where Dame Janet commandingly conveys the genuine bitterness and anger of Orpheus at Eurydice's death.

That most famous of Gluck's arias comes over fresh and clear with no sentimentality whatever, and conversely the display aria which brings Act I to a close has passion and expressiveness even in the most elaborate coloratura. Elisabeth Speiser as Eurydice and Elizabeth Gale as Amor are both disappointing but, as in the theatre, the result is a complete and moving experience centring round a great performance from Dame Janet. The complete ballet-postlude is included, delightful celebration music. The recording has been enhanced in the CD transfer, bright and vivid without edginess, with the modern orchestral strings sounding both fresh and warm. At mid-price this makes a clear first choice.

The surprise of the Decca set is the conducting of Georg Solti, which combines his characteristic brilliance and dramatic bite with warm sympathy for the eighteenth-century idiom. Where often in this opera the progress of the drama can be forgotten, here the experience is riveting, the more so when Solti and Horne opt to conclude Act I, not as the Gluck score prescribes, but with a brilliant display aria, *Addio, o miei sospiri*, taken from the contemporary opera, *Tancredi*, by Ferdinando Bertoni. That may sound like cavalier treatment for Gluck, but stylistically Solti justifies not only that course but his whole interpretation, which combines drama with delicacy. Marilyn Horne makes a formidably strong Orfeo, not as deeply imaginative as Dame Janet Baker but wonderfully strong and secure, with fine control of tone. Pilar Lorengar sings sweetly, but is not always steady, while Helen Donath is charming in the role of Amor. Recording quality is outstandingly fine.

The big attraction of the Capriccio version is the inspired singing of the German counter-tenor Jochen Kowalski in the title-role. The main shortcoming can be assessed at the very start, when the washy acoustic obscures rapid figuration in the overture, and the whole scale of the performance seems too big. Haenchen, with a good chamber orchestra using modern instruments, opts for the Vienna version of the opera, using Italian, more compact than the later, Paris score; but he provides as an appendix the Paris ballet with its *Dance of the blessed spirits*, an essential item.

The extra sharpness of the Vienna score is unfortunately countered not only by the recording and the conductor's occasionally heavy direction, but also by the murkiness of the large-sounding chorus. None of these shortcomings needs weigh very heavily against the glories of the solo singing, notably that of Kowalski who, with his firm, characterful voice, generally warm-toned in a masculine way, creates an exceptionally convincing portrait of the bereaved Orpheus. More than usual he brings out the full poignant agony of the hero's situation. *Che farò* is taken effectively fast, but tenderly and with big rallentandos, and his intensity is matched by the fresh vehemence of his Eurydice, Dagmar Schellenberger-Ernst. Having a boy-treble as Amor is more controversial, but it is justified when Christian Fliegner's voice is so pure and true. He comes from the Tölzer Boy Singers, and sings with commendably clean attack, fine rhythmic sense and no hooting.

Bernius, a fine Gluck conductor, with his period group, Tafelmusik, opts for the original, Vienna version of this operatic landmark, omitting all the material Gluck wrote later for Paris. The impact of the opera is all the sharper, but it is disappointing not to have the *Dance of the blessed spirits*. Sony should have included it as a supplement with the rest of the Paris ballet music, as the Capriccio version does.

As it is, it makes very short measure to have only 83 minutes of music on two full-price discs.

Just as the Capriccio set has the outstanding German counter-tenor Jochen Kowalski in the title-role, so this one has the leading British counter-tenor, Michael Chance, dominating the whole performance, with his voice full and forward. The focus of the sound is far sharper than on the disconcertingly distanced Capriccio. Nancy Argenta is a sweet-toned Eurydice, and Amor is taken by the confident German boy-treble, Stefan Beckerbauer. With such sprightly playing from Tafelmusik, using period instruments, this is an even more stylish version than its Capriccio rival, but the price is very high.

Clearly, if you have a mezzo as firm and sensitive as Shirley Verrett, then there is much in favour of using the original Italian version rather than the later, Paris version with tenor. Quite apart from making a sensible decision over the text, Fasano in the mid-priced reissue of his vintage RCA set uses an aptly scaled orchestra (of modern instruments) and adopts an appropriately classical style. Anna Moffo and Judith Raskin match Verrett in clean, strong singing, and the Rome Polyphonic Chorus is far more incisive than most Italian choirs. The recording is vivid and atmospheric, but on CD the close balance of the voices emphasizes the music's dramatic qualities rather than its tenderness.

Hager's Munich version, recorded in 1986 in full and atmospheric, if slightly distanced sound, brings a good, enjoyable middle-of-the-road performance. Marjana Lipovšek has a beautiful, rich mezzo inclined to fruitiness, which yet in this breeches role is well able to characterize Orfeo strongly and positively. So *Che farò* is warm and direct in its expressiveness, with Lipovšek avoiding distracting mannerism both here and in recitative. Lucia Popp makes a delightful Eurydice and Julie Kaufmann, though less distinctive, is fresh and bright as Amor. The chorus is on the heavyweight side for Gluck, but that adds to the power of the performance, which uses the 1762 Vienna version of the score, though with instrumental numbers added from the Paris version.

With period instruments and a counter-tenor in the title-role, Kuijken's set – using the original Italian version of 1762 – provides a fair alternative for those looking for an 'authentic' performance. Jacobs is especially impressive as Orfeo; however, exceptionally *Che farò*, taken very slowly, is disappointing, and not everyone will like his ornamentation. Marjanne Kweksilber makes an appealing Eurydice; but generally, with authentic style sounding a degree self-conscious, the whole performance lacks a necessary degree of involvement. This is *Orfeo* coolly dissected. Good recording.

Muti chose to record the relatively severe 1762 version of *Orfeo ed Euridice* which eliminates some much-loved passages added later, but then opted for a most unstylish approach, sleek and smooth but full of romantic exaggerations. The pity is that the trio of principals was one of the strongest on record. Sadly, even Agnes Baltsa cannot make *Che farò* sound stylish when the speed is so leaden. The recording is warm and rounded and the sound generally first class. This set has been withdrawn in the UK.

Orfeo ed Eurydice (abridged version, sung in Italian).
(M) (**) Decca mono 433 468-2. Glyndebourne Festival Ch., Southern PO, Stiedry.
  Orfeo (Kathleen Ferrier), Euridice (Ann Ayars), Amor (Zoë Vlachopoulos).

This much-abridged version of Gluck's opera was recorded soon after the Glyndebourne performances of 1947 and is valuable only for Kathleen Ferrier's magnificent contribution. Even so, it is obvious that this was only a first attempt by a great artist to scale a formidable part. At that time she was not entirely at ease singing in Italian, and when Fritz Stiedry chose a very fast tempo for the big aria, *Che farò*, she was less impressive – in spite of the vocal freshness – than in her later recording of the aria with Sargent. That is available on one of the ten discs of the Kathleen Ferrier Edition (Decca 433 470-2; *433 470-4*). Decca have little to be proud of in this reissue; apart from the fact that Stiedry's imaginative contribution with chorus and orchestra is no more than adequate, the bright transfer is edgy and the sound not always completely secure.

Paride ed Elena: complete.
Withdrawn: (*) Orfeo Dig. C 118842 (3) [id.]. Schoenberg Ch., Austrian R. Ch. & SO, Zagrosek.
  Paris (Franco Bonisolli), Helen (Ileana Cotrubas).

Paride ed Elena, dating from 1770, fell between early and late operatic styles in Gluck's output. Alfred Einstein describes it as 'a curious and daring work [in which] Calzabigi made a wholly unheroic transformation of the abduction of Helen', the act that triggered the Trojan War.

Helen is Queen of Sparta and is betrothed to Menelaus. Paris lands on the Peloponnesian coast to claim the fairest woman in Greece as the prize for his judgement in favour of Venus. Helen receives him correctly: a Spartan martial ballet is mounted, but otherwise he is treated coolly.

Indeed, such is her lack of ardour that he has a fainting fit. Only on his feigned departure does she reveal her real feelings. Pallas appears in the clouds and prophesies the fatal consequences of an elopement, but the pair take consolation in Cupid's favours and protection.

Though it contains many beautiful numbers, such as Paris's Serenade in Act III, it was never a success even in the composer's lifetime; nowadays it presents formidable problems of presentation which this performance with its highly anachronistic style does little to solve. The central objection is to the casting of Franco Bonisolli in the role of Paris, originally designed for a high soprano castrato.

To transfer what was intended to be eerily penetrating and exotic to the tones of a lusty modern Verdi tenor with little or no idea of classical style and who regularly attacks notes from below, is to undermine the whole project. Ileana Cotrubas, a delightful, stylish soprano as a rule, here sounds dispirited, and the balance in favour of the voices brings out the vocal faults all the more. Zagrosek's conducting is efficient, and the choral singing solidly effective, but the lack of authentic style prevents anything more than a listing of the recording for the interest of the work itself.

La rencontre imprévue (opéra-comique).
*** Erato/Warner Dig. 2292 45516-2 (2) [id.]. Lyon Op. O, Gardiner.

> Rezia (Lynne Dawson), Balkis (Claudine Le Coz), Dardané (Catherine Dubosc), Amine (Sophie Marin-Degor), Ali (Guy De Mey), Osmin (Jean-Luc Viala), Sultan (Guy Flechter), Vertigo (Jean-Philippe Lafont), Calender (Gilles Cachemaille), Chef de Caravane (Francis Dudziak).

La rencontre imprévue is based on *Le pèlerins de la Mecque* ('The Pilgrims for Mecca') of 1726 by Alain-René Lesage, as adapted by Louis Hurtant Dancourt. The plot is related to Mozart's *Die Entführung aus dem Serail* and tells of Prince Ali's constancy in his love for Princess Rezia.

The match is opposed by Rezia's father. Ali and his servant, Osmin, arrive in Cairo, where Rezia is held captive in the Sultan's harem: they plan to escape, disguised as pilgrims to Mecca, but their stratagem is betrayed and they are threatened with death. Many tests are made of Ali's fidelity and, on learning of their long devotion, the sultan (magnanimous, as in all similar operatic farragos set in the 'mystic' East) takes pity on them.

This is another of the revelatory recordings of Gluck that John Eliot Gardiner has made with the Lyon Opera. Here he demonstrates that one of Gluck's comic operas – a genre long disparaged for bad timing and poor invention – can come up as freshly as the great reform operas like the two *Iphigénie* works he previously recorded. It is true that *Les pèlerins de la Mecque* – as Gardiner prefers to call it, rather than using its duller, more usual title, given above – has nothing like the comic timing of Mozart. Yet the brief 'Turkish' overture with its jingles has a breeziness that rivals that of *Entführung*, and all through the brisk sequence of arias and ensembles Gardiner gives the lie to the idea of the score being banal.

The story may be disjointed but, with dialogue neatly edited and with some excellent singing, these three 35-minute Acts make delightful entertainment on record. The sweet-toned Lynne Dawson is charming as the heroine, Rezia, and Guy de Mey as the hero, Ali, is one of the few tenors who could cope effortlessly with the high tessitura, even though the voice does not sound quite young enough. Pierre Cachemaille sings powerfully in an incidental role, and other excellent members of the Lyon team include the tenor, Jean-Luc Viala, and the baritone, Francis Dudziak. The Lyon acoustic, as usual, is on the dry side, as recorded, but that has many advantages in comic opera.

Opera arias from *Alceste; Armide; Iphigénie en Aulide; Iphigénie en Tauride; Orfeo ed Euridice; Paride ed Elena; La rencontre imprévue.*
(M) *** Ph. 422 950-2; *422 950-4.* Janet Baker, ECO, Leppard.

Helped by alert and sensitive accompaniments, Dame Janet Baker's singing of Gluck completely undermines any idea of something square or dull. The most famous arias bring unconventional readings – *Divinités du Styx* from *Alceste* deliberately less commanding, more thoughtful than usual – but the rarities are what inspire her most keenly: the four arias from *Paride ed Elena*, for example, are vividly contrasted in their sharply compact form. Outstanding recording, vividly remastered.

Goldmark, Karl (1830–1915)

Die Königin von Saba.
** Hung. HCD 12179/81 [id.]. Hungarian State Op. Ch. and O, Fischer.
   Queen of Sheba (Klára Takács), Assad (Siegfried Jerusalem), Sulamith (Veronika Kincses),
   King Solomon (Sándor Sólyom-Nagy), Astaroth (Magda Kalmár), Baal-Hanan (Lajos Miller),
   High Priest (József Gregor), Watchman (László Polgár).

Goldmark's most successful works all came within a relatively short span in his career, with this long opera the most ambitious of them. *Die Königen von Saba* was first performed in Vienna in 1875; it stayed in the repertory for some time after that and was conducted by, among others, Mahler, Richard Strauss and Bruno Walter.

The biblical story takes place in the tenth century BC and opens with the Queen of Sheba visiting Solomon in his palace. Assad, who is betrothed to Solomon's daughter, Sulamith, is sent as envoy to meet the queen and falls in love with her without realizing who she is. On arrival at Solomon's court, she removes her veil and he rushes to embrace her but is repulsed, the queen prudently saying that she has never set eyes on him before.

Solomon reminds everyone of the wedding to come on the morrow; but the queen is in love with Assad and is not willing to lose him to Sulamith. Assad meets her in the gardens that evening, and their ardour reasserts itself. The following morning the wedding ceremony is about to begin when the queen arrives. Assad is so smitten he throws the wedding ring away and declares that the queen is the only woman he will marry.

Solomon arranges another feast and the queen pleads on Assad's behalf. Now Solomon's daughter appears, and the contrast between her innocence and the queen's machinations is very striking. Solomon reprieves Assad but banishes him to the desert. The queen follows him but they are both exhausted and dying of exposure in the fierce sunlight. Assad pushes the queen away as Sulamith arrives and expires in the arms of his betrothed.

With the Queen of Sheba representing evil and the lovely Sulamith representing good, its theme links directly with that of Wagner's *Tannhäuser*, but in style Goldmark rather recalls Mendelssohn and Gounod, with a touch of Meyerbeer. In the tenor role of Assad, Siegfried Jerusalem gives a magnificent performance, not least in his aria, *Magische Töne*. Klára Takács is dramatic and characterful as the Queen of Sheba, but on top the voice is often raw. Sándor Nagy is an impressive Solomon, and Adám Fischer, one of the talented family of conductors, draws lively performances from everyone. The recording is very acceptable, but even on CD there are many details which do not emerge as vividly as they might. The documentation is acceptable, although shortened. It offers a full translation, but is in no way comparable with the splendid booklet offered with the original LP set.

Gounod, Charles (1818–93)

Faust (complete).
*** EMI Dig. CDS7 54228-2 (3) [Ang. CDCC 54228]. Ch. & O of Capitole de Toulouse, Plasson.
   Faust (Richard Leech), Marguérite (Cheryl Studer), Méphistophélès (José Van Dam),
   Valentin (Thomas Hampson).
(M) **(*) EMI CMS7 69983-2 (3) [Ang. CDMC 69983]. Paris Nat. Op. Ch. and O, Cluytens.
   Faust (Nicolai Gedda), Marguérite (Victoria De los Angeles), Méphistophélès (Boris
   Christoff), Valentin (Ernest Blanc).
**(*) Ph. Dig. 420 164-2 (3) [id.]. Bav. R. Ch. and SO, C. Davis.
   Faust (Francisco Araiza), Marguérite (Kiri Te Kanawa), Méphistophélès (Evgeny
   Nesterenko), Valentin (Andreas Schmidt).
** EMI CDS7 47493-8 (3) [Ang. CDCC 47493]. Paris Op. Ch. & O, Prêtre.
   Faust (Plácido Domingo), Marguérite (Mirella Freni), Méphistophélès (Nicolai Ghiaurov),
   Valentin (Thomas Allen).
(M) ** Decca 421 240-2 (3) [id.]. Amb. S., Highgate School Ch., LSO, Bonynge.
   Faust (Franco Corelli), Marguérite (Joan Sutherland), Méphistophélès (Nicolai Ghiaurov),
   Valentin (Robert Massard).
(M) *(*) Erato/Warner 2292 45685-2 (3) [id.]. Ch. of Op. du Rhin, Strasbourg PO, Lombard.
   Faust (Giacomo Aragall), Marguérite (Montserrat Caballé), Méphistophélès (Paul Plishka),
   Valentin (Philippe Huttenlocher).

Although Berlioz and Boito, among others, have successfully dramatized the Faust legend in music, it is Gounod's sometimes ingenuous version of the story with which the public have consistently identified.

As the curtain rises the ageing Dr Faust, alone in his study, is about to drain a poisoned goblet of wine when he hears cheerful young voices. As they recede, he bewails his failing powers and instead calls on the powers of darkness to aid him. Mephistopheles makes a spectacular entrance and offers to do Faust's bidding. Faust above all desires youth and Mephistopheles cunningly conjures up before him a vision of the beautiful Marguerite. Anticipating that she can be his, Faust no longer hesitates to sign away his soul to Mephistopheles. He is immediately transformed into a gallant youth and shares his eager anticipation with his new master.

In the Kermesse the crowd is merry and the wine flows. Valentin, Marguerite's brother, regrets that he must leave his sister unguarded while he goes to war. Siebel, who admires Marguerite, promises to protect her. Mephistopheles exuberantly sings his cynical *Calf of gold* aria and predicts ill-fortune for both Valentin and Siebel: every flower that Siebel touches will fade and die.

Flamboyantly conjuring wine from the inn sign, Mephistopheles drinks to Marguerite. Valentin, angered, draws his sword but finds himself transfixed. The crowd, realizing that devilry is afoot, form the sign of the cross with their swords and Mephistopheles recoils, temporarily foiled. A waltz begins and, when Faust enters, Mephistopheles introduces him to Marguerite. Faust proffers his arm but Marguerite refuses politely. Siebel finds his way blocked by Mephistopheles.

We now move to Marguerite's garden where Siebel is picking flowers which promptly wither; he then dips his hand in holy water and the flowers retain their bloom. He departs. Mephistopheles and Faust enter, and Mephistopheles procures a jewel-box for Marguerite, who is captivated by its contents. Soon Faust's courtship achieves the hoped-for response and Marguerite invites her lover to join her in the house, to Mephistopheles' sardonic amusement.

Faust deserts Marguerite after she has borne his child. Siebel's love is steadfast, but it is Faust Marguerite loves. In church she prays for forgiveness, but Mephistopheles intervenes in sinister fashion as her conscience. The soldiers now return from the war and Valentin is with them. He rejects Marguerite and challenges Faust to a duel; Mephistopheles intervenes and Valentin is killed.

The interpolated ballet scene brings Walpurgis Night revels in the Harz mountains, where Faust has a vision of Marguerite with blood forming a halter round her neck. He demands to be taken to her. She is in prison, condemned for murdering her child in a fit of despairing madness. Faust enters and takes her in his arms, begging her to escape with him. She dreamily recalls their early happiness together, but when she sees Mephistopheles – who believes her soul now to be his – she rejects Faust and prays to heaven to forgive her, and a chorus of angels declares that she is saved.

Recordings of *Faust* have been dogged by ill-luck, with major flaws regularly preventing a full recommendation, but Plasson with his excellent cast headed by three American singers comes nearer than anyone to scotching the jinx. Ironically, it is the French-speaking singer among the four principals who might worry traditionalists, for José van Dam's gloriously dark, finely focused bass-baritone yet does not have the heft of a full-blooded bass voice, such as is associated with the role of Mephistopheles.

That said, it is a masterly performance, more searching and sinister than almost any, with the singer projecting superbly and consistently exploiting his idiomatic French, so different from the Slavonic singers who are his rivals in the other main sets. The *Calf of gold* solo has a lift in its jolly, bouncing rhythms that makes it all the more sinister, and it is good to have as one of the four previously unrecorded offerings in the Appendix on the third disc an early, discarded aria intended for the same point in the opera. All three of the American principals are outstanding stylists, very much in sympathy with the idiom.

Cheryl Studer, while exploiting the power of her soprano, conveys the girlishness of Marguerite, managing to lighten her voice, using the widest range of dynamic and colour. In the *Jewel song* she is brighter and jollier than any of her main rivals, helped by Plasson's understanding accompaniment. If Richard Leech's voice, on a par with van Dam's, might in principle seem too lightweight for the role of Faust, the lyrical flow and absence of strain, coupled with fine projection, make his singing consistently enjoyable. As Valentin, Thomas Hampson is strongly cast, with his firm, heroic baritone.

As for the ensemble and choral writing and Plasson's direction generally, he is more successful than any latterday rival in giving a rhythmic lift to Gounod's score, bringing out the jollity of the Kermesse scene and building the final trio the more compellingly by keeping power in reserve till the final stanza. The sound has a good sense of presence, set in a pleasantly reverberant acoustic which does not obscure necessary detail. In addition to the supplementary numbers – which also include a trio for Faust, Siebel and Wagner as well as a duet for Marguerite and Valentin – the appendix offers the complete ballet music.

The vintage (1960) EMI recording at mid-price was a re-make of an earlier, mono set, with the contributions of De los Angeles, Gedda and Christoff all generally improved. The seductiveness of De los Angeles's singing is a delight and, as she had twice shown before on record, she has all the agility required in the *Jewel song*. It is a pity that the recording hardens the natural timbre slightly. Christoff is magnificently Mephistophelian. The dark, rich, bass voice with all its subtle shadings of tone-colour is perfect for the part, at once musical and dramatic.

Gedda, though showing some signs of strain, sings intelligently, and among the other soloists Ernest Blanc has a pleasing, firm voice, which he uses to make Valentin into a sympathetic character. Cluytens's approach is competent but somewhat workaday. He rarely offers the extra spring needed to bring out the full charm of Gounod's score, and he shows a tendency to over-drive in the more dramatic passages. The recording is generally well balanced, although at times some of the soloists are oddly placed on the stereo stage. Apart from the slight hardening on the vocal timbre, the CD transfer is generally well managed, increasing the vividness and presence, with the offstage passages well caught within a convincing choral perspective. The layout of the five Acts over three CDs is just as it should be, and the libretto includes a full translation.

Sir Colin Davis, with his German orchestra and with no French singer among his principals, gives a performance which, from the very measured account of the opening onwards, relates back to the weight of Goethe as much as to French opera. As in his other recordings of French opera – notably another Goethe inspiration, Massenet's *Werther* – he removes the varnish of sentimentality. It may not always be idiomatic but, with fine singing from most of the principals, it is a refreshing version.

Dame Kiri, more than you might expect, makes a light and innocent-sounding Marguerite, with the *Jewel song* made to sparkle in youthful eagerness leaping off from a perfect trill. Evgeni Nesterenko as Mephistopheles is a fine, saturnine tempter; Andreas Schmidt as Valentin sings cleanly and tastefully in a rather German way; while Pamela Coburn as Siebel is sweet and boyish. The big snag is the Faust of Francisco Araiza, a disappointing hero with the voice, as recorded, gritty in tone and frequently strained. He underlines the simple melody of *Salut, demeure*, for example, far too heavily, not helped by a syrupy violin solo. The sound is first rate, with the voices cleanly focused and well balanced against the orchestra, giving a fine sense of presence.

Though Prêtre working with a French orchestra has claims to a more idiomatic approach than most of his current rivals, the playing is relatively coarse and lacking in intensity. Among the soloists Plácido Domingo produces golden tone, rich and heroic, even if the characterization is rather anonymous. Thomas Allen makes an outstanding Valentin, both firm and imaginative, but Mirella Freni too often sounds strained, and Nicolai Ghiaurov is less rich and resonant than he was in his earlier Decca recording under Richard Bonynge. The 1979 recording is full and warm, and the CD transfer is laid out most conveniently on the three CDs, with very generous banding.

Decca provide a performance of *Faust* with only one Frenchman in the cast (Robert Massard as Valentin); in the event, it is not surprising if the flavour is only intermittently authentic. Richard Bonynge's conducting is fresh and stylish – the most consistently successful contribution – but much of the singing, including Sutherland's, falls short. It goes without saying that the heroine produces some exquisite sounds, but too often she indulges in her 'mooning' style, so that *Le Roi de Thule* provokes unclean attack all through, and ends with a disagreeable last phrase on *Et doucement*. Corelli's faults are more than those of style, and his French is excruciating. Ghiaurov also hardly sounds at home in the music. But when Gounod's aim is clear, then all the singers' efforts click into place, and the final trio is wonderfully rousing. There is also a memorable contribution from Monica Sinclair as Martha. The text is more complete than that in most versions and the quality of the sound is of Decca's best.

The Erato set is one of the disappointments in their normally excellent 'Affordable Opera' series, and it is not one of Alain Lombard's successes as an opera conductor. The unatmospheric recording and singing (either unstylish or dull) do not help. Caballé is the chief offender, plainly seeing herself as a prima donna whose vagaries and self-indulgences have to be wooed. Aragall produces some beautiful sounds, but he does not seem completely happy in French, and Paul Plishka lacks flair and devilry as Mephistopheles.

Faust: highlights.
(M) ** EMI CDM7 63090-2; *EG 763090-4* (from above recording with Domingo, Freni, Ghiaurov; cond. Prêtre).

With the reappearance of the De los Angeles/Gedda/Christoff set at mid-price, there seems little point in recommending highlights from the much less recommendable Prêtre set, except perhaps to Domingo admirers, for his contribution is vocally superb, even if the characterization is not especially individual. The late-1970s recording sounds well.

Roméo et Juliette (complete).
Withdrawn: *** EMI Dig. CDS7 47365-8 (3) [Ang. CDCC 47365]. Midi-Pyrénées Regional Ch., Capitole Toulouse Ch. and O, Plasson.
  Roméo (Alfredo Kraus), Juliette (Catherine Malfitano)

Although Gounod's *Roméo et Juliette* follows the outline of Shakespeare's plot, it has its own minor variants. The opening scene is of a masked ball in the palace of the Capulets. Count Paris is engaged to Juliet Capulet, but appearing at the ball, their identities concealed, are Romeo, Mercutio and Benvolio and their followers from the house of Montague.

Gertrude, Juliet's nurse, is called away and Romeo takes his opportunity to approach Juliet, and in a moment they are entranced with each other. When Romeo removes his mask, Tybalt realizes that he is the scion of the house of Montague, sworn enemies of the Capulets. Full of hospitality, Count Capulet orders that peace shall be sustained.

Later, Juliet is on her balcony; Romeo appears below and they declare their love with great ardour. They go to Friar Lawrence who marries them secretly in his cell, hoping the union will unite the two warring households. But a quarrel develops between Mercutio and Tybalt; they fight; Mercutio is slain and Romeo, avenging his death, kills Tybalt. The Duke of Verona banishes Romeo, who then seeks Juliet in her room. When morning comes, he departs.

Friar Lawrence has not revealed the news of Juliet's marriage to Romeo and her father begins the arrangements for her wedding with Count Paris. He instructs the friar to tell Juliet of the wedding plans. Instead, the friar gives Juliet a potion after swallowing which she will appear to be dead for several hours.

A ball is once more in progress at the palace. Juliet drinks the potion and falls unconscious. Romeo hears that Juliet is dead. He returns from exile, enters her tomb and in despair turns his dagger on himself. Juliet, recovering from the effects of the potion, plunges his dagger into her own breast.

The Plasson set, well sung and vividly recorded, makes an excellent choice for an opera that has been unlucky on record. Kraus may no longer be youthful-sounding in the role of Roméo, but the range and finesse of expression are captivating, while Malfitano proves a delectably sweet and girlish Juliette. Excellent contributions too from Gino Quilico and José van Dam, beautifully set against ripely sympathetic playing from the Capitole orchestra, and atmospherically recorded. Plasson's setting of scenes is most persuasive, whether in the love music or the big ensembles. The fairly resonant recording has produced improved focus and firmer outlines than on the original LPs, and there is slightly greater body to the sound. The documentation and cueing are good, although track 5 of the second disc includes more music than the booklet suggests.

Grieg, Edvard (1843–1907)

VOCAL MUSIC

(i) *Bergliot, Op. 42;* (ii) *Den Bergtekne (The mountain spell), Op. 32;* (iii; iv) *Foran sydens kloster (Before a Southern Convent);* (ii; iii) *7 Songs with orchestra: Den første møde; Solveigs sang; Solveigs vuggesang; Fra Monte Pincio; En svane; Våren; Hnerik Wegeland.*
*** DG Dig. 437 519-2 [id.]. (i) Rut Tellefsen; (ii) Håkan Hagegård; (iii; iv) Barbara Bonney; (iii) Randi Stene, Gothenburg SO, Neeme Järvi.

As can be seen below, *Peer Gynt* was essentially a play with music, not much of it vocal, and the nearest that Grieg came to writing a full opera was *Olav Trygvason*. But the melodrama, *Bergliot*, has a certain interest in any survey of dramatic word-setting, especially as neither the cantata, *Foran sydens kloster* ('Before a southern convent'), nor *Bergliot*, both to words of Bjørnstjerne Bjørnson, are hardly mainstream repertoire. Nor is *Den bergtekne* ('The Mountain Spell'), for baritone, two horns and strings, the simple reason that performances and records are very rare.

All three works arrive on a Gothenburg record, together with seven songs with orchestra, sung by Barbara Bonney and Håkan Hagegård. *Before a Southern Convent* dates from 1871, three years after the *Piano Concerto*, and was dedicated to Liszt. *Before a Southern Convent* is also based on a Bjørnson poem which tells how Ingigerd, the daughter of a chieftain, has seen her father murdered by the villainous brigand, Arnljot. He was on the verge of raping her but relented and let her go. In spite of what she has suffered, she feels a certain attraction for Arnljot and now seeks expiation by entering a foreign convent.

The piece is in dialogue form. When she is questioned, she speaks openly to the nuns of her feelings of guilt, and the piece ends with a chorus of nuns who admit her to their number. While not great Grieg, it has a lot going for it; it is well worth investigating, very naturally balanced with plenty of air round the sound. The singers are well placed and not right on top of you. Generally speaking, the quality on all these DG recordings is excellent – which is not surprising, as they're made by the same Gothenburg team that have recorded for the BIS label.

(i) *Landkjenning (Land-sighting), Op. 31;* (i; ii) *Olav Trygvason, Op. 50; Peer Gynt Suites Nos. 1 & 2.*
*** DG Dig. 437 523-2 [id.).(i) Anne Gjevang; (ii) Randi Stene; (i; ii) Håkan Hagegård; Gothenburg SO, Neeme Järvi.

The great enthusiasm which greeted *Before a Southern Convent* prompted Bjørnson to plan an opera, *Olav Trygvason*. *Landtjenning* ('Land-sighting') and the three scenes that survive from the opera are here coupled together with the two *Peer Gynt* suites. Set in the tenth century, Bjørnson's poem tells of Olav Trygvason, the first king to convert Norway to Christianity. The three tableaux that survive come closer to being a cantata than an opera.

The first is set in a pagan temple near Trondheim, where an anxious throng is awaiting the arrival of the evil Olav, herald of the new faith. In the second a priestess appears; she utters sinister incantations and chants magic formulae, casting runic characters into the holy fire. The priestess is sung by Anne Gjevang, the Erda in the Haitink *Ring* on EMI; some may find her vibrato a bit excessive. The other soloists, Randi Stene and Håkan Hagegård, acquit themselves well, as does the Gothenberg Orchestra and Chorus under Neeme Järvi. The *Peer Gynt* suites are not new, though two of the numbers have been re-recorded. Recommended.

Peer Gynt (incidental music), *Op. 23* (complete).
(M) *** Unicorn UKCD 2003/4 [id.]. Toril Carlsen, Vessa Hanssen, Kåre Bjørkøy, Asbjørn Hansli, Oslo PO Ch., LSO, Dreier.

Peer Gynt (incidental music), *Op. 23* (complete); *Sigurd Jorsalfar* (incidental music), *Op. 56* (complete).
*** DG Dig. 423 079-2 (2) [id.]. Barbara Bonney, Marianne Eklöf, Urban Malmberg, Carl Gustaf Holmgren; Kjell Magnus Sandve, Foss, Maurstad, Stokke (speakers); Gösta Ohlin's Vocal Ens., Pro Musica Chamber Ch., Gothenburg SO, Järvi.

Peer Gynt is, of course, a play with extensive incidental music and no single performance included everything Grieg composed. The story follows Peer, not the most attractive of heroes, from youth into old age, and perhaps into the next world, for the closing scenes are ambiguous.

He begins by leaving his widowed mother, Aase, at the worst possible moment – harvest time – and he elopes with Ingrid, just as she is about to marry someone else. He soon leaves her abandoned, for he has also discovered the lovely Solveig, who is to be the enduring love of his life.

Next, with his overflowing libido, Peer meets and seduces three mountain girls (who are very willing) and a green woman who, he soon discovers, is the Mountain King's daughter. As she becomes pregnant, he is expected to marry her, but he escapes from the kingdom of the Trolls, meeting a strange creature called the Boyg on the way, perhaps his own id. He now revisits Aase, who is dying, and he gently kisses her farewell.

Travelling through foreign lands, he trades in African slaves and Chinese artefacts. He lives in Africa and Arabia, where he is mistaken for a prophet (the famous *Morning* represents dawn in the North African desert). It is in the Arab lands that he meets the seductive Anitra, and she is the one woman who comes out on top, for she leaves with his horse and nearly all his possessions. He then returns to Solveig.

But Peer is still restless and many other experiences follow, including a visit to a lunatic asylum; after a shipwreck, he finally returns to Norway in a small boat. He is the only survivor, for he cruelly lets his companion, the cook, drown in the sea. Re-encountering Solveig, he hears her singing but cannot face her. Now he finds himself on a desolate moor at night-time and the ghost of Aase reproaches him. So does a strange maker of buttons, who unflatteringly suggests that Peer's character is flawed and (like nearly all men) that he is irresponsible rather than evil. For the first time Peer faces despair, yet his irrepressible libido recovers, and in the final scene even Solveig forgives him when she gently takes him in her arms, as a mother would a child, and the Pentecost hymn is heard in the distance.

Neeme Järvi's well-documented set comes as close as possible to Grieg's declared wishes and is also closer to the original than its competitor in including spoken dialogue, as one would have expected in the theatre. The set has the additional advantage of the complete *Sigurd Jorsalfar* score, which includes some splendid music. The performances by actors, singers (solo and choral) and orchestra alike are exceptionally vivid, with the warm Gothenberg ambience used to creative effect. The vibrant histrionics of the spoken words undoubtedly add to the drama; indeed there is an added dimension here, for the perspective of the recording has striking depth as well as breadth (the choral sounds are particularly lovely). These CDs are undoubtedly in the demonstration class.

Those who prefer not to have the Norwegian spoken dialogue can rest content with the excellent Unicorn analogue set from the end of the 1970s, which sounds admirably fresh in its CD format, the sound untampered with in the transfer. Per Dreier achieves very spirited results from his soloists, the Oslo Philharmonic Chorus and our own LSO, with some especially beautiful playing from the woodwind; the recording is generally first class, with a natural perspective between soloists, chorus and orchestra. The Unicorn set (without *Sigurd Jorsalfar*) may be thought less generous, but it includes 32 numbers in all, including Robert Henrique's scoring of the *Three Norwegian Dances*. Whichever version one chooses, this music, whether familiar or unfamiliar, continues to astonish by its freshness and inexhaustibility.

Peer Gynt: extended excerpts.
*** DG Dig. 427 325-2; [id.]. Barbara Bonney, Marianne Eklöf, Urban Malmberg, Maurstad, Foss, Gothenburg Ch. & SO, Järvi.
*** Decca Dig. 425 448-2 [id.]. Urban Malmberg, Mari Anne Häggander, San Francisco Ch. & SO, Blomstedt.
(M) *** Sony Dig. MK 44528 [id.]. Barbara Hendricks, Oslo PO, Salonen.

(i) *Peer Gynt:* extended excerpts; *Overture In Autumn, Op. 11; Symphonic dance No. 2; Variations on an old Norwegian folksong.*
(M) *** EMI CDM7 64751-2 [id.]. (i) Ilse Hollweg, Beecham Ch. Soc.; RPO, Beecham.

All the single-disc compilations from *Peer Gynt* rest under the shadow of Beecham's, which is not ideal as a recording (the choral contribution lacks polish and is rather too forwardly balanced) but which offers moments of magical delicacy in the orchestral playing. Beecham showed a very special feeling for this score, and to hear *Morning*, the gently textured *Anitra's dance* or the eloquent portrayal of the *Death of Aase* under his baton is a uniquely rewarding experience. Ilse Hollweg too is an excellent soloist.

The recording dates from 1957 and, like most other Beecham reissues, has been enhanced by the remastering process. The orchestral sound is full and warm, and if the choral image remains too robust, the fierceness has been tamed. In short this is not to be missed, particularly at mid-price. The most delectable of the *Symphonic Dances*, very beautifully played, makes an ideal encore after *Solveig's lullaby*, affectingly sung by Hollweg. The *Overture In Autumn*, not one of Grieg's finest works, is most enjoyable when Sir Thomas is so affectionately persuasive, and the attractive *Variations on an old Norwegian folksong* has been generously added. Again the recording is made to seem more expansive than in its old LP format, with a firmer bass, and glowing colour from the woodwind and horns.

Neeme Järvi's disc offers more than two-thirds of the 1875 score, and the performance has special claims on the collector who wants one CD rather than two (half the second CD of the set is taken up by *Sigurd Jorsalfar*).

Decca's set of excerpts makes a useful alternative to the Järvi disc. All but about 15 minutes of the complete score is here and the spoken text is included too, all admirably performed. Perhaps the Gothenburg acoustic is to be preferred to the Davies Hall, San Francisco, and there is a marginally greater sense of theatre in the Swedish account. However, there is really not much to choose between them, and the Decca recording approaches the demonstration class.

Salonen's selection is generous too, offering some 17 numbers: all those included in the suites plus one or two more than have previously been included in single-disc highlights. Anyone investing in this version with Barbara Hendricks and the Oslo Philharmonic is unlikely to be disappointed. Salonen has a good feeling for this repertoire and he draws sensitive playing from his Norwegian forces and receives well-detailed recording.

(i) *Sigurd Jorsalfar, Op. 22:* incidental music; *Funeral march in memory of Rikard Nordraak* (orch. Halvorsen); (i) *Den Bergtekne (The Mountain Spell), Op. 32.*
(M) *** Unicorn UKCD 2019. (i) Kåre Bjørkøy; Oslo Philharmonic Ch., LSO, Per Dreier.

Grieg composed his incidental music for *Sigurd Jorsalfar* (*Sigurd the Crusader*) in 1872 for a production of Björnson's historical drama in Christiania (as Oslo was then known), though neither he nor the dramatist was particularly satisfied with it. The score comprised five movements in all, from which Grieg drew the familiar suite; but there were additional sections as well, most importantly the moving *Funeral march in memory of Nordraak* which is given here in Halvorsen's orchestral transcription. *The Mountain Spell* (or 'thrall', as it is sometimes translated) is somewhat later than *Sigurd Jorsalfar* and was one of Grieg's favourite pieces. It is a song of great beauty, and is alone worth the price of the CD. It is also available on DG at full price – see above. The Oslo Philharmonic Choir give a spirited account of themselves, as do the LSO, who play sensitively for Per Dreier. Kåre Bjørkøy is an excellent soloist with well-focused tone. The recording is very good indeed and the perspective is agreeably natural.

Hába, Alois (1893–1973)

Mother (complete).
Sup. 10 8258-2 (2) [id.]. Prague Nat. Theatre Ch. & O, Jiří Jirouš.
    Křen (Oldřich Spisar), Maruša (Vlasta Urbanová), Francka (Marcela Lemariová), Nanka (Marta Sandtnerová), Maruša, a daughter (Jana Políková).

The Czech avant-gardist, Alois Hába, the apostle of micro-tones, known to older record-collectors for an item on 78s in the old Columbia History of Music, here offers a full-length opera using quarter-tones. *Mother* was completed in 1929. The composer drew his scenario from his own native region in Moravia and his libretto details the life of a poor farmer who remarries and whose second wife eventually assumes a dominating role in his life. At the opening, Křen, the farmer, and his sister-in-law stand with the children by the coffin of his first wife, Anča. She has died in childbirth, having been worked rigorously by her husband right up to the time the latest baby was born. The neighbours arrive and echo the problem of having six children without a mother. There is general mourning and Anča is duly buried.

A year later Křen is alone with his children whom he has put to work, just as his wife was hard-driven by the needs of poverty. His brother-in-law arrives and is told that Křen, while travelling round the villages as a folk musician, has found a new bride-to-be. Maruša is nearly thirty but she is pretty and has plenty of common sense. She found the prospect of six children intimidating but agreed to become his wife the following Tuesday.

Křen journeys to fetch his bride, conscious of his own masculine strength, and he longs to press a warm body against his own again. Now the marriage ceremony is over, there is dancing and Maruša tells how she escaped the attentions of the young men from her own village in favour of her new husband. Křen praises her robust beauty, but her misgivings about caring for six children still remain.

Two years now pass, and Maruša laments that, as yet, she has no child of her own, though not for her husband's lack of interest in her body. She has been to see a doctor, who has told her there is no reason why she should not become pregnant, and she blames her husband for not wanting to extend the family. Křen responds sympathetically and puts his arms round her; they go off to bed.

A decade later and Maruša has her coveted baby son, Toneček, and is now visited by his godmother; they wonder what the boy will be when he grows up. The other children discuss the problem of another mouth to feed and the further dilution of any dowry. Křen enters and chases them back out to work. He tries to make love to his wife but she refuses him, slapping his face twice when he persists. He complains, but she is the victor and suckles her infant instead.

The children grumble about the meagre food and their meatless diet; two of the boys decide to leave home after the harvest. Maruša contines her endless chores and caring and wonders if the children will ever appreciate what a mother's love means. But she nurtures them and knows they need her. The following morning their father rouses them early, but again Maruša stands in the way of his bullying.

Ten more years pass, and the family have all left home, except for Maruša's own young son who remains to care for them in their old age. Křen apologizes to his wife for his roughness and insensitivity when a younger man. Both are fairly content with their lot. All the children have gained from the rigours of their childhood: the daughters are married; the boys studied hard; the two who left have successfully emigrated to America; all were nurtured with love. Even the little farm is prospering modestly. All is well.

Well constructed and well written, commendably lyrical, *Mother* can yet be recommended only to devotees of the composer or to listeners who are tone-deaf. The use of quarter-tones, as well as being ugly, has a totally disorientating effect. It is not so much as if everyone was singing and playing out of tune, but rather as if the turntable was rotating eccentrically. When some of the soloists have vibratos that are wider than a quarter-tone, the absurdity of the thesis behind Hába's writing is quickly exposed. Yet this is a bold experiment and, as far as one can tell, the piece is very well performed and certainly well recorded.

Halévy, Jacques Fromental (1799–1862)

La juive: complete.
*** Ph. Dig. 420 190-2 (3). Amb. Op. Ch., Philh. O, Almeida.
> Eléazar (José Carreras), Rachel (Julia Varady), Princess Eudoxia (June Anderson), Cardinal de Brogni (Ferruccio Furlanetto), Prince Léopold (Dalmacio Gonzalez).

La juive ('The Jewess') was the piece which, along with the vast works of Meyerbeer, set the pattern for the epic French opera, so popular in the last century. Eléazar was the last role that the great tenor, Enrico Caruso, tackled, and it was in this opera that he gave his very last performance. Yet it was probably never performed in its entirety on a single night, nor is the Philips recording absolutely complete, even if much more is included here than you will find in the published edition.

The cuts are mainly of crowd scenes, drinking choruses and the like, many of which simply hold up the action. As it is, over three hours of music on three CDs makes an attractive package. There are three great character-roles: not just the tenor role of Eléazar, the Jew, and that of the heroine, Rachel, his adoptive daughter, but also the dark bass role of Cardinal de Brogni, who in this story of the Spanish Inquisition pronounces anathema on these Jewish infidels.

The story begins in the square in the city of Constance in Switzerland. Eléazar, a Jewish goldsmith and jeweller, is hard at work while the *Te Deum* is heard from the cathedral. Léopold, a young general in diguise and going under the name of Samuel, is working for Eléazar and is in love with his daughter, Rachel. The festivity is in honour of the emperor's state visit; he has formed a council aimed at uniting all Christians in a single faith. Ruggiero the provost announces a public holiday.

The goldsmith's work is interrupted as he is dragged out for interrogation with his daughter. He tells his inquisitors that his sons were killed by Christians. Ruggiero says that he too must die, but at that moment Cardinal de Brogni passes by, recognizes Eléazar and prays that Jewish unbelievers should abandon their faith in favour of Christianity.

Léopold (as the workman Samuel and believed to be Jewish) serenades Rachel. The crowd turn on them and Eléazar faces them with courage, but the crowd determines to throw him in the lake. At this point Albert, a sergeant in the army of the emperor, recognizes Samuel as Léopold, and the latter prevails upon the mob to disperse; Rachel is astonished at Samuel's seeming power over the Christians. Later, inside Eléazar's house where the Passover is being celebrated, Rachel notices that Samuel does not eat the unleavened bread and this worries her.

A knock at the door causes a sudden dispersal of the assembled company and ritual glasses are hastily hidden. Eléazar asks Léopold to remain. Princess Eudoxia enters and asks Eléazar for a gold chain which had once belonged to the Emperor Constantine; she wishes to give it to her husband, Léopold, whom she expects to return soon from the Hussite wars. She orders that the chain be brought to the palace the next day. Léopold still does not reveal his identity but is ashamed of his deception.

The princess departs and the returning Rachel asks 'Samuel' how he was able to control the crowd. He confesses he is a Christian but tells her of his love. Eléazar then enters and angrily discovers that Léopold is a Christian, but at Rachel's pleading he agrees to their betrothal. Léopold, however, states that he cannot marry her.

In the emperor's garden, when Eléazar and Rachel bring the chain to Eudoxia she places it round the neck of Léopold, her husband. Rachel snatches it off and declares that he has committed the crime of consorting with herself, a Jewess.

All three, Eléazar, Rachel and Léopold, are condemned to death, but Eudoxia, still loving her husband, begs Rachel to retract her damning statements and she does so out of charity. Cardinal de Brogni pleads with both father and daughter to renounce their faith and adopt Christianity.

Eléazar then reminds de Brogni that when the cardinal's house was ablaze, all perished except a daughter who was rescued from the flames by a Jew. He refuses to name her whereabouts and will die with his secret. Léopold is banished and Eléazar, himself condemned and torn with doubts and hatred towards the Christians, watching Rachel go to her death, begs her to become a Christian and save herself.

Firmly refusing, she is thrown into a flaming cauldron and Eléazar cries to the vengeful Cardinal de Brogni, 'Your daughter died in those flames.' The final scene vies with that of *Il Trovatore* in its melodrama.

The greater part of the recording was completed in 1986, but that was just at the time when José Carreras was diagnosed as having leukaemia. The recording was made without him, and it was only in 1989 that he contributed his performance through 'overdubbing'. It is a tribute to the Philips engineers that the results rarely if ever betray that deception, sounding naturally balanced even when Carreras is contributing to the many complex ensembles. He sings astonishingly well, but the role of the old Jewish father really needs a weightier, darker voice, such as Caruso had in his last years. Julia Varady as Rachel makes that role both the emotional and the musical centre of the opera, responding both tenderly and positively.

In the other soprano role, that of Princess Eudoxia, June Anderson is not so full or sweet in tone, but she is particularly impressive in the dramatic coloratura passages, such as her Act III *Boléro*. Ferruccio Furlanetto makes a splendidly resonant Cardinal in his two big solos, and the Ambrosian Opera Chorus brings comparable bite to the powerful ensembles. Antonio de Almeida as conductor proves a dedicated advocate. Halévy is more lyrical in his writing than his contemporary, Meyerbeer, writing melodies that almost – but not quite – stick in the mind. As a massive music-drama, this is at least as impressive and moving as anything Meyerbeer wrote. As a recording, it is a formidable achievement.

Handel, George Frideric (1685–1759)

In surveying the music of Handel, it would seem perverse to omit those oratorios which are based on biblical drama. Handel, willing impresario as well as composer, turned to writing oratorio in English in order to meet the demands of an eager public that required the interplay of characters to be readily understandable in their own tongue, when the convention of the time required that opera be sung in Italian. Handel's masques spring from a tradition carried over from Purcell's time, while many of the cantatas are operatic in feeling.

Aci, Galatea e Polifemo (masque/opera).
*** HM Dig. HMC 90 1253/4; *HMC 40 1253/4* [id.]. L. Bar., Medlam (with: *Recorder sonatas in F; C & G* (trans. to *F*) – Michel Piquet, John Toll).
  Aci (Emma Kirkby), Galatea (Carolyn Watkinson), Polifemo (David Thomas).

Handel first set the mythological tale of Acis and Galatea in a format which he described as a 'Serenata a tre', and it was premièred in Naples in 1708. *Aci, Galatea e Polifemo* proves to be quite a different work from the always popular English masque, *Acis and Galatea*, with only one item even partially borrowed. In effect it is a one-Act opera, full of delightful brief numbers, far more flexible in scale and layout than later full-scale Italian operas. The participants are in many ways more fully characterized than in the later, more famous version.

Polifemo, the monster/villain, has a much bigger – indeed, more serious – part to play. Aci, a shepherd, and Galatea, a sea nymph, are first shown together, blissfully sharing their idyllic love, but Galatea expresses foreboding at the furious, revengeful Polifemo: 'He keeps for me his poisoned lips.'

Aci is bravely protective of his beloved but Polifemo sends a great rock bouncing down which crushes him to death. Galatea then resourcefully changes her dead lover into a river so that he can flow down to the ocean, she can join him and he can embrace her. It is Polifemo who relates the final scene, clearly realizing his own ugliness and inadequacies and moved by Galatea's loving constancy.

Charles Medlam directs London Baroque in a beautifully sprung performance with three excellent soloists, the brightly characterful Emma Kirkby as Aci, Carolyn Watkinson in the lower-pitched role of Galatea (often – a little confusingly – sounding like a male alto), and David Thomas coping manfully with the impossibly wide range of Polifemo's part. The three recorder sonatas are comparably delightful, a welcome makeweight. Excellent sound, full of presence.

Acis and Galatea (masque).
*** DG 423 406-2 (2) [id.]. E. Bar. Soloists, Gardiner.
    Acis (Anthony Rolfe Johnson), Galatea (Norma Burrowes), Damon (Martyn Hill), Polyphemus (Willard White).

(i) *Acis and Galatea;* (ii) *Cantata: Look down, harmonious saint.*
*** Hyp. Dig. CDA 66361/2; *KA 66361/2.* (ii) Ainsley; King's Cons., Robert King.
    (i) Acis (John Mark Ainsley), Galatea (Claron McFadden), Damon (Rogers Covey-Crump), Polyphemus (Michael George).
(M) *** Decca 436 227-2 (2) [id.]. St Anthony Singers, L. Philomusica, Boult (with Arias: *Alcina: Tornami a vagheggiar; Ah! Ruggiero crudel . . . Ombre pallide.* BONONCINI: *Giselda: Per la gloria.* PAISIELLO: *Nel cor più non mi sento.* PICCINI: *La buona figliuola: Furia di donna.* ARNE: *Love in a village: The traveller benighted. Artaxerxes: The soldier tir'd.* SHIELD: *Rosina: When William at eve; Whilst with village maids; Light as thistledown.* Joan Sutherland, with Philomusica O, Anthony Lewis or Granville Jones).
    Acis (Peter Pears), Galatea (Joan Sutherland), Damon (David Galliver), Polyphemus (Owen Brannigan).

Handel's later masque, *Acis and Galatea*, was one of his most popular works. The story, taken from Dryden's translation of the 13th Book of Ovid's *Metamorphoses*, is here treated more genially than in the composer's earlier version, and Polyphemus almost becomes a pantomime villain. The story remains broadly the same. The opening rural prospect sets a scene of Arcadian delight. Acis and Galatea pine romantically for each other and finally meet joyfully, while Polyphemus looks on lustfully – 'I rage, I melt, I burn' – and describes Galatea appreciatively as 'ruddier than the cherry'. But there is an additional character, Damon, who tries to bring them all down to earth.

He urges the monster to proceed with discretion if he would 'gain the tender beauty' he covets. But the headstrong Acis is ready to meet Polyphemus head on, even though Damon urges caution. After Acis has been crushed by the great boulder, Galatea turns him into a fountain and the deified hero appears within its flowing waters, providing a distinctly upbeat ending.

Robert King directs a bluff, beautifully sprung reading of the masque that brings out its domestic jollity. Using the original version for five solo singers and no chorus, this may be less delicate in its treatment than John Eliot Gardiner's reading of the original version on DG Archiv but, at speeds generally a little faster and with warmer, fuller sound, it is if anything even more winning. The soloists are first rate, with John Mark Ainsley among the most stylish of the younger generation of Handel tenors and the bass, Michael George, characterizing strongly as Polyphemus, yet never at the expense of musical values. Claron McFadden's vibrant soprano is girlishly distinctive. This Hyperion issue scores somewhat on price too and provides a valuable makeweight in the florid solo cantata, thought to be originally conceived as part of *Alexander's Feast*, nimbly sung by Ainsley.

Certain of John Eliot Gardiner's tempi are idiosyncratic (some too fast, some too slow), but the scale of the performance, using original instruments, is beautifully judged, with the vocal soloists banding together for the choruses. The acoustic is rather dry, the balance fairly close, but the soloists are consistently sweet of tone, although the singing is less individually characterful than in some previous versions. Willard White is a fine Polyphemus, but his *O ruddier than the cherry* has not quite the degree of genial gusto that Owen Brannigan brought to it. The authentic sounds of the English Baroque Soloists are finely controlled and the vibrato-less string timbre is clear and clean without being abrasive. A thoroughly rewarding pair of CDs.

In 1959 Boult provided the début stereo recording of Handel's masque. The starry cast obviously relish the high level of Handel's inspiration; Joan Sutherland, in fresh, youthful voice, makes a splendid Galatea, sparkling in the florid passages, warmly sympathetic in the lyrical music. Peter Pears, too, is at his finest and, although David Galliver is less striking, his contribution is still a good one; while Owen Brannigan was surely born to play Polyphemus, who comes over as a very genial one-eyed giant, the villainy muted.

We are given the opportunity to enjoy his splendid account of *O ruddier than the cherry* twice (where he almost makes a virtue of intrusive aspirates) for it is included as an appendix in the alternative version with treble recorder. Anyone hearing it who can resist a smile must be stony-hearted indeed. Although tempi are more relaxed than we would expect today, Boult's sympathetic direction ensures that the music-making has a lift throughout; the recording sounds as vivid as ever.

Although the remastering has brought some thinness to the violins, the voices are given a natural presence. The documentation includes the full text, and the recital used to fill out the second CD is admirably chosen. These recordings were made at the same time as the complete set, when Joan Sutherland was achieving her first international success. Though the full beauty of the voice is not always fully captured, the freshness and clarity are stunning. She went on to record some items again, such as *Light as thistledown*, but these early performances are cherishable.

Agrippina (opera; complete).
*** HM Dig. HMU 907063/5 (3). Capella Savaria, McGegan.
  Agrippina (Sally Bradshaw), Nero (Wendy Hill), Poppea (Lisa Saffer), Claudius (Nicholas Isherwood), Otho (Drew Minter), Pallas (Michael Dean), Narcissus (Ralf Popken), Lesbo (Béla Szilágyi), Juno (Gloria Banditelli).

Though based, like *Giulio Cesare*, on Roman history, *Agrippina* presents a total contrast with that later opera from Handel's full maturity. Written for Venice in 1710, it is delightfully light-hearted, the astonishingly brilliant inspiration of the young Handel. The libretto by Cardinal Grimani avoids the stiffness of most librettos of the period. That plainly encouraged the adventurous young composer to experiment with an even more fluid, less formalized structure than in most of his later operas for London. There is no number quite so striking as the finest in the later masterpieces, but the opera is magnetic in its fanciful telling of the intrigues between the Emperor Claudius, his wife Agrippina, Nero (her son) and Poppea, as well as Otho (Ottone) and Pallas (Pallante).

The setting is Rome, *c.* AD 50. The Emperor Claudius is in Britain and his death is reported. His wife, Agrippina, secures the throne for Nero, her son by an earlier marriage. Her plans are thwarted by the return of Claudius: his life has been saved by Ottone, to whom Claudius has promised the succession as a reward. Agrippina uses Claudius's passion for Poppea, who is also the object of Nero's and Ottone's affections, to turn his mind against Ottone. Ottone is denounced as a traitor but convinces Poppea that he is faithful to her.

Poppea contrives for her three lovers to enter in succession, each hiding as the next arrives. She exposes Nero to Claudius as his rival and Agrippina's machinations are also revealed. The latter skilfully persuades Claudius that she was acting in his best interest; he promises the succession to Ottone and Poppea to Nero. The latter complains that it would be a double punishment to gain a wife and lose an empire. Claudius goes back on his decision, giving Ottone to Poppea and the succession to Nero. Juno descends to bless the nuptials.

Nicholas McGegan is markedly more sympathetic in his European recordings of Handel with the Budapest-based Capella Savaria than in those he has made in California, supported by a less unhelpfully dry acoustic. *Agrippina* was recorded in the studio at the time of the 1991 Göttingen Festival. With a fine bloom on voices and instruments, notably the brass, the performance is exhilaratingly fresh and alert. The cast is first rate, led by the silvery Sally Bradshaw as Agrippina, the bright Nero of Wendy Hill and the seductive Poppea of Lisa Saffer, all well contrasted in their equally stylish ways.

(i) *Alceste* (incidental music); (ii) *Comus* (incidental music).
*** O-L 421 479-2 [id.]. (i) Judith Nelson, Emma Kirkby, Paul Elliott; (i; ii) Margaret Cable, David Thomas; (ii) Patrizia Kwella; AAM, Hogwood.

Commissioned to write incidental music for a play by Smollett, the composer was stopped in his tracks by the abandonment of the whole project. Nevertheless there is much to enjoy in what he wrote for *Alceste*, not just solo items but also some simple tuneful choruses, all introduced by an impressive, dramatic overture in D minor. The incidental music for *Comus* makes equally refreshing listening, intended as it was to be an epilogue for a performance of the Milton masque. Performances of all this music have the freshness and vigour one associates with the Academy under Hogwood at their finest. The sound, too, is first rate.

Alcina (opera; complete).

*** EMI Dig. CDS7 49771-2 (3) [Ang. CDCB 49771]. Opera Stage Ch., City of L. Bar. Sinfonia, Hickox.

Alcina (Arleen Augér), Ruggiero (Della Jones), Bradamante (Kathleen Kuhlmann), Morgana (Eiddwen Harrhy), Oberto (Patrizia Kwella), Oronte (Maldwyn Davies), Melisso (John Tomlinson).

Richard Hickox's superb recording of one of Handel's greatest operas, the text complete, was based on a staged production at the Spitalfields and Cheltenham festivals, later taken to Los Angeles. That stage experience adds dramatic sharpness to what – for all the beauty of individual numbers – can seem a very long sequence of *da capo* arias following a convoluted storyline. The enchantress, Alcina, lives on a magic island with her sister, Morgana, who is loved by General Oronte, commander of Alcina's troops. Alcina, who is somewhat misanthropic, habitually changes her suitors into animal or other forms. As the opera opens, Bradamante, dressed in male attire, posing as her own brother and calling herself Ricciardo, is shipwrecked on the island, accompanied by her guardian, Melisso.

Bradamante is searching for her betrothed, Ruggiero; he has disappeared and is Alcina's latest captive. He is enchanted by Alcina in both senses of the word, and his infatuation, alas, blots out memories of Bradamante.

Morgana complicates matters further by falling in love with Bradamante (as Ricciardo), whom Ruggiero fails to recognize. General Oronte jealously tells Ruggiero that Alcina is attracted to Ricciardo; he warns him also of her habit of changing her prospective lovers into alien forms, but Alcina denies that she is fickle and expresses her passionate love for Ruggiero.

Bradamante and Melisso now vainly try to convince Ruggiero that his supposed rival, Ricciardo, is in fact his betrothed true love. Unheeding of their pleas, Ruggiero asks Alcina to get rid of Ricciardo. Melisso now appears to Ruggiero disguised as his old tutor, chastizes him and convinces him as to the true situation, giving him a magic ring to rid himself of Alcina's spell. It works and he lovingly recognizes Bradamante. To escape from Alcina, he arranges to go hunting.

Meanwhile a young nobleman, Oberto, asks Alcina to help him find his missing father. She agrees but does not tell him that the father is already her captive. General Oronte now informs Alcina that Ruggiero has fled, armed with a magic sword and shield, and he tells Morgana that she too has lost her 'lover', Ricciardo. They fall out, then Morgana begs Oronte to forgive her fickle behaviour.

Alcina, in a subterranean cavern, evokes her gods and the spirits which control her sorcery, but her efforts to regain her power over Ruggiero are of no avail and a chorus is heard foretelling both the union of the true lovers and that they will found a great dynasty. Oberto now pleads with Alcina to release his father.

Treacherously she agrees on condition that he will slay a lion; luckily, he discovers in the nick of time that the lion is his father. Thwarted, Alcina makes one final attempt to part the lovers, but Ruggiero intervenes by smashing the urn which holds the key to Alcina's magic and at once all her ex-suitors, including Oberto's father, are restored to their human shapes and the opera ends with dancing and general rejoicing.

Hickox underlines the contrasts of mood and the speed of events, conveying the full range of emotion. It would be hard to devise a septet of Handelian singers more stylish than the soloists here. Though the American, Arleen Augér, may not have the weight of Joan Sutherland (who in a much-edited text sang the title-role both at Covent Garden and on record), she is just as brilliant and pure-toned, singing warmly in the great expansive arias. Even next to her, Della Jones stands out in the breeches role of Ruggiero, with an extraordinary range of memorable arias, bold as well as tender. Eiddwen Harrhy as Morgana is just as brilliant in the aria, *Tornami a vagheggiar*, usually 'borrowed' by Alcina, while Kathleen Kuhlmann, Patrizia Kwella, Maldwyn Davies and John Tomlinson all sing with a clarity and beauty to make the music sparkle. As for the text, it is even more complete than any known performance ever, when it includes as appendices two charming items that Handel cut even at the première. There are few Handel opera recordings to match this, with warm, spacious sound, recorded at EMI's Abbey Road studio.

(i) *Alcina* (complete); (ii) *Giulio Cesare (Julius Caesar):* highlights.
(M) **(*) Decca 433 723-2 (3) [id.]. (i) LSO; (ii) L. New SO; both cond. Bonynge.

(i) Alcina (Joan Sutherland), Ruggiero (Teresa Berganza), Bradamante (Monica Sinclair), Oronte (Luigi Alva), Morgana (Graziella Sciutti), Oberto (Mirella Freni), Melisso (Ezio Flagello).

(ii) Cleopatra (Joan Sutherland), Cesare (Margreta Elkins), Cornelia (Marilyn Horne), Sesto (Richard Conrad).

Although the 1962 Decca *Alcina* is less complete than the newer EMI set, it is has the advantage of including some 50 minutes of highlights from *Giulio Cesare*, made a year later, which Sutherland did not undertake in a complete version. *Alcina*, however, represents the extreme point of what can be described as Sutherland's dreamy, droopy period. The fast arias are stupendous. Bonynge does not spare her at all, and in the brilliant Act I finale he really does rush her too fast, the result dazzling rather than musically satisfying. But anything slow and reflective, whether in recitative or in aria, has Sutherland mooning about the notes, with no consonants audible at all and practically every vowel reduced to 'aw'.

It is all most beautiful of course, but she could have done so much better. Of the others, Berganza is completely charming in the castrato part of Ruggiero, even if she does not manage trills very well. Monica Sinclair shows everyone up with the strength and forthrightness of her singing. Both Graziella Sciutti and Mirella Freni are delicate and clear in their two smaller parts. Richard Bonynge draws crisp, vigorous playing from the LSO. Only in those rushed showpiece arias for his wife does he sound too inflexible. The 30-year-old Walthamstow recording is vintage Decca, and the CD transfer only hints at its age in the orchestral string sound.

Not surprisingly the *Giulio Cesare* highlights are used as a vehicle for Sutherland, and her florid elaborations of melodies turn da capos into things of delight and wonder. There is some marvellous singing from Marilyn Horne and Monica Sinclair too, and Bonynge conducts with a splendid sense of style. As a sample try *V'adoro pupile* – Cleopatra's seduction aria. Full translations are provided in both works.

Alessandro (opera; complete).
(M) **(*) HM/BMG GD 77110 (3) [77110-2-RG]. La Petite Bande, Kuijken.

Alessandro (René Jacobs), Rossane (Sophie Boulin), Lisaura (Isabelle Poulenard), Clito (Jean Nirouët), Leonato (Stephen Varcoe), Cleone (Guy De Mey).

Sigiswald Kuijken directs his team of period-performance specialists in an urgently refreshing, at times sharply abrasive reading of one of Handel's key operas, the first in which he wrote roles for the rival prima donnas, Faustina and Cuzzoni, not to mention the celebrated castrato, Senesino. The plot is as complicated and extraordinary as in almost any Handel opera, but essentially its message is that invincibility has gone to Alexander's head and he seems to love whichever of the two women in his life he turns to at each particular convolution of the story, inspiring less confidence in his fidelity than in his ability to win battles.

Alexander the Great has had a triumphant Asian campaign, and is the first enemy general ever to invade the city of Sidrach. Suddenly he finds himself in mortal danger but is rescued by his Macedonian supporters, Clitus, Leonatus and Cleon. In the camp, two rival women are both concerned for Alexander's safety, Lisaura, a Scythian princess, and the Persian princess, Roxana, who is a prisoner. Alexander appears to love them both, and has not decided which of them he will choose. Taxiles, the Indian king, arrives with the news that Alexander is safe.

Although both princesses are overjoyed, Taxiles is dismayed: he is himself in love with Lisaura but owes both his throne and his life to Alexander and would not choose to be his rival in love. When Alexander returns, he greets both princesses with ardour, in each case inspiring jealousy in the breast of the other and rage in the heart of Cleon, who also loves Roxana. While he and his friends are in the temple of Jupiter, Alexander encourages his friends to worship him as a deity. Clitus alone refuses; although he honours Alexander as king and for his valour, he will reserve his worship for Jupiter alone. Alexander knocks him down in his anger, but the others finally appease him.

Still trying to win Alexander's heart, Roxana begs him to free her. He fears he may lose her but consents. Leonatus and his followers plot to overthrow Alexander, so great has his arrogance become. As all are assembled, Alexander announces his intention of dividing his conquered territories among them, his supporters. He himself is content with his glory as the son of Jupiter. Clitus once again confronts Alexander, denying his divinity, at which the king is so enraged that he prepares to attack Clitus with a spear.

At this moment the conspirators cause the great canopy over the throne to collapse. No one is injured and Alexander concludes that his divinity has saved his life. He orders Cleon to imprison Cletus. Alexander overhears Roxana weeping. She believes he has been killed. He is moved by her love and decides at last that she is the one for him. Now Leonatus, still conspiring, comes with urgent news, reporting to Alexander that there has been an uprising. Alexander goes off to join his army.

Cleon is guarding Clitus but Leonatus succeeds in freeing him and has Cleon imprisoned instead. The conspirators now plan to defeat Alexander in battle, with loyal Macedonians to support them. Alexander sees Lisaura again and manages to convince her that he must give her up in favour of his great friend, King Taxiles, who loves her dearly. Taxiles is overjoyed. The conspirators have joined all their forces together, but Alexander is supported by Taxiles and his troops, and he defeats them in a brief battle. They all implore him to have mercy and the great Alexander forgives magnanimously.

As a high counter-tenor, René Jacobs copes brilliantly with the taxing Senesino role of Alexander himself. His singing is astonishingly free and agile, if too heavily aspirated. Among the others, Isabelle Poulenard at her best sounds a little like a French Emma Kirkby, though the production is not quite so pure and at times comes over more edgily. The others make a fine, consistent team, the more effective when the recording so vividly conveys a sense of presence with sharply defined directional focus. Even though reissued at mid-price, the set is well documented and with full translation: the printing apparently uses period-style fonts. The three CDs have 70 separate points of access.

Alexander's Feast (oratorio; complete).
*** Collins Dig. 7016-2 (2). Nancy Argenta, Ian Partridge, Michael George, The Sixteen Ch., The Sixteen O, Christophers (with: *Harp concerto, Op. 4/6; Organ concerto, Op. 4/1* – Lawrence-King, Tragicomedia; or Nicholson, The Sixteen O, Christophers).
**(*) Ph. Dig. 422 053-2 (2) [id.]. Carolyn Watkinson, Nigel Robson, Donna Brown, Ashley Stafford, Stephen Varcoe, Monteverdi Ch., E. Bar. Soloists, Gardiner (with *Alexander's Feast concerto grosso*).

Alexander's Feast is Handel's vivid account of a banquet held by Alexander the Great in celebration of the conquest of Persia. Alexander sits with his mistress, Thais, while Timotheus the musician entertains the party by playing the flute and lyre and singing. So powerful is Timotheus' music that, with Thais's co-operation, Alexander is in turn charmed, intoxicated, downcast and made lovesick. At last he is roused to avenge the Greeks slain in earlier battles with Persia by setting alight the Persian capital of Persepolis.

In a reflective conclusion, St Cecilia is credited with bringing a new dimension to music through the invention of the organ, and in the Collins recording the *Organ concerto*, Op. 4/1, is appropriately placed before the final chorus. The *Harp concerto*, Op. 4/4, is used equally appropriately to represent Timotheus' contribution to Alexander's banquet.

Harry Christophers directs a lively, sympathetic account of Handel's extended cantata, very well sung and recorded. The sound effectively sways the balance of advantage between this and Gardiner's Göttingen version on Philips which, recorded live, lacks bloom on the voices. The three soloists – Nancy Argenta, Ian Partridge and Michael George – are all first rate, making a more consistent team than the quintet used by Gardiner. The bass, Michael George, is satisfyingly firm and dark in the two big bass arias, both of them among Handel's greatest, *Bacchus ever bright and fair* and *Revenge, Timotheus cries*. As Christophers also provides two of the related Opus 4 concertos, he omits the *Alexander's Feast concerto grosso* offered by Gardiner.

Gardiner's version of *Alexander's Feast* was recorded live at performances given at the Göttingen Festival. The sound is not distractingly dry, but it is still harder than usual on singers and players alike, taking away some of the bloom. What matters is the characteristic vigour and concentration of Gardiner's performance, which winningly explains how this now neglected piece could, in Handel's lifetime, have been his most frequently performed work after *Messiah* and *Acis and Galatea*. Among the most striking numbers are the two big arias for the bass, both with brilliant brass obbligato: the drinking song *Bacchus ever fair and young* (with two horns) and the Victorian favourite, *Revenge, Timotheus cries* (with trumpet). Stephen Varcoe may lack the dark resonance of a traditional bass, but he projects his voice well. Nigel Robson's tenor suffers more than do the others from the dryness of the acoustic. The soprano, Donna Brown, sings with boyish freshness, and the alto numbers are divided very effectively between Carolyn Watkinson and the soft-grained counter-tenor, Ashley Stafford. The two discs also include the

Concerto grosso in C that was given with the oratorio at its first performance and which still bears its name.

L'allegro, il penseroso, il moderato (oratorio; complete).
*** Erato/Warner 2292 45377-2 (2). Michael Ginn, Patrizia Kwella, Marie McLaughlin, Jennifer Smith, Maldwyn Davies, Martyn Hill, Stephen Varcoe, Monteverdi Ch., E. Bar. Soloists, Gardiner.

Taking Milton as his starting point, Handel illustrated in music the contrasts of mood and character between the cheerful and the thoughtful. Then, prompted by his librettist, Charles Jennens, he added compromise in *Il moderato*, the moderate man. The final chorus may fall a little short of the rest (Jennens's words cannot have provided much inspiration), but otherwise the sequence of brief numbers is a delight, particularly in a performance as exhilarating as this, with excellent soloists, choir and orchestra. The recording is first rate.

Alpestre monte; Mi palpita il cor; Tra le fiamme; Tu fedel? Tu costante? (Italian cantatas).
*** O-L Dig. 414 473-2 [id.]. Emma Kirkby, AAM, Hogwood.

The four cantatas here each have a certain operatic manner of expression. They are all for solo voice with modest instrumental forces, are nicely contrasted, with the personality of the original singer by implication identified with *Tu fedel*, a spirited sequence of little arias rejecting a lover. Even 'a heart full of cares' in *Mi palpita il cor* inspires Handel to a pastorally charming aria, with a delectable oboe obbligato rather than anything weighty, and even those limited cares quickly disperse. Light-hearted and sparkling performances to match.

Amadigi (opera; complete).
*** Erato/Warner Dig. 2292 45490-2 [id.]. Musiciens du Louvre, Minkowski.
Amadigi (Nathalie Stutzmann), Oriana (Jennifer Smith), Melissa (Eiddwen Harrhy), Dardano (Bernarda Fink), Orgando (Pascal Bertin).

Written in 1715, *Amadigi* was the fifth of the Italian operas that Handel wrote for London, following up the success of the first, *Rinaldo*, and rounding off his early period of operatic experimentation. The plot is one of the most convoluted in his operatic output, but its twists and turns are admirably handled (no pun intended) by an inspired score.

The curtain rises to find Amadigi, the hero, and Dardanus, the Prince of Thrace, in the garden of the sorceress, Melissa. They are awaiting nightfall, when they will make their escape. As they are about to depart, Dardanus discovers that Amadigi is in love with Princess Oriana, whom Dardanus himself also secretly loves. Before they can escape, Melissa enters. She hopes to win the heart of Amadigi with her caresses, but when he resists she threatens him.

Amadigi and Dardanus must now rescue Oriana, imprisoned by the sorceress in a tower protected by flames. Only Amadigi succeeds in passing through the fire, while Dardanus calls to Melissa for help, ever jealous that Amadigi may win the love of Oriana. Oriana is freed from her enchantment by Amadigi's rescue, and the two are reunited in the presence of a great company of enchanted knights and ladies. The lovers declare their enduring love and fidelity but, before they can escape together, the vengeful Melissa enters and sends her furies to detain Amadigi and take Oriana to Dardanus.

In Act II, Amadigi visits the Fountain of True Love in Melissa's palace garden. Desperate for reassurance that Oriana is faithful to him, he asks the fountain to reveal the truth but, deceived by Melissa's magic, he has a false vision of Oriana in the arms of Dardanus, and faints. Melissa calls for Oriana to appear, then arouses Amadigi, whereupon he reproaches her for her faithlessness. She protests bitterly and leaves, saying he'll regret having offended her. In despair, Amadigi now attempts to kill himself, but Melissa intervenes.

Amadigi continues to resist the sorceress's approaches. She changes the scene to a place of horror, a cave of monsters and furies, to torment him, but the hero is undaunted. Meanwhile Dardanus is dismayed that Oriana continues to flee from him. Melissa encourages him and changes his form so that he appears to be Amadigi. What does it matter, she asks, if he feels loved again, that it is through deceit? Oriana is taken in by the deception and forgives and declares her love again.

However, at this moment Amadigi himself appears and, although he doesn't see his rival, Dardanus has spotted him, and follows him in a passion, determined on murder. But in the ensuing fight Amadigi is victorious and Oriana is left to wonder what is happening, when Melissa returns to report the death of Dardanus at the hand of Amadigi. Melissa, still determined to have Amadigi for herself, threatens Oriana anew, but the latter scorns her now and says she no longer fears her powers, so strong and confident is she in her love.

In the final Act, Melissa, still hoping to win Amadigi, has Oriana brought forth with devils and threatens her with death. It doesn't work. Oriana says she'll be happy to die for her love; it will only heighten her passion. The sorceress then brings the two together in chains. They each beg that the other be spared, and the desperate Melissa, her thoughts only on vengeance, calls on the shade of Dardanus to come to aid in her revenge. Dardanus's ghost, however, brings her the dismal news that the gods are now protecting these faithful lovers.

Melissa's powers are at an end. As she attempts to dispatch Oriana, she finds herself prevented by a divine force and, condemning herself as most unfortunate, stabs herself and dies. Unhappy Melissa, says Amadigi. The scene changes to a palace of great beauty and the enchanter Orgando, uncle to Oriana, arrives to announce the end of the lovers' torment and a happy wedding. Shepherds and shepherdesses dance, Oriana and Amadigi swear their eternal love, and a chorus sings 'Rejoice, O loving hearts'.

Much of the opera's initial success was owed to the lavishness (by the standards of the time) of the staging but, perhaps surprisingly, it involves only five high voices, with no tenor or bass among the soloists, but that hardly limits the variety or vigour of Handel's inspiration. Handel provides some of his most brilliant arias, for Prince Dardano of Thrace in particular, superbly sung by Bernarda Fink. Nathalie Stutzmann sings Amadigi's gentle arias most affectingly, notably the lovely *Sussurate, onde vezzose*, and the two women characters, Amadigi's lover, Melissa and Princess Oriana, are well taken by Eiddwen Harrhy and Jennifer Smith. As in his splendid recording of Charpentier's music for *Le malade imaginaire*, Marc Minkowski directs an electrifying performance, which is given greater impact by the closeness of the recording. That also brings an abrasiveness to the period strings, but not disagreeably so; rather, the impression is of a performance on an intimate scale, and the more involving for that.

Aminta e Fillide (cantata).
*** Hyp. CDA 66118 [id.]. Gillian Fisher, Patrizia Kwella, L. Handel O, Darlow.

In writing for two voices and strings, Handel presents a simple encounter in the pastoral tradition over a span of ten brief arias which, together with recitatives and final duet, last almost an hour. The music is as charming and undemanding for the listener as it is taxing for the soloists. This lively performance, beautifully recorded with two nicely contrasted singers, delightfully blows the cobwebs off a Handel work till now totally neglected.

Apollo e Dafne (cantata).
**(*) HM HMC 90 5157 [id.]. Judith Nelson, David Thomas; Hayes, San Francisco Bar. O, McGegan.

Apollo e Dafne is one of Handel's most delightful cantatas, with at least two strikingly memorable numbers: a lovely siciliano for Dafne with oboe obbligato and an aria for Apollo, *Come rosa in su la spina*, with unison violins and a solo cello. Both soloists are first rate, and Nicholas McGegan is a lively Handelian, though the playing of the orchestra could be more polished and the sound more firmly focused.

Atalanta (opera; complete).
*** Hung. Dig. HCD 12612/4 [id.]. Savaria Vocal Ens. and Capella, McGegan.
   Atalanta (Katalin Farkas), Meleagro (Eva Bartfai-Barta), Irene (Eva Lax), Aminta (János Bándi), Nicandro (József Gregor), Mercury (László Polgár).

It is welcome to find Hungary producing – with the help of a British conductor and continuo-player, Nicholas McGegan – so stylish an authentic performance of a Handel opera on period instruments. The fresh precision of the string playing of the Capella Savaria demonstrates – even without the help of vibrato – what Hungarian string quartets have been proving for generations, a super-fine ability to match and blend. Though it is odd that a then-Communist country should have lighted on an opera expressly written to celebrate a royal occasion (the wedding of Frederick, Prince of Wales, whose long-standing animosity towards Handel promptly evaporated), it proves an excellent choice, crammed with dozens of sparkling light-hearted numbers to match a plot which continually changes, with miscommunications galore. There is no lapse in the inspiration, the very opposite of weighty Handel. The story goes as follows.

King Meleagro of Aetolia is living a carefree life in the guise of a shepherd, Tirsi. As the opera begins, he is looking for Atalanta, whom he loves. He meets Aminta, another shepherd, and each complains of his lover's cruelty. Irene, Aminta's beloved, enters and chastizes him bitterly, doubting his love. Aminta swears that he will go away and die if it will please her, but even in death he'll remain faithful to his love. In fact, Irene soon confesses to her father, Nicandro, that she does love Aminta but she wants to test his love for her before they are married. Her father warns her not to be too cruel to one who seems so sincere in asking for her love. On her own, Irene suggests that, like a turtle-dove, her lover will have to yearn, wait and suffer, before his day of joy arrives!

Atalanta appears. She is really the Princess of Arcadia, but is posing as a shepherdess, Amarilli. All are preparing to go hunting and Meleagro would like to stay near Atalanta to protect her, but she urges him away, even while confessing to herself that she does love him. Aminta enters and is quite ready to throw himself in front of an approaching wild boar to prove his love for Irene, but he is held back by the other shepherds, and Atalanta wounds the boar with her spear (Meleagro, having missed, greatly admires Atalanta's skill and hopes her heart is as tender as her arms are strong). On his own, Meleagro has fears and doubts but also hopes, through the constancy of his love, that Atalanta will find him the object of her own.

While nymphs and shepherds are celebrating, Atalanta is brooding over her love for Meleagro. Meleagro overhears her and is overwhelmed to discover that Atalanta is herself in disguise and dares not show her feelings for Tirsi because she thinks he is a shepherd. He wishes to tell her that he is in fact a king, but both he and Atalanta are unable to speak directly, about either their love or their status. Consequently it is not clear that there are no obstacles to their love. Atalanta leaves and Irene enters, pretending to love Meleagro as a further torment to Aminta. Meleagro promises to love her if she will take a ribbon to Atalanta, and she volunteers to speak to Atalanta on his behalf.

Once she has gone, Meleagro confesses that he cares for Irene only in as much as she helps him to win Atalanta's heart. Meanwhile Irene pretends that Meleagro has given her the ribbon and allows Aminta to see her kissing it. Aminta emerges, dying of jealousy. Irene tells him he'll just have to get over it, and she leaves. Atalanta shows up and asks Aminta to help her by taking an arrow to her love but without saying it has come from her.

Aminta would have Atalanta deliver his bitter reproaches to Irene, but changes his mind as hope softens his heart again. He departs and Meleagro returns to try to talk to Atalanta, but she rejects him. Meleagro now knows his lover's secret, so he departs not unhappily, proclaiming his love. Atalanta, now alone, is sad that she must feign coldness when she feels such love.

A change of scene, and Irene now presents Atalanta with Meleagro's ribbon. Delighted but hesitant, she tells Irene that Meleagro may discover the secrets of her heart from Aminta. Irene goes to find Aminta and discovers him with Atalanta's arrow, intended for Meleagro, but useful now to incite a bit of jealousy in Irene's teasing breast.

Irene is frantic that she might lose her Aminta to Atalanta as a result of all her contrivances and begins to retrace her steps. When Meleagro appears, she hurriedly confesses that she only feigned love for him to torture her adored Aminta, but Meleagro, believing that Atalanta has now given her heart to Aminta, falls down in despair and sleeps.

Atalanta comes along. She is examining the ribbon and remarks that it looks like the one her father gave to King Meleagro. She notices the sleeping Meleagro, who is tossing with anxiety, and prays that he may have some peace. Meleagro awakens, and Atalanta is no longer able to contain her feelings. She confesses her love and the happy pair embrace at last. Along comes Nicandro with Irene and Aminta, who have by now admitted their mutual passion. Nicandro reveals the true identities of the royal pair, who exclaim that fate has bound them as securely as their love. Mercury now descends on a cloud, accompanied by the Graces and many small Cupids, to give Jupiter's blessing to the marriage of these earthly beings. All glorify the young couple, while bonfires and cries of jubilation mark the celebration and the end of the opera.

Led by the bright-toned Katalin Farkas in the name-part, the singers cope stylishly, and the absence of Slavonic wobbles confirms the subtle difference of Magyar voices; József Gregor with his firm, dark bass is just as much in style, for example, as he regularly is in Verdi. First-rate recording.

Athalia (oratorio; complete).
*** O-L Dig. 417 126-2 (2) [id.]. New College, Oxford, Ch., AAM, Hogwood.
    Athalia (Joan Sutherland), Josabeth (Emma Kirkby), Joad (James Bowman), Joas (Aled Jones).

Athalia was Handel's third English oratorio, completed in 1733, and, although not written for a London theatre, it was given at Covent Garden five times in 1735. With a libretto by Samuel

Humphreys, based on Racine's play, *Athalie*, the oratorio opens with the worship of Jehovah at a Jewish festival by the high priest, Joad, and his wife, Josabeth.

We now meet the queen, Athalia, who – in a symbolic dream – is first warned by her mother, Jezebel; then a young boy appears and plunges a dagger into Athalia's breast. She awakens in terror and a search is instituted for the boy. Meanwhile Joad and Josabeth decide to tell the people that the boy they have brought up is Joas, the rightful heir to the throne. Joad seeks and receives a promise of allegiance to the true king from Abner, captain of the Jewish army. Athalia approaches and asks the boy's identity and is told he is Eliakim, an orphan.

The young Joas does not know his real identity but he refuses to go with the queen as she is a disciple of Baal. Joad now foretells the downfall and death of the queen, and Joas declares that, if he were a king, David would be his model. He is duly enthroned and Athalia is denounced by Abner, and all give praise to Jehovah.

As Queen Athalia, an apostate Baal-worshipper who comes to no good, Dame Joan Sutherland sings boldly with a richness and vibrancy to contrast superbly with the pure silver of Emma Kirkby, not to mention the celestial treble of Aled Jones, in the role of the boy-king, Joas. That casting is perfectly designed to set the Queen aptly apart from the good Israelite characters led by the priest, Joad (James Bowman in a castrato role), and Josabeth (Kirkby). Kirkby's jewelled ornamentation is brilliant too, and Aled Jones's singing – despite a few moments of caution – is ethereally beautiful, if only a little more remarkable than that of the three trebles from the Christ Church choir who sing the little trios for Three Virgins at the end of Act II. Christopher Hogwood with the Academy brings out the speed and variety of the score that has been described as Handel's first great English oratorio. The recording is bright and clean, giving sharp focus to voices and instruments alike.

Belshazzar (oratorio; complete).
*** DG Dig. 431 793-2 (3) [id.]. E. Concert Ch. & O, Pinnock.

Belshazzar (Anthony Rolfe Johnson), Nitocris (Arleen Augér), King Cyrus (Catherine Robbin), Daniel (James Bowman).

After Walton, any musical treatment of the ominous writing on the wall is bound to seem tame, but Handel's oratorio, written two years after *Messiah* with the *Messiah*'s librettist, Charles Jennens, supplying the words, contains rich inspirations. Handel modified the work over the years, and Pinnock has opted, not for the earliest, but for the most striking and fully developed text.

Daniel, leader of the captive Jews in Babylon, assures Queen Nitocris, mother of King Belshazzar, that submission to the will of God is always rewarded. Meanwhile Cyrus is besieging the city; he plans to divert the river which provides its water supply and enter over the dry riverbed. His attack is timed to coincide with the day of a Babylonian feast when Belshazzar and his soldiers will be too drunk to resist. The feast duly takes place, in spite of the queen's pleas for restraint, and the king, against her further warning, orders that sacred temple vessels belonging to the Jews shall be used at the feast as drinking goblets.

The Euphrates is diverted and Cyrus and his troops enter the city at the height of the hedonistic feast. Belshazzar's sacrilege is answered by the famous writing on the wall and everyone is terrified. Daniel is summoned to translate: Belshazzar's days are numbered; he is weighed and found wanting; his kingdom shall be divided between the Medes and the Persians. Cyrus advances on the palace and in the brief battle that follows Belshazzar is killed but Nitocris and Daniel are spared. The temple at Jerusalem is to be rebuilt and the Jews released from captivity. Cyrus confirms his allegiance to the God of Israel.

The cast is starry, with Arleen Augér at her most ravishing as the Babylonian king's mother, Nitocris, Anthony Rolfe Johnson in the title-role, James Bowman as the prophet, Daniel, and Catherine Robbin as King Cyrus, all excellent. Full, well-balanced sound.

(i) *Cecilia vogi un sguardo* (cantata); *Silete venti* (motet).
*** DG Dig. 419 736-2 [id.]. Jennifer Smith, John Elwes, E. Concert, Pinnock.

These two fine cantatas come from a later period than most of Handel's Italian-language works in this genre. Both reveal him at his most effervescent, a quality superbly caught in these performances with excellent singing and playing, most strikingly from Jennifer Smith whose coloratura has never been more brilliantly displayed on record. Excellent recording.

Esther (oratorio; complete).
**(*) O-L Dig. 414 423-2 (2) [id.]. Westminster Cathedral Boys' Ch., AAM Ch. & O, Hogwood.

Esther (Patrizia Kwella), Ahasuerus (Anthony Rolfe Johnson), Mordecai (Ian Partridge), Haman (David Thomas), Israelite woman (Emma Kirkby), 1st Israelite (Paul Elliott).

Hogwood has opted for the original 1718 score with its six compact scenes as being more sharply dramatic than the 1732 expansion. The biblical story itself is certainly not lacking in drama or characterful personalities.

In Persia, King Ahasuerus has divorced his wife and married Esther, an Israelite in exile. Esther was raised by her relative, Mordecai, to whom the king is also indebted for saving his life. Mordecai has refused to bow down to the king's chief minister, the arrogant Haman, because Haman is a descendant of the ancient Israelite enemy, the Amalekites. In revenge, Haman plans to persecute the Israelites. He dismisses a plea for mercy from one of his officers and orders the massacre. The Persian soldiers shout their approval.

The Israelites are celebrating Esther's marriage to Ahasuerus, praising God and expressing their hope for an end to persecution and idol-worship. However, their priest brings news of Haman's plans and the mood of celebration turns to one of despair. The priest fears they may never be able to return to the homeland of Jordan. Mordecai then tells Esther that he is the cause of this persecution and asks her to go to the king to plead their cause. This will put Esther in danger, as it is punishable by death to approach the king unsummoned. Esther agrees, hoping that her tears and the king's love will soften his anger.

When she enters the throne room, the king is at first angry, but when he recognizes his queen he forgives and welcomes her. She faints in fear, but the king shows his concern for her and assures her that he will grant her anything. Her request is that he and Haman both join her for dinner in her apartment. He is charmed and agrees. The Israelites are sure that Esther's virtues will protect her and they call on Jehovah to bring his wrath to bear on their enemies.

At Esther's banquet, the king asks her to explain her purpose in inviting them. She asks that her people be spared and reminds Ahasuerus of the debt he owes to Mordecai. When the king wants to know more, Haman's personal motives for decreeing the persecution are exposed, and his fate is sealed. The king condemns him to death, and even Esther rejects his pleas for mercy. Mordecai is honoured, and the Israelites are overjoyed at their new acceptance. They praise God and anticipate the time when they will rebuild their temple in the Holy Land.

Handel's response to Esther's courage and resourcefulness in this, his first English oratorio, is full of imaginative touches, and the choruses are particularly fine. Hogwood's rather abrasive brand of authenticity goes well with the bright, full recorded sound which unfortunately exaggerates the choir's sibilants. The Academy's own small chorus is joined by the clear, bright trebles of Westminster Cathedral Choir, and they all sing very well (except that the elaborate passage-work is far too heavily aspirated, at times almost as though the singers are laughing). The vigour of the performance is unaffected and the team of soloists is strong and consistent, with Patrizia Kwella sounding distinctive and purposeful in the name-part.

Flavio (opera; complete).
*** HM Dig. HMC 901312/13 (2) [id.]. Ens. 415, Jacobs.

Flavio (Jeffrey Gall), Guido (Derek Lee Ragin), Emilia (Lena Lootens), Tedata (Bernarda Fink), Vitige (Christina Högman), Ugone (Gianpaolo Fagotto), Lotario (Ulrich Messthaler).

Based on a staging of this unjustly neglected Handel opera at the 1989 Innsbrück Festival, René Jacobs' recording vividly captures the consistent vigour of Handel's inspiration. Unlike most Handel operas, this one has principal soloists in all four registers and keeps well within modern ideas of length, with some two and a half hours of music squeezed on to the two CDs. That and the quality of invention make it surprising that *Flavio* has never enjoyed popular success, even in Handel's time. The plot is no stiffer or more improbable than most of the period, although its twists and turns could surely win a prize for their complexity, the more so as the whole action of the opera takes place within the span of a single day. It opens just before daybreak.

Teodata, daughter of King Flavio's counsellor, Ugone, and Vitige, her lover, say their farewells so he may steal away unnoticed. His duties tonight will prevent him from being at the wedding celebration of her brother, Guido, who is a knight and is today to marry Emilia, daughter of the king's second counsellor, Lotario. Early in the day, Guido and Emilia exchange their vows in the presence of relatives assembled for the wedding and, after the ceremony, they separate until the time of the evening celebration.

Ugone takes Teodata to the castle and presents her to the king. Ugone is anxious that his daughter become a lady-in-waiting at court so she won't be lonely, unaware that she already has a lover in Vitige, who is the king's adjutant. Flavio is more than willing to accept her at court. He is smitten with her beauty and sends her to be with his wife, Ernelinda.

Lotario arrives and is inviting the king to the wedding feast when Vitige brings a letter from the Governor of England, which is part of Flavio's realm. Narsete, who is now bedridden and too old to continue his duties, has written asking to return to Lombardy. Flavio's first instinct is to appoint Lotario in his place, and indeed Lotario anticipates this since he – of the two counsellors under consideration – is still in his prime.

But the king suddenly changes his mind and appoints Ugone, realizing that Ugone's absence will make it easy for him to woo Teodata. Lotario is enraged that he has been slighted and abruptly leaves. Flavio now tells Vitige of his passion for Teodata, and Vitige conceals his own relationship with her by denying her attractions.

In the courtyard of the castle, Ugone finds his son and shows him that Lotario has just struck his cheek in his rage over the king's appointment. Their code of honour requires that the insult be avenged, and Ugone asks Guido to challenge Lotario. This sets Guido between his love for Emilia, whom he has just married, and the honour of his family. Meanwhile, inside the castle, Flavio is courting Teodata. They are interrupted by Ugone, who is terribly distressed. The king leaves them together, and Ugone speaks wildly about the loss of family honour. Teodata immediately jumps to the conclusion that her relationship with Vitige has been discovered and she quickly confesses everything. Ugone now sees himself as doubly dishonoured.

Lotario orders Emilia to forget about her wedding celebration. Guido is the son of his hated rival and is now unworthy. Guido arrives, looking for Lotario, and finds Emilia alone. He doesn't tell her what has happened but asks that she leave him alone for a few minutes.

At the castle, Flavio asks Vitige to bring Teodata to him and to encourage her affection towards the king. When Vitige goes to Teodata she tells him that her father has discovered their secret love. Vitige enlists her deception for the moment. She will pretend, with a twinkle and a smile, to fall in love with the king. Vitige assures her that she will be his before the sun sets in the west.

In the courtyard of Lotario's house, Guido challenges Lotario to a duel. Lotario is experienced and mocks Guido, but he is the one who falls. Emilia finds her father lying in a pool of blood. Before he dies, he tells her that it was Guido's sword that pierced him. In her agony she cries out for revenge but is not sure whether she wants to punish her beloved or rather to die herself to end her suffering. Back in the castle, Emilia and Ugone are together with the king. The daughter calls for justice for her father's murder, while the father pleads for his son's life. This is the first Emilia has heard of her father's insult to Ugone and of Guido's challenge.

Flavio is stunned and needs time to consider. He sends them away. While he is thinking of how much this tragedy touches him personally, Vitige enters and presents Teodata to him. Overwhelmed by her beauty, the king loses his courage and asks Vitige to speak for him. When Vitige's attempts seem only half-hearted, Flavio takes over, calling Teodata his queen and gaining her acceptance of his love. This inspires furious jealousy in Vitige, who is quite desperate at the thought of this imminent loss of Teodata's love.

Emilia is in mourning, ranting against Guido, who appears with the sword that slew her father and offers it to Emilia so that she may take her revenge on him. She raises the sword, but cannot strike. Left alone together briefly, Vitige and Teodata quarrel about letting the situation with the king get so serious. Entering quietly, Flavio has overheard all this, and they have to admit, abashedly, that they are lovers. Flavio's hopes are dashed.

Guido then comes to the king, asking for death if Emilia still despises him. Ugone protests that it was his fault. Flavio calls for Emilia so that she may pronounce his decision, but as she approaches he directs Guido to hide himself, and he proceeds to tell Emilia that Guido has been been sacrificed as penance for her father's death. Frantic, she begs for death for herself as well. Her faithfulness pleases the king and Ugone, and Guido is restored to her and he asks for forgiveness. She forgives, but asks that her suffering heart should have time to mourn her loss.

Flavio now turns to Vitige; it is decreed that he must marry Teodata. Ugone must accept his new son-in-law and go to rule Britain. At the end of the opera all are apparently happily reconciled, and peace is restored, but Flavio does not outwardly acknowledge his own responsibility for what happened. Deep in his heart he must realize that his own ill-judged impulsiveness precipitated all the trauma, which in turn led to the tragic death of Lotario.

Handel's score was brilliantly written for some of the most celebrated singers of the time, including the castrato, Senesino. His four arias are among the highspots of the opera, all sung superbly here by the warm-toned and charactertul counter-tenor, Derek Lee Ragin. The first three are brilliant coloratura arias; but the last, in the rare key of B flat minor, touches a darker, more tragic note. The other tragic aria is for the heroine, Emilia, again in a distant key, F sharp minor; but almost every other aria is open and vigorous, with the whole sequence rounded off in a rousing ensemble. René Jacobs' team of eight soloists is a strong one, with only the strenuous tenor of Gianpaolo Fagotto occasionally falling short of the general stylishness. Full, clear sound.

Giulio Cesare (opera; complete).
*** HM Dig. HMC 901385/7 [id.]. Concerto Köln, Jacobs.
  Giulio Cesare (Jennifer Larmore), Cleopatra (Barbara Schlick), Cornelia (Bernarda Fink), Sextus (Marianne Rørholm), Ptolemy (Derek Lee Ragin), Achillas (Furio Zanasi), Curio (Olivier Lallouette), Nirenus (Dominique Visse).

Handel's most famous opera was first performed in London in 1724. Based on an often confusing libretto by Nicola Haym, it takes place during the year 48 BC at Pharsalus, where Caesar is victorious over his rival, Pompey.

By the side of the Nile the Egyptians prudently hail the conquering Romans and Caesar appears to celebrate his triumph. Pompey's widow, Cornelia, and her son, Sesto, beg for Caesar's mercy while General Achillas, counsellor to Ptolemy, offers hospitality to Caesar on behalf of the Egyptian king. He had been Pompey's military aide, but he now displays Pompey's severed head as proof of his newfound loyalty to Caesar, who immediately condemns such treacherous cruelty.

Cornelia attempts suicide, scorning the offered love of the Roman tribune, Curio, and lamenting her misery and loneliness. Her son promises revenge. Meanwhile Cleopatra, Ptolemy's sister, who has designs upon the throne, decides to seduce Caesar, convinced that her beauty far outweighs Achillas' macabre gift from her brother.

Achillas offers to slay Caesar but craves in return the hand of the lovely Cornelia. Ptolemy agrees to the bargain. Caesar now meets Cleopatra, who tells him that she is Lydia, one of the Queen's companions, and Caesar is overcome by her physical charms. Cornelia and Sesto argue over who is to take vengeance on Ptolemy, who instigated her husband's murder.

In his palace Ptolemy, disguising his true feelings, welcomes Caesar while Achillas covets Cornelia, who supports Sesto as he challenges Ptolemy. Both are seized by the guards. Sesto is imprisoned; Cornelia is taken to the king's harem where Achillas offers her her freedom if she will marry him. She will not!

In the garden, taking part in a staged vision of Mount Parnassus, Cleopatra appears disguised as a goddess, and her seduction of Caesar is complete as he expresses his desire for her. They meet to consummate their passion in her boudoir but are interrupted by Curio with the news that Egyptian soldiers are coming to kill Caesar. Cleopatra, filled with love for Caesar, reveals her true identity and implores him to save himself.

Meanwhile Nerino, Cleopatra's aide, has taken Sesto to Ptolemy; Sesto attempts to stab the king, but Achillas intervenes, announcing that Caesar has escaped by plunging into the harbour. Cleopatra and her soldiers mount a coup against Ptolemy; Achillas defects to join her when Ptolemy denies him Cornelia's hand in marriage (he wants her for himself). Sesto, after unsuccessfully attempting suicide and urged on by Cornelia, joins them. But Ptolemy's army is victorious and Cleopatra is imprisoned.

Achillas, dying from his wounds, presents Sesto with a signet ring which will ensure that hidden Egyptian troops will obey his commands. Caesar arrives to rescue Cleopatra and frees her; Ptolemy reveals his love for Cornelia, who scorns him and threatens his life with a dagger. Sesto intervenes and kills Ptolemy in a duel. Thus Sesto and Caesar are reconciled, Cleopatra takes the throne as Egyptian queen by Caesar's side and the opera ends in general rejoicing.

Astonishingly, with what is probably Handel's greatest and most popular opera, this Harmonia Mundi set is the very first CD version to offer a really complete text. The previous ones were based on theatre productions, seriously cut. The counter-tenor, René Jacobs, now conductor of the German group, Concerto Köln, is a warmly expressive rather than a severe period performer. With a cast of consistently fresh voices and with rhythms sprung infectiously, he also allows the broadest expansion on the great reflective moments. So Caesar's mourning for Pompey in Act I brings the most darkly intense account of his aria, *Alma del gran Pompeo*, and the two greatest and most beautiful of Cleopatra's arias, *V'adoro pupille* and *Piangero*, are similarly expansive without being over-romanticized.

The casting of the pure, golden-toned Barbara Schlick as Cleopatra proves outstandingly successful, when she encompasses so commandingly the sharp contrasts between the heroine's eight arias, bringing out different sides of the character from girlish vivacity to tragic intensity. Jennifer Larmore, too, a fine, firm mezzo with a touch of masculine toughness in the tone, makes a splendid Caesar. Together they crown the whole performance with the most seductive account of their final duet. Others both stylish and characterful include the American counter-tenor, Derek Lee Ragin, excellent in the sinister role of Tolomeo (Ptolemy), Bernarda Fink as Cornelia and Marianne Rørholm as Sesto, with the bass, Furio Zanasi, as Achille.

Jacobs' expansive speeds mean that the whole opera will not fit on three CDs, but the fourth disc, at 18 minutes merely supplementary, comes free as part of the package and includes an extra aria for the servant, Nireno, delightfully sung by the French counter-tenor, Dominique Visse. Firm, well-balanced sound.

Giulio Cesare (abridged).
(M) ** BMG/RCA GD 86182 (2) [6182-2-RG]. NY City Op. Ch. & O, Julius Rudel.
   Giulio Cesare (Norman Treigle), Cleopatra (Beverly Sills), Cornelia (Maureen Forrester), Sextus (Beverly Wolff), Ptolemy (Spiro Malas), Achillas (Dominic Cossa).

This RCA recording of *Julius Caesar* (first issued on LP in 1968) is based on a New York stage production, using a reasonably complete text. With some distinguished singing from the women principals, its merit is its vigour, reflecting stage experience. The conductor's approach is fresh and intelligent, but by latterday standards this is grossly inauthentic, with the title-role amazingly taken by a baritone, following the old-fashioned German practice. The set is more valuable as a memento of the New York City Opera at a vintage period than as a recording, though the CD transfer offers vivid sound.

Giulio Cesare: highlights.
(M) **(*) Teldec Dig. 2292 42410-2 [id.]. Schoenberg Ch., VCM, Harnoncourt.
   Giulio Cesare (Paul Esswood), Cleopatra (Roberta Alexander), Cornelia (Marjana Lipovšek), Seste (Ann Murray).

Instead of issuing Harnoncourt's complete set on CD, Teldec offer just short of an hour of highlights. The opera is strongly cast with Marjana Lipovšek and Ann Murray both making fine contributions. Paul Esswood as Cesare sings pleasingly, especially in *Va tacito e nascosto* with its horn obbligato, but ideally one wants more striking differentiation between the voices. Roberta Alexander takes readily to Cleopatra's coloratura, although curiously she is replaced by Lucia Popp in the closing bourrée, *Ritorni omai.* Harnoncourt directs the proceedings with plenty of rhythmic spirit and makes the most of the *Sinfonia bellica.* Good, bright recording with plenty of resonant atmosphere.

Julius Caesar (opera; complete, in English).
(M) *** EMI Dig. CMS7 69760-2 (3). ENO Ch. & O, Mackerras.
   Julius Caesar (Janet Baker), Cleopatra (Valerie Masterson), Cornelia (Sarah Walker), Sextus (Della Jones), Ptolemy (James Bowman), Achillas (John Tomlinson).

Julius Caesar, particularly in English translation, as in this set based on the ENO stage production at the Coliseum, really does bear out what specialists have long claimed concerning Handel's powers of characterization in opera. With Mackerras's lively and sensitive conducting, this is vivid and dramatically involving in a way rare with Handel opera on record. Dame Janet, in glorious voice and drawing on the widest range of expressive tone-colours, shatters the old idea that this alto-castrato role should be transposed down an octave and given to a baritone. Valerie Masterson makes a charming and seductive Cleopatra, fresh and girlish, though the voice is caught a little too brightly for caressing such radiant melodies as those for *V'adoro pupille* (*Lamenting, complaining*) and *Piangero* (*Flow my tears*).

Sarah Walker sings with powerful intensity as Pompey's widow; James Bowman is a characterful counter-tenor Ptolemy and John Tomlinson a firm, resonant Achillas, the other nasty character. The ravishing accompaniments to the two big Cleopatra arias amply justify the use by the excellent English National Opera Orchestra of modern, not period, instruments. The full, vivid studio sound makes this one of the very finest of the invaluable series of ENO opera recordings in English sponsored by the Peter Moores Foundation. Well transferred, the CD version brings the advantage that each of the three Acts is accommodated on a single disc, with the first exceptionally well filled.

Julius Caesar: highlights (in English).
(M) *** EMI Dig. CDM7 63724-2 [id.] (from above recording; cond. Mackerras).
   A well-selected, generous compilation (68 minutes) for those not wanting the complete set.

Hercules (opera; complete).
*** DG Dig. 423 137-2 (3) [id.]. Monteverdi Ch., E. Bar. Soloists, Gardiner.
   Hercules (John Tomlinson), Dejanira (Sarah Walker), Hyllus (Anthony Rolfe Johnson), Iole (Jennifer Smith), Lichas (Catherine Denley), Priest of Jupiter (Peter Savidge).

Though the English libretto has its unintentional humour (the jealous Dejanira tells her husband Hercules to 'Resign thy club', meaning his knobkerrie not the Athenaeum), this is a great opera, more dramatically convincing than many of its kind based on Greek legend.

Hercules has been so long gone from Trachis that his wife Dejanira fears he will never return. Her son, Hyllus, returns from consulting the oracle, where the temple shook and was plunged into darkness. Even the priest foretold the death of Hercules. Dejanira is reconciled to not seeing her dear husband again until the afterlife, but Hyllus is determined to go out and search for his father.

Before he can set off, Lichas, the herald, announces that Hercules is returning from Oechalia with many captives, including the Princess Iole, daughter of Euryptus, whom Hercules has slain. In the palace square Hercules declares that his labours are finally over; he has appeased Juno's rage. He frees Iole but she is not interested, still thinking only of her father's death. Hercules lays down his arms and awaits the joy of returning to Dejanira's love.

Iole wishes she had never been born a princess and longs for a simple life. Dejanira enters, her mind full of suspicion. Iole's great beauty has convinced her that Hercules' attack on Oechalia was the result of his desire for the princess, which Iole firmly refutes. Nevertheless Dejanira believes that Hercules is false and rebukes him bitterly. He defends himself, telling her not to heed a jealousy so completely without cause.

Now thinking to retrieve herself and secure her husband's love, Dejanira remembers a magic garment, given to her by the centaur Nessus after it was mortally wounded by Hercules; its powers were supposed to rekindle fading love. She directs Lichas to take it to Hercules as a pledge of reconciliation. Iole approaches and Dejanira tells her how sorry she is to have suspected her. Iole weeps, and Dejanira comforts her.

Lichas appears, bringing the disastrous news of Hercules, who, having passed through every danger during his long labours, has now become the victim of a woman's jealousy. Dejanira's gift was Nessus' revenge, and Hercules the prey. The magic garment consumes the great hero in fire. He cries out to his son to build him a funeral pyre at the summit of Mount Oeta, that he may arise to the gods on wings of flame. Dejanira suffers great torment.

The priest of Jove soon announces that Hercules has risen to the court of Jove, guided by an eagle which came to light on his funeral pyre. Jove is also deeply concerned about the welfare of Iole, and decrees that Hyllus and she shall marry.

Gardiner's generally brisk performance using authentic forces may at times lack Handelian grandeur in the big choruses, but it superbly conveys the vigour of the writing, its natural drama. Writing in English, Handel concentrated on direct and involving human emotions more than he generally did when setting classical subjects in Italian. Numbers are compact and memorable, and the fire of this performance is typified by the singing of Sarah Walker as Dejanira in one of her finest recordings. John Tomlinson makes an excellent, dark-toned Hercules, with florid passages well defined except for very occasional sliding. Youthful voices consistently help in the clarity of the attack – Jennifer Smith as Iole, Catherine Denley as Lichas, Anthony Rolfe Johnson as Hyllus and Peter Savidge as the Priest of Jupiter. Refined playing and outstanding recording quality, with the CDs bringing a gripping immediacy and realistic projection to this admirably alive music-making.

Israel in Egypt (oratorio; complete).
(m) **(*) DG 429 530-2 (2) [id.]. Heather Harper, Patricia Clark, Paul Esswood, Alexander Young, Michael Rippon, Christopher Keyte, Leeds Festival Ch., ECO, Mackerras.

(i) *Israel in Egypt;* (ii) *The Ways of Zion* (funeral anthem).
**(*) Erato/Warner 2292 45399-2 (2) [id.]. (i) Jean Knibbs, Julian Clarkson, Paul Elliott, Stephen Varcoe; (ii) Norma Burrowes, Charles Brett, Martyn Hill, Varcoe; Monteverdi Ch. & O, Gardiner.

Israel in Egypt was written in 1738 and first heard at the King's Theatre in London's Haymarket. Although initially not one of Handel's great successes, the work has since become a favourite, mainly because of its dramatic choruses. The oratorio opens sombrely with the lamentations of the Israelites for the death of Joseph. The burden of the Israelites is related, and the succession of plagues which led the Egyptians to release them, followed by their departure from Egypt and their escape across the Red Sea. Finally, the Israelites celebrate the miracle of this escape and their wondrous liberation.

Though the solo singing, shared between principals in the chorus, is variable on Erato, the choruses are what matter in this work, making up a high proportion of its length, and the teamwork involved brings tingling excitement. This was one of Gardiner's earlier Handel recordings, using not the period instruments of the English Baroque Soloists but the Monteverdi Orchestra. It is also welcome to have the moving funeral anthem as an extra item. The DG/Mackerras account may have more distinctive solo contributions, but Gardiner's chorus remains the finer.

Mackerras's performance represents a dichotomy of styles, with the English Chamber Orchestra crisp, stylish and lightweight set against the fairly large amateur choir, singing with impressive weight rather than incisively. The grandeur of the work rather than its athletic vigour comes over. Though the sound is strongly projected on CD, the recording balance is variable. The chorus is almost drowned at times by the orchestra in the epic pieces, then suddenly comes to the fore for the lighter moments of the score. The solo singing is distinguished, but the style is refined rather than earthy and the choruses are the main glory.

Jephtha (oratorio; complete).
*** Ph. Dig. 422 351-2 (3) [id.]. Monteverdi Ch., E. Bar. Soloists, Gardiner.
   Jephtha (Nigel Robson), Iphis (Lynne Dawson), Storge (Anne Sofie Von Otter), Hamor (Michael Chance), Zebul (Stephen Varcoe).

Whatever Handel's personal trials in writing what, in all but name, is a biblical opera, the result is a masterpiece, containing some magnificent music, not least in the choruses. There are only three *da capo* arias out of ten, and the beautiful accompanied recitatives – not least Jephtha's celebrated *Deeper and deeper still* in Act II – give a cohesion to the whole story.

The Israelites are being oppressed by the Ammonites and need a strong leader. Jephtha, a strong and courageous warrior, is most likely to bring them success, but he has been disinherited and has gone into exile as a result of his illegitimate birth. Invited back to be their commander, Jephtha agrees, but only if they will make him their leader after his victory.

Jephtha's daughter, Iphis, is betrothed to one of her father's soldiers, Hamor. Iphis agrees to marry him if they win the battle. Jephtha privately makes a vow that, if the battle ends in victory, the first person he sees on his return will be sacrificed to God. Jephtha's wife, Storge, knows nothing of these plans, but has premonitions of some evil waiting to take place. After determining that the Ammonite king will indeed not end his oppression, Jephtha proceeds with the battle he feels secure in winning.

When Hamor returns to announce their great victory, Iphis is doubly joyful and joins together with her maidens to prepare a welcome celebration to greet her father. She is the first he sees and he recoils in horror, then tells her of his vow. Iphis resigns herself to death and Jephtha dutifully makes preparations to carry out the sacrifice of his only child. However, at the last moment, an angel appears and announces that the Holy Spirit which inspired Jephtha to make such a vow would rather see it fulfilled in Iphis's dedication to God than in her death. Thus Iphis can remain a virgin and live. Hamor, too, is resigned, and all sing praise to God.

John Eliot Gardiner's recording was made live at the Göttingen Festival in 1988 and, though the sound does not have quite the bloom of his finest studio recordings of Handel, the exhilaration and intensity of the performance come over vividly, with superb singing from both chorus and an almost ideal line-up of soloists. Nigel Robson's tenor may be on the light side for the title-role, but in such a lovely aria as *Waft her, angels* the clarity of sound and the sensitivity of expression are very satisfying. Lynne Dawson, with her bell-like soprano, sings radiantly as Iphis; and the counter-tenor, Michael Chance, as her beloved, Hamor, is also outstanding. Anne Sofie von Otter is powerful as Storge, and Stephen Varcoe with his clear baritone, again on the light side, is a stylish Zebul. As for the Monteverdi Choir, their clarity, incisiveness and beauty are a constant delight.

Joshua (oratorio; complete).
⊛ *** Hyp. Dig. CDA 66461/2; *KA 66461/2* [id.]. New College, Oxford, Ch., King's Consort, King.
   Achsa (Emma Kirkby), Othniel (James Bowman), Joshua (John Mark Ainsley), Caleb (Michael George).

Written in 1747, five years after *Messiah* first appeared, *Joshua* was almost equally successful.

Although its storyline is altogether more operatic, in this grandly military oratorio, based on the Book of Joshua, Handel makes sure that his audience knows that the outcome is essentially motivated by the will of God.

The Israelites are rejoicing over their conquest of Canaan and their crossing of the River Jordan. Joshua is most confident and Caleb's flattery inspires him to act the more so. However, Achsah, Caleb's daughter, wistfully remembers the suffering during their captivity in Egypt. Joshua directs Caleb to oversee the establishment of a suitable monument to ensure that the miraculous escape is recorded for posterity.

Othniel, a young soldier betrothed to Achsah, appears and is startled to find himself in the company of an angel, who announces that he has come from God and that Joshua is to defeat and destroy Jericho, where some of its citizens are worshipping idols. All make haste to carry out Joshua's orders to prepare for battle, but Achsah and Othniel meet and have a quiet moment together before the trumpet sounds.

For six days Joshua has been laying siege to Jericho. Finally, on the seventh day, the walls of the city are levelled. Caleb sets about destroying the rest of the city. Achsah tries to put in a word of caution about how the Israelites have experienced sadness more than triumph, but the confident soldiers are in no mood to heed her. Soon news arrives that their soldiers have been defeated at Ai, and all mourn.

Joshua tries to arouse courage in his men with reminders of the victory at Jericho. Othniel goes off in search of Achsah. She has missed him, too. But Caleb is angry that Othniel has let his soldiering lapse while succumbing to thoughts of love, and he sends Achsah away. Caleb now unites the troops to defend an ally against the Canaanites who, defeated, disperse and flee from the victorious Israelites.

Joshua is again the mighty hero. Even Achsah is happy in the security of freedom. Joshua proposes to divide the conquered land among the tribes of Israel, and Caleb is given the land of Hebron. Othniel reminds Caleb that one city is as yet unconquered. Caleb finds his strength declining and proposes to give the hand of Achsah to the soldier who will pursue this last conquest. Othniel rises to the challenge, confident that he cannot fail. All pray that he will be successful, and Joshua soon returns with the news that Othniel has indeed achieved this victory for his people. Achsah is jubilant. Caleb welcomes Othniel as his son. All praise God.

Joshua's popularity owed much to two numbers, which at once gained currency outside the opera house, the chorus *See, the conqu'ring hero comes* and the brilliant soprano aria *O, had I Jubal's lyre*. In the context of the whole oratorio, heard in quick succession in the triumphant third Act, their magnetism is enhanced, with the patriotic chorus atmospherically bringing louder, grander repetitions, and with Emma Kirkby here ideally sparkling and light in the solo. Her Act I aria too is a delight, *Hark, 'tis the linnet*, full of delightful bird noises. She has the role of Achsah, daughter of the patriarchal leader, Caleb (taken here by the bass, Michael George). Her love for Othniel, superbly sung by James Bowman, successfully provides the romantic interest.

The brisk sequence of generally brief arias is punctuated by splendid choruses, with solo numbers often inspiring choral comment. The call to arms in Act I is particularly effective, with the brass silent until that moment. Act II then tells the story of the siege of Jericho, leading up to Joshua's stopping of the sun in the astonishingly original *O thou bright orb*. In that final number of the Act for tenor and chorus, first high violins then the rest of the strings are eerily stilled to represent the miracle, with the chorus finally fading away at the end of the Act. The sounds of victory are then left for Act III. The singing is consistently strong and stylish, with the clear, precise tenor, John Mark Ainsley, in the title-role giving his finest performance on record yet. Robert King and his Consort crown their achievement in other Hyperion issues, notably their Purcell series, with polished, resilient playing, and the choir of New College, Oxford, sings with ideal freshness. Warm, full sound. On two well-packed discs, it makes an exceptionally attractive Handel issue.

Judas Maccabaeus (oratorio; complete).
(M) **(*) Van. 08 4072.72 (2). Amor Artis Ch., Wandsworth School Boys' Ch., ECO, Somary.
　　Israelite Woman (Heather Harper), Israelite Man (Helen Watts), Judas Maccabaeus
　　(Alexander Young), Simon (John Shirley-Quirk).

Judas Maccabaeus, though its popularity has been eclipsed, contains much fine and noble music, and Johannes Somary's vital performance underlines this. The choruses of lamentation for the Israelites in Act I and strong, heroic solos and choruses all through – the tenor's *Sound an alarm* typical of them – make for a work which may be long but has much to hold the attention. The solo singing is excellent, with Alexander Young a ringing tenor, and Helen Watts singing the opening aria in Act III exquisitely. Very good recording – the choruses could ideally have a crisper focus, but the effect is wholly natural – and a sense of commitment throughout from all departments. The most famous chorus, *See the conqu'ring hero comes*, takes the horns up to a high G *in alt*. (one note above the instrument's normal compass) and there is a famous (and true) story told about the great horn-player, Aubrey Brain (father of Dennis), who at rehearsals would wear his bowler hat and, each time he reached the high note, would raise it with one hand (and a genial smile).

(i) *Nell'Africane selve; Nella stagion che, dio viole e rose* (Italian cantatas). Duets: *Quel fior che all'aba ride; No, di voi non vo' fidarmi; Tacete ohimè, tacete!;* Trio: *Se tu non lasci amore.* (ii) *The Alchemist* (incidental music): suite. Theatre songs: *Universal passion: I like the am'rous youth. The Way of the World: Love's but the frailty of the mind. The What d'ye call it: 'Twas when the seas were roaring.*

*** O-L 430 282-2 [id.]. (i) Emma Kirkby, Judith Nelson, David Thomas; Hogwood (harpsichord); Sheppard (cello); (ii) Patrizia Kwella, Margaret Cable, D. Thomas, AAM, Hogwood.

This attractive reissue combines almost all the contents of two highly recommended analogue LPs recorded in 1980/81. The most ear-catching items among the Italian cantatas are those which Handel later drew on in *Messiah* for such numbers as *His yoke is easy, For unto us a child is born* and *All we like sheep.* Emma Kirkby and Judith Nelson sing them brilliantly; and one of the melodically less striking pieces nevertheless prompts an amazing virtuoso display from the bass, David Thomas, who is required to cope with an enormous range of three octaves. In the fast movements Hogwood favours breathtaking speeds (in every sense), yet the result is exciting, not too hectic, and the recording is outstanding. The coupled selection of Handel's theatre music contains more delightful rarities, and the performances by the Academy under Hogwood have all the freshness and vigour one associates with his companion set of Purcell theatre music. The transfers to CD are sophisticated: the sound is first class throughout.

Orlando (opera; complete).
*** O-L Dig. 430 845-2 (3) [id.]. AAM, Hogwood.
   Orlando (James Bowman), Angelica (Arleen Augér), Medoro (Catherine Robbin), Dorinda (Emma Kirkby), Zoroastro (David Thomas).

Hogwood and his fine team made this recording immediately after taking this opera on tour in the United States, giving semi-staged performances. Based on Ariosto's *Orlando furioso* and, more closely, on a libretto earlier used by Domenico Scarlatti, Handel's *Orlando* was radically modified to provide suitable material for individual singers, as for example the bass role of the magician, Zoroastro, specially created for a member of Handel's company.

Even so, the title-role seems to have failed to please the celebrated castrato, Senesino, for whom it was intended, probably because of Handel's breaks with tradition, notably in the magnificent mad scene in the Underworld which ends Act II on the aria, *Vaghe pupille*, with the simple ritornello leading to amazing inspirations. That number, superbly done here by James Bowman, with appropriate sound-effects, is only one of the virtuoso vehicles for the counter-tenor. This was written in 1732, after Handel had begun to compose English oratorios, and that experience evidently encouraged him to be more adventurous in his handling of operatic form.

Orlando himself is a strange central character, more mad than sane and torn between the equal attractions of love and his frenzied impulse to do battle with everyone in sight. Zoroastro, the magician, who presides over Orlando's destiny, is scornful of his interest in love and creates a vision showing mythological heroes being lulled to sleep by Cupid. But remembering the amorous exploits of Hercules and others, Orlando is not convinced.

Of the other characters in the story, Dorinda, the shepherdess, is in love with Medoro, an African prince. So is Angelica, Queen of Cathay. Medoro returns her feelings and, to spare Dorinda, he pretends Angelica is a relative – which she doubts but for the moment accepts.

Orlando's latest escapade has resulted in his rescuing a princess, Isabella, and Angelica demands that he must not see Isabella again, thus proving his constancy to her. Medoro, hidden behind a fountain, overhears all this but Angelica persuades him not to make an issue of it, for she knows Orlando is a dangerous opponent. She reassures Medoro that it is him she really loves. Their parting embrace is in turn seen by Dorinda, and Angelica tells her that she and Medoro are now betrothed, and she gives Dorinda a jewelled bracelet.

Dorinda, however, is inconsolable, even though both Angelica and Medoro try to be kind to her. Later, Orlando and Dorinda meet and Orlando angrily recognizes the bracelet which he once gave to Angelica. He is made even more angry when Dorinda tells him that Medoro is his rival for Angelica's affections. Zoroastro warns Angelica and Medoro of the dangers of upsetting the unstable Orlando and urges them to depart and escape his vengeful wrath. Not very sensibly, Medoro first carves their names together on a tree. However, Zoroastro brings his magic to bear on the situation and Angelica is borne off on a protective cloud.

Orlando, seeing the names of Medoro and Angelica carved on the tree, goes mad and – in a remarkably forward-looking passage of music, even involving a 5/8 metre on the strings – imagines himself taken across the River Styx by Charon to Pluto's domain, where he is attacked by the Furies, one of whom appears in the form of Medoro who is taken into the embrace of Proserpine (Pluto's wife). Her tears (in a famous aria) move Orlando momentarily, then his rage returns and finally he is carried off in Zoroastro's magic chariot. At Angelica's bidding, Medoro goes to Dorinda and asks her to hide him in her house.

Orlando then reappears and declares his love for Dorinda with such exaggerated ardour that it is obvious he is still unhinged; his mental faculties then become even more deranged and he leaves in confusion. Everyone is concerned until Zoroastro arrives, promising that Orlando's sanity shall be restored. But Orlando, still on the rampage, destroys Dorinda's house, and the hidden Medoro is engulfed in the ruins. As if that were not enough, Orlando next throws Angelica into a dark cavern, then he falls into an exhausted sleep.

Zoroastro again intervenes and restores Orlando's mind with a magical liquid contained in a vessel provided by the eagle of Jupiter. Orlando wakes up, discovers what has happened and promptly wants to kill himself. Angelica intervenes, and it turns out that Zoroastro managed to arrive in time to save Medoro, so he and Angelica can at last be united as husband and wife. Orlando manages to stay sane long enough to give the couple his blessing and Dorinda is reconciled to the match.

For the jewelled sequences of arias and duets, Hogwood has assembled a near-ideal cast, with Arleen Augér at her most radiant as the queen, Angelica, and Emma Kirkby characteristically bright and fresh in the lighter, semi-comic role of the shepherdess, Dorinda. Catherine Robbin assumes the role of Prince Medoro strongly, though the recording sometimes catches an unevenness in the voice. Though a weightier bass would be preferable, David Thomas sings stylishly as Zoroastro. Acclaimed as Hogwood's first complete opera set, this is one of his finest achievements on record, taut, dramatic and rhythmically resilient. Vivid, open sound. The three Acts might just have been squeezed on to two discs, but the three-disc layout allows each Act to occupy a single disc, if at considerable extra expense.

Ottone, re di Germania (opera; complete).
*** Hyp. Dig. CDA 66751/3 [id.]. King's Consort, Robert King.
     Ottone (James Bowman), Teofane (Claron McFadden), Gismonda (Jennifer Smith), Matilda (Catherine Denley), Adelberto (Dominique Visse), Emireno (Michael George).
**(*) HM Dig. HMU 907073/5 [id.]. Freiburg Bar. O, Nicholas McGegan.
     Ottone (Drew Minter), Teofane (Lisa Saffer), Gismonda (Juliana Gondek), Matilda (Patricia Spence), Adelberto (Ralf Popken), Emireno (Michael Dean).

Ottone, one of Handel's lesser-known Italian operas for London, dates from 1722, just before *Giulio Cesare*. Previously unrecorded, it simultaneously prompted these two versions, both of which have their points of advantage. Nicholas McGegan continues his impressive Handel series for Harmonia Mundi in a recording with the Freiburg Baroque Orchestra and with Drew Minter taking the title-role, while Robert King with his King's Consort offers a version on Hyperion with James Bowman as Ottone.

When the women principals in McGegan's version have purer, firmer voices than their rivals, there is a strong case for preferring his set. This is the piece – with a plot even more absurdly involved than most – which first introduced the temperamental soprano, Francesca Cuzzoni, to London, prompting the story of Handel trying to push the difficult prima donna out of a window. As the heroine, Teofane, Lisa Saffer for McGegan is markedly sweeter and clearer than Claron McFadden for King.

When it comes to the key castrato roles taken by counter-tenors, it is quite different. For McGegan, Drew Minter, a stylish singer, no longer has the power to give the many bravura arias the thrust they need, whereas Bowman for King with his far richer tone continues to sing with enormous panache and virtuoso agility. Dominique Visse as the duplicitous Adelberto on King's set tends to overcharacterize, but again the singing makes the rival version seem colourless. Add to that the extra richness and bloom on the instrumental sound in the Hyperion version, and the balance clearly goes in its favour. This may not be as distinctive as some of Handel's later Italian operas but, as ever, the sequence of brief numbers has an irresistible freshness.

Partenope (opera; complete).
(M) *** HM/BMG GD 77109 (3) [77109-2-RG]. La Petite Bande, Kuijken.
   Partenope (Krisztina Laki), Arsace (René Jacobs), Armindo (John York Skinner), Ormonte (Stephen Varcoe), Rosmira (Helga Müller-Molinari), Emilio (Martyn Hill).

By the time he wrote *Partenope* in 1730, Handel was having to cut his cloth rather more modestly than earlier in his career. In its limited scale this opera has few heroic overtones, yet a performance as fresh and alert as this amply demonstrates that the result can be even more invigorating.

Partenope is a fictional romance set in the Court of Queen Partenope, the legendary founder of Naples. In Act I, Partenope invokes the blessing of Apollo on the newly founded Naples in the presence of Arsace, Prince of Corinth, and Armindo, Prince of Rhodes. Rosmira, disguised as a man, introduces herself as Prince Eurimene, the only survivor of a shipwreck, but she and Arsace recognize each other. Ormonte enters and announces that Prince Emilio of Cuma is approaching with an army.

Rosmira learns that Prince Armindo is in love with Partenope but will never reveal it because Partenope has pledged her allegiance to Arsace. Rosmira pretends that she, too, is in love with Partenope. Emilio then appears and asks Partenope to be his queen, saying his troops are there to honour her; when she declines, he declares war. Partenope appoints Arsace as her commander, to the consternation of her generals and princes.

In Act II, Armindo of Rhodes saves Partenope, and Arsace rescues Rosmira (Eurimene) as she is being attacked by Emilio, whom he captures. A dispute arises between Rosmira and Arsace as to who has captured Emilio, and Rosmira challenges Arsace to single combat. Partenope places Eurimene under guard, eventually releasing him (her) on condition that he never approaches him again.

In the last Act, Eurimene (Rosmira) reveals the reasons for his quarrel with Arsace: he wishes to avenge his treatment of Princess Rosmira. Her true identity finally emerges when Arsace insists that they fight bare-chested. Partenope presents Rosmira to Arsace, marries Armindo, and allows Emilio, with whom she forms an alliance, to return to Cuma.

One problem for Handel was that at this time his company could call on only one each of soprano, tenor and bass; with an excellent team of counter-tenors and contralto, however, this performance makes light of that limitation. With the exception of René Jacobs, rather too mannered for Handel, the roster of soloists is outstanding, with Krisztina Laki and Helga Müller-Molinari welcome additions to the team. Though ornamentation is sparse, the direction of Sigiswald Kuijken is consistently invigorating, as is immediately apparent in the *Overture*. The 1979 recording sounds excellent in its CD format, and the only irritation is that the English translation is printed separately – in an old-style font – from the Italian original. Each is cued, however – there are 74 points of access – so it is fairly easy to link the two.

Il pastor fido (opera; complete).
**(*) Hung. Dig. HCD 12912 (2) [id.]. Savaria Vocal Ens., Capella Savaria, McGegan.
   Mirtillo (Paul Esswood), Amarilli (Katalin Farkas), Dorinda (Márta Lukin), Silvio (Gábor Kállay), Eurilla (Mária Flohr), Tirenio (József Gregor).

Drawn largely from material originally written for other operas, and using a libretto by Giacomo Rossi after the play by Battista Guarini, *Il pastor fido* was revised three times by Handel, with still more mixing of sources. The action takes place in Arcadia, which is enjoying the displeasure of the goddess Diana. The Arcadians believe that only the marriage of Amarilli to the young huntsman, Silvio, both of divine ancestry, will placate her. Amarilli nurses a secret love for the shepherd, Mirtillo, while Silvio only cares about hunting. Another shepherdess, Dorinda, is also in love with him. Eurilla, who is also in love with Mirtillo, traps Amarilli in a compromising situation for which the punishment is death.

While hunting, Silvio shoots Dorinda in mistake for an animal and wounds her; her devotion remains unchanged and he now falls in love with her. By the orders of the goddess Diana, Amarilli is reprieved and united with Mirtillo, Eurilla is forgiven and Silvio with Dorinda share their joy.

It is an unpretentious pastoral piece which charms gently rather than compelling attention. Though there is some fussiness in the orchestral playing (on period instruments) in this welcome recording, Nicholas McGegan demonstrates what talent there is in Budapest, among singers as

among instrumentalists. Singers better known in much later operatic music translate well to
Handel, for example the celebrated bass, József Gregor, but the most stylish singing comes from
the British counter-tenor, Paul Esswood, in the castrato role of Mirtillo. Good sound and
excellent documentation.

La Resurrezione (oratorio; complete).
Withdrawn: *** O-L Dig. 421 132-2 (2) [id.]. Emma Kirkby, Patrizia Kwella, Carolyn
  Watkinson, Ian Partridge, David Thomas, AAM, Hogwood.
*** Erato/Warner Dig. 2292 45617-2 [id.]. Nancy Argenta, Barbara Schlick, Guillemette
  Laurens, Guy De Mey, Klaus Mertens, Amsterdam Bar. O, Ton Koopman.

Though *La Resurrezione* does not have the great choral music which is so much the central
element of later Handel oratorios, it is a fine and many-faceted piece. Hogwood directs a clean-
cut, vigorous performance with an excellent cast of singers highly skilled in the authentic
performance of Baroque music. Emma Kirkby is at her most brilliant in the coloratura for the
Angel, Patrizia Kwella sings movingly as Mary Magdalene and Carolyn Watkinson as Cleophas
adopts an almost counter-tenor-like tone. Ian Partridge's tenor has a heady lightness as St John
and, though David Thomas's Lucifer could have more weight, he too sings stylishly. Excellent
recording, well balanced and natural in all respects, with an attractive ambient bloom.

Koopman's recording of this oratorio provides a valuable alternative to the fine Hogwood
version on Oiseau-Lyre. Koopman's cast of soloists is just as strong, with Barbara Schlick as the
Angel outstandingly fine and Klaus Mertens as Lucifer weightier and stronger than his opposite
number. Koopman's approach is lighter and more resilient, allowing more relaxation, though
the recording is less well focused, with voices less full and immediate.

Rinaldo (opera; complete).
* Nuova Era Dig. 6813/4 (2). La Fenice O, John Fisher.
  Rinaldo (Marilyn Horne), Almirena (Cecilia Gasdia), Goffredo (Ernesto Palacio), Armida
  (Christine Weidinger).

Rinaldo was the first opera that Handel wrote after settling in London, a piece full of
memorable numbers and with four starring roles, Goffredo, the Crusader general, putting
Jerusalem to siege, his daughter Almirena, the hero, Rinaldo, and Armida, Queen of Damascus
and also a sorceress.

Goffredo has promised that Rinaldo shall marry Almirena, assuming his victory in Jerusalem
is assured. The lovers are mutually enamoured of this idea (not always the case in opera).
However, a Saracen herald arrives to ask that Goffredo will parley with Argante, King of
Jerusalem. He arrives in splendid style and is granted a three-day truce. Argante is infatuated
with Armida, and he relies on her wily charms to gain victory over his Christian foes.

Armida arrives in a chariot drawn by dragons and invokes the Furies. She tells Argante that if
he is to obtain the defeat of the Crusaders Rinaldo must be eliminated, a task she herself will
perform. Rinaldo and Almirena, happily in love, are unaware that evil is afoot until Almirena is
suddenly abducted. The grieving Goffredo and Eustazio (Goffredo's brother) wonder if a
Christian magician could help, and Rinaldo swears vengeance. Meanwhile Argante receives
Almirena and declares his love for her, but she disdains him.

However, Armida's plans are altered when she herself falls in love with Rinaldo. To ensure her
favourable reception, she appears before him in the form of Almirena but, suspecting that all is
not what it seems, Rinaldo resists the attempted seduction and Armida is furious. Argante now
enters and also protests his love for the supposed Almirena, imprudently promising to deliver
her from Armida's spell.

Armida, now very angry indeed, immediately reveals her true identity; the two quarrel and,
not surprisingly, she withdraws her co-operation. With good timing and the help of the duly
recruited Christian magician, Goffredo now leads an assault on Armida's magic castle. At first
he is repelled by monsters, but superior Christian magic aids the escape both of his daughter and
of Rinaldo, who then prevents Armida from killing Almirena.

Yet Armida still has a final card up her sleeve: the Furies intervene to save the sorceress from
Rinaldo's sword. Her powers are then of no further avail. A Christian magic incantation causes
the evil castle to vanish and the city of Jerusalem appears in its place. After a final battle the
Christians are completely victorious. Argante and Almira are vanquished and Rinaldo is at last
able to marry Almirena.

This vigorous Venice performance of June 1989, recorded live, provides the star names, but it
is very much an adaptation to modern stage conditions, with plentiful cuts and a performing

style leaning towards the romantic, such as one might more normally have encountered 30 years ago. Marilyn Horne remains a formidable Handelian, with voice strong and flexible, though not as fresh as before. Cecilia Gasdia sings warmly and affectingly as Almirena, but attack is not always clean enough, as in the bird-song aria, *Augelletti*, or the lovely *Lascia ch'io piango*. Christine Weidinger makes a powerful Armida, strong in coloratura, but the voice is edgy; and Ernesto Palacio has his coarse moments. Particularly with its stage-noises, this cannot compare with the excellent 1977 CBS set with a first-rate cast under Jean-Claude Malgoire, which Sony should certainly reissue on CD.

Rodelinda, Regina de Langobardi (opera; complete).
**(*) HM/BMG Dig. RD 77192 (3) [77192-2]. La Stagione, Schneider.
  Rodelinda (Barbara Schlick), Eduige (Claudia Schubert), Bertarido (David Cordier), Unulfo (Kai Wessel), Grimoaldo (Christoph Prégardien), Garibaldo (Gotthold Schwarz).
** Decca Dig. 414 667-2 (2) [id.]. WNO O, Bonynge.
  Rodelinda (Joan Sutherland), Eduige (Isobel Buchanan), Bertarido (Alicia Nafé), Unulfo (Huguette Tourangeau), Grimoaldo (Curtis Rayam), Garibaldo (Samuel Ramey).

In February 1725 Handel produced *Rodelinda*, following up the enormous success of *Giulio Cesare* of a year earlier and using the same librettist, Nicola Francesco Haym, who again provided him with a melodramatic – not to say convoluted – narrative.

As the story begins, Rodelinda, Queen of Lombardy, is alone in her palace apartments mourning her dead husband, Bertarido. He is in fact alive and hoping for revenge on Grimoaldo, who has deposed him. When Grimoaldo enters her chambers to ask for her hand in marriage, Rodelinda turns angrily from him, for Grimoaldo is already betrothed to Bertarido's sister, Eduige. The latter also derides him when she discovers that his new plan is to aspire to the throne alongside her 'late' brother's wife. Grimoaldo now consults his scheming friend, Garibaldo, on how to secure Rodelinda's hand, and they hatch a plan together.

The scene now changes to a cypress wood where Bertarido in disguise – accompanied by his faithful friend, Unulfo (who alone knows of his survival) – views his own tomb in the traditional burial ground for the kings of Lombardy. He sings of his longing for his wife in one of Handel's most famous and loveliest arias, *Dove sei*.

Rodelinda and her son, Flavio, arrive to lay a wreath. Unulfo prevents Bertarido from revealing that he is alive. Garibaldo now enters as Grimoaldo's emissary and tells Rodelinda that, unlesss she weds Grimoaldo, her son will die. She is compelled to agree, but swears revenge. The despairing Bertarido overhears this exchange and realizes that his wife believes him to be dead. Unulfo comforts him, but he comes increasingly to believe that Rodelinda has betrayed him and calls upon the brooks and fountains to share his sorrow.

It is in this mood that the revengeful Eduige finds him and is amazed to discover that her brother is alive. She and Unulfo convince him that Rodelinda is totally faithful. Within the palace, Rodelinda changes her mind and tells Grimoaldo that she will marry him only *after* he has killed her son, surmising that he will thus reveal himself to the Lombardians as the monster he is. The weak Grimoaldo is nonplussed, but the scheming Garibaldo tells him to obey Rodelinda's command. Unulfo now appears and tells Rodelinda that Bertarido is alive, and the two are promptly and joyfully united.

As they embrace, however, Grimoaldo enters unexpectedly and angrily tells Bertarido that prison and death shall be his fate. He leaves husband and wife together to make their last farewells in one of Handel's greatest love-duets. Now Eduige intervenes: by securing a duplicate key to Bertarido's dungeon she and Unulfo plan his rescue.

In the prison Bertarido again bemoans his fate (he is not exactly the most resourceful of heroes); as he does so, a sword is thrown through the window by Unulfo, who then enters and is promptly wounded for his trouble by Bertarido, which leads to more confusion. They escape by a secret passage, whereupon Rodelinda and Eduige arrive and discover a bloodstained cloak, and they make the assumption that Bertarido has been murdered.

In the garden Bertarido bandages Unulfo's wound and rejoices in his freedom. Grimoaldo is also there and his conscience is troubled; when he falls asleep, the treacherous Garibaldo arrives. He has designs on the throne for himself and is about to kill Grimoaldo when Bertarido at last takes matters into his own hands and slays Garibaldo. Grimoaldo, highly relieved at the turn of events, renounces the throne and Rodelinda and her husband are reunited to a joyful closing chorus.

As in *Giulio Cesare*, so in *Rodelinda*, Handel modified the strict operatic conventions of the time, notably in the most celebrated of the arias, *Dove sei*, inaccurately translated as 'Art thou troubl'd?'. That emerges without pause from the accompanied recitative before it, surprising the ear the more with its beauty. On the German recording from Michael Schneider and La Stagione it is tenderly sung with plaintive tone by the British counter-tenor, David Cordier, matching the rest of the excellent, otherwise all-German cast. Barbara Schlick is pure and golden in the title-role and the tenor, Christoph Prégardien, is also outstanding as Grimoaldo. Schneider is a lively and fresh Handelian, not afraid of expressiveness but often adopting a clipped, abrasive manner. He encourages generous ornamentation in *da capo* repeats. Each Act fits neatly on a single CD, but inconveniently the libretto prints Italian text and English translation separately. First-rate, clean sound.

Rodelinda is an opera which, in 1959 during the Handel bicentenary celebrations, was given by the Handel Opera Society in London with the newly emergent Joan Sutherland dazzling in the name-part. It is the greatest of pities that that historic rendering was not recorded at once. Here in the late 1980s she finally tackled the role on record and, quite apart from the style now seeming dated, much more romantic than has become acceptable in this age of 'authentic' performance, Dame Joan's voice has developed a beat which obscures its beauty in slow numbers. Not only that, the slow speeds go with a rhythmic slackness and over-affectionate expressive style that undermine the classical purity. Even so, the flexibility of this still-glorious voice is thrilling in the fast arias, and one welcomes an opera in which the protagonist has so many important numbers.

Scholars will also argue over the aptness of ornamentation as Richard Bonynge has devised it, though that will trouble the non-specialist listener less. Outstanding among the others is Alicia Nafé as Bertarido, the main castrato role. Her account of the best-known aria in the opera, *Dove sei?*, is most beautiful, firm and even. Curtis Rayam, in one of the earliest of tenor parts, copes confidently with the role of the usurper, Grimoaldo, and Samuel Ramey's dark bass is similarly effective in the villain's role of Garibaldo. Isobel Buchanan sings freshly, but is not at her sweetest, while Huguette Tourangeau is most disappointing, far too wobbly for Handel. The playing of the Welsh National Opera Orchestra is vigorous but not always polished; and the recording, though full and bright, has the voices too close.

Samson (oratorio): complete.
(M) *** Erato/Warner 2292 45994-2 (3) [id.]. L. Voices, ECO, Raymond Leppard.
  Samson (Robert Tear), Dalila (Janet Baker), Micah (Helen Watts), Manoah (John Shirley-Quirk), Harapha (Benjamin Luxon), Philistine Woman (Norma Burrowes), Messenger / Israelitish Woman (Felicity Lott), Philistine Man (Philip Langridge), Israelitish Man (Alexander Oliver).

Leppard directs a highly dramatic account of Handel's most dramatic oratorio, one which translates very happily to the stage. Newburg Hamilton's libretto uses Milton's *Samson Agonistes* as its basis and the oratorio begins with Samson already in prison, chained and blind. Unlike the opera of Saint-Saëns, Handel's oratorio does not centre on the spectacle of the destruction of the Philistine Temple, but relates to Samson's psychological development and his reactions to meetings with his father (Manoah), his seductive wife Dalila (whom he rejects), and with the giant, Harapha (representing physical rather than spiritual power), so that at the dénouement Samson's heroism becomes a triumph of the spirit.

The work's exultant culmination, *Let the bright Seraphim*, is here beautifully sung by Felicity Lott. But the moment when the orchestra interrupts a soloist in mid-sentence to indicate the collapse of the Temple (which happens offstage) is more vividly dramatic than anything in a Handel opera. Leppard handles that and much else with total conviction. Robert Tear as Samson produces his most heroic tones – rather too aggressively so in *Total eclipse* – and the rest of the cast could hardly be more distinguished. Dame Janet Baker – not by nature a seductress in the Dalila sense – sings with a lightness totally apt for such an arias as *With plaintive notes*, and the others are in excellent voice. The recording is outstanding, atmospheric and naturally balanced, and it has transferred to CD with splendid body, realism and presence.

Saul (oratorio; complete).
*** Ph. Dig. 426 265-2 (3) [id.]. Monteverdi Ch., E. Bar. Soloists, Gardiner.
  Saul (Alistair Miles), Jonathan (John Mark Ainsley), David (Derek Lee Ragin), Merab (Donna Brown), Michal (Lynne Dawson).
** Teldec/Warner 2292 42651-2 (3) [id.]. V. State Op. Ch., VCM, Harnoncourt.
  Saul (Dietrich Fischer-Dieskau), Jonathan (Anthony Rolfe Johnson), David (Paul Esswood), Merab (Julia Varady), Michal (Elizabeth Gale).

Completed some three years before *Messiah*, *Saul* had the same librettist, Charles Jennens, and represents Handel's full emergence as a great oratorio composer, with the widest range of emotions conveyed. The alternation of mourning and joy in the final sequence of numbers is startlingly effective.

As the oratorio opens, David has just slain Goliath and the Philistines have been defeated. Saul honours David and asks him to stay in his royal household and to marry his daughter, Merab. Jonathan, son of Saul, pledges his friendship to David, but Merab is less than happy about becoming David's wife. She cannot refuse her father but considers it a dishonour to ally herself with someone with such a plebeian background as David.

In the ensuing celebrations, more praise is heaped on David than on Saul and the king becomes jealous. Nothing calms him and in a rage he throws his spear at David, but misses. He commands Jonathan to take David's life, but Jonathan determines that their friendship is sacred, and he will defend David at all costs.

There emerges a most powerful chorus regarding the destructive power of envy. Jonathan finds David and tries to console him over the strange way events have turned against him. Saul has even betrothed Merab to another. But David, aware of Merab's scorn of him, is not aggrieved. Saul approaches and appears to be pacified by Jonathan's appeal to his reason. The king welcomes David again and affiances him to his second daughter, Michal, who (in contrast to her sister) has long adored David for his great virtue.

It becomes apparent that Saul's reconciliation with David is a ruse and that he is still plotting David's end. Michal sends David away just in time, as Saul has summoned him to court, intending to kill him. The king's rage is uncontrolled, and in desperation he seeks counsel from a witch, whom he asks to call up the spirit of Samuel. The prophet tells Saul that in his disobedience God has forsaken him, and that by the next day he and his sons will be dead, their kingdom lost.

There is now a great battle, and when it is over David speaks with an Amalekite, who tells him that Saul and Jonathan are dead, the king despatched by the Amalekite himself. Angry that the man has dared to kill God's anointed king, David has the Amalekite slain. Israel mourns the loss of Saul and Jonathan. The high priest entrusts David with the restoration of the Hebrew honour.

Made at the Göttingen Festival in 1989, Gardiner's version of this magnificent oratorio offers a live recording far more sympathetic than Harnoncourt's on Teldec. Gardiner's performance is typically vigorous in what is rather a biblical opera than an oratorio. With choruses leavening the sequence of arias and with the confrontation of David and Saul most dramatically treated, it is more obviously approachable for the modern listener than most Handel operas. With Derek Lee Ragin in the counter-tenor role of David, with Alistair Miles as Saul, Lynne Dawson as Michal and John Mark Ainsley as Jonathan, it is not likely to be surpassed on disc for a long time.

Harnoncourt's version was recorded live at the Handel tercentenary celebrations in Vienna in 1985 and, whatever the advantages of period performance, the extraneous noises of coughs and creaks, together with the odd slip of execution, seriously reduce its merits. Dietrich Fischer-Dieskau in the name-part is most characterful, but his expressive style is very heavy for Handel, particularly in the recitatives. It is still for the most part a rich and noble performance, and Julia Varady, though not quite idiomatic, is individual too, with tone cleanly focused. The English members of the cast sing stylishly, notably Anthony Rolfe Johnson as Jonathan and Paul Esswood as David. Elizabeth Gale's bright soprano is not always sweetly caught by the microphones, but it is a sympathetic performance. Harnoncourt's direction is lively, but he misses much of the grandeur of the work, and some of the cuts he makes are damaging. The Vienna State Opera Concert Choir are responsive, but they never quite sound at home coping with English words.

Semele (opera; complete).
*** DG Dig. 435 782-2 (3) [id.]. Amb. Op. Ch., ECO, Nelson.
    Semele (Kathleen Battle), Juno (Marilyn Horne), Cadmus / Somnus (Samuel Ramey), Jupiter (John Aler), Iris (Sylvia McNair), Athamas (Michael Chance), Apollo (Neil Mackie).
**(*) Erato/Warner 2292 45982-2 (2). Monteverdi Ch., E. Bar. Soloists, Gardiner.
    Semele (Norma Burrowes), Juno (Della Jones), Cadmus (Robert Lloyd), Somnus (David Thomas), Jupiter (Anthony Rolfe Johnson) Iris (Patrizia Kwella), Athamas (Timothy Penrose), Apollo (Maldwyn Davies).

DG's new digital recording of *Semele* turns away from current fashion in using modern rather than period instruments, but the balance of advantage lies very much in its favour, compared with the Erato set of Gardiner – even period fanatics may well find it the better choice. Nelson follows the rules of baroque performance as closely as most period performers, and his starry cast brings not only flair and character but a keen sense of style. Surprisingly, the Nelson performance is generally crisper and faster than Gardiner's, with rhythms sprung just as infectiously.

Most importantly, he opens out the serious cuts made by Gardiner, following the old, bad tradition. If *Semele* – dating from 1744, three years after *Messiah* – is as a rule known only by its most celebrated aria, *Where'er you walk*, it contains many other superb numbers and, more than any of his other English-language works, even *Samson*, it is a genuine opera rather than an oratorio, using a witty send-up of a classical plot, based on a play by Congreve. Handel was aiming to satirize George II's mistress, Lady Yarmouth, in his portrayal of the central character of Semele – a self-regarding princess, seduced by Jupiter, who through him seeks to become immortal, just as Lady Yarmouth wanted to become queen.

The story of *Semele* derives from Ovid's *Metamorphoses*, and Congreve's libretto was written in 1708. As the piece opens, Cadmus, King of Thebes, is trying to persuade his daughter Semele not to delay her marriage to Athamas, but she resists as she is already pregnant with Jupiter's child. Athamas loves Semele but is forced by the gods to marry instead her sister, Ino, and bring up Bacchus, bastard child of Zeus and Semele. (Later the vengeful Juno induces them to murder their own children while mad.)

Juno now arrives on Earth with Iris and they discuss the problems of dealing with Semele, who is well protected, while Semele, awakened from her slumbers to sing her famous *O sleep why dost thou leave me?*, is assured by Jupiter of his love. But in Act III we meet Somnus, who is called on by the jealous Juno to put the guardian dragons to sleep so that she can visit Semele in the form of Ino. Then Juno shows Semele her reflection in a magic mirror, which makes her seem ravishingly lovely, and the goddess cunningly suggests to Semele that she is beautiful enough to reject Jupiter's advances unless he in return appears to her as a god rather than in human form; thus she will become a goddess alongside him.

Juno then exits, knowing that she has arranged Semele's destruction. When Jupiter arrives, Semele strikes just this bargain with him and Jupiter is forced to agree, knowing that the result will be disastrous. The story ends with Juno celebrating her revenge and Semele, too late, realizing that she has connived at her own destruction.

Norma Burrowes for Gardiner makes the character sweetly innocent, but Kathleen Battle with alluringly rich tone is more provocative, giving the brilliant aria, *Myself I shall adore*, something of the tongue-in-cheek quality you find in the G&S heroines, notably Yum-Yum in *Mikado*. Another of Semele's arias is the celebrated *O sleep, why dost thou leave me?* which Battle sings with a sensuous beauty to outshine her rival easily. The material restored by Nelson in the opened-out cuts, far from being dull, includes such marvellous numbers as three magnificent arias for Athamas, Semele's suitor, a counter-tenor role that is almost eliminated in the Gardiner set.

On stage there is a case for such cuts, but not on disc, particularly when you have Michael Chance as the superb singer. Marilyn Horne defies the years as a fire-snorting Juno, if anything even more characterful than the splendid Della Jones for Gardiner. Though Anthony Rolfe Johnson as Jupiter for Gardiner is a more stylish, fuller-toned tenor than John Aler for Nelson, the DG cast is not only starrier but generally more consistent, to confirm a strong recommendation whatever your preference in baroque performance.

The Erato reissue, in the Libretto series, of John Eliot Gardiner's 1981 version of *Semele* offers a period performance with the English Baroque Soloists using an excellent cast of British specialist singers. Very well recorded, it has the very practical advantage of coming on only two mid-price discs, and the extensive cuts which make that possible are the traditional ones, some of them sanctioned by Handel himself. Though this was an early EBS recording, not quite as polished as more recent ones, Gardiner's ability to use period performance with warmth and imagination makes it consistently compelling. Norma Burrowes is a sweet, pure Semele and Anthony Rolfe Johnson is outstanding as Jupiter, singing *Where'er you walk* with a fine sense of line and excellent pacing.

Solomon (oratorio; complete).
⊛ *** Ph. Dig. 412 612-2 (2) [id.]. Monteverdi Ch., E. Bar. Soloists, Gardiner.
      Solomon (Carolyn Watkinson), The Queen (Nancy Argenta), Queen of Sheba (Barbara Hendricks).

Among the very greatest of all Handel's oratorios, *Solomon* is conceived on the largest scale, and it is very theatrical both in conception and in its sense of drama. The plot is based on the Second Book of Chronicles and the incident of the judgement from the First Book of Kings, as well as using as some ideas taken from Josephus' *Antiquities of the Jews*. Solomon's temple is completed and dedicated, and his happiness in his marriage to the Pharaoh's daughter is apparent. We see his wisdom when he has to judge which woman is the mother of a disputed infant, and the visit of the Queen of Sheba brings her admiration both for his sagacity and for the splendour of his court. In essence, the work represents Handel's vision of Solomon's court as an ideal society.

Gardiner's DG version is in every way worthy of Handel's inspired music. With panache, he shows how authentic-sized forces can convey Handelian grandeur even with clean-focused textures and fast speeds. The choruses and even more magnificent double-choruses stand as cornerstones of a structure which may have less of a story-line than some other Handel oratorios – the Judgement apart – but which Gardiner shows has consistent human warmth.

Thus in Act I, the relationship of Solomon and his queen is delightfully presented, ending with the ravishing Nightingale chorus, *May no rash intruder*; while the Act III scenes between Solomon and the Queen of Sheba, necessarily more formal, are given extra warmth by having in that role a singer who is sensuous in tone, Barbara Hendricks. Carolyn Watkinson's pure mezzo, at times like a male alto, is very apt for Solomon himself (only after Handel's death did baritones capture it), while Nancy Argenta is clear and sweet as his Queen.

In the Judgement scene, Joan Rodgers is outstandingly warm and characterful as the First Harlot, but the overriding glory of the set is the radiant singing of Gardiner's Monteverdi Choir. Its clean, crisp articulation matches the brilliant playing of the English Baroque Soloists, regularly challenged by Gardiner's fast speeds, as in the *Arrival of the Queen of Sheba*; and the sound is superb, coping thrillingly with the problems of the double choruses.

Susanna (oratorio; complete).
**(*) HM Dig. HMU 90 7030/2 [id.]. U. C. Berkeley Chamber Ch., Philh. Bar. O, McGegan.
    Susanna (Lorraine Hunt), Joachim (Drew Minter), Daniel (Jill Feldman).

This is the first ever recording of a superb oratorio, written right at the end of Handel's composing career. The richness of inspiration comes very near to matching that of the other biblical piece he wrote earlier in the summer of 1748, *Solomon*. It is a much more intimate piece and, if it has failed to achieve the impact it deserves, that is largely because choruses are very few, making it unappealing to choral societies. Yet the wealth of arias and the refreshing treatment of the Apocrypha story of Susanna and the Elders make it ideal for records.

When Joachim, her husband, is forced to leave on a journey, two of the Elders watch Susanna bathing and, filled with lust, try to rape her. When she strenuously resists, they publicly accuse her of adultery and she is condemned to death. Fortunately young Daniel has witnessed the attempted seduction and speaks up for her. Joachim returns and learns what has happened in his absence, and the chorus concludes that a virtuous wife is more precious than a golden crown.

McGegan's performance does not quite match those of his earlier Handel recordings, made in Budapest. This one was done live with a talented period group from Los Angeles. The main snag is that the dry acoustic brings an abrasive edge to the instrumental sound and takes away bloom from the voices. It also underlines a certain squareness in the rhythmic treatment, with tension often low, even in such a magnificent number as the chromatic chorus which follows the *Overture*. Yet with fine soloists including Lorraine Hunt (Susanna), Drew Minter (Joacim) and Jill Feldman (Daniel), this is far more than a mere stop-gap.

Tamerlano (opera; complete).
(M) *** Erato/Warner Dig. 2292 45408-2 (3) [id.]. E. Bar. Soloists, Gardiner.
    Tamerlano (Derek Lee Ragin), Bajazet (Nigel Robson), Asteria (Nancy Argenta), Andronico (Michael Chance), Irene (Jane Findlay), Leone (René Schirrer).

Tamerlano takes place in Prusa, capital of Bithinia, at the very beginning of the fifteenth century. The Ottoman Emperor, Bajazet, is held prisoner by the Tartar ruler, Tamerlane (Tamerlano), who has conquered his empire. Tamerlane is betrothed to Irene, Princess of Trabisond, but has not as yet had the pleasure of seeing his prospective bride. However, he does see Bajazet's daughter, Asteria, and promptly falls in love with her, renouncing his obligation to Irene. A Greek prince, Andronicus, friend of Tamerlane, also loves Asteria and she returns his feelings.

In Tamerlane's palace Andronicus is instructed to free Bajazet from his chains, but the latter mistrusts Tamerlane's motives and would kill himself, were it not for his protective love for his daughter. However, Tamerlane now sends Andronicus to offer Bajazet his freedom and at the same time convey his feelings to Asteria. If he is successful, Andronicus will be offered as a reward the throne of Greece and marriage to Princess Irene.

Not surprisingly, Bajazet scorns Tamerlane's conditional promise of freedom; on receiving Andronicus's offer of love on behalf of Tamerlane, Asteria is dismayed, thinking that Andronicus has betrayed their own mutual passion. But her love remains steadfast. The unfortunate Andronicus now has to inform Irene that, instead of marriage to Tamerlane, she has to marry him instead, and he suggests that, as Tamerlane has not seen her, she could pretend to be Irene's confidante and intercede with him before the double marriage ceremony takes place, which no one but Tamerlane wants.

Irene, in disguise, pleads her cause with Tamerlane, who listens calmly but is unimpressed; Asteria reveals to Irene her true feelings towards Andronicus. Suddenly matters are brought to a head: Bajazet determines to prevent Asteria from joining the Tartar Emperor on his throne, and Andronicus rebels and threatens vengeance against Tamerlane before committing suicide.

In a scene around the throne Bajazet apparently kneels in homage to Tamerlane as Asteria attempts to assassinate him, saying that her wedding gift is a dagger. She fails and Tamerlane orders her execution alongside that of her father. Bajazet and Asteria resolve to commit suicide, using poison they have concealed. However, Tamerlane cannot bring himself to carry out the death sentences and vacillates between begging for Asteria's love and releasing Bajazet, and humiliating them both, with Asteria to become a slave.

Once more Asteria is determined to have recourse to poison, this time in a final attempt to despatch Tamerlane, but Irene knocks it from her hand. Her punishment for attempted murder is to be sent to the common seraglio, with her father witnessing her disgrace.

Bajazet surreptitiously swallows the poison himself and, bidding his daughter farewell, threatens Tamerlane that his ghost will haunt him for ever. He departs to die, escorted by Andronicus and Asteria, who then returns to beg for her own death as she can never give herself to Tamerlane. He is horrified by the cruel results of his actions and finally pardons everyone. Tamerlane and Irene come together and the tale ends with the expression of subdued happiness.

Recorded at a live concert performance for West German Radio, immediately after a staging in Lyon and Göttingen, John Eliot Gardiner's Erato set of *Tamerlano* presents a strikingly dramatic and immediate experience. One has no doubt whatever that this is one of Handel's most masterly operas. The pacing of numbers and of the recitative is beautifully thought out, and with a singing cast notable for clean, precise voices the result is electrifying, the more so when, more than usual, in this opera Handel wrote ensemble numbers as well as solo arias, most of them crisp and compact.

Leading the cast are two outstanding counter-tenors whose encounters provide some of the most exciting moments: Michael Chance as Andronicus, firm and clear, Derek Lee Ragin in the name-part equally agile and more distinctive of timbre, with a rich, warm tone that avoids womanliness. Nigel Robson in the tenor role of Bajazet conveys the necessary gravity, not least in the difficult, highly original G minor aria before suicide; and Nancy Argenta sings with starry purity as Asteria. The only serious snag is the dryness of the sound, which makes voices and instruments sound more aggressive than they usually do in Gardiner's recordings with the English Baroque Soloists. Even that flaw might be thought to add to the dramatic impact.

Teseo (opera; complete).
*** Erato/Warner Dig. 2292 45806-2 (2) [id.]. Les Musiciens du Louvre, Minkowski.
  Teseo (Eirian James), Medea (Della Jones), Agilea (Julia Gooding), Egeo (Derek Lee Ragin), Clizia (Catherine Napoli), Arcane (Jeffrey Gall).

Dating from December 1712, *Teseo* was only the second opera that Handel wrote for London, and the first after he had established himself here. Using an Italian translation of a French libretto originally written for Lully 40 years earlier, Handel uniquely produced a hybrid between an Italian *opera seria* and a French tragédie lyrique, with the classical story of Theseus and Medea told dramatically in a brisk sequence of short arias.

Teseo, commander-in-chief of the Athenian armies, in love with Agilea, leaves for battle. He is victorious, but meanwhile King Egeo has decided to make Agilea his own wife. She refuses his offer to become queen. Medea, the sorceress, who has designs on the throne for herself, also loves Teseo, and she is distraught when Egeo come to tell her of his decision, saying that Medea shall marry his son instead.

Arcane warns the king that Teseo may seek to usurp the throne. Medea in turn warns Teseo that he may be in danger; she tells him that she alone can manipulate the king to change his mind. Arcane comes to Egeo for permission to marry Clizio.

Teseo now returns in triumph, joyful at being reunited with his beloved Agilea. But Arcane tells him of the king's plan to take Agilea for himself. Medea, furious at her plans being thwarted, turns the city into a wilderness. Then she tries to persuade Agilea to accept the king's offer. Agilea refuses until the sorceress conjures up the sleeping Teseo surrounded by ghosts. Fearing for her lover's life, she agrees to marry the king and in tears tells Teseo she no longer loves him.

Medea is so moved by Agilea's devotion and willingness to sacrifice her own happiness that she decides that, after all, Teseo shall have this woman who loves him so much. But not for long. Despairingly jealous, Medea changes her mind and, aided and abetted by Egeo, decides to kill Teseo with poison. Before drinking, however, Teseo declares his absolute loyalty to the king and Egeo, ashamed, dashes the chalice from his hand. Medea flees. The nuptials of Teseo and Agilea, and of Arcane and Clizio, are confirmed. But we have not heard the last of Medea. She returns in fury to make one last attempt to destroy the palace by fire, and it is only Minerva's intervention from on high that saves the day.

Sadly, after its initial run of 13 performances, *Teseo* was never produced again until the present century. The score may not contain great Handel melodies, but it is characteristically fresh and imaginative. Marc Minkowski, the liveliest of period-performance specialists in France, brings out the inventiveness, helped by an excellent cast, dominated by British and American singers. These include Della Jones as Medea, Eirian James in the castrato role of Teseo, Julia Gooding as Agilea and characterful counter-tenors, Derek Lee Ragin and Jeffrey Gall, as Egeo and Arcane.

Theodora (oratorio; complete).
**(*) Teldec/Warner Dig. 2292 46447-2 (2) [id.]. Schönberg Ch., VCM, Harnoncourt.
   Theodora (Roberta Alexander), Didymus (Jochen Kowalski), Irene (Jard Van Nes), Septimius (Hans-Peter Blochwitz), Valens (Anton Scharinger).
(M) **(*) Van. 08.4075.72 (2). Amor Artis Ch., ECO, Somary.
   Theodora (Heather Harper), Didymus (Maureen Forrester), Irene (Maurene Lehane), Septimius (Alexander Young), Valens (John Lawrenson).

Theodora, first heard in 1750, was one of the very last of Handel's oratorios, with only *Jephtha* of the major works to come. There is much to praise in both available CD versions, and there is certainly a great deal to enjoy in the lively Teldec account, with fresh, clean textures typical of the Concentus Musicus, and with Harnoncourt thrusting in manner, occasionally to the point of being heavy-handed. The story – bowdlerized during the Victorian era to avoid the references to prostitution – is set in the Antioch of Diocletian (284–345).

The Christian community has refused to participate in a feast celebrating the Roman gods, and the Roman governor, Valens, decrees various cruel punishments, including consigning Theodora to a military brothel. Didymus, a Roman officer, asks that the sentence be less severe for those who hold beliefs which do not permit them to celebrate in Roman ways. But Valens is not interested in the defence of Christians, and Didymus rues the effect this edict will have both on the Christians and on those who will have to persecute them, such as his fellow officer, Septimius. This good friend, though not a Christian, would prefer mercy to Roman discipline but, without such choice, can only provide pity.

Theodora and Irene are resigned to the afflictions they suffer for their faith; suffering makes them feel nearer to heaven. A messenger arrives to tell them to flee from the heathen and possible death, but Irene sees no need, the Lord's protection will be with her wherever she is. Septimius fears they are quite misguided to flaunt the President's decree. Didymus now comes looking for Theodora, whom he loves, and Irene tells him that she has been taken away by a Roman soldier. Didymus prays for the courage and inventiveness necessary to free her.

Valens calls for the sacrificial celebrations to begin and sends Septimius off to check on Theodora. She must make an offering to the gods before nightfall if she desires her freedom, otherwise she will be raped by the vilest of Valens' guards. Didymus conspires with Septimius to visit Theodora in her cell, changing costumes with her to enable her escape. But when he finds her, Theodora wants Didymus to kill her with his sword. He refuses and insists on freeing her, no matter that he himself will suffer.

Theodora returns to Irene. Grateful that her honour has been spared, she robes herself and goes back to defend Didymus. Unafraid of facing death, she confronts Valens in her effort to save him. Valens conveniently changes Theodora's sentence from loss of chastity to execution, so Theodora can be a martyr. Rather uselessly, she gives herself up, and both lovers are condemned together.

On Teldec the solo casting is strong, though this team of international singers does not always sound at home, either stylistically or singing in English. Roberta Alexander sings with characteristic warmth in the title-role of the noble and beautiful Christian. Though a purer voice would have been even more apt, she is the finest of the soloists, with the counter-tenor Jochen Kowalski exceptionally warm of tone but hardly sounding Handelian in the role of Didymus, the centurion converted to Christianity. Jard van Nes is warm and fruity as Irene and Hans-Peter Blochwitz is light and fresh as Septimius. The Schönberg Choir sings with apt weight and freshness. The jollity of the choruses of heathens is nicely distinguished from the far more solemn choruses for Christians, though words are often unclear. Bright, full recording.

The Triumph of Time and Truth (oratorio; complete).
**(*) Hyp. CDA 66071/2 [id.]. Gillian Fisher, Emma Kirkby, Charles Brett, Ian Partridge, Stephen Varcoe, L. Handel Ch. and O, Darlow.

Darlow's performance of Handel's very last oratorio, with the London Handel Choir and Orchestra using original instruments, has an attractive bluffness. The soloists all seem to have been chosen for the clarity of their pitching – Emma Kirkby, Gillian Fisher, Charles Brett and Stephen Varcoe, with the honey-toned Ian Partridge singing even more beautifully than the others, but with a timbre too pure quite to characterize 'Pleasure'. Good atmospheric recording; though the chorus is a little distant, the increase in overall immediacy which has come with the CD transfer makes this less striking.

COLLECTIONS

Arias: *Aci, Galatea, e Profumo: Qui l'augel di pianta in pianta. Floridante: Bramo te sola; Se dolce m'era già. Giulio Cesare in Egitto: Se in fiorito ameno prato; Va tacito. Orlando: Ah Stigie larve/Vaghe pupille; Fammi combattere. Partenope: Furibondo spira il vento. Radamisto: Ombra cara di mi sposa. Rinaldo: Cara sposa, amante cara.*
*** BMG/RCA Dig. 09026 61205-2 [id.]. Nathalie Stutzmann, Hanover Band, Goodman.

Nathalie Stutzmann is both characterful and brilliant in this valuable collection of arias from ten Handel operas, recorded in London with Roy Goodman and the Hanover Band. With Stutzmann so positive a singer, each item emerges as a winner, strikingly memorable. Military rhythms are a feature in several, including the opening item, *Fammi combattere*, from *Orlando*, which is like a trial run for *Let the bright Seraphim* from *Samson*. The sequence ends with the most tragic of the arias, *Ombra cara* from *Radamisto*, in which Stutzmann and her accompanists give the darkly chromatic writing the fullest expressive weight.

Opera arias: *Agrippina: Bel piacere. Orlando: Fammi combattere. Partenope: Funbondo spira il vento. Rinaldo: Or la tromba; Cara sposa; Venti turbini; Cor ingrato; Lascia ch'io pianga. Serse: Frondi tenere; Ombra mai fù.*
(M) **(*) Erato/Warner Dig. 2292 45186-2 [id.]. Marilyn Horne, Sol. Ven., Scimone.

Horne gives virtuoso performances of a wide-ranging collection of Handel arias. The flexibility of her voice in scales and trills and ornaments of every kind remains formidable, and the power is extraordinary down to the tangy chest register. The voice is spotlit against a reverberant acoustic. Purists may question some of the ornamentation, but voice-fanciers will not worry. The recording sounds well.

Arias: *Alexander's Feast: The Prince, unable to conceal his pain; Softly sweet in Lydian measures. Atalanta: Care selve. Giulio Cesare: Piangero. Messiah: Rejoice greatly; He shall feed his flock. Rinaldo: Lascia ch'io pianga. Samson: Let the bright Seraphim.*
**(*) Delos Dig. D/CD 3026 [id.]. Arleen Augér, Mostly Mozart O, Schwarz (with BACH: *Arias* **(*)).

Arleen Augér's bright, clean, flexible soprano is even more naturally suited to these Handel arias than to the Bach items with which they are coupled. The delicacy with which she tackles the most elaborate divisions and points the words is a delight, and the main snag is that the orchestral accompaniment, recorded rather too close, is coarse, though the sound is bright and clear.

Haydn, Josef (1732–1809)

L'anima del Filosofo (Orfeo ed Euridice).
** BMG/RCA Dig. RD 77229 (2) [77229-2]. Netherlands Chamber Ch., La Stagione, Frankfurt, Michael Schneider.
　Euridice (Marilyn Schmiege), Orfeo (Christoph Prégardien), Genio (Claron McFadden), Creonte (Gotthold Schwarz).

Haydn wrote his Orpheus opera in 1791 for performance in London. He was just completing it after his arrival when the whole project had to be abandoned: George III refused to license the theatre when its patron was his son, the Prince of Wales (later George IV). Though the subject of the Orpheus story failed signally to draw from Haydn the sort of tragic music that it requires, there are many delightful numbers. What one also seriously misses are the big solo numbers for the main characters that no doubt Haydn would have added before the first performance; they would have added dramatic interest as well as musical substance. This first CD recording is generally well sung, with the clean-toned tenor, Christoph Prégardien, as Orfeo, the warm, expressive Marilyn Schmiege as Euridice and the baritone, Gotthold Schwarz, a resonant Creonte. Unfortunately, Michael Schneider and La Stagione, Frankfurt, lively in the brisk numbers, too often make heavy weather of the broader, more spacious passages. A more crisply focused recording would also have helped in adding bite.

Armida (complete).
*** Ph. 432 438-2 (2) [id.]. Lausanne CO, Dorati.
　Armida (Jessye Norman), Rinaldo (Claes Hakon Ahnsjö), Zelmira (Norma Burrowes), Idreno (Samuel Ramey), Ubaldo (Robin Leggate), Clotarco (Anthony Rolfe Johnson).

Armida, considered in Haydn's time to be his finest opera, was the last he produced at Esterháza and the one most frequently performed there. It is a piece in which very little happens. Rinaldo, a crusader seduced away from crusading by the sorceress Armida, who is heavily disguised as a goody, takes three Acts to decide to cut down the myrtle tree which will undermine Armida's wicked power.

There is a sub-plot: on the way to try to rescue Rinaldo, Clotarco, one of Rinaldo's knights, meets Zelmira, daughter of the Sultan of Egypt, who has been sent by Armida to seduce him too, but at the sight of him she experiences love at first sight and promptly leads him to safety. Armida's wicked uncle, Idreno, then tries to enlist Zelmira's help to lure Clotarco and his fellow knight, Ubaldo, into an ambush on their way back to camp, but Zelmira steadfastly refuses to co-operate and saves her lover instead.

In the final Act Rinaldo is given heavy treatment by Armida in an enchanted forest. He is headily pursued by nymphs (among them an image of Zelmira) and later the thwarted Armida turns the Furies and the powers of darkness on our Christian hero, but he stands firm to the end.

More than most works in this form, *Armida* presents a psychological drama, with the myrtle tree the most obvious of symbols. On CD it makes a fair entertainment, with splendid singing from Jessye Norman, even if she scarcely sounds malevolent. Claes Ahnsjö as the indecisive Rinaldo does better than most tenors in coping with the enormous range.

The whole team of soloists is one of the most consistent in Dorati's Haydn opera series, with Norma Burrowes particularly sweet as Zelmira. As well as some advanced passages, *Armida* also has the advantage that there is little secco recitative. The 1978 recording quality is outstanding and the transfer on to a pair of CDs is characteristic of the high standard of this pioneering Philips series, with the one break quite conveniently placed in the middle of the second of the three Acts.

Armida: excerpts; *La vera constanza*: excerpts.
(M) *** Ph. 426 641-2. Jessye Norman, Claes Hakon Ahnsjö, Lucerne CO, Dorati.

With both these operas returned to the catalogue as we go to press, this set of arias and duets is the more attractive, to whet the musical appetite for the complete works. Jessye Norman's voice is superbly captured in fine recording, with Claes Hakon Ahnsjö also impressive in two duets. Lively and sympathetic conducting from Dorati.

La fedeltà premiata (complete).
*** Ph. 432 430-2 (3) [id.]. SRO Ch., Lausanne CO, Dorati.
　Celia / Fillide (Lucia Valentini Terrani), Fileno (Tonny Landy), Amaranta (Frederica Von

Stade), Perrucchetto (Alan Titus), Nerina (Ileana Cotrubas), Lindoro (Luigi Alva), Melibeo (Maurizio Mazzieri), Diana (Kari Lövaas).

The operatic mastery of Mozart has always dogged the reputation of Haydn in this field, but *La fedeltà premiata* shows its composer on his finest form. It may have a preposterous plot, but this sparkling performance suggests that in all the complications of who is in love with whom, Haydn was sending up classical conventions with tongue firmly in cheek, almost like eighteenth-century G&S. That at least would tie in with the concept of court entertainment at Esterháza, designed for particular singers and players performing before a select and familiar group of patrons. We can only guess what private jokes were involved but, above all in the extended finales to the first and second Acts, one finds Haydn as opera composer setting a dramatic and musical pattern not so far different from Mozart.

In the opening scene Amaranta, a lady with the arrogance of high birth, arrives at the temple of Diana with two doves as a sacrifice. She is welcomed by the priest, Melibeo. On the temple wall is an inscription demanding a yearly sacrifice of a pair of faithful lovers until a hero offers his own life in their place. Tempting him with false promises of love, she asks Melibeo to arrange for her brother, Lindoro, to marry Celia, which will suit Lindoro very well. Count Perrucchetto now arrives, flustered after being robbed on his journey. He is obviously attracted to Amaranta, which does not please Melibeo a bit, but Amaranta is flattered.

Now we meet Fileno and a nymph, Nerina. Both are very upset and they commiserate with each other: Nerina's love (Lindoro) has been usurped by Celia, while Fileno's lover (Fillide) has been bitten by a deadly poisonous snake. Neither knows that Celia and Fillide are one and the same person. They depart topether and Celia now appears, equally distraught, for her Fileno has vanished. She had adopted the name of Celia while trying to find him. She falls asleep, to be watched over by Lindoro.

When Nerina and Filento arrive, Lindoro is soon chased off and Celia awakens to rejoice at the return of her true love. But in the background she suddenly notices Melibeo looking on and realizes their joint danger of being sacrificed at the temple as a truly faithful pair of lovers. So to his consternation she denies Fileno. However, Melibeo suspects the deception and gives Celia the alternative of either becoming Lindoro's wife or being the next sacrifice.

Celia asks the jealous Nerina to warn Fileno that he too is under threat, but Nerina fails to understand the point of the subterfuge – and in any case the arrival of the ever-amorous Count Perrucchetto takes her mind off everything as she responds to his initial advances. At that moment Amaranta enters and is furious at the count's flagrant philandering.

In the opera's central Act Fileno, in despair, determines to commit suicide but first carves a message on a tree, telling why. Celia comes in and reads his words and is equally distraught at his apparent death. The cunning Melibeo now arranges to have Celia and Perrucchetto caught together in a cave and assigned as the next joint lovers' sacrifice.

Amaranta decides to try to intervene, for after all a philandering count as husband is better than nothing. However, she is powerless to prevent the sacrifice and the protesting couple are led to the Temple by Melibeo, only to be saved when Fileno, out of his great love for Celia and despite her apparent infidelity, offers himself as a voluntary sacrifice. The goddess Diana is so moved by his brave gesture that all can end happily. Fileno can marry Fillide (Celia) and Count Perrucchetto shall be Amaranta's doubtful prize. The villain of the piece, Melibeo, is dispatched to the Underworld.

This was the first of Dorati's series of Haydn opera recordings for Philips, launched with characteristic effervescence, helped by an excellent Haydn-sized orchestra and a first-rate cast. The proud Aramanta is superbly taken by Frederica von Stade, while Haydn's unconventional allocation of voices brings a fine baritone, Alan Titus, to match her as the extravagant Count Perrucchetto. But the sweetest and most tender singing comes from Ileana Cotrubas as the fickle nymph, Nerina. The recording is intimate but with plenty of atmosphere. It is well transferred to CD, but at times one feels the cueing could be more generous.

(i) *L'incontro improviso* (complete). Arias for: (ii) *Acide e Galatea*. (iii) SARTI: *I finti eredi*. (iv) TRAETTA: *Ifigenia in Tauride*. (ii–iv) Terzetto from: PASTICCIO: *La Circe, ossia L'isola incantata*.

*** Ph. 432 416-2 (3) [id.]. (ii) Michael Devlin; (iii) Aldo Baldin; (iv) Ahnsjö; Lausanne CO, Dorati.

    (i) Ali (Claes Hakon Ahnsjö), Rezia (Linda Zoghby), Osmin (Domenico Trimarchi), Calandro (Benjamin Luxon), Balkis (Margaret Marshall), Dardane (Della Jones), Sultan (Jonathan Prescott).

In eighteenth-century Vienna the abduction opera involving Moorish enslavement and torture became quite a cult – a strangely masochistic taste when Turkish invasions were not that distant. The greatest instance is Mozart's *Entführung*, but this example of the genre from Haydn, a light entertainment for Prince Esterházy's private theatre, is worthy of comparison with its very similar story.

Prince Ali, forced to flee his homeland by his unscrupulous brother, arrives in Persia where he has been befriended by the king. He falls in love with the king's daughter, Rezia, and she with him, but their match is hopeless as she is promised to another suitor. The lovers elope by sea but are captured and separated by pirates. Now Prince Ali arrives in Cairo where Rezia is already a slave in the Sultan's harem. Osmin is Ali's servant, but his gluttony tempts him to join Calandro and a group of dervishes who seem to have an inexhaustible supply of good things to eat.

Rezia is already one of the Sultan's favourites even though (unbelievably) she has managed to stay out of his bed. She sees her lover from a window and, determining to test his fidelity, sends her slave Balkis with an assignation without naming the lady in question. Ali rejects the temptation but, rather than appear rude, accompanies Balkis and takes Osmin with him who relishes the offered feast.

A further assignation is then offered in the form of a beautiful slave, Dara, but when this is refused the reassured Rezia enters and takes her lover in her arms, reassuring him that the Sultan has left her unmolested. With Calandro's help they all plan to escape down a secret staircase and Calandro has a storehouse where they can hide.

The Sultan offers a substantial reward for their capture, and in consequence Calandro is tempted to reveal their hiding place to the Sultan's soldiers, and the use of disguise proves a failure. Yet, just as the lovers are awaiting execution, they are saved by the Sultan's humane clemency. He pardons them, and instead the treacherous Calandro is condemned to death. However, even this death sentence is commuted at the lovers' request; instead, Calandro is exiled and the happy pair can be married, amid general rejoicing.

In 47 generally brief numbers, but with finales of almost Mozartian complexity, the opera may lack depth of characterization (Haydn was using a libretto also set by Gluck), but the result is musically delightful. The most heavenly number of all is a trio for the three sopranos in Act I, *Mi sembra un sogno*, which, with its high-flown legato phrases, keeps reminding one of *Soave sia il vento* in *Così fan tutte*. The tenor's trumpeting arias are beautifully crisp and the vigorous canzonettas for the two *buffo* basses include a nonsense song or two. Benjamin Luxon and Domenico Trimarchi are delectable in those roles. Claes Ahnsjö is at his finest, resorting understandably to falsetto for one impossible top E flat; the role of the heroine is superbly taken by Linda Zoghby, and she is well supported by Margaret Marshall and Della Jones.

The secco recitatives are rather heavy, as ever contradicting Dorati's well-sprung style in Haydn. The recording conveys a most convincing theatre atmosphere, well transferred to CD, though voices are not always as cleanly focused as in some of this fine series. An indispensable set, just the same. The layout places each of the three Acts on a single CD and makes room on the third for two arias which Haydn devised for other men's operas, plus one for his own *Acide e Galatea*. The selection ends with an amazing eating and drinking trio.

L'infedeltà delusa (complete).
*** Ph. 432 413-2 (2) [id.]. Lausanne CO, Dorati.
    Vespina (Edith Mathis), Sandrina (Barbara Hendricks), Filippo (Aldo Baldin), Nencio (Claes Hakon Ahnsjö), Nanni (Michael Devlin).
**(*) HM/BMG RD 77099 (2) [77099-2-RC]. La Petite Bande, Sigiswald Kuijken.
    Vespina (Nancy Argenta), Sandrina (Lena Lootens), Filippo (Christoph Prégardien), Nencio (Markus Schäfer), Nanni (Stephen Varcoe).

L'infedeltà delusa ('Infidelity outwitted') was the last of the admirable Philips series of Haydn operas recorded with Antal Dorati and the Lausanne Chamber Orchestra, providing an important nucleus of the works written for performance at Esterháza. This one, a rustic comedy, may not be dramatically the most imaginative, but by the standards of the time it is a compact piece, punctuated by some sharply memorable ideas.

The opera is set in Filippo's house in the country and at the opening the main characters sing together of the restful beauty of the evening. Filippo and his rich neighbour, Nencio, are then seen completing a transaction. Sandrina (Filippo's daughter) comes in and her father announces that he has arranged a suitable marriage for her – to Nencio. Sandrina is dismayed, for she loves

Nanni, even though he is poor, but for the moment she yields to her father, until he says she must not see Nanni again.

Sandrina and Nanni now discuss their situation and Nanni is both angered and determined not to lose Sandrina. Nanni returns home and tells his sister what has happened; it is a blow for both of them, for she in turn loves Nencio. Nencio now sings a serenade to Sandrina, overheard by Vespina and Nanni, and says that if necessary he will take her as his wife with or without her agreement.

Vespina emerges from hiding and lets him know what she thinks of him. Later she conceives a plan to put matters to rights and, dressed as an old woman, she tells Filippo that she is looking for her daughter's husband, one Nencio, who has abandoned her. Sandrina is appalled and Filippo isn't exactly pleased either.

Nencio (who knows nothing of this) is now approached by Vespina in yet another disguise, that of a servant. She tells him that her employer, the Marquis of Ripafratta, will shortly appear, expecting to marry Filippo's daughter. Nencio is nonplussed and angrily seeks confirmation from Filippo; but before he can do so, Vespina reappears in yet another disguise as the marquis himself and states that Sandrina is socially beneath him and is intended as a wife for one of his servants.

Nencio is delighted that he can assist in making a fool of Filippo and offers to be a witness for the notary. Filippo, still thinking his daughter is sought in marriage by a marquis, is trying to persuade her as to the benefits that come with such a match, when Vespina appears transformed yet again. She is now a notary, followed by a disguised Nanni pretending to be Sandrina's husband-to-be, which he then becomes in his own right. Afterwards the truth comes out, and now Vespina and the humbled Nencio can also plight their troth in a double celebration of nuptials.

The opera brings many memorable numbers such as a laughing song for Nencio (on Philips the admirable Claes Ahnsjö) and a song of ailments for the spirited and resourceful heroine, Vespina (Edith Mathis, lively and fresh). Vespina is first cousin to Despina in Così fan tutte, and there is a splendid, Mozartian anticipation when in the finale of Act I she slaps Nencio's face, Susanna-style. Dorati draws vigorous, resilient performances from everyone (not least from the delightful Barbara Hendricks). The Philips recording is splendidly full-blooded and neatly transferred on to a pair of CDs, with one Act complete on each.

More than Haydn's other operas, L'infedeltà delusa makes one wonder whether Mozart and Da Ponte had access to it before they created their three supreme operatic masterpieces. When the Act I finale is launched by the jealous Vespina slapping her beloved's face, it might almost be Susanna in Figaro. As there, the effect is totally refreshing, with sudden realism in the midst of formality, and some of the scenes are also very complex for their period. Musically, the surprises come less in the melodic writing – which, in one jolly number after another, is relatively conventional – than in ear-catching twists and striking instrumental effects. Haydn was proud of the Esterházy horns, for example, and they have some marvellous whooping to do.

The plot of the opera is unusual for the time in giving the role of the heavy father to the tenor (well taken on RCA by Christoph Prégardien), reflecting the fact that it was expressly designed for Karl Friberth, literary adviser to Prince Esterhazy as well as a singer. This performance on period instruments nicely captures the flavour of a semi-domestic performance in the prince's country palace. Both the RCA sopranos, Nancy Argenta and Lena Lootens, are agile and precise, if a little edgy. Both tenors, Markus Schäfer as well as Prégardien, are stressed by the range demanded but, like the bass, Stephen Varcoe, they have clean voices, apt for Haydn on a small scale. The scale of the whole work, much shorter than was common in the late eighteenth century, makes it the more apt for revival today. L'infedeltà delusa may be no Così fan tutte, but this is a most enjoyable set, even if Dorati's pioneering version for Philips using modern instruments, more strongly cast, is a powerful contender.

L'isola disabitata (complete).
*** Ph. 432 427-2 (2) [id.]. Lausanne CO, Dorati.
  Costanza (Norma Lerer), Silvia (Linda Zoghby), Gernando (Luigi Alva), Enrico (Renato Bruson).

By eighteenth-century standards L'isola disabitata ('The uninhabited island') is an extremely compact opera. Costanza, her husband, Gernando, and her sister, Silvia, are shipwrecked on an island; Gernando has been kidnapped by pirates and the two ladies are left behind, sure that they have been abandoned. Thirteen years later Gernando returns with his friend, Enrico. Silvia, in hiding, spots them but does not recognize them.

The two men discover an inscription on a rock, but it is unfinished and they wonder whether this indicates that Costanza is dead. Enrico now encounters Silvia (she has worn well) and they fall in love, but when Gernando finally meets and tries to take Costanza in his arms, she rejects him bitterly and falls in a faint. Needless to say, when Enrico is able to confirm her husband's explanation, all is well. General rejoicing.

Were it not for the preponderance of accompanied recitative over set numbers this would be an ideal Haydn opera to recommend to the modern listener. As it is, many passages reflect the *Sturm und Drang* manner of middle-period Haydn – and this is hinted at immediately in the overture – often urgently dramatic, with tremolos freely used. But in Act I it is only after twenty minutes that the first aria appears, a delightful piece for the heroine with a hint of *Che farò* in Gluck's *Orfeo*.

Vocally, it is the second soprano here, Linda Zoghby, who takes first honours, though the baritone, Renato Bruson, is splendid too. The piece ends with a fine quartet of reconciliation, only the eighth number in the whole piece. The direction of recitatives is unfortunately not Dorati's strong point – here, as elsewhere in the series, rather too heavy – but with excellent recording, very vividly transferred to CD, and with just the right degree of ambience, this makes a fascinating issue. The two Acts are given a CD apiece.

(i) *Il mondo della luna* (complete). (ii) Arias for: Cantata: *Miseri noi, misera patria*; Petrarch's sonnet from *Il Canzoniere: Solo e pensoso*. BIANCHI: *Alessandro nell'Indie*. CIMAROSA: *I due supposti conti*. GAZZANIGA: *L'isola di Alcina*. GUGLIELMI: *La Quakera spiritosa*. PAISIELLO: *La Frascatana*. PASTICCIO: *La Circe, ossia l'Isola incantana*.
*** Ph. 432 420-2 (3) [id.]. (i) Lausanne CO, Dorati ; (ii) Edith Mathis, Lausanne CO, Jordan.
    (i) Buonafede (Domenico Trimarchi), Ecclitico (Luigi Alva), Lisetta (Frederica Von Stade), Flaminia (Arleen Augér), Clarice (Edith Mathis), Ernesto (Lucia Valentini Terrani), Cecco (Anthony Rolfe Johnson).

Il mondo della luna ('The world on the moon') is better known (by name at least) than the other Haydn operas that the Philips series has disinterred. Written for an Esterházy marriage, it uses the plot of a naïve but engaging Goldoni comedy. A bogus astronomer (played by Luigi Alva) hoodwinks the inevitable rich old man (Domenico Trimarchi, sparkling and stylish in comic vocal acting) into believing he has been transported to the moon. All this is in aid of getting the rich man's lovelorn daughter the hero of her choice.

The opera opens in Ecclitico's observatory, where he and four students are observing the moon through a telescope. Enter Buonafede who desires to make his own lunar survey and, on doing so, describes much engaging human activity on the distant planet, and pays well for the privilege. But Ecclitico reveals that his main interest lies in Buonafede's daughter, Clarice, while Ernesto is in love with Flaminia, Buonafede's other daughter.

To complete the lovers' sextet, Cecco, Ernesto's valet, fancies Lisetta, Buonafede's serving-maid. Ecclitico now confides to Buonafede that he has been invited to visit the moon by its emperor and that he means to do so by using a magic elixir. He agrees to share the potion and take the old man with him.

Ecclitico dresses up his garden into a fantastic moonscape and Buonafede wakes up from a drugged sleep and is very impressed by everything he sees, including a dance divertissement in which he is brought lavish garments to wear. The 'emperor of the moon' now arrives (Cecco in disguise) and agrees to have Clarice and Flaminia transported from Earth but he insists that Lisetta shall be his and subsequently proclaims her 'empress', to Buonafede's consternation. Clarice and Flaminia are spectacularly flown in and (by a ruse) are given in hand to Ecclitico and Ernesto respectively. Back on Earth the nuptial matches are confirmed under a degree of duress, but in the end, needless to say, there is general rejoicing.

Although the plot is simple by the standards of the time, it takes an age in the resolving. Much of the most charming music comes in the brief instrumental interludes, and most of the arias are correspondingly short. That leaves much space on the discs devoted to secco recitative and, as on his other Haydn opera issues, Dorati proves a surprisingly sluggish harpsichord player. Nevertheless, with splendid contributions from the three principal women singers, this is another Haydn set which richly deserves investigation by anyone devoted to opera of the period. The eight substitution arias (including *Solo e pensoso*, the lovely setting of Petrarch's twenty-eighth sonnet – the last Italian aria Haydn wrote) are simply and stylishly sung by Edith Mathis. The 1977 recording is first class throughout, as is the CD transfer, and the layout, with one Act allotted to each of the three CDs, leaves room for the eight substitution arias (recorded three years later) on the last disc.

Orlando paladino (complete).
*** Ph. 432 434-2 (3) [id.]. Lausanne CO, Dorati.
    Angelica (Arleen Augér), Eurilla (Elly Ameling), Alcina (Gwendoline Killebrew), Orlando (George Shirley), Medoro (Claes Hakon Ahnsjö), Rodomonte (Benjamin Luxon), Pasquale (Domenico Trimarchi), Caronte (Maurizio Mazzieri), Licone (Gabor Carelli).

One might infer from this delightful send-up of a classical story in opera that Haydn in his pieces for Esterháza was producing sophisticated charades for a very closed society. Though long for its subject-matter, this is among the most delightful of all, turning the legend of Roland and his exploits as a medieval champion into something not very distant from farce. Roland's madness (*Orlando furioso*) becomes the amiable dottiness of a Disney giant with a club.

As the opera begins, Rodomonte, King of Barbary, asks the shepherdess Eurilla if she knows where he can find Angelica, Queen of Cathay, and her lover, Medoro. They are both hiding from Orlando's destructive fury and Angelica isn't very pleased about it. Rodomonte now meets Pasquale, Orlando's amiable squire, and Eurilla prevents them falling out. Meanwhile Orlando is seen obsessed by Angelica and desperately jealous of Medoro.

When the altercation between Orlando and the feisty Rodomonte finally comes, the sorceress Alcina comes to Rodomonte's rescue and Orlando is magically confined in a cage. Later he is freed and Rodomonte is about to challenge him again when Eurilla arrives to announce that Angelica and Medoro have escaped.

Orlando dashes off to find them. Meanwhile Eurilla and Pasquale have fallen in love. Medoro and Angelica become separated, and Angelica, after searching everywhere for him, is convinced Medoro is dead. She is about to jump off a clifftop when Alcina once more comes to the rescue and Angelica miraculously finds herself in her lover's arms again. Orlando catches up with them, of course, but the resourceful and indefatigable Alcina keeps him in check with a pair of monsters.

This proves not permanent enough, and in desperation Alcina first turns Orlando to stone, then mistakenly relents, and he pursues her angrily, to find himself entombed within the rock-face. Finally, with the assistance of Charon, the famous ferryman, Alcina lifts Orlando's madness with water from the river Lethe. All ends happily and the two couples can unite in peace.

There are plenty of touches of parody in the music: the bass arias of the King of Barbary suggest mock Handel and Charon's aria (after Orlando is whisked down to the Underworld) brings a charming exaggeration of Gluck's manner. Above all the Leperello-like servant figure, Pasquale, is given a series of numbers which match and even outshine Mozart, including a hilarious duet when, bowled over by love, he can only utter monosyllables – cue for marvellous *buffo* singing from Domenico Trimarchi. The overall team is strong, with Arleen Augér as the heroine outstandingly sweet and pure. George Shirley as Orlando snarls too much in recitative, but it is an aptly heroic performance; and Elly Ameling and Gwendoline Killebrew in subsidiary roles are both excellent. The recitatives here, though long, are rather less heavily done than in some other Dorati sets, and the 1976 recording is first rate and splendidly transferred to three CDs, one for each Act.

La vera costanza (complete).
*** Ph. 432 424-2 (2) [id.]. Lausanne CO, Dorati.
    Rosina (Jessye Norman), Lisetta (Helen Donath), Count Errico (Claes Hakon Ahnsjö), Villotto Villano (Wladimiro Ganzarolli), Masino (Domenico Trimarchi), Baroness Irene (Kari Lövaas), Marchese Ernesto (Anthony Rolfe Johnson).

Written, like most of Haydn's operas, for private performance at Esterháza, *La vera costanza* keeps an elegantly urbane tone of voice, illustrating what is on the face of it a preposterous story of a shipwreck and a secret marriage.

The opening scene brings ashore the haughty Baroness Irene, the Marquis Ernesto (who has her in mind for his wife), a rich but vapid courtier, Villotto, and the Baroness's maid, Lisetta, all crammed into a small boat. Much the worse for wear, they are offered shelter by lovely Rosina and her brother, Masino.

This is doubly opportune, for the baroness has been worried that her nephew, Count Errico, had been captivated by the said Rosina and planned to make a highly unsuitable marriage with her. She intends to marry Rosina off to the fop, Villotto, instead, who is enraptured with the idea of such a beautiful prize.

Alas, Baroness Irene does not know that Rosina is not only already the wife of the count but that she has borne him a son and heir. The count now arrives and makes plain to Villotto that he must keep away from Rosina, but the baroness threatens Rosina's brother with death unless he persuades Rosina to accept Villotto. At the same time Lisetta adds to Masino's confusion by making it plain that she is very attracted to him.

The count now decides to test Rosina's constancy and speaks unfeelingly to her. Rosina confides in Lisetta and is willing to die rather than be coerced into accepting Villotto. Now the count relents and takes Rosina into his arms, but the baroness enters with a portrait of the woman she wants him to marry and, when he innocently expresses admiration for her, poor Rosina does not know where she is!

Later Ernesto (who will not be allowed to marry the baroness until the nuptials of her nephew are settled to her satisfaction) tries to persuade Rosina that only she can bring him his desired happiness. He is overheard by both the count and the baroness, both of whom, reasonably enough, jump to the conclusion that he is now courting Rosina. Villotto and Lisetta also reject her when they hear what has happened. The count is furious enough with Rosina to want to have Villotto kill her and her brother, until Lisetta, realizing the mistake, convinces him that Rosina remains faithful.

But by now Rosina has fled with her child. Masino comes looking for her and Villotto follows him and is about to murder him, on the count's orders when Lisetta again saves the situation. The count finally discovers the whereabouts of Rosina through her son and begs her forgiveness. The baroness makes one last attempt to part Rosina and her nephew with forged letters, but she fails: this time they trust each other, and the opera ends with the family reunited and the baroness ready, finally, to go to the altar with Ernesto.

Like Mozart's *Marriage of Figaro*, the piece has serious undertones, if only because it is the proletarian characters who consistently inspire sympathy while the aristocrats come in for something not far short of ridicule. The individual numbers may be shorter-winded than in Mozart, but Haydn's sharpness of invention never lets one down, and the big finales to each of the first two Acts are fizzingly impressive, pointing clearly forward to *Figaro*. Overall the opera is nicely compact. In every way bar one this is a delectable performance.

The conducting of Dorati sparkles, Jessye Norman is superb as the virtuous fisher-girl, Rosina, while the others make up an excellent team, well cast in often difficult roles designed for the special talents of individual singers at Esterháza. The snag is the continuo playing of Dorati himself, heavy and clanguorous, holding up the lively singing of the secco recitatives. Apart from some discrepancy of balance between the voices and a touch of dryness in the acoustic, the recorded sound is excellent. The CD transfer is first rate, too, and the opera fits snugly on a pair of CDs.

Heise, Peter (1830–79)

Drot og Marsk (King and Marshal) (complete).
*** Chan. Dig. CHAN 9143/5 (3) [id.]. Danish Nat. R. Ch. & RSO, Michael Schønwandt.
King Erik (Poul Elming), Stig Andersson (Bent Norup), Fru Ingeborg (Eva Johansson), Rane Johnsen (Kurt Westi), Count Jakob (Christian Christiansen), Jens Grand (Aage Haugland), Arved Bengsten (Ole Hedegaard), Aase (Inge Nielsen), Herald (Ronnie Johansen).

Heise is best known for his contribution to the literature of Danish song: he composed about 300. His opera, *Drot og Marsk*, composed in the mid-1870s not long before his untimely death, was his first major attempt at the genre, though it was not the first time he addressed himself to the theme of the unsolved murder of King Erik Glipping in Jutland in 1286. (There is an earlier Overture, *Marshal Stig*, whose first performance Gade conducted and which he substantially revised for the opera!)

The plot itself is straightforward and tells how Marshal Stig Andersson and his fellow-conspirators murder Erik V at Finderup to avenge his seduction of the marshal's wife, Ingeborg. Unable to bear the shame, Ingeborg takes her own life and the marshal is banished.

Heise's opera is a delight from beginning to end, full of charm and fertile melodic invention; it has plenty of variety and, given Heise's lack of orchestral experience, is very well scored. The liveliness and freshness of its inspiration are well conveyed in this excellent performance; there are hardly any weaknesses in the cast, and the orchestral playing under Michael Schønwandt is eminently alive and sensitive. The Chandos recording, made in collaboration with Danish Radio, is excellently balanced with the voices recorded truthfully and with plenty of air round the sound. *Drot og Marsk* may not be the equal of either of the Nielsen operas, but it is dramatically effective and has abundant charm. An eminently enjoyable set.

Henze, Hans Werner (born 1926)

Die Bassariden (The Bassarids).
*** Koch Schwann 314 006-2 (2) [id.]. Berlin RIAS Chamber Ch. & RSO, Albrecht.
   Dionysus / Voice (Kenneth Riegel), Penthus (Andreas Schmidt), Cadmus (Michael Burt),
   Tiresias (Robert Tear), Captain (William Murray), Agave (Karan Armstrong), Autonoe
   (Celina Lindsley), Beroe (Ortrun Wenkel).

In a massive single Act of almost two hours, Henze's *The Bassarids*, based on the *Bacchae* of Euripides, is among the most powerful of modern operas. It is not just more deeply emotional than is usual with Henze, it tellingly and involvingly presents a contrast of rival philosophies between the Dionysiac and the Apollonian, the sensual and the intellectual.

With its well-constructed libretto by W. H. Auden and Chester Kallman (who also did *The Rake's Progress* for Stravinsky) it becomes on disc a massive dramatic symphony, full of inventive vigour. But in order to understand the narrative it is important to know the mythological background to the story.

Thebes was founded by Cadmus (son of the King of Tyre, brother of Europa, who was loved by Zeus disguised as a bull), who was also responsible for the Sown Men (fire warriors) who sprang from dragon's teeth. Directed by Cadmus, they built the city and founded its noble families. One of the Sown Men, Echion, married Cadmus's daughter, Agave. Another of his daughters, Semele, was courted by Zeus as a mortal. At her death, her unborn son, Dionysus, was sown into Zeus's thigh and was born from his body.

Semele's tomb then became a shrine of pilgrimage for followers of the cult of Dionysus, but it was said by unbelievers that Semele's lover, and the father of Dionysus, was not Zeus but a mortal, bringing scorn on the cult. Cadmus abdicated and his grandson, Pentheus, became King of Thebes and, torn between the two explanations concerning his ancestry, was yet afraid of bringing down the wrath of Dionysus upon himself.

The opera opens in the courtyard of the royal palace in Thebes. A flame burns on the altar of the tomb of Semele. The Bassarids (citizens) gather in homage to the new king, Pentheus. A voice is heard in the distance announcing that Dionysus is at hand. The crowd disperses and Cadmus, Beroe (a slave, nurse to both Semele and Pentheus), Agave and Tiresias (an old blind prophet) enter the now empty courtyard. Tiresias expresses his fervent desire to worship Dionysus and visit Mount Cythaeron.

Cadmus exclaims that there is no proof that Dionysus is a god and that Pentheus rages at the sound of his name. The Bassarids are heard in the distance and the captain of the guard approaches Agave and her sister, Autonoe, who has also just appeared. Both are captivated by this handsome man. Beroe instructs him to proclaim that Semele was not loved by an immortal, that her offspring could therefore not be a god, and that Thebans are forbidden to believe otherwise.

Pentheus now enters, scorns the flame burning on the tomb and extinguishes it with his cloak. He is angry that the Bassarids are not in the square to witness his action and Agave tells him that they have gone to Cythaeron. Pentheus departs in fury. The voice of Dionysus is heard singing ecstatically of Cythaeron, and Agave and Autonoe are hypnotized by what they hear and they dance off. Pentheus returns and Cadmus is horrified to hear him announce an even sterner enforcement of his proclamation.

He orders the guards to bring prisoners back from Cythaeron, and when they arrive they include Agave, Autonoe, Tiresias and a youthful stranger (who is in fact Dionysus), all apparently in a state of trance. Exasperated, Pentheus orders that they be taken away and questioned under torture. The prisoners say nothing and obviously feel no pain when tortured.

Agave and Autonoe are sent back to the palace, and the captain of the guard is ordered to demolish Tiresias's house. Pantheus grows angrier and angrier as he questions the young stranger, believing him to be a priest of Dionysus.

The stranger at last tells the story of a slave ship on which Dionysus caused a vine to grow from the deck and serpents to appear. The seamen, leaping overboard in terror, were turned into dolphins. Pentheus orders the whipping of the stranger, whereupon tremors of an earthquake shake the city, the cloak flung on Semele's tomb moves aside and the flame rekindles itself.

The prisoners escape, shouting as they run towards Cythaeron. Pentheus orders that all followers of Dionysus be eradicated, but the stranger advises caution and shows Pentheus his mother's mirror. In it he sees reflected the flame from the tomb. Agave and Autonoe laugh helplessly at Pentheus and the Bassarids can also be heard joining in the mirth.

After an interlude – an extended charade, performed by Agave, Autonoe and the captain, with Tiresias playing the part of Calliope – there is more laughter. Then the stranger warns Pantheus of great danger as he makes ready to travel to Mount Cythaeron. He is advised to disguise himself as a woman, and he does so, dressed in one of Agave's gowns. Beroe now enters, addresses the stranger as Dionysus and begs him to spare Pentheus. Dionysus refuses.

Beroe and Cadmus lament the loss of the king and the downfall of Thebes. Dionysus organizes the Bassarids to hunt for a trespasser in their midst. Pentheus hides in the foliage, but a shaft of light falls on him, as from his mother's mirror. He calls on her for help to no avail and dies, screaming. Agave now enters the courtyard carrying the head of Pentheus and demanding to see the king. She believes she is carrying the head of a lion and is appalled when she recognizes her own son.

Pentheus's mangled body is now brought in by the captain and the guards. Autonoe disclaims any part in the murder, but Agave now realizes that she is responsible and begs Cadmus, her father, to kill her with Pentheus' sword. Dionysus now appears and banishes Cadmus, Agave and Autonoe from Thebes. He restores Semele to her formal place on the tomb and his own statue stands there too. Thus he has achieved his revenge for their treatment of his mother. The Bassarids sing his praises.

With its meaty musical argument and consciously symphonic shape, *The Bassarids* is an opera that has cried out for a complete recording, and this fine account from Berlin fits the bill well, amply confirming the work's power. The cast is first rate, including Kenneth Riegel, Andreas Schmidt, Robert Tear and Karen Armstrong, and the 1986 sound is full and well balanced, giving weight and warmth to the taut playing of the Berlin Radio Symphony Orchestra. The choral writing adds greatly to the impact, splendidly realized here by the RIAS Choir. One unnecessary snag is that the CDs provide separate tracks only for the four movements (Acts), not for individual sections.

Herrmann, Bernard (1911–75)

Wuthering Heights: complete.
(M) *** Unicorn UKCD 2050/2 [id.]. Elizabethan Singers, Pro Arte O, composer.
 Catherine Earnshaw (Morag Beaton), Heathcliffe (Donaldson Bell), Hindley Earnshaw (John Kitchiner), Isabella Linton (Pamela Bowden), Edgar Linton (Joseph Ward), Nelly Linton (Elizabeth Bainbridge), Joseph (Michael Rippon), Mr Lockwood (David Kelly), Hareton Earnshaw (Mark Snashall).

Bernard Herrmann, best known for his film scores and as conductor, spent many years working on his operatic adaptation of Emily Brontë's novel and, though it inevitably gives an over-simplified idea of the tensions in the original story, the result is confident and professional. Much of the writing is fittingly atmospheric, though Herrmann detracts from the final effect by going on too long (3½ hours) and keeps the pace of the music consistently slow. Though the writing is purely illustrative rather than musically original, this performance, strongly conducted by the composer, makes for a colourful telling of the story. The solo singing is consistently good and the recording beautifully clear. The Elizabethan Singers come in rather incongruously as highly civilized 'carollers from Gimmerton'. Perhaps the whole drama is too civilized to represent stark Brontë emotions, but it is good to have on CD a complete recording of an ambitious modern opera, as yet unstaged.

Hindemith, Paul (1895–1963)

(i) *Cardillac:* complete; (ii) *Mathis der Maler:* excerpts.
(M) *** DG 431 741-2 (2) [id.]. (i) Cologne R. Ch. & SO, Keilberth; (ii) Fischer-Dieskau, Grobe, Pilar Lorengar, Berlin RSO, Ludwig.
 Cardillac (Dietrich Fischer-Dieskau), Cardillac's Daughter (Leonore Kirchstein), Officer (Donald Grobe), Gold Merchant (Karl Christian Kohn).

Taken from a radio performance, this reissue of *Cardillac* shows Hindemith at his most vigorous. In the story of a Parisian goldsmith who resorts to murder in order to keep his own creations, Hindemith uses academic forms such as fugue and passacaglia with Bachian overtones in the idiom but to striking dramatic effect.

The opera's opening scene takes place in a busy Paris street where a mob has gathered. A series of murders has occurred and the king's edict is proclaimed that, when found, the murderer shall be burned alive. The crowd disperses leaving a lone figure: it is Cardillac, the goldsmith, a much respected and highly skilled artist.

A conversation between a woman and a cavalier, an officer of the king's guard, reveals a curious link between the goldsmith's work and the murders: before dying, each victim has purchased something made by Cardillac. She offers to give herself to the cavalier if in return he will bring her the finest artefact from Cardillac's workshop. The cavalier decides that a night of love is worth the risk of dying. Later in her bedchamber the lady is languorously preparing for her new lover's visit, and when he arrives he brings her a magnificent golden belt.

As they are about to consummate their passion, a cloaked and masked figure enters, stabs the cavalier to death and disappears, taking the belt with him. The local gold merchant is understandably suspicious of the connection between Cardillac and the murders but, on seeking to do business with the craftsman, is told that the gold he offers to supply is impure. They leave together and Cardillac's daughter is now alone, awaiting her lover, with whom she plans to elope – though torn by a sense of duty towards her father.

When Cardillac returns, it is with a supply of pure gold: he is thrilled by its quality, and his daughter is convinced that he loves this gleaming metal more than he loves her. Cardillac explains that each piece of his work renews his zest for life, but is sympathetic to her betrothal. The king now looks over Cardillac's choicest pieces, the bloodstained gold belt among them, but is discouraged by the goldsmith from making a purchase. Even the king is vulnerable to obsessive retribution.

An officer now enters and asks for Cardillac's permission to marry his daughter. Accepted, he then buys a golden chain from his reluctant prospective father-in-law. When he leaves with his purchase, the officer is followed by a masked figure, dressed all in black. It is night and the street is crowded, yet the officer strolls along with his new acquisition displayed round his neck. He is aware of the figure following him. It is Cardillac who stabs him but inflicts only a minor wound then escapes.

The guards are called and Cardillac is dragged back in, but the officer refuses to accuse him and suggests that the gold merchant could be the possible attacker. Cardillac now battles with his conscience. At first he suggests that the gold merchant is merely an accomplice, that he has watched the real murderer but will not identify him. The angry crowd threatens to demolish his workshop if he refuses to name the killer and, to save his beloved artefacts, Cardillac admits to the murders and the crowd beats him to death.

As he lies dying, the officer returns and asks why the mob took matters so far, acting as judge and executioner, when Cardillac was so obviously a victim of madness. As he dies, Cardillac tries to kiss the chain, and the opera closes with a threnody lamenting the tragedy of his heroic obsession with the works of art he had created.

Fischer-Dieskau as the goldsmith has a part which tests even his artistry and, though the other soloists are variable in quality, the conducting of Keilberth holds the music together strongly. This is the original, 1926 version of the score, fresher and more effective than Hindemith's later revision.

As a generous and ideal coupling, the second disc contains an hour of excerpts from Hindemith's even more celebrated opera, *Mathis der Maler*, which is concerned with the conflict in Germany between the Lutherans and Papists at the time of the Reformation.

Mathis is a painter working on frescos in the St Anthony Monastery in Mainz. He is attracted to Regina, the daughter of Schwalb, the leader of the peasants' rebellion, whom he aids. He lovingly gives Regina a ribbon to bind her hair. The Cardinal Archbishop of Mainz, who seeks to burn the religious literature of the Lutheran movement, has his own personal temptation – to renounce celibacy so that he can marry Ursula, daughter of Riedlinger, a rich Lutheran burgher of Mainz, a marriage which could also bring considerable financial advantages to the church treasury.

Schwalb dies in a bloody peasant insurrection in which Mathis is caught up but from which he escapes alongside the distraught and grieving Regina. Finally the cardinal learns a degree of tolerance from Ursula, and he and she go their own ways and retain their respective faiths. The key central scene of the opera reflects the Temptations of St Anthony: Mathis is tempted by luxury, success and martydom, and the cardinal (as St Paul) tells Mathis (as St Anthony) to be true to himself and his talent and to dedicate his work to God. Regina dies, imagining she has seen her father's image in Mathis's painting of the Resurrection but first asking Ursula to return to Mathis the hair ribbon he once gave her. Mathis is left to find satisfaction in his artistic achievements alone.

Again with Fischer-Dieskau taking the lead, and with Donald Grobe in a supporting role, the DG performance is highly impressive. The selection concentrates on Mathis's solos and on his duets with his beloved, Regina, a role beautifully sung by Pilar Lorengar. The 1960s recordings of both operas are excellently transferred, with voices full and fresh. No texts are given, but instead there are detailed summaries of the plots, with copious quotations.

Holst, Gustav (1874–1934)

(i) *The Wandering Scholar* (opera, ed. Britten and I. Holst; complete); (ii) *Choral hymns from the Rig Veda* (Group 2), *H. 98; Hymn of Jesus, Op. 37; Ode to Death, Op. 38.*
Withdrawn: * *** EMI CDC7 49409-2. (i) E. Op. Group, ECO, Bedford; (ii) London Symphony Ch., St Paul's Ch., LPO, Groves.
Norma Burrowes, Robert Tear, Michael Rippon, Michael Langdon

The one-Act comic opera *The Wandering Scholar* works delightfully on stage, but on record its galumphing humour is less than sparkling. It is a very late work which the composer himself never saw produced, and the score required a certain amount of intelligent editing before it was given modern performances. Whatever one's response to the comedy, the musical inspiration has the sharp originality and economy one associates with Holst's last period, a fascinating score.

Otherwise this generous CD (71 minutes 42 seconds) offers an indispensable collection of mostly little-known Holst. The recording of *The Hymn of Jesus* is on the whole finer than Boult's older, Decca account which has served collectors well over the years. Sir Charles Groves brings great sympathy and conviction to this beautiful and moving score whose visionary quality has never paled.

The *Ode to Death* is from the same period, written in memory of Holst's friends killed in the 1914–18 war. A setting of Whitman, it must be accounted one of Holst's most inspired and haunting works, comparable in quality with the *Choral Fantasia*.

The second group of the *Rig Veda hymns* are less of a novelty: they were written in the immediate wake of Holst's Algerian visit of 1909 which also produced *Beni Mora*. They are on familiar Holstian lines, though they make considerable demands on these singers. The recordings all come from the mid-1970s and were of very high quality, but the CD is something of a revelation in opening up the choral sound, while still retaining the atmosphere and bloom of the analogue originals. The words of the soloists in *The Wandering Scholar* are also clear. An outstanding reissue in every way.

(i) *Sávitri* (complete); (ii) *Dream city* (song cycle, orch. Matthews).
**(*) Hyp. Dig. CDA 66099 [id.]. (i) Hickox Singers; (ii) Patrizia Kwella; City of L. Sinfonia, Hickox.
Sávitri (Felicity Palmer), Satyaván (Philip Langridge), Death (Stephen Varcoe).

Few chamber operas are as beautifully scaled as Holst's *Sávitri*. The simple story is taken from a Sanskrit source – Sávitri, a woodcutter's wife, cleverly outwits Death, who has come to take her husband – and Holst, with beautiful feeling for atmosphere, sets it in the most restrained way.

Sávitri hears her husband Satyaván's song, serenading her beauty, as he journeys home. She knows that Death is waiting to take him from her. He is young and strong but she fears that Death, the summoner, will not be stayed. She cries out a warning and her husband, arming himself with an axe, faces the dark stranger. But the axe falls from his grasp and, calling his wife's name, he falls to the ground.

Sávitri holds him in her arms and addresses Death with gentle courage. Because of her quiet welcome, he offers to grant her a boon, but not Satyaván's life. She asks for her own life instead. Death points out that she already has her own life, but she responds that without her husband she will have no life of her own and will become 'an image floating on the waters of memory'. Death retreats and Satyaván is restored to his loving and resourceful wife.

With light texture and many slow tempi, this is a work which can fall apart in an uncommitted performance, but the Hyperion version makes an excellent alternative to Imogen Holst's earlier Argo/Decca recording with Dame Janet Baker (currently withdrawn from the catalogue), bringing the positive advantage of fine digital recording. Felicity Palmer is more earthy, more vulnerable as Sávitri, her grainy mezzo well caught. Philip Langridge and Stephen Varcoe both sing sensitively with fresh, clear tone, though their timbres are rather similar. Hickox is a thoughtful conductor both in the opera and in the orchestral song-cycle arranged by Colin Matthews (with Imogen Holst's approval) from Holst's settings of Humbert Wolfe poems. Patrizia Kwella's soprano at times catches the microphone rather shrilly.

Honegger, Arthur (1892–1955)

Jeanne d'Arc au bûcher.
✪ *** DG Dig. 429 412-2 [id.]. Marthe Keller, Georges Wilson, Pierre-Marie Escourrou, Françoise Pollet, Michèle Command, Nathalie Stutzmann, R. France Ch., Fr. Nat. O, Seiji Ozawa.

Jeanne d'Arc au bûcher, Honegger's 1935 setting of the Claudel poem, is one of his most powerful and imaginative works, full of variety of invention, colour and textures. It was commissioned by Ida Rubinstein, whom we also have to thank for Debussy's *Le Martyre de Saint Sébastien*. While many of its episodes make a strong effect, the work is more than the sum of its parts.

Joan awaiting death looks back through her life. The music dramatizes its conflicts and, in a concise panorama of French history, describes the main events which led her to the stake. At the end, a parallel is drawn between her experience and that of Christ on the cross.

Using a strong cast of both singers and actors, this DG account is much more successful than Ozawa's 1970s recording in English for CBS, with the merit of being given in the original French. The Joan of Marthe Keller is outstanding, and the singers, too, are all excellent, while the choir and the six soloists of the Maîtrise of Radio France match the orchestra in excellence. The DG engineers cope splendidly with the large forces and the acoustic of the Basilique de Saint-Denis. There is a fine perspective, with plenty of detail and presence, as well as a wide dynamic range. A powerful and important work, performed with dedicated artistry and recorded with splendid realism.

Judith.
*** Van. 08.9054.71 [id.]. Madeleine Milhaud (nar.), Salt Lake Symphonic Ch., Utah SO, Abravanel.
　　Judith (Netania Davrath), Maidservant (Blanche Christiansen).

Judith dates from 1925, four years after *Le roi David*. It was composed to a libretto by the Swiss poet, René Morax, to whom Honegger had turned for his more celebrated oratorio. He calls it 'a biblical music drama' and its form, like that of its predecessor, is a dramatic vocal/orchestral concert work with interspersed narration. This was premièred at the Théâtre du Jurat in Mézières, Switzerland, in 1925. Honegger was subsequently persuaded to turn it into an opera, replacing narration with sung recitative, in which form it was first performed the following year in Monte Carlo. Abravanel uses the first version of the score.

The plot tells how the Assyrians have laid siege to Bethulie and have cut off their water; if the Lord does not replenish the water in the coming five days they will surrender. Judith and her servant go into the wilderness and cross into Holophernes' camp where they are well received. She ingratiates herself into his favour and when, during their festivities on the eve of the planned attack, they are overcome by wine, he dismisses his servants so that he is alone with Judith, who slays him. On her return with his severed head in her hand, she urges the Israelites into battle and victory. In some respects it scores over *Le roi David* in musical concentration, variety of pace and range of musical devices; some passages are marvellously imaginative and atmospheric (the Choral invocation to protect Judith on her voyage through the valley of fear to cross into the Assyrian lines is quite chilling). The performance dates from 1964 and is totally committed; the only let-down is in some of the choral singing, which could be stronger. The work is short (just under 45 minutes) and it would have added to the competitiveness of the issue to have provided a fill-up. But if it is short on quantity, it is long on musical and dramatic interest.

Le roi David (oratorio).
(M) *** Erato/Warner 2292 45800-2 [id.]. Christiane Eda-Pierre, Jeannine Collard, Eric Tappy, Bernard Petel, Simone Valère, Jean Desailly, Philippe Caillard Ch., Ens. Instrumental, Dutoit.

(M) *** Van. 08.4038.71 [OVC 4038]. Netania Davrath, Marvin Sorensen, Jean Preston, Martial Singher, Madeleine Milhaud, Utah University Ch., Utah SO, Abravanel.

Withdrawn: (M) ** Decca 425 621-2 [id.]. Audel (nar.), Suzanne Danco, Marie-Luise De Montmollin, Mireille Martin, Michel Hamel, Ch. & SRO, Ansermet.

(i) *Le roi David. Mouvement symphonique No. 3; La Tempête: Prélude.*
**(*) Sup. Dig. 110132-2 [id.]. (i) Christiane Eda-Pierre, Martha Senn, Tibere Raffalli, Daniel Mesguich, Annie Gaillard, Prague Philharmonic Ch., Kuhn's Children's Ch., Czech PO, Serge Baudo.

Le roi David is a powerful, dramatic canvas for narrators and soloists which in the course of its three short Acts recounts the slaying of Goliath, the jealousy of Saul, and David's coronation and reign. The music is highly imaginative, if perhaps a bit short-breathed. Charles Dutoit's *Le roi David* uses the original instrumental forces and not the full orchestra favoured by most of his rivals. In this he has single wind with flute alternating with piccolo, oboe with cor anglais and so on, horn, trumpets and trombone, no strings apart from cello and double-bass, percussion with celeste, organ and piano. The recording dates from 1970, but no one coming to it afresh would guess that. It is a compelling performance of strong dramatic coherence.

Listening to the present digital transfer of the Vanguard version, it is difficult to believe that the recording was made in 1961. It is remarkably vivid, well detailed and present, and the playing of the Utah Symphony under Maurice Abravanel is in many respects superior to that of the Suisse Romande for Ansermet. The recording also stands up well to the comparison, though one would welcome greater back-to-front perspective and slightly more air round the soloists. Netania Davrath is excellent, and so is Madeleine Milhaud, the composer's wife, as the Witch of Endor, and this reissue is thoroughly recommendable, emerging in a much stronger light than it did in its original LP form.

The score's savagery, colour and poetry are splendidly conveyed under Baudo and the balance is excellent. Though the acoustic of the House of Artists is over-reverberant and slightly glassy on top, this can certainly be recommended to those looking for digital sound. However, it costs more than its competitors.

Ansermet's Decca recording dates from the mid-1950s and the sound lacks the body of the Supraphon set. (Decca misleadingly list their reissue as dating from 1970, which was when the stereo version first appeared, but it was originally issued in mono in 1957.) Ansermet fully reveals the vivid detail of Honegger's rich tapestry, and has the advantage of Danco, of course, a strong cast, and amazingly good sound. Judged by the highest standards, the orchestral playing is a little wanting in finish, but Ansermet fully reveals the vivid detail of Honegger's rich tapestry. It is a pity that this version has been withdrawn.

Humperdinck, Engelbert (1854–1921)

Hänsel und Gretel (complete).
*** EMI Dig. CDS7 54022-2 (2) [Ang. CDCB 54022]. Tölz Boys' Ch, Bav. RSO, Tate.
    Hänsel (Anne Sofie Von Otter), Gretel (Barbara Bonney), Mother (Hanna Schwarz), Father (Andreas Schmidt), Sandman (Barbara Hendricks), Dew Fairy (Eva Lind), Witch (Marjana Lipovšek).
(M) (***) EMI mono CMS7 69293-2 (2) [Ang. CDMB 69293]. Children's Ch., Philh. O, Karajan.
    Hänsel (Elisabeth Grümmer), Gretel (Elisabeth Schwarzkopf), Mother (Maria Von Ilosvay), Father (Josef Metternich), Sandman / Dew Fairy (Anny Felbermayer), Witch (Else Schürhoff).
(M) *** Sony M2K 79217 (2) [M2K 35898]. Cologne Op. Children's Ch., Cologne Gürzenich O, Pritchard.
    Hänsel (Frederica Von Stade), Gretel (Ileana Cotrubas), Mother (Christa Ludwig), Father (Siegmund Nimsgern), Sandman (Kiri Te Kanawa), Dew Fairy (Ruth Welting), Witch (Elisabeth Söderström).
**(*) Decca 421 111-2 (2) [id.]. V. Boys' Ch., VPO, Solti.
    Hänsel (Brigitte Fassbaender), Gretel (Lucia Popp), Mother (Júlia Hamari), Father (Walter Berry), Sandman (Norma Burrowes), Dew Fairy (Edita Gruberová), Witch (Anny Schlemm).

Humperdinck's delightful opera, first heard in 1893, faithfully follows the events of the famous fairy story. Straight away we meet the two children chatting together; Gretel is knitting and Hansel is making brooms, for that is his father's profession. They sing and dance vigorously in order to try to forget their hunger. Their mother, angry to find that they are not working, sends them out into the woods to collect strawberries. Once alone, she worries how to feed her family. Father returns after a good day at the market and unpacks a large basket of food. He is horror-struck to hear that the children have gone into the woods and tells of a witch who cooks and eats little children. They both rush out to make a search.

In the forest the children are happy, Gretel making garlands, Hansel picking strawberries, which they eat in their hunger. Darkness falls and the wood grows mysterious with strange shapes and eerie echoes. But the Sandman appears and gently sings them to sleep. A dream pantomime shows angels in white guarding the two children. They are awakened by a Dream Fairy and, coming upon a gingerbread house, they approach it and start to nibble. Suddenly the witch comes out, throws a rope round Hansel and takes them both inside. She offers them delicious food, but they are not allowed to leave and Hansel is put in a cage.

The witch tells Gretel that Hansel needs fattening. Hansel pretends to sleep and overhears the witch's plan to push Gretel into the oven to cook her. The witch goes off on a broomstick ride and, on returning, feeds Hansel again. Then she tells Gretel to look into the oven. Gretel asks her to demonstrate, then resourcefully pushes the witch inside, slamming the door shut. At the witch's death all her previous childish victims reappear and sing joyfully of her demise. The parents of Hansel and Gretel now arrive and all join together in a cheerful song of thanks to God for the children's deliverance.

Tate brings a Brucknerian glow to the *Overture*, then launches into a reading of exceptional warmth and sympathy at speeds generally faster than those in rival versions. Karajan in his vintage EMI recording may be more rapt, finding more mystery in the *Evening hymn* and *Dream pantomime*, but the freshness of Tate avoids any hint of sentimentality, giving the *Evening hymn* the touching simplicity of a children's prayer. He relates the opera to the Wagner of Act II of *Die Meistersinger*, rather than to anything weightier. The Witch of Marjana Lipovšek is the finest of all, firm and fierce, using the widest range of expression and tone without any of the embarrassing exaggerations that mar, for example, Elisabeth Söderström's strong but controversial reading for Pritchard on Sony, and without any of the fruitiness of the conventional readings provided on the other sets.

The chill that Lipovšek conveys down to a mere whisper makes one regret, more than usual, that the part is not longer. All the casting matches that in finesse, with no weak link. Barbara Bonney as Gretel and Anne Sofie von Otter as Hänsel are no less fine than the exceptionally strong duos on the rival sets, notably Schwarzkopf and Grümmer on the splendid mid-priced Karajan set, or Cotrubas and von Stade on the excellent alternative from Pritchard. The main difference is that Bonney and von Otter have younger, fresher voices. The casting of the parents also reflects that young approach: Hanna Schwarz and Andreas Schmidt.

There is only a slight question mark over the use of the Tölzer Boys' Choir for the gingerbread children at the end. Inevitably they sound what they are, a beautifully matched team of trebles, and curiously the heart-tug is not quite as intense as with the more childish-sounding voices in the rival choirs. That is a minimal reservation, however, when the breadth and warmth of the recording add to the compulsion of the performance, giving extra perspectives in focus and dynamic, compared with any other version.

Karajan's classic 1950s set of Humperdinck's children's opera, with Schwarzkopf and Grümmer almost peerless in the name-parts, is enchanting; this was an instance where everything in the recording went right. The original mono LP set was already extremely atmospheric. One notices that the main image stays centrally situated between the speakers, but in all other respects the sound has as much clarity and warmth as rival recordings made in the 1970s. There is much to delight here; the smaller parts are beautifully done and Else Schürhoff's Witch is memorable. The snag is that the digital remastering has brought a curious orchestral bass emphasis, noticeable in the *Overture* and elsewhere, but notably in the *Witch's ride*.

Beautifully cast, the Pritchard version from Sony/CBS was the first in genuine stereo to challenge the vintage Karajan set. Cotrubas – sometimes a little grainy as recorded – and von Stade both give charming characterizations, and the supporting cast is exceptionally strong, with Söderström an unexpected but refreshing and illuminating choice as the Witch. Pritchard draws idiomatic playing from the Gürzenich Orchestra; though the recording has not the sharply focused brilliance of Solti's Decca sound, it is pleasingly atmospheric and very realistically balanced, making it preferable.

Solti with the Vienna Philharmonic directs a strong, spectacular version, emphasizing the Wagnerian associations of the score. Solti does the *Witch's ride* very excitingly, and the VPO are encouraged to play with consistent fervour throughout. The result, though rather lacking in charm, is well sung, with the two children both engagingly characterized. Edita Gruberová is an excellent Dew Fairy and Walter Berry is first rate as Peter. Anny Schlemm's Witch is memorable if vocally unsteady, and there are some imaginative touches of stereo production associated with *Hocus pocus* and her other moments of magic. The recording is even more vivid in its CD transfer.

Hänsel und Gretel: highlights.
*** EMI Dig. CDC7 54327-2 [id.] (from above recording with Von Otter, Bonney; cond. Tate).

The highlights disc of Tate's EMI version is generous, well selected to contain more than half of the opera (73 minutes) and most of the key passages, though not the overture.

Königskinder (complete).
(M) *** EMI CMS7 69936-2 (3). Bav. R. Ch., Tolz Boys' Ch., Munich R. O, Wallberg.
King's Son (Adolf Dallapozza), Goose-girl (Helen Donath), Minstrel (Hermann Prey), Witch (Hanna Schwarz), Woodcutter (Karl Ridderbusch), Broom-maker (Gerhard Unger).

The success of *Hänsel und Gretel* has completely overshadowed this second fairy-tale opera of Humperdinck. The composer had expanded his incidental music to a play in order to make the opera, which was given its première in New York in 1910. It tells the story of a king's daughter put under the spell of a witch; she is forced to become a goose-girl in the forest. The witch intends to teach her all the magic arts and makes her bake a magic loaf, death to anyone eating it. One day a prince travelling through the forest stops to talk to the goose-girl. He is the first human being she has seen, apart from the witch, and he tells her about the outside world. They fall in love and he gives her his crown. But she cannot leave with him, for the spell holds her imprisoned in the forest.

A woodcutter, a broom-maker and a wandering fiddler now arrive at the witch's hut to ask her to predict who is to be king, as the townspeople wish to know. They are told that it will be the first person to enter the city gates after the noon bells toll on the following day, a festival day. The minstrel senses that the goose-girl is of royal blood and she tells him about the prince. With the fiddler's help the witch's spell is broken. Down in the town of Hellabrunn the people dance as they await the arrival of the new king. The prince had arrived at midnight and his abode is a pigsty at the inn. The innkeeper's daughter is very attracted to the handsome young man, but he can think of no one but the goose-girl, and he has accepted a job as a swineherd.

The woodcutter and broom-maker are in the waiting crowd and the broom-maker's youngest daughter offers to sell a broom to the prince. He has no money but offers to dance with her instead. The prince now suggests that, when he arrives, the king may not be sumptuously attired but could be in simple garments. The crowd laugh at this suggestion and the innkeeper's daughter scorns this man who does not pay for anything. At noon the goose-girl arrives through the city gates. She wears the crown and is followed by her geese and also by the fiddler. The prince greets her as his queen, but he is ridiculed and the crowd turn upon them. The fiddler too is beaten. Too late, the broom-maker's daughter cries out that they were indeed the king and queen.

It is now midwinter, bitterly cold and with persistent snow. Despondently the fiddler lives alone in the witch's dilapidated hut. The broom-maker and his children arrive and ask him to return to the town. The prince and the goose-girl approach, desperately cold and hungry. The woodcutter at first refuses to shelter them in the hut and the prince becomes angry, but his anger changes to sorrow as the goose-girl tries to sing and dance to prove she is well. The prince offers his crown to the woodcutter in exchange for some bread – but it is the magic loaf. The lovers eat it together and die in each other's embrace. The children of Hellabrunn and the fiddler take their bodies back to town on a litter, and the fiddler sings his last song.

Königskinder contains much fine music, notably in the love-duets, the fiddler's songs and the preludes to the three Acts. In an entertainment for children the sadness and cruelty of a typical German fairy-tale, not to mention the heavy vein of moralizing, are a serious disadvantage, and as the fine English National Opera staging demonstrated, the piece is on the long side. Yet those drawbacks are minimized in a recording, and this fine, refreshing performance under Wallberg, very well cast, is most welcome. Good, full-toned recording.

Janáček, Leoš (1854–1928)

The Cunning Little Vixen (complete); *Cunning little vixen* (suite, arr. Talich).
*** Decca Dig. 417 129-2 (2) [id.]. V. State Op. Ch., Bratislava Children's Ch., VPO, Mackerras.
     Vixen (Lucia Popp), Fox (Eva Randová), Forester (Dalibor Jedlička), Schoolmaster
     (Vladimir Krejčík).

Janáček's highly original fairytale opera, mixing the lives of humans and animals so
enchantingly, is based on a short story, with the libretto developed by the composer. The
opening evocation of summer introduces the forester who finds an appropriate spot for an
afternoon nap. Animals and insects dance, a blue dragonfly hovers and a badger smokes his
pipe. A vixen cub (Sharpears) pounces on a frog, which leaps on to the forester's nose. He wakes
up, grabs the vixen and carries her away . . .

It is now autumn and the forester's wife feeds milk to the dachshund and the fox cub,
intended as a pet for their child. The dog (Lapàk) half-heartedly approaches the vixen with
amorous intent, but she chatters vividly about the starlings – she is not interested in the dog's
advances. The farmer's son and a friend tease the fox, and she inflicts a sharp nip on her
principal tormentor, only to be tied up by the forester and left outside in misery. As night falls it
is as if she was a human girl, and the orchestra passionately expresses her longing for freedom.

When morning comes the forester's wife feeds the chickens and the vixen begins a peroration.
The hens ignore her so she feigns death. The chickens are duly fooled, and she suddenly springs
to life and bites off the heads of several of them. The forester's wife is horrified and her husband
beats the vixen, but she bites through her leash and escapes into the woods. She teases the
badger, who goes off in a temper, and she takes up residence in his sett . . . We now return to the
humans, the forester and schoolmaster, playing cards and discussing the schoolmaster's possible
marriage to Terynka, who has also had her eye on the unpopular local priest . . . We are in the
woods at night: a bridge can be seen in the moonlight. First the drunken schoolmaster lumbers
along, then the priest and finally the forester, all thinking about Terynka and all watched by
Sharpears, the vixen. Shots ring out and the frightened priest and schoolmaster fear that the
forester may shoot at them . . . Sharpears is now seen in her earth, courted by Goldenmane, a
handsome dog-fox. They mate ecstatically and in the morning, with the vixen already pregnant,
they visit the woodpecker to be married . . .

Time passes, and on another fine spring morning the forester greets the pedlar, Harašta, who
is going to marry Terynka. The forester then sets a trap for the foxes. Sharpears and
Goldenmane soon appear, still deeply attached, with a young family of cubs. Harašta returns
with some chickens he has stolen but, taunted by Sharpears, he trips and drops his catch which
the cubs eagerly devour. The forester shoots wildly at them but, by protecting her young with her
body, only the vixen falls dead . . .

The wedding of Terynka and Harašta is being celebrated at the village inn. The schoolmaster
and the forester are philosophical about the turn of events . . . It is now spring again and the
forester is once more in the woods. He falls asleep, nostalgically remembering the springtime of
his own life. He sees a vixen cub and, as at the beginning of the story, tries to catch her, but again
finds a frog in his hand.

Mackerras's thrusting, red-blooded account of the opera is spectacularly supported by a digital
recording of outstanding demonstration quality. His determination to make the piece more than
quaint is helped by the Viennese warmth of playing. That Janáček deliberately added the death
of the vixen to the original story points very much in the direction of such a strong, purposeful
approach. The inspired choice of Lucia Popp as the vixen provides charm in exactly the right
measure, a Czech-born singer who delights in the fascinating complexity of the vixen's character:
sparkling and coquettish, spiteful as well as passionate. The supporting cast is first rate, too.
Talich's arranged orchestral suite (two movements) is offered as a bonus in a fine new recording.

(i) *The Cunning Little Vixen* (sung in English); (ii) *Taras Bulba*.
*** EMI CDS7 54212-2 (2) [id.]. (i) ROHCG Ch. & O; (ii) Philh. O; Simon Rattle.
     (i) Vixen (Lilian Watson), Fox (Diana Montague), Forester (Thomas Allen), Schoolmaster
     (Robert Tear).

Simon Rattle's recording came as a spin-off – generously sponsored by the Peter Moores
Foundation – of the outstanding Covent Garden production of the opera in June 1990. For
anyone who wants the work in English, it provides an ideal answer, with Rattle's warmly
expressive approach to the score giving strong support to the singers, who equally have gained in

expressiveness from singing their roles on stage in the theatre. The cast is outstanding, with Lilian Watson delightfully bright and fresh as the Vixen and Thomas Allen firm and full-toned as the Forester. The characterizations of both humans and animals are all strongly individual – again reflecting stage experience by such individual singers as Robert Tear and Gwynne Howell. Rattle's reading provides a clear-cut contrast with that of Sir Charles Mackerras on the splendid Decca version with the Vienna Philharmonic and a Czech cast. If Mackerras's Janáček style is more angular and abrasive, bringing out the jagged, spiky rhythms and unexpected orchestral colours, Rattle's is more moulded, more immediately persuasive, if less obviously idiomatic. The English words are splendidly clear, set against a warm, well-balanced recording of the orchestra. Though the EMI booklet is less informative than the exceptionally fine Decca one, the number of CD tracks is greater and their identification much clearer. The coupling of *Taras Bulba* – taken from Rattle's fine earlier recording with the Philharmonia – is also marginally more generous than the two movements of the so-called *Little Vixen suite* which Mackerras adds.

(i) *From the House of the Dead;* (iii) *Mládí* (for wind sextet); (ii; iii) *Říkadla* (for Chamber Ch. & 10 instruments).
*** Decca Dig. 430 375-2 (2) [id.]. (i) V. State Op. Ch., VPO, Mackerras; (ii) L. Sinf. Ch.; (iii) L. Sinf., Atherton.
  Goryanchikov (Dalibor Jedlička), Luka (Jiří Zahradníček), Skuratov (Ivo Žídek), Shishkov (Václav Zítek).

With fine digital recording adding to the glory of the highly distinctive instrumentation, the Decca version of Janáček's last opera outshines even the earlier recordings in Mackerras's series. By rights, this piece – based on Dostoevsky – should be intolerably depressing in operatic form, but, as this magnificent performance amply demonstrates, the mosaic of sharp response, with sudden hysterical joy punctuating even the darkest and most bitter emotions, is consistently uplifting.

At the brutal opening Alexander Petrovich Goryanchikov, a political prisoner, is brought out into the prison grounds to be flogged on the orders of the Camp Commandant. It is winter and the prisoners stand aimlessly about arguing and quarrelling so that his cries of pain are barely noticed, exccept by Alyeya, a young Tartar. An eagle with a broken wing, kept in a cage, is a symbol of the prisoners' plight and an old man contrasts the eagle's pride with the low mentality of mankind. The prisoners return to work and Skuratov, a homesick cobbler from Moscow, entertains his fellows with a folksong. He and his companion, Luka Kuzmich, are obviously at odds with each other, and we learn that Luka stabbed to death his tyrannical commanding officer and in consequence was beaten and tortured. Goryanchikov rejoins the other prisoners.

The sun is shining on the river Irtysh where prisoners are hammering away on its banks as they break up an old boat. Goryanchikov befriends the youthful Alyeya, asks about his sister and offers to teach him to read and write. Skuratov now tells of his love for a German girl, whose aunt made her choose a richer suitor. His narration is interrupted by a drunken prisoner crying out, 'It's lies!' but Skuratov continues to tell how he shot his rival and received a life sentence. He does not say what happened to the girl but calls out her name emotionally.

The prisoners are given a break in their labours and a lay is performed featuring Don Juan and his servant Kedril; the other characters include the various wives he seduces, variously belonging to a miller and a priest. The mood of the play is remarkably light-hearted. Afterwards Goryanchikov and Alyeya are drinking tea together when a prisoner attacks Alyeya, wounding his hand. He is taken to the prison hospital where Goryanchikov visits him. Alyeya can now read, and he has been reading the Bible. He says how unimpressed he is by its teaching that men should love their enemies.

Skuratov in a fever is obsessed with memories of his beloved Luisa and Luka lies, dying. Against this background Shishkov tells his own story. He had married a young girl called Akulka, believed to have lost her honour to a previous lover, Filka Morosov. Yet on their wedding night Shishkov had found out that she was a virgin, wrongly accused and beaten by her parents. On Filka's later departure into army service, Akulka devastated her husband by saying that she had been unfaithful to him and now loves Filka. Shishkov, agonized by her confession, had cut her throat. At this point in Shishkov's confession, Luka cries out and dies, and Shishkov realizes that he is really Filka. He curses the corpse as it is taken away.

Now Goryanchikov is taken to the prison commandant who apologizes to him and begs his forgiveness for the flogging. He is to be freed and he tries to comfort Alyeya, who is heartbroken at his friend's departure. The prisoners symbolically free the eagle. Now that Goryanchikov has departed, the normal prison routine reasserts itself in the House of the Dead and Alyeya is left alone, still wearing his hospital gown.

With one exception the cast is superb, with a range of important Czech singers giving sharply characterized vignettes. The exception is the raw Slavonic singing of the one woman in the cast, Jaroslav Janska as the boy, Alyeya, but even that fails to undermine the intensity of the innocent relationship with the central figure, which provides an emotional anchor for the whole piece. The chamber-music items added for this reissue are both first rate: *Mládí*'s youthful sparkle comes across splendidly in the London Sinfonietta's fine version, as does *Říkadla*, a rarity for chamber choir and ten instruments.

Jenůfa (complete).
⊛ *** Decca Dig. 414 483-2 (2) [id.]. V. State Op. Ch., VPO, Mackerras.
    Jenůfa (Elisabeth Söderström), Laca (Wieslaw Ochman), Kostelnička (Eva Randová), Števa (Peter Dvorský), Karolka (Lucia Popp).
**(*) Sup. 10 2751/2 [id.]. Brno Janáček Op. Ch. & O, Jílek.
    Jenůfa (Gabriela Beňačková), Laca (Vilém Přibyl), Kostelnička (Naděžda Kniplová), Števa (Vladimir Krejčík), Grandmother (Anna Barová), Stárek / The Miller (Karel Berman).

This is the warmest and most lyrical of Janáček's operas, but it is useful to understand the opera's narrative background, before the action begins. Grandmother Buryjova bore two sons, both now dead. The older of the two, a miller, married the widow Klemen, whose son was Laca. Števa was the son of Buryja and the miller and is the family heir. Tomas, the younger son, had a daughter by his first wife, Jenůfa. He married Kostelnička when his first wife died and she brought up Jenůfa.

We first meet Jenůfa as she waits impatiently for Števa, fearing that he might have been recruited into the army. Pregnant with his child, she both loves him and fears the consequences if he cannot marry her fairly soon. Laca comes by and sneeringly implies that Števa has always been his grandmother's favourite – his mood is bitter. The shepherd boy, Jano, taught by Jenůfa, reveals that he can now read, and Grandmother Buryjova comments that, like her stepmother, she has a teacher's skills.

The mill foreman now appears, and Laca gives him his knife to be ground. Laca and Jenůfa quarrel, the tensions between them essentially caused by Laca's jealousy of Števa, for he wants Jenůfa for himself. Števa arrives, the worse for drink, and calls for singing and dancing to celebrate his proposed future with Jeňfa, and he compels her to dance with him. Kostelnička, a formidable lady, tells Števa that if he persists in excessive drinking he will not be able to marry Jenůfa. The grandmother finally sends the musicians packing and lectures her granddaughter about life's sorrows and disappointments.

Although Jenůfa reassures Števa concerning her love for him, he becomes petulant when he discovers that she is carrying his child, and she loses patience with him. Yet when Laca arrives and criticizes his behaviour, she springs to Števa's defence. The jealous Laca then tells her that her rosy cheeks are her only attraction for Števa – then, without warning, he slashes her face with his knife and she runs off, screaming. He immediately regrets his action and tries to pretend it was an accident. Time passes, the baby is born, and Jenůfa is sitting, sewing, with Kostelnička in her living room. Kostelnička cannot forgive Števa, who has been absent for months, and the shame of her step-daughter's situation has become obsessive, but Jenůfa dotes upon her child whom Števa has not seen. Her face is still disfigured by her wound and Kostelnička gives her a drug to make her sleep. Kostelnička now confronts Števa about the baby. He rebels, upset that Jenůfa's beauty is spoilt, but agrees to help finance the child's upbringing as long as no one knows that he is the father, since he has contracted to marry Karolka, the mayor's daughter.

He leaves Kostelnička in despair. Laca now enters and begs to see Jenůfa. She tells him about the baby and declares that if he marries her he will have to accept Števa's child as his own, which he seems unwilling to do. Kostelnička panics, brings the baby from his crib wrapped in her shawl and determines to kill him. Jenůfa wakes up much later, thinking that Kostelnička is showing the baby to Števa, but presently Kostelnička tells her that she has been in a drugged sleep for two days and that the baby has died and is buried. Laca now enters and asks Jenůfa to live out her life with him; she is urged to do so by Kostelnička. She admits to feeling tenderness for him. A chilling wind outside brings with it a feeling of uneasiness and a bad portent for the future.

Now Jenůfa is preparing for her wedding to Laca. She has persuaded her prospective husband to invite Števa as a guest and he arrives with the flighty Karolka. Jenůfa teases Števa and makes him uneasy; Laca's devotion is unswerving. The village girls bring flowers and grandmother adds her blessing, when suddenly Jano rushes in to say that the murdered baby has been found in the millstream. A mob gathers, ready to stone Jenůfa when she agrees that the baby is hers, but Kostelnička admits to the crime and explains her reasons for it. Jenůfa understands and manages somehow to forgive her. Laca reasserts his feelings for her and now at last she is able to return his love.

Jenůfa inspires a performance from Mackerras and his team which is both deeply sympathetic and strongly dramatic. After Mackerras's previous Janáček sets, it was natural to choose Elisabeth Söderström for the name-part. Mature as she is, she creates a touching portrait of the girl caught in a family tragedy. Where this set scores substantially over previous ones is in the security and firmness of the voices, with no Slavonic wobblers. The two rival tenors, Peter Dvorský and Wieslav Ochman as the half-brothers Števa and Laca, are both superb; but dominating the whole drama is the Kostelnička of Eva Randová. For the first time on record one can register the beauty as well as the power of the writing for this equivocal central figure. Some may resist the idea that she should be made so sympathetic but, particularly on record, the drama is made stronger and more involving. The CDs give great clarity and fine definition to the warm, wide-ranging Vienna recording, the voices caught with special vividness.

The Supraphon version of *Jenůfa* lacks the concentration of the Mackerras set, but the performance is fresh, sharp and very enjoyable. The role of Jenůfa is played by a fine, creamy-toned soprano with no hint of Slavonic wobble, Gabriela Beňačková, and her singing gives much pleasure. As Števa, the tenor Vladimir Krejčík confirms the excellent impression he made in the Decca set of *The Makropulos Affair*. The rest of a strong cast is headed by two veteran singers, Vilém Přibyl as Laca and Naděžda Kniplová as Kostelnička; their singing is most assured but their voices are often raw for the gramophone. So too with most of the singers in the small parts. František Jílek brings out the opera's lyrical warmth and the performance certainly does not lack drama. It is helped by a CD transfer that is particularly smooth and natural, with a well-focused chorus, an excellent balance and a very believable theatrical atmosphere. The libretto/booklet is clearly printed and the CDs are reasonably generously cued.

(i) *The Makropulos Affair (Věc Makropulos)*: complete; (ii) *Lachian dances*.
*** Decca 430 372-2 (2) [id.]. (i) V. State Op. Ch., VPO, Mackerras; (ii) LPO, Huybrechts.
   (i) Emilia Marty (Elisabeth Söderström), Albert Gregor (Peter Dvorský), Hauk-Sendorf (Beno Blachut).

Mackerras and his superb team provide a thrilling new perspective on an opera which is far more than the bizarre dramatic exercise it once seemed, with its weird heroine preserved by a magic elixir well past her three-hundredth birthday. The story begins in the office of Dr Kolenatý where he has been discussing with his chief clerk, Vítek, the case of Gregor versus Prus, which has been going on for many years. Albert Gregor now arrives, as does Vítek's daughter, Kristina; she talks enthusiastically of a prima donna, Emilia Marty, who then arrives.

She is vastly interested in the Gregor – Prus case and she shows an astonishing knowledge of its detail. Dr Kolenatý relates its background, dating from 1827 when Baron Prus had died, apparently childless and intestate. The prima donna contradicts this, saying that Ferdinand MacGregor was his son and names his mother as Ellian MacGregor. She suggests proof could be found in the archives of the present Baron Prus. As the opera progresses it becomes increasingly apparent that the singer has intimate knowledge of many liaisons and events of years gone by and especially those concerning Ellian MacGregor, Eugenia Montez and Elina Makropulos.

Finally the remarkable truth is revealed: she is in fact herself Elina Makropulos, born in Crete in 1549. Her father, an alchemist and physician to King Rudolph II, had brewed an elixir and, in order to prove to the king that it was not poisoned, had insisted that his daughter drink it. She it was who registered her son by Baron Prus 100 years ago as Ferdinand Makropulos. Her theatrical *nom de plume* was Ellian MacGregor and she was also known variously as Elsa Muller and Ekaterina Myshkin. She had acquired the prescription for the life-giving elixir, whose effect lasts 300 years, by coaxing it out of Baron Prus, and she planned to give it to her son.

Every sixty years or so she had been compelled to change her identity, but always her initials had remained the same – E. M. For so long she has wanted to die as everything about her that seemed unnatural had continuously worried those around her. Now the time has come either to drink afresh of the elixir or else to die, and she begins to age rapidly and is at last ready to find her release. She is finally persuaded to give the elixir to Kristina who throws it into the fire.

In most performances the character of the still beautiful Emilia seems mean beyond any sympathy, but here the radiant Elisabeth Söderström sees it rather differently, presenting from the first a streak of vulnerability. She is not simply malevolent: irritable and impatient rather, no longer an obsessive monster. Framed by richly colourful singing and playing, Söderström amply justifies that view, and Peter Dvorský is superbly fresh and ardent as Gregor. The recording, like others in the series, is of the highest Decca analogue quality. The performance of the *Lachian dances* by the London Philharmonic under the Belgian conductor, François Huybrechts, is highly idiomatic and effective and makes a good bonus.

Osud (complete).
*** EMI Dig. CDC7 49993-2 [Ang. CDC 49993]. WNO Ch. & O, Mackerras.
Kathryn Harries, Bronder, Kale
  Živný (Philip Langridge), Míla (Helen Field)

This single-disc recording of Janáček's most unjustly neglected opera is very welcome. Richly lyrical, more sustained and less fragmented musically than his later operas, it is not just a valuable rarity but makes an ideal introduction to the composer. It is a piece that was for generations rejected as being unstageable, thanks to the oddities of the libretto; that was until the English National Opera presented it at the Coliseum in London in an unforgettable production by David Pountney.

Before the opera begins, Živný, its composer hero, has had an affair with Míla, and Míla is pregnant. Míla's mother strongly disapproves of the relationship and has introduced Míla to another man, hoping to separate her from Živný, who becomes extremely bitter about the situation, writing of his resentment in an opera on which he is working.

Osud then opens with a happy scene in a lovely spa town. Students and their friends are gathered together and are dancing in the morning sunshine. Míla sees Živný approaching and asks if he has come to see their son. Meanwhile Miss Stuhlá, a schoolteacher, tries in vain to organize a choral rehearsal. Dr Suda and Lhotský encourage a bagpiper to play and guests sit down for a meal. Míla's mother pushes through the crowd, looking for her daughter, upset that Živný is also in evidence. Dr Suda and Miss Stuhlá depart and the crowd disperses. Živný and Míla are drawn together and she reasserts her love for him as the father of her child, although she is obviously still worried about her mother's disapproval. The happy crowd returns and sings of summer romance.

When we meet Míla and Živný again, they have been married four years and her mother's influence still hangs over their relationship. The couple are both students and Zivný is continuing his opera, which is autobiographical and in Act I portrays his mistrust of his wife. Their son, Doubek, is heard playing and is sent off to his nanny's care. Živný is composing at the piano and longs for Míla to have faith in his work: he is torn by the portrayal of their relationship which it embodies, unsure how to express the truth. Now the young Doubek asks about love – the behaviour of his nanny and her boyfriend have awakened his curiosity – and he questions his mother. At this, Míla's mother loses all control and rushes at Míla; in the resulting mêlée her daughter and Doubek both fall over the balcony. Míla dies and the child and his father are left devastated.

Eleven years pass and now Živný's opera chorus is being rehearsed by students. Its composer tells them that his work is finished, except for the finale which, he says, is in God's hands. The baritone, Verrva, tells the company that the opera's hero is Živný and that Doubeck and his nanny are also in the story. Živný now enters and in a soliloquy dwells on Míla and her beauty and on his own conflicting feelings. He collapses and his son gives him water as he murmurs snatches of the opera, but repeating that the last act is in God's hands.

Though this recording, one of the series sponsored by the Peter Moores Foundation, was made with Welsh National Opera forces, its success echoes the ENO production too, with Philip Langridge, as at the Coliseum, superb in the central role of the composer, Živný, well supported by Helen Field as Míla, the married woman he loves, and by Kathryn Harries as her mother – a far finer cast than was presented on a short-lived Supraphon set. That was done in the original Czech, whereas this performance, following ENO, uses Rodney Blumer's excellent English translation, adding to the immediate impact. Sir Charles Mackerras matches his earlier achievement in the prize-winning series of Janáček opera recordings for Decca, capturing the full gutsiness, passion and impetus of the composer's inspiration, from the exhilarating opening waltz ensemble onwards, a passage that vividly sets the scene in a German spa at the turn of the century. The warmly atmospheric EMI recording, made in Brangwyn Hall, Swansea, brings out the unusual opulence of the Janáček sound in this work written immediately after *Jenůfa*, yet it allows words to come over with fine clarity. With a playing-time of nearly 80 minutes, the single disc comes complete with English libretto and excellent notes.

Joplin, Scott (1868–1917)

Treemonisha (opera: arr. and orch. Schuller): complete.
(M) **(*) DG 435 709-2 (2) [id.]. Houston Grand Op. Ch. and O, Schuller.
> Treemonisha (Carmen Balthrop), Monisha (Betty Allen), Remus (Curtis Rayam), Ned (Willard White).

The tragic story of Scott Joplin's life hinges on his desire to flee from composing the rags which gave him a degree of fame, and to write a full-blown opera. In the end, having completed the score of *Treemonisha*, he managed to sponsor a single performance in an obscure hall in Harlem in 1915, only to be faced with a total flop. He died two years later. Three-quarters of a century later, with Joplin's rags popular once more, Günther Schuller orchestrated and edited the surviving piano score, and the result was presented on stage in Houston and New York.

This well-rehearsed performance on record stems from that live production, and something of a live occasion is conveyed. The deliciously ingenuous score will not appeal to all tastes, with its mixture of choral rags, barber's shop quartets, bits of diluted Gilbert and Sullivan, Lehár and Gershwin, and much that is outrageously corny, but – to some ears – irresistibly so. The story (with libretto by Joplin himself) tells of a black girl who fights with all too ready success against the primitive superstitions of her race. For this to have bitten as it should, one would need a far sharper portrayal of evil. Nevertheless, taken as a folk-opera, the piece really works.

The background to the narrative is told in Monisha's long Act I monologue. She and Ned, a childless couple, found a two-day-old baby under a tree and decided to keep it. They drove in their mule cart to friends living 20 miles away and there little Treemonisha stayed for two months; then the 'parents' returned home and their new 'daughter' was accepted by their friends amid general congratulations. Monisha bargained with a white family to educate her daughter in return for doing their laundry while Ned chops the wood, for the schoolhouse is too far away. Treemonisha grows up to be a teacher and is determined to educate her own people.

The dramatic climax of the opera is the conflict between innocence (represented by the community) and evil in the form of black conjurors, for whom the people's ignorance is very lucrative. They abduct the heroine and plan to murder her by throwing her into a hornet's nest; fortunately the appropriately named Remus, dressed as a scarecrow, intervenes and saves Treemonisha in the nick of time. She is accepted as the leader of her people and the opera ends with 'A Real Slow Drag', with very careful instructions included by the composer in his libretto as to just how it should be managed.

Thus the work has the ethos of the musical rather than of the opera house. But (with the exception of some unlovable singing from Betty Allen as Monisha) the performance and recording are first class and many will find themselves warming to the spontaneity of Joplin's invention.

Kabalevsky, Dmitri (1904–87)

Colas Breugnon (complete).
*** Olympia OCD 291 A/B (2) [id.]. Stanislavsky & Nemirovich-Dantchnenko Moscow Music Theatre Ch. & O, Georgy Zhemchuzhin.
> Colas Breugnon (Leonid Boldin), Selina (Nina Isakova), Jacqueline (Valentina Kayevchenko), Gifflard (Eugene Maksimenko), Curé Chamaille (Georgy Duradev), Robinet (Nilokai Gutorovich), Duke d'Asnois (Anatole Mishchevski).

Few pieces this century can match in high spirits the overture which the Russian, Dmitri Kabalevsky, wrote for his opera, *Colas Breugnon*. It has an effervescence comparable to that of Bernstein's *Candide* or Walton's *Scapino*. Yet the opera which it introduces has remained virtually unknown in the West, except for a promising suite of genre pieces. This complete recording, made in Russia in the 1970s, confirms that the overture is not just a flash-in-the-pan but part of an exceptionally winning piece, rhythmically inventive and full of good tunes, many of them drawn from French folksong. There is a patter-song for the hero in Act I directly based on one of the jaunty themes of the overture.

Colas Breugnon was the master carver and sculptor of the Burgundian town of Clamecy in the sixteenth century, a bluff and energetic character, as the overture indicates. The opera, based on a novel of Romain Rolland, tells of Breugnon's fight as man and artist with the tyrannical duke who rules the town, as well as with his officials. You can see why the novel was so popular in

Soviet Russia in the 1930s and why the young Kabalevsky responded to it. Latterly the irony emerged ever more clearly in Russia that the attack was at least as much on bureaucracy as on aristocracy.

The snag is that between Acts I and II in the three-Act layout there is a story gap of 40 years. Enough of the same characters are still around to maintain continuity, but youthful effervescence is less apt for aged characters in Acts II and III. Nevertheless the Russian performance and recording, made by members of the Moscow Music Theatre, is most convincing, with a cast superbly led by the baritone, Leonid Boldin, in the title-role. The other male singers are first rate too, with splendidly alert singing from the chorus (which in good proletarian fashion plays a key part in the opera).

The women soloists are raw-toned in a very Russian way, and the whole performance under Georgy Zhemchuzhin reflects the confidence of experience on stage. The 1973 recording, rather dry but with fine presence, catches the voices splendidly, though the orchestra is backwardly placed. But reservations can be put to one side; this is a thoroughly worthwhile set.

Kálmán, Emmerich (1882–1953)

Countess Maritza: highlights (in English).
*** That's Entertainment CDTER 1051. Marilyn Hill Smith, Ramon Remedios, Lynn Barber, Laureen Livingstone, Tudor Davies, Julian Moyle, New Sadler's Wells Op. Ch. and O, Wordsworth.

The label, 'That's Entertainment', has brought out an enterprising series of recordings of stage musicals. Here it adds a recording based on the New Sadler's Wells production (in English) of Kálmán's operetta. Voices are fresh, playing and conducting are lively and the recording excellent. Much recommended for those who prefer their operetta in English, for the CD has fine presence.

Kern, Jerome (1885–1945)

Show Boat (complete recording of original score).
⊛ *** EMI Dig. CDS7 49108-2 (3) [Ang. CDC 49108]. Amb. Ch., L. Sinf., McGlinn.
    Magnolia Hawks (Frederica Von Stade), Gaylord Ravenal (Jerry Hadley), Julie LaVerne (Teresa Stratas), Joe (Bruce Hubbard), Queenie (Karla Burns), Frank Schultz (David Garrison), Ellie May Chipley (Paige O'Hara).

Show Boat (excerpts).
(**(*)) Sony mono SK 53330 [id.]. 1946 Broadway cast. Ch. & O, Edwin McArthur.
    Magnolia Hawks (Jan Clayton), Gaylord Ravenal (Charles Fredericks), Julie LaVerne (Carol Bruce), Joe (Kenneth Spencer), Queenie (Helen Dowdy), Ellie May Chipley (Colette Lyons).

Show Boat, the first great musical, virtually created a new theatrical genre overnight. To quote Didier Deutsch, the writer of the notes and synopsis for the Sony New York cast reissue, 'it changed the face of Broadway' and redefined the American musical theatre 'in terms that were entirely the product of the American experience'. The storyline, incredibly daring in America in 1927, does not shirk the problem of miscegenation and, in giving Joe his anguished monologue, *Ol' man river*, created one of the very first racial protest songs. Moreover the scene (often cut) showing Joe's domestic situation demonstrates the results of the emasculation by the whites of the American black male slave, with his wife inevitably becoming the family matriarch.

The curtain rises on the show boat of the title, moored at the quay in Natchez, Mississippi. Cap'n Andy, the ebullient owner/impresario, introduces the cast for the evening's melodrama, notably the husband-and-wife players, Julie La Verne and Steve Baker, who are his star performers, with Ellie and Frank (also the dance team) in support. Frank is the villain of the play. During this presentation, Pete, one of the crew, has made a pass at Julie, whom he loves, and is fired by Cap'n Andy for creating a disturbance.

In the crowd is the young, handsome gambler, Gaylord Ravenal, who has been given twenty-four hours to leave town by the sheriff. He is instantly captivated by the charm of Magnolia, Andy's pretty young daughter, and they discreetly reveal their burgeoning feelings of love in a famous duet, *Make believe*. We now meet Joe who tells of his gruelling life working alongside *Ol' man river*.

Magnolia and Julie are confidantes, and Magnolia tells Julie of her new-found love; she is given due warning by her friend that in such matters all may not be what it seems. The theatrical performance now takes place, interrupted by the sheriff. The angry Pete has betrayed Julie: she has black blood in her veins and thus is illegally married. She and her husband leave hastily, and Cap'n Andy's problem of finding new romantic leads is solved (against his wife's better judgement) by Ravenal joining the cast, with daughter (Magnolia) as juvenile lead. In due course they are married.

Three years pass. Magnolia and Gaylord now live in Chicago, still in love, and they have a young daughter, Kim. But things have been going badly for Gaylord's finances and he decides he is merely a drag on his wife and daughter and, sadly, he leaves. Mother and daughter are now found in very reduced circumstances by Frank and Ellie, who are doing well and are in Chicago for a New Year gala performance. They encourage Magnolia to try for a singing job at the club where they are among the supporting acts.

The current star turns out to be Julie, looking older and sadder. Her husband has left her. She sings her great number, *Bill*, and then, seeing that Magnolia has arrived for an audition, she unselfishly slips away and disappears. Julie, hesitant at first, still lands the job and becomes a star. More years pass, and we return to the moored *Cotton Blossom*, a relic of a past era. Here Julie's repentant husband eventually finds her and his young daughter, and they are all happily reunited.

In faithfully following the original score, this superb set at last does justice to a musical of the 1920s which is both a landmark in the history of Broadway and musically a work of strength and imagination hardly less significant than Gershwin's *Porgy and Bess* of a decade later. Even with spoken scenes cut and dialogue drastically pruned, the recording lasts for almost four hours – and that includes a fascinating appendix of variants and extra items alone lasting over an hour. The original, extended versions of important scenes are included, as well as various numbers written for later productions. In the modern 'crossover' manner, this recording is operatically cast, but with far more concern for idiomatic performance than usual.

As the heroine, Magnolia – who dauntingly has to age 37 years between beginning and end – Frederica von Stade gives a meltingly beautiful performance, totally in style, bringing out the beauty and imagination of Kern's melodies, regularly heightened by wide intervals to make those of most of his Broadway rivals seem flat. The first half-hour alone brings a clutch of hit numbers – *Make believe*, *Ol' man river* and *Can't help lovin' dat man* among them – which one would be lucky to find in a whole season of Broadway musicals today. The London Sinfonietta plays with tremendous zest and feeling for the idiom, while tuba bass and banjo regularly add spice to the ensemble; the Ambrosian Chorus sings with joyful brightness and some impeccable American accents.

Opposite von Stade, Jerry Hadley makes a winning Ravenal, and Teresa Stratas is charming as Julie, giving a heartfelt performance of the haunting number, *Bill* (words by P. G. Wodehouse). Above all, the magnificent black bass, Bruce Hubbard, sings *Ol' man river* and its many reprises with a firm resonance to have you recalling the wonderful example of Paul Robeson, but for once without hankering after the past. The cast of actors is also distinguished, with the late Lillian Gish, a star since her first appearance on the silent screen, as an old lady on the levee, right at the end. Beautifully recorded to bring out the piece's dramatic as well as its musical qualities, this is a heart-warming issue.

The 1946 Broadway cast record can be merely regarded as an appendix. The content is singularly ungenerous, omitting much that is important, though interpolating *Nobody else but me* (a solo spot for Magnolia at the end of the show). This was composed for the present production and was Kern's very last song. Having said that, the key numbers are very well done, notably Kenneth Spencer's resonant and deeply felt *Ol' man river*, while Carol Bruce's two numbers, *Can't help lovin' dat man* and (especially) *Bill*, are very successful. No complaints about the mono sound or the excellent CD transfer, and the documentation is good, including one stiffly stylized 'still' photograph of the final scene which is surely a collector's item!

Songs: *Centennial: Summer; All through the day. Cover Girl: Long ago and far away. High wide and handsome: The folks who live on the hill. Lady be Good: The last time I saw Paris. Music in the air: The song is you. Roberta: Smoke gets in your eyes; Yesterdays. Sally: Look for the silver lining. Show Boat: Bill; Can't help lovin' dat man. Swing Time: A fine romance; The way you look tonight. Very warm for May: All the things you are. You were never lovelier: I'm old fashioned.*
*** EMI Dig. CDC7 54527-2 [id.]. Kiri Te Kanawa, L. Sinf., Jonathan Tunick.

This handsomely packed recital offers a backing orchestra of 57 players and new orchestrations. Jonathan Tunick has unashamedly and with considerable skill rescored each song to suit his soloist's style. All 14 are heard complete, with original introduction, verse and ending, and several of them (usually written for movies, where their treatment was often cavalier) are heard complete for the first time on record. As with her previous recital of Gershwin songs with John McGlinn, Dame Kiri is at her most relaxed and, if there could be more variety of pacing, she clearly relishes the (often unfamiliar) words of the introductions, and her languorous vocalism is very seductive. Songs like *Smoke gets in your eyes* and *The last time I saw Paris* and, especially, the sultry *Long ago and far away* suit her approach, and in the Paris nostalgia she lightens her manner nicely in the middle section. *The way you look tonight* swells out gloriously, and *All the things you are* has a similar sense of rapture, while *A fine romance* swings along most appealingly.

As titled above, *Bill* was written – by P. G. Wodehouse – not for *Show Boat* but for a much earlier musical, and Dame Kiri's freshly soaring lyricism must be close to the original conception, although the Hammerstein revision of the words is used. Her timing is immaculate and she is equally appealing in her rather similar transformation of *Can't help lovin' dat man*, although here both the manner of singing and the accompaniment reflect the character, Magnolia, who so touches the audience with the song's heartfelt lyric in *Show Boat*.

Knussen, Oliver (born 1952)

Where the Wild Things are (complete).
*** Unicorn Dig. DKPCD 9044; *DKPC 9044* [id.]. L. Sinf., composer.
   Max (Rosemary Hardy), Mama / Tzippy (Mary King), Bearded Wild Thing / Goat Wild Thing (Hugh Hetherington), Horned Wild Thing (Stephen Richardson), Rooster Wild Thing (Stephen Rhys-Williams), Bull Wild Thing (Andrew Gallacher).

In a closely argued score, which yet communicates immediately and vividly, Oliver Knussen has devised a one-Act opera that beautifully matches the grotesque fantasy of Maurice Sendak's children's book of the same name, with its gigantic monsters or Wild Things which prove to have hearts of gold and make the naughty boy, Max, their king. After being cheeky to his mother, Max is sent to his bedroom without supper.

The Wild Things have been threatening his toy soldiers, and he jumps out at his mother as she vacuums; after their violent altercation (when she calls him a 'wild thing'), the vacuum-cleaner chases him to his bedroom. The room changes to a forest; then water appears and he climbs into a boat. A great sea-monster rises up but is quelled by Max's command. When he moors the boat, the Wild Things appear. They crown him and the celebratory Wild Rumpus starts as Max rides around on a bull's back.

Finally Max stops the riot, despatches the Wild Things to bed and climbs back into his boat. Once back in his room, he can smell the aroma of delicious hot soup wafting up from the kitchen.

On stage at Glyndebourne and elsewhere, the fun and ingenuity of Sendak's own designs and costumes tended to distract attention from the score's detailed concentration, but the record compensates here, while still presenting the piece with the bite and energy of a live performance. It helped that the sessions took place immediately after a series of stage performances. The final rumpus music, which Knussen managed to complete only after the rest, here feels like the culmination intended. Rosemary Hardy makes a superb Max, not just accurate but giving a convincing portrait of the naughty child with little or no archness. Mary King sings warmly in the small part of the Mother. The CD is particularly convenient to use, with no fewer than 26 separate bands. Any particular passage is promptly spotted, in a work of such detail, so that it feels far longer than 40 minutes. The brilliant recording vividly conveys a sense of presence and space, with the excellent chrome cassette closely matched.

Kodály, Zoltán (1882–1967)

Háry János (musical numbers only).
Withdrawn: **(*) Hung. HCD 12837/8-2 [id.].   Sándor Sólyom-Nagy, Takács, Sudlik, Póka, Mészöly, Gregor, Palcsó, Hungarian R. & TV Children's Ch., Hungarian State Op. Ch. and O, Ferencsik.

When originally issued on LP, this Hungarian recording of the complete *Háry János* included a full hour of spoken dialogue in Hungarian. For the CD transfer the dialogue has been cut out, which means that there is no dramatic continuity; but when Kodály's score is so colourful – not just in the movements of the well-known suite but in many other numbers too – the piece becomes a rich chocolate-box of delights.

Háry's escapades are familiar to all Hungarians: he is at once a simple peasant, a swashbuckling hero in his own eyes, but also something of a Quixote character – a dreamer and poet. Háry's first adventure, accompanied by his betrothed, Örzse, is as a handsome Hussar. They are at the border between Muscovy and Galicia. It is a bitter winter's day and Marie-Louise, Napoleon's wife, arrives with her retinue but is not allowed over the border by the guard. János solves the problem by assembling the group in the sentry-box itself and dragging it across to safety. They celebrate in song, then all proceed to Vienna, after Háry has insisted that his horse be fed and that Örzse go with them.

János is now made a sergeant and has further adventures, including breaking in a not too dangerous horse and providing a cure for the emperor's gout. The Viennese musical clock strikes noon, and Örzse feeds the eagle on the imperial crest. János has trouble with the knight, Ebelastin, a practical joker, but soon he is in Italy with the army near Milan, and the general seeks his advice. The mock battle with Napoleon begins and Napoleon begs Háry for mercy. Marie-Louise would now like to divorce her failed emperor-husband and take Háry instead, and she quarrels with Örzse.

Háry is offered Napoleon's empire if he agrees, but he whispers to his beloved that he will arrange matters in Vienna, whither they now all return. Marie-Louise prepares for the nuptials, Háry is given splendid accommodation, and a banquet is held in his honour. Örzse sadly arrives to say goodbye, but instead Háry returns home to Hungary with his beloved, as a great patriot. The story ends as it begins, with János a peasant, humble but happy.

Ferencsik's performance with Hungarian singers and players is committedly idiomatic, with strong singing, not always ideally well characterized but very stylish, from some of the most distinguished principals of the Budapest Opera. The CD transfer gives extra clarity and a sense of presence to the original recording.

Kokkonen, Joonas (born 1921)

The Last Temptations: complete.
**(*) Finlandia FACD 104 (2) [id.]. Savonlinna Op. Festival Ch. & O, Söderblom.
   Paavo Ruotsalainen (Martti Talvela), Riitta (Ritva Auvinen), Juhana (Seppo Ruohonen), Jaakko Högman (Matti Lehtinen).

The Last Temptations tells of a revivalist leader, Paavo Ruotsalainen, from the Finnish province of Savo, and of his inner struggle to discover Christ. The opera is dominated by the personality of Martti Talvela, and its invention for the most part has a dignity and power that are symphonic in scale. Too much of the opera takes place in the same tonal area, but overall the work makes a strong impact. All four roles are well sung, and the performance under Ulf Söderblom is very well recorded indeed (in 1977).

Korngold, Erich (1897–1957)

Die tote Stadt (complete).
(M) *** BMG/RCA GD 87767 (2) [7767-2-RG]. Bav. R. Ch., Tölz Ch., Munich R. O, Leinsdorf.
   Paul (René Kollo), Marietta (Carol Neblett), Frank (Benjamin Luxon), Fritz (Hermann Prey).

At the age of twenty-three Korngold had his opera, *Die tote Stadt*, presented in simultaneous world premières in Hamburg and Cologne! It may not be a great work, but in a performance like this, splendidly recorded, it is one to revel in on the gramophone. The story is set in Bruges at the end of the nineteenth century. Paul, its hero, is mourning the loss of his young wife, Marie, in a city which, with its still, silent canals, old, crumbling buildings and its medieval atmosphere, emphasizes everything that is past. His introspection is centred on a room in the house where he keeps mementoes of his past relationship, notably a lock of his wife's golden hair.

He tells his friend, Frank, that he has met Marietta, a dancer from Lille, who resembles Marie uncannily. She arrives and dances, and he tries to embrace her. She sees what appears to be her own portrait. When she departs for the theatre, Paul has a vision of his wife. He pleads his loyalty to her memory, but the vision urges him to rejoin the mainstream of life, that another calls to him. Paul – still in his dream – wanders out into the city and watches Frank approaching Marietta's lodging to seduce her. He seizes the key from him.

Now a group of singers and dancers approaches on a canal boat. Marietta is seen with the dancer, Gaston, and a rehearsal of Meyerbeer's *Robert le Diable* is begun, in which Marietta plays Hélène; all this is staged against ghostly sounds from the nearby cathedral. Marietta's friends wander off and Paul tells her that he loves her only as an image of his dead wife. Marietta determines to banish the ghost of her predecessor from his consciousness and uses all her seductive power to arouse his passion. She is finally successful and he takes her back to the house that was once Marie's, and they spend the night in each other's arms.

The next morning Marietta stands triumphant before the picture which represents both the women in Paul's life. Outside, a religious procession is taking place, with the townspeople dressed in medieval costumes like ghosts from the city's past. Paul falls to his knees, affected by religious feeling. Marietta mocks him and offers him her body in the most flagrantly erotic gesture, to profane his sacred mood. She derides his religious feelings as superstition, accusing him of hypocrisy. Paul defends his faith and his loyalty to the past, and orders her out of the house. But she discovers the braid of his wife's hair and, tauntingly placing it round her neck, begins a sensuous dance. He strangles her using the braid.

Slowly morning dawns and everything is as it was before. Paul's visionary dream is over. The braid is back in its box. Marietta re-enters. She left her umbrella behind when she came the day before. She leaves and meets Frank on the way out. She will not return, and Paul will no longer stay in Bruges, in that way breaking free of the past.

The score includes many echoes of Puccini and Richard Strauss, but its youthful exuberance carries the day. Here René Kollo is powerful, if occasionally coarse of tone, Carol Neblett sings sweetly in the equivocal roles of the wife's apparition and the newcomer, and Hermann Prey, Benjamin Luxon and Rose Wagemann make up an impressive cast. Leinsdorf is at his finest.

Violanta (complete).
(M) **(*) Sony MK 79229 [MK 35909]. Bav. R. Ch., Munich R. O, Janowski.
     Violanta (Eva Marton), Alfonso (Siegfried Jerusalem), Simone Troval (Walter Berry), Giovanni Bracca (Horst Laubenthal), Bice (Gertraut Stoklassa), Barbara (Ruth Hesse).

Korngold was perhaps the most remarkable composer-prodigy of this century; he wrote this opera at the age of seventeen. It was given its first triumphant performance under Bruno Walter, and even Ernest Newman seriously compared Korngold to Mozart.

Violanta takes place in fifteenth-century Venice at the time of the carnival. Its beautiful heroine is the wife of the autocratic Simone Trovai, the republic's military commander. Violanta's sister, Nerina, was seduced and raped by Alfonso, Prince of Naples, and she subsequently committed suicide. Violanta seeks vengeance and has already expressed her angry frustration by refusing her husband access to her bedroom.

Giovanni Bracca, an artist, is about to take Simone to the carnival when Violanta appears, covered in confetti. She orders Bracca to go, then tells her husband that she has enticed Alfonso to come to the house. He will arrive shortly, and then her husband must kill him. She promises that if he does so he can return to the marital bed; if he refuses, maybe she'll give herself to Alfonso instead.

Simone agrees to carry out the murder and conceals himself. Alfonso arrives, praising Violanta's beauty. She insists that he remove his cloak and sword, then reveals her intention to avenge her sister. He offers no resistance and tells her to give the sign for the murder. But Violanta is struck dumb and realizes that she is in love with him. She orders him to leave but instead they fall into each other's arms, and Simone rushes in to discover them in passionate embrace.

He tries to kill Alfonso, but Violanta gets in his way and herself receives the mortal blow. At that moment Bracca and a group of revellers burst in to take Simone to the carnival. They find Violanta dying in her husband's arms and Alfonso sobbing.

Though luscious of texture and immensely assured, the writing lets one down by an absence of really memorable melody; but, with a fine, red-blooded performance and with Siegfried Jerusalem a youthfully fresh hero, it makes a fascinating addition to the recorded repertory. Eva Marton, not always beautiful of tone, combines power and accuracy in the key role of the heroine, suddenly floating high pianissimos with unexpected purity. The recording is quite full if not especially refined.

Das Wunder der Heliane (complete).

*** Decca Dig. 436 636-2 (3) [id.]. Berlin R. Ch. & RSO, Mauceri.

Heliane (Anna Tomowa-Sintow), Der Herrscer (Hartmut Welker), Der Fremde (John David De Haan), Die Botin (Reinhild Runkel), Der Pförtner (René Pape), Der Schwertrichter (Nicolai Gedda), Der junge Mensch (Martin Petzoid).

Like the Decca set of Krenek's *Jonny spielt auf*, this Korngold opera, also first performed in Vienna in 1927, comes in a series devoted to works banned by the Nazis, '*Entartete Musik*', so-called 'decadent music'. Far more exotic, *Das Wunder der Heliane* was the opera which was initially presented in direct confrontation with the Krenek. Korngold's father, Julius, as the leading Viennese critic, vilified the Krenek piece so bitterly (ironically bringing in the Nazis as allies) that there was a backlash, and this symbolic fairytale opera with opulent orchestration to out-Strauss Strauss was quickly withdrawn. The story itself is full of overt eroticism.

As the curtain rises we meet the chained stranger, sitting alone in his cell. The old porter enters with his bread and water and we learn that the condemned revolutionary has incited the people against the king, but Queen Heliane is a more sympathetic figure to their cause. The porter removes the chains and foretells a visitor. The gaunt ruler now enters and questions the stranger's right to foment unrest and confirms his death sentence. The ruler leaves and the stranger now enters the adjacent chapel where Queen Heliane appears. She grieves for mankind, is powerless to save him, but expresses love for him in his predicament. He kisses her feet and, expressing his love in return, asks that she give herself to him. At first she refuses but then she slips out of her gown and he embraces her ecstatically.

The ruler now returns, offering the stranger a reprieve in return for the secret of his power over men's minds and particularly over the queen, whom the ruler has not conquered. He offers a ring in reward. But the stranger prefers death. The ruler suggests that the stranger should go that night to the queen's bedroom and bend her will to accept her husband's advances. The queen now reappears, still virtually naked, and the ruler realizes what has just taken place. The guards are called and the stranger protects her temporarily, but she is seized.

The scene now changes to the ruler's castle; the judges and hangman are summoned through a female messenger, previously the ruler's mistress. We hear of others being sought and condemned for profligacy. The judges now enter, led by one who is blind (Heliane's father) and they immediately decree a death sentence for a wife caught in adultery. The king tells of the queen's faithlessness with the stranger and Heliane relates how she gave herself to him, not out of desire but in pity and sorrow, so her love was pure. The ruler gives her a dagger so that she can kill herself, but she refuses. The stranger is led in and asks to be left alone with the queen, and his request is granted.

Everyone leaves but the two lovers, and the stranger asks the queen to strangle him with her girdle. She refuses but he tells her that he does not wish to live without her, takes her into his arms, kisses her in a long embrace and then stabs himself with the dagger. A crowd breaks in, seeking the stranger. The ruler now calls on the queen to bring the stranger back to life, if her purity gives her the power to work such a miracle, otherwise she will go to the scaffold.

The queen, now suffused with growing passion, bends over her dead lover while the crowd forces its way into the hall. They believe that resurrection is possible, that God will intervene. Heliane calls on the stranger to stand up in the name of God then suddenly draws back, realizing that she now loves him in all the fullness of human passion.

She continues, control abandoned, to urge him back to life. The crowd are now against her in their disbelief and call for her death. The ruler offers to save her if she will be united with him. She refuses; there is then a tremendous thunderclap and everyone is spellbound as the stranger rises from his bier. The couple's love is transcendent and the ruler, in agonized jealousy, kills Heliane with his sword then staggers from the scene, leaving the crowd joyously celebrating their freedom from his tyranny. In the final scene the lovers, transfigured, approach the gates of heaven in a close embrace.

Though the plot, with its tyrannical ruler, his wife and a mysterious stranger, is unconvincing, Decca's magnificent recording amply confirms the view that this is Korngold's masterpiece, musically even richer than his better-known opera, *Die tote Stadt*. The opening prelude, with its exotic harmonies and heavenly choir, will seduce anyone with a sweet tooth and, though in three Acts of nearly an hour each, it is overlong, Korngold – who had just emerged from his years as a child prodigy to rival Mozart – sustains the story with a ravishing score. Puccini as well as Strauss is often very close, with one passage in the big Act I love-duet bringing languorous echoes of the end of *Fanciulla del West*. Korngold's lavish Hollywood scores of the 1930s are thin by comparison. John Mauceri draws glorious sounds from the Berlin Radio Symphony Orchestra, and the cast is headed by three outstanding singers, the soprano Anna Tomowa-Sintow at her richest, an impressive American Heldentenor John David de Haan as the stranger, and Hartmut Welker as the ruler.

Křenek, Ernst (1900–1991)

Jonny spielt auf (complete).
**(*) Decca Dig. 436 631-2 (2) [id.]. Leipzig Op. Ch., Leipzig GO, Zagrosek.
   Max (Heinz Kruse), Anita (Alessandra Marc), Jonny (Krister St Hill), Daniello (Michael Kraus), Yvonne (Marita Posselt).

Read any musical history of the 1920s written at the time, and Ernst Křenek's opera, *Jonny spielt auf* ('Jonny plays on'), will have a prominent place. It was acclaimed as the first jazz opera, even though the composer always resisted that description. In Berlin in 1927 it scored a phenomenal success, reviled by the critics but loved by the public, and within the year there had been 50 productions throughout Europe. Yet it all proved to be a flash in the pan. Paris was unimpressed, and back in Germany it was quickly banned by the Nazi regime, who condemned it as '*Entartete Musik*', decadent music. Křenek (not a Jew) found refuge in America, and in New York the piece was a flop. It did not help that as late as 1938 the singer taking the role of Jonny had to be a 'blacked-up' white man. However, Jonny does not make his entry until the third scene.

At the beginning of the story, Max has met and fallen in love with the singer Anita while climbing on a glacier in the Alps. He presents her with the manuscript of his new opera but wants her to give up her travelling career and stay with him. She refuses and goes on to Paris alone, where the opera is being performed. Here Anita meets Jonny, a jazz musician, and Daniello, a virtuoso classical violinist, who seduces her. She gives him a ring as a memento, since she must return to Max. Meanwhile Jonny, with the help of the chambermaid, Yvonne, steals Daniello's violin and hides it in Anita's banjo case. When the loss is discovered, Yvonne is sacked from the hotel and becomes instead Anita's personal maid. The angry Daniello passes on the ring to Yvonne as proof of Anita's seduction.

Meanwhile Max waits for Anita and longs for the security of her love as he knew it, on the glacier. When Yvonne shows him the ring, he guesses the truth and rushes off to seek solace on that very glacier. Jonny, following on after the others, now appropriates the missing violin, but when his band broadcasts, Daniello recognizes its timbre and tells the police of his loss. Max journeys to rejoin Anita; Jonny, now on the run from the police, hides the violin in Max's luggage at the station. Max is arrested.

The jealous Daniello tries to prevent Yvonne from clearing Max's name, then falls under a train! Yvonne and Jonny – who is still trying to get the violin back – meet outside the police station. Jonny promises to help Max, and so he does by overpowering their police escort. Max now determinedly rejoins Anita on the train on her way to America and Jonny remains behind, playing his new jazz music on the violin belonging to the culture of the old world.

Hearing the opera now in a fine recording based on a 1990 Leipzig production – made just before the composer died at the age of ninety – it stands as more than a historical curiosity. Contradicting its reputation, it is a lyrical post-romantic piece. As can be seen from the story, it is primarily about a frustrated musician, Max, in which the story of Jonny stealing a violin is merely a sub-plot, and the jazzy passages – blues, tango and so on – are superimposed, like cherries on a cake.

One's first disappointment is that it hardly matches the Kurt Weill operas. The idiom is far milder, with syncopations used more gently in the jazzy passages and with the instrumentation less abrasive. The cavortings of Jonny, complete with Keystone Kops-style chases, were what originally attracted attention, and in the recording – helped by spectacular sound-effects – they come over with colour and energy, but Max (symbolically addicted to exploring glaciers) and his process of self-discovery, touchingly treated, provides a far more important element.

Though the Leipzig Gewandhaus Orchestra under Lothar Zagrosek does not always sound at home in the jazzy sequences, the recording provides the most convincing evidence yet that the piece deserves reappraisal. Heinz Kruse as Max sustains his long monologues impressively, and Krister St Hill as Jonny also sings well, even if the microphone catches an unevenness in their voices. It is Alessandra Marc as the heroine, Anita, who emerges as the main star, relishing lush Křenek melodies that yet never quite stick in the mind.

Kuhlau, Friedrich (1786–1832)

Elverhøj (The Elf Hill), Op. 100.
** Dacapo Dig. DCCD 8902 [id.]. Bodil Gøbel, Gurli Plesner, Mogens Schmidt Johansen, Danish R. Ch. & SO, John Frandsen.

Kuhlau's incidental music to J. L. Heiberg's play, *Elverhøj*, was composed for a production to mark the marriage of the daughter of King Frederik VI in 1829, and the present CD accommodates 21 numbers from it, including its splendid overture. Unlike his opera *Lulu*, composed five years before, it was an immediate success and has retained its popularity in Denmark down to the present day. The usual influences – Beethoven, Weber, Cherubini, Mendelssohn and so on – are to be found, but the overall impression is endearingly fresh. Not so the recording, however. This comes presumably from the 1970s (it was issued on the DMA label – Dansk Musik Antologi) and sounds really rather dryish as if recorded in a packed concert hall. The music has great charm and the performance under John Frandsen is also very sympathetic.

Lulu: complete.
*** Kontrapunkt/HM 32009/11 [id.]. Danish R. Ch. & SO, Schonwandt.
    Lulu (Risto Saarman), Sidi (Anne Frellesvig), Vela (Tina Kiberg), Dilfeng (Ulrik Cold).

Kuhlau is best remembered as a composer for the piano and the flute, but he made an important contribution to opera or, more particularly, to singspiel. The libretto is an adaptation of Wieland's *Lulu oder die Zauberflöte* – though there is little likelihood of this opera being confused with either Alban Berg or Mozart. This *Lulu* comes from 1824 and enjoyed some success in its day; it would probably have enjoyed more, but contemporary audiences complained that both the text and the music were too long. They certainly had a point: the spoken passages are omitted here but, even so, the music lasts for three hours.

The opening of Act II has overtones of the Wolf's Glen scene in *Der Freischütz*, while the dance of the black elves in the moonlight is pure Mendelssohn – and has much charm. The invention is generally fresh and engaging, though no one would claim that it has great depth. Unlike Schikaneder's and Mozart's Sarastro, the sorcerer Dilfeng, splendidly portrayed by Ulrik Cold, lacks any redeeming features or even a trace of nobility, and Periferihme, unlike the Queen of the Night, is good.

The largely Danish cast cope very capably with the not inconsiderable demands of Kuhlau's vocal writing, and the title-role, sung by the Finnish tenor, Risto Saarman, is admirable. The weakest member of the cast is Anne Frellesvig's rather white-voiced Princess Sidi. The Danish Radio recording is eminently truthful and vivid, and Michael Schonwandt draws excellent results from the Danish Radio Chorus and Orchestra. Despite its longueurs, this is a pleasant surprise and can be recommended to collectors willing to venture off the beaten track.

Lalo, Eduard (1823–92)

Le roi d'Ys (complete).
*** Erato/Warner Dig. 2292 45015-2 (2) [id.]. Fr. R. Ch. & PO, Jordan.
    Rozenn (Barbara Hendricks), Margared (Delores Ziegler), Mylio (Eduardo Villa), Le Roi (Jean-Philippe Courtis), Karnac (Marcel Vanaud).

Lalo's *Le roi d'Ys*, first heard in 1788, was initially a considerable success in Paris, but then came to be performed less and less often, and has not been staged there since the 1950s. Its melodramatic story opens on the palace terrace of the King of Ys, on Christmas morning. Prince Karnac is about to marry Margared, the king's daughter, and the populace are looking forward to a period of peace and prosperity.

Rozenn, Margared's sister, is now concerned that Margared is looking shaky and unhappy. Margared says that she seeks to suffer in silence and will do her duty, for the marriage will bring political stability. Finally she declares her love for their childhood companion. She means Mylio, but Rozenn thinks she means his friend. Both men left by sea together, apparently never to return. Margared declares that she hates her prospective husband.

At that very moment Mylio appears. He had been captured by enemies but is now victorious. He leaves as Karnac enters with the king, who is pleased that the marriage means he will lose a rival and gain a son. Margared now tells her sister of the good news about Mylio and it is obvious that Rozenn is deeply in love with him. When they meet, he returns her ardour.

Gathering all her courage, Margared tells her father that she will not marry Karnac. There is uproar, both from her own people and from the offended warriors of Karnac. The prince casts down his gauntlet to declare war. Mylio rushes forward and picks it up and we see that he has his own soldiers with him. The people of Ys now give their support to Mylio. Karnac threatens great carnage but is given safe conduct to depart with his men.

Later that day Margared looks out of her window and sees that the city is put to siege. The king commands Mylio to take his troops into battle on the morrow. Mylio tells Rozenn and Margared that he has had a vision of Saint-Corentin, Patron of Brittany, offering protection, and the king is sure that heaven is on the side of the defenders. But just as Mylio is about to go off to battle, Margared reveals the truth to her sister that she is in love with the same man! When the king promises Rozenn to Mylio if he is victorious, Margared's jealous fury knows no bounds.

Rozenn is appalled and says that the heavens favour her love for Mylio, but Margared determines on revenge: she would rather see her sister dead than in Mylio's embrace. Karnac's army is duly routed but Karnac himself survives. Margared seeks him out and tells him she has come to avenge him, that his hate has passed into her soul. She determines to open the sluice-gates which hold the sea back from the city, but she is not physically strong enough to do so without his help. They pass the chapel of Saint-Corentin, and Margaret blasphemously defies the saint to bring a miracle to save the city. As they go off, the sky darkens, the saint appears and curses them both, while a heavenly voice urges repentance.

The distressed Rozenn has locked herself in her bedchamber. Young couples arrive to try and persuade her to open the door and take Mylio as her husband. Mylio says he will stay by her door for ever, if necessary. Rozenn finally gives in and accepts him as her lord and master. Meanwhile the nervous Karnac and Margared are in the chapel while the choir sings a *Te Deum*. He reminds her of her promise to lead him to the sluice-gates but, as the chorus becomes more insistent, Margared refuses to commit so dreadful a crime against God. Karnac recalls their joint determination for vengeance.

As Mylio and his bride Rozenn leave the chapel after their marriage ceremony, Karnac cunningly anticipates their shared delights as they go off to celebrate their nuptial bliss together. The wedded pair are heard to declare their great love for each other. Margared's jealousy now gets the better of her. 'Let them die!' she says, and she and Karnac depart quickly together. Mylio leaves Rozenn with the king. Rozenn assures her father that she has prayed for her sister and that God will surely pardon her.

Noise and shouting is heard outside the church, and Margared comes back in and confronts her sister. The sluice-gates have been opened. Mylio has killed Karnac, but the flood is almost upon them. They all flee the church and are later seen on a flat hilltop, while the sea rages around them. The water is still rising. Margared dramatically declares her responsibility for the catastrophe, and the crowd call for her death. The king declares that vengeance shall be God's alone. There is a great thunderclap, and Margared rushes away and climbs the highest rock then throws herself into the waves. From where she is engulfed the gleaming figure of Saint-Corentin rises up, the sky clears and the waters begin to abate.

The Erato version gains enormously in presenting this opulent score in sumptuous modern sound, with Jordan underlining the colourful, dramatic contrasts between the exotic scene-setting and the sharply rhythmic choruses. The women soloists are particularly fine, preferable to those on previous sets. The American mezzo-soprano, Delores Ziegler, is very convincingly cast in what – thanks to the celebrated example of Rosa Ponselle, among others – used to be counted a soprano role. Her dramatic, unfruity voice is perfectly contrasted against the ravishing Rozenn of Barbara Hendricks. Eduardo Villa as the hero, Mylio, may not be as stylish as his recorded predecessors, not delicate enough in the famous *Aubade*, but his heady tenor has no trouble with the high tessitura. Jean-Philippe Courtis as the King, in this improbable Breton legend of medieval chivalry, and Marcel Vanaud as the villain, Karnac, have dark, weighty voices, marred at times by flutter.

Leclair, Jean-Marie (1697–1764)

Scylla et Glaucus: complete.
⊛ *** Erato/Warner Dig. 2292 45277-2 (3) [id.]. Monteverdi Ch., E. Bar. Soloists, Gardiner.
    Scylla (Donna Brown), Glaucus (Howard Crook), Circé (Rachel Yakar), Vénus (Agnès Mellon).

A younger contemporary of Rameau, Jean-Marie Leclair regrettably wrote only this one opera. First heard at the Paris Opéra in 1746, it follows the formal pattern of the tragédie-lyrique laid down by Lully and developed by Rameau, involving an allegorical prologue and five Acts. The style is more direct, less elaborate than Rameau's, and the speed with which the brief numbers follow each other – some arias as brief as a minute long – give the piece a freshness which easily sustains its length of nearly three hours.

In 1979 John Eliot Gardiner was responsible for the first performance (at St John's, Smith Square, London) anywhere in modern times, followed by a broadcast. Here with a different cast of principals in a production sponsored by Lyon Opéra, of which he is music director, Gardiner crowns that achievement, demonstrating this to be one of the neglected masterpieces of late French Baroque, every bit as worthy to be remembered as Rameau's operas.

Quite apart from Gardiner's characteristically electrifying direction, the playing and singing can hardly be faulted. Donna Brown makes a sweet-toned Scylla, who yet rises to the extra challenge of her longer numbers. Howard Crook is superb in the tenor role of Glaucus, headily beautiful, never strained by the highest tessitura; while Rachel Yakar characterizes the malevolent role of the sorceress, Circe, without ever transgressing the bounds of classical stylishness. With all these singers, ornamentation becomes a natural point of expression, never clumsy or forced, and the recording, made in St Giles, Cripplegate, is brightly atmospheric, full and clear.

Lehár, Franz (1870–1948)

The Count of Luxembourg (highlights, in English).
*** That's Entertainment CDTER 1050. Marilyn Hill Smith, Neil Jenkins, Vivien Tierney, Harry Nicoll, Lawrence Richard. New Sadler's Wells Op. Ch. and O, Wordsworth.

Like its companion disc of selections from Kálmán's *Countess Maritza*, this record from That's Entertainment presents lively and fresh performances from the cast of the New Sadler's Wells Opera production. Particularly in the general absence of records of operetta in English, this is very welcome. Bright, digital sound, which is given plenty of presence on CD.

The Land of Smiles (Das Land des Lächelns; complete in German).
Withdrawn: *** EMI Dig. CDS7 47604-8 (2). Bav. R. Ch., Munich RO, Boskovsky.
Sou-Chong (Siegfried Jerusalem), Lisa (Helen Donath).
Withdrawn: (M) (***) EMI mono CHS7 69523-2 (2). Philh. Ch. & O, Ackermann.
Sou-Chong (Nicolai Gedda), Lisa (Elisabeth Schwarzkopf).

The Land of Smiles (Das Land des Lächelns): highlights.
(M) *** EMI Dig. CDM7 69597-2 [id.] (from above recording with Jerusalem, Donath; cond. Boskovsky).

Even by the standards of Viennese operetta, *Land of Smiles*, a revamped version of an earlier failed work, *The Yellow Jacket*, has an offbeat plot, with its uncomfortable clash of East and West. Coming to it after hearing Johann Strauss, one cannot help being struck by the seriousness of emotion. These are real characters, not machinery in an elaborate charade, even if the situation comes dangerously close to the sentimental.

The story is relatively straightforward. Lisa, the daughter of Count Lichtenfel, has an ardent suitor in Gustl, a young Hussar officer, but instead she falls in love with a Chinese diplomat, Prince Sou-Chong; when he suddenly returns home as President of China, she accompanies him as his wife.

At first the couple are happy together, until Lisa discovers that he already has four other wives! However, in the famous *Dein ist mein ganzes Herz* he assures her that she is the only one who counts. But Gustl now re-enters Lisa's life. Having been appointed military attaché in Peking, he meets and is attracted to the prince's sister, Mi (a modern Chinese girl, who wears tennis shorts!).

When the prince and Lisa finally fall out over his polygamy and Lisa is made a prisoner in her quarters, Gustl is on hand to plan their escape, with the help of Mi. But they come face to face with Sou-Chong. Realizing that he cannot force her love and that their cultures are too far apart, he reluctantly but graciously lets her return home with Gustl.

Completed in 1929, this was relatively late Lehár, and some of his writing seems to have reflected serious models, though fascinatingly the parallels with Richard Strauss's *Arabella* (both musical and dramatic) are in Lehár's favour, for *Land of Smiles* came four years before the opera. The piece proved a great success, thanks in good measure to the tailoring of the central role of the Chinese prince to the needs of Richard Tauber, who promptly made the song *Dein ist mein ganzes Herz* his own enormously popular signature-tune.

Siegfried Jerusalem, who plays Sou-Chong in the stereo version (currently withdrawn, but with a highlights disc offered for the moment instead), has nothing like the same charm as Tauber, but it is a strong and sympathetic reading, lacking only a vein of implied tragedy, the wistfulness behind the smile. Helen Donath sings sweetly as his beloved Lisa, and the whole ensemble is admirably controlled in a colourful performance, warmly recorded, by Willi Boskovsky. The CD adds extra clarity and an enhanced presence to the sound.

Though, equally, Gedda does not have quite the passionate flair of Tauber in his famous *Dein ist mein ganzes Herz*, his thoughtful artistry matches a performance which effortlessly brings out the serious parallels without weighing the work down. Schwarzkopf and Kunz sing delectably and the stereo transcription brings out the ravishing sounds of Lehár's often Puccini-like invention. The transfer to CD is very lively and full of presence.

The Merry Widow (Die lustige Witwe; complete in German).
⊛ *** EMI CDS7 47178-8 (2) [Ang. CDCB 47177]. Philh. Ch. and O, Matačić.
   Hanna Glawari (Elisabeth Schwarzkopf), Danilo (Eberhard Waechter), Mirko Zeta (Josef Knapp), Camille (Nicolai Gedda), Valencienne (Hanny Steffek), Raoul (Hans Strobhauer), Cascada (Kurt Equiluz).
(M) (***) EMI mono CDH7 69520-2 [id.]. Philh. Ch. & O, Ackermann.
   Hanna Glawari (Elisabeth Schwarzkopf), Danilo (Erich Kunz), Mirko Zeta (Anton Niessner), Camille (Nicolai Gedda), Valencienne (Emmy Loose), Raoul (Josef Schmidinger), Cascada (Otakar Kraus).
(M) ** DG 435 712-2 (2) [id.]. German Op. Ch., BPO, Karajan (with SUPPÉ: Overtures: *Beautiful Galathea; Jolly robbers; Light cavalry; Morning, noon and night in Vienna; Pique dame; Poet and peasant ***).
   Hanna Glawari (Elizabeth Harwood), Danilo (René Kollo), Mirko Zeta (Zoltan Kélémen), Camille (Werner Hollweg), Valencienne (Teresa Stratas), Raoul (Werner Krenn), Cascada (Donald Grobe).
Withdrawn: (M) *(*) EMI CMS7 69940-2 (2). Bav. R. Ch., Munich R. O, Wallberg.
   Hanna Glawari (Edda Moser), Danilo (Hermann Prey), Mirko Zeta (Benno Kusche), Camille (Siegfried Jerusalem), Valencienne (Helen Donath).
(*) Denon Dig. DC-8103/4 [id.]. V. Volksoper Ch. and O, Bibl.
   Hanna Glawari (Mirjana Irosch), Danilo (Peter Minich), Mirko Zeta (Herbert Prikopa), Camille (Ryszard Karczykowski), Valencienne (Dagmar Koller), Raoul (Kurt Ruzicka), Cascada (K. Huemer).

Lehár's *Merry Widow* (the greatest of all operettas, if one regards Johann Strauss's *Die Fledermaus* as a fully fledged opera) was first heard in 1905. The première was in Vienna, the city whose ambience it epitomizes – even though the story is actually set in Paris. Its characters may be lightweight but its theme of love triumphing over everything is the very stuff of which operetta is made.

The heroine, Hanna Glawari, and hero, Count Danilo, were friends in their youth and had been parted when Hanna married the wealthy Glawari. She now arrives in Paris and Baron Zeta connives that Danilo should marry the rich widow and secure her fortune for their country, Pontevedro. Danilo, however, is still a romantic and does not want Hanna to think his intentions are financially motivated.

Meanwhile Camille de Rossignole has improper designs on the Baron's attractive young wife, Valencienne. They are in love, but Valencienne prudently decides that Camille should instead marry Hanna. But Hanna has other plans: her eye is on Count Danilo, and during a party she tests his feelings towards her. Camille and Valencienne have made a secret rendezvous in the garden pavilion and Hanna arrives just as they are discovered by Zeta and Danilo.

They are disconcerted when Hanna appears with Camille and announces that they are engaged to be married. Danilo is jealously furious and Hanna now knows where his heart lies. She informs the assembled company that when she remarries she will lose her fortune. Thus when Danilo at last makes his proposal she knows he truly loves her for herself.

Von Matačić provides a magical set, guaranteed to send shivers of delight through any listener with its vivid sense of atmosphere and superb musicianship. It is one of Walter Legge's masterpieces as a recording manager. He had directed the earlier *Merry Widow* set, also with his wife, Elisabeth Schwarzkopf, as Hanna, and realized how difficult it would be to outshine it. But outshine it he did, creating a vivid sense of theatre. If the Decca approach to opera was always to conceive it in terms of a new medium, Legge went to the opposite view and produced something that is almost more theatrical than the theatre itself. No other opera record more vividly conveys the feeling of expectancy before the curtain rises than the preludes to each Act here. The CD opens up the sound yet retains the full bloom, and the theatrical presence and atmosphere are something to marvel at. The layout is less than ideal, however, and only two bands are provided on each CD, though there is generous indexing.

It was the Ackermann mono set of the early 1950s which established a new pattern in recording operetta. Some were even scandalized when Schwarzkopf insisted on treating the *Viljalied* very seriously indeed at an unusually slow tempo, but the big step forward was that an operetta was treated with all the care for detail normally lavished on grand opera, and the result had heightened character, both dramatic and musical, with high polish and sharp focus the order of the day. Ten years later in stereo Schwarzkopf was to record the role again, if anything with even greater point and perception, but here she has extra youthful vivacity, and the *Viljalied* – ecstatically drawn out – is unique. Some may be troubled that Kunz as Danilo sounds older than the Baron, but it is still a superbly characterful cast, and the transfer to a single CD is bright and clear.

'Brahms's *Requiem* performed to the tunes of Lehár' was how one wit described the Karajan version of *The Merry Widow*, with its carefully measured tempi and absence of sparkle. The reverberant recording has been dried out a little, but this means that the choral focus is not always quite clean, although the solo voices have plenty of presence. Karajan's brilliant recordings of six Suppé overtures are added to fill out the space on the second disc, but DG would have done better to have cut the recording a little, so that it would fit on a single CD. There is, however a highlights disc – see below.

With the two principals (Edda Moser as Hanna Glawari, Hermann Prey as Danilo) both seriously lacking in charm, the Wallberg version is hardly a serious competitor, though the direction is idiomatic, the recording very good and the contributions of the second pair of lovers, Helen Donath as Valencienne and Siegfried Jerusalem as Camille, are outstanding.

Recorded live in a stage performance given in Tokyo in 1982, the Vienna Volksoper version is easily idiomatic, but lacks the polish and finesse to make Lehár's charming operetta sparkle. With singing generally too rough to give much pleasure on record (shrill from the women, strained and wobbly from the men), the result is jolly but coarse. The recorded sound does not help, thin in the middle, lacking body. Banding is limited to beginnings of Acts, which is the more irritating when there is so much spoken dialogue to wade through.

The Merry Widow: highlights.
** DG 415 524-2 [id.] (from above recording with Harwood, Kollo; cond. Karajan).

This CD selection of highlights is generous, some 68 minutes, and all the important numbers are included; but also on a single CD you can get the first of Schwarzkopf's two recordings complete. Recommended for those who want a memento of Elizabeth Harwood's charming if hardly commanding portrait of Hanna Glawari. There is a synopsis but no libretto.

The Merry Widow (English version by Christopher Hassall): abridged.
(B) ** CfP CD-CFP 4485; *TC-CFP 4485*. Sadler's Wells Op. Ch. and O, William Reid.
   Hanna Glawari (June Bronhill), Danilo (Thomas Round), Mirko Zeta (Denis Dowling), Camille (William McAlpine), Valencienne (Marion Lowe).

The performance on Classics for Pleasure does not always have an *echt*-Viennese flavour, but it says much for the achievement of the Sadler's Wells production in the 1950s that their version is so magnetic. For many, the deciding factor will be the English words, sung in an admirable translation. The Sadler's Wells cast is strongly characterized; only in Howell Glynne's approach is there a suspicion of Gilbert and Sullivan. Thomas Round is an appropriately raffish Danilo, though it is a pity that the recording tends to exaggerate the unevenness in his voice. William McAlpine as the second tenor, Camille de Rosillon, comes over much better, and his *Red as the rose* is exquisitely sung. The chorus is outstandingly good (especially the men) in the big scenes. The 1959 recording sounds fresh, if slightly dated, but the voices and diction are clear and, though there is a touch of shrillness on top, there is an agreeable ambient feeling.

The Merry Widow (English version by Bonynge): highlights.
(M) **(*) Decca 421 884-2; *421 884-4* [id.]. Joan Sutherland, Werner Krenn, Regina Resnik,

Valerie Masterson, Graeme Ewer, John Brecknock, John Fryatt, Francis Egerton, Amb. S., Nat. PO, Bonynge.

Although not everyone will take to Sutherland's Widow, this is generally an attractive English version. The exuberantly breezy overture (arranged by Douglas Gamley) introduces all the hits seductively, to set the mood of the proceedings; the slightly brash recording (the sheen on the strings sounding digitally bright, even though this is a remastered 1977/8 analogue recording) is determinedly effervescent. The chorus sings with great zest and the ensembles are infectious. The whole of the closing part of the disc – the Finale of Act II, Njegus's aria (nicely done by Graeme Ewer), the introduction of the girls from Maxim's and the famous *Waltz duet* – is certainly vivacious; the Parisian atmosphere may seem a trifle overdone, but enjoyably so. Earlier, Sutherland's *Vilja* loses out on charm because of her wide vibrato, but the *Waltz duet* with Krenn is engaging.

Leoncavallo, Ruggiero (1858–1919)

La Bohème (complete).
* Nuova Era Dig. 6917/19 [id.]. Ch. & O del Teatro La Fenice, Latham-Koenig.
   Mimì (Lucia Mazzaria), Rodolfo (Jonathan Summers), Marcello (Mario Malagnini), Musette (Martha Senn), Schaunard (Bruno Praticò), Colline / Paolo (Pietro Spagnoli), Barbemuche (Silvano Pagliuca), Durand / Gaudenzio (Romano Emili), Eufemia (Cinzia Mola).

Jan Latham-Koenig makes a persuasive case for this 'other' *Bohème*, drawing lively, sharply pointed playing from his Venice orchestra. The plot, although it contains the same basic characters, is quite different from the Puccini version until the last Act, and Mimì, the heroine, is an altogether less innocent character who, like Musetta, acquires a wealthy lover before the end of the story.
   Leoncavallo's Act I takes us straight to the Café Momus, where Gaudenzio, its proprietor, is taking the musician, Schaunard, to task. His Bohemian friends use the restaurant entirely for their own ends, eating little and seldom paying for it. Schnaunard promises to make amends. Indeed that very evening he and his colleagues are having a celebration which should be profitable for Gaudenzio. In due course the poet Rodolfo, the painter Marcello, and the philosopher Colline appear, with their respective mistresses. The laundress Eufemia belongs to Schaunard; Mimì, Rodolfo's mistress, is a flower girl. She brings Musetta, a seamstress, with her. Marcello falls heavily for Musetta as soon as they meet.
   Eventually the bill arrives, and Barbemuche, an intellectual and teacher who would like to join the Bohemians on a permanent basis, offers help. But they refuse his gift and instead make the bill a wager on a game of billiards between Barbemuche and Schaunard. The game is played as if it were a great drama, with everyone participating eagerly (except Marcello and Musetta, who are too busy staring into each other's eyes). Fortunately Schaunard wins, so Gaudenzio is pleased too.
   Musetta has been living with a rich banker but has now deserted him in favour of Marcello. So Durand, understandably, has withdrawn his financial support; all her personal possessions and furniture are being taken away to the pawnshop. As Musetta has invited friends to her flat for a meal, it is decided to hold the dinner party in the courtyard. In the course of the evening, Mimì decides to leave Rodolfo for a richer admirer, Count Paolo, and she quietly disappears. The sleeping residents are not well pleased with the noise generated by the Bohemians' carousing, and finally they are ejected from the courtyard.
   Schaunard and Marcello are penniless and decide to seek work and earn some cash. When Marcello has gone, Musetta follows Mimì's example and she departs to find a richer lover, but first she writes Marcello a farewell letter. Mimì, on the other hand, has come looking for Rodolfo and would like to return to him, but he rejects her. Marcello is also angry with Mimì, as he thinks she has been influential in Musetta's departure.
   It is now Christmas Eve, and Schaunard, Marcello and Rodolfo are once more sharing a meal, remembering the women in their lives who are no longer present. Marcello has invited Musetta to eat with them, but it is Mimì who arrives first, exhausted and desperate. She has been abandoned by Count Paolo, is too ill to work and cannot pay for hospital treatment. Musetta finally enters and pawns her jewellery to pay for a doctor and medicine for Mimì, but she is too late, Mimì, having made up her quarrel with Rodolfo, dies before they have finished their meal.
   The plot seems well laid out, yet in its timing and dramatic layout – with Mimì in the mezzo

role stealing the final scene from the soprano–tenor duo of Musetta and Marcello – this cannot compare with Puccini. Despite the vigour, and some good singing from the men – Bruno Praticò as Schaunard, Mario Malagnini as Marcello and Jonathan Summers as the baritone Rodolfo – this is a seriously flawed set. The stage noises in this live recording are thunderous, the prompter keeps interrupting, and the orchestra is backwardly balanced with voices dry and close. Worst of all, Martha Senn makes a shrill and fluttery Musetta, and the mezzo, Lucia Mazzaria, is barely more acceptable as Mimì. The opera is extravagantly laid out on three discs, when Acts II and III could easily have been contained on a single disc.

I Pagliacci (complete).
*** DG 419 257-2 (3) [id.]. La Scala, Milan, Ch. & O, Karajan – MASCAGNI: *Cavalleria rusticana.* ***
    Canio (Carlo Bergonzi), Nedda (Joan Carlyle), Tonio (Giuseppe Taddei), Silvio (Rolando Panerai), Beppe (Ugo Benelli).
(M) *** EMI CMS7 63967-2 (2) [Ang. CDMB 62967]. La Scala, Milan, Ch. & O, Matačić – MASCAGNI: *Cavalleria rusticana.* **(*)
    Canio (Franco Corelli), Nedda (Lucine Amara), Tonio (Tito Gobbi), Silvio (Mario Zanasi), Beppe (Mario Spina).
(M) *** BMG/RCA GD 60865 (2) [60865-2]. John Alldis Ch., LSO, Santi – PUCCINI: *Il Tabarro.* **(*)
    Canio (Plácido Domingo), Nedda (Montserrat Caballé), Tonio (Sherrill Milnes), Silvio (Barry McDaniel), Beppe (Leo Goeke).
(***) EMI CDS7 47981-8 (3) [Ang. CDCC 47981]. La Scala, Milan, Ch. & O, Serafin – MASCAGNI: *Cavalleria rusticana.* (***)
    Canio (Giuseppe Di Stefano), Nedda (Maria Callas), Tonio (Tito Gobbi), Silvio (Rolando Panerai), Beppe (Nicola Monti).
(B) **(*) Naxos Dig. 8.660021 [id.]. Slovak Philh. Ch., Czech RSO, Alexander Rahbari.
    Canio (Nicola Martinucci), Nedda (Miriam Gauci), Tonio (Eduard Tumagian), Silvio (Boje Skovhus), Beppe (Miroslav Dvorsky).
(M) **(*) EMI CMS7 63650-2 (2). Amb. Op. Ch., Philh. O, Muti – MASCAGNI: *Cavalleria rusticana.* **(*)
    Canio (José Carreras), Nedda (Renata Scotto), Tonio (Kari Nurmela), Silvio (Thomas Allen), Beppe (Ugo Benelli).
(M) (**(*)) Nimbus mono NI 7843/4 [id.]. La Scala Ch. & O, Ghione – MASCAGNI: *Cavalleria rusticana.*
    Canio (Beniamino Gigli), Nedda (Iva Pacetti), Tonio (Mario Basiola), Silvio (Leone Paci), Beppe (Giuseppe Nessi).
** Decca 414 590-2 (2) [id.]. L. Voices, Finchley Children's Group, Nat. PO, Patanè – MASCAGNI: *Cavalleria rusticana.* **(*)
    Canio (Luciano Pavarotti), Nedda (Mirella Freni), Tonio (Ingvar Wixell), Silvio (Lorenzo Saccomani), Beppe (Vincenzo Bello).
(M) ** Decca 421 807-2 (2). Rome St Cecilia Ac. Ch. & O, Molinari-Pradelli – MASCAGNI: *Cavalleria rusticana.* *(*)
    Canio (Mario Del Monaco), Nedda (Gabriella Tucci), Tonio (Cornell MacNeil), Silvio (Renato Capecchi), Beppe (Piero De Palma).
*(*) Ph. 411 484-2 (2). La Scala, Milan, Ch. & O, Prêtre.
    Canio (Plácido Domingo), Nedda (Teresa Stratas), Tonio (Juan Pons), Silvio (Alberto Rinaldi), Beppe (Florindo Andreolli).
* Ph. Dig. 434 131-2 [id.]. Westminster Symphonic Ch., Phd. Boys Ch., Phd. O, Muti.
    Canio (Luciano Pavarotti), Nedda (Daniella Dessì), Tonio (Juan Pons), Silvio (Paolo Coni), Beppe (Ernesto Gavazzi).

Pagliacci, the very stuff of verismo opera, was first heard in Milan in 1892. Its earthy realism is emphasized by the hunchback Tonio's famous Prologue, when he steps in front of the curtain to tell the audience that the entertainment they are about to see depicts a real-life story. A group of travelling actors arrives in a small Sicilian village. Canio, the leader of the troupe, thanks the villagers for their welcome and announces that a performance will take place that night at eleven o'clock.

Tonio, who is in love with Canio's wife, Nedda, tries to help her alight from the wagon but Canio pushes him away and aids Nedda himself. The crowd laugh at the humiliated Tonio, who quietly vows vengeance.

The troupe are invited to enter the local tavern. Tonio declines and a villager coarsely jokes that he is staying behind to make love to Nedda. Canio says that, whereas in a play that would be entertaining, in real life it is not to be thought of.

Evening bells ring and Nedda, left alone, suddenly faces Tonio who declares his love. She mocks him and strikes him across the face and he departs in pain, once more vowing revenge. Silvio, Nedda's real lover, now appears, they embrace and she agrees to go away with him. Tonio, hidden, hears and sees the meeting and fetches Canio; the latter, too late to glimpse Silvio, overhears Nedda declare, 'Tonight and for ever I am thine.'

Nedda refuses to name her love and in fury Canio almost knifes her then and there but Beppe, his fellow actor, intercedes and takes him away. Canio, watching for his rival, now has to get ready for the performance and he sings his famous aria 'Vesti la giubba'. While the audience are assembling, Nedda and Silvio manage to speak briefly to each other.

The curtain of the stage within a stage now rises against the musical background of an eighteenth-century minuet. Nedda, dressed as Columbina, tells the audience that her husband, Pagliacco (Canio), is away and the clown, Taddeo, is at the market, and we hear Beppe (as Arlecchino) singing a serenade. Tonio (as Taddeo) now enters and makes a grotesque avowal of love for Nedda.

Arlecchino enters and throws Taddeo out, but the hunchback-clown promises to watch for the return of Pagliacco. When his warning is delivered, Arlecchino leaves hastily and Columbina is singing 'Tonight and for ever I am thine', as Pagliacco enters, words he had heard before in a different context. Pagliacco (still acting) accuses Columbina of unfaithfulness.

She brings in Taddeo to reassure him, but Taddeo plays his part with a sneer and Canio, suddenly abandoning the play, demands to know the name of Columbina's real lover. She tries to laugh the situation off. The audience are enraptured by such splendid and believable acting. Nedda tries to retrieve the play but the audience become electrically aware that this is no longer mere playacting. Canio in rage stabs Nedda and, as Silvio rushes to help, kills him too. Canio then turns to the audience, who now sense the depth and horror of the tragedy, and sings, 'La commedia è finita!'

The Italian opera traditionalists may jib at Karajan's treatment of Leoncavallo's melodrama – and for that matter its companion piece. He does nothing less than refine them, with long-breathed, expansive tempi and the minimum of exaggeration. One would expect such a process to take the guts out of the drama, but with Karajan the result is superb. One is made to hear the beauty of the music first and foremost, and that somehow makes one understand the drama more. Passions are no longer torn to tatters, Italian-style – and Karajan's choice of soloists was clearly aimed to help that – but the passions are still there; and rarely if ever on record has the La Scala Orchestra played with such beautiful feeling for tone-colour.

Bergonzi is among the most sensitive of Italian tenors of heroic quality, and it is good to have Joan Carlyle doing a major operatic role on record, touching if often rather cool. Taddei is magnificently strong, and Benelli and Panerai could hardly be bettered in the roles of Beppe and Silvio. The opulence of Karajan's performance is well served by the extra clarification given on CD, with voices more sharply defined. As a filler on this three-disc set, DG provides not only the usual coupling of Cavalleria rusticana, but also a splendid collection of operatic intermezzi from Manon Lescaut, Suor Angelica, Schmidt's Notre Dame, Giordano's Fedora, Cilea's Adriana Lecouvreur, Wolf-Ferrari's Jewels of the Madonna, Mascagni's L'amico Fritz, plus the Méditation from Thaïs (with Michel Schwalbé), and the Prelude to Act III of La Traviata.

The EMI (originally Columbia) recording under Lovro von Matačić dates from the early 1960s and is especially notable for the contribution of the tenor, Franco Corelli, as Canio. He is not as imaginative as some of the great singers of the past, yet, with his glorious tenor at its thrilling peak, he shows a natural feeling for the phrases. Gobbi is a predictably magnificent Tonio; there may be some threadbare patches towards the top of the voice, but Gobbi uses a thrillingly wide tonal range to powerful dramatic effect. Lucine Amara gives a thoroughly sound performance as Nedda, both vocally and dramatically, and the recording has a vivid sense of atmosphere and movement. The coupled Cav. is dramatically not quite so striking, but this still makes a clear first choice in the mid-priced range for those who want the pairing with Mascagni.

For those who do not want the obvious coupling with Cavalleria rusticana, the RCA set at mid-price is a first-rate recommendation, with fine singing from all three principals, vivid playing and recording, and one or two extra passages not normally included – as in the Nedda–Silvio duet. Milnes is superb in the Prologue, the young Domingo is in thrilling voice and, though Caballé does not always suggest a young girl, this is technically the most beautiful account of Nedda available on record. The 1971 recording was made at Walthamstow Town

Hall and the CD transfer has plenty of atmosphere and increased vividness. A full translation is provided.

It is thrilling to hear *Pagliacci* starting with the *Prologue* sung so vividly by Tito Gobbi on EMI. The bite of the voice and its distinctive timbres are unique. Di Stefano, too, is at his finest, but the performance inevitably centres on Callas. She never attempted the role of Nedda on the stage, and the flashing-eyed characterization is never conventional. There are many points at which she finds extra intensity, extra meaning, so that the performance is worth hearing for her alone. Serafin's direction is strong and direct. The mono recording is dry, like the others made at La Scala, with voices placed well forward but with choral detail blurred (if not unacceptably so), a balance underlined in the clarity and definition of CD.

Alexander Rahbari conducts his Slovak forces in a vigorous, red-blooded reading which, with first-rate solo singing, makes an excellent bargain recommendation, very well recorded, if with the chorus a little distant. Miriam Gauci is a warmly vibrant Nedda with plenty of temperament, and Eduard Tumagian is an outstanding Tonio, not only firm and dark of tone but phrasing imaginatively. As Canio, Nicola Martinucci has an agreeable tenor that he uses with more finesse and a better line than many more celebrated rivals, even though his histrionics at the beginning and end of *Vesti la giubba* are unconvincing.

Under Muti's urgent direction, both *Cav.* and *Pag.* represent the music of violence. In both he has sought to use the original text, which in *Pag.* is often surprisingly different, with many top notes eliminated and Tonio instead of Canio delivering (singing, not speaking) the final *La commedia è finita*. Muti's approach represents the antithesis of smoothness, and the coarse rendering of the *Prologue* in *Pag.* by the rich-toned Kari Nurmela is disappointing. Scotto's Nedda goes raw above the stave, but the edge is in keeping with Muti's approach, with its generally brisk speeds. Carreras seems happier here than in *Cav.*, but it is the conductor and the fresh look he brings which will prompt a personal choice here. The sound is extremely vivid.

The Nimbus transfer of the classic 1934 recording with Gigli focuses the voices effectively enough, giving them a mellow bloom, though the orchestra, often rather recessed, is relatively muffled. Gigli is very much the centre of attention, with Iva Pacetti as Nedda clear and powerful rather than characterful.

Pavarotti links the latest Decca recordings of *Cav.* and *Pag.*, both of them beefy performances, very well recorded. In *Pag.*, Pavarotti gives a committed performance, though in both operas he seems reluctant to sing any way but loud. Voices are recorded rather close, which exaggerates this fault, and Freni is not helped by the balance either, not sounding as sweet as she usually does. Wixell as Tonio is somewhat out of character, giving a Lieder-style performance, full of detail. The vivid CD transfer places the set on a pair of discs.

The dramatic force of Mario del Monaco's performance so dominates the early Decca set, aided by vintage Decca recording with its genuine opera-house atmosphere and sense of realism, that one is persuaded to accept singing that would otherwise seem undistinguished. Yet Cornell MacNeil is a splendid Tonio and Gabriella Tucci a sweet-voiced Nedda, if without much imagination. However, coupled with a less than electrifying account of *Cavalleria rusticana* under Serafin, this can hardly be considered a strong contender and it is not surprising that Decca have now withdrawn it.

The Prêtre version is taken from the soundtrack of Zeffirelli's film of the opera, and is principally remarkable for the large-scale heroic performance, superbly sung, of Plácido Domingo as Canio. Much of the rest is less recommendable. Juan Pons sings the *Prologue* impressively and exploits his fine baritone as Tonio; but Teresa Stratas and Alberto Rinaldi (Silvio) both suffer from uneven vocal production, with Stratas's earthy timbres going raw under pressure. The CD transfer manages to place the opera complete on a single disc, although the extra clarity and presence serve only to underline the vocal flaws.

The Philips set with Riccardo Muti conducting the Philadelphia Orchestra and a cast headed by Luciano Pavarotti is spliced together from live concert performances in the unhelpful acoustic of the Music Academy in Philadelphia, with sound that is muddy in the bass and harsh at the top. The tenor's tone is glorious but unremittingly loud, with effortful grunts at the end of each phrase. He sings better in his earlier, Decca set, and Muti is less effortful too in his earlier, EMI recording, timing the dramatic conclusion more effectively. What then puts this version out of court is the Nedda of Daniella Dessì, recalling the classic phrase of Philip Hope-Wallace describing sopranos who, when Nedda is communing with the birds, 'sound like a jungle locomotive scaring the macaws'. Dessì is one such, disturbing the vocal line with squally, unsteady notes and sounding much too hefty for the delicate passages. Juan Pons sings with strong, forthright tone as Tonio (and in the Prologue) but, like Paolo Coni as Silvio, is dramatically unconvincing.

I Pagliacci: highlights.
(M) ** Decca 421 870-2; *421 870-4* [id.] (from above recording with Freni, Pavarotti; cond. Patanè) – MASCAGNI: *Cavalleria rusticana*: highlights. **

On Decca, a reasonably generous coupling of excerpts from *Cav.* and *Pag.* with about half an hour from each opera. The sound is extremely lively and vivid, even if the performances are flawed.

Liszt, Franz (1811–86)

Don Sanche (complete).
Withdrawn: **(*) Hung. Dig. HCD 12744/5-2 [id.]. Hungarian R. & TV Ch., Hungarian State Op. O, Támas Pál.
Don Sanche (Gérard Garino), Elzire (Júlia Hamari).

At the age of thirteen, well before Beethoven died, the child prodigy Liszt sought to demonstrate in this fairytale opera that he was a composer as well as a pianist. *Don Sanche or The Castle of Love*, first given in Paris in 1825, was the boy's first essay at a stage work; it was totally forgotten for a century and a half until it was revived (in Britain) in 1977. The piece tells of a magic castle of love ruled over by a sinister magician and how the knight, Don Sanche, finally wins the love of the disdainful Elzire.

The only really Lisztian quality is the way the boy composer lights on instruments relatively exotic at the time, loading piccolos and trombones on to writing which suggests Weber or Rossini with dashes of Haydn, Schubert or even an occasional watered-down echo of Beethoven's *Fidelio*.

The pity is that, after a promising start, the 90-minute one-Acter tails off, with invention growing thinner and thinner, suggesting that childish enthusiasm for an improbable subject waned, and he wanted to get it over with.

Támas Pál conducts a lively performance, with some stylish singing from the lyric tenor, Gérard Garino, in the name-part. Other principals are variable, including Júlia Hamari as the hard-hearted heroine; as long as you keep firmly in mind that this is the work of a thirteen-year-old, however, it will give much pleasure. The sound is bright and close.

Lloyd Webber, Andrew (born 1948)

Cats.
*** Polydor 817 810-2 (2) [id.]. Original London cast, including Elaine Page, Paul Nicholas, Brian Blessed, Wayne Sleep, Sarah Brightman, Susan Jane Tanner, Stephen Tate, Jeff Shankley, O, Harry Rabinowitz.

Although it could be argued that T. S. Eliot's *Old Possum's Book of Practical Cats* does not need music, *Cats* is, alongside *Phantom*, Lloyd Webber's most successful show. Seen live, the choreography, inventive though it is, produces longueurs for some viewers, although women seem to enjoy the piece rather more than men. But the score is individual and inventive, and if *Macavity* in some ways recalls Mancini's *Pink panther*, *Bustopher Jones* (Brian Blessed) is another number to remain in the memory alongside the other two hit-songs, *Mr Mistoffelees* and the famous *Memory* (Elaine Page).

The original cast projects everything with much conviction and enthusiasm, and words are admirably clear. Harry Rabinowitz retains the freshness. The full score is included here – some 96 minutes of music. The sound is forward and bright, but the documentation is poor and indifferently printed, with no cues given, even though each number is separately banded.

The Phantom of the Opera (complete).
*** Polydor 831 273-2 (2) [id.]. Michael Crawford, Sarah Brightman, Steve Barton, Ch. & O of original London cast, Michael Read.

The Phantom of the Opera: highlights.
*** Polydor 831 563-2 (from above recording).

The worldwide success of *The Phantom of the Opera* means that the recording of the score needs no advocacy from us. It can be said, however, that there are more good tunes in it than the ubiquitous *Music of the night*, and the chromatic *Phantom theme* is the real stuff of melodrama. As the anti-hero of the piece was a neglected composer, Lloyd Webber needed to write some pastiche opera for him, and this he does very skilfully. The vividly recorded highlights will be the best way to approach this score, but the complete set is also surprisingly compulsive. Extraordinarily, there are no internal cues on the CDs.

Loesser, Frank (1910–69)

Guys and Dolls.
*** BMG/RCA Dig. 09026 61317-2 [61317-2]. New Broadway cast. Ch. & O, Edward Strauss.
   Sarah Brown (Josie De Gutzman), Sky Masterson (Peter Gallagher), Miss Adelaide (Faith Prince), Nathan Detroit (Nathan Lane), Nicely Nicely Johnson (Walter Bobbie), Rusty Charlie (Timothy Shew), Arvide Abernathy (John Carpenter).

Guys and Dolls is that rare experience, a virtually perfect musical. The book, based on Damon Runyon's *Idyll of Miss Sarah Brown* but with a wonderful clutch of additional fake gangland characters, is wittily sentimental as all good musicals must be, but heart-warmingly so, and the music – Loesser's greatest score – is a joy. There are enough good things in Act I, but when in Act II *Luck be a lady*, *Sue me* – and Nicely Nicely Johnson's guaranteed show-stopper, *Sit down, you're rocking the boat*, all come in quick succession, the exhilarated audience becomes aware they are in the presence of a theatrical masterpiece, and the reprise of the superb title-number rounds the evening off splendidly.

The unlikely love-story between the confirmed gambler, Sky Masterson, and the Salvation Army proselytizer, Sarah Brown, is balanced by the humour of the secondary couple, the promoter of floating crap games, Nathan Detroit, and the nightclub chantootsie to whom he has been engaged for fourteen years. Altogether they are as likeable a quartet of lovers as you will find in any show.

Of course one does not forget the great film version with Frank Sinatra (for whom the part of Nathan was a natural), Marlon Brando and Jean Simmons, but the present Broadway revival cast is pretty good too. Josie de Gutzman (Sarah) and Peter Gallagher (Sky) are convincingly romantic in *I've never been in love before*, and they manage their brief moments of dialogue particularly well. Faith Prince's Miss Adelaide is (properly) squeakily abrasive – one understands why Nathan hesitates to take the plunge!

The set pieces go fizzingly throughout, even if Walter Bobbie's boat-rocking is perhaps a fraction on the fast side. The recording, as so often with musicals, is up-front and could have used more bass (especially in the big numbers), but has plenty of theatrical atmosphere.

The Most Happy Fella (complete).
*** Sony mono S2K 48010 (2)[id.]. Original Broadway cast. Ch. & O, Herbert Greene.
   Tony (Robert Weede), Rosabella / Amy (Jo Sullivan), Cleo (Susan Johnson), Joe (Art Lund), Herman (Shorty Long), Marie (Mona Paulee).

The Most Happy Fella (extended excerpts).
**(*) BMG/RCA Dig. 09026 61294-2 [61294-2]. New Broadway cast. Tim Stella and Michael Rafter (pianists), Ch., Tim Stella.
   Tony (Spiro Milas), Rosabella / Amy (Sophie Hayden), Cleo (Liz Larsen), Joe (Charles Pistone), Herman (Scott Waara), Marie (Claudia Catania).

Frank Loesser's ambitious *Most Happy Fella* has all the hallmarks of a musical – hits like the title-number, the irresistible *Standing on the corner*, the charming *Happy to make your acquaintance*, and the rousing *Big 'D'*, yet its very musical breadth brings it near to the opera house and it certainly has a direct inheritance from the German Singspiel. Because of its scope it is in danger of not finding an audience. As the harpist in the large orchestra for the London production (dominated by the superb Inia Te Wiata) commented to the writer: 'It's too highbrow for the lowbrows, and too lowbrow for the highbrows.' Perhaps it is, but for the open-minded it makes a splendid entertainment.

Based on a Pulitzer Prize-winning novel and play by Sidney Howard, *They Knew What They Wanted*, *The Most Happy Fella* centres on Tony, a genially successful sixty-year-old Napa Valley wine-maker. On a visit to San Francisco he falls in love (from a distance) with Amy, a waitress. He woos her by mail, only too successfully – as Rosabella – but his self-confidence fails him in the matter of identity, and instead of his own picture he sends her a photo of his good-looking foreman, Joe.

When Rosabella arrives to marry him, she is bitterly disillusioned but cuts her losses and decides to go ahead with the wedding when Tony is badly injured in a road accident. Her new husband incapacitated, Joe consoles her and his tenderness turns to passion.

With an ironical twist to the story, Rosabella spends the night in the arms of the foreman photograph-lover. When, two months later, she begins to fall in love with Tony, she is already two months pregnant. After telling her husband what has happened she packs her bags, but Tony has a big heart; he forgives her, asks her to stay and assures her he will keep her secret – they will raise the child as their own.

With an elaborate layout – orchestral preludes for each of the three Acts and imaginative orchestrations by Don Walker, the score is of consistently high quality. One of its gems is the Act III Madrigal, *Song of a summer night*, highly original and all too short. Here one thinks first of the Gilbert and Sullivan glees, but Loesser's development of this format is all his own.

The 1956 Sony set – the first time a Broadway musical was ever recorded complete – does it full justice. Robert Weede is a totally believable Happy Fella. He looks middle-aged, but one can believe that Amy could eventually succumb to his warmth, innocence and humanity. Jo Sullivan sings most appealingly as the heroine, and the two subsidiary characters, Cleo and Herman, are admirably portrayed by Susan Johnson and Shorty Long. They have at least two of the best songs, which are used by Loesser to create a vibrant American ethos to balance the strong Italian flavour of the celebratory dance numbers. Smaller parts are all well taken and in this splendidly atmospheric recording the whole score springs vividly to life. Absolutely no apologies have to be made for the mono sound-quality and the CD transfer is expert. Excellent documentation and lots of photographs complement a highly distinguished reissue.

The New Broadway cast recording suffers from two main drawbacks. It has only a two-piano accompaniment and, although the playing of Tim Stella and Michael Rafter is full of vitality, the music loses a dimension, particularly in the spectacular scenes and, of course, in the lovely *Song of a summer night*. The other problem is the very forward digital recording, with the voices right on top of the microphones, which often brings an edgy kind of presence. Liz Larsen is a vibrant Cleo, but her opening *Ooh my poor feet* and the following duet, with the equally personable Sophie Hayden as Amy, becomes positively abrasive.

The microphones are often not kind to Spiro Milas. He is a properly appealing and larger-than-life Happy Fella but is at times robbed of vocal charm. The show has plenty of life, Scott Waara is an inimitable Herman (it is a gift of a part), and *Standing on the corner, Fresno beauties* and, especially, *Happy to make your acquaintance* project very vividly. There are 74 minutes of music offered on this generously filled CD, but, although the result is certainly not lacking in verve, the score's lyrical opulence is certainly diminished.

Loewe, Frederick (born 1904)

Brigadoon.
*** EMI Dig. CDC7 54481-2 [id.]. Amb. Ch., L. Sinf., John McGlinn.
Tommy Albright (Brent Barrett), Meg Brockie (Judy Kaye), Fiona MacLaren (Rebecca Luker), Charlie Dalrymple (John Mark Ainsley), Jean (Jackie Morrison) Mr Lundie (Frank Middlemass).

The Lerner/Loewe musical, *Brigadoon*, was the first show to establish this famous team of composer/lyricist. But by the standards of their later successes there is a good deal of milk-and-water in the writing. However, if one of its principal hits, *Come to me, bend to me*, belongs to the world of operetta rather than to the post-war musical, *Almost like being in love* looks forward rather than back and could almost be a Rodgers and Hammerstein hit. The scenario of an idyllic love-affair in a Scottish village which reappears only once every hundred years is based on a German short story by Friedrich Gerstäcker: the original village was called Germelshausen. Here the Scottish musical whimsy of Lerner's adaptation fits in well with the new name. The performance, brightly directed by John McGlinn, is admirable. Rebecca Luker as Fiona and Brent Barrett as Tommy are an agreeable pair of lovers; the second Scottish pair, Charlie (John Mark Ainsley) and Jean (Jackie Morrison), who is nicely serenaded in *Come to me, bend to me*, are also very believable, and the spiritedly flirtatious role of Meg is given plenty of vitality by Judy Kaye – perhaps she even over-projects at times. Frank Middlemass is a convincing Mr Lundie, the village schoolmaster who stays on hand to provide the promise of a happy ending.

With its choruses emerging from the mists and with animated dance sequences, the recording is vivid enough: the performance will grip all those who can respond to its old-fashioned romantic sentimentality. There is no doubting the hold the piece has on a modern audience, and *Brigadoon* certainly contains much engaging music, together with some of Loewe's finest lyrics. The CD is splendidly documented, with full lyrics included.

My Fair Lady (musical).
*** Decca Dig. 421 200-2 [id.]. Kiri Te Kanawa, Jeremy Irons, John Gielgud, Warren Mitchell, Jerry Hadley, London Voices, LSO, Mauceri.

Hoping to follow the great success of Bernstein's recording of *West Side Story*, Decca set up a starry cast to make a brand-new digital version of Loewe's splendid music. Alas, it did not work out quite as planned, and the issue was not the hoped-for bestseller, perhaps because of Kiri Te Kanawa's difficulty with Eliza's cockney persona. Although she sings *I could have danced all night* ravishingly, memories of Julie Andrews are not banished; and Jeremy Irons, who gives a forceful portrayal of Higgins, does not match Rex Harrison's elegant timing, especially in his first, early, mono recording. Clearly this is a studio production.

Having said that, it is a joy to hear the music presented with such vigour and sophistication. Warren Mitchell's Doolittle is endearingly crusty and Jerry Hadley sings *On the street where you live* very engagingly. One realizes just how many good tunes there are. If the original cast is forgotten, the interplay between the characters here works very well and, with spirited direction from John Mauceri, this is a first-class entertainment, with the recording giving depth as well as presence.

Lully, Jean-Baptiste (1632–87)

Atys (opera; complete).
*** HM Dig. HMC 901257/9 (3). Les Arts Florissants Ch. & O, Christie.
   Iris / Sangaride (Agnès Mellon), Atys (Guy De Mey), Doris (François Semellaz), Cybèle (Guillemette Laurens), Mélisse (Noémi Rime), Célénus (Jean-François Gardeil).

Harmonia Mundi's valuable set of *Atys* brings the first ever complete recording of a Lully opera to be issued commercially. As was normal at the time, it has a symbolic Prologue in which Flora, goddess of spring, and Time vie with each other to pay homage to King Louis XIV. But Melpomene sends them off and the Muse then entertains with the story of Atys.

It is dawn and its hero welcomes the goddess, Cybèle, who is to preside over the marriage of Célénus, King of Phrygia, and Sangaride, who really loves Atys. He does not at first return her feelings but then surprises her by tenderly declaring his love, even though by so doing he is being untrue to his friend, Célénus. Cybèle adds her support to Atys and Sangaride, even though we soon discover that she loves Atys herself. She still has designs on him. Though as queen of the gods she cannot declare her passion openly, Cybèle arranges for Atys to fall into a deep sleep, and she woos him in his dreams with apparitions helping to support her cause. When he awakens, understandably confused, Sangaride distractedly reminds him of their mutual declaration of love.

Alone, Cybèle is desolate that her planned seduction of Atys is not succeeding. Sangaride does not realize that Cybèle is a deity, thinking her a normal rival, but Atys disillusions her and the two swear to be true to each other, come what may. Meanwhile Cybèle's high priest goes to seek Sangaride's father (Sangarius) to enlist his support for the goddess's cause and to ask him to cancel the wedding arrangements.

King Célénus and Cybèle now agree that Atys must pay a dire penalty for seducing Sangaride away from her marriage with the king. Cybèle inflicts a fit of madness on the errant hero and, thinking he sees a monster, he stabs Sangaride. When he regains his senses and realizes what he has done, he tries to commit suicide, but Cybèle intervenes and transforms him into a pine tree, then laments his own loss.

Like Charpentier's *Médée*, earlier recorded for Harmonia Mundi by William Christie and Les Arts Florissants, this authentic performance demonstrates from first to last that French opera of this early period need not seem stiff and boring. Consistently Christie and his excellent team give life and dramatic speed to the performance, so much so that, though this five-Act piece lasts nearly three hours, one keeps thinking of Purcell's almost contemporary masterpiece on quite a different – miniature – scale, *Dido and Aeneas*.

Invention is only intermittently on a Purcellian level, but there are many memorable numbers, not least those in the sleep interlude of Act III. Outstanding in the cast are the high tenor, Guy de Mey, in the name-part and Agnès Mellon as the nymph, Sangaride, with whom he falls in love. The three well-filled discs are very conveniently laid out, with the Prologue and Act I on the first, and the other two each containing two Acts complete.

Le bourgeois gentilhomme (comédie-ballet; complete).
(M) *** HM/BMG GD 77059 (2) [77059-2-RG]. Siegmund Nimsgern, Dorothea Jungmann, Dirk Schortemeier, René Jacobs, Tölz Ch., La Petite Bande, Leonhardt – CAMPRA: *L'Europe galante.* ***

Entertainment rather than musical value: in itself, Lully's score offers no great musical rewards. The melodic invention is unmemorable and harmonies are neither original nor interesting; but if the music taken on its own is thin stuff, the effect of the entertainment as a whole is quite a different matter. This performance puts Lully's music into the correct stage perspective and, with such sprightly and spirited performers as well as good 1973 recording, this can hardly fail to give pleasure. The orchestral contribution under the direction of Gustav Leonhardt is distinguished by a splendid sense of the French style.

Madetoja, Leevi (1887–1947)

The Ostrobothnians (Pohjalaisia).
*** Finlandia 511002 (2) [id.]. Finnish Nat. Op. O & Ch., Panula.
    Jussi Harri (Jorma Hynninen), Antti (Eero Erkkilä), Maija (Maija Lokka).

Madetoja's opera was first produced in Helsinki in 1924 and is an adaptation by the composer himself of a play by Artturi Järviluoma. The setting is the western Finnish plains of Ostrobothnia (which Madetoja knew well), and its central theme is the Bothnian farmer's love of personal liberty and his abhorrence of all authoritarian restraints.

The nationalist tone of the original play was prompted by the growing Russification of Finland in the period leading up to and including the First World War. In the nineteenth century, the peasantry had been prepared to co-operate with a centrally appointed governor or sheriff, but the brutal authority into which it had turned inspired strong hostility.

Against the background of these tensions is set a simple love story. Antti, one of the farmers, is imprisoned after a stabbing incident; Act I centres on his relationship with Maija, and the increased tension between her brother, Jussi, and the sheriff. In Act II, Antti escapes during an attack by the sheriff's thugs, whose leader is soundly beaten by Jussi. In the last Act a chance remark leads the sheriff mistakenly to believe that Jussi was implicated in the escape, and the opera ends with Jussi's death at the sheriff's hands.

The opera is also interspersed with humorous elements that lighten the mood and lend the work variety. Unlike Merikanto's *Juha*, composed at much the same time, Madetoja's language is not ahead of its time: it springs from much the same soil as most Scandinavian post-nationalists. However, the score often makes imaginative use of folk material, and Madetoja's sense of theatre and his lyrical gift are in good evidence. Although it is unlikely to find a place on the international opera circuit, *Pohjalaisia* is a good work that rewards attention; this 1975 performance has the benefit of excellent teamwork from the soloists, and keen and responsive playing from the orchestra. The analogue recording is very good indeed.

Magnard, Albéric (1865–1914)

Guercoeur: complete.
Withdrawn: *** EMI CDS7 49193-8 (3). Orféon Donostiarra, Toulouse Capitole O, Plasson.
        Guercoeur (José Van Dam) Vérité (Hildegard Behrens), Heurtal (Gary Lakes), Giselle (Nadine Denize).

Following up the success of his prizewinning record of Magnard's *Fourth Symphony*, Plasson here presents with similar warmth and conviction the large-scale opera on an ambitious theme that occupied the composer over his early thirties from 1897 to 1901.

Acts I and III are set in Heaven, where Vérité (Truth) rules. Guercoeur, the hero and saviour of his people in a medieval city-state, has died, and in Act I pleads to be allowed to return to earth. Act II on earth finds him disillusioned that his friend, Heurtal, having become the lover of his wife, Giselle, plans to use his power to restore the dictatorship.

Though Act III brings a beautiful, inspired ensemble towards the end, inevitably the return to Heaven in disillusionment makes a downbeat conclusion. With its distant echoes of Wagner's *Tristan*, its warm lyricism and superbly crafted writing, it makes a fine offering on record, almost as rich and distinctive as Magnard's symphonies. It echoes specific passages in Wagner less than Chausson's *Le roi Arthus*, the other fine French opera of the period now restored through recording; but Magnard's lyricism is almost too rich, so regularly heightened that the key moments stand out too little.

José van Dam makes a magnificent hero, the ideal singer for the role with his firm, finely shaded baritone. Hildegard Behrens makes a similarly powerful Vérité. Though some of the soprano singing among the attendant spirits in Heaven is edgily French, the casting is generally strong, with Gary Lakes a ringing Heurtal and Nadine Denize a sweet-toned Giselle. A rich rarity, warmly recorded.

Martin, Frank (1890–1974)

Le vin herbé (oratorio).

*(**) Jecklin Disco JD 581/2-2 [id.]. Basia Retchitzka, Nata Tuscher, Adrienne Comte, Hélène Morath, Marie Luise De Montmollin, Vera Diakoff, Oleg De Nyzankowskyi, Eric Tappy, Hans Jonelli, Heinz Rehfuss, André Vessières, Derrik Olsen, composer, Winterthur O (members), Desarzens.

Martin's oratorio on the Tristan legend is laid out for a madrigal choir of twelve singers, who also assume solo roles, and a handful of instrumentalists, including the piano, played here by the septuagenarian composer himself. It is powerfully atmospheric and sounds like a distant relative of *Pelléas et Mélisande*, having all the pale, dimly lit but at times luminous colouring of Debussy's world. It is powerful and hypnotic, and there is some fine singing here from Nata Tuscher (Isolde), Eric Tappy (Tristan) and Heinz Rehfuss (King Mark). The instrumental playing, though not impeccable, is dedicated (and the same must be said for the choral singing). The 1960s sound ideally needs a bit more space round it but is much improved in the CD format. *Le vin herbé* is a masterly and compelling work and is strongly recommended.

Martinů, Bohuslav (1890–1959)

Ariane.

** Sup. Dig. 10 4395-2 (2) [id.]. Czech PO, Vaclav Neumann.
Ariane (Celina Lindsley), Theseus (Norman Phillips), Burun (Vladimir Doležal), Minotaur (Richard Novák), Guard (Miroslav Kapp), Old Man (Ludek Vale).

Ariane is a slight work to which Martinů turned as a relaxation from *The Greek Passion*. It is based on the play, *Le voyage de Thésée*, by his friend, Georges Neveux, with whom he had collaborated on what is probably his operatic masterpiece, *Julietta*. As Jaroslav Mihule points out in his notes, in making his adaptation of the play, Martinů cast it in the form of a baroque monody with three sinfonias and and three self-contained dramatic sequences plus a closing aria. Apparently the demanding role of Ariane was inspired by Callas. It is all quite engaging and high-spirited though without being Martinů at his very best. Written in the course of a month, it is a short piece, no longer than forty-three minutes, though it is housed in a two-CD format so as to accommodate a multi-lingual booklet and libretto. The singers (and in particular Celina Lindsley) are very good indeed: only Richard Novák's wide vibrato is problematic. Decent rather than outstanding recording quality. Attractive music but not quintessential Martinů.

The Epic of Gilgamesh (oratorio).

⊛ *** Marco Polo Dig. 8.223316 [id.]. Eva Děpoltová, Štefan Margita, Iván Kusnjer, Ludek Vele, Milan Karpíšek, Slovak Ph. Ch. & O, Zdeněk Košler.

The Epic of Gilgamesh comes from Martinů's last years and is masterly: it has vision, depth and power. Like Honegger's *King David*, it is for narrator, soloists, chorus and orchestra, and it similarly evokes a remote and distant world, full of colour and mystery. *Gilgamesh* is the oldest poem known to mankind: it predates the Homeric epics by 1,500 years, which places it at 7000 BC or earlier.

The story survives in fragmentary form and tells, in the first part of Martinů's oratorio, how Gilgamesh, King of Uruk, hears of the great warrior, Enkidu, a primitive who is at home with the world of nature and of animals. The king befriends him, they quarrel and fight, before their friendship is finally sealed.

The second part tells of Enkidu's death and of Gilgamesh's grief; and the third addresses the themes of death and immortality, Gilgamesh's plea to the gods and his encounter with Enkidu's spirit. The final pages are awesome, even chilling, and the work abounds in invention of the highest quality and of consistently sustained inspiration. The performance is committed and sympathetic and the recording very natural in its balance. A powerful and gripping work – indeed, one of the most imaginative choral works of the present century.

OPERA

The Greek Passion (sung in English).
*** Sup. Dig. 10 3611/2 [id.]. Kuhn Children's Ch., Czech PO Ch., Brno State PO, Mackerras.
Manolios (John Mitchinson), Katerina (Helen Field), Grigoris (John Tomlinson), Kostandis (Phillip Joll), Fotis (Geoffrey Moses), Yannakos (Arthur Davies), Lenio (Rita Cullis), Nikolios / Old Woman (Catherine Savory).

Written with much mental pain in the years just before Martinů died in 1959, this opera was the work he regarded as his musical testament. Based on a novel by Nikos Kazantzakis (author of *Zorba the Greek*), it tells in an innocent, direct way of a village where a Passion play is to be presented; the individuals – tragically, as it proves – take on qualities of the New Testament figures they represent.

At the very opening there is a hymn-like prelude of diatonic simplicity, and what makes the work so moving – given occasional overtones of Janáček, Mussorgsky and Britten – is Martinů's ability to simplify his message both musically and dramatically. On stage, the degree of gaucheness can be hard to present effectively, but on record it is quite another matter.

This extraordinarily vivid recording – with exceptionally clear focus for the soloists – was made by a cast which had been giving stage performances for the Welsh National Opera; the singing is not only committed but accomplished too. The Czechs in 1981 were happy to record the opera in what is in effect the original language of Martinů's libretto, English. Virtually every word is crystal clear and the directness of communication to the listener is riveting, particularly as the choral perspectives are so tellingly and realistically managed.

The combination of British soloists with excellent Czech choirs and players is entirely fruitful. As a Czech specialist, Mackerras makes an ideal advocate, and the recording is both brilliant and atmospheric – for instance, the scena with the accordion in Act III is handled most evocatively. With the words so clear, the absence of an English libretto is not a serious omission, but the lack of any separate cues within the four Acts is a great annoyance. But in its simple way *The Greek Passion* makes a most moving experience, and on CD the projection gives the listener the impression that the tragedy is being played out 'live' in the area just behind the speakers.

Julietta (complete).
*** Sup. 10 8176-2 (3) [id.]. Prague Nat. Theatre Ch. & O, Jaroslav Krombholc.
Julietta (Maria Tauberová), Michel (Ivo Žídek), Inspector (Antonín Zlesák), Man with the Helmet (Adenék Otava), Man in the Window (Václav Bednář),Litte Arab (Ivana Mixová), Old Arab (Vladimir Jedenáctík), Bird-seller (Jaroslava Procházková), Fishmonger (Ludmilla Hanzalíková), Palmist (Vera Soukupová), Memory-dealer (Jinřich Jindrák), Old Sailor (Jaroslav Veverka), Young Sailor (Zdeněk Švehla), Forest Warden (Antonín Zlesák), Errand-boy (Marcela Lemariová), Beggar (Karel Berman).

Described by the composer as a Dreambook, *Julietta* was given first in Prague in March 1938, the year which brought the Munich Agreement and the dismemberment of Czechoslovakia at the hands of Hitler, itself a surreal period for the Czech nation.

Julietta is based on a play by Georges Neveux, and takes place in a bizarre dream-world, where there is no reality. Michel, its central figure, is the only character able to retain his memory and relate events to what has gone before. The story takes place against the background of a small but imaginary seaside town. As the opera begins, Michel, returning to the town he last visited three years previously, asks the little Arab the way to the Hotel Mariner. He is told it does not exist but the old Arab comes out of his house and takes Michel inside, telling him, 'It's here.'

The fishmonger and bird-seller now emerge from their shops and discuss what they have overheard. The man in the window plays his accordion, and the man with the helmet looks for his ship. From within the Arab's house Michel's voice is heard crying for help – the old Arab has a knife. The inspector enters; Michel's cries can still be heard and the inspector knocks at the door. Michel appears and says he was forced to relate his childhood at knife-point. The inspector tells him that everyone in the town has lost their memory. There is a good deal of confusion before Michel is appointed captain of the town as he is the only one with a reliable memory.

Michel wants to leave as he came, by train, but is told there is no train and no station. Dusk falls. Michel and the man with the helmet sit down and talk together. Michel relates how as a travelling bookseller he once visited a small town and heard the sound of a woman's voice coming from a window: she was very beautiful and he was afraid he would fall in love with her, so he left on the first train in the morning. Now he has returned to find her. He searches for her in the shops, but they shut up. The man with the helmet departs and Julietta's voice is heard from an upper window, singing of her lost love. They recognize each other. She has not changed. She implores him not to leave her again and goes back into the house.

The inspector reappears; he has now become the postman and cannot remember appointing Michel captain of the town. They play a game of cards, which is drawn. Julietta now comes out, pleased that Michel has not left. He declares his love and she asks him to meet her by the crossroads, at the well. He waits for her as instructed, and three gentlemen approach, formally attired. They are lost and they stop and talk with him, then depart. An old man arrives; he puts up a sign and offers Michel a glass of wine; a grandfather and grandmother arrive together. They sit and recall their past; then a palmist offers to read Michel's hand. He warns of danger and disappears. So does the old man with the wine.

At last Julietta arrives and pleads with Michel to reassure her that he never left her. She admits her love for him, but when he tries to embrace her she holds back. Voices from the wood echo their declarations of love. The memory-dealer arrives and displays a photograph-album of Julietta and Michel in Spain (where they have never been together). Michel sends him off. He is in favour of reality and retells Julietta the story of the first time he saw her. Suddenly she wishes to depart and Michel tries to restrain her; as she runs off he pulls a pistol from his pocket and shoots after her; there is a cry, then silence.

Michel considers the situation in disbelief. He runs after her. All the characters from the earlier scenes reappear and accuse him, and Michel again retells his story, now including the fantasy visit to Spain. They all disappear together into the wood. Michel reappears and meets the forest warden, who has heard a gunshot but says it was he who fired – at a snipe. Michel returns to the town, where he meets two sailors whom he directs to the wood, asking them to bring back Julietta's body. The sailors go off and Michel now discovers he no longer has the pistol.

The man with the helmet returns and offers to take Michel with him on his ship. The sailors return with a stretcher, but there is no body on it, only a veil. They did not find Julietta. The sailors disappear into the ship which is bound for Spain.

Michel impulsively knocks on the door of Julietta's house and the old lady opens the door. She denies Julietta's existence and slams the door in his face. The younger of the two sailors now returns and asks to keep the veil. Michel agrees and he returns to the ship, and Michel begins to follow him. Then he hears Julietta's voice once more coming from the window. Michel, apparently no longer remembering the past, mounts the gangplank and disappears inside the ship.

The scene partly changes to what appears to be a travel agency, but part of Julietta's house can still be observed in the background. Michel questions the clerk and discovers he is in the central dream office; the clerk suggests that all that has happened to him is a dream. An errand boy arrives, searching for Buffalo Bill (there are shots and noises of horses offstage), and a beggar seeks a visit to the tropics with a lady. Her name is Julietta. The errand boy returns, having enjoyed his fantasy, and he too mentions Julietta. Michel continues to wait patiently. Now a convict enters asking for a cell with bars that disintegrate at a touch, and the engine driver of the Orient Express who had fallen asleep at a red light seeks a photograph of his dead daughter.

The clerk disappears and Julietta's voice calls from the distance, pleading with Michel to wait for her, but the nightwatchman warns him of danger and suggests he leave. Julietta's voice is heard for the last time and Michel calls back to her passionately, but he cannot reach her through the door for it will not open. The dream office recedes, and Julietta's house dominates the final brief scene. The little Arab and old Arab redirect Michel to the Hotel Mariner and he enters again, like a recurring dream.

This vintage Supraphon recording, made in 1964, captures that surreal quality vividly. One would never guess the date of the recording, for the ear is magnetized from the very start, when the howling of a high bassoon introduces the astonishingly original prelude. The voices as well as the orchestra are then presented with a bright immediacy which reinforces the power and incisiveness of Krombholc's performance. The sharpness of focus adds to the atmospheric intensity, as when in the first Act the Man in the Window plays his accordion. Ivo Žídek gives a vivid portrait of the central character, Michel, perplexed by his dream-like search, and there is no weak link in the rest of the cast. The snag is that the set stretches extravagantly to three discs, when the opera could have been fitted on two, though that layout brings the advantage of having each Act complete on a single disc. Informative notes and libretto come with multiple translations.

Mascagni, Pietro (1863–1945)

L'Amico Fritz (complete).
Withdrawn: *** EMI CDS7 47905-8 (2) [Ang. CDCB 47905]. ROHCG Ch. and O, Gavazzeni.
   Fritz (Luciano Pavarotti), Suzel (Mirella Freni), David (Vicente Sardinero).

L'Amico Fritz, which was first heard in Rome in 1891, failed to repeat the success of *Cavalleria rusticana*, which had firmly established its composer in the operatic firmament the previous year. It is a simple tale of rustic love, but without the drama of betrayal, and has altogether more refinement than the previous work. The Italian public, no doubt disappointed by a milk-and-watery situation, refused to take to the piece.

As it opens, David, a rabbi, leaves Fritz's house to tell two neighbours that Fritz will provide a dowry for their wedding. Fritz himself apparently has no time to consider this happy state for himself, though sighing for female attention. His two friends, Hanezò and Frederica, together with Caterina, his housekeeper, wish him luck on his fortieth birthday. David prophesies that, whatever Fritz thinks, before the year is over he will be married. Fritz laughs scornfully at such a suggestion.

Caterina then ushers in Suzel, daughter of one of Fritz's tenant farmers, and she gives him flowers. Beppe the gypsy plays his fiddle and entertains the company with song. He praises Fritz's charitable disposition. Suzel leaves and everyone comments on her fresh beauty now she is almost grown up. Fritz's response is that she is only a girl, and David says that nevertheless she will soon be finding a husband. He repeats his prophecy that Fritz too will soon be married and, when Fritz demurs, this is turned into a wager with Fritz's vineyard at stake.

We now move outside to find Suzel picking cherries from a tree. She throws them down to Fritz, which occasions the opera's most famous number. Friends arrive and a countryside drive is planned, but David stays behind. Suzel offers him water to drink and he is reminded of the biblical story of Rebecca and Isaac. He makes her read and understand the significance of the passage. When Fritz returns, David says he has found a suitable husband for Suzel, with her father approving. Fritz is stunned by this news and finally has to admit to himself that he wants Suzel for himself, but he dashes away in embarrassed confusion. Suzel is disconcerted and upset, and David offers words of comfort.

Mascagni's second most famous Intermezzo introduces the opera's culminating scene. Fritz has not encountered the agonies of love before and is undermined by the experience which he shares with Beppe, already familiar with the problem. David now approaches Fritz for his consent to Suzel's marriage (not to himself!) and is refused. Suzel arrives with fruit for Fritz, but is very sad; Fritz asks for her confirmation that she is to marry another. She says she does want this arranged marriage, and pleads for his help, which he readily provides with his own declaration of love. General rejoicing in Fritz's new-found happiness.

The haunting *Cherry duet* from this opera whets the appetite for more, and it is good to hear so rare and charming a piece, one that is not likely to enter the regular repertory of British opera houses. Disappointingly, no other number in the opera approaches that famous duet in memorability, and for all the opera's innocent charm the plot and libretto lack sharpness, standing in total contrast to *Cavalleria rusticana*. Though this performance could be more refined, Freni and Pavarotti – early in their careers in 1969 – sing freshly and attractively, with the Covent Garden Orchestra giving warm-hearted support; the recording is clear and atmospheric, and has transferred very successfully to CD.

Cavalleria rusticana (complete).
*** BMG/RCA RD 83091. Amb. Op. Ch., Nat. PO, Levine.
   Santuzza (Renata Scotto), Turiddù (Plácido Domingo), Alfio (Pablo Elvira), Lola (Isola Jones), Mamma Lucia (Jean Kraft).

*** DG 419 257-2 (3) [id.]. Ch. & O of La Scala, Milan, Karajan – LEONCAVALLO: *I Pagliacci* *** (also with collection of *Operatic intermezzi* ***).

Santuzza (Fiorenza Cossotto), Turiddù (Carlo Bergonzi), Alfio (Giangiacomo Guelfi), Lola (Adriane Martino), Mamma Lucia (Maria Garcia Allegri).

(***) EMI mono CDS7 47981-8 (3) [Ang. CDCC 47981]. Ch. & O of La Scala, Milan, Serafin – LEONCAVALLO: *I Pagliacci.* (***)

Santuzza (Maria Callas), Turiddù (Giuseppe Di Stefano), Alfio (Rolando Panerai), Lola (Anna Maria Canali), Mamma Lucia (Ebe Ticozzi).

(B) **(*) Naxos Dig. 8.660022 [id.]. Slovak Philh. Ch., Czech RSO, Alexander Rahbari.

Santuzza (Stefka Evstatieva), Turiddù (Giacomo Aragall), Alfio (Eduard Tumagian), Lola (Anna Di Mauro), Mamma Lucia (Alzbeta Michalková).

**(*) DG Dig. 429 568-2 [id.]. ROHCG Ch., Philh. O, Sinopoli.

Santuzza (Agnes Baltsa), Turiddù (Plácido Domingo), Alfio (Juan Pons), Lola (Susanne Mentzer), Mamma Lucia (Wiera Baniewicz).

**(*) Decca 414 590-2 (2) [id.]. L. Op. Ch., Nat. PO, Gavazzeni – LEONCAVALLO: *I Pagliacci.* **

Santuzza (Julia Varady), Turiddù (Luciano Pavarotti), Alfio (Piero Cappuccilli), Lola (Carmen Gonzales), Mamma Lucia (Ida Bormida).

(M) **(*) EMI CMS7 63967-2 (2) [Ang. CDMB 64967]. Rome Op. Ch. & O, Santini – LEONCAVALLO: *Pagliacci.* ***

Santuzza (Victoria De los Angeles), Turiddù (Franco Corelli), Alfio (Mario Sereni), Lola (Adriana Lazzarini), Mamma Lucia (Corinna Vozza).

(M) **(*) Decca 425 985-2 [id.]. Maggio Musicale Fiorentino Ch. & O, Erede.

Santuzza (Renata Tebaldi), Turiddù (Jussi Bjoerling), Alfio (Ettore Bastianini), Lola (Lucia Dani), Mamma Lucia (Rina Corsi).

(M) **(*) EMI CMS7 63650-2 (2). Amb. Op. Ch., Southend Boys' Ch., Philh. O, Muti – LEONCAVALLO: *I Pagliacci.* **(*)

Santuzza (Montserrat Caballé), Turiddù (José Carreras), Alfio (Matteo Manuguerra), Lola (Júlia Hamari), Mamma Lucia (Astrid Varnay).

(M) (***) BMG/RCA mono GD 86510 [RCA 6510-2-RG]. Robert Shaw Chorale, RCA O, Cellini.

Santuzza (Zinka Milanov), Turiddù (Jussi Bjoerling), Alfio (Robert Merrill), Lola (Carol Smith), Mamma Lucia (Margaret Roggero).

(M) (**) Nimbus mono NI 7843/4 [id.]. La Scala Ch. & O, composer – LEONCAVALLO: *I Pagliacci.* (**(*))

Santuzza (Lina Bruna Rasa), Turiddù (Beniamino Gigli), Alfio (Gino Bechi), Lola (Maria Marcucci), Mamma Lucia (Giulietta Simionato).

*(*) Ph. 416 137-2 [id.]. La Scala, Milan, Ch. & O, Prêtre.

Santuzza (Elena Obraztsova), Turiddù (Plácido Domingo), Alfio (Renato Bruson), Lola (Axelle Gall), Mamma Lucia (Fedora Barbieri).

(M) *(*) Decca 421 807-2 (2). Rome St Cecilia Ac. Ch. & O, Serafin – LEONCAVALLO: *Pagliacci.* **

Santuzza (Giulietta Simionato), Turiddù (Mario Del Monaco), Alfio (Cornell MacNeil), Lola (Ana Raquel Satre), Mamma Lucia (Anna Di Stasio).

*(*) Ph. Dig. 432 105-2; *432 105-4* [id.]. Paris Ch. & O, Bychkov.

Santuzza (Jessye Norman), Turiddù (Giuseppe Giacomini), Alfio (Dmitri Hvorostovsky), Lola (Martha Senn), Mamma Lucia (Rosa Laghezza).

Cavalleria rusticana, with its ironic title ('Rustic chivalry'), was Mascagni's only great and enduring success, and perhaps he was lucky that Leoncavallo wrote a companion-piece with which it could naturally pair. Moreover the central *Intermezzo* became one of the most famous of all romantic orchestral melodies to emerge from the opera house. During the overture another indelible theme is heard from behind the curtain, Turiddù's secret serenade to his illicit love, Lola, who is Alfio's wife.

The opera opens on Easter Day. Church bells ring and the people are making their way to church. Santuzza arrives at the inn to ask Mamma Lucia, the inn-keeper, if her son, Turiddù, is there. Mamma Lucia says he is away purchasing wine. But Santuzza points out that he was seen in the village the previous evening. Alfio now enters, obviously in good spirits, and he asks Lucia for wine. She repeats the story that Turiddù is away to replenish the cellar, and again doubts are expressed as Turiddù had also been observed near Alfio's cottage that very morning. The Resurrection hymn is heard from the church.

Santuzza now goes over her misfortunes with Mamma Lucia. Turiddù had been engaged to Lola before he went away to war. By the time he had returned Lola had married Alfio. Santuzza then became Turiddù's lover, but now Lola once again is showing affection and desire and is jealous of Santuzza. Turiddù now enters and Santuzza complains of his faithlessness – which he at first denies but then tells her not to bother him any longer. Lola approaches, mocks Santuzza and invites Turiddù to enter the church with her. Santuzza pleads with him, but he says there is nothing left between them and, when she remonstrates, he throws her to the ground.

Alfio arrives and the spurned Santuzza tells him angrily of Lola's infidelity. He swears to avenge his honour. The stage empties and the strains of the famous *Intermezzo* fill the silent square. When the service is over, Turiddù asks Lola to join the gathering outside his mother's inn and he sings a drinking song. Alfio arrives and refuses the wine Turiddù offers and the women, scenting trouble, take Lola away. Turiddù and Alfio exchange bitter words, then Turiddù bites Alfio's ear, the traditional Sicilian challenge to a duel. Turiddù exonerates Lola from any blame in the affair. Fearing for Santuzza, he asks Mamma Lola to look after her if the worst should happen and he begs his mother's blessing. It does happen – offstage – and, on hearing of Turiddù's death, both women collapse to the ground.

The RCA issue was the first to appear on a single CD (libretto included) and, on balance, in performance remains the best current recommendation, with Domingo giving a heroic account of the role of Turiddù, full of defiance. Scotto, also strongly characterful though not always perfectly steady on top, gives one of her finest performances, and James Levine directs colourfully with splendid pacing, drawing red-blooded playing from the National Philharmonic. The recording is first rate, with a striking feeling of presence on CD.

Karajan's direction of the other half of the inevitable partnership matches that of *Pagliacci*. He pays Mascagni the tribute of taking his markings literally, so that well-worn melodies come out with new purity and freshness, and the singers have been chosen to match that. Cossotto quite as much as Bergonzi keeps a pure, firm line that is all too rare in this much-abused music. Together they show that much of the vulgarity lies in interpretations rather than in Mascagni's inspiration. Not that there is any lack of dramatic bite (except marginally, because of the recording balance in some of the chorus work). On CD, voices are generally more sharply defined, while the spacious opulence is retained. Karajan's fine performances of various opera-interludes make a welcome filler on the three-CD set.

Though on stage Maria Callas sang Santuzza in *Cav.* only as a young teenager, she gives a totally distinctive characterization, matched by few others on disc. Dating from the mid-1950s, these performances reveal the diva in her finest voice, with edginess and unevenness of production at a minimum and with vocal colouring at its most characterful. The singing of the other principals is hardly less dramatic and Panerai, here at the beginning of his long career, is in firm, well-projected voice. This powerful team is superbly controlled by Serafin, a master at pacing this music, giving it full power while minimizing vulgarity. However, with Callas providing the central focus, the performance seems to centre round the aria, *Voi lo sapete*, wonderfully dark and intense, and one soon adjusts to the fact that the restricted range means that choruses sound rather mushy; the solo voices, however, are vividly projected on both CD and the very acceptable mid-priced cassettes.

As in his parallel recording of *Pag.*, Alexander Rahbari conducts a red-blooded reading of *Cav.*, making it a first-rate super-bargain choice. Stefka Evstatieva is a warmly vibrant Santuzza, well controlled, no Slavonic wobbler, and Giacomo Aragall as Turiddù, not quite as fresh-sounding as he once was, yet gives a strong, characterful performance, with Eduard Tumagian excellent as Alfio, firm and dark. Well-focused digital recording. This set is a real bargain.

Highly individual, passionately committed, only occasionally wilful, Sinopoli's reading is quite unlike any other. Traditionalists may well not like it, and they will be able to test that soon enough when the opening prelude, very flexible in its rubato, shows the conductor at his most extreme. This performance has the sort of high emotional tension which marks Sinopoli's readings of Elgar, and he is superbly backed by the Philharmonia, the strings in particular playing with a luminous warmth. Regularly Sinopoli brings out markings in the score that are usually neglected, and among the soloists it is Domingo, the keenest musician, who thrives on them most, giving a superb, imaginative performance, vocally as rich as ever. The characterful timbres of Baltsa's mezzo are not ideally suited to the role of Santuzza: there is little sense of vulnerability in her tough sound, even though her vehemence is apt. Juan Pons as the carter, Alfio, sings well, but there is no snarl in the voice, and Susanne Mentzer rather lacks sparkle in Lola's solo. Yet with rich, spacious sound this single disc provides a warm and refreshing experience.

With Pavarotti loud and unsubtle as Turiddù – though the tone is often most beautiful – it is left to Julia Varady as Santuzza to give the Decca version under Gavazzeni its distinction. Though her tone is not heavyweight, the impression of youth is most affecting; the sharpness of pain in *Voi lo sapete* is beautifully conveyed, and the whole performance is warm and authentic. Cappuccilli's Alfio is too noble to be convincing, and as in the companion *Pag.* the main claim to attention lies in the brilliant forward recording, equally impressive. The coupling with *Pagliacci* is economically issued on a pair of CDs.

Though not as vibrant as Von Matačić's *Pagliacci* coupling, Santini's essentially lyrical EMI performance, beautifully sung, is satisfying enough, provided the bitterness of Mascagni's drama is not a first consideration. Like the coupling, it shows Corelli in good form; both he and De los Angeles are given scope by Santini to produce soaring, Italianate singing of Mascagni's richly memorable melodies. The recording is suitably atmospheric.

The early (1957) Decca recording with Tebaldi offers a forthright, lusty account of Mascagni's blood-and-thunder piece with three excellent soloists. Tebaldi is most moving in *Voi lo sapete*, and the firm richness of Bastianini's baritone is beautifully caught. As always, Bjoerling shows himself the most intelligent of tenors, and it is only the chorus that is seriously disappointing. The choristers are enthusiastic and accurate enough when accompanying Bjoerling's superb account of the drinking scene, but at other times they are undisciplined. At mid-price this is well worth considering by admirers of Tebaldi and Bjoerling.

There are fewer unexpected textual points in the EMI *Cav.* with Caballé than in the companion version of *Pag.*, but Muti's approach is comparably biting and violent. He brushes away the idea that this is a sentimental score, but runs the risk of making it vulgar. The result is certainly refreshing, with Caballé – pushed faster than usual, even in her big moments – collaborating warmly. So *Voi lo sapete* is geared from the start to the final cry of *Io son dannata*, and she manages a fine snarl on *A te la mala Pasqua*. Carreras does not sound quite so much at home, though the rest of the cast is memorable, including the resonant Manuguerra as Alfio and the veteran Astrid Varnay as Mamma Lucia. The recording is forward and vivid.

On a single mid-price CD in the Victor Opera series, RCA offers a vintage version recorded in New York in mono in the early 1950s with soloists from the Met. The sound is surprisingly full and vivid for its age, but none of the documentation gives any clue to the date of recording. Though Zinka Milanov starts disappointingly in the *Easter hymn*, the conjunction of three of the outstanding Met. principals of the period brings a warmly satisfying performance. Admirers of Milanov will not want to miss her beautiful singing of *Voi lo sapete*, and in the duet Merrill's dark, firm timbre is thrilling. Bjoerling brings musical and tonal subtlety to the role of Turiddù, while Cellini's conducting also minimizes the vulgarity of the piece.

EMI's vintage 1940 version of *Cav.*, conducted by the composer with Gigli as Turiddù, came out from EMI on CD in an ungenerous two-disc package, and we await its reissue. It is good to have it again available on CD from Nimbus, along with the curious little speech of introduction that Mascagni himself recorded. Yet the composer's sluggish speeds mean that this opera has to start awkwardly at the end of the *Pag.* disc. Nimbus's transfer captures the voices well, giving them a mellow bloom, though the focus is not nearly as sharp as on the old EMI transfer, and the orchestral sound becomes muzzy.

Taken from the soundtrack of a Unitel television film (like the companion version of *Pag.*), the Prêtre set can be recommended to those who want a reminder of the film, and maybe also to those who want to hear Domingo in ringing voice; but otherwise the flaws rule it out as a serious contender. Obraztsova's massive and distinctive mezzo is certainly characterful but sounds edgy and uneven, hardly apt for the role. One or two moments are memorable – for example, the agonized utterance of the curse *A te la mala Pasqua*, not fire-eating at all – but she, like some of the others, equally unsteady, looked better than they sound. Fedora Barbieri, a veteran of veterans among mezzos, makes a token appearance as Mamma Lucia. The recording is full and atmospheric with the sound-effects needed for television. The single-disc CD format brings a libretto in a slipcase.

The comparatively restrained tone of the earlier Decca performance is set by Serafin. Simionato is not ideal as Santuzza: her *Easter hymn* should be steadier than this. Cornell MacNeil is an efficient but unimaginative Alfio. As with the coupling, the redeeming feature is the Decca recording, with its vivid theatrical presence and atmosphere. This set has been withdrawn just as we go to press.

Jessye Norman produces glorious sounds and dominates Bychkov's whole performance. It is almost comic the way that after the conductor's funereal pace for the introduction to *Voi lo sapete* she instantly gets the music moving, adding electricity. Plainly she should have been conducting too. Hvorostovsky produces beautiful sounds as Alfio, but the whip-cracking song is limp, and Giuseppe Giacomini proves a prosaic, colourless Turiddù. Star-casting here lets the listener down.

Cavalleria rusticana: highlights.
(M) ** Decca 421 870-2; *421 870-4* [id.] (from above recording with Varady, Pavarotti; cond. Gavazzeni – LEONCAVALLO: *I Pagliacci*: highlights. **

The Decca excerpts from *Cavalleria rusticana* include *Santuzza's prayer* and *Voi lo sapete*, very welcome because Julia Varady is the most individual member of the cast. Pavarotti is not far short of being coarse as Turiddù, though the tone is often beautiful. The recording is brilliant, with striking presence and fine atmosphere.

Iris (complete).
(M) *** Sony Dig. M2K 45526 (2) [id.]. Bav. R. Ch., Munich R. O, Patanè.
   Iris (Ilona Tokody), Osaka (Plácido Domingo), Kyoto (Juan Pons), Blind Man (Bonaldo Giaiotti).

Iris is the opera – first given in 1898 – which, with its story of Old Japan and a heroine-victim, prompted the ever-competitive Puccini to turn his attention to the East and write *Madama Butterfly*. It has often been said that, but for *Butterfly*, *Iris* would have stayed in the repertory – but even as committed a performance as this hardly sustains such an idea. Amid the early plaudits for an opera which aims far higher than *Cavalleria rusticana*, Puccini put his finger on the central weakness: a lack of interesting action.

Iris is young and beautiful. When we first meet her it is dawn and the mountain, Fujiyama, is glowing in the morning sunlight. But she has not slept peacefully, having had bad dreams of monsters trying to attack her sleeping doll. She is a simple girl and loves her blind father. But Osaka, a wealthy rake, desires her and Kyoto plots to obtain her for him. He and Osaka bring a marionette show to the house, and as Iris watches enthralled she is carried off and, since money is left behind for her father, the abduction becomes legal. But her father, enraged, begins a search for her, even though he is led to believe that she left voluntarily.

Inside the green house of the Yoshiwara Iris awakens, watched by Kyoto and Osaka. She believes she is waking from death, but death should bring paradise and she feels no sense of happiness. Osaka places jewels beside her and tries unsuccessfully to woo her. He is splendidly garbed and she thinks he is Jor, the sun god, but he says he is Pleasure. She believes death and pleasure are one, so she is very uneasy. Finally Osaka is weary of her innocence and he leaves. But Kyoto, in an effort to lure him back, places Iris on a balcony dressed in transparent clothes.

Crowds in the street praise her beauty; passing by, her father assumes she is an inmate of her own free will. She calls happily to him, but he throws mud at her and curses her. Terrified, she leaps from a window into the sewer below. Later the ragpickers and scavengers drag her body from the sewer. They tear off her jewels but flee when she seems to be alive. Warmth and light spring from the mountain Fujiyama as she slowly regains consciousness. Spirit voices are heard whispering of the conflicts of her life, the treachery of Kyoto, the lust of Osaka, and the selfish wishes of her father for her caring ministrations.

Enough strength returns to her for her to appreciate the warmth of the sun – the expression of Nature's love – and the opera ends as it began in a pantheistic glow.

This heroine-as-victim is totally passive, much put upon by everyone. The rich hero, Osaka, makes advances to her in Act II, behaves insensitively and promptly finds himself bored by the reactions of a frightened child. How different that delayed duet is from the love-duet in *Butterfly*. Iris's one positive act is to throw herself to her death when even her blind father turns against her – through an implausible misunderstanding, needless to say. Illica as librettist falls sadly short of his achievement for Puccini. Musically, *Iris* brings a mixture of typical Mascagnian sweetness and a vein of nobility often echoing Wagner. So the long symbolic prelude representing night and dawn has obvious echoes of Wagner's dawn music in the prologue to *Götterdämmerung*, and it returns at the end of the opera to represent the dead heroine's transfiguration. The comparison with the dawn interlude in *Butterfly* is also pointful, when Puccini, realistic and unsymbolic, is so much more involving.

With a strong line-up of soloists including Domingo, and with Giuseppe Patanè a persuasive conductor, this recording makes as good a case for a flawed piece as one is ever likely to get. Domingo's warm, intelligent singing helps to conceal the cardboard thinness of a hero who expresses himself in generalized ardour. The most celebrated passage from the opera, the Neapolitan-like *Apri la tua finestra*, proves to be just a stylized item in a play within the play, not the hero's personal serenade at all. The Hungarian soprano, Ilona Tokody, brings out the tenderness of the heroine but, with dramatic tone, also expansively makes her into a plausible Butterfly figure, singing beautifully except when under pressure. Juan Pons, sounding almost like a baritone Domingo, is firm and well projected as Kyoto, owner of a geisha-house, and Bonaldo Giaiotti brings an authentically dark Italian bass to the role of Iris's father. Full, atmospheric recording.

Lodoletta (complete).
*** Hung. Dig. HCD 31307/8 [id.]. Hungarian State Op. Children's Ch., Hungarian R. & TV Ch. & State O, Charles Rosekrans.
    Lodoletta (Maria Spacagna), Mad Woman (Andrea Ulbrich), Maud (Zsuzsanna Bazsinka), La Vanard (Jolán Sánta), Flammen (Péter Kelen), Giannotto (Károly Szilágyi), Franz (Mihály Kálmándi), Antonio (László Polgár).

Lodoletta was first heard in Rome in 1917, some 27 years after *Cavalleria rusticana* had established its composer's reputation. The plot, based on *Two little wooden shoes* by Ouida, is so soft-centred that the shrewd Puccini firmly gave up his option to set it, having considered it closely. The scene-setting, as at the very start in Holland, is often delightful. As the opera opens, it is Lodoletta's birthday. Everyone brings gifts; Antonio, her foster-father, had planned to give her a pair of clogs but he has no money. Flammen, an artist, now wants to buy a picture of the Holy Virgin which belongs to the heroine; when he is told it is not for sale, he asks if instead he can borrow it and make a copy. He offers a gold piece, and Antonio is well satisfied.

But then Antonio is killed, falling out of a tree, and Flammen, though not exactly a model character, decides, with the best intentions, to try and adopt the orphaned girl. Lodoletta has a village boy-friend, Giannotto, but she does not love him; however, she is feeling the beginnings of real ardour for Flammen.

Suddenly an amnesty is granted by Napoleon to expatriates who want to return to France, and Flammen decides to take advantage of the decree. Lodoletta follows him back to Paris, to offer herself as his mistress, but, when she arrives, looking through the window she sees him surrounded by attractive women. She falls, exhausted, in the snow; later, when walking into the garden, Flammen comes upon her dead body.

Although the melodies rarely stick in the mind, this valuable first recording from Hungaroton makes a persuasive case for Mascagni's unashamed mixture of charm and sentimentality. As the little Dutch girl, Lodoletta, Maria Spacagna sings most sensitively, even if the voice is too warm and full to suggest extreme youth. As the dissolute painter who unwittingly drives her to her death Péter Kelen proves a stylish and heady-toned lyric tenor, singing his big Act I solo, the *Song of the flowers*, very beautifully. The American, Charles Rosekrans, makes a very sympathetic conductor, in charge of a strong cast from the Hungarian State Opera. In vivid sound and with some excellent singing this is well worth trying.

Massenet, Jules (1842–1912)

Cendrillon (complete).
(M) **(*) Sony MK 79323 (2) [M2K 35194]. Amb. Op. Ch., Philh. O, Rudel.
    Cendrillon (Frederica Von Stade), Prince Charming (Nicolai Gedda), Mme de la Haltière (Jane Berbié), Pandolfe (Jules Bastin), Fairy (Ruth Welting).

Julius Rudel directs a sparkling, winning performance of Massenet's Cinderella opera, very much a fairy story in which the magic element is vital. The opera follows Charles Perrault's famous narrative closely enough but adds a few twists of its own. At the opening, Madame de la Haltière and her two daughters are getting dressed for the ball, hoping that the prince will notice them among the many guests. Pandolfe, her husband, bitterly regrets his second marriage and is distressed that his wife and her two daughters treat Lucette (Cendrillon) so badly; he determines, not very convincingly, to be master in his own household. Lucette, left behind when the others set off, is so tired by her hard day's work that she falls asleep and her fairy godmother takes the opportunity to dress her sumptuously in moonbeams, starlight and colours from the rainbow; she provides a suitable carriage, using hummingbirds and butterflies to form the entourage. Cinderella promises to return on the stroke of midnight and off she goes.

She makes a splendid entrance and is much admired. Prince Charming is melancholy and no efforts of the doctors can cheer him up. But (at the discreet instructions of the king), as the prince approaches Cinderella, the ballroom clears and it is love at first sight. Alas, the midnight bell tolls and Cinderella departs in haste, leaving the prince more desolate than ever. As everyone knows, in her hurry she loses a slipper.

Later her stepmother and stepsisters display their chagrin at the intruder at the ball and tell Cinderella (quite falsely) that the king has decreed that the mystery woman should be punished with death. Cinderella goes pale; Pandolfe comforts her and orders his family from the room. He decides to take Cinderella away with him, but she is torn between her feelings, faith in the prince and the threat supposedly hanging over her. She rushes out into the night. Magic comes to the rescue, for the fairies bring the two lovers together in the forest, separated by a dense wall of clover. They are at first not aware of each other's identity, but soon discover that they had previously met at the ball. Overjoyed, they ask that the wall of flowers be dissolved and then they fervently embrace. Finally they fall asleep in a magic slumber.

Cinderella is found in the forest and brought safely home and her father lovingly cares for her. Months have now passed and she is convinced that it was all a dream. At last there is news of a further palace reception at which the slipper is be tried on by all the ladies of rank who attend. Once more her fairy godmother comes to the rescue so that Cinderella can attend, and the couple meet again and declare their mutual love. Pandolfe moves forward to embrace his daughter, but Madame de la Haltière rudely brushes him aside and, with the words, 'My own daughter,' she embraces Cinderella. Pandolfe whimsically addresses the audience instead, conveying his pleasure at the outcome of the tale.

In Massenet's opera the Fairy Godmother is a sparkling coloratura (here the bright-toned Ruth Welting) and Cendrillon a soprano in a lower register. Von Stade gives a characteristically strong and imaginative performance, untroubled by what for her is high tessitura. The pity is that the role of the prince, originally also written for soprano, is here taken by a tenor, Gedda, whose voice is no longer fresh-toned. Jules Bastin sings most stylishly as Pandolfe, and the others make a well-chosen team. The recording is vivid and spacious.

Chérubin (complete).
⊛ *** RCA/BMG Dig. 09026 60593-2 (2) [60593-2]. Bav. State Op. Ch., Munich RSO, Pinchas Steinberg.
   Chérubin (Frederica Von Stade), Le Philosophe (Samuel Ramey), L'Ensoleillad (June Anderson), Nina (Dawn Upshaw).

What Massenet did in this delightful comédie chantée of 1903 (he was sixty at the time) was to follow up what happened to Cherubino after the *Marriage of Figaro*. There is none of the social comment of Beaumarchais, or of da Ponte or Mozart, just a frothy entertainment, one brimming with ear-tickling ideas, from the dazzlingly witty overture onwards. The inconsequential plot involves Cherubino having a fling with a celebrated dancer, favourite of the king, only to return at the end to the simple girl who adores him.

As the opera opens, the dashing young Cherubino is celebrating his seventeenth birthday. He has invited the illustrious dancer, L'Ensoleillad, to perform at his party. Meanwhile Nina confesses to her tutor, Jacopo (who regards himself as a philosopher), that she is in love with Cherubino, as indeed is almost every other female in sight. Certainly the countess is, and Cherubino is happy to respond, leaving a poetic love-letter for her in a hollow tree. Unfortunately it is the count who finds it, but he is made to believe it was intended for Nina. But Cherubino's first choice is the actress/dancer, who duly arrives.

We now move to the inn, which is crowded as it is the time of fiesta. The best rooms are reserved for L'Ensoleillad. Cherubino unwisely makes a pass at one of the officers' mistresses and is challenged to a duel. A masked woman arrives and Cherubino brusquely gives her a kiss but has to apologize, for it is the famous dancer. But L'Ensoleillad is not really displeased and eventually the two go off into the woods together. Later Cherubino manages by a ruse to get his lover back into her room without her identity being discovered, so it is unclear who accompanied him for the assignation.

The next morning three different jealous men want to fight a duel with Cherubino. However, he now admits that his lover was L'Ensoleillad and she reluctantly leaves him to return to dance at the duke's court. Nina now arrives to bid farewell, before taking her vows at a convent. Cherubino relents, begs her to forgive him for his various amours and pledges to love her exclusively for ever, even though he still has the countess's ribbon peeping out of his coat pocket!

What matters is that the characterization, though plain, is convincing, with each of the main figures sharply contrasted, both dramatically and musically. So Cherubino, as in Mozart, is taken by a high mezzo; L'Ensoleillad, the dancer, by a dramatic soprano; and the ingénue, Nina, by a soubrettish soprano. The only other main character is Cherubino's tutor, the Philosopher.

In this superb RCA recording the cast is both starry and ideal, with June Anderson powerful and flamboyant as the dancer, Dawn Upshaw sweet and pure as Nina and Samuel Ramey warm and firm as the Philosopher. Yet finest of all is Frederica von Stade in the title-role. Cherubino is a perky figure, much more self-confident and pushy than in Mozart, master of his own household, though still full of youthful high spirits. The delight is to find one tiny gem of an aria after another, with Massenet at this late stage in his career able to establish a mood and make a dramatic point even in a solo of just a minute or so. What seals this as an exhilarating experience is the conducting of Pinchas Steinberg with the Munich Radio Symphony Orchestra, strong and thrustful yet responsive to the dramatic subtleties, plainly a conductor who should be used more often in recordings. The sound is fresh and atmospheric, bringing out the sparkle and fantasy of the piece.

Le Cid (complete).
(M) ** Sony MK 79300 (2) [M2K 34211]. Byrne Camp Chorale, NY Op. O, Queler.
  Chimène (Grace Bumbry), Infanta (Eleanor Bergquist), King (Jake Gardner), Rodrigue (Plácido Domingo), Don Diegue (Paul Plishka).

The hero of Massenet's opera is Rodrigo Diaz de Bivar (1026–99), known as El Cid ('the conqueror'), equally famous in Spanish history and legend. The story of the opera has little to do with history. Rodrigo, valiant Spanish warrior, is to be knighted, while Count Gormas is to become guardian of the king's son. Chimène, Gormas's daughter, loves Rodrigo and receives her father's blessing for their marriage. The Infanta of Spain also loves Rodrigo but there is no rivalry between the two ladies because, as he is not of royal blood, the princess cannot marry him.

The king duly dubs Rodrigo a knight but, to the consternation of Gormas, the king simultaneously announces that Don Diego (Rodrigo's father) has been chosen as the prince's guardian. The furious count provokes a quarrel with Diego, which leads to a duel in which Diego is humiliated. He tells his son and asks for his honour to be avenged. Imprudently, Rodrigo agrees, before discovering that the perpetrator is the father of his betrothed Chimène! Nevertheless a second duel takes place and Gormas dies.

This incurs the extreme distress of Chimène, who demands Rodrigo's execution. Diego points out that Rodrigo was only defending his father's honour and a decision on Rodrigo's fate is withheld while he goes off to defend his country against a sudden Moorish attack. Rodrigo bids Chimène farewell and she relents enough to tell him she still loves him. She very nearly forgives him but remembers her duty to her father. When he retorts that he will die in the forthcoming battle, she promises she will be his if he saves his country from the Moors, but her conflict of loyalties leaves her in confused shame.

Rodrigo is now seen on the battlefield, exhorting his men while understanding their fears of defeat. He prays, and in a vision is assured of victory. The battle commences.

Back at the palace, Don Diego is informed by deserters that his son is dead. Chimène is sad but also philosophical. Her dilemma – the choice between love and honour – is resolved. She can't be more wrong. The king proclaims that Rodrigo is not only alive but that he has saved Spain. He returns and asks for the royal decision concerning the death of Gormas. The king passes on the judgement to Chimène. In her confusion she refuses to condemn him but she cannot forgive his act. In despair, Rodrigo makes a move to stab himself, and she instantly relents. For once a story of Spanish honour ends relatively happily.

The CBS recording is taken from a live performance in New York and suffers from boxy recording-quality. Only with the entrance of Domingo in the second scene does the performance begin to take wing, and the French accents are often comically bad. Even so, the attractions of Massenet's often beautiful score survive all shortcomings and this makes a valuable addition to the CD catalogue. Domingo, not always as stylish as he might be, is in heroic voice and Grace Bumbry as the proud heroine responds splendidly. The popular ballet music is given a sparkling performance. It is disappointing not to have this reissue at mid-price.

Cléopâtre (complete).
**(*) Koch/Schwann Dig. 3 1032-2 (2). Festival Ch., Nouvel O de Saint-Étienne, Fournillier.
  Cléopâtre (Kathryn Harries), Octavie (Danielle Streiff), Charmion (Martine Olmeda), Marc-Antoine (Didier Henry), Spakos (Jean-Luc Maurette), Ennius (Mario Hacquard).

Cléopâtre was the very last of Massenet's operas, written in 1912, the year he died. Reacting against a Shakespeare adaptation that had just proved a failure, he and his librettist deliberately made the plot and characterization simple and direct to suit operatic needs. With exotic choruses, fanfares, dances and marches, it makes one regret that Massenet – unlike Erich Korngold – did not live to become a Hollywood composer: *Cléopâtre* has much of the easy opulence of a film spectacular. It is sad that it has never been appreciated as a major addition to the Massenet canon. It had to wait until 1914, two years after the composer's death, for its première, and then it was given in a garbled form with the role of Cleopatra modified to suit a soprano. Yet with its echoes of Verdi's *Aida*, as well as of Wagner, it could yet prove viable on stage.

The opera begins after the death of Caesar. Marcus-Antonius (Marc-Antoine) makes camp on the banks of the Cydnus and, having accepted various tributes from the conquered peoples, welcomes Cleopatra who arrives in spectacular style, as if she were Venus personified, in her extravagantly decorated barge. He is easily seduced by her alluring manner and physical beauty and, ignoring calls from the Senate to return to Rome, joins her on the barge, which sets off into the languorous night, with the new lovers thinking only of their own pleasure.

But the call from Rome cannot be resisted for long, and Marcus-Antonius returns to his previously planned marriage to Octavia. The ceremony is about to proceed when news comes that Cleopatra is consoling herself with another lover, Spakos. Driven out of his mind with jealousy, Marcus-Antonius leaves Octavia and returns to Alexandria. Here Cleopatra is seeking venal pleasures in a tavern, accompanied by Spakos. Her response to the physical attractions of a dancing youth angers Spakos and he tries to strangle the boy, but Cleopatra reveals her identity and intervenes to prevent the murder. News comes that Marcus-Antonius has returned to Egypt and she rushes off to find him.

They meet at a party where he is in oriental disguise. She offers herself to any man who would first drink poison. Marcus-Antonius objects to such cynical cruelty but remains enamoured of the Egyptian queen. Octavia arrives and tries to persuade him to return as a Roman, but he decides instead to fight at Cleopatra's side. Cleopatra's army is defeated and she prepares to commit suicide. She sends a message to Marcus-Antonius but, because of Spakos' intervention, it never arrives; hearing instead that Cleopatra is dead, Marcus-Antonius falls on his own sword and he is brought back to her, mortally wounded.

Meanwhile Cleopatra has discovered Spakos's deceit and has killed him personally. Marcus-Antonius dies in her arms and Cleopatra then uses the asp to ensure that she joins her lover in the next world.

This première recording was taken from a live performance at the Massenet Festival in Saint-Étienne in 1990, with Patrick Fournillier conducting. The cast has no serious weakness, and the two principal roles are splendidly taken, with Didier Henry firm and responsive as Mark Antony and Kathryn Harries demonstrating what a rich role for a singing actress this Cleopatra is, a woman who consciously breaks men's hearts, toying with them. Miss Harries with her rich mezzo should be used more on record, when her expressive intensity here in her big solos is magnetic. That is particularly so in the concluding scenes.

Mark Antony's death-throes bring first an extended love-duet leading to what becomes a Massenet equivalent of Isolde's *Liebestod*. The excellent notes in the well-produced booklet and libretto even suggest that Massenet, anticipating his own death, was composing an equivalent to Mahler's *Tenth Symphony*, written at exactly the same time. The Koch live recording is not helped by the dryness of the orchestral sound, though only the brass is seriously affected, and the voices are vividly caught.

Don Quichotte (complete).
(M) *** Decca 430 636-2 (2) [id.]. SRO Ch & O, Kord.
    Don Quichotte (Nicolai Ghiaurov), Sancho Pança (Gabriel Bacquier), Dulcinée (Régine Crespin).

Massenet's operatic adaptation of Cervantes' classic novel gave him his last big success, written as it was with Chaliapin in mind for the title-role. It is a totally captivating piece with not a jaded bar in it, suggesting that Massenet might have developed further away from his regular romantic opera style.

The opera opens at a Spanish fiesta, with all the revelry and noise one would expect from such an occasion. Dulcinea addresses two of her admirers – Rodriguez and Juan – coquettishly from her balcony, and in return her charms are ardently extolled. They notice the arrival of Don Quixote, strangely garbed. Juan mocks him, but Rodriguez sees warmth and kindness in his mien and the crowd delight in his appearance together with his companion, Sancho Panza. He holds his lance aloft and distributes a small amount of money.

The Don sends Sancho off to an inn to quench his thirst while he proceeds to serenade

Dulcinea. Juan tries to prevent this, but Quixote draws his sword; Dulcinea intervenes and praises the verses of his serenade and, thoroughly enchanted, the Don vows to recover a necklace stolen from her by Ténébrun, a bandit. Morning dawns to find Sancho Panza ruefully remembering the Don's exploit of the previous day – charging a flock of sheep and some black pigs. He is fed up with the idea of seeking out the bandit, and he riles against Dulcinea and indeed all women. At that moment the Don catches sight of some giants ahead and charges at them, his lance levelled, spurring on his steed, Rosinante. They are of course windmills, as Sancho had realized, and we see the Don caught on their sails by the seat of his pants.

The Don then meets up with the bandits and they overpower him, but the bandit chief, Ténébrun, is affected by his personality. Quixote prays, then says to the bandits, 'Je suis le chevalier errant,' and tells them his task is to right all wrongs, love the poor, and even honour bandits who are proud of their bearing. The amazing result is the return of Dulcinea's jewellery and then the bandits leave, extolling the Knight of the Long Countenance.

Don Quixote now returns to Dulcinea who has been dreaming of an idealized love. He presents her with the necklace and she delightedly rewards him with a grateful kiss. The result is a flowery expression of Quixotish love and a marriage proposal. Everyone is highly amused, but not Dulcinea. She tenderly refuses him: he is an old man and she feels too warmly towards him to marry him. She will not allow the crowd to mock him; Sancho Panza too springs to his defence then embraces him affectionately.

Time passes and the Don is now dying in the forest, with Sancho watching over him. The Don thinks Sancho longs for his native village far away, and he tells him he only fought for the good things: he meant to reward his servant and companion with castles and islands. He refuses to allow Sancho to remove his armour and looks up to the stars as he hears Dulcinea's voice singing in the distance.

There is genuine nobility as well as comedy in the portrait of the knight, and that is well caught here by Ghiaurov, who refuses to exaggerate the characterization. Bacquier makes a delightful Sancho Panza, but it is Régine Crespin as a comically mature Dulcinée who provides the most characterful singing, flawed vocally but commandingly positive. Kazimierz Kord directs the Suisse Romande Orchestra in a performance that is zestful and electrifying, and the recording is outstandingly clear and atmospheric.

Esclarmonde (complete).
(M) *** Decca 425 651-2 (3) [id.]. Alldis Ch., Nat. PO, Bonynge.
    Esclarmonde (Joan Sutherland), Roland (Giacomo Aragall), Parseis (Huguette Tourangeau), Eneas (Ryland Davies), Bishop of Blois (Louis Quilico), King Cléomer (Robert Lloyd), Emperor Phorcas (Clifford Grant).

Esclarmonde, the grandest of Massenet's operas with its Wagnerian echoes and hints of both Verdi and Berlioz, is set in Byzantium. The opening scene is at the Basilica, where the Emperor/Sorcerer Phorcas abdicates in favour of his daughter, Esclarmonde, to whom he has given the secrets of his magic powers. But there is a snag: he declares that she will retain her mystical gifts only if she remains veiled until the age of twenty. Then her hand in marriage shall be given to the winner of a great tournament and with it the kingdom. Her sister, Parseis, is appointed Esclarmonde's guardian.

In no time at all Esclarmonde is bemoaning her father's restrictions, for she has fallen in love with a French knight, Roland, without his knowledge. Parseis reminds her of her magical powers and suggests that they be put to good use to bring Roland to her.

Learning that Roland is soon to marry the King of France's daughter, Esclarmonde quickly invokes her powers to convey Roland to a magic island, where she promptly joins him while he is asleep. Awakening him with a kiss, she declares her love and confesses he has been abducted by means of her magical powers. Fortunately he loves her in return but he is warned that he must never attempt to raise her veil.

At that moment, news arrives that France is being attacked by the Saracens, led by the cruel Sarwegur, and now Roland must go to lift the siege on the capital, Blois. Esclarmonde promises him that she will magically transport herself to join him each night, and he is also provided with the Sword of St George which will make him invincible, as long as he holds to his vow to her to keep her identity secret. Meanwhile the lustful Sarwegur has demanded from King Cléomer a tribute of 100 virgins, no less, if he is not to sack the city.

In the nick of time Roland rides in and challenges Sarwegur to single combat. The virgins, no doubt, sigh a multiple sigh of relief, for Roland is victorious and as a reward the king offers him the hand of his daughter, Bathilde. Roland refuses the honour and proves unable to disclose his reasons. He is excused by the king but the Bishop of Blois is determined to find out why such a prize has been rejected. Roland, however, is thinking of the coming night which he is to spend in the arms of Esclarmonde.

The bishop now demands that Roland reveal his secret, urging him to confess in the name of God or he will be excommunicated and face the fires of eternal damnation. Roland will only tell of an unknown woman who visits him nightly and the bishop bides his time, then bursts in on the lovers and, believing her to be a consort of the devil, tears the veil from Esclarmonde's face. She is appalled at her betrayal and, when Roland raises the great sword in her defence, it splinters. Esclarmonde disappears, cursing her lover's disloyalty.

Phorcas in retirement lives as a hermit and anchorite. Parseis arrives and tells the tragic story of Esclarmonde's encounter with Roland. The angry Phorcas retrieves his magical powers and summons Esclarmonde before him. She makes a spectacular, flaming entrance and Phorcas punishes her with the loss of her throne and tells her that Roland too will die unless she renounces her love for him. Roland arrives and she forgives him. He suggests that they escape together but Phorcas appears and reminds her of her promise. Despairingly, she spurns Roland and she and her father promptly disappear in a puff of smoke. Poor Roland, wishing for nothing but death, sets off back to Byzantium.

We now return to its Basilica. Phorcas is back on the throne and the tournament has been won by a knight in black armour who is to be given Esclarmonde (by now, presumably, having reached the age of twenty). Without raising his visor the black knight says his name is Despair; he had hoped to die in the tournament and he refuses his prize. But Esclarmonde recognizes the voice – it is none other than Roland! He, in turn, now recognizes Esclarmonde and they can be joyfully united.

The opera's central role calls for an almost impossible combination of qualities. Joan Sutherland at her peak commandingly encompasses all the demands – great range, great power and brilliant coloratura – giving a performance closely akin to that on her recording of Puccini's *Turandot*. Aragall is an excellent tenor, sweet of tone and intelligent, and the other parts, all of them relatively small, are well taken too. Richard Bonynge draws passionate singing and playing from chorus and orchestra, and the recording has both atmosphere and spectacle.

Manon (complete).
Withdrawn: (M) (*(**)) EMI mono CMS7 63549-2 (3) [Ang. CDMC 63549]. Opéra-comique, Monteux (with C H A U S S O N: *Poème de l'amour et de la mer* (***)).
   Manon (Victoria De los Angeles), Des Grieux (Henri Legay), Lescaut (Michel Dens), Comte Des Grieux (Jean Borthayre).
Withdrawn: *** EMI Dig. CDS7 49610-2 (3) [Ang. CDCC 49610]. Ch. & O of Capitole, Toulouse, Plasson.
   Manon (Ileana Cotrubas), Des Grieux (Alfredo Kraus), Lescaut (Gino Quilico), Comte Des Grieux (José Van Dam).

Massenet's most warmly approachable opera was first heard in Paris in 1884 and it remains his most successful work. The courtyard of Amiens is the scene of the opening. Two friends, Guillot and de Brétigny, arrive at the inn accompanied by three supposed actresses, really Guillot's mistresses. Their meal is ready and they enter. The stage coach is due at any minute. Lescaut and his two friends appear; they go inside while Lescaut, a member of the Royal Guard, awaits the arrival of his cousin, Manon, on her way to a convent.

There is bustle and confusion as the coach arrives and Lescaut greets Manon, commenting on her beauty, then goes off to arrange the porterage of her luggage. Guillot appears and promptly offers to elope with her, but she manages to laugh this off; nevertheless Guillot puts his own coach at her service before returning to his friends. Lescaut now warns Manon against such propositions. He goes off to play cards and she is left alone.

Enter the Chevalier des Grieux, about to meet his father and seeing Manon instead. It is rapturous love at first sight for both of them and they depart for Paris, using Guillot's coach. Lescaut and Guillot now come out of the inn and Lescaut accuses Guillot of abducting Manon. The innkeeper relates how Manon left with a young man, Guillot vows vengeance and the bystanders ridicule him.

The scene now moves to Paris where Des Grieux and Manon live together. Des Grieux writes to his father to ask permission to marry her (she is only sixteen). The maid ushers in two men, Lescaut and de Brétigny (also dressed as a guardsman), and Manon recognizes him. Lescaut and Des Grieux quarrel but de Brétigny pleads restraint and Des Grieux assures Lescaut of his honourable intentions towards Manon and, to prove it, shows him the letter to his father.

But Des Grieux's father has other plans for his son: he means to remove him from Paris that very evening. De Brétigny informs Manon of this and asks, would she not prefer a life of luxury with him? Des Grieux returns after posting his letter and finds Manon unhappy. As he tells her of a happy dream he has had, there is a knock at the door, a sudden scuffle and he is taken away.

Time has passed and we now move to the fashionable Cours-la-Reine. Guillot arrives, then de Brétigny who now lives with Manon, and finally Manon herself, much admired by all those present. De Brétigny now discovers from the Comte des Grieux that his son has entered a seminary to train for the priesthood. Manon overhears this conversation and, not revealing her identity, speaks to the count and discovers that his son is desperately unhappy and is trying to escape from the world.

Guillot arrives and seeks to impress Manon, hoping to win her from de Brétigny, but Manon asks Lescaut to call her carriage and goes off to St Sulpice. At the seminary the Comte des Grieux is trying without success to dissuade his son from taking his final vows as a priest, but Manon's arrival changes his mind. He loves her as much as ever, and they depart together.

Back in Paris, the profligate life of easy living and gambling continues. Manon persuades Des Grieux to enter a game against Guillot. Des Grieux wins but Guillot suggests he has been cheated and Des Grieux challenges him. Yet the crowd seems on Guillot's side and he returns with the police, who arrest Des Grieux with Manon as his accomplice. The Comte des Grieux enters and his son shows remorse. Guillot delights in his revenge.

The count promises that his son will soon be freed, but Manon is led away to be deported among a group of prostitutes. Lescaut arrives and bribes a sergeant to let him take Manon, who is dying, and he leaves her with Des Grieux who hopes to contrive her release. She nostalgically remembers her former happiness with him and, too ill to escape, she dies and Des Grieux falls over her body in despair and grief.

The combination of Victoria de los Angeles singing the role of the heroine with Pierre Monteux conducting is unbeatable in Massenet's most warmly approachable opera. There has never been a more winning Manon than De los Angeles, deliciously seductive from the start, making her first girlish solo, *Je suis encore tout étourdie*, sparkle irresistibly. The meeting with Des Grieux is then enchanting, with the hero's youthful wonderment breathtakingly caught by Henri Legay in his light, heady tenor.

Though there are cuts – for example the end of Act I – this is a unique performance that defies the limitations of ancient mono recording. Unfortunately, the CD transfer emphasizes the top registers unduly while giving little body to lower registers. Voices can be made to sound vivid, but the orchestra remains thin and edgy. The original four LPs have been transferred to three CDs, with the bonus of De los Angeles' recording of the delightful Chausson cantata.

Plasson's set, recorded in Toulouse, presents a stylish performance well characterized and well sung. Ileana Cotrubas is a charming Manon, more tender and vulnerable than De los Angeles on the earlier set, but not so golden-toned and with a more limited development of character from the girlish chatterbox to the dying victim. Alfredo Kraus betrays some signs of age, but this is a finely detailed and subtle reading with none of the blemishes which marred his *Werther* performance for EMI. Gino Quilico has a delightfully light touch as Lescaut, and José van Dam is a superb Comte Des Grieux. The warm reverberation of the Toulouse studio is well controlled to give bloom to the voices, and though Plasson is rougher with the score than Monteux, he has a fine feeling for French idiom.

Le Roi de Lahore (complete).
⚜ (M) *** Decca Dig. 433 851-2 (2) [id.]. L. Voices, Nat. PO, Bonynge.
  Sitâ (Joan Sutherland), Alim (Luis Lima), Scindia (Sherrill Milnes), Indra (Nicolai Ghiaurov), Timour (James Morris), Kaled (Huguette Tourangeau).

With a libretto that sets high melodrama against an exotic background, *Le Roi de Lahore* was Massenet's first opera for the big stage of L'Opéra in Paris and marked a turning point in his career, even introducing the supernatural with one Act set in the Paradise of Indra. Scindia, the king's first minister, has fallen in love with his niece Sitâ, a priestess, but she has been experiencing a 'visionary' midnight visitor who has spoken of love but never touched her. He turns out to be Alim, the king, who bids her follow him as he leads his army into battle against invaders. In the ensuing conflict Alim is mortally wounded by the jealous and treacherous Scindia, and he dies in Sitâ's arms.

In the Paradise of Indra, Alim begs to be allowed to return to earth and his beloved Sitâ. The god grants his request, but he must return as a humble commoner, although still protected by Indra, and can remain on earth only while Sitâ lives. Scindia has now taken over the royal palace and plans to add Sitâ to his conquests, but now Alim reappears and the lovers are briefly reunited, before, fearing Scindia's power, Sitâ desperately stabs herself and thus seals Alim's fate too. But they are reunited, transfigured, in Indra's Paradise.

The characters may be stock figures out of a mystic fairy tale, but in the vigour of his treatment Massenet makes the result red-blooded in an Italianate way. This vivid performance under Bonynge includes passages added for Italy, notably a superb set-piece aria which challenges Sutherland to some of her finest singing. Massenet's idea of the exotic extends to a saxophone waltz (here made deliciously Parisian), but generally the score reflects the eager robustness of a young composer stretching his wings for the first time. Sutherland may not be a natural for the role of the innocent young priestess, but she makes it a magnificent vehicle with its lyric, dramatic and coloratura demands. Luis Lima as the King is somewhat strained by the high tessitura, but he is a ringing tenor, clean of attack. Sherrill Milnes as the heroine's wicked uncle sounds even more Italianate, rolling his 'r's ferociously; but high melodrama is apt, and with digital recording of demonstration splendour and fine perspective this shameless example of operatic hokum could not be more persuasively presented on CD.

Werther (complete).
*** Ph. 416 654-2 (2) [id.]. Children's Ch., O of ROHCG, C. Davis.
    Werther (José Carreras), Charlotte (Frederica Von Stade), Albert (Thomas Allen), Sophie (Isobel Buchanan), Magistrate (Robert Lloyd).
(M) *** DG 413 304-2 (2) [id.]. Cologne Children's Ch. and RSO, Chailly.
    Werther (Plácido Domingo), Charlotte (Elena Obraztsova), Albert (Franz Grundheber), Sophie (Arleen Augér), Magistrate (Kurt Moll).
Withdrawn: (M) **(*) EMI CMS7 63973-2 (2) [Ang. CDMB 63973]. Voix d'Enfants de la Maîtrise de l'ORTF, O de Paris, Prêtre.
    Werther (Nicolai Gedda), Charlotte (Victoria De los Angeles), Albert (Roger Soyer), Sophie (Mady Mesplé), Magistrate (Jean-Christoph Benoit).
Withdrawn: (M) ** EMI CMS7 69573-2 (2). Ch. & LPO, Plasson.
    Werther (Alfredo Kraus), Charlotte (Tatiana Troyanos), Albert (Matteo Manuguerra), Sophie (Christine Barbaux).

Werther followed eight years after *Manon* and was first produced in Vienna in 1892. It takes place at Christmas, but the seasonal spirit does not prevent a tragic dénouement to the story, which opens in the garden of the Magistrate's house where the children are rehearsing a seasonal song. The Magistrate comments that if Charlotte were there the singing would be better and, true enough, at the arrival of Charlotte the singing improves. Johann and Schmidt, two friends of the Magistrate, are also listening and then they remind him of their meeting that night at the Raisin d'Or. Sophie (Charlotte's sister) then enters and both Werther the poet and Albert are talked of, and Schmidt suggests that Albert would make a splendid husband for Charlotte.

Schmidt and Johann now retire and the others go into the house. Werther now appears, extolling the joys of the countryside, and finds his way to the Magistrate's house. Charlotte is busying herself preparing supper for the children, although she is already dressed for the ball, and Werther is most impressed by the family scene. Later, at the ball, Werther and Charlotte become strongly attracted, and Werther declares his love. Their dream is shattered when the Magistrate announces that Albert is back – the prospective husband for Charlotte chosen by her mother before she died. Werther is shattered.

Time passes and we see Johann and Schmidt drinking at the inn, while in the church the village pastor is celebrating his golden wedding. Charlotte and Albert have now been married for three months. The unhappy Werther first talks with Albert then, coming face to face with Charlotte, throws caution to the winds and once again declares his great love for her. She begs him to leave and tells Sophie he is leaving for ever.

It is now Christmas Day and Charlotte, re-reading Werther's letters, realizes how very much she is in love with him: she is overcome by misery and depression and prays for strength. Werther reappears and they relive their happier times in each other's company: the books they read together, the music they shared. They embrace and Charlotte rushes from the room. Albert returns and grasps the general situation.

A servant then enters with a request from Werther for the loan of Albert's pistols; Albert tells Charlotte to give them to the servant and she obeys him, understanding the implication of the request. We now move to Werther's apartment. Charlotte finds him dying and, somewhat late in the day, tells him she loved him from their very first moment together. As he dies, the children's voices are heard singing their Christmas carol.

Sir Colin Davis has rarely directed a more sensitive or more warmly expressive performance on record than his account of *Werther*. The magic of sound hits the listener from the opening prelude onwards, and the refined recording, together with a superb performance based on a stage production at Covent Garden, is consistently compelling. Frederica von Stade makes an enchanting Charlotte, outshining all current rivals on record, both strong and tender, conveying the understanding but vulnerable character of Goethe's heroine. Carreras, matching almost every rival, uses a naturally beautiful voice freshly and sensitively. Others in the cast, including Thomas Allen as Charlotte's husband Albert and Isobel Buchanan as Sophie, her sister, are also excellent. The CD transfer on two discs has been highly successful, with a single serious reservation: the break between the two compact discs is badly placed in the middle of a key scene between Werther and Charlotte, just before *Ah! qu'il est loin ce jour!*. Otherwise this is one of the very finest French opera sets on CD.

With a recording that gives fine body and range to the sound of the Cologne orchestra, down to the subtlest whisper from the pianissimo strings, the DG version stands at an advantage, particularly as Chailly proves a sharply characterful conductor, one who knows how to thrust home an important climax as well as how to create evocative textures, varying tensions positively. Plácido Domingo in the name-part sings with sweetness and purity as well as strength, coping superbly with the legato line of the aria *Pourquoi me réveiller?*. Elena Obraztsova, though richer and firmer than usual, is often rough vocally, giving a generalized portrait, sharply contrasted against the charming Sophie of Arleen Augér. The others make up a very convincing team.

Victoria de los Angeles, who has already given us a delectable portrayal of Manon, is equally attractive depicting Charlotte in *Werther*. Her golden tones which convey pathos so beautifully are ideally suited to Massenet's gentle melodies and, though she is recorded too closely (closer than the other soloists), she makes a tenderly appealing heroine, matching the sweetness of the piece. Gedda makes an intelligent romantic hero, though Prêtre's direction is often unsubtle. This set has been withdrawn as we go to press.

It is sad that Alfredo Kraus, as a rule one of the most stylish of tenors, came to record *Werther* so late in his career. His account of *Pourquoi me réveiller?* brings effortful underlining, making him almost unrecognizable. Elsewhere the strained tone is less distracting, and his feeling for words is generally most illuminating. Troyanos makes a volatile Charlotte, but the voice as recorded is grainy. Manuguerra produces rich tone as the Bailiff, but the engineers have not been kind to the LPO strings, which sound thin. Plasson is a stylish conductor but here fails to convey the full power of the piece.

Maxwell Davies, Peter (born 1934)

The Martyrdom of St Magnus.
*** Unicorn Dig. DKPCD 9100 [id.]. Scottish Chamber Op. Ens., Michael Rafferty.
   Blind Mary / Ingerth / Mary O'Connell (Tasmin Dives), Earl Magnus (Christopher Gillett), Norse Herald / King of Norway / Keeper / Lifolf (Paul Thomson), Welsh Herald / Tempter (Richard Morris), Bishop of Orkney / Earl Hakon (Kelvin Thomas).

Lasting just over 70 minutes, this chamber opera, based on the novel *Magnus* by George Mackay Brown, fits neatly on to a single CD. The five soloists – taking multiple parts – belong to Music Theatre Wales, whose director, Michael McCarthy, was responsible for the stage production which forms the basis of this fine recording, made in the concert hall of the Royal College of Music in London. With Gregorian chant providing an underlying basis of argument, Maxwell Davies has here simplified his regular idiom. The musical argument of each of the nine compact scenes is summarized in the interludes which follow. The story is baldly but movingly presented, with St Magnus translated to the present century as a concentration camp victim, finally killed by his captors. Outstanding among the soloists is the tenor, Christopher Gillett, taking among other roles that of the Prisoner (or saint).

Meale, Richard (born 1932)

Voss: complete recording.
*** Ph. 420 928-2 (2) [id.]. Australian Op. Ch., Sydney SO, Challender.
   Voss (Geoffrey Chard), Laura Trevelyan (Marilyn Richardson), Frank Le Mesurier (Robert

Gard), Palfreyman (John Pringle), Harry Robarts (Gregory Tomlinson), Judd (Robert Eddie), Mr Bonner (Clifford Grant).

Johann Ulrich Voss was a German explorer whose expedition crossing the Australian continent is celebrated in a novel by Patrick White. Richard Meale was inspired by the novel to tackle this difficult subject and to write an opera about Voss to a libretto, by David Malouf, which enhances the hero's mythic status.

Act I has Voss in Sydney, nobly singing about his ambitions, finding love with Laura, the niece of the rich businessman who is financing the venture, and setting off on the expedition in 1845.

The second half brings obvious staging problems, with Voss on his expedition and those back in Sydney presented on opposite sides of the stage, periodically coming together with one scene superimposed on the other, notably in the climactic scene where Voss is killed and decapitated by an Aboriginal servant.

The opera is rounded off with an epilogue which takes place 20 years after the main action and which sets Voss's exploit in context.

In Act I, the libretto has Voss regularly uttering nobly uplifting sentiments, often to banal words set to heightened cantilena which is more grateful to the voice (and ear) than most in modern opera. Meale, having returned to a conservative style after earlier experimentation, has written a strong and skilful score, atmospherically decorated with authentic Australian quadrilles from the middle of the last century.

It may not be a great opera, but it is a warmly expressive one; here, under the sensitive control of Stuart Challender, it is given a colourful, strongly committed performance. Geoffrey Chard is outstanding in the taxing role of Voss himself, and though the microphone brings out occasional unevenness in Marilyn Richardson's soprano as the heroine, Laura, there is no weak link anywhere among the principals from the Australian Opera's stage production. The recording, made in the studios of ABC in Sydney, is clear and generally well balanced.

Mendelssohn, Felix (1809–47)

VOCAL MUSIC

Elijah (oratorio), *Op. 70.*
*** Chan. Dig. CHAN 8774/5; *DBTD 2016* [id.]. Willard White, Rosalind Plowright, Linda Finnie, Arthur Davies, London Symphony Ch., LSO, Hickox.

Richard Hickox with his London Symphony Chorus and the LSO secures a performance that both pays tribute to the English choral tradition in this work and presents it dramatically as a kind of religious opera. Though in Victorian times this was an oratorio which was notoriously treated as sentimental, Hickox shows what fresh inspiration it contains, what a wealth of memorable ideas, treated imaginatively, as for example in the way that numbers merge one into the next, with dramatic emphasis given to each incident in the story of the prophet. The choice of soloists reflects that approach.

Willard White may not be ideally steady in his delivery, sometimes attacking notes from below, but he sings consistently with fervour, from his dramatic introduction to the overture onwards. Rosalind Plowright and Arthur Davies combine purity of tone with operatic expressiveness, and Linda Finnie, while not matching the example of Dame Janet Baker in Frühbeck de Burgos's classic EMI recording, sings with comparable dedication and directness in the solo, *O rest in the Lord*. The chorus fearlessly underlines the high contrasts of dynamic demanded in the score. The Chandos recording, full and immediate, yet atmospheric too, enhances the drama. The old EMI set should by rights be reissued on CD; even when it is, the modern digital sound as well as the performance here will make this Chandos version a keen contender.

A Midsummer Night's Dream: Overture, Op. 21; Incidental music, Op. 61.
*** EMI CDC7 47163-2 [id.]. Lilian Watson, Delia Wallis, Finchley Children's Music Group, LSO, Previn.
*** BMG/RCA Dig. RD 87764 [7764-2-RC]. Lucia Popp, Marjana Lipovšek, Bamberg Ch. & SO, Flor.
(B) *** CfP Dig. CD-CFP 4593; *TC-CFP 4593*. Edith Wiens, Sarah Walker, LPO Ch. & O, Litton.

The magical incidental music for *A Midsummer Night's Dream*, written by an incredibly gifted teenage composer, is one of the miracles of musical history. On EMI, Previn offers a wonderfully refreshing account of the complete score; the veiled pianissimo of the violins at the beginning of the *Overture* and the delicious woodwind detail in the *Scherzo* certainly bring Mendelssohn's fairies into the orchestra. Even the little melodramas which come between the main items sound spontaneous here, and the contribution of the soloists and chorus is first class. The *Nocturne* (taken slowly) is serenely romantic and the *Wedding march* resplendent. The recording is naturally balanced and has much refinement of detail. The CD brings the usual enhancement, with the fairy music in the *Overture* given a most delicate presence.

Claus Peter Flor's account omits the little melodramas, which is a pity; but for those who require the major items only, this beautiful RCA CD could well be a first choice. Recorded in the warmly resonant acoustics of the Dominikanerbau, Bamberg, the orchestra is given glowingly radiant textures; but Flor's stylish yet relaxed control brings the kind of intimacy one expects from a chamber group. The very opening of the *Overture*, with its soft flute timbre and diaphanous violins, is agreeably evocative and, later, the *Wedding march*, played with much vigour and élan, expands splendidly. The lightly rhythmic *Scherzo*, taken not too fast, is another highlight; and Lucia Popp's vocal contribution is delightful, especially when she blends her voice so naturally with that of Marjana Lipovšek in *You spotted snakes*.

Andrew Litton also includes the melodramas and, like Previn, he uses them most effectively as links, making them seem an essential part of the structure. He too has very good soloists; in the *Overture* and *Scherzo* he displays an engagingly light touch, securing very fine wind and string playing from the LPO. The wide dynamic range of the recording brings an element of drama to offset the fairy music. Both the *Nocturne*, with a fine horn solo, and the temperamental *Intermezzo* are good examples of the spontaneity of feeling that permeates this performance throughout and makes this disc a bargain.

St Paul, Op. 36.
(M) *** EMI CMS7 64005-2 (2) [Ang. CDMB 64005]. Helen Donath, Hanna Schwarz, Werner Hollweg, Dietrich Fischer-Dieskau, Boys' Ch., Dusseldorf Musikverein & SO, Frühbeck de Burgos.
**(*) Ph. 420 212-2 (2). Gundula Janowitz, Rosemarie Lang, Hans-Peter Blochwitz, Gothart Stier, Hermann Christian Polster, Theo Adam, Leipzig R. Ch. & GO, Masur.
(M) **(*) Erato/Warner Dig. 2292 45279-2 (2) [id.]. Rachel Yakar, Brigitte Balleys, Markus Schäfer, Thomas Hampson, Lisbon Gulbenkian Foundation Ch. & O, Michel Corboz.

St Paul (or, in German, *Paulus*) was for long notorious as one of the most sanctimonious of Victorian oratorios. This sympathetic performance under the conductor who helped us review our ideas on *Elijah* – the return of his outstanding EMI/Philharmonia set, with gorgeous singing from Dame Janet Baker, cannot be far away – gives the lie to that, a piece full of ideas well worthy of the composer of the *Italian Symphony*. Like *Elijah* ten years later, *Paulus* – completed in 1836 – was Mendelssohn's substitute for opera. In youthful zest it erupts in great Handelian choruses, and a Bachian style of story-telling is neatly updated in its choral interjections and chorales, with the soprano joining the traditional tenor in the narration.

The story tells of the defiance and stoning to death of Stephen, Saul's subsequent journey to Damascus, his vision, blindness and conversion. He meets Ananias and his sight is restored. His preaching as a Christian leader follows, the miracle restoring the cripple at Lystra, and finally his departure by ship to Jerusalem.

What reduces the dramatic effectiveness is that Mendelssohn, ever the optimist, comes to his happy resolution of the plot far too quickly and with too little struggle involved. This performance glows with life. Fischer-Dieskau takes the name-part (as he did for *Elijah*), leading an excellent team of soloists and with admirable support from the Dusseldorf choir and orchestra. The recording is full and atmospheric, its vividness enhanced on CD.

Masur, always a persuasive interpreter of Mendelssohn, here directs a performance which, without inflating the piece or making it sanctimonious, conveys its natural gravity. Theo Adam is not always steady, but otherwise the team of soloists is exceptionally strong, and the chorus adds to the incandescence, although placed rather backwardly. The Leipzig recording is warm and atmospheric.

The newest set from Lisbon is also very successful, with a fine team of soloists. Thomas Hampson is preferable to Theo Adam on Philips, and there is excellent choral singing. Many will prefer this set for its naturally balanced digital recording, but the chorus itself, because of the resonance, is not very sharply focused, nor is it as immediate as would be ideal. The performance is very enjoyable but has marginally less impact and individuality of character than the Masur version.

Menotti, Gian-Carlo (born 1911)

Amahl and the Night Visitors: complete.
*** That's Entertainment CDTER 1124. ROHCG Ch. & O, David Syrus.
    Amahl (James Rainbird), Mother (Lorna Haywood), King Kaspar (John Dobson), King Melchior (Donald Maxwell), King Balthazar (Curtis Watson), Page (Christopher Painter).

Recorded under the supervision of the composer himself, this Royal Opera House production of what was originally a television opera brings a fresh and highly dramatic performance, very well sung and marked by atmospheric digital sound of striking realism. With voices very firmly placed on (and off) a believable stage, it vividly succeeds in telling the sentimental little story of the cripple-boy who offers his crutch to the three Kings to take to the Infant Jesus.

As the opera begins, we meet Amahl playing his pipe outside the small shepherd's hut where he lives. His home-made crutch lies beside him on the ground. His mother listens to his playing, then calls him. He doesn't obey but instead exasperates her, trying to persuade her to come outside to see the brilliant new star in the heavens 'as large as a window and with a glorious tail'. She refuses to come and instead scolds him for lying – it is just another of his stories! Then she cries quietly to herself at the thought of begging again next day. They retire to bed.

The voices of the three Kings are now heard outside. A black page walks in front of them lighting the way. He is laden with bundles, a jewel box, a parrot in a cage. King Melchior knocks at the door of the hut and Amahl opens it, then runs to his mother. Three times she thinks he is lying but eventually is persuaded to come to the door, whereupon the Kings bid her a dignified good evening. She offers her impoverished hospitality, in some awe of her royal visitors. They accept with gratitude; Kaspar is effusive in his thanks and jauntily the Kings enter, sitting on a bench. The page places their treasures on a rug and the mother goes off to find firewood.

In spite of his mother's caution not to pester the visitors, Amahl – as he watches King Balthazar feeding his parrot – is all agog with his questions. What is contained in King Kaspar's box? Precious stones to guard against misfortune, he is told solemnly. Then off he goes to fetch the shepherds who are also looking for a newly born child, 'the colour of dawn'. Amahl leads the shepherds in. Laden with simple gifts from the fields, vegetables and fruit, they too are overawed by the resplendent scene of the three Kings. They dance, bow, and go on their way. Amahl asks Kaspar if by chance he has a magic stone to cure a crippled boy, but Kaspar affects not to hear his question. Amahl lies down on his straw bed, low in spirits, and everyone sleeps until dawn, excepting Amahl's mother who lies awake, feeling that it is unfair that such wealth should go to this unknown child, when her Amahl is almost starving.

She tries to steal one of the bundles, waking the page, and they struggle. Amahl flies to his mother's defence and King Kaspar orders the page to let the mother go. The Child has no need of gold, he says, the mother can keep it. She is now ashamed and, indeed, enthralled by the King's words about the Christ Child; she wants instead to make her own gift to the baby, but she has nothing to give. Amahl offers his crutch and, lifting it up, suddenly takes a step without it. At first nobody can believe the miracle, but then the Kings give thanks to God and Amahl dances round in glee. He now begs to accompany the Kings and, having been showered with maternal advice by his mother, sets off with them, happily playing his pipe.

In the note accompanying the record, Menotti touchingly tells how the work came to be written: of his fascination with the story of the three Kings as a child in Italy (where they take on something of the role of Father Christmas); of his characterization of them in his mind then; and of his sudden inspiration many years later on seeing Bosch's 'Adoration of the Magi'. This helps to explain the extraordinary immediacy and effectiveness of the piece. The dramatic timing is masterly, beautifully brought out by the conductor, David Syrus, in this performance which – though recorded in the studio – followed a run of the staged production at Sadler's Wells Theatre.

Central to the success of the performance is the astonishingly assured and sensitively musical singing of the boy treble, James Rainbird, as Amahl, purposefully effective even in the potentially embarrassing moments. Lorna Haywood sings warmly and strongly as the Mother, with a strong trio of Kings. The realism of the recording makes the chamber size of the string section sound thin at the start, but the playing is both warm and polished.

Merikanto, Aarre (1893–1958)

Juha: complete.
**(*) Finlandia FACD 105 (2) [id.]. Finnish Nat. Op. Ch. and O, Ulf Söderblom.

> Juha (Matti Lehtinen), Marja (Raili Kostia), Shemeikka (Hendrik Krumm), Anja (Taru Valjakka), Mother-in-law (Maiju Kuusoja).

Merikanto composed *Juha* in the early 1920s, at a time when opera in Finland was in its infancy. After its rejection by the conservative-minded Board of the Finnish Opera who had commissioned it, he made no effort to get it performed and became embittered. It was not in fact staged until the 1960s, a decade after his death. In spite of the folk setting (the action takes place in Karelia), there is little sense of the Nordic world. The musical language reflects his more international sympathies – one is reminded fleetingly of Puccini, Strauss, Scriabin, Schreker, Debussy and Janáček – and yet the music is far more than merely eclectic. It is atmospheric and highly expert in scoring and, in its way, bears a quite distinctive stamp. This performance derives from the early 1970s and, though not ideal (there is not quite enough space round the orchestra and not a deep enough perspective), every detail registers and the words are clearly projected. The singing on the whole is more than respectable, and Matti Lehtinen in the title-role is outstanding. The opera is not long – under two hours – and is very well worth investigating.

Messager, André (1853–1929)

Fortunio (complete).
⊛ (M) *** Erato/Warner Dig. 2292 45983-2 (2) [id.]. Ch. & O of L'Opéra de Lyon, Gardiner.

> Fortunio (Thierry Dran), Jacqueline (Colette Alliot-Lugaz), Clavaroche (Gilles Cachemaïlle), Landry (Francis Dudziak), Maître André (Michel Trempont), Maître Subtil (Patrick Rocca).

Dating from 1907, *Fortunio*, based on a play by Alfred de Musset, has all the effervescence and heady lyricism of an operetta combined with the strength and subtlety of a full opera. The tuneful score has ravishing solos for the lovelorn hero – with the heady-toned Thierry Dran very well cast – which are beautifully woven into the through-composed structure in four compact Acts. Its story of the triumph of youthful love and the outwitting of the older generation – husband and paramour alike – by a personable and essentially innocent hero, was bound to appeal to the Parisian public.

The piece opens with an animated scene of drinking and a game of boules. Landry (Fortunio's practical and hedonistic cousin) is the inebriated winner. Fortunio enters with his uncle, Maître Subtil, who explains why they left home to seek their fortunes in the big city, and that he is to be apprenticed as a clerk working for the lawyer, Maître André. This is not what Fortunio wants at all; he is a dreamer and loves beauty and poetry. But Landry, who already works in the same office, tries to reassure him.

Captain Clavaroche now appears, very much a ladies' man, and after discussing the possible local conquests he decides to make a bid for the favours of Jacqueline. She is the wife of the notary, Maître André, described as 'a pearl without a blemish'; Maître André, self-opinionated and highly conceited, certainly doesn't deserve her. She and Clavaroche are duly introduced and, declining his flattery, she tells him that her husband, over sixty, is a father figure to her. Clavaroche immediately declares his love, tries to hold her hand and is rebuffed.

But Maître André asks to be introduced to the captain, and his wife obliges. Fortunio, too, is greatly attracted to Jacqueline and changes his mind about working for her husband. Now Maître André becomes suspicious of Jacqueline, as Guillaume, his other clerk, has reported seeing a man slipping through her window.

She prevaricates, suggesting first to her husband that he must be ill, then declaring that he does not love her as he once did, vehemently denying the accusation, suggesting that Guillaume was imagining things.

The nocturnal visitor is of course Clavaroche, and the lovers discuss what course of action to take over the suspicious husband. If a duel is to be avoided, then what about a decoy instead? The innocent Fortunio is ready-made to play such a role, and Jacqueline agrees that she might flirt with him a little. Jacqueline consults her maid, Madelon, and finds that Fortunio is just a dreaming child whom the maid rather fancies. The clerks now all arrive with flowers to celebrate Jacqueline's wedding anniversary and praise her beauty, all longing for her favours.

Jacqueline meets Fortunio privately and makes him promise to keep their friendship a secret. He readily agrees and speaks to her with tender, admiring innocence and with much poetic feeling. He agrees with a glad heart to be her solicitous friend and a servant to her needs. He then, less innocently, questions Guillaume about Jacqueline's nocturnal visitor, whom he envies, but says that he would not betray the lovers.

Meanwhile Jacqueline and the captain are pleased with the success of their plan, for her husband has been duly taken in by the decoy. Fortunio is asked to entertain them with a love-song, in which he tenderly unburdens the deepest feelings of his heart, yet declares that he would never reveal the identity of his beloved.

By now Jacqueline is very taken indeed with her young page and she praises his delicacy of feeling and his discretion. He reveals that his song was written for her, and together they nostalgically recall their first meeting. He declares his love with passion and Jacqueline returns his feelings but tells him that, for that very reason, they must part.

Clavaroche now returns to report that Maître André is to set an ambush to catch his wife's seducer and that Clavaroche himself is to be one of the four armed men who are to lie in wait for the usurper. He suggests that their weapons should be turned on the decoy. Jacqueline at first does not fully comprehend his implication, but Fortunio, who has been eavesdropping, does. He is aghast that Clavaroche is the lover in question.

Jacqueline now sends a note via Madelon to warn Fortunio, but this does not reach him in time and Fortunio duly arrives and reveals to Jacqueline his knowledge and hurt about her liaison with Clavaroche. He attempts to leave, knowing that an ambush is awaiting him, yet wishing to save her honour. Now Jacqueline, overcome by his passionate generosity, reveals the depth of her feelings for him.

The piece culminates in a delicious send-up of the close of the love-duet in Wagner's *Tristan* translated into bedroom farce. The old husband returns with the captain, but with far-from-tragic results. '*C'est moi!*' he announces prosaically, as he comes through the door, then hilariously fails to find Fortunio in his hiding-place. He is full of apologies for not trusting her, promising to sack Guillaume for his false accusations and determining that Fortunio shall be promoted to take his place. 'Mind you lock your door in future,' he warns his wife as he leaves her. Love-making joyously resumes as the curtain falls. No wonder the opera was a great success!

Gardiner is in his element, and the Lyon Opera cast includes such outstanding singers as Colette Alliot-Lugaz, rich-toned and characterful as the vivaciously provocative heroine, Jacqueline, and Thierry Dran as Fortunio, with Gilles Cachemaille as the handsome Captain Clavaroche, rival suitor for the heroine's attentions. On two mid-priced discs in Erato's Libretto series, it makes an ideal rarity to recommend not just to opera-lovers, but also to those who normally limit themselves to operetta.

Meyerbeer, Giacomo (1791–1864)

Il Crociato in Egitto (complete).
*** Opera Rara OR 10 (4). Geoffrey Mitchell Ch., RPO, David Parry.
    Aladino (Ian Platt), Adriano (Bruce Ford), Armando (Diana Montague), Palmide (Yvonne Kenny), Felicia (Della Jones), Alma (Linda Kitchen), Osmino (Ugo Benelli).

This was the sixth and last opera which the German-born Meyerbeer wrote for Italy. It was enthusiastically applauded in Venice in 1824, a work which was credited at the time with breaking Rossini's dominance in Italian opera. It may sound very Rossinian to us today, but there is an extra weight in the orchestral writing which points forward to Verdi and later Italian opera. The musical invention may not often be very distinctive, but the writing is consistently lively, notably in the ensembles.

During the Crusades, Armando d'Orville of Provence, after defeat in battle, mingled with the enemy under the assumed name of Elmiro and found an opportunity to save the life of Aladino, Sultan of Dalmietta. The sultan received him into his family and Armando fell in love with the sultan's daughter, Palmide. He secretly instructed her in Christianity and married her, and now they have a son, all without her father knowing. Peace comes between the warring factions and Christian emissaries are expected to open an embassy in Aladino's kingdom.

The opera opens as Elmiro returns from another campaign, to be welcomed by Palmide, who tells him that her father plans marriage festivities in accordance with his own religion. Simultaneously the Christian knights offering peace arrive by ship. With them is Felicia in male attire. She is the girl Armando/Elmiro left behind in Provence; she assumes her betrothed is dead.

The leader of the Christian party, Adriano, recognizes Armando as his missing nephew. He is in disgrace for cohabiting with the 'enemy' and Adriano takes his sword from him and tells him that if he wishes to redeem himself he must reveal his real identity to the sultan, and then return to Provence with Felicia. Armando tells his uncle of his new amorous commitment but is sternly ordered to renounce his beloved.

Felicia now meets Palmide with her young son, Mirva, and discovers the identity of his father. The women share their feelings: both still love Armando and suffer together and for each other. Armando returns and embraces Palmide but tears himself away. He then asks Palmide to kill him, but she reminds him of their child. Felicia forgives him.

Aladino frees the Christian slaves and the lavish wedding celebrations begin. The foreigners are invited. But Armando enters, dressed in the regalia of a Christian knight, and tells Palmide it is his duty to return to where he came from. The astonished Aladino hails him as a traitor and draws his dagger. Felicia, saying she is Armando's brother, shields him with her body and bravely draws her sword against the sultan. Aladino casts Armando into a dungeon and declares war on the Christians. The slaves are put back in chains. Felicia meets secretly with the Emir and is told she may still be able to save Armando.

Aladino now discovers that his daughter has a young son by Armando and sends for the father. Adriano is also confronted with his nephew's offspring. He is horrified and unmercifully condemns Armando, who then persuades Palmide to declare that she has converted to the Christian faith five years previously. This alters the situation entirely. Adriano is overjoyed and Felicia welcomes her as a sister. However, the furious Aladino decrees that they shall all die.

The Christians accept their fate, breaking their swords, ready to become martyrs. Osmino, the Grand Vizier, who throughout has hovered, plotting, in the background, now seeks to usurp Aladino's throne and rearms the Christian knights so that they can support him in his coup. But Armando stands by Aladino's side – he will not side with traitors. The other Christian knights follow his lead and Osmino is killed. The sultan, greatly moved, welcomes the Christian knights as his friends, and Armando looks forward to a joyous return to Provence with his wife and son.

With one exception – Ian Platt, ill-focused in the role of the Sultan – the cast is a strong one, with Diana Montague outstanding in the castrato role of the Crusader-Knight, Armando. Della Jones, too, in the mezzo role of Felicia, whom Armando has abandoned in favour of Palmide, the Sultan's daughter, sings superbly, with agile coloratura and a rich chest register. Yvonne Kenny is brilliant as Palmide. Bruce Ford, with his firm, heroic tone, and Ugo Benelli are very well contrasted in the two tenor roles. Though the chorus is small, the recording is clear and fresh.

Les Huguenots (complete).
(M) *** Decca 430 549-2 (4) [id.]. New Philh. O, Bonynge.
  Marguerite (Joan Sutherland), Valentine (Martina Arroyo), Urbain (Huguette Tourangeau), Comte de Saint Bris (Gabriel Bacquier), Comte de Nevers (Dominic Cossa), Raoul de Nangis (Anastasios Vrenios), Marcel (Nikola Ghiuselev).
** Erato/Warner Dig. 2292 45027-2 (4) [id.]. Montpellier Op. Ch. & PO, Diederich.
  Marguerite (Ghyslaine Raphanel), Valentine (Françoise Pollet), Urbain (Danielle Borst), Comte de Saint Bris (Boris Martinovich), Comte de Nevers (Gilles Cachemaille), Raoul de Nangis (Richard Leech), Marcel (Nikola Ghiuselev).

Meyerbeer's once-popular opera of epic length was a favourite with Dame Joan Sutherland. At the Sydney Opera House it was the subject of her last operatic appearance before retirement. Vast in scale, it is a disconcertingly episodic piece even for Meyerbeer, with many passages musically uninspired and with melodic invention often square.

The plot is very complicated, and the opera is often heard in revised and curtailed versions, but the outline of the story is as follows. In Touraine, the Comte de Nevers, a Catholic leader, is holding a banquet for his friends. The Huguenot nobleman, Raoul de Nangis, is one of them; his retainer, Marcel, is an even more fanatical Huguenot. Everyone must toast Raoul's love – she is an unknown lady whom he rescued from over-enthusiastic students and he hopes to meet her again. Meanwhile Marcel sings Luther's hymn, *Ein' feste Burg*, and follows it with a Huguenot battle-song. The Catholic guests are simply amused.

Comte de Nevers now proceeds to the garden to meet a lady who has asked to speak with him. Raoul recognizes her as the participant in the encounter with the students and realizes that he loves her; he fears a liaison might exist between her and the Comte de Nevers. He is right. She is

Valentine, daughter of the Catholic nobleman, Comte de St Bris, and she is pledged to de Nevers. However, the Queen, Marguerite de Valois, reasons that the differences between the Catholics and the Huguenots could be softened if Valentine would marry Raoul, and de Nevers is asked to release her from her engagement, to which he agrees.

The leaders of the Catholic group present also agree to the plan, and Raoul is led, blindfolded, by her page, Urbain, and brought before the queen. Valentine now enters and, knowing she is the woman the Comte de Nevers met in the garden but knowing nothing of their earlier betrothal, Raoul judges her to be unchaste and refuses her hand. Swords are drawn at his impugning her honour, but the queen prevents a fight.

We now proceed to the nuptial cortège in Paris, where, after all, the Comte de Nevers and Valentine are to marry. There is general uneasiness among the population, but representatives of both Royalists and Huguenots are present. Valentine remains in the chapel to pray. De Nevers and his companions are still seething over Raoul's seemingly shameful attitude towards Valentine and they conspire to ambush and murder him. Valentine overhears their plot, informs Marcel and a street fight develops. The queen arrives and Raoul now learns that he had refused the hand of a woman who loved him and that Valentine's meeting with de Nevers in the garden was specifically to ask for her release from her obligation to the count.

Raoul is devastated and now seeks out Valentine to hear her confirmation of the queen's words; Valentine, even though she is now married to de Nevers, concurs. She hides him when her husband enters unexpectedly, together with St Bris and other Catholic noblemen, who propose a plan to kill Raoul and massacre the Huguenots. It is to be carried out that very night, the Night of St Bartholomew. But, to his credit, the Comte de Nevers refuses to take part, relinquishes his sword to St Bris and is led away, a prisoner of the insurgents.

The priests now bless the remaining swords, St Bris and his followers swear loyalty to the cause and the great bell from St Germain tolls to signal the launch of the enterprise. Raoul must now notify his Huguenot friends of their peril. Valentine tries to prevent him leaving and says she loves him, but he leaps from a window. Covered in blood, he rushes to the Huguenot leaders gathered together to celebrate the marriage of Marguerite de Valois and Henri IV.

The scene now changes to a churchyard where Raoul and Marcel are resting. Valentine arrives and begs Raoul to adopt her faith. De Nevers has died nobly and she is free to marry him. He refuses to abandon his faith. Valentine says she will die with him, and the fanatical Marcel gives both of them his blessing. Later, in a square in Paris, Raoul is severely wounded. Marcel and Valentine are again with him. St Bris approaches with his followers. He calls out 'Who goes there?' and Raoul answers with his remaining strength, 'Huguenots!' There is a volley and Raoul, Valentine and Marcel fall dead. St Bris has murdered his own daughter! Heady stuff – but this ending is sometimes omitted, though not on either of the two recordings here.

Yet in a performance like the Decca it can be a powerful end to a powerfully convincing closing scene. Richard Bonynge prepared for this 1970 recording a concert performance in the Royal Albert Hall, and both then and in the recording itself his own passionate belief in the music is very clear. It is good too to have Sutherland augmenting the enticing sample of the role of the queen which she gave in one of her earlier recorded recitals ('*The art of the Prima Donna*' – see below). The result is predictably impressive, with the voice both rich and agile, if with an occasional hint of a 'beat' in it. The rest of the cast is uneven. Gabriel Bacquier and Nikola Ghiuselev are fine in their roles and, though Martina Arroyo is below her best as Valentine, the star quality is unmistakable. The tenor, Anastasios Vrenios, has too small a voice for the heroic part of Raoul, but he copes well with the extraordinarily high tessitura and florid divisions. Fine recording to match this ambitious project, well worth investigating by lovers of French opera. The excellent Decca recording comes up very freshly on CD.

Montpellier in the south of France, scene of a lively annual festival, prompted this alternative CD version of the most successful of Meyerbeer's blockbuster operas, recorded live in concert in the autumn of 1988. Though inevitably it is flawed, with the soloists very variable, there is much to enjoy, with the engineers capturing the atmosphere of the occasion very vividly. The five substantial Acts are neatly contained on the four discs, with the first three Acts each complete on a disc, and with Acts IV and V together on the final CD. Outstanding among the singers is the soprano, Françoise Pollet, who sings the role of Valentine, one of the two heroines.

Hers is a warm, full voice, which she uses most imaginatively, with fine clean attack in her big Act IV aria and in the long duet with the hero, Raoul, which follows. In that role Richard Leech has a light, pleasing tenor, but his style is too lachrymose. Ghyslaine Raphanel as the other heroine, Queen Marguerite de Valois, attacks the dauntingly difficult Act II aria with total assurance in coloratura, but the voice is shrill and tweety in a very French way; and though

Danielle Borst in the breeches role of the page, Urbain, is sweeter on the ear and agile, she cannot match her predecessor on record, Huguette Tourangeau in the Decca set with Joan Sutherland. Singing the role of the Huguenot soldier, Marcel (in both the new set and the old Decca), is Nikola Ghiuselev; but in almost twenty years the voice has grown much less steady, even though the comedy of his Act I solo, *Piff-Paff*, is again beautifully caught.

Le Prophète (complete).
(M) **(*) Sony M3K 79400 (3) [id.]. Boys' Ch. of Haberdasher's Aske's School, Amb. Op. Ch., RPO, Henry Lewis.
  Fidès (Marilyn Horne), Jean de Leyden (James McCracken), Berthe (Renata Scotto), Comte d'Oberthal (Jules Bastin), Zacharie (Jerome Hines), Jonas (Jean Dupouy).

This recording of Meyerbeer's second most famous stage piece anticipated the 1977 production at the New York Met. with the same conductor and principal soloists. The opera is set in Dordrecht, in Holland, and in Münster, in 1534/5.

Fidès, mother of John of Leyden, arrives at Count Oberthal's castle to gain permission for her son to marry Bertha, who carries John's betrothal ring. Simultaneously three Anabaptists arrive: their aim is to arouse revolt against tyranny. The count appears and recognizes Jonas, leader of the Anabaptists, as a steward he had once dismissed, and he orders the man to be beaten by his soldiers. Bertha pleads with the count and tells him that John had rescued her from the river Meuse and they have loved each other ever since. The count refuses his permission for the marriage and instead Bertha is seized and taken to his castle to serve his own pleasure. The populace are furious about this turn of events and they seek the leadership of the Anabaptists.

Now in Leyden, John dreams of his marriage. The three Anabaptists see in him a remarkable similarity to the picture of King David in Münster Cathedral. John mentions a dream wherein he stood in a temple with the people kneeling before him, and the Anabaptists see this as evidence that he will mount a throne. But he refuses to join them. His love is for Bertha, not political ambition. Bertha escapes and begs John to hide her, but the count and his soldiers arrive; the count has taken Bertha's mother prisoner and threatens her life if Bertha is not returned to him.

John hands over Bertha to Oberthal and her mother is released. John then joins the Anabaptists and in Münster, where the people have risen, he is proclaimed a prophet of God and he leads the revolt besieging the city. The fanatical Anabaptists capture Oberthal and call for his execution, but John decrees that Bertha shall decide Oberthal's fate. Meanwhile, the Anabaptists try to attack Münster without John, and it is only when his authority is restored that victory is achieved. John now decides to become emperor. But his mother is duped by the Anabaptists (who do not want her to know that her son is the prophet).

Shown some of his clothes stained with blood, she believes he is dead and, meeting Bertha, she tells her that her son has been murdered. Bertha vows vengeance on the prophet. However, during the coronation of the new emperor, Fidès hears John's voice in the cathedral and cries out, 'My son!' John fears that if the people think that this woman is his mother they will murder him. He tells his followers to kill him with their swords if the woman repeats her claim that she is his mother and Fidès, to save him, disowns him.

The German emperor is now moving towards Münster with his army and, fearing John's power, makes a pact with the three original Anabaptists: if they will hand over the prophet to him they will be pardoned. As they had only used John to attain their initial objective, they willingly agree to this bargain. Fidès and John now meet secretly at the palace. He begs his mother's forgiveness which she grants, believing that his motivation all along has been vengeance for Bertha's abduction.

Meanwhile Bertha, still not knowing the prophet's identity, has determined to blow up the palace and has set a slow fuse; when the prophet and his followers dine, the powder magazine will blow up. She then hears that the German emperor and his army are at the palace gates, that the prophet is betrayed and that he and John are one and the same person. Horrors! In despair and remorse she plunges a dagger into her own heart. John, now willing to die, joins the revellers in the banqueting hall, Fidès accompanies her son and they die all together in the explosive holocaust which follows.

This is an opera that needs a performance of the greatest conviction to be entirely convincing. That the Sony sessions had more than their share of crises is reflected in the final result, with a performance lacking the last degree of assurance. But even if none of the soloists is quite at peak form, they make a strong team, and with vigorous direction from Henry Lewis – rather brutal in the Coronation scene – there is much to enjoy. The recording is vividly transferred to CD but would have benefited from a more atmospheric acoustic.

Mondonville, Jean-Joseph Cassanea de (1711–72)

Titon et L'Aurore (complete).
*** Erato/Warner Dig. 2292 45715-2 (2) [id.]. Les Musiciens du Louvre, Minkowski.
    Titon (Jean-Paul Fouchécourt), L'Aurore (Catherine Napoli), Prométhée / Eole (Philippe Huttenlocher), Palès (Jennifer Smith), Amour / Nymphe (Ann Monoyios).

Described as a 'heroic-pastoral', *Titon et L'Aurore* was presented in Paris in the mid-eighteenth century as a masthead work by the advocates of opera in French, countering the Italian-language traditionalists. Mondonville, no heavyweight, fluently pours forth a sequence of crisp ideas in each of the three Acts of this formal classical tale of the mortal, Titon, who has the temerity to fall in love with Aurora, goddess of the dawn. In the customary Prologue, Prometheus brings to life the statues which are displayed throughout his palace. Cupid then bestows on these newly created beings the delights and joys of human love.

As the curtain rises in Act I, Titon is waiting for his Dawn goddess. But soon after she arrives and they have celebrated their mutual passion, Aeolus arrives. He too is enamoured of Aurora and determines that this impertinent mortal must die. Pales, who is herself attracted to Titon, suggests as an alternative that she take on the shepherd herself. In response Aeolus orders the North Winds to carry Titon off.

But this action does him no good: Aurora remains steadfast in her love for Titon. Pales then suggests to Aeolus that Titon should be freed from his shackles. He is lavishly entertained, but nothing can lift his melancholy and Pales, furious that she cannot have him for herself, is forced to let him go. But she inflicts him with premature ageing. Even so, Aurora remains faithful to him, and finally the God of Love brings an end to his afflictions so that he can be united with Aurora.

Some of Mondonville's instrumental effects are most vivid. After the formal Prologue featuring Prometheus, Act 1 opens in total darkness with low bassoons and double-basses in duet, before a sustained crescendo heralds the arrival of the goddess. The three Acts then bring a courtly entertainment which may miss the emotional intensity of a Rameau but which is full of charming ideas, presented with freshness and vigour. Marc Minkowski proves an ideal interpreter, directing a performance of the highest voltage, which yet allows the singers a full range of expressiveness. Jean-Paul Fouchécourt in the almost impossibly high tenor role of Titon proves an outstanding example of the French *haute-contre*, sustaining stratospheric lines with elegance and no strain. Catherine Napoli is bright and clear, if shallow at times as Aurore, while Ann Monoyios sings with ideal sweetness as L'Amour. Fitting neatly on two CDs, it makes an enticing set, very well recorded.

Monteverdi, Claudio (1567–1643)

(i) Il ballo delle ingrate; (ii) *Il combattimento di Tancredi e Clorinda* (opera-ballets).
Withdrawn: (M) *** Ph. 426 451-2; *426 451-4*. (i) Heather Harper, Anne Howells, Lilian Watson, Stafford Dean; Amb. S.; (ii) Harper, Luigi Alva, John Wakefield; ECO, Leppard.

Monteverdi's mastery in these pioneering essays in sung drama is brought out powerfully in the finely sung performances under Leppard, recorded before period instruments became obligatory in this repertory. The famous dramatic narrative of *Tancredi and Clorinda*, brother and sister, tragically and unknowingly matched in mortal combat, comes off particularly well on record. Tancredi, a Christian knight, engages in battle with a powerful Saracen warrior who, clothed in male armour, has burned down a Christian fortification. As she returns from this victorious assault, Tancredi sees and pursues her. He thinks she is male and challenges her to mortal combat. A narrator comments throughout the drama and the music describes first the horseback pursuit, then a melody praising the beauty of the night gives way to phrases representing battle. At its peak both combatants rest, momentarily exhausted, and Tancredi seeks to know the name of his opponent. Clorinda answers that it is one of the two who burned the Christian fortification. They resume the fight and when Clorinda lies dying she begs for Christian baptism. Tancredi brings her water and raises the visor of her helmet and is horrified to discover the identity of the dying woman. But he baptizes her, and as her soul rises to heaven she sings a last soaring phrase.

On Philips, *Tancredi and Clorinda* is perfectly coupled with *Il ballo delle ingrate*, which tells of the 'ungrateful' ladies who were condemned to the domain of Pluto, not for profligacy but for refusing to yield to their lovers' caresses. (Clearly the 'moral' of the story was aimed directly at the bride of the Duke of Mantua, at whose nuptial celebrations the work received its première.) The poignant climax to this remarkably expressive piece comes with the beautiful aria sung by a 'lost spirit', who stays behind to plead the cause of her companions. The recorded sound is very beautiful, the balance excellent and the vocal projection very present and natural against an attractively warm ambience. It is a great pity that this virtually ideal set has been for the moment withdrawn.

Il ballo delle ingrate; Sestina: Lagrime d'amante al sepolcro dell'amata.
**(*) HM Dig. HMC 90 1108 [id.]. Les Arts Florissants, Christie.

William Christie directs refreshingly dramatic accounts of both *Il ballo delle ingrate* and the *Sestina*, using the period instruments of his talented Paris-based company. His singers have been chosen for character and bite rather than for beauty of tone, and the final lament of *Il ballo* is spoilt by exaggerated plaintiveness, but (particularly in the *Sestina*) the boldness of Christie's interpretation makes for very compelling performances, beautifully recorded. The note on the CD version irritatingly omits details of the soloists.

Il combattimento di Tancredi e Clorinda. L'Arianna: Lasciatemi Morire (Ariadne's lament) (with FARINA: *Sonata (La Desperata).* ROSSI: *Sonata sopra l'aria di Ruggiero.* FONTANA: *Sonata a tre violini.* MARINI: *Passacaglia a 4. Sonata sopra la Monica; Eco a tre violini.* BUONAMENTE: *Sonata a tre violini*).
**Withdrawn: **(*) DG 415 296-2 [id.]. Patrizia Kwella, Nigel Rogers, David Thomas, Carolyn Watkinson; Col. Mus. Ant., Goebel.

Under Reinhard Goebel, the Cologne Musica Antiqua using original instruments has built up a formidable reputation on record, and these tasteful performances of two masterly Monteverdi settings, coupled with sonatas by Monteverdi's contemporaries, are welcome. Carolyn Watkinson's singing of the *Lament* is finely controlled and certainly dramatic. So too is the performance of the touching and powerfully imaginative narrative about the battle of Tancredi and Clorinda, which understandably moved the audience to tears at its première. The other pieces are of more mixed appeal. Highlights are Fontana's engaging *Sonata for three violins* and Marini's ingenious *Eco a tre violini*, which is performed here to great effect, with the imitations echoing into the distance. Elsewhere, the slightly spiky sounds produced by the string players, with the close microphones bringing a touch of edginess, may not appeal to all tastes. The transfers of the 1979 analogue recordings are impeccably managed. Full texts and notes are provided.

L'Incoronazione di Poppea.
*** Virgin/EMI Dig. VCT7 90775-2 (3) [id.]. City of L. Bar. Sinfonia, Hickox.
    Poppea (Arleen Augér), Nerone (Della Jones), Ottavia (Linda Hirst), Ottone (James Bowman).
**(*) HM Dig. HMC 901330/2 [id.]. Concerto Vocale, Jacobs.
    Poppea (Danielle Borst), Nerone (Guillemette Laurens), Ottavia (Jennifer Larmore), Ottone (Axel Köhler).
(M) **(*) Teldec/Warner 2292 42547-2 (4) [id.]. VCM, Harnoncourt.
    Poppea (Helen Donath), Nerone (Elisabeth Söderström), Ottavia (Cathy Berberian), Ottone (Paul Esswood).

Monteverdi's *Coronation of Poppea* has appeared in a number of versions over the years, and its Prologue, sometimes omitted, sees the coquettish flaunting of the Goddesses of Fortune and Virtue, with the Goddess of Love outshining them both.

The opera opens as the rays of the dawn sun are just appearing. Two guards are asleep outside Poppea's house. Ottone, her lover, approaches but sees the soldiers and realizes that his place has been taken by Nero. Inside the house, Poppea and Nero have spent the night in each other's arms and Nero finds it difficult to leave her. Poppea presses for marriage, for Nero to put aside the Empress Octavia in her favour. Nero half promises to meet her wishes; Arnalto, Poppea's nurse, urges caution, but Poppea feels that the Goddess of Love is on her side.

Meanwhile Octavia in her palace laments her situation and calls on Jove to punish Nero for his infidelity. Seneca the philosopher urges her to rise above the blows of fortune and exult in her own glory. She responds that glory is cold comfort.

When alone, Seneca has a vision in which Pallas, Goddess of Wisdom, appears. She warns that to interfere between Nero and Octavia will bring about his death. Seneca has no fear of death, indeed would welcome it, but then Nero tells his old tutor and current adviser that he will set his wife aside and marry Poppea. Seneca warns Nero that both the Senate and populace will be against him. They part in anger. Nero rejoins Poppea and she denounces Seneca and sneeringly suggests that Nero's rule has hitherto depended on Seneca's guidance. Inflamed by this, Nero orders Seneca's immediate execution.

Ottone once more desperately seeks to regain Poppea's love but she spurns him. He turns for comfort instead to Drusilla, Octavia's lady-in-waiting, for she is in love with him. She cannot quite believe it when he declares his love in return but she is only too ready to respond to his desire for her.

Liberto, Captain of the Guard, now informs Seneca of Nero's decree that he must die. Seneca tells his students that the moment has come for him to prove his stoical theories and accept his fate. On his death Nero carouses with his friend, Lucano, whom he tells of his great love for Poppea. Meanwhile Octavia threatens Ottone that, unless he kills Poppea, she will blacken his character. His reluctance is expressed in evasions.

Drusilla is happy in her love for Ottone, and he secures her help to commit what he regards as his shameful crime, by the loan of her garments as a disguise. She willingly accedes.

In her garden Poppea rejoices with Arnalta that Seneca is dead. She requires Love to guide her safely to harbour, and the goddess descends and promises her protection. Ottone enters, disguised as Drusilla, but the goddess intervenes. Poppea awakens. She and Arnalta think that the threatening intruder is 'Drusilla' and Arnalta organizes pursuit.

The real Drusilla is arrested for an attempt on Poppea's life. She insists she is innocent and is about to be taken to her death when Ottone appears and confesses to the deception. Nero banishes him; Drusilla elects to accompany him.

Nero now decrees his divorce of Octavia and determines to exile her in turn. Telling Poppea that Ottone not Drusilla had attempted murder, he says that Drusilla is at the very least implicated and must be exiled too. Octavia now bids a dignified farewell to Rome in her famous *Lament*, and Poppea and Nero are left to reign together in triumph.

The tender expressiveness of Arleen Augér in the title-role of Monteverdi's elusive masterpiece goes with a performance from Richard Hickox and the City of London Sinfonia which consistently reflects the fact that it was recorded in conjunction with a stage production. Hickox, following the latest scholarship, daringly uses a very spare accompaniment of continuo instruments, contrasting not just with the opulent score presented at Glyndebourne by Raymond Leppard, but with the previous period performance on record, that of Nikolaus Harnoncourt and the Concentus Musicus of Vienna, who has a far wider, more abrasive range of instrumental sound. Hickox overcomes the problems of that self-imposed limitation by choosing the widest possible range of speeds. So the exuberant Nero–Lucano duet after the death of Seneca is very fast and brilliant, while the heavenly final duet of the lovers (apparently not by Monteverdi at all) is extremely slow, rapt and gentle.

The purity of Augér's soprano may make Poppea less of a scheming seducer than she should be, but it is Monteverdi's music for the heroine which makes her so sympathetic in this oddly slanted, equivocal picture of Roman history, and one that has never sounded subtler or more lovely on record than here. Taking the castrato role of Nero, Della Jones sings very convincingly with full, rather boyish tone, while Gregory Reinhart is magnificent in the bass role of Seneca. James Bowman is a fine Ottone, with smaller parts taken by such excellent young singers as Catherine Denley, John Graham-Hall, Mark Tucker and Janice Watson. Linda Hirst sounds too raw of tone for Ottavia, making her a scold rather than a sympathetic, suffering widow. Squeezed on to three well-filled CDs, the opera comes with libretto, translation and excellent notes by Clifford Bartlett.

Like the Virgin set conducted by Richard Hickox, the one directed by René Jacobs was recorded immediately after stage performances. This helps to give it fluency, though neither the characterization nor the timing of dialogue gives quite the same illusion of staging. Danielle Borst as Poppea and the Nerone of Guillemette Laurens are both fresh and stylish, if not quite as sharply distinctive as their counterparts. With the exception of a tremulous counter-tenor as Ottone, this is a strong cast, with such fine singers as Guy de Mey and Dominique Visse in subsidiary roles, and with Jennifer Larmore as the wronged Ottavia far richer and more sympathetic than her opposite number. Jacobs' restoration of instrumental ritornellos between scenes is welcome, even if Hickox's balder treatment often brings extra gravity. Excellent, clear recording, but the Virgin set, with Arleen Augér a tenderly expressive Poppea, remains first choice.

Nikolaus Harnoncourt's well-paced and dramatic version makes a welcome reappearance at mid-price in Teldec's Harnoncourt series. First issued in 1974, it offers a starry cast, with Elisabeth Söderström as Nero (imaginative but not always ideally steady), Helen Donath pure-toned as Poppea and Cathy Berberian as the most charactered and moving Ottavia on disc. Others include Paul Esswood and Philip Langridge, and Harnoncourt's bold and brassy instrumentation adds to the bite. The snag is that, unnecessarily, the set stretches to four discs instead of three, which cancels out the price advantage over the excellent rival sets from Richard Hickox and René Jacobs.

Orfeo: complete.
*** DG Dig. 419 250-2 (2) [id.]. Monteverdi Ch., E. Bar. Soloists, Gardiner.
   Orfeo (Anthony Rolfe Johnson), Euridice (Julianne Baird), Music (Lynne Dawson), Messenger (Anne Sofie Von Otter), Nymph (Nancy Argenta).
Withdrawn: *** EMI Dig. CDS7 47142-8 (2) [Ang. CDCB 47141]. Chiaroscuro, L. Bar. Ens., L. Cornett & Sackbutt Ens., Rogers & Medlam.
   Orfeo (Nigel Rogers), Euridice (Patrizia Kwella), Music (Emma Kirkby), Proserpina (Jennifer Smith).
*** O-L Dig. 433 545-2 (2) [id.]. New London Consort, Pickett.
   Orfeo (John Mark Ainsley), Euridice (Julia Gooding), La Musica / La Messaggiera / Proserpina (Catherine Bott), Nymph (Tessa Bonner).
** Teldec/Warner 2292 42494-2 (2) [id.]. Munich Capella Antiqua, VCM, Harnoncourt.
   Orfeo (Lajos Kozma), Euridice (Rotraud Hansmann), Messaggiera / Speranza (Cathy Berberian), Proserpina (Eiko Katanosaka), Plutone (Jacques Villisech), Apollo (Max Van Egmond).

The Prologue of Monteverdi's first opera opens with an arresting clarion call, followed by La Musica demonstrating her powers of creating narrative atmosphere. We move to a scene of rejoicing. Orfeo and Euridice sing of their love, there are contributions from a nymph and two shepherds and the wish is expressed that these lovers' happiness will not dissolve in misfortune. And indeed Orfeo's delight is short-lived. His mood becomes apprehensive at the envy of the gods, then he is stunned when the Messenger brings the news of the death of Euridice.

The shepherds are also appalled, and Orfeo sings his great *Lament*. But now Orfeo is resolved to do something about his situation. He determines to seek Euridice in Hades and at that moment is confronted by Hope. Indeed he is hoping that his singing prowess will gain him admission to the Underworld. Charon listens to Orfeo and yields and there is a solemn chorus of acceptance from the spirits below.

Pluto, King of the Underworld, finally agrees to release Euridice, but of course Orfeo may not look back at her on his journey to safety – which he does, with disastrous results. Orfeo now roams the plains of Thrace in despair. He summons Nature to mourn with him. Apollo, Orfeo's father, descends from heaven and tells Orfeo that he will receive divine immortality and meet Euridice in the heavenly firmament, and Apollo and Orfeo duly ascend into the heavens.

John Eliot Gardiner very effectively balances the often-conflicting demands of authentic performance – when this pioneering opera was originally presented intimately – and the obvious grandeur of the concept. The very atmospheric recording vividly conveys the impression of some hall in a prince's palace, much more likely as a venue than a small room, and lively enough to give bloom to the voices and to the colourful instrumentation. So the Monteverdi Choir, twenty-one strong, conveys on the one hand high tragedy to the full, yet sings the lighter commentary from nymphs and shepherds with astonishing crispness, often at top speed. However, Gardiner is strong on pacing. He does not simply race along in the way that authentic performance has tended to encourage but gives full and moving expansion to such key passages as the messenger's report of Euridice's death, sung with agonizing intensity by Anne Sophie von Otter.

It intensifies that narration that the singer is heard first from a distance, then gradually approaches. Lynne Dawson is also outstanding as the allegorical figure of Music in the Prologue, while Anthony Rolfe Johnson shows his formidable versatility in the title-role. Though rival tenors with smaller voices have been more flexible in the elaborate *fioriture* of the Act III aria, presenting it more urgently, it is an advantage having a fuller-bodied voice that can yet focus cleanly. This is a set to take you through the story with new involvement. Though editing is not always immaculate, the recording on CD is vivid and full of presence.

Nigel Rogers – who recorded the role of Orfeo ten years earlier for DG Archiv – in the EMI version has the double function of singing the main part and acting as co-director. In the earlier recording under Kurt Jürgens, ample reverberation tended to inflate the performance but, this time in a drier acoustic, Rogers has modified his extraordinarily elaborate ornamentation in the hero's brilliant pleading aria before Charon and makes the result all the freer and more wide-ranging in expression, with his distinctive fluttering timbre adding character. With the central singer directing the others, the concentration of the whole performance is all the greater, telling the story simply and graphically.

The sound of thunder that fatefully makes Orpheus turn around as he leads Euridice back to earth is all the more dramatic for being drily percussive; and Euridice's plaint, beautifully sung by Patrizia Kwella, is the more affecting for being accompanied very simply on the lute. The other soloists make a good team, though Jennifer Smith as Proserpina, recorded close, is made to sound breathy. The brightness of the cornetti is a special delight, when otherwise the instrumentation used – largely left optional in the score – is modest. Excellent, immediate recording, at its finest on CD.

Philip Pickett and the New London Consort triumphantly establish how vibrantly alive this music of 1607 can be. Thoughtful and scholarly as he is, Pickett has not tried to treat *Orfeo* with kid gloves but has aimed above all to bring out its freshness. Compared with John Eliot Gardiner, whose DG Archiv recording combines precision and alertness in presenting the drama, Pickett is rougher, not caring quite so much about pinpoint ensemble, preferring less extreme speeds and characteristically relying more on dramatic contrasts in instrumentation. So in the dark *Sinfonia* with its weird chromatic writing which at the opening of Act III represents Orfeo's arrival in the Underworld, Pickett cuts out strings and uses brass instruments alone. He has the cornetts, sackbutts and a rasping regal organ playing at a lower pitch than usual, deducing that transposition from Monteverdi's use of high clefs. The result is all the more darkly menacing. While planning his recording, Pickett visited the Gonzaga Palace in Mantua, scene of the first performances of *Orfeo*, trying to establish in which room precisely the event took place. That has dictated both the scale and the acoustic chosen for the recording, drier than Gardiner's DG, with the performers placed more immediately.

As Orfeo, John Mark Ainsley may have a less velvety tenor than Anthony Rolfe Johnson on the Gardiner set, but his voice is more crisply flexible in the elaborate decorations of *Possente spirto*, Orfeo's plea to Charon. Outstanding among the others, establishing the characterful style of the solo singing from the start, is Catherine Bott, who was also the vocal star of Pickett's exciting set, *The Pilgrimage to Santiago*. In *Orfeo* she not only sings the elaborate role given to La Musica in the Prologue, sensuously beautiful and seductive in her coloration, but also the part of Proserpina and the key role of the Messenger, who graphically describes the death of Euridice. Excellent among the others are Julia Gooding as Euridice, the counter-tenor Christopher Robson as Hope and Tessa Bonner as the Nymph.

In Harnoncourt's version, the ritornello of the Prologue might almost be by Stravinsky, so sharply do the sounds cut. He is an altogether more severe Monteverdian than Nigel Rogers. In compensation, the simple and straightforward dedication of this performance is most affecting, and the solo singing, if not generally very characterful, is clean and stylish. One exception to the general rule on characterfulness comes in the singing of Cathy Berberian as the Messenger. She is strikingly successful and, though differing slightly in style from the others, she sings as part of the team. Excellent restrained recording, as usual in Harnoncourt's remastered Telefunken CD series, projecting the performance even more vividly than on LP. The extra clarity and sharpness of focus – even in large-scale ensembles – add to the abrasiveness from the opening *Toccata* onwards, and the 1969 recording certainly sounds immediate, with voices very realistic.

Il ritorno d'Ulisse in patria (complete).
*** HM Dig. HMU 90 1427/9 (3) [id.]. Concerto Vocale, René Jacobs.
    Ulisse (Christoph Prégardien), Penelope (Bernarda Fink), Telemaco (Christina Högman), Minerva / Fortuna (Lorraine Hunt), Pisandro / L'Umana fragilità (Dominique Visse), Anfinomo (Mark Tucker), Antinoo (David Thomas).
(M) **(*) Teldec/Warner 2292 42496-2 (3) [id.]. Junge Kantorei, VCM, Harnoncourt.
    Ulysses / Human Frailty (Sven Olaf Eliasson), Penelope (Norma Lerer), Telemachus (Kai Hansen), Melantho / Fortune (Margaret Baker-Genovesi), Athene (Rotraud Hansmann),

Pisandrus (Kurt Equiluz), Anfinomus (Paul Esswood), Antinous / Time (Walker Wyatt), Eurimacus (Nigel Walters), Eumaeus (Max Van Egmond), Euryclea (Anne-Marie Mühle).

The second of Monteverdi's three surviving operas, *Il ritorno d'Ulisse in patria*, neglected for so long in the CD catalogue, is here treated to a most enjoyable version with René Jacobs employing the same cast as in the Montpellier Festival. Following up Jacobs' earlier set of Monteverdi's *Il coronazione di Poppea*, also from Montpellier, it offers a scholarly performance that is not afraid of being warmly expressive. This is not just a far longer opera than *Orfeo*, it contains much more of what one might describe as madrigal material – relatively brief solos and ensembles that form landmarks amid Monteverdi's free-running recitative.

In the Prologue of Monteverdi's setting of the Ulysses story, characters representing the inexorable progress of Time, blind and deaf Fortune, and Love, against which there is no defence, exert their influence over the Frailty of Man. Then, as the story begins, we join Penelope, wife of Ulysses, still pining for her husband for whom she has waited so long. He lies asleep on a beach in Ithaca after long conflict with the gods. He is now able to return home. Athene instructs him to return disguised in the clothes of a beggar.

Meanwhile Penelope's maid, Melantho, is trying to persuade her mistress to give herself to one of her other suitors, Anfinomus, Pisandrus or Antinous. All would like to possess her and Ulysses' realm too. On his journey Ulysses meets the loyal swineheard, Eumaeus, and Athene leads Telemachus, Ulysses' son, to Eumaeus, who tells him of his father's immediate arrival. The news is also conveyed to the palace, and the traitorous suitors plan to do battle and to kill Telemachus. They offer presents to Penelope.

Now Eumaeus appears at the palace with an old beggar (Ulysses in disguise). Penelope, not recognizing her husband, is at her wits' end as to how to defeat her suitors. Resourcefully she declares that she will give herself to whoever can bend Ulysses' bow. Nobody is able to do so until Ulysses steps forward, bends the bow and shoots the suitors dead. Penelope, still influenced by Melantho, cannot believe her eyes, and Eumaeus and Telemachus are unable to convince her that she has just met her husband.

The gods Athene and Hera ask Zeus to intercede on behalf of Ulysses, and Poseidon agrees also to pardon Ulysses for blinding his son, Polyphemus. Athene is the catalyst of the reconciliation. Ulysses now enters the palace in his normal form, but Penelope believes that he is someone else who has magically taken on her husband's image. Euryclea, Ulysses' nurse, comes to the rescue; she knows of a wound which Ulysses received when fighting a wild boar, and she identifies the scar. Yet only when Ulysses reminds her how she once had a uniquely patterned quilt on her bed – which only he could have seen – does Penelope concede that he really is her husband, and her doubt turns to joy.

Jacobs as a singer himself is most understanding of the need to give his soloists free rein, and they make a first-rate team, with the clear-toned German tenor, Christoph Prégardien, splendid as Ulisse, firm and heroic but light enough to cope with the elaborate ornamentation. Bernarda Fink with her rich, firm mezzo gives full weight to Penelope's agony, and it is encouraging to find such excellent British singers as the tenors Martyn Hill and Mark Tucker and the baritone David Thomas taking character roles. The French counter-tenor Dominique Visse is excellent too, both as Human Frailty in the Prologue and as one of Penelope's suitors, with Guy de Mey in the comic role of the glutton, Iro. The five Acts fit neatly on the three CDs of around an hour each, with no internal breaks within Acts. Jacobs explains that, with the surviving manuscripts raising dozens of textual questions, he decided to return to the original five-Act division of the text which, as he suggests, is better balanced. He also inserts music by Rossi and Caccini for the choruses included in the text but missing from the score, all adding to the impact of the whole piece.

Harnoncourt's 1971 recording of *Il ritorno d'Ulisse* brings a sympathetic performance, generally not quite as brisk as Jacobs in his recording from the Montpellier Festival, and rather more square in rhythm, but bringing a keener sense of repose, important in Monteverdi. The solo singing is not as characterful as that on the Jacobs set, nor as Harnoncourt's *Poppea*, though Norma Lerer makes a touching Penelope, with Sven Olaf Eliasson a stylish Ulisse, not ideally pure of timbre.

Ballet e balletti: *Orfeo: Lasciate i monti; Vieni imeneo; Ecco pur ch'a voi ritorno; Moresca. Tirsi e Clori: ballet. Scherzo musicali: Il ballo delle ingrate; De la belleza la dovute lodi; Volgendo il ciel.*
(*) Erato/Warner Dig. 2292 45984-2 [id.]. Patrizia Kwella, Anthony Rolfe Johnson, Laurence Dale, Alan Woodrow, Monteverdi Ch., E. Bar. Soloists, Gardiner.

This is in effect a Monteverdi sampler; while the mosaic from *Orfeo*, for instance, may not suit the specialist listener, it makes delightful listening when the singing is so fresh. The music from the famous *Il ballo delle ingrate* is very short (about 3½ minutes) and seems pointless out of context; but all the rest, notably the choral ballet from *Tirsi e Clori*, is most engaging with its changes of mood: sometimes dolorous, sometimes gay and spirited. Gardiner's direction, as always, is vivid and his pacing lively; there is much to titillate the ear in the spicy vocal and orchestral colouring. The balance is fairly close, but the overall perspective is well defined, within a warm acoustic.

Mozart, Wolfgang Amadeus (1756–91)

Apollo et Hyacinthus (complete).
(M) *** Ph. 422 526-2 (2) [id.]. Salzburg Chamber Ch. & Mozarteum O, Hager.
   Apollo (Cornelia Wulkopf), Hyacinthus (Edith Mathis), Oebalus (Anthony Rolfe Johnson),
   Melia (Arleen Augér), Zephyrus (Hanna Schwarz).

Apollo et Hyacinthus was written when Mozart was eleven, with all but two of the parts taken by schoolchildren. It is essentially an Intermezzo, written and designed to be performed within Father Rufinus Wild's mythological tragedy, *Clementi Croesi*; yet it stands up admirably on its own. The story (from Euripides' *Helen*) tells how Apollo accidentally kills the youth Hyacinth, whom he loves, with a discus and then, heartbroken, creates a flower of great beauty to grow from the grave. But in Mozart's setting Apollo is not personally responsible for the death of Hyacinth.

As the story begins, Hyacinth prepares a sacrifice to Apollo, and Zephyr questions his special loyalty to this particular god. Oebalus and Melia (Hyacinth's father and sister) enter and the sacrificial fire is kindled. But black stormclouds gather in the sky, lightning destroys the altar, and all wonder whether they have in some way offended the god. Hyacinth urges courage and is philosophical about his destiny being regulated by the whims of the deities. Apollo now arrives in the garb of a shepherd and apologizes for Jove's anger in the heavens. They all praise him and he promises his favour. Hyacinth and Apollo go off together, and Oebalus tells his daughter that Apollo desires to marry her. She cannot believe her luck and readily consents to become a goddess – all Apollo has to do is ask.

Zephyr now returns to relate the tragic news of Hyacinth's demise: he was killed by Apollo's discus thrown directly at his head. The angry Oebalus wants to banish Apollo from his kingdom; Melia is now doubtful about marrying her brother's murderer. Zephyr, who has designs on Melia, is himself responsible for the murder and he encourages Oebalus' imprudent anger. Melia now questions Zephyr as to why Apollo should have killed the youth for whom he has professed such deep feelings, and Zephyr describes the god as sly, cruel and capricious. He offers himself as an alternative suitor but is rejected.

Zephyr is terrified as Apollo now approaches – rightly so, for the god knows everything and, as a punishment, turns Zephyr into a breeze, and he floats away. Apollo now tries to placate Melia but she rejects him totally. Meanwhile Oebalus has gone in search of his son and the dying Hyacinth reveals the real killer's identity, confirming Apollo's innocence. Oebalus' fury knows no bounds and when Melia enters, incensed that Apollo has now dispatched Zephyr too, her father informs her what really happened.

They are both appalled that each has unjustly accused Apollo, but he returns and creates the lovely flower where Hyacinth is buried. Melia and Oebalus beg his forgiveness and Melia now fervently offers herself as his bride. She is accepted and, as together they celebrate the coming nuptials, the god's favour in the future is assured.

The style of the writing and vocalization is rather simpler than in other dramatic works of the boy Mozart, but the inspiration is still remarkable, astonishingly mature. The orchestration is assured and full of imaginative touches. Specially delightful is the eighth of the nine numbers, a duet between the heroine Melia and her father, after her brother Hyacinthus has died. The accompaniment of muted violins with pizzicato second violins and bass with divided violas is magical. The performance here is stylish and very well sung. If, as so often in early Mozart, recitatives seem too long, the CD banding allows one to make one's own selection if not requiring the whole opera. Excellent, clear and well-balanced recording, originally made by DG in Salzburg in 1971, and admirably transferred to CD. The voices are forward but not excessively so.

Ascanio in Alba (complete).
(M) **(*) Ph. 422 530-2 (3) [id.]. Salzburg Chamber Ch., Salzburg Mozarteum O, Hager.
   Ascanio (Agnes Baltsa), Silvia (Edith Mathis), Aceste (Peter Schreier), Venere (Lilian Sukis),
   Fauno (Arleen Augér).

Mozart provided this '*Festa teatrale*' as a festive entertainment for the coronation of the
Archduke Ferdinand to an Italian princess in Milan in 1771. Written when he was fifteen, it
came between the boy composer's two other Milan commissions, *Mitridate* and *Lucio Silla*.

The opera has a pastoral setting in the mythical Alba, populated by nymphs, shepherds and
the Graces, a kingdom much enjoyed by Venus. Her son, Ascanio, is to rule in her name, and
Silvia, a nymph, is to be his bride. Ascanio wonders if she will love him, but is reassured to hear
that for four years Cupid, in Ascanio's form, has paid court to Silvia in her dreams. Ascanio may
now meet his future wife but, to test her, he must not reveal his identity.

Venus returns to the heavens and Ascanio remains as a stranger awaiting the priest and Silvia.
Fauno warns him to respect her modesty. The loving pair meet and Silvia confesses her love for
someone very special to her. Venus reappears and promises a further test of Silvia's virtue;
meanwhile a splendid new city will be created as the couple's new home. Ascanio badly wants to
tell Silvia who he is, but she thinks she recognizes him as her dream lover. Fauno, acting as
chaperone, misleads her into thinking she is mistaken. She immediately becomes pale and
listless in her distress. Ascanio may still not reveal himself and, when he addresses her, she flees.
Thus her virtue is confirmed, and Venus reappears once more. Silvia's trials are at an end and
the two lovers can at last be united. Their heirs will prosper.

At 2¾ hours it is a comparatively expansive piece, though as a classical celebration of
marriage – with Ascanio representing the young Archduke and the nymph Silvia representing
the bride he had never previously seen, Maria Beatrix d'Este – it lacks the dramatic qualities of
Mozart's two other Milanese examples of *opera seria*. At its first performance it scored an
immediate success with its unquenchable inventiveness, completely eclipsing the other newly
commissioned work for the coronation, an opera by Hasse. Though it hardly compares with
what Mozart was to do later, it brings one delightful number after another. Interspersed between
the arias are choruses of comment, far more so than is usual in an *opera seria*. The final trio
leads on, very imaginatively for the time, to a recitative and separate cabaletta, before the final
brief chorus. Hager makes an excellent start with an exceptionally lively account of the delightful
Overture, but then the choruses seem relatively square, thanks to the pedestrian, if generally
efficient singing of the Salzburg choir. Hager's speeds are sometimes on the slow side, but the
singing is excellent, with no weak link in the characterful cast, though not everyone will like the
distinctive vibrato of Lilian Sukis as Venus. The analogue recording, made in collaboration with
Austrian Radio in 1976, is full and vivid.

Bastien und Bastienne (complete). Concert arias: *Mentre ti lascio, o figlia, K.513; Misero! o
sogno . . . Aura, che intorno spiri, K.431. Le nozze di Figaro: Giunse alfin il momento . . . Deh
vieni; Un moto di gioia.*
*** Sony Dig. SK 45855 [id.]. Liszt CO, Leppard.
   Bastien (Vinson Cole), Bastienne (Edita Gruberová), Colas (László Polgár).

Bastien und Bastienne (complete); Lieder: *Komm, liebe Zither, komm; Die Zufriedenheit.*
(M) **(*) Ph. Dig. 422 527-2 [id.]. V. Boys' Ch., VSO, Harrer.
   Bastien (Georg Nigl), Bastienne (Dominik Orieschnig), Colas (David Busch).

Bastien and Bastienne, completed in 1768, was written when Mozart was twelve and is his
first German Singspiel. (The term describes a modest stage work, usually sung in German and
well laced with popular airs, featuring spoken dialogue, arias, duets, trios and small ensembles.)
The libretto was adapted from Jean-Jacques Rousseau's *Le devin du village* and tells of
Bastienne, a shepherdess, who has just been deserted by her lover, Bastien. She turns to Colas, a
magician of doubtful credentials but with a great deal of practical common sense, and she is told
that Bastien has succumbed to temptation in the form of a noble lady who wants him for herself.

Colas suggests that a little flirting might help to retrieve her lover and make him refocus his
attentions in the right direction. In fact, after more of Colas's good advice, Bastien has already
come to his senses and, when he hears that Bastienne is also looking elsewhere, he is horrified.
Colas's help with a little bit of magic is obviously the answer, and a suitable spell is contrived to
redirect her affections. The two lovers meet again, but she is not easily placated, and when

Bastien threatens to drown himself she suggests that a cold bath might be quite enjoyable. Finally she is persuaded to forgive him, they are united, and Colas offers his blessing.

Leppard, too long neglected by the record companies, here conducts for Sony a near-ideal performance of the twelve-year-old Mozart's charming little one-Acter, very well recorded. The trio of soloists is excellent. Edita Gruberová is delectably fresh and vivacious as the heroine, Vinson Cole is a sensitive and clean-voiced Bastien, and László Polgár is full of fun in the *buffo* role of Colas. The dialogue is excellently directed, and the Liszt Chamber Orchestra of Budapest plays with dazzling precision, bringing wit to the opening with its anticipation of Beethoven's *Eroica*. As a generous fill-up, the three soloists sing Mozart arias, including the big scena for tenor, *Misero! o sogno*, and a replacement aria for Susanna, specially written for the 1789 production of *Le nozze di Figaro: Un moto di gioia*.

On Philips the opera is performed by boy trebles instead of the soprano, tenor and bass originally intended. Members of the Vienna Boys' Choir give a refreshingly direct performance under Uwe Christian Harrer, missing little of the piece's charm, though a recording with adult singers is preferable. The two songs with mandolin accompaniment, also sung by one of the trebles, make an attractive fill-up. First-rate 1988 digital sound.

La clemenza di Tito (complete).
(M) *** Ph. 422 544-2 (2) [id.]. ROHCG Ch. & O, Sir Colin Davis.
    Tito (Stuart Burrows), Vitellia (Janet Baker), Sesto (Yvonne Minton), Annio (Frederica Von Stade), Servilia (Lucia Popp), Publio (Robert Lloyd).
*** DG Dig. 431 806-2 (2). Monteverdi Ch., E. Bar. Soloists, Gardiner.
    Tito (Anthony Rolfe Johnson), Vitellia (Julia Varady), Sesto (Anne Sofie Von Otter), Annio (Catherine Robbin), Servilia (Sylvia McNair), Publio (Cornelius Hauptmann).
(M) *** DG 429 878-2 (2) [id.]. Leipzig R. Ch., Dresden State O, Boehm.
    Tito (Peter Schreier), Vitellia (Julia Varady), Sesto (Teresa Berganza), Annio (Marga Schiml), Servilia (Edith Mathis), Publio (Theo Adam).
(M) ** Decca 430 105-2 (2) [id.]. VPO Ch. & O, Kertész.
    Tito (Werner Krenn), Vitellia (Maria Casula), Sesto (Teresa Berganza), Annio (Brigitte Fassbaender), Servilia (Lucia Popp), Publio (Tugomir Franc).

Mozart's *opera seria*, *La clemenza di Tito*, was written in 1791 while he was composing *Die Zauberflöte*. It was commissioned for the coronation of Leopold II, written over a period of less than three weeks, then duly performed in Prague. The story centres on Vitellia, who is the daughter of the deposed Emperor, Vitellius. Sextus, a young Roman patrician, is in love with her. But she, though enamoured of the Emperor Titus, mainly has her eye on the throne and is not pleased when she hears that Titus plans to marry Berenice, the daughter of Agrippa the First of Judaea.

Vitellia therefore plans a conspiracy and enlists the aid of Sextus, who agrees to help her. Then suddenly Vitellia discovers that Berenice has been sent back to Judaea, for Titus has changed his mind and is now planning to make a Roman marriage.

Sextus has a friend, Annius, who wishes to marry his sister, Servilia, and Annius begs Sextus to ask the emperor's permission for the marriage to take place. But Titus announces that he wishes to marry Servilia himself. With commendable honesty Servilia tells the emperor that she is already in love with Annius and the emperor thereupon decides to marry Vitellia instead. Vitellia, knowing nothing of all this, sends Sextus off to complete her planned rebellion: he is to set fire to the Capitol and murder Titus.

The moment Sextus has left, Vitellia learns that she is to marry Titus. Sextus completes the first part of the plan but someone wearing Titus's cloak is slaughtered instead. Confusion reigns. Titus now learns of the plot against him. Annius advises Sextus to beg for mercy from Titus, but Vitellia, frightened that her part in the plot may be discovered, begs Sextus instead to leave the country.

Publius, however, steps in to arrest Sextus before he can escape. He is tried by the Senate and condemned to death. Titus confronts Sextus with proof of his part in the plot, yet is willing to reprieve him, provided he reveals who is behind the conspiracy. But Sextus keeps his silence, and he and his conspirators are in danger of being thrown into the arena where the wild beasts wait. However, Vitellia is unable to bear her guilt a moment longer and confesses her part in the plot. The magnanimous Emperor Titus forgives them all.

It was a revelation, even to dedicated Mozartians, to find in the 1970s Covent Garden production that *La clemenza di Tito* had so much to offer. Sir Colin Davis's superb set, among the finest of his many Mozart recordings, sums up the achievement of that stage production and adds still more, for, above all, the performance of Dame Janet Baker in the key role of Vitellia has deepened and intensified. Not only is her singing formidably brilliant, with every roulade and exposed leap flawlessly attacked; she actually makes one believe in the emotional development of an impossible character, one who develops from villainy to virtue with the scantiest preparation. Whereas earlier Dame Janet found the evil hard to convey on stage, here the venom as well as the transformation are commandingly convincing. The two other mezzo-sopranos, Minton as Sesto and Von Stade in the small role of Annio, are superb too, while Stuart Burrows has rarely if ever sung so stylishly on a recording as here; he makes the forgiving emperor a rounded and sympathetic character, not just a bore. The recitatives add to the compulsion of the drama – here they are far more than mere formal links – while Davis's swaggering manner in the pageant music heightens the genuine feeling conveyed in much of the rest, transforming what used to be dismissed as a dry *opera seria*. Excellent recording, which gains in brightness and immediacy in its CD format. There is excellent internal access.

Following the pattern of his prize-winning recording of Mozart's other great *opera seria*, *Idomeneo*, Gardiner's recording was done live at performances in Queen Elizabeth Hall, London. Again, with his vitality and bite he turns the piece into a genuinely involving drama. One keeps marvelling how Mozart developed *opera seria* conventions, not how he was limited by them. Though the team of soloists is not quite so consistent as on Sir Colin Davis's 1977 recording, Anthony Rolfe Johnson is outstanding in the title-role, making the wise, forgiving emperor a rounded character in the mould of Idomeneo. Any blandness in the story is then dispelled by the vivid characterizations of both Anne Sofie von Otter as Sesto, the Roman nobleman who rebels, and of Julia Varady as Vitellia, who here becomes the equivalent of the violent Elettra in *Idomeneo*. Sylvia McNair is an enchanting, pure-toned Servilia, and Catherine Robbin a well-matched Annio, though the microphone catches an unevenness in the voice, as it does with Cornelius Hauptmann in the incidental role of Publio. More seriously, DG's vivid, immediate recording picks up a distracting amount of banging and thumping on stage in the Sussmayr recitatives, which with fair judgement are substantially pruned – more so than on the Davis version.

In his mid-eighties Karl Boehm at last managed to record *La clemenza di Tito*, and he gave the work warmth and charm, presenting the piece more genially than we have grown used to. The atmospheric recording helps in that, and the cast is first rate, with no weak link, matching at every point that of Sir Colin Davis on his Philips set. Yet, ultimately, even Julia Varady for Boehm can hardly rival Dame Janet Baker for Davis, crisper and lighter in her coloratura. Davis's incisiveness, too, has points of advantage; but, to summarize, any Mozartian can safely leave the preference to his feelings about the two conductors, the one more genial and glowing, the other more urgently dramatic.

Kertész attacks Mozart's last opera with fine dramatic directness, but over the span of this formal *opera seria* one cannot help missing a more individual interpretative hand. He seems to have no idea about the grammar of the *apoggiatura*, for the endings of phrases requiring them are regularly left blunt. The recitative too is taken ponderously and one longs to have more pace and contrast in the story-telling. But with very vivid recording and production, generally excellent singing – particularly from Teresa Berganza as Sesto – and strong playing, this might be considered, although Davis's version and Boehm's mellower DG set in the same price-range are far more persuasive.

Così fan tutte.
⓭ (M) *** EMI CMS7 69330-2 (3) [Ang. CDMC 69330]. Philh. Ch. & O, Boehm.
　　Fiordiligi (Elisabeth Schwarzkopf), Dorabella (Christa Ludwig), Despina (Hanny Steffek), Ferrando (Alfredo Kraus), Guglielmo (Giuseppe Taddei), Don Alfonso (Walter Berry).
*** Ph. Dig. 422 381-2; *422 381-4* (3) [id.]. Amb. Op. Ch., ASMF, Marriner.
　　Fiordiligi (Karita Mattila), Dorabella (Anne Sofie Von Otter), Despina (Elzbieta Szmytka), Ferrando (Francisco Araiza), Guglielmo (Thomas Allen), Don Alfonso (José Van Dam).
⓭ (M) (***) EMI mono CHS7 69635-2 (3) [Ang. CDHC 69635]. Philh. Ch. & O, Karajan.
　　Fiordiligi (Elisabeth Schwarzkopf), Dorabella (Nan Merriman), Despina (Lisa Otto), Ferrando (Léopold Simoneau), Guglielmo (Rolando Panerai), Don Alfonso (Sesto Bruscantini).
*** EMI Dig. CDS7 47727-8 (3) [Ang. CDCC 47727]. Glyndebourne Ch., LPO, Haitink.
　　Fiordiligi (Carol Vaness), Dorabella (Delores Ziegler), Despina (Lilian Watson), Ferrando (John Aler), Guglielmo (Dale Duesing), Don Alfonso (Claudio Desderi).
(M) *** Ph. 422 542-2 (3) [id.]. ROHCG Ch. & O, Sir Colin Davis.

Fiordiligi (Montserrat Caballé), Dorabella (Janet Baker), Despina (Ileana Cotrubas), Ferrando (Nicolai Gedda), Guglielmo (Wladimiro Ganzarolli), Don Alfonso (Richard Van Allan).

(M) *** Erato/Warner 2292 45683-2 (3) [id.]. Rhine Op. Ch., Strasbourg PO, Lombard.

Fiordiligi (Kiri Te Kanawa), Dorabella (Frederica Von Stade), Despina (Teresa Stratas), Ferrando (David Rendall), Guglielmo (Philippe Huttenlocher), Don Alfonso (Jules Bastin).

**(*) O-L Dig. 414 316-2 (3) [id.]. Drottningholm Court Theatre Ch. & O, Östman.

Fiordiligi (Rachel Yakar), Dorabella (Alicia Nafé), Despina (Georgine Resick), Ferrando (Gösta Winbergh), Guglielmo (Tom Krause), Don Alfonso (Carlos Feller).

Withdrawn: (M) **(*) EMI Dig. CMS7 69580-2 (3). V. State Op. Ch., VPO, Muti.

Fiordiligi (Margaret Marshall), Dorabella (Kathleen Battle), Despina (Agnes Baltsa), Ferrando (Francisco Araiza), Guglielmo (James Morris), Don Alfonso (José Van Dam).

**(*) DG Dig. 423 897-2 (3) [id.]. Concert Group of Vienna State Op., VPO, Levine.

Fiordiligi (Kiri Te Kanawa), Dorabella (Ann Murray), Despina (Marie McLaughlin), Ferrando (Hans-Peter Blochwitz), Guglielmo (Thomas Hampson), Don Alfonso (Ferruccio Furlanetto).

(M) **(*) Decca 417 185-2 (2) [id.]. V. State Op. Ch., VPO, Boehm.

Fiordiligi (Lisa Della Casa), Dorabella (Christa Ludwig), Despina (Emmy Loose), Ferrando (Anton Dermota), Guglielmo (Erich Kunz), Don Alfonso (Paul Schoeffler).

(M) **(*) DG 429 874-2 (2) [id.]. V. State Op. Ch., VPO, Boehm.

Fiordiligi (Gundula Janowitz), Dorabella (Brigitte Fassbaender), Despina (Reri Grist), Ferrando (Peter Schreier), Guglielmo (Hermann Prey), Don Alfonso (Rolando Panerai).

**(*) Teldec/Warner Dig. 9031 71381-2 [id.]. Netherlands Op. Ck., Concg. O, Harnoncourt.

Fiordiligi (Charlotte Margiono), Dorabella (Delores Ziegler), Despina (Anna Steiger), Ferrando (Deon Van der Walt), Guglielmo (Gilles Cachemaille), Don Alfonso (Thomas Hampson).

Withdrawn: (M) (***) EMI mono CHS7 63864-2 (2) [Ang. CDHB 63864]. Glyndebourne Festival Ch. & O, Fritz Busch.

Fiordiligi (Ina Souez), Dorabella (Luise Helletsgruber), Despina (Irene Eisinger), Ferrando (Heddle Nash), Guglielmo (Willi Domgraf-Fassbaender), Don Alfonso (John Brownlee).

(M) **(*) BMG/RCA GD 86677 (3) [6677-2-RG]. Amb. Op. Ch., New Philh. O, Leinsdorf.

Fiordiligi (Leontyne Price), Dorabella (Tatiana Troyanos), Despina (Judith Raskin), Ferrando (George Shirley), Guglielmo (Sherrill Milnes), Don Alfonso (Ezio Flagello).

Withdrawn: (M) **(*) EMI CMS7 63845-2 (3) [Ang. CDMC 63845]. Alldis Ch., New Philh. O, Klemperer.

Fiordiligi (Margaret Price), Dorabella (Yvonne Minton), Despina (Lucia Popp), Ferrando (Luigi Alva), Guglielmo (Geraint Evans), Don Alfonso (Hans Sotin).

(M) ** Decca 430 101-2 (3) [id.]. ROHCG Ch., LPO, Solti.

Fiordiligi (Pilar Lorengar), Dorabella (Teresa Berganza), Despina (Jane Berbié), Ferrando (Ryland Davies), Guglielmo (Tom Krause), Don Alfonso (Gabriel Bacquier).

(B) ** Naxos Dig. 8.660008/10 [id.]. Slovak Philharmonic Ch., Capella Istropolitana, Johannes Wildner.

Fiordiligi (Joanna Borowska), Dorabella (Rohangiz Yachmi), Despina (Priti Coles), Ferrando (John Dickie), Guglielmo (Andrea Martin), Don Alfonso (Peter Mikuláš).

*(*) Erato/Warner Dig. 2292 45475-2 (3) [id.]. Berlin RIAS Chamber Ch., BPO, Barenboim.

Fiordiligi (Lella Cuberli), Dorabella (Cecilia Bartoli), Despina (Joan Rodgers), Ferrando (Kurt Streit), Guglielmo (Ferruccio Furlanetto), Don Alfonso (John Tomlinson).

Mozart's *Così fan tutte*, first performed in Vienna in 1790, has had a chequered history. Initially it was thought somewhat too frivolous, while the Victorians considered it little short of immoral. Even the title, which might be translated as 'They all do it', was thought to be in singularly bad taste. In today's world the plot is quite unbelievable, but modern audiences usually enter willingly into the spirit of Don Alfonso's unlikely fidelity test, and simply enjoy the delightful music. When, at the opening of the piece, he questions the constancy of the fair sex, Ferrando and Guglielmo – officers and gentlemen both – express complete faith in their closely related brides-to-be, Dorabella and Fiordiligi respectively. They willingly agree to bet on their ladies' honour against whatever temptations Don Alfonso might care to put in their way.

We then meet the two sisters in the garden, gazing admiringly at the two miniature portraits they carry of their lovers. Don Alfonso arrives and tells them that the two officers have been ordered away to war, and in due course they depart after an affectionate farewell. In the background we hear Don Alfonso's cynical laughter. He now takes the maid, Despina, into both his confidence and his pay, and she discovers her mistresses moaning that they cannot exist without their lovers; they are so lonely. To fill the void, two Albanian noblemen – none other than Ferrando and Guglielmo heavily disguised – now enter. Don Alfonso 'recognizes' them as old friends and makes the appropriate introductions. But both ladies scorn their attentions and Fiordiligi asserts, in a famous aria, that she is as firm as a rock.

Alfonso and Despina plan the next move: both men, upon rejection, take poison and collapse. In the nick of time a doctor appears (Despina in disguise, speaking bogus Latin). She waves a large magnet – 'an invention of Doctor Mesmer' – over the two prone Albanians and they return to the world of the living, asking for kisses as further restoratives. Despina now schemes that Dorabella shall be aligned with the dark one, Guglielmo, and Fiordiligi with the fair one, Ferrando; so each chooses the other's previous bridegroom.

Soon Guglielmo is making considerable progress with Dorabella and he begs a keepsake (her miniature of Ferrando); in return he presents her with a heart-shaped locket. Ferrando meets with more opposition from Fiordiligi; she admits to fond feelings for him but declares her loyalty to her absent lover. When the two men subsequently meet, Ferrando learns that his Dorabella has weakened, and this is confirmed when he is shown the portrait of himself given to his comrade. Guglielmo is reassured by Fiordiligi's continuing resistance, but Ferrando is not amused by the turn of events.

Fiordiligi now determines that female honour must be saved and plans to follow their fiancés wearing the military uniforms they have left behind. But Ferrando returns to the attack and Fiordiligi at last yields to his amorous protestations. A nuptial party is planned and Don Alfonso announces the arrival of the notary (Despina in another disguise). But a chorus of soldiers heralds the return of the regiment, and the two 'Albanians' hastily resume their normal military attire. They immediately unmask the lawyer, Despina, and the ladies unhappily admit they were preparing for a wedding. The full details of the plot are now revealed, to the temporary discomfiture of almost everyone. But this is the world of opera and, with each pair of lovers reunited, the piece ends happily – especially for Don Alfonso, who wins his bet.

Così fan tutte has been lucky on records, but first choice remains with Boehm's classic EMI set on three mid-priced CDs, with its glorious solo singing, headed by the incomparable Fiordiligi of Schwarzkopf and the equally moving Dorabella of Christa Ludwig, a superb memento of Walter Legge's recording genius. With Boehm at his most genially perceptive, it still stands comparison with any other recordings, made before or since, though, in keeping with earlier practice, there are cuts in the recitative.

Marriner directs a fresh and resilient performance, beautifully paced, often with speeds on the fast side, and with the crystalline recorded sound adding to the sparkle. Though the women principals (Karita Mattila a warm Fiordiligi, Anne Sofie von Otter a characterful Dorabella and Elzbieta Szmytka a light, charming Despina) make a strong team, the men are even finer: Francisco Araiza as Ferrando, Thomas Allen as Guglielmo and José van Dam as Don Alfonso all outstanding. Individual as they are, they work together superbly to produce the crispest possible ensembles so that, though the reading is lighter in weight than those of Boehm, Karajan, Haitink or Davis, it has more fun in it, bringing out the laughter in the score. For those wanting a modern digital recording, this could well be a first choice; but the classic Boehm set and Karajan's sparkling mono version both remain indispensable.

Karajan has rarely made an opera recording more felicitous than his 1954 set of *Così fan tutte*. Commanding as Schwarzkopf is as Fiordiligi in the 1962 Boehm set, also with the Philharmonia, the extra ease and freshness of her singing in the earlier version makes it even more compelling. Nan Merriman is a distinctive and characterful Dorabella, and the role of Ferrando has never been more mellifluously sung on record than by Léopold Simoneau, ravishing in *Un aura amorosa*. The young Rolando Panerai is an ideal Guglielmo, and Lisa Otto a pert Despina; while Sesto Bruscantini in his prime brings to the role of Don Alfonso the wisdom and artistry which made him so compelling at Glyndebourne. Karajan has never sparkled more naturally in Mozart than here, for the high polish has nothing self-conscious about it. The little trio for Fiordiligi, Dorabella and Don Alfonso, *O soave sia il vento*, has never been more seductive. Though the mono recording is not as clear as some others of this period, the subtleties of the music-making are very well caught. In such a performance, one hardly worries that some recitative and one or two numbers are cut. An essential purchase for Mozartians as a supplement to the Boehm set.

With speeds often more measured than usual, Haitink's EMI version yet consistently conveys the geniality and sparkle of live performances at Glyndebourne. Haitink has rarely sounded quite so relaxed on record. As in his prize-winning version of *Don Giovanni*, similarly based on a Peter Hall production at Glyndebourne, the excellent teamwork, consistently conveying humour, makes up for a cast-list rather less starry than that on some rival versions. This is above all a sunny performance, sailing happily over any serious shoals beneath Da Ponte's comedy. Claudio Desderi as Don Alfonso more than anyone among the singers helps to establish that Glyndebourne atmosphere, with recitatives superbly timed and coloured. They are consistently made to sound as natural as ordinary conversation, with the variety of pace compensating for any tendency to slowness in the set numbers. If Carol Vaness and Delores Ziegler are rather too alike in timbre to be distinguished easily, the relationship becomes all the more sisterly when, quite apart from the similarity, they respond so pointfully to each other. John Aler makes a headily unstrained Ferrando, beautifully free in the upper register; and two Glyndebourne regulars, Lilian Watson and Dale Duesing, make up a strong team. The digital recording gives fine bloom and an impressive dynamic range to voices and orchestra alike.

Sir Colin Davis has rarely if ever made a more captivating record than his magical set of *Così fan tutte*. His energy and sparkle are here set against inspired and characterful singing from the three women soloists, with Montserrat Caballé and Janet Baker proving a winning partnership, each challenging and abetting the other all the time. Cotrubas equally is a vivid Despina, never merely arch. The men too make a strong team. Though Gedda has moments of rough tone, his account of *Un aura amorosa* is honeyed and delicate, and though Ganzarolli falls short in one of his prominent arias, it is a spirited, incisive performance, while Richard van Allan here naturally assumes the status of an international recording artist with flair and imagination. Sparkling recitative (complete) and recording which has you riveted by the play of the action. The transfer to CD has brought an even greater sense of presence and the set is generously cued.

Kiri Te Kanawa made her first, Erato recording of *Così* in 1977, more than a decade before her digital set with Levine. Her voice sounds radiant, rich and creamy of tone; she is commanding in *Come scoglio*, and tenderly affecting in *Per pietà*, which is more moving here than with Levine. Lombard is a sympathetic accompanist, if not always the most perceptive of Mozartians; some of his tempi are on the slow side, but his sextet of young singers makes up a team that rivals almost any other. Frederica von Stade's Dorabella is distinguished, with fine detail and imaginative phrasing, David Rendall is a fresh-toned tenor and the others, too, give firm, appealing performances. With warm recording of high quality, naturally transferred to CD, this is most enjoyable and could be a first choice for any who follow the singers in question.

Arnold Östman has established a formidable reputation conducting authentic performances of Mozart in the beautiful little court opera house at Drottningholm, near Stockholm. Except that soloists of international standing have been introduced – an aptly fresh-voiced team, stylishly Mozartian – this recording aims to reproduce one of the most successful of his productions. The point initially to marvel at is the hectic speed of almost every number. The wonder is that with light-toned period instruments and with singers sufficiently agile, the anticipated gabble does not take place, and Östman refreshingly establishes a valid new view. Few Mozartians would want to hear *Così fan tutte* like this all the time, but with no weak link in the cast and with the drama vividly presented it can be recommended to those who enjoy authentic performance and to all who are prepared to listen afresh. The sound is clear and immediate, and whatever the lack of charm and geniality, Östman's set remains compulsive listening throughout.

Muti's recording of *Così fan tutte* was planned and executed by EMI producers and engineers in an exceptionally short time, when in the summer of 1982 it was decided at a few days' notice to take advantage of the success of the Salzburg Festival production. It was possible to record only three of the live performances, and one of those had a different tenor. When Michael Hampe's production was elaborate, with plenty of stage movement, the job of the engineers was formidable, and in effect the third of three performances was the one which provided almost all the finished recording. The result is vivid, vigorous and often very beautiful. Ensemble is not always flawless, but this is far more polished than Boehm's eightieth-birthday performance, also recorded live (for DG) at the Kleines Festspielhaus. Muti's vigour is infectiously captured, and also his ability to relax into necessary tenderness. Though purists will prefer the extra precision of a studio performance, this EMI version gives an irresistible flavour of the theatre and the sparkle of Mozartian comedy, even if the sound is rough and lacks body. (This set is currently withdrawn.)

Levine's view of *Così fan tutte* is brisk and bright rather than charming or frothy. His conducting, rhythmically rather square, hardly rivals the very finest sets. Instead of sparkling, the score fizzes vigorously. There are vocal delights in the singing of Dame Kiri Te Kanawa in one of her finest Mozart performances on record; and there the conductor's taut discipline has inspired the singer to give one of the most dazzling accounts of *Come scoglio*, even if *Per pietà* lacks a full heartache. The recording was made over a concentrated period of ten days, adding to the cohesion of the whole, and with recitatives made more genial with a fortepiano instead of a harpsichord. Outstanding besides Dame Kiri is Thomas Hampson as Guglielmo, rich, firm and characterful. It is good to have his longer, more searching Act I aria included, with the usual one, *Non ti ritrasi*, given as an appendix on the same disc, so that it can be programmed instead. Hans-Peter Blochwitz is pallid by comparison but sings with heady beauty; Ferruccio Furlanetto is an urbane, rather fruity Don Alfonso, and Marie McLaughlin is a superb Despina, no mere soubrette but a strong character matching Don Alfonso. The main disappointment concerns Ann Murray's Dorabella, well characterized but with the voice straining uncomfortably above *mezzo forte*.

Boehm's 1955 Decca set is not as polished a performance as the later one for EMI, and the persistent cutting of brief passages from the ends of arias is irritating, but it remains a thoroughly likeable and convincing account of the frothiest of Mozart's comedies and has a strong vocal cast. Lisa della Casa is less characterful than Schwarzkopf but is strong and sweet-toned, and the rest are often sparklingly good. Paul Schoeffler was nearing the end of his career when the recording was made, but in the role of Don Alfonso his singing is most appealing. This was one of Decca's earliest stereo experiments, and there is little attempt at stage production, but the result is still surprisingly vivid and atmospheric.

Boehm's third recording makes a delightful memento and, offered on a pair of mid-priced CDs, it is worth considering, despite its obvious flaws. It was recorded live during the Salzburg Festival performance on the conductor's eightieth birthday, and though the zest and sparkle of the occasion come over delightfully, with as splendid a cast as you could gather, the ensemble is not ideally crisp for repeated listening. The balance favours the voices, with stage noises made the more prominent on CD.

As in his other Mozart opera recordings, Harnoncourt, the period-performance specialist, here favours an orchestra of modern instruments, while adopting aspects of period-style. His is a quirkily magnetic reading, with speeds eccentric in both directions, slow as well as fast. Though even the lovely terzetto *O soave sia il vento* is raced along, Fiordiligi's great Act II aria, *Per pietà*, is taken impossibly slowly. Even so, Charlotte Margiono sustains the line immaculately, and she is similarly accommodating over another of Harnoncourt's eccentricities, making the emphatic opening of Fiordiligi's other big aria, *Come scoglio*, into a hushed meditation. With Deon van der Walt sweetly caught as Ferrando and Delores Ziegler an outstanding Dorabella (as she is in Haitink's EMI set), the casting has no weak link, though this remains a performance to hear once rather than repeatedly.

Available during the LP era for only a very brief period as an import from France, this legendary Glyndebourne performance, the first ever recording of *Così fan tutte*, is the finest of the three pioneering sets recorded on 78s in the mid-1930s with the newly founded Glyndebourne company. The sound in the CD transfer, though limited, is amazingly vivid, with voices very well focused and with a keener sense of presence than on many recordings of the 1990s. Busch at the time was a progressive Mozartian, preferring athletic treatment – occasionally to excess, as in the concluding ensemble of Act I – but this is as effervescent as any more recent recording, and nowadays even the use of a piano for the recitatives instead of a harpsichord seems less outlandish with the emergence of the fortepiano. John Brownlee as Don Alfonso is very much the English aristocrat, with 'fruffly-fruffly' English vowels instead of Italianate ones, but he is a fine, stylish singer. Ina Souez and Luise Helletsgruber as the two sisters outshine all but the very finest of their successors on record, technically superb; and Heddle Nash and Willi Domgraf-Fassbaender as their lovers are at once stylish and characterful, with Irene Eisinger a delightfully soubrettish Despina. Cuts are made in the recitatives according to the custom of the time and, more seriously, four numbers disappear – including, amazingly, Ferrando's *Tradito, schernito* and Dorabella's *E amore un ladroncello*. The bonus is that, with those cuts, the opera fits on to only two mid-price CDs.

On the RCA set, Leinsdorf is not an elegant Mozartian, but he was at his most relaxed in his 1967 recording of *Così fan tutte*, using a sextet of some of the finest American singers of the time. With Leontyne Price scaling her voice down well as Fiordiligi, with fine playing from the Philharmonia and with recording full of presence, it is a viable mid-price version, even though it can hardly match – except in its more complete text – its direct EMI rivals from Karajan and Boehm.

Klemperer's last opera set was predictably idiosyncratic. When the record company jibbed at his suggestion of recording this sparkling comedy, he is alleged to have protested (aged eighty-six at the time), 'What do you want? A posthumous interpretation?' The result proved by no means as funereal as had been predicted, with fine rhythmic pointing to lighten the slow tempi. There is fine singing too from the whole cast (Alva alone at times disappointing) to make the whole a satisfying entertainment, a different view of Mozart to be heard at least once. It is a pity the recitatives are not more imaginatively done. An excellent transfer to CD, but this has been withdrawn as we go to press.

Solti's set will please those who want high voltage at all costs even in this most genial of all Mozart comedies. There is little relaxation and little charm, which underlines the shortcomings of the singing cast, notably of Pilar Lorengar, whose grainy voice is not treated kindly by the microphone and who here in places conveys uncertainty. It is a pity that the crackling wit of Solti's Covent Garden performances was not more magically captured on record. Brilliant recording.

On three budget-price CDs (each costing slightly more than this super-bargain label's orchestral and instrumental repertory) the Naxos version comes out at a price comparable to the Glyndebourne two-disc set, yet provides a text without the omissions of the latter, and the modern digital recording is fresh and bright. But with the exception of Joanna Borowska as a strong, stylish Fiordiligi, the Czech cast is in a different league. After Borowska, Peter Mikuláš is the most successful of the soloists, a forthright, clean-toned Don Alfonso. John Dickie, as recorded, sounds rather too throaty as Ferrando and Rohangiz Yachmi as Dorabella has too fruity a vibrato for Mozart. After a gabbled overture, Wildner directs a well-played, generally well-paced performance. It is worth remembering that for the price of these discs one would be well pleased to come across such a performance in the opera house, be it in Bratislava or elsewhere.

Barenboim has a first-rate cast – with Joan Rodgers as Despina making a very welcome recording début in a major operatic role – but some are well below their best. Ferruccio Furlanetto is miscast as Guglielmo, sounding far too venerable, and even Lella Cuberli, a fine Fiordiligi, has her powerful, agile singing in the big test of *Come scoglio* seriously undermined by limp accompaniment. Generally the Berlin Philharmonic sounds too thick and heavy, lacking resilience. The playing sounds breathless and unsprung when Barenboim, in his erratic choice of speeds, opts to take a number fast. Dull recording does not help.

Così fan tutte: highlights.
(M) (***) EMI mono CD-EMX 2211; *TC-EMX 2211* (from above recording with Schwarzkopf, Merriman, Otto; cond. Karajan).
(M) **(*) DG Dig. 431 290-2; *431 290-4* [id.] (from above recording with Te Kanawa, Murray, McLaughlin; cond. Levine).
**(*) Teldec/Warner Dig. 9031 76455-2 [id.] (from above recording with Margiono, Ziegler, Steiger; cond. Harnoncourt).
(M) ** DG 429 824-2 [id.] (from above recording with Janowitz, Fassbaender, Grist; cond. Boehm).

The selection from Karajan's sparkling 1954 set, with many jewelled items, will readily suit those who have a stereo version of the complete opera. At 73 minutes, the selection is even more generous.

A generous selection (75 minutes) from Levine's brisk, rather unsmiling *Così*, especially useful for sampling Dame Kiri's Fiordiligi, one of her finest Mozartian performances on record, and Thomas Hampson's characterfully rich portrayal of Guglielmo. Marie McLaughlin is a splendid Despina, so there is much to enjoy here, although Ann Murray's Dorabella is a disappointment.

Many may enjoy the highlights from Harnoncourt's characterful but somewhat eccentric version, rather than the complete set. The selection includes the controversially fast *O soave si il vento*, Fiordiligi's *Come scoglio* and *Per Pietà* within a generally comprehensive and well-selected 74-minute sampler. However, this would have been even more enticing at mid-price.

Although an hour's playing time is indicated on the back liner-leaflet, this selection from Boehm's live 1974 Salzburg Festival recording (his third) runs to over 72 minutes, and the sparkle of the occasion is well conveyed. This is a good way of approaching a set where ensemble is at times less than perfect, but which offers a splendid cast and some fine individual contributions. Unusually for DG, however, the documentation is wholly inadequate.

Don Giovanni (complete).
*** EMI CDS7 47260-8 (3) [Ang. CDCC 47260]. Philh. Ch. & O, Giulini.
Don Giovanni (Eberhard Waechter), Donna Anna (Joan Sutherland), Donna Elvira

(Elisabeth Schwarzkopf), Zerlina (Graziella Sciutti), Don Ottavio (Luigi Alva), Leporello (Giuseppe Taddei), Masetto (Piero Cappuccilli), Commendatore (Gottlob Frick).

(M) *** Decca 411 626-2 (3). V. State Op. Ch., VPO, Krips.

Don Giovanni (Cesare Siepi), Donna Anna (Suzanne Danco), Donna Elvira (Lisa Della Casa), Zerlina (Hilde Gueden), Don Ottavio (Anton Dermota), Leporello (Fernando Corena), Masetto (Walter Berry), Commendatore (Kurt Boehme).

*** EMI Dig. CDS7 47037-8 (3) [Ang. CDCC 47036]. Glyndebourne Ch., LPO, Haitink.

Don Giovanni (Thomas Allen), Donna Anna (Carol Vaness), Donna Elvira (Maria Ewing), Zerlina (Elizabeth Gale), Don Ottavio (Keith Lewis), Leporello (Richard Van Allan), Masetto (John Rawnsley), Commendatore (Dimitri Kavrakos).

*** EMI Dig. CDS7 54255-2 (3) [Ang. CDCC 54255]. V. State Op. Konzertvereinigung, VPO, Muti.

Don Giovanni (William Shimell), Donna Anna (Cheryl Studer), Donna Elvira (Carol Vaness), Zerlina (Susanne Mentzer), Don Ottavio (Frank Lopardo), Leporello (Samuel Ramey), Masetto (Natale De Carolis), Commendatore (Jan-Hendrik Rootering).

*** DG Dig. 419 179-2 (3) [id.]. German Op. Ch., Berlin, BPO, Karajan.

Don Giovanni (Samuel Ramey), Donna Anna (Anna Tomowa-Sintow), Donna Elvira (Agnes Baltsa), Zerlina (Kathleen Battle), Don Ottavio (Gösta Winbergh), Leporello (Ferruccio Furlanetto), Masetto (Alexander Malta), Commendatore (Paata Burchuladze).

(M) *** Ph. 422 541-2 (3) [id.]. ROHCG Ch. & O, Sir Colin Davis.

Don Giovanni (Ingvar Wixell), Donna Anna (Martina Arroyo), Donna Elvira (Kiri Te Kanawa), Zerlina (Mirella Freni), Don Ottavio (Stuart Burrows), Leporello (Wladimiro Ganzarolli), Masetto (Richard Van Allan), Commendatore (Luigi Roni).

(M) (***) EMI mono CHS7 63860-2 (3) [Ang. CDHB 63860]. V. State Op. Ch., VPO, Furtwängler.

Don Giovanni (Cesare Siepi), Donna Anna (Elisabeth Grümmer), Donna Elvira (Elisabeth Schwarzkopf), Zerlina (Erna Berger), Don Ottavio (Anton Dermota), Leporello (Otto Edelmann), Masetto (Walter Berry), Commendatore (Deszö Ernster).

**(*) Ph. Dig. 432 129-2 (3); *432 129-4* (2) [id.]. Amb. O Ch., ASMF, Marriner.

Don Giovanni (Thomas Allen), Donna Anna (Sharon Sweet), Donna Elvira (Karita Mattila), Zerlina (Marie McLaughlin), Don Ottavio (Francisco Araiza), Leporello (Simone Alaimo), Masetto (Claudio Otelli), Commendatore (Robert Lloyd).

(M) **(*) Sony M3K 35192 (3) [id.]. Paris Op. Ch. & O, Maazel.

Don Giovanni (Ruggero Raimondi), Donna Anna (Edda Moser), Donna Elvira (Kiri Te Kanawa), Zerlina (Teresa Berganza), Don Ottavio (Kenneth Riegel), Leporello (José Van Dam), Masetto (Malcolm King), Commendatore (John Macurdy).

Withdrawn: (M) **(*) DG 413 282-4 (2) [id.]. V. State Op. Ch., VPO, Boehm.

Don Giovanni (Sherrill Milnes), Donna Anna (Anna Tomowa-Sintow), Donna Elvira (Teresa Zylis-Gara), Zerlina (Edith Mathis), Don Ottavio (Peter Schreier), Leporello (Walter Berry), Commendatore (Dale Duesing).

Withdrawn: (M) **(*) EMI CMS7 63841-2 (3) [Ang. CDMC 63841] New Philh. O & Ch., Klemperer.

Don Giovanni (Nicolai Ghiaurov), Donna Anna (Claire Watson), Donna Elvira (Christa Ludwig), Zerlina (Mirella Freni), Don Ottavio (Nicolai Gedda), Leporello (Walter Berry), Masetto (Paolo Montarsolo), Commendatore (Franz Crass).

**(*) O-L Dig. 425 943-2 (3) [id.]. Drottningholm Court Theatre Ch. & O, Östman.

Don Giovanni (Håkan Hagegård), Donna Anna (Arleen Augér), Donna Elvira (Della Jones), Zerlina (Barbara Bonney), Don Ottavio (Nico Van der Meel), Leporello (Gilles Cachemaille), Masetto (Bryn Terfel), Commendatore (Kristin Sigmundsson).

(M) **(*) DG 437 341-2 (3) [id.]. Berlin RIAS Chamber Ch & RO, Fricsay.

Don Giovanni (Dietrich Fischer-Dieskau), Donna Anna (Sena Jurinac), Donna Elvira (Maria Stader), Zerlina (Irmgard Seefried), Don Ottavio (Ernst Haefliger), Leporello (Karl Christian Kohn), Masetto (Ivan Sardi), Commendatore (Walter Kreppel).

(M) (***) EMI mono CHS7 61030-2 (3). Glyndebourne Festival Ch. & O, Fritz Busch.

Don Giovanni (John Brownlee), Donna Anna (Ina Souez), Donna Elvira (Luise Helletsgruber), Zerlina (Audrey Mildmay), Don Ottavio (Koloman Von Pataky), Leporello (Salvatore Baccaloni), Masetto (Roy Henderson), Commendatore (David Franklin).

(M) ** DG 429 870-2 (3) [id.]. Prague Nat. Theatre Ch. & O, Boehm.

Don Giovanni (Dietrich Fischer-Dieskau), Donna Anna (Birgit Nilsson), Donna Elvira

(Martina Arroyo), Zerlina (Reri Grist), Don Ottavio (Peter Schreier), Leporello (Ezio Flagello), Masetto (Alfredo Mariotti), Commendatore (Martti Talvela).

(M) ** Decca 425 169-2 (3) [id.]. London Op. Ch., LPO, Solti.

Don Giovanni (Bernd Weikl), Donna Anna (Margaret Price), Donna Elvira (Sylvia Sass), Zerlina (Lucia Popp), Don Ottavio (Stuart Burrows), Leporello (Gabriel Bacquier), Masetto (Alfred Sramek), Commendatore (Kurt Moll).

*(*) Teldec/Warner Dig. 2292 44184-2; *2292 44184-4* (3) [id.]. Netherlands Op. Ch., Concg. O, Harnoncourt.

Don Giovanni (Thomas Hampson), Donna Anna (Edita Gruberová), Donna Elvira (Roberta Alexander), Zerlina (Barbara Bonney), Don Ottavio (Hans-Peter Blochwitz), Leporello (László Polgár), Masetto (Anton Scharinger), Commendatore (Robert Holl).

Withdrawn: (M) *(*) EMI CMS7 63976-2 (3) [Ang. CDMC 63976]. Scottish Op. Ch., ECO, Barenboim.

Don Giovanni (Roger Soyer), Donna Anna (Antigone Sgourda), Donna Elvira (Heather Harper), Zerlina (Helen Donath), Don Ottavio (Luigi Alva), Leporello (Geraint Evans), Masetto (Alberto Rinaldi), Commendatore (Peter Lagger).

Lorenzo da Ponte described his libretto for *Don Giovanni*, as a '*dramma giocoso*'. Mozart's masterly setting, first heard in Prague in 1787, has extraordinary validity for today's audiences. The balance between the moral and jocular aspects of this Don Juan narrative is finely drawn, yet the Don remains a heroic figure – at the close of the opera he descends to hell with courageous dignity and maintains his defiance of popular morality to the end. The opera opens in a spirit of high drama. Leporello is found waiting outside Donna Anna's house. His master is within in the very act of seduction. But suddenly he appears, masked, with Donna Anna in hot pursuit, desperately trying to identify her seducer. Her father, the Commendatore, follows and furiously insists on a duel, in which he is however killed. Don Giovanni and Leporello escape.

Donna Anna turns to Don Ottavio, her betrothed, and makes him swear vengeance on the unknown masked intruder. We follow Leporello and the Don and he is already approaching another possible conquest, but he recognizes her as Donna Elvira, a previous mistress whom he had deserted. He manages to slip away, leaving Leporello to list his famous catalogue of his master's countless previous liaisons.

In a nearby village Masetto and Zerlina are to be married. Don Giovanni arrives, Leporello is instructed to entice Masetto away, and this leaves the Don free to charm Zerlina; but fortunately Donna Elvira arrives in time to warn her of her danger. Donna Anna now enters with Don Ottavio and Donna Elvira re-states her warning; Don Giovanni's denial of her accusations comes to naught when Donna Anna recognizes the voice of her masked seducer and she passionately urges Don Ottavio to take revenge.

We move to the Don's residence, where a party is to be held. Masetto and Zerlina are invited, and the masked figures of Donna Anna, Donna Elvira and Don Ottavio come too. While Leporello is attempting to decoy Masetto, the Don is busy trying to rape Zerlina. She calls for assistance and the Don is confronted by the masked trio. Ever resourceful, drawing his sword he escapes.

He now attempts the seduction of Donna Elvira's maid. Once more he courts then betrays Donna Elvira, sending her off with Leporello, effectively disguised in the Don's cloak. Left alone, he serenades the maid but Masetto appears with a group of peasant supporters, after his blood. But the Don is wearing Leporello's cloak and they mistake him for his own servant. He sends Masetto's supporters off with directions on where to search, then thrashes Masetto. Zerlina arrives in time to comfort her wounded lover. Donna Anna and Don Ottavio now come upon Donna Elvira and Leporello, who have lost their way in the darkness; Zerlina and Masetto also join the group, and Leporello removes his disguise in order to extricate himself. Don Ottavio comforts the others, who are again thwarted.

Don Giovanni and Leporello are now reunited in the cemetery and there discover a statue of the murdered Commendatore, whom the Don jokingly invites to supper. The statue first nods then voices his acceptance, and Leporello is terrified. We again meet briefly Donna Anna and Don Ottavio, who again declares his feelings; she apologizes for continuing to delay her marriage to him. In the final scene, Don Giovanni is discovered enjoying his supper. Donna Elvira enters and makes one last entreaty to her ex-lover, then turns and screams: the statue has arrived. The Commendatore knocks to demand entry and is welcomed by Don Giovanni. He demands repentance but to no avail, and he drags the Don down to hell.

Thus the various couples are left to replan their future lives. Donna Elvira will enter a convent; Donna Anna will, a year hence, marry Don Ottavio; Zerlina and Masetto think of earthly pleasures; Leporello will seek a new master. All join to ponder on the implications of the fate of the unrepentant lover of all women.

The return of the classic Giulini EMI set, lovingly remastered to bring out even more vividly the excellence of Walter Legge's original sound-balance, sets the standard by which all other recordings have come to be judged. Not only is the singing cast more consistent than any other; the direction of Giulini and the playing of the vintage Philharmonia Orchestra give this performance an athletic vigour which carries all before it. The whole production owes so much to the work of Walter Legge, uncredited in the original issue but the prime mover behind this and so many other Philharmonia issues.

Legge's wife, Elisabeth Schwarzkopf, as Elvira, emerges as a dominant figure to give a distinctive but totally apt slant to this endlessly invigorating drama. No wilting sufferer she, but the most formidable of women, who flies at the Don with such cries as *Perfido mostro!* unforgettably sung. The young Sutherland may be relatively reticent as Anna but, with such technical ease and consistent beauty of tone, she makes a superb foil. Taddei is a delightful Leporello, and each member of the cast – including the young Cappuccilli as Masetto – combines fine singing with keen dramatic sense. Recitatives are scintillating, and only the occasional exaggerated snarl from the Don of Eberhard Waechter mars the superb vocal standards. Even that goes well with his fresh and youthful portrait of the central character.

Krips's recording, from the very earliest days of stereo, of this most challenging opera has kept its place as a mid-priced version which is consistently satisfying, with a cast of all-round quality headed by the dark-toned Don of Cesare Siepi. The women are not ideal, but they form an excellent team, never overfaced by the music, generally characterful, and with timbres well contrasted. To balance Siepi's darkness, the Leporello of Corena is even more saturnine, and their dramatic teamwork is brought to a superb climax in the final scene – quite the finest and most spine-tingling performance of that scene ever recorded. The 1955 recording – genuine stereo – still sounds remarkably well. As usual with Decca, the CDs reveal how good it was, now with added definition and presence.

Haitink's set superbly captures the flavour of Sir Peter Hall's memorable production at Glyndebourne, not least in the inspired teamwork. The only major change from the production on stage is that Maria Ewing comes in as Elvira, vibrant and characterful, not ideally pure-toned but contrasting characterfully with the powerful Donna Anna of Carol Vaness and the innocent-sounding Zerlina of Elizabeth Gale. Keith Lewis is a sweet-toned Ottavio, but it is Thomas Allen as Giovanni who – apart from Haitink – dominates the set, a swaggering Don full of charm and with a touch of nobility when, defiant to the end, he is dragged to hell – a spine-chilling moment as recorded here. Rarely has the Champagne aria been so beautifully sung, with each note articulated – and that also reflects Haitink's flawless control of pacing, not always conventional but always thoughtful and convincing. Excellent playing from the LPO – well practised in the Glyndebourne pit – and warm, full recording, far more agreeable than the dry sound in the old auditorium at Glyndebourne.

Muti's EMI version is a strong contender, based as it is on the performances he has conducted at Salzburg, though with important changes of casting. It is on a bigger scale than such immediate rivals as Marriner's Philips set or Haitink's EMI, but is refreshingly alert, using a fortepiano continuo. Shimell makes a rather gruff Don, not as insinuatingly persuasive as he might be, and like the others he is not helped by the distancing of voices. With Samuel Ramey, Karajan's chosen Don for his DG recording, convincingly translated here to the role of Leporello, and Cheryl Studer an outstanding Donna Anna, the rest of the casting is strong and satisfying.

With the presence of all the singers demanded at all sessions – something unheard-of elsewhere in the recording world – Karajan achieved an unusually spontaneous result, by deciding only at the very last minute on each day just which passages he would record. Though ensemble was at times imperilled by that free-and-easy approach, and the final scene of Giovanni's descent into hell goes off the boil a little, the end result has fitting intensity and power, with a cast of eight highly distinctive principals. This is a performance of extremes, not as smooth as much of Karajan's earlier Mozart. Though the very opening is extraordinarily slow and massive, the rest of the performance is just as remarkable for fast, exhilarating speeds as for slow.

Though in the pacing of recitatives Karajan was plainly thinking of a big auditorium, having Jeffrey Tate as continuo player helps to keep them moving and to bring out word-meaning. The starry line-up of soloists is a distinctive one, with all four bass-baritone roles taken by singers who have played Giovanni himself. Samuel Ramey is the one chosen for the title-role, a noble rather than a menacing Giovanni, consistently clear and firm. Ferruccio Furlanetto's beautiful timbre as Leporello may not be contrasted quite enough, but both his style of singing – with sing-speech allowed into recitative – and his extrovert acting provide the necessary variation. The dark, firm bass of Paata Burchuladze as the Commendatore is thrillingly incisive, and Alexander Malta makes a bluff, mature Masetto, sharply contrasted with the fresh, sweet and innocently provocative Zerlina of Kathleen Battle.

Anna Tomowa-Sintow has rarely if ever sung so animatedly on record as here in the role of Donna Anna, with *Or sai chi l'onore* showing her as a fire-eating obsessive, even while the tone remains beautiful. She is well matched by the virile Ottavio of Gösta Winbergh, unusually positive for a character who can seem limp. Most individual of all is the Donna Elvira of Agnes Baltsa. The venom and bite of her mezzo timbre go with a touch of vulnerability, so that even when – as in *Mi tradi* – ensemble falls apart, the result is memorable. Recording and editing are erratic, but the result is full and vivid.

The final test of a recording of this most searching of operas is whether it adds up to more than the sum of its parts. Sir Colin Davis's certainly does, with a very strong singing cast. Martina Arroyo controls her massive dramatic voice more completely than one would think possible, and she is strongly and imaginatively contrasted with the sweetly expressive Elvira of Kiri Te Kanawa and the sparkling Zerlina of Freni. As in the Davis *Figaro*, Ingvar Wixell and Wladimiro Ganzarolli make a formidable master/servant team with excellent vocal acting, while Stuart Burrows sings gloriously as Don Ottavio, and Richard Van Allan is a characterful Masetto. Davis draws a fresh and immediate performance from his team, riveting from beginning to end, and the recording, now better defined and more vivid than before, is still refined in the recognizable Philips manner.

The historic Furtwängler performance was recorded live by Austrian Radio at the 1954 Salzburg Festival, barely three months before the conductor's death. Far from taking a weightily Germanic view, he consistently brings out the sparkle in this '*dramma giocoso*', to use da Ponte's term on the title-page. Though speeds are often slow by today's standards, his springing of rhythm never lets them sag. Even the very slow speed for Leporello's catalogue aria is made to seem charmingly individual. With the exception of a wobbly Commendatore, this is a classic Salzburg cast, with Cesare Siepi a fine, incisive Don, dark in tone, Elisabeth Schwarzkopf a dominant Elvira, Elisabeth Grümmer a vulnerable Anna, Anton Dermota a heady-toned Ottavio and Otto Edelmann a clear and direct Leporello. Stage noises often suggest herds of animals lumbering about, but both voices and orchestra are satisfyingly full-bodied in the CD transfer, and the sense of presence is astonishing.

Marriner has the benefit of outstandingly fine recorded sound, full and well balanced. His direction is well paced and resilient, with far keener feeling for dramatic pacing than his earlier recording of *Figaro*. Vocally the star is Thomas Allen as the Don, even more assured than he was for Haitink in his EMI Glyndebourne version. The others make a strong team, with Simone Alaimo an attractive, young-sounding Leporello, though Sharon Sweet is occasionally raw-toned as Donna Anna.

Whatever the inhibitions and influences of preparing his CBS recording as a soundtrack for the Losey film of *Don Giovanni*, Lorin Maazel directs a strong and urgent performance, generally very well sung. An obvious strength is the line-up of three unusually firm-toned basses: José van Dam a saturnine Leporello, not comic but with much finely detailed expression; Malcolm King a darkly intense Masetto, and Ruggero Raimondi a heroic Giovanni, not always attacking notes cleanly but on balance one of the very finest on record in this role. Among the women, Kiri Te Kanawa is outstanding, a radiant Elvira; Teresa Berganza as a mezzo Zerlina generally copes well with the high tessitura; and though Edda Moser starts with some fearsome squawks at her first entry, the dramatic scale is certainly impressive and she rises to the challenge of the big arias. Unfortunately the recording, made in a Paris church, has the voices close against background reverberation and this is something the remastering for CD has not been able substantially to alter.

Recorded in 1977 at a sequence of live performances in the Kleines Festspielhaus at Salzburg, Karl Boehm's second recording of this opera has an engaging vigour. The tempi are sometimes on the slow side, but the concentration is unfailing, and the whole reading centres round an assumption of the role of the Don which is richly heroic and far more sympathetic in characterization than is common. Sherrill Milnes sings with a richness and commitment which match his swaggering stage presence. Anna Tomowa-Sintow as Donna Anna is generally creamy-toned, only occasionally betraying a flutter, while Teresa Zylis-Gara as Elvira controls her warm voice with delicacy. These are stylish performances without being deeply memorable. Edith Mathis sings with her usual intelligence, but the tone is not always perfectly focused. Firm, reliable performances from the men. Unlike Boehm's Salzburg *Così fan tutte*, where the ensembles were distractingly ragged, this live *Giovanni* presents a strong and consistently enjoyable experience distinct from that on any other set. The recording – favouring the voices but amazingly good under the conditions – is especially vivid in the culminating scene. This set has one savouring the unique flavour of Mozart opera in Salzburg with remarkable realism and with few distractions.

The lumbering tempo of Leporello's opening music will alert the listener to the predictable Klemperer approach and at that point some may dismiss his performance as 'too heavy' – but the issue is far more complex than that. Most of the slow tempi which Klemperer regularly adopts, far from flagging, add a welcome breadth to the music, for they must be set against the unusually brisk and dramatic interpretation of the recitatives between numbers. Added to that, Ghiaurov as the Don and Berry as Leporello make a marvellously characterful pair. In this version, the male members of the cast are dominant and, with Klemperer's help, they make the dramatic experience a strongly masculine one. Nor is the ironic humour forgotten with Berry and Ghiaurov about, and the Klemperer spaciousness allows them extra time for pointing. Among the women, Ludwig is a strong and convincing Elvira, Freni a sweet-toned but rather unsmiling Zerlina; only Claire Watson seriously disappoints, with obvious nervousness marring the big climax of *Non mi dir*. It is a serious blemish but, with the usual reservations, for those not allergic to the Klemperer approach, this stands as a good recommendation – at the very least a commanding experience. However this set has been withdrawn as we go to press.

Östman follows up his earlier recordings of *Così fan tutte* and *Le nozze di Figaro* with this period performance of *Don Giovanni*. This time, with a far darker score, he has modified his stance. Though speeds are still often fast, this time they rarely seem breathless. The tough sound of period instruments sharpens the drama, even if scrawny violins are at times a trouble. Exceptionally, some speeds are unusually slow – as for example the rustic ensembles – but rhythms are well sprung and the intimate scale of a Drottningholm production is well caught. Håkan Hagegård as Giovanni could be sweeter-toned, but his lightness and spontaneity, particularly in exchanges with the vividly alive Leporello of Gilles Cachemaille, are most winning, with recitative often barely vocalized. Arleen Augér is a radiant Donna Anna, while two Welsh singers also make fine contributions: Della Jones a full-toned Elvira and Bryn Terfel a resonant Masetto. Understandably, the original Prague text is used, which means that each of the two Acts can be fitted complete on to a single disc, an obvious advantage. Such essential additions as Ottavio's *Dalla sua pace* (beautifully sung by Nico van der Meel) and Elvira's *Mi tradi* are given in an appendix on the third disc.

As he has shown in his recording of *Die Zauberflöte*, Fricsay is a forceful, dramatic Mozart conductor. This might suggest that *Don Giovanni* is exactly the Mozart opera best suited to his talents. In fact, though there is fine crispness throughout and the ensembles are superb, the absence of charm is serious. This is mainly felt in some ridiculously fast speeds. Zerlina, Masetto and their rustic friends are hustled unmercifully along in 6/8, and poor Zerlina has an even worse time when it comes to her aria, *Batti batti*. Seefried being the superb artist she is, her charm comes through, but how much more charming it would be if she were allowed more time to breathe. The cast is generally strong, but unfortunately there is a serious blot in the Donna Elvira of Maria Stader. She is made to sound shrill and some of her attempts to get round the trickier florid passages leave a good deal to be desired. Yet most of the singing is most stylish. Haefliger shows himself as one of the finest Mozart tenors of the time, Karl Christian Kohn is a fine, incisive Leporello, Ivan Sardi an exceptionally rich-voiced Masetto, and Seefried a truly enchanting Zerlina.

As so often on records, Jurinac is not quite as thrilling here as one remembers her in the flesh; the timbre of the voice is harder – but what wonderful singing this is nonetheless. Fischer-Dieskau is a particularly interesting choice of Don, his characterization proving powerful and forwardly projected: there is no suspicion of his singing being mannered, even if at the beginning of *Là ci darem* his tone is not as pure as it normally is. Yet with all these plus points, the set does not quite add up to the sum of its parts, even though there is much to enjoy. The 1958 recording was made in the Berlin Jesus Christus-Kirche and so the stereo is remarkably atmospheric, although Zerlina's scream at the end of Act I is decidedly disappointing (not Seefried's fault either) and that because it is too loud rather than too soft.

Those whose memories stretch back to the age of short-playing 78-r.p.m. records will remember the almost mystical quality surrounding the first ever Mozart opera recordings, made for EMI's Society Edition, of the three Da Ponte operas. In those days such opera sets were not only very expensive but mightily inconvenient to play, for this very first complete recording of *Don Giovanni* stretched originally to no fewer than 23 records! The wonder is that it has stood the test of time so well; and one can understand that there are those who still count it the finest version of all. Certainly the process of recording in short, four-minute takes has not at all affected the concentration of the whole performance, with Fritz Busch an inspired Mozartian, pointing the music with a freshness and absence of nineteenth-century heaviness rare at the time.

It will come as a shock to the modern listener to find that a piano is used for the *secco* recitatives, and that the chords are played very baldly and without elaboration; but the interplay of characters in those exchanges has never been caught more infectiously on disc. We have to remember that this recording, like the companion ones of *Così fan tutte* and *Figaro* (with recitatives cut), was made in the opera house at the end of the Glyndebourne season, when these same singers had been rehearsing and performing this music under the producer, Carl Ebert, as well as under Busch, with an intensity that has rarely been matched for a recording, before or since. Nor is there any hint of staleness, for this recording was a great adventure, as comes out clearly from first to last.

The cast is a strong one, with singers consistently fresh, firm and well focused in the best manner of the time, technically immaculate in almost everything. John Brownlee as Giovanni may have a rather British-stiff-upper-lip Italian accent (noticeable for the most part in the recitatives), but it is a noble performance, beautifully sung, and he is brilliantly set against the lively, idiomatically Italian Leporello of Salvatore Baccaloni. The three ladies are both contrasted and well matched, with Mrs John Christie, Audrey Mildmay, as Zerlina a delightful foil for the excellent, if otherwise little-known, Ina Souez and Luise Helletsgruber. Koloman von Pataky uses his light, heady tenor well as Ottavio, and the British stalwarts, David Franklin (later to become well known as a broadcaster) and Roy Henderson, are both first rate as the Commendatore and Masetto respectively. Altogether the set is a delight, and Keith Hardwick's digital transfers are astonishingly vivid, with very little background noise, bringing the singers right into your presence with a realism that is all too rare even in modern recordings. It adds to the pleasures of using the CDs that they have such copious cueing.

The Boehm set chosen for reissue is the earlier of his two versions for DG, recorded in Prague, with Dietrich Fischer-Dieskau singing powerfully if sometimes roughly in the title-role. Birgit Nilsson does wonders in scaling down her Wagnerian soprano for the needs of Mozart, making a characterful if hardly a flawless Donna Anna. Similarly, the Verdian, Martina Arroyo, is characterful as Elvira, even if she has ungainly moments. The partnership between Fischer-Dieskau and Ezio Flagello as Leporello is most appealing, and Reri Grist makes a charming Zerlina. A flawed set, enjoyable but scarcely matching the others in the Boehm cycle.

Solti directs a crisp, incisive performance, with generally fast tempi and very well-directed recitatives. If it shows no special signs of affection, it contains one glorious performance in Margaret Price's Anna, pure in tone and line but powerfully dramatic too, always beautiful. Next to her, Sylvia Sass as a somewhat gusty Elvira sounds rather miscast, characterful though her singing is. The two baritones, Bernd Weikl and Gabriel Bacquier, are clearly contrasted as Giovanni and Leporello respectively, though the microphone is not kind to either. The recording is brilliant in its realistic clarity.

Harnoncourt's version with the Concertgebouw rather falls between two stools. He persuades the orchestra's reduced strings to play with a lighter, more detached style than usual and with little vibrato, but the heavily over-reverberant recording removes any advantages; Harnoncourt's fast speeds, unlike Östman's, tend to sound perverse instead of helpful. Thomas Hampson as Don Giovanni is splendid, the archetypal seducer; and the others are generally good too, but Edita Gruberová is a surprisingly squally and often raw Donna Anna, no match for most rivals.

Barenboim's (currently withdrawn) recording is directly based on the stage production at the 1974 Edinburgh Festival, but the often slack and unsparkling performance recorded here can scarcely reflect the live account. Surprisingly, Barenboim seems to be echoing Klemperer in his steady approach and exaggeratedly slow tempi. However, with Klemperer himself there was a granite-like solidity; with Barenboim, uncharacteristically, the rhythms sag. Roger Soyer's performance as the Don is refreshingly youthful in feeling, and the set is well worth hearing for Sir Geraint Evans's Leporello alone, but Luigi Alva's Ottavio is distressingly unsure. Heather Harper as Elvira and Helen Donath as Zerlina battle well against the tempi, but Antigone Sgourda as Anna uses her big, floppy voice in hit-or-miss fashion.

Don Giovanni: highlights.
(M) *** DG Dig. 431 289-2; *431 289-4* [id.] (from above recording with Ramey, Tomowa-Sintow; cond. Karajan).
(M) *** EMI CDM7 63078-2; *EG 763078-4* (from above recording with Waechter, Schwarzkopf; cond. Giulini).
(M) **(*) DG 429 823-2 [id.] (from above recording with Milnes, Tomowa-Sintow; cond. Boehm).
(M) ** EMI CD-EMX 2193; *TC-EMX 2193* (from above complete recording with Soyer, Sgourda; cond. Barenboim).
(M) *(*) Decca 421 875-2. Cesare Siepi, Birgit Nilsson, Leontyne Price, Eugenia Ratti, Cesare Valletti, Fernando Corena, V. State Op. Ch., VPO, Leinsdorf.

A particularly generous selection from Karajan's digital set, most of the favourite items included and all the principals given a chance to shine, in solos, duets and ensembles. The selection opens with the *Overture* and closes with the powerful final scene. There is a good matching chrome tape, although the resonance does bring slight clouding to the upper range.

EMI offer at mid-price an outstanding sampler of the classic Giulini set recommended above. Not surprisingly, it concentrates on Sutherland as Donna Anna and Schwarzkopf as Donna Elvira, so that the Don and Leporello get rather short measure; but Sciutti's charming Zerlina is also given fair due. With the recording sounding well, it can be recommended to those who already own a different complete set.

Like its companion collection of highlights from *Così fan tutte*, Boehm's selection is very generous (76 minutes) and is taken from live performances at Salzburg (recorded in 1977). It makes a welcome representation of a set centring round Sherrill Milnes's unusually heroic assumption of the role of the Don, and he sings with a richness and commitment to match his swaggering stage presence. The rest of the cast give stylish performances without being deeply memorable but, unlike *Così* where ensembles were less than ideally crisp, this live *Giovanni* presents strong and consistently enjoyable teamwork. The balance again favours the voices but is especially vivid in the culminating scene. However, the documentation, as with *Così*, offers only period pictures and a list of contents.

Barenboim's EMI version from the early 1970s is by no means a front runner, but admirers of Sir Geraint Evans will surely welcome his Leporello, and Roger Soyer is a personable Don. Among the ladies Heather Harper (Elvira) and Helen Donath as Zerlina both shine (*Là ci darem la mano* is very pleasing). The selection is generous (77 minutes).

Although the selection is again fairly generous (70 minutes), there is little else to recommend in Leinsdorf's 1960 recording. It begins with a fierce, fast version of the *Overture* and elsewhere has drama without charm, for Leinsdorf's direction is largely uninspired. Nilsson again makes a gusty Donna Anna and Leontyne Price is equally poorly cast. Siepi and Corena are reliable but are better served in the Krips version. The sound is vivid but lacks bloom.

Die Entführung aus dem Serail (complete).
*** DG Dig. 435 857-2 (2) [id.]. Monteverdi Ch., E. Bar. Soloists, Gardiner.
Constanze (Luba Orgonasova), Blonde (Cyndia Sieden), Belmonte (Stanford Olsen), Pedrillo (Uwe Peper), Osmin (Cornelius Hauptmann).
(M) *** DG 429 868-2 (2) [id.]. Leipzig R. Ch., Dresden State O, Boehm.
Constanze (Arleen Augér), Blonde (Reri Grist), Belmonte (Peter Schreier), Pedrillo (Harald Neukirch), Osmin (Kurt Moll).
*** Teldec/Warner Dig. 2292 42643-2 (3) [id.]. Zurich Op. Ch. & Mozart O, Harnoncourt.
Constanze (Yvonne Kenny), Blonde (Lilian Watson), Belmonte (Peter Schreier), Pedrillo (Wilfried Gahmlich), Osmin (Matti Salminen).
**(*) O-L Dig. 430 339-2 (2) [id.]. AAM & Ch., Hogwood.
Constanze (Lynne Dawson), Blonde (Marianne Hirsti), Belmonte (Uwe Heilmann), Pedrillo (Wilfried Gahmlich), Osmin (Günther Von Kannen).
**(*) Decca Dig. 417 402-2 (2) [id.]. V. State Op. Ch., VPO, Solti.
Constanze (Edita Gruberová), Blonde (Kathleen Battle), Belmonte (Gösta Winbergh), Pedrillo (Heinz Zednik), Osmin (Martti Talvela).
(M) ** Ph. 422 538-2 (2) [id.]. Alldis Ch., ASMF, Sir Colin Davis.
Constanze (Christiane Eda-Pierre), Blonde (Norma Burrowes), Belmonte (Stuart Burrows), Pedrillo (Robert Tear), Osmin (Robert Lloyd).

Die Entführung aus dem Serail (complete). (i) Arias from: *La clemenza di Tito; Die Entführung; Idomeneo.*

Withdrawn: (M) **(*) EMI stereo/mono CHS7 63715-2 (2). (i) Léopold Simoneau; Beecham Ch. Soc., RPO, Beecham.

Constanze (Lois Marshall), Blonde (Ilse Hollweg), Belmonte (Léopold Simoneau), Pedrillo (Gerhard Unger), Osmin (Gottlob Frick), Bassa Selim (Hansgeorg Laubenthal).

Mozart's Seraglio adventure was premièred in Vienna in 1782, four years before *Le nozze di Figaro*. The plot is made preposterous by its unexpectedly happy ending, but the music more than compensates for this with its brilliantly contrived special 'Turkish' percussion effects. One willingly suspends disbelief when the opera produces two personable pairs of lovers, a strong heroine, Constanze, and in Osmin one of the most delectable *buffo* parts in all opera.

We first meet Belmonte, a Spanish nobleman, outside a large Turkish country house, owned by the Pasha Selim. He questions Osmin, the pasha's overseer, as to the whereabouts of Constanze, his lost beloved, whom he is seeking. Osmin ignores his questions and speaks instead of his hatred for Pedrillo (Belmonte's former servant) who is now the pasha's gardener. It is from Pedrillo that Belmonte learns that Constanze, though held against her will by the pasha, has been able to remain faithful to him. He decides he might prove of service to the pasha if he poses as an eminent visiting architect.

We now meet Constanze and the pasha together. She has been able to resist, or at least to postpone, his advances and says that she loves another. Belmonte is announced and the pasha accepts his proffered services, much to Osmin's disgust. Osmin makes his own advances to Constanze's maid, Blonde, but his coarseness is abhorrent to her and she firmly dismisses him. Constanze, too, declares her own resistance to the pasha, even under threat of torture. Pedrillo now plies Osmin with a great deal of wine and he passes out in a drunken stupor.

The field is clear for Belmonte to greet Constanze rapturously, and Blonde, having boxed Pedrillo on the ears for suggesting she might not be true to him, also warms to him; all four now express loving sentiments together. An escape is planned and attempted, but it is thwarted by Osmin. Unhappily, the pasha now discovers Belmonte's true identity, and matters are made worse by the fact that at one time Belmonte's father had wronged the pasha. The captives shall be tortured. Osmin is overjoyed.

Then there is an astonishing *volte face*. The pasha reappears and announces that he so despises Belmonte's father that he has no desire to follow his example, and he sets the captives free. All four now join in giving thanks to the pasha for his magnanimity, Osmin actually joining in, though in reality he is the only one who is not pleased at all.

Unlike *Idomeneo* and *La clemenza di Tito*, the first two in Gardiner's series of Mozart opera recordings with the English Baroque Soloists, *Entführung* was not recorded live but in the studio immediately after a concert performance. With a comedy like this, studded with spoken dialogue, that was a wise decision. The direct comparison in a period performance of the opera is with Christopher Hogwood and the Academy of Ancient Music and, like him, Gardiner includes some minor additions to the text, sanctioned by recent scholarship. The overture immediately establishes the extra zest of the Gardiner performance, with wider dynamic contrasts, more body in the sound and with more spring in the rhythm and a keener sense of fun. Though Gardiner's speeds are often fast, they never sound breathless, thanks to his rhythmic flair, making the music lift and allowing time for imaginative phrasing. So Constanze's great heroic aria, *Martern aller Arten*, has tremendous swagger, and, thanks also to glorious singing from Luba Orgonasova, at once rich, pure and agile, the close is triumphant.

Curiously Gardiner exaggerates the *ad lib.* markings in the first half of that climactic aria. Orgonasova sounds far richer than Lynne Dawson, the outstanding Constanze for Hogwood, and in the other great aria, *Traurigkeit*, she is warmer too, less withdrawn. As Belmonte, Stanford Olsen for Gardiner is firmer and more agile than the fluttery Uwe Heilmann for Hogwood; though Cornelius Hauptmann, Gardiner's Osmin, lacks a really dark bass, he too is firmer and more characterful than the unsteady Günther von Kannen for Hogwood. Add to that a recording which gives a clearer idea of staging, and you have a version of *Entführung* to be recommended as first choice even for those who would not normally go for a period performance.

Boehm's is a delectable performance of this delightful farrago, superbly cast and warmly recorded. Arleen Augér early in her career is outstanding in the role of Constanze, girlish and fresh, yet rich, tender and dramatic by turns, with brilliant, almost flawless coloratura. The others are also excellent, notably Kurt Moll whose powerful, finely focused bass makes him a superb Osmin, one who relishes the comedy too. Boehm with East German forces finds a natural, unforced Mozartian expression which carries the listener along in glowing ease. The warm recording is beautifully transferred, to make this the most sympathetic version of the opera on CD, setting out the action vividly before the listener, with the added attraction of being at mid-price.

Based on a celebrated stage production in Zurich with these same forces, Harnoncourt's version establishes its uniqueness at the very start of the overture, tougher and more abrasive than any previous recording. What Harnoncourt contends is that Mozart wanted more primitive sounds than we are used to in his Turkish music, with the jingle of cymbals, Turkish drums and the like more than living up to the nickname 'kitchen department', with the stove itself seemingly included. It is not a comfortable sound, compounded by Harnoncourt's often fast allegros, racing singers and players off their feet. Another source of extra abrasiveness is the use of a raw-sounding flageolet instead of a piccolo.

Once you get used to the sound, however, the result is refreshing and lively, with the whole performance reflecting the fine rapport built up in stage performance. Slow passages are often warmly expressive, but the stylishness of the soloists prevents them from seeming excessively romantic, as in Schreier's charming singing of *O wie ängstlich* in Act I. The other men are excellent, too: Wilfried Gahmlich both bright and sweet of tone, Matti Salminen outstandingly characterful as an Osmin who, as well as singing with firm dark tone, points the words with fine menace. Yvonne Kenny as Constanze and Lilian Watson as Blonde sound on the shrill side – partly a question of microphones – but they sing with such style and point that one quickly accepts that. *Martern aller Arten* prompts the most brilliant coloratura from Kenny, with the coda including some extra bars, now authorized by scholarship, but doubtfully effective, one of the many textual niceties of the set. Good, clean, dryish recording.

Christopher Hogwood in the first period recording of *Entführung* offers a bonus number, discovered as a result of keen detective work. It is a march which precedes the *Chorus of Janissaries*, very useful for producers wanting to get supernumeraries on stage. Hogwood has rarely sounded so relaxed on record, though the excellent cast is let down by one unwise choice, the ill-focused Osmin of Günther von Kannen. Otherwise Lynne Dawson is a dazzling Constanze, relying on fine projection rather than weight in the big arias, and contrasting well with the soubrettish Blonde of Marianne Hirsti. The tenor Uwe Heilmann as Belmonte here completely avoids the fluttery tone which mars his performance as Tamino in the Solti set of *Zauberflöte*.

Though Solti's speeds are disconcertingly fast at times – as in Pedrillo and Osmin's drinking duet, *Vivat Bacchus* – and the manner is consequently often too tense to be comic, the performance is magnetic overall, with the big ensembles and choruses electric in their clean, sharp focus. Gruberová makes a brilliant Constanze, but the edge on the voice is not always comfortable. Exciting as *Martern aller Arten* is, with a fire-snorting coda and some beautiful shading for contrast (surprising with so bright a voice), the edge on the voice is underlined by the recording. She is more appealing elsewhere. Gösta Winbergh makes an ardent, young-sounding Belmonte, Kathleen Battle a seductive, minxish Blonde and Heinz Zednik a delightfully light and characterful Pedrillo, with Martti Talvela magnificently lugubrious as Osmin. With brilliant recording this makes a fresh and compelling reading, but not one likely to make you smile often.

There is much to treasure in Beecham's vivid but idiosyncratic reading, not least the incomparable portrayal of Osmin by the great German bass, Gottlob Frick, thrillingly dark and firm, characterizing superbly. His aria, *O wie will ich triumphieren*, like the *Overture* and the *Chorus of Janissaries* in Act I, finds Beecham fizzing with energy, spine-tingling in intensity. Léopold Simoneau as Belmonte has rarely been matched on record for mellifluous beauty and flawless line, and Gerhard Unger is a charming Pedrillo, not least in the spoken dialogue. The two women soloists are more variable. Lois Marshall is technically fine as Constanze, but the voice has a hint of rawness, while Ilse Hollweg, bright and clear, could be more characterful too.

The oddity of the set lies in the text. Beecham, dissatisfied with the heroine's two big arias following each other so closely, moved the second, heroic one, *Martern aller Arten*, to Act III, and he also made an unwarranted cut in *Traurigkeit*. He additionally moved Belmonte's *Wenn der Freude* to the beginning of Act III, where it replaces *Ich baue ganz*, a curious decision. The transfer of early stereo sound is first rate. The four mono recordings of Mozart arias sung by Simoneau – including the missing *Ich baue ganz* – make an excellent bonus. We hope this set will be restored to the catalogue in due course.

Sir Colin Davis, using a smaller orchestra, the St Martin's Academy, than he usually has in his Mozart opera recordings, produces a fresh and direct account, well but not outstandingly sung.

There are no performances here which have one remembering individuality of phrase, and even so characterful a singer as Robert Tear does not sound quite mellifluous enough in the role of Pedrillo, while Robert Lloyd as Osmin is outshone by a number of his rivals, especially the incomparable Gottlob Frick in the deleted Beecham set. Crisp as the ensembles are, Davis's reading rather lacks the lightness and sparkle, the feeling of comedy before our eyes, which makes Boehm's DG set so memorable.

La finta giardiniera (complete).
(M) *** Ph. 422 533-2 (3) [id.]. Salzburg Mozarteum O, Hager.
Sandrina (Judy Conwell), Podestà (Ezio Di Cesare), Belfiore (Thomas Moser), Arminda (Lilian Sukis), Ramiro (Brigitte Fassbaender), Serpetto (Jutta-Renate Ihloff), Nardo (Barry McDaniel).

Die Gärtnerin aus Liebe (*La finta giardiniera* sung in German) (complete).
(M) **(*) Ph. 422 534-2 (3) [id.]. N. German R. Ch. & SO, Schmidt-Isserstedt.
Sandrina (Helen Donath), Podestà (Gerhard Unger), Belfiore (Werner Hollweg), Arminda (Jessye Norman), Ramiro (Tatiana Troyanos), Serpetto (Ileana Cotrubas), Nardo (Hermann Prey).

This is the only *opera buffa* written by Mozart in his youth that can be regarded as a preparation for *Figaro*, particularly as you find Mozart at nineteen confidently using techniques in the extended finales which he was to perfect in the Da Ponte masterpiece. In the manner of the time, every possible excuse is used to prevent true love from being fulfilled until the end of Act III; yet, with Mozart, the more improbable the story the more inspired the music.

The story is certainly unconvincing. Before it begins, Count Belfiore has attacked his mistress, the Marchioness Violante Onesti, in jealous rage. He thinks she is dead and he leaves hastily. Violante (in disguise as Sandrina) sets out to find him with Robert, her servant, who is disguised as Nardo. Both become employed as gardeners by the Podestà (Governor) of Lagonero on the Black Sea. The Podestà immediately falls in love with his unexpectedly fair gardener, while Nardo fancies Serpetto, the governor's housekeeper.

To complicate matters further, the knight Ramiro is a guest of the Podestà: he is the former lover of the governor's niece, Arminda. The local inhabitants of the Lagonero estate await Arminda who is betrothed to Count Belfiore. The Podestà tries to make advances to Sandrina but she eludes him. Arminda arrives, is welcomed by the count, and Sandrina faints when she tells her she plans to marry Belfiore. Arminda now meets her former lover, Ramiro.

There is general confusion, with reproaches and misunderstandings all round. Ramiro produces a document which states that Belfiore is the murderer of the Countess Violante and requests an investigation. Arminda's wedding is postponed, but Sandrina comes to the count's rescue, revealing who she really is and saying she was not killed but only wounded. No one believes her, but the count tells her that he loves her. Sandrina now seeks safety in a cave. More confusion during which the count and Sandrina go mad and think they are gods. Fortunately they fall asleep, and when they wake up their madness has departed and they recognize each other. Arminda now decides she will marry Ramiro, and Serpetto and Nardo also are united. The Podestà agrees to stay single until another Sandrina turns up!

By the time Leopold Hager came to record the opera in 1980 with Salzburg Mozarteum forces, the text of the recitatives in Italian had been rediscovered and he was able to use the original language. He has a strong vocal team, with three impressive newcomers taking the women's roles – Jutta-Renate Ihloff, Judy Conwell (in the central role of Sandrina, the marquise who disguises herself as a garden-girl) and Lilian Sukis (the arrogant niece). Brigitte Fassbaender sings the castrato role of Ramiro, and the others are comparably stylish. It is a charming – if lengthy – comedy, which here, with crisply performed recitatives, is presented with vigour, charm and persuasiveness. The recording, made with the help of Austrian Radio, is excellent and has been brightly and freshly transferred to CD.

Hans Schmidt-Isserstedt's set was made in Hamburg a decade earlier, and he was forced to record the version that used the clumsy German Singspiel translation, in use until the discovery of the Italian recitatives. However, though this performance is slow in getting off the ground, it readily makes up for this later, with particularly delightful performances from Ileana Cotrubas and Hermann Prey in the roles of the two servants. The sound too is very pleasing, although the violin tone is a little on the thin side; but the CD transfer does not exaggerate this and retains an attractive ambience.

La finta semplice (complete).
(M) *** Ph. Dig. 422 528-2 (2) [id.]. C. P. E. Bach CO, Schreier.
   Rosina (Barbara Hendricks), Don Cassandro (Siegfried Lorenz), Don Polidoro (Douglas Johnson), Giacanta (Ann Murray), Ninetta (Eva Lind), Fracasso (Hans-Peter Blochwitz), Simone (Andreas Schmidt).

Peter Schreier draws sparkling playing from the C. P. E. Bach Orchestra of East Berlin, so that, with an excellent cast, this completely new recording (made for the Philips Complete Mozart Edition) is one of the most delectable of all the sets of early Mozart operas. The plot, adapted from a Goldoni comedy, is a conventional one of love and intrigue, involving two rich, unmarried brothers, Don Cassandro and Don Polidoro (both described as 'foolish gentlemen'), and the trickery of the women in each getting the man of her choice.

Captain Fracasso and his Sergeant Simone have been quartered on the brothers, and the captain is in love with Giacanta, their sister, while Simone has been trying his luck with her maid, Ninetta. For the moment these amours must be kept from the brothers. Don Cassandro is a tyrannical misogynist who keeps a tight rein on Don Polidoro, a natural philanderer, but something of a simpleton and not to be taken too seriously. Ninetta feels that the solution to the problem is to ensure that the brothers each find a responsive lover.

Rosina, Fracasso's resourceful sister, is staying at the local inn, as Don Cassandro won't have her residing in his house. In spite of his obduracy, Fracasso makes a wager with Don Cassandro that he will be smitten sooner or later. Rosina is then persuaded by Ninetta to make *both* the foolish brothers fall in love with her. First she makes approaches to Don Polidoro then to Don Cassandro, and she is so successful that the latter reluctantly gives her a ring then invites her to stay.

After dinner the two brothers, thoroughly inebriated, are discussing their 'conquests'. Rosina rejects the clumsy approaches of Don Polidoro; the brothers quarrel, and Don Cassandro then makes his proposal but is also put off. He falls into a drunken stupor and Rosina replaces the ring on his finger. When he wakes up, she tells him that her affections are divided between the two of them, and there is further feuding over the ring.

Simone now plans to elope with Giacanta, with Ninetta in tow, but the brothers go after them, thinking she is taking all the household valuables with her. Finally all is resolved, Ninetta and Giacanta are able to marry their chosen lovers; Rosina has prudently decided that it is Don Cassandro she wants, but she encourages Don Polidoro's expectations one last time before accepting Don Cassandro's hand. Don Polidoro is finally left to enjoy bachelor solitude.

What is astonishing is the way Mozart responds to this amorous mix-up. Indeed the invention of the twelve-year-old composer is no less winning than that of anything he wrote in his early teens, starting with an overture guaranteed to raise the spirits. In every way Schreier's version replaces the earlier, Orfeo full-priced set from Leopold Hager, particularly when it comes at mid-price on two discs instead of three. The digital recording is wonderfully clear, with a fine sense of presence, capturing the fun of the comedy. Ann Murray has never sung more seductively in Mozart than here as Giacanta, and the characterful Barbara Hendricks is a delight in the central role of Rosina.

Idomeneo (complete).
※ *** DG Dig. 431 674-2 (3) [id.]. Monteverdi Choir, E. Bar. Soloists, Gardiner.
   Idomeneo (Anthony Rolfe Johnson), Idamante (Anne Sofie Von Otter), Ilia (Sylvia McNair), Elettra (Hillevi Martinpelto), Arbace (Nigel Robson), High Priest (Glenn Winslade), Oracle (Cornelius Hauptmann).
(M) *** DG 429 864-2 (3) [id.]. Leipzig R. Ch., Dresden State O, Boehm.
   Idomeneo (Wieslaw Ochman), Idamante (Peter Schreier), Ilia (Edith Mathis), Elettra (Julia Varady), Arbace (Hermann Winkler), High Priest (Eberhard Büchner), Oracle (Siegfried Vogel).
*** Decca Dig. 411 805-2 (3) [id.]. V. State Op. Ch., VPO, Pritchard.
   Idomeneo (Luciano Pavarotti), Idamante (Agnes Baltsa), Ilia (Lucia Popp), Elettra (Edita Gruberová), Arbace (Leo Nucci), High Priest (Timothy Jenkins), Oracle (Nikita Storojev).
(M) **(*) Teldec/Warner 2292 42600-2 (3) [id.]. Zürich Op. O, Harnoncourt.
   Idomeneo (Werner Hollweg), Idamante (Trudeliese Schmidt), Ilia (Rachel Yakar), Elettra (Felicity Palmer), Arbace (Kurt Equiluz), High Priest (Robert Tear), Oracle (Simon Estes).
Withdrawn: (M) **(*) EMI CMS7 63990-2 (3) [Ang. CDMC 63990]. Leipzig R. Ch., Dresden State O, Schmidt-Isserstedt.

Idomeneo (Nicolai Gedda), Idamante (Adolf Dallapozza), Ilia (Anneliese Rothenberger), Elettra (Edda Moser), Arbace (Theo Adam), High Priest (Peter Schreier).

Withdrawn: (M) (***) EMI mono CHS7 63685-2 (2) [Ang. CDHB 63685]. Glyndebourne Festival Ch. & O, Pritchard.

Idomeneo (Richard Lewis), Idamante (Léopold Simoneau), Ilia (Sena Jurinac), Elettra (Lucille Udovick), Arbace (James Milligan), High Priest (William McAlpine), Oracle (Hervey Alan).

(M) ** Ph. 422 537-2 (3) [id.]. Bav. R. Ch. & RSO, Sir Colin Davis.

Idomeneo (Francisco Araiza), Idamante (Susanne Mentzer), Ilia (Barbara Hendricks), Elettra (Roberta Alexander), Arbace (Uwe Heilmann), High Priest (Werner Hollweg), Oracle (Harry Peeters).

** Ph. 420 130-2 (3) [id.]. BBC Ch. & SO, C. Davis.

Idomeneo (George Shirley), Idamante (Ryland Davies), Ilia (Margherita Rinaldi), Elettra (Pauline Tinsley), High Priest (Robert Tear).

Idomeneo, Mozart's setting of classical Greek mythology, was first heard in Munich in 1781, the year before *Die Entführung*. Its central character, Idomeneo, the Cretan king, is fighting in the Trojan wars and has been absent from home for many years. One of the prisoners he has sent back to Crete is Ilia, and she has fallen in love with his son, Idamante.

As the opera opens, Ilia compares her hatred for her conquerors with her love for Idamante. He enters, hints that his feelings for her are reciprocal, then announces that all Trojan prisoners are to be freed in honour of his father's impending return home. Arbace, Idomeneo's friend and confidant, now enters and says that Idomeneo's vessel has sunk. In the following confusion we find that Elettra, a Greek princess, is also in love with Idamante. She is furious as she feels that with Idomeneo's death nothing will prevent or delay an immediate marriage of Idamante and Ilia.

Idomeneo, very much alive, now enters, and we find that he made a pact with Neptune and thus the storm which would have wrecked his ship was calmed. In return for his escape from death, he has unwisely vowed to sacrifice the first living creature he meets on dry land. It is, of course, his son who is there at the unpropitious moment of his arrival, although the king does not recognize him at first – he was only an infant when his father had departed from Crete. Appalled, Idomeneo dismisses Idamante, who fails to understand his father's displeasure.

Idomeneo now confides his awesome obligation to Arbace, who suggests that Idamante be sent away forthwith, so Idomeneo instructs his son to escort Elettra back to Greece. Ilia now enters and tells Idomeneo how happy she has become in Crete, finding in him a second father. Idomeneo realizes that she loves his son, yet he fears that Neptune will claim as victims not only Idamante but also Ilia and himself.

Elettra, accompanied by Idamante, is now ready to depart, but as they make their farewells a ferocious storm develops at sea and a great monster rises from the angry waves, a sign of the fury of the gods. Idomeneo accepts that the guilt for this manifestation lies squarely on his shoulders. Ilia and Idamante now both openly declare their mutual passion but Idomeneo, having withheld knowledge of his sacrificial vow from his son, now says he must leave, never to return. Ilia is devastated, Elettra seethes with anger over the imminent departure of the man she loves. But the rampaging monster has killed thousands in the city and in the temple Idomeneo confesses his vow to Neptune, and the High Priest says that the vow must be fulfilled.

They offer a prayer to Neptune, then there is a sudden commotion. Idamante has slain the monster but, learning of his father's predicament, comes forward to offer himself as the sacrifice. Ilia wishes to take his place. Opportunely, Neptune's oracle intervenes. Idomeneo must be deposed and Idamante shall be king in his place, with Ilia as his bride. Elettra leaves, still as furious as ever, and Idomeneo presents his son to the rejoicing populace.

Gardiner's revelatory recording, taken from live performances at Queen Elizabeth Hall in June 1990, was the first on period instruments. With its exhilarating vigour and fine singing it will please many more than period-performance devotees. Using period instruments 'played with gusto', Gardiner says, the result in this opera is 'earthier and emotionally raw'. He also suggests that this is 'the most orchestrally conceived of all Mozart's operas', and the recording substantiates both these claims. Gardiner's aim has been to include all the material Mozart wrote for the original, 1781 production, whether it was finally used or not. It is astonishing to find that, with all the variants and amendments, the music for Act III alone lasts an hour and three-quarters, and he recommends the use of the CD programming device for listeners to select the version they prefer, with supplementary numbers put at the end of each disc.

The abrasiveness is modified by Gardiner's Mozartian style, well sprung and subtly moulded rather than severe, and his choice of singers puts a premium on clarity and beauty of production rather than weight. Even Hillevi Martinpelto, the young soprano chosen to sing the dramatic role of Elettra, keeps a pure line in her final fury scene, avoiding explosiveness – a passage given in alternative versions. The other principals sing beautifully too, notably Anne Sofie von Otter as Idamante and Sylvia McNair as Ilia, while Anthony Rolfe Johnson, a tenor on the light side for the role of Idomeneo in a traditional performance, is well suited here, with words finely projected. The electrifying singing of the Monteverdi Choir adds to the dramatic bite, and the sound is excellent, remarkably fine for a live performance in a difficult venue.

Textually Boehm's version of *Idomeneo* gives grounds for regrets. The score is snipped about and, like previous recordings, it opts for a tenor in the role of Idamante. That said, however, it is a highly successful and richly enjoyable set. Boehm's conducting is a delight, often spacious but never heavy in the wrong way, with lightened textures and sprung rhythms which have one relishing Mozartian felicities as never before. As Idomeneo, Wieslaw Ochman, with tenor tone often too tight, is a comparatively dull dog, but the other principals are generally excellent. Peter Schreier as Idamante also might have sounded more consistently sweet, but the imagination is irresistible. Edith Mathis is at her most beguiling as Ilia, but it is Julia Varady as Elettra who gives the most compelling performance of all, sharply incisive in her dramatic outbursts, but at the same time precise and pure-toned, a Mozartian stylist through and through. Hermann Winkler as Arbace is squarely Germanic, and it is a pity that the *secco* recitatives are done heavily; whatever incidental reservations have to be made, however, this is a most compelling set which leaves one in no doubt as to the work's status as a masterpiece. The first-class recording has transferred vividly to CD.

More than any previous recorded performance, the Decca version conducted by Sir John Pritchard – who did the first ever recording of the opera with a Glyndebourne cast over thirty years earlier – centres round the tenor taking the name-part. It is not just that Pavarotti has the natural magnetism of the superstar but that he is the only tenor at all among the principal soloists. Not only is the role of Idamante given to a mezzo instead of a tenor – preferable, with what was originally a castrato role – but that of the High Priest, Arbace, with his two arias is taken by a baritone, Leo Nucci. The wonder is that though Pavarotti reveals imagination in every phrase, using a wide range of tone colours, the result remains well within the parameters of Mozartian style. On balance this is not only the most heroic and the most beautiful but also the best controlled performance of this demanding role that we have on record.

Casting Baltsa as Idamante makes for characterful results, tougher and less fruity than her direct rivals. Lucia Popp as Ilia tends to underline expression too much, but it is a charming, girlish portrait. Gruberová makes a thrilling Elettra, totally in command of the divisions as few sopranos are; owing to bright Decca sound, the projection of her voice is a little edgy at times. As to Pritchard, he has relaxed a little since his Glyndebourne days – this is a bigger view than before – and (with text unusually complete) more than most current rivals brings light and shade to the piece.

Using a text very close to that of the Munich première of Mozart's great *opera seria*, and with the role of Idamante given to a soprano instead of being transposed down to tenor register, Harnoncourt presents a distinctive and refreshing view, one which in principle is preferable to general modern practice. The vocal cast is good, with Hollweg a clear-toned, strong Idomeneo, and no weak link. Felicity Palmer finds the necessary contrasts of expression as Elettra. On LP, the voices were sometimes given an unpleasant edge, but, with the CD remastering, the sound is transformed and the edginess smoothed without loss of presence. It is surprising that, in an account which aims at authenticity, appoggiature are so rarely used. This is hardly a performance to warm to, but it is refreshing and alive.

Schmidt-Isserstedt's version of Mozart's great essay in *opera seria* dates from 1971 and was first issued as a timely memorial soon after the conductor's death. Though not perfect, it is most stylishly performed and at the time was the most complete version available. It was a pity that the role of Idamante was given to a tenor, and the decision is the more irritating when Adolf Dallapozza is by far the least accomplished soloist. Otherwise the cast is strong, with Gedda heroic as Idomeneo, Rothenberger an appealing Ilia and Edda Moser a richly characterful Elettra. Altogether this is a very commanding version with fine concern for detail and very good recording, full and warm as well as vivid in its CD transfer.

The very first 'complete' recording of the opera, recorded in 1955 with Glyndebourne forces under John Pritchard, makes a timely reappearance on CD. Though it uses a severely cut text and the orchestral sound is rather dry, it wears its years well. The voices still sound splendid, notably Sena Jurinac as a ravishing Ilia, Richard Lewis in the title-role, and Léopold Simoneau so delicate he almost reconciles one to the casting of Idamante as a tenor (from Mozart's compromised Vienna revision). The cuts mean that the whole opera is fitted on to two (mid-price) discs instead of three.

To have a major new opera-set like this, issued from the start on a mid-priced label, is generous, but Sir Colin Davis's second version of Mozart's great *opera seria* was designed as part of the Philips Complete Mozart Edition and is priced accordingly. It comes with the fine qualities of presentation associated with the series; the text aims at completeness, with an appendix on the third disc containing major numbers like Arbace's two arias, omitted in the main text, as well as the ballet music designed to be performed after the drama is over. It also has the advantage over Davis's previous recording that the role of Idamante is given to a mezzo instead of a tenor, following Mozart's original Munich text. Such a number as the great Quartet of Act III benefits much by that – but unfortunately, as in Davis's previous version, there are flaws in the casting; his reading has also grown smoother and less incisive, less fresh than before, if now at times grander.

Francisco Araiza's efforts to produce the heroic tone needed often sound strained, and he is not clean enough in his attack; while Barbara Hendricks as Ilia adopts an even less apt Mozartian style, with too much sliding and under-the-note attack, missing the purity needed for this character. Uwe Heilmann as Arbace is also disappointing, and it is as well that his arias are left to the appendix. Others in the cast are far finer, but the total result is less than completely satisfactory, particularly arriving so soon after John Eliot Gardiner's brilliant and dramatic full-priced version for DG Archiv using period instruments. The Philips recording is full and warm, but the Gardiner set is well worth its extra cost.

Sir Colin Davis's earlier version was his first complete Mozart opera recording, and the casting was flawed. His direction is exceptionally fresh and stylish, with the drama of the piece tellingly brought out. The orchestra responds with vitality, but the singers when taxed with their important arias lack a degree of polish and refinement. Pauline Tinsley, seriously neglected on record, is fine in the part of Elettra, but the voice has an uncomfortable edge. George Shirley as Idomeneo and Ryland Davies as Idamante are well contrasted in timbre, but having a tenor in that second role makes for oddities of balance in the ensembles. Margherita Rinaldi is a sweet-voiced Ilia. The Philips recording comes up freshly on CD.

Lucio Silla (complete).
(M) *** Ph. 422 532-2 (3) [id.]. Salzburg R. Ch. & Mozarteum Ch. & O, Hager.
    Lucio Silla (Peter Schreier), Giunia (Arleen Augér), Cecilio (Julia Varady), Lucio Cinna (Edith Mathis), Celia (Helen Donath), Aufidio (Werner Krenn).

Lucio Silla (slightly abridged).
*** Teldec/WEA Dig. 2292 44928-2 (2). Schoenberg Ch., VCM, Harnoncourt.
    Lucio Silla (Peter Schreier), Giunia (Edita Gruberová), Cecilio (Cecilia Bartoli), Lucio Cinna (Yvonne Kenny), Celia (Dawn Upshaw).

The sixteen-year-old Mozart wrote his fifth opera, on the subject of the Roman dictator Sulla (Silla), in double quick time; and although the formal story has its longueurs (the total timing is 3½ hours) the speed of the composition is electrically communicated, with most of the arias urgently fast and strong symphonic ideas developed at surprising length.

At the opening, Senator Cecilio, who has been exiled from Rome by its despotic ruler, Lucio Silla, is on the banks of the river Tiber looking for his betrothed, Giunia. Here Cecilio meets his friend, Lucio Cinna, and hears that Silla has falsely told Giunia of his death as he wants her for himself. The angry Cecilio journeys to the grave of Giunia's father to wait for her. At the palace Silla is courting Giunia, with his sister, Celia's help. The tribune Aufidio urges his ruler to be more forceful in his conquest. But Giunia refuses all Silla's approaches. She will not have him, even if her lover is dead; she mocks Silla, who is deeply chagrined and decides that if her love is not to be his, he will have revenge instead. The melancholy Giunia now arrives at her father's grave, but Cecilio appears and sadness turns to joy.

Back at the palace, Aufidio persuades Silla to make a public proclamation of his marriage to Giunia and, although he has moments of remorse, he tells his sister that the marriage will take place immediately and moreover that she shall marry the patrician, Lucio Cinna. Cinna restrains Cecilio from taking precipitous action when he hears the news. Then Celia comes in and joyfully tells Cinna that Lucio Silla has given permission for their own marriage. But Cinna is for the moment more concerned with Giunia's situation and tells her of Silla's real plans. He suggests that she should go through with the marriage and kill her tyrannical husband on their wedding night. Giunia refuses, so Cinna decides to murder him instead.

Silla makes one more attempt to persuade Giunia to be his wife voluntarily, but she again rejects him; she would rather die. Silla warns her ominously that not only her life is forfeit if she refuses. Cecilio comes to offer his protection, but she urges him to escape and he leaves, sensibly if reluctantly. Celia comforts Giunia. At the Capitol, Silla now announces the wedding to popular acclaim, but Giunia publicly refuses him. Cecilio enters fruitlessly, with drawn sword, is overpowered and chained. Cinna also arrives but behaves more prudently.

All seems lost but Celia still hopes to change her brother's mind, and Cinna offers to marry her if she is successful. Giunia comes to the prison to die alongside her lover. In the extraordinary final scene at the Capitol, Giunia publicly denounces Silla and he relents. He pardons Cecilio, gives his blessing to the marriage of Cinna and Celia, further pardons all those in opposition to his rule and abdicates. The crowd hail his decision as just and wise.

In spite of the twists and turns of the story and its preposterous dénouement, there are many pre-echoes in the score of later Mozart operas, not just of the great *opera seria*, *Idomeneo*, but of *Entführung* and even of *Don Giovanni*. Though the formal limitations inhibit ensembles, there is a superb one at the end of Act I, anticipating the Da Ponte masterpieces. A rousing chorus is interrupted by an agonized G minor lament for the heroine and leads finally to an ecstatic reunion duet. In Hager's set the castrato roles are splendidly taken by Julia Varady and Edith Mathis, and the whole team could hardly be bettered. The direction is fresh and lively, and the only snag is the length of the *secco* recitatives. However, with CD one can use these judiciously. The 1975 analogue recording (originally DG) has been vividly and naturally remastered, although it is a pity that, in fitting the work on to CD, the first break had to come nine minutes before the end of Act I, in the middle of the scena described above, just before the duet.

What Harnoncourt has done is to record a text which fits on to two generously filled CDs, not just trimming down the recitatives but omitting no fewer than four arias, all of them valuable. Yet his sparkling direction of an outstandingly characterful team of soloists brings an exhilarating demonstration of the boy Mozart's genius, with such marvels as the extended finale to Act I left intact. Anyone not over-concerned about completeness will find Harnoncourt's two CDs a vivid experience. As in the earlier set, Schreier is masterly in the title-role, still fresh in tone, while Dawn Upshaw is warm and sweet as Celia, and Cecilia Bartoli is full and rich as Cecilio. The singing of Edita Gruberová as Giunia and Yvonne Kenny as Cinna is not quite so immaculate, but still confident and stylish. The Concentus Musicus of Vienna has rarely given so bright and lightly sprung a performance on record. Excellent digital sound.

Mitridate, rè di Ponto (complete).
(M) **(*) Ph. 422 529-2 (3) [id.]. Salzburg Mozarteum O, Hager.
> Mitridate (Werner Hollweg), Aspasia (Arleen Augér), Sifare (Edita Gruberová), Farnace (Agnes Baltsa), Ismene (Ileana Cotrubas), Marzio (David Kuebler), Arbate (Christine Weidinger).

Mozart at fourteen attempted his first full-scale *opera seria* and showed that he could fully encompass the most ambitious of forms. *Mitridate* was written for Milan and was first performed in 1767. Mitridate, who reigned *c.* 135–65 BC, is at the centre of the story, but the plot is more concerned with his problems as a father. He has two sons, Farnace and Sifare, and all three characters are enamoured of the same woman, the young Aspasia. Mitridate is currently engaging on one of his frequent forays against Rome (the historically correct feature of the story) and has left Aspasia, his betrothed, and his two sons behind. Arbate, the city governor, sides with the younger son, Sifare, whose political sympathy lies with the Greeks rather than the Romans. Aspasia asks Sifare to intervene when Farnace, who favours the Romans, forces his attentions on her, and she is amazed to hear that Sifare loves her too. The brothers' quarrel leads to violence, but Aspasia is able to restrain them; she is not sure which of the two she favours. It is agreed that their mutual feelings shall be concealed from their father. His return is now announced. Having suffered defeat at the hands of Rome, he is bringing with him Ismene, daughter of the King of Parthia, as a bride for Farnace.

Ismene is disillusioned by her reception; Arbate tells the king that his older son favours the Romans and that Farnace also wants Aspasia for himself. The king decides that Farnace must be exiled. Ismene had been expecting Farnace to welcome her but is cruelly told that his former love for her has evaporated. She is full of anger. Mitridate sympathizes with her, decreeing that his son will pay for this betrayal with his life. He suggests Sifare as an alternative suitor and reminds Aspasia that she is expected to remain faithful to her vows. She and Sifare are already in love, but both put duty first and resolve to part.

The two sons arrive at Mitridate's camp at the same time as the Roman tribune, Marzio, who has come to sue for peace. Farnace urges his father to accept the offer and is threatened with imprisonment. Ismene intercedes and Farnace now tells his father that Sifare, too, loves Aspasia. To test her fidelity the king tells her he is willing to release her from her engagement to him and offers her Sifare instead. Aspasia at first refuses but finally admits her true feelings, only to discover from Mitridate's rage that the offer was false.

Despairingly she beseeches Sifare to kill her, but he urges her to accept his father as husband and become the queen. She refuses, and the two lovers face possible death together. But Aspasia desperately pleads for Mitridate's mercy and Ismene adds her own passionate plea for his change of heart. Aspasia is told that she can save Sifare only by giving herself to the king, but again she refuses.

The sudden dramatic arrival of the Roman fleet in the harbour and the simultaneous vanquishing of Mitridate's army puts a different complexion on the situation. Aspasia is about to take poison, but Sifare arrives just in time to stop her; now he will fight to the bitter end alongside his father. Farnace also makes a *volte face* and decides he will join them, in spite of the Roman consul's promise that the Romans will offer him the throne if he co-operates with the enemy.

In the ensuing battle Mitridate, rather than suffer defeat, throws himself on his own sword. He is reconciled with his sons and gives Aspasia to Sifare. Farnace is a hero, having taken a torch to the Roman ships so that they are in retreat. The opera ends with stirring quintet refusing to yield to tyranny, and praising freedom.

Not all the 22 arias are of the finest quality; some are too long for their material, and the Metastasio libretto is hardly involving dramatically. But a fresh and generally lively performance (the rather heavy recitatives excepted) brings splendid illumination to the long-hidden area of the boy Mozart's achievement. Two of the most striking arias (including an urgent G minor piece for the heroine, Aspasia, with Arleen Augér the ravishing soprano) exploit minor keys most effectively. Ileana Cotrubas is outstanding as Ismene, and the soloists of the Salzburg orchestra cope well with the often important obbligato parts. Like the others in Hager's series, this has a DG source. The recording is bright and fresh, the CD transfer vivid and forward and a little lacking in atmosphere.

Le nozze di Figaro (complete).
*** Decca Dig. 410 150-2 (3). LPO & Ch., Solti.
    Figaro (Samuel Ramey), Susanna (Lucia Popp), Count Almaviva (Thomas Allen), Countess Almaviva (Kiri Te Kanawa), Cherubino (Frederica Von Stade), Marcellina (Jane Berbié), Bartolo (Kurt Moll), Don Basilio (Robert Tear).
⊛ (B) *** CfP CD-CDPD 4724; *TC-CFPD 4724* (2). Glyndebourne Ch. & Festival O, Gui.
    Figaro (Sesto Bruscantini), Susanna (Graziella Sciutti), Count Almaviva (Franco Calabrese), Countess Almaviva (Sena Jurinac), Cherubino (Risë Stevens), Marcellina (Monica Sinclair), Bartolo (Ian Wallace), Don Basilio (Hugues Cuénod).
(M) *** EMI CMS7 63266-2 (2) [Ang. CDMB 63266]. Philh. Ch. & O, Giulini.
    Figaro (Giuseppe Taddei), Susanna (Anna Moffo), Count Almaviva (Eberhard Waechter), Countess Almaviva (Elisabeth Schwarzkopf), Cherubino (Fiorenza Cossotto), Marcellina (Dora Gatta), Bartolo (Ivo Vinco), Don Basilio (Renato Ercolani).
(M) *** Ph. 422 540-2 (3) [id.]. BBC Ch. & SO, Sir Colin Davis.
    Figaro (Wladimiro Ganzarolli), Susanna (Mirella Freni), Count Almaviva (Ingvar Wixell), Countess Almaviva (Jessye Norman), Cherubino (Yvonne Minton), Marcellina (Maria Casula), Bartolo (Clifford Grant), Don Basilio (Robert Tear).
(M) **(*) Decca 417 315-2 (3) [id.]. V. State Op. Ch., VPO, Erich Kleiber.
    Figaro (Cesare Siepi), Susanna (Hilde Gueden), Count Almaviva (Alfred Poell), Countess Almaviva (Lisa Della Casa), Cherubino (Suzanne Danco), Marcellina (Hilde Rössl-Majdan), Bartolo (Fernando Corena), Don Basilio (Murray Dickie).
(M) *** DG 429 869-2 (3) [id.]. German Op. Ch. & O, Boehm.
    Figaro (Hermann Prey), Susanna (Edith Mathis), Count Almaviva (Dietrich Fischer-Dieskau), Countess Almaviva (Gundula Janowitz), Cherubino (Tatiana Troyanos), Marcellina (Patricia Johnson), Bartolo (Peter Lagger), Don Basilio (Erwin Wohlfahrt).
**(*) EMI Dig. CDS7 49753-2 (3) [Ang. CDCC 49753]. Glyndebourne Ch., LPO, Haitink.
    Figaro (Claudio Desderi), Susanna (Gianna Rolandi), Count Almaviva (Richard Stilwell),

Countess Almaviva (Felicity Lott), Cherubino (Faith Esham), Marcellina (Anne Mason), Bartolo (Artur Korn), Don Basilio (Ugo Benelli).

(M) (**(*)) EMI mono CMS7 69639-2 (2) [Ang. CDMB 69639]. V. State Op. Ch., VPO, Karajan.

Figaro (Erich Kunz), Susanna (Irmgard Seefried), Count Almaviva (George London), Countess Almaviva (Elisabeth Schwarzkopf), Cherubino (Sena Jurinac), Marcellina (Elisabeth Höngen), Bartolo (Marjan Rus), Don Basilio (Erich Majkut).

Withdrawn: (M) **(*) EMI CMS7 63849-2 (3) [Ang. CDMC 63849]. Alldis Ch., New Philh. O, Klemperer.

Figaro (Geraint Evans), Susanna (Reri Grist), Count Almaviva (Gabriel Bacquier), Countess Almaviva (Elisabeth Söderström), Cherubino (Teresa Berganza), Marcellina (Annelies Burmeister), Bartolo (Michael Langdon), Don Basilio (Werner Hollweg).

** Ph. Dig. 416 370-2 (3) [id.]. Amb. Op. Ch., ASMF, Marriner.

Figaro (José Van Dam), Susanna (Barbara Hendricks), Count Almaviva (Ruggero Raimondi), Countess Almaviva (Lucia Popp), Cherubino (Agnes Baltsa), Marcellina (Felicity Palmer), Bartolo (Robert Lloyd), Don Basilio (Aldo Baldin).

** Decca 421 125-2 (3) [id.]. V. State Op. Ch., VPO, Karajan.

Figaro (José Van Dam), Susanna (Ileana Cotrubas), Count Almaviva (Tom Krause), Countess Almaviva (Anna Tomowa-Sintow), Cherubino (Frederica Von Stade), Marcellina (Jane Berbié), Bartolo (Jules Bastin), Don Basilio (Heinz Zednik).

** EMI Dig. CDS7 47978-8 (3) [Ang. CDCC 47978]. V. State Op. Ch., VPO, Muti.

Figaro (Thomas Allen), Susanna (Kathleen Battle), Count Almaviva (Jorma Hynninen), Countess Almaviva (Margaret Price), Cherubino (Ann Murray), Marcellina (Mariana Nicolesco), Bartolo (Kurt Rydl), Don Basilio (Alejandro Ramirez).

** DG Dig. 431 619-2 (3) [id.]. NY Met. Op. Ch. & O, Levine.

Figaro (Ferruccio Furlanetto), Susanna (Dawn Upshaw), Count Almaviva (Thomas Hampson), Countess Almaviva (Kiri Te Kanawa), Cherubino (Anne Sofie Von Otter), Marcellina (Tatiana Troyanos), Bartolo (Paul Plishka), Don Basilio (Anthony Laciura).

** Decca Dig. 421 333-2 (3) [id.]. Drottningholm Theatre Ch. & O, Östman.

Figaro (Petteri Salomaa), Susanna (Barbara Bonney), Count Almaviva (Håkan Hagegård), Countess Almaviva (Arleen Augér), Cherubino (Alicia Nafé), Marcellina (Della Jones), Bartolo (Carlos Feller), Don Basilio (Edoardo Gimenez).

Withdrawn: (M) ** EMI CMS7 63646-2 (3) [Ang. CDMC 63646]. Alldis Ch., ECO, Barenboim.

Figaro (Geraint Evans), Susanna (Judith Blegen), Count Almaviva (Dietrich Fischer-Dieskau), Countess Almaviva (Heather Harper), Cherubino (Teresa Berganza), Marcellina (Birgit Finnila), Bartolo (William McCue), Don Basilio (John Fryatt).

** Erato/Warner 2292 45501-2 (3) [id.]. Berlin RIAS Ch., BPO, Barenboim.

Figaro (John Tomlinson), Susanna (Joan Rodgers), Count Almaviva (Andreas Schmidt), Countess Almaviva (Lella Cuberli), Cherubino (Cecilia Bartoli), Marcellina (Phyllis Pancella), Bartolo (Günther Von Kannen), Don Basilio (Graham Clark).

(M) ** DG 437 671-2 (3) [id.]. Berlin RIAS Chamber Ch. & RSO, Fricsay.

Figaro (Renato Capecchi), Susanna (Irmgard Seefried), Count Almaviva (Dietrich Fischer-Dieskau), Countess Almaviva (Maria Stader), Cherubino (Hertha Töpper), Marcellina (Lilian Benningsen), Bartolo (Ivan Sardi), Don Basilio (Paul Kuen).

*(*) BMG/RCA Dig. RD 60440 (3) [60440-2-RC]. Bav. R. Ch. & SO, C. Davis.

Figaro (Alan Titus), Susanna (Helen Donath), Count Almaviva (Ferruccio Furlanetto), Countess Almaviva (Julia Varady), Cherubino (Marilyn Schmiege), Marcellina (Cornelia Kallisch), Bartolo (Siegmund Nimsgern), Don Basilio (Heinz Zednik).

Mozart's *Nozze di Figaro*, first heard in Vienna in 1786, is surely the most perfect among comic operas. It carries a very human story with three-dimensional characters, and Lorenzo da Ponte's libretto, modelled on a Beaumarchais play, does not minimize the underlying semi-revolutionary sentiments. For it is the servants who, displaying greater wit and resource than their 'betters', continually triumph over their aristocratic master.

As the curtain rises, Figaro, personal attendant to Count Almaviva, and Susanna, the countess's maid, are eagerly anticipating their forthcoming marriage. Susanna tries on a hat, while Figaro measures the room for a bed. But while the apartment is conveniently situated for their duties, Figaro has misgivings and Susanna feels insecure: their abode is only too near the count's bedroom. Although Count Almaviva has officially renounced his privilege of *droit du seigneur*, he is not to be trusted.

Figaro leaves and Dr Bartolo enters to add his support to Marcellina (once his housekeeper and probably more than that) whom Figaro had some time ago offered to marry because of a debt. He had wriggled out of his obligation, but Marcellina still has designs on him, and she is jealous of Susanna. The two ladies spar verbally. Marcellina leaves as Cherubino, the count's young page, enters, full of youthful passion for the countess. He asks Susanna for help (as he is in danger of dismissal) and hides when the count enters, thus overhearing the count ask for a secret liaison with Susanna.

The count in turn is forced to hide when the voice of Don Basilio is heard: he is the music master and general organizer of intrigue in the household. Both Cherubino and the count choose the same chair; the former, concealed by a gown, curls up on top of it, the latter is concealed behind it. Basilio stirs things up by insinuating that Cherubino has been openly flirting with both Susanna and the countess. Immediately the count comes out from his hiding place and angrily declares he will dismiss Cherubino, for he personally had recently discovered the amorous page making advances to the gardener's daughter, Barbarina. He pulls away the gown and Cherubino is revealed.

Everyone intercedes for Cherubino, but the count is adamant that he must leave and finally decides that Cherubino shall be made an officer in the count's regiment and shall depart almost immediately. Figaro then cheerfully relates to Cherubino the pains and pleasures of being a soldier.

We now meet the countess in her chamber and learn of her misgivings and doubts: she feels that her husband no longer loves her. Figaro is unhappy too, for he has learned that the count is withholding his consent to his marriage. Susanna enters and confides her suspicions of the count's intentions towards her, and together they plan to outwit him. They will send Cherubino, disguised as Susanna, to make an assignation with the count. Cherubino now comes in and sings of his amorous feelings and he tries on his disguise. Suddenly the count is heard outside the door. Susanna and Cherubino both hide, with Cherubino locked in an inner room.

The perturbed countess now welcomes her husband into the room. But he is highly suspicious of the locked inner door and insists that the countess accompany him to find tools to open it. Susanna now dashes from her hiding place, unlocks the door and takes Cherubino's place, while he jumps out of the window into the garden. On their return the countess admits that Cherubino is in the inner room but, when the count draws his sword, opens the inner door and confronts Susanna, the countess (although nearly as startled as he by the sudden turn of events) resourcefully explains that her confession was a pretence to shame him.

He is reluctantly forced to beg for her forgiveness. But Antonio, the gardener, now enters, stating that a man has jumped from the window and damaged his plants. In the nick of time, Figaro arrives and declares that it was he who jumped. But in his haste Cherubino had dropped his officer's commission, so poor Figaro now has to explain this latest embarrassment away. He does so by saying that the commission was invalid as it was unsealed. To add to the confusion, Basilio and Bartolo arrive with Marcellina, who is still seeking Figaro's hand in marriage, and so once again his planned nuptials with Susanna seem at risk.

Now the plan to outwit the count's designs on Susanna takes a further step forward as Susanna arranges a nocturnal meeting with him in the garden; after she has left, the count soliloquizes about his frustration in his own situation, while his servants can apparently be happy in matters of love. Figaro is indeed in high spirits, for it is now discovered that Bartolo and Marcellina are his parents (he is identified by a birthmark on his arm), so he cannot possibly marry his own mother! He embraces her and Susanna arrives and jealously boxes his ears; however, she too is delighted when she learns the truth of the matter. Meanwhile the countess, alone, is again lamenting her husband's cruel lack of feeling for her, remembering her past happiness.

So, in furtherance of the plan to catch him out in an act of infidelity, she dictates a letter to Susanna to arrange the meeting in the garden. A pin, fastening the letter, is to be returned as a sign that the rendezvous will be kept. Figaro and Susanna, Marcellina and Dr Bartolo now approach the count to ask his blessing on their respective marriages, and Susanna takes the opportunity to slip the letter into Almaviva's hand. Reading it and looking forward to seducing Susanna that very evening, he seals the note with a pin, confirming the assignation, and entrusts the pinned reply to Barbarina, who promptly loses the pin. Figaro arrives and, overhearing her distress at the loss, deduces that Susanna is to meet the count that very night. He is not aware that all is not as it seems and angrily asks Bartolo and Basilio to come with him to witness her faithless behaviour.

Susanna and the countess now exchange cloaks and the count arrives and makes a passionate declaration of love to his own wife in disguise. Susanna, meanwhile, having rapturously declared her own feelings for her husband-to-be, then meets Figaro and is nonplussed when he (teasing her) pretends to make love to her as the countess. But she soon forgives him; when the count appears, he quickly discovers his own mistake and is humbled in front of the gathered company. Magnanimously he pardons them for their deception and touchingly begs the countess for forgiveness, which she happily gives. Few operas end more happily, yet with greater underlying pathos about the flawed nature of the human condition.

Solti's exuberant version of *Figaro* starts with a controversially fast account of the *Overture*, matching Karajan in the 'egg-timer' race. Elsewhere Solti opts for a fair proportion of extreme speeds, slow as well as fast, but they never intrude on the happiness of the entertainment. Rejecting the idea of a bass Figaro, Solti has chosen in Samuel Ramey a firm-toned baritone, a virile figure. He is less a comedian than a lover, superbly matched to the most enchanting of Susannas, Lucia Popp, who gives a sparkling and radiant performance to match the Pamina she sang in Haitink's recording of *Zauberflöte*. Thomas Allen's Count is magnificent too, tough in tone and characterization but always beautiful on the ear. Kurt Moll as Dr Bartolo sings an unforgettable *La vendetta* with triplets very fast and agile 'on the breath', while Robert Tear far outshines his own achievement as the Basilio of Sir Colin Davis's amiable recording. Frederica von Stade, as in the Karajan set, is a most attractive Cherubino, even if *Voi che sapete* is too slow; but crowning all is the Countess of Kiri Te Kanawa, challenged by Solti's spacious tempi in the two big arias but producing ravishing tone, flawless phrasing and elegant ornamentation throughout. With superb, vivid recording this makes a clear first choice for a much-recorded opera.

The most effervescent performance of *Figaro* on disc, brilliantly produced in early but well-separated stereo, the 1955 Glyndebourne recording makes a bargain without equal on only two CDs from CfP. The transfer on CD brings sound warmer, more naturally vivid and with more body than on many modern recordings. There is no added edginess, as occurs on so many CD transfers involving voices (in that respect it is far superior to the disappointing Decca CD transfer of the vintage Decca Kleiber set from the same period). The realistic projection instantly makes one forget any minimal tape-hiss, and the performance, recorded in the studio immediately after a vintage Glyndebourne season, offers not only unsurpassed teamwork, witty in its timing, but a consistently stylish and characterful cast.

Just as Sesto Bruscantini is the archetypal Glyndebourne Figaro, Sena Jurinac is the perfect Countess, with Graziella Sciutti a delectable Susanna and Risë Stevens a well-contrasted Cherubino, vivacious in their scenes together. Franco Calabrese as the Count is firm and virile, if occasionally stressed on top; and the three character roles have never been more vividly cast, with Ian Wallace as Bartolo, Monica Sinclair as Marcellina and the incomparable Hugues Cuénod as Basilio. The only regret is that Cuénod's brilliant performance of Basilio's aria in Act IV has had to be omitted (as it so often is on stage) to keep the two discs each within the 80-minute limit. There is no libretto, but a detailed synopsis is provided with cueing points conveniently indicated.

Like his set of *Don Giovanni* – also recorded in 1959 – the Giulini version is a classic, with a cast assembled by Walter Legge that has rarely been matched, let alone surpassed. If the fun of the opera is more gently presented by Giulini than by some others, he provides the perfect frame for such a characterful line-up of soloists. Taddei with his dark bass-baritone makes a provocative Figaro; opposite him, Anna Moffo is at her freshest and sweetest as Susanna. Schwarzkopf as ever is the noblest of Countesses, and it is good to hear the young Fiorenza Cossotto as a full-toned Cherubino. Eberhard Waechter is a strong and stylish Count. On only two mid-priced discs instead of the original four LPs, it makes a superb bargain, though – as in the other EMI two-disc version, the Gui on CfP – Marcellina's and Basilio's arias are omitted from Act IV. The break between discs is neatly managed towards the end of the Act II finale. The transfer is excellent, giving a focus and sense of presence often not achieved in modern digital recordings. Unlike many mid-priced opera sets from EMI, this one comes in a slip-case, complete with full libretto and translation, bringing an advantage over the CfP set.

The pacing of Sir Colin Davis has a sparkle in recitative that directly reflects experience in the opera house, and his tempi generally are beautifully chosen to make their dramatic points. Vocally the cast is exceptionally consistent. Mirella Freni (Susanna) is perhaps the least satisfying, yet there is no lack of character and charm. It is good to have so ravishingly beautiful a voice as Jessye Norman's for the Countess, making one of her earliest opera-recordings. The Figaro of Wladimiro Ganzarolli and the Count of Ingvar Wixell project with exceptional clarity and vigour, and there is fine singing too from Yvonne Minton as Cherubino, Clifford Grant as Bartolo and Robert Tear as Basilio. The 1971 recording has more reverberation than usual, but the effect is commendably atmospheric and on CD the voices have plenty of presence. The CD transfer is altogether smoother than Decca have managed for the Kleiber set, with the break in the middle of Act II coming earlier and much better placed. This remains one of the most enjoyable versions of this opera from the analogue era.

Kleiber's famous set was one of Decca's offerings in 1956 for the bicentenary of Mozart's birth. It remains an outstanding bargain at mid-price, an attractively strong performance with much fine singing. Gueden makes an enchanting Susanna, singing characterfully with golden tone, and her voice both blends and contrasts beautifully with Della Casa's as the Countess. Danco as Cherubino and Della Casa are both at their finest. A dark-toned Figaro in Siepi brings added contrast and, if the pace of the recitatives is rather slow, this is not inconsistent within the context of Kleiber's overall approach. It is a pity that the Decca remastering, in brightening the sound, has brought a hint of edginess to the voices, though the basic atmosphere remains. Also, the layout brings a less than felicitous break in Act II, which Kleiber shapes with authoritative inevitability. In this respect the cassettes (no longer available) were superior – and they had smoother sound, too.

Boehm's DG set offers one of the most consistently assured performances available. The women all sing most beautifully, with Janowitz's Countess, Mathis's Susanna and Troyanos's Cherubino all ravishing the ear in contrasted ways. Prey is an intelligent if not very jolly-sounding Figaro, and Fischer-Dieskau gives his dark, sharply defined reading of the Count's role. The timing, not just from the singers, but above all from the conductor, is masterly. The fine playing and recording are all the more vivid on CD.

As in his other Glyndebourne recordings, Haitink's approach to Mozart is relaxed and mellow, helped by beautifully balanced orchestral sound. Where in *Così* the results were sunny, here in *Figaro* there is at times a lack of sparkle. There is much fine singing and excellent ensemble, and the set is well worth hearing, in particular for Claudio Desderi's idiomatically pointed and characterful Figaro, a vintage Glyndebourne performance. Yet next to the finest versions, as for example, Solti's, this falls short in the line-up of soloists. That even applies to Felicity Lott as the Countess. Though she sings *Dove sono* with melting simplicity, the voice is not as well caught as it can be, and she does not match such a rival as Kiri Te Kanawa. Gianna Rolandi as Susanna and Faith Esham as Cherubino are both stylish without being specially characterful, and the microphone gives an edge to their voices.

Recorded in 1950, Karajan's first recording of *Figaro* offers one of the most distinguished casts ever assembled; but, curiously at that period, they decided to record the opera without the *secco* recitatives. That is a most regrettable omission when all these singers are not just vocally immaculate but vividly characterful – as for example Sena Jurinac, later the greatest of Glyndebourne Countesses, here a vivacious Cherubino. The firmness of focus in Erich Kunz's singing of Figaro goes with a delightful twinkle in the word-pointing, and Irmgard Seefried makes a bewitching Susanna. Schwarzkopf's noble portrait of the Countess – not always helped by a slight backward balance of the microphone placing for her – culminates in the most poignant account of her second aria, *Dove sono*. Erich Majkut is a delightfully bright-eyed Basilio. Karajan at this early period was fresher as a Mozartian than later, sometimes hurrying his singers but keeping a necessary lightness. The sound, though obviously limited, presents the voices very vividly. Conveniently, each of the CDs contains two Acts.

Klemperer may seem to have been the most solemn of conductors but he had a great sense of humour. Here he shows very clearly how his humour fits in with the sterling characteristics we all recognize. Though the tempi are often slow, the pointing and shading are most delicate and the result, though hardly sparkling, is full of high spirits. A clue to the Klemperer approach comes near the beginning with Figaro's aria *Se vuol ballare*, which is not merely a servant's complaint about an individual master but a revolutionary call, with horns and pizzicato strings strongly defined, to apply to the whole world: 'I'll play the tune, sir!'

Geraint Evans is masterly in matching Klemperer; though his normal interpretation of the role of Figaro is more effervescent than this, he is superb here, singing and acting with great power. Reri Grist makes a charming Susanna and Teresa Berganza is a rich-toned Cherubino. Gabriel Bacquier's Count is darker-toned and more formidable than usual, while Elisabeth Söderström's Countess, though it has its moments of strain, gives ample evidence of this artist's thoughtful intensity. Though this is not a version one would regularly laugh over, it represents a unique experience. The recording has transferred very well to CD but, like the other Klemperer Mozart operas sets (except *Die Zauberflöte*), this has been withdrawn.

After his sparkling set of the other Figaro opera, Rossini's *Barbiere di Siviglia*, Sir Neville Marriner this time in Mozart falls down on his dramatic timing, and the result fails to lift. As an instance, the delicious duet between Susanna and the Count at the beginning of Act III, *Crudel!*

perche finora, is made lugubrious thanks to Raimondi, who is then superbly well focused in his big aria. Though Lucia Popp gives a deeply felt performance as the Countess, the strain on the voice tends to imperil the legato. Barbara Hendricks makes an attractively girlish Susanna and Van Dam a formidable Figaro, though one inclined to be too emphatic, not comic; even *Non più andrai* is too heavy. The final disappointment of the set is Marriner's failure to convey the necessary sense of resolution in the closing scene, with little or no poignancy conveyed. Despite the excellent recording in both formats, this could not be a first choice.

With Karajan on Decca, the speed and smoothness of the *Overture* establish the character of the whole performance. Too much is passed over with a deftness which quickly makes the result bland, despite superb singing and playing. Only Frederica von Stade as Cherubino establishes the sort of individuality of expression that is the very stuff of operatic drama; she alone emerges as a rounded character. With a bloom on the sound and added presence in the CD transfer, the performance is a joy to the ear but is likely to leave any Mozartian unsatisfied.

The Muti set of *Figaro* with the Vienna Philharmonic is disappointing for the cloudiness of focus in the recording, and the singing from a starry line-up of soloists is very variable. Margaret Price is a powerful, firm Countess, not quite as nobly distinctive as she might be, and Kathleen Battle is a sparkling Susanna. Commanding as Thomas Allen is as Figaro, this is not a comic figure, dark rather, and less than winning, more a Count translated. Hynninen is relatively uncharacterful as the Count and Ann Murray makes an edgy Cherubino. Muti's timing, often too fast, conveys little feeling for the comedy.

Levine's DG recording with forces from the Met. in New York brings some outstanding individual performances – notably Anne Sofie von Otter as a delightful Cherubino – but overall it lacks the effervescence needed for this opera. Dame Kiri Te Kanawa's Countess is far better appreciated in the Solti Decca set, Dawn Upshaw is too pert a Susanna, and Ferruccio Furlanetto's resonant Figaro is not helped by the roughness of Levine's accompaniment, as in *Non più andrai*.

Östman's version (based on the production at the Drottningholm Court Theatre but with different principals, like his earlier recording of *Così fan tutte*) is the first to use period instruments; also like *Così*, it brings generally hectic speeds. Far more than in *Così*, such treatment undermines both the fun and the dramatic point. Östman refuses to pause or even to broaden for a second in passages which cry out for it, whether it be in the ensemble where Susanna realizes that Marcellina is Figaro's mother or – most seriously – in the Act IV finale, when the Countess enters and the Count is confounded – a key moment which here is flicked through with minimal easing. Over and over again, with such a metrical beat even the most sparkling moments lose their brightness, and charm is far away. Nevertheless the cast is impressive.

The Susanna of Barbara Bonney is delightful, and though Petteri Salomaa is rather dry-toned, he makes an engaging young Figaro. Håkan Hagegård is a splendid Count, and Arleen Augér a pure-toned Countess who manages (against the odds) to mitigate the effect of Östman's cruelly fast speeds for *Dove sono* and the *Letter duet* – though both are made merely pretty rather than moving. Among the others, too, there are no weak links at all, and the set is valuable for generously including variant numbers that Mozart incorporated in productions at different times. Among them is a variant version of *Dove sono* and a higher version of the Count's aria; very sensibly, each is included on the relevant disc, so that on CD they can be programmed as alternatives to the regular number. Full and well-balanced recording.

For so lively a Mozartian, Barenboim takes a strangely staid view of *Figaro* in both his recordings. His EMI one, now reissued at mid-price, was recorded soon after live performances at the Edinburgh Festival and with substantially the same cast. Though recitatives are sharp enough, the result lacks sparkle, despite the characterful – if at times unsteady – Figaro of Sir Geraint Evans, in a classic characterization. The others too, on paper a fine, starry team, fail to project at full intensity, often thanks to slow speeds and unlifted rhythms. Those interested in individual singers might consider the set, but there are far finer versions than this.

In Barenboim's Berlin recording for Erato he takes a similar approach, with speeds again on the slow side and rhythms stodgy. On the question of scale this new version loses out in relation to the EMI, when a relatively large orchestra is set in a big, boomy acoustic. Superbly as the Berlin Philharmonic plays, that seriously undermines the sparkle of the piece. These shortcomings are the more regrettable when the cast is a strong one. The singer who most completely overcomes the problems, to give an enchanting performance, is Joan Rodgers as Susanna. John Tomlinson as Figaro sings strongly too, but he makes a rather dour figure. Cecilia Bartoli is a characterful Cherubino, but the voice remains disconcertingly feminine in its richness, not at all boyish. There is less need for sparkle in the roles of Count and Countess, and Andreas Schmidt and Lella Cuberli both sing well, but even they suffer from the curious focus of the sound.

Fricsay's account, for all its vitality, cannot match his splendid *Zauberflöte*. Tempi are consistently fast, and this contributes to the brilliance, while at the same time the sense of urgency produces some fine teamwork. Vocally the disappointment of the set is the Susanna of Irmgard Seefried; plainly she was not in the best of voice when the set was recorded. Fischer-Dieskau's commanding assumption of the role of the Count makes some amends, but a *Figaro* with an under-par Susanna cannot receive a very strong recommendation and the overall level of the singing generally falls well below that on the best of the rival mid- and bargain-priced sets.

Sir Colin Davis's RCA version comes as a disappointment after his excellent Philips set. Though his pointing of Mozart is as finely judged as ever, the result does not sparkle as it did, not helped by the colourless Figaro of Alan Titus. There are some fine individual performances, but this hardly matches the finest versions.

Le nozze di Figaro: highlights.
*** Decca Dig. 417 395-2 [id.] (from above recording with Ramey, Popp, Allen, Te Kanawa; cond. Solti).
(M) *** DG 429 822-3 [id.] (from above recording with Prey, Mathis, Fischer-Dieskau, Janowitz; cond. Boehm).
(M) **(*) Decca 421 317-2 [id.] (from above recording with Van Dam, Cotrubas, Krause, Tomowa-Sintow; cond. Karajan).
** DG Dig. 435 488-2 [id.] (from above recording with Furlanetto, Upshaw, Hampson, Te Kanawa; cond. Levine).

Solti's highlights disc remains at full price and, though it is a good selection, one can buy the virtually complete Glyndebourne recording of the opera on Classics for Pleasure for less than the cost of this Decca CD.

Boehm's selection includes many of the key numbers, but with a little over an hour of music it is less generous than its companion highlights discs. Like them, it is inadequately documented but the singing is first class and the sound vivid.

Though overall Karajan's Decca Vienna recording of *Figaro* with its wilful speeds is too slick for so fizzing a comedy, such polish and refinement deserve to be sampled – notably Frederica von Stade's Cherubino. This selection, vividly recorded, does the job admirably.

Levine's highlights disc gives one a chance to sample Anne Sofie von Otter's Cherubino (with *Non so più* and *Voi che sapete* included) and Ferruccio Furlanetto's striking Figaro, but Dame Kiri's Countess projects more effectively with Solti on Decca. The 67-minute selection is well balanced, including the *Overture* and finale.

L'Oca del Cairo (complete).
(M) *** Ph. Dig. 422 539-2 [id.]. Berlin R. Ch. (members), C. P. E. Bach CO, Schreier – *Lo sposo deluso.* ***
  Pippo (Dietrich Fischer-Dieskau), Celidora (Edith Wiens), Biondello (Peter Schreier), Calandrino (David Johnson), Lavina (Pamela Coburn), Chicchibio (Anton Scharinger), Auretta (Inge Nielsen).

We owe it to the Mozart scholar and Philips recording producer, Erik Smith, that these two sets of Mozartian fragments, *L'Oca del Cairo* and *Lo sposo deluso*, have been prepared for performance and recorded. Dating from 1783–4, they anticipate the great leap forward in the history of comic opera represented by *Le nozze di Figaro* in 1786. Though it is doubtful whether even Mozart could have developed the ideas they contain into comparable masterpieces, the incidental delights are many.

What there is of the story of *L'Oca del Cairo* tells of Celidora and her friend Lavina being imprisoned in a tower by the aged Marchese Don Pippo, who intends Lavina for his bride (though she has her sights on Calandrino), while Celidora is intended for Count Lionetto, instead of her own choice (Biondello). In the main household, the maid Auretta flirts with various tradesmen and her lover, the butler (Chicchibio), is jealous. Finding Don Pippo is taking a nap, Calandrino makes a pass at Auretta but they are caught in the act by Chicchibio. Don Pippo thinks that Biondello's rescue plan will fail, and the ladies are able to get out of the tower into the garden.

Thus the two principal pairs of lovers can discuss their mutual feelings and the forthcoming escape. Auretta and Chicchibio now rush in to give warning of Don Pippo's approach; he is angry to find the ladies in the garden . . . That is as far as the plot is developed, and Mozart was in two minds whether or not he could accept the planned outline for Act II, which in Abate Varesco's libretto rather doubtfully involved a goose, and the project was apparently abandoned.

L'Oca del Cairo ('The Cairo goose'), containing roughly twice as much music as *Lo sposo deluso*, involves six substantial numbers, most of them ensembles, including an amazing finale to the projected Act I. It is as extended as the comparable finales of *Figaro* and *Così fan tutte*, with contrasted sections following briskly one after the other. The score left by Mozart has the vocal parts virtually complete, as well as the bass line and the occasional instrumental indications. Smith has sensitively filled in the gaps to make a satisfying whole, very well conducted by Peter Schreier, who also takes part as one of the soloists. Dietrich Fischer-Dieskau takes the *buffo* old-man role of Don Pippo, and Anton Scharinger is brilliant in the patter aria in tarantella rhythm for the major-domo, Chicchibio, bringing a foretaste of Donizetti.

Lo sposo deluso, for which Smith did his completion much earlier, involves only four numbers, preceded by a splendid overture, but their invention is sharper and even more clearly anticipates the style of Mozart's Da Ponte operas. Sir Colin Davis directs an excellent (mainly British) cast, with the 1975 analogue recording as fresh and bright as the 1990 digital recording for *L'Oca del Cairo*.

Il rè pastore (complete).
(M) **(*) Ph. Dig. 422 535-2 (2) [id.]. ASMF, Marriner.

   Aminta (Angela Maria Blasi), Elisa (Sylvia McNair), Tamiri (Iris Vermillion), Alessandro (Jerry Hadley), Agenore (Claes Hakon Ahnsjö).

Il rè pastore, the last of Mozart's early operas, is best known for the glorious aria, *L'amerò*, one of the loveliest he ever wrote for soprano. The whole entertainment, described as a 'Serenata, on the subject of the shepherd-king nominated by Alexander the Great as his successor', is among the most charming of his early music, a gentle piece which works well on record.

The shepherd Aminta loves Elisa and, after assuring him of her reciprocal feelings, she leaves to get her parents' consent to the marriage. Alessandro, ruler of Macedonia, and his confidant, Agenore, admire the pastoral life which Aminta enjoys, but Alessandro recognizes that Aminta is the heir to the throne of Sidon (recently liberated from the tyrant, Strato) who has been living humbly, unaware of his real identity.

Meanwhile Agenore meets his beloved, Tamiri, the daughter of the deposed tyrant, also in a shepherd's garb, hiding from Alessandro. She refuses to believe that Alessandro is a just ruler who means her no harm. Elisa now returns with permission for her marriage to Aminta. Aminta is then dismayed to discover – through Agenore, who was his guardian as a child – that he is heir apparent to Sidon and that his real name is Abdolonimo. He refuses to give up Elisa and she reaffirms her feelings for him.

Alessandro and Aminta now consult about the future, Agenore turns Elisa away from the tent, but Aminta appears and refuses to put royal duty before his love for her. Alessandro – without realizing that Agenore is in love with Tamiri – asks his help to arrange a marriage between Tamiri and Aminta to consolidate the throne. But Aminta has gone into retreat, determined to refuse the crown. Everyone is unhappy. Elisa thinks Aminta has deserted her and Tamiri is equally appalled at the arrangements made for her future. Finally Tamiri begs Alessandro not to part two pairs of lovers, and the great ruler wisely brings each couple back together. Thus the shepherd finally becomes king, but with Elisa by his side.

The newest version of this delightful piece, by Marriner and the Academy, has a first-rate cast. Brisk and bright, with plenty of light and shade, and superbly played, it yet does not efface memories of the 1979 DG version conducted by Leopold Hager, which offered even purer singing. Here Angela Maria Blasi, despite a beautiful voice, attacks notes from below, even in *L'amerò*. Excellent sound.

Der Schauspieldirektor (The Impresario; opera): complete.
Withdrawn: (M) *** DG 429 877-2; *3371 002* (3) [id.]. Dresden State O, Boehm – *Die Zauberflöte*. **(*)

   Mme Herz (Reri Grist), Mlle Silberklang (Arleen Augér), Vogelsang (Peter Schreier), Buff (Kurt Moll).
(M) **(*) Ph. 422 536-2 (2) [id.]. LSO, Sir Colin Davis – *Zaïde*. ***

   Mme Herz (Ruth Welting), Mlle Silberklang (Ileana Cotrubas), Vogelsang (Anthony Rolfe Johnson), Buff (Clifford Grant).

(iv; vii) *Der Schauspieldirektor*. Concert arias: (ii; vi; viii) *Misera, dove son!, K.369; Un moto di gioia, K.579; Schon lacht der holde Frühling, K.580.* (i; vi; viii) *Vado, ma dove? oh Dei!, K.583; Bella mia fiamma, addio, K.529; Nehmt meinen Dank, ihr holden Gonner!* (iii; v; ix) *Die Entführung: Ha! Wie will ich triumpheren.* (iv; vii) *Le nozze di Figaro: Overture.*
*** Decca Dig. 430 207-2 [id.]. (i) Te Kanawa, (ii) Gruberová, (iii) Jungwirth; (iv) VPO; (v) Vienna Haydn O; (vi) Vienna CO; (vii) Pritchard; (viii) Fischer; (ix) Kertész.
   Mme Herz (Edita Gruberová), Mlle Silberklang (Kiri Te Kanawa), Vogelsang (Uwe Heilmann), Buff (Manfred Jungwirth).

Mozart's scenario for *Der Schauspieldirektor* has a wonderfully knowing cynicism about theatrical mores and the egotism of artists. Its impressario hero, Frank, is to establish a new company devoted to *buffo* Singspiel in Salzburg. Buff, his principal actor, gives him good advice: as long as the ensemble is large, its quality is less important. Good taste can go out of the window because – so far as the musical public is concerned – the 'worst pieces are the best'. Besides giving the press free tickets, they must also be supplied with supper, and lunch with the most attractive lady star. In any case financial backing is dependent on the star role going to the banker's mistress, Madame Pfeil.

At the audition, she is to perform the closing scene of *The Outraged Husband*. The actor, Herz, and Madame Krone are now introduced. She specializes in tragedy, with chaste emotional feeling, and with her colleague performs an excerpt from *Bianca Capello*. Next comes comedy and Madame Vogelsang joins Buff in a scene from *The Amorous Country Girl*. They both introduce relations who also seek to display their talents.

Franz's wife offers a sentimental ballad. Now Mlle Silberklang comes on with a demonstration of spectacular coloratura; when both sopranos are engaged, they quarrel about money, and Madame Pfeil joins in. The distraught Frank now abandons his plans through lack of sufficient finance, and all the artists join in a declaration that money is not as important as being able to demonstrate their glittering talents for the public to judge.

This Decca recording of the four musical numbers from *Der Schauspieldirektor* (presented 'dry' with no German dialogue) was made only six months before Sir John Pritchard died, an apt last offering from him, a great Mozartian. Having two such well-contrasted star sopranos adds point to the contest, and the performances are a delight, though the recorded sound is not as well focused as usual from this source. The *Figaro overture*, also conducted by Pritchard, is another completely new item. The rest is reissue material, with three concert arias each from Gruberová and Dame Kiri, taken from Decca's 1981 boxed set of the collected arias. Manfred Jungwirth's bitingly dark account of Osmin's aria from *Entführung* dates from ten years before that, a welcome extra. The single disc is boxed with texts and notes.

The DG performance of *Der Schauspieldirektor* is also without dialogue, so that it is short enough to make a fill-up for Boehm's *Zauberflöte*. Reri Grist's bravura as Madame Herz is impressive, and Arleen Augér is pleasingly fresh and stylish here. The tenor and bass make only minor contributions, but Boehm's guiding hand keeps the music alive from the first bar to the last.

There is no contest whatsoever between the two rival prima donnas presented in the Philips recording. *Ich bin die erste Sängerin* ('I am the leading prima donna'), they yell at each other; but here Ileana Cotrubas is in a world apart from the thin-sounding and shallow Ruth Welting. Davis directs with fire and electricity a performance which is otherwise (despite the lack of spoken dialogue) most refreshing and beautifully recorded (in 1975) in a sympathetic acoustic.

Il sogno di Scipione (complete).
(M) *** Ph. 422 531-2 (2) [id.]. Salzburg Chamber Ch. & Mozarteum O, Hager.
   Scipio (Peter Schreier), Costanza (Lucia Popp), Fortuna (Edita Gruberová), Publio (Claes Hakon Ahnsjö), Emilio (Thomas Moser), Licenza (Edith Mathis).

Mozart described this early piece as a *serenata* or *azione teatrale* rather than an opera: it was written for the enthronement in Salzburg of Archbishop Colloredo, with whom Mozart later had his celebrated dispute. It has an allegorical plot in which Scipio has to choose between Fortune and Constancy. The principal character, Roman commander and conqueror of Carthage, is transported through various experiences so that he can properly make up his mind. From the Elysian Fields he moves on to Elysium, where he meets the spirits of both his father and grandfather. Both insist that duty is paramount and he discovers that heroes have been rewarded in Elysium with beautiful dwellings. Fortune now reminds him of the importance of good luck in any human life, but Scipio is sceptical about trusting only to luck rather than seeking a path of virtue, and this invokes Fortune's wrath. Scipio wakes up and realizes it was all a dream and Licenza confirms his steadfastness.

Mozart's setting consists of a sequence of 11 extended arias using three tenors and two sopranos. As a modern entertainment it outstays its welcome, but a recording as stylish and well sung as this certainly has its place. Given the choice of present-day singers, this cast could hardly be finer, with Edita Gruberová, Lucia Popp and Edith Mathis superbly contrasted in the women's roles (the latter taking part in the epilogue merely), and Peter Schreier is joined by two of his most accomplished younger colleagues. Hager sometimes does not press the music on as he might, but his direction is always alive, and the Salzburg Mozarteum Orchestra plays with fine point and elegance – witness the winningly sprightly violins in the *Overture*. With fine recording, vividly and atmospherically transferred to CD, the set is not likely to be surpassed in the immediate future.

Lo sposo deluso.
(M) *** Ph. 422 539-2 [id.]. LSO, Sir Colin Davis – *L'Oca del Cairo*. ***
  Eugenia (Felicity Palmer), Bettina (Ileana Cotrubas), Pulcherio (Robert Tear), Don Asdrubale (Anthony Rolfe Johnson), Bocconio (Clifford Grant).

The music presented here from *Lo sposo deluso* ('The disappointed bridegroom') is all that survives from an unfinished opera written in the years before *Figaro*, and it contains much that is memorable. The situation it presents is conventional but promising. The elderly Bocconio is dressing in finery proper for his marriage to his young bride, Eugenia. Pulcherio thinks it is all a great joke and feels sorry for her. Bocconio's niece, Bettina, and her husband, Don Asdrubale, sit playing cards. Eugenia arrives, and her fresh beauty is appreciated by Pulcherio, who anticipates what will happen when she is disillusioned after the wedding; he is glad he is single. In the final *Trio* Bocconio, Eugenia and Don Asdrubale all react personally to the probable outcome.

The *Overture*, with its trumpet calls, its lovely slow middle section and recapitulation with voices, is a charmer, while the two arias, reconstructed by the recording producer and scholar, Erik Smith, are also delightful: the one a trial run for Fiordiligi's *Come scoglio* in *Così*, the other (sung by Robert Tear) giving a foretaste of Papageno's music in *The Magic Flute*.

Zaïde (complete).
(M) *** Ph. 422 536-2 (2) [id.]. Berlin State O, Klee – *Der Schauspieldirektor*. **(*)
  Zaïde (Edith Mathis), Gomatz (Peter Schreier), Allazim (Ingvar Wixell), Sultan Soliman (Werner Hollweg), Osmin (Reiner Süss).
** Orfeo Dig. C 055832 I (2) [id.]. Salzburg Mozarteum O, Hager.
  Zaïde (Judith Blegen), Gomatz (Werner Hollweg), Allazim (Wolfgang Schöne), Sultan Soliman (Thomas Moser), Osmin (Robert Holl).

Zaïde, written between 1779 and 1780 and never quite completed, was a trial run for *Entführung*, based on a comparable story of love, duty, escape and forgiveness in the seraglio. It has nothing like the same dramatic sharpness of focus, which may perhaps account for Mozart's failure to complete the piece when within sight of the end. For whatever reason, he left it minus an overture and a finale, but it is simple enough for both to be supplied from other sources, as is done here: the Symphony No. 32 makes an apt enough overture and a *March* (K.335/1) rounds things off quickly and neatly.

The story is easily ascertained from the text of the 15 numbers. Act I opens with a cheerful slaves' chorus. However, the mood soon changes: their leader, Gomatz, stops what he is doing and complains of his desperate plight. Then as he lies down under a tree, Zaïde, the sultan's favourite, appears. She secretes a picture of herself and a purse in Gomatz's pocket. When he wakes up, he falls in love with her image. Zaïde reappears and together they plan to escape. Allazim, the slaves' overseer, now enters and surprises the lovers with his sympathy. He offers to help them escape and says he will accompany them.

Act II brings the entry of the enraged sultan, already missing Zaïde. Osmin then boldly enters to report that Allazim has also absconded; he urges the sultan not to be upset by Zaïde's departure: as a procurer of slaves he can offer ready replacements. But the sultan seeks revenge, and soon we find Zaïde in a dungeon, defiant but anticipating her execution alongside Gomatz. Allazim now pleads for the lives of the captives. There is a grand quartet for the sultan, Allazim and the lovers, in which they all declare their conflicting feelings, and we are left to imagine the ending for ourselves. Remembering *Die Entführung aus dem Serail*, one suspects that the sultan will relent and pardon everyone.

Much of the music is superb, and melodramas at the beginning of each Act are strikingly effective and original, with the speaking voice of the tenor in the first heard over darkly dramatic writing in D minor. Zaïde's arias in both Acts are magnificent: the radiantly lyrical *Ruhe sanft* is hauntingly memorable, and the dramatic *Tiger aria* is like Constanze's *Martern aller Arten* but briefer and more passionate. Bernhard Klee on Philips directs a crisp and lively performance, with excellent contributions from singers and orchestra alike – a first-rate team, as consistently stylish as one could want. The 1973 recording is most refined, and the CD transfer retains the appealingly warm ambient atmosphere, making this an attractively compact Mozartian entertainment.

The Orfeo performance is generally well sung and well recorded. The CDs have presence and atmosphere. However, this version does not quite match the earlier, Philips set, either in playing or in singing. The Sultan of the earlier version, Werner Hollweg, here becomes the hero, Gomatz, free-toned and stylish, if hardly passionate. Judith Blegen makes an appealing Zaïde, though the voice could be steadier, and Robert Holl is a fine, dark-toned Osmin.

Die Zauberflöte (complete).
*** Ph. Dig. 426 276-2; *426 276-4* (2) [id.]. Amb. Op. Ch., ASMF, Marriner.
  Pamina (Kiri Te Kanawa), Queen of the Night (Cheryl Studer), Tamino (Francisco Araiza), Papageno (Olaf Bär), Sarastro (Samuel Ramey), Speaker (José Van Dam), Monostatos (Aldo Baldin), Papagena (Eva Lind), 3 Ladies (Yvonne Kenny, Iris Vermillion, Anne Collins).
⊕ (M) (***) DG mono 435 741-2 (2). Berlin RIAS Ch. & SO, Fricsay.
  Pamina (Maria Stader), Queen of the Night (Rita Streich), Tamino (Ernst Haefliger), Papageno (Dietrich Fischer-Dieskau), Sarastro (Josef Greindl), Speaker (Kim Borg), Monostatos (Martin Vantin), Papagena (Lisa Otto), 3 Ladies (Marianna Schech, Liselotte Losch, Margarete Klose).
(M) *** EMI CMS7 69971-2 (2) [Ang. CDMB 69971]. Philh. Ch. & O, Klemperer.
  Pamina (Gundula Janowitz), Queen of the Night (Lucia Popp), Tamino (Nicolai Gedda), Papageno (Walter Berry), Sarastro (Gottlob Frick), Speaker (Franz Crass), Monostatos (Gerhard Unger), Papagena (Ruth-Margret Pütz), 3 Ladies (Elisabeth Schwarzkopf, Christa Ludwig, Marga Höffgen).
(M) (***) EMI mono CHS7 69631-2 (2) [Ang. CDHB 69631]. V. State Op. Ch., VPO, Karajan.
  Pamina (Irmgard Seefried), Queen of the Night (Wilma Lipp), Tamino (Anton Dermota), Papageno (Erich Kunz), Sarastro (Ludwig Weber), Speaker (George London), Monostatos (Peter Klein), Papagena (Emmy Loose), 3 Ladies (Sena Jurinac, Friedl Riegler, Else Schürhoff).
*** EMI Dig. CDS7 47951-8 (3) [Ang. CDCC 47951]. Bav. R. Ch. & SO, Haitink.
  Pamina (Lucia Popp), Queen of the Night (Edita Gruberová), Tamino (Siegfried Jerusalem), Papageno (Wolfgang Brendel), Sarastro (Roland Bracht), Speaker (Norman Bailey), Monostatos (Heinz Zednik), Papagena (Brigette Lindner), 3 Ladies (Marilyn Richardson, Doris Soffel, Ortrun Wenkel).
*** Telarc Dig. CD-80302 (2). SCO & Ch., Mackerras.
  Pamina (Barbara Hendricks), Queen of the Night (June Anderson), Tamino (Jerry Hadley), Papageno (Thomas Allen), Sarastro (Robert Lloyd), Speaker (Gottfried Hornik), Monostatos (Helmut Wildhaber), Papagena (Ulrike Steinsky), 3 Ladies (Petra Maria Schnitzer, Gabriele Sima, Julia Bernheimer).
*** DG Dig. 410 967-2 (3) [id.]. German Op. Ch., Berlin, BPO, Karajan.
  Pamina (Edith Mathis), Queen of the Night (Karin Ott), Tamino (Francisco Araiza), Papageno (Gottfried Hornik), Sarastro (José Van Dam), Speaker (Claudio Nicolai), Monostatos (Heinz Kruse), Papagena (Janet Perry), 3 Ladies (Anna Tomowa-Sintow, Agnes Baltsa, Hanna Schwarz).
Withdrawn: (M) **(*) DG 429 877-2; *3371 002* (3) [id.]. Berlin RIAS Chamber Ch., BPO, Boehm
  – *Der Schauspieldirektor.* ***
  Pamina (Evelyn Lear), Queen of the Night (Roberta Peters), Tamino (Fritz Wunderlich), Papageno (Dietrich Fischer-Dieskau), Sarastro (Franz Crass), Speaker (Hans Hotter), Monostatos (Friedrich Lenz), Papagena (Lisa Otto), 3 Ladies (Hildegard Hillebrecht, Cvetka Ahlin, Sieglinde Wagner).
(***) Pearl mono GEMM CDS 9371 (2) [id.]. Ch. & BPO, Beecham.
  Pamina (Tiana Lemnitz), Queen of the Night (Erna Berger), Tamino (Helge Roswaenge), Papageno (Gerhard Hüsch), Sarastro (Wilhelm Strienz), Speaker (Walter Grossmann), Monostatos (Heinrich Tessmer), Papagena (Irma Beilke), 3 Ladies (Hilde Scheppan, Elfriede Marherr-Wagner, Rut Berglund).

(M) (**) EMI mono CHS7 61034-2 (2) [id.]. Ch. & BPO, Beecham.
Cast as above.
(M) (*(*)) Nimbus mono NI 7827/28; *NC 7827/28* [id.]. Ch. & BPO, Beecham.
Cast as above.
**(*) Decca Dig. 433 210-2 (2). V. State Op. Ch., VPO, Solti.
Pamina (Ruth Ziesak), Queen of the Night (Sumi Jo), Tamino (Uwe Heilmann), Papageno (Michael Kraus), Sarastro (Kurt Moll), Speaker (Andreas Schmidt), Monostatos (Heinz Zednik), Papagena (Lotte Leitner), 3 Ladies (Adrianne Pieczonka, Annette Kuettenbaum, Jard Van Nes).
**(*) Decca 414 568-2 (3) [id.]. V. State Op. Ch., VPO, Solti.
Pamina (Pilar Lorengar), Queen of the Night (Cristina Deutekom), Tamino (Stuart Burrows), Papageno (Hermann Prey), Sarastro (Martti Talvela), Speaker (Dietrich Fischer-Dieskau), Monostatos (Gerhard Stolze), Papagena (Renata Holm), 3 Ladies (Hanneke Van Bork, Yvonne Minton, Hetty Plümacher).
(M) ** Decca 414 362-2; *414 362-4* (2) [id.]. V. State Op. Ch., VPO, Boehm.
Pamina (Hilde Gueden), Queen of the Night (Wilma Lipp), Tamino (Léopold Simoneau), Papageno (Walter Berry), Sarastro (Kurt Boehme), Speaker (Paul Schoeffler), Monostatos (August Jaresch), Papagena (Emmy Loose), 3 Ladies (Judith Hellwig, Christa Ludwig, Hilde Rössl-Majdan).
(M) ** BMG/RCA GD 86511 (3) [RCA 6511-2-RG]. Leipzig R. Ch., Dresden State O, Suitner.
Pamina (Helen Donath), Queen of the Night (Sylvia Geszty), Tamino (Peter Schreier), Papageno (Günther Lieb), Sarastro (Theo Adam), Speaker (Siegfried Vogel), Monostatos (Harald Neukirch), Papagena (Renate Hoff), 3 Ladies (Hanne-Lore Kuhse, Gisela Schröter, Annelies Burmeister).
** Teldec/Warner Dig. 2292 42716-2 (2) [id.]. Zurich Op. Ch. & O, Harnoncourt.
Pamina (Barbara Bonney), Queen of the Night (Edita Gruberová), Tamino (Hans-Peter Blochwitz), Papageno (Anton Scharinger), Sarastro (Matti Salminen), Speaker (Thomas Hampson), Monostatos (Peter Keller), Papagena (Edith Schmid), 3 Ladies (Pamela Coburn, Delores Ziegler, Marjana Lipovšek).
** EMI Dig. CDS7 54287-2 [Ang CDCB 54287]. L. Classical Ch. & Players, Norrington.
Pamina (Dawn Upshaw), Queen of the Night (Beverley Hoch), Tamino (Anthony Rolfe Johnson), Papageno (Andreas Schmidt), Sarastro (Cornelius Hauptmann), Speaker (Olaf Bär), Monostatos (Guy De Mey), Papagena (Catherine Pierard), 3 Ladies (Nancy Argenta, Eirian James, Catherine Denley).
(M) *(*) Ph. Dig. 422 543-2 (3) [id.]. Dresden Kreuzchor, Leipzig R. Ch., Dresden State O, Sir Colin Davis.
Pamina (Margaret Price), Queen of the Night (Luciana Serra), Tamino (Peter Schreier), Papageno (Mikael Melbye), Sarastro (Kurt Moll), Speaker (Theo Adam), Monostatos (Robert Tear), Papagena (Maria Venuti), 3 Ladies (Marie McLaughlin, Ann Murray, Hanna Schwarz).
Withdrawn: *(*) EMI CDS7 47827-8 (2). Bav. State Ch. & O, Sawallisch.
Pamina (Anneliese Rothenberger), Queen of the Night (Edda Moser), Tamino (Peter Schreier), Papageno (Walter Berry), Sarastro (Kurt Moll), Speaker (Theo Adam).

Die Zauberflöte, Mozart's curious but inspired mixture of masonic ritual and humorous pantomime, works by using a basic concept which is fundamentally both noble and full of humanity. While the story has moments of great charm and delightful touches of humour, it also has the right degree of added gravitas, partly afforded by the use of the German language. The opera made a profound impression when it first appeared in Vienna in 1791, scarcely a year after the lightweight *Così fan tutte*, and proved to be Mozart's greatest theatrical success, even though he was to die little more than two months after the première.

Prince Tamino, the opera's personable hero, first enters, pursued by a monstrous black serpent, and faints. But three ladies-in-waiting to the Queen of the Night appear and dispatch the evil snake with their spears. They express intense admiration for the good-looking prince but depart as he recovers. The strangely attired Papageno now approaches, his feathered apparel revealing his trade as a bird catcher, also in the service of the Queen of the Night. He boasts to Tamino that it was he who killed the snake, and the three ladies return and place a padlock on his mouth to punish him for the untruth. They then show Tamino a miniature portrait of Pamina, daughter of the Queen of the Night, and he at once falls in love with her. Tamino is told that she is a prisoner of Sarastro, the high priest, the inference being that he must be evil. Tamino resolves to rescue her.

The Queen of the Night now descends from the clouds, lamenting the loss of her beloved daughter. She promises Tamino that he shall marry Pamina if he can rescue her. After the queen has retired, the three ladies, Tamino and Papageno assess the situation, but the best that the poor padlocked Papageno can contribute is 'Hm, hm, hm', so the padlock is removed. Tamino is given a magic flute which he can use if in difficulties or danger; the ladies also give Papageno – who is now assigned to aid Tamino – a magic chime of bells. Finally they assure them both that three genii (young boys) will show them the way.

In Sarastro's palace the imprisoned Pamina is being wooed by Monostatos, the Captain of the Guard, when Papageno enters, disturbing his unwelcome attentions. Both are equally taken aback by the other's appearance and the Moor flees, thinking Papageno is the devil in a strange new form. Papageno tells Pamina that she will soon be rescued by someone who loves her and in turn Pamina consoles Papageno, who above all would like to be loved himself.

The three genii now lead Tamino to the Temple of Wisdom, which has three doors. A voice from within the first two doors abjures him to stand back. But the Speaker now emerges from the third door and he suggests to Tamino that Sarastro is not wicked but noble, and that he has rescued Pamina from the evil designs of her mother. Tamino now plays his flute, hoping that Pamina will hear him. Papageno and Pamina respond but Monostatos tries to intercept and arrest them. The resourceful Papageno remembers his magic bells and Monostatos' retinue of slaves are distracted and begin to dance.

Sarastro now makes his solemn entrance and emphasizes to Pamina that she is held captive for her own good. Monostatos brings in Tamino under duress and he and Pamina enjoy a brief, enraptured recognition. Pamina describes the ugly treatment she has received from Monostatos and, when the latter asks Sarastro for a reward for his vigilance in preventing an attempted abduction of Pamina, Sarastro orders that he shall be beaten instead.

Sarastro's priests now enter in a solemn procession and Sarastro announces that, before Tamino can marry Pamina, he must prove his worthiness to share their joint destiny, and the ritual trials begin. The first is of maintaining silence, especially in the presence of the fair sex, and the three ladies confront them once more and try to induce a conversation. Papageno nearly succumbs, but Tamino manages to stop him breaking their pledge.

Meanwhile Pamina is asleep and Monostatos approaches with amorous intent, but the Queen of the Night appears and instructs Pamina to kill Sarastro with a dagger, or she will be unable to rejoin Tamino. But the queen is more concerned with her own revenge. She disappears. Monostatos again approaches Pamina, but Sarastro intervenes and Pamina begs Sarastro not to take revenge on her mother. He answers that in the temple there is no thought of revenge.

Tamino and Papageno await the next stage of their ordeal. An old crone approaches Papageno and says she is his sweetheart and he is thus induced to speak. He is amused but does not guess the true identity of the lady he addresses. The three genii bring Tamino his flute and Papageno his bells. Tamino, seeing Pamina, cannot speak to her, and she is grief-stricken when he appears to ignore her. Sarastro now tells Tamino that his endurance is to be rewarded, but Pamina still thinks he does not love her. Papageno meanwhile sighs for someone to love.

The old crone reappears, and this time makes him swear to be true to her, and she is immediately revealed to be young and attractive, and feathered, just as he is. Then, just as he is about to embrace her, she eludes him again.

Pamina, heartbroken, is about to take her own life, but the three boys (genii) restrain her. Two men in armour arrive to oversee Tamino's last ordeal, by fire and by water, and now Pamina may join him. Tamino plays his flute and they find their way safely between the wall of fire and the rushing torrent. It is Papageno now who is contemplating suicide at the apparent loss of his love, but the three boys urge him to play his magic bells.

Papagena now reappears and the feathered couple charmingly plight their troth together by singing 'Pa-pa-pa-pa' 48 times. The Queen of the Night, with Monostatos in attendance still lusting after Pamina, once more tries to defeat Sarastro, but her dark powers are overcome in a great storm. The radiant Tamino and Pamina now enter Sarastro's Temple of the Sun and Sarastro's guidance ensures that wisdom and goodness shall prevail.

Die Zauberflöte is exceptionally well represented on CD, but for those wanting first-class modern sound, Marriner's set has a great deal to recommend it. He directs a pointed and elegant reading of Mozart's unique amalgam of pantomime and Masonic ritual, bringing out all the fun of the piece. It lacks weight only in the overture and finale, and the cast is the finest in any modern recording. Dame Kiri – who could have sounded grand rather than girlish – lightens her voice delightfully, and consistently sings with fine control. Olaf Bär, vividly characterful, brings the Lieder-singer's art to the role of Papageno, as Gerhard Hüsch and Dietrich Fischer-

Dieskau did in earlier vintage recordings. Araiza's voice has coarsened since he recorded the role of Tamino for Karajan, but this performance is subtler and conveys more feeling. Cheryl Studer is quite the finest Queen of the Night on any modern recording; and Samuel Ramey, not quite as rich and firm as usual, yet gives a generous and wise portrait of Sarastro. José van Dam, Karajan's Sarastro, is here a superb Speaker. With spoken dialogue directed by August Everding, this the finest digital version, superbly recorded, and on only two discs.

From the early LP era Fricsay's is an outstandingly fresh and alert *Die Zauberflöte*, marked by generally clear, pure singing and well-sprung orchestral playing at generally rather fast speeds. In some ways Fricsay anticipates the Mozart tastes of a later generation, even if his approach to ornamentation is hardly in authentic-period style. So the duet, *Bei Männern*, and Pamina's big aria, *Ach, ich fühl's*, are taken at flowing speeds, with Maria Stader and Dietrich Fischer-Dieskau phrasing most beautifully. The most spectacular singing comes from Rita Streich as a dazzling Queen of the Night – after Hempel (see Vocal Recitals) the finest on record – and the relatively close balance of the voice gives it the necessary power such as Streich generally failed to convey in the opera house. Ernst Haefliger, too, is at his most honeyed in tone as Tamino, and only the rather gritty Sarastro of Josef Greindl falls short – and even he sings with a satisfyingly dark resonance. This was the first version to spice the musical numbers with brief sprinklings of dialogue, just enough to prevent the work from sounding like an oratorio. Even including that, DG has managed to put each of the Acts complete on a single disc. The transfer of the original 1954 mono recording (made in the Berlin Jesus Christus-Kirche) is remarkably full-bodied, with a pleasant ambience and sense of presence. There are few CD transfers of mono recordings that approach this in natural realism, and the quality of the production lets one appreciate why DG had such a high reputation for excellence in the early days of mono LP.

Klemperer's inspired conducting of *The Magic Flute* is one of his finest achievements on record, when he gives the dramatic music Beethovenian breadth and strength. But he does not miss the humour and point of Papageno's music, and to a surprising degree he achieves the best of both worlds. The cast is outstanding – the Three Ladies alone could not be more distinguished – but curiously it is that generally most reliable of all the singers, Gottlob Frick as Sarastro, who is slightly disappointing, not quite so firm and dark as usual. Lucia Popp in her earlier opera-recording makes a fresh, agile Queen of the Night, and Gundula Janowitz sings Pamina with a creamy beauty that is breathtaking. Walter Berry too is a firm-voiced Papageno. The recording was made in the summer of 1964 at the time of the Philharmonia crisis when it was threatened with disbandment, but from the results you would never know that. It is a pity the dialogue is not included, but on that point Klemperer was insistent, and the set remains his triumph. The transfer to a pair of mid-priced CDs is managed superbly, wonderfully fresh, with balance strikingly good. A translation is provided with the libretto, to make this another of EMI's outstanding operatic bargains.

As with the companion mono version of *Così fan tutte*, there has never been a more seductive recording of *Zauberflöte* than Karajan's mono version of 1950. The Vienna State Opera cast here has not since been matched on record: Irmgard Seefried and Anton Dermota both sing with radiant beauty and great character, Wilma Lipp is a dazzling Queen of the Night, Erich Kunz as Papageno sings with an infectious smile in the voice, and Ludwig Weber is a commanding Sarastro. There is no spoken dialogue; but on two mid-priced CDs instead of three LPs, it is a Mozart treat not to be missed, with mono sound still amazingly vivid and full of presence.

Haitink in his first ever opera recording was inspired to direct a rich and spacious account of *Zauberflöte*, superbly recorded in spectacularly wide-ranging digital sound. There is a sterling honesty in Haitink's approach to every number. With speeds generally a shade slower than usual, the point of the playing and the consistent quality of the singing present this as a Mozart masterpiece that is weighty as well as sparkling. The dialogue – not too much of it, nicely produced and with sound-effects adding to the vividness – frames a presentation that has been carefully thought through. Popp makes the most tenderly affecting of Paminas (as she did in the Salzburg production) and Gruberová has never sounded more spontaneous in her brilliance than here as Queen of the Night: she is both agile and powerful. Jerusalem makes an outstanding Tamino, both heroic and sweetly Mozartian; and though neither Wolfgang Brendel as Papageno nor Bracht as Sarastro is as characterful as their finest rivals, their personalities project strongly and the youthful freshness of their singing is most attractive. The Bavarian chorus too is splendid, and the recording's perspectives featuring the chorus are extraordinarily effective, particularly in the superb Act I finale.

Though the recording puts a halo of reverberation round the sound, Mackerras and the Scottish Chamber Orchestra find an ideal scale for the work. His speeds are often faster than usual, not least in Pamina's great aria of lament, *Ach, ich fühl's*, but they always flow persuasively. This is the version among recent ones which best conveys the fun of the piece as well as its power, with the orchestral textures even clearer and more detailed than those of Norrington and his period players. Jerry Hadley makes a delightfully boyish Tamino, with Thomas Allen the most characterful Papageno, singing beautifully. Robert Lloyd is a noble Sarastro, and though June Anderson is a rather strenuous Queen of the Night, it is thrilling to have a big, dramatic voice so dazzlingly agile. Barbara Hendricks is a questionable choice as Pamina, not clean enough of attack, but the tonal quality is golden. Unlike his rivals, Mackerras offers in an appendix an extra duet for Tamino and Papageno, though the conductor justifiably pours cold water on its credentials. Among modern recordings this is a set to put beside Haitink's very enjoyable EMI version, despite the reverberant sound.

Zauberflöte has also inspired Karajan to one of his freshest, most rhythmic Mozart performances for DG, spontaneous-sounding to the point where vigour is preferred to immaculate precision in ensembles. The digital recording is not always perfectly balanced, but the sound is outstandingly fresh and clear. The CDs add presence and refine detail but also underline the variable balances. There are numbers where the tempi are dangerously slow (Tamino's *Dies Bildnis*, both of Sarastro's arias and Pamina's *Ach, ich fühl's*), but Karajan's concentration helps him to avoid mannerism completely. The choice of soloists may seem idiosyncratic, and in principle one would want a darker-toned Sarastro than José van Dam, but the clarity of focus and the fine control, not to mention the slow tempi, give the necessary weight to his arias. Francisco Araiza and Gottfried Hornik make impressive contributions. Karin Ott has a relatively weighty voice for the Queen of the Night, but she is helped by Karajan's considerate tempi. The Pamina of Edith Mathis has many beautiful moments, her word-pointing always intelligent.

One of the glories of Boehm's DG set is the singing of Fritz Wunderlich as Tamino, a wonderful memorial to a singer much missed. Passages that normally seem merely incidental come alive, thanks to his beautiful, intense singing. Fischer-Dieskau, with characteristic word-pointing, makes a sparkling Papageno on record (he was always too big of frame, he says, to do the role on stage) and Franz Crass is a satisfyingly straightforward Sarastro. The team of women does not match this standard – Lear taxed cruelly in *Ach, ich fühl's*, Peters shrill in the upper register (although her singing is exciting), and the Three Ladies not blended well – but the direction of Boehm is superb, light and lyrical, yet weighty where necessary and always glowing and compelling. Fine recording, with the considerable bonus on this three-disc set, of Boehm's admirable account of *Der Schauspieldirektor*.

Recorded in Berlin between November 1937 and March 1939, Beecham's recording of *Zauberflöte* was also the first opera set produced by Walter Legge. It brings a classic performance, and though Helge Roswaenge was too ungainly a tenor to be an ideal Tamino, the casting has otherwise been matched in only a few instances on record. Beecham too was at his peak, pacing each number superbly. Like other early recordings of this opera, this one omits the spoken dialogue; but the vocal delights are many, not least from Tiana Lemnitz as a radiant Pamina, Erna Berger as a dazzling Queen of the Night, and Gerhard Hüsch as a delicately comic Papageno, bringing the detailed art of the Lieder-singer to the role.

Of the three currently available transfers of this Beecham recording to CD, the Pearl is the one which captures the original 78 recording most naturally, with the keenest sense of presence for the voices, even if it leaves it with plentiful surface hiss. The orchestra too has more body than on the EMI transfer, though the price is rather higher and Pearl, unlike EMI, provides no libretto. A useful essay is included, filling in the background of the recording. The disappointment of the EMI alternative, transferred by the CEDAR process, is the dryness of the sound, with a limited top, little sense of presence and no bloom on the voices. The Nimbus attempt finds that company's re-recording process, using an acoustic gramophone, less effective than it can be. The orchestral sound is made thin, almost disembodied, and though the voices have bloom on them, they often jangle.

Solti directs the Vienna Philharmonic in a well-paced and strong reading of *Zauberflöte* that misses some of the fun. There are snags too in his cast. Though Ruth Ziesak as Pamina and Sumi Jo as the Queen of the Night both sing with beguiling sweetness and elegance, and Kurt Moll is gloriously firm and dark as Sarastro, the other male principals are disappointing. Both the Tamino of Uwe Heilmann and the Papageno of Michael Kraus are too fluttery and unsteady to give pleasure, though the latter characterizes well. Full, well-balanced Decca sound.

Dating from 1971, Solti's earlier analogue reading is tough, strong and brilliant but totally lacking in charm. For all the vitality of the drama, the full variety of Mozart's inspiration is lacking. On the male side the cast is very strong indeed, with Stuart Burrows stylish and rich-toned. Martti Talvela and Fischer-Dieskau as Sarastro and the Speaker respectively provide a stronger contrast than usual, each superb in his way, and Hermann Prey rounds out the character of Papageno with intelligent pointing of words. The cast of women is less consistent. Pilar Lorengar's Pamina is sweetly attractive as long as your ear is not worried by her obtrusive vibrato, while Cristina Deutekom's Queen of the Night is technically impressive, though marred by a curious warbling quality in the coloratura, almost like an intrusive 'w' where you sometimes have the intrusive 'h'. The brilliant and lively sound has been well transferred.

The principal attraction of the Decca mid-price Viennese reissue from the earliest days of stereo is the conducting of Karl Boehm. With surprisingly good recording quality (vintage 1955), vivid, warm and full in the bass, that might well be counted enough recommendation, in spite of the absence of dialogue, particularly when the Tamino of Léopold Simoneau and the Papageno of Walter Berry are strongly and sensitively sung. But the rest of the singing is variable, with Hilde Gueden a pert, characterful Pamina unhappy in the florid divisions, Wilma Lipp an impressive Queen of the Night, but Kurt Böhme a gritty and ungracious Sarastro. For its age the sound is remarkably atmospheric.

In Suitner's Dresden version the sound is full and forward, the reading plain but generally lively, to make it a fair bargain recommendation at mid-price in the Victor Opera series. The cast has one notable flaw in the Sarastro of Theo Adam, unsteady if not as wobbly as he sometimes is; and the Papageno of Günther Lieb is undercharacterized; but Peter Schreier is at his finest as Tamino, and Helen Donath is a lovely, girlish-sounding Pamina, with Sylvia Geszty a satisfyingly rich-toned Queen of the Night.

In Mozart, Nikolaus Harnoncourt is always unpredictable, sometimes harking back to his period-performance background, sometimes weighting the music excessively; in *Zauberflöte* he manages to do both simultaneously. The very opening, with sforzandos exaggerated and violin-tone thinned down in the overture, demonstrates the period-performance tendencies, but thereafter the speeds are not only on the slow side as a rule, they have a rhythmic squareness which removes much of the charm of the music. Hans-Peter Blochwitz makes a fresh and youthful Tamino, his lightness for this role compensated by the closeness of balance in the full, bright recording. Barbara Bonney, an enchanting Pamina, similarly benefits from that closeness when the voice is caught with such consistent sweetness; she even manages to cope with Harnoncourt's impossibly slow speed for the duet, *Bei Männern*.

With the Papageno of Anton Scharinger and the Sarastro of Matti Salminen, the closeness is less flattering, the one sounding heavy in comedy, the other not given the space for bloom to develop on the voice. At Harnoncourt's speed Sarastro's second aria is very sluggish. With Edita Gruberová the outstanding Queen of the Night of her generation, the closeness adds to the dramatic bite of her singing, but with rawness developing. Although such a number as the little Act II quintet between Tamino, Papageno and the Three Ladies has all the jollity one could wish for, too often Harnoncourt's fussiness as well as his slow speeds undermine the comedy – even though, like his earlier Mozart opera recordings in Zurich, this one was done in conjunction with a Zurich Opera House production. Disconcertingly, the story is told – in German – by a female narrator, Gertraud Jesserer, with dialogue reduced to the odd phrase.

Norrington in his period performance linked his recording with a live concert but left too long a period between them, so that the sparkle of the live event disappeared. Fast speeds become fierce and unsmiling when rhythms can no longer be lifted seductively. The cast is strong but not ideal, chosen mainly for lightness and clarity rather than character. It is good to have Anthony Rolfe Johnson's stylish Tamino on disc, but Cornelius Hauptmann is distractingly wobbly as Sarastro.

The last of Sir Colin Davis's recordings of Mozart's major operas, and the only one made outside Britain, is also the least successful. With speeds often slower than usual and the manner heavier, it is a performance of little sparkle or charm, one which seems intent on bringing out serious, symbolic meanings. Thus, although Margaret Price produces a glorious flow of rich, creamy tone, she conveys little of the necessary vulnerability of Pamina in her plight. Luciana Serra sings capably but at times with shrill tone and not always with complete security; while Peter Schreier is in uncharacteristically gritty voice as Tamino, and Mikael Melbye as Papageno is ill-suited to recording, when the microphone exaggerates the throatiness and unevenness of his production. The greatest vocal glory of the set is the magnificent, firm and rich singing of Kurt Moll as Sarastro. The recording is excellent.

Sawallisch's Munich set of the early 1970s is recorded in thin sound, and though Sawallisch is a thoughtful Mozartian, the cast is flawed. The outstanding performance comes from Kurt Moll as Sarastro, and Walter Berry is a delightful Papageno. But even Peter Schreier sounds strained as Tamino, with bloom lacking on the voice. Edda Moser is a strong Queen of the Night but on the fruity side, and Anneliese Rothenberger is disturbingly fluttery as Pamina.

Die Zauberflöte: highlights.

(M) *** EMI CDM7 63451-2 (from above recording with Janowitz, Popp, Gedda; cond. Klemperer).

(M) *** DG Dig. 431 291-2; *431 291-4* [id.] (from above recording with Mathis, Ott, Araiza; cond. Karajan).

*** EMI Dig. CDC7 47008-2 [id.] (from above recording with Popp, Gruberová, Jerusalem; cond. Haitink).

(M) **(*) DG 429 825-2; *429 825-4* [id.] (from above recording with Lear, Peters, Wunderlich; cond. Boehm).

(M) ** Ph. Dig. 432 618-2; *432 618-4* (from above recording with M. Price, Serra, Schreier; cond. Sir Colin Davis).

** Decca Dig. 433 667-2 [id.] (from above recording with Ziesak, Sumi Jo, Heilmann; cond. Solti).

(M) ** Decca 421 302-2; *421 302-4* (from above recording with Lorengar, Deutekom, Burrows; cond. Solti).

** RCA/BMG Dig. RCD 14621 [RCD1 4621]. Eric Tappy, Martti Talvela, José Van Dam, Peter Weber, Ileana Cotrubas, Rachel Yakar, Zdislawa Donat, Elisabeth Kales, Christian Boesch, V. State Op. Ch., VPO, Levine.

Those looking for a first-rate set of highlights from *Die Zauberflöte* will find the mid-priced Klemperer disc hard to beat. It makes a good sampler of a performance which, while ambitious in scale, manages to find sparkle and humour too. The selection is well balanced and fairly generous, although it is a pity it does not include the passage most characteristic of Klemperer with the Armed Men. However, it does include the ensemble *Hm, hm, hm* between Papageno, Tamino and the Three Ladies, with Schwarzkopf, Ludwig and Höffgen at their very finest. The chief glory of the set vocally is the singing of the women; Gedda's Tamino and Frick's Sarastro are by comparison disappointing. A synopsis details each individual excerpt, and in this case the inclusion of the *Overture* is especially welcome. The remastered sound has plenty of presence, but atmosphere and warmth too.

The Karajan set is reasonably generous (61 minutes); it includes the *Overture* and most of the key numbers, including the Papageno/Papagena items, and it demonstrates the overall strength of a generally first-rate cast. At mid-price this is probably a best buy for a highlights disc from this opera, alongside the Klemperer selection.

Haitink's disc makes a good sampler with the Papageno/Papagena music well represented to make a contrast with the lyrical arias and the drama of the Queen of the Night.

The hour of (very inadequately documented) excerpts from Boehm's recording is not obviously directed towards bringing out its special qualities. One would have liked more of Wunderlich's Tamino, one of the great glories of the set. However, the key arias are all included and the sound is fresh and full.

A highlights disc is probably the best way to approach Sir Colin Davis's 1984 digital *Zauberflöte*, and it includes Sarastro's two principal arias, the most memorable items in a 65-minute selection. However, only a list of titles is included by way of documentation.

The selection from Solti's recent digital set offers only 58 minutes of music and is a premium-price CD. The disc is mainly notable for Sumi Jo's two Queen of the Night arias and the items featuring Ruth Ziesak (Pamina) and Kurt Moll (Sarastro). The disc was issued as part of Solti's birthday celebrations and includes a thick illustrated booklet detailing his career.

The Solti analogue highlights disc displays the characteristics of the complete set from which it is taken; the reading is tough, strong and brilliant, and it is arguable that in this opera these above all are the required qualities, but the almost total absence of charm is disconcerting. The drama may be consistently vital, but ultimately the full variety of Mozart's inspiration is not achieved.

The RCA highlights CD offers 15 excerpts and has a certain charm in detailing each in a lurid English translation; thus the Queen of the Night's second aria (*Die Hölle Rache*) is given as 'The vengeance of Hell boils in my heart'. It is variably sung. Zdzislawa Donat's contribution is one of the few outstanding performances here, alongside Cotrubas's Pamina – her aria *Ach, ich fühl's* is equally fine. Neither artist is named on the insert leaflet; however, this does provide a synopsis of 'The Plot'. There is nothing special about the CD sound, apart from the background silence. However, the dialogue which weighed down the complete LP set is omitted here.

OPERA RECITALS

Arias from: *Davidde penitente; Così fan tutte; La clemenza di Tito; La finta giardiniera; Don Giovanni; Die Entführung aus dem Serail; Idomeneo; Le nozze di Figaro; Die Zauberflöte.*
**(*) EMI Dig. CDC7 54329-2 [id.]. Plácido Domingo, Munich R. O, Kohn.

Domingo's years singing Otello and other big heroic roles have taken their toll of his powers of projecting the upper voice gently, however firm and beautiful the sound generally remains. The slight distancing of the voice in the recording spectrum hardly alleviates the problem and, paradoxically, the most enjoyable, happy and relaxed performances here are of the two unheroic 'character' roles. Domingo gives a delicious little portrait of Don Basilio in *Figaro* and as Pedrillo in *Entführung* sings the 'Into Battle' aria with superb contrasts as a miniature heroic piece. There are obvious thrills in Domingo's singing of Idomeneo's big aria, *Fuor del mar*, while the Emperor's brief solo in *La clemenza di Tito* suits his heroic style too. Domingo's sense of line never deserts him, but most of the great items here demand much gentler handling tonally. The welcome rarities are the aria from *La finta giardiniera* and the tenor aria which Mozart added to his material from the *C minor Mass* for the oratorio, *Davidde penitente*, intending it for the first Belmonte.

'Famous arias': from *La clemenza di Tito; Così fan tutte; Don Giovanni; Le nozze di Figaro; Il rè pastore; Zaïde; Die Zauberflöte.*
(M) **(*) Decca 421 311-2 [id.]. Teresa Berganza, Pilar Lorengar, Nicolai Ghiaurov, Tom Krause, Stuart Burrows, Gabriel Bacquier, Brigitte Fassbaender, Anna Tomowa-Sintow, Lucia Popp, Werner Krenn, Cristina Deutekom.

This Decca compilation provides nearly 64 minutes and 14 Mozart arias, including many favourites. It is the men who provide the most memorable singing: Stuart Burrows melting in *Il mio tesoro* from *Don Giovanni*, Gabriel Bacquier hardly less engaging in the *Serenade (Deh! vieni alla finestra)* from the same opera, and Ghiaurov bringing a sparkle to the *Catalogue song*. Among the ladies, Brigitte Fassbaender does not let us forget that Cherubino is a breeches role when she sings *Voi che sapete* stylishly but very directly; and Anna Tomowa-Sintow's account of the Countess's *Dove sono*, also from *Figaro*, is a trifle cool too. Yet Pilar Lorengar is very moving in *Per pietà* from *Così fan tutte*, an outstanding performance; and Lucia Popp's contributions from *Il rè pastore* and *Zaïde* leaven an otherwise popular collection; the recording adds a suspicion of hardness to her voice but is mostly vividly atmospheric. The recital ends with Cristina Deutekom's sharply dramatic account of the Queen of the Night's aria, *Der Hölle Rache*, from *Die Zauberflöte*.

Arias: *La clemenza di Tito: S'altro che lagrime. Così fan tutte: Ei parte . . . Sen . . . Per pietà. La finta giardiniera: Crudeli fermate . . . Ah dal pianto. Idomeneo: Se il padre perdei. Lucio Silla: Pupille amate. Il rè pastore: L'amerò, sarò costante. Zäde: Ruhe sanft, mein holdes Leben. Die Zauberflöte: Ach ich fühl's, es ist verschwunden.*
*** Ph. Dig. 411 148-2 [id.]. Kiri Te Kanawa, LSO, C. Davis.

Kiri Te Kanawa's is one of the loveliest collections of Mozart arias on record, with the voice at its most ravishing and pure. One might object that Dame Kiri concentrates on soulful arias, ignoring more vigorous ones, but with stylish accompaniment and clear, atmospheric recording, beauty dominates all.

Mussorgsky, Modest (1839–81)

Boris Godunov (original version; complete).
**(*) Ph. 412 281-2 (3) [id.]. USSR TV and R. Ch. and SO, Fedoseyev.
Boris (Alexander Vedernikov), Grigory (Vladislav Piavko), Marina (Irina Arkhipova), Pimen (Vladimir Matorin), Varlaam (Artur Eisen), Shuisky (Andrei Sokolov), Missail (Anatoli Mishutin), Rangoni (Yuri Mazurok), Feodor (Glafira Koroleva), Xenia (Elena Shkolnikova).
** Sony Dig. S3K 45763 (3) [id.]. Sofia Nat. Op. Ch., Sofia Festival O, Tchakarov.
Boris (Nicolai Ghiaurov), Grigory (Mikhail Svetlev), Marina (Stefka Mineva), Pimen (Nikola Ghiuselev), Varlaam (Dimiter Petkov), Shuisky (Joseph Franck), Missail (Angel

Petkov), Rangoni (Boris Martinovich), Feodor (Rossitza Troeva-Mircheva), Xenia (Ludmila Hadjieva), Simpleton (Mincho Popov).
** Erato/Warner Dig. 2292 45418-2 (3) [id.]. Washington Ch. Arts Soc. & Ontario Soc., Nat. SO, Rostropovich.
Boris (Ruggero Raimondi), Grigory (Vyacheslav Polozov), Marina (Galina Vishnevskaya), Pimen (Paul Plishka), Varlaam (Romuald Tesarowicz), Shuisky (Kenneth Riegel), Missail (Misha Raitzin), Rangoni (Nikita Storojev), Feodor (Matthew Adam Fish), Xenia (Catherine Dubosc), Simpleton (Nicolai Gedda).

Mussorgsky's great epic opera takes place in Russia and Poland between 1598 and 1605. The scene of the Prologue is a courtyard outside the Monastery of Novodevichy. A crowd has gathered and the Secretary of the State council, Shchelkalov, announces reluctantly that, despite the wishes of the nobles and the church and the prayers of the people, Boris Godunov has declined the throne. Pilgrims arrive and enter the monastery, and the crowd are then instructed to reassemble at dawn outside the Kremlin. There, in front of the people, Prince Shuisky hails Boris, who has changed his mind, and the crowd join in praise for the new Tsar, while Boris, in an introspective mood, prays for the guidance of God in the great task before him. The coronation proceeds in a spirit of jubilation.

At Chudor, in a monastery, Pimen, the old monk, is writing his chronicle of Russia. Dawn comes and chanting is heard from the chapel. A young monk, Grigory, asks for Pimen's blessing, then tells how he is haunted by a dream of crowds in Moscow pointing at him with scorn. Pimen then tells Grigory that, twelve years before, he saw the body of the son of late Tsar, Feodor. The young Prince Dmitri had been killed by the usurper, Boris Godunov. Grigory is extremely impressed. Pimen adds that if the young prince were alive he would be the same age as Grigory.

We move to a roadside inn. Two vagabond monks arrive, Varlaam and Missail; with them is Grigory, dressed as a peasant. Varlaam declaims boisterously about the reputation of Tsar Ivan. Grigory is uneasy. He is planning to pose as Dmitri in order to claim the Russian throne; but first he must cross the frontier into Lithuania (part of Poland at that time). Frontier guards now enter with a warrant for his arrest but by a clever ruse he escapes, indicating Varlaam as the fugitive, although Varlaam manages to extricate himself from this accusation.

The scene now changes to the Kremlin where Xenia, daughter of Boris, weeps for her dead fiancé. A mechanical clock delights her young brother. The old nurse tries to comfort Xenia with a song about a gnat, and Feodor joins the nurse in a further children's song but is interrupted by the entry of Boris. Xenia and the nurse leave. Proudly the young Feodor shows Boris the position of Russia on a globe. Boris sends his son away; when alone, he contemplates the future with foreboding: he is haunted by the memory of Dmitri's murder. A boyar enters to report that Prince Shuisky has caused a civil disturbance. Boris now accuses Shuisky of plotting, but he replies that a pretender has emerged in Lithuania with the name of Dmitri. The shattered Boris begs Shuisky to confirm that the true Dmitri is indeed dead. Alone, Boris has the fantasy that the mechanical clock, as it strikes, is a vision of the murdered child.

At Sandomir Castle in Poland, Princess Marina is being adorned by her handmaidens. Unimpressed by their flattery, she is more interested in deeds of war and politics than in romantic imagery. Nevertheless she is attracted to the pretender, Dmitri, and visualizes herself as his Tsarina in Moscow. The Jesuit Rangoni tells her she must use all her female powers to win Dmitri so that Russia can become converted to the faith of Rome. Later in the castle gardens Dmitri waits for Marina, passionately smitten with desire for her. She first insults him, damaging his pride, so that he is put into a frame of mind arrogantly to lead an army into Moscow. Once this is decided, she is willing to return his love, and Rangoni reappears to seek acceptance as a spiritual guide.

The following scene in front of St Basil's Cathedral in Moscow is sometimes omitted. Like the opera's closing sequence, this also begins and ends with the simpleton, tormented by the cruelty of children and contemplating the melancholy destiny of Mother Russia. Boris and his supporters emerge from the cathedral and the women beg for alms. The simpleton suggests that Boris order his young tormentors be killed as Boris once had the infant Dmitri murdered. When Shuisky tries to have the simpleton arrested, Boris cancels the order and asks the simpleton to remember him in his prayers. But the simpleton refuses, comparing Boris with Herod.

The dramatic climax of the story now approaches. The State Council of Boyars meets in the Kremlin. Shchelkalov announces that Boris has demanded that all should rally to his support against the pretender. Shuisky is suspected of duplicity. He enters and tells how, spying on Boris, he has watched him trembling and unhinged, calling out in his fear that he sees the ghost of the murdered Dmitri and using the words 'Out child!' Boris, now ill and demented with guilt, stumbles in and speaks those very same words. The boyars are visibly shocked, but Boris then recovers somewhat and Shuisky asks if he may bring in a monk who wishes to speak with the Tsar. Pimen enters and declares that he was blind but has been miraculously cured when he visited the murdered Dmitri's grave.

Boris can take no more and falls, dying. He dismisses the boyars and leads his young son to the throne. He tells Feodor not to trust the boyars but to uphold the people and the Russian church. Then he falls dead, leaving the fearful Feodor to await what the future has to bring. We soon discover that Feodor has no place in it.

In a forest near Kromy, an unruly mob are baiting Krushchov, a captured boyar who had supported Boris. A simpleton enters and is mocked by the urchins among the crowd. Missail and Varlaam are also seen; they lead the crowd in support of Dmitri, the pretender. Two Jesuits also praise Dmitri, but in Latin, and are taken off to be hanged. Dmitri then enters ceremoniously, orders that the boyar and the Jesuits be set free, and the whole entourage sets off for Moscow. The simpleton is left to himself, singing of the tragic fate of Russia.

On Philips, Fedoseyev conducts a powerful performance of Mussorgsky's masterpiece in its original scoring, using the composer's own 1872 revision, as near an 'authentic' solution as one can get with a problematic score that never reached definitive form. Some may miss the brilliance of the Rimsky-Korsakov revision, which still generally holds sway in the opera house and did so for a generation on record; but the earthy strength of the score comes over superbly, far more bitingly than it did in EMI's disappointing version recorded in Poland, now deleted. Ideally for records, one needs a firmer singer than the mature Vedernikov as Boris, but this is a searingly intense performance which rises commandingly to the big dramatic moments, conveying the Tsar's neurotic tensions chillingly. Arkhipova is also too mature for the role of Marina, but equally her musical imagination is most convincing. The rest of the cast is a mixed bag, with some magnificent Russian basses but a few disappointing contributions, as from the whining tenor, Vladislav Piavko, as the Pretender. Though the recording was made over a period of years, the sound is full and satisfying, if not always ideally balanced.

Though Ghiaurov gives a magnificent performance as Boris, as fine in its way as his recording for Karajan of 20 years earlier, and Tchakarov brings out the reflective side of the score well, the whole Sony recording seriously lacks power. It is partly a question of backward orchestral and choral balance, partly a lack of bite in the actual performance. Without the necessary earthy quality the score fails to make its full impact. The intensity of Boris's big monologues and above all the death scene, with Ghiaurov singing beautifully, rarely snarling in sing-speech, hardly compensates for such a shortcoming.

Among the others, Stefka Mineva is typically fruity as Marina, with a pronounced vibrato, and Mikhail Svetlev as the Pretender, Grigory, produces characteristic Slavonic sound too with his clean, tight-toned tenor. Among the basses Nikola Ghiuselev is magnificent as Pimen, but Dimiter Petkov is a disappointing, unsteady Varlaam. As on the Philips set, the 'original' 1872 text is used, but with the 1869 St Basil's Scene provided as a supplement before the death scene. The definitive Kromy Forest scene then comes after that, ending again with the Simpleton. Solo voices come over well and, though the orchestra sounds too distant, the recording allows fine clarity.

Recorded live in Washington, Rostropovich's version of Mussorgsky's original score, unadulterated by Rimsky-Korsakov, is no more successful at providing the ideal version than its predecessors. It sounds very much what it was: a well-drilled concert performance with some fine choral singing, making this great pageant-opera into an oratorio, and the choice of Ruggero Raimondi to sing the name-part is consistent with this. It is good to have so warmly Italianate a voice bringing out the lyricism of lines more often barked or grunted. Boris's death scene is refined and beautiful, wonderfully controlled in hushed intensity, but the Tsar's inner agony is missing. Even the grand Coronation scene lacks weight, though that may have something to do with the composer's own orchestration being much more subdued than Rimsky's.

Taking the role of Marina, as she did in the Karajan set of twenty years earlier, is Rostropovich's wife, Galina Vishnevskaya, giving a masterly demonstration of how to eke out a voice no longer young; it remains a most vivid portrait. Of the others, Paul Plishka is a disappointingly unsteady Pimen, but Romuald Tesarowicz is a first-rate Varlaam and Vyacheslav Polozov as Grigory is far less strained than his counterpart on the Philips Russian set. Kenneth Riegel is an excellent Shuisky and the veteran, Nicolai Gedda, makes a touching Simpleton. The sound is full and faithful, far more consistent than the Philips analogue set, but capturing the atmosphere of a concert hall, not an opera.

Boris Godunov (arr. Rimsky-Korsakov).
*** Decca 411 862-2 (3) [id.]. V. Boys' Ch., Sofia R. Ch., V. State Op. Ch., VPO, Karajan.
   Boris (Nicolai Ghiaurov), Grigory (Ludovic Spiess), Marina (Galina Vishnevskaya), Pimen
   (Martti Talvela), Varlaam (Anton Diakov), Shuisky / Simpleton (Alexei Maslennikov),
   Missail (Milen Paunov), Rangoni (Zoltan Kélémen), Feodor (Olivera Miljakovic), Xenia
   (Nadejda Dobrianowa).
** EMI CDS7 47993-8 (3). Sofia Nat. Op. Ch., Paris Conservatoire O, Cluytens.
   Boris / Pimen / Varlaam (Boris Christoff), Marina (Evelyn Lear).

If Ghiaurov in the title-role lacks some of the dramatic intensity of Christoff on the EMI set,
Karajan's superbly controlled Decca version, technically outstanding, comes far nearer than
other recordings of the Rimsky-Korsakov edition to conveying the rugged greatness of
Mussorgsky's masterpiece. Only the Coronation scene lacks something of the weight and
momentum one ideally wants. This makes a clear first choice on CD, even if Vishnevskaya is far
less appealing than the lovely non-Slavonic Marina of Evelyn Lear on EMI.

The EMI set is chiefly valuable for the resonant contribution of Boris Christoff, for a
generation unmatched in the role of Boris. Here he takes the part not only of the Tsar but of
Pimen and Varlaam too, relishing the contrast of those other, highly characterful, bass roles. It is
good that this glorious voice is so vividly caught on CD, but sadly the overall performance under
Cluytens does not quite add up to the sum of its parts, as the earlier mono recording with
Christoff did.

Khovanshchina (complete).
*** DG Dig. 429 758-2 (3) [id.]. V. State Op. Ch. & O, Abbado.
   Ivan Khovansky (Aage Haugland), Andrey Khovansky (Vladimir Atlantov), Golitsin
   (Vladimir Popov), Shaklovity (Anatolij Kotscherga), Dosifey (Paata Burchuladze), Marfa
   (Marjana Lipovšek), Susanna (Brigitte Poschner-Klebel), Scribe (Heinz Zednik), Emma
   (Joanna Borowska).
**(*) Ph. Dig. 432 147-2 (3) [id.]. Kirov Theatre Ch. & O, Gergiev.
   Ivan Khovansky (Bulat Minjelkiev), Andrey Khovansky (Vladimir Galusin), Golitsin (Alexei
   Steblianko), Shaklovity (Valery Alexeev), Dosifey (Nikolai Ohotnikov), Marfa (Olga
   Borodina), Susanna (Evgenia Tselovalnik), Scribe (Konstantin Pluzhnikov), Emma (Jelena
   Prokina).
** Sony Dig. S3K 45831 (3) [id.]. Sofia Nat. Op. Ch. & O, Tchakarov.
   Ivan Khovansky (Nicolai Ghiaurov), Andrey Khovansky (Zdravko Gadjev), Golitsin (Kaludi
   Kaludov), Shaklovity (Stoyan Popov), Dosifey (Nikola Ghiuselev), Marfa (Alexandrina
   Milcheva), Susanna (Maria Petrova Popova), Scribe (Angel Petkov), Emma (Martya
   Dimchewska).
(**) Chant du Monde LDC 2781024-6 (3) [id.]. Bolshoi Op. Ch. & O, Khaikin.
   Ivan Khovansky (Alexei Krivtchenia), Andrey Khovansky (Vladislav Piavko), Golitsin
   (Alexei Maslennikov), Shaklovity (Victor Netchipailo), Dosifey (Alexander Ognivtsiev),
   Marfa (Irina Arkhipova).

Mussorgsky's second greatest opera, in which the action takes place towards the end of the
seventeenth century, is concerned with the conflicts between the religious and political
reactionaries of the past and a 'new' Russia identified with the reign of Peter the Great. The
composer did not live to finish his work and it has been completed by others, notably by Rimsky-
Korsakov, and more recently by Shostakovich, who tried to keep more closely to the original,
although both composers brought their own musical personalities to bear on their adaptations of
the score as the composer left it.

Although the story of the opera might seem overtly concerned with politics, the music is full of
melody and consistently inspired, and the piece certainly has no lack of drama. The work opens
with a wonderfully beautiful orchestral evocation of dawn over the Kremlin in Moscow. A
passing patrol sees Kouzka, a musketeer, and they all converse. It is said that the Streltsy
(political reactionaries motivated by Prince Ivan Khovansky) were out during the night killing
their opponents in the city.

The scrivener (public letter-writer) sits in his place in the square; the boyar Shaklovity dictates
an anonymous letter to the Tsar and his Council, warning them that the prince plots to become
Tsar; he is aided by his son and the so-called Old Believers (reactionaries who have refused to
accede to reform of any kind).

A mob gathers and the scrivener is compelled by them to read out a proclamation placed in the square by the Streltsy. Prince Ivan Khovansky arrives and the scrivener leaves hastily. The prince tells the populace that he is determined to crush the enemies of the Tsar and stamp out any signs of treason. He orders the Streltsy to patrol the city. Emma, a young German girl, now enters, followed by Khovansky's son, Andrey; she resists as he tries to kiss her. Marfa, once deserted by this same prince, comes to Emma's aid and when she intercedes he angrily draws out his dagger. Marfa, also armed, parries the blow. Andrey's father (Prince Ivan) steps in to end the quarrel and, admiring Emma's appearance, orders his guards to take her. His son would prefer to kill her rather than see her held by the Streltsy, but Dosifey, leader of the Old Believers, steps in and restores peace. Marfa departs with Emma. Prince Ivan Khovansky and his Streltsy enter the Kremlin. The Old Believers pray.

Prince Golitsin, council member and once the lover of the Tsarevna, sits in his apartment reading a love-letter from her. He realizes he cannot trust the favour of the Tsar. His attendant, Varsonofiev, announces the arrival of a Lutheran pastor who complains of Emma's ill-treatment by the Khovanskys. Golitsin says he cannot interfere. Marfa arrives at Golitsin's apartment to cast his horoscope and she foretells his fall from grace. Angrily he orders her away, then secretly instructs that she is to be seized and drowned. He broods over his past services to Russia.

Old Prince Khovansky enters, complaining of Golitsin's interference in his capacity as adviser to the Tsarevna. Dosifey arrives and advises reconciliation and a return to government based on ancient customs. Marfa rushes in, (ironically) asking for Golitsin's protection from a servant who tried to drown her. He was foiled in the attempt by Petrortsy, a member of the bodyguard of Peter the Great. The prince is alarmed to hear that the Tsar's troops are in the capital and is even more worried when the boyar Shaklovity enters to announce that the Khovanskys have been denounced to Tsar Peter as traitors.

In the Streltsy quarter, Marfa sits near Prince Andrey's house and nostalgically recalls her past love-affair, but Susanna (an Old Believer) accuses her of irredeemable sin. Dosifey offers comfort. They leave. Shaklovity expresses the hope that Russia may shake off its oppressive government. The Streltsy are heard approaching and he hides. The scrivener tells how he has seen foreign mercenaries attacking women and children not very far away, and the Streltsy appeal to Prince Khovansky to lead them against the culprits. The prince advises obedience to the rule of Tsar Peter.

Varsonofiev arrives at the residence of Prince Ivan Khovansky, bearing a message from Prince Golitsin warning him of threatening danger. Khovansky, unheeding, orders Persian slaves to dance for him. As the dancing ends, boyar Shaklovity enters to invite Khovansky to attend the Tsarevna's council. As he leaves the room, Shaklovity stabs him in the back. In the square in front of St Basil's Cathedral, Moscow, Prince Golitsin, guarded by troops, leaves for exile.

Dosifey laments the downfall of both Golitsin and Khovansky. He speaks briefly to Marfa, and Prince Andrey asks if she has any news of Emma. Marfa says she is safe, possibly now married. The prince threatens her with death at the hands of the Streltsy archers, but she defies him. They arrive, but in a melancholy procession, carrying blocks on which they are to be beheaded. Marfa takes Andrey away to safety and the Tsar's guards announce that – in spite of the demands of the crowd – they are pardoned.

In a pine wood near Moscow the Old Believers have arrived for their last visit to their hermitage. Their cause has failed and they are persecuted all over Russia. Soldiers surround them, but they will die rather than yield. Marfa and Andrey are with them. They build a funeral pyre and ascend it as it bursts into flames; the troops arrive, too late to arrest them.

Abbado's live recording brings the most vivid account of this epic Russian opera yet on disc, giving cohesion to a sequence of scenes even more episodic than those in *Boris Godunov*. With the text left incomplete and in a fragmentary state at the composer's death, there is no clear answer to the work's textual problems, but Abbado's solution is more satisfying than any other: he uses the Shostakovich orchestration (with some cuts), darker and harmonically far more faithful than the old Rimsky-Korsakov version, now regarded as a travesty by Mussorgskians. Yet Abbado rejects the triumphant ending of the Shostakovich edition and follows instead the orchestration that Stravinsky did for Diaghilev in 1913 of the original, subdued ending as Mussorgsky himself conceived it.

When the tragic fate of the Old Believers, immolating themselves for their faith, brings the deepest and most affecting emotions of the whole opera, that close, touching in its tenderness, is far more apt. One is left sharing the pain of their stoic self-sacrifice, instead of being brought back to automatic praise of Mother Russia. Lipovšek's glorious singing as Marfa, the Old Believer with whom one most closely identifies, sets the seal on the whole performance. Aage

Haugland is a rock-like Ivan Khovansky and, though Burchuladze is no longer as steady of tone as he was, he makes a noble Dosifey. Stage noises sometimes intrude and voices are sometimes set back, but this remains a magnificent achievement.

Though Gergiev's Kirov version is less compelling than Abbado's live Vienna recording, it provides a viable alternative, broader and more rugged, if less persuasive. Gergiev does not disguise the squareness of much of the writing, and such a number as the *Dance of the Persian slave-girls* in Act IV lacks the flair and brilliance of Abbado. Unlike either Abbado or Tchakarov on Sony, Gergiev stays faithful to the Shostakovich version of the score throughout, notably at the very end. There he simply adds a loud repetition of the *Old Believers' chorale* on unison brass, a less subtle ending than either Abbado's fascinating Stravinsky version or Tchakarov's reference back to the *Dawn on the Moscow River prelude*. The soloists from the Kirov may not have such starry names as those on Abbado's version, but they make a fine, consistent team, with Olga Borodina magnificent as Marfa, both rich and firm. Nikolai Ohotnikov with his dark bass is splendidly firm too as Dosifey, and though Bulat Minjelkiev as Ivan Khovansky has a pronounced vibrato, its rapidity prevents it from developing into a wobble. The two tenors are very well contrasted – Vladimir Galusin as Andrey lighter and brighter than the weighty Alexei Steblianko as Golitsin.

The Sony version, one of that company's series recorded in Sofia, like the Philips set, presents the text as Shostakovich restored and arranged it, absolutely complete. Unlike Abbado, Tchakarov accepts the triumphant ending, adding a reference back to the Moscow River theme; but his conducting is dull, not only in comparison with Abbado's but next to his own colourful account of Borodin's *Prince Igor*. There is some fine singing, notably from Alexandrina Milcheva as Marfa, Nicolai Ghiaurov as Ivan Khovansky and the characterful Nikola Ghiuselev as Dosifey. The recording is first rate.

The old Bolshoi version, using the Rimsky-Korsakov text, is valuable for letting us hear the commanding Marfa of Irina Arkhipova, but the close balance undermines the subtleties in her singing. The Bolshoi basses are splendid, matching those on more recent versions; but the coarseness of the recorded sound is all the more obvious on CD.

Sorochinsky Fair: complete.
*** Olympia OCD 114 A/B (2) [id.]. Stanislavsky Theatre Ch. & O, Esipov (with BORODIN, arr. Glazunov: *Petite suite* ***).
    Cherevik (Vladimir Matorin), Khirria (L. Zakharenko), Parassia (L. Chernikh), Gritzko (Anatole Mishchevski), Priest's Son (V. Voinarovski), Cherevik's Crony (O. Klenov), Gypsy (V. Temichev).

When Mussorgsky drank himself into an early grave, he left behind two major unfinished opera projects: not only *Khovanshchina*, which has long been in the regular repertory but also *Sorochinsky Fair*, which was much further from completion and required a lot more work on it. This first complete recording uses the edition prepared by Vissarion Shebalin; on this showing, in the colourful and vigorous performance by the company of the Stanislavsky Theatre in Moscow, it is an entertainment that should be imported into the West. Though the most striking passage, *St John's Night* at the beginning of Act III, is the original choral version of what Rimsky-Korsakov turned into *Night on the bare mountain*, this is not at all a grim piece but a folk-comedy that is full of fun, as charming and attractive as any, its score spiced with characteristically individual Mussorgskian progressions.

Cherevik has brought his daughter, Parassia, to a country fair for the first time and she is suitably excited. An old gypsy calls out greetings but warns the crowd that the ground where they stand is cursed: the devil appears periodically in the form of a pig seeking the sleeve of a red garment which he lost and never recovered. During the gypsy's story, Parassia has found her young suitor, Gritzko, who then asks Cherevik for his daughter's hand in marriage.

Cherevik gives the couple his blessing, then retires to the inn to get drunk. Khirria, his wife, appears; she does not approve of a prospective son-in-law whom she has not even seen. Gritzko is upset at this turn of events but the old gypsy offers to help him. He will ensure that both Cherevik and Khirria approve of the match, in return for a good bargain connected with the oxen Gritzko has for sale. Gritzko happily accepts the offer.

Khirria is now found busy in her kitchen. Cherevik is asleep, but when he wakes up they quarrel about the sale of farm produce. Cherevik leaves and Khirria waits impatiently for her lover, the priest's son. She has prepared delicious food, which she knows he cannot resist. He now arrives, a contradictory and grotesque figure, for his surface piety contrasts with his carnal intentions. A sudden noise interrupts them and, only just in time, Khirria hides him for her husband is returning with his cronies.

They are noisy and a bit scared too at being anywhere near where the devil's red sleeve could be. When the hidden priest knocks over a tin can, they imagine it is the work of the red sleeve. One crony again recites the tale and at the climax the window blows open and the head of a pig is seen. Consternation reigns. In his terror the priest's son falls into the midst of the assembled company, covered by Khirria's nightdress. All is revealed, to much hilarity.

The following morning in the village square Gritzko lies asleep on the ground, dreaming of the kingdom of darkness (the music is familiar as the *Night on a bare mountain*). Parassia arrives, happily singing and dancing, and wakes up her lover. Cherevik comes out of his cottage and confirms his agreement to the marriage, and even Khirria cannot spoil the pair's happiness with her disapproval. In any case her husband has now acquired a fresh purpose and dignity following her disgrace with the priest's son, and he is now the one who makes the decisions about such matters.

In the Olympia version, the piece ends joyfully with an exhilarating choral version of the famous *Gopak*, here brilliantly sung. The full-ranging Melodiya recording has fine immediacy and presence, though the impression is much more one of a studio than of the theatre, with voices sharply focused. That does not diminish the impressiveness of a company who have performed the piece on stage, with the bass, Vladimir Matorin, outstanding as the village elder, Cherevik. An English translation of the libretto is included in the booklet. The two discs generously offer not only the opera (just under 105 minutes) but also Borodin's *Petite suite*, which at 30 minutes may be thought mistitled but which in fact consists of Glazunov's orchestrations of Borodin piano pieces. The *Petite suite*, which Glazunov orchestrated after Borodin's death, is a colourful if undemanding work and makes a generous coupling, very well played and recorded.

Nicolai, Carl Otto (1810–49)

The Merry Wives of Windsor (Die lustigen Weiber von Windsor): complete.
Withdrawn: (M) **(*) EMI CMS7 69348-2 (2) [Ang. CDMB 69348]. Ch. & O of Bav. State Op., Heger.
  Falstaff (Gottlob Frick), Herr Fluth (Ernst Gutstein), Herr Reich (Kieth Engen), Fenton (Fritz Wunderlich), Dr Cajus (Carl Hoppe), Frau Fluth (Ruth-Margret Pütz), Frau Reich (Gisela Litz), Anna Reich (Edith Mathis).

This version from Munich of Nicolai's frothy Shakespearean comedy was originally issued in 1963. Nicolai's opera opens in the gardens between the houses of Messrs Ford and Page. Their respective wives compare love letters they have received from Sir John Falstaff.

Page has promised the hand of his daughter, Anne, to Slender, despite the pleadings of two other suitors, Doctor Caius and Fenton. Mistress Ford, now inside her own house, receives Falstaff and, as he begins making advances to her, her husband arrives, together with witnesses to her supposed betrayal. Falstaff is to be dumped in the river but hides in a laundry basket. Mistress Ford scolds her husband for his suspicions.

The scene now changes to the Garter Inn where Falstaff is carousing. Ford arrives, calling himself 'Brook', seeking to find out more about his wife's affair. Three suitors, Dr Caius, Slender and the more romantic Fenton, now serenade Mistress Page in her garden; then we move back to Ford's house, where he angrily warns his wife that he will catch her out. Falstaff is smuggled in under her husband's nose, dressed as an old woman and pretending to be deaf.

The final scene is in Windsor Forest, near Herne the Hunter's Oak. Falstaff makes advances to both wives but is not taken seriously. Anne and Fenton make a proper couple in their costumes of Titania and Oberon, and the musical setting is familiar from the opera's famous overture.

The opera has a flimsy storyline, but the great glory of the EMI recording is the darkly menacing Falstaff of Gottlob Frick in magnificent voice, even if he sounds baleful rather than comic. It is good too to have the young Fritz Wunderlich as Fenton opposite the Anna Reich of Edith Mathis. Though the others hardly match this standard – Ruth-Margret Pütz is rather shrill as Frau Fluth – they all give enjoyable performances, helped by the production which conveys the feeling of artists who have experienced performing the piece on stage. The engineers have also captured the natural feeling of stage perspectives.

The effectiveness of the comic timing is owed in great measure to the conducting of the veteran, Robert Heger, best known on record perhaps as the conductor of the classic pre-war recording of *Rosenkavalier* excerpts. From the CD transfer one could hardly tell the age of the recording, with the voices particularly well caught.

Nielsen, Carl (1865–1931)

Maskarade (opera; complete).
**(*) Unicorn DKPCD 9073/4 [id.]. Danish R. Ch. & SO, Frandsen.
  Jeronimus (Ib Hansen), Magdelone (Gurli Plesner), Leander (Tonny Landy), Henrik (Mogens Schmidt Johansen), Arv (Christian Sørensen), Leonard (Gert Bastian), Leonora (Edith Brodersen), Master of the masquerade (Aage Haugland).

Maskarade is new to the gramophone: only the overture and a handful of interludes have been recorded before. It is Nielsen's second and last opera and must be accounted a triumphant success in this recording. The libretto derives from Holberg's comedy of 1724, which Nielsen himself shaped into operatic form, with the literary historian, Vilhelm Andersen, as collaborator.

The story is innocently simple. Leander awakens the morning after his first visit to the Copenhagen Masquerade, with Henrik, his servant. He fell in love the night before and must return to find the girl in question. Henrik knows that, some years before, Jeronimus, Leander's father, had promised his son as a prospective husband to Leonora, the daughter of a prominent fellow citizen, Mr Leonard. He warns Leander of the severity of the law concerning breach of promise. Magdelone, Leander's mother, is envious of her son's visit to the Masquerade; she loves to dance and wishes she could have been there too. But her severe husband does not approve.

Henrik tells of Leander's new affair of the heart; then Mr Leonard arrives to say that his daughter has refused the match with Leander, and the two fathers make plans to avert a scandal. Jeronimus asks Leander to explain his behaviour of the night before and insists that his son apologize to Mr Leonard, but Leander rebels and resists his father's control.

The next night Henrik, who likes to socialize, again accompanies Leander to the Masquerade. Magdelone and Mr Leonard (together), Leonora in disguise (and in a sedan chair) and her maid, Penille, are all there too. Realizing his son and Henrik are missing from home, Jeronimus goes off to buy a suitable mask. Thus disguised, he interrupts a flirtation between his wife and Mr Leonard (without recognizing either) then, after being plied with alcohol by his son, finally lets his hair down and flirts with a dancing girl. At the end of the opera there are explanations all round and the household is never quite the same again.

Recounting the bare bones of the plot does scant justice to the charm and interest of the opera. *Maskarade* is a buoyant, high-spirited score full of strophic songs and choruses, making considerable use of dance and dance rhythms, and having the unmistakable lightness of the *buffo* opera. It is excellently proportioned: no Act outstays its welcome, one is always left wanting more, and the scoring is light and transparent. The performance here is delightful, distinguished by generally good singing and alert orchestral support. The disappointment is the CD transfer which, in trying to clarify textures, has in fact made the focus less clean.

Saul and David (opera; complete).
⊛ *** Chan. Dig. CHAN 8911/2; *DBTD 2026* (2) [id.]. Ch. & Danish Nat. RSO, Järvi.
  Saul (Aage Haugland), David (Peter Lindroos), Michal (Tina Kiberg), Jonathan (Kurt Westi), Witch of Endor (Anne Gjevang).

Nielsen's first opera comes from the same period as the *Second Symphony*; most collectors have known it in the English-language version, made in 1972, with Boris Christoff as Saul and with Jascha Horenstein conducting. This Chandos version under Järvi is in every way a vast improvement: the sound is glorious, it is sung in the original language, which is as important with Nielsen as it is with Janáček, and it has the merit of an outstanding Saul in Aage Haugland. The opera centres on Saul: his is the classic tragedy concerning the downfall of a heroic figure through some flaw of character.

In Gigal, King Saul of Israel and his son, Jonathan, await the arrival of the prophet, Samuel. They are ready to make a sacrifice to God in return for help against the Philistines. But Samuel interrupts the ritual, upbraids Saul and, designating him an outcast, proclaims that his rule is over and that Israel will survive. Jonathan brings his friend David, a shepherd boy, to the court and David falls in love with Michal, Saul's daughter.

Act II brings the famous battle between David and Goliath. David bids farewell to Michal and, armed only with a sling and five smooth stones, sets off to meet his giant adversary. The progress of the fight is described by Michal and her retainers, then Jonathan rides in with the news of David's victory. Just as Saul is giving David permission to marry Michal, a cry is heard lamenting that 'Saul has slain thousands and David tens of thousands'. Saul hurls a javelin at David and banishes him. But David returns, enters the camp and disarms Saul.

The prophet Samuel proclaims that God has ordained David to be King of the Israelites and anoints him, then falls dead. Saul tries to have David arrested but the latter leaves, unharmed, and Michal defies her father and goes with him. In the battle that follows on Mount Gilboa, Jonathan is mortally wounded, but Saul has time to proclaim David 'Blest of the Lord' before – cursing God – he dies by his own sword. David arrives with Michal and is proclaimed king, 'chosen of God'.

The Chandos cast is very strong and the powerful choral writing is well served by the Danish Radio Chorus. The opera is replete with wonderful and noble music, the ideas are fresh and abundant and full of originality. The opera convinces here in a way that it rarely has before, and the action is borne along on an almost symphonic current that disarms criticism. A marvellous set.

Nyman, Michael (born 1944)

The man who mistook his wife for a hat (chamber opera).
(M) *(*) Sony Dig. MK 44669 [id.]. O, composer.
    Dr S., the Neurologist (Emile Belcourt), Mrs P. (Sarah Leonard), Dr P. (Frederick Westcott).

The plot and theme of Michael Nyman's curious chamber opera are evident enough from the title, which is taken from a book by Oliver Sacks investigating the case of a doctor with visual agnosia or 'mental blindness'. Nyman has turned this psychiatric study into what one might call a cabaret opera, with a small instrumental ensemble (string quintet and harp, led by the piano) accompanying the three soloists. Sadly this recording, close-miked in the dry, aggressive acoustic of the CBS studios, gives a very limited idea of the work. Even the words of the narration, spoken by Dr S., the neurologist, at the start are seriously masked by the piano; and the English text is consistently needed if you are to follow the contortions of the story. The composer, playing the piano, makes an eager leader of the ensemble; but the singing is flawed, with Emile Belcourt (as the neurologist) often strained, Frederick Westcott (as the man of the title, Dr P.) throaty of tone, and Sarah Leonard (as his wife) too shrill.

Offenbach, Jacques (1819–80)

La Belle Hélène (complete).
*** EMI CDS7 47157-8 (2) [Ang. CDCB 47156]. Capitole Toulouse Ch. and O, Plasson.
    Hélène (Jessye Norman), Paris (John Aler), Ménélas (Charles Burles), Agamemnon (Gabriel Bacquier), Calchas (Jean-Philippe Lafont), Oreste (Colette Alliot-Lugaz).

Offenbach's *Belle Hélène*, first produced in Paris in 1864, characteristically pokes fun at the whims of the mythological deities. In Sparta, just before the Trojan war, Calchas the high priest enters, concerned at the Spartans' current lack of enthusiasm for religious ritual and sacrifices to the gods. Venus, however, is in receipt of considerable popular esteem. She has promised the beautiful Helen (the king's wife) to Paris, a shepherd but in fact one of the sons of the King of Troy. In return he is to reward Venus with the golden apple.

Helen and Paris are enamoured of each other and when, having defeated the kings of Greece, his identity is finally revealed in a test of wisdom, she is delighted to find that Venus has provided her with such an attractive suitor.

Calchas now arranges a thunderstorm to suggest a decree from Jupiter and sends Menelaus (Helen's husband) off to Crete, to leave the coast clear for the new match. Helen, having dressed modestly, welcomes the visiting royalty to a banquet, and at a game of chance (at which Calchas cheats) she retires. Calchas has promised she shall dream of Paris, but he takes the opportunity to turn up in her bedroom in person. Alas, their amours are interrupted by the return of Menelaus. Helen grumbles that he should have announced his return, but Paris is told to leave.

The court now moves to the seaside at Nauplia. Venus is none too pleased that matters have so gone awry, and Agamemnon decides that the king must be prepared to fit in with her plans. A ship arrives in the harbour with a bearded figure aboard; he says he is an emissary of Venus, come to take Helen to Cythera. Menelaus has no option but to give his consent and, after the ship has embarked once more, Paris reveals himself then sails away to Troy with his beloved Helen.

The casting of Jessye Norman in the name-part of *La Belle Hélène* may seem too heavyweight, but the way the great soprano can lighten her magisterial voice with all the flexibility and sparkle the music calls for is a constant delight, and her magnetism is irresistible. John Aler, another American opera-singer who readily translates to the style of French operetta, makes a heady-toned Paris, coping superbly with the high tessitura in the famous Judgement couplets and elsewhere. The rest of the cast is strong too, not forgetting Colette Alliot-Lugaz as Oreste, who had such dazzling success in the central role of Chabrier's *L'étoile* in John Eliot Gardiner's brilliant recording.

Michel Plasson here produces similarly fizzing results, with excellent ensemble from the choir and orchestra of the Capitole. Excellent recording, less reverberant than in some other discs from this source, and especially lively and present in its CD format. Indeed it is very important not to set the volume level too high or the spoken dialogue will seem unrealistically close.

Les brigands (complete).
**(*) EMI Dig. CDS7 49830-2 (2). Lyon Opera Ch. & O, Gardiner.
  Falsacappa (Tibere Raffalli), Fiorella (Ghyslaine Raphanel), Fragoletto (Colette Alliot-Lugaz), Pietro (Michel Trempont), Comte de Gloria-Cassis (Jean-Luc Viala), Duke of Mantua (Thierry Dran), Baron de Campotasso (François LeRoux), Antonio (Bernard Pisani).

This is one of Gardiner's delectably frothy French offerings, in which the Lyon Opera Company re-enacts in the studio a stage presentation. *Les brigands* has a Gilbertian plot about brigands and their unlikely association with the court of Mantua, with the carabinieri behaving very like the police in *The Pirates of Penzance*.

The bandit chief is Ernesto Falsacappa, who, to distract his men from being depressed by their limited criminal success, brings back to the camp eight young peasant girls to provide entertainment and solace. Falsacappa's daughter, Fiorella, is in love with Fragoletto, an honest farmer whose farm the brigands have recently raided. She had gone with them and now Fragoletto, seeking her out, is only too pleased to be captured.

He asks for her hand but is told that if he is to join the band he must show what he is made of. They are impressed with him, for he captures a courier plus diplomatic bag. Inside is a portrait of the Princess of Granada with details of her coming marriage to the Prince of Mantua. Part of her dowry is the settlement of a three-million debt between Mantua and Granada. Falsacappa puts his daughter's portrait in place of that of the princess and sends the courier off to complete his assignment. Fragoletto is now made a full member of the band, the wine flows freely and the arrival of the carabinieri is no embarrassment at all, for they can find nothing incriminating.

In an inn on the border of Granada and Mantua the innkeeper, Pipo, his wife, Pipa, and their daughter, Pipetta, await the arrival of the two advance wedding parties. The brigands also arrive and take over the inn, including the kitchen. The two marital deputations arrive separately, and the Mantuans are put out of the way in the cellar with the carabinieri; the Granadans are kept in their bedrooms. Falsacappa in the uniform of the chief of carabinieri takes charge and, when the innkeeper breaks free, the carabinieri in the cellar are too inebriated to have any effect on the situation.

At the palace of the Duke of Mantua, the prince is getting ready for his wedding and pays reluctant farewell to those ladies who have brought romantic pleasure to his youthful years. He is impressed with the portrait of the bride, whom he recognizes as a lady who once helped him find his way when he was lost in the mountains. What he does not know is that the Mantuan treasury has been robbed by the treasurer, Antonio, to pay for his many mistresses, so there is no money to repay the national debt.

The brigands purporting to be the Granadan delegation now arrive and, though they seem a motley crew, the prince is certainly delighted with his 'bride'. Falsacappa, discovering that the expected money has been embezzled, is furious; so too are the members of the real delegation, which now appears. All ends happily. Falsacappa is pardoned (because of his daughter's influence with the prince, after his mountain rescue by her) and will reform; Fiorella and Fragoletto can be married, and so can the prince and princess, for Antonio finds a way of arranging a loan to reimburse the treasury coffers.

Les brigands may not be quite such a charmer as its predecessors in Gardiner's Lyon sequence, Chabrier's *L'étoile* (EMI) for instance, and the tone of the principal soprano, Ghyslaine Raphanel, is rather edgily French, but the rest of the team is splendid. Outstanding as ever is the characterful mezzo, Colette Alliot-Lugaz as Fragoletto, in another of her breeches roles. Warm, well-balanced recording.

Les Contes d'Hoffmann (The Tales of Hoffmann): complete.
⊛ *** Decca 417 363-2 (2) [id.]. R. Suisse Romande and Lausanne Pro Arte Ch., SRO, Bonynge.
  Hoffmann (Plácido Domingo), Olympia / Giulietta / Antonia / Stella (Joan Sutherland), Nicklausse / Muse (Huguette Tourangeau), Lindorf / Coppélius / Dapertutto / Dr Miracle (Gabriel Bacquier).
Withdrawn: * EMI CDS7 49641-2 (3) [Ang. CDCC 49641]. Ch. & O of Nat. Op., Brussels, Cambreling.
  Hoffmann (Neil Shicoff), Olympia (Luciana Serra), Giulietta (Jessye Norman), Antonia (Rosalind Plowright), Stella (Dinah Bryant), Nicklausse / Muse (Ann Murray), Lindorf / Coppélius / Dapertutto / Dr Miracle (José Van Dam).
**(*) Ph. 422 374-2 (3) [id.]. Dresden Ch. & State O, Tate.
  Hoffmann (Francisco Araiza), Olympia (Eva Lind), Giulietta (Cheryl Studer), Antonia (Jessye Norman), Nicklausse / Muse (Anne Sofie Von Otter), Lindorf / Coppélius / Dapertutto / Dr Miracle (Samuel Ramey).
** DG Dig. 427 682-2 (2). Fr. R. Ch., Fr. Nat. O, Ozawa.
  Hoffmann (Plácido Domingo), Olympia / Giulietta / Antonia (Edita Gruberová), Nicklausse / Muse (Claudia Eder), Lindorf (Andreas Schmidt), Coppélius (Gabriel Bacquier), Dapertutto (Justino Diaz) Dr Miracle (James Morris).

Offenbach did not live to finalize his masterpiece or to see its extraordinary success, and in consequence it is performed in several different versions, with the ordering of Acts II and III often reversed. The composer's original intention was that the three principal soprano roles, and also that of Stella in the Prologue, be taken by the same singer, and similarly, the various manifestations of evil can be personified by a single male artist; it is no accident that the most consistently successful recorded version carries out the composer's wishes.

The Prologue takes place in Luther's beer-cellar, situated adjacent to the Nuremberg opera house where the celebrated prima donna, Stella, is appearing in Mozart's *Don Giovanni*. The evil Councillor Lindorf is pursuing Stella, and he bribes Stella's servant into handing over to him a letter intended for the poet, Hoffmann, together with a key to her room. He intends to keep the assignation in the place of Hoffmann, who now enters with his companion, Nicklausse.

The gathered students prevail on him to sing the tale of the dwarf, Kleinsach, who clicks his knees together, but Hoffmann is in a strange mood; in the middle of his story he falls into a reverie about his beloved, then pulls himself together and finishes his song. He recognizes Lindorf, who for him symbolizes the malignant spirit which has always dogged his happiness. Luther warns that Act II of the opera is about to start but Hoffmann, instead of returning to the theatre, relates to the assembled company the story of the three great loves of his life.

The first was Olympia, the amazing mechanical creation of the inventor, Spalanzani, who hoped to make a fortune by demonstrating his 'daughter', but feared that Coppélius (who had a part in the doll's construction) might claim a share. His bank, Elias, went broke. Hoffmann, Spalanzani's pupil, observing Olympia at a distance, thinks she is human but Nicklausse tries to warn him that Spalanzani is a famous inventor of lifelike dolls. Coppélius arrives. His 'magic eyes' are the secret of the automaton's success, and he sells a pair of magic spectacles to Hoffmann, which confirms the poet's illusion that Olympia is real.

Coppélius, as Spalanzani suspected, has come for his share of the money, and Spalanzani pays him with a cheque on the now-defunct bank. Olympia dances and sings for the assembled guests, with Spalanzani discreetly and hastily 'winding her up' every time her clockwork mechanism runs down. Hoffmann is in love; Olympia first eludes him but at last he is able to dance with her. He is whirled around furiously and his magic glasses fall off and break, just as the furious Coppélius returns without his money and smashes the doll to pieces.

In the second (or third, according to the chosen order) story, Hoffmann is in Venice. We hear the famous *Barcarolle* shared by Nicklausse and the courtesan, Giulietta. Hoffmann is in love with her, but she currently favours Schlemil, who is enslaved to the sorcerer, Dapertutto (in league with the devil). Hoffmann's soul is in danger, for Dapertutto bribes Giulietta with a diamond: she is to capture Hoffmann's reflection in a mirror, which she manages to do by persuading him to look at the glass so that she can retain his image there for ever. He is aghast to find the mirror does not show his reflection.

The *Barcarolle* steals in once more and Nicklausse tries to persuade the demented Hoffmann to leave; but Hoffmann demands the key to Giulietta's room from Schlemil. They fight a duel which, through Dapertutto's evil influence, Schlemil cannot win, and Hoffmann kills him. He then sees Giulietta in a gondola with Pittichinaccio, her hunchback alternative lover, and Nicklausse manages to drag his friend away to safety.

The episode which makes the most effective climax for the opera takes place in Munich. Antonia, loved by Hoffmann, is a singer, like her mother before her. Crespel, her father, reminds her that she has promised not to sing for, along with her mother's voice, she has inherited her tuberculosis. Crespel does not favour Hoffmann's visits and he instructs his servant, Franz, to forbid him entry. But Franz is deaf and so disobeys his master. Hoffmann and Antonia embrace and plan their future together. She grows faint and he hides when her father returns.

Crespel announces the arrival of Dr Miracle. He was in attendance at the death of Crespel's wife, but insists on treating Antonia, and by magic diagnoses her illness in her absence. He instructs her to sing and Crespel drives him out. Hoffmann and Antonia meet again and Hoffmann now begs her to forget her dream of becoming a prima donna. But his urging is in vain, for Dr Miracle returns and chides her for wasting her talents, promising her a dazzling future. She looks at her mother's portrait as if for guidance, and its face is suddenly alive and imploring her to sing. Dr Miracle bizarrely produces a violin to accompany what becomes a great soaring climax as Antonia (aided and abetted by the spirit of her mother) sings her heart out, then collapses. Dr Miracle pronounces her dead.

We now return to Luther's tavern. Hoffmann has finished his history of love and is exhausted. In the adjacent theatre Stella is taking her curtain calls; cheers and applause can be heard. Lindorf quietly slips away. Nicklausse explains that Stella is the embodiment of Hoffmann's three loves, and all drink to Stella. Hoffmann slumps in a drunken stupor on the table. In a vision, the Muse of Poetry appears to console him – that is where his destiny lies. But, in the real world, Stella makes her entrance on Lindorf's arm and, seeing Hoffmann is drunk, goes off with his rival. The students continue their carousing as the curtain falls.

Decca's sparkling CD transfer of the Bonynge set (with its economical layout on a pair of CDs, each playing for over 70 minutes) makes Offenbach's inspired score sound consistently refreshing, with the immediacy of the action very striking and the acoustics of Victoria Hall, Geneva, adding fullness and warmth to the vividness. Joan Sutherland gives a virtuoso performance in three heroine roles, not only as Olympia, Giulietta and Antonia but also as Stella in the Epilogue, which in this version – very close to that originally prepared by Tom Hammond for the English National Opera – is given greater weight by the inclusion of the ensemble previously inserted into the Venice scene as a septet, a magnificent climax.

Bonynge opts for spoken dialogue and puts the Antonia scene last, as being the most substantial. His direction is unfailingly sympathetic, while Sutherland is impressive in each role, notably as the doll, Olympia, and in the pathos of the Antonia scene. As Giulietta she hardly sounds like a *femme fatale* but still produces beautiful singing. Domingo gives one of his finest performances on record, and so does Gabriel Bacquier. It is a memorable set in every way, much more than the sum of its parts. One's only real criticism concerns the cueing, which could be more generous in Acts II and III.

The EMI version broke new ground. Sylvain Cambreling with his Belgian forces opted for the complete text of Fritz Oeser's edition, putting together nearly all the material which Offenbach failed to sort out before his untimely death. This is rather like Oeser's expanded version of *Carmen*, only more so, for much of the material omitted from the regular Choudens edition is of dubious quality. A good deal of that comes in the Venice scene which, as it usually stands, seems too short to sustain the sequence's dramatic weight.

Here the expansions are the more attractive and the more weighty, when the commanding Giulietta is Jessye Norman. Rosalind Plowright brings extra – and satisfying – power to the Antonia episode without losing charm, and Luciana Serra, as at Covent Garden, is a bright, clear Olympia. Neil Shicoff as Hoffmann makes a confident Domingo-substitute (often sounding very like that model), and Ann Murray is, as ever, everyone's favourite Nicklausse, though the voice regularly loses focus above the stave. José van Dam sings with splendid firmness in the four villainous roles, if too nobly; while Robert Tear is excellent in the four character-tenor roles.

Offenbach devotees will want to hear this performance; as a general recommendation, the Decca version, with Sutherland assuming all three heroine roles, remains preferable, with the Choudens edition expanded as at the English National Opera but on one CD fewer than this EMI set. Not that EMI sells anyone short, with no less than 214 minutes of music on the three discs. The recording is pleasantly atmospheric in both media, if not as cleanly focused as the Decca.

Jeffrey Tate in this textually troubled work uses a new edition prepared by Michael Kaye that takes account of the discovery of 350 more manuscript pages in addition to those which expanded the Oeser edition to Wagnerian lengths. One big difference here from the complete Oeser edition, as presented by Cambreling on his deleted EMI set, is that dialogue replaces all the recitatives written by Ernest Guiraud. The Prologue is more extended, showing the transformation of the Muse into Nicklausse, with extra material in the Olympia and Antonia Acts too, such as the striking trio for Hoffmann, Nicklausse and Coppélius. Also, Tate points out that 'the Giulietta act contains music that shows conclusively that Offenbach would have wanted a single voice to embody all of Hoffmann's female infatuations'.

A fascinating illustration of that comes in the jaunty couplets, *L'amour lui dit: la belle*, leading into exchanges and a duet reprise with Hoffmann. It is a jolly little piece, close in style to earlier Offenbach, which in its lightness and use of high coloratura radically alters one's conception of the character of the Venetian *femme fatale*. Needless to say, Cheryl Studer has no problems here over high coloratura, but in context it seems inconsistent with the character as we know it. It is a pity that the logic of the project was not carried through, with a single singer chosen for all the heroines, as in both the Bonynge/Sutherland and the Ozawa/Gruberová sets. As it is, Jessye Norman, the Giulietta of the Cambreling set, has here become the Antonia of the new one. Though she cunningly lightens her voice, making it sound as girlish as she can, and she urges the music on at a brisker speed than usual in the charming duet, *C'est une chanson d'amour*, it is still hard to imagine her as the fragile young girl destined to die. Tate's determination to adopt an authentic text leads him to reject the septet, based on the *Barcarolle* theme, not even including it in an appendix (as Cambreling does). Nor is Dapertutto's *Scintille, diamant* included, drawn originally from another Offenbach work, when the authentic *Tourne, tourne miroir*, is restored at that point.

As a recording, the set's drawback is that it does not feel very theatrical, thanks partly to being recorded in a church but also to the very sparing use of sound effects, with the chorus's contributions sounding rather oratorio-like. The spoken dialogue does not help when, among the principals, only Georges Gautier, in the four grotesque roles, has a French-speaking background, though Jessye Norman's spoken French is a delight. The new set, unlike the Cambreling, uses the sour alternative ending to the Venice Act, with Giulietta accidentally taking poison. Samuel Ramey sings very well in all four villainous roles, with satisfyingly firm, dark tone, even if he finds it hard to sound really sinister, but principal vocal honours go to Anne Sofie von Otter as a superb Muse and Nicklausse, making one relish all the extra music given the character in this version. Eva Lind is bright and clear, if a little edgy and shallow, as Olympia, perfectly doll-like in fact; and Cheryl Studer is technically very strong and confident, even if she does not quite sound in character. Not always helped by the recorded sound, refined and rather lacking in weight, Riccardo Cassinelli, Georges Gautier and Boris Martinovitch give enjoyable but rather undercharacterized performances, and the student leaders in the Prologue sound far too mature. Francisco Araiza makes an agreeable Hoffmann, but he lacks the flair of his finest rivals, and the voice tends to lose its focus under pressure.

Jeffrey Tate secures fine ensemble. He tends to pace on the slow side, but by contrast presses the celebrated *Barcarolle* on faster than usual – a conflation of the vocal and entr'acte versions – with woodwind soloists who in their literal way miss the magic. Even with reservations there is a very strong textual case for this set, and admirers of the opera will surely want to have it alongside the first choice with Sutherland, Domingo and Bacquier.

In his autobiography Plácido Domingo devotes special attention in whole chapters to two operatic roles only: not just Otello – which one would expect – but Hoffmann in Offenbach's opera. He finds something of Beethoven and of the mocked hunchback, Rigoletto, in the character; and DG's set, conducted by Ozawa, justifies itself first and last by the intelligence and strength of Domingo's performance. Yet there is no denying that the voice is no longer as fresh as it was when he recorded the same role for Decca opposite Dame Joan Sutherland, a version which, unlike this, was consistently well cast. Edita Gruberová is one of the few sopranos today who could attempt to match Sutherland's feat of singing all the strongly contrasted heroine roles. Yet even in the coloratura role of the doll, Olympia, which should suit her perfectly, she gives a limited portrait; though she sings strongly and intelligently in the other two roles, the timbre of the voice is no help. The others in the cast are disappointing, even Gabriel Bacquier, who sang all four villain roles for Decca, but here is limited to Coppélius. Though he is still characterful, he is far less firm of voice. Ozawa, generally sympathetic, makes an intelligent choice of the options now presented by the very full Oeser edition, but Bonynge's choice in the Decca set works even better, based on the text originally suggested by Tom Hammond and used by English National Opera, among others. Full, warm recording, on the reverberant side for this work.

Les Contes d'Hoffmann: highlights.
(M) *** Decca 421 866-2; *421 866-4* (from above recording with Domingo, Sutherland; cond. Bonynge).
(M) **(*) DG Dig 435 402-2 [id.] (from above recording, with Domingo, Gruberová; cond. Ozawa).
Withdrawn: (M) ** EMI CDM7 63448-2 [id.]; *EG 763448-4*. Nicolai Gedda, Gianna D'Angelo, Elisabeth Schwarzkopf, Victoria De los Angeles, Nikola Ghiuselev, George London, Ernest Blanc, Duclos Ch., Paris Conservatoire O, Cluytens.

The Decca highlights disc is one of the finest compilations of its kind from any opera. With over an hour of music, it offers a superbly managed distillation of nearly all the finest items and is edited most skilfully.

The DG highlights – which is also part of the 'Domingo Edition' – is certainly generous (72 minutes) and includes much more of the Prologue than on Decca (25 minutes), and well-chosen excerpts from the other three Acts, rounding off with the touching *Malheureux, tu ne comprends donc pas* from the Epilogue. Offered at mid-price, this has the advantage of modern digital sound (though rather a reverberant acoustic), and those who want to sample Gruberová in the three soprano roles should find this a useful appendix to the Decca complete set. Those without the complete opera who want just a selection will still find the admittedly shorter Decca highlights the more rewarding.

With such a starry cast-list it is disappointing that the earlier EMI set was not more successful. In particular André Cluytens proved quite the wrong conductor for this sparkling music. Fortunately, most of the best moments are included in the highlights disc, including the Schwarzkopf/Gedda duet from the Venetian scene, not to mention the famous *Barcarolle* and the brilliant septet. De los Angeles (sadly out of voice) and George London (unpleasantly gruff-toned) provide the vocal disappointments.

(i) *Mesdames de la Halle*. (ii) *Monsieur Choufleuri*. (iii) *Pomme d'Api* (complete recordings).
Withdrawn: *** EMI Dig. CDS7 49361-2 (2). (i–iii) Mady Mesplé, Jean-Philippe Lafont; (i; ii) Charles Burles, Michel Trempont, Michel Hamel; (i; iii) Leonard Pezzino; Laforge Ch. Ens., Monte Carlo PO, Rosenthal.

All three of these sparkling one-Act operettas make delightful listening, idiomatically performed under Manuel Rosenthal. *Pomme d'Api* has the usual triangle between an old man, his nephew and the girl they both fancy. *Monsieur Choufleuri* involves a party scene with imitations of grand opera; while *Mesdames de la Halle* is a knockabout farce with three characters in drag, set in the Parisian fruit-market. The proportion of French spoken dialogue may be rather high for repeated listenings – however, it is separately banded, so can be cued out – but the zest of the many musical numbers is well worth investigating. Mady Mesplé is less shrill of tone than she has sometimes been, hardening only on top. Like the other principals she has the right style. Outstanding among the others is the baritone, Jean-Philippe Lafont. Atmospheric recording, with the CDs bringing added presence but not detracting from the ambient warmth.

Orphée aux enfers (Orpheus in the Underworld; 1874 version).
*** EMI CDS7 49647-2 (2). Petits Chanteurs à la Croix Potencée, Toulouse Capitole Ch. and O, Plasson.
Orpheus (Michel Sénéchal), Eurydice (Mady Mesplé), Aristeus / Pluto (Charles Burles), Jupiter (Michel Trempont), Juno (Danièle Castaing), Public Opinion (Jane Rhodes), Cupid (Jane Berbié).

Offenbach's most famous operetta – and not just because of its *Overture* – was first heard in Paris in 1858. Another mythological send-up, it also good-humouredly parodies local political and social conditions. Public Opinion introduces the plot. The setting is rustic and this particular Orpheus and Eurydice are far from model lovers. Both have been unfaithful, and Eurydice reveals that she detests his fiddle-playing. Never theless he threatens her with his latest and very long violin concerto.

Eurydice's current lover is Pluto. He appears disguised as a shepherd and bee-keeper under the name of Aristaeus. He warns that to love him is to risk being transported to the Underworld. Eurydice is only too willing to accompany him there and leaves a note for Orpheus telling him that she is dead. Orpheus is about to breathe a sigh of relief when Public Opinion threatens him with scandal if he fails to follow his wife and rescue her. So Orpheus reluctantly sets off for Hades.

On Mount Olympus the gods are quarrelling. Jupiter has changed Acteon into a stag and is worrying that Diana is compromising herself over him. Mercury arrives and relates what has happened to Eurydice. Jupiter rebukes Pluto, who defends himself vigorously.

The gods in chorus rebel against the monotony of eternal nectar and ambrosia and remind Jupiter of his own previous transgressions. Orpheus and Public Opinion arrive, Pluto denies hiding Eurydice; Orpheus, urged on by Public Opinion, requests her return and, to his dismay, Jupiter orders Pluto to give her up and himself descends to Hades to look after her interests. Everyone else decides to come as well.

Down in the Underworld, John Styx, in charge of the prison, looks after Eurydice. Jupiter arrives and is very taken with her. There is a chorus, provided by twenty small policemen, then, on the advice of Cupid, Jupiter disguises himself as a fly, to get intimately near to Eurydice, and they buzz together. Jupiter then reveals his identity.

Eurydice is now seen transformed into a bacchante, and the famous *Can-can* is danced, to unleash everyone's inhibitions. Pluto stops Jupiter from going off with Eurydice, and at that moment Orpheus and Public Opinion arrive. Eurydice is restored to Orpheus, but with the famous proviso that he must not look back at her. Jupiter, ever wily, hurls a thunderbolt, and in shock Orpheus turns around. Eurydice is lost to him for ever. Everyone is highly delighted; Orpheus returns happily alone to Thebes, and Eurydice remains as a bacchante with a ready choice of godly lovers.

Plasson recorded his fizzing performance – the first complete set in French for 30 years – in time for the Offenbach centenary. He used the far fuller four-Act text of 1874 instead of the two-Act version of 1858, so adding such delectable rarities as the sparkling *Rondo* of Mercury and the *Policemen's chorus*. Mady Mesplé as usual has her shrill moments, but the rest of the cast is excellent, and Plasson's pacing of the score is exemplary. The recording is brightly atmospheric and the leavening of music with spoken dialogue just enough.

Orpheus in the Underworld: abridged version of Sadler's Wells production (in English).
(B) **(*) CfP TC-CFP 4539. June Bronhill, Eric Shilling. Sadler's Wells Op. Ch. and O, Faris.

With a single reservation only, this is highly recommendable. Without visual help, the recording manages to convey the high spirits and genuine gaiety of the piece, plus – and this is an achievement for a non-Parisian company – the sense of French poise and precision. June Bronhill in the *Concerto duet* is infectiously provocative about her poor suitor's music. One's only complaint is that Alan Crofoot's King of the Boeotians is disappointing vocally. The sound is full and brilliant, with plenty of atmosphere, and there is no doubt that this reissue of a vintage recording dating from 1960 is very successful.

Orpheus in the Underworld: highlights of ENO production (in English).
**(*) That's Entertainment Dig. CDTER 1134. Stuart Kale, Lilian Watson, Richard Angas, Shelagh Squires, Bonaventura Bottone, Cathryn Pope, Emile Belcourt, ENO Ch. & O, Mark Elder.

The English National Opera production, lively and provocative with its grotesque scenery and costumes in political cartoon style by Gerald Scarfe, here spawned a comparably lively collection of highlights, enterprisingly recorded by That's Entertainment Records. It starts not with the conventional *Overture* but with a prelude, over which the invented character, Public Opinion, delivers a moral in unmistakable imitation of the then Prime Minister. From then on, the whole entertainment depends a lot for its fun on the racy new adaptation and translation by Snoo Wilson and the ENO producer, David Pountney. It will delight all those who enjoyed the original show at the Coliseum; but Offenbach devotees should be warned: there is little of Parisian elegance in this version and plenty of good knockabout British farce, brilliantly conveyed by the whole company. For this kind of performance one really needs a video, when even Bonaventura Bottone's hilariously camp portrait of a prancing Mercury is not nearly so much fun when simply heard and not seen. Bright, vivid recording to match the performance.

La Périchole (complete).
(M) *** Erato/Warner 2292 45686-2 (2) [id.]. Rhine Op. Ch., Strasbourg PO, Lombard.
Périchole (Régine Crespin), Piquillo (Alain Vanzo), Don Andrès (Jules Bastin), Miguel de Panatellas (Gérard Friedmann), Don Pedro (Jacques Trigeau).

**Withdrawn: **(*) EMI Dig. CDS7 47362-8 (2) [Ang. CDCB 47361]. Toulouse Capitole Ch. and
O, Plasson.

Périchole (Teresa Berganza), Piquillo (José Carreras), Don Andrès (Gabriel Bacquier),
Miguel de Panatellas (Michel Sénéchal), Don Pedro (Michel Trempont).

La Périchole has an exotic setting but its plot is nothing to do with mythology and its bitter-
sweet romanticism has more substance than usual in an Offenbach operetta. It opens in the
public square in Lima in front of The Three Cousins. As it is the birthday of the viceroy, Don
Andrès, wine is free. He wanders around incognito, and the populace humour him in his
deception. Across the street La Périchole and Piquillo, her lover, are attempting to make an
impression on the crowd, but the collection is small; anyway Piquillo looks fiercely at any man
who wants to give money to his mistress. A circus passes.

Piquillo goes off and Don Andrès now approaches La Périchole and asks if she would like to
become one of the viceroy's ladies-in-waiting. She is hungry and accepts, but first she must write
a note to tell Piquillo and bid him farewell. Only married women are accepted as ladies-in-
waiting at the palace so Panatellas, the lord-in-waiting, is ordered to find a husband for La
Périchole. Piquillo is about to hang himself when he receives the farewell letter; at the same time
he finds himself arbitrarily chosen by Panatellas as the prospective husband of the viceroy's new
lady-in-waiting. He is to be handsomely paid, so he agrees to the bargain.

The marriage goes ahead as planned, but while La Périchole, who has become tipsy to dull the
pain of her enforced matrimony, suddenly delightedly recognizes her lover, Piquillo is too drunk
to know what is happening to him and he explains that he loves someone else. In the palace the
new Countess of Tabago (none other than La Périchole) arrives to be presented by her husband.

The ladies of the court sneer at her because of her lowly birth. Piquillo finally recognizes her
and he loses his temper at his betrayal, for how could she have known that he would be picked to
be her count? The viceroy orders him to be put in prison among other recalcitrant husbands, and
La Périchole asks permission to visit him there. But the viceroy, disguised as a jailer, hears of a
plan for escape and orders La Périchole to be chained up opposite her husband. She will be freed
only if she gives herself to the viceroy instead.

The plot now borrows from *The Count of Monte Cristo*: an old prisoner burrows through to
the cell and helps free the lovers from their chains. They agree that La Périchole will fool the
viceroy into thinking she will be his. He comes in, full of expectancy, and is promptly tied up in
their place. The escapees hide in The Three Cousins but finally decide to give themselves up and
throw themselves on the viceroy's mercy. Magnanimously, he grants them their freedom and
their new titles too.

Dating from 1976, this Erato recording of one of Offenbach's most delectable scores features
in the principal roles two of the singers who represent the French tradition at its very finest.
Though both Régine Crespin in the title-role and Alain Vanzo as her partner, Piquillo, were past
their peak at that time, their vocal control is a model in this music, with character strongly
portrayed but without any hint of vulgar underlining. That is strikingly true of Crespin's account
of the most famous number, the heroine's tipsy song, *Ah! quel dîner*, which makes its point with
delectable slyness. Crespin is fresh and pointed too in the letter song in waltz-time which
precedes it, an equally celebrated number.

Vanzo, firm and clear and betraying few signs of age, produces heady tone in his varied arias,
some of them brilliant. Jules Bastin is characterful too in the subsidiary role of Don Andrès,
Viceroy of Peru. Lombard secures excellent precision of ensemble from his Strasbourg forces,
only occasionally pressing too hard. The recorded sound is vivid and immediate, and the only
disappointment is that spoken dialogue is omitted, even in numbers described as *Melodrame*.
Instead, the libretto provides a detailed synopsis of the action between the texts and translations
of numbers.

The alternative EMI version – currently withdrawn from the catalogue – certainly has its
merits. Though the sound (as usual in Toulouse) is over-reverberant, the CD remastering has
sharpened the impact and ensemble work is excellent, with diction surprisingly clear against full
orchestral sound. The incidental roles are superbly taken, but it is odd that Spaniards were
chosen for the two principal roles. José Carreras uses his always lovely tenor to fine effect but is
often unidiomatic, while Teresa Berganza – who should have made the central character into a
vibrant figure, as Régine Crespin used to – is surprisingly heavy and unsparkling. The CD disc-
break is well placed between Acts, but cueing might have been more generous.

La vie parisienne (complete).

*** EMI CDS7 47154-8 (2) [Ang. CDCB 47154]. Régine Crespin, Mady Mesplé, Luis Masson, Michel Sénéchal, Michel Trempont, Ch. and O of Capitole, Toulouse, Plasson.

Hardly less effervescent than the parallel version of *Orpheus in the Underworld*, also conducted by Michel Plasson for EMI, *La vie parisienne* is a scintillating example of Offenbach's work, an inconsequential farce around the heady days of the International Exhibition in Paris. The opening scene is the approach to the Saint-Lazare railway station.

Raoul de Gardefeu and Bobinet are both in love with the demi-mondaine, Métella, and each has independently come to meet her. When she arrives, she fails to recognize either of them, as she has yet another admirer travelling with her. The two spurned lovers make friends.

Gardefeu's manservant, Joseph, is acting as a guide for the Swedish Baron de Gondremarck and his very pretty wife. Gardefeu tips Joseph generously and takes over his customers; bringing them to his own house, he says it is a hotel annexe. So that he can have uninterrupted access to the baroness, he puts them in separate bedrooms. The baron does not object, as he is bored with his wife and is looking for Métella. Opportunely, she now arrives, seeking reconciliation with Gardefeu, but is told that her rooms are being used by the baroness. She leaves very angrily.

Gardefeu connives to get rid of the baron so that he can have the baroness to himself. He arranges with some disguised tradespeople to take de Gondremarck off to a celebrity dinner. Bobinet has access to his aunt's house (she is away on a visit) and will be host, while the servants can masquerade as distinguished guests, and the chambermaid, disguised as an admiral's wife, will seduce the baron, to keep him from returning home to his wife. As everyone becomes very inebriated, the whole thing goes with a swing.

Meanwhile a masked ball is in progress at the Café Anglais, and Métella, anxious to restore her relationship with Gardefeu, plots with the baroness who wants to remove her husband from the temptations of Parisian life. All ends well, with Métella and Gardefeu reunited, and Bobinet indicating that he is also still in love with her, which she regards as a bonus. All join together in toasting *La vie parisienne*, where the wine sparkles and 'lovers and mistresses love each other happily'.

Though the EMI recording is not quite as consistent as the one of *Orphée aux enfers*, the performance and presentation sparkle every bit as brilliantly, with the spoken dialogue for once a special attraction. Régine Crespin in a smaller role is just as commanding, and though the cast lacks the excellent Vanzo and Massard, the style is captivatingly authentic. The CD transfer is vivid, without loss of ambient atmosphere.

Orff, Carl (1895–1982)

Antigonae (complete).

(M) **(*) DG 437 721-2 (3) [id.]. Bav. R. Ch. & RSO, Ferdinand Leitner.

Antigonae (Inge Borkh), Ismene (Claudia Hellman), Kreon (Carlos Alexander), Guard (Gerhard Stolze), Haemon (Fritz Uhl), Tiresias (Ernst Haefliger), Messenger (Kim Borg), Eurydice (Hetty Plümacher).

Antigonae was the first of three works in which Orff sought to relate opera back to Greek origins. The story opens as Antigone, Oedipus' daughter (in defiance of King Creon) tries to ensure a proper burial for her brother, Polynices, and to get her frightened sister to help her. Creon is furious when he hears she has tried to cover the corpse with earth using her bare hands. She is seized, along with Ismene, and both are thrown into prison. Haemon, the king's son, seeks mercy for the two sisters, but Creon at first refuses.

When Haemon declares that he is determined to commit suicide, Creon reluctantly releases Ismene but confines Antigone in a rocky cave. Tiresias, the blind prophet, now foretells disaster for Creon and counsels him to release Antigone and give Polynices a burial proper to his rank. Creon agrees, but too late: Antigone has already hanged herself and Haemon dies by his own hand at her side. To complete the tragedy, Creon's wife, Eurydice, now also kills herself.

Using an orchestra full of percussion (including grand pianos), Orff reminds us, on the one hand, of Stravinsky's *Les noces* and, on the other, of Stravinsky's much greater operatic setting of the Oedipus legend. The baldness of the writing brings few of the delights of such a work as *Carmina burana*, but the splendid performance here of Inge Borkh – one of her finest on record – makes it an important set. The 1961 recording was made in the Munich Hercules-Saal and has plenty of atmosphere, but the percussive sounds grow a little wearing after a time, since the opera runs for 160 minutes.

De temporum fine comoedia.
(M) (***) DG 429 859-2 [id.]. Christa Ludwig, Peter Schreier, Josef Greindl, Cologne R. Ch., RIAS Chamber Ch., Tölz Boys' Ch., Cologne RSO, Karajan.

Some may find merit in a tiresome, meretricious work. Musical invention is not its strong suit; the simplicity and melodic spontaneity that one encounters in *Carmina burana* are not to be found here. The performance offers the very highest standards and the recording is extremely lively and vivid, but musically this is a very thin brew, whatever impact it may have had as theatre.

(i) *Die Kluge;* (ii) *Der Mond.*
Withdrawn: (M) *** EMI CMS7 63712-2 (2) [Ang. CDMB 63712]. Philh. Ch. & O, Sawallisch.
(i) King (Marcel Cordes), Peasant (Gottlob Frick), Peasant's Daughter (Elisabeth Schwarzkopf), Jailer (Georg Wieter), Man with donkey (Rudolf Christ), Man with mule (Benno Kusche).
(ii) Narrator (Rudolf Christ), 1st Young Man (Karl Schmitt-Walter), 2nd Young Man (Helmut Graml), 3rd Young Man (Paul Kuen), 4th Young Man (Peter Lagger), Petrus (Hans Hotter).
(M) **(*) BMG/Eurodisc GD 69069 (2) [69069-2-RG]. (ii) Kiermeyer Kinderchor; Bavarian R. Ch., Munich R. O, Kurt Eichhorn.
(i) King (Thomas Stewart), Peasant (Gottlob Frick), Peasant's Daughter (Lucia Popp), Jailer (Richard Kogel), Man with donkey (Manfred Schmidt), Man with mule (Claudio Nicolai).
(ii) Narrator (John Van Kesteren), 1st Young Man (Heinz Friedrich), 2nd Young Man (Richard Kogel), 3rd Young Man (Ferry Gruber), 4th Young Man (Benno Kusche).

Sawallisch's pioneering Orff recordings of the mid-1950s were regularly used as demonstration records in the early days of stereo; the sound, well balanced, is still vivid and immediate on CD, with such effects as the thunderbolt in *Der Mond* impressive still. *Der Mond* brings the tale of the land where there was no moon and the night sky was as dark as pitch. But four young men on their travels in another country see the white globe in the sky; they steal it and bring it home with them. They are declared Keepers of the Moon and decide that, as they grow old and die, each shall have a quarter of the moon buried with him. When the last one dies, darkness again blankets the landscape at night.

When the four young men reach the Underworld, they put the moon's four quarters together again, and all the rest of the dead reawaken and are soon thoroughly enjoying themselves in the most licentious ways. Hearing the noise, St Peter comes down to investigate. The dead continue to carouse until they are all exhausted and fall asleep. St Peter takes the moon away and puts it up in the heavenly firmament where it remains.

The story of *Die Kluge* is less spectacular, telling of a peasant who, while ploughing his field, finds a golden mortar. Paying no heed to his daughter's warning that he will be under suspicion if he reveals his discovery, the poor man finds himself in prison. The king has the daughter brought before him and asks her three riddles. If she can solve them, her father will be saved. She solves them without difficulty and the king promptly marries her.

Two men, vagabonds, now enter, one riding a donkey, the other a mule. The king and his wife are playing chess but he stops the game to give judgement on their dispute over ownership of a foal. It is a baby donkey, but the king makes his verdict in favour of the mule's owner. The queen consoles the donkey's owner and gives him some instructions; he is seen later dragging a fishing net across the land. In reply to the king's surprised question, he says that if a mule can bear a foal it is possible to catch fish on dry land.

In a fit of anger the king banishes his wife but tells her she can take with her one chest full of the possessions she treasures most. The next morning the donkey owner is freed from prison, and the king awakens from a drugged sleep to find himself imprisoned inside the chest. The king is so impressed and touched by her interpretation of his decree, he praises her cleverness. She retorts: 'Nobody can be in love and clever both at the same time,' and the old Peasant wryly comments, 'She has found the pestle which belongs to the mortar.'

The recording producer of the EMI set was Walter Legge, using all his art of presentation, and the casts he assembled would be hard to match. His wife, Elisabeth Schwarzkopf, is here just as inspired in repertory unusual for her as in Mozart, characterful and dominant as the clever young woman of the title in *Die Kluge*. It is good too to hear such vintage singers as Gottlob

Frick and Hans Hotter in unexpected roles. Musically, these may not be at all searching works but both short operas provide easy, colourful entertainment, with Sawallisch drawing superb playing from the Philharmonia. No texts are provided, but the discs are very generously banded.

Eichhorn's Eurodisc version of the early 1970s provides an excellent alternative, with casts equally consistent. *Der Mond* is given in Orff's revised, 1970 version, and the composer himself is credited with having supervised the production of the recordings. Certainly their great merit lies in the fun and jollity they convey, beautifully timed if not always quite as crisp of ensemble as the EMI versions. The sound as transferred is shriller and brighter than the 1950s EMI, rather wearingly so, with voices not quite so cleanly focused. German texts are given but no translation.

Oedipus der Tyran (complete).
(M) ** DG 437 029-2 (2) [id.]. Bav. Rad. Ch. & SO, Kubelik.
    Oedipus (Gerhard Stolze), Jokasta (Astrid Varnay), Kreon (Kieth Engen), Tiresias (James Harper), Priest (Karl Christian Kohn).

In discussing composition with twelve notes, Schoenberg once said that there was 'a great deal of good music to be written in C'. So indeed there is, but this is not it! At least *Carmina burana* has the merit of a certain earthy vitality and some rousing moments. Those who think it thin and repetitive should wait until they hear this! Three hours of declamation on and around middle C may do wonders for your German but it doesn't offer much in the way of musical substance.

Orff set Hölderlin's *Oedipus der Tyran* in 1958, so it is a relatively late piece, the second of his trilogy of Greek-based operas, coming a decade after *Antigonae*. Huge forces are involved: a large percussion section (including specially constructed stone chimes, wooden blocks, gongs, tambourines, bass drums, castanets and a Javanese gong), no strings except nine double-basses, flutes, oboes, trombones, harps and six grand pianos); despite all this, its sound-world remains austerely monochrome and, as so often with this composer, offers plentiful reminders of Stravinsky's *Les noces*.

But there is more music in a page of the latter than there is in any of the five Acts under discussion, and it is a scrappy piece for a setting of the searingly horrifying tragedy of Oedipus, who unwittingly marries his own mother (after unknowingly killing his father) and who, after she hangs herself, blinds himself with the pins from the golden brooches on her dress. No quarrels with the performances: Astrid Varnay's Jokasta and Gerhard Stolze's Oedipus are strongly characterized, and the Bavarian Radio forces under Kubelik are exemplary.

The vintage 1966 recording emanates from the Herculesaal in Munich, an excellent acoustic, and still sounds very impressive. The DG CDs – like the original LP issue – offer no English translation. Only Hölderlin's original translation of Sophocles is provided with the records to act as synopsis, so the recording is in any case recommendable only to those who readily understand German, for it is very much a dialogue opera with choral interjections, in spite of the exotic and spectacular percussive effects. Three stars minus for the performance and recording, but several minus stars for the piece itself!

Pacius, Fredrik (1809–91)

Kung Karls Jakt (King Charles's Hunt): complete.
(M) *** Finlandia Dig. FACD 107. Jubilate Ch., Finnish Nat. Op. O, Söderblom.
    Leonora (Pirkko Törnqvist), Jonathan (Peter Lindroos), Reutercrantz (Tom Krause), Gyllenstjerna (Walton Groenroos).

Fredrik Pacius was German-born and studied with Spohr, before settling in Helsinki. Here he became known as 'the father of Finnish music', for he brought the Finnish capital, then a provincial backwater, into contact with the mainstream of European music. His opera *King Charles's Hunt* was composed in 1851–2 but Pacius made no fewer than three subsequent revisions, the fourth and last version being staged as late as 1880. Although it is hailed as the first Finnish opera, it is by a German and to a Swedish-language text, exhibiting little sign of nationalism except in its choice of subject. Although the second version was staged in Stockholm, it has never entered the repertoire abroad and has maintained no more than a peripheral hold on the stage in Finland itself.

The plot is simple and tells of how an attempt on the sixteen-year-old Charles XI of Sweden, on a hunting trip in the Åland islands, is thwarted by a young fisherman's daughter, whose fiancé had shot one of the king's elks (a capital offence) but who is subsequently pardoned. The musical ideas are pretty simple too, some are pleasant but there is little evidence of much individuality; Pacius's Danish contemporaries, Hartman and Heise, are far more distinctive. There is some fine singing from Pirkko Törnqvist as the fisherman's daughter, Leonora, Peter Lindroos as her fiancé, and from Walton Grönroos as the coup leader, Gustaf Gyllenstjerna. The young king is a speaking role. Much care has been lavished on the production and Ulf Söderblom holds things together admirably. No masterpiece is uncovered but it will be of interest to collectors with a specialist interest in the beginnings of opera in the northern countries.

Paisiello, Giovanni (1740–1816)

Il barbiere di Siviglia: complete.
*** Hung. Dig. HCD 12525/6-2 [id.]. Hungarian State O, Adám Fischer.
   Figaro (Istvan Gáti), Rosina (Krisztina Laki), Dr Bartolo (József Gregor), Don Basilio (Sándor Sólyom-Nagy), Count Almaviva (Dénes Gulyás).

Paisiello's *Barbiere di Siviglia* may for many generations have been remembered only as the forerunner of Rossini's masterpiece of a Beaumarchais adaptation, but latterly stage revivals have helped to explain why, before Rossini, the opera was such a success. The plot follows the same basic lines as the Rossini version (detailed below).

Figaro and Count Almaviva meet outside old Bartolo's house. Figaro had previously been in the count's employ and, since he left, has become an apothecary's assistant and barber with a horse-doctor in the cavalry. He says that he was dismissed because he wrote sonnets, odes and madrigals, then travelled widely, but now he is down on his luck. He is happy to help the count achieve his aim of thwarting Bartolo and marrying Bartolo's ward, Rosina.

They are interrupted as she opens her window to throw her note down for Almaviva, whom she knows as Lindoro. (He wants to be sure she will marry him for himself and not for his title.) With Figaro's help, Lindoro gains admittance, first as a soldier looking for a billet then as a music master and student of theology. Basilio proposes his counterplan to Bartolo to slander Almaviva, but later, after the misunderstanding between the lovers is resolved, money works wonders; Basilio is witness to the wedding contract, and Bartolo has to accept the marriage as a *fait accompli.*

The libretto may be much more of a muddle than the one Rossini used, over-complicated and with untidy ends, and the musical inspiration may too often be short-winded, but the invention is full of vitality, and that is captivatingly reflected in this Hungarian performance under Adám Fischer. On Hungaroton opera sets one has come to recognize the sterling strength of the stars of the Budapest Opera, and this brings another excellent example of their teamwork and consistency. József Gregor, for example, is a vividly characterful Bartolo, a role more important here than in Rossini, while Istvan Gáti is a strong, robust Figaro. Krisztina Laki is a brilliant Rosina and Dénes Gulyás a clean, stylish Almaviva, relishing his Don Alonso imitation. Full, vivid recording.

Pepusch, Johann Christian (1667–1752)

The Beggar's Opera – see John Gay, above

Pergolesi, Giovanni (1710–36)

La serva padrona: complete recording (includes alternative ending and insertion arias).
*** Hung. HCD 12846-2 [id.]. Capella Savaria, Németh.
   Serpina (Katalin Farkas), Uberto (József Gregor).

Pergolesi's two-Act Intermezzo was first heard in Naples in 1733. The plot is simple enough. As the curtain rises, we find Uberto dressing to go out but still waiting for his breakfast chocolate after three hours. He complains to Serpina, the maid, but she answers him in kind and takes it out on the mute servant, Vespone, who cannot answer back. Serpina then tells Uberto that it is too late to go out.

Thoroughly fed up with his situation, Uberto declares he will get married. Serpina thinks herself the ideal candidate, but that thought is furthest from Uberto's mind. However, Serpina is not to be put off, and she plans to trap Uberto into marrying her.

She tells him she has found a prospective soldier husband, Captain Tempest, but that he is intolerably bad-tempered, and it transpires also that her suitor is demanding a very large dowry to take Serpina off Uberto's hands. Needless to say, in the end Serpina gets her way, Uberto finally grants that he loves her, and she is duly installed as prospective mistress of the house.

Lasting just an hour and involving only two voices, *La serva padrona* is ideally suited to disc, and on this Hungaroton issue receives a delightful, sparkling performance well sung by two of the most characterful singers we have come to know from Budapest recordings and with the excellent period-performance group, Capella Savaria. József Gregor sings with splendid *buffo* stylishness, while Katalin Farkas, as Serpina the maid, brings out the fun of the writing, with the shrewishness of the character kept in check. Bright, clean recording.

Pfitzner, Hans (1869–1949)

Palestrina: complete.
(M) *** DG 427 417-2 (3) [id.]. Tölz Boys' Ch., Bav. R. Ch. & SO, Kubelik.
  Pope Pius IV / Christoph Madruscht (Karl Ridderbusch), Morone (Bernd Weikl), Borromeo (Dietrich Fischer-Dieskau), Count Luna (Hermann Prey), Palestrina (Nicolai Gedda), Ighino (Helen Donath), Silla (Brigitte Fassbaender).

Kubelik's magnificent complete recording of Pfitzner's epic opera on the subject of Palestrina's fight for artistic freedom at the Council of Trent makes a superb reappearance on CD in DG's mid-price 20th-Century Classics series. It was originally issued in 1973 and, despite universal praise, quickly disappeared from the catalogue.

We first meet Palestrina at home with a pupil, Silla. The great composer's son, Ighino, arrives and comments on his father's melancholy. He has written nothing since his wife's death and his life seems to be at an end. Cardinal Borromeo now arrives from Rome and the Council of Trent; he is in a dictatorial mood. The church is in a dilemma about what music is suitable for future ecclesiastical use. He is against the return to the use of Gregorian chant. All other sacred music must be burned. It is necessary for a contemporary composer to write a Mass sufficiently fine and spiritually pure to convince the pope and his council, and so ensure the future of church music.

Palestrina offers his regrets but he cannot take on such a commission – his artistic powers are declining. The angry cardinal accuses him of blasphemy and departs. Palestrina has a vision of composers from the past. They remind him of his youth and suggest that his musical destiny is not yet fulfilled. A new vision of angels now provides the inspiration for a Mass.

At the climax of their visit, Palestrina's wife, Lucretia, reappears to give him succour and new confidence in himself, and Palestrina senses the supreme exaltation of artistic creation. At dawn the bells of Rome are heard and Silla and Ighino are delighted to discover the sheets of music written during the night – an entire mass. The boys gather up the papers.

The scene now moves to Cardinal Madruscht's palace at Trent. Borromeo arrives and says he has been unable to persuade Palestrina to write the required Mass and he is unable to break the composer's self-imposed silence. There is discussion about the problem of music in the church. More delegates arrive and there is much bickering and suspicion of each other's interests and quarrels about order of precedence.

The papal delegate, Morone, prays for wisdom and tries to calm things down. But the large meeting slowly degenerates into a chaos of nationalist disagreement, and the fracas which develops eventually becomes a fight. The guard is called and ordered to open fire. The Church's council must not be defiled: any survivors will be tortured.

We now return to Palestrina's room. He awakens and Ighino tells him that the new Mass is being performed at the pope's palace. They explain that he and Silla collected the manuscript sheets and how the music was taken from them. Suddenly there are cries from the street indicating that the pope is coming. He arrives to offer his personal congratulations on the success of the Mass which has made an enormous impression on him. He decrees that Palestrina must remain in the service of the Church until his life ends.

The pope and his retinue of cardinals depart and Ighino, greatly impressed, asks his father if he is not the happiest man in the world. Perhaps, says Palestrina, but he is old and not so exuberant. He stands quietly before the portrait of his wife; he then walks over to the organ and plays softly. From outside come the shouts of praise from the crowd.

This rich and glowing performance goes a long way towards explaining why in Germany the mastery of this unique opera is trumpeted so loudly, and on record the scale of Pfitzner's achievement is all the easier to appreciate and enjoy. Though Pfitzner's melodic invention hardly matches that of his contemporary, Richard Strauss, his control of structure and his drawing of character through music (using his own patiently written, if at times ungainly, libretto) make an unforgettable impact. It is the central Act, a massive and colourful tableau representing the Council of Trent, which lets one witness the crucial discussion on the role of music in the church.

The outer Acts – more personal and more immediately compelling – show the dilemma of Palestrina himself and the inspiration which led him to write the *Missa Papae Marcelli*, so resolving the crisis, both personal and public. At every point Pfitzner's response to this situation is illuminating, and this glorious performance with a near-ideal cast, consistent all through, could hardly be bettered in conveying the intensity of an admittedly offbeat inspiration. This CD reissue captures the glow of the Munich recording superbly. Though this is a mid-price set, DG has not skimped on the accompanying booklet, in the way some other companies have tended to do with sets of rare operas. The libretto has useful background information and an English translation along with the German original.

Ponchielli, Amilcare (1834–86)

La Gioconda (complete).
*** Decca Dig. 414 349-2 (3) [id.]. L. Op. Ch., Nat. PO, Bartoletti.
    La Gioconda (Montserrat Caballé), La Cieca (Alfreda Hodgson), Enzo Grimaldo (Luciano Pavarotti), Alvise (Nicolai Ghiaurov), Laura (Agnes Baltsa), Barnaba (Sherrill Milnes).
*** EMI CDS7 49518-2 (3) [Ang. CDCC 49518]. La Scala, Milan, Ch. & O, Votto.
    La Gioconda (Maria Callas), La Cieca (Irene Companeez), Enzo Grimaldo (Pier Miranda Ferraro), Alvise (Ivo Vinco), Laura (Fiorenza Cossotto), Barnaba (Piero Cappuccilli).
(M) ** Decca 433 770-2 (2) [id.]. Ch. & O of Maggio Musicale Fiorentino, Gavazzeni.
    La Gioconda (Anita Cerquetti), La Cieca (Franca Sacchi), Enzo Grimaldo (Mario Del Monaco), Alvise (Cesare Siepi), Laura (Giulietta Simionato), Barnaba (Ettore Bastianini).

Each of the four Acts of Ponchielli's epic opera has its own title. Act I, called 'The Lion's Mouth', is set in the grand courtyard of the Venetian ducal palace. On one side of the courtyard one of the historic lions' mouths, a stone monolith, has the following inscription cut ominously into the wall: 'For secret denunciations to the Inquisition, against any person, with impunity, secrecy, and benefit to the state'.

But it is springtime and the courtyard is filled with a busy crowd in holiday mood. Barnaba (a spy for the Inquisition) leans back against a column, a small guitar slung round his neck. The crowd rushes off to watch the regatta and Barnaba observes them disdainfully. Gioconda tenderly leads in La Cieca, her blind mother. Barnaba is in love with Gioconda but she continually repulses him. She loves Enzo, a Venetian nobleman who has been proscribed by the Venetian authorities but who is nevertheless in the city in the guise of a sea captain, with his ship waiting in the Fusina Lagoon. Barnaba again presses his attentions on Gioconda, but she runs off.

The crowd returns from the regatta. The boatman Zuane, their hero, has been defeated, but he comes in with Gioconda and Enzo. Barnaba infers that La Cieca is a witch and that Zuane has been beaten because of her sorcery. Amidst rising antagonism La Cieca is dragged from the church steps. Enzo calls on his sailor friends to help him save her. Alvise Badoero, one of the heads of the State Inquisition, and his masked wife, Laura, descend from the palace steps and demand an end to the rioting. Barnaba notices that Laura is gazing at Enzo and that he recognizes her despite the mask. Gioconda now kneels before Alvise, begging mercy for her mother; when Laura also intercedes on La Cieca's behalf, it is granted.

La Cieca gives Laura a rosary as token of her thanks. She asks her name and, as she is identified, Enzo exclaims, 'Tis she!' Everyone departs except Barnaba and Enzo, whereupon Barnaba addresses him as Enzo Grimaldo, Prince of Santa Fior. The spy knows that at one time Laura and Enzo were betrothed, but on their separation she was obliged to marry Alvise; Barnaba realizes that they are still passionately involved with each other.

Now the nefarious Barnaba seeks to show Gioconda that Enzo is false to her and he arranges for Laura to go aboard Enzo's boat, ready to depart with him. Enzo leaves. Gioconda, hidden behind a pillar with her mother, overhears Barnaba dictate a letter to Isepo the scribe, that a wife will elope that night with Enzo. Fearing that Enzo has betrayed her, Gioconda and La Cieca enter the church. Isepo leaves and Barnaba posts the letter into the lion's mouth. La Cieca comforts her daughter.

Act II, 'The Rosary', takes us to an uninhabited island with a moored vessel. It is night. Barnaba and Isepo, disguised as fishermen, sit in a small boat. Enzo waits in eager anticipation for Laura and she arrives with Barnaba. They will sail away as soon as the moon sets. But Gioconda now steals on board and confronts Laura. Angrily, she tries to stab her but Alvise and his guards arrive in time to prevent the murder. Laura makes a plea to the Virgin, raising the rosary La Cieca had given her, and, recognizing her mother's gift, Gioconda helps Laura to escape in another boat, with Alvise in hot pursuit. Enzo arrives on deck looking for Laura and confronts Gioconda instead. Rather than have his boat impounded by the authorities, Enzo sets fire to it.

Act III, 'The House of Gold', opens in the home of Alvise; he has condemned Laura for her betrayal of his honour. He summons her, accuses her of unfaithfulness and gives her a phial of poison, coldly pointing to a funeral bier held in readiness for her body. But Gioconda is hiding in the palace and, finding Laura, gives her a narcotic which, when taken, will immediately simulate the appearance of death. Gioconda pours the poison into her own phial. Alvise now returns to check that Laura is dead and is convinced by the deception.

At this point comes the famous ballet of the *Dance of the hours*, symbolizing a struggle between darkness and light. When it is concluded, Barnaba drags in La Cieca, and Enzo also manages to enter. A bell tolls and Alvise draws back a curtain to reveal Laura, prostrate. Enzo rushes at Alvise with a dagger but is restrained by guards.

The final Act, 'The Orfano Canal', takes us to the vestibule of a ruined palace on the island of Giudecca. Two men arrive carrying the supine Laura, swathed in a black cloak. Gioconda motions them to place the cloaked figure on the couch behind a screen at the back of the room. Gioconda has promised to give herself to Barnaba if he will help Enzo escape from prison and guide him to the Orfano Canal. She is obsessed with her own suicide and weeps. Enzo enters.

She infuriates him by saying that she has hidden Laura's body where he will never find it, but suddenly Laura's voice is heard calling Enzo from behind the screen. She revives, and the reunited pair thank Gioconda for the boat in which they escaped. Barnaba now reappears and Laura despairingly remembers her agreement with him. Pretending to adorn herself with jewellery, she snatches up a dagger from the table and stabs herself. He is furious and as she expires he shouts in her ear: 'Last night thy mother did offend me and I have strangled her!' But she is already dead, and does not hear his words.

The colourfully atmospheric melodrama of this opera gives the Decca engineers the chance to produce a digital blockbuster, one of the most vivid opera recordings yet made, with CD enhancing the presence of both voices and orchestra to involve the listener strongly. The casting could hardly be bettered, with Caballé just a little overstressed in the title-role but producing glorious sounds. Pavarotti, for long immaculate in the aria *Cielo e mar*, here expands into the complete role with equally impressive control and heroic tone. Commanding performances too from Milnes as Barnaba, Ghiaurov as Alvise and Baltsa as Laura, firm and intense all three. Bartoletti proves a vigorous and understanding conductor, presenting the blood and thunder with total commitment but finding the right charm in the most famous passage, the *Dance of the hours*.

Maria Callas gave one of her most vibrant, most compelling, most totally inspired performances on record in the title-role of *La Gioconda*, with flaws very much subdued. The challenge she presented to those around her is reflected in the soloists – Cossotto and Cappuccilli both at the very beginning of distinguished careers – as well as the distinctive tenor Ferraro and the conductor Votto, who has never done anything finer on record. The recording still sounds well, though it dates from 1959. The remastering increases the vocal presence yet retains the bloom.

Although no match for the digital Caballé set, the 1957 Decca *La Gioconda* has much to commend it. The cast is generally distinguished with Cerquetti very powerful in the name-part; although Gavazzeni is not always the most dramatic of conductors, the performance has many fine moments and is satisfying as a whole. The recording, though clear enough, is not one of Decca's very best.

Porter, Cole (1891 – 1964)

Aladdin (excerpts).
**(*) Sony SK 48205 [id.]. Introduction: the composer. Ch. & O, Robert Emmett Dolan.
  Magician (Cyril Ritchard), Astrologer (Dennis King), Emperor / Chamberlain (George Hall),
  Aladdin (Sal Mineo), Princess (Anna Maria Alberghetti).

It would be too easy to dismiss this score, written for a television production at the very end of
an illustrious career, and it certainly isn't vintage Cole Porter. But in the *Emperor's song* it
includes the last lyrics the composer/lyricist ever penned (in November 1957). He had problems
with this number, since he got the impression from his researches that the only thing oriental
potentates ever did was to have their subjects beheaded! So he chose a fun 'on holiday' theme
instead, and the result is genial, and nothing like Gilbert's conception of the Mikado. The main
lyrical number, *I adore you*, is very pleasing too, and Cyril Ritchard's *No wonder taxes are so
high*, if more sub-G&S, becomes the score's catchy highlight.

All the cast make the very most of their opportunities and it is fascinating to hear the sleek
kitsch of the American late-1950s pop-choral style, so firmly dated in its moment in time. The
CD is transferred from excellent stereo tapes, never used before, and the sound is remarkably
smooth and vivid. As a novelty appendix, four more items have been added. Four alternative
versions of the key songs, they were originally intended for a demo disc, recorded by unnamed
and unknown but very professional session soloists.

Best of all is the inclusion of the composer's own spoken introduction, sounding amazingly
strong and up-beat for a man who had endured 31 operations for a serious injury incurred from
a 1937 horse-riding accident. Both his legs were badly broken, and Porter's right leg was finally
amputated at about the time his show appeared on television to a hostile press reception.

Anything goes (musical).
*** EMI Dig. CDC7 49848-2 [id.]. Amb. Ch., LSO, McGlinn.
  Reno Sweeney (Kim Criswell), Billy Crocker (Cris Groenendaal), Hope Harcourt (Frederica
  Von Stade).

John McGlinn, with a scholarly concern for original sources comparable to that of a baroque
specialist, here reconstructs the original (1934) version of Cole Porter's brilliant score, with the
plot following the characters on a liner sailing the Atlantic in the 1930s. McGlinn firmly
demonstrates the extra vigour and point of this version over the radical revisions made after the
Second World War, when other numbers were introduced and the orchestration was radically
altered. McGlinn had the benefit of working with Hans Spialek, one of the original
orchestrators, just before he died at the age of 89.

In the original production Ethel Merman had her first big Broadway success in the unlikely
role of ~Reno, evangelist-turned-nightclub-singer, and here Kim Criswell proves a superb
successor. In the very first number, *I get a kick out of you*, she commandingly establishes her star
quality, and she remains the focus of the whole piece, though Frederica von Stade is equally
winning as the second heroine, Hope. One of the other hit numbers, *You're the top*, is presented
in a clipped way that follows the original rather than what has become traditional practice. The
well-filled single disc includes as an appendix three extra numbers cut from the 1934 score, one
of them, *There's no cure like travel*, a more elaborate version of the chorus, *Bon voyage*,
involving a counter-theme in descant. Full, satisfying beefy sound, bringing out the vigour of
playing and singing.

Can-Can.
(M) *** EMI ZDM7 64664-2 [id.]. Original Broadway cast. Ch. & O, Milton Rosenstock.
  La Môme Pistache (Lilo), Judge Aristide Forestier (Peter Cookson), Boris Adzinidzinadze
  (Hans Conried), Claudine (Gwen Verdon).

The trouble with *Can-Can* is that the French insouciance is laminated on and the champagne
fizz of a piece like Offenbach's *La vie parisienne* is replaced with a harder – admittedly zestful –
transatlantic rhythmic aggressiveness. Moreover the lead in the original Broadway show was
played by an imported star without a surname, Mlle Lilo. She is genuinely French but self-
consciously so, not unlike a kind of female Maurice Chevalier, but without that smile in the
voice which helped him get away with his preposterous accent. Nevertheless Lilo's presentation
of Cole Porter's justly acclaimed string of hits, the waltz song *Never give anything away*, *C'est
magnifique* (almost a caricature), *Live and let live* (with splendid lyrics), *Every man is a stupid*

man and the gorgeous *I love Paris*, do have a plangent, pseudo-chanteuse colouring, and Lilo can articulate *Allez-vous en* authentically enough.

The title-number has undoubted mid-Atlantic pep, but the highlight of the disc is not given to the star but to the engaging Gwen Verdon as the sexy Claudine, who shares *If you loved me – truly* quite unforgettably with Peter Cookson. He camps up the part of Judge Aristide Forestier very agreeably. The story centres on the judge seeking to prosecute the can-can dancers for obscenity (they usually wore no panties and very little else) and who ends up falling in love with the owner of a dance-hall (La Môme Pistache). She is no better than she ought to be and he is disgraced by his association with her, becomes part-owner in a new club, and finally defends the very licentiousness he had set out to eradicate. The recording is described as stereo and it certainly sounds like it. If so, it must derive from one of the earliest of all commercial stereo master-tapes, for the recording date is given as 17 May 1953. No complaints about the documentation.

Kiss me Kate (musical).
*** EMI Dig. CDS7 54033-2 (2) [Ang. CDC 54033]. Amb. Ch., L. Sinf., John McGlinn.
  Lilli Vanessi / Katharine (Josephine Barstow), Fred Graham / Petruchio (Thomas Hampson), Lois Lane / Bianca (Kim Criswell), Bill Calhoun / Lucentio (George Dvorsky), Hattie (Karla Burns), Paul (Damon Evans).
(M) **(*) EMI ZDM7 64760-2 [id.]. Original Broadway cast. Ch. & O, Pembroke Davenport.
  Lilli Vanessi / Katharine (Patricia Morison), Fred Graham / Petruchio (Alfred Drake), Lois Lane / Bianca (Lisa Kirk), Bil Calhoun / Lucentio (Harold Lang), Hattie (Annabelle Hill), Paul (Lorenzo Fuller), Mobsters (Aloysius Donovan, Alexis Dubroff).

It may seem extravagant for a Cole Porter musical to stretch to two discs but, as in his previous recordings for EMI, McGlinn has delved into the archives and has rescued the originally neglected material, so providing a substantial and fascinating appendix, unearthing such lovely songs as the heroine's *We shall never be younger*. There is also a nicely judged sprinkling of dialogue between numbers. Having two opera-singers, Josephine Barstow and Thomas Hampson, in the principal roles of the ever-argumentative husband-and-wife team who play Kate and Petruchio in *The Taming of the Shrew* also works excellently, both strong and characterful.

There is little of the inconsistency of style which made the choice of Dame Kiri Te Kanawa so controversial in *West Side Story*. Kim Criswell is delectable as Lois Lane, brassy but not strident in *Always true to you, darling, in my fashion*. Strong characterization too from George Dvorsky, Damon Evans and Karla Burns, with the London Sinfonietta – as in the prize-winning set of *Show Boat* – playing their hearts out. The recording is full and vivid with enough atmosphere to intensify the sense of presence.

After the newer and extended EMI recording, the 1959 version using most of the original Broadway cast (with 46 minutes of music) is a much smaller beer. *Another opening, another show*, and *Wunderbar* go well enough, Lisa Kirk's *Why can't you behave* has a sultry period flavour, and *Always true to you, darling, in my fashion* is splendidly zippy , but Alfred Drake's *I've come to wive it wealthily in Padua* seems curiously stagy and slightly self-conscious, and the stereo recording does not help by being a little edgy; his ballad, *So in love*, has similar problems. Patricia Morison's *I hate men* is lyrical rather than venomous and her *I am ashamed that women are so simple* obviously dates from before the time of 'Women's lib.' However, Lorenzo Fuller's *Too darn hot* is suitably peppy and nicely accompanied, and the Aloysius Donovan/Alexis Dubroff *Brush up your Shakespeare*, with its characteristically witty lyrics, is most winningly done. Overall, Pembroke Davenport's direction has plenty of spirit. Good documentation.

Nymph Errant (musical).
Withdrawn: * EMI Dig. CDC7 54079-2 [id.]. Kaye Ballard, Emile Belcourt, Fiona Fullerton, Patricia Hodge, Larry Kent, Lisa Kirk, Andrea McArdle, Maureen McGovern, Virginia McKenna, Liliane Montevecchi, Patrice Munsel, Marie Santell, Alexis Smith, Derek Waring, Elisabeth Welch, Stephen Hill Singers, O, Pippin & Firman.

Unlike most other EMI sets of Broadway musicals, this one is a live recording of a charity concert, given at Drury Lane in May 1989, with the numbers shared between a wide range of soloists. Only two numbers have survived to become standards, *Entertainment* and *Solomon* – the latter inimitably done by the veteran, Elisabeth Welch, who rightly receives an ovation – but there is plenty of charm and point in the rest. There is also an appendix of five more numbers to add to the regular fifteen. The sound, though less sophisticated in balance than in EMI's studio recordings, is pleasantly atmospheric, and the single disc comes with an excellent booklet and libretto.

Poulenc, Francis (1899–1963)

Dialogue des Carmelites (complete).
*** Virgin/EMI Dig. VCD7 59227-2 (2). Lyon Opéra O, Kent Nagano.
Blanche de la Force (Catherine Dubosc), Mme de Croissy (Rita Gorr) Mme Lidoine (Rachel Yakar), Constance (Brigitte Fournier), Marquis de la Force (José Van Dam), Chevalier de la Force (Jean-Luc Viala), Mère Marie (Martine Dupuy).

The opening of Poulenc's *Dialogue des Carmelites* with its very Stravinskian ostinatos for a moment suggests a minimalist opera written before its time. Yet the relative ease of the idiom, even sounding trivial, conceals a genuine depth, superbly brought out by Kent Nagano and Lyon Opéra forces in this recording made by Virgin in collaboration with Radio France. It fills an important gap, when the only previous version, recorded soon after the première in 1957, has not been generally available.

Much is owed to the dynamic Nagano, who gives an extra momentum and sense of contrast to a work which, with its measured speeds and easily lyrical manner, can fall into sameness. That the male casting is so strong, with the principal roles taken by José van Dam and the tenor, Jean-Luc Viala, compensates for any lack of variety in having women's voices predominating in an opera about nuns. Catherine Dubosc, in the central role of the fear-obsessed, self-doubting Blanche, is fresh and appealing, with Brigitte Fournier charming as the frivolous nun, Constance, and the veteran Rita Gorr as the old prioress and Rachel Yakar as the new prioress both splendid. The vivid recording, helped by a stage production in Lyon, culminates in a spine-chilling rendering of the final execution scene, with the sound of the guillotine ever more menacing.

La voix humaine (complete).
** Chan. Dig. CHAN 8331 [id.]. Adelaide SO, Serebrier.
La femme (Carole Farley).

This virtuoso monodrama, just one woman and a telephone, is ideally suited to a record if, as here, the full text is provided. Where on stage few singers can project the French words with ideal clarity to make every detail apparent, both the brightness of Carole Farley's soprano and the recording balance present the whole scena in vivid close-up.

A young woman is abandoned by her lover after expecting to marry him on the morrow, so she attempts suicide. The listener assumes that her present telephone conversation will be her last communication with him. Throughout, she gravitates between expressing the known feelings shared in a long relationship and desperate awareness of her present predicament.

She fears he will hang up on her; first she assures him of her trust in him; then she becomes the betrayed lover. She cannot accept reality and plays for sympathy; yet her mood changes quixotically to angry despair. Finally the dialogue ends abruptly, and the receiver drops from her hand. Banality and sentimentality have overshadowed the depth of the betrayal.

Ms Farley's French is clear but not quite idiomatic-sounding, and that rather applies to the playing of the Adelaide orchestra, crisply disciplined and sharply concentrated as it is. The result has little of French finesse. The 15 bands of the CD are very helpful in finding one's way about the piece.

Prokofiev, Serge (1891–1953)

(i) *Alexander Nevsky* (cantata), *Op. 78;* (ii) *Ivan the Terrible, Op. 116* (film music, arr. Lankester).
*** Sony Dig. S2K 48387 (2) [id.]. (i) Dolora Zajic; (ii) Christopher Plummer (nar.), Tamara Sinyavskaya, Sergei Leiferkus, London Symphony Ch., LSO, Rostropovich.

Rostropovich's set offers not the usual cantata version of Prokofiev's music for the Eisenstein film but one, more comprehensive, prepared by Michael Lankester, which tells the story of the tsar by way of an elaborate narration, dotted with biblical quotations. Having snatches of music joined by spoken narration suits this subject well, though there are occasional bizarre echoes of *Peter and the wolf*, and having so much speech means that the piece spreads to a second disc.

Particularly moving is the humming chorus which starts the second of the two discs, a hushed and meditative version of the great surging melody which later became a central theme in Prokofiev's epic opera, *War and Peace*, representing General Kutuzov's patriotic defiance. Christopher Plummer is the oratorical narrator, with Sergei Leiferkus and the fruity-toned Tamara Sinyavskaya the excellent soloists, and the London Symphony Chorus both powerful and refined.

As a fill-up on the second disc comes the ideal coupling, the *Alexander Nevsky* cantata, arranged by Prokofiev himself from the music he wrote for another great Eisenstein historical film. Dolora Zajic is the moving mezzo soloist in the great *Lament for the Dead* after the *Battle on the ice*, with Rostropovich again drawing an inspired performance from the LSO and Chorus.

L'amour des trois oranges (The Love for 3 oranges): complete.
**(*) Virgin/EMI Dig. VCD 791084-2 (2) [id.]. Lyon Opera Ch. & O, Kent Nagano.

King of Clubs (Gabriel Bacquier), Prince (Jean-Luc Viala), Truffaldino (Georges Gautier), Fata Morgana (Michèl Lagrange), Ninetta (Catherine Dubosc), Cook (Jules Bastin).

Previous recordings of Prokofiev's sparkling charade, *The Love for three oranges*, have always been in Russian. Very reasonably, however, Virgin opted for the alternative of French, as being the original language: that was the language used when the opera was given its first, lavish production in Chicago in December 1921. French inevitably brings a degree of softening in vocal texture, but most listeners will understand far more of the words; and the brilliant young conductor, Kent Nagano, and his Lyon Opera House team make up for any loss in knife-edged precision of ensemble.

In the Prologue we meet the chorus – representing the audience – not only commenting on the changing dramatic situations of the narrative, but even interfering with its course. Already they are disputing about what kind of entertainment they are seeking. Suddenly masked announcers tell them that, however much they harangue, they are to watch a play concerning 'The love for three oranges', and a herald announces that the story relates to the hypochondria of the prince, son of the King of Clubs.

The curtain now rises on the palace where doctors tell the king that his son is incurable. The king laments the lack of a proper successor, for his unattractive niece, Clarissa, is no substitute. The spectators are perturbed at the king's lack of dignity, but the monarch decides that if the prince could be made to laugh, he would be restored to normality. Pantaloon suggests that a theatrical performance and a feast might do the trick. The jester, Truffaldino, will make the arrangements. However the prime minister, Leandro, for his own reasons has no wish to see the prince recover.

The stage darkens and, against a cabbalistic background, Tchelio (a magician, protector of the king) and Fata Morgana (a witch, in the employ of Leandro) play against each other, using gigantic cards. Little devils surround them. Tchelio loses. In the king's palace Clarissa (who has her eye on the throne) and Leandro scheme together: they are plotting the prince's demise. In return Leandro shall become Clarissa's husband, with obvious advantages.

Leandro is sure he can cause the prince's death by filling him full of tragic verse and prose. At this point the spectators try to interfere and Clarissa demands action. The pair discover that Smeraldina (Fata Morgana's black servant) is eavesdropping and they threaten her with death. But she is clearly on their side and tells them that Tchelio guards the prince and may yet manage to make him laugh; Fata Morgana will do her best to interfere. They must be sure that the witch is invited to the festivities.

We now move to the prince's quarters where he is discovered, very bored, with a compress on his head. Truffaldino's antics fail to raise a glimmer of a smile. Eventually he is persuaded to attend the festivities, and the famous *March* introduces the following scene in the great hall of the palace. Everyone is present, the prince dressed in furs lest he catch cold. Truffaldino stages a mock battle without moving the prince in the least. But when Fata Morgana arrives, surrounded by her little devils, and Truffaldino tries to eject her, she loses her balance and somersaults, and the prince finds this hilarious.

Everyone is happy, except of course Leandro and Clarissa. But Fata Morgana, composing herself, puts a curse on the prince: he will fall in love with three oranges and pursue them to the ends of the earth. The prince sets off on his travels with Truffaldino and with Farfarello, one of the devils, wafting them on their way with his bellows.

We next find them in the desert, and the magician appears to warn them that when they discover the oranges they may cut them open only near water. The terrible Creonte also arrives in the form of a massive cook. Tchelio gives Truffaldino a magic ribbon to distract the giant while the prince steals the oranges. Farfarello once again uses his bellows and the prince and Truffaldino are blown away to the music of the opera's familiar orchestral *Scherzo*.

The enormous cook (Creonte) now appears from her kitchen and is duly captivated by the ribbon round Truffaldino's neck. The prince creeps into the kitchen and emerges with three huge oranges. Truffaldino gives Creonte her ribbon, she dances with delight and the pair make their escape.

Back in the desert, the three oranges appear bigger than ever. The prince falls asleep and the thirsty Truffaldino cuts into one of the oranges. Out steps Princess Linetta who tells him she will die of thirst unless he can provide water. She expires. From the second orange, when cut, Princess Nicoletta appears. She also dies. Unable to awaken the prince, the appalled Truffaldino rushes off despairingly into the desert. The prince finally stirs, and without emotion orders four soldiers (who conveniently appear) to bury the two bodies with all due reverence. He then cuts open the third orange and the beauty who emerges is Princess Ninetta, the girl he has been waiting for all his life. She sinks into his arms in distress, as her urgent demand for water is fecklessly ignored. Fortunately the exasperated spectators come to the rescue, a bucket of water is produced and her life is saved.

Princess Ninetta is now left alone to make a suitable dress for her meeting with the king, but Smeraldina appears and the spectators in the box again become agitated when they see Fata Morgana's shadow. Smeraldina sticks a long magical pin into Ninetta's head. She groans and turns into a rat. The spectators return to their seats while Fata Morgana instructs Smeraldina that she must take Ninetta's place for the meeting with the king. He duly arrives in procession, and the prince becomes very upset at the witch's clumsy deception, flatly refusing to marry the attractive, dark-skinned substitute. But the king instructs him to take her back to the palace.

Again we return to the cabbalistic background, to find Morgana and Tchelio bickering. Morgana seems to be winning her argument and the alarmed spectators leave their boxes, surround her and shut her away. Smoke and fire can be seen, and it seems that Tchelio is the victor. Leandro is preparing the royal throne-room for the reception, and when the curtains round the throne are pulled away a large rat is revealed.

The somewhat inept Tchelio makes huge efforts at magical metamorphosis in reverse and finally he manages it: Princess Ninetta stands before them. The prince is overjoyed, Smeraldina and Clarissa are revealed as Leandro's accomplices, and the three are accused of treason and promptly condemned to death. Truffaldino pleads in vain for mercy. There is much confusion as the miscreants try to escape, Fata Morgana reappears, a trap-door opens and the culprits disappear below. A cry goes up praising the king and he changes it to a toast to the happy future for the prince and princess.

The only star names in the cast of the Virgin recording are the basses in the two main character-roles, Gabriel Bacquier as the King and Jules Bastin as the monstrous Cook, guardian of the three oranges. They are well matched by the others, including Jean-Luc Viala as an aptly petulant Prince and Catherine Dubosc as a sweetly girlish Princess Ninette. A snag with the recorded sound is that the commenting chorus – very much a part of the action in commedia dell'arte style – is focused too vaguely, a pity when the timing is so crisp. Happily the focus for the solo voices is clearer. On the whole, Virgin's enterprise in going to Lyon and its outstanding new music director – successor to John Eliot Gardiner – has paid off impressively. However, it is irritating that there are so few cueing points on the CDs (just one for each scene), even if this is very much an ensemble opera, with few set solos.

The Fiery Angel (complete).
*** DG Dig. 431 669-2 (2) [id.]. Ohlin Vocal Ens., Gothenburg Pro Musica Chamber Ch., Gothenburg SO, Järvi.
   Renata (Nadine Secunde), Ruprecht (Siegfried Lorenz), Inquisitor (Kurt Moll).

Like Prokofiev's even earlier one-Act opera, *Maddalena*, *The Fiery Angel* centres on a neurotically obsessed woman, the tragic Renata, whose hysterical visions finally get her condemned as a witch. She appears at the very beginning of the story, when Ruprecht (a knight) goes to his room in a ramshackle inn and immediately hears hysterical cries coming from behind a seemingly unused door. Renata, utterly distraught, throws herself into his arms for protection, simultaneously defending herself from an imagined attacker. Ruprecht makes the sign of a cross with his sword and, exhausted, Renata grows calmer.

She relates her life story and tells how when she was eight years old an angel, Madiela, dressed in white and with golden hair and blue eyes, appeared to her, surrounded by flames. The angel told her that she was to be a saint and reappeared, day and night, to emphasize her destiny. At seventeen she desired to experience physical love and this drove him away, but in a dream she was assured that he would return. She then met Count Heinrich and knew he was Madiela in human form. The count denied this, and she experienced a year of happiness with him before he abandoned her. Since then she has been pursued by nightmare visions from which, she says, Ruprecht has saved her.

The hostess and her servant arrive and suggest that Renata is a profligate woman, having troubled the villagers and bewitched the count. Ruprecht, however, decides that she is very attractive and must be his. He tries to seduce her but fails. She cannot forget Heinrich, and Ruprecht, too, is caught up in her need to find her former lover. The hostess arrives with a fortune-teller/sorceress, who makes overt references to Renata's guilt in preferring to exert her own physical attractions, instead of accepting her destiny.

The action moves to Cologne. Renata is consulting a book of magic and Jacob Glock arrives with more books on the subject, but Ruprecht complains that even with their help Heinrich is elusive. Ruprecht again declares his love for Renata but she pours scorn on him and burns magic herbs acquired from the sorceress. Suddenly a knocking is heard on the wall. Anticipating the arrival of Heinrich, the door is opened, but no one is there. Renata weeps and Ruprecht, determined to help her, goes off with Glock to consult a philosopher-magician.

They come upon the coldly diabolical Agrippa von Nettlesheim in his rooms, surrounded by human skeletons, magic treatises, bottles of elixir, plus three black dogs. He flatly refuses his help. Renata now learns where Heinrich is living, but is rejected by him – she is a woman possessed by the devil. Ruprecht returns from his visit to Agrippa and finds that Renata no longer loves Heinrich, believing him to be an impostor and not the embodiment of her angel, Madiela. She offers herself to Ruprecht if he will kill her seducer and, while he is demanding entrance to Heinrich's house, she prays to Madiela for forgiveness for her mistaken identification.

Through a window Ruprecht can be seen challenging Heinrich, who suddenly becomes the incarnation of Madiela, a true angel of fire. Immediately Renata countermands her orders for his death but a duel follows in which Ruprecht is seriously wounded. As he lies, exhausted, on the bank of the Rhine, Renata declares her love for him; if he should die, she will enter a convent. They are now obviously obsessed with each other, even if Ruprecht is in delirium. A doctor is called who asserts that Ruprecht will live.

Ruprecht has scarcely recovered when Renata changes her mind again and tells him she must leave him and take the veil to achieve salvation. He protests, she tries to commit suicide and attacks him when he weakly endeavours to intervene; Mephistopheles and Faust watch over the scene. A pot-boy brings them wine and is swallowed up by Mephistopheles for his trouble. The innkeeper intervenes and Mephistopheles restores the boy to life. He and Faust befriend Ruprecht and ask him to show them the beauties of Cologne.

Meanwhile Renata has become a nun, and the Mother Superior questions her about the visions. Are they evil spirits? Since she arrived at the convent, there has been a frenzy of strange noises, with the sisters attacked by dark spirits. The inquisitor now questions Renata, asking for proof that her visions are not inspired by hell. She retorts that her visitor is from heaven and always speaks words of virtue. Immediately there is general turmoil, ghostly noises are heard. The inquisitor pronounces Renata a witch and a heretic and sentences her to death at the stake. The nuns are satisfied with his verdict.

Though the story is largely distasteful, the score is masterly, containing passages as rich and warm as anything Prokofiev ever wrote before his return to Soviet Russia, as, for example, some of the duetting in Act III between Renata and her lover, the knight Ruprecht. What reinforces the impact of the work is its compactness, telling a complicated story in five crisply tailored Acts, with the first two Acts on the first CD, the remaining three on the second. Prokofiev's vivid orchestration adds colour and atmosphere, as when in Act IV Mephistopheles is conjured up, along with Faust, and proceeds to eat an offending serving lad – cue for horrific whoopings on the horns. After that, the final scene with the Inquisitor (Kurt Moll ever sinister) and chattering nuns does not quite rise to the expected climax. This fine recording easily outshines the only previous version, which was recorded in 1957 with a cast singing in French. Nadine Secunde for Järvi sings passionately as Renata, well supported by Siegfried Lorenz as Ruprecht. With such warm advocacy one can fully appreciate the work's mastery, even if the reasons for its failure to get into the repertory remain very clear.

The Gambler: complete.
*(*) Olympia OCD 162 A/B (2) [id.]. Ch. & O of USSR Bolshoi Theatre, Lazarev.

General (Alexander Ognivtsiev), Pauline (M. Kasrashvili), Alexis (Alexei Maslennikov), Marquis (D. Korolev), Blanche (Galina Borisova), Grandmother (Larissa Avdeyeva).

The Gambler, based on Dostoevsky, has never really established itself in the repertory, though it has been staged in the UK. It is earlier than *Love for Three Oranges*; indeed, Prokofiev had finished scoring it by 1916, though it did not receive its première until the Théâtre de la Monnaie mounted it in 1929. The action of the story takes place in Roulettenberg, a German gambling spa, midway through the nineteenth century.

A Russian general, living with his children and his ward, Pauline, has gambled away virtually all his money. There are mortgages too, and he awaits his grandmother's death for a legacy to pay off a French marquis to whom he owes a great deal. He can then marry the demi-mondaine, Blanche. The marquis seduces Pauline, who herself has a relationship with the central character, Alexis, tutor to the governor's children. Pauline offers Alexis the money received from her pawned jewellery to gamble, and he loses it all. The relationship between them wavers between fondness and contempt.

After a fracas with a baroness, the general dismisses Alexis, and both he and the marquis, using a letter of support from Pauline, try to persuade Alexis not to cause further trouble. The general's grandmother now arrives and she plays the tables continually until all her money is lost. She borrows her fare for the journey home from Alexis. Blanche abandons the general and leaves him in despair.

Now Alexis finds that the marquis has also abandoned Pauline and, to help her, he goes to the roulette table and wins and wins, amassing a huge sum of money and breaking the bank at two tables. He is now obsessed with gambling; Pauline refuses his offer of help and leaves, throwing the money in his face. Alexis returns to the tables.

There are many characteristic ideas here, several of which are included in the *Four Portraits* which Prokofiev subsequently made for orchestra. This performance is the only one we have currently and there may not be another. The opera is well worth investigating and the playing is thoroughly idiomatic, though the singers are characteristically Slavonic. At times the recording inclines towards the strident, and the balance is pretty disastrous, placing the singers very forward so that, if orchestral detail is to come into its own, one has to listen at an uncomfortable level. Few of the singers vary their dynamic level, which is usually high. Recommendable with caution and only *faute de mieux*.

Maddalena: complete.
**(*) Olympia Dig. OCD 215 [id.]. Male group of State Chamber Ch., MoC SO, Rozhdestvensky. Maddalena (E. Ivanova), Genaro (A. Martynov), Stenio (S. Yakovenko), Gemma (N. Koptanova), Romeo (V. Rumyantsev).

Maddalena is an opera which Prokofiev wrote in 1911, two years after graduating, but he then failed to finish the scoring. It was left to the conductor, Edward Downes, to complete the orchestration over 60 years later, revealing a fascinating example of Russian Grand Guignol.

The opera is set in Venice. Maddelena waits at sunset in the house of the painter, Genaro, for her husband to return. Two friends, Gemma and Romeo, approach in a gondola and ask Maddelena to come with them, but she refuses. Genaro finally arrives and declares his love, which she returns. There is a sudden knock on the door and Maddelena hides. It is Stenio, an alchemist, and he tells his friend about a woman with whom he has had the most passionate relationship over the past three months so that now he is a slave to her sexual power – yet he does not know her name.

The wind blows aside the curtain behind which Maddelena is hidden, and Stenio recognizes her as the woman who has seduced him. Genaro in turn discovers that the pearls he gave Maddalena at her wedding are in Stenio's possession. She tells them together that she has loved them both: with Stenio her love was full of sinful, physical passion; with her husband it was good. Both draw their daggers, and Maddalena encourages her husband to kill first Stenio then her. The two men throw themselves on each other and Stenio dies, while Genaro is mortally wounded. He tries to kill his wife but fails.

Though Prokofiev orchestrated only the first and shortest of the four scenes, Downes's contribution has a true Prokofiev ring, with distinctive colouring. His edition is here adopted by these Russian performers for the first recording. Any disappointment with the work lies more in the relative lack of melodic distinction in the vocal writing which, for the most part, flows in an easy cantilena.

Nevertheless, this 50-minute piece very ably tells the horrific story of the predatory

Maddalena and her savage way with men. Rozhdestvensky, with his fine orchestra of young players, directs a persuasive performance, even if some of the singing is indifferent. Ivanova is a bright, precise soprano, with Martynov singing splendidly in the tenor role of her wronged husband, Genaro. By contrast, Yakovenko in the baritone role of Maddalena's lover is disappointingly wobbly. Full, forward sound, not always refined. The disc comes with libretto, translation and notes.

War and peace (complete).

⊛ (M) *** Erato/Warner 2292 45331-2 (4) [id.]. Fr. R. Ch. & Nat. O, Rostropovich.

Prince Andrei Bolkonsky (Lajos Miller), Natasha (Galina Vishnevskaya), Sonya (Katherine Ciesinski), Maria (Mariana Paunova), Count Rostov (Dimiter Petkov), Pierre Bezoukhov (Wieslaw Ochman), Hélène (Stefania Toczyska), Anatol Kuragin (Nicolai Gedda), Dolokhov (Vladimir De Kanel), Denissov (Malcolm Smith), Marshal Kutuzov (Nikola Ghiuselev), Napoleon (Eduard Tumagian).

*** Ph. Dig. 434 097-2 (3) [id.]. Kirov Theatre Ch. & O, Valery Gergiev.

Prince Andrei Bolkonsky (Alexandr Gergalov), Natasha (Jelena Prokina), Sonya (Svetlana Volkova), Maria (Ludmilla Kanunnikova), Count Rostov (Sergei Alexashkin), Pierre Bezoukhov (Gegam Gregoriam), Hélène (Olga Borodina), Anatol Kuragin (Yuri Marusin), Dolokhov (Alexandr Morozov), Denissov (Mikhail Kit), Marshal Kutuzov (Nikolai Ohotnikov), Napoleon (Vassily Gerelo).

That the Soviet Union over 70 years spawned so many musical masterpieces despite the frightening restrictions of the system is a tribute to the purest genius, above all to that of Prokofiev and Shostakovich. And no single work encompasses that triumph over restriction, the demand to create people's music, more completely than Prokofiev's opera, *War and Peace*. That any composer could even think of capturing in an opera the essence of Tolstoi's vast novel is remarkable enough: all the more astonishing that Prokofiev, struggling against illness in his final years, achieved it to produce one of the very greatest modern operas. *War and Peace* is not just aptly epic in scale but warmly approachable, with a fund of melody rarely matched this century. In this opera more than anywhere, Prokofiev squared the impossible Soviet circle. He achieved his purpose by dividing the narrative into thirteen scenes, the first seven dealing with the principal characters during times of peace, and the remainder of the opera showing Russia at war and finally victorious over Napoleon.

The first scene, a moonlight night in May 1806, is set in Count Rostov's estate at Otradnoye. Prince Andrei Bolkonsky, a widower visiting on business, cannot sleep. He thinks of Natasha Rostova and of spring. Natasha cannot sleep either and complains to her cousin, Sonya. They are both in a romantic mood.

Scene II takes place four years later at a New Year's Eve ball in St Petersburg. Count Rostov enters with his daughter, Natasha, and Sonya is with her. Count and Countess Bezoukhov are also present. Madame Akhrisimova compliments Natasha, but the beauty of Hélène Bezoukhova arouses less complimentary remarks.

The Tsar enters. Count Bezoukhov (Pierre) suggests to his friend, Prince Andrei, that he should ask the young Natasha to dance as it is her first ball. After the dance, Prince Andrei is in exalted mood. He is in love and hopes he can persuade Natasha to become his wife. However, the reprobate Prince Anatol Kuragin also has designs on Natasha and had earlier asked his sister Hélène Bezoukhova to arrange an introduction for him.

Before the third scene Prince Andrei has already proposed to Natasha. It is February 1812, and Count Rostov brings his daughter to meet Prince Nikolai Bolkonsky, Andrei's father, who insists that, before settling down, his son must spend a year abroad. The prince refuses to meet his visitors, but his daughter, Princess Maria (Andrei's sister), is willing to receive them. Count Rostov departs and suddenly the old prince appears in dressing gown and nightcap. Maria excuses his testy behaviour but Natasha is sure that he objects to the marriage and, although Maria tries to make conversation when Rostov returns, Natasha feels uncomfortable with this haughty family.

The fourth scene takes us to a dance in Pierre Bezoukhov's house in May of the same year. Natasha, though engaged to Andrei, is present and Hélène mentions that her brother pines with love for Natasha. Prince Anatol arrives and woos Natasha passionately; she is fascinated and flattered by him. He kisses her and gives a her a letter arranging an assignation.

She is deeply impressed but retains her love for Andrei. A month passes and the fifth scene moves to the apartments of the officer, Dolokhov. Natasha is to elope with Anatol. The prince waits for the prearranged time for the rendezvous. Dolokhov tries to convince him that the elopement is madness but Anatol cannot be persuaded to abandon his plans. Balaga, a troika driver, arrives and the three men drink to adventure, Moscow and to Matriosha, Anatol's gypsy mistress.

In the sixth scene Natasha is staying at Maria Dmitrievna Akhrosimova's house while her father is away. She awaits the arrival of Prince Anatol, her bag packed, but the maid appears and tells her that Sonya has revealed the planned elopement. The butler bars Anatol's entry and he goes off with Dolokhov. Natasha is left in despair. The butler announces the arrival of Pierre (Count Bezoukhov). He offers his friendship and tells her she has had a lucky escape as Anatol is already married, but he says that if he himself were free he would be on his knees asking her to marry him instead. He rushes away in confusion. Sonya fears that Natasha will not forgive her betrayal, but Natasha desperately asks for her help and sympathy.

In the final peacetime scene Hélène is entertaining at her house. Among the guests is Anatol; Pierre arrives and insists that he leave at once: his conduct was infamous and unforgivable.

The opera now moves to the wartime defence of Russia against the French invasion later that same year. The Russian people are fortunate in being led by Field Marshal Mikhail Kutuzov who, although he is a prince, is also a master of strategy. As the eighth scene opens, soldiers and peasants are working together preparing the country's defences. Prince Andrei has trained his own regiment and discusses a plan to harass Napoleon's troops. Much has already happened: Russia is being devastated by the advancing French troops; Andrei's father has been killed. Pierre enters, but as a spectator, and he and Andrei embrace. Pierre departs as the great Marshal Kutuzov arrives. Prince Andrei declines to join the Marshal's staff.

The ninth scene introduces Napoleon. Moscow now appears to be at his mercy and he broods on the future: if he shows clemency, history will praise him. The tenth scene shows Marshal Kutuzov's dilemma: if he should defend Moscow, his army will be decimated; if he retreats, the city will be open to the invader. He orders retreat: only through the sacrifice of Moscow can there be any hope of eventual victory.

In the eleventh scene the people of Moscow set fire to their city rather than surrender. Pierre is caught up in the turmoil around him. The Rostovs have left and taken their wounded with them. Pierre intervenes when citizens are harassed. He is taken prisoner by the French, accused of being an incendiary. Napoleon progresses through the smoking city, impressed at the courage and resolve of its inhabitants.

In the twelfth scene we meet the principal characters of the peacetime story once again. Prince Andrei lies wounded and Natasha is at his side. He is delirious and she begs forgiveness; he tells her that he loves her, that there shall be a new beginning if he should survive. She tries to reassure him but, dreaming of their first dance together, he slips away into death.

The opera's great final scene depicts Napoleon's famous retreat from Moscow. The French troops marching wearily through the snow have taken their prisoners with them, including Pierre and Karataev, an old soldier. He is shot as a straggler. The Russian guerrillas attack from all sides, and Pierre is rescued. Colonel Denissov, commanding the guerrillas, recognizes Pierre and tells him that Andrei is dead and that Natasha is in Moscow. The Russian advance guard now appears, led by the victorious Marshal Kutuzov. All join in a thankful celebration of the indomitable Russian spirit.

A really complete rendering of Prokofiev's text – never heard by the composer in its finished form – shows triumphantly how the components cohere into an opera of epic achievement. The English National Opera's stage production at the Coliseum proved that beyond doubt, and here Rostropovich's similarly complete account on record, flawed in some of the casting, nevertheless confirms beyond doubt that this is one of the great operatic masterpieces of the century. Prokofiev was never more prolific in his tune-writing than here: one melody follows another, almost as in a musical. However, no one should be deceived by the ease of listening into thinking that the writing lacks strength or intensity; rather, Prokofiev, in his game with the Soviet authorities, was submitting to the impossible restrictions of writing a 'people's opera' and succeeding masterfully, knowing that only he could have done it.

In Rostropovich's powerful reading one revels – thanks also to the lively Erato recording – in the vividness of the atmosphere, both in the evocative love-scenes and ball scenes of the first half (Peace) and the high tensions of the battle scenes in the second half (War). The opera culminates in a great patriotic chorus, using the most haunting tune of all, earlier sung by Marshal Kutuzov after the Council of Fili, and the emotional thrust is overwhelming. The French Radio Choir sings that chorus with real Russian fervour – though anyone remembering the ENO production will be disconcerted to find the opera starting, not with the shattering choral epigraph which hit so hard at the Coliseum, but with a pot-pourri overture airing some of the main themes. Prokofiev wrote it as an option, and what Rostropovich has done, with fair logic, is to reserve the choral epigraph – telling of the invasion of Russia – for the beginning of the second half and the scenes of war.

Even with a total playing time of over four hours, the opera yet seems compact and fits on the four CDs very neatly, with the scenes of peace on the first two, the scenes of war on the second pair, and without a single scene being broken in the middle. It was natural that Rostropovich's wife, Galina Vishnevskaya, should sing the central role of Natasha, as she did in the earlier, much cut, Bolshoi recording. It is extraordinary how convincingly this mature soprano in her early sixties characterizes a young girl; there may be raw moments, but she is completely inside the role. The Hungarian baritone, Lajos Miller, not flawless either, is a clear-voiced Andrei, and Wieslaw Ochman is a first-rate Pierre, with the veteran, Nicolai Gedda, brought in as Kuragin. Katherine Ciesinski is a warm-toned Sonya, but Dimiter Petkov is disappointingly unsteady as Natasha's father, Count Rostov. The small role of Napoleon is strongly taken by Eduard Tumagian, while Nikola Ghiuselev is a noble Kutuzov, in some ways the most impressive of all.

The bite, energy and warmth which run through the whole performance are owed above all to Rostropovich, who promised the composer not long before the latter died that he would do all he could to get this masterpiece – his own final favourite among Prokofiev's works – fully recognized in its definitive form. This recording could hardly provide a more vital contribution to that process. The libretto contains French and English translations, but no Russian transliteration, only the Cyrillic text in a separate section.

On Philips, the company of the Kirov Theatre in St Petersburg offers a rival version, recorded at a sequence of live performances in the theatre, using the production that was also seen on television. The comparisons with Rostropovich are fascinating. Almost inevitably with such large projects, the corners show in both recordings. The Kirov sound is on the dry side, faithful no doubt to the theatre's acoustic but hardly allowing as full an expansion as the Erato for the big, stirring climaxes, notably those using the great patriotic theme associated with Marshal Kutuzov.

The Kirov performance under Valery Gergiev, at rather more urgent speeds than Rostropovich's, may be less warmly expressive and atmospheric, but it brings the advantage of having in the principal roles younger voices. Many will prefer the Kirov Natasha, Jelena Prokina, to the controversially cast Vishnevskaya on the Rostropovich set. The voice is fresher as well as younger-sounding, though under pressure the tone becomes hard, losing any sweetness. Alexandr Gergalov, Prince Andrei in the Kirov performance, is attractively young-sounding too, lighter and more lyrical than Rostropovich's principal, Lajos Miller.

Otherwise the Kirov principals, including Nikolai Ohotnikov as Kutuzov, are almost all as characterful and assured as their generally starrier rivals on Erato, and the sense of purpose from a very large company, well drilled in the music, counterbalances in part, though not entirely, the unhelpful dryness of the sound. The economical layout on three CDs may seem to favour Philips, but there is no price-advantage, when Rostropovich's Erato comes at mid-price in the Libretto series. Not only that, there are far too few entry points on Philips, with only one track per scene (some lasting over half an hour). The Erato version provides a generous number, and the four-disc format brings a positive advantage in neatly dividing the seven scenes of peace from the six scenes of war, two discs apiece. The three-disc format on Philips is made possible by Gergiev's faster speeds and a briefer text for the final patriotic chorus, though the breaks between discs come awkwardly in the middle of scenes.

Puccini, Giacomo (1858–1924)

La Bohème (complete).

⊛ (***) EMI mono CDS7 47235-8 (2) [Ang. CDCB 47235]. RCA Victor Ch. & O, Beecham.

　　Mimì (Victoria De los Angeles), Rodolfo (Jussi Bjoerling), Musetta (Lucine Amara), Marcello (Robert Merrill), Colline (Giorgio Tozzi), Benoit / Alcindoro (Fernando Corena).

*** Decca 421 049-2 (2) [id.]. German Op. Ch., Berlin, BPO, Karajan.

　　Mimì (Mirella Freni), Rodolfo (Luciano Pavarotti), Musetta (Elizabeth Harwood), Marcello (Rolando Panerai), Colline (Nicolai Ghiaurov), Benoit / Alcindoro (Michel Sénéchal).

(M) *** Decca 425 534-2 (2). St Cecilia Ac. Ch. & O, Serafin.

　　Mimì (Renata Tebaldi), Rodolfo (Carlo Bergonzi), Musetta (Gianna D'Angelo), Marcello (Ettore Bastianini), Colline (Cesare Siepi), Benoit / Alcindoro (Fernando Corena).

**(*) BMG/RCA RD 80371 [RCD2 0371]. Alldis Ch., Wandsworth School Boys' Ch., LPO, Solti.

Mimì (Montserrat Caballé), Rodolfo (Plácido Domingo), Musetta (Judith Blegen), Marcello (Sherrill Milnes), Colline (Ruggero Raimondi).

(M) **(*) EMI CMS7 69657-2 (2) [Ang. CDMB 69657]. La Scala, Milan, Ch. & O, Schippers.

Mimì (Mirella Freni), Rodolfo (Nicolai Gedda), Musetta (Mariella Adani), Marcello (Mario Sereni), Colline (Ferruccio Mazzoli).

(***) EMI mono CDS7 47475-8 (2) [Ang. CDCB 47475]. La Scala, Milan, Ch. & O, Votto.

Mimì (Maria Callas), Rodolfo (Giuseppe Di Stefano), Musetta (Anna Moffo), Marcello (Rolando Panerai), Colline (Nicola Zaccaria), Benoit / Alcindoro (Carlo Badioli).

(B) ** CfP CD-CFP 4708; *CD-CFP 4708* (2). Trinity Boys' Ch., Amb. Op. Ch., Nat. PO, Levine.

Mimì (Renata Scotto), Rodolfo (Alfredo Kraus), Musetta (Carol Neblett), Marcello (Sherrill Milnes), Colline (Paul Plishka).

** Erato Dig. 2292 45311 (2) [id.]. Ch. & O Nat. de France, Conlon.

Mimì (Barbara Hendricks), Rodolfo (José Carreras), Musetta (Angela Maria Blasi), Marcello (Gino Quilico), Colline (Francesco Ellero D'Artegna), Benoit / Alcindoro (Federico Davià).

(M) ** BMG/RCA GD 83969 (2) [RCA-3969-2-RG]. Rome Opera Ch. & O, Leinsdorf.

Mimì (Anna Moffo), Rodolfo (Richard Tucker), Musetta (Mary Costa), Marcello (Robert Merrill), Colline (Giorgio Tozzi).

** Ph. 416 492-2 (2) [id.]. ROHCG Ch. & O, C. Davis.

Mimì (Katia Ricciarelli), Rodolfo (José Carreras), Musetta (Ashley Putnam), Marcello (Ingvar Wixell), Colline (Robert Lloyd).

** DG Dig. 423 601-2; *423 601-4* (2) [id.]. St Cecilia Ac., Rome, Ch. & O, Bernstein.

Mimì (Angelina Réaux), Rodolfo (Jerry Hadley), Musetta (Barbara Daniels), Marcello (Thomas Hampson), Colline (Paul Plishka).

Withdrawn: (M) (**) EMI mono CHS7 63335-2 (2) [Ang. CDHB 63335]. La Scala, Milan, Ch. & O, Berrettoni.

Mimì (Licia Albanese), Rodolfo (Beniamino Gigli), Musetta (Tatiana Menotti), Marcello (Afro Poli), Colline (Dullio Baronti), Benoit / Alcindoro (Carlo Scattola).

(M) (**) BMG/RCA GD 60288; *GK 60288* (2) [60288-2-RG; *60288-4-RG*]. NBC Ch., NBC SO, Toscanini.

Mimì (Licia Albanese), Rodolfo (Jan Peerce), Musetta (Anne McKnight), Marcello (Frank Valentino), Colline (Nicola Moscona), Benoit / Alcindoro (Salvatore Baccaloni).

(B) ** Naxos Dig. 8.66000-3/4 [id.]. Slovak Philharmonic Ch., Slovak RSO (Bratislava), Will Humburg.

Mimì (Luba Orgonasova), Rodolfo (Jonathan Welch), Musetta (Carmen Gonzales), Marcello (Fabio Previati), Colline (Ivan Urbas).

EMI Dig. CDS7 54124-2 (2). Piccolo Coro dell'Antoniano, Bologna Teatro Comunale Ch. & O, Gianluigi Gelmetti.

Mimì (Daniella Dessì), Rodolfo (Giuseppe Sabbatini), Musetta (Adelina Scarabelli), Marcello (Paolo Gavanelli), Colline (Carlo Colombara).

(M) DG 435 715-2 (2) [id.]. Ch. & O of Maggio Musicale Fiorentino, Votto.

Mimì (Renata Scotto), Rodolfo (Gianni Poggi), Musetta (Jolanda Meneguzzer), Marcello (Tito Gobbi), Colline (Giuseppe Modesti).

The four Acts of Puccini's greatest opera are constructed with consummate skill, and are laid out as an equivalent of the four movements of a symphony, complete with scherzo (coming second) and slow movement. The reprise, in the finale, of the Bohemian motifs of the opening scene is made essential by the story itself. The opera opens and closes in a rooftop garret in Paris where four artistic friends co-exist together. Rodolfo is a poet, Marcello a painter, Colline a philosopher and Schaunard a musician; none of them could be described as materially successful.

It is very cold and, with no fuel for the stove, they argue about what they can burn and finally settle on Rodolfo's play manuscript. As soon as the sheets are consumed by the flames, Schaunard enters with food, wine and fuel. He has earned some cash by giving music lessons to an Englishman and insists that as it is Christmas Eve they must all dine out together. But Benoit, the landlord, interrupts their celebration by arriving to ask for the rent. They ply him with wine then, by a ruse, chase him out. All go off to the Café Momus except Rodolfo, who stays behind to finish an article.

There is a gentle knock on his door. It is Mimì, a seamstress, who occupies an adjacent room.

She is very frail but perhaps more resourceful than she seems. She appears almost to faint, her candle goes out and she drops her key (perhaps on purpose?).

Astonishingly, both their candles are extinguished and they have to search for the key in the darkness. As their hands touch comes one of the most magical moments in all opera (*Che gelida manina*), and the love scene which follows is unsurpassed in its sweep of romantic passion. Rodolfo is at first captivated by her simple charm. He asks her name and she tells him about her work embroidering flowers. Then, by one of those simple miracles of stage production, a light is turned on and Rodolfo sees her face in the moonlight: he is rapturously in love and he sings the justly famous *O soave fanciulla*. The voices of his friends drift up from outside, reminding them of the call of supper, and they go off to the Café Momus together.

The second Act is the opera's brilliant scherzo and takes place in the city's Latin Quarter. Crowds gather in the modest square outside the café: Marcello flirts with passing girls; Schaunard buys a horn; Colline buys books; Parpignol, the toy-seller, delights the children besieging his stall. Rodolfo and Mimì arrive and Rodolfo buys her a pretty bonnet; then Musetta makes her grand entrance, accompanied by an elderly admirer, Alcindoro.

She sees Marcello, once her lover, and coquettishly sits nearby. Marcello, obviously still in love with her, is jealous. They enjoy their meal; then Alcindoro is capriciously sent off on an errand and Musetta and Marcello are able to embrace. The guards now parade past, followed by the children, and in the confusion the Bohemians, together with Musetta and Mimì, are able to make good their escape, leaving Alcindoro to foot the bill.

The opera's third scene takes place two months later at the Barrière d'Enfer, one of the gates of Paris. It is early morning and flakes of snow are drifting down. Musetta's voice can be heard singing (through an open window) in a nearby inn. Mimì arrives seeking Rodolfo. She meets Marcello, who tells her that he and Musetta have been living together for a month. She is teaching singing and he is working as a jobbing painter.

As she asks for Rodolfo, Mimì breaks down in tears. They still love each other as much as ever, but he is insanely jealous. She coughs persistently. Rodolfo now appears but Mimì hides and she overhears him tell his friend that she is very ill and that their cold attic room is the last place in which she should be staying. Mimì's coughing and weeping betray her presence and in a great quartet, while she and Rodolfo tenderly renew their expressions of love, Marcello and Musetta quarrel over Musetta's repeated and unrepentant unfaithfulness.

The four friends are again together in their garret apartment on the rooftops of Paris. The two women have left. Rodolfo does not know what has happened to Mimì, but Marcello knows that Musetta has a rich lover. They try to forget their feelings and indulge in uninhibited horseplay. Colline arrives with four loaves and a herring for a banquet. Suddenly Musetta enters; her mood is one of despair as she helps Mimì inside. Mimì is evidently dying. With no food, they all pool their resources and Musetta offers her earrings to buy medicine and a muff to warm Mimì's frozen hands.

Schaunard and Colline leave, Colline bidding an eloquent farewell to his old coat which is to be pawned. Rodolfo and Mimì, left alone together, recall their first happy meeting. She still has her little bonnet. Mimì coughs convulsively. Musetta and Marcello return, Mimì is comforted by the muff and falls asleep. Musetta quietly prays. Colline returns with money for a doctor who is already on his way. But it is too late. Schaunard whispers to Marcello that Mimì is dead. Rodolfo at first thinks she is sleeping peacefully, then their faces tell him the truth and he flings himself on the bed, sobbing over her dead body.

Beecham recorded his classic interpretation of *Bohème* in 1956 in sessions in New York that were arranged at the last minute. It was a gamble getting it completed, but the result was incandescent, a unique performance with two favourite singers, Victoria de los Angeles and Jussi Bjoerling, challenged to their utmost in loving, expansive singing. Its magic is vividly caught on CD, triumphing over any limitations in the mono sound. The voices are far better treated than the orchestra, which is rather thinner-sounding than it was on LP, though as ever the benefits of a silent background are very welcome in so warmly atmospheric a reading. With such a performance one hardly notices the recording, but those who want fine modern stereo can turn readily to Karajan.

The rich sensuousness of Karajan's highly atmospheric reading is all the more vivid on CD, with the clean placing of voices enhancing the performance's dramatic warmth. He too takes a characteristically spacious view of *Bohème*, but there is an electric intensity which holds the whole score together as in a live performance – a reflection no doubt of the speed with which the recording was made, long takes the rule. Karajan unerringly points the climaxes with full force, highlighting them against prevailing pianissimos. Pavarotti is an inspired Rodolfo, with comic flair and expressive passion, while Freni is just as seductive a Mimì as she was in the Schippers set ten years earlier. Elizabeth Harwood is a charming Musetta, even if her voice is not as sharply contrasted with Freni's as it might be. Fine singing throughout the set. The reverberant Berlin acoustic is glowing and brilliant in superb Decca recording.

The earlier Decca set with Tebaldi and Bergonzi was technically an outstanding recording in its day. Vocally the performance achieves a consistently high standard, Tebaldi as Mimì the most affecting: she offers some superbly controlled singing, but the individuality of the heroine is not as indelibly conveyed as with De los Angeles, Freni or Caballé. Carlo Bergonzi is a fine Rodolfo; Bastianini and Siepi are both superb as Marcello and Colline, and even the small parts of Benoit and Alcindoro (as usual taken by a single artist) have the benefit of Corena's magnificent voice. The veteran Serafin was more vital here than on some of his records. The recording, now nearly 30 years old, has its vividness and sense of stage perspective enhanced on CD, with minimal residue tape-hiss, though the age of the master shows in the string timbre above the stave.

The glory of Solti's set of *Bohème* is the singing of Montserrat Caballé as Mimì, an intensely characterful and imaginative reading which makes you listen with new intensity to every phrase, the voice at its most radiant. Domingo is unfortunately not at his most inspired; *Che gelida manina* is relatively coarse, though here as elsewhere he produces glorious heroic tone, and never falls into vulgarity. The rest of the team is strong, but Solti's tense interpretation of a work he had never conducted in the opera house does not quite let the full flexibility of the music have its place or the full warmth of romanticism. However, the RCA recording – disappointing on LP – acquires extra brightness and clarity in the digital transfer to CD, to give extra point and sparkle to the performance.

Freni's characterization of Mimì is so enchanting that it is worth ignoring some of the less perfect elements. The engineers placed Freni rather close to the microphone, which makes it hard for her to sound tentative in her first scene, but the beauty of the voice is what one remembers, and from there to the end her performance is conceived as a whole, leading to a supremely moving account of the Death scene. Nicolai Gedda's Rodolfo is not rounded in the traditional Italian way, but there is never any doubt about his ability to project a really grand manner of his own. Thomas Schippers' conducting starts as though this is going to be a hard-driven, unrelenting performance, but quickly after the horseplay he shows his genuinely Italianate sense of pause, giving the singers plenty of time to breathe and allowing the music to expand. The resonant, 1964 recording has transferred vividly to CD.

Callas, flashing-eyed and formidable, may seem even less suited to the role of Mimì than to that of Butterfly, but characteristically her insights make for a vibrantly involving performance. The set is worth getting for Act III alone, where the predicament of Mimì has never been more heartrendingly conveyed in the recording studio. Though Giuseppe di Stefano is not the subtlest of Rodolfos, he is in excellent voice here, and Moffo and Panerai make a strong partnership as the second pair of lovers. Votto occasionally coarsens Puccini's score – as in the crude crescendo in the closing bars of Act III – but he directs with energy. The comparatively restricted dynamic range means that the singers appear to be 'front stage', but there is no lack of light and shade in Act II. The orchestra sounds full and warm, and the voices are clearly and vividly caught, the more so on CD, though the mono sound cannot match in its perspectives the range of the best stereo versions.

At bargain price on CfP comes the 1980 EMI set, conducted by James Levine. Alfredo Kraus's relatively light tenor sets the pattern at the very start for a performance that is strong on comedy. One registers the exchanges more sharply than usual on record, and though Kraus (no longer as sweet of timbre as he was) tends to over-point in the big arias, it is a stylish performance. Scotto – who first recorded the role of Mimì for DG in 1962 – is not flatteringly recorded here, for the rawness and unevenness which affect her voice at the top of the stave are distracting, marring an affectionate portrait. Milnes makes a powerful Marcello and Neblett a strong Musetta, a natural Minnie in *Fanciulla* transformed into a soubrette. Levine, brilliant in the comic writing of Acts I and IV, sounds less at home in the big melodies. The recording has plenty of warmth and atmosphere, sounding very well on CD, and its resonance has not blunted the tape transfer too much: the voices ride naturally over the rich orchestral texture.

Following up the big box-office success of its *Carmen* film, with its attendant recording used for the sound-track, Erato provided an equivalent recording of *Bohème* for its Luigi Comencini film of the opera. It is a characterful reading, fluently conducted by James Conlon, though with sticky, over-exaggerated passages that may have been influenced by the two principal singers. José Carreras gives a far freer, more varied and detailed account of Rodolfo's part than he did for Sir Colin Davis on the Philips set. There are moments of strain in *Che gelida manina* but a resonantly rich conclusion, which is reinforced by the close placing of the voice. Barbara Hendricks makes a provocative Mimì, at times minx-like, vulnerable but not in any way an innocent. Much of her singing is seductive to match the character, but with her the closeness of balance brings out any unevenness in the production, with some ungainly portamento, as in *Sì, mi chiamano Mimì*. Through the closeness of recording there is a hint of breathiness, as there also is with the Musetta of Angela Maria Blasi, a singer who might easily have been chosen as Mimì, warm and appealing but not really contrasted enough with Hendricks. Gino Quilico makes a magnificent, dark-toned Marcello, but the other two Bohemians are undistinctive, and Federico Davià's Benoit takes aged grotesquerie to the limit. With the orchestral sound set back and lacking a little in body, the recording has an edge that to a degree detracts from realism and presence.

Leinsdorf's version from the 1960s has a well-matched, reliable cast. Moffo is an affecting Mimì, Mary Costa a characterful Musetta, while Merrill and Tozzi provide strong support. Tucker gives a positive characterization as Rodolfo, though as ever he has lachrymose moments. Sadly, Leinsdorf's rigid direction, with speed fluctuations observed by instruction and never with natural expression, sets the singers against a deadpan, unsparkling accompaniment. Dated but acceptable recording.

The CD transfer in its clarity and sharp focus underlines the unidiomatic quality of Davis's reading, with un-Italianate singers like Ingvar Wixell and Ashley Putnam in key roles. As in *Tosca*, Sir Colin Davis here takes a direct view of Puccini, presenting the score very straight, with no exaggerations. The result is refreshing but rather lacking in wit and sparkle; pauses and hesitations are curtailed. Ricciarelli's is the finest performance vocally, and Davis allows her more freedom than the others. *Sì, mi chiamano Mimì* is full of fine detail and most affecting. Carreras gives a good generalized performance, wanting in detail and in intensity, and rather failing to rise to the big moments. Wixell makes an unidiomatic Marcello, rather lacking in fun, and Robert Lloyd's bass sounds lightweight as Colline. Ashley Putnam makes a charming Musetta, but at full price this is not really a competitive set.

Bernstein's is a very distinctive but flawed version of *La Bohème*. He decided to work not with opera stars but with a team of young singers, mostly American. Live performances in Rome were edited together, following the recording pattern Bernstein latterly preferred, and that seems to have encouraged him to draw out Puccini's sparkling score as expansively as possible, with rallentandos so extreme they tax even the longest-breathed of his young soloists. Bernstein's characteristic rhythmic flair keeps the music from stagnating, but it means that many expressive points are underlined too heavily, and flow is impaired. Unfortunately, the Mimì of Angelina Réaux and the Musetta of Barbara Daniels are less impressive than they might be, when the microphone exaggerates the pronounced vibrato in their voices. Réaux at least does sound Italianate. Jerry Hadley sings freshly, only occasionally straining, but is quite un-Italianate, and James Busturud makes a disagreeably gritty Schaunard. It is Thomas Hampson as Marcello who shines out from the team in the one performance of real quality; but it is the conductor's personality above all which dominates everything. Set in an ample acoustic, the recording of voices and orchestra has an agreeable bloom and spaciousness, with generally good balance.

The pre-war EMI set conducted by Berrettoni is dominated – as was planned at the time of recording – by the great tenor, Beniamino Gigli, a superstar of his day. The way he spices the role of Rodolfo with little Gigli chuckles is consistently charming. From first to last his facial expression comes over vividly in his strongly characterized singing, and the pity is that he is not well served by the conducting (unimaginative) or the recording, which is markedly less vivid than in the parallel recording of *Tosca* with Gigli as Cavaradossi. Licia Albanese, later to sing the same role for Toscanini in his 1946 concert performance and recording, is tenderly affecting but, thanks to the recording, the voice is recessed. Afro Poli sings firmly, but proves a colourless Marcello, and Tatiana Menotti is an edgy, fluttery Musetta.

Toscanini's set is taken from the first of his concert performances of opera in New York, recorded in 1946. The sound is even drier than most from this source, but the voices are vivid in their forward placing, and fortunately the singers had been chosen for their clean focus. Albanese, though held in an expressive straitjacket by the conductor, sounds fuller and sweeter as Mimì than in her earlier recording with Gigli; indeed she is delightfully fresh, even though no pianissimos are possible in the NBC acoustic. Jan Peerce as Rodolfo and Frank Valentino as Marcello are reliable rather than imaginative – not surprising with the conductor such a disciplinarian – and Anne McKnight makes a bright, clear Musetta. Toscanini is heavy-handed and often rigid in his direction, but his love of this score, which he knew from its earliest performances, shines out all through, not least in his loud and endearing vocal obbligatos during the big tunes.

With good digital recording and fresh, clear sopranos taking the roles of Mimì and Musetta, the Naxos set makes a viable bargain issue, despite prosaic conducting. Luba Orgonasova and Carmen Gonzales both sing with fine control of the soaring vocal lines, but Jonathan Welch as Rodolfo is coarse, his tenor throaty and at times unsteady. Fabio Previati is a firm if unimaginative Marcello.

Recorded live in Bologna in 1990, the Gelmetti/EMI set balances the voices behind the orchestra, which may be just as well when the singing is so indifferent. When Giuseppe Sabbatini sings above a cooing *mezza voce* his tenor becomes strangulated, while Daniella Dessì makes a colourless Mimì, fluttery and effortful. Gelmetti's conducting brings rough-and-ready ensemble in the larking of the Bohemians, with the score alternately overdriven and languorously soupy. Add to that a vinegary Musetta and a Marcello who blurts like a foghorn, and one wonders how this set ever came to appear as a premium-price issue. The only possible excuse is that the revised Ricordi score is used, for the first time on record.

We also wonder why DG decided to reissue their Florence recording of *Bohème*, and we list it here in case any collector might be tempted by the cast and the medium price. It is, in fact, totally unrecommendable. Even Gobbi is less than a success as Marcello: do we really want to hear a Bohemian snarling? Scotto's voice is not at all well caught, and as for Poggi, he makes the most frightful noises!

La Bohème: highlights.
*** Decca 421 245-2 [id.] (from above recording with Freni, Pavarotti; cond. Karajan).
(M) **(*) Decca 421 301-2 [id.] (from above recording with Tebaldi, Bergonzi; cond. Serafin).
(M) **(*) EMI CDM7 63932-2; *EG 763932-4* (from above recording with Freni, Gedda; cond. Schippers).

It is a pity to cut anything from so taut an opera as *La Bohème*; but those who feel they can make do with a single CD instead of two will find this selection from the Karajan set ideal. However, most collectors will surely want a reminder of the vintage set with Tebaldi and Bergonzi at the height of their powers. The selection is well made, and the disc is competitively priced. The selection from the Schippers set is reasonably generous (60 minutes) and contains most of the key items; it is certainly well transferred.

La Fanciulla del West (The Girl of the Golden West) complete.
❀ (M) *** Decca 421 595-2 (2) [id.]. St Cecilia Ac., Rome, Ch. & O, Capuana.
   Minnie (Renata Tebaldi), Dick Johnson (Mario Del Monaco), Jack Rance (Cornell MacNeil), Jake Wallace (Giorgio Tozzi).
*** DG 419 640-2 (2) [id.]. ROHCG Ch. and O, Mehta.
   Minnie (Carol Neblett), Dick Johnson (Plácido Domingo), Jack Rance (Sherrill Milnes), Jake Wallace (Gwynne Howell).
** BMG/RCA Dig. 09026 60597-2 (2) [id.]. Bav. R. Ch., Munich RO, Slatkin.
   Minnie (Eva Marton), Dick Johnson (Dennis O'Neill), Jack Rance (Alain Fondary), Jake Wallace (Brian Montgomery).
Withdrawn: (M) ** EMI CMS7 63970-2 (2) [Ang. CDMB 63970]. La Scala, Milan, Ch. & O, Von Matačić.
   Minnie (Birgit Nilsson), Dick Johnson (João Gibin), Jack Rance (Andrea Mongelli), Jake Wallace (Nicola Zaccaria).
(**) Nuova Era 2324/5 (2) [id.]. Trieste Teatro Verdi Ch. & O, Arturo Basile.
   Minnie (Magda Olivero), Dick Johnson (Gastone Limarilli), Jack Rance (Lino Puglisi), Jake Wallace (Vito Susca).
*(*) Sony Dig. S2K 47189 (2) [id.]; *40-47189.* La Scala, Milan, Ch. & O, Maazel.
   Minnie (Mara Zampieri), Dick Johnson (Plácido Domingo), Jack Rance (Juan Pons), Jake Wallace (Mario Chingari).

Like *Madama Butterfly*, 'The Girl', as Puccini called it in his correspondence, was based on a play by the American, David Belasco. The composer wrote the work with all his usual care for detailed planning, both of libretto and of music. In idiom the music marks the halfway stage between *Butterfly* and *Turandot*.

The story of the opera takes place in a Californian mining camp around 1849/50. It opens in the Polka Tavern where the miners gather, drinking and playing cards. They are entertained by Jake Wallace, a travelling ballad singer. Homesickness affects them all, and Jim Larkins in particular yearns for his old home in Cornwall. There is a whip-round for money to pay his fare. Sid, another miner, cheats and the sheriff (Jack Rance) is forced to intervene to prevent the men from hanging him. The Wells Fargo agent announces a reward for the capture of the bandit, Ramirrez. Rance announces that Minnie, the tavern's proprietess, is to marry him. Sonora, jealous of Jack, fires his pistol, but Minnie's entry quietens everyone. Nick, the bartender, has wrongly told both Sonora and Trin, another miner, that Minnie favours them. Sonora pays his outstanding account with gold.

Minnie now starts her 'school' with the miners, reading from the Psalms about the pure in heart. She orders Billy Jackrabbit to marry Wowkle (Minnie's American-Indian servant), for he is the father of her child. Finally Jack Rance is able to be alone with Minnie and he courts her, but she repulses him. He offers $1,000 dollars for a kiss, but Minnie recalls the love her mother knew; Jack Rance has a wife already. Dick Johnson now enters and is given a much warmer welcome, and he leads Minnie off to a nearby dance-hall.

The sheriff is angry. Castro, a half-caste member of Ramirrez's gang, has been captured and is brought in as an informer. Discreetly he tells Dick Johnson (who is Ramirrez) that the gang is nearby. As Castro is taken off, Minnie and Johnson feel love awakening between them, but a signal (a shrill whistle) warns Johnson to depart. Regretfully he leaves Minnie behind.

The scene now changes to Minnie's cabin. Billy Jackrabbit comes in and confirms his promise to marry Wowkle, who sits rocking their baby. Minnie orders supper for two and waits for Dick Johnson to arrive. She has doubts about him, concerning a girl called Nina who is no better than she ought to be. But when he arrives, Johnson denies that Nina had been his mistress and as the snow is falling heavily outside Minnie offers the use of her bedroom to her visitor. Outside men are heard seeking Ramirrez. Minnie hides Johnson, then lets the members of the posse enter.

She is informed that Johnson and Ramirrez are one and the same person and that Nina, his former lover, has betrayed him. Johnson tries to leave after the men have gone but is shot as he gets outside the door; Minnie hides him again, in her loft. Rance enters and tells Minnie he wants her; as he is declaring his feelings, blood drips from the ceiling betraying Ramirrez's presence. Minnie now offers Rance a game of poker. If she wins, she and Johnson go free; if she loses, Rance can have them both. Minnie cheats but her sleight-of-hand remains undiscovered and so she wins. Rance leaves.

The hunt is now on for Johnson, alias Ramirrez, and he is finally captured. The men rejoice. He is condemned to be hung and asks for a little grace, as his head is being placed in the noose. Minnie rushes in, armed with a pistol. She makes a desperate appeal to the miners for whom she has done so much. Sonora capitulates and the others follow, and the men join together, mourning their great loss as she leaves the camp on Johnson's arm.

Like Karajan's classic 1961 *Tosca* (see below), the Decca set of *La Fanciulla del West* has been remastered for CD with spectacular success. The achievement is the more remarkable when one considers that the original recording was made in 1958; but this is vintage Decca sound, both atmospheric and vivid, and now offered on a pair of discs with the Acts uninterrupted by breaks, making a clear first choice for this opera on CD. Tebaldi gives one of her most warm-hearted and understanding performances on record, and Mario del Monaco displays the wonderfully heroic quality of his voice to great – if sometimes tiring – effect. Cornell MacNeil as the villain, Sheriff Rance, sings with great precision and attack, but unfortunately lacks a villainous-sounding voice to convey the character fully. Jake Wallace's entry and the song *Che faranno i viecchi miei* is one of the high spots of the recording, with Tozzi singing beautifully. Capuana's expansive reading is matched by the imagination of the production, with the closing scene wonderfully effective. The two discs are generously cued (45 points of entry in all) and a full libretto is provided.

DG took the opportunity of recording the opera when Covent Garden was staging a spectacular production in 1977. With one exception, the cast remained the same as in the theatre and, as so often in such associated projects, the cohesion of the performance in the recording is enormously intensified. The result confirms that – whatever doubts may remain over the subject, with its weeping goldminers – Puccini's score is masterly, culminating in a happy ending which brings one of the most telling emotional coups that he ever achieved. Mehta's manner – as at the very start – is on the brisk side, not just in the cakewalk rhythms but even in refusing to let the first great melody, the nostalgic *Che faranno i viecchi miei*, linger into sentimentality. Mehta's tautness then consistently makes up for intrinsic dramatic weaknesses (as, for example, the delayed entries of both heroine and hero in Act I).

Sherrill Milnes as Jack Rance was the newcomer to the cast for the recording, and he makes the villain into far more than a small-town Scarpia, giving nobility and understanding to the Act

I *arioso*. Domingo, as in the theatre, sings heroically, disappointing only in his reluctance to produce soft tone in the great aria *Ch'ella mi creda*. The rest of the Covent Garden team is excellent, not least Gwynne Howell as the minstrel who sings *Che faranno i viecchi miei*; but the crowning glory is the singing of Carol Neblett as the Girl of the Golden West herself, gloriously rich and true and with formidable attack on the exposed high notes. Full, atmospheric recording to match, essential in an opera full of evocative offstage effects. The CD transfer captures the fullness and boldness of the original DG recording, but the slight drying-out process of the digital sound adds some stridency in tuttis, readily acceptable with so strong a performance.

Leonard Slatkin conducts a strong and well-paced performance of Puccini's wild-west opera, taking a spacious, sympathetic view. It is good to have Dennis O'Neill taking the principal tenor role in a major international recording, bringing out the lyrical side of Dick Johnson's role very persuasively. He also rises well to the challenge of the final scene, with the aria, *Ch'ella mi creda*, and the hero's disappearance with Minnie into the sunset. Alain Fondary's firm, dark baritone makes Sheriff Rance less of a villain than usual, conveying wronged nobility. Eva Marton manages to sing far more gently for much of the time than she usually does on disc, and she copes well with the big dramatic moments, but it is still a voice that quickly grows raw, with too many loud, unpitched notes. For all its qualities this is not among the most recommendable versions.

The difference between the Rome and Milan performances is obvious from the very first bar: Capuana on Decca is the more refined, Matačić the more passionate. The EMI sound is closer and not so atmospheric, though it has excellent directional separation too. Nilsson makes a formidable Minnie, not as warm-toned as Tebaldi, nor as gloriously expansive as Carol Neblett on DG, but thrilling as a budding Brünhilde was bound to be (she recorded this in 1959). João Gibin is a degree more imaginative than Del Monaco and has a good, distinctive timbre, and Mongelli's Rance is a splendid characterization. One or two brief passages are omitted, whereas the Decca (and full-priced DG) versions are complete, so this must be very much a third choice.

Recorded at a live performance in 1965, this historic recording offers the legendary Magda Olivero in a role for which she was ideally suited. In the command of her singing she consistently gives life to the fire-eating, gun-toting Minnie who yet has the softest, most vulnerable heart. Sadly, the sound is depressingly thin and dry, and stage noises often submerge the music in the many crowd scenes. The tenor, Gastone Limarilli, matches Mario del Monaco in coarseness, without offering so thrilling a voice, but Lino Puglisi makes a firm, dark Jack Rance, and the conducting of Basile builds up to a moving climax in Act III, though Limarilli's milking of applause at the end of *Ch'ella mi creda* is hilarious.

After a long gap Maazel here resumed his projected Puccini cycle for Sony/CBS with a live recording of an opera that presents more snags than usual using that technique. Intrusive stage noises from the miners as they charge around, bad balances with voices consistently subordinated to orchestra, and the inconsistent inclusion of applause from the over-enthusiastic audience all prevent this from being a viable competitor with the finest studio recordings. Though the orchestra is placed forward of the voices, it fails to carry the necessary weight at climaxes, and the dry Scala acoustic is unkind to instruments and voices alike, dulling their edge.

As a Puccinian, Maazel has mellowed since his earlier recordings, and he moulds Puccini melodies affectionately, but the dramatic bite is dulled, thanks only in part to the recording. Even Domingo's heroic voice has a slight unevenness exposed at the start, though as ever he rises superbly to the big moments. Even so, his studio recording with Mehta on DG is far preferable. Juan Pons sounds far too gentlemanly and sympathetic to be the unforgiving Sheriff Rance, and in some ways Mara Zampieri fares best with her bright, cleanly projected voice bringing the occasional hint of a hoot. A disappointment.

La Fanciulla del West: highlights.
(M) *** DG 435 407-2; *435 407-4* [id.] (from above recording with Neblett, Domingo, Milnes; cond. Mehta).

This is most welcome as the only current set of highlights from *Fanciulla del West*, essentially representing the hero (as part of the 'Domingo Edition') but covering the whole opera generously with 75 minutes of music. No libretto, but a good track synopsis.

Gianni Schicchi (complete) (see also under *Il Trittico*).
*** Ariola-Eurodisc Dig. 258404 [id.]. Munich R. O, Patanè.
    Gianni Schicchi (Rolando Panerai), Lauretta (Helen Donath), Rinuccio (Peter Seiffert).
**(*) Hung. Dig. HCD 12541 [id.]. Hungarian State Op. O, Ferencsik.

Gianni Schicchi (Gyôrgy Melis), Lauretta (Magda Kalmár), Rinuccio (Dénes Gulyás).

Gianni Schicchi takes place in Florence in 1299. Buoso Donati lies dead; relatives surround him with prayers and laments. Betto, his brother-in-law, says that it is rumoured that Buoso has left all his money to a monastery and not to his relatives. A frantic search takes place for Buoso's will and Rinuccio finds it. Before it is opened, he asks to marry Lauretta, Schicchi's daughter. Zita, his aunt, consents with some reluctance.

Gianni Schicchi is now sent for, together with Lauretta. Meanwhile the relatives read the will in dismay. Rinuccio says that Schicchi is their only hope. He arrives with his daughter, and she and Rinuccio greet each other quickly but warmly. Zita now withdraws her permission for Lauretta to marry Rinuccio as there is no dowry. They all quarrel and Schicchi threatens to leave. But Rinuccio asks his help in circumventing the will so that he and Lauretta can marry, and she adds her heartfelt plea, *O mio babbino caro*.

Schicchi studies the will then checks carefully to ensure that no one outside the room knows of Buoso's death. He instructs the relatives to move the body and re-make the bed. A knock is heard on the door. Spinelloccio, a doctor from Bologna, enters as they hastily darken the room. Schicchi manages an accurate imitation of Buoso's voice and asks the doctor to return in the evening, as he is sleepy; the doctor departs. Schicchi tells the assembled relatives that he will pose as the dying Buoso and a notary will take down 'his last will and testament'. Zita sends Rinuccio to fetch the notary, and quarrels now recommence about the content of the new document.

Schicchi dresses himself in Buoso's night attire, and various relatives offer him bribes to make certain items over to them. As he climbs into bed, he dramatically warns them all of the legal punishment for falsifying a will – the loss of a hand and exile. Amantio, the notary, enters with two witnesses. Schicchi now begins dictating the will and comments that when people leave large sums of money to the church (which was Donati's intention) they are too often suspected of having come by such money dishonestly. He first leaves the five specific smaller items to the relatives, as requested earlier, then moves on to the main bequests and, carefully detailing each important possession (the mule, the house, the mills), leaves everything to – Gianni Schicchi!

There is a riot when the notary and witnesses leave and the house is ransacked. Schicchi defends himself with a stick. Rinuccio and Lauretta embrace outside on the balcony. Schicchi grins wickedly and turns to the audience to ask: who could think of a better use for the money? He continues by whimsically suggesting that for his escapade he could be condemned to eternal damnation, but with Dante's permission, if the audience have enjoyed themselves, perhaps he may plead extenuating circumstances.

Like the parallel version of *Il Tabarro*, the first of the three *Trittico* one-Acters, the Ariola Eurodisc record of *Gianni Schicchi* brings a co-production with Bavarian Radio, and the recording is similarly vivid and well balanced. Again Patanè conducts a colourful and vigorous performance, very well drilled in ensembles, even when speeds are dangerously fast, and with the voices nicely spaced to allow the elaborate details of the plot to be appreciated by ear alone. Central to the performance's success is the vintage Schicchi of Rolando Panerai, still rich and firm. He confidently characterizes the Florentine trickster in every phrase, building a superb portrait, finely timed.

Peter Seiffert as Rinuccio gives a dashing performance, consistently clean and firm of tone, making light of the high tessitura and rising splendidly to the challenge of the big central aria. Helen Donath would have sounded even sweeter a few years earlier, but she gives a tender, appealing portrait of Lauretta, pretty and demure in *O mio babbino caro*. Though Italian voices are in the minority, it is a confident team. Like *Il Tabarro*, the single disc comes in a double jewel-case and sadly, like that companion issue, has only two tracks, the second starting immediately after, not before, *O mio babbino caro*. Why will record companies not wake up to the necessary facilities of CD?

Ferencsik conducts all-Hungarian forces in an energetic and well-drilled account of Puccini's comic masterpiece, which makes up for some unidiomatic rigidity with red-blooded commitment. The singing is variable, with the incidental characters including some East European wobblers. Gyôrgy Melis is not always perfectly steady, but his is a fine, characterful reading, strongly projected; though Magda Kalmár sounds too mature for the girlish Lauretta, the tone is attractively warm and finely controlled, as is Dénes Gulyás's tenor in the role of Rinuccio. It is a pity that the CD has no banding whatever.

Madama Butterfly (complete).
*** Decca 417 577-2 (3) [id.]. V. State Op. Ch., VPO, Karajan.

Madama Butterfly (Mirella Freni), Pinkerton (Luciano Pavarotti), Sharpless (Robert Kerns), Suzuki (Christa Ludwig).

*** DG Dig. 423 567-2; *423 567-4* (3) [id.]. Amb. Op. Ch., Philh. O, Sinopoli.

Madama Butterfly (Mirella Freni), Pinkerton (José Carreras), Sharpless (Juan Pons), Suzuki (Teresa Berganza).

(M) *** EMI CMS7 69654-2 (2). Rome Op. Ch. & O, Barbirolli.

Madama Butterfly (Renata Scotto), Pinkerton (Carlo Bergonzi), Sharpless (Rolando Panerai), Suzuki (Anna Di Stasio).

(M) *** BMG/RCA GD 84145 (2) [4145-2-RG]. Rome Op. Ch. & O, Leinsdorf.

Madama Butterfly (Anna Moffo), Pinkerton (Cesare Valletti), Sharpless (Renato Cesari), Suzuki (Rosalind Elias).

(M) **(*) EMI CMS7 63634-2 (2) [Ang. CDMB 63634]; *TC-CFPD 4446*. Rome Op. Ch. & O, Santini.

Madama Butterfly (Victoria De los Angeles), Pinkerton (Jussi Bjoerling), Sharpless (Mario Sereni), Suzuki (Miriam Pirazzini).

(M) **(*) Decca 425 531-2 (2) [id.]. St Cecilia Ac. Ch. & O, Serafin.

Madama Butterfly (Renata Tebaldi), Pinkerton (Carlo Bergonzi), Sharpless (Enzo Sordello), Suzuki (Fiorenza Cossotto).

(M) **(*) Sony M2K 35181 (2) [id.]. Amb. Op. Ch., Philh. O, Maazel.

Madama Butterfly (Renata Scotto), Pinkerton (Plácido Domingo), Sharpless (Ingvar Wixell), Suzuki (Gillian Knight).

(***) EMI mono CDS7 47959-8 (2) [Ang. CDCB 47959]. La Scala, Milan, Ch. & O, Karajan.

Madama Butterfly (Maria Callas), Pinkerton (Nicolai Gedda), Sharpless (Mario Borriello), Suzuki (Lucia Danieli).

Withdrawn: (***) EMI mono CDS7 49575-2 (2). Rome Op., Gavazzeni.

Madama Butterfly (Victoria De los Angeles), Pinkerton (Giuseppe Di Stefano), Sharpless (Tito Gobbi), Suzuki (Anna Maria Canali).

Withdrawn: (M) (***) EMI mono CHS7 69990-2 (2) [Ang. CDHB 69990]. Rome Op. Ch. & O, Serafin.

Madama Butterfly (Toti Dal Monte), Pinkerton (Beniamino Gigli), Sharpless (Mario Basiola), Suzuki (Vittoria Palombini).

** BMG/RCA RD 86160 [RCA 6160-2-RC]. RCA Italiana Ch. & O, Leinsdorf.

Madama Butterfly (Leontyne Price), Pinkerton (Richard Tucker), Sharpless (Philip Maero), Suzuki (Rosalind Elias).

Withdrawn: ** Hung. HCD 12256-7 [id.]. Hungarian State Op. Ch. & O, Patanè.

Madama Butterfly (Veronika Kincses), Pinkerton (Peter Dvorský), Sharpless (Lajos Miller), Suzuki (Tamara Takács).

(B) ** Naxos Dig. 8.660015/6 (2). Ch. & Slovak RSO (Bratislava), Rahbari.

Madama Butterfly (Miriam Gauci), Pinkerton (Yordi Ramiro), Sharpless (Georg Tichy), Suzuki (Nelly Boschkowá).

It is surprising to discover that Puccini's most popular opera, *Madama Butterfly*, was not an instant success at its La Scala, Milan, première in 1904. But the composer withdrew and revised the score, and three months later, at Brescia, it began its triumphant conquest of the opera houses of the world. The story pays innocent homage to both American and Japanese cultures.

As it opens, Lieutenant Pinkerton, an American naval officer temporarily stationed in Nagasaki, is being shown around a house he is renting to be his matrimonial home in Japan. Goro, the marriage-broker, is with him, as are three Japanese servants, including Suzuki, who is to be hand-maiden to Cio-Cio-San, known as Butterfly, Pinkerton's intended bride. The American Consul, Sharpless, now joins Pinkerton, and Goro is sent to fetch Butterfly.

The consul becomes uneasy when Pinkerton drinks to 'a real wife from America'. Butterfly, who is deeply in love with her lieutenant and has just been baptized as a Christian, enters and makes a profound impression on Sharpless for both her simplicity and her obvious devotion. He warns Pinkerton not to trifle with her.

The Imperial Commissioner reads the marriage contract and it is duly signed by all concerned. But the happy atmosphere is temporarily broken by the entry of the Bonze, Butterfly's uncle, who accuses Butterfly of renouncing her family and religion. Everyone is scandalized, and friends and family all depart, leaving Butterfly weeping. But Pinkerton takes her into his arms and, as night falls, the lovers retire to consummate their mutual passion.

Three years pass, and we discover Butterfly again in distress, and the faithful Suzuki praying with a prayer-bell. Pinkerton was called back to America fairly soon after the wedding, but there is now a small child, a son, as witness to their liaison. Butterfly believes her husband will return, and in her great aria (*Un bel dì*) visualizes in her imagination the great day when his boat will re-enter the harbour. Sharpless comes to see her, with Goro, knowing that Pinkerton is returning with an American wife, but Butterfly's enthusiastic chatter prevents him from telling her or imparting the contents of Pinkerton's letter. Instead, she asks about the time of year robins nest in America, for Pinkerton had promised to return at nesting-time.

The imposingly suave Prince Yamadori is now introduced by Goro. He wants to marry Butterfly, and Goro tells her that under Japanese law she could divorce Pinkerton. Butterfly innocently declares her feelings and asserts her American citizenship; she is dismayed when Sharpless hints that Pinkerton may not return. She shows him her young son and says that, if deserted, she only has two choices: a return to her life as a geisha or death.

Very much affected by his encounter, Sharpless leaves, promising to tell Pinkerton of the existence of the child. A cannon-shot is heard from the harbour: it is an American ship. Butterfly and Suzuki decorate the house with flowers, and while Suzuki and the child fall asleep, Butterfly maintains her vigil throughout the night, watching for her lover's return.

Daylight comes and Sharpless and Pinkerton arrive, but when Suzuki tells him that Butterfly had stayed up all night waiting for him, Pinkerton lacks the courage to face his Japanese 'wife'. Kate, Pinkerton's American bride, can be seen outside; when Sharpless chides Pinkerton for his heartless behaviour, he at last shows signs of remorse. Kate and Suzuki now enter and Kate promises that, if she adopts the child, she will bring the boy up as her own.

Butterfly at last grasps her true situation and says she will hand over her son in an hour's time if Pinkerton will come for the boy himself. When they have departed, Butterfly takes her father's suicidal knife from its case and reads aloud the inscription: 'Death with honour is better than life with dishonour'. Suzuki guesses Butterfly's intention as she gives the child a last kiss and an American flag. Then, as Pinkerton and Sharpless enter, Butterfly thrusts the knife into her own body, stumbles, points desperately to her son and dies in Pinkerton's arms.

The sensuousness of Karajan's gloriously rich reading comes out all the more ravishingly on CD. Though the set is extravagantly laid out on three discs instead of two for most of the rival sets – slow speeds partly responsible – there is the clear advantage that each Act is complete on a single disc. Karajan inspires singers and orchestra to a radiant performance which brings out all the beauty and intensity of Puccini's score, sweet but not sentimental, powerfully dramatic but not vulgar. He pays the composer the compliment of presenting each climax with precise dynamics, fortissimos surprisingly rare but those few presented with cracking impact. Freni is an enchanting Butterfly, consistently growing in stature from the young girl to the victim of tragedy, sweeter of voice than any rival on record. Pavarotti is an intensely imaginative Pinkerton, actually inspiring understanding for this thoughtless character, while Christa Ludwig is a splendid Suzuki. The recording is one of Decca's most resplendent, with the Vienna strings producing glowing tone.

With speeds that in principle are eccentrically slow, Sinopoli's reading is the most idiosyncratic on record, but also one of the most powerful and perhaps the most beautiful of all, certainly in the ravishing orchestral sound. However expansive his speeds, Sinopoli is never sentimental or self-indulgent. Puccini's honeyed moments are given, not sloppily, but with rapt intensity – as at the poignant close of the *Flower duet*, when '*sola e rinnegata*' is recalled from Act I. They are then set the more movingly against the biting moments, from the opening fugato of Act I, sharply incisive, through to the final aria, tough and intense, where the trumpet monotone as Butterfly dies (marked to be played as a solo but rarely done that way) nags the nerves as never before. As she was for Karajan in his classic Decca set, Freni is a model Butterfly; though the voice is no longer so girlish, she projects the tragedy even more weightily than before. José Carreras is similarly presented as a large-scale Pinkerton, Juan Pons is a virile Sharpless and Teresa Berganza an equally positive, unfruity Suzuki. This is a set which in its spacious but intensely concentrated way brings a unique and unforgettable experience.

Sir John Barbirolli had some apprehensions before going to Rome in 1966 to make his first major recording of a complete opera, but at the very first session he established his mastery. The result is a performance in which, against all the rules, the conductor emerges as the central hero, not through ruthlessness but by sheer love. Players and singers perform consistently with a dedication and intensity rare in opera recordings made in Italy, and the whole score – orchestrated with masterly finesse – glows more freshly than ever. One has only to hear a passage such as the nostalgic duet between Pinkerton and Sharpless in the first scene to realize how Barbirolli reinforces the work of the singers, drawing them out to their finest.

There is hardly a weak link in the cast. Bergonzi's Pinkerton and Panerai's Sharpless are both much more sensitively and beautifully sung than one expects these days; Anna di Stasio's Suzuki is more than adequate, and Renata Scotto's Butterfly has a subtlety and perceptiveness in its characterization that more than make up for any shortcoming in the basic beauty of tone-colour. It is on any count a highly individual voice, used here with great intelligence to point up the drama to its tragic climax. The set has been successfully remastered, and the sound freshened, for its mid-price reissue on a pair of CDs. The violins have lost a little of their original opulence, but in all other respects the recording combines vividness with atmosphere. A full translation is provided in the accompanying libretto.

Anna Moffo's set of *Madama Butterfly* was recorded before the other RCA version, with Leontyne Price (RD 86160 [6160-2-RC] – also made in Rome under Leinsdorf) and is superior to that version in almost every way. Moffo's Butterfly proves delightful, fresh and young-sounding but without any of the heavy coyness that marred Price's characterization. *Un bel dì* has some sliding at the beginning, but the end is glorious, and the *Flower duet* with Rosalind Elias is enchanting. Valletti's Pinkerton has a clear-voiced, almost Gigli-like charm – preferable to most rivals – and with Corena as the Bonze the only blot on the set vocally is the unimaginative Sharpless of Renato Cesari. Leinsdorf is efficient and undistracting, and with vivid recording (balanced in favour of the voices) this – like the Barbirolli set – makes a first-class mid-priced recommendation.

In the late 1950s and early 1960s, Victoria de los Angeles was the most memorable of Butterflies, and her 1960 recording displays her art at its most endearing, with golden tone-colour lovingly exploited. The voice is well recorded if rather close. Opposite her, Jussi Bjoerling was making one of his very last recordings and, though he shows few special insights, he produces a flow of rich tone to compare with that of the heroine. Mario Sereni is a full-voiced Sharpless, but Miriam Pirazzini is a disappointingly wobbly Suzuki; while Santini is a reliable, generally rather square conductor who rarely gets in the way. With recording quality freshened, this fine set is most welcome either on a pair of mid-price CDs or, still sounding bright and clear, in its bargain-priced cassette format (offered in a chunky box with a synopsis rather than a libretto).

Serafin's sensitive and beautifully paced reading finds Tebaldi at her most radiant. Though she was never the most deft of Butterflies dramatically (she never actually sang the role on stage before recording it), her singing is consistently rich and beautiful, breathtakingly so in passages such as the one in Act I where she tells Pinkerton she has changed her religion. The excellence of the Decca engineering in 1958 is amply proved in the CD transfer, with one serious exception. The very opening with its absence of bass brings a disagreeably shrill and thin sound, promptly corrected once the orchestration grows fuller, with voices very precisely and realistically placed.

The digital transfer of the Sony/CBS recording underlines the clarity and incisiveness of Maazel's reading, making it sound less persuasively natural, all too tautly controlled. Scotto, who assumes the title-role, had recorded the opera previously with Barbirolli, but this later version catches her in better voice. Her soprano – always inclined to spread a little on top at climaxes – had acquired extra richness and was recorded with a warmer tonal bloom. Maazel is both powerful and unsentimental, with a fine architectural control and feeling for Puccini's subtle orchestration. Plácido Domingo sings heroically as Pinkerton but arguably makes him too genuine a character for such a cad. Wixell's voice is not ideally rounded as Sharpless, but he sings most sensitively, and Gillian Knight makes an expressive Suzuki. Among the others, Malcolm King as the Bonze is outstanding.

The idea of the flashing-eyed Maria Callas playing the role of the fifteen-year-old Butterfly may not sound convincing, and certainly this performance will not satisfy those who insist that Puccini's heroine is a totally sweet and innocent character. But Callas's view, aided by superbly imaginative and spacious conducting from Karajan, gives extra dimension to the Puccinian little woman, and with some keenly intelligent singing too from Gedda as Pinkerton (a less caddish and more thoughtful character than usual) this is a set which has a special compulsion. The performance projects the more vividly on CD, even though the lack of stereo in so atmospheric an opera is a serious disadvantage. Yet the powerful combination of Callas and Karajan – each challenging the other both in expressive imagination and in discipline – makes a powerful effect on the listener; unlike Karajan's later and more sumptuous Decca version with Freni, this one is fitted on to two CDs only.

Victoria de los Angeles' first recording of *Madama Butterfly*, a role which for a decade and more she made her own, was done in mono in 1954. Never reissued in the days of LP, it makes a welcome return on CD, when it has many advantages over the later, stereo version. De los

Angeles' tone is even more meltingly beautiful, Di Stefano is a more ardent Pinkerton, and Tito Gobbi, unexpectedly cast as a rugged Sharpless, uses that small role to point some of the set's most memorable moments, notably the Act I toasting duet with Pinkerton and the Act II confrontation with Butterfly. The mono sound is full of presence, with voices and orchestra both vividly caught. The only disappointment is that the set is offered at full price.

There has never been as endearing a portrait of Pinkerton on record as Gigli's. The perennial smile in his voice makes one immediately forget how totally caddish the American lieutenant's behaviour is. One simply revels in the beauty of the sound and the imagination of the phrasing, only occasionally self-indulgent. The Butterfly of Toti dal Monte is something of an acquired taste. The 'little-girl' sound is often exaggerated, but it is a classic performance nevertheless. Serafin, as ever, is a master of timing; but this mono recording of 1939, sounding very well for its age, is a set to get above all for the great tenor and his unique performance.

Leontyne Price was in glorious voice when, in July 1962, she recorded this opera under Erich Leinsdorf. This is a weighty portrait of Butterfly, with Price's gloriously rich, creamy tone seamlessly controlled, even if occasionally she indulges in unwanted portamenti. The obvious snag is that some of the vocal acting sounds too crude for Puccini's little woman, and Tucker is at times similarly coarse as Pinkerton. Added to that, what puts the set finally out of court is Leinsdorf's metrical and unresilient conducting, and with that rigidity comes a straitjacketing of emotion. At full price it is not competitive.

Recorded in 1981 in analogue sound, vividly remastered for CD, the Hungaroton set presents a warm, idiomatically conducted reading with dramatically convincing performances from the principals. Peter Dvorský's clear, fresh tenor takes well to recording; he gives an attractively lyrical performance as Pinkerton, sweet and concerned rather than an ardent lover in Act I. He remains a recessive character next to the Butterfly of Veronika Kincses, who emerges as an attractively girlish figure with facial expression made clear in every phrase.

For all the natural vibrancy there is no suspicion of a wobble, and it is only when the voice is pressed in the upper register that the tone hardens in vocal as well as dramatic terms from girlish tones through increasing warmth and on to growing maturity in Act II. Sadly, the least attractive singing comes in the final suicide aria, but Patanè's commitment carries one over that. Lajos Miller makes a young-sounding Sharpless, pleasing of tone, while Tamara Takács is a fruity, positive Suzuki and József Gregor a firmly resonant Bonze, impressive in the curse.

Rahbari conducts a warm, well-paced reading of *Butterfly* with an excellent young Maltese soprano in the name-part, Miriam Gauci. She sings with a warm vibrato which yet does not disturb her attractively girlish portrait. The light-toned Yordy Ramiro is here more successful in Puccini as Pinkerton than he is in his Verdi recordings for Naxos. Though Georg Tichy makes a colourless Sharpless and the final suicide scene is lacking in orchestral bite, this makes an enjoyable, atmospherically recorded version. As with other Naxos operas, there is a full text but no translation. The tracking is exceptionally generous, neatly linked with a detailed synopsis.

Madama Butterfly: highlights.
*** Decca 421 247-2 [id.] (from above recording with Freni, Pavarotti; cond. Karajan).
(M) *** EMI CDM7 63411-2; *EG 763411-4* (from above recording with Scotto, Bergonzi; cond. Barbirolli).
(M) ** Decca 421 873-2; *421 873-4* [id.] (from above recording with Tebaldi, Bergonzi; cond. Serafin).

The Karajan disc is an obvious first choice for a highlights CD from *Butterfly* (if the purchase of the complete set – ungenerously presented on three CDs – is felt to be uneconomical), since it includes the *Humming chorus*, omitted from the mid-priced Tebaldi/Bergonzi selection. The remastered sound is excellent.

The EMI selection (54 minutes) offers only slightly more music than the Tebaldi selection, and also includes the essential *Humming chorus*. For those owning another complete set, it offers a fine sampler of Barbirolli's deeply felt performance with its admirably consistent cast. Scotto's Butterfly was one of her finest recorded performances. The transfer does reveal the age of the 1966 recording in the orchestral sound, but the voices are full and vividly projected.

The Tebaldi/Bergonzi Decca set dates from 1958 but the sound is rich in ambience, and the dated upper string sound is seldom distracting, for the voices are vividly projected. The magnetism of the singing is very compelling, but the 51 minutes' selection is ungenerous and still omits the *Humming chorus*.

Madame Butterfly: highlights (sung in English).
(B) **(*) CfP CD-CFP 4600; *TC-CFP 4600.* Marie Collier, Charles Craig, Ann Robson, Gwyn
   Griffiths, Sadler's Wells O, Brian Balkwill.

This 1960 recording was the first of a series of Sadler's Wells highlights discs of operas in
English. There are few better examples, for the clear recording lets the listener hear almost every
word and this is achieved without balancing things excessively in favour of the voices. Marie
Collier got inside the part very well; she had a big, full voice and she sings most movingly.
Charles Craig is a splendid Pinkerton, his singing achieving international standards, and he was
in particularly fresh voice when this record was made. As to the choice of extracts, the one
omission which is at all serious is the entry of Butterfly. As it is, the duet of Pinkerton and
Sharpless cuts off just as she is about to come in. The recording wears its years lightly; just
occasionally the bright CD transfer brings a touch of peakiness in the vocal climaxes, but the
performance remains very involving.

Manon Lescaut (complete).
*** DG Dig. 413 893-2 (2) [id.]. ROHCG Ch., Philh. O, Sinopoli.
   Manon Lescaut (Mirella Freni), Des Grieux (Plácido Domingo), Lescaut (Renato Bruson).
*** Decca Dig. 421 426-2; *421 426-4* (2) [id.]. Ch. & O of Teatro Comunale di Bologna, Chailly.
   Manon Lescaut (Kiri Te Kanawa), Des Grieux (José Carreras), Lescaut (Paolo Coni).
*** Naxos Dig. 8.660019/20 (2) [id.]. BRT Philh. Ch. & O, Alexander Rahbari.
   Manon Lescaut (Miriam Gauci), Des Grieux (Kaludi Kaludov), Lescaut (Vicente Sardinero).
(M) (***) BMG/RCA mono GD 60573 (2) [60573-2-RG]. Rome Op. Ch. & O, Perlea.
   Manon Lescaut (Licia Albanese), Des Grieux (Jussi Bjoerling), Lescaut (Robert Merrill).
(M) **(*) Decca 430 253-2 (2) [id.]. St Cecilia Ac., Rome, Ch. & O, Molinari-Pradelli.
   Manon Lescaut (Renata Tebaldi), Des Grieux (Mario Del Monaco), Lescaut (Mario
   Borriello).
(M) (***) EMI mono CDS7 47393-8 (2) [Ang. CDCB 47392]. La Scala, Milan, Ch. and O,
   Serafin.
   Manon Lescaut (Maria Callas), Des Grieux (Giuseppe Di Stefano), Lescaut (Giulio
   Fioravanti).
Withdrawn: ** EMI CDS7 47736-8 (2) [id.]. Amb. Op. Ch., New Philh. O, Bartoletti.
   Manon Lescaut (Montserrat Caballé), Des Grieux (Plácido Domingo).
* Sony S2K 48474 (2) [id.]. La Scala, Milan, Ch. & O, Maazel.
   Manon (Nina Rautio), Des Grieux (Peter Dvorský), Lescaut (Gino Quilico).

Manon Lescaut, Puccini's first fully successful opera, was first heard in Turin in 1893. Its text
is based on the Abbé Prévost novel, also used by Massenet and Auber, among others. Like the
Massenet setting, Puccini's version of the opera opens at an inn in Amiens.

The Chevalier des Grieux, not in the happiest of moods, Lescaut, Sergeant of the King's
Guard, Geronte di Ravoir (Treasurer-General) and Manon all arrive together. Lescaut is
escorting his sister to a convent. He notices that the wealthy Geronte is admiring Manon and
looks the other way when the latter plots with the landlord to abduct her.

Des Grieux is also attracted and asks her name. It is he to whom she is immediately drawn,
and soon it is obvious they are in love. Made aware of the abduction plot, Des Grieux persuades
Manon to elope with him and they drive away in the carriage Geronte had ordered. When they
have gone, Lescaut observes that Des Grieux is not wealthy and he suggests to Geronte that it
will not be difficult to entice her back, for Manon loves luxury.

As predicted, Manon leaves Des Grieux for Geronte, but at the same time she longs for her
more humble and loving existence with Des Grieux (*In quelle trine morbide*). While Manon
enjoys a dancing lesson, Lescaut goes off to inform Des Grieux of her new address. Des Grieux,
who has made money gambling, arrives and reproaches Manon, but her beauty overcomes him
and they passionately re-declare their mutual love.

Geronte discovers them together and goes off to fetch the police. Manon delays their
departure while she gathers up her jewels. Des Grieux chides her – and indeed her love of luxury
is her downfall, for the police arrive, the jewels are seen and she is arrested, charged by Geronte
as a prostitute.

Manon is banished to the then French colony of Louisiana. The journey to Le Havre is
represented by an Intermezzo. In a square near the harbour, Des Grieux and Lescaut have come
to try and free Manon, but in vain, and Des Grieux, beside himself with grief, begs the guard and
then the ship's captain to be allowed to travel with her. His request is granted.

In the final scene Manon and Des Grieux have arrived at and then left New Orleans; now they are travelling across arid, open country and Manon is exhausted. Des Grieux goes off to find help and, when he returns, she is dying; he collapses beside her.

Sinopoli's brilliant version of Puccini's passionately romantic opera provides in almost every way the answer most Puccinians have been waiting for. With his concern for detail, his love of high dramatic contrasts, and the clear pointing of changes of mood, along with sharp control of tension, the plan of each Act is presented with new precision, reflecting the composer's own careful crafting. This is also the most sensuous-sounding reading on record, thanks also to the fine playing of the Philharmonia, taking over in what is in most respects a recording of the Covent Garden production. Plainly the chorus has benefited from having also worked with Sinopoli in the opera house, and Plácido Domingo's portrait of Des Grieux is here far subtler and more detailed, with finer contrasts of tone and dynamic, than in his earlier, EMI recording opposite Caballé. The nicely shaded legato of *Donna non vidi mai* in Act I contrasts with an Othello-like outburst on *No, no pazzo son*, making a shattering conclusion to Act III. Freni, taking the place of Kiri Te Kanawa in the stage production, proves an outstanding choice. Her girlish tones in Act I rebut any idea that she might be too mature. *In quelle trine morbide*, in Act II, retains freshness of tone with fine concern for word detail, while the long duet and aria of the last Act present a most moving culmination, not feeling like an epilogue.

Freni and Sinopoli together bring a ravishing change of mood on the unexpected modulation from F minor to D flat on *Terra de pace* in that scene, a wonderful moment of stillness to heighten the impact of *Non voglio morir*. Of the others, a first-rate team, Renato Bruson nicely brings out the ironic side of Lescaut's character, and having Brigitte Fassbaender just to sing the madrigal adds to the feeling of luxury, as does John Tomlinson's darkly intense moment of drama as the ship's captain, bringing the happy resolution in Act III. The voices are more recessed than is common, but they are recorded with fine bloom, and the brilliance of the orchestral sound comes out particularly impressively on CD.

In the Chailly version of *Manon Lescaut*, Dame Kiri is in ravishing voice as the heroine; the relative merits of this Decca issue and the earlier DG set under Sinopoli could make for a difficult choice for Dame Kiri's admirers. Creamier of tone than Mirella Freni on DG, she also gives an affecting characterization, at times rather heavily underlined but passionately convincing in the development from innocent girl to fallen woman. Freni's is the subtler performance and, in the final aria, *Sola, perduta, abbandonata*, Sinopoli's ominously steady tread helps to give her the greater intensity. Sinopoli directs a more sharply focused performance than that of his rival, and the playing from Chailly's Bologna orchestra cannot quite match that of the Philharmonia. Yet Chailly is a degree more idiomatic in his pacing. Both tenors are good but Carreras, recorded just before his illness, sounds a little strained at times. The Decca sound, with voices further forward, is the more vivid.

On the super-bargain Naxos issue, Miriam Gauci gives one of the most sensitive performances of this role on any set. Her Act II aria *In quelle trine morbide* is beautifully poised, and her monologue in the Death scene, *Sola perduta, abbandonata*, is the more moving for being restrained at the start, building from there in intensity without sacrificing musical values. The young Bulgarian, Kaludi Kaludov, is a clean-cut, virile Des Grieux, opening up impressively in his big moments. Vicente Sardinero makes a powerful Lescaut, and Rahbari, as in his Bratislava recordings of *Cav.* and *Pag.*, is a red-blooded interpreter of Italian opera, generally pacing well, even if at the very start he is disconcertingly hectic. Though the Brussels orchestra plays with refinement – the strings in particular – the sound is thinner than in the Slovakian recordings, with the orchestra set slightly back. This is the least expensive *Manon Lescaut* in the catalogue – but even if it cost more, it would still be very recommendable.

Perlea's 1954 recording of *Manon Lescaut*, well paced, fresh and vigorous, makes a valuable addition to the excellent Victor Opera series at mid-price. The mono sound may be limited (with the orchestra in this transfer not given the body it originally had on LP), but no Puccinian should miss it, when Jussi Bjoerling gives the finest ever interpretation on record of the role of Des Grieux. This is one of Bjoerling's best recordings, passionately committed and gloriously sung; and Robert Merrill too is superb as Manon's brother, giving delightful irony to the closing scene of Act I which has rarely sounded so effervescent. The Manon of Licia Albanese is sensitively sung, but the voice is not at all girlish, even less so than in her two classic recordings as Mimì in *Bohème*: with Gigli in 1939 and in Toscanini's concert performance in 1946.

At mid-price, the Decca set with Tebaldi, dating from the mid-1950s, is still worth considering. The Decca recording still sounds well, with good detail, and the direction of Molinari-Pradelli is warm and intense. While Tebaldi is not quite the little woman of Puccini's dreams, she produces a flow of gorgeous, rich tone. Only the coarseness of Mario del Monaco as Des Grieux mars the set, but this is exciting, red-blooded singing and he does not overwhelm Tebaldi in the duet sequences.

The early La Scala mono set partnering Callas and Di Stefano has striking individuality and dramatic power. It is typical of Callas that she turns the final scene – which often seems an excrescence, a mere epilogue after the real drama – into the most compelling part of the opera. Serafin is here electrifying, and Di Stefano too is inspired to one of his finest complete opera recordings. The cast-list even includes the young Fiorenza Cossotto, impressive as the singer in the Act II madrigal. The recording – still in mono, not a stereo transcription – is boxy but gives good detail. The CD transfer refines the boxiness a degree further than the LPs, but for once the new medium loses out when, unlike the LPs, a break is involved in Act II between the two discs, where LP had that Act complete on one side.

The EMI version conducted by Bartoletti is chiefly valuable for the beautiful performance of Montserrat Caballé as the heroine, one of her most affecting, with the voice alluringly beautiful. Her account of *In quelle trine morbide* is lightly flowing, while the big Act IV aria is strong and positive. Otherwise the set is disappointing, with Plácido Domingo unflattered by the close acoustic, not nearly as perceptive as in his much later, DG performance under Sinopoli. Bartoletti's conducting is also relatively coarse, with the very opening forced and breathless. The digital transfer on CD adds to the harsh glare of the 1972 analogue recording.

In the latest Sony version with the company of La Scala, the title-role is taken by a newcomer, Nina Rautio, who sings with full, creamy tone but with perilously little expression, consistently underplaying the meaning and with words barely identifiable. When at their first meeting she tells Des Grieux her name, she might be answering a civil service questionnaire, and the tenor, Peter Dvorský, often excellent in Slavonic opera, proves coarse here in Puccini, too loud and with no roundness of tone. Lorin Maazel, always on the stiff side in Puccini, sounds particularly square in this exuberantly youthful score, not helped by the dry Milan acoustic.

Manon Lescaut: highlights.
(M) *** DG Dig. 435 408-2; *435 408-4* [id.] (from above recording with Freni, Domingo; cond. Sinopoli).

With 66 minutes of music offered, most of the important music is included, so this selection from the highly recommendable Sinopoli set will certainly tempt collectors who already have another recording of the complete opera. An adequate synopsis with track cues is provided in lieu of a libretto.

La Rondine (complete).
(M) *** Sony Dig. M2K 37852 [id.]. Amb. Op. Ch., LSO, Maazel.
   Magda (Kiri Te Kanawa), Ruggero (Plácido Domingo), Lisetta (Mariana Nicolesco), Prunier (David Rendall), Rambaldo (Leo Nucci).
(M) ** BMG/RCA GD 60459 (2) [4801-2-RG]. RCA Italiana Op. Ch. & O, Molinari-Pradelli.
   Magda (Anna Moffo), Ruggero (Daniele Barioni), Lisetta (Graziella Sciutti), Prunier (Piero De Palma), Rambaldo (Mario Sereni).

La Rondine was a product of the First World War, and though nothing could be less grim in subject than this frothy tale told in Viennese-operetta style, the background to its composition and production may have had their effect. It has never caught on, and a recording like this will almost certainly surprise anyone by the mastery of the piece.

The story is based on a watered-down *Traviata* situation, culminating not in tragedy but in a sad-sweet in-between ending such as the Viennese (for whom it was written) loved. It opens in Magda's luxurious house in Paris. She is Rambaldo's mistress; they are entertaining friends, including Prunier, a poet. Rambaldo now produces a necklace for Magda, the envy of those around her.

The maid then asks if Rambaldo will see a young man, Ruggero, the son of an old friend, who has waited in the hall for over two hours. He agrees and, while he is gone, Magda tells of her former days of innocence, when she went to Bulliers' café and had her first experience of love with a man whom she can never forget, yet whose name she does not know. Ruggero is brought in and Prunier starts to tell fortunes: Magda's future is that she will migrate from Paris like a swallow to find love.

Ruggero decides to spend his first evening in Paris at Bullier's café. Lisetta, Magda's maid, cheekily agrees that his choice is excellent. As it is her day off, she dresses in Magda's clothes and, having met Prunier on the balcony, they set off together. The story continues in the

Ballroom at *chez* Bullier. Ruggero sits alone. Magda now enters, dressed as a grisette, and dances with him. Prunier and Lisetta come in, and Lisetta thinks she recognizes her mistress. Rambaldo now also arrives and asks Magda to come home with him. She refuses and says she has left him for ever. He leaves, preserving his dignity, and Ruggero and Magda go off together.

For a period they live happily together in Nice. Ruggero tells her that he has sought his father's consent to their marriage and that he is sure the family will welcome her. Magda wonders how to tell him the details of her past life. Prunier and Lisetta now reappear; Lisetta has attempted a stage career, but unsuccessfully, and now wants to return to her position with Magda. Magda agrees. Prunier thinks they might all return to Paris; he declares that he is finished with Lisetta but takes care to discover where she will be staying that night. Rambaldo still wants his mistress back.

A letter now arrives for Magda from Ruggero's mother and she realizes that she can deceive him no longer: the time has come to reveal her past life as a courtesan. She cannot marry him or face his mother who expects a virgin bride. She leaves with Lisetta to return to her old way of life.

With a captivating string of catchy numbers, *La Rondine* makes a delightful entertainment. It is not just a question of Puccini taking Viennese waltzes as a model but all kinds of other suitable dances such as tangos, foxtrots and two-steps. Not aggressively at all, for, as with so much that this most eclectic of composers 'cribbed', he commandeered them completely, to make the result utterly Puccinian. If there is a fault, it lies in the inability of the story to move the listener with any depth of feeling, but a recording does at least allow one to appreciate each tiny development with greater ease than in the theatre.

Maazel's is a strong, positive reading, crowned by a superb, radiant Magda in Dame Kiri Te Kanawa, mature yet glamorous. From the stratospheric phrases in *Il sogno di Doretta* which are headily beautiful, her performance has one spellbound. Domingo, by age too mature for the role of young hero, yet scales his voice down most effectively in the first two Acts, expanding in heroic warmth only in the final scene of dénouement. Sadly, the second pair are far less convincing, when the voices of both Mariana Nicolesco and David Rendall take ill to the microphone. Others in the team are excellent and, though Maazel launches the very opening too aggressively, the rest is most sympathetically done, with fine playing from the LSO. Though the CD transfer is excellent, there is a serious lack of access within the opera itself. Acts I and II are on the first disc, Act III on the second, but there are no cues to find individual passages.

The alternative set from RCA has a price advantage. Anna Moffo leads a good cast, and the performance, though not ideal, is still highly enjoyable, with understanding direction from Molinari-Pradelli, more warmly expressive than Maazel's. The recording too has come up well, but the Sony/CBS set remains first choice.

Suor Angelica (complete) (see also under *Il Trittico*).
**(*) Hung. Dig. HCD 12490 [id.]. Hungarian State Op. Ch. and O, Gardelli.
    Suor Angelica (Ilona Tokody), Princess (Eszter Póka), Abbess (Zsuzsa Barlay), Mistress of the Novices / Infirmary Sister (Tamara Takács).

Suor Angelica is the second of the three operas which make up Puccini's *Il Trittico,* and the working out of its narrative is, regretfully, highly imbued with sentimentality, for which the music fails to make amends. Angelica, the daughter of a noble Florentine family, is the (unmarried) mother of a young child. She has taken the veil to expiate the scandal and has spent seven years in the peace of the convent.

The abbess tells her that she has a visitor, the princess (her aunt), who unemotionally requires her signature on a legal document which will allow the money allotted for Angelica's dowry to pass to her sister on her forthcoming marriage. Suor Angelica asks for news of her child and is told that the infant died two years ago. Angelica resolves to take her own life and concocts a poisonous liquid from various herbs. She prays that she may not die in mortal sin and, seemingly in answer to her prayer, the Virgin Mary appears in a vision, leading a little child towards her. She dies.

Gardelli conducts a beautifully paced reading, marked by effective characterization from the Hungarian cast (suggesting stage experience) and vivid, lifelike, digital sound. Ilona Tokody makes an attractively girlish-sounding Angelica, but above the stave her voice is shrill. The Zia Principessa of Eszter Póka is breathy and wobbly and not even formidable, the one unconvincing characterization.

Il Tabarro (complete) (see also under *Il Trittico*).
(M) **(*) BMG/RCA GD 60865 (2) [60865-2]. John Alldis Ch., New Philh. O, Leinsdorf –
    LEONCAVALLO: *I Pagliacci*. ***
    Michele (Sherrill Milnes), Giorgetta (Leontyne Price), Luigi (Plácido Domingo).
**(*) Ariola Eurodisc Dig. 258 403 [7775-2-RC]. Munich R. O, Patanè.
    Michele (Siegmund Nimsgern), Giorgetta (Ilona Tokody), Luigi (Giorgio Lamberti).

The unforgettably atmospheric colouring in Puccini's essay in Grand Guignol is beautifully
caught by the atmospheric RCA recording, made in Walthamstow Town Hall in 1971. The
opera takes place on Michele's barge, moored on the Seine with Notre Dame visible in the
distance.

The story begins in the early evening. Stevedores are finishing a job on the boat and Giorgetta,
Michele's wife, suggests that they be offered a drink before they go. Michele tries to kiss his wife
but she merely offers her cheek, and he disconsolately leaves for the shore. The men crowd
round her, and an organ-grinder plays a catchy dance tune. One of the workers, Tinca, offers
himself as a dancing partner, but another, Luigi, seeing how clumsy Tinca is, takes his place.
Michele reappears as the dancing ends. A trip to Rouen is planned and Tinca, Talpa and Luigi
are to come along.

A song-seller on the shore is trying to sell his ballads and he sings a song about Mimi – which
gives Puccini a chance to quote from *La Bohème*. Frugola, Talpa's wife (a rag-picker), arrives
with her day's pickings and she talks to Giorgetta of her beloved cat. The stevedores come up
from below and they drink together. Talpa and Frugola dream of owning the cottage in the
country they will never be able to afford. Giorgetta, too, would like to give up their nomadic
existence and remembers earlier happiness in Paris.

Now she and Luigi are alone and their mutual passion flares up. She warns him that Michele
will soon return. He does but, when he goes into the cabin, the lovers declare their feelings again.
They plan an assignation for an hour later; Giorgetta will light a match to indicate that the coast
(or, rather, the boat) is clear. Luigi departs, and when Michele again tries to caress his wife he is
rebuffed and told they are both getting old. Nothing has been the same since their child died.

Giorgetta goes to bed and Michele curses his wife as a whore. He realizes she is still dressed
and agonizes over who her lover can be. He lights his pipe with a match. Luigi, seeing the agreed
signal, boards the barge and Michele seizes him by the throat and forces out his confession; then
he strangles him, swiftly wrapping the body in his cloak.

Giorgetta comes back in, disturbed by the noise. She apologizes for her earlier coldness and
asks to come closer to her husband. As she does so, he allows the body to fall by undoing his
cloak. He seizes his wife and pushes her against her dead lover's face.

Leontyne Price may not be ideally cast as the bargemaster's wife, but she is fully in character,
even though she does not point word-meanings in enough detail. Sherrill Milnes is rather young-
sounding for the bargemaster, but he sings memorably in the climactic aria, *Nulla silenzio*,
sustaining an unusually slow tempo. Plácido Domingo makes a fresh-voiced and well-
characterized young stevedore, while Leinsdorf is at his most sympathetic, and the refinement of
the New Philharmonia playing is an added attraction. The CD transfer increases the sense of
presence, yet retains the ambience. A full translation is provided.

Puccini's *Il Tabarro* also comes in a powerful performance from Munich forces under Patanè,
a co-production between Ariola Eurodisc and Bavarian Radio. Patanè in his larger-than-life
direction may at times run the risk of exaggerating the melodrama, but the result is richly
enjoyable, less delicately atmospheric than it can be in its dark picture of the Seine under the
bridges of Paris, but satisfyingly red-blooded. Ilona Tokody, already well known from
Hungaroton opera sets, makes a powerful, strongly projected Giorgetta, somewhat showing up
the relative weakness of the tenor, Giorgio Lamberti, as her lover, Luigi. His over-emphatic
underlining mars his legato, but the main love-duet comes over with gutsy strength.

Siegmund Nimsgern makes a powerful Michele, a shade too explosive in the climactic final
aria, but generally firm and clean in his projection, losing nothing in conviction by the un-
Italianate timbre of the voice, rather making the character more sinister. The full and brilliant
recording has voices set convincingly on a believable stage and well balanced against the
orchestra, though it is a pity that the 51 minutes' span brings only two tracks, one for each scene,
where separate indexing of sections should have been a high priority. The single disc comes with
libretto in a double-disc jewel-box.

Tosca (complete).
⊛ *** EMI CDS7 47175-8 (2) [Ang. CDCB 47174]. La Scala, Milan, Ch. and O, De Sabata.
    Tosca (Maria Callas), Cavaradossi (Giuseppe Di Stefano), Scarpia (Tito Gobbi).
(M) *** Decca 421 670-2 (2) [id.]. V. State Op. Ch., VPO, Karajan.
    Tosca (Leontyne Price), Cavaradossi (Giuseppe Di Stefano), Scarpia (Giuseppe Taddei).
*** DG Dig. 431 775-2 (2). ROHCG Ch., Philh. O, Sinopoli.
    Tosca (Mirella Freni), Cavaradossi (Plácido Domingo), Scarpia (Samuel Ramey).
*** DG 413 815-2 (2) [id.]. German Op. Ch., BPO, Karajan.
    Tosca (Katia Ricciarelli), Cavaradossi (José Carreras), Scarpia (Ruggero Raimondi).
(B) *** Ph. 438 359-2 (2) [id.]. ROHCG Ch. and O, C. Davis.
    Tosca (Montserrat Caballé), Cavaradossi (José Carreras), Scarpia (Ingvar Wixell).
**(*) Decca Dig. 414 597-2 (2) [id.]. WNO Ch., Nat. PO, Solti.
    Tosca (Kiri Te Kanawa), Cavaradossi (Giacomo Aragall), Scarpia (Leo Nucci).
**(*) EMI Dig. CDS7 49364-2 (2) [Ang. CDCB 49364]; (B) CfP *TC-CFPD 4715*. Amb. Op. Ch.,
    St Clement Danes School Boys' Ch., Philh. O, Levine.
    Tosca (Renata Scotto), Cavaradossi (Plácido Domingo), Scarpia (Renato Bruson).
Withdrawn: (M) (***) EMI mono CHS7 63338-2 (2) [Ang. CDHB 63338]. Rome Op. Ch. & O,
    Fabritiis.
    Tosca (Maria Caniglia), Cavaradossi (Beniamino Gigli), Scarpia (Armando Borgioli).
(M) ** BMG/RCA GD 84514 (2) [RCA 4514-2-RG]. Rome Op. Ch. & O, Leinsdorf.
    Tosca (Zinka Milanov), Cavaradossi (Jussi Bjoerling), Scarpia (Leonard Warren).
(M) ** Decca 411 871-2 (2) [id.]. St Cecilia Ac., Rome, Ch. & O, Molinari-Pradelli.
    Tosca (Renata Tebaldi), Cavaradossi (Mario Del Monaco), Scarpia (George London).
** Decca 414 036-2 (2) [id.]. Wandsworth School Boys' Ch., L. Op. Ch., Nat. PO, Rescigno.
    Tosca (Mirella Freni), Cavaradossi (Luciano Pavarotti), Scarpia (Sherrill Milnes).
(M) ** EMI CMS7 69974-2 (2) [Ang. CDMB 69974]. Paris Op. Ch. & Conservatoire O, Prêtre.
    Tosca (Maria Callas), Cavaradossi (Carlo Bergonzi), Scarpia (Tito Gobbi).
(B) *(*) Naxos Dig. 8. 660001/2 [id.]. Slovak Philharmonic Ch., Slovak R. SO (Bratislava),
    Alexander Rahbari.
    Tosca (Nelly Miricioiu), Cavaradossi (Giorgio Lamberti), Scarpia (Silvano Carroli).
* Sony Dig. S2K 45847 (2) [id.]. Hungarian State R. & TV Ch. & State O, Tilson Thomas.
    Tosca (Eva Marton), Cavaradossi (José Carreras), Scarpia (Juan Pons).

Puccini's *Tosca* is based on a melodrama by Sardou, but Puccini enhanced its dramatic force by creating three-dimensional characters – even Baron Scarpia, the Chief of Police, is far more than the conventional villain lusting after the heroine – while the torture scene in Act II, although unpleasant, is the more acceptable for being kept offstage.

The opera opens in the Rome church of Sant'Andrea della Valle. An escaped political prisoner, Angelotti, runs in, unkempt and exhausted. Under the image of the Virgin he finds a key, left for him by his sister, the Marchesa Attavanti. He opens the door of the family chapel and disappears within. The sacristan enters and is surprised that Cavaradossi, the painter, is not there. The Angelus sounds and Cavaradossi enters and uncovers his unfinished painting at the back of the church. The sacristan views it uneasily; it resembles a lady he has often seen praying in the chapel. Cavaradossi tells him the painting is to be of Mary Magdalene and that he has used the Marchesa Attavanti as a model, but as he paints he studies a miniature of Tosca. The sacristan leaves and Angelotti, thinking the church is empty, re-emerges. He sees Cavaradossi and recognizes him as a supporter of his own Republican party.

Tosca's voice is heard outside and Cavaradossi rushes Angelotti back into the chapel with a basket of food prepared for himself. As she enters, Tosca suspects her lover is not alone: perhaps he was with another woman; she is desperately jealous. When she sees a likeness of the marchesa in the painting, she is even more suspicious, and Cavaradossi has great difficulty in reassuring her. But he declares his love ardently and they arrange to meet again later that night.

After she leaves, Cavaradossi lets Angelotti out of the chapel. (He had taken part in an abortive uprising to make Rome a republic.) Cavaradossi arranges to hide him in his villa and will take him there immediately. A cannon shot is heard, denoting that a prisoner's escape has been discovered, and the pair hurry off. The sacristan returns and Scarpia enters with Spoletta, his police henchman, who questions the sacristan about the unlocked Attavanti Chapel.

They find a fan belonging to the marchesa and the empty food basket, and Scarpia realizes that Angelotti is being helped by Cavaradossi. Tosca returns and is puzzled by Cavaradossi's absence. Scarpia shows her the fan and suggests that Cavaradossi has gone to meet its owner, the marchesa. Tosca's jealousy flairs up and she rushes off to Cavaradossi's villa with Spoletta following. The church fills, a *Te Deum* is sung in which Scarpia joins while he considers his own objectives, the death of Angelotti and the possession of Tosca.

In his study in the Farnese Palace, Scarpia sends a note to Tosca asking her to come and see him after her performance that evening. Spoletta has followed her to Cavaradossi's villa, but an extensive search has not revealed Angelotti. Cavaradossi is brought in and questioned. Tosca now enters and embraces her lover and he whispers to her, asking her not to reveal what she knows. Scarpia has Cavaradossi taken away to be tortured until he reveals Angelotti's whereabouts. As he questions Tosca, Cavaradossi's cries of pain can be heard, and they increase in intensity.

Unable to remain silent any longer, Tosca reveals that Angelotti is concealed in a well in the garden of the villa. Cavaradossi is brought in, badly injured from his treatment. Scarpia sends Spoletta off to find Angelotti and Cavaradossi realizes that Tosca has betrayed them both, and he turns from her. A messenger now arrives to announce that Napoleon has defeated the royal troops and Cavaradossi cries out, 'Vittoria!' condemning himself as a republican sympathizer. He is taken away.

Tosca pleads with Scarpia to spare Cavaradossi's life and he cynically agrees to do so if she will give herself to him. She refuses. Spoletta now reports that Angelotti killed himself when he was about to be recaptured and Scarpia – calmly eating his supper – repeats to Tosca his price for Cavaradossi's life and freedom. Tosca has no choice but to consent, and Scarpia writes a letter of safe-conduct and orders Spoletta to stage a supposed mock execution for Cavaradossi 'as in the manner of Count Palmieri'. Spoletta goes off and, left alone with Scarpia, Tosca picks up a knife and plunges it into his heart. She takes the safe-conduct pass from his hand, places a crucifix on his body and four candles round it. Then she quietly leaves the room.

Cavaradossi is to be executed on the ramparts of the Castle St Angelo on a beautiful starry night. He enters, writes a last letter to Tosca and thinks about the past. Then Tosca rushes in with the safe-conduct and tells him about the 'mock execution'; she emphasizes that he must fall down at the shots and not stand up again too soon.

The firing squad arrives and she watches while they shoot him. The soldiers go off and Cavaradossi still does not move. The execution was real. At that moment Spoletta arrives: Scarpia's death has been discovered. Tosca pushes him away and springs up on to the parapet, throwing herself to her death below, shrieking that she will meet Scarpia in front of God.

There has never been a finer recorded performance of *Tosca* than Callas's first, with Victor de Sabata conducting and Tito Gobbi as Scarpia. One mentions the prima donna first because, in this of all roles, she was able to identify totally with the heroine and turn her into a great tragic figure, not merely the cipher of Sardou's original melodrama. Gobbi too makes the unbelievably villainous police chief into a genuinely three-dimensional character, and Di Stefano as the hero, Cavaradossi, was at his finest. The conducting of De Sabata is spaciously lyrical as well as sharply dramatic, and the mono recording is superbly balanced in Walter Legge's fine production. The CD remastering brings an extension of range at both ends of the spectrum, with a firm, full bass to balance the extra brightness and clarity in the treble. Though there is inevitably less spaciousness than in a real stereo recording, there is no lack of bloom, even on the violins, and the voices are gloriously caught. Only in the big *Te Deum* scene at the end of Act I does the extra clarity reveal a hint of congestion, and this is minimal.

The Decca/Karajan set from the early 1960s sounds splendid in its digitally remastered CD format, with the voices vividly projected within a warm ambience; the whole effect combines presence and atmosphere in an ideal way. Offered at mid-price, this for many will be an obvious first choice. Karajan deserves equal credit with the principal singers for the vital, imaginative performance, recorded in Vienna. Some idea of its quality may be gained from the passage at the end of Act I, just before Scarpia's *Te Deum*. Karajan takes a speed far slower than usual, but there is an intensity which takes one vividly to the Church of San Andrea while at the same time building the necessary tension for the depiction of Scarpia's villainy. Taddei himself has a marvellously wide range of tone-colour, and, though he cannot quite match the Gobbi snarl, he has almost every other weapon in his armoury. Leontyne Price is at the peak of her form and Di Stefano sings most sensitively. The sound of the Vienna orchestra is enthralling – both more refined and richer than usual in a Puccini opera.

With a trio of soloists that could hardly be more starry, what above all marks out the DG version as exceptional is the conducting of Sinopoli. Even more than the Puccini operas he had previously recorded – always with spacious, finely moulded treatment – *Tosca* seems to match his musical personality. The big chords of the Scarpia motif at the very start have never come over with greater power than here, helped by DG recording of spectacular weight and range, with an involving sense of immediacy. Sinopoli then sets the mood of each section of the opera very vividly, often pointing rhythms to lighten the texture, as in the Act I love-duet or in moments when Scarpia affects to conceal his sinister side.

Not that Ramey's is a conventional portrait of the evil police chief. The natural timbre of his glorious bass is noble, with no snarl in it. Inevitably one misses many of the sinister or villainous overtones, but the role has rarely been sung with more sheer beauty, with such a climax as the *Te Deum* at the end of Act I sounding thrilling in its firmness and power. Domingo's heroic power is formidable too, and, unlike many of his opera recordings for DG, this one presents him in close-up, not distanced. Freni's is not naturally a Tosca voice, and her singing here is less firm and even than it was on her earlier Decca recording, but it is still a powerful, heartfelt performance. Among the others the Welsh bass, Bryn Terfel, makes a formidable international opera recording début as Angelotti, clear-cut and positive.

Karajan's later, superbly unified reading for DG presents *Tosca* as very grand opera indeed, melodrama at its most searingly powerful. For Karajan, the police chief, Scarpia, seems to be the central character, and his unexpected choice of singer, a full bass, Raimondi, helps to show why, for this is no small-time villain but a man who in full confidence has a vein of nobility in him – as in the *Te Deum* at the end of Act I or the closing passage of the big solo addressed to Tosca, *Già mi dicon venal*. Detailed illumination of words is most powerful, and Karajan's coaching is evident too in the contribution of Katia Ricciarelli – another singer who had not taken the role on stage before the recording. She is not the most individual of Toscas, but the beauty of singing is consistent, with *Vissi d'arte* outstanding at a very slow tempo indeed. Carreras is also subjected to slow Karajan tempi in his big arias and, though the recording brings out an unevenness in the voice (this is not as sweet a sound as in the performance he recorded with Sir Colin Davis for Philips), it is still a powerful, stylish one. The recording is rich and full, with the stage picture clearly established and the glorious orchestral textures beautifully caught. The CD transfer improves definition but also, and more importantly, increases the feeling of spaciousness, putting more air round the voices and adding bloom to the orchestral sound. The wide dynamic range, however, means that care has to be taken to select a playing level which strikes a compromise between general immediacy and containment of the expansive climaxes.

Pacing the music naturally and sympathetically, Sir Colin Davis proves a superb Puccinian, one who not only presents Puccini's drama with richness and force but gives the score the musical strength of a great symphony. Davis rarely if ever chooses idiosyncratic tempi, and his manner is relatively straight; but it remains a strong and understanding reading as well as a refreshing one. In this the quality of the singing from a cast of unusual consistency plays an important part. Caballé may not be as sharply jealous a heroine as her keenest rivals but, with the purity of *Vissi d'arte* coming as a key element in her interpretation, she still presents Tosca as a formidable siren-figure ('*Mia sirena*' being Cavaradossi's expression of endearment).

Carreras reinforces his reputation as a tenor of unusual artistry as well as of superb vocal powers. Though Wixell is not ideally well focused as Scarpia, not at all Italianate of tone, he presents a completely credible lover-figure, not just the lusting ogre of convention. The 1976 analogue recording is full as well as refined, bringing out the beauties of Puccini's scoring. It is given a strikingly successful CD transfer, with three-dimensional placing of voices. The overall effect is more consistent and certainly more spacious than on the remastered Karajan set – especially noticeable at the big choral climax at the end of Act I. As a bargain reissue in the Philips Duo series, this is now very competitive indeed.

Sir Georg Solti's is a colourful and robust reading of Puccini's great melodrama, recorded in exceptionally vivid digital sound with a heroine who may not be a natural Tosca but who has magnetic star quality. Rarely has Solti phrased Italian melody so consistently *con amore*, his fiercer side subdued but with plenty of power when required. Even so, the timing is not always quite spontaneous-sounding, with transitions occasionally rushed. Scarpia's entry is presented with power but too little of the necessary menace. Nucci in that role sings strongly but not very characterfully. Aragall as Cavaradossi produces a glorious stream of heroic tone, vocally reliable from first to last, and the incidental characters are strongly cast too, with Spiro Malas giving an unusually resonant and firm account of the Sacristan's music, not at all doddery.

But the principal *raison d'être* of the set must be the casting of Dame Kiri as the jealous opera-singer. Her admirers will – as with Aragall – relish the glorious stream of beautiful tone, but the jealous side of Tosca's character is rather muted. Her recognition of the fan shown to her by Scarpia, *E L'Attavanti!*, has no snarl of anger in it, even though she later conveys real pain in her half-tones, as Scarpia's poison begins to work. One distinctive point in the unusually vivid recording is that in the Prelude to Act III the bells have actually been recorded from churches and clocks, not conventionally in the orchestra, though that adds less atmosphere than you might expect.

With extreme speeds, both fast and slow, and fine playing from the Philharmonia Orchestra, Levine directs a red-blooded performance which underlines the melodrama. Domingo here reinforces his claim to be the finest Cavaradossi today, while the clean-cut, incisive singing of Renato Bruson presents a powerful if rather young-sounding Scarpia. Renata Scotto's voice is in many ways ideally suited to the role of Tosca, certainly in its timbre and colouring; as caught on record, however, the upper register is often squally. The digital recording is full and forward. This has much to offer in its CD format; but readers will note that it is also available in a chunky tape-box on Classics for Pleasure at a fraction of the cost and sounding very well, if without quite the presence and range of the compact discs; on a car journey, however, it would prove ideal, and the value is obvious.

Collectors with long memories will be nostalgic about what inevitably, if illogically, must be described as 'the Gigli *Tosca*'; in the days of 78s, it was one of the glories of Puccini representation in the catalogue. The transfer brings astonishingly vivid sound, as in the rasping trombones on the opening Scarpia chords, along with a fine sense of presence. The great tenor dominates the whole performance, his facial expressiveness consistently beaming out through his voice, while Maria Caniglia, not characterful enough to be a memorable Tosca, sings with warmth and total commitment. Armando Borgioli is a young-sounding, virile Scarpia, forceful and upstanding rather than sinister. The conducting of Fabritiis brings far more natural and convincing timing than you find on many a more recent recording.

At mid-price in RCA's Victor Opera Series, Leinsdorf's version makes a fair bargain, despite dated 1950s recording and the conductor's heavy style. Jussi Bjoerling was at the peak of his form as Cavaradossi; though Zinka Milanov was past her best and was sometimes stressed by the role, there is much beautiful singing here from a great soprano who recorded all too little. Leonard Warren was another characterful veteran, but the furry edge to his voice makes him a less-than-sinister Scarpia.

Tebaldi's early stereo *Tosca* is outclassed by most later versions, yet, with a voice naturally suited to the role, she is splendidly dramatic and often sings very affectingly. The set is well worth hearing for her classic assumption of the role, but unfortunately the other two principals do not match her.

The action of the drama is caught superbly in the vividly recorded Decca version under Nicola Rescigno. The three principals were originally lined up for a Karajan recording on Decca, but plans turned in other directions. Pavarotti is a bright-eyed Cavaradossi, but it is only in Act III that the voice acquires its full magic. As Tosca, Freni sounds rather taxed, so that even *Vissi d'arte* produces her stressed tone rather than even, lyrical sound. Milnes as Scarpia gives a fresh, direct performance, with words finely enunciated, a good characterization. The big snag is Rescigno's conducting, for his control of rubato sounds forced and unspontaneous, strange from an Italian conductor. At full price this is hardly competitive, except perhaps for Pavarotti fans.

The Callas stereo *Tosca* is exciting and disappointing in roughly predictable proportions. There are few points of improvement over the old mono set, with Callas in the title-role and De Sabata conducting far more imaginatively than Prêtre here. When it comes to vocal reliability, the comparison is just as damaging. Gobbi is magnificent still, but no more effective than he was before, and Bergonzi's Cavaradossi, intelligent and attractive, is not helped by an unfavourable recording balance. Callas's mono set remains the one to have.

The Naxos version at budget price is worth hearing for the vibrant and strong performance of Nelly Miricioiu as Tosca, a soprano who deserves to be recorded far more. She is not helped by the principals around her and least of all by the conductor, Alexander Rahbari, whose preference for slow speeds undermines any tension the soprano builds up. Yet she both brings echoes of Maria Callas in her dramatic moments and gives a beautifully thoughtful and inward account of *Vissi d'arte*, finely controlled at a spacious speed. Giorgio Lamberti is a coarse-grained Cavaradossi, hammy in his underlining, and Silvano Carroli, despite a fine, weighty voice, is a rough-edged Scarpia, too often shouting rather than vocalizing. Good digital sound and refined playing.

Eva Marton makes a coarse and often unsteady Tosca on the Sony set. José Carreras sings well as Cavaradossi, but not as well as on his two previous versions, for Karajan and Colin Davis. Juan Pons is a lightweight Scarpia, not sinister enough. Such vocal shortcomings undermine the thrust of Tilson Thomas's direction, making it a disappointing version all round.

Tosca: highlights.
*** DG Dig. 437 547-2 [id.] (from above recording with Freni, Domingo, Ramey; cond. Sinopoli).
*** DG 423 113-2 [id.] (from above recording with Ricciarelli, Carreras, Raimondi; cond. Karajan).
*** EMI Dig. CDC7 54324-2 [id.] (from above recording with Scotto, Domingo, Bruson; cond. Levine).
**(*) Decca Dig. 421 611-2 [id.] (from above recording with Te Kanawa, Aragall, Nucci; cond. Solti).
(M) ** Decca 421 888-2; *421 888-4* [id.] (from above recording with Freni, Pavarotti, Milnes; cond. Rescigno).

Over an hour of excerpts is offered from the splendid DG set with Domingo, Ramey and Sinopoli on top form, Freni perhaps marginally less so. This selection is at full price.

So too is the selection from Karajan's powerful, closely recorded Berlin version, which is also welcome. The breadth of Karajan's direction is well represented in the longer excerpts – for example the opening of Act I up to the end of the love-duet and Act III from *E lucevan le stelle* to the end of the opera. There is also Tosca's *Vissi d'arte*, but Scarpia's music is under-represented (the torture scene of Act II plus the duet with Tosca). That is a pity, when Raimondi made such a distinctive Scarpia with his dark bass timbre. Bright vivid sound.

Domingo first recorded *Tosca* for EMI rather than DG, and Cavaradossi is one of his most impressive roles. So this selection fits in well with DG's 'Domingo Edition', although (unlike that series of highlights) it is issued at full price and, even so, offers only 65 minutes of excerpts, although all the key items are here.

The generous selection from Solti's robust and colourful set will be of interest mainly to fans of Dame Kiri Te Kanawa. She sings with glorious tone, as does Aragall.

A not especially generous (63 minutes) selection from Rescigno's 1978 Decca set is mainly notable for offering a sampler of Pavarotti's assumption of the role of Cavaradossi and *E lucevan le stelle* is undoubtedly the highlight. As Tosca, Freni sounds rather taxed, so that even *Vissi d'arte* produces her stressed tone rather than even, lyrical sound. Milnes is quite well represented in the Act II excerpts: his Scarpia is fresh and direct, with words finely enunciated, a fine characterization. However, Rescigno's conducting, for all his control of rubato, sounds forced and unspontaneous, strange from an Italian conductor. The Decca sound has characteristic brilliance and atmosphere.

Il Trittico: (i) *Il Tabarro;* (ii) *Suor Angelica;* (iii) *Gianni Schicchi.*
(M) *** EMI mono/stereo CMS7 64165-2 (3) [Ang. CDMC 64165]. Rome Op. Ch. & O; (i) Bellezza; (ii) Serafin; (iii) Santini.
    (i) Michele (Tito Gobbi), Giorgetta (Margaret Mas), Luigi (Giancinto Prandelli).
    (ii) Suor Angelica (Victoria De los Angeles), La Zia Principessa (Fedora Barbieri).
    (iii) Gianni Schicchi (Tito Gobbi), Lauretta (Victoria De los Angeles), Rinuccio (Carlo Del Monte).
(M) **(*) Sony M3K 79312 (3) [M3K 35912]. (ii) Desborough School Ch.; (iii) Amb. Op. Ch.; (i; ii) Nat. PO; (iii) LSO, Maazel.
    (i) Michele (Ingvar Wixell), Giorgetta (Renata Scotto), Luigi (Plácido Domingo).
    (ii) Suor Angelica (Renata Scotto), Princess (Marilyn Horne), Abbess (Patricia Payne), Mistress of the Novices (Ann Howard), Suor Genovieffa (Ileana Cotrubas), Infirmary Sister (Elizabeth Bainbridge).
    (iii) Gianni Schicchi (Tito Gobbi), Lauretta (Ileana Cotrubas), Rinuccio (Plácido Domingo).
(M) **(*) RCA/Eurodisc Dig. GD 69043 (3) [7775-2-RC: *Il Tabarro*; 7806-2-RC: *Suor Angelica*; 7751-2-RC: *Gianni Schicchi*]. Bav. R. Ch., Munich R. O, Patanè.
    (i) Michele (Siegmund Nimsgern), Giorgetta (Ilona Tokody), Luigi (Giorgio Lamberti).
    (ii) Suor Angelica (Lucia Popp), Princess (Marjana Lipovšek), Abbess (Marga Schiml), Mistress of the Novices (Birgit Calm).
    (iii) Gianni Schicchi (Rolando Panerai), Lauretta (Helen Donath), Rinuccio (Peter Seiffert).
(M) ** Decca 411 665-2 (3). Maggio Musicale Fiorentino Ch. & O, Gardelli.
    (i) Michele (Robert Merrill), Giorgetta (Renata Tebaldi), Luigi (Mario Del Monaco).
    (ii) Suor Angelica (Renata Tebaldi), Princess (Giulietta Simionato), Abbess / 2nd Lay Sister (Lucia Danieli), Mistress of the Novices / Infirmary Sister (Anna Di Stasio).

(iii) Gianni Schicchi (Fernando Corena), Lauretta (Renata Tebaldi), Rinuccio (Agostino Lazzari).

Puccini's three one-Act operas show him musically and dramatically at the peak of his achievement. They are balanced like the movements of a concerto: *Il Tabarro*, sombre in its portrait of the cuckolded bargemaster, but made attractive by the vividness of the atmosphere and the sweetness of the love music; *Suor Angelica*, a lyrical slow movement with its picture of a nunnery, verging on the syrupy but never quite falling; and *Gianni Schicchi*, easily the most brilliant and witty one-Act comedy in the whole field of opera.

The classic EMI set of *Il Trittico* has dominated the catalogue since the earliest days of LP. This vividly atmospheric and brilliantly contrasted group of one-Acters has never been more richly and characterfully presented on record, with Tito Gobbi giving two of his ripest characterizations. The central role of the cuckolded bargemaster, Michele, in *Il Tabarro*, inspires him to one of his very finest performances on record. Though this version of Puccini's Grand Guignol opera is a mono recording, not stereo, it conveys the sense of horror far more keenly than any, with Gobbi's voice vividly caught on CD.

The central panel of the triptych, *Suor Angelica*, brings a glowing performance from Victoria de los Angeles, giving a most affecting portrayal of Angelica, the nun ill-treated by her noble family, with Fedora Barbieri formidable as her unfeeling aunt, the Zia Principessa.

De los Angeles reappears, charmingly girlish as Lauretta, in *Gianni Schicchi*, where the high comedy has never fizzed so deliciously outside the opera house. She and Gobbi come together just as characterfully in this final opera. Though Gobbi's incomparable baritone is not by nature comic-sounding, he is unequalled as Schicchi, sardonically manipulating the mourning relatives of Buoso Donati as he frames a new will for them. Puccini, the master of tragedy, here emerges a supreme master of comic timing too. Only *Gianni Schicchi*, recorded last in 1958, is in genuine and excellent stereo; *Il Tabarro* (1955) and *Suor Angelica* (1957) are mono, but all the transfers are expert, clear and convincingly balanced.

Maazel's performances of the three *Trittico* operas together underline his consistency. *Il Tabarro* may most seriously lack atmosphere, but his directness is certainly refreshing, and in the other two operas it results in powerful readings; the opening of *Gianni Schicchi*, for example, has a sharp, almost Stravinskian bite. In the first two operas, Scotto's performances have a commanding dominance, presenting her at her finest.

In *Gianni Schicchi* the veteran Tito Gobbi gives an amazing performance, in almost every way as fine as his EMI recording of 20 years earlier – and in some ways this is even more compelling. The generally close recording has a full range and the immediacy is increased by the vivid CD transfers. The only snag is the lack of cueing; there is only one track for the whole of *Il Tabarro* and only two each for *Gianni Schicchi* and *Suor Angelica*, the second in each case being used to indicate the main soprano aria.

Patanè's Munich recordings of the three *Trittico* one-Acters first appeared separately, but here come, attractively packaged, on three mid-price CDs. Patanè directs consistently well-paced, idiomatic performances of all three operas, well played and atmospherically recorded. Neither Lucia Popp as Angelica nor Marjana Lipovšek as the vindictive Zia Principessa is ideally cast in the central opera of the triptych – the one overstressed, the other sounding too young – but these are both fine artists who sing with consistent imagination. Nimsgern as Michele in *Tabarro* gives a memorable, well-projected performance, and so does the characterful Rolando Panerai as Schicchi in the comic final opera, both central to the success of the performances. Though the cueing on CD is not generous, it is far more helpful than on the rival Maazel set. In the USA the three operas are available separately but at premium price.

On grounds of recording, the Decca set remains very impressive, but the performances are variable. Fernando Corena's Schicchi is too coarse-grained, both vocally and dramatically. This is *buffo*-bass style with too much parlando 'acting'. Nor is Tebaldi entirely at home in the open-eyed part of the young Lauretta, though she sings *O mio babbino caro* very sweetly. She is more at home in the role of Sister Angelica and gives a rich-voiced and affecting portrayal, only slightly troubled by the top notes at the end.

Simionato makes a fine, firm Zia Principessa: one can really believe in her relentlessness, while Gardelli keeps the performance moving forward gently but firmly, and in a somewhat static piece this is most important. The scene of *Il Tabarro* is set on a barge on the banks of the Seine, in Paris, and though the Decca production team capture all of Puccini's background effects, the result has not so much a Parisian flavour as the acoustic of an empty opera-house. Merrill sings very strongly as the cuckolded bargemaster, and Tebaldi and del Monaco are good in a conventional, whole-hogging Italian way. The recording has been effectively remastered and sounds a shade drier than when first issued, but the voices are vividly projected on CD, and the sense of atmosphere remains.

Turandot (complete).

⊛ *** Decca 414 274-2 (2) [id.]. Alldis Ch., Wandsworth School Boys' Ch., LPO, Mehta.
  Turandot (Joan Sutherland), Calaf (Luciano Pavarotti), Liù (Montserrat Caballé), Timur (Nicolai Ghiaurov), Emperor (Peter Pears).

(M) *** EMI CMS7 69327-2 (2) [Ang. CDMB 69327]. Rome Op. Ch. & O, Molinari-Pradelli.
  Turandot (Birgit Nilsson), Calaf (Franco Corelli), Liù (Renata Scotto), Timur (Bonaldo Giaiotti), Emperor (Angelo Mercuriali).

(***) EMI mono CDS7 47971-8 (2) [Ang. CDCB 47971]. La Scala, Milan, Ch. & O, Serafin.
  Turandot (Maria Callas), Calaf (Eugenio Fernandi), Liù (Elisabeth Schwarzkopf), Timur (Nicola Zaccaria), Emperor (Giuseppe Nessi).

**(*) DG Dig. 423 855-2 (2) [id.]. V. State Op. Ch., V. Boys' Ch., VPO, Karajan.
  Turandot (Katia Ricciarelli), Calaf (Plácido Domingo), Liù (Barbara Hendricks), Timur (Ruggero Raimondi), Emperor (Piero De Palma).

(M) ** Sony M2K 39160 (2) [id.]. V. State Op. Ch. & O, Maazel.
  Turandot (Eva Marton), Calaf (José Carreras), Liù (Katia Ricciarelli), Timur (John Paul Bogart), Emperor (Waldemar Kmentt).

(M) *(*) Decca 433 761-2 (2) [id.]. Santa Cecilia, Rome, Ch. & O, Erede.
  Turandot (Inge Borkh), Calaf (Mario Del Monaco), Liù (Renata Tebaldi), Timur (Nicola Zaccaria), Ping (Fernando Corena), Pang (Mario Carlin), Pong (Renato Ercolani).

Puccini left his last opera unfinished, but his pupil, Franco Alfano, completed the final scene very effectively, using the composer's draft sketches, and the result provides a remarkably vivid theatrical experience.

The Princess Turandot of Peking will marry only if a royal suitor can solve her three chosen riddles. The Prince of Persia has just failed to do so and death is his reward. The crowd call for the executioner, Pu-Fin-Pao, to come forth and do his work. In the crush an old man falls to the ground and Liù, a slave girl, calls for help. The unknown prince recognizes the old man as Timur, his father; both are fugitives from Tartary, where a usurper has taken the throne.

Timur had thought his son, Calaf, was dead and, knowing the boy's life was forfeit if discovered, he has kept his birth and name a secret. He now tells his son of his flight. Calaf asks Liù why she risked so much for the old man and is told in reply that once in the palace he had smiled upon her.

As the moon rises, the Prince of Persia is led in procession up the hill to his execution, and the crowd changes its mood and expresses sympathy. Voices calling for his pardon are heard, including that of Calaf. But Turandot appears on the balcony and makes a decisive gesture. Death for the unfortunate prince! Calaf is struck by Turandot's great beauty and desires her. He will submit to the test. His father and Liù, who loves him, beg him to withdraw, and the three Ministers of the Royal Household, Ping, Pang and Pong, who wear grotesque masks, also try to dissuade him.

Calaf calls Turandot's name three times and sounds the three strokes on the gong that commit him as a suitor. Ping, Pang and Pong prepare simultaneously for both a wedding and a funeral, whichever may be required, and reminisce about happier days before Turandot's bloody reign. The crowds gather in the square and the Emperor Altoum, on a huge throne, dominates the scene. He too, in ailing voice, tries to talk Calaf out of the hopeless competition.

Turandot appears, clad in gold. She explains that her savage edict is in revenge for an event a thousand years earlier, when a princess was taken away and cruelly ravished by a barbarian. She too suggests that Calaf should withdraw but he refuses. She sets the first riddle and he answers promptly, 'Hope.' He takes longer to answer the second, but his answer is correct: 'Blood.'

The third riddle, 'What is the ice that gives you fire?', brings even longer hesitation, but then he answers, 'Turandot.' He has triumphed. The princess protests wildly when the crowd insists that her oath is binding. But she asks whether her suitor is prepared to take her by force. Now Calaf in turn offers Turandot a riddle. He gives her the opportunity to escape her obligation: if she can discover his name by morning, he is prepared to die.

From the palace gardens heralds can be heard proclaiming Turandot's decree that none shall sleep tonight (*Nessun dorma*) on pain of death, until the prince's name is discovered. Ping, Pang and Pong endeavour to bribe Calaf to abandon his suit, but he remains firm in his resolve. Soldiers drag in Timur and Liù, but the prince says they know nothing. Turandot is summoned.

Ping offers to torture the name from them. Liù now steps forward. She alone, not the old man, knows the name. Turandot asks her how she can endure torture and she replies that it is because of her love.

They are about to torture her again when she says she will speak and she does so directly to Turandot, declaring that Turandot will capitulate to the prince and that she herself must die. She seizes a dagger and kills herself at the prince's feet. Timur holds her hand tenderly as she dies, but the secret of the prince's name is still undisclosed. The crowd are repentant. (Puccini's music ends here.)

The prince and Turandot are now alone and he upbraids her for her cruelty. Then he impulsively snatches away her veil and kisses her passionately. Her thoughts of revenge evaporate, her spirit seems broken. She begs Calaf to go and take his secret with him. But he refuses and reveals his identity. In the throne room, Turandot assembles the courtiers in front of the emperor and declares, 'I have discovered the stranger's secret and his name is – Love.'

On CD the Mehta set, in vividness, clarity and immediacy of sound, brings an astonishing tribute to Decca engineering in the early 1970s. In every way it outshines the later, digital recordings of Karajan and Maazel, and the reading remains supreme. The role of Turandot, the icy princess, is not one that you would expect to be in Joan Sutherland's repertory, but here on record she gives an intensely revealing and appealing interpretation, making the character far more human and sympathetic than ever before. This is a character, armoured and unyielding in *In questa reggia*, whose final capitulation to love is a natural development, not an incomprehensible switch. Sutherland's singing is strong and beautiful, while Pavarotti gives a performance equally imaginative, beautiful in sound, strong on detail. To set Caballé against Sutherland was a daring idea, and it works superbly well; Pears as the Emperor is another imaginative choice. Mehta directs a gloriously rich and dramatic performance, superlatively recorded.

The EMI set brings Nilsson's second assumption on record of the role of Puccini's formidable princess. As an interpretation it is very similar to the earlier, RCA performance, but its impact is far more immediate, thanks to the conducting of Molinari-Pradelli – much warmer than Leinsdorf's for RCA – thanks also to the more forward if less refined recording quality. The climax of *In questa reggia* is far more telling when the conductor pushes forward beforehand with a natural – if unexaggerated – *stringendo*. There are many similar effects to notice. Corelli may not be the most sensitive prince in the world – Bjoerling is far better on detail – but the voice is in glorious condition. Scotto's Liù is very beautiful and characterful too. With vividly remastered sound, this makes an excellent mid-priced recommendation, though the documentation does not include an English translation.

Having Maria Callas, the most flashing-eyed of sopranos, as Turandot is – on record at least – the most natural piece of casting. With her the icy princess is not just an implacable man-hater but a highly provocative female. One quickly reads something of Callas's own underlying vulnerability into such a portrait, its tensions, the element of brittleness. In the arioso from Alfano's completion, *Del primo pianto*, the chesty way she addresses Calaf as *Straniero!* in the opening phrase is unforgettable in its continuing threat. With her the character seems so much more believably complex than with others. It was sad that, except at the very beginning of her career, Callas felt unable to sing the role in the opera house, but this 1957 recording is far more valuable than any memory of the past, one of her most thrillingly magnetic performances on disc. It is made the more telling, when Schwarzkopf provides a comparably characterful and distinctive portrait as Liù, sweet and wilting.

Even more than usual one regrets that the confrontation between princess and slave is so brief. Schwarzkopf's meticulous observance of dynamic markings in Liù's arias reinforces their fine-spun Straussian quality. Next to such sopranos, it was unkind of Walter Legge as producer to choose so relatively uncharacterful a tenor as Eugenio Fernandi as Calaf, but his timbre is pleasing enough. By contrast, Serafin's masterly conducting exactly matches the characterfulness of Callas and Schwarzkopf, with colour, atmosphere and dramatic point all commandingly presented. The Ping, Pang and Pong episode of Act II has rarely sparkled so naturally. With such a vivid performance the 1957 mono sound will for many, if not most, opera-lovers hardly matter. The CD transfer makes it satisfyingly full-bodied, not boxy, even though the acoustic is rather dry, with solo voices balanced forward and with the choral sound tending to overload at climaxes.

Karajan takes a characteristically spacious view of Puccini's last opera. His tempi are regularly slower than those in rival versions, yet his concentration is irresistible and he relishes the exotic colourings of the sound, just as he puts an unusual slant on the vocal colouring as well as the dramatic balance by his distinctive casting of the two contrasted heroines. Both the Liù of Barbara Hendricks and the Turandot of Katia Ricciarelli are more sensuously feminine than is usual. With her seductively golden tone, Hendricks is almost a sex-kitten, very different from the usual picture of a chaste slave-girl.

Ricciarelli is a far more vulnerable figure than one expects of the icy princess, and the very fact that the part strains her beyond reasonable vocal limits adds to the dramatic point, even if it subtracts from the musical joys. By contrast, Plácido Domingo is vocally superb, a commanding prince; and the rest of the cast presents star names even in small roles. The sound is full and brilliant, if at times rather close in the manner of DG engineers working in the Berlin Philharmonie. Ensemble is not always as crisp as one expects of Karajan with Berlin forces, though significantly the challenge of the manifestly less inspired completion of Alfano has him working at white heat. The compact discs bring added presence, although balance is not always good.

Turandot brings the warmest and most sensuous performance in Maazel's Puccini series, thanks in good measure to its being a live recording, made in September 1983 at the Vienna State Opera House. Applause and stage noises are often distracting, and the clarity of CD tends to make one notice them the more. Recording balances are often odd, with Carreras – in fine voice – suffering in both directions, sometimes disconcertingly distant, at others far too close. Karajan's Turandot here becomes Liù, and the result is predictably heavyweight, though the beat in her voice is only rarely apparent. The strengths and shortcomings of Eva Marton as the icy princess come out at the very start of *In questa reggia*. The big, dramatic voice is well controlled, but there is too little variation of tone, dynamic or expression; she rarely shades her voice down. In the closing Act, during the Alfano completion, Marton's confidence and command grow impressively, with her heroic tone ever more thrilling. Recommendable to those who relish a live performance. Annoyingly, the CDs contain no bands within the Acts.

Inge Borkh is not the most biting of princesses, and the early (1955) Decca recording is a little unkind to her upper register, bringing out the unevenness there. Tebaldi sings beautifully as Liù, but the characterization is rather too hefty. And Mario del Monaco is his own loud-voiced self as the stranger prince. What a wonderfully heroic voice this is, yet how consistently del Monaco seeks to use it with blundering lack of restraint. The Ping, Pang and Pong are excellent. There are undoubtedly enjoyable things here, but the performance overall lacks atmosphere and sheer vitality; nor does the singing match that on the other sets.

Turandot: excerpts.
Withdrawn: (M) (***) EMI mono CDH7 61074-2. Eva Turner, Giovanni Martinelli, Licia Albanese, Mafalda Favero, Giulio Tomei, Octave Dua, ROHCG Ch., LPO, Barbirolli.

The Références issue of Dame Eva Turner in extracts from *Turandot* has live recordings made at Covent Garden during the Coronation season of 1937, with Sir John Barbirolli conducting and with Giovanni Martinelli as a unique Calaf. For many years this was a legendary recording, debarred from official issue by copyright problems which were solved finally after half a century. These excerpts, recorded at two separate performances and fascinatingly duplicating most of the items, are vividly communicative, with the second performance in each pair marginally more spacious and helpful in sound, and generally warmer and more relaxed as a performance. Martinelli's heroic timbre may be an acquired taste, but he is stirringly convincing, and Dame Eva Turner gloriously confirms all the legends, even more commanding than in her earlier studio accounts of the big aria, *In questa reggia*. Keith Hardwick's excellent transfers, for all the obvious limitations of recording on stage at Covent Garden, give a superb sense of presence.

Turandot: highlights.
*** Decca 421 320-2; *421 320-4* [id.] (from above recording with Sutherland, Pavarotti; cond. Mehta).
(M) *** DG Dig. 435 409-2; *435 409-4* [id.] (from above recording with Ricciarelli, Domingo; cond. Karajan).
(M) *** EMI CD-EMX 2208; *TC-EMX 2208* (from above recording with Nilsson, Corelli, Scotto; cond. Molinari-Pradelli).
(M) **(*) EMI CDM7 63410-2; *EG 763410-4*. Montserrat Caballé, José Carreras, Mirella Freni, Paul Plishka, Michel Sénéchal, Rhine Op. Ch., Strasbourg PO, Lombard.

A generous and shrewdly chosen collection of excerpts from the glorious Decca set of *Turandot*. *Nessun dorma*, with Pavarotti at his finest, is here given a closing cadence for neatness. The vintage Decca sound is outstandingly full and vivid.

Domingo is at his very finest on DG, and he is exceptionally well represented in this 70-minute selection of highlights (part of the 'Domingo Edition'), as indeed is the chorus. The opera's narrative is cued with track references, which serves instead of a translation.

Nilsson's portrait of the icy princess on EMI is memorable and the Eminence selection offers some 69 minutes from the opera, including not only the major part of Turandot's music in Act III, but also the important arias of both Calaf and Liù. The recording is suitably atmospheric.

Caballé's Turandot is well worth having on disc, even if, like the others in EMI's Puccini highlights series, the selection (52 minutes) is far from generous. All the singers are recorded very close, which is not always flattering, and Lombard is not a very idiomatic Puccinian. But the combination of Caballé and Freni (as Liù) is a fascinating one: it works well dramatically, and not in the most predictable way.

Le Villi: complete.
(M) *** Sony MK 76890 [MK 36669]. Amb. Op. Ch., Nat. PO, Maazel.
   Guglielmo (Leo Nucci), Anna (Renata Scotto), Roberto (Plácido Domingo), Narrator (Tito Gobbi).

Le Villi ('The witches') was Puccini's first opera. It was premièred in Milan as part of a triple bill in May 1884, but Ricordi, the composer's publisher-to-be, urged its expansion into two Acts, and that later version was first heard in Turin in December of the same year, although it was a mixed success and never became established in the repertory.

The story, about the ghosts of young girls abandoned by their betrothed before marriage, comes from the same source as Adam's *Giselle*, but Ferdinando Fontana's libretto handles the legend less convincingly than the famous ballet. Roberto, the hero, not the brightest of characters, comes up from the country to Mainz just before his marriage, having suddenly inherited a fortune. Before he leaves, the betrothed pair declare their mutual love, and Anna gives her beloved a bouquet of flowers as 'forget-me-nots'. He promises faithfully to return.

An orchestral intermezzo indicates his journey, and a narrator tells how the feckless Roberto was seduced by another and lured to an orgy of pleasure, while Anna, waiting for him in vain, was cut down 'like a lily'. We then hear of the legend of the Villis, who wait to catch such a culprit and dance with him until he dies of exhaustion. Act II opens with Anna's funeral and the despair of her father, Guglielmo, and his wish for the Villis to avenge his daughter. Then comes Roberto's conscience-stricken return and frightened awareness of the vengeful ghosts, and finally Anna's reappearance as a spirit and the retribution in a climactic wild dance.

Maazel directs a performance so commanding, with singing of outstanding quality, that one can at last assess Puccini's first opera on quite a new level. Its weaknesses have always been the feeble, over-simplified story and the cardboard characterization. With such concentration, and with musical qualities emphasized, the weaknesses are minimized and the result is richly enjoyable. Puccini's melodies may be less distinctive here than they later became, but one can readily appreciate the impact they had on early audiences, not to mention the publisher, Giulio Ricordi. Scotto's voice tends to spread a little at the top of the stave but, like Domingo, she gives a powerful performance, and Leo Nucci avoids false histrionics. A delightful bonus is Tito Gobbi's contribution, reciting the verses which link the scenes; he is as characterful a reciter as he is a singer. The recording is one of CBS's best.

COLLECTIONS

Love duets from: *Manon Lescaut,* Act II (with Intermezzo); *La Bohème,* Act I; *Tosca,* Act III; *Madama Butterfly,* Act I.
(M) ** EMI CDM7 64195-2. Lenora Lafayette, Richard Lewis, Hallé O, Barbirolli (with VERDI: *La forza del destino: Overture; La traviata: Preludes, Acts I & III.* MASCAGNI: *Cavalleria rusticana: Intermezzo **).

It is unexpected casting to have Richard Lewis (recorded in 1958) singing the big Puccini roles. The voice is in good condition and he sings warmly, intelligently and (especially in the *Bohème* excerpt) touchingly. Perhaps this is no substitute for the Italianate temperament of a Pavarotti but the freshness is in no doubt, and Lenora Lafayette makes a good partner, an interesting soprano with an Albanese-like quality. The four duets are more sizeable than might strictly be imagined: the *Manon Lescaut* excerpt goes from Des Grieux's entry to the entry of Geronte; the *Bohème* excerpt starts well before *Che gelida manina* and moves on to the end of the Act; the *Tosca* goes from *E lucevan le stelle* to just after the outburst on *Trionfal*; the *Butterfly* from *Viene la sera* to the end of the Act. The recording is very good and Barbirolli is obviously relishing his day back in the opera pit. The programme opens with a vibrant Verdi *Forza del destino* overture and the Hallé strings are equally intense in the *Traviata Preludes*; indeed they play impressively throughout.

Arias from: *La Bohème; Fanciulla del West; Gianni Schicchi; Madama Butterfly; Manon Lescaut; Suor Angelica; Tosca; Turandot.*
(B) ** CfP CD-CFP 4569; *TC-CFP 4569*. Nicolai Gedda; Renata Scotto; Giuseppe Campora; Antonietta Stella; Mirella Freni; Montserrat Caballé; Bernabé Marti; Charles Craig; Floriana Cavalli; Franco Corelli; Amy Shuard; ROHCG Ch. & O, Gardelli.

Nicolai Gedda opens this Classics for Pleasure recital with a characteristically sensitive *Che gelida manina*, although he is not quite heroic enough in *Nessun dorma*. Charles Craig, one of the few British tenors to make a name in Italian opera, sings strongly in excerpts from *Manon Lescaut* and *Tosca*, but the remastering of these 1959 recordings does not flatter the voice. On the other hand, Amy Shuard's 1962 *In questa reggia* is thrillingly projected, and Mirella Freni is on fine form both in Liù's farewell from the same opera and in the most famous *Butterfly* aria. The rest is less distinctive, though the women are more refined than the men. As so often, a collection of histrionics like this needs singing of the highest quality to make an enjoyable continuous entertainment.

'Favourite Puccini': (i) *La Bohème: Mi chiamano Mimì; Donde lieta usci;* (ii) *Musetta's waltz song. Gianni Schicchi: O mio babbino caro. Madama Butterfly: Un bel dì;* (iii; iv) *Spira sul mare; Flower duet; Con onor muore . . . Tu, tu.* (ii) *Manon Lescaut: In quelle trine morbide;* (iii) *Sola, perduta, abbandonata.* (ii) *La Rondine: Chi il bel sogno di Doretta. Suor Angelica:* (iii) *Senza mamma, O bimbo, tu sei morto.* (i) *Tosca: Vissi d'arte. Turandot: Tu, che di gel sei cinta;* (i; v) *In questa reggia. Le Villi: Se come voi.*
(M) *** Sony Analogue/Dig. SMK 48094 [id.]. (i) Eva Marton; (ii) Kiri Te Kanawa; (iii) Renata Scotto; (iv) with Ingvar Wixell and Gillian Knight; (v) with José Carreras.

Kiri Te Kanawa's six ravishing contributions are the highlight of this collection – there is currently no more luscious Puccini singing than this – but the others are very characterful too, even if Eva Marton's Mimì is a shade forceful; she is better suited to the role of Turandot. However, *In questa reggia*, which ends the disc excitingly, then delivers a damp squib by fading out. Before that there is much to enjoy, not least Scotto's beautiful *Senza mamma* from *Suor Angelica*, and the two moving excerpts (Butterfly's entrance and the opera's climax) from Maazel's complete set of *Madama Butterfly*. The sound is excellent throughout, although sometimes the vocal balance is very forward. There is no back-up documentation, except a list of titles and performers.

Arias: *La Bohème: Quando m'en vo' soletta. Gianni Schicchi: O mio babbino caro. Madama Butterfly: Un bel dì. Manon Lescaut: In quelle trine morbide. La Rondine: Chi il bel sogno di Doretta. Tosca: Vissi d'arte. Le Villi: Se come voi piccina.*
*** Sony Dig. CD 37298 [id.]. Kiri Te Kanawa, LPO, Pritchard – VERDI: Arias. ***

The creamy beauty of Kiri Te Kanawa's voice is ideally suited to these seven lyrical arias – including rarities like the little waltz-like song from *Le Villi*. Expressive sweetness is more remarkable than characterization, but in such music, well recorded and sounding especially believable on CD, who would ask for more?

'Puccini heroines'; *La Bohème: Sì, mi chiamano Mimì; Donde lieta usci; Musetta's waltz song. Edgar: Addio, mio dolce amor. La Fanciulla del West: Laggiù nel Soledad. Gianni Schicchi: O mio babbino caro. Madama Butterfly: Bimba, bimba non piangere* (Love duet, with Plácido Domingo); *Un bel dì. Manon Lescaut: In quelle trine morbide; Sola, perduta, abbandonata. La Rondine: Ore dolci a divine. Tosca: Vissi d'arte. Turandot: In questa reggia. Le Villi: Se come voi piccina.*
*** BMG/RCA RD 85999 [RCA 5999-2-RC]. Leontyne Price, New Philh. O or LSO, Downes; Santi.

With three extra items added to the original recital LP, this collection, running for 70 minutes, is a formidable demonstration of the art of Leontyne Price at the very peak of her career, still marvellously subtle in control (the end of Tosca's *Vissi d'arte* for example), powerfully dramatic, yet able to point the *Rondine* aria with delicacy and charm. The Love duet from *Butterfly* in which she is joined by Domingo is particularly thrilling, and there is much else here to give pleasure. The remastering is extremely vivid and the voice is given fine bloom and presence. A Puccinian feast!

Arias: *La Bohème; Sì, mi chiamano Mimì; Donde lieta uscì. Gianni Schicchi: O mio babbino caro. Madama Butterfly: Un bel dì; Tu, tu piccolo Iddio. Manon Lescaut: In quelle trine morbide; Sola, perduta, abbandonata. La Rondine: Chi il bel sogno di Doretta. Tosca: Vissi d'arte. Turandot: Signore, ascolta!; Tu che di gel sei cinta. Le Villi: Se come voi piccina.*
*** EMI CDC7 47841-2 [id.]. Montserrat Caballé, LSO, Mackerras.

Montserrat Caballé uses her rich, beautiful voice to glide over these great Puccinian melodies. The effect is ravishing, with lovely recorded sound to match the approach. This is one of the loveliest of all operatic recital discs and the comparative lack of sparkle is compensated for by the sheer beauty of the voice. The CD transfer is extremely successful, vivid yet retaining the full vocal bloom.

Arias and duets from: *La Bohème; Gianni Schicchi; Madama Butterfly; Manon Lescaut; Tosca; Turandot.*
(B) *** EMI CDZ7 62520-2. Montserrat Caballé, Plácido Domingo, Giuseppe Di Stefano, Nicolai Gedda, Mirella Freni, Ghena Dimitrova, Renato Bruson, Victoria De los Angeles, Jussi Bjoerling, Renata Scotto, Franco Corelli.

Plácido Domingo opens with *Donna non vidi mai* from *Manon Lescaut* and is equally stirring in *Recondita armonia* from *Tosca*; Caballé is often ravishing in arias from *Manon Lescaut*, *Bohème*, a splendid *Vissi d'arte* from *Tosca*, *Un bel dì* from *Butterfly* and *Tu che di gel sei cinta*. Gedda and Freni join passionately for *O soave fanciulla*, and Victoria de los Angeles and Jussi Bjoerling offer the Love scene from *Butterfly*. Room is also found for a fine 1957 mono version by Giuseppe di Stefano of *Che gelida manina*. The voices are given strong presence; the orchestral sound is vivid but not sumptuous. Excellent bargain value with 70 minutes of music.

'Great arias' from: *La Bohème; La Fanciulla del West; Gianni Schicchi; Madama Butterfly; Manon Lescaut; La Rondine; Suor Angelica; Tosca; Turandot.*
(M) *** Decca 421 315-2 [id.]. Mirella Freni, Luciano Pavarotti, Elizabeth Harwood, Renata Tebaldi, Sherrill Milnes, Montserrat Caballé, Franco Corelli, Birgit Nilsson, Joan Sutherland, Maria Chiara.

Opening with Freni's *One fine day* and following with Pavarotti's *Che gelida manina* and Freni returning for *Si, mi chiamano Mimì*, this recital begins splendidly and offers many highlights, including Caballé's *Signora ascolta* and Sutherland's *In questa reggia* (both from *Turandot*). Maria Chiara is melting in arias from *Manon Lescaut* and *Suor Angelica*; and Tebaldi reminds us how ravishingly she could turn a phrase in *O mio babbino caro* from *Gianni Schicchi*, which ends this 61-minute collection. Vivid sound throughout and no real disappointments, though Franco Corelli's *Tosca* arias are merely forthright and dramatic.

'The world of Puccini': excerpts from *La Bohème; La Fanciulla del West; Gianni Schicchi; Madama Butterfly; Manon Lescaut; La Rondine; Suor Angelica; Tosca; Turandot.*
(M) ** Decca 433 865-2; *433 865-4* [id.]. Mirella Freni, Luciano Pavarotti, Elizabeth Harwood, Leona Mitchell, Bruno Previdi, Renata Tebaldi, Carlo Bergonzi, Fiorenza Cossotto, Maria Chiara, Virginia Zeani, Joan Sutherland, James McCracken, Giuseppe Di Stefano.

After the inspired choice of Decca's 'World of Verdi', this is a disappointment, mainly because of the roster of artists. All the singing is sympathetic and often stirring, but easily the most distinctive section of the disc is the Love scene from Act I of *La Bohème*, with Freni and Pavarotti (also included above); here also Elizabeth Harwood adds on *Musetta's waltz song*. There are also extended excerpts (24 minutes) from the Tebaldi/Bergonzi *Butterfly*, but the thin violins may prove a drawback to the novice seeking a fuller, more modern Puccini sound. Joan Sutherland's *Vissi d'arte* is a rare example of her as Tosca and Giuseppe di Stefano's *Nessun dorma* ends the programme excitingly.

'Heroines': (i) *La Bohème: Musetta's waltz song;* (ii) *Sì, mi chiamano Mimì.* (iii) *Edgar: D'ogni dolor.* (i) *Gianni Schicchi: O mio babbino caro. Madama Butterfly: Un bel dì. Manon Lescaut: In quelle trine morbide;* (iii) *Sola, perduta, abbandonata.* (i) *La Rondine: Chi il bel sogno di Doretta.* (iii) *Suor Angelica: Senza mamma, o bimbo.* (i) *Tosca: Vissi d'arte.* (iv) *Turandot: Tu che di gel sei cinta* (*Death of Liù*); (v) *In questa reggia.* (i) *Le Villi: Se come voi piccina.*
(M) **(*) Sony MK 39097 [id.]. (i) Kiri Te Kanawa; (ii) Ileana Cotrubas; (iii) Renata Scotto; (iv) Katia Ricciarelli; (v) Eva Marton; (iv; v) José Carreras.

The Sony compilation of Puccini 'heroines' neatly gathers together some fine performances out of its series of complete Puccini opera sets, plus other items such as the two *Bohème* arias taken from recitals. Vocally these are not always immaculate performances, but the quintet of sopranos represented is exceptionally characterful, contrasting strongly with one another, where Puccini recitals from a single soprano can lack variety. However, the layout does not make as much as possible of the interplay of different voices, as Kiri Te Kanawa's seven contributions are all placed together at the start of the collection. They come from her recital with Pritchard – see above – and have the character of concert performances. Ileana Cotrubas's assumption of Mimì has greater feeling of the opera house; other highlights include Katia Ricciarelli's *Death of Liù* and Renata Scotto's beautiful *Senza mamma* from *Suor Angelica*. The thrilling climax of *In questa reggia* (Eva Marton and José Carreras) is spoiled by a fade-out at the end, particularly unfortunate as it is the closing item. The CD gives the voices plenty of presence, but the variations in ambience and balance are made the more striking.

Arias from: *La Bohème; Gianni Schicchi; Madama Butterfly; Manon Lescaut; La Rondine; Suor Angelica; Tosca; Turandot; Le Villi.*
(M) ** Sony Dig. MK 42167 [id.]. Eva Marton, Munich RSO, Patanè.

Eva Marton's recital covers a formidable range of 14 Puccini arias, taking her well away from the big dramatic repertory which has generally been counted her forte. Surprisingly, she is at her most effective when totally unstressed in lyrical arias, regularly producing clear, creamy and beautifully scaled tone, as in Manon's *In quelle trine morbide* or in Mimì's two arias. What the microphone exposes too often is a forcing of tone and with it an ugly widening of vibrato when the voice is under pressure. Characterization is less varied than it might be, with *Turandot* – Marton's regular role – made more convincing than the rest. It is good to have the waltz-like aria from *Le Villi* and Magda's Act I aria from *La Rondine* included with the better-known arias. Warm, well-balanced recording.

'Great operatic duets': *La Bohème:* (i; ii) *Che gelida manina . . . Sì, mi chiamano Mimì . . . O soave fanciulla;* (ii; iii) *In un coupé . . . O Mimì tu più non torni.* (i; ii) *Madama Butterfly: Viene la sera.* (iv; v) *Manon Lescaut: Oh, sarò la più bella . . . Tu tu amore? Tu?.* (iv; vi) *Tosca: Mario! Mario! Mario!.* (vii; ii) *Turandot: Principessa di morte.*
(M) *** Decca Analogue/Dig. 421 896-2. (i) Mirella Freni; (ii) Luciano Pavarotti; (iii) Rolando Panerai; (iv) Kiri Te Kanawa; (v) José Carreras; (vi) Giacomo Aragall; (vii) Joan Sutherland.

Puccini duets don't come any better than this – a 70-minute recital to show the great strength of the Decca catalogue in the music of Puccini. The opening love scene from *Madama Butterfly* is fine enough, but the meeting of Rodolfo and Mimì in Act I of *La Bohème* brings a glorious sequence of three aria/duets that is surely unsurpassed in romantic opera. Freni and Pavarotti sing with great ardour and beauty, and Kiri Te Kanawa does not disappoint in her scenes from *Tosca* and *Manon Lescaut*. Finally Pavarotti forms an equally memorable partnership with Sutherland in *Turandot*. The sound, mostly analogue, is well up to Decca's expected high standards.

Arias: *Manon Lescaut: Cortese damigella . . . Donna non vidi mai; Presto! In filia! . . . Guardate, pazzo son. Turandot: Non piangere Liù . . . Ah! Per l'ultima volta; Nessun dorma.*
*** DG Dig. 413 785-2 [id.]. Plácido Domingo – VERDI: *Arias.* ***

These Puccini items, taken, like the Verdi, from earlier recordings made by Domingo for DG, make a fine heroic supplement, when he was challenged to some of his finest, most imaginative singing by Sinopoli and Karajan. The sound is consistently vivid.

Purcell, Henry (1659–95)

STAGE WORKS AND THEATRE MUSIC

Dido and Aeneas (complete).
⊛ (M) *** Decca 425 720-2; *425 720-4* [id.]. St Anthony Singers, ECO, Anthony Lewis.
Dido (Janet Baker), Aeneas (Raimund Herincx), Belinda (Patricia Clark), Sorceress (Monica Sinclair), Sailor (John Mitchinson).
*** Teldec/Warner Dig. 4509 91191-2 [id.]. St James's Singers & Baroque Players, Ivor Bolton.

Dido (Della Jones), Aeneas (Peter Harvey), Belinda (Donna Dean), Sorceress (Susan Bickley), Sailor (Andrew Murgatroyd).
*** Ph. Dig. 416 299-2 [id.]. ECO and Ch., Leppard.

Dido (Jessye Norman), Aeneas (Thomas Allen), Belinda (Marie McLaughlin), Sorceress (Patricia Kern), Sailor (Patrick Power).
*** Chan. Dig. CHAN 0521; *EBTD 0521* [id.]. Taverner Ch. & Players, Parrott.

Dido (Emma Kirkby), Aeneas (David Thomas), Belinda (Judith Nelson), Sorceress (Jantina Noorman), Sailor (Tessa Bonner).
**(*) DG Dig. 427 624-2 [id.]. Ch. & E. Concert, Pinnock.

Dido (Anne Sofie Von Otter), Aeneas (Stephen Varcoe), Belinda (Lynne Dawson), Sorceress / Sailor (Nigel Rogers).
Withdrawn: (M) (***) EMI mono CDH7 61006-2 [id.]. Mermaid Theatre Singers & O, Geraint Jones.

Dido (Kirsten Flagstad), Aeneas (Thomas Hemsley), Belinda (Elisabeth Schwarzkopf), Sorceress (Arda Mandikian), Sailor (David Lloyd).
Withdrawn: (M) ** Ph. 422 485-2; *422 485-4* [id.]. Alldis Ch., ASMF, C. Davis.

Dido (Josephine Veasey), Aeneas (John Shirley-Quirk), Belinda (Helen Donath), Sorceress (Elizabeth Bainbridge).
** HM HMC 90 5173 [id.]. Les Arts Florissants, Christie.

Dido (Guillemette Laurens), Aeneas (Philippe Cantor), Belinda (Jill Feldman), Sorceress (Dominique Visse), Sailor (Michel Laplénie).
** Erato/Warner 2292 45263-2 [id.]. ECO Ch., ECO, Leppard.

Dido (Tatiana Troyanos), Aeneas (Richard Stilwell), Belinda (Felicity Palmer), Sorceress (Patricia Kern), Sailor (Philip Langridge).
*(*) Teldec/Warner Dig. 2292 42959-2 [id.]. Schoenberg Ch., VCM, Harnoncourt.

Dido (Ann Murray), Aeneas (Anton Scharinger), Belinda (Rachel Yakar), Sorceress (Trudeliese Schmidt), Sailor (Josef Köstlinger).

Purcell's *Dido and Aeneas* – the first great English opera – premièred in London in 1689, had a considerable influence on the rapid development of the genre in England, even though, when Handel arrived in 1710, he looked to the Italian Neapolitan tradition for his operatic style, rather than following in Purcell's footsteps. Nevertheless, as Handel was so often to do, Purcell used a classical Greek legend as the basis for his plot.

Its heroine, Dido, is not the happiest person, troubled by her love for Prince Aeneas, who was forced to flee from the sack of Troy and who is a guest at court. Belinda, her lady-in-waiting, tries to cheer her up. She is urged to marry Aeneas and so unite the thrones of Carthage and Troy. The courtiers depart on a hunting expedition and Aeneas enters and declares his love for Dido.

But trouble is brewing, in the form of a sorceress who, with her companion witches, seeks the downfall of both Carthage and Troy. A false spirit disguised as Mercury is conjured up to persuade Aeneas to leave. Additionally, the manifestation of a thunderstorm will spoil the hunt and bring the royal group back to court. Meanwhile Aeneas has killed a boar.

The false Mercury now appears and tells him that Jove has commanded that he abandon Dido and sail away that very night. Aeneas is in despair but he must obey the command of the gods. The ships, with Aeneas on board, are now ready for departure, and the sorceress and her coven of witches watch with glee, then join the sailors in a dance.

Dido is heartbroken to discover that Aeneas means to leave her and, when he suggests he will stay after all, she turns away and angrily dismisses him. Left to die, she laments bitterly in her great aria, *When I am laid in earth*, with the words 'Remember me' poignantly repeated.

It was Janet Baker's 1961 recording of *Dido* for the Oiseau-Lyre label that established her as a recording star of the front rank: it is a truly great performance. The radiant beauty of the voice is obvious enough, but here she goes beyond that to show what stylishness and insight she can command. The emotion is implied, as it should be in this music, not injected in great uncontrolled gusts. Listen to the contrast between the angry, majestic words to Aeneas, *Away, away!* and the dark grief of the following *But death alas I cannot shun*, and note how Baker contrasts dramatic soprano tone-colour with darkened contralto tone. Even subtler is the contrast between the opening phrase of *When I am laid in earth* and its repeat a few bars later: it is a model of graduated *mezza voce*. Then with the words *Remember me!*, delivered in a monotone, she subdues the natural vibrato to produce a white tone of hushed, aching intensity.

When this record was first issued, we suggested that it would be surprising if a more deeply satisfying interpretation were recorded within the foreseeable future, and so it has proved: three decades later, this reissue still occupies the top of the recommended list. Anthony Lewis chooses fast speeds, but they challenge the ECO (Thurston Dart a model continuo player) to produce the crispest and lightest of playing, which never sounds rushed.

The other soloists and chorus give very good support. Herincx is a rather gruff Aeneas, but the only serious blemish is Monica Sinclair's Sorceress. She overcharacterizes in a way that is quite out of keeping with the rest of the production. Generally, by concentrating on musical values, Lewis and his singers and instrumentalists make the clear, simple dramatic point of the opera all the more telling, and it proves a most moving experience. Like most vintage Oiseau-Lyre recordings, this was beautifully engineered: the remastering thins out the upper range a little, but the effect is to increase the feeling of authenticity, for the ambient bloom remains.

Ivor Bolton and the St James's Singers and Players present a period performance, intimately scaled, which avoids the snags of earlier versions, with Della Jones as Dido giving her finest recorded performance yet. She has a weightier mezzo than her rivals in other period performances, yet her flexibility over ornamentation is greater, and *Dido's Lament* is the more moving when, unlike Von Otter on DG Archiv, she is restrained over expressive gestures, keeping a tender simplicity. She shades her voice tonally very much as Dame Janet Baker did in her classic recording with Sir Anthony Lewis and the ECO, made in 1961, long before period manners were adopted.

Ivor Bolton's team, recorded with bright immediacy, has no weak link, with Peter Harvey as Aeneas, Susan Bickley as a clear-toned Sorceress, Donna Dean as a characterful Belinda, and Andrew Murgatroyd as the Sailor a tenor who plays no stylistic tricks. Setting the seal on the performance's success, the choir is among the freshest and liveliest, and the use of a guitar continuo as well as brief guitar interludes (suggested by the original libretto) enhances the happy intimacy of the presentation.

'Like *Tristan und Isolde* in a pint pot,' says Raymond Leppard of *Dido and Aeneas*; on Philips, he provides crisply disciplined backing for the most magnificently expansive rendering of *Dido* since Kirsten Flagstad recorded it over 40 years ago. Authenticists should keep away, but Jessye Norman amply proves that this amazingly compressed setting of the epic *Aeneid* story has a dramatic depth and intensity to compare with Berlioz's setting – or, for that matter, with Wagner's *Tristan*. The opening phrase of *Ah Belinda* brings the most controversial moment, when Norman slows luxuriantly. But from then on the security and dark intensity of her singing make for a memorable performance, heightened in the recitatives by the equally commanding singing of Thomas Allen as Aeneas. The range of expression is very wide – with Jessye Norman producing an agonized whisper in the recitative just before Dido's *Lament* – but the inauthentic element must not be exaggerated.

By most yardsticks this is finely poised and stylish singing, even if in the last resort Norman cannot match Dame Janet Baker in conveying the aching vulnerability of the love-lorn Dido. Marie McLaughlin is a pure-toned Belinda, Patrick Power a heady-toned Sailor, singing his song in a West Country accent, while Patricia Kern repeats her performance as the Sorceress, using conventionally sinister expression. The warm-toned counter-tenor, Derek Lee Ragin, makes the Spirit Messenger into an eerie, other-worldly figure. Leppard's direction this time is a degree plainer and more direct than it was in his Erato version, again with some slow speeds for choruses. Excellent recording in both formats.

Andrew Parrott's concept of a performance on original instruments has one immediately thinking back to the atmosphere of Josias Priest's school for young ladies, where Purcell's masterpiece was given its first known performance. The voices enhance that impression, not least Emma Kirkby's fresh, bright soprano, here recorded without too much edge but still very young-sounding. It is more questionable to have a soprano singing the tenor role of the Sailor in Act III; but anyone who fancies the idea of an authentic performance need not hesitate. The CD is exceptionally refined, the sound well focused, with analogue atmosphere yet with detail enhanced. The tape transfer, too, is fresh and clean, retaining the recording's bloom.

As in his other Purcell recordings, Pinnock pursues authenticity with more concern for the non-specialist listener than most. Significantly, an essay accompanying the libretto for this disc puts the case that the first performance of *Dido* was probably given as a Court entertainment rather than in Dr Josias Priest's girls' school in Chelsea, as has long been thought. Pinnock seeks to reproduce just such a performance at Court, rather than a school-sized entertainment; and though the reading is not as inspired as many that Pinnock has given of Purcell, the scale is attractive. Pinnock's choice of singers for the two principal women's roles is outstandingly successful, when both Anne Sofie von Otter and Lynne Dawson have voices that are at once warm and aptly pure for authentic performance.

Von Otter as Dido, both fresh and mature-sounding, sings her two big arias with a combination of weight, gravity and expressive warmth which are yet completely in scale. The final lament, while faster than in traditional performances, still conveys the full tragic intensity of this epic in microcosm. Much more questionable is the casting on the male side, and that includes a tenor taking the role of the Sorceress. Nigel Rogers, not in his sweetest voice, takes that role as well as that of the Sailor. Confusingly, almost immediately after the Sailor's jolly song at the start of Act III, Rogers reappears as the Sorceress in quite a different mood, making much too quick a change. Stephen Varcoe is a rather unheroic-sounding Aeneas, but the chorus of the English Concert produces fresh, alert singing. Instead of a repetition of the final chorus, Pinnock opts for an instrumental reprise to provide an epilogue.

Bernard Miles's inspiration in inviting Kirsten Flagstad to sing in Purcell's miniature epic at his original Mermaid Theatre in St John's Wood led in due course to this classic recording, in which Elisabeth Schwarzkopf added another characterful element, equally unexpected. In this excellent mid-price CD transfer on EMI's historic Références series the surprise is that, even in this age of period performance, this traditional account under Geraint Jones sounds fresh and lively still, not at all heavy. Though Flagstad's magnificent voice may in principle be too weighty for this music – one might point to the latterday equivalent of Jessye Norman – she scales it down superbly in her noble reading, which brings beautiful shading and masterly control of breath and tone. Schwarzkopf is brightly characterful as Belinda, and though Thomas Hemsley is not ideally sweet-toned as Aeneas, he sings very intelligently. The mono sound, obviously limited, yet captures the voices vividly, and this above all is Flagstad's set.

Sir Colin Davis's version is fresh and enjoyable but hardly inspired. It was an interesting idea to have the same Dido here in Purcell as Davis chose for Berlioz's great opera on the same subject; and Veasey sings most reliably, but next to others she sounds a little stiff and unsympathetic. Good remastered sound on both CD and cassette.

A version of *Dido and Aeneas* such as the Harmonia Mundi issue with a predominantly French cast may seem an oddity but, with trifling exceptions, English accents are more than acceptable; William Christie, as in his recordings of other early operas, provides direction on an authentic chamber scale that makes the results both dramatic and intense. Particularly impressive – and an interesting idea for casting – is having the role of the Sorceress taken by the outstanding French counter-tenor, Dominique Visse. The shortcoming is that Guillemette Laurens makes a disappointing Dido, not strong or positive enough. First-rate recording.

On the Erato disc Leppard directs a consistently well-sprung, well-played performance, as one would expect, but the overall impression is disappointing, largely because the climax of the opera fails to rise in intensity as it should. Tatiana Troyanos, stylish elsewhere, misses the tragic depth of the great lament of Dido, and without that focus the impact of the rest falls away. Philip Langridge sings the Sailor's song freshly and the recording is excellent, clear yet full and atmospheric.

Harnoncourt's idiosyncratic rhythmic style in Purcell, often in exaggerated marcato, as well as his extreme speeds in both directions, undermines the effectiveness of the whole performance, presenting the authentic view far less imaginatively than his direct rivals. Ann Murray sings beautifully as Dido but has to struggle against the funereal speed for the *Lament*. The chorus is excellent and the other soloists consistently good, well trained in English but still distractingly foreign-sounding, even the heady-toned Sailor of Josef Köstlinger. Rachel Yakar is an agile Belinda, but she does not always blend well with Dido, and Trudeliese Schmidt makes a resonant, fire-eating Sorceress.

Dioclesian; Timon of Athens.
*** Erato/Warner 2292 45327-2; *2292 45327-4* (2) [id.]. Lynne Dawson, Gillian Fisher, Rogers Covey-Crump, Paul Elliott, Michael George, Stephen Varcoe, Monteverdi Ch., E. Bar. Soloists, Gardiner.

On his two-disc Erato set, John Eliot Gardiner rescues some of the most colourful and memorable of Purcell's theatre music. It is tragic that such inspired writing should by its very format have fallen out of the current repertory, when these pieces illustrate plays that are totally non-viable on the stage today. Gardiner's collection brings typically vigorous and understanding performances of the so-called semi-opera, *Dioclesian* – taking up rather more than one disc – and of Thomas Shadwell's adaptation of Shakespeare's *Timon of Athens*. The martial music, shining with trumpets, is what stands out from *Dioclesian* – the adaptation of a Jacobean play, first given in 1622 – while the *Timon* music contains such enchanting inventions as *Hark! how the songsters of the grove*, with its '*Symphony of pipes* imitating the chirping of birds'. This is music which Gardiner consistently brings to life, recorded here in vivid, agreeably atmospheric sound.

The Fairy Queen (complete).
*** DG Dig. 419 221-2 (2) [id.]. Eiddwen Harrhy, Jennifer Smith, Judith Nelson, Timothy
    Penrose, Ashley Stafford, Wynford Evans, Martyn Hill, Stephen Varcoe, David Thomas,
    Monteverdi Ch., E. Bar. Soloists, Gardiner.
*** HM Dig. HMC 90 1308/9 [id.]. Nancy Argenta, Lynne Dawson, Charles Daniels, Bernard
    Loonen, Jérôme Corréas, Les Arts Florissants, William Christie.
(M) *** Decca 433 163-2 (2) [id.]. Jennifer Vyvyan, James Bowman, Peter Pears, Mary Wells,
    Ian Partridge, John Shirley-Quirk, Owen Brannigan, Norma Burrowes, Amb. Op. Ch., ECO,
    Britten.
(B) **(*) HM HMP 390257/58 (2) [id.]. Honor Sheppard, Jean Knibbs, Maurice Bevan, Norman
    Platt, Alfred Deller, Neil Jenkins, Mark Deller, John Buttrey, Christina Clarke, Stour Music
    Ch. & O, Deller.

Purcell's setting of Shakespeare's *Midsummer Night's Dream*, following in the wake of the great success of *Dido and Aeneas*, was written in 1692. The revised plot broadly follows the original play but the wedding of Hippolyta and Theseus is omitted. Hippolyta also finds herself on the cutting-room floor, while Theseus becomes the Duke of Athens. The music takes the form of five masques, each symbolizing one aspect of the play, and mythical characters or fairies introduce each of the scenes, with a curious 'Chinese' evocation of marital paradise in the last Act, combined with the entry of Hymen, god of marriage.

The Fairy Queen provides a classic example of a masterpiece, made non-viable by changed conditions, which happily records can help to keep alive, a score which is crammed with the finest Purcellian inspiration. The masque follows and elaborates on the story of Shakespeare's *Midsummer Night's Dream*, adding in characters from Greek mythology for good measure. One wonders whether, with the resources of modern technology, it would be possible today to stage the piece with the kind of spectacle that delighted Purcell's audiences.

In Act I the Fairies entertain Titania's Indian page by making fun with three drunken poets.

Act II details the quarrel between Titania and Oberon and brings the first major transformation scene, in which Titania changes the woodland into fairyland. Four allegorical figures, Night, Mystery, Secresie and Sleep, appear, to provide a ballet, then Oberon sprinkles the magic juice in Titania's eyes.

Act III brings Titania's embarrassing love-affair with Bottom and another spectacular transformation scene, with dances from fauns, dryads and, later, four savage, leprechaun-like creatures. Finally the Shepherd, Coridon, tries to steal a kiss from his consort, Mopsa.

Act IV follows Shakespeare's Act III, with the mix-up involving the two pairs of lovers, Hermia and Lysander, Helena and Demetrius. The awakening of Titania and Bottom by Oberon is an excuse for another spectacle, a garden of fountains, with Phoebus on a cloud, greeting the dawning of Oberon's birthday.

Finally there is a ballet of the Four Seasons. Act V winds up the plot, with Theseus introduced to approve the marriages of the mortals, after the two pairs of human lovers have been reunited. To impress Theseus, Oberon now lays on a final display of magic, featuring Juno in his heavenly chariot, and a Chinese garden representing paradise, lit by Hymen's torch.

Gardiner's performance is a delight from beginning to end, for, though authenticity and completeness reign, scholarship is worn lightly and the result is consistently exhilarating, with no longueurs whatever. The fresh-toned soloists are first rate, while Gardiner's regular choir and orchestra excel themselves with Purcell's sense of fantasy brought out in each succeeding number. Performed like this, *The Fairy Queen* has a magic equivalent to *A Midsummer Night's Dream*, of which it usually seems so strange a distortion. Beautifully clear and well-balanced recording, sounding all the fresher on CD. The layout places the first three Acts complete on disc one and the remaining two Acts on the second CD.

William Christie made his recording of *The Fairy Queen* immediately after a highly successful production on stage at the Aix-en-Provence Festival, also involving a presentation of Shakespeare's *Midsummer Night's Dream* text, judiciously pruned and given by the Peter Hall Theatre Company. It is a pity that not even a smattering of Shakespeare is included here – but, that said, the robust vigour of Christie's treatment is most compelling; he uses a far bigger team of both singers and instrumentalists than John Eliot Gardiner on the rival (DG Archiv) set, allowing a wider range of colours. The drunken poet episode, for example, uses a glissando bassoon so that, in its earthiness, that sequence makes Gardiner's version sound too refined by comparison.

The bite of the performance is increased by the relative dryness of the recorded sound. Some of the voices need more air round them to sound their best, and Gardiner's extra elegance goes with warmer, more congenially atmospheric recording. Among Christie's soloists two sopranos, well known in Britain, are outstanding, Nancy Argenta and Lynne Dawson; and the whole team is a strong one. The number of singers in solo roles allows them to be used together as chorus too – an authentic seventeenth-century practice. This makes a vigorous and refreshing alternative to the fine Gardiner set; but the Harmonia Mundi booklet is most inadequate: ingeniously, it has you chasing around in three places instead of one to identify both which number is where and who is singing. Any table of contents should be detailed enough to answer all questions.

Britten's version from the early 1970s used a newly reshaped arrangement of the music made by Britten himself in collaboration with Imogen Holst and Peter Pears. The original collection of individual pieces is here grouped into four satisfying sections: *Oberon's birthday*, *Night and silence*, the *Sweet passion* and the *Epithalamium*. This version was first heard at the Aldeburgh Festival in 1967, and here the authentic glow of a Maltings performance (1971 vintage) is beautifully conveyed in the playing, the singing and the recording. Philip Ledger's imaginative harpsichord continuo is placed too far to one side, but otherwise the sound can scarcely be faulted. The cast is consistently satisfying, with Peter Pears and Jennifer Vyvyan surviving from the much earlier mono version of Anthony Lewis on Oiseau-Lyre.

Deller's set was recorded – very well too – at the Stour Music Festival in 1972 and, although the balance is rather forward, the acoustic is pleasingly warm and the voices and orchestra combine effectively. All the solo singing is of a high standard, with Honor Sheppard particularly memorable as Night in Act II, well matched by Jean Knibbs's Mystery in some of Purcell's most evocative writing. Norman Platt is a suitably bucolic Drunken Poet in Act I and becomes one of a pair of West Country haymakers (Alfred Deller obviously enjoying himself as his companion, Mopsa) in Act III. The many ensembles are eloquently sung and, although this has not quite the sophistication of Gardiner's set, its robust warmth and Deller's considerable concern for detail make for an enjoyable entertainment, well worth its modest price when so smoothly and vividly transferred to CD.

The Indian Queen (incidental music; complete).
*** HM HMC 90243 [id.]. Deller Singers, King's Musick, Deller.
   Ismeron / High Priest / Envy (Maurice Bevan), Orazia / God of Dreams / Aerial Spirit (Honor Sheppard), Boy / Follower of Envy (Mark Deller), Fame / Aerial Spirit (Paul Elliott), Aerial Spirit (Alfred Deller).
**(*) Erato/Warner 2292 45556-2; *2292 45556-4* [id.]. Monteverdi Ch., E. Bar. Soloists, Gardiner.
   Ismeron (Stephen Varcoe), Orazia (Jennifer Smith), Boy / God of Dreams (Martyn Hill), Fame / 1st Aerial Spirit (John Elwes), Girl (Rosemary Hardy), 3rd & 4th Aerial Spirit (Gillian Fisher), Follower of Envy (Ashley Stafford), Envy / High Priest (David Thomas) Aerial Spirit (Diana Harris).

The Indian Queen is one of the Purcellian entertainments that fit into no modern category, a semi-opera. Convention dictated that the main human characters in the story were spoken parts; only the supernatural beings could sing. An exception is made in the Prologue, however, for here an Indian Boy and Girl celebrate Mexico's peace before the brutal invasion to come.

Act I is without music, so the recording then moves to Act II in a celebratory masque for Zempoalla, in which Fame and Envy vie with each other.

In Act III, Zempoalla has a visionary dream, so Ismeron is required to call on 'twice ten hundred deities' and bring forth the God of Dreams to offer some sort of explanation. But he is unable to help with any interpretation concerning the future. The Aerial spirits now arrive, delighting in their freedom from human failings and temptations. Zempoalla responds in a famous aria by attempting 'from love's sickness to fly'.

Act IV ends with Montezuma and Orazia in chains awaiting death. It contains only one love-song from Orazia, that does not seem to be closely connected with the story, and Act V also contains only one section of solemn, ceremonial music, for the rest of the story, with the deaths of Acasis and Zempoalla, and Montezuma's confirmation as the true ruler of Mexico, is entirely spoken. If there was intended to be a spectacular closing masque, it has not survived.

The impossible plot matters little. Purcell's music contains many delights, and indeed the score seems to get better as it proceeds. John Eliot Gardiner's Erato version is very well cast and uses an authentic accompanying baroque instrumental group. The choral singing is especially fine, with the close of the work movingly expressive. Gardiner's choice of tempi is apt and the soloists are all good, although the men are more strongly characterful than the ladies; nevertheless the lyrical music comes off well. The recording is spacious and well balanced, and the performance consistently reflects Gardiner's imagination.

The Harmonia Mundi set – with fine individual contributions from Maurice Bevan, Honor Sheppard and Paul Elliott, as well as from Deller himself – is also lively and characterful. *Ye twice ten hundred deities* is splendidly sung by Maurice Bevan; and the duet for male alto and tenor, *How happy are we* (with Deller himself joined by Paul Elliot), as well as the best-known item, the soprano's *I attempt from love's sickness to fly* (Honor Sheppard), are equally enjoyable.

(i) *The Indian Queen* (incidental music); (ii) *King Arthur* (complete).

⊛ (M) *** Decca 433 166-2 (2) [id.]. (i) April Cantelo, Wilfred Brown, Robert Tear, Ian Partridge, Christopher Keyte, St Anthony Singers, ECO, Mackerras; (ii) Elsie Morison, Heather Harper, Mary Thomas, John Whitworth, Wilfred Brown, David Galliver, John Cameron, Trevor Anthony, Hervey Alan, St Anthony Singers, Philomusica of L., Lewis.

This Decca Serenata (originally Oiseau-Lyre) version of *The Indian Queen* dates from 1966 and the recording, from a vintage era, remains first rate. With stylish singing and superb direction and accompaniment (Raymond Leppard's harpsichord continuo playing must be singled out), this is an invaluable reissue. Charles Mackerras shows himself a strong and vivid as well as scholarly Purcellian.

The Rosette, however, is for the pioneering 1959 set (also Oiseau-Lyre) of *King Arthur*, fully worthy to stand alongside the companion recording of *Dido and Aeneas*, made three years later – see above. Here the success of the interpretation does not centre on the contribution of one inspired artist but rather on teamwork among a number of excellent singers and on the stylish and sensitive overall direction of Anthony Lewis. Oiseau-Lyre's excellent stereo also plays a bit part.

This was an early set, but one would never guess it from the pleasing ambience and the sophistication of the antiphonal effects. A very happy example is the chorus *This way, that way*, when the opposing spirits (good and evil) make a joint attempt to entice the king, while the famous freezing aria will surely send a shiver through the most warm-blooded listener. Indeed *King Arthur* contains some of Purcell's most memorable inspiration, not just the items mentioned above and the famous song, *Fairest isle*, but a whole range of lively and atmospheric numbers which are admirably realized here by a very strong cast.

King Arthur (complete).

*** Erato/Warner 2292 45211-2 (2) [id.]. Jennifer Smith, Gillian Fischer, Elizabeth Priday, Gill Ross, Ashley Stafford, Paul Elliott, Stephen Varcoe, E. Bar. Soloists, Gardiner.

*** DG Dig. 435 490-2 (2) [id.]. Nancy Argenta, Julia Gooding, Linda Perillo, Jamie MacDougall, Mark Tucker, Brian Bannatyne-Scott, Gerald Finley, Ch. & E. Concert, Pinnock.

It is a tragedy that this magnificent work presents such difficulties of staging, not to mention textual problems, that it is unlikely to be given publicly as often as it deserves. *King Arthur* dates from 1691 and its patriotic tone was no doubt dictated by the historical background, with William III busy at the time fighting the French in Flanders at the head of the Grand Alliance.

As the story opens, King Arthur has recaptured all of his British kingdom except Kent from the Saxon king, Oswald. Both monarchs seek the hand of Emmeline, the blind daughter of the Duke of Cornwall. Oswald has his magician, Osmond, to help him, whose assistants are the spirits of earth and air, Grimbald and Philidel, respectively. However, Arthur has a trump card in Merlin, whose wizardry finally proves superior.

In Act II Philidel is persuaded by Merlin to go over to the Brits, and so, in the delightful chorus, *Hither, this way, this way bend*, he triumphs over Grimbald who tries to lead our heroes down the wrong path.

In Act III, with both Oswald and Osmond making overtures to Emmeline, Philidel, following Merlin's instructions, restores her sight; Osmond then tries to impress her by magically freezing everything up and showing that, with Cupid's help, love can thaw even the most frosty situation.

In Act IV Osmond again endeavours to turn Arthur from his true path, with two sensuous sirens. But Arthur, a true Englishman, is not to be seduced so easily, and he draws his sword, striking at a large tree to counter the spell. The tree changes into the bleeding Emmeline, and

Arthur is just bringing her succour when Philidel appears, touches her with his wand and lo! – she proves to be Grimbald in disguise! Arthur then strikes the tree again, the spell is finally broken, and Grimbald becomes his prisoner.

In the last Act, Osmond again teams up with Oswald when the latter fights a final duel with Arthur who, needless to say, wins hands down, and takes Emmeline as his reward.

The piece ends resplendently, with a spectacular patriotic tableau. Aeolus commands Britannia to rise up from the sea. Everyone celebrates, Venus with her '*Fairest isle*', Honour invoking St George and with all joining in to match even the 'Last night of the Proms' in flag-waving fervour.

Gardiner, with his combination of stylishness and electricity of the highest voltage, presents a performance on record which in almost every way provides the clear modern answer to the problems this work presents. *King Arthur* may be cumbersome on stage, but here its episodic nature matters hardly at all; one can simply relish the wealth of sharply inspired and colourful numbers. Gardiner's solutions to the textual problems carry complete conviction, as for example his placing of the superb *Chaconne in F* at the end instead of the start. Solo singing for the most part is excellent, with Stephen Varcoe outstanding among the men. As the Cold Genius he helps Gardiner to make the Frost scene far more effective than usual. He is also one of the trio that give a delightfully roistering account of *Harvest home*. *Fairest isle* is treated very gently after that, with Gill Ross, boyish of tone, reserved just for that number. Throughout, the chorus is characteristically fresh and vigorous, and the instrumentalists marry authentic technique to pure, unabrasive sounds beautifully. The recording vividly captures a performance in an aptly intimate but not dry acoustic.

Pinnock opens with the *Chaconne*, which is placed before the *Overture*. His performance is consistently refreshing and can be recommended alongside – though not in preference to – Gardiner's. Linda Perillo makes a charming Philidel (one cannot imagine Arthur's soldiers having any doubt about their direction when she leads the famous *Hither, this way* chorus) and later her Sirens' duet with Julia Gooding, *Two daughters of this aged stream*, is captivating. Brian Bannatyne-Scott is superb in Aeolus's *Ye blust'ring brethren*, and in his *Frost aria* (where Pinnock's sharply articulated accompaniment anticipates *Winter* in Vivaldi's *Four Seasons*) he achieves an unusual if controversial effect by beginning his series of shakes from slightly under the note. Not surprisingly, Nancy Argenta sings beautifully in the double roles of Cupid and Venus, and her *Fairest isle* will not disappoint. The *Harvest home* sequence is every bit as exuberant here as it is with Gardiner, and both chorus and orchestra sing and play throughout with consistent vitality. The DG recording is first class, but why no coupling? The second CD plays for only 39 minutes.

King Arthur: highlights.
(M) *** Erato/Warner Dig. 2292 45919-2 (from above recording; cond. Gardiner).
(B) ** HM HMA 90200 [id.]. Honor Sheppard, Jean Knibbs, Rosemary Hardy, Alfred Deller, Mark Deller, Paul Elliott, Leigh Nixon, Maurice Bevan, Nigel Bevan, Deller Ch., King's Musick, Alfred Deller.

A well-chosen 64-minute selection from John Eliot Gardiner's recording which can be strongly recommended, for it contains a great deal of the music, including the famous stereophonic chorus, *Hither this way*.

It was sensible of Harmonia Mundi, faced with the competition of Lewis's outstanding complete set, to choose to reissue a bargain disc of highlights from Deller's 1978 version. This has considerable merit, not least a stylish accompaniment from the King's Musick, using original instruments effectively and not too abrasively, and a spacious recording which has transferred realistically to CD. Deller's solution to performing problems will satisfy almost everyone and, though the solo singing is not always polished, the performance has a refreshing vigour; Deller pioneered the idea of singing the *Harvest home* chorus in Act V in a rousing West Country accent. But a highlights disc without the famous opening scene of Act II (*Hither this way*), with its opposing spirits, is almost unbelievably bad planning, when there would have been plenty of room for it.

The Tempest (incidental music; complete).
*** Erato/Warner 2292 45555-2; *2292 45555-4* [id.]. Monteverdi Ch. & O, Gardiner.
    Amphitrite (Jennifer Smith), Dorinda (Rosemary Hardy), Ariel (Carol Hall), Aeolus (John Elwes), Neptune (Stephen Varcoe), 1st Devil (David Thomas), 2nd Devil (Roderick Earle).

Whether or not Purcell himself wrote this music for Shakespeare's last play (the scholarly arguments are still unresolved), John Eliot Gardiner demonstrates how delightful it is, a masterly collection, in performances both polished and stylish and with excellent solo and choral singing. At least the *Overture* is clearly Purcell's, and that sets the pattern for a very varied collection of numbers, including three *da capo* arias and a full-length masque celebrating Neptune for Act V. The recording, full and atmospheric, has transferred vividly to CD.

Theatre music (collection).

Disc 1: *Abdelazar: Overture and suite. Distressed Innocence: Overture and suite. The Gordian Knot Untied: Overture and suite; The Married Beau: Overture and suite. Sir Anthony Love: Overture and suite.*

Disc 2: *Bonduca: Overture and suite. Circe: suite. The Old Bachelor: Overture and suite. The Virtuous Wife: Overture and suite.*

Disc 3: *Amphitrion: Overture and suite; Overture in G min.; Don Quixote: suite.*

Disc 4: *Overture in G min. The Double Dealer: Overture and suite. Henry II, King of England: In vain, 'gainst love, in vain I strove. The Richmond Heiress: Behold the man. The Rival Sisters: Overture; 3 songs. Tyrannic Love: Hark my Damilcar!* (duet); *Ah! how sweet it is to love. Theodosius:* excerpts. *The Wives' Excuse:* excerpts.

Disc 5: *Overture in D min.; Cleomenes, the Spartan Hero: No, no, poor suff'ring heart. A Dialogue between Thirsis and Daphne: Why, my Daphne, why complaining? The English Lawyer: My wife has a tongue:* excerpts. *A Fool's Preferment:* excerpts. *The History of King Richard II: Retir'd from any mortal's sight. The Indian Emperor: I look'd and saw within. The Knight of Malta: At the close of the ev'ning. The Libertine:* excerpts. *The Marriage-hater Match'd: As soon as the chaos . . . How vile are the sordid intregues. The Massacre of Paris: The genius lo* (2 settings). *Oedipus:* excerpts. *Regulus: Ah me! to many deaths. Sir Barnaby Whigg: Blow, blow, Boreas, blow. Sophonisba: Beneath the poplar's shadow. The Wives' excuse:* excerpts.

Disc 6: *Chacony; Pavans Nos. 1–5; Trio sonata for violin, viola de gamba and organ. Aureng-Zebe: I see, she flies me. The Canterbury Guests: Good neighbours why? Epsom Wells: Leave these useless arts. The Fatal Marriage: 2 songs. The Female Virtuosos: Love, thou art best. Love Triumphant: How happy's the husband. The Maid's Last Prayer:* excerpts. *The Mock Marriage: Oh! how you protest; Man is for the woman made. Oroonoko: Celemene, pray tell me. Pausanius: Song (Sweeter than roses) and duet. Rule a Wife and Have a Wife: There's not a swain. The Spanish Friar: Whilst I with grief.*

(M) *** O-L 425 893-2 (6) [id.]. Emma Kirkby, Judith Nelson, Elizabeth Lane, Joy Roberts, Robert Lloyd, James Bowman, Martyn Hill, Rogers Covey-Crump, Paul Elliott, Alan Byers, Peter Bamber, David Thomas, Christopher Keyte, Geoffrey Shaw, Michael George, Taverner Ch., AAM, Hogwood.

This set of six CDs creates an anthology from the contents of a selective but wide-ranging series of LPs recorded between 1974 and 1983. Most of the music Purcell wrote for the theatre is relatively little heard, and one must remember that the 'suites' assembled here were not originally intended for continuous performance. If in the earlier discs they do not provide the variety and range one would expect from works conceived as a whole, much of the music comes up with striking freshness in these performances using authentic instruments.

As well as the charming dances and more ambitious overtures, as the series proceeds we are offered more extended scenas with soloists and chorus, of which the nine excerpts from *Theodosius*, an early score (1680), are a particularly entertaining example. Before that, on Disc 3 we have already had the highly inventive Overture and incidental music for *Don Quixote*.

Purcell was one of three contributors on this occasion (there were three plays to service, all by Thomas D'Urfey and based on Cervantes' famous novel). Though the music was written at high speed, much of it was attractively lively and it deserves to be resurrected in such stylish performances, with much enchanting singing from both the soprano soloists, Emma Kirkby and Judith Nelson. Disc 4 also includes a delightful duet from *The Richmond Heiress*, representing a flirtation in music.

There are other attractive duets elsewhere, for instance the nautical *Blow, blow, Boreas, blow* from *Sir Barnaby Whigg*, which could fit admirably into *HMS Pinafore* (Rogers Covey-Crump and David Thomas) and the jovial *As soon as the chaos* from *The Marriage-hater Match'd*. In *Ah me! to many deaths* from *Regulus*, Judith Nelson is at her most eloquent while, earlier on Disc 5, she sings charmingly the familiar *Nymphs and shepherds*, which comes from *The Libertine*, a particularly fine score with imaginative use of the brass. The equally famous *Music for a while*, beautifully sung by James Bowman, derives from *Oedipus*.

The last disc again shows Judith Nelson at her finest in a series of arias, but it also includes a splendidly boisterous Quartet from *The Canterbury Guests*. The collection is appropriately rounded off by members of the Academy giving first-class performances of some of Purcell's instrumental music, ending with the famous *Chacony*.

The sharpness of inspiration comes over very compellingly on original instruments, though Hogwood tends to prefer tempi faster than one might expect. Throughout, the sound is admirably fresh, with clean transfers retaining the warmth and bite of the original analogue recordings, yet without adding any abrasive edge. The discs are comprehensively documented and with full texts included.

Rachmaninov, Sergei (1873–1943)

Aleko: complete.
Withdrawn: (B) **(*) AVM AVMCD 1011; *AVMC 1011* [id.]. Plovdiv PO, Raichev.
   Aleko (Nikola Ghiuselev), Zemfira (Blagovesta Karnobatlova), Young gypsy (Pavel Kourchoumov), Old gypsy (Dimiter Petkov).

Rachmaninov's early one-Act opera is based on a Pushkin tale of love and jealousy set in a gypsy camp. The story takes place during a single night. Aleko, a fugitive from justice, arrives at a Bessarabian settlement. He adapts immediately to the easy-going life-style and the casual attitude to responsibility of the gypsies, and he marries his gypsy lover, Zemfira. Her father warns him that she may not be constant, for Zemfira's mother was unfaithful to him.

Later that same evening, Aleko finds Zemfira *in flagrante delicto* with a younger man and, in jealous anger, kills them both. He is immediately ejected from the settlement for not accepting the gypsies' free attitude to love-making, consistent with everything else in their culture.

The opera never quite lives up to its promise of Russian *verismo*. Even the climactic passage, in which Aleko comes upon his gypsy wife in the arms of another, fails to bite, but there is some colourful, atmospheric writing and some yearning melodies. Nikola Ghiuselev sings nobly in his cavatina, and Pavel Kourchoumov brings a fresh, light tenor to the role of the Young Gypsy. Dimiter Petkov, past his best but resonant, is aptly cast as the Old Gypsy. Slavonic shrillness prevents Blagovesta Karnobatlova's singing as the heroine, Zemfira, from being as attractive as it promises. The recording, though not ideally atmospheric, is agreeable enough. This set currently has no distributor, but may reappear in the lifetime of this book and so is included *faute de mieux*.

(i) *Monna Vanna* (incomplete opera: Act I, orch. Buketoff); (with (ii) *Piano concerto No. 4* (original version)).
**(*) Chan. Dig. CHAN 8987 [id.]. (i) Sherrill Milnes, Seth McCoy, Blythe Walker, Nickolas Karousatos, Jon Thorsteinsson; (ii) William Black; Iceland SO, Buketoff.

Monna Vanna is the fragment of an opera based on Maeterlinck which Rachmaninov wrote around the inspired period of his *Second Symphony*. He composed the piano score of Act I complete during an exceptionally happy stay in Dresden in 1907 but was prevented from continuing it at the time by other commitments. Maeterlinck then refused to let him have the rights for setting the play, but Rachmaninov thought so well of the fragment that it was the one score he brought away from Russia after the Revolution. Igor Buketoff, who knew the composer, has rescued this Act I score and orchestrated it very sensitively to make an interesting curiosity. In its ripely romantic manner – very different from Debussy setting Maeterlinck – it may not have big tunes, but the writing has lyrical warmth and flows freely, thrusting home climactic moments with the same sureness as Rachmaninov's symphonies. The snag is the wordy libretto and improbable story, set in fifteenth-century Pisa, which is surrounded by the Florentine army and has been under siege for three months.

As the opera opens, Guido, commander of the defending army, is in consultation with his lieutenants, Torello and Borso. With supplies of food and ammunition all but exhausted, and with reinforcements prevented from getting through, the situation is desperate. Guido has requested surrender terms and sent his elderly father, Marco, as token of his good faith, and they cannot understand why the enemy, led by Prinzivalle, does not either communicate or storm the city. They decide to tell the people that the situation is hopeless.

Then Guido's father appears. He was received by the enemy with courtesy and respect, but Prinzivalle's terms are apparently unacceptable. Giovanna, Guido's wife, must come to Prinzivalle's tent, wearing only a mantle, and spend the night with him. He promises to return her safely in the morning, when the city will receive fresh supplies. Guido is furious and assures his father that Vanna will never consent, only to discover that she has already been consulted and the Pisa Council is meeting at that very moment to discuss the demand.

The cries of the people now indicate that Vanna is arriving. She turns to Marco and says she is prepared to sacrifice herself to save the city; moreover she will not take her opportunity to kill Prinzivalle, as that would only lead to the sacking of Pisa. Guido desperately tries to persuade her not to go, saying first that he will renounce her then threatening her with death, but she is determined and begs him to realize that her love for him is greater than ever. Guido dismisses her and, sadly, she departs. (This is where Rachmaninov's music ends.)

The resolution of the plot in the remaining two Acts is as follows. Vanna enters Prinzivalle's tent, conforming to his conditions regarding her attire. He grasps her hand and passionately declares his love for her, reminding her that they were childhood sweethearts in Venice. Later his father took him to Africa and, after many experiences, he returned to discover his beloved had married another. Vanna's memories and affections are reawakened and the night passes tenderly.

But Prinzivalle only kisses her hand and does not attempt to take advantage of his situation. Dawn comes and she is still chaste. News comes from Florence which appears to indicate that Prinzivalle's life is in great danger. Vanna suggests that he accompany her back to Pisa as her prisoner.

We return now to the jealous, bitter Guido, who is sure he has been betrayed. Vanna approaches, accompanied by Prinzivalle. She is repulsed by her husband and, when she tries to explain to him that she has returned untouched, just as she left, her father accepts her word, but not her husband.

Guido furiously condemns Prinzivalle to death, and Vanna makes a dramatic *volte face*: she now says she was subject to a night of carnal degradation at Prinzivalle's hands and gives him an ironically passionate kiss in front of Guido. She asks for the keys to his cell, so that she can supervise an appropriate punishment, and gives the keys to Marco for safe keeping. The suggestion is that she will abandon her husband and fly with Prinzivalle, probably taking her father with her.

Buketoff's performance with the Iceland Symphony is warmly convincing, but the singing is flawed, with Sherrill Milnes, as Monna Vanna's jealous husband, standing out from an indifferent team, otherwise thin-toned and often wobbly. That enjoyable rarity is unexpectedly but attractively coupled with Buketoff's resurrection of the original score of the *Fourth Piano concerto*, rather more expansive than the text we know. William Black is the powerful soloist, though the piano sound, unlike that of the orchestra, lacks weight.

Rameau, Jean Philippe (1683–1764)

OPERA-BALLET AND OPERA

Anacréon (complete).
*** HM HMC 90 1090 [id.]. Les Arts Florissants, Christie.
Anacréon (René Schirrer), L'amour (Agnès Mellon), Prêtresse (Jill Feldman), Agathocle (Dominique Visse), Convive (Michel Laplénie).

Rameau composed two works on the theme of the ancient Greek poet, Anacreon, famed for his devotion to Cupid and Bacchus. This is the second, originally designed as an *acte de ballet* to a libretto by P.-J. Bernard and composed in 1757. The music has charm, even if it is not Rameau at his most inventive; the performance is as authoritative and stylish as one would expect from William Christie's group. Those with an interest in the period will certainly want it – and it has moments of great appeal. The recording is admirable.

Castor et Pollux (complete).
(M) *** Teldec/Warner 2292 42510-2 (3) [id.]. Stockholm Chamber Ch., VCM, Harnoncourt.
Castor / Amour (Zeger Vandersteene), Pollux (Gérard Souzay), Phébé (Norma Lerer), Minerva (Jeanette Scovotti), Venus (Märta Scheele), Mars (Rolf Leanderson), Jupiter (Jacques Villisech).

Harnoncourt and his Viennese colleagues went to Stockholm in 1972 to record this richly varied score, the second of Rameau's tragédies lyriques, telling the mythological story of Castor and Pollux, the heavenly twins.

In the Prologue the Arts and Minerva together persuade Amour to subdue Mars with love, and peace reigns. Then we move to the tombs of the Spartan kings where there is general lamentation for the recent death of King Castor, slain by Linceus. Pollux, his brother, has in turn avenged Castor by killing Linceus and now comforts Telaira (who loved Castor) for he loves her also. She asks him to prove his feelings for her by going to the Underworld to bring Castor back with him.

Pollux is torn between love for his brother and his passion for Telaira. He asks his father, Jupiter, to restore Castor but is told that such a restoration can only come about if Pollux takes his brother's place. Jupiter then tempts his son to remain on Earth with a seductive dance entertainment arranged by Hebe, the Goddess of Eternal Youth.

Phoebe, who in turn loves Pollux, tries to stop him on his way to the Underworld by evoking the demons, but Telaira thwarts her and Pollux tells Phoebe that his affections lie elsewhere, news which does not please her at all.

In Elysium, Castor is pining for Telaira. When his brother appears to rescue him, he is overjoyed until he discovers the necessary sacrifice. He says that after 24 hours he will return to the Underworld and thus restore Pollux to life. Castor and Telaira are now joyously reunited and the desperate Phoebe commits suicide.

But Castor, having enjoyed his loving reunion, cannot be persuaded to return and so restore his brother to life. Yet help is at hand.

Suddenly a great storm develops and Jupiter appears. He makes both brothers immortal, to take their place in the heavens. In return Pollux generously offers his brother Telaira, who will now become a goddess. The final rejoicing brings in everyone, including stars and gods as well as mortals.

With many interludes for choral and ballet divertissements, Harnoncourt is a direct rather than a persuasive interpreter. He brings as much edge as elegance to the music, underlining detail and contrasts of colour with his refusal to smooth over lines in expressive legato. The result is fresh and immediate and very compelling, helped by a strong singing cast and a very good recording, bright, atmospheric and well balanced. It sounds freshly minted in its CD transfer and certainly not over two decades old. The documentation is excellent.

Les Fêtes d'Hébé: 3rd Entrée: La Danse.
(M) *** Erato/Warner 2292 45985-2 [id.]. Monteverdi Ch. & O, Gardiner.
   Églé (Jill Gomez), A Shepherd (Anne-Marie Rodde), Mercury (Jean-Claude Orliac).

Les Fêtes d'Hébé was first staged in 1739 in Paris; it was the fourth major work Rameau had composed for the lyric stage and his second in the opera-ballet genre, *Les Indes galantes* being the first. In its complete form *Les Fêtes d'Hébé* consists of a prologue and three Acts dedicated to poetry, music and finally the dance. This last is a pastoral interspersed with dances in which Mercury courts the shepherdess Églé.

Few people have done more in recent years for Rameau's music than John Eliot Gardiner and this performance is distinguished by his great feeling for this composer and an alive sensitivity. He secures excellent playing and singing from his forces and the music itself is inventive and delightful. In short, this is a record not to be missed, particularly if you are a newcomer to Rameau. It is beautifully recorded and the CD transfer is smooth with lovely textures, choral and orchestral, both warm and transparent, with the soloists most naturally balanced.

Platée (complete).
** Erato/Warner Dig. 2292 45028-2 (2) [id.]. Ens. Vocale Françoise Herr, Musiciens du Louvre, Minkowski.
   Platée (Gilles Ragon), La folie / Thalie (Jennifer Smith), Thespis / Mercure (Guy De Mey), Jupiter / Satyr (Vincent Le Texier), Junon (Guillemette Laurens), Cithéron / Momus (Bernard Delétré), L'amour / Clarine (Véronique Gens), Momus (Michel Verschaeve).

Platée, written in 1745, is described as a '*ballet bouffon*', in fact a comic opera comprising a Prologue and three short Acts, based on a classical theme. The central character, the nymph Platée (Plataea), is a drag role taken by a tenor, a favourite comic device of the time, as Raymond Leppard's realization of Cavalli's *La Calisto* brought out.

The Prologue opens with Thespis lying asleep, while dancing celebrating the wine harvest goes on around him and a satyr comments on Bacchus' gratification. Thespis awakens and is urged to open his heart to Thalia with the help of Eros and create a new entertainment.

Act I then moves to a pastoral setting, with Mount Kithaeron in the background, on whose summit is a temple dedicated to Bacchus. Mercury arrives to see Kithaeron, noted for his wisdom, and tells him that Juno is jealous over Jupiter's inconstancy and she cannot be calmed. Jupiter needs a means of placating his spouse. Mercury adds that the affair has humorous possibilities.

Kithaeron tells of a nymph, 'blindly unaware of her comic countenance', who lives in a nearby marsh and has daily hopes of the attention of lovers. He suggests that Jupiter should pay court to her and that Juno be made aware of the affair. We now meet Plataea who immediately professes love for Kithaeron, but his response, though respectful, is distinctly cool. Mercury arrives, and Kithaeron tells Plataea of Jupiter's admiration.

In Act II Mercury reports on Juno's expected jealous anger and Jupiter arrives in a chariot, appearing first to Plataea as a four-footed creature, garlanded with flowers, then changing himself into a bird and flying away. Then, after a thunderclap, he appears as himself, accompanied by Momus, and seeks to make an impression on Plataea by launching several thunderbolts. He declares his ardour and offers the possibility of marriage. Folly now appears as part of the ballet and comments on Jupiter's commitment to Plataea.

Act III brings in Juno, seething with anger and jealousy, but Mercury suggests that she put her jealous feelings aside since Jupiter really cares only for her. Meanwhile Plataea is impatient for Jupiter's fullest avowal of his passion, but Momus arrives in the place of Eros (who has business elsewhere) and offers only tears and weeping and, at the best, hope.

Kithaeron returns to tell the nymph that her conquest has created a local sensation. Before taking further action, Jupiter awaits Juno, who finally arrives, throws herself on Plataea and, tearing off her veil, sees for herself that she is no rival. Jupiter, smirking, says glibly, 'You see now your mistake! Can you have doubts about my love for you?' Juno exits in high dudgeon, while Plataea vows vengeance for her humiliation, and blames Kithaeron.

With such a send-up of classical tradition, the performers here understandably adopt comic expressions and voices, which in a recording, as opposed to a stage performance, become rather wearing on the listener. It is like being nudged in the ribs, prompted to laugh, when the joke is not subtle. Also surprisingly with such stylish singers as the tenor Guy de Mey, almost all the soloists aspirate heavily in florid passages. Within that convention this is a lively, brisk performance, very well conducted by Marc Minkowski, but marred by the dryness of the recording. As a joint project with French Radio, it was made in what sounds like a small Paris studio: though the sense of presence is very vivid, the sound of period instruments reminds one of the abrasiveness of much earlier recordings. Minkowski writes of the distinctive instrumentation that Rameau devised, all top and bottom, and the aggressive acoustic emphasizes that. But as a work, *Platée* certainly provides a fascinating side-glance at Rameau's mastery.

Pygmalion (complete).
(M) **(*) HM/BMG GD 77143 [77143-2-RG]. John Elwes, Mieke Van der Sluis, François Vanhecke, Rachel Yakar, Paris Chapelle Royal Ch., La Petite Bande, Leonhardt.

Leonhardt's 1980 account with John Elwes as Pygmalion and Mieke van der Sluis as Céphise is welcome in the catalogue in this inexpensive format. Leonhardt's direction is rather leisurely, but his soloists make a good team. The use of period instruments brings attractive transparency of texture and, thanks to the excellence of the original recording, this is enhanced on CD. The documentation (including full translation) is first class.

Zoroastre (complete).
(M) **(*) HM/BMG GD 77144 (3) [77144-2-RG]. Ghent Coll. Vocale, La Petite Bande, Kuijken. Zoroastre (John Elwes), Amélite (Greta De Reyghere), Erinice (Mieke Van der Sluis), Céphie (Agnès Mellon), Abramane (Gregory Reinhart).

Zoroastre was the last but one of Rameau's tragédies-lyriques. It appeared 15 years before his final masterpiece, *Les Boréades*; but the original 1749 score was drastically revised to produce the text of 1756, recorded here. It is a piece giving great opportunities for spectacle and the fullest use of stage machinery.

The narrative celebrates the battle between Zoroastre (an Abraham-like figure, but also the founder of the magic arts) and his evil adversary, Abramane, whose power comes from the spirits of darkness. With Rameau here abandoning the old convention of an allegorical Prologue, the opera opens in the gardens of the kings of Bactria after a violent thunderstorm.

The villainous High Priest, Abramane, announces that, rather than the ungrateful Amélite, the heir presumptive (who has spurned him), Princess Erinice shall become queen of Bactria, and he hopes to share the crown. Erinice in turn has tender feelings for Zoroastre, but they too are rejected (Zoroastre loves Amélite), so she stifles them in her determination to seek revenge.

Abramane and Erinice decide to join forces. 'I want to see my rival tremble,' cries Erinice, and Abramane breaks his magic ring in two and gives one half to Erinice as pledge of their bond. Zoroastre has been outlawed and has departed the kingdom. Amélite sorely misses him and she is consoled by Céphie, her handmaiden. Erinice enters and brutally tells Amélite of her dire predicament, and the spirits of cruelty drag her off.

Act II moves to the palace of Oromases, King of the Genies, but its pleasures can do nothing to assuage Zoroastre's grief, for he sorely misses Amélite. Oromases tells him that he must return to rescue her, and Zoroastre is tenderly fearful for her safety. The spirits of the elements are conjured up to help their cause and Oromases urges Zoroastre to be steadfast and unfearful in his task, giving him the Book of Life to help him out of danger.

We now return to Bactria to find Amélite chained and guarded by demons who declare that innocence is powerless against the prince of hell. Erinice enters and gives Amélite an ultimatum: renounce the throne or die! Amélite defies her and Erinice hurls herself at her with a dagger, but a great door suddenly bursts open and there stands Zoroastre, arriving in the nick of time to prevent the murder. The demons dematerialize. Erinice is thwarted. Amélite and Zoroastre now greet each other passionately and Amélite tells him that her love for him is more important than her kingdom.

Zoroastre invokes his magic and the cell walls disappear and the crowded central square of Bactria becomes visible. He tells the gathered citizens that Amélite is now restored to them, and Céphie and the crowd give her a rousing welcome. The following ballet celebrates the triumph of love, its joys proclaimed by Amélite who says that happiness can arrive suddenly, like lightning in a storm, born in the midst of hardship. Zoroastre, somewhat prematurely, urges the citizens to fear Abramane and his crew no longer: victory is assured and love has triumphed.

We now move to a nearby riverbank before sunrise. Abramane is lying in wait to trap Zoroastre: 'His tomb is prepared and I shall guide him to it.' The angry Erinice is determined on revenge; her simmering love-hate feeling for Zoroastre is submerged by anger that he prevented her from stabbing her rival. Abramane is not fooled and he sees that her real motivation is that of a lover spurned and, sensing her to be an unreliable ally, he sends her off in a cloud. As the first light of dawn appears, he is obsessed with vengeance.

Zoroastre and Amélite and their retinues now arrive, still romantically celebrating their loving feelings and looking forward to their wedding day. A ballet of nubile girls and young mountain-dwelling couples brings a sexist call from Zoroastre to the dancing maidens to give full rein to their desires and passions – 'for marriage will fulfil your expectations, with one delight after another'.

This is heady stuff and, needless to say, it is suddenly interrupted by reality. A thunderclap is heard, the earth shakes and the vengeful Abramane flies in, bringing terror and destruction all round him. The people take flight and Zoroastre finds Amélite, apparently dying, and all but loses his resolve. Then he summons up the beneficent spirits who surround her and bear her off. At the same time, the city is ravaged by fire.

Act IV takes us to the Underworld, ruled over by Ariman. Zopire tells Abramane that his enemy is triumphant, for Zoroastre's magic has caused Abramane's soldiers to turn their swords on themselves. Erinice enters, feeling herself irretrievably bound up in Abramane's evil schemes. He calls on her to harden her resolve. Despair, he tells her, is only the lot of unfortunate wretches without power. But what can she hope for, with Amélite alive and adored by Zoroastre; indeed she is consumed with envy at their happiness.

Within a temple, 'with a double door of thickest bronze', Abramane, Erinice, Zopire and the assembled priests now call upon the powers of darkness to come to their aid, and appropriate sacrifices are made. Throngs of evil spirits fill the stage, dominated by Revenge, armed with a huge club, studded with iron spikes. Erinice recovers her confidence and imagines her rival's death at her own hands. Revenge is sweet, says Abramane, and the evil spirits attack a statue of Zoroastre with fearful incantations, and the statue is engulfed in flames. Revenge celebrates victory over the beneficent powers.

The last Act moves to the domain of Zerodoust, where the kings of Bactria are crowned. Erinice is still smitten with Zoroastre and fearful for his life. But Zoroastre scorns her warnings of Abramane's invocation of the powers of hell. His confidence increases her uneasiness – all she wants is for him to stay alive. Sounds are heard of the people calling for Amélite, and Erinice goes off in fresh despair. Céphie now appears, to tell Zoroastre the dire news that, while in the midst of the celebrating crowd, a whirlwind has carried off Amélite.

It looks as if Erinice and Abramane have triumphed after all, for when they enter with their followers (Abramane riding on a fiery cloud), Amélite is revealed at Abramane's feet, in chains. But Zoroastre calls on heaven, a flash of lightning strikes his enemies asunder and they all disappear into the bowels of the earth.

There is a great transformation scene, and the Temple of Light appears, signifying the munificent virtues of Zoroastre's power. The benign spirits bring Amélite and Zoroastre together, and Oromases congratulates him on his virtue and perseverance. The couple are crowned with flowers and again declare their mutual love. Amélite has the final word: 'Cupid comes a-flying at the sound of oboes. The sweet sounds of his voice are accompanied by your bagpipers.'

Zoroastre may not have quite the inspiration of *Les Boréades* in modifying once rigid conventions; but frequently, as in the monologue of the villain Abramane in Act III, Rameau was clearly taking a leaf out of Gluck's book in the dark originality of the instrumentation, here made transparent in finely detailed recording. Though Kuijken's characteristically gentle style with his excellent authentic group, La Petite Bande, lacks a little in bite and urgency, it is a fine presentation of a long-neglected masterpiece, with crisp and stylish singing from the soloists, notably John Elwes in the name-part and Gregory Reinhart as Abramane. The Ghent Collegium Vocale, placed rather close, sings with vigour in the choruses, but the individual voices fail to blend. The five Acts are now offered on three CDs against the original set on four LPs. The excellent documentation (144 pages, including translations) puts the mid-priced issues of many of the large international companies to shame.

Ravel, Maurice (1875–1937)

L'enfant et les sortilèges.
Withdrawn: *** EMI Dig. CDC7 47169-2 [id.]. Amb. S., LSO, Previn.
  Child (Susan Davenny Wyner), with Jocelyne Taillon, Jane Berbié, Jules Bastin, Philippe Huttenlocher, Philip Langridge, Arleen Augér, Linda Finnie.

Previn's dramatic and highly spontaneous reading of *L'enfant* brings out the refreshing charm of this miniature masterpiece, and it is a great pity that it is currently withdrawn from the catalogue. Helped by a strong and stylish team of soloists, including Arleen Augér and Philip Langridge in multiple roles, and marred only by the rather raw timbre of Susan Davenny Wyner as the Child, this makes superb entertainment. On CD, the precision and sense of presence of the digital recording comes out vividly, with subtle textures clarified and voices – including the odd shout – precisely placed. That precision goes well with Previn's performance, crisply rhythmic rather than atmospherically poetic. The original issue of this 44-minute piece had only one band, divided only by index markings, unusable on many machines. We must hope this can be rectified when the recording is reissued at mid-price.

(i) *L'enfant et les sortilèges;* (ii) *L'heure espagnole* (complete).
(M) ****(*)** Decca stereo/mono 433 400-2 (2) [id.]. (i) Motet de Genève; (i; ii) SRO, Ansermet (with DEBUSSY: *Le Martyre de Saint-Sébastien* – Suzanne Danco, Nancy Waugh, Marie-Luise De Montmollin, Union Chorale de la Tour-de-Peilz).
  (i) The Child (Flore Wend) with Marie-Luise De Montmollin, Geneviève Touraine, Adrienne Migliette, Suzanne Danco, Juliette Bise, Hugues Cuénod, Pierre Mollet, Lucien Lovano.
  (ii) Concepción (Suzanne Danco), Gonzalve (Paul Derenne), Torquemada (Michel Hamel), Ramiro (Heinz Rehfuss), Don Inigo Gomez (André Vessières).

L'enfant et les sortilèges (complete).
**(*) DG 423 718-2 [id.]. RTF Ch. & Boys' Ch., RTF Nat. O, Maazel.
  Child (Françoise Ogéas), with Jeannine Collard, Jane Berbié, Sylvaine Gilma, Colette Herzog, Heinz Rehfuss, Camille Maurane, Michel Sénéchal.

L'heure espagnole (complete).
**(*) DG 423 719-2 [id.]. Paris Op. O, Maazel.

Concepción (Jane Berbié), Gonsalve (Michel Sénéchal), Torquemada (Jean Giraudeau), Ramiro (Gabriel Bacquier), Inigo Gomez (José Van Dam).

Ravel wrote a pair of highly theatrical yet charming one-Act operas, which are remarkably contrasted, yet complementary, so that they make a diverting double bill. The scene of *L'enfant et les sortilèges* ('The child and the magic spells') is the living room of an old Norman country house. The child – about six or seven years old – is sitting lazily, avoiding doing his lessons. His mother, bringing in his tea, is vexed that he is not working and has made a blot on the tablecloth. She tries to make him go back to work and he puts his tongue out rudely.

As soon as she departs, an orgy of destruction begins. He smashes the cup and teapot, pricks his pet squirrel with his pen, pulls the cat's tail, flourishes the poker and upsets the kettle into the fire. Then, using the poker as a sword, he attacks the wallpaper with its design of shepherds and shepherdesses, and pulls long strips from the wall. Opening the grandfather clock, he swings on the pendulum and pulls it off then turns to his books, which are torn up with gleeful abandon.

Then suddenly the magic spell begins. The chair on which he sits moves away from him, and as it joins another Louis XV chair in a grotesque dance, the two converse, saying that they will never again have to endure the pranks of a naughty child.

The sofa, ottoman, settle and wicker chair all agree; the mutilated clock complains of his lack of balance and strikes uncontrollably; the Chinese cup and teapot cry out in nonsense words – a mixture of English and pseudo-Chinese – and then indulge in a foxtrot. The fire now spits back at the child, pursues it round the room and says that warmth is only for those who are good; bad children will be burnt.

The wallpaper shepherds and shepherdesses dance and the fairy princess rises from the torn book. From an arithmetic learner an old man emerges, covered in symbols, and reels off mathematical problems to torment the child, who sits down with his head in his hands. The child then addresses the cat, and it too spits at him; a second white cat appears, and the two join in a cat love-duet then frenziedly leap out of the window.

Following them into the moonlit garden, the child soon finds his peace is shattered when the tree complains that his flanks have been cut. A dragonfly calls for her lost mate, pinned to the wall in the child's room. A bat has also been killed, leaving its family uncared for. Frogs dance round the pool and one lays its head on the child's lap. A squirrel warns it to take no risks with such a dangerous creature, for her mate is captive in a cage. The child explains that he loves the squirrel's beautiful eyes, but the squirrel begs for freedom for her partner.

The animals race round him, pushing him, and he cries out, '*Maman!*' A wounded squirrel limps towards him and the child binds up its paw. All at once the animals' hostility dies away and they sense the child's loneliness. They echo his call for '*Maman*'. He is led gently back to the house, where the windows light up and he repeats his cry more confidently, '*Maman!*'

L'heure espagnole is set in eighteenth-century Toledo, where the absent-minded clock-maker, Torquemada, has a shop. Today is the day and this is the hour when he visits the town hall to service the clocks in his care. His wife, Concepción, makes the most of this regular opportunity to enjoy a visit from one of her lovers. Just as Torquemada leaves, Ramiro, a muleteer, arrives to have his watch repaired, a much-prized family heirloom. Concepción is annoyed when her husband invites Ramiro to wait until he returns, but she arranges for him to carry a large clock up to her room, which her husband says is too heavy for him to lift.

Gonsalve, Concepción's poetic lover, now arrives, but he talks too much and does not make the most of his amorous opportunities. Rather similarly, when a further prospective lover arrives, the ungainly banker, Don Inigo Gomez, Concepción is again disappointed by his lack of practical ardour. She hides both of them, one in each of two grandfather clocks, and the agreeable muleteer carries both upstairs.

Admiring his strength, Concepción transfers her attentions to her willing clock-porter, has the clocks brought back down again into the shop, then retires with him contentedly to her bedroom. At length Torquemada returns, finds two dejected philanderers in his clocks and sells one to each. Concepción now re-enters with Ramiro, and her smile indicates that carrying clocks is not his only talent. So everyone is happy, and the moral of the tale supposedly comes from Boccaccio: '*Entre tous les amants, seul amant efficace; il arrive un moment, dans les déduits d'amour, où le muletier a son tour!*' This, freely translated, suggests that among all lovers there comes the need for loving to be effective, so that the moment arrives when the demands of love ensure that the muleteer will have his day!

Maazel's recordings of both the operas were made in the early 1960s (*L'enfant* in 1961, *L'heure espagnole* four years later) and, though the solo voices in the former are balanced too close, the sound is vivid and the performances are splendidly stylish. Neo-classical crispness of articulation goes with refined textures that convey the tender poetry of the one piece, the ripe humour of the other. The CD remastering has been very successful and both performances are given striking presence, without loss of essential atmosphere. Unlike this CD issue, the last incarnation of these recordings (paired together) was at mid-price and, though this time full librettos are included, collectors may well feel that the present offering is unreasonably expensive.

In Ansermet's vintage recordings, the two Ravel operas are accommodated on one disc apiece and Debussy's *Le martyre* is split between the two. They were recorded in 1953–4 and were the mainstay of the catalogue, largely (it must be admitted) on account of Decca's superior engineering and their enlightened policy of keeping them in the catalogue. *L'enfant et les sortilèges* is stereo; *L'heure espagnole* is mono. Not that Ansermet's performances are wanting in style or insight. The mono *L'heure espagnole* was not quite as atmospheric as René Leibowitz's Vox recording, which had an incomparable Concepción in Janine Linda (Lindemeier), while the Ansermet *L'enfant et les sortilèges* did not quite match Ernest Bour's pioneering set in subtlety and finesse. Strangely enough, the latter has never been reissued on LP in this country (though it has been available on the continent), nor has it been singled out for transfer to CD.

Ansermet is an objective interpreter of impressionist music and these are among the most winning recordings he ever made, with casts that add to the feeling of totally idiomatic performances; there is no lack of tenderness on the one hand, incisiveness on the other, with the charm of the pieces never underplayed. *L'enfant*, recorded in October 1954, brings an astonishingly vivid example of early stereo, with voices sharply focused, even if occasionally balances are odd – as with the most characterful soloist, Hugues Cuénod, whose voice is backwardly placed. The fresh, bright singing of Flore Wend as the Child contrasts strongly with some later interpreters.

Recorded a year earlier, *L'heure espagnole* comes in mono sound that is not only less atmospheric but also rather duller, with too little bloom on the voices. Yet Suzanne Danco is enchanting as the provocative wife who opts for the virile muleteer over her other, inadequate suitors, with a slight flicker in the voice adding to its distinctively French timbre. Heinz Rehfuss sings with incisive clarity as the muleteer and, as in *L'enfant*, Hugues Cuénod gives a vivid character-study, this time as the old clockmaker-husband. Role for role, however, neither account matches the later records made by Lorin Maazel and French Radio forces, either in terms of characterization or atmosphere. Ansermet's recording of 50 minutes of Debussy's incidental music for *Le martyre de Saint-Sébastien* is a generous makeweight. The main omissions are the mélodrames with spoken narration. Like *L'enfant*, it is in early stereo, though the sound is duller.

Respighi, Ottorino (1879–1936)

La Fiamma (complete).
*** Hung. Dig. HCD 12591/3 [id.]. Hungarian R. and TV Ch., Hungarian State O, Gardelli.
    Eudossia (Klára Takács), Basilio (Sándor Sólyom-Nagy), Donello (Péter Kelen), Silvana (Ilona Tokody).

La Fiamma, a tale of witchcraft and the early church set in seventh-century Ravenna, might be described as Puccini updated – though the setting does also give Respighi plenty of opportunities to draw on his medievalist side, not just his love of exotic sounds.

We are in the palace of the exarch (one rank down from a patriarch), Basilio. Eudossia, his mother (severe and uncompromising), and Silvana, his young second wife, are engaged in embroidery. Eudossia leaves and the atmosphere lightens, but Silvana complains to her favourite serving maid, Monica, that she feels imprisoned.

Agnes di Cervia now rushes in, in flight, accused of witchcraft. Having been convinced that Agnes is not in league with the devil, Silvana hides her. Donello, Silvana's stepson, now returns from Byzantium. He has not met his father's new wife until now but he remembers that his childhood friend was aided by the young Silvana when thrown from his horse. She had taken the boy to Agnes's hut to be succoured. Eudossia returns and receives the gifts her grandson has brought from the Empress Irene. They are interrupted by the mob, seeking Agnes. The crowd is led by the Church Exorcist, who enters the palace, discovers her hiding place, and drags Agnes off, cursing.

At the opening of Act II it becomes obvious that Monica is in love with Donello, and Silvana (who fancies him for herself) peremptorily banishes her favourite lady-in-waiting to a convent. Basilio now arrives. A strict orthodox, he is determined to do battle with the pope. Meanwhile Agnes has been burnt at the stake, and has not only betrayed Silvana's complicity in hiding her but has revealed that Silvana's mother used witchcraft to arrange her daughter's marriage to the exarch.

The angry Basilio issues a decree that anyone who repeats this story shall have his tongue cut out. But he confesses to Silvana that it is true, saying that, although he may have been seduced originally by magic, now he truly loves her and has since been penitent about his earlier readiness to gratify his carnal desires. Silvana is curious to know if the genes passed down to her include any of her mother's skills in witchcraft.

To try herself out, she successfully invokes Donello and receives an ardent and thoroughly illicit kiss. Soon the lovers are spending the night in Donello's room, caught up in abandoned passion. Dawn comes and, experiencing *coitus triste*, Donello seeks to escape from Silvana's sinful embrace. But his ecstasy proves too strong for him and, when Eudossia encounters the couple *in flagrante dilecto*, she threatens her daughter-in-law with her husband's wrath.

When Basilio enters, it is obvious that the news of his wife's unfaithfulness has devastated him. He tells Donello of the latter's recall by Empress Irene and, although at first reluctant, Donello goes off, sighing in relief that he has extricated himself from such a potentially disastrous situation. When Silvana and Basilio are left alone, the thwarted Silvana suddenly reveals her suppressed hatred for her husband and Basilio dies of shock and despair. Silvana calls out for help and Eudossia accuses her of witchcraft.

She is brought for trial before the church tribunal and pleads that, although she transgressed in her love for Donello, she did not murder her husband. Donello adds his support to her plea. Eudossia, however, recalls Agnes's statement on the scaffold about Silvana's mother being involved in witchcraft and, when Donello also turns against her, the speechless Silvana is unable to make her required assertion of innocence on a reliquary before the bishop. She is declared a witch by the appalled watching crowd.

Richly atmospheric, with choruses and ensembles both mysterious and savage, *La fiamma* makes a fine impact in this excellent first recording, idiomatically conducted by Lamberto Gardelli. The Hungarian cast is impressive, with Ilona Tokody producing Callas-like inflexions in the central role of Silvana, who falls in love with her stepson, shocks her husband into falling down dead, and then cannot find tongue to deny a charge of witchcraft. Sándor Sólyom-Nagy is impressive as Basilio, Péter Kelen is aptly light-toned as the stepson, but it is the formidable Klára Takács as the interfering Eudossia who personifies the grit in the oyster, providing high melodrama. The playing is warmly committed and, apart from some distancing of the chorus, the sound is first rate, atmospheric but also precisely focused.

Semirama (complete).
*** Hung. Dig. HCD 31197/8 [id.]. Hungarian State O, Gardelli.
    Semirama (Eva Marton), Merodach (Lando Bartolini), Susiana (Veronika Kincses).

Imagine a cross between *The Pines of Rome* and Puccini's *Turandot*, and you have a fair idea of Respighi's *Semirama*. In this, his first opera, the daring young Italian composer saw no reason to hold back. The year was 1910, and in the atmosphere of abandon after the operatic scandals of Strauss's *Salome* and *Elektra*, the score goes over the top. Very differently from Rossini in *Semiramide*, Respighi treats the story as a sort of Oedipus in reverse: the lascivious Queen Semirama seduces the young Babylonian general, Merodach, and then finds that he is her son.

The opera was an instant success with the first Bologna audience – and no wonder, when Respighi offers such consistently sumptuous sounds, along with an almost endless flow of melody. At that time Puccini was still the reigning monarch of Italian opera, but after *Butterfly* in 1904 he faltered, wondering where to go next, and it is surprising that the claims of Respighi in this formidable first opera did not bring it into the repertory. With the outbreak of the First World War, the climate turned against lavish operas about exotic figures from antiquity.

This first recording of *Semirama*, made in Budapest with Lamberto Gardelli pacing the score masterfully, should help to bring the opera back from oblivion, perhaps even encourage stage productions. The surprise is that this highly accomplished score dates from well before any of the works for which Respighi is usually known, including *The Pines of Rome* (1924). He also anticipates Puccini. One passage, when the queen questions her victim with an imperiously repeated '*Rispondi!*', is so like the Riddle scene in *Turandot* that plainly Puccini was the one who copied, not the young Respighi.

This recording, like so many previous opera sets from Budapest, offers splendid playing from the Hungarian State Orchestra, with fine singing from the Radio and Television Chorus and a strong cast of soloists. Eva Marton makes a powerful queen, and the voice, so often unsteady and ill-focused in recordings, is here firmer than usual in the soaring melodies. Lando Bartolini produces clear, heroic tone as Merodach, though he is reluctant to scale the voice down. Veronika Kincses as the Chaldaean princess, Susiana, caresses the Respighi melodies with her sweet, pure tone but then grows rather edgy for the more dramatic moments. The booklet looks skimpy but efficiently provides libretto, translation and the necessary background.

Rimsky-Korsakov, Nikolay (1844–1908)

The Tsar's Bride (complete).
** Chant du Monde Dig. LDC 288 056/57 [id.]. Sveshnikov Russian Ac. Ch., Bolshoi Theatre O, Chistiakov.

Vassili Stépanovitch Sobakine (Piotr Gluboky), Marfa, his daughter (Ekaterina Kudriavchenko), Grigori Grigorivitch Maliouta Skouratov (Nikolai Nizienko), Ivan Sergueïevitch Lykov (Arkadi Michenkin), Liubacha (Nina Terentieva).

One by one, the 15 operas of Rimsky-Korsakov are emerging from obscurity. The Chant du Monde set of Rimsky's ninth opera, *The Tsar's Bride*, first given in St Petersburg in 1899, provides a fair stopgap, an unhelpfully dry recording of a performance by a Bolshoi cast. Rimsky, ever attentive to musical fashion, was in part reflecting the then recent arrival of Puccini and others, for his heroine, Marfa, is as vulnerable as Mimì or Butterfly.

Yet Rimsky's easy, colourful music hardly reflects the darkness of this story of conspiracy, betrayal and poison, set in the days of Ivan the Terrible. For him, it seems, writing operas was all too easy, and he here showed little or none of Puccini's power to involve. The Bolshoi performance under Andrei Chistiakov is amiable to match, conveying few stage tensions. As Marfa Ekaterina Kudriavchenko is firmer than most Russian sopranos but has moments of rawness, and she is rather upstaged by the fine mezzo, Nina Terentieva, in the villainous role of Liubacha. Unlike most of the others, she produces beautiful tone despite the dryness. The four Acts are squeezed on to two very well-filled CDs.

Rodgers, Richard (1902–79)

No strings.
(M) **(*) EMI CDM7 64694-2 [id.]. Ch. & O, Peter Matz.

Barbara Woodruff (Diahann Carroll), David Jordan (Richard Kiley), Louis de Pourtal (Mitchell Gregg), Jeanette Valmy (Noelle Adam), Mollie Plummer (Polly Rowles), Comfort O'Connell (Bernice Massi), Mike Robinson (Don Chastain).

This *fin de siècle* post-Hammerstein show dates from 1962. Oscar Hammerstein had died of cancer two years earlier and the great tunesmith never found a replacement for him. So in *No strings* he wrote his own lyrics for a bittersweet story about a Parisian affair between a black fashion model and an American expatriate writer. There were no racial implications; rather, Rodgers' confidence in the show's star, Diahann Carroll, underlined the modern view that the skin of real talent was colourless.

The very opening flute solo has a certain delicacy and *The sweetest sounds*, the show's charming hit song, avoids the ripe sentimentality of the Rodgers/Hammerstein *oeuvre*. Indeed all the music, seldom indelible but always catchy, is easily melodic and has a certain pastiche quality, as if Rodgers had been listening to others, including Loewe. *Look no further*, even if it has just a hint of *South Pacific*, brings an engaging melancholy, but *How sad to be a woman, women are stuck with men* immediately recalls *My Fair Lady*, without any direct crib. *Maine, Eager beaver* and the happy waltz-song, *Love makes the world go round*, all represent the comments and experiences of subsidiary characters and cleverly bring the necessary upbeat contrast. The show's two stars are admirably partnered. Because of the usual close microphones Richard Kiley's voice is given a slightly abrasive edge, but otherwise the recording matches the score's sophistication. Rodgers certainly hadn't lost his touch and, while *No strings* is far from a coach party show, its music affords a lot of pleasure.

Rodgers and Hammerstein, Oscar II (1895–1960)

Carousel (excerpts).
(M) ** EMI ZDM7 64692-2 [id.]. Film soundtrack recording. Ch. & O, Alfred Newman.
  Carrie Pipperidge (Barbara Ruick), Julie Jordan (Shirley Jones), Billy Bigelow (Gordon MacRae), Cousin Nettie Fowler (Claramae Turner), Mr Enoch Snow (Robert Rounseville), Jigger Craigin (Cameron Mitchell).

Carousel is flawed, its songs combining the best and most sentimental of the Rodgers and Hammerstein *oeuvre*. The freshness of the writing of a delightful number like *Mister Snow*, the warmth of the romantic ballad, *If I loved you*, and the exuberance of *June is bustin' out all over* have to be balanced against the mawkish *You'll never walk alone*, and the problem of the central character remains unsolved. Billy Bigelow is hardly sympathetic, a fairground barker who dies during an abortive robbery by falling on his own knife, leaving the heroine pregnant. He is allowed to return from heaven for his daughter's graduation to offer reassurance.

In the film Billy, a wife-beater, is all too sympathetically played by Gordon MacRae, and it is left to Barbara Ruick as Carrie (whose *Mister Snow* is charmingly sung) and Shirley Jones as the ill-treated heroine to carry the show, helped by Robert Rounseville as a personable Mr Snow. Alfred Newman as musical director makes the most of his opportunities, notably in the opening *Carousel waltz*. But the early stereo recording is at times edgy and unkind to the male voices.

The King and I.
*** Ph. Dig. 438 007-2; *438 007-4* [id.] [id.]. Members of the Los Angeles Master Ch., Hollywood Bowl O, John Mauceri.
  Anna Leonowens (Julie Andrews), The King (Ben Kingsley), Tuptim (Lea Salonga), Lun Tha (Peabo Bryson), Lady Thiang (Marilyn Horne).
*** Sony SK 53328 [id.]. Ch. & O, Lehman Engel.
  Anna Leonowens (Barbara Cook), The King (Theodore Bikel), Tuptim (Jeanette Scovotti), Lun Tha (Daniel Ferro), Lady Thiang (Anita Darian).
(M) *** EMI ZDM7 64693-2 [id.]. Film soundtrack recording. Ch. & O, Alfred Newman.
  Anna Leonowens (Marni Nixon / Deborah Kerr), The King (Yul Brynner), Tuptim (Rita Moreno), Lun Tha (Carlos Rivas), Lady Thiang (Terry Saunders).

The King and I, enormously successful both on the stage and as a film, was based on a book by Margaret Landon, *Anna and the King of Siam*. This was discovered by Gertrude Lawrence (the first Broadway Anna) who herself recommended it to Rodgers and Hammerstein as the basis for a musical. They remained unconvinced until they saw the film dramatization (without songs) starring Rex Harrison and Irene Dunne, and the musical owes a good deal to the screenplay.

Landon's book drew on an earlier account by Anna Leonowens (published as *An English Governess at the Siamese Court*) of her visit as governess to the King of Siam to tutor the Crown Prince, where she supposedly persuaded the king into the British (colonial) way of doing things. The fact that the story was apparently true added some credence to Hammerstein's somewhat sentimental characterization of the relationship between Anna and the king. Recent research has suggested that the story may have comparatively little basis in fact – but, never mind, it is the very stuff of popular folklore.

To be convincing, the king has to have a special kind of presence, and for many Yul Brynner was uniquely believable in the role. But his charisma is strongly visual, and on record the electricity between the king and the elegant governess, winningly personified by Deborah Kerr, projects rather less strongly. However, with Alfred Newman in charge of the arrangements and a great Hollywood orchestra to hand, the result is sumptuously involving in its Hollywood way.

Helped by the opulent Capitol stereo sound, the 6½-minute *Overture* is especially welcome. The originally uncredited Marni Nixon ghosted the songs on the soundtrack – in the places where Deborah Kerr participates in the vocal numbers it is easy to spot where the voices change over – and she sings with great charm. The secondary lovers croon their numbers in the pop style of the time, which will not be to all tastes, but Terry Saunders is a dignified and convincing Lady Thiang. The CD transfer is excellently managed and the documentation properly includes an account of the Nixon/Kerr collaboration.

For many, the film soundtrack will be first choice, if only for reasons of familiarity. Yet the American studio recording has a special kind of freshness. All the songs spring forward, newly minted. Barbara Cook is a delightfully vivacious – if American – Anna, and Theodore Bikel projects his dryer portrayal of the king very convincingly. The subsidiary lovers, Jeanette

Scovotti and Daniel Ferro, are altogether more attractive in their vocal style than the artists on the soundtrack version, and Lehman Engel, using new arrangements by Philip Lang, finds plenty of sparkle in the orchestra. Altogether enjoyable, and a refreshing change. Documentation is well up to the standard of this excellent Sony Broadway series.

It seems remarkable that Julie Andrews – so famous as a governess, either Mary Poppins or Maria in *The Sound of Music* – never played Anna on the stage, yet she is a natural for the role and in the Philips recording, with her wonderfully crisp diction and natural sense of musical line, she readily upstages her competitors. Remarkably, the famous voice retains its bloom, and the eagerness of the characterization is a joy. *Hello, young lovers,* one of Rodgers' very finest songs, with its subtle interplay between 6/8 and waltz time, is splendidly done, and both in her vehement soliloquy, *Shall I tell you what I think of you,* and in her interplay with the king there is just the right degree of tension.

Ben Kingsley's King is an eccentric but a strongly projected one, and it was an inspired idea to choose Marilyn Horne as Lady Thiang to sing *Something wonderful.* She doesn't disappoint. John Mauceri directs with aplomb, using the Newman orchestrations, and the recording was made, appropriately, on the MGM sound-stage at Culver City. As usual, the singing style of of Lun Tha (Peabo Bryson) is very pop-orientated and it seems strange that the ballet (*The small house of Uncle Tom*) was omitted, but otherwise the 65-minute selection contains much more music than its competitors and makes an obvious first choice.

Oklahoma!

(M) ******* EMI ZDM7 64691-2 [id.]. Ch. & O, Jay Blackton.

    Curly (Gordon MacRae), Laurey (Shirley Jones), Aunt Eller (Charlotte Greenwood), Will Parker (Gene Nelson), Ado Annie Carnes (Gloria Grahame), Jud Fry (Rod Steiger), Andrew Carnes (James Whitmore).

(***) Sony mono SK 53326 [id.]. Ch. & O, Lehman Engel.

    Curly (Nelson Eddy), Laurey (Virginia Haskins), Aunt Eller (Portia Nelson), Will Parker (Wilton Clary), Ado Anne Carnes (Kaye Ballard), Jud Fry (Lee Cass).

Like *Show Boat, Oklahoma!* changed the face of the Broadway musical, and Rodgers and Hammerstein never matched, let alone bettered, its score. The sentimental streak that slips into all their other shows is here kept at bay by the sheer vitality and breeziness of the invention, and Jud Fry – a weird, offbeat villain – has more than a little in common with Dick Deadeye in *HMS Pinafore.*

The film, made for the wide screen, certainly blew the action up out of proportion a little, but the excellence of the performers more than redeemed this inflation of a simple farm love-story. Gordon MacRae and Shirley Jones are perfectly cast as the ranch-hand, Curly, and his girlfriend, Laurey. MacRae's opening *Oh what a beautiful morning* has just the right degree of charm, and in *The surrey with the fringe on top* the gentle close is beautifully handled. Gene Nelson and Gloria Grahame project the folksy subsidiary couple with robust vitality (*I cain't say no* and *All er nothin'* are genuine highlights), and Rod Steiger, with little to do musically, provides the necessary black dourness as Jud. The big title-number goes with the required zest, and the 1955 soundtrack recording offers remarkably full and well-focused stereo.

The alternative studio recording centres on Nelson Eddy's assumption of the role of Curly. It was not an obvious casting, even though he had done it before on 78-r.p.m. discs in 1944, but it succeeds triumphantly because of the sheer quality of the voice, still fresh and blooming. The rest of the cast measures up well and the fizzing liveliness of the whole score is tribute to the conductor, Lehman Engel, and the producer, Goddard Lieberson. Eddy's *Beautiful morning* and *Surrey with the fringe* are memorable, and he teams up most successfully with Virginia Haskins, an engaging Laurey. Lee Cass, as Jud Fry, has an additional number not included in the film, *Lonely room,* which fills out the character. The mono sound is first class.

The Sound of Music.

(M) ******* BMG/RCA ND 90368. Film soundtrack recording. Ch. & O, Irwin Kostal.

    Maria (Julie Andrews), The Captain (Christopher Plummer), Mother Abbess (Peggy Wood), Rolf (Dan Truhitte).

Having been turned down for the part of Eliza in the movie of *My Fair Lady,* Julie Andrews bounced back to confound the Hollywood moguls who had ignored her talent, and she turned *The Sound of Music* into the greatest success story in the history of filmed musicals. It was shown on and off for more than a decade in many theatres. In one cinema in Blackpool, the Lancashire holiday resort, the projectionist carefully nurtured his copy and it played, week in and week out, apparently endlessly. When it was finally and reluctantly taken off, the cinema itself closed. For many (mainly women) cinemagoers who returned to see it again and again, Julie Andrews' assumption of the role of Maria was a reassurance that such an untainted, simple, romantic figure could continue to exist in a world in which moral standards and attitudes seemed to its audience to have collapsed altogether.

Today, for all its inherent sentimentality – and one must remember that the story on which the musical is based is essentially true – the Rodgers and Hammerstein songs come up with remarkable freshness. The title-song soars, the lighter numbers, *Sixteen going on seventeen*, *My favourite things*, the charming *Edelweiss* and, of course, the brilliant children's number, *Do-re-me*, which it is too easy to take for granted, are all delightful. Peggy Wood as Mother Abbess delivers *Climb ev'ry mountain* with restrained sonorous conviction. Christopher Plummer is adequate.

But Julie Andrews' infectious enthusiasm, helped by her uniquely crisp diction, comes over with refreshing sincerity, while the strength of her personal charm carries the plot with complete conviction, never more so than in the children's yodelling number, which goes like a bomb. When we first discussed the LP in Volume IV of the original *Stereo Record Guide*, we observed that 'future generations will almost certainly find the idiom nostalgic and even quaint, rather than scented with hearts and flowers'. And so it is. Hammerstein's lyrics, especially in a Gilbertian song like *My favourite things*, are a major asset, and Irwin Kostal's overall musical direction is refreshingly spontaneous and zestful. The soundtrack quality is also good and has lost only a little of its opulence in the CD remastering.

The presentation, however, is barely adequate, a folded leaflet, just four times the size of a CD jewel case, including five poorly focused colour stills from the film, three more in black and white, and a personable (if indistinct) photograph of composer and librettist. There are other recordings, notably Mary Martin's exuberant Broadway cast record, while someone at Warner had the bright idea of gathering together the disbanded Trapp singing group (on whose family history the musical was based). They added their own European flavour to the music, producing an engaging naivety in the performance. But that record has long disappeared – and anyway, it remains Julie Andrews' show.

South Pacific.
(M) ***** BMG/RCA ND 83681. Film soundtrack recording. O, Alfred Newman.
  Nellie Forbush (Mitzi Gaynor), Emile de Becque (Giorgio Tozzi), Bloody Mary (Juanita Hall), Lt Cable (John Kerr).
(***) Sony mono SK 53327. Original Broadway cast. Ch. & O, Salvatore Dell'Isola.
Nellie Forbush (Mary Martin), Emile de Becque (Ezio Pinza), Bloody Mary (Juanita Hall), Lt Cable (William Tabbert).

It seems extraordinary that in the late 1940s Oscar Hammerstein conceived a popular musical whose plot was rooted in cultural racial problems – although, of course, two decades before that, *Show Boat* had set an honourable precedent in bringing miscegenation into the subplot.

In *South Pacific*, however, the heroine, Nellie Forbush, becomes reconciled to the fact that her cultured European lover, Emile de Becque, has previously been married to a Polynesian Islander who, though now dead, had first given him two Eurasian children. First she wants to 'wash that man right outta my hair', but in the end there is no doubt that she will share his 'enchanted evenings', in spite of her small-town American prejudices.

That lavishly romantic song is perhaps a little over-ripe as delivered by Giorgio Tozzi on the soundtrack recording (he sounds at times like an ageing Maurice Chevalier) but the actual quality of the voice is in no doubt. Mitzi Gaynor brings Nellie Forbush vividly to life as she first resists, then discovers what is important to her in the lilting *I'm in love with a wonderful guy*.

Alas, the subsidiary lovers are not so lucky, and Lieutenant Cable, having initially revelled in the fact that the girl he has fallen for is ravishingly *Younger than springtime*, finally explains why, in his low-key soliloquy: 'You've got to be taught . . . to be afraid of people whose eyes are oddly made and people whose skin is a different shade'. (The issue of a mixed marriage between the Lieutenant and Bloody Mary's daughter, Liat, is avoided, thanks to his death towards the end of the story.)

Juanita Hall is a properly larger-than-life Bloody Mary (the local fixer of various male needs) and her big production number, *Bali Ha'i*, with its sumptuous floating chorus, is Hollywood sound at its most resonantly spectacular – the film won an Academy Award for its sonic quality. But even better is the exhilarating male chorus, *There is nothing like a dame*, sung with heartfelt yet good-natured American raunchiness.

Much of the success of the record is due to the superb orchestral playing under Alfred Newman, who is in his element. The CD transfer retains the orchestral opulence and the voices, though forward, are never edgy. The presentation is a disgrace, and so different from the original, properly extravagant, LP sleeve. The CD has a cover picture and a list of titles, but is not even dignified by a cast list.

Many will opt for the alternative Sony disc by the original Broadway cast with the irrepressible Mary Martin, whose *Cock-eyed optimist, I'm gonna wash that man* and, especially, *Honey bun* have an unforgettable exuberance. Ezio Pinza's voice, too, sounds fresher and younger than Giorgio Tozzi on the later record, and the rest of the cast is excellent. Salvatore Dell'Isola keeps the pot bubbling in the orchestra and, if the *Overture* is inevitably less sumptuous in a mono recording, the sound is still very good indeed, while the stereo is hardly missed in the solo vocal numbers.

The first-class CD transfer of the 1949 recording was made using the original master tapes, whereas the LP was apparently taken from acetate discs. The improvement in vividness is remarkable. As an appendix we are offered two cut-outs (*My girl back home*, which is in the film, and a later Mary Martin version of *Loneliness of the evening*), and Ezio Pinza closes the disc with a resonant version of *Bali Ha'i*, which, of course, is not his to sing in the show. With excellent documentation, including vintage black-and-white photographs and a synopsis, the presentation puts the RCA CD to shame.

'The Rodgers and Hammerstein Songbook': Carousel: (i) *Waltz. Cinderella:* (ii) *In my own little corner;* (ii; iii) *Do I love you because you're beautiful. Flower Drum Song:* (iv) *I enjoy being a girl;* (iv; v) *Sunday. The King and I:* (vi) *I whistle a happy tune; Getting to know you;* (vi; vii) *Shall we dance? Oklahoma!:* (viii) *Oh what a beautiful morning;* (viii; ix; x) *The surrey with the fringe on top; People will say we're in love;* (ix) *Out of my dreams. The Sound of Music:* (xi; xii) *My favourite things;* (xi) *Do-Re-Mi;* (xii) *Climb ev'ry mountain;* (?) *Edelweiss. South Pacific:* (xiii) *Some enchanted evening;* (xiv) *There is nothin' like a dame;* (xi) *A wonderful guy;* (xv) *Younger than springtime.*

*** Sony mono/stereo SK 53331 [id.]. (i) NYPO, composer; (ii) Julie Andrews; (iii) Jon Cypher; (iv) Pat Suzuki; (v) Larry Blyden; (vi) Barbara Cook; (vii) Theodore Bikel; (viii) Nelson Eddy; (ix) Portia Nelson; (x) Virginia Haskins; (xi) Mary Martin; (xii) Patricia Neway; (xiii) Ezio Pinza; (xiv) Men's chorus; (xv) William Tabbert.

This admirable 77-minute collection not only shows the sheer melodic fecundity of the Rodgers and Hammerstein partnership but also its relatively limited range of human sentiment. That said, there are many splendid songs here, often in performances which are unsurpassed. It is good that the *Oklahoma!* excerpts were taken from the Nelson Eddy selection (see above), for there is something special about his *Surrey with the fringe on top* which includes some cornball dialogue (brought off with a touching, folksy spontaneity) before the captivatingly gentle close. It is good to have the composer conducting his *Carousel waltz* in an extended version with the New York Philharmonic, and to have Julie Andrews as Cinderella, investing a second-rate number with great charm. The contributions of Mary Martin and Barbara Cook are essential supplements to any CD show collection which does not include the complete recordings from which they are derived. *There is nothin' like a dame* has enormous verve and enthusiasm here, and it was a happy idea to end the programme with the indelible *Edelweiss* (sung very simply, presumably by Theodore Bikel, but uncredited), the last lyric Oscar Hammerstein ever penned; he died of cancer six months after *The Sound of Music* was premièred. As always in this series, the excellence of the CD transfers is matched by the documentation.

Rodgers and Hart, Lorenz (1895–1943)

The Boys from Syracuse.
(***) Sony mono SK 53329 [id.]. Ch. & O, Lehman Engel.
    Adriana (Portia Nelson), Antipholus of Syracuse and Ephesus (Jack Cassidy), Luce / Courtesan (Bibi Osterwald), Luciana (Holly Harris), Dromio of Syracuse and Ephesus (Stanley Prager), Singing policeman (Bob Shaver).

George Abbot's book for *The Boys from Syracuse* is based on Shakespeare's *Comedy of Errors*, although the script contains but one quote actually by the bard: 'The venom clamours of a jealous woman / Poisons more deadly than a mad dog's tooth', and when it was delivered in the original (1938) Broadway show someone shouted the word 'Shakespeare!' from the wings, to remind the audience of its source.

If the musical softens the edges of the original play, there is plenty of fun; the score, with its felicitous lyrics by Lorenz Hart, produced a more sophisticated measure of sentimentality than the shows in which Richard Rodgers later collaborated with Oscar Hammerstein II.

The present studio recording, brightly directed by Lehman Engel, is sung by a cast assembled by the producer, Goddard Lieberson, in 1953, and they bring a distinctive 1950s pop style to the delivery of the principal numbers. So this CD is essentially a period piece.

The pleasant-voiced Jack Cassidy (as the Antipholuses) croons agreeably in *When you cast your shadow on the sea*. He is well teamed with Holly Harris in *This can't be love*, with its rippling, rhythmic backing, while Bibi Osterwald and Stanley Prager make a suitably dry pair in the roles of the Dromios and Luce. Their collaboration in *What can you do with a man* and the dialogue duet, *He and she* (Hart's lyrics at their most ingenious), are two of the best lighter numbers, alongside Bibi Osterwald's catchy *O Diogenes* (which is a bit like Gershwin's *'Swonderful*). Portia Nelson's rendering of the main hit song, *Falling in love with love*, with its warbling vibrato, belongs to the world of light operetta, although she leads the engaging trio, *Sing for your supper*, very effectively.

The bright orchestrations give pleasure in themselves: Rodgers' brief ballet sequence even introduces a snippet of Debussy's *Prélude à l'après-midi d'un faune*. The mono sound is excellent, faithful to orchestra and voices alike, and the documentation is as impressive as usual with this valuable Sony series.

On Your Toes.
**(*) That's Entertainment Dig. CD-TER 1063 [id.]. (1983) Broadway cast. Ch. & O, John Mauceri.
  Frankie Frayne (Christine Andreas), Phil Dolan III Jr (Philip Arthur Ross), Sergei Alexandrovitch (George S. Irving), Peggy Porterfield (Dina Merrill), Hank J. Smith (Michael Vita).

On Your Toes has an exceptionally flimsy plot combining a vaudeville act called The Three Dolans with the Russian ballet, and even including gangsters, plus an attempted murder, to the final ballet sequence. However, the score does include several genuine Rodgers and Hart hits, notably *There's a small hotel*, *It's got to be love* and the charming *Quiet night*. Although the presentation here is authentic, the cast has no really big star-name to carry the show and, while the songs are enjoyable enough, this is not a record to raise the temperature very high.

John Mauceri uses the original Spialek orchestrations and, in his note, comments on the skill with which, in the orchestral title-number, *On your toes*, the tune is constantly repeated and embroidered for eight minutes. But the recording here is spiced up with closely miked taps, and the ear wearies before the end of this sequence. *La Princesse Zenobia ballet* is also pretty threadbare, and even the famous *Slaughter on 10th Avenue*, which forms the show's climax, sounds just a bit thin, using the original 25-piece ensemble. We are used to this piece (containing two of Rodgers' very best tunes) sounding more opulent on a bigger band. Overall the studio recording is rather dry and lustreless, and it adds nothing in the way of atmosphere. In many respects this CD is worth having; but it remains a disappointment, and the reduced artwork and small print of the flimsy liner is an unattractive presentation for a full-priced record.

Pal Joey.
(M) (***) EMI mono ZDM7 64696-2 [id.]. New York cast. Ch. & O, Max Meth.
  Joey Evans (Dick Beavers), Vera Simpson (Jane Froman), Linda English (Pat Northrop), Gladys Bumps (Helen Gallagher), Melba Snyder (Elaine Stritch).
** That's Entertainment CD-TER 1005 [id.]. London Cast, Ch. & O, Trevor York.
  Joey Evans (Denis Lawson), Vera Simpson (Sian Phillips), Linda English (Danielle Carson), Gladys Bumps (Helen Gallagher).

Like the character of Nathan Detroit in *Guys and Dolls*, *Pal Joey* remains in the mind primarily as a vehicle for Frank Sinatra, who so readily identified with its principal role and who gave the plot a slightly more upbeat ending, as he finally decides not to let the ingenue heroine, Linda, go out of his life.

The Rodgers and Hart musical is based on a short story by John O'Hara, who initially offered to collaborate with George Abbott – who revised and re-wrote his draft – but then O'Hara lost interest. Set in Chicago in the late 1930s, the story centres on an all-time loser, a small-time vaudeville artist and hustler, fought over by two women, one of whom, Vera Simpson (described as 'Mrs Chicago Society'), he needs to become the patron of the nightclub in which he works – in order to win a bet. Without the dialogue, the show loses a lot of its ambience, but it has some memorable Rodgers and Hart numbers, notably *Bewitched, bothered and bewildered* and *I could write a book*. *Pal Joey* has enough vitality to merit regular revival, and it did better on its second Broadway appearance in 1952 than when it first appeared, 12 years earlier.

The New York recording is described as by the 'Broadway cast' but is in fact a 1952 studio job, with the two leads taken by Jane Froman, a popular radio star of the time, with a fair degree of charm and very good diction, and Dick Beavers, who also sings very much in the style of the period. Helen Gallagher is a suitably brassy Gladys (*That terrific rainbow*). However, the scoop was to get Elaine Stritch to sing *Zip*, with its amusingly sharp lyrics. Don Walker's orchestrations emerge vividly, and overall the music projects well. The mono sound is first rate for its period, and there is good documentation.

The 1980 London cast version has the advantage of stereo but suffers from fake New York accents and a thin-sounding orchestra, although the recording itself has plenty of warmth and atmosphere. The performance is lively enough, and the dusky timbre and potent delivery of Sian Phillips as Vera Simpson remind one a little of Marlene Dietrich in *What is a man?* and *Bewitched*. Denis Lawson comes over as an appealing, easy-going Joey (especially good in *Happy hunting horn*) and Danielle Carson, with little to sing, is a sympathetic Linda. Darlene Johnson does a good job with *Zip*. But the documentation unforgivably is non-existent.

Romberg, Sigmund (1887–1951)

The Student Prince (complete).
**(*) That's Entertainment Dig. CDTER 1172 (2) [id.]. Amb. Ch., Philh. O, Owen Edwards.
  Prince Karl Franz (David Rendall), Kathie (Marilyn Hill Smith), Dr Engel (Norman Bailey), Ruder (Jason Howard), Gretchen (Rosemary Ashe), Von Asterberg (Neil Jenkins), Detlef (Bonaventura Bottone), Lucas (Donald Maxwell), Princess Margaret (Diana Montague), Tarnitz (Stephen Page).

The story of the prince who, as a student at Heidelberg, falls in love with Kathie, the innkeeper's daughter, but has to relinquish her to make a royal marriage when the king dies, is the very stuff of operetta. The book works better than *The Desert Song*, Romberg's other famous piece, which has even more indelible tunes. But the famous *Drinking song* and *Deep in my heart* ensure that *The Student Prince* will always be remembered, even if (like its companion piece) it is most likely to be staged by amateurs.

The present cast is certainly professional, and Marilyn Hill Smith with her clear and true, if somewhat shrill, soubrette soprano and David Rendall as a stentorian prince make a convincing pair of lovers, although Mario Lanza's famous contribution to the otherwise uninspired film version remains obstinately in the memory. As always, the dialogue offers problems; however, the important closing scene, when the prince returns to bid his last farewell to Kathie, comes off reasonably convincingly. It is good to hear Romberg's orchestrations played by the Philharmonia, and the Ambrosians make a lusty contribution to the drinking song. The studio recording, bright, close and immediate, is not always flattering to the voices but certainly does not lack vividness.

Rossi, Luigi (1597–1663)

Orfeo (opera; complete).
**(*) HM Dig. HMC 90 1358/60 (3) [id.]. Les Arts Florissants, Christie.
  Orfeo (Agnès Mellon), Euridice (Monique Zanetti), Nutrice / Bacco (Dominique Favat), Aristeo (Sandrine Piau), Vecchia / Giove (Jean-Paul Fouchécourt), Endimione (Jérôme Corréas), Augura / Plutone (Bernard Delétré), Caronte / Momo (Jean-Marc Salzmann).

Luigi Rossi's *Orfeo* was written in 1647, exactly 40 years after Monteverdi's pioneering masterpiece on the same subject. It has a much more complex classical story than the Monteverdi, yet in its artificial way it is less effectively dramatic. The symbolic Prologue depicts the victory of France as being a battle of good over evil, and the victory of Orfeo over the Underworld is seen as a comparable victory of Love and Faith.

The opera itself opens with Endymion, father of the bride, dwelling on the apparent conflict between love and happiness, but he is hopeful that love will triumph as Orfeo and Euridice are about to be married. Orfeo sees the union as perfect, but Aristeo, in love with Euridice himself and rejected, bemoans his fate to his satyr friend and asks that Venus should aid him.

The matter is further argued between Love and the Graces and it is decided that Venus will disguise herself to take Aristeo's side and Orfeo's love shall be redirected. The wedding takes place in the presence of Momus, the god of slander, but Apollo and Endymion are on the side of the bridal couple. However, all lights are extinguished at the height of the ceremony, an inauspicious omen. Nevertheless Orfeo and Euridice reaffirm their love and confidence in each other.

Venus is now found transformed into an old woman and, together with Aristeo, she tries in vain to persuade Euridice to give up Orfeo. Aristeo is desolate; the satyr suggests abduction. Momus, Juno and Apollo intervene with Love to give firm support to the married couple, and Love then reveals to Orfeo Aristeo's compact with Venus; Orfeo rushes off to warn Euridice.

When Venus discovers her betrayal, she determines on revenge but Juno promises her protection to the married pair. Yet, while Euridice is asleep, she is bitten by a monstrous serpent and, refusing the aid of Aristeo, she dies before Orfeo can arrive. Now the Fates determine to guide Orfeo to the Underworld to retrieve his bride. Aristeo is attacked by the ghost of Euridice in the form of a wild creature, and he goes mad and finally commits suicide.

Juno summons Jealousy and Suspicion, who set off to make Proserpina believe that Euridice is a rival and thus encourage her expulsion from the Underworld. Proserpina and Charon intercede with Pluto and Orfeo captivates everyone with his playing. Proserpina feels better when Pluto agrees that Orfeo can take Euridice with him – as long he does not turn to look back at her.

Of course he does just that, but Pluto promises that Euridice shall be sent to the Elysian Fields. From her point of view, Proserpina is not sure that this is an ideal solution. Venus tries to interfere again and tells Bacchus of the death of his son (Aristeo), and the Bacchants are ordered to tear Orfeo apart. Orfeo accepts death and Jupiter changes both lovers and the lyre into heavenly constellations. In the Epilogue, Mercury tells the audience that Orfeo's lyre stands for the Lily of France, that the reunion of Orfeo and Euridice is a representation of the Resurrection. Long live the king!

Even if the opera's narrative line is convoluted, it offers such incidental delights as a slanging match between Venus (enemy of Orfeo, when he represents marital fidelity) and Juno. That hint of a classical send-up adds sparkle, contrasting with the tragic emotions conveyed both in Orfeo's deeply expressive solos and in magnificent Monteverdi-like choruses. Rossi, when composing the opera in Paris, heard of the death of his young wife back in Italy, and the bereavement affected what he wrote, even though the serious element is limited in the original libretto.

William Christie draws characteristically lively and alert playing from Les Arts Florissants, but his cast is not as consistent as he usually has in his Harmonia Mundi recordings. Too many of the singers sound fluttery or shallow, and even Agnès Mellon as Orfeo is less even and sweet of tone than usual. Nevertheless, with excellent documentation and first-rate sound, this makes a most welcome recording of an important rarity.

Rossini, Gioacchino (1792–1868)

Armida (complete).
*** Koch Europa Dig. 350211 [id.]. Amb. Op. Ch., I Sol. Ven., Scimone.
   Armida (Cecilia Gasdia), Goffredo / Carlo (William Matteuzzi), Ubaldo / Gernando (Bruce Ford), Rinaldo (Chris Merritt), Eustazio (Charles H. Workman), Idraote / Astarotte (Ferruccio Furlanetto).

Armida is one of the most distinctive of the serious operas that Rossini wrote for Naples in the years after the *Barber of Seville*. In 1817, when it was first performed, the piece ran into the criticism that it was too 'German', but to modern ears the writing is characteristically Rossinian, with the delights of Armida's magic garden remaining very much in the clear light of Italian day, with no mystery conveyed at all. The ballet at the end of Act II (the only one Rossini included in any of his Italian operas) is bright and jolly, not other-worldly at all. Hardly presented as sinister, the sorceress Armida becomes what Richard Osborne in his book on Rossini aptly describes as one of the first great operatic *femmes fatales* of the nineteenth century.

The opera opens in the Crusaders' camp where Dudone, their leader, is to be buried. Armida, who is in love with Rinaldo, enters and requests the aid of ten champions, as she says (untruthfully) that her throne in Damascus has been usurped. Goffredo agrees, but insists that Dudone's successor be determined. Eustazio suggests Rinaldo as the obvious choice, and in so doing provokes the resentment of Gernando. A duel is fought and Gernando is killed.

Act II opens with a chorus of demons devoted to Astarotte. Armida and Rinaldo arrive on a cloud and find themselves first in a beautiful garden, then in a magic castle.

In Act III, Ubaldo and Carlo, two paladins, arrive in the enchanted garden, having resolved to rescue Rinaldo from Armida's clutches. They hide when Armida approaches but, as she leaves, they approach Rinaldo. He finally comes to his senses and the angry sorceress destroys the magic garden and departs spectacularly in her chariot at the centre of a group of demons.

Rossini provides the sorceress with some marvellous fire-eating moments of display, particularly in the last Act, when the knight, Rinaldo, finally manages to resist her magic and escape. Her realization of defeat, dramatically conveyed in a repeated monotone, is intensely human. Other remarkable numbers include a quartet in Act I, in which at a key moment Rossini quotes (whether intentionally or not) Caldara's song, *Caro mio ben*.

This first studio recording from Europa in every way matches the quality of comparable opera sets from the big international companies, not only in recorded sound but in casting too. As Armida, Cecilia Gasdia may not be strikingly characterful (Maria Callas knew the role) but her singing is both powerful and agile, firm and bold in Rossini's brilliant coloratura. As for the problem of finding three high *bel canto* tenors capable of tackling elaborate ornamentation, Europa offers a trio as fine as any available today.

One of the high spots comes in Act III, when Rinaldo is joined by two fellow-knights intent on saving him from Armida, and they sing a radiant ensemble. William Matteuzzi and Bruce Ford more than match Chris Merritt as Rinaldo. Though the principal, he is the least gainly of the three, but still impressive, notably in the love-duets with Armida, one of them in Act II introduced by a long, romantic cello solo. Ferruccio Furlanetto is excellent in two bass roles, and a fourth tenor, Charles Workman, might well have stood in for any of the others. The three Acts are squeezed on to two extremely well-filled CDs. The booklet includes an introduction in English, but no translation of the Italian libretto.

L'assedio di Corinto (The siege of Corinth; complete).
(M) **(*) EMI CMS7 64335-2 (3). Amb. Op. Ch., LSO, Schippers.
   Pamira (Beverly Sills), Neocle (Shirley Verrett), Maometto (Justino Diaz), Cleomene (Harry Theyard), Jero (Gwynne Howell), Omar (Robert Lloyd).

The siege of Corinth, like other Rossini operas, had a chequered history. In its final form (*Le siège de Corinthe*, in French) it was produced in Paris in 1826, a reworking of an earlier *opera seria, Maometto II*, given in Naples six years earlier. The story of beleaguered Greeks besieged by the Turks in 1459 has stirring qualities.

The heroine, Pamira, is the daughter of Cleomene, Governor of Corinth, and he has chosen Neocle to be her husband and protector, but she has other ideas. Her initial choice is Almanzor, who is in fact Maometto, leader of the Turks, who had previously spent some time incognito in Greece and had fallen in love with Pamira.

However, after the first victory of the Turks, Pamira's patriotism prevails and she returns with Neocle to receive her father's blessing and await the final assault on the city. As the Turks are finally victorious, Pamira, anticipating the slaughter of Neocle, kills herself rather than submit to the conquering Maometto.

Thomas Schippers, the conductor here, first edited the score for a revival at La Scala, Milan, in 1969, and then made this recording in London in 1974 in preparation for another production at the Met. in New York with virtually the same cast. The pity is that he has encouraged the coloratura prowess of the prima donna, Beverly Sills, at the expense of Rossini's final thoughts, with display material from the earlier version. Many Rossinians will no doubt remain untroubled by academic points, in gratitude that so much inspired music has been brought to the gramophone.

Some of the most striking passages are the patriotic choruses, recognizably Rossinian but not at all in the usual vein. Sills, as so often on record, is variable, brilliant in coloratura but rarely sweet of tone, and she is completely upstaged by Shirley Verrett, singing magnificently as Neocle. Some strong singing too among the others, though not all the men are very deft with ornamentation. The recording, made at All Saints, Tooting, has plenty of atmosphere and has achieved a very satisfactory CD transfer.

Il barbiere di Siviglia (complete).
*** Ph. Dig. 411 058-2 (3) [id.]. Amb. Op. Ch., ASMF, Marriner.
  Figaro (Thomas Allen), Rosina (Agnes Baltsa), Almaviva (Francisco Araiza), Doctor Bartolo
  (Domenico Trimarchi), Don Basilio (Robert Lloyd).
(M) *** EMI CMS7 64162-2 (2) [id.]; (B) CfP *TC-CFPD 4704*. Glyndebourne Festival Ch., RPO,
  Gui.
  Figaro (Sesto Bruscantini), Rosina (Victoria De los Angeles), Almaviva (Luigi Alva), Doctor
  Bartolo (Ian Wallace), Don Basilio (Carlo Cava).
*** Decca Dig. 425 520-2 (3) [id.]. Ch. & O of Teatro Comunale di Bologna, Patanè.
  Figaro (Leo Nucci), Rosina (Cecilia Bartoli), Almaviva (William Matteuzzi), Doctor Bartolo
  (Enrico Fissore), Don Basilio (Paata Burchuladze).
*** EMI CDS7 47634-8 (2) [Ang. CDCB 47634]. Philh. Ch. & O, Galliera.
  Figaro (Tito Gobbi), Rosina (Maria Callas), Almaviva (Luigi Alva), Doctor Bartolo (Fritz
  Ollendorff), Don Basilio (Nicola Zaccaria).
(M) *** BMG/RCA GD 86505 (3) [RCA 6505-2-RG]. Met. Op. Ch. & O, Leinsdorf.
  Figaro (Robert Merrill), Rosina (Roberta Peters), Almaviva (Cesare Valletti), Doctor Bartolo
  (Fernando Corena), Don Basilio (Giorgio Tozzi).
**(*) DG Dig. 435 763-2 (2) [id.]. Ch. of La Fenice Theatre, Venice, COE, Abbado.
  Figaro (Plácido Domingo), Rosina (Kathleen Battle), Almaviva (Frank Lopardo), Doctor
  Bartolo (Lucio Gallo), Don Basilio (Ruggero Raimondi).
**(*) DG 415 695-2 (2) [id.]. Amb. Ch., LSO, Abbado.
  Figaro (Hermann Prey), Rosina (Teresa Berganza), Almaviva (Luigi Alva), Doctor Bartolo
  (Enzo Dara), Don Basilio (Paolo Montarsolo).
(M) **(*) Decca 417 164-2 (2) [id.]. Rossini Ch. & O of Naples, Varviso.
  Figaro (Manuel Ausensi), Rosina (Teresa Berganza), Almaviva (Ugo Benelli), Doctor Bartolo
  (Fernando Corena), Don Basilio (Nicolai Ghiaurov).
*(*) Sony S3K 37862 (3) [id.]. La Scala, Milan, Ch. & O, Chailly.
  Figaro (Leo Nucci), Rosina (Marilyn Horne), Almaviva (Paolo Barbacini), Doctor Bartolo
  (Enzo Dara), Don Basilio (Samuel Ramey).

Rossini's most famous opera, *Il barbiere di Siviglia*, premièred in Rome in 1816, was a success
from its very first performance and has maintained its supremacy in the world of Italian *opera
buffa* to the present day. The story, which sparkles with witty opportunities for its characters,
opens in the street outside Dr Bartolo's house.

Count Almaviva, aided by musicians provided by Fiorello, serenades Rosina, the doctor's rich
ward. Figaro now enters and flamboyantly reveals his calling as a barber-factotum. As he has
access to Dr Bartolo's house, he agrees to help the count. Rosina and Bartolo appear on the
balcony; she drops a note into the street and asks Bartolo to go down and pick it up, saying it is
music for a song. Almaviva intercepts the note, which asks for his name and he tells her:
Lindoro. For the moment he wishes to remain incognito.

After a little money exchanges hands, Figaro agrees to introduce the count into the Bartolo
household as an inebriated soldier requiring a billet. We now move indoors, where Rosina is
singing her famous *Una voce poco fa*, thinking affectionately of her new lover but very
determined to have her own way while still affecting mildness of temperament. Don Basilio,
both music master and scandal-monger, hears from Bartolo that Count Almaviva is Rosina's
suitor. Basilio suggests spreading scandal about the count to ruin his reputation. The whisper, he
suggests, will grow into a thunderclap (*La calunnia*).

Figaro now contrives to let Rosina know of Lindoro's ardour and asks: will she write a note to
him? But one is already written! Bartolo warns Rosina not to try to deceive him, just as the
'drunken' soldier arrives. Bartolo tries to eject the military intruder and the police are called, but
when he whispers his real identity, instead of making an arrest, the police salute him.

An unknown 'music master' is now introduced into the household by Figaro. Garbed as a
cleric, the new arrival blesses everyone *ad lib*. He states that he is Don Basilio's substitute, that
gentleman being very sick. It is, of course, Almaviva and he gives Rosina a singing lesson. Figaro
now arrives to shave Bartolo, and the lovers take their opportunity to behave less discreetly.
There is consternation when Don Basilio arrives. However, as with Figaro, a little money works
wonders and, when Almaviva slips a purse into his hand, Basilio agrees that he is really sick and
happily wishes everyone *Buona sera* – more than once!

The resourceful Figaro now plans an elopement for that very night, and Berta, the elderly
maidservant, comments scornfully on Bartolo's wish to marry Rosina himself – he is sixty! The

suspicious Bartolo now confides to Rosina his suspicion that Figaro and the 'music master' are conspiring to abduct her in order to hand her over to Count Almaviva. Rosina, still unaware of her lover's true identity, angrily exposes the elopement plan and agrees to marry Bartolo.

A summer storm interrupts the action, then Figaro and Almaviva enter and explain the truth to Rosina. A notary, hired by Bartolo for his own wedding, conveniently officiates at the marriage ceremony between Rosina and Almaviva, with Basilio – at pistol point – and Figaro the necessary witnesses. Bartolo arrives with soldiers – too late to prevent the nuptials – but he orders the arrest of Figaro and the false music master. However, when identities are finally disclosed, the situation is very different, and Bartolo philosophically accepts the inevitable.

Il barbiere was Sir Neville Marriner's first opera recording and he finds a rare sense of fun in Rossini's witty score. His characteristic polish and refinement – beautifully caught in the clear, finely balanced recording – never get in the way of urgent spontaneity, the sparkle of the moment. So for example in the big Act II quintet, when the wool is being pulled over Don Basilio's eyes, there is an ideal balance between musical precision and dramatic presentation. Thomas Allen as Figaro – far more than a *buffo* figure – and Agnes Baltsa as Rosina – tough and biting, too – manage to characterize strongly, even when coping with florid divisions, and though Araiza allows himself too many intrusive aitches he easily outshines latterday rivals, sounding heroic, not at all the small-scale tenorino but never coarse either. Fine singing too from Robert Lloyd as Basilio. On CD, the theatrical feeling and sense of atmosphere are enhanced, with the placing of the singers strikingly clear.

Victoria de los Angeles is as charming a Rosina as you will ever find: no viper this one, as she claims in *Una voce poco fa*, but an enchantress. Musically hers is a relaxed performance which consistently brings out the fun, with Rossini's brilliant *fioriture* done lovingly, with no sense of fear or danger. That matches the gently rib-nudging humour of what is otherwise a recording of the Glyndebourne production of the early 1960s, a masterly example of the way Gui could make Rossini sparkle as few rivals ever have. Sesto Bruscantini is a delight as Figaro, heading an exceptionally characterful team that is both polished and relaxed. With elaborate stage direction in the stereo production, reflecting the Glyndebourne production, it is an endearing performance, which in its line is unmatched. The recording still sounds well, with voices and instruments full and well focused. Tape collectors should be very well satisfied with the CfP issue which is at bargain price on two cassettes in a chunky box, with synopsis instead of libretto. The transfer is kind to the voices and generally vivid.

Giuseppe Patanè made his recording of *Il Barbiere* only months before his untimely death, but it is a performance that brims with life, very much a team effort with a cast – Burchuladze very much excepted – entirely of native Italian-speakers. Patanè is a relaxed Rossinian, generally favouring unrushed speeds, timing the delectably pointed recitatives with a keen concern for stage action. With helpful sound-effects and full and vivid sound, it makes a happy new digital recommendation for a much-recorded opera. What sets it apart is the exciting choice of singer as the heroine, Rosina.

Cecilia Bartoli made this recording when she was still in her early twenties, a mezzo with a rich, vibrant voice who not only copes brilliantly with the technical demands but who also gives a sparkling, provocative characterization. In her big Act I aria, *Una voce poco fa*, she even outshines the memorable Agnes Baltsa on the excellent Marriner set. Like the conductor, Bartoli is wonderful at bringing out the fun. So is Leo Nucci, and he gives a beautifully rounded portrait of the wily barber, even though the voice is less firm and less expansive than it was, showing signs of wear. Thomas Allen for Marriner sings much better and gives a more youthful characterization.

Burchuladze, unidiomatic next to the others, still gives a monumentally lugubrious portrait of Basilio, and the Bartolo of Enrico Fissore is outstanding, with the patter song wonderfully articulated at Patanè's sensible speed. The lyrical, rounded quality of William Matteuzzi's tenor makes him an attractive, if hardly memorable Almaviva. In keeping with the idiomatic style of the performance, the text is the traditional Italian one rather than the scholarly reconstruction of Alberto Zedda; but this makes a superb entertainment.

Gobbi and Callas were here at their most inspired and, with the recording quality nicely refurbished, the EMI is an outstanding set, not absolutely complete in its text, but so crisp and sparkling it can be confidently recommended. Callas remains supreme as a minx-like Rosina, summing up the character superbly in *Una voce poco fa*. In the final ensemble, despite the usual reading of the score, Rosina's verse is rightly given premier place at the very end. Though this was not among the cleanest of Philharmonia opera recordings, the early stereo sound comes up very acceptably on a pair of CDs, clarified to a degree, presenting a uniquely characterful performance with new freshness and immediacy.

In the Victor Opera series, with a near-complete text and a performance consistently well sung, the Leinsdorf set from the late 1950s makes a good bargain CD version to rival the Gui Glyndebourne version. Roberta Peters is a sparkling Rosina, a singer too little known in Europe who here lives up to her high reputation at the Met., dazzling in coloratura elaborations *in alt*. Robert Merrill may not be a specially comic Figaro, but the vocal characterization is strong, with the glorious voice consistently firm and well focused. Valletti, Corena and Tozzi make up a formidable team, and Leinsdorf conducts with a lightness and relaxation rare for him on record. Good, clear sound of the period, set against a reverberant, helpful acoustic.

The casting of Plácido Domingo as Figaro in Rossini's *Barber of Seville* suggests some mistake. But no, Domingo, the superstar tenor – who started out as a baritone many years ago, and whose Otello has grown weightier with the years – has here recorded the role of Rossini's barber. On the cover of the DG set, guitar in hand, he is pictured cheerily wearing the regulation costume, heading a cast that would be hard to beat today, including Kathleen Battle, Frank Lopardo and Ruggero Raimondi, with Claudio Abbado conducting the Chamber Orchestra of Europe, as he did in his prize-winning set of Rossini's *Il viaggio a Reims*. So far from being just a gimmick, the irony is that Domingo is the set's biggest success.

Compared with his earlier self, Abbado is freer and more spontaneous-sounding, but his touch, as conveyed in dry, close-up sound, is much heavier-handed, missing much of the sparkle of his earlier DG set, with ensemble work surprisingly rough. Even Raimondi as Basilio in his big aria, *La calunnia*, is relatively undisciplined, if spontaneous-sounding, and the big bangs at the climax are completely miscalculated. Kathleen Battle makes a minx of a Rosina, coy but full of flair, and Frank Lopardo is a stylish Almaviva, though not well contrasted with Domingo.

Abbado in his earlier DG version directs a clean and satisfying performance that lacks the last degree of sparkle. Berganza's interpretation of the role of Rosina remains very consistent with her earlier performance on Decca, but the Figaro here, Hermann Prey, is more reliable, and the playing and recording have an extra degree of polish. The text is not absolutely complete, but the omissions are of minimal importance. With fresh recorded sound and plenty of immediacy, this remains competitive.

Vocally the 1964 Decca set, also with Teresa Berganza who proves an agile Rosina, is very reliable, and Silvio Varviso secures electrifying effects in many of Rossini's high-spirited ensembles. There remain important reservations, however. Manuel Ausensi as Figaro himself is rather gruff, both vocally and dramatically, though he was chosen specifically because of the authenticity of having a darker-toned voice than usual in the part. Ugo Benelli is charming as the Count, a free-voiced 'tenorino', though he sounds nervous in his first aria. Corena's fine Dr Bartolo is well known, and Ghiaurov sings with characteristic richness as Basilio. This version, while textually not quite complete, does contain much more than usual, including the often omitted Act II tenor aria which uses the *Non più mesta* theme from *Cenerentola*. It is very well recorded – the sound is noticeably fuller than the earlier, RCA version.

Chailly's CBS version is a generally coarse and disappointing set, not helped by indifferent playing by the orchestra of La Scala. Marilyn Horne makes a formidable Rosina, the voice still agile if not as cleanly focused as once it was, but Paolo Barbacini is unacceptably rough as Almaviva. As Figaro, Leo Nucci is vocally inconsistent. All the singers are more impressive in ensembles than in solo items. The CD transfer is vivid and clear.

Il barbiere di Siviglia: highlights.
*** Ph. Dig. 412 266-2 [id.] (from above recording with Allen, Baltsa, Araiza; cond. Marriner).
(M) *** EMI CDM7 63076-2; *EG 763076-4* (from above recording with Gobbi, Callas, Alva; cond. Galliera).
*** Decca Dig. 440 289-2 [id.] (from above recording with Bartoli, Nucci, Matteuzzi; cond. Patanè).
(M) *** BMG/RCA GD 60188; *GK 60188* [60188-2-RG; *60188-4-RG*] (from above recording with Merrill, Peters, Valletti; cond. Leinsdorf).

The Philips highlights are well chosen and admirably reflect the qualities of Marriner's complete set, the sound particularly sparkling in the delightful Act II finale.

Those who already have Marriner's version will certainly want to sample the Callas set; this mid-priced selection, though at 56 minutes not as generous as some highlights discs, offers most of the key solo numbers from Act I, while in Act II it concentrates on Rossini's witty ensembles, including the extended Second Act *Quintet*. The *Overture* is included and, while it is stylishly played, it would have been better to have offered more of the vocal music. The leaflet includes a useful synopsis but no translation.

The selection from the Patanè set is at full price, but it contains more music (66 minutes) than the Callas/Gobbi version and does not waste space on the *Overture*. It is a most entertaining disc, with Bartoli's sparkling *Una voce poco fa* matched by Nucci's *Largo al factotum*, while the ensembles never go off the boil. First-rate modern, digital sound.

The selection from the Leinsdorf *Barber* is generous (71 minutes) and well chosen, and the documentation relates the excerpts to an excellent synopsis. The 1958 recording sounds a little shrill in the treble (the violins in the *Overture* are thin), but it responds to the controls.

La cambiale di matrimonio; L'inganno felice; L'occasione fa il ladro; La scala di seta; Il Signor Bruschino (all complete).
(M) ** Claves Dig. CD 50-9200 (8). Soloists (see below), ECO or I Filarmonico di Torini, Marcello Viotti.

The Claves versions of all five of Rossini's one-Act operas, discussed below, here come in a useful package, with the eight discs selling for the price of five. That offer is not specially generous when the performances are so variable and with the works taking two discs instead of one, each lasting only just over 80 minutes. Like the individual issues, they come with Italian librettos but only summaries of the plots in English.

La cambiale di matrimonio (complete).
* Claves Dig. CD 50-9101 [id.]. ECO, Viotti.
    Tobia Mill (Bruno Praticò), Fanny Mill (Alessandra Rossi), Edoardo Milfort (Maurizio Comencini), Slook (Bruno De Simone), Norton (Francesco Facini), Clarina (Valeria Baiano).

This was the first of the Claves series to be recorded in London, and unfortunately the venue chosen was the reverberant All Saints, Tooting. The voices have fair bloom on them, but the orchestra, rather recessed, sounds washy, a significant flaw in such intimately jolly music, with ensembles suffering in particular.

As the opera opens, Tobia Mill, a businessman, is trying, not very successfully, to find his way around a map of the world. Norton, his manager, arrives with a letter from their American agent, Slook. He is looking for a wife, under thirty, with a charming nature and unsullied reputation. Moreover, he is willing to pay well for the right introduction. Mill arbitrarily decides that his daughter, Fanny, fits the description and shall be promised as the bride. Norton is appalled. Of course, Fanny already has a lover, Edoardo, and when she tells him of her father's plan he is rightly angry, too.

Mill now enters and, to prevent trouble, Edoardo is introduced as the firm's new book-keeper. Mill shows the correspondence and the marriage contract to his daughter as a *fait accompli*. Slook now arrives and Fanny tries to persuade him to withdraw from the contract. Edoardo has some difficulty in keeping his temper but he, too, argues with Slook and is told that money has already exchanged hands as part of the arrangement.

Fed up with the whole affair, Slook withdraws from the arrangement, and now it is Mill who is angry, and he challenges Slook to a duel. But his agent is a sentimental American and, when he sees the lovers' warm feelings for each other so openly displayed, he picks up the wedding contract and writes 'Edoardo' in place of his own name. As the duel has not been called off, Mill re-enters and is furious when he discovers that the contract has been rewritten. But Slook remonstrates with him for treating his daughter like a product to be bought and sold, and all ends happily when the father is reconciled to the course of true love.

Viotti is a relaxedly stylish Rossinian, drawing pointed playing from the ECO, but the singing is poor. The tenor, Maurizio Comencini, sounds unsteady and strained, while Alessandra Rossi as the heroine, agile enough, is too shrill for comfort. The best singing comes from the *buffo* baritone, Bruno Praticò, as the heroine's father.

La Cenerentola (complete).
*** Ph. Dig. 420 468-2; *420 468-4* (2) [id.]. Amb. Op. Ch., ASMF, Marriner.
    Angelina (Agnes Baltsa), Don Ramiro (Francisco Araiza), Dandini (Simone Alaimo), Don Magnifico (Ruggero Raimondi), Clorinda (Carol Malone).
(M) (***) EMI mono CMS7 64183-2 (2) [Ang. CDMB 64183]. Glyndebourne Festival Ch. & O, Gui.
    Angelina (Marina De Gabarain), Don Ramiro (Juan Oncina), Dandini (Sesto Bruscantini), Don Magnifico (Ian Wallace), Clorinda (Alda Noni).

** DG 423 861-2 (2) [id.]. Scottish Op. Ch., LSO, Abbado.
   Angelina (Teresa Berganza), Don Ramiro (Luigi Alva), Dandini (Renato Capecchi), Don Magnifico (Paolo Montarsolo), Clorinda (Margherita Guglielmi).
** Sony S2K 46433 (2) [id.]; *40-46433*. W. German R. (male) Ch., Cappella Coloniensis, Ferro.
   Angelina (Lucia Valentini Terrani), Don Ramiro (Francisco Araiza), Dandini (Domenico Trimarchi), Don Magnifico (Enzo Dara), Clorinda (Emilia Ravaglia).
(M) *(*) Decca 433 030-2 (2) [id.]. Ch. & O of Maggio Musicale Fiorentino, Fabritiis.
   Angelina (Giulietta Simionato), Don Ramiro (Ugo Benelli), Dandini (Sesto Bruscantini), Don Magnifico (Paolo Montarsolo), Clorinda (Dora Carral).

La Cenerentola, Rossini's tenth opera, followed a year after *Il Barbiere*, and was first heard in Rome in 1817. The plot has considerable variants on the traditional story, and is without the midnight clock and the lost slipper – a bracelet serves instead, rather less romantically. But the opera brings some charmingly comic moments, and its coloratura makes even greater demands on the vocal resources of the heroine than its predecessor.

Predictably, the curtain rises in the kitchen of the household of Don Magnifico, an impoverished nobleman. Cinderella is busy with household chores. Her half-sisters, Clorinda and Tisbe, are preening themselves. Alidoro, Prince Ramiro's tutor and philosopher (the equivalent of the Fairy Godmother), now enters, disguised as a beggar. Cinderella takes pity on him and gives him food, which angers her two sisters, who disdain him. They announce the prince's forthcoming visit, and he is expected to invite the family to the ball, where he will choose his bride. The sisters demand that Cinderella help them adorn themselves and the bustle disturbs Don Magnifico from his dreams of a successful marriage for one of his daughters.

Alidoro persuades the prince to dress himself as his own valet, Dandini, and, so disguised, he enters Don Magnifico's household, where Alidoro suggests that one of the baron's daughters would be the best bride he could choose. He immediately encounters Cinderella, the serving maid (as he thinks). They are both enamoured of each other. Don Magnifico and Dandini (masquerading as the prince) now enter, and Clorinda and Tisbe and their father are all impressed by Dandini's deportment and grand manner and take little notice of the real prince. Dandini proffers invitations to the ball. Cinderella begs to be included but Don Magnifico peremptorily refuses her request.

The ubiquitous Alidoro now reappears as an official taking a population census and asks about Don Magnifico's third daughter. He is told that she has died, but no one quite believes this, and when the others have departed Alidoro amazes Cinderella by telling her that she is invited to the ball and reveals his magical powers. He provides a suitable ballgown, adorned with jewels, and a fairy coach to transport her.

Back in the palace and alone with the prince, Dandini states that Clorinda and Tisbe (with whom he flirted) are both stupid. The two sisters arrive and Dandini tells them that he will marry one and give the other to his squire (Ramiro). Both men enjoy the joke, especially as the sisters are both horrified at the suggestion that either of them would want to marry a servant! Cinderella now appears and, after removing her mask, dazzles everyone with her beauty. All are struck by her resemblance to Don Magnifico's serving maid. Dandini falls in love with Cinderella but she tells him that she loves his squire (Ramiro). Ramiro overhears and claims her for himself. She gives him a bracelet, tells him he must discover its companion, and leaves.

The prince now reassumes his true identity and, with his courtiers, goes off to find the girl he loves. By now Cinderella is back in her kitchen, dressed in her shabby clothes. Her family return from the ball. There is a storm (always a useful device in Rossini operas) and Alidoro engineers matters so that the prince's coach breaks down outside Don Magnifico's house. The prince enters, recognizes Cinderella and, identifying the bracelet she is wearing, claims her as his own true love.

He also reminds Clorinda and Tisbe of their snobbish scorn when they thought him merely a courtier and he leaves with Cinderella. Back at the palace he makes her his princess and bride, and she forgives her father and sisters. She recalls that she was born to a life that was lonely (*Nacqui all'affano*) but the opera ends sparklingly with her happiness (*Non più mesta al fuoco* – 'Now no longer by the cinders').

Marriner's set of *Cenerentola*, following the pattern of his first opera recording of *Il barbiere di Siviglia*, conveys Rossinian fun to the full. As in *Barbiere*, the role of heroine is taken by the formidable Agnes Baltsa – not so aptly cast this time in a vulnerable Cinderella role – and that of the hero by Francisco Araiza, sweet and fresh of tone, though still allowing too many aspirates in passage-work. Ruggero Raimondi's commanding and resonant singing as Don Magnifico is very satisfying, and there is no weak link in the rest of the cast. Above all, Marriner in his rhythmic control avoids the metrical fierceness which has marred performances by some star conductors, not least by distinguished Italians. The sound is first class in all respects, nicely resonant with plenty of atmosphere.

Dating from 1953, Gui's recording of *Cenerentola* has mono sound of amazing clarity and immediacy. Sadly the text is seriously cut, but the effervescence of Gui's live performances at Glyndebourne has been infectiously caught, making this – at mid-price – a viable alternative to the really complete versions. Juan Oncina produces the most sweet-toned singing as the Prince, with the vintage baritone, Sesto Bruscantini, a vividly characterful Dandini, almost another Figaro. The title-role is sung by the Spanish mezzo, Marina de Gabarain, a strikingly positive singer with a sensuous flicker in the voice, very much in the style of the legendary Conchita Supervia.

Unlike *The Barber*, *La Cenerentola* has not been lucky on record, and the DG set, although enjoyable, lacks the extrovert bravura and sparkle of an ideal performance. The atmosphere in places is almost of a concert version, with excellent balance between the participants, helped by the fine recording. The recitative in general has plenty of life, particularly when Dandini (Renato Capecchi) is involved. Berganza, agile in the coloratura, seems too mature, even matronly, for the fairy-tale role of Cinderella. Alva sings well enough but is somewhat self-conscious in the florid writing. Abbado, though hardly witty in his direction, inspires delicate playing throughout. The CD transfer of the 1972 analogue recording brings an admirable feeling of freshness, with plenty of presence for the voices and a good balance with the lively orchestral sound.

Ferro, one of the ablest of Rossini scholars who earlier recorded *L'Italiana in Algeri* impressively, on Sony conducts an easy-going, at times pedestrian account of *La Cenerentola*, well played and well sung but lacking some of the fizz essential in Rossini. Even the heroine's final brilliant aria hangs fire, and that in spite of warm, positive singing from Lucia Valentini Terrani, whose stylish contribution is spoilt only by a high quota of intrusive aitches. The rest of the cast is strong and, apart from backward placing of the orchestra, the digital transfer is full and realistic.

With never very refined singing from any of his soloists, Fabritiis in the early Decca set makes the piece sound longer and less interesting than it is. Simionato is well below her best vocally, wobbling far more than she ought to, and it is small consolation that the sound is brilliant.

Le Comte Ory (complete).
⊛ (M) (***) EMI mono CMS7 64180-2 (2) [Ang. CDMB 64180]. Glyndebourne Festival Ch. & O, Gui.
  Comte Ory (Juan Oncina), Adèle (Sari Barabas), Gouverneur (Ian Wallace), Isolier (Cora Canne-Meijer), Raimbaud (Michel Roux), Ragonde (Monica Sinclair), Alice (Jeannette Sinclair).
⊛ *** Ph. Dig. 422 406-2 (2) [id.]. Lyon Op. Ch. & O, Gardiner.
  Comte Ory (John Aler), Adèle (Sumi Jo), Gouverneur (Gilles Cachemaille), Isolier (Diana Montague), Raimbaud (Gino Quilico), Ragonde (Raquel Pierotti), Alice (Maryse Castets).

Gui's classic recording of *Le Comte Ory*, with the same Glyndebourne forces who gave this sparkling opera on stage, has claims to being the most indispensable of all Rossini opera recordings, bringing pure delight.

This is the piece which tells of the wicked Count Ory's attempt to seduce the virtuous Countess Adèle while her protective brother is away at the Crusades. Ory and his dissolute young friend, Raimbaud, wait outside the castle gates for a chance to enter, dressed as hermits. Ragonde, a companion to the Comtesse Adèle, comes out to silence levity among the crowd, for the comtesse is disconsolate at her brother's absence. Ragonde decides that they will consult the hermits, who might alleviate their distress.

The profligate Count Ory now declares his interest in ladies requiring husbands. He is pleased to hear that Adèle has vowed to shun all men until her brother, Le Comte de Formoutiers, returns; moreover, that she is depressed and longing for his advice. Meanwhile Isolier, Ory's page, arrives, together with the count's tutor.

Isolier is in love with Adèle, who is his cousin. Although the tutor suspects Ory's identity, Isolier for the moment fails to recognize the count and unburdens his secret to him, telling him he plans to gain admittance to the castle disguised as a hermit. Count Ory decides he will do likewise.

Adèle now consults with the 'Hermit' (Ory) and is told that to counteract her depression she must fall in love. He absolves her from her vow to shun the opposite sex and she looks warmly at her cousin, Isolier. The 'hermit' then warns her about the scheming and notorious Count Ory. But the tutor recognizes Ory publicly and everyone is scandalized at the deception. At the same time Adèle learns of her brother's imminent return. Ory reflects that time is short if he is to win Adèle over.

Within the castle, the ladies celebrate their escape from the machinations of the wicked Count Ory. A pilgrims' chant is heard, and Ragonde is sent out to investigate. Adèle is ever hospitable to travellers, and a group of nuns enter, stating that they are fleeing from the notorious Ory. Their Mother Superior is in fact the wicked count in disguise, and 'she' expresses gratitude for the offered hospitality, mentioning in passing that it is known that Ory truly loves Adèle. The latter is highly indignant at such a suggestion.

Left alone, the nuns regale themselves with wine, but they appear subdued when Adèle reappears to announce that their accommodation is prepared. Isolier now comes in to announce that Adèle's brother is expected back at any moment; when he hears about the nuns, his suspicions are aroused and he warns Adèle that she may be sheltering Ory himself. He volunteers to save her from a fate worse than death.

Ory arrives and tries to seduce Adèle, but in the dark Isolier takes her place and intercepts him. Trumpets are heard, the Crusaders are returning. Ory emerges and Isolier counters his master's fury by threatening to expose his wickedness to his father; then he helps Ory to make his getaway, and the story ends with the return of the Comte de Formoutiers and his followers.

In this opera, Rossini deftly uses much of the brilliant material he had written for the occasional celebration opera, *Il viaggio a Reims*. In this re-using, Rossini even introduces extra point – not surprising when the hilarious complications of the plot involve such farcical situations as the count, disguised as a nun, believing he is addressing Countess Adèle, when it is in fact his page (played by a woman), who is himself (herself) in love with the countess. Rossini handles such complications with unrivalled finesse.

With musical argument more sustained than in other comic pieces of the period, *Le Comte Ory* stands out even among Rossini operas, as frothy as any, helped by the witty, unconventional plot. In limited but clearly focused mono sound, Gui conveys an extra sparkle and resilience, even over Gardiner's brilliant Philips version. There is a natural sense of timing here that regularly has you laughing with joy, as in the dazzling finale of Act I, one of the most infectiously witty of all recordings of a Rossini ensemble.

Gui even more than Gardiner capitalizes on the great asset of this piece even against Rossini's Italian comic operas, the extended numbers, often almost as complex as Mozart's finales for the da Ponte operas. The farcical story offers character as well as wit, with such incidental delights as the *Nuns' drinking chorus* of Act II, when the wicked Count Ory and his followers in disguise penetrate the Countess Adèle's castle. Juan Oncina in his prime as the Count, the Hungarian Sari Barabas as the Countess Adèle and Michel Roux as the Count's friend are superbly matched by Monica Sinclair as the Countess's housekeeper and Ian Wallace as the count's tutor. Some ten minutes of text have been cut, but that allows the complete opera to be fitted on two CDs, each containing a complete Act.

Gardiner's set provides a splendid answer for those who insist on a stereo recording in modern digital sound. It is beautifully and sparklingly sung, with ensembles finely balanced, as in the delectable Act II trio. Gardiner tends to be rather more tense than Gui was, with speeds on the fast side, and he allows too short a dramatic pause for the interruption to the Nuns' drinking choruses. But the precision and point are a delight, with not a single weak link in the casting, which is more consistent than Glyndebourne's. Though John Aler hardly sounds predatory enough as the Count, the lightness of his tenor is ideal, and Sumi Jo as Adèle and Diana Montague as the page, Isolier, are both stylish and characterful. So is the clear-toned Gino Quilico as the friend, Raimbaud. With the cuts of the old Glyndebourne set opened out and with good and warm, if not ideally crystal-clear, recording, this set takes its place as another jewel of a Rossini issue.

La Donna del lago (complete).
*** Sony Dig. S2K 39311 (2) [id.]. Prague Philharmonic Ch., COE, Pollini.
   Elena (Katia Ricciarelli), Malcolm (Lucia Valentini Terrani), Uberto / Giacomo (Dalmacio Gonzalez), Rodrigo di Dhu (Dano Raffanti), Douglas d'Angus (Samuel Ramey).

La Donna del lago – adapted with extreme freedom from Scott's *Lady of the Lake*, published not long before – may doubtfully be effective on stage, as the 1985 Covent Garden production suggested; on record, in a lively and understanding performance, it is a Rossini rarity to cherish.

Philip Gossett, the Rossini scholar, has described it as 'by far the most romantic of Rossini's Italian operas and perhaps the most tuneful'. The 'historical' basis of the story is derived from the life of King James V of Scotland (1512–42) who was imprisoned for five years by the Earl of Angus. When he escaped in 1528, the earl fled to England. The king took revenge on his relatives.

As the opera begins, the earl has returned to Scotland and is protected by Roderick Dhu, who is in opposition to the young king. Roderick has been promised to the earl's daughter, Ellen. We are on the shores of Loch Katrine. Ellen hopes that Malcolm, her young lover, will be with the hunting party she can hear approaching. Hubert (King James V) arrives alone, incognito and lost, and she offers him shelter.

The hunters return. Ellen reveals to Hubert that her father has been exiled. She tells him she is promised to Roderick, who loves her, but that her heart is already given to someone else. Hubert hopes it might be he. Ellen and Malcolm now greet each other passionately.

Later, in a nearby valley, with his troops, Roderick declares his love for Ellen and she tries to hide her true feelings. Malcolm, with his followers, joins Roderick, who now speaks of Ellen as his bride-to-be. Ellen stops Malcolm from revealing his love for her and word comes that the enemy is approaching. Hubert, however, is thoroughly smitten by Ellen and gives her a ring, saying that it is from the King of Scotland, whose life she unwittingly saved. It can be used to secure the king's help, should she ever be in danger.

Roderick overhears all this, challenges Hubert and tries to discover his identity. Hubert merely says enigmatically that he does not fear the king's enemies. The attack now comes and Hubert and Roderick prepare for battle. In the upshot, Ellen's father is imprisoned in Stirling Castle, and Ellen sets forth with the ring to seek the king's promised help. She is astounded when she meets Hubert, but he pardons Malcolm and releases her father.

With Rossini echoing if not quoting the inflexions of Scottish folksong, whether in the Scottish snaps in the jolly choruses or in the mooning melodies given to the heroine, the music is certainly distinctive. Maurizio Pollini, forsaking the keyboard for the baton, draws a fizzing performance from the Chamber Orchestra of Europe, suggesting fascinating foretastes not just of Donizetti but of Verdi: of the *Anvil chorus* from *Il Trovatore* in the Act I March and of the trombone unisons of *La forza del destino* later in the finale.

Though Pollini keeps his singers on a tight rein, there are three outstanding and characterful performances. Katia Ricciarelli in the title-role of Elena, Lady of the Lake, has rarely sung so stylishly on record, the voice creamy, with no suspicion of the unevenness which develops under pressure, and very agile in coloratura. Lucia Valentini Terrani with her warm, dark mezzo is no less impressive in the travesti role of Elena's beloved, Malcolm; while Samuel Ramey as Elena's father, Douglas, makes you wish the role was far longer with his darkly incisive singing. Of the two principal tenors, Dalmacio Gonzalez, attractively light-toned, is the more stylish; but Dano Raffanti as Rodrigo di Dhu copes with equal assurance with the often impossibly high tessitura. The recording, made at the end of a series of performances in the 1983 Rossini Festival in Pesaro, is clear and generally well balanced, and is given added immediacy in CD format, complete on two discs.

Elisabetta, Regina d'Inghilterra (complete).
(M) *** Ph. 432 453-2 (2) [id.]. Amb. S., New Philh. O, Masini.
    Elisabetta (Montserrat Caballé), Leicester (José Carreras), Matilde (Valerie Masterson), Enrico (Rosanna Creffield), Norfolk (Ugo Benelli), Guglielmo (Neil Jenkins).

The first surprise in this lively operatic setting of the Elizabeth and Leicester story comes in the *Overture*, which turns out to be the one which we know as belonging to *Il barbiere di Siviglia*. It is one of a whole sequence of self-borrowings which add zest to a generally delightful score. When Queen Elizabeth's big aria in Act II wanders into music which we know as the cabaletta to Rosina's *Una voce poco fa*, it may seem strange to have the formidable Tudor monarch associated with comedy, but in their different ways both ladies were certainly vipers.

At the Palace of Westminster the Duke of Norfolk is seized with jealousy for the Earl of Leicester (commander of the army) whose military triumphs are being celebrated. Leicester has brought hostages with him, the sons of the Scottish nobility, and is astonished to see Matilda, his secret wife, among them. They are all made courtiers.

Matilda is related to Mary, Queen of Scots, and this places Leicester in some danger. Norfolk reveals Leicester's secret to the queen, who is furious, as she had planned to marry him herself. She instructs Fitzwilliam (Captain of the Royal Guard) to bring the hostages to her. Matilda is easily identified from her obviously worried manner. The queen then confronts Leicester, proposing that he shall become her consort. He has no choice but to refuse, the queen flies into a rage, and he is arrested.

Elizabeth now demands that Matilda shall sign a renunciation of her status with Leicester; in return Leicester and her brother, Henry, will be freed. Leicester enters and tears up the document, and the queen orders Norfolk to be banished. Outside the Tower of London, Norfolk tries to stir up the populace against the queen, then he offers Leicester a false promise of help.

When the queen arrives to see Leicester before his execution, Norfolk hides. Matilda and Henry are also present when Norfolk draws a dagger and attempts to kill the queen. Matilda intervenes by throwing herself between them. The queen forgives both Leicester and Matilda, and Norfolk is condemned to death in Leicester's place.

There are passages in the opera where Rossini's invention is not at its peak, and the libretto is typically unconvincing, but in a well-sprung performance like this, with beautiful playing from the LSO and some very fine singing, it is a set for any Rossinian to investigate. Of the two tenors, José Carreras proves much the more stylish as Leicester, with Ugo Benelli, in the more unusual role of a tenor-villain, singing less elegantly than he once did. Caballé produces some ravishing sounds, though she is not always electrifying. Lively conducting and splendid recording.

Ermione.
(M) ***** Erato/Warner Dig. 2292 45790-2 (2) [id.]. Prague Philharmonic Ch., Monte Carlo PO, Scimone.
> Ermione (Cecilia Gasdia), Andromaca (Margarita Zimmermann), Pirro (Ernesto Palacio), Oreste (Chris Merritt), Pilade (William Matteuzzi), Fenicio (Simone Alaimo).

Ermione is the one Rossini opera never revived after its first production. First given in Naples in 1819, this *opera seria* is an adaptation of Racine's great tragedy, *Andromaque*; as the title suggests, it is slanted with Hermione at the centre and Andromaque (Andromaca in Italian) taking the subsidiary mezzo role.

As in the play, Ermione loves Pirro, who has agreed to be faithful to her, but who loves Andromaca. Oreste is enamoured of Ermione, and agrees to act on her behalf. But she only half-wants him to kill Pirro and, when he has done so, she demands that the Eumenides despatch him in revenge. At the end of the story, Ermione (unlike Hermione in the original play), survives.

The opera begins very strikingly with an off-stage chorus, introduced in the slow section of the *Overture*, singing a lament on the fall of Troy. The use of dramatic declamation, notably in the final scene of Act II, also gives due weight to the tragedy; however, not surprisingly, Rossini's natural sparkle keeps bursting through, often a little incongruously. The piece is interesting too for its structure, working away from the set aria towards more flexible treatment, allowing, for example, Oreste's cavatina in the third scene to have a duetting commentary from the principal tenor's companion, Pilade.

That makes three important tenor roles in the opera, Pirro (Pyrrhus) and Pilade as well as Oreste, reflecting the abundance of tenors in the Naples opera at the time.

The formidable technical demands of the writing for tenor present the principal stumbling-block for performance today. Though the three tenors in this Monte Carlo set from Erato are good by modern standards – Ernesto Palacio (Pirro), Chris Merritt (Oreste) and William Matteuzzi (Pilade) – they are uncomfortably strained by the high tessitura and the occasional stratospheric top notes. Cecilia Gasdia makes a powerful Ermione, not always even enough in her production but strong and agile; while Margarita Zimmermann makes a firm, rich Andromaca. Scimone, not always imaginative, yet directs a strong, well-paced performance.

On this showing, *Ermione* certainly does not deserve the century and a half of neglect it has received, with brickbats even from Rossini specialists who should have known better. Rossini himself, asked to explain the poor audiences for *Ermione* in Naples, said it was written for posterity. Now at last, thanks to Erato, posterity can fully judge. The recording is rather dry on the voices, but the hint of boxiness is generally undistracting. The break between the two discs comes before the final scene of Act I.

La gazza ladra (complete).
(**) Sony Dig. S3K 45850 (3) [id.]; *40-45850*. Prague Philharmonic Ch., Turin RAI SO, Gelmetti.
> Ninetta (Katia Ricciarelli), Gianetto (William Matteuzzi), Gottardo (Samuel Ramey), Pippo (Bernadette Manca Di Nissa), Lucia (Luciana D'Intino), Fernando Villabella (Ferruccio Furlanetto).

La gazza ladra is fascinating, an *opera semiseria*, with passages of romantic melodrama set against sparkling music such as one expects from the *Overture*. The story takes place in a village near Paris.

In the courtyard of Fabrizio's residence a magpie sits in an open cage. Fabrizio is a rich merchant; his son, Gianetto, is expected back from the wars. A voice calls out 'Pippo' (the name of a servant in Fabrizio's employ) and we realize that it belongs to the magpie. Lucia, Fabrizio's wife, asks the magpie who shall marry her son. 'Ninetta,' is the reply, and Lucia is displeased; she is inclined to blame Ninetta (their maidservant) for anything and everything, even for the loss of a silver fork.

Ninetta enters, carrying strawberries, and sings happily of Gianetto's return. She loves him and when he finally arrives it is clear that he loves her, too. Ninetta's father, Fernando, now appears; he is a tragic figure: having infringed military law, he has been condemned to death. Ninetta greets him; he is penniless, but he gives Ninetta some silver spoons to sell on his behalf and arranges that the money shall be left in a secret hiding place. When the mayor approaches, Fernando is forced to hide.

The mayor is conceited, pompous and no longer young, but he pays court to Ninetta. When an important message arrives for him, he asks Ninetta to read it out loud, as he does not have his spectacles. This enables her to alter its content, for it's about her father, reporting him as a deserter – to be apprehended. She changes the name and description. The mayor then proposes to Ninetta and she firmly rejects him; Fernando is drawn into the altercation and supports her vigorously. Both now leave and the magpie snatches one of the Fabrizio family's spoons and flies off with it.

Ninetta successfully sells her father's spoons to Isaac, a pedlar; as she is about to be paid, Gianetto and Fabrizio appear and Fabrizio approves of their marriage. Lucia, who is less well pleased, now checks the family silver and discovers a spoon is missing. 'Who can be the thief?' Gianetto asks. 'Ninetta,' the magpie answers. The mayor now discovers the deception over the name and description of Ninetta's father and that his daughter had shielded him. Ninetta's money now falls to the ground and Lucia asks where it came from. Pippo confirms that it came from Isaac the pedlar, to whom the spoons were sold; they can be identified by the initials 'F V' (for Fernando Villabella). But the pedlar has now resold the spoons, so this cannot be proved and, at the insistence of Lucia and the mayor, Ninetta is marched off as a criminal. Execution is the punishment for a servant caught stealing.

In prison Gianetto tries to comfort her and she affirms her innocence. The mayor arrives and says she should trust him and she might be saved, but he is treacherous: his help is dependent on her accepting his hand. Pippo also arrives. Ninetta gives him the three crowns she received from the sale of the spoons and tells him the whereabouts of the secret hiding-place. She also gives her silver cross to him, while her ring must go back to Gianetto. Fernando tries to save his daughter and is himself arrested, while she goes off to her death. But, in the nick of time, the magpie is discovered to be the thief, and his hoard is found. The king conveniently pardons Fernando, and Ninetta and Gianetto can be united.

Sadly, this live Sony recording, made at the Rossini Festival in Pesaro in 1989, is too rough and unstylish to recommend with great enthusiasm, though it is valuable as a complete recording of a Rossini rarity, usually remembered for its overture alone. Often with distractingly slipshod ensemble from the singers, the whole work is coarsened. The sound too is dry and unflattering, and Gelmetti proves a vigorous but often rigid Rossinian, with a tendency to press too hard. Those shortcomings are the more frustrating when the cast is a strong one, with four excellent singers in the principal roles.

Guglielmo Tell (William Tell: complete, in Italian).
*** Decca 417 154-2 (4) [id.]. Amb. Op. Ch., Nat. PO, Chailly.
   Guglielmo Tell (Sherrill Milnes), Matilde (Mirella Freni), Arnoldo (Luciano Pavarotti), Walter Furst (Nicolai Ghiaurov).
** Ph. Dig. 422 391-2 (4) [id.]. La Scala, Milan, Ch. & O, Muti.
   Guglielmo Tell (Giorgio Zancanaro), Matilde (Cheryl Studer), Arnoldo (Chris Merritt), Walter Furst (Giorgio Surjan).

Rossini wrote his massive opera about William Tell in French, and the first really complete recording (under Gardelli on EMI) used that language. But Chailly and his team here put forward a strong case for preferring Italian, with its open vowels, in music which glows with Italianate lyricism. Chailly's is a forceful reading, particularly strong in the many ensembles, and superbly recorded. The opera takes place in thirteenth-century Switzerland. Before it begins we need to know that Arnold, the son of the venerable Swiss leader Melchthal, has saved Princess Mathilde von Hapsburg – the sister of the hated tyrant, Gessler – from drowning. Mathilde and Arnold are in love.

Guillaume Tell's house is by the side of Lake Lucerne. It is a beautiful May morning and by ancient custom the venerable Melchthal blesses betrothed couples at the shepherds' festival. But Gessler and his men are approaching. Leuthold, a shepherd, cries that, in order to protect his daughter from being raped by one of these men, he had to kill him. He is now being tracked down and because a storm is brewing in the mountains, no one will take him across the lake to safety. Tell comes to his rescue and when Gessler's henchmen cannot find Leuthold they take old Melchthal instead.

In the valley, Arnold and Mathilde meet to declare their love. She wants him to be loyal to Austria, but Tell and Walter arrive and Arnold discovers that Melchthal has been murdered at Gessler's orders. Arnold now firmly knows which side he is on. The three men swear an oath to free Switzerland and throw off the heavy yoke of Austria.

At the marketplace of Altdorf there is to be dancing on the hundredth anniversary of Austrian rule. The villagers are instructed to bow down to Gessler's hat, placed on a pole. Tell, his young son, Jemmy, with him, refuses to pay homage to the hat and he is recognized as the man who saved Leuthold. In the famous contest, Gessler orders Tell to shoot an apple from Jemmy's head, which he does. He then tells Gessler that, had his first arrow missed, the second would have been for him. Tell is arrested and taken off.

While a storm rages on the lake, Arnold decides to rescue Tell. Mathilde takes Jemmy home. Gessler's men free Tell from his bonds so that he can pilot the boat taking Gessler and his guards across the stormy lake. On reaching the shore, he leaps out and pushes the boat hard out into the middle of the lake. Meanwhile Tell's house has been set on fire by Jemmy, but this is a signal for the rebellion to commence. Gessler manages to save himself from the lake, but Tell now uses that second arrow to kill him, and the Swiss enter triumphantly from all sides, to vanquish the remaining Austrians.

Milnes makes a heroic Tell, always firm, and though Pavarotti has his moments of coarseness he sings the role of Arnoldo with glowing tone. Ghiaurov too is in splendid voice, while subsidiary characters are almost all well taken, with such a fine singer as John Tomlinson, for example, finely resonant as Melchthal. The women singers too are impressive, with Mirella Freni as the heroine Matilde providing dramatic strength as well as sweetness. The recording, made in 1978 and 1979, is one of the finest of Decca's late-analogue vintage and comes out spectacularly on CD. In the four-disc layout, Acts III and IV are each complete on the last two discs, so that only the long Act I has any break. The *Pas de six* ballet music is here banded into its proper place in Act I.

Recorded live, the Philips alternative provides a welcome memento of Muti's enterprise as music director at La Scala in presenting the grandest of Rossini's operas absolutely complete on stage for the first time in many generations. In the theatre longueurs were not avoided, even with Muti's electric direction, when the stage production was uninspired and visually bizarre. Sadly, the performance captured here on record is vocally too flawed to inspire a full recommendation. Muti is forceful, but his rhythmic thrust tends to work against lyrical warmth. The much-praised Chris Merritt is sadly strained in the tenor role of Arnoldo, no match for Pavarotti on Decca's studio recording, who is musically more imaginative too. Giorgio Zancanaro is a strong, generally reliable Tell but is outshone by Sherrill Milnes on the earlier set. Even Cheryl Studer, warm and sympathetic as Mathilde, is below her best. The recording conveys a vivid, atmospheric impression of a performance at La Scala but, quite apart from erratic balances, inevitably suffers from the acoustic of the theatre, difficult for recording.

Guillaume Tell (William Tell) (sung in French).
(M) *** EMI CMS7 69951-2 (4). Amb. Op. Ch., RPO, Gardelli.
  Guillaume Tell (Gabriel Bacquier), Mathilde (Montserrat Caballé), Arnold (Nicolai Gedda), Walter Furst (Kolos Kováts).

The great interest of this fine 1973 EMI set is that it is sung in the original French. It is fortunate too that Gardelli is such an imaginative Rossini interpreter, allying his formidable team to vigorous and sensitive performances. Bacquier makes an impressive Tell, developing the character as the story progresses; Gedda is a model of taste, and Montserrat Caballé copes ravishingly with the coloratura problems of Mathilde's role. While Chailly's more forceful Decca set puts forward a strong case for using Italian with its open vowels, this remains an excellent alternative, with excellent CD sound. The one considerable snag is that no English translation is provided.

L'inganno felice (complete).
*(*) Claves Dig. CD 50-9211 [id.]. ECO, Viotti.

Batone (Natale De Carolis), Isabella (Amelia Felle), Bertrando (Iorio Zennaro), Tarabotto (Fabio Previati), Ormondo (Danilo Serraiocco).

Among the one-Act *farse* that Rossini wrote between 1810 and 1813 for the Teatro San Moise in Venice this is in many ways the most attractive of all. It badly needed a recording, but unfortunately this one is only a stop-gap. The plot is melodramatic and does not seem the stuff of farce, but it is surprisingly effective when filled out with Rossini's music.

Tarabotto, a miner, finds a beautiful girl lying senseless on the beach. He does not at first know her identity, so he tells everyone she is his niece, Nisa. Later, when he finds a locket containing a picture of her husband, he discovers that she is Isabella, the wife of Duke Bertrando.

The villain of the piece is not the duke but Ormondo who, having unsuccessfully tried to seduce Isabella, had ordered his henchman, Batone, to throw her into the sea to drown. As is the way in Italian opera, Duke Bertrando and his soldiers now arrive at the mine. Everyone in the party is put on edge by the sight of 'Nisa', Bertrando because he still loves his wife, Batone because of his guilty conscience and Ormondo because he was never sure whether Isabella perished or not.

To be quite sure, Ormondo orders Batone to abduct her again! When night arrives, Nisa disappears. Tarabotto and the duke lie in wait for the plotters, Isabella reappears in the clothes in which she was found on the beach, Ormondo confesses, and the duke is reunited with his wife who magnanimously forgives Batone.

The opera is stylishly and energetically conducted by Viotti with sprung rhythms and polished playing, but with a flawed cast. As the heroine, Amelia Felle is agile but too often raw-toned, even if on occasion she can crown an ensemble with well-phrased cantilena. As the hero, Bertrando, Iorio Zennaro has an agreeable natural timbre, but his tenor is not steady enough and strains easily. The *buffo*, Fabio Previati, is the soloist who comes closest to meeting the full challenge. The recorded sound has a pleasant bloom on it, but the orchestra is too recessed, and though the recitatives are briskly done, with crisp exchanges between the characters, the degree of reverberation is a serious drawback.

L'Italiana in Algeri (complete).
⊛ *** DG 427 331-2 (2) [id.]. V. State Op. Konzertvereinigung, VPO, Abbado.

Isabella (Agnes Baltsa), Lindoro (Frank Lopardo), Taddeo (Enzo Dara), Mustafà (Ruggero Raimondi).

*** Sony Dig. S2K 39048 (2) [id.]. Cologne R. Ch., Capella Coloniensis, Ferro.

Isabella (Lucia Valentini Terrani), Lindoro (Francisco Araiza), Taddeo (Enzo Dara), Mustafà (Wladimiro Ganzarolli).

(M) *** Erato/Warner 2292 45404-2 (2) [id.]. Prague Ch., Sol. Ven., Scimone.

Isabella (Marilyn Horne), Lindoro (Ernesto Palacio), Taddeo (Domenico Trimarchi), Mustafà (Samuel Ramey).

(M) **(*) Decca 417 828-2 (2) [id.]. Maggio Musicale Fiorentino Ch. & O, Varviso.

Isabella (Teresa Berganza), Lindoro (Luigi Alva), Taddeo (Rolando Panerai), Mustafà (Fernando Corena).

Withdrawn: (M) (**) EMI mono CHS7 64041-2 (2) [Ang. CDHB 64041]. La Scala O & Ch., Giulini.

Isabella (Giulietta Simionato), Lindoro (Cesare Valletti), Taddeo (Marcello Cortis), Mustafà (Mario Petri).

L'Italiana in Algeri has been extraordinarily successful on record, and it says a great deal that Abbado's brilliant version, recorded in conjunction with a new staging by the Vienna State Opera, with timing and pointing all geared for wit on stage, is the most captivating of all recordings of the opera.

At the opening we find ourselves in the palace of Mustafa, the Bey of Algiers. Eunuchs are discussing the miserable lot of women, and this thought is echoed by Elvira, Mustafa's wife, and her confidante, Zulma, for the bey has rejected Elvira and is seeking an Italian wife instead. Lindoro, one of the bey's Italian slaves, is pining for his beloved Isabella, when lo! a shipwreck occurs, and she appears with the ageing Taddeo. But meanwhile Mustafa has offered money to Lindoro to take Elvira off his hands.

Elvira confides in Lindoro that she still loves her difficult husband but Lindoro tells her that, if she accompanies him to Italy, she will find a remarkably wide choice of husbands and lovers. Isabella now arrives at the palace, and she and Lindoro recognize each other; but when she discovers that the bey is discarding his wife, she is highly indignant.

Alone with Lindoro, Isabella chides him for agreeing to help Mustafa dispose of Elvira, but Lindoro reaffirms his love for her, and they plan to escape. The bey, who has his sights on Isabella, tells Taddeo, whom he believes to be her uncle, that he will invest him as the Grand Kaimaken of Algeria, but he must bring Isabella to him and leave them alone together.

The bey is now persuaded to join the noble order of 'Pappatici' (eat and be silent) which implies a complacent and contented husband. He willingly enrols, thinking it a great honour. They make a fool of him and, discovering that he has been hoodwinked, Mustafa returns to Elvira and says that Italians were only a passing fancy.

In this splendid DG recording, Agnes Baltsa is a real fire-eater in the title-role, and Ruggero Raimondi with his massively sepulchral bass gives weight to his part without undermining the comedy. The American tenor, Frank Lopardo, proves the most stylish Rossinian, singing with heady clarity in superbly articulated divisions, while both *buffo* baritones are excellent too. This DG set has all the sparkle of Abbado's scintillating live recording of *Il viaggio a Reims*, plus first-rate studio sound, and uses the authentic score, published by the Fondazione Rossini in Pesaro.

Like the Abbado version, the Sony set uses the critical edition of the score but goes further towards authenticity in using period instruments, including a fortepiano instead of harpsichord for the recitatives (well played by Georg Fischer). Though Ferro can at times be sluggish in slow music (even in the opening of the *Overture*), he is generally a sparkling Rossinian, pacing well to allow a rhythmic lift to be married to crisp ensemble. The set also gains from forward and bright digital recording, more immediate than in previous sets, and the cast is a fine one.

Lucia Valentini Terrani here gives her strongest performance on record to date with her rich, firm voice superbly agile in coloratura. She may not be as tough and forceful as Agnes Baltsa or Marilyn Horne on the Erato set but, with a younger, sunnier voice, she is very seductive. Francisco Araiza as Lindoro peppers the rapid passagework with intrusive aitches, but the strength of the voice makes the performance heroic. Ganzarolli treats the role of the Bey, Mustafa, as a conventional *buffo* role, with a voice not ideally steady but full of character; the rest of the cast is strong, too. Excellent digital sound.

Scholarship as well as Rossinian zest have also gone into Scimone's highly enjoyable version, which in addition has the advantage of economy. It is beautifully played and recorded with as stylish a team of soloists as one can expect nowadays. As with the DG and Sony sets, the text is complete, the original orchestration having been restored (as in the comic duetting of piccolo and bassoon in the reprise in the *Overture*), and alternative versions of certain arias are given as an appendix. Marilyn Horne makes a dazzling, positive Isabella, and Samuel Ramey is splendidly firm as Mustafa. Domenico Trimarchi is a delightful Taddeo and Ernesto Palacio an agile Lindoro, not coarse, though the recording does not always catch his tenor timbre well. Nevertheless the sound is generally very good indeed, and the fullness and atmosphere come out the more vividly on CD. A good medium-price choice.

The Decca set is offered at mid-price too. Under Varviso the opera has Rossinian sparkle in abundance and the music blossoms readily. Teresa Berganza makes an enchanting Italian girl, and the three principal men all sing with agility and a fair feeling for Rossinian style. The 1963 recording is vintage Decca, vividly remastered, and adds greatly to the sparkle of the performance. With excellent documentation this is a fair bargain at mid-price.

Set in a dry, intimate acoustic, Giulini's mono version is effective enough in this CD reissue, with the rhythmic point of his conducting bringing plenty of sparkle. But the characterful Simionato, in one of her most cherished roles as Isabella, is relatively disappointing, lacking charm. Her powerful mezzo is made to sound a little fluttery, less flatteringly caught than in her Decca recordings and with coloratura plentifully aspirated. Mario Petri produces woolly tone as the Bey, Mustafa, but the tenor, Cesare Valletti, a pupil of Tito Schipa, is excellent, and the Taddeo of Marcello Cortis is fresh and clear, while Graziella Sciutti is a delight in the role of Mustafa's wife, Elvira. The text is seriously cut, and the booklet gives only the Italian text without translation.

L'Italiana in Algeri: highlights.
*** DG Dig. 429 414-2 [id.] (from above recording with Baltsa, Lopardo, Dara, Raimondi; cond. Abbado).

This 67-minute selection of highlights provides an admirable and sparkling sampler with well-chosen excerpts, even if the complete recording on two CDs is an even better investment.

Maometto II (complete).
*** Ph. Dig. 412 148-2 (3) [id.]. Amb. Op. Ch., Philh. O, Scimone.
  Anna (June Anderson), Calbo (Margarita Zimmermann), Erisso (Ernesto Palacio), Maometto (Samuel Ramey), Condulmiero / Selimo (Laurence Dale).

Maometto II is set in Negroponte, a Venetian outpost in Greece, in the middle of the fifteenth century. It is being besieged by the Turks. In the palace of the governor, Paolo Erisso, the community's leaders have to decide whether or not to surrender. Erisso's daughter, Anna, is offered the chance to marry the young General Calbo and have his special protection.

But Anna loves another, Uberto, from Mytilene, whom she says she met in Corinth during her father's absence on a visit to Venice. Erisso is astonished at this statement, for Uberto had been with him on his Venetian trip, and Anna now realizes that the man she loves is an impostor.

Noise of the battle interrupts this revelation and the two men go out to fight; Anna retires to the church to pray. As danger threatens, Erisso gives his daughter a dagger with which to commit suicide if taken captive by the Turks.

At sunrise the Turks appear, with Mahomet at their head. His strategy shows an obvious knowledge of the city and he tells his vizier, Selim, that he has been in Greece before as a spy, and also – here he is suitably nostalgic – visited Corinth.

The Venetians have now been defeated, and Calbo and Erisso appear in chains. When Mahomet discovers Erisso's identity and that he was once governor of Corinth, and a father, he offers to spare the prisoners' lives if the city gates are opened.

But both refuse his offer and are about to be taken away and tortured when Anna rushes in. Mahomet recognizes her, and she realizes that he is the supposed Uberto. She draws her dagger and threatens to die there and then unless Mahomet is willing to release her father and Calbo, whom she describes as her 'brother'. Mahomet agrees, Calbo is grateful, but Erisso spurns his daughter.

Anna now shares Mahomet's tent but not, apparently, his bed. Mahomet loves her and wishes to make her his queen, but Anna weeps, refusing his offer. Now Mahomet is to lead the final assault on the city and, to protect Anna, he gives her a royal seal of authority. Erisso and Calbo are hiding in the crypt of the church. Anna appears and swears fidelity to her father, giving him Mahomet's seal. They rush off to encourage the Venetian defenders to make one last effort.

Anna says she must stay behind, but first she marries Calbo, as her father had previously arranged. News now comes of the unexpected victory of the Venetians, spurred on by the reappearance of their two leaders. The sultan and his army have been defeated and are fleeing, but Anna is warned that the Turks are hunting for her, intent on revenge. She awaits their arrival, and they are so impressed by her calm acceptance of her fate that they are unable to kill her.

The angry Mahomet now arrives and demands that Anna give him back his seal. Anna, dagger in hand, informs the sultan that she gave it to her father and her 'husband'; then, before he can stop her, she kills herself, and falls lifeless on her mother's tomb.

Claudio Scimone here repeats the success of his earlier set for Philips of *Mosé in Egitto*. But where he chose the most compressed of Rossini's three versions of that opera, here he chooses the most expansive early version of a work which the composer also radically revised for Paris as *Le siège de Corinthe*. There are cogent reasons for approving Scimone's preference in each instance. This account of *Maometto II* has Samuel Ramey magnificently focusing the whole story in his portrait of the Muslim invader in love with the heroine. The nobility of his singing makes Maometto's character all the more convincing, even if the opera is made the less tense dramatically from having no villain.

The other singing is less sharply characterized but is generally stylish, with Margarita Zimmermann in the travesti role of Calbo, June Anderson singing sweetly as Anna, not least in the lovely prayer which comes as an interlude in a massive Trio or Terzettone in Act I. Laurence Dale is excellent in two smaller roles, while Ernesto Palacio mars some fresh-toned singing with his intrusive aitches. Excellent recording, made the more attractive on CD.

Mosè in Egitto (complete).
(M) *** Ph. 420 109-2 (2) [id.]. Amb. Op. Ch., Philh. O, Scimone.
  Mosè (Ruggero Raimondi), Elcia (June Anderson), Amaltea (Zehava Gal), Aronne (Salvatore Fisichella), Osiride (Ernesto Palacio), Faraone (Siegmund Nimsgern).

For a century and more it was assumed that Rossini's later thoughts on the subject of a Moses opera – his expanded version for Paris – were the ones to be preferred. It is good that Scimone took scholarly advice and, in a direct and understanding reading, presents the second and far preferable of the two Italian versions. So here the last and briefest of the three Acts is strongly expanded with a big ensemble based on Moses' prayer to make it almost a forerunner of another great chorus for the children of Israel, *Va pensiero* from Verdi's *Nabucco*. Other Verdian parallels come out, for some of the ceremonial writing suggests a much later Egyptian opera, *Aida*, as well as a masterpiece written at that same period, the *Requiem*. Clearly Scimone justifies his claim that the 1819 version is dramatically more effective than both the earlier Italian one and the later Paris one.

As the opera opens, Pharaoh has refused to free the Israelites from their Egyptian slavery, and the Hebrew God has turned Egypt into a place of stygian darkness. Pharaoh finally sends for Moses and desperately promises the children of Israel their freedom if daylight returns. Aaron is suspicious of Pharaoh's reliability, but Moses waves his rod and calls on the Lord to dispel the darkness. He is then told by the Pharaoh that the Israelites must depart immediately.

Meanwhile the Pharaoh's son, Osiris, has seduced an Israeli girl, Elcia, and does not want her to leave. He persuades the high priest, Mambre, to warn the Egyptians that the departure of their slaves is highly inconvenient and undesirable. Mambre, who hates and envies Moses, readily agrees. But Elcia comes to bid Osiris a sad goodbye.

Mambre's efforts, which are well financed, are highly successful and soon the Pharaoh is once again forced to withdraw his agreement that the Israelites should leave. Pharaoh's queen, Amaltea, is also involved, as she has secretly been converted to the Jewish faith and now sympathizes with Moses. When the edict is made, Moses again demonstrates the power of the Hebrew God, calling down fire and hailstones, which wreak havoc, destroying the Egyptian farmland.

The pragmatic, if vacillating Pharaoh realizes that something has to be done, so he agrees that the Israelites should get ready to depart at once, and he also arranges for his son to marry a princess from Armenia. He is surprised when Osiris fails to welcome the proposed wedding. But Aaron and Moses know why, as they have learned of the affair between Elcia and Osiris, and they pass this news on to Amaltea.

Osiris and Elcia meet in a dark cave and he suggests that they live the simple life together, but the queen and Aaron now arrive together to put an end to his impractical dream. Nevertheless the lovers refuse to part, and Osiris says he will give up the Egyptian throne rather than lose his beloved.

The Pharaoh, under further pressure, changes his mind again and, with their departure once more in abeyance, Moses now decrees that all the first-born of Egypt will be struck by lightning. The furious Pharaoh puts him in chains and, saying that his son shall now rule alongside himself, tells Osiris to order Moses' execution. Elcia comes to the rescue by revealing her love for Osiris and begging for the release of Moses and his people. Osiris flatly refuses, sentences Moses to death and is immediately struck down by lightning.

Elcia is in despair, but at least now she can return to the Promised Land with her people. So, though they are fearful, the children of Israel pass through the wilderness, and Moses invokes the help of the Lord in a prayer of great power and solemnity. He then leads the Israelites onwards and, just as the Egyptians arrive to attack them, a passage opens in the Red Sea and they pass through safely. The Egyptians, including the Pharaoh and Mambre, follow but the waters close over their heads and they are engulfed.

Rossini's score brings much fine music and, among the soloists, Raimondi relishes not only the solemn moments like the great invocation in Act I and the soaring prayer of Act III, but the rage aria in Act II, almost like Handel updated if with disconcerting foretastes of Dr Malatesta in Donizetti's *Don Pasquale*. The writing for the soprano and tenor lovers (the latter the son of Pharaoh and in effect the villain of the piece) is relatively conventional, though the military flavour of their Act I cabaletta is refreshingly different. Ernesto Palacio and June Anderson make a strong pair, and the mezzo, Zehava Gal, is another welcome newcomer as Pharaoh's wife. Siegmund Nimsgern is a fine Pharaoh, Salvatore Fisichella an adequate Arone (Aaron). The well-balanced recording emerges most vividly on CD.

Mosè (complete recording of Paris version).
** Hung. HCD 12290/2-2 [id.]. Hungarian R. & TV Ch., Hungarian State Op. O, Gardelli.
    Mosè (József Gregor), Elcia (Magda Kalmár), Amaltea (Júlia Hamari), Aaron (Ferenc Begányi), Faraone (Sándor Sólyom-Nagy).

The Hungarian version of *Mosè*, using the Paris text of 1827 but translated back into Italian, has the merit of Gardelli's understanding conducting. Much of the singing is pleasing too, but when the far more vital 1819 text of *Mosè in Egitto* has been recorded on an excellent Philips set, this is hardly competitive, particularly when Act II scene iii is omitted. The Philips recording, strongly directed by Scimone, is in every way preferable.

L'occasione fa il ladro (complete).
**(*) Claves Dig. CD 50-9208/9 [id.]. ECO, Viotti.
> Berenice (Maria Bayo), Don Parmenione (Natale De Carolis), Conte Alberto (Iorio Zennaro), Ernestina (Francesca Provvisionato), Martino (Fabio Previati), Don Eusebio (Fulvio Massa).

On two discs this is one of the longer one-Acters in the Claves series, bringing one of the more recommendable performances, with Viotti at his most relaxed.

Count Alberto and Don Parmenione are both staying at a country inn. Alberto is en route for Naples to meet his betrothed; Parmenione seeks the sister of a friend who has run off. Alberto leaves, and by mistake his valet takes Parmenione's travelling case and leaves the count's bag behind. Parmenione and his servant, Martino, unscrupulously rifle the count's bag and discover a picture of a woman whom Don Parmenione thinks is Alberto's bride-to-be. Parmenione is smitten and, as the count's passport is also among the contents, Parmenione decides to substitute himself for the count.

At the home of Marquise Berenice, wedding plans are well advanced. But Berenice, who was promised to her husband-to-be by her father and who has never met him, is not sure if she wants to go through with her marriage. With the support of her uncle and guardian, Don Eusebio, she exchanges identities with her maid, Ernestina, to find out what sort of man her count really is. Parmenione now arrives, elaborately dressed, and meets Ernestina, in the guise of the marquise. They fall in love, even though he is surprised that she does not look a bit like her portrait. All is tidied up at the end. Alberto and Berenice find happiness with each other, and the picture turns out to be of Alberto's sister.

Maria Bayo as the heroine sings warmly and sweetly, with no intrusive aspirates in the coloratura. The soubrette role of Ernestina is also charmingly done, and the *buffo* characters sing effectively, though the tenor, Iorio Zennaro, is hardly steady enough for Rossinian cantilena. This is a piece that the Buxton Festival presented with success; as the only available recording, the Claves set can be recommended. The two discs come in a single hinged jewel-box at upper mid-price.

Otello (complete).
(M) *** Ph. 432 456-2 (2) [id.]. Amb. S., Philh. O, Lopez-Cobos.
> Otello (José Carreras), Desdemona (Frederica Von Stade), Iago (Gianfranco Pastine), Rodrigo (Salvatore Fisichella), Emilia (Nucci Condò), Elmiro (Samuel Ramey).

The libretto of Rossini's *Otello* bears remarkably little resemblance to Shakespeare – virtually none at all until the last Act.

At the opening of the story the Moor, Otello, returns in triumph to Venice and is crowned by the Doge with a laurel wreath. Meanwhile the jealous Iago and the Doge's son, Rodrigo, plan to destroy his power. Iago has a letter from Desdemona which will help them. Desdemona, longing for Otello to return to her, is at the same time fearful of her father's disapproval of her marriage. But she fears that Otello is unsure of her love for him, as a token of her feelings (a lock of her hair) and a letter have been intercepted by her father. He thought they were intended for Rodrigo and she did not disillusion him.

Iago, who had previously but unsuccessfully paid court to Desdemona, now approaches, and Desdemona and her maid and friend, Emilia, avoid him. He joins Rodrigo and Elmiro (Desdemona's father) who offers Rodrigo Desdemona's hand. They all hate the Moor and their joint efforts should be able to arrange his downfall. Elmiro suggests that Rodrigo might tell his father (the Doge) that Otello is plotting to overthrow him. Meanwhile Iago is ordered to make the wedding arrangements.

Alone, Elmiro determines to be revenged on Otello and when his daughter comes in he tells her that he has found her a husband. Desdemona assumes that her father means Otello and that he has become reconciled to him. Only at the wedding ceremony does she discover her mistake and is appalled to find that she is to marry Rodrigo. Her father tells her to trust his decision, but Desdemona still loves Otello, and Roderigo senses that he is entering a loveless marriage. Otello now arrives and holds everything, demanding Desdemona for his own bride. The Moor asks her to confirm that she loves him and she immediately and willingly does so. Elmiro angrily takes his daughter off.

Rodrigo now finds Desdemona in the garden and discovers that she is already married to Otello. Desdemona then tells Emilia she is not sure of her husband but she would go off with him if he asked her. Meanwhile Otello too is full of doubts about his own intentions, and these are encouraged by Iago, whom Otello trusts. He asks Iago to find proof of Desdemona's betrayal. But he also threateningly warns Iago not to betray him.

Iago produces the missing letter and Otello reads it, not realizing it was originally addressed to him. Iago then caps the matter by presenting Otello with the lock of Desdemona's hair. The Moor is now overwhelmed by what he thinks is evidence of his wife's betrayal and a desperate personal need for revenge.

Rodrigo enters and tries to make friends with Otello, with no success; Desdemona also comes in, and both men turn on her, then leave to fight. Otello wins the duel and the faithful Emilia comes to warn her mistress. At that moment Elmiro also arrives and furiously castigates his daughter.

The grieving Desdemona and Emilia are alone together in Desdemona's bedroom. A storm is rising, and the wind breaks the window, surely an omen, and Emilia leaves, distraught. Alone, Desdemona prays that Otello will come to her, and sure enough he does, dagger in hand, through a secret entrance, led by Iago. When he sees Desdemona sleeping, at first he draws back, but she murmurs an expression of love for him in her sleep, and he is instantly suspicious. Before he can stab her, she is awakened by a lightning flash.

Otello tells her that Iago has already killed Rodrigo, and she suddenly realizes who is at the bottom of the plot against her. As the storm becomes more violent, Otello, still believing it is Rodrigo she loves, stabs her. There is a knock on the door and a retainer announces that Rodrigo is alive; that instead Iago has died, having confessed his guilt. Now the doge, Elmiro, and Rodrigo enter the bedchamber together. Realizing the awful crime he has committed, Otello re-uses his dagger to take his own life.

Rossini's layout of voices is odd. Not only is Otello a tenor role, so is Rodrigo (second in importance), and Iago too. It is some tribute to this performance, superbly recorded, and brightly and stylishly conducted by Lopez-Cobos, that the line-up of tenors is turned into an asset, with three nicely contrasted soloists. Carreras is here at his finest – most affecting in his recitative before the murder, while Fisichella copes splendidly with the high tessitura of Rodrigo's role, and Pastine has a distinctive timbre to identify him as the villain. Frederica von Stade pours forth a glorious flow of beautiful tone, well matched by Nucci Condò as Emilia. Samuel Ramey is excellent too in the bass role of Elmiro. *Otello*, Rossini style, is an operatic curiosity, but this recording helps to explain why it so ensnared such a sensitive opera-lover as the novelist Stendhal.

La pietra del paragone (complete).
(M) **(*) Van. 08 9031 73 (3) [id.]. Clarion Concerts Ch. & O, Newell Jenkins.
　　Marchesina Clarice (Beverly Wolff), Conte Asdrubale (John Reardon), Giocondo (José Carreras), Macrobio (Andrew Foldi), Baroness Aspasia (Elaine Bonazzi), Donna Fulvia (Anne Elgar), Pacuvio (Justino Diaz), Fabrizio (Raymond Murcell).

This recording of the *opera buffa*, *La pietra del paragone*, made by Vanguard in New York in 1972, presents the young José Carreras in an incidental role, just one in an attractively fresh-voiced cast of soloists. It is given a vigorous, if occasionally hard-pressed performance under Newell Jenkins with what is called the Clarion Concerts Orchestra and Chorus. This was an early piece, written when Rossini was only twenty. Glyndebourne presented it as long ago as 1964 but in the process scandalized that company's great Rossinian, Vittorio Gui, when they used 'a Germanized travesty'. Not so this recording. The plot of disguises and deceit is a throwback to artificial eighteenth-century conventions, involving a house-party with a couple of poets and a venal critic brought in. For modern performance the problem is the length, though on disc that evaporates when Rossini's invention is at its peak in number after number.

La scala di seta (complete).
*** Claves Dig. 50-9219/20 [id.]. ECO, Viotti.
　　Germano (Alessandro Corbelli), Giulia (Teresa Ringholz), Dorvil (Ramón Vargas), Blansac (Natale De Carolis), Lucilla (Francesca Provvisionato), Dormont (Fulvio Massa).

The overture is among the best known of all that Rossini wrote, and here Viotti establishes his individuality with an unusually expansive slow introduction, leading to a brisk and well-sprung allegro, scintillatingly played by the ECO.

The story sparkles, like the overture. It begins as Giulia, the heroine, waits for Germano to leave. Giulia is impatiently waiting to embrace Dorvil, whom she has recently married in secret, but Germano, her guardian's servant, is with her and Germano must not see Dorvil or he would tell his master, Dormont. Germano is about to depart when Lucilla, Giulia's cousin, arrives, so he stays. Finally Giulia gets rid of both of them and Dorvil comes out of the closet.

He reveals that his wealthy friend, Blansac, wants to marry her, but she reassures him of her love, and he escapes down a silken ladder just as Dormont comes in to announce Blansac. Giulia now decides to arrange a meeting between Lucilla and Blansac, hoping they will fall in love, and suggests that Germano might spy on Blansac to see if he is already paying court to Lucilla. Germano at first thinks she is interested in him, but eventually agrees to do what she asks.

Giulia departs and Blansac and Dorvil enter. Dorvil tries to talk Blansac out of the wedding, saying Giulia is unresponsive to his attentions, but Blansac is confident enough to think he can seduce her and invites Dorvil to observe his progress. Dorvil, none too pleased, agrees, if only to test his wife's constancy. He is forced to hide again as Giulia comes back. She in turn wants to test Blansac and, to determine whether he is a gentleman or a profligate, she turns the full force of her charms on him, with her husband watching! Germano – the appointed spy – also watches the course of events and realizes that he is not alone.

Everyone now comes out into the open and Germano gets the blame. All depart, except Blansac who stays behind to try again to seduce Lucilla, this time with rather more success. Germano finds out that Giulia is awaiting a lover that evening, who will climb up the silk ladder to her room and, as he is sure it must be Blansac, he tells him about the ladder. Then he also tells Lucilla, who is jealous of Blansac and decides to spy in her own right. Germano, too, determines to hide himself to see what transpires.

Midnight strikes, and Giulia lets down the silken ladder. Dorvil then appears, with Blansac close on his heels. Poor Dorvil has to hide, yet again! Now Dormont, the guardian, also comes by and angrily discovers the silk ladder. He bumps into each of the participants in the comedy in turn, one at a time. The truth has to come out. Dorvil and Giulia declare they are husband and wife, Blansac proposes to Lucilla, and the old man gives his blessing, as he has had a letter from Giulia's aunt recommending her match with Dorvil.

The cast here is stronger vocally than those in the rest of the Claves series, with Teresa Ringholz delightful as the heroine, Giulia, warm and agile, shading her voice seductively. She and the *buffo*, Germano, have the biggest share of the solo work, and the *buffo*, Alessandro Corbelli, is also first rate. The tenor Ramón Vargas sings without strain – rare in this series – and the mezzo, Francesca Provvisionato, sings vivaciously as the heroine's cousin, Lucilla, with a little aria in military rhythm a special delight. Warm sound with good bloom on the voices.

Semiramide (complete).
(M) *** Decca 425 481-2 (3) [id.]. Amb. Op. Ch., LSO, Bonynge.
　　Semiramide (Joan Sutherland), Arsace (Marilyn Horne), Assur (Joseph Rouleau), Idreno (John Serge), Oroe (Spiro Malas).

The story of *Semiramide* is certainly improbable, involving the love which almost all the male characters bear for the Princess Azema, a lady who, rather curiously, appears very infrequently in the opera.

Semiramide, Queen of Babylon, has murdered her husband, Nino, aided by Prince Assur, who hopes to take Nino's place on the throne. The queen has a son, and only the chief priest of the temple, Oroe, knows that Arsace, the victorious commander of her army, is he. Even the queen herself does not realize who he truly is, and he is generally believed to be a Scythian.

Arsace is Princess Azema's most important lover. At a gathering in the temple the gates of Nino's tomb mysteriously swing open. The ghost of Nino announces that his successor shall be Arsace, who is summoned. He must visit the tomb at midnight to learn the secret of Nino's assassination.

Prince Assur is angry at this revelation and determines to enter the tomb himself at the appointed hour. Semiramide, having now discovered that Arsace is her son, comes to the tomb to warn him against Assur. All three people involved gather in the tomb area. Arsace tries to stab Assur, but Semiramide throws herself between them and herself receives the death blow. Arsace has thus avenged his father's murder and is proclaimed king.

Rossini's setting concentrates on the love of Queen Semiramide for the Prince Arsace (a mezzo-soprano), and musically the result is a series of fine duets, superbly performed here by

Sutherland and Horne (in the mid-1960s when they were both at the top of their form). What a complete recording brings out, however, is the dramatic consistency of Rossini's score, with the music involving the listener even when the story falls short. In Sutherland's interpretation, Semiramide is not so much a Lady Macbeth as a passionate, sympathetic woman and, with dramatic music predominating over languorous cantilena, one has her best, bright manner. Horne is well contrasted, direct and masculine in style, and Spiro Malas makes a firm, clear contribution in a minor role. Rouleau and Serge are variable but more than adequate, and Bonynge keeps the whole opera together with his alert, rhythmic control of tension and pacing. The vintage Decca recording has transferred brilliantly to CD.

Semiramide: Scenes and duets: Act I: *Mitrane! E che rechi? . . . Serbami ognor sì fido; Alle più calde immagini.* Act II: *No: non ti lascio . . . Ebben . . . a te, ferisci . . . Giorno d'orre; Madre – addio.*
(M) *** Decca 436 303-2 [id.]. Semiramide (Joan Sutherland), Arsace (Marilyn Horne), Mitrane (Leslie Fyson), LSO, Bonynge – BELLINI: *Norma: Scenes & duets.* **(*)

Serbami ognor, from the complete set of *Semiramide,* provides one of the finest examples of duet singing ever recorded. Even Sutherland and Horne have never surpassed this in their many collaborations. With other excerpts included, plus duets from *Norma,* this reissue is most attractive, and the vintage Decca recording from 1965/6 does not disappoint.

Il Signor Bruschino (complete).
Claves Dig. CD 50-8904/5 [id.]. I Filarmonico di Torino, Viotti.
   Bruschino (Natale De Carolis), Sofia (Patrizia Orciani), Gaudenzio (Bruno Praticò), Florville (Luca Canonici), Filiberto (Pietro Spagnoli), Marianna (Katia Lytting), Bruschino's son / Police Commissioner (Fulvio Massa).

This was recorded first in the Claves series, and acoustically the Turin sound provides an extreme contrast with the rest, dry to the point of rasping. It gives no help to the singers and exaggerates the flaws in the playing of the Turin orchestra.
   The story, based on a French farce, *Le fils par hasard,* tells how a young blade, Florville, impersonates Bruschino's son in order to win the hand of Sofia, the ward of Gaudenzio, and to do this he has to try to fool Bruschino himself about his identity.
   Bruschino, who is not entirely convinced, protests against the deception, which is even accepted by the police commissioner, so that the old man even begins to wonder if he is going mad. But then his real son arrives, a libertine and gambler who until that moment has been kept under lock and key by an innkeeper to whom he owes money. All, of course, ends happily and Florville and Sofia are happily united.
   Viotti springs rhythms very persuasively, but the fun of the piece still fails to come over. The tenor, Luca Canonici, sounds strained, and the rapid patter-numbers bring a storm of aspirated singing from all concerned.

Tancredi (complete).
** Sony S3K 39073 (3) [id.]. Ch. and O of Teatro la Fenice, Weikert.
   Tancredi (Marilyn Horne), Amenaide (Lella Cuberli), Argirio (Ernesto Palacio), Orbazzano (Nicola Zaccaria), Isaura (Bernadette Manca Di Nissa), Roggiero (Patricia Schuman).

Tancredi, first heard in the Teatro la Fenice in 1813, was enormously popular in its day, so famous that Wagner many years later quoted from it in *Die Meistersinger,* knowing his audience would appreciate the source.
   The story is set in Syracuse in AD 1005. Tancredi has been banished for many years (because of a family feud) but is loved by Amenaide, who is now required to marry Orbazzano. She writes and implores Tancredi to return and liberate Syracuse and meanwhile tries to postpone the wedding. Tancredi and his followers now reappear, but in disguise.
   Argirio, Amenaide's father, tells her that both the Saracens and Tancredi are near, and the city is in peril. He orders her to marry Orbazzano forthwith. Tancredi comes to see her; to protect him, she repulses him and begs him to flee from what she feels is certain death. The wedding celebrations continue and the disillusioned Tancredi, assuming his beloved is now Orbazzano's lover, asks Argirio if he can join in the forthcoming battle against the Saracen hordes. He is accepted, but then Amenaide refuses to go ahead with the wedding and the furious Orbazzano produces the incriminating letter, assuming it to have been intended for Solamir, leader of the Saracens.
   Everyone now considers Amenaide to be beyond the pale. Unable to tell the truth, her

protestations of innocence are of no avail. After much heart-searching, her father sentences her to death. Once more she proclaims her innocence to Orbazzano, who publicly asks if there is anyone who will defend her cause in a duel. Tancredi – though still believing her unfaithful – agrees to do so and he also accuses Orbazzano of being a tyrant.

Tancredi is triumphant in the duel, but because he does not trust poor Amenaide he now makes ready to leave Syracuse. As he departs, he receives news of the impending attack of the Saracens and instead returns to lead the battle against them. He is mortally wounded. Amenaide comes to comfort him, and Argirio at last reveals that the letter was addressed to Tancredi. So the lovers can be married before Tancredi finally expires.

The chief glory of this live recording from Venice is the enchanting singing of Lella Cuberli as the heroine, Amenaide. The purity and beauty of her tone, coupled with immaculate coloratura and tender expressiveness, make it a memorable performance, confirming the high opinions she won from the DG set of *Il viaggio a Reims*. Marilyn Horne, though not quite as fresh-sounding as earlier in her career, gives a formidable performance in the breeches role of Tancredi, relishing the resonance of her chest register, but finding delicacy too in her big aria, *Di tanti palpiti*. Ernesto Palacio is an accomplished Rossini tenor, commendably agile in the role of Argirio, but the tone tends to grow tight; and Zaccaria as Orbazzano sings with fuzzy, sepulchral tone. The conducting is efficient rather than inspired, failing to make the music sparkle or to bring the drama to life. The recording gives a realistic idea of a dryish theatre acoustic.

Il Turco in Italia (abridged).
*** Ph. Dig. 434 128-2 (2) [id.]. Amb. Op. Ch., ASMF, Marriner.
    Selim (Simone Alaimo), Fiorilla (Sumi Jo), Geronio (Enrico Fissore), Narciso (Raúl Giménez), Zaida (Susanne Mentzer).
Withdrawn: (*******) EMI mono CDS7 49344-2 (2). Ch. & O of La Scala, Milan, Gavazzeni.
    Selim (Nicola Rossi-Lemeni), Fiorilla (Maria Callas), Geronio (Franco Calabrese), Narciso (Nicolai Gedda), Zaida (Jolanda Gardino).
**(*) Sony Dig. S2K 37859 (2). Amb. Op. Ch., Nat. PO, Chailly.
    Selim (Samuel Ramey), Fiorilla (Montserrat Caballé), Geronio (Enzo Dara), Narciso (Ernesto Palacio), Zaida (Jane Berbié).

Il Turco in Italia followed hot on the heels of *L'Italiana in Algeri* and was first heard in Milan in the summer of 1814. The Turk in question is Selim, loved by Zaida. But he does not appear at the beginning of the story.

We first meet Zaida with Albazar, two other runaway Turks in a gypsy encampment on the outskirts of Naples. We also encounter the poet, Prosdocimo, who must produce a stage comedy for his patron and who has come to the camp for inspiration.

At that moment Geronio appears, looking for a gypsy to give him advice on how to cope with his young wife, Fiorilla. Zaida tells Prosdocimo that she was driven away from her master, Selim Damelec of Erzerum, by intrigue. Prosdocimo has heard that a Turkish pasha is currently due to arrive in Naples, but it is Fiorilla who meets the Turkish ship.

Selim emerges and is attracted to her. But Fiorilla already has a young lover, Narciso (to say nothing of her ailing husband). Prosdocimo watches all that is going on and sees in it a theme for his comedy. Fiorilla now amorously entertains Selim to coffee in her apartments. Geronio enters but Fiorilla manages to prevent a serious confrontation. Narciso is disgruntled by the turn of events. Selim arranges an assignation with Fiorilla that night by the harbour. Geronio regrets his marriage to someone much younger than he, and Prosdocimo's advice to be firm seems to have little effect.

Selim arrives in the gypsy quarter to discover whether the omens are propitious for an elopement with Fiorilla, and Zaida recognizes him. Then Fiorilla arrives, pursued by her husband, with Narciso following close behind. Zaida and Fiorilla confront each other and Prosdocimo feels that this might be a good finale for his play. However, there is more to come.

Prosdocimo suggests that Geronio needs to catch Selim and Fiorilla together, while Selim is now forced to choose between Fiorilla and Zaida. Prosdocimo suggests a plan: at that evening's masked ball Selim must carry off Fiorilla. But he arranges with Geronio and Narciso that Zaida should go disguised in Fiorilla's place. In addition Geronio must dress as Selim. In the event the desperate Narciso decides to appear as a second Selim. Much confusion follows, but Fiorilla decides to return to Geronio, Selim will go back to Turkey with Zaida, and Narciso must simply profit from experience. Prosdocimo has the dénouement for his play.

On Philips, Sumi Jo as Fiorilla, the sharp-tongued heroine, unhappily married to old Don Geronio, is no fire-eater, as Callas was in her vintage recording, but she sparkles delightfully, a more believable young wife than her other rival on disc. That is the heavyweight Montserrat Caballé on the CBS/Sony set, conducted by Riccardo Chailly. What seals the success of the Philips set is the playing of the St Martin's Academy under Sir Neville Marriner, consistently crisper and lighter than their predecessors, wittily bringing out the light and shade in Rossini's score and offering an even fuller text than Chailly. The big snag with the old Callas set was that it was severely cut by more than half an hour of music. As for the rest of the Philips cast, Simone Alaimo as the visiting Turkish prince, Selim, may lack the sardonic weight of Samuel Ramey on Sony, but it is a fine voice; and the *buffo* of Geronio finds Enrico Fissore agile and characterful in his patter numbers. Raúl Giménez is the stylish tenor in the relatively small role of Narciso, which happily acquires an extra aria. Altogether a most welcome follow-up to Marriner's excellent set of the *Barber*.

With quite a different slant on the balance of characters, the Chailly version – very well conducted and with a good feeling for theatrical timing – provides a good alternative to the Marriner, its early digital sound bright and clear. Montserrat Caballé as Fiorilla, a weighty heroine, is far less girlish than Sumi Jo, while Samuel Ramey is a strong, rather straight-faced Selim. His singing is superb, but the comedy is minimized, and Leo Nucci too as the Poet is not quite at ease in a *buffo* style, though ensembles – so important in this work – go well. The tenor, Ernesto Palacio, sings stylishly though the voice is a little pinched. The bright-toned harpsichord used for *secco* recitatives is less attractive than the mellow fortepiano in the Marriner version. There is also an awkward break in the finale of Act I, far more distracting than the one in the Philips set. The text is full and scholarly, including an aria from the original score for the incidental character, Albazar, even though it is not by Rossini. Marriner has the advantage there by including instead a tenor aria written for a production in Rome in 1815.

Callas was at her peak when she recorded this rare Rossini opera in the mid-1950s. As ever, there are lumpy moments vocally, but she gives a sharply characterful performance as the capricious Fiorilla, married to an elderly, jealous husband and bored with it. Nicola Rossi-Lemeni as the Turk of the title is characterful too, but the voice is ill-focused, and it is left to Nicolai Gedda as the young lover and Franco Calabrese as the jealous husband to match Callas in stylishness. It is good too to have the veteran Mariano Stabile singing the role of the Poet in search of a plot. Walter Legge's production has plainly added to the sparkle. On CD the original mono recording has been freshened and given a degree of bloom, despite the closeness of the voices. It is a vintage Callas issue, her first uniquely cherishable essay in operatic comedy.

Il viaggio a Reims (complete).
*** DG Dig. 415 498-2 (2) [id.]. Prague Philharmonic Ch., COE, Abbado.
  Corinna (Cecilia Gasdia), Madama Cortese (Katia Ricciarelli), Contessa di Folleville (Lella Cuberli), Marchesa Melibea (Lucia Valentini Terrani), Cavalier Belfiore (Edoardo Gimenez), Conte di Libenskof (Francisco Araiza), Lord Sidney (Samuel Ramey), Don Profondo (Ruggero Raimondi), Barone di Trombonok (Enzo Dara), Don Alvaro (Leo Nucci).

Rossini wrote this fizzing piece of comic nonsense as a gala piece for the coronation of Charles X in Paris. The opera has virtually no story, with the journey to Rheims never actually taking place, only the prospect of it. The wait at the Golden Lily hotel at Plombières provides the opportunity for the ten star characters to perform, each in turn.

First the hotel doctor, Don Prudenzio, and the efficient Maddalena arrive to check the menu and instruct the servants. Madame Cortese directs that every guest is to receive individual attention. The Countess of Folleville now concerns herself with the proper clothes for the forthcoming journey, for her dress has been spoilt on the way; her maid comes to the rescue with a new bonnet.

Don Profondo, academician, and the Spanish admiral, Don Alvaro, are followed by an impetuous Russian general, Count Libenskof, and a duel between the latter pair is averted only at the last minute.

Lord Sidney suffers from unrequited love, delivering daily flowers to the lady of his desires, Corinna, a famous Roman poetess. She in turn receives unwanted overtures from Chevalier Belfiore. Don Profondo now makes a list of all the valuables belonging to the guests. Now it seems the journey must be cancelled, for there are no horses to be had.

However, Madame Cortese offers alternative rooms in Paris (where the king's arrival is expected) and the journey can be accomplished by coach. Meanwhile there is to be a banquet that very evening where they are. The lovers' quarrel between Marquise Melibea and Count Libenskof is now resolved by male tenderness, and the occasion ends with the promised banquet, where Corinna entertains poetically with a historical theme centring on – Charles X, King of France.

Rossini's score was painstakingly reconstructed and given its first modern performance at the 1984 Pesaro Festival. This recording was edited together from various performances which the DG engineers put on tape; the result is one of the most sparkling and totally successful live opera recordings available, with Claudio Abbado in particular freer and more spontaneous-sounding than he generally is on disc, relishing the sparkle of the comedy. One hardly wonders that after the first performances Rossini refused ever to allow a revival, on the grounds that no comparable cast could ever be assembled. Instead, he used some of the material in his delectable comic opera, *Le Comte Ory*, and it is fascinating here to spot the numbers from it in their original form.

Much else is delightful, and the line-up of soloists here could hardly be more impressive, with no weak link. Established stars like Lucia Valentini Terrani, Katia Ricciarelli, Francisco Araiza, Samuel Ramey and Ruggero Raimondi, not to mention the *buffo* singers, Enzo Dara and Leo Nucci, hardly need commendation; in addition the set introduced two formidable newcomers in principal roles, Cecilia Gasdia as a self-important poetess (a nice parody of romantic manners) and, even finer, Lella Cuberli as a young fashion-crazed widow. The rich firmness and distinctive beauty of Cuberli's voice, coupled with amazing flexibility, proclaims a natural prima donna.

Inconsequential as the sequence of virtuoso numbers may be, ensembles as well as arias, the inspiration never flags, and Abbado's brilliance and sympathy draw the musical threads compellingly together with the help of superb, totally committed playing from the young members of the Chamber Orchestra of Europe. The CDs bring extra precision and clarity.

Zelmira (complete).
*** Erato/Warner Dig. 2292 45419-2 (2) [id.]. Amb. S., Sol. Ven., Scimone.
   Zelmira (Cecilia Gasdia), Emma (Bernarda Fink), Ilo (William Matteuzzi), Antenore (Chris Merritt).

Zelmira, the last-but-one opera that Rossini wrote in Italy before going off to live in Paris, has always had a bad press, but this recording, well sung (with one notable exception) and very well recorded, lets us appreciate that Rossinian inspiration had certainly not dried up, even if the plot's absurdities make it hard to imagine a modern staging.

The opera takes place on the island of Lesbos. Its king is Polydorus and his daughter is Zelmira, the heroine of the story. She is married to Ilos who, before the opera commences, goes off to war, leaving the island defenceless. Azor, Lord of Mytilene, takes over but Zelmira, rightly fearing for her father's life, resourcefully hides Polydorus in the vault of the Lesbosian kings and lets it be known that he is hidden in the temple. Azor burns the temple down so that everyone believes Polydorus to be dead. Now Antenor usurps the throne of Mytilene and, helped by Leucippus, kills Azor.

The curtain goes up as the soldiers mourn the loss of their leader, Azor, without knowing who the culprit is. Leucippus plans that Antenor shall become the new ruler, but first he must get rid of Zelmira and her young son. He spreads the word that she is responsible for Polydorus's death. Meanwhile Zelmira, with Emma, her confidante, is comforting her father in the tomb. Ilos returns, victorious, and his wife lovingly greets him, but she is not sure whether to tell him about everything that has happened since he left. Emma gives the impression that Antenor has accused Zelmira of the death of Azor, and Antenor and Leucippus persuade Ilos that his wife cannot be trusted. Despite her protestations that she is guilty of nothing, she is taken to prison.

Antenor is now sure that Polydorus is alive and he has Zelmira watched. Outside the city, Ilos is in despair about his wife's behaviour when Polydorus comes to him with the truth. But Antenor captures Polydorus, and Zelmira is forced to offer her own life for that of her father. Emma discovers that the usurpers plan to kill everyone and promptly warns Ilos. He frees his wife, and the villainous Antenor and Leucippus duly take her place in the dungeon.

Scimone conducted the recording immediately after a concert performance in Venice, and that obviously helped to give vitality to the substantial sequences of accompanied recitative. He takes a generally brisk view of both the arias and the ensembles but never seems to race his singers. Though the story of murders and usurpations in the royal family of Lesbos is too ill-motivated to be involving, it gives some splendid excuses for fine Rossini arias. There is precious little distinction in musical tone of voice between the goodies and the baddies in the story, with the usurping Antenore given some of the most heroic music, for example the first aria. That is a tenor role, more robust than that of Ilo, husband of the wronged heroine, Zelmira.

In this performance the choice of singers underlines the contrast between the two principal tenor-roles. Chris Merritt combines necessary agility with an almost baritonal quality as the scheming Antenore, straining only occasionally, and William Matteuzzi sings with heady beauty and fine flexibility in florid writing as Ilo. Star of the performance is Cecilia Gasdia in the name-part, projecting words and emotions very intensely in warmly expressive singing. She is well matched by the mezzo, Bernarda Fink, as her friend, Emma, and only the wobbly bass of José Garcia as the deposed Polidoro mars the cast. On two generously filled CDs, with libretto in four languages and first-rate notes, this makes an attractive set for Rossinians, not least because of the fine ensembles such as the two quintets, one at the end of Act I, the other at the climax of Act II.

COLLECTIONS

L'assedio de Corinto: Avanziam . . . Non temer d'un basso affeto! . . . I destini tradir ogni speme . . . Signormche tutto puio . . . Sei tu, che stendi; L'ora fatal s'appressa . . . Giusto ciel. La Donna del lago: Mura Felici; Tanti affetti. Otello: Assisa a pie d'un salice. Tancredi: Di tanti palpiti.
⊛ (M) *** Decca 421 306-2 [id.]. Marilyn Horne, Amb. Op. Ch., RPO, Henry Lewis.

Marilyn Horne's generously filled recital disc in Decca's mid-price Opera Gala series brings one of the most cherishable among all Rossini aria records ever issued. It is taken from two earlier LP discs, recorded when Horne was at the very zenith of her powers. The voice is in glorious condition, rich and firm throughout its spectacular range, and is consistently used with artistry and imagination, as well as brilliant virtuosity in coloratura. By any reckoning this is thrilling singing, the more valuable for mostly covering rarities – which, with Horne, make you wonder at their neglect. The sound is full and brilliant, hardly at all showing its age.

Arias: La Cenerentola: Non piu mesta. La Donna del Lago: Mura felici . . . Elena! O tu, che chiamo. L'Italiana in Algeri: Cruda sorte! Amor tiranno! Pronti abbiamo . . . Pensa all patria. Otello: Deh! calma, o ciel. La Pietra del Paragone: Se l'Italie contrade . . . Se per voi lo care io torno. Tancredi: Di tanti palpiti. Stabat Mater: Fac ut portem.
*** Decca Dig. 425 430-2 [id.]. Cecilia Bartoli, Arnold Schoenberg Ch., V. Volksoper O, Patanè.

Cecilia Bartoli is one of the most exciting coloratura mezzo-sopranos to have arrived in many years, a successor to Berganza, Horne and Baltsa. She is the more remarkable for having achieved so much so young. The voice is full, warm and even in its richness, which yet allows extreme flexibility. This recital of Rossini showpieces brings a formidable demonstration not only of Bartoli's remarkable voice but of her personality and artistry. As yet, she is not so much a sparkler as a commander, bringing natural warmth and imagination to each item without ever quite making you smile with delight. That may well follow, but in the meantime there are not many Rossini recitals of any vintage to match this. Vocally, the one controversial point to note is the way that Bartoli articulates her coloratura with a half-aspirate, closer to the Supervia 'rattle' than anything else, but rather obtrusive. Accompaniments under the direction of Patanè in one of his last recordings are exemplary, and Decca provided the luxury of a chorus in some of the items, with hints of staging. Full, vivid recording. Recommended.

'Rossini heroines': Arias from: La donna de lago; Elisabetta, Regina d'Inghilterra; Maometto II; Le nozze di Teti e Peleo; Semiramide; Zelmira.
*** Decca Dig. 436 075-2; *435 075-4* [id.]. Cecilia Bartoli, Ch. & O of Teatro la Fenice, Marin.

Cecilia Bartoli follows up the success of her earlier Rossini recital-disc with this second brilliant collection of arias, mostly rarities. The tangy, distinctive timbre of her mezzo goes with a magnetic projection of personality to bring to life even formal passage-work, with all the elaborate coloratura bright and sparkling. The portrait of Queen Elizabeth I in the final scene from *Elisabetta, Regina d'Inghilterra* is fierce and commanding, with the lighter and more vulnerable sides of the character presented rather less effectively. The rarest item of all is an aria for the goddess Ceres from the classically based entertainment, *Le nozze di Teti e Peleo*, making a splendid showpiece. The collection is crowned by a formidably high-powered reading of *Bel raggio* from *Semiramide*, with Bartoli excitingly braving every danger. A characterful disc from an artist who, though still young, is already among the most positive operatic mezzos of today.

Roussel, Albert (1869–1937)

Padmâvatî (opera; complete).
*** EMI Dig. CDS7 47891-8 (2). Orféon Donostiarra, Toulouse Capitole O, Plasson.

Padmâvatî (Marilyn Horne), Ratan-Sen (Nicolai Gedda), Ala-uddin (José Van Dam), Nakamti (Jane Berbié), Brahmin (Charles Burles), Gora (Marc Vento), Badal (Laurence Dale).

Padmâvatî, rich and exotic in its Indian setting, was inspired by Roussel's visit – as it happened, in the company of Ramsay MacDonald – to the ruins of Chitoor in Rajputana. Padmâvatî is the wife of the Prince of Chitoor. Before the opera begins, a Brahmin priest had fallen in love with her, and consequently was banished from Chitoor. The priest is now serving Ala-uddin, the Mogul ruler of Delhi. To reap revenge on Prince Ratan-Sen, the Priest persuades Ala-uddin to attack Chitoor.

As the curtain rises, crowds are gathered in the square in front of the palace. Ala-uddin and his envoys are expected to arrive to discuss peace with Ratan-Sen. Gora, the palace steward, learns that the Mogul army is not far away, drawn up on the plain beyond the city. Ala-uddin arrives, and the Brahmin priest accompanies him. The sovereigns greet each other, and Gora says that the rulers should confer alone, but Ala-uddin insists that his Brahmin adviser remain.

Ala-uddin, having inspected the palace dancers, asks to see the beautiful Padmâvatî, and the Brahmin sings her praises. Ratan-Sen has misgivings, but his wife appears on the balcony. Ala-uddin departs without signing the treaty. The Brahmin now delivers his master's message: if Padmâvatî is not brought to Ala-uddin's quarters, the Mogul army will annihilate Chitoor. Ratan-Sen refuses, and the crowd lynches the Brahmin, who dies prophesying death and destruction for Chitoor and its people. Padmâvatî prays for death rather than separation from her husband. Ratan-Sen now leads his army against the Moguls but he is defeated.

The threat remains: Chitoor will be sacked if Padmâvatî is not handed over. Ratan-Sen arrives at the temple. He is wounded and his wife believes that her fate at the hands of Ala-uddin will be far worse than death. She stabs Ratan-Sen in the heart, knowing this will mean that she will die on her husband's funeral pyre. She prepares for death amid general mourning. The funeral pyre is lit and Padmâvatî is led in. Ala-uddin bursts into the temple but too late: all he sees is smoke.

That simple plot gives Roussel the opportunity to write colourful, richly atmospheric music not just in the symbolic preludes to each of the two Acts but in sequences which seek to combine full-scale ballet with opera – an entertainment for the sultan in Act I and the rites of Siva's daughters in Act II. It is a heady mixture, with Plasson drawing warmly sympathetic playing from the Toulouse orchestra.

In an excellent cast, José van Dam is superb as the evil, deceptive Sultan and, though Marilyn Horne sounds rather too mature for the name-part, hers is a powerful, convincing performance as the wife who, rather than submit to being given to the soft-speaking but predatory Mogul sultan, Ala-uddin, stabs her beloved and commits *suttee*. One remarkable feature of the opera is the profusion of principal tenors required, and here Gedda as the Prince is splendidly matched with contrasted soloists in smaller roles, Charles Burles, Thierry Dran and Laurence Dale. Warm, convincingly balanced sound. This is well worth exploring.

Saint-Saëns, Camille (1835–1921)

Samson et Dalila: complete.
*** EMI CDS7 54470-2 (2) [Ang. CDCB 54470]. L'Opéra-Bastille Ch. & O, Myung-Whun Chung.

Samson (Plácido Domingo), Dalila (Waltraud Meier), Priest (Alain Fondary), Abimelech (Jean-Philippe Courtis).

(M) **(*) DG 413 297-2 (2) [id.]. Ch. & O de Paris, Barenboim.

Samson (Plácido Domingo), Dalila (Elena Obraztsova), Priest (Renato Bruson), Abimelech (Pierre Thau), Old Hebrew (Robert Lloyd).

**(*) Ph. Dig. 426 243-2; *426 243-4* (2) [id.]. Bav. R. Ch. & RSO, C. Davis.

Samson (José Carreras), Dalila (Agnes Baltsa), Priest (Jonathan Summers), Abimelech (Simon Estes), Old Hebrew (Paata Burchuladze).

Withdrawn: ** EMI CDS7 47895-8 (2) [Ang. CDCB 47895]. Choeurs René Duclos, Paris Nat. Op. O, Prêtre.

Samson (Jon Vickers), Dalila (Rita Gorr), Priest (Ernest Blanc), Abimelech / Old Hebrew (Anton Diakov).

Saint-Saëns's *Samson et Dalila* was first performed in the Weimer Court Theatre in Germany in 1877. Although, to our ears, the piece now sounds very French, it was originally considered Wagnerian, and it was some time before the Paris Opéra was won over to its considerable merits.

The story is set in Gaza in Palestine in 1150 BC. Samson calls on the Israelites to take arms against their oppressors, and he kills Abimelech with his own sword when he arrives with his guards and slanders the God of Israel. The high priest of Dagon swears to be revenged. Samson is flattered by the attentions of nubile young Philistine girls; among them is Delilah, who sets out to seduce him for reasons of her own. She succeeds later that evening, in her house in the valley of Sorek ('*Mon coeur s'ouvre à ta voix*').

But first the high priest has come to her and asked that she discover the reason for Samson's uncanny strength. Surrendering to her passionate embrace, he tells her his secret and later she cuts off his hair and summons the Philistine soldiers, who overpower him and take him away. Confined to a dungeon, his hair shorn and his eyes put out, he is a pitiable figure and he prays for God's help for himself and his people.

Now the Philistines are celebrating a festival in their temple of Dagon. A young boy brings in the blind Samson, and Delilah mocks him, saying that her passion was only simulated. The carousing becomes a bacchanale and finally an orgy. Samson manoeuvres himself between the two main pillars supporting the temple's domed roof and embraces one column with each arm. Then, praying to God, he recovers his strength and succeeds in bringing down the whole edifice and crushing his enemies.

When the vintage DG set with Plácido Domingo as Samson offers Daniel Barenboim as conductor, it was a neat move by EMI to present the opera again with Domingo as the hero, but with Barenboim's successor at the Bastille Opéra in Paris, Myung-Whun Chung. Chung's view is altogether more volatile, more idiomatic, which helps Domingo to give a more imaginative and varied interpretation, even more detailed than before, with the voice still in glorious condition. So in the big Act III aria, when the blind Samson is turning the millstone, Domingo with Chung gives a deeper, more thoughtful performance, broader, with greater repose and a sense of power in reserve.

When the big melody appears in Dalila's seduction aria, *Mon coeur s'ouvre*, Chung's conducting encourages a tender restraint, where others produce a full-throated roar. Meier may not have an ideally sensuous voice for the role, with some unwanted harshness in her expressive account of Dalila's first monologue, but her feeling for words is strong and the characterization vivid. Generally Chung's speeds are on the fast side, yet the performance does not lack weight, with some first-rate singing in the incidental roles from Alain Fondary, Samuel Ramey and Jean-Philippe Courtis. Apart from backwardly placed choral sound, the recording is warm and well focused.

Barenboim proves as passionately dedicated an interpreter of Saint-Saëns here as he did in the *Third Symphony*, sweeping away any Victorian cobwebs. It is important, too, that the choral passages, so vital in this work, be sung with this sort of freshness, and Domingo has rarely sounded happier in French music, the bite as well as the heroic richness of the voice well caught. Renato Bruson and Robert Lloyd are both admirable too; sadly, however, the key role of Dalila is given an unpersuasive, unsensuous performance by Obraztsova, with her vibrato often verging on a wobble. The recording is as ripe as the music deserves.

When the role of Samson is not one naturally suited to Carreras, it is amazing how strong and effective his performance is, even if top notes under stress grow uneven. Particularly after his near-fatal illness, the very strain seems to add to the intensity of communication, above all in the great aria of the last Act, when Samson, blinded, is turning the mill. Unevenness of production is more serious with Agnes Baltsa as Dalila. The microphone often brings out her vibrato, turning it into a disagreeable judder, and the changes of gear between registers are also underlined.

She remains a powerful, characterful singer, but hers is hardly the seductive portrait required in this role, and it is a shortcoming that, like the rest of the cast, she is not a native French-speaker. Both Burchuladze as the Old Hebrew and Simon Estes as Abimelech equally seem intent on misusing once-fine voices, but Jonathan Summers as the High Priest of Dagon is far more persuasive. Despite all these reservations, the inspired conducting of Sir Colin Davis, with splendid choral singing, helped by refined and atmospheric recording, makes this preferable to the EMI set conducted by Georges Prêtre, also seriously flawed.

EMI's earlier set – currently withdrawn – was conducted by Prêtre and dates from the beginning of the 1960s. As transferred to CD, the warm, atmospheric sound is very acceptable, even if the recording shows signs of age, with the occasional touch of distortion on the voices. Jon Vickers and Rita Gorr are in commanding form, both recorded at their vocal peak. Ernest Blanc characterizes well as the High Priest, but other soloists are undistinguished. The main snag is the contribution of Prêtre. He presents the big moments of high drama effectively enough, but is coarse-grained at too many points.

Samson et Dalila: highlights.
(M) ** EMI CDM7 63935-2; *EG 763935-4* (from above recording with Gorr, Vickers; cond. Prêtre).

This 53-minute EMI selection just about passes muster, even if Prêtre is below his best form. Jon Vickers and Rita Gorr sing vibrantly and make an appealing duo, and the 1962 recording has plenty of atmosphere.

Salieri, Antonio (1750–1825)

Les Danaïdes (complete).
Withdrawn: *** EMI Dig. CDS7 54073-2 (2). Stuttgart RSO, Gelmetti.
Hypermnestre (Margaret Marshall), Danaus (Dimitri Kavrakos), Lyncée (Raúl Giménez).

This recording, the first ever of a tragic Salieri opera, offers a piece written for Paris in 1784 to a libretto originally intended for Gluck. The result is very Gluckian in the racy way it sets a classical subject, rejecting the formality of *opera seria* in favour of a much freer structure. The setting is ancient Greece.

Danaus and his daughters, the Danaids, swear friendship to the sons of Aegyptus, brother and enemy of Danaus. The eldest of Aegyptus' sons, Lyncée (Lynceus) now heads the family (Aegyptus is dead) and, as part of their agreement, Lynceus and his brothers all marry the Danaids, Lynceus marrying Hypermnestra. Danaus then tells of his plans to avenge the wrongs committed by Aegyptus and orders his daughters to murder their husbands.

All but Hypermnestra agree. Danaus confronts her with a prophecy: if his vengeance is not completed, he himself will be murdered. After the wedding celebrations, Hypermnestra comes close to telling Lynceus of the plot but merely urges him to leave. He flees amid the cries of his brothers who are being murdered off stage.

On discovering that Lynceus has escaped, Danaus is furious: Lynceus attacks the palace and slaughters the Danaids; Hypermnestra faints. The palace is destroyed in flames and in the last scene the Danaids are seen imprisoned in the underworld, Danaus chained to a rock, his entrails being devoured by a vulture. The Furies promise them unending torment.

This emerges as a direct successor to Gluck's last two Iphigénie operas, compact and fast-moving; and the musical invention, though hardly on a Mozartian level, is on balance livelier and more sharply memorable than in all but the greatest Gluck operas. Though the language is French and the composer Italian, there is a Germanic feel to much of the writing, in the often surprising 'symphonic' modulations and in the line of many of the arias, which at times are almost Schubertian.

The five Acts last a mere hour and three-quarters, centring on the conflict of loyalty felt by the heroine, Hypermnestre, between her love for Lyncée and the command from her father, Danaus, that in line with her sisters she must slaughter her husband. The speed masks the enormity of the story, with brisk exchanges in accompanied recitative, brief set numbers – including some charming duets – and, above all, powerful comment from the chorus.

Margaret Marshall as the heroine surpasses all she has done so far on record. She sings with superb attack and brilliant flexibility, as well as with tender intensity when Hypermnestre pleads with her father. Dimitri Kavrakos is not always adequately sinister-sounding as Danaus, but the voice is warmly focused. Raúl Giménez in the tenor role of Lyncée is first rate too, straining only occasionally, and so is Clarry Bartha as one of Danaus's younger daughters. Gelmetti secures a crisp, stylish performance from the Stuttgart Radio Orchestra and the excellent South German Radio Choir. The booklet contains notes in English but no translation of the French libretto.

Falstaff: complete.
*** Hung. Dig. HCD 12789/91 [id.]. Salieri Chamber Ch. & O, Tamás Pál.
Falstaff (József Gregor), Mistress Ford (Mária Zempléni), Master Ford (Dénes Gulyás),

Master Slender (Istvan Gáti), Mistress Slender (Eva Pánczél), Bardolf (Tamás Csurja), Betty (Éva Vámossy).

It is fascinating to find Salieri – unfairly traduced in the play and film, *Amadeus* – writing as lively a setting as this of Shakespeare's *Merry Wives of Windsor* almost a hundred years before Verdi. First given in 1799, *Falstaff* (full title: *Falstaff ossia Le tre burle*), written to a libretto by Carlo Prospero Defranchesi, is one of his many comic operas. Like Verdi, Salieri and his librettist ignore the Falstaff of the histories. They tell the story (minus the Anne and Fenton sub-plot and without Mistress Quickly) within the framework of the conventional two-Act opera of the period. Mrs Ford comes to Falstaff as a German girl, speaking a comic mixture of German and Italian.

Dozens of little arias and duets are linked by brisk recitative, leading to substantial finales to each Act, involving deftly handled comic interplay, and with the Act II finale bringing moments of tenderness and delicacy to nudge one forward towards Verdi. Though the opera is long, the speed is fast and furious, with the set numbers bringing many delights, as in the charming little duet, *La stessa, stessissima*, for the two wives reading their identical letters (Beethoven wrote variations on it) or Falstaff's first aria, swaggering and jolly, introduced by a fanfare motif, and a delightful laughter trio in Act II.

None of the ideas, however charming or sparkling, is developed in the way one would expect in Mozart, but it is all great fun, particularly in a performance as lively and well sung as this. József Gregor is splendid in the name-part, with Dénes Gulyás equally stylish in the tenor role of Ford. Mária Zempléni as Mistress Ford and Eva Pánczél in the mezzo role of Mistress Slender (not Page) are both bright and lively. The eponymous chorus and orchestra also perform with vigour under Tamás Pál; the recording is brilliant, with a fine sense of presence. Enjoyment is greatly enhanced by the exceptionally generous CD banding of the discs.

Sallinen, Aulis (born 1935)

Kullervo: complete.
*** Ondine Dig. ODE 780-3T [id.]. Finnish Nat. Op. Ch. & O, Ulf Söderblom.
Kullervo (Jorma Hynninen), Kalervo, his father (Matti Salminen), Smith's young wife (Anna-Lisa Jakobsson), Kimmo (Jorma Silvasti), Sister (Satu Vihavainen).

Sallinen's fourth opera occupied him between 1986 and 1988 and was written for the Los Angeles Opera, who premièred it in 1992. The action is set in primitive times against a background of clan feuds and violence. Although the theme will be familiar from Sibelius's early symphony of the same name, Sallinen based his *Kullervo* on the play by Aleksis Kivi and wrote the libretto himself. The plot emerges from a mixture of narration, in which the chorus plays a central role, and dreams.

Put crudely, the feud between two brothers, Kalervo and Unto, culminates in the burning of Kalervo's house. Kullervo, Kalervo's son, is abducted and sold into slavery; he destroys the smith's cattle and kills his young wife. Now a fugitive, Kullervo comes upon his parents who have survived the fire, but they reject him when it emerges that he has unwittingly slept with his sister.

Kullervo determines to exact vengeance on Unto, but on his way there Kimmo, his childhood friend and a fellow-slave for a time, intercepts him and reveals that his parents and sister have been killed. Kullervo decides to kill all Unto's family, and the opera ends with him going in search of Kimmo and finding that, as a result of his experiences, he has lost his sanity. Kullervo commits suicide.

The opera is a compelling musical drama, far more atmospheric and musically effective than its immediate predecessor, *The King goes forth to France*. Sallinen's musical language owes debts to composers as diverse as Britten (shadows of the '*Sunday morning*' interlude in *Peter Grimes* briefly cross the score in Kullervo's dream at the beginning of Act II), Puccini, Debussy even, though they are synthesized into an effective vehicle for a vivid theatrical imagination.

There is impressive variety of pace and atmosphere, and the black voices of the Finnish Opera Chorus resonate in the memory. So, too, do the impressive performances of Jorma Hynninen as Kullervo and Anna-Lisa Jakobsson as the smith's young wife, and indeed the remainder of the cast and the Finnish National Opera Orchestra under Ulf Söderblom. While *Kullervo* may not be a great opera, it is gripping and effective musical theatre, and the Ondine recording has excellent presence and detail.

Ratsumies (The Horseman): opera; complete.
** Finlandia FACD 101 (2). Savonlinna Op. Festival Ch. & O, Söderblom.
   Antti (Matti Salminen), Anna (Taru Valjakka), Merchant of Novgorod (Eero Erkkilä),
   Merchant's Wife (Anita Välkki), Judge (Martti Wallén).

Sallinen's first opera, *The Horseman* (1972–5), was a landmark in the recent renaissance of
opera in Finland. It is both more atmospheric and musically more interesting than either of its
immediate successors (though admittedly that is not difficult). Its plot is convoluted and heavy
with political symbolism. The first Act opens at Easter in Novgorod. Antti and his wife, Anna,
are bonded servants in the house of a merchant who is determined to seduce Anna. She is not
unwilling but asks for payment. The merchant retorts he has paid for her already. Anna asks if a
bear comes to the house at Eastertime. She is told that the bear comes in search of a maiden but
that she need not worry as she is not a maiden.
   They leave together but the merchant is suspicious of his own wife. He is right to suspect her,
for she goes out to meet the approaching horseman. It is the returning Antti. He is searching for
Anna and must now put on the skin of a bear. The merchant returns with Anna, who chides her
husband and says that bears who are so forward and talkative are liable to be hanged.
   The merchant means to discover if his wife has slept with Antti. He instructs Antti to tie her
hands together. He will then know, from her expression, whether or not she is guilty. Antti asks
the merchant to test the strength of the rope and so traps him, and Anna and Antti then escape
together.
   A court scene then follows in which a woman admits to killing a bastard child. The father was
a dark man who rode the highway. It seems likely that the horseman was Antti. As her husband
has disappeared, Anna claims she is a widow and requires official recognition, but she has to
wait a year and a day for her widowhood to be recognized.
   The horseman (her husband) now reappears, disguised as an old man, and wishes to
corroborate Anna's story. The judge is suspicious and orders them, plus two other witnesses, a
woman and a yeoman, to be confined. The judge comes to question them further, and they trick
him and escape.
   Anna, the horseman and their companions are now living together as outlaws. Anna tries to
persuade the horseman to leave with her, unsuccessfully. The opera's political undertones now
become more overt, as there is talk about war between Russia and Sweden and a plan to create a
new forest buffer state to lie between the two countries. The group are to take part in a plot to
capture the royal manor at Liistonsaari.
   Incredibly, the women are to make a large cake and Antti will be placed inside it! It is to be
delivered to the sheriff at the manor. Antti will escape and open the gates. The plan goes wrong.
They are repulsed and shots are fired. Antti is left dying, as the women lament.
   The opera has something of the symbolism that distinguished *The King goes forth to France*,
and its libretto by Paavo Haavikko has the same deep-seeming quality that afflicts the later
opera. It is strong on atmosphere and holds the listener: at times it calls to mind Britten, but its
sound-world, with constant recourse to the evocation of bells, is undoubtedly imaginative, and
there are a few moments of real power. A good performance, though the rather dry acoustic
environment and stage noises diminish its appeal. Sallinen's operas will not (one suspects) hold
the stage in the future, but they are nevertheless better than most modern opera after Britten
(and that wouldn't be very difficult either).

Saxton, Robert (born 1953)

Caritas (opera; complete).
*** Collins 1350-2 (id.]. E. N. Philh. O, Diego Masson.
   Christine (Eirian Davies), Bishop of Norwich (Jonathan Best), Robert Lonie (Christopher
   Ventris), Agnes (Linda Hibberd), William (Roger Bryson), Richard Lonie / Travelling Priest
   (David Gwynne).

Coming from a Jewish background, Robert Saxton yet finds regular inspiration in Christian
ritual. From outside the church his music echoes religious experience – often, as here, in the
most complex way. Arnold Wesker's play of the same name sets up an intricate web of
sympathies and associations, faithfully reflected in Saxton's score. Wesker directly relates the
intolerance of the medieval church to the reactionary politics of the English monarchy in

brutally putting down the Peasants' Revolt in 1381. It tells the story of Christine, the daughter of a carpenter, who became an anchoress.

The opening scene with its monastic choruses shows her as she is walled up in her cell. Only then does she find out too late that she has no vocation. Amid incidental developments of stomach-turning brutality, her pleas to be freed from her confinement are rejected and madness finally takes over.

It is as disagreeable a plot as could be imagined, with the kinship between extreme religious practice and sexual perversion brought home. Yet, thanks to Saxton's approachable, evocative and generally well-paced score, it is a highly involving piece. It is the more disturbingly pointful for its political overtones, set alongside the religious, making it finally an opera of protest. Saxton subtly differentiates his echoes of early church music to heighten individual characterization.

The recording was made live at the 1991 Huddersfield Festival, with Diego Masson directing the English Northern Philharmonia and an excellent cast, movingly headed by Eirian Davies as Christine, the anchoress. The whole piece is the more telling when Saxton's scheme is so compact, with an hour-long first act in 12 brisk scenes, followed without a pause by a second act of 20 minutes devoted to the painful last monologue of Christine. The stereo sound is of spectacular range and spread, adding greatly to the work's impact.

Scarlatti, Alessandro (1660–1725)

La Giuditta (oratorio).
Withdrawn: *** Hung. Dig. HCD 12910 [id.]. Capella Savaria, McGegan.
  Judith (Mária Zádori), Prince Ozias (Katalin Gémes), Holofernes (Drew Minter), Captain Achior (Guy De Mey).

La Giuditta, telling the biblical story of Judith, is a fascinating example of pre-Handelian oratorio as it was developing in Italy at the end of the seventeenth century. The story takes place partly in Bethulia, the Jewish castle under siege, and partly in the camp of Holofernes, the besieging general.

Judith, the heroine, is a young widow whose moral superiority is established at the very opening. (For what she has to do later in the story, she must be above suspicion.) The ruling prince, Ozias, is shown as an altogether weaker character, but Judith conveys her own confidence and faith that it is possible to hold the castle.

Meanwhile General Holofernes, their evil adversary, is portrayed as uncouth and not even very bright, when he first fails to heed the warning that Captain Achior, the leader of the Ammonites, might change sides. But when this finally sinks in, Holofernes has the captain taken to the enemy walls, sure that he will be killed. In so doing he plays into the hands of his enemies.

Now Judith's plan is put into operation. She goes to see Holofernes in his tent, and he naïvely assumes that he is attractive enough, both as a power figure and as a man, for her to fall readily into his embrace. At the same time the captain is being welcomed within Bethulia and he tells Ozias and the high priest of Judith's plan. He predicts that if they join together, victory will be speedy.

We return to join Judith as she responds cunningly to Holofernes' expressions of ardour but persuades him to rest and sleep. She prays and Holofernes interrupts her twice, complaining that she is too melancholy; somehow he has a premonition that all is not well. But eventually he falls into the slumber which is to be his very last. Judith beheads him.

Back at the castle, Ozias and the high priest are beginning to lose their nerve, and the priest is sure that the captain has betrayed them, which is hotly denied. Judith now makes her momentous entry, bearing the head of Holofernes which she hands to Ozias. Everyone now joins in the vocal celebration, even the dead head of the villain!

Nicholas McGegan, who has made several successful period-performance recordings for Hungaroton, here directs a fresh and stylish account, with three Hungarian principals joined by the soft-grained but agile American counter-tenor, Drew Minter, as Holofernes, and the excellent French tenor, Guy de Mey, as the captain. The two main principals, Mária Zádori as Judith and Katalin Gémes as Prince Ozias, both have attractively bright, clear voices. Very well recorded in clean, immediate sound and with libretto and notes included in the package, it makes a most attractive disc, generously filled.

Schmidt, Franz (1874–1939)

Das Buch mit sieben Siegeln (The Book with 7 seals): oratorio.
**(*) Orpheus Dig. C 143862H (2). Peter Schreier, Robert Holl, Sylvia Greenberg, Carolyn Watkinson, Thomas Moser, Kurt Rydl, V. State Op. Ch., Austrian RSO, Zagrosek.

Das Buch mit sieben Siegeln has much music of substance and many moments of real inspiration. Peter Schreier's St John is one of the glories of this set, and there are fine contributions from some of the other soloists. This performance was recorded in the somewhat unappealing acoustic of the ORF studios and is wanting in the transparency that the score deserves. Detail is less vivid than it might be and the dynamic range is somewhat compressed; however, the sound is more than acceptable.

Schnittke, Alfred (born 1934)

Leben mit einem Idioten (Life with an idiot) complete.
*** Sony Dig. S2K 52495 (2) [id.]. Vocal Ens. & Rotterdam PO, Rostropovich.
I (Dale Duesing / Romain Bischoff), Wife (Teresa Ringholz), Vova (Howard Haskin), Guard (Leonid Zimnenko), Marcel Proust (Robin Leggate).

This is a live recording, with Mstislav Rostropovich conducting, of the world première production of Schnittke's first opera, *Life with an idiot*, staged by Netherlands Opera in Amsterdam in the spring of 1992. Predictably, the piece defies operatic convention, which means that it is at least as effective on disc as when seen in the theatre. This is an adaptation not of Dostoyevsky but of a story by a fellow dissident, Victor Erofeyev, who, like Schnittke, spent some of his youth in the West. It is an allegory of Soviet oppression.

As punishment for poor performance at work, the central character (unnamed), with his wife (also unnamed), has to take an idiot, Vova, into his home. The first Act tells how 'Vova becomes me', and the second how 'I become him'. The Russian text is down to earth and full of banal domestic detail, often expressed in profanities and off-colour slang; but basically this is a Kafka-esque nightmare, with descriptions of Vova's impossible behaviour generally taking the place of action.

As an opera it hardly works, but Schnittke's often violent, always energetic score characteristically heightens nerve-jangling situations in the home to make it an involving personal cantata, with incidental musical echoes of Stravinsky's comparably stylized domestic cantata, *The Wedding*.

Rostropovich draws a vigorous performance from the Rotterdam Philharmonic with Dale Duesing and Teresa Ringholz, as the central character and his wife, both excellent and with Howard Haskin providing peremptory interjections as Vova. One hardly expected Schnittke's first opera to be in any way conventional in its approach to the genre, but with a composer whose music is so naturally dramatic one hopes he will before long apply himself to a less surreal story with stage action in it, not just a nightmare fantasy.

Schoenberg, Arnold (1874–1951)

Erwartung, Op. 17.
*** Decca Dig. 417 348-2 (2) [id.]. Anja Silja, VPO, Dohnányi – BERG: *Wozzeck.* ***

(i) *Erwartung.* (ii) Cabaret songs: *Arie aus dem Spiegel von Arcadien; Einfältiges Lied; Galathea; Der genügsame Liebhaber; Jedem das Seine; Mahnung; Nachtwandler* (with trumpet, piccolo & snare drum).
*** Ph. Dig. 426 261-2; *426 261-4* [id.]. Jessye Norman; (i) Met. Op. O, Levine; (ii) James Levine (piano).

The monodrama, *Erwartung* – 'Expectation' – may be among the least appealing of Schoenberg's formidable *oeuvre*, but Jessye Norman and James Levine present it on a disc which could well win the composer more friends than any ever issued before. The neurotic tensions behind this dramatic monologue have never been in doubt, involving a woman who, lost in a forest, finds the dead body of her lover.

The libretto of Marie Pappenheim, a young doctor drawn into Schoenberg's Viennese circle, could easily have come from a Freudian case-history. We have heard many performances that have presented the piece powerfully, but always so as to leave an unpleasant taste afterwards. With Jessye Norman it is quite different. She herself has said that Erwartung is 'technically the most difficult thing I have ever sung' but that, having learnt it, she found it 'immensely singable'. That clearly accounts for the warmth, intensity, range of expression and sheer beauty that she and Levine bring to this score. Levine draws ravishing sounds from the Metropolitan Opera Orchestra, to relate this not just to Schoenberg's early romantic string-piece, Verklaerte Nacht, but also to the closing scenes of Berg's Wozzeck and even to Debussy's Pelléas et Mélisande. Jessye Norman's singing, beautiful and totally secure over the widest range of expression and dynamic, is a revelation too. So far from leaving a nasty aftertaste, this brings a fulfilment. Compare this with Anja Silja, accompanied by Christoph von Dohnányi on their fine Decca issue, and the extra depth, range of emotion and refinement of the New York performance come out at every point.

The impact of this Erwartung is brilliantly heightened by the total contrast of the Schoenberg coupling. Accompanied by Levine at the piano – a sparkily individual partner – Jessye Norman sings all eight of the cabaret songs, the Brettl-Lieder, that Schoenberg wrote when he was working in Berlin. In these witty, pointed, tuneful songs Schoenberg was letting his hair down in a way that to his detractors must be almost unimaginable. These are art-songs that yet completely belong to the half-world of cabaret.

Jessye Norman projects her personality as masterfully as a latterday Marlene Dietrich. And it is astonishing how she can colour her voice, slinkily inflecting it, scaling it down, so as as to capture the authentic style. The swagger with which she sings the comic song about the heart beating faster (boom, boom, boom!) is irresistible and, unlike any rival on record, she includes the final military song, Nachtwandler ('Night Wanderer'), with extra accompaniment of piccolo, trumpet and drum.

Schoenberg's searingly intense monodrama makes an apt and generous coupling for Dohnányi's excellent version of Berg's Wozzeck. As in the Berg, Silja is at her most passionately committed. The sound under pressure may be raw, but the self-tortured questionings of the central character come over grippingly, and the digital sound is exceptionally vivid.

Gurrelieder.
*** Decca Dig. 430 321-2 (2) [id.]. Siegfried Jerusalem, Susan Dunn, Brigitte Fassbaender, Hermann Becht, Pater Haage, Hans Hotter, St Hedwig's Cathedral Ch., Berlin, Düsseldorf State Musikverein, Berlin RSO, Chailly.
*** Ph. 412 511-2 (2) [id.]. James McCracken, Jessye Norman, Tatiana Troyanos, Werner Klemperer, Tanglewood Festival Ch., Boston SO, Ozawa.
** Denon Dig. CO 77066-67 (2) [id.]. Paul Frey, Elizabeth Connell, Jard Van Nes, Walton Groenroos, Volker Vogel, NDR Choir, Bav. R. Ch., Frankfurt State Op. Ch., Frankfurst RSO, Inbal.

Chailly's magnificent recording of Schoenberg's massive Gurrelieder effectively supplants all existing versions, even Ozawa's impressive Boston set, recorded live. This Berlin recording not only brings richer, fuller, more detailed and better-balanced sound, but it conveys a natural dramatic tension not easy to find in studio conditions. Chailly has a finer team of soloists than on any rival set, with Siegfried Jerusalem as Waldemar not only warmer and firmer of tone than his rivals but more imaginative too. Susan Dunn makes a sweet, touchingly vulnerable Tove, while Brigitte Fassbaender gives darkly baleful intensity to the message of the Wood-dove. Hans Hotter is a characterful Speaker in the final section. The impact of the performance is the more telling with sound both atmospheric and immediate, bringing a fine sense of presence, not least in the final choral outburst.

Ozawa also directs a gloriously opulent reading. The playing of the Boston Symphony has both warmth and polish and is set against a resonant acoustic; among the soloists, Jessye Norman gives a performance of radiant beauty, at times reminding one of Flagstad in the burnished glory of her tone-colours. As the wood-dove, Tatiana Troyanos sings most sensitively, though the vibrato is at times obtrusive; and James McCracken does better than most tenors at coping with a heroic vocal line without barking. The luxuriant textures are given a degree more transparency, with detail slightly clearer on CD.

Inbal directs a convincing, well-paced reading, but with Paul Frey strained and rough-toned as Waldemar and Elizabeth Connell as Tove less well focused than her rivals, this is no match for either Chailly or Ozawa. Jard van Nes is effective in the Wood-dove's song, but tensions are lower than in the rival sets, not helped by slightly distanced recording.

Moses und Aron.
*** Decca Dig. 414 264-2 (2) [id.]. Chicago Ch. and SO, Solti.

Moses (Franz Mazura), Aron (Philip Langridge), Priest (Aage Haugland), Young Girl (Barbara Bonney).

Recorded in conjunction with concert performances, working very much against the clock and with the whole opera completed in fourteen hours, Solti gives Schoenberg's masterly score a dynamism and warmth which set it firmly – if perhaps surprisingly – in the grand romantic tradition. This is no mere intellectual exercise or static oratorio, as it can seem, but a genuine drama.

As the work opens Moses is at prayer and a spoken chorus provides his answers from the burning bush: he must lead the Israelites from bondage in Egypt. Moses replies that he is no orator, but the answer comes that his brother, Aaron, will speak for him. The two brothers then meet and both view the task differently, Moses conscious of the power and the personal guiding hand of God, Aaron needing a simple, more easily understandable image to which the people can relate.

Together they take God's message to the Israelites and, when Moses feels that words are not enough to hold the people together, Aaron takes a rod and performs miracles. A rod turns into a serpent; the Nile waters turn red. There is great religious fervour and the people prepare for the journey through the desert. Moses now ascends Mount Horeb to receive instructions concerning God's laws.

With Moses absent, Aaron and seventy elders gather before the Mountain of Revelation. The Israelites are assembled below Mount Sinai, but the people have turned against Moses. Aaron assumes that Moses is interceding with God but feels that they must take positive action quickly. He gives the people a chance to return to older beliefs. Gold is brought in and the golden calf is cast. There is a religious orgy. Wild animals are sacrificed, great riches are offered; there are even human sacrifices by old men. It all gets out of hand as enormous tension mounts. A youth is slaughtered as he tries to prevent this idolatry. There is rape and destruction until exhaustion sets in.

Finally a cry is heard. Moses is descending from the mountain. He appears, carrying the tablets with the ten commandments in his hands, and at his command the golden calf disintegrates. Aaron tries to vindicate himself and the people. But in despair Moses breaks the stone tablets. A pillar of fire then leads the Children of Israel on their march towards the promised land with Aaron at their head. Moses is left alone in despair but still praying.

The uncompleted Third Act brings another dialogue between Moses and Aaron, with Aaron in chains. Moses declares that Aaron failed God but Aaron tries to defend himself, is released and falls dead. Moses underlines his belief that a direct communication with God is the only way forward.

Solti instructed his performers to 'play and sing as if you were performing Brahms', and here *Moses und Aron* can almost be regarded as the opera which Brahms did not write – if with the 'wrong notes'. Particularly when two fine previous versions remain unavailable – Boulez on CBS, Gielen on Philips – Solti's broad romantic treatment presents a splendid alternative. This is a performance which in its greater variety of mood and pace underlines the drama, finds an element of fantasy and, in places – as in the *Golden Calf* episode – a sparkle such as you would never expect from Schoenberg. It is still not an easy work.

The Moses of Franz Mazura may not be as specific in his sing-speech as was Gunter Reich in the two previous versions – far less sing than speech – but the characterization of an Old Testament patriarch is the more convincing. As Aaron, Philip Langridge is lighter and more lyrical, as well as more accurate, than his predecessor with Boulez, Richard Cassilly. Aage Haugland with his firm, dark bass makes his mark in the small role of the Priest; Barbara Bonney too is excellent as the Young Girl. Above all, the brilliant singing of the Chicago Symphony Chorus matches the playing of the orchestra in virtuosity. More than ever the question-mark concluding Act II makes a pointful close, with no feeling of a work unfinished. The brilliant recording shows little or no sign of the speed with which the project was completed, and the CD adds an even sharper focus.

Schreker, Franz (1878-1934)

Der Schatzgräber: complete.
**(*) Capriccio Dig. 60 010-2 (2) [id.]. Hamburg State O, Gerd Albrecht.
   Elis (Josef Protschka), Els (Gabriele Schnaut), King (Harald Stamm), Fool (Pater Haage).

Completed at the very end of the First World War, *Der Schatzgräber* ('The treasure-digger') had phenomenal success in the following six years, being given in Germany and Austria many hundreds of times. The attractions of Schreker's sweet-sour treatment of a curious morality fairy-story then waned. Schreker was forced by the Nazis to resign from his Berlin posts in 1933, and he died the following year.

The Prologue tells of the queen's illness; the magic jewels that lend her beauty and fertility have disappeared. All the king's efforts to discover them have come to nought and he sends for the Fool, who tells him about a treasure-seeker called Elis. His magic lute points out all hidden treasure to him. The king promises him a wife if he can find Elis.

In Act I, Els, daughter of a tavern keeper, is to be married off to a rich but brutal nobleman whom she loathes. She has him murdered by her servant, Albi, but, before he does so, Elis appears and is to entertain the wedding party. His songs please only Els and he presents her with an ornament he has found near the corpse of the young nobleman. Els meanwhile has become the object of the bailiff's attentions, and he has Elis, for whose charms she has fallen, arrested.

In Act II, Elis is to be hanged but the king's Fool, who has been searching for him, promises to save him. At the gallows Elis is to sing a ballad but, fearing that his lute will reveal the hidden treasure, Els orders Albi to steal it. Nevertheless Elis is saved.

Act III opens in Els's room. In a night of rapture with Elis, Els reveals the jewels and, out of love, gives them to him, asking him never to reveal their provenance. In Act IV, the queen has recovered her jewellery and there are great festivities. Elis has to explain how he found the jewels, but instead sings a ballad, whose music reminds him of his night with Els.

The bailiff enters and announces that he has extracted a confession from Albi, revealing the murder, and demands Els's execution. But the Fool, reminding the king of his promise, claims her as his bride. Els implores Elis' forgiveness, but he turns away in silence. Els is dying and only the Fool has remained with her; he fetches the minstrel and Elis sings a last ballad to ease her death, but his art fails.

In idiom the comedy scenes owe much to the Wagner of *Meistersinger*, only with fewer tunes. The love music is more freely lyrical, with Schreker giving his central character, Elis – a roving minstrel with magical powers – a series of charming ballads. In Act III, before the great night of love between Elis and the heroine, Els – an innkeeper's daughter with a knack for dispatching unwanted suitors – Schreker has the temerity to have her quote her mother's simple cradle-song, a moment almost too sweet for comfort, and maybe an indication that Freudian motivation had hardly entered the composer-librettist's mind, either there or elsewhere.

This first recording was made live at the Hamburg State Opera in 1989, though there are very few signs of the audience's presence, with no applause, even at the end. Josef Protschka sings powerfully as Elis, hardly ever over-strenuous, but Gabriele Schnaut finds it hard to scale down her very bright and powerful soprano and seems happiest when she is scything your ears with loud and often unsteady top notes; yet she is certainly dramatic in this equivocal role. Outstanding among the others is Pater Haage as the court jester, who in the end is the only one to take pity on the disgraced Els, even though Elis is finally persuaded to sing a ballad as she dies. *Der Schatzgräber* may be hokum, but it is enjoyable hokum and, with Albrecht drawing committed performances from the whole company, this well-made recording is most welcome.

Schubert, Franz (1797-1828)

Fierabras (complete).
*** DG Dig. 427 341-2 (2) [id.]. Schoenberg Ch., COE, Abbado.
   Fierabras (Josef Protschka), Emma (Karita Mattila), Charlemagne (Robert Holl), Roland (Thomas Hampson), Eginhard (Robert Gambill), Boland (László Polgár), Florinda (Cheryl Studer).

Few operas by a great composer have ever had quite so devastatingly bad a press as *Fierabras*. However, in Vienna in 1988 Claudio Abbado conducted for a staging which, against all the odds, proved a great success; and the present recording was taken live from that. As with so many operas, the libretto is the main problem, absurd and cumbersome even by operatic standards. Yet the relationships between the central characters are clear enough, in this story from the days of chivalry. Schubert may often let his musical imagination blossom without considering the dramatic effect, so that there are jewels in plenty in this score; for example, the tenor *Romance* for Eginhard, the second hero, at the start of the Act I finale, magically turns from minor to major when his beloved, Emma, takes over the tune. Later in Act II the other heroine, Florinda, transforms an already lovely melody by adding a mezzo-soprano descant.

Many solos and duets develop into delightful ensembles, and the influence of Beethoven's *Fidelio* is very striking, with spoken melodrama and offstage fanfares bringing obvious echoes. By the standards of 1823 this was an adventurous opera, and it is sad that Schubert never saw it staged, so that he might have learnt to time the drama more effectively. A recording is the ideal medium for such buried treasure, and Abbado directs a performance as electrifying as his earlier one of Rossini's *Viaggio a Reims*, also with the Chamber Orchestra of Europe. Both tenors, Robert Gambill and Josef Protschka, are on the strenuous side, but have a fine feeling for Schubertian melody. Cheryl Studer and Karita Mattila sing ravishingly, and Thomas Hampson gives a noble performance as the knight, Roland, who finally wins Florinda. Only Robert Holl as King Karl (Charlemagne) is unsteady at times. The sound is comfortably atmospheric, outstanding for a live recording.

Schumann, Robert (1810–56)

Das Paradies und das Peri, Op. 50 (oratorio: complete).
**(*) Erato/Warner Dig. 2292 45456-2 (2). Edith Wiens, Sylvia Herman, Anne Gjevang, Robert Gambill, Christoph Prégardien, SRO Ch. & O, Jordan.

Schumann described this oratorio as 'my greatest and, I hope, my best work'. Though in the modern repertory it has almost sunk without trace, it is an important pioneering venture: as the first fully romantic oratorio using a secular text, it marked a breakthrough. Based on a quest poem by Thomas Moore, it centres on the heroine's search for gifts as a passport to heaven. From this fine recording one can understand both why the composer was so excited and why the piece has failed to gain a foothold.

This was the work which rounded off Schumann's extraordinary period of creative activity, prompted by his marriage to Clara, starting with the miraculous 'Year of Song', 1840. The richness and the fluency of the writing carry you on with no let-up, strongly argued, but the melodic invention is less striking than in Schumann's songs, with themes plain rather than memorable. Armin Jordan draws first-rate singing and playing from his Suisse Romande forces, helped by warmly atmospheric recording. The soloists are reliable, but not very distinctive – Edith Wiens, Anne Gjevang, Robert Gambill and Christoph Prégardien.

Scenes from Goethe's Faust.
⊛ (M) *** Decca 425 705-2 (2) [id.]. Elizabeth Harwood, Peter Pears, John Shirley-Quirk, Dietrich Fischer-Dieskau, Jennifer Vyvyan, Felicity Palmer, Aldeburgh Festival Singers, ECO, Britten.

Britten made this superb recording of a major Schumann work, long neglected, in 1973, soon after a live performance at the Aldeburgh Festival. Though the reasons for neglect remain apparent – this episodic sequence of scenes is neither opera nor cantata – the power and imagination of much of the music, not least the delightful garden scene and the energetic setting of the final part, are immensely satisfying. Britten inspired his orchestra and his fine cast of singers to vivid performances, which are outstandingly recorded against the warm Maltings acoustic. The CD remastering has effectively retained the ambience yet added to the projection of both solo voices and chorus. This is magnificent music, and readers are urged to explore it – the rewards are considerable.

Shostakovich, Dmitri (1906–75)

Lady Macbeth of Mtsensk (complete).
⊛ *** EMI CDS7 49955-2 (2) [Ang. CDCB 49955]. Amb. Op. Ch., LPO, Rostropovich.
Ekaterina Lvovna Ismailova (Galina Vishnevskaya), Sergey (Nicolai Gedda), Boris

Timofeyevich Ismailov (Dimiter Petkov), Zinovy Borisovich Ismailov (Werner Krenn), Shabby peasant (Robert Tear).

Rostropovich, in one of his very finest recordings, proves with thrilling conviction that this first version of Shostakovich's greatest work for the stage is among the most original operas of the century. In text *Lady Macbeth* may not be radically different from the revised version, *Katerina Ismailova*, but it has an extra sharpness of focus that transforms what is much more than just a sordid love-story involving three murders by the heroine.

When the story begins, Katerina has already been five years in a loveless marriage to Zinovy Borisovich Ismailov. Her father-in-law, Boris Timofeyevich, enters and complains that she has not given his son an heir. No doubt she would like a lover, but he will prevent that. Zinovy is called to go and repair a dam which has burst, and his father demands that Katerina swear an oath to be faithful to her husband while he is away. We now meet Sergei, Zinovy's personal servant, and Aksinya, who is attracted to him. Sergei had been dismissed from his previous post because of a relationship with his employer's wife. The bored Katerina has an altercation with Aksinya which turns into a fight, and Boris threatens to tell his son about Katerina's uncontrolled behaviour.

She returns to her bedroom, where she is joined by Sergei, and soon they are sharing a passionate embrace. Unfortunately as he leaves through the bedroom window he is observed by Boris, who has him flogged and locked up. Katerina brings Boris a supper of poisoned mushrooms. He is in agony, a priest is called and, as he dies, he accuses Katerina of his murder. But she mourns his death most convincingly.

Back together with Katerina in the bedroom, Sergei now says he fears Zinovy's return which will mean the end of their liaison. The ghost of Boris appears and terrifies Katerina. Steps are heard outside the bedroom door; it is Zinovy. Accusing his wife of infidelity, he picks up a belt to beat her. Sergei takes the opportunity to try to escape while Katerina grabs her husband and, between them, they manage to strangle him. The body is hidden in the cellar, then they return to their love-making. Now Katerina and Sergei are to be married, but they still brood about Zinovy's murder. Unfortunately for them, a drunk prowling in the cellar discovers the body and Katerina and Sergei are arrested by the police.

Katerina and Sergei are condemned to exile in Siberia and are in a transit camp together. Katerina bribes a guard to let her go to Sergei, but he repulses her and instead turns to the younger Sonyetka, who demands a pair of warm stockings in return for her body. Sergei wheedles them out of Katerina; when she realizes why he wants them, she awaits her moment, then seizes Sonyetka while she is standing on the parapet of a bridge and takes her down into the river with her. The current is too strong for rescue and the two women are drowned. The remaining convicts, including Sergei, form up into their marching column.

In this EMI recorded performance the brutality of the love-affair between the rich merchant's wife and Sergei, the roving-eyed servant, has maximum punch; and Rostropovich, helped by superlative recording, all the more vivid on CD, gives a performance of breathtaking power. Vishnevskaya is inspired to give an outstanding performance and provides moments of great beauty alongside aptly coarser singing; and Gedda matches her well, totally idiomatic. As the tyranical father-in-law, Petkov is magnificent, particularly in his ghostly return, and there are fine contributions from Robert Tear, Werner Krenn, Birgit Finnilä and Alexander Malta.

Sibelius, Jean (1865–1957)

The Maiden in the tower. Karelia suite, Op. 11.
*** BIS Dig. CD 250 [id.]. Mari Anne Häggander, Jorma Hynninen, Erland Hagegard, Tone Kruse, Gothenburg Ch. and SO, Järvi.

Sibelius abandoned his first operatic venture, *Veneen luominen* ('The building of the boat') after visiting Bayreuth in 1894, only two years after *Kullervo*, though some of its material found its way into the *Lemminkäinen Legends*; indeed, the first version of *The Swan of Tuonela* originally served as its Prelude. Only two years later came the present work, which was performed in Helsinki in 1897 and was never revived in the composer's lifetime. The feeble libretto has been blamed for the opera's failure, but this is only part of the problem. The plot itself does not rise above Victorian melodrama and the layout of the opera is scarcely convincing. It falls into eight short scenes and lasts no more than 35 minutes.

Its short Prelude is not unappealing but does not promise great things – any more than the ensuing scene delivers them. But the orchestral interlude between the first two scenes brings us the real Sibelius, and the second scene is undoubtedly impressive; there are echoes of Wagner, such as we find in some of the great orchestral songs of the following decade, and the vocal line has the wide tessitura and dramatic flexibility of such masterpieces as *Höstkväll* and *Jubal*. All the same, Sibelius's refusal to permit its revival was perfectly understandable, for it lacks something we find in all his most characteristic music: quite simply, a sense of mastery.

Yet even if it must be admitted that this is neither good opera nor good Sibelius, there is enough musical interest to warrant the attention of more than just the specialist collector. There are telling performances, too, from Mari Anne Häggander and Jorma Hynninen and the Gothenburg orchestra. Neeme Järvi's account of the *Karelia suite* is certainly original, with its opening rather impressive in its strange way. It is difficult to imagine a more spacious account of the *Intermezzo*, which is too broad to make an effective contrast with the ensuing *Ballade*. Järvi's account of this movement is so slow that it sags. However, this is obviously a record that the Sibelian will want to investigate, and BIS have put us in their debt by making it.

Sinopoli, Giuseppe (born 1946)

Lou Salome; suites Nos. 1 and 2.
*** DG Dig. 415 984-2 [id.]. Lucia Popp, José Carreras, Stuttgart RSO, composer.

Giuseppe Sinopoli as composer writes in an approachable Bergian style, colourful and energetic by turns. You might know from the lyrical lines – not just for the voices – that this is an Italian composer. In this opera, first produced in Munich in 1981, the use of the orchestra is unfailingly imaginative. It follows the life and loves of the heroine of the title, Lou Salome, a real-life figure closely associated with such characters as the philosopher Nietzsche and the poet Rilke. The two suites are quite distinct. The first one, after an atmospheric prelude, presents a big duet between Lou and her lover, Paul Ree; the second consists of a sequence of colourful genre pieces illustrating Lou's relationships with her partners. Under the composer's direction, the performance is passionately committed and the recording full and brilliant.

Smetana, Bedřich (1824–84)

The Bartered Bride (complete, in Czech).
*** Sup. Dig. 10 3511-2 (3) [id.]. Czech Philharmonic Ch. and O, Košler.
   Mařenka (Gabriela Beňačková), Jeník (Peter Dvorský), Vašek (Miroslav Kopp), Kečal (Richard Novák), Esmeralda (Jana Jonášová).

The digital Supraphon set under Košler admirably supplies the need for a first-rate Czech version of this delightful comic opera which takes place in spring in a Bohemian village. The villagers are in good spirits because of a forthcoming dance. But Mařenka and Jeník are downcast. They are in love, but Mařenka's parents want her to have a wealthy husband.

Mařenka's parents arrive with a marriage broker. He suggests that Mařenka should marry the son of their rich neighbour, Tobias Micha Krušina. Mařenka's father knows Micha but cannot remember the names of the two sons. Kečal replies that there is only one son; the other, the offspring of Micha's first marriage, has long since disappeared and is presumed dead. Ludmilla, Mařenka's mother, feels that Mařenka should decide for herself. Mařenka does just that: she joins her parents and Kečal and announces that she is now engaged to Jeník. Her parents' reaction is unfavourable, but she knocks the marriage contract out of Kečal's hand.

Mařenka enters the inn and meets Vašek, who stammers and is completely guileless. She realizes that this is the prospective bridegroom her parents have picked out for her and is horrified. She tells him that she is very sorry to hear that he is engaged to Mařenka, a flighty trollop who will give him no peace if he marries her. She points a pretty girl out to him and he readily agrees to give up Mařenka. Kečal now sets to work to buy off Jeník, but to no avail until Jeník says that he is willing to renounce his claim to Mařenka, but only in favour of the eldest son of Tobias Micha. Moreover the bribe from Kečal is not reclaimable under any circumstances.

Kečal goes off happily and, as Jeník knows that he is in fact the missing eldest son of Micha, he is satisfied with the bargain. Kečal returns with the document for Jeník to sign, and the whole village is up in arms that he has traded Mařenka for 300 Gulden. The forlorn Vašek grieves that he cannot find the lovely girl who gave him such good advice. But the circus comes to town, and among them is the glamorous Esmeralda and a real live American bear. The comedians enter too, but at last Vašek is left alone with Esmeralda.

A clown rushes in and says that the circus troupe member who wears the bear's costume is drunk. Esmeralda suggests Vašek as a replacement, and he is delighted to oblige. He is practising for his part when his mother enters, wishing him to meet his bride, Mařenka. He flatly refuses to accept her and goes off. Mařenka enters, lamenting that Jeník has betrayed her.

But, of course, everything ends well. Everyone gathers to witness the betrothal of Mařenka and 'the eldest son of Micha' and, as soon as Jeník speaks, his father recognizes him as the long-lost son. Jeník now asks Mařenka if she will wed Vašek or the eldest son of Micha, and Kečal is furious when she makes the obvious choice. A bear comes in, but it is only Vašek, and his mother drags him off.

The Supraphon recording acoustic may be rather reverberant for comedy, but the orchestral sound is warm and the voices are given good presence, while the performance sparkles from beginning to end, with folk rhythms crisply enunciated in an infectiously idiomatic way. The cast is strong, headed by the characterful Gabriela Beňačková as Mařenka and one of the finest of today's Czech tenors, Peter Dvorský, as Jeník. Miroslav Kopp in the role of the ineffective Vašek sings powerfully too. As Kečal the marriage-broker, Richard Novák is not always steady, but his swaggering characterization is most persuasive. The CDs offer some of the best sound we have yet had from Supraphon, fresh and lively. The voices are placed well forward in relation to the orchestra, and there is occasionally just a hint of digital edge on the vocal peaks. But the effect overall has fine presence. The discs are generously banded. The libretto is of poor quality, badly printed in minuscule type, offering a choice of Czech, English and Japanese.

The Bartered Bride (complete): sung in German.
Withdrawn: (M) ***** EMI CDM7 64002-2 (2). Berlin RIAS Chamber Ch., Bamberg SO, Kempe.
    Mařenka (Pilar Lorengar), Jeník (Fritz Wunderlich), Kečal (Gottlob Frick).

The Bartered Bride sung in German seems an unlikely candidate for a recommendation, yet this vivacious set is a remarkable success. This is an opera where the choruses form a basic platform on which the soloists can build their performances, and here they are sung with splendid lilt and gusto, and Kempe's warm, guiding hand maintains the lyrical flow perfectly. The discipline of the chorus and the lack of rigidity in the melodic line almost completely compensate for the absence of the idiomatic colouring that the Czech language can bring, and certainly the soloists here offer far more refined singing than from most Czech casts.

Pilar Lorengar is most appealing as Mařenka and Fritz Wunderlich in one of his all-too-few recordings is outstanding as Jeník. Gottlob Frick gives a strong, earthy characterization of Kečal, the marriage-broker. The whole production is full of high spirits. The recording is bright and vivid, yet has plenty of depth. This is not an opera that calls for much 'production', but the entry of the comedians is particularly well managed. The digital remastering produces some occasional sibilance and thinness on top – but nothing to worry about, when the attractive ambience remains.

Libuše (complete).
**(*) Sup. Dig. 1116 4211/4 [id.]. Prague Nat. Theatre Ch. & O, Košler.
    Libuše (Gabriela Beňačková), Přemysi (Václav Zítek), Chrudoš (Antonín Svorc), Štáhlav (Leo Marian Vodička).

Recorded live at the Prague National Theatre in 1983, this performance vividly communicates the fervour of nationalist aspirations, more intense when shared with an audience. Yet this opera, written for the opening of the National Theatre of Prague in 1881, inevitably has a limited appeal for the non-Czech listener, with a plot concerning the Czech royal dynasty.

Two brothers, Chrudoš and Štáhlav, are in dispute over their dead father's estate. Their sister, Radmilla, informs the Princess Libuše who, as her father's only child, is the ruler of Bohemia. Krasava, a cousin of the brothers, is very concerned about the outcome of the disputed territory. Libuše prays majestically and leaves for the council chamber.

In an open place at Vyšehrad the brothers and their uncle, Lutobar, await the arrival of Libuše, and the brothers quarrel. Libuše arrives in procession and publicly states the purpose of the meeting. Chrudoš angrily declares that in his view the elder brother should inherit the entire estate, as is determined by German law. Štáhlav, more amenably, agrees to abide by the consensus of opinion.

Libuše announces that, according to ancient custom, the estate can be managed jointly or divided between the brothers. Chrudoš objects and Libuše suggests that the council make the final decision. Radovan, leader of the council, says that the elders agree with Libuše's proposal. Chrudoš angrily rejects Libuše as a judge, describing her as merely a weak woman, and storms off, followed by his uncle and brother.

Libuše decides to abrogate her personal power and bids the people choose a suitable husband for her, who may rule in her stead. But the assembly passes this choice back to her and she determines on Přemysi, her childhood sweetheart whom she has continued to love through the years.

Krasava now confesses to her father, Lutobor, that she loves Chrudoš. He tells her to persuade her lover to bend more readily to Libuše's decisions. Chrudoš enters, still venting his spleen against the princess, and he is angry with Krasava, too: he thinks she loves his brother. Krasava persuades him that he is very wrong and, relenting, he declares the depth of his passion for her, which is returned. Radmilla (his sister), Lutobor and Štáhlav overhear these mutual confessions of love and are delighted. The brothers embrace each other.

The scene changes to Přemysi's farmhouse at Stadice. The voices of the harvesters are heard, and Přemysi is obviously in a reverie of love, both for the beautiful countryside and for Libuše. When it is discovered that he is to be her consort, there is general rejoicing. However, he has misgivings about the reaction of Chrudoš to the news. In Libuše's court she awaits her chosen bridegroom, the reconciliation of the two brothers is legally solemnized, and the betrothal of Chrudoš and Krasava is determined.

Back in the open square at Vyšehrad, the crowd gathers to await Libuše and Přemysi. When they arrive, the gods are asked to bless their nuptials. Chrudoš finally bows the knee and Přemysi embraces him eagerly. Libuše now gazes into the future, foretelling the destiny of her people in 'six pictures' (the composer's own description), ending with a scene of grandeur. The opera closes with a great patriotic chorale.

The cast here is even stronger than that of the previous recording under Krombholc, with Gabriela Beňačková-Čápová as Libuše memorable in her prophetic aria in Act III, while Václav Zitek as Přemysi, her consort, provides an attractive lyrical interlude in Act II which, with its chorus of harvesters, has affinities with *The Bartered Bride*. In Act I there is some Slavonic wobbling, notably from Eva Děpoltová as Krasava, but generally the singing is as dramatic as the plot-line will allow. Košler directs committedly; with the stage perspectives well caught, an unintrusive audience, and no disturbing stage noises with such a static plot, the recording is very satisfactory. The libretto booklet is clear, even if the typeface is minuscule. But with only 16 cues provided to an opera playing for not far short of three hours, internal access is poor.

Sondheim, Stephen (born 1930)

Assassins.
*** BMG/RCA Dig. RD 60737. Assassins O, Paul Gemignani.
  Proprietor (William Parry), Balladeer (Patrick Cassidy), John Wilkes Booth (Victor Garber), Lee Harvey Oswald (Jace Alexander), Leon Czolgosz (Terence Mann), John Hinckley (Greg Germann), Charles Guiteau (Jonathan Hadary), Giuseppe Zangara (Eddie Korbich), Samuel Byck (Lee Wilkof), Lynette 'Squeaky' Fromme (Annie Golden), Sarah Jane Moore (Debra Monk), David Herold (Marcus Olson), James Garfield (William Parry), James Blaine (John Jellison), Billy (Michael Shulman), Gerald Ford (William Parry).

This extraordinarily powerful and compressed piece survived only 73 performances in a Playrights Horizons production in the winter of 1990/91; it was seen by just over 10,000 theatregoers. Yet it is a remarkable example of Sondheim at his most dramatically compelling, emotionally and politically dedicated, and perhaps least commercial. It has a pungent, eclectic score, drawing on many sources from Copland to Sousa, and, if there are no hits in the normally accepted sense of the word, Sondheim's own musical personality dominates the piece and constantly involves the listener.

The narrative line is closely wedded to the music and the spoken dialogue is equally forceful, especially in the climactic scene in which Lee Harvey Oswald, sitting on a pile of books on the sixth floor of the Texas School Book Depository in Dallas, is joined first by John Wilkes Booth (who assassinated Abraham Lincoln) and then by his fellow presidential assassins (whom we have met individually earlier in the show) and persuades Lee of his complex reasons and motives for shooting JFK. 'You have the power of Pandora's Box,' says Booth, and the others express envy for the magnitude of Oswald's act and the fame it will bring him. After the gunshot, it is his predecessors who have the last word.

One of the most sinisterly haunting verbal images relates to the simplicity of using a gun, as expressed in Booth's words to Czolgosz (who killed President McKinley in 1901): 'All you have to do is move your little finger and you can change the world.' Victor Garber makes a strong Booth, Jace Alexander a convincing Lee Harvey Oswald and Patrick Cassidy as the Balladeer sings of the earlier assassinations to great effect. The recording is vividly forward – words are admirably clear – and its presence is telling in projecting the drama, yet there is no lack of theatrical atmosphere. A full text is provided.

Follies.
(M) *** EMI ZDM7 64666-2 [id.]. Original Broadway cast. Ch. & O, Harold Hastings.
> Sally Durant Plummer (Dorothy Collins), Hattie (Ethel Shutta), Dimitri Weismann (Edwin Steffe), Roscoe (Michael Bartlett), Benjamin Stone (John McMartin), Buddy Plummer (Gene Nelson), Phyllis Stone (Alexis Smith), Emily Whitman (Marcie Stringer), Theodore Whitman (Charles Welch), Solange (Fifi D'Orsay), Carlotta Campion (Yvonne De Carlo), Stella Deems (Mary McCarthy), Heidi Schiller (Justine Johnson), Young Buddy (Harvey Evans), Young Ben (Kurt Peterson), Young Sally (Marti Rolph), Young Phyllis (Virginia Sandifer).

When *Follies* opened in London in 1987, it was entirely rewritten (not an unusual thing for musicals). Controversy surrounded the original, though it ran for 521 performances on Broadway. Its plot-line, about two former chorus girls whose marriages have been unsuccessful and who meet again at a Follies reunion (with flashbacks and interpolations to recall their youth), was considered too meagre. It supported a series of spectacular numbers, many of them essentially Broadway pastiche, sung by a large and expensive cast, and the long, dream-like re-creation of the Weismann Follies (like a divertissement in a ballet) is effective enough musically.

Anyway, the score is the thing on a show record, and there are some splendid numbers here – set off by the opening chorus, *Beautiful girls.* They are performed with panache by artists of the calibre of Yvonne de Carlo (*I'm still here*), John McMartin and Dorothy Collins (*Too many mornings*), Gene Nelson (*The right girl*, splendidly timed), Alexis Smith (*The story of Lucy and Jessie* and the charming waltz, *Could I leave you?*), while the combined *Ah! Paris/Broadway Baby* (Fifi D'Orsay and Ethel Shutta) and of course, Dorothy Collins's touching *Losing my mind* are also memorable. As a memento of a brilliant theatrical experience, this is distinctly preferable to the more elaborate BMG/RCA offering below, and it is far better balanced and recorded. Harold Hastings' musical direction is first class. Excellent documentation, too.

(i) *Follies* (in concert); (ii) *Stavisky* (film score).
*(**) BMG/RCA Dig. RD 87128 (2). Ch. & NYPO, Paul Gemignani.
> (i) Sally Durant Plummer (Barbara Cook), Hattie (Elaine Stritch), Dimitri Weismann (André Gregory), Roscoe (Arthur Rubin), Benjamin Stone (George Hearn), Buddy Plummer (Mandy Patinkin), Phyllis Stone (Lee Remick), Emily Whitman (Betty Comden), Theodore Whitman (Adolph Green), Solange (Liliane Montevecchi), Carlotta Campion (Carol Burnett), Stella Deems (Phyllis Newman), Heidi Schiller (Licia Albanese), Young Buddy (Jim Walton), Young Ben (Howard McGillan), Young Sally (Liz Callaway), Young Phyllis (Daisy Prince).

This BMG/RCA set offers a live gala performance of *Follies,* recorded in the Avery Fisher Hall in September 1985. The composer had a hand in selecting the cast, which includes many starry names, and the performance has the genuine zing and razzmatazz of Broadway. If the close microphones (in a difficult venue) and the digital recording bring not only a brilliant presence but also a degree of edginess to the sound and especially to the voices, which needs taming, the vitality and star-calibre of the presentation are undeniable, and there are hits and potential hits galore, among them the ensemble numbers, *Beautiful girls* and (especially) the catchy *Waiting for the girls upstairs* (which has much in common with Loesser's *Standing on the corner watching all the girls go by*).

Betty Comden and Adolph Green are unforgettable in the engaging *Rain on the roof,* and if Elaine Stritch's *Broadway baby,* with its tremendous audience reaction, almost stops the show, Barbara Cook's haunting *In Buddy's eyes* is equally memorable, as is her hauntingly nostalgic *Losing my mind.* Carol Burnett (as Carlotta) delivers a vibrantly strident *I'm still here* and Lee Remick (as Phyllis) is very personable in the charming *Could I leave you?* with its splendid pay-off: 'Guess!' and she later handles the equally famous *Story of Lucy and Jessie* with enormous verve.

Licia Albanese was specially imported from the Met. for the coloratura pastiche number, *One more kiss* (with the orchestra obviously relishing the accompaniment). The snag is that the second CD has only the last five items (about 20 minutes) and is then filled out with a very slight film-score written for Alain Resnais's movie, *Stavisky*. It uses a chamber orchestra, and the thin, often ill-focused sound is unflattering.

Into the Woods.
*** BMG/RCA Dig. RD 86796. O, Paul Gemignani.
  Narrator / Mysterious Man (Tom Aldredge), Cinderella (Kim Crosby), Jack (Ben Wright), Baker (Chip Zien), Baker's wife (Joanna Gleason), Cinderella's stepmother (Joy Franz), Little Red Riding Hood (Danielle Ferland), Witch (Bernadette Peters), Wolf / Cinderella's Prince (Robert Westenberg), Rapunzel (Pamela Winslow), Rapunzel's Prince (Chuck Wagner).
*** BMG/RCA Dig. RD 60752. O, Peter Stanger.
  Narrator (Nicholas Parsons), Cinderella (Jacqueline Dankworth), Jack (Richard Dempsey), Baker (Ian Bartholomew), Baker's wife (Imelda Staunton), Cinderella's stepmother (Ann Howard), Little Red Riding Hood (Tessa Burbridge), Witch (Julia McKenzie), Wolf / Cinderella's Prince (Clive Carter), Rapunzel (Mary Lincoln), Rapunzel's Prince (Mark Tinkler), Mysterious Man (John Rogan).

Into the Woods creates an uneasy mixture of innocence and cynicism, picking up the ethos of fairyland and placing it within the world of stark reality. James Lapine's book brings together favourite storybook characters and takes them on a woodland journey in which, to quote Little Red Riding Hood, they learn that 'Nice is different than good'.

The first half of the show is light-hearted and makes fun of the traditional predicaments of its characters, who slowly become more resourceful and worldly. In the second Act, catastrophes abound and, in the ensuing havoc, violence erupts which not everyone survives. Romanticism is temporarily deserted and even Cinderella's Prince betrays her. Finally the characters band together. United, they despatch the giant, and the moral of the tale is obvious.

The two recordings faithfully reflect the British and transatlantic approaches. The very opening 'Once upon a time' is much more urgent and graphic in New York (Tom Aldredge), while Nicholas Parsons' narration is distinctly urbane. Although – not unexpectedly – Julia McKenzie is a stunning witch, overall the American cast project with an added tang. The music is a characteristically integrated Sondheim score and, apart from the quite catchy title-number, which we hear a lot (perhaps too much), and the lyrically nostalgic *Agony*, there are no obvious hits, although both *Any moment* and *No one is alone*, which comes near the *Candide*-like close of the show, are touching, if without the sheer memorability of a song like *You'll never walk alone* from *Carousel*.

This is perhaps a piece to see first, rather than to remember from its score alone, although its drama certainly comes across on record. Both CDs are impressively vivid and atmospheric, but the New York Cast version is much better documented. It comes (like its competitor) on a single disc, but in a two-CD jewel-case to make room for the generously illustrated booklet, which includes a full text of the songs.

Marry me a little.
*** BMG/RCA Dig. GD 87142. Musical direction: E. Martin Perry.
  Man (Craig Douglas), Woman (Suzanne Henry).

Marry me a little shows Sondheim at his most intimately stylish. Conceived as a duologue with simple piano accompaniment, this revue/conversation piece was put together during the rehearsals of *Sweeney Todd* (using already-written material, including cut-outs dropped from other shows). It opened in October 1980 and later moved off Broadway to the Actors' Playhouse.

The scenario centres on two singles who find themselves alone in New York on a Saturday night, and the opening number celebrating that day of meeting is distinctly inviting. *Bang* is rather irritating, and one can understand why it was dropped from *A Little Night Music*, but the nostalgic *Silly people* was well worth saving. *Can that boy foxtrot!*, very well done here, has hit potential, as have the title-song, *The girls of summer*, and *So many people*, while the duets, *A moment with you* and the catchy *Little white house*, both show the composer's light vocal interplay at its most charmingly whimsical. *There won't be trumpets* has that haunting feeling for a phrase that makes a song sit in the memory.

Both Craig Douglas and Suzanne Henry are completely at one with the mood of the show; although the end effect is slight, the score is consistently appealing in its unostentatious sophistication. The piano accompaniments, from an unnamed pianist, are splendid and the recording makes a perfect balance between presence and intimacy.

A Little Night Music.
(M) *** BMG/RCA GD 85090. O, Ray Cook.
 Fredrik Egerman (Joss Ackland), Desirée Armfeldt (Jean Simmons), Madame Armfeldt (Hermione Gingold), Anne Egerman (Veronica Page), Petra (Diane Langton), Count Carl-Magnus Malcolm (David Kernan), Countess Charlotte Malcolm (Maria Aitken), Quintet: Mrs Nordstrom (Chris Melville), Mrs Segstrom (Jacquey Chappell), Mrs Anderson (Liz Robertson), Mr Erlanson (David Bexton), Mr Linquist (John J. Moore).
**(*) That's Entertainment Dig. CDTER 1179 [id.]. O, John Owen Edwards.
 Fredrik Egerman (Eric Flynn), Desirée Armfeldt (Sian Phillips), Madame Armfeldt (Elisabeth Welch), Anne Egerman (Janis Kelly), Petra (Maria Friedman), Count Carl-Magnus Malcolm (Jason Howard), Countess Charlotte Malcolm (Susan Hampshire), Quintet: Dinah Harris, Hilary Western, Susan Flannery, Michael Bulman, Martin Nelson.

Stephen Sondheim's most successful and enduring stage piece, *A Little Night Music*, with its neo-eighteenth-century elegance, was based on Ingmar Bergman's film, *Smiles of a Summer Night*. The result, immensely civilized yet lyrically heady, is as much a masque as an operetta, with a French insouciance in Hugh Wheeler's light handling of a story in which almost everyone makes love to someone else's partner, although the maid, Petra, has to be content with the butler.

After the sophisticated opening quintet and the deliciously nostalgic *Night waltz*, Madame Armfeldt (in a part that was surely custom-made for Hermione Gingold) presides over all that follows. She tells her young granddaughter of the three 'smiles of the summer night', the first for the young who know nothing, the second for the fools who do not know enough, and the third for the old who, like herself, know too much.

The actress-heroine, Desirée, belongs to the second group and is particularly endearing when, in Act I, she welcomes back her former lover, Fredrik. He left her and married a much younger woman. Genuinely horrified when she hears that his pretty new wife, Anne, flatly refuses to consummate the marriage, she warmly embraces him in her own bedroom. She then realizes that she wants him on a permanent basis; when he is unwilling to give Anne up, sadly defeated Desirée sings the wonderfully touching *Send in the clowns*.

But later Anne herself discovers the delights of love, but with Fredrik's son, Henrik, and runs off with him instead. So in the end Desirée and Fredrik are thrown back together, and for once in a musical the reprise of its most famous number becomes central to the exposition of the plot. Before that the score, consistently melodic in the Singspiel tradition, and with Sondheim's wryly mordant lyrics, is rich in duets (*You must meet my wife*, with Desirée's ironic comments), trios (*Perpetual anticipation*) and small ensembles (*The glamorous life* and the catchy hit-song, *A weekend in the country*).

The music is technically difficult, but the excellent London cast, a splendid team, bring it off with sparkle and finesse. Glynis Johns in the original Broadway cast made *Send in the clowns* very much her own, but Jean Simmons sings it simply and touchingly. Joss Ackland is a vocally sympathetic Fredrik, and Hermione Gingold's monologue, *Liaisons*, is unforgettable. As so often with recordings of musicals, the balance is rather too forward, but the remastering for CD of a 1975 recording is expertly managed.

The alternative, more recent, digital version from That's Entertainment offers what is essentially the 1989 Chichester Festival Theatre production, which later transferred to London. For both practical and financial reasons, a reduced orchestration was used, but Jonathan Tunick's scoring is clever enough for that not to be a drawback. The recording is more recessed (the exception is Henrik's *Later*, which at its climax bursts uncomfortably out of the speakers). This gives a smoother effect to the ensembles, but the singing, though well integrated, has not quite the same degree of sparkling polish of the earlier, London cast record.

Nevertheless there is much to enjoy. Elisabeth Welch's Madame Armfeldt is a more restrained characterization than Hermione Gingold's but is still telling, and the key numbers all have plenty of vitality. If Sian Phillips is rather more deadpan in *Send in the clowns*, one of the surprises of the show is Susan Hampshire's Countess Charlotte. Her *Every day a little death* is beautifully done, and she emerges as an individual voice in the infectious *A weekend in the country*. Excellent, atmospheric recording.

Sunday in the Park with George.
*** BMG/RCA RD 85042. O, Paul Gemignani.

George (Mandy Patinkin), Dott / Marie (Bernadette Peters), Jules (Charles Kimbrough), Yvonne (Dana Ivey), Old Lady (Barbara Bryne).

Sunday in the Park with George celebrates the work of the French neo-impressionist painter, Georges Seurat, and in particular his most famous pointillist work, *A Sunday afternoon on the Island of La Grande Jatte.*

Act I is essentially about the creation of the picture, and though there is much additional detail, including the pregnancy of his mistress, Dott, the painting dominates everything and itself becomes the closing tableau.

In Act II the painting is finished and in a museum, and a new George comes to see the picture with his very old grandmother, Marie, the daughter of Dott and the artist. He is to lecture on Seurat's work and this brings the opportunity for spectacular projections of the paintings.

The final scene returns to the island of La Grande Jatte, where everything now looks different, with high-rise blocks in place of the trees. With the aid of a book passed on to Marie by her daughter, Dott reappears and the painting is re-created. The visual part of the show is obviously of the greatest importance; however, Sondheim's score, sometimes abrasive but always pertinent to the action, stands up well on its own, especially the duet, *Colour and light,* the vivacious ensemble celebrating *The day off,* and the brilliantly conceived promenade of the various characters from the painting which opens Act II. Later, *Children and art,* Marie's monologue, with George looking over her shoulder, is very touching. Bernadette Peters is equally impressive as the vibrant mistress who has to take second place to a painting and, later, as Marie, and Mandy Patinkin is an appropriately characterful George. As ever, Paul Gemignani's musical direction is full of life and the recording has the right degree of presence.

COLLECTIONS

Side by Side (revue, including songs from: *Anyone can whistle; Company; Evening Primrose; Follies; A funny thing happened on the Way to the Forum; A little night music; Pacific overtures; The 7 percent solution;* BERNSTEIN: *West Side Story.* STYNE: *Gypsy.* Richard RODGERS: *Do I hear a waltz?* Mary RODGERS: *The Mad Show.*

(M) **(*) BMG/RCA GD 81851 (2). Millicent Martin, Julia McKenzie, David Kernan; Tim Higgs and Stuart Pedlar (pianos).

Side by Side is a feast of Sondheim, but perhaps essentially one for British ears. Millicent Martin and (especially) Julia McKenzie can be as abrasive as anyone, and there is no lack of bravura (*Getting married today*). But mostly the presentation here has the laid-back sophistication of a late-night revue, even if the sparkling numbers from *Company* and *Follies* have no lack of fizz, and Julia McKenzie's riotous *Broadway baby* is splendidly individual. The delicious trio, *You could drive a person crazy,* shows the team at their most exhilarating, and David Kernan's lightly etched vocalism is especially effective in the intimate interchange of *You must meet my wife* (*A Little Night Music*). It is good that songs were included from several shows, famous and otherwise, to which Sondheim contributed only the lyrics. Excellent, natural sound, with good projection and presence, gives a very real effect: the singers are almost at the other end of the room. If you enjoy these artists, you will like this a lot.

'A musical tribute': Overture; Entr'acte. Anyone can whistle: (i) *Me and my town; A parade in town;* (ii) *Anyone can whistle.* Company: (iii) *You could drive a person crazy;* (iv) *The little things you do together;* (v) *Getting married today;* (vi) *Another hundred people;* (vii) *Happily ever after; Being alive;* (viii) *Side by side by side.* Evening primrose: (ix) *Evening primrose; Take me to the world;* (x) *I remember.* Follies: (x; xi) *One more kiss;* (xii) *Broadway baby;* (xiii; xiv) *Pleasant little kingdom; Too many mornings;* (xv) *Buddy's blues.* (xvi) *Beautiful girls;* (xvii) *I'm still here;* (xviii) *Could I leave you?;* (xiii) *Losing my mind.* A funny thing happened on the way to the forum: (xix) *Love is in the air;* (xx) *Your eyes are blue.* A Little Night Music: (xxi) *Silly people;* (x; xxii) *Two fairy tales.* Saturday night: (xxiii) *So many people.* BERNSTEIN: *West Side Story:* (xxiv; vi) *America.* STYNE: *Gypsy:* (xxv) *If mama were married.* RODGERS: *Do I hear a waltz?:* (xxvi) *Do I hear a waltz?;* (xxvii) *We're gonna be alright.*

**(*) BMG/RCA RD 60515 (2) [id.]. (i) Angela Lansbury (with Harvey Evans, Tony Stevens); (ii) composer; (iii) Donna McKechnie, Pamela Myers, Susan Browning; (iv) Mary McCarthy; (v) Beth Howland, Terri Ralston, Steve Elmore; (vi) Pamela Myers; (vii) Larry Kert; (viii) The entire company; (ix) Marti Rolph; (x) Victoria Mallory; (xi) Justine Johnson; (xii) Ethel Shutta; (xiii) Dorothy Collins; (xiv) John McMartin; (xv) Larry Blyden (with Donna McKechnie and Chita Rivera); (xvi) Ron Holgate; (xvii) Nancy Walker; (xviii) Alexis Smith;

(xix) Larry Blyden, Susan Browning; (xx) Harvey Evans, Pamela Hall; (xxi) George Lee Andrews; (xxii) Mark Lambert; (xxiii) Susan Browning, Jack Cassidy; (xxiv) Chita Rivera; (xxv) Alice Playten, Virginia Sandifer; (xxvi) Dorothy Collins; (xxvii) Laurence Guittard and Terri Ralston; O, Paul Gemignani.

The present tribute took place on 11 March 1973, when 33 Broadway celebrities gathered together to provide a restrospective of Sondheim's work until then, from his early lyrics for Bernstein's *West Side Story*, Jule Styne's *Gypsy* and Richard Rodgers' *Do I hear a waltz?* through his own shows of the early 1970s, notably *Company*, *Follies* and *A little night music*. Only actors/singers who had enjoyed stage parts in Sondheim productions were invited to perform, including most of the original cast of *Company* plus a round half-dozen from *Follies*. Jack Cassidy was the odd man out: he had been cast in a production of *Saturday night* which never opened, because the producer died and the backers backed out.

The snag with these live occasions is the audience; they certainly add to the atmosphere and help to pump up the artists' adrenalin, but they usually clap too much and overdo the laughter. That happens here, notably in Ethel Shutta's exuberant *Broadway baby*. But mostly the performances are worthy of the applause. *Follies* is particularly well represented. Justin Johnson warbles a bit in *One more kiss*, but Dorothy Collins and John McMartin make a great team in their two numbers, and *Buddy's blues* is an irresistible combined effort (Larry Blyden, joined by Donna McKecknie and the inimitable Chita Rivera).

Among the solos, Alexis Smith's *Could I leave you?* is matched by Nancy Walker's *I'm still here*, beginning intimately and building to a dynamic climax. *Company* brings the winningly frothy trio, *You could drive a person crazy* (Donna McKechnie, Pamela Myers and Susan Browning), while Mary McCarthy's *Little things you do together* is a delight, followed by *Getting married today*, with breath-catching vocal bravura from Beth Howland.

The two numbers from the little-known *Evening primrose* – *Take me to the world* (Marti Rolph) and (especially) *I remember* (Victoria Mallory) – are memorably nostalgic, and the duet, *Love is in the air*, from *A funny thing happened on the way to the forum* has comparable charm (Larry Blyden and Susan Browning). Angela Lansbury opens the second half with lively aplomb (*Me and my town*) and, before the final number, Sondheim offers his own version of *Anyone can whistle*. Considering these are live recordings, with no chances for second takes, the recording is very well managed, and the presentation includes plenty of photographs.

'*Sondheim Songbook*': excerpts from: *Anyone can whistle*; *Company*; *A Little Night Music*. BERNSTEIN: *West Side Story*. STYNE: *Gypsy*. Richard RODGERS: *Do I hear a waltz?* Mary RODGERS: *The boy from*.
*** Sony SK 48201 [id.]. Lee Remick, Angela Lansbury, Harry Guardino, Elaine Stritch, Glynis Johns, Len Cariou, Hermione Gingold, Larry Kert, Ethel Merman, Linda Lavin and others.

Stephen Sondheim was just as importantly a lyricist as a song-writer. Leonard Bernstein, with whom he worked for *West Side Story*, said, 'His contribution was just enormous. What made him so valuable was that he was also a composer and so I could explain musical problems to him and he'd understand immediately.' Here is a selection of some of Sondheim's best songs, not only from his own shows but also those with music by others. The programme opens with two from *West Side Story* and carries on through to his own early musicals, notably four superb numbers from *Company*, dominated by the gravel-voiced Elaine Stritch, and five from *A Little Night Music*. *You must meet my wife* shows him at his wittiest and the swinging *Weekend in the country* demonstrates equally his ready facility for ensemble writing. Hermione Gingold is unforgettable in *Liaisons* and the disc ends with the memorable *Send in the clowns*, sung with haunting nostalgia by Glynis Johns. Before that there are many individual highlights from other shows, notably the two Richard Rodgers numbers from *Do I hear a waltz?*, the delightful ballad *Moon in my window* and the catchy *We're gonna be alright*.

Spohr, Ludwig (1784–1859)

Die letzten Dinge (The Last Judgement): oratorio.
Withdrawn: *** Ph. Dig. 416 627-2 [id.]. Mitsuko Shirai, Marjana Lipovšek, Josef Protschka, Matthias Hölle, Stuttgart Ch. & RSO, Kuhn.

Spohr's picture of the Apocalypse was designed to please rather than to startle, and the gentle first half of his oratorio comes as an amiable preparation for the Judgement Day music in the second, launched in a vigorous Handelian chorus, followed by contemplation and rejoicing. The elaborate fugal writing is very skilled (Handel the main influence). Spohr's horror music too readily relies on conventional chromatic progressions, and the gently flowing tempi provide too little contrast; well performed, as here, this historical curiosity does prove well worth reviving. Among the soloists Mitsuko Shirai is outstanding, with Matthias Hölle, an imposing bass, also impressive. Good, atmospheric recording.

Spontini, Gasparo (1774–1851)

Olympie: complete.
**(*) Orfeo Dig. C 137862H (3) [id.]. Berlin RIAS Chamber Ch., German Op. Male Ch., Berlin RSO, Albrecht.
   Olympie (Julia Varady), Statira (Stefania Toczyska), Cassandra (Ferruccio Tagliavini), Antigonè (Dietrich Fischer-Dieskau), L'Hiérophante (George Fortune), Hermas (Josef Becker).

Spontini's *Olympie*, based on a historical play by Voltaire about the daughter of Alexander the Great, had the misfortune to be superseded in popular fashion by Weber's *Der Freischütz* almost as soon as it appeared. Yet a modern revival shows that it looks forward in operatic history as well as back, presenting the story strongly and dramatically, with even the occasional hint of Berlioz, who himself admired the piece. The principal characters are Olympie, Alexander's daughter, and Statire, his widow, with rival suitors for Olympie's hand setting off the dramatic conflict: the tenor, Cassandre, as the goody and the baritone, Antigone, as the baddy.

At the beginning of the story Cassandre and Antigone have made peace. As the Hiérophante (who might be described as the presiding priest) gives Aménaïs (with whom Antigone is in love) to Cassandre as his wife, Alexander's widow, Statire, realizes that this is the man who murdered her husband. Cassandre begs her forgiveness and reveals that Aménaïs is really her daughter, Olympie.

At this point Antigone takes him prisoner but he manages to escape and succeeds in overthrowing his captor. Fearing Cassandre's vengeance, Statire stabs herself and Olympie, who still loves him, commits suicide. The tragic ending is resolved by an apotheosis of Statire, Alexander and Olympie.

The 1819 version ran to only seven performances, and Spontini revised it for performance in Berlin in E. T. A. Hoffmann's translation, altering the plot so that Antigone becomes the murderer of Alexander. He returned to the happy ending in the 1826 Paris version.

The writing is lively and committed and, despite flawed singing, so is this performance. Julia Varady is outstanding in the name-part, giving an almost ideal account of the role of heroine, but Stefania Toczyska is disappointingly unsteady as Statira and Ferruccio Tagliavini is totally out of style as Cassandra. Even Dietrich Fischer-Dieskau is less consistent than usual, but his melodramatic presentation is nevertheless most effective. The text is cut to fit on to three CDs, but only scholars need worry.

Stockhausen, Karlheinz (born 1928)

Donnerstag aus Licht (complete).
Withdrawn: **(*) DG 423 379-2 (4). Soloists, Cologne RSO Ch.; Hilversum R. Ch. & O, W. German R. Ens., Ens. Intercontemporain, composer; Eötvös.

One needs patience to appreciate so enormous a project as *Licht*, Stockhausen's seven-day operatic cycle, still in process of completion. This Thursday episode, sharply eventful, has obvious concentration in its direct musical expression. The central character is the Archangel Michael, with Act I devoted to his childhood, 'moon-eve' and examination, Act II to Michael's journey round the Earth (with trumpet and orchestra), and Act III to Michael's return home, representing finally Judgement Day and the end of time. The recording (made on different occasions, mainly at live performances) is hardly a substitute for the full visual experience, but the originality of Stockhausen's aural imagination, not least in his use of voices, is brilliant.

The digital transfer to CD adds superbly to the immediacy and atmospheric realism of the recording with its often spectacular spatial effects. It is good that the *Greeting* and *Farewell* which frame any performance of the opera are now allotted their rightful places, instead of being consigned to a supplement, as on LP. The same notes are given as with the LP set, but the complete text is again omitted, and the synopsis is not always detailed enough for the action to be followed fully, a pity in a work which is baffling enough already.

Stradella, Alessandro (1644–82)

San Giovanni Battista (oratorio).
⊛ *** Erato/Warner Dig. 2292 45739-2 [id.]. Catherine Bott, Christine Batty, Gérard Lesne, Richard Edgar-Wilson, Philippe Huttenlocher, Musiciens du Louvre, Minkowski.

Stradella's oratorio on the biblical subject of John the Baptist and Salome is an amazing masterpiece, in effect (like many early oratorios) an opera for church performance. Written in 1675 by this notorious libertine of a composer, its compact structure of 37 sections lasting just over an hour offers unashamedly sensuous treatment of the story. Insinuatingly chromatic melodic lines for Salome (here described simply as Herodias' daughter) are set against plainer, more forthright writing for the castrato role of the saint, a seventeenth-century equivalent of Richard Strauss.

There is one amazing phrase for Salome, gloriously sung here by Catherine Bott, which starts well above the stave and ends after much twisting nearly two octaves below with a glorious chestnote, a hair-raising moment. Salome's brief arias cover an extreme range of moods, both vigorous and pathetic, and there is one beautiful trio she has with her mother and the tenor Counsellor which brings striking echoes of Monteverdi's *Lamento della ninfa*, one of the most languorously beautiful of all madrigals.

Herod's anger arias bring reminders of both Purcell and Handel, and at the end Stradella ingeniously superimposes Salome's gloating music and Herod's expressions of regret, finally cutting off the duet in mid-air as Charles Ives might have done, bringing the whole work to an indeterminate close.

Quite apart from Catherine Bott's magnificent performance, at once pure and sensuous in tone and astonishingly agile, the other singers are most impressive, with Gérard Lesne a firm-toned counter-tenor in the title-role and Philippe Huttenlocher a clear if sometimes gruff Herod. Marc Minkowski reinforces his claims as an outstanding exponent of period performance, drawing electrifying playing from Les Musiciens du Louvre, heightening the drama. Excellent sound. Not to be missed.

La Susanna (oratorio).
Withdrawn: (M) **(*) EMI CMS7 63438-2 (2) [id.]. Bar. Instrumental Ens., Curtis.
Susanna (Marjanne Kweksilber), Daniele (Judith Nelson), Testo (René Jacobs), Galudice II / Judge II (Martyn Hill), Glaudice I / Judge I (Ulrik Cold).

Recorded in Amsterdam in 1978, this period performance of Stradella's biblical oratorio, based on the story of Susanna and the Elders, begins disconcertingly. That was the time when baroque strings (the group here is violin, cello and violone, with theorbo, chittarone and harpsichord) used an abrasive squeeze technique on sustained notes. The slow *Prelude*, recorded close, is unpleasantly abrasive, but then the fine qualities of this lively performance emerge more and more.

As in *San Giovanni Battista*, Stradella's characterization is strong. Its heroine is depicted as being sensitive in nature yet with underlying strength, showing an element of heroism for, although at first intimidated, she firmly resists the advances of the lecherous Elders, who come upon her while she is swimming.

With an excellent cast of soloists, including the aptly named Marjanne Kweksilber silver-toned in the title-role, the listener is certainly involved in the drama of the famous biblical story. The oratorio is in two sections, lasting just over an hour and a half in all, and including no fewer than 25, mainly brief, numbers, linked by fluid recitative. Outstanding are the three substantial arias for Susanna near the beginning of Part Two, including a lament lasting nearly seven minutes. With its simple descending ground bass and languishing melodic lines, it directly echoes Monteverdi's celebrated *Lamento della ninfa*.

That is not the only likeness to the earlier composer, with many brief duets and trios also recalling Monteverdi's madrigals. Though the booklet provides a helpful essay about Stradella himself, there is too little information specifically about *La Susanna*, no text and not even a synopsis, though with bright, close-up sound the Italian words are exceptionally clear.

Strauss, Johann Jnr (1825-99)

Die Fledermaus (complete; gala performance).
**(*) Decca 421 046-2 (2) [id.]. (With guest artists: Birgit Nilsson, Renata Tebaldi, Fernando Corena, Joan Sutherland, Giulietta Simionato, Ljuba Welitsch, Teresa Berganza, Leontyne Price), V. State Op. Ch., VPO, Karajan.
Rosalinde (Hilde Gueden), Adèle (Erika Köth), Eisenstein (Waldemar Kmentt), Alfred (Giuseppe Zampieri), Doctor Falke (Walter Berry), Orlovsky (Regina Resnik), Frank (Eberhard Waechter).

Die Fledermaus (complete).
*** Ph. Dig. 432 157-2; *432 157-4* (2) [id.]. V. State Op. Ch., VPO, Previn.
Rosalinde (Kiri Te Kanawa), Adèle (Edita Gruberová), Eisenstein (Wolfgang Brendel), Alfred (Richard Leech), Doctor Falke (Olaf Bär), Orlovsky (Brigitte Fassbaender), Frank (Tom Krause).
(M) (***) EMI mono CHS7 69531-2 (2) [Ang. CDHB 69531]. Philh. Ch. & O, Karajan.
Rosalinde (Elisabeth Schwarzkopf), Adèle (Rita Streich), Eisenstein (Nicolai Gedda), Alfred (Helmut Krebs), Dr Falke (Erich Kunz), Orlovsky (Rudolf Christ), Frank (Karl Dönch).
Withdrawn: (M) *** EMI CMS7 69354-2 (2) [id.]. V. State Op. Ch., VSO, Boskovsky.
Rosalinde (Anneliese Rothenberger), Adèle (Renata Holm), Eisenstein (Nicolai Gedda), Alfred (Adolf Dallapozza), Dr Falke (Dietrich Fischer-Dieskau), Orlovsky (Brigitte Fassbaender), Frank (Walter Berry).
(B) **(*) CfP CD-CFPD 4702 (2) [Ang. CDMB 62566]; *TC-CFPD 4702*. Philh. Ch. & O, Ackermann.
Rosalinde (Gerda Scheyrer), Adèle (Wilma Lipp), Eisenstein (Karl Terkal), Alfred (Anton Dermota), Dr Falke (Eberhard Waechter), Orlovsky (Christa Ludwig), Frank (Walter Berry).
Withdrawn: **(*) EMI Dig. CDC7 47480-8 (2) [Ang. CDCB 47480]. Bav. R.Ch., Munich Op. O, Domingo.
Rosalinde (Lucia Popp), Adèle (Eva Lind), Eisenstein (Peter Seiffert), Alfred (Plácido Domingo), Dr Falke (Wolfgang Brendel), Orlovsky (Agnes Baltsa), Frank (Kurt Rydl).
*(*) DG 415 646-2 (2) [id.]. Bav. State Op. Ch. & O, Carlos Kleiber.
Rosalinde (Julia Varady), Adèle (Lucia Popp), Eisenstein (Hermann Prey), Alfred (René Kollo), Dr Falke (Bernd Weikl), Orlovsky (Ivan Rebroff), Frank (Benno Kusche).
* Denon Dig. C37 7305/6 [id.]. V. Volksoper Ch. & O, Binder.
Rosalinde (Mirjana Irosch), Adèle (Melanie Holliday), Eisenstein (Waldemar Kmentt), Alfred (Ryszard Karczykowski), Dr Falke (Robert Granzer), Orlovsky (Dagmar Koller), Frank (Hans Kraemmer).

If *Die Fledermaus* is regarded as operetta, rather than as opera – and in this instance the line is difficult to draw – then it is unsurpassed in the genre, with the proviso that the final Act is dramatically weak, relying too much on the comic skills of the actor who plays Frosch, the jailer. The work was premièred in 1874 in Vienna (where it takes place) and has been in the international repertory ever since.

The story opens in Eisenstein's house. His wife, Rosalinde, is being serenaded (from outside) by Alfred, an old flame. Adèle, her precocious maid, reads aloud a letter from her sister, Ida, who as a member of the ballet is invited that very night to Prince Orlovsky's ball. If Adèle can find a dress, she proposes to join her sister for the occasion, but she also needs to have the night off, so she asks Rosalinde if she can visit her sick aunt.

Unfortunately Rosalinde cannot spare her: Eisenstein, her husband, is due to start a five-day prison sentence, so Adèle must produce and serve a good supper. Adèle departs for the kitchen; meanwhile Alfred enters and tells Rosalinde that, as her husband will be away for some days, he will keep her company. She is not sure if she can resist the advances of a tenor who can sing a top 'A'. Eisenstein enters, blaming his attorney that his sentence has now been increased to eight days. Adèle is still weeping crocodile tears over her sick aunt. Rosalinde goes to look for old clothes suitable as prison garments.

Dr Falke comes in; he has a genuine grievance against Eisenstein, with whom he recently attended a carnival. The doctor had been dressed as a bat (*Fledermaus*) and Eisenstein left him to find his own way home in broad daylight, still wearing his ridiculous costume. Falke seeks revenge, but for the moment he tries to persuade Eisenstein to go to Prince Orlovsky's ball with him. He suggests his prison incarceration might be postponed until the following morning. Eisenstein thinks the idea a capital one.

Rosalinde decides she will go to the ball too – suitably masked. She does not know her husband's plan, and is amazed to find him going to prison in evening dress. But she is even more concerned that Alfred may take his opportunity and turn up at the house that evening. Adèle therefore gets her night off.

Eisenstein departs and Alfred enters, borrows Eisenstein's dressing gown, eats the prepared supper and drinks his fill (*Trinke, Liebchen, trinke schnell*). Now Frank, the new prison governor, makes his entrance. He has come to escort Eisenstein to jail, and assumes that the figure sitting at the table is he. Alfred at first denies this, until Rosalinde asks him how she could possibly be at supper so late with anyone but her husband; so as not to compromise her, Alfred lets Frank hurry him off to the cells – for Frank, too, is going to the ball.

The party at Prince Orlovsky's house is in full swing. Eisenstein is introduced as Marquis Renard. He suspects that the pretty masked girl in what appears to be one of his wife's dresses must be Adèle, the maid, but this suggestion provokes only hilarity among the guests. However, Eisenstein does not recognize his masked wife, who is masquerading as a Hungarian countess and sings a Csárdás to prove it.

Regarding her as a new conquest, he shows her his watch, which he uses as bait for his seductions, and his masked companion resourcefully manages to purloin it. The gaiety continues, the prince proposes a toast to champagne, then finally – Cinderella fashion – a clock strikes, not midnight, but 6 a.m., and Eisenstein remembers his date with the prison jailer.

At the prison, Frosch, the jailer, completely inebriated, has found Alfred's singing – to relieve his own boredom – somewhat tiresome. Frank now appears, and so do Adèle and her sister, whom the amorous governor has promised to take under his wing. Adèle fancies herself as an actress, which was not what Frank had in mind; to get rid of them, they are consigned to a cell.

The 'Marquis Renard' appears next, and he and Alfred are equally astonished at discovering their joint deception. Another lady is announced and, suspecting it to be Rosalinde, Eisenstein borrows the gown, wig and spectacles of his attorney, Dr Blind, as a disguise. But he soon abandons his disguise and then grows stern with both his wife and Alfred, admonishing them for their flagrant behaviour.

Rosalinde turns the tables on him by producing the watch. Finally all ends well, everyone is reconciled, and the hitherto bored Prince Orlovsky says he will look after Adèle's future career. They all drink to the cause of all their mishaps, and one of life's greatest pleasures – champagne.

André Previn has a special relationship with the Vienna Philharmonic, and the collaboration works here to produce an enjoyably idiomatic account of Strauss's masterpiece, yet one which is tautly controlled. This may be a plainer reading than some, avoiding a few traditional hesitations and accelerations when the score plainly indicates '*a tempo*', but it is one which consistently conveys the work's exuberant high spirits. Dame Kiri Te Kanawa's portrait of Rosalinde brings not only gloriously firm, golden sound but also vocal acting with star quality, and the fact that her German accent is less than perfect is turned to advantage. She becomes an Anglo-Saxon Rosalinde, with the occasional phrase or two of English slipped deftly into the dialogue.

Brigitte Fassbaender is the most dominant Prince Orlovsky on disc; for her alone it is worth hearing this set. Singing with a tangy richness and firmness, she emerges as the genuine focus of the party scene, no effete dandy but a tough figure. Her spoken dialogue, throatily delivered, has all the command of Marlene Dietrich in her prime. Edita Gruberová is a sparkling, characterful and full-voiced Adèle, stunningly brilliant in her Act III Couplets. The men soloists are vocally just as strong as the women, though not as characterful. Wolfgang Brendel as Eisenstein and Olaf Bär as Dr Falke both sing very well indeed, though their voices sound too alike. Richard Leech as Alfred provides heady tone and a hint of parody, and the odd opera snippets he trots out in Acts I and III are not overdone.

Tom Krause makes a splendid Frank, the more characterful for no longer sounding young. Anton Wendler as Dr Blind and Otto Schenk as Frosch the jailer give vintage Viennese performances, with Frosch's cavortings well tailored and not too extended.

This now goes to the top of the list of latterday *Fledermaus* recordings, though with one serious reservation. The Philips production in Act II adds a layer of crowd noise as background throughout the Party scene, even during Orlovsky's solos. Such a host would have been furious at being ignored so blatantly, with women shrieking behind. Strauss's gentler moments are then seriously undermined by the sludge of distant chatter and laughter, as in the lovely chorus *Bruderlein und Schwesterlein*, yearningly done.

The only number exempted from background chatter is Rosalinde's great *Heimat* solo and Csárdás, with Dame Kiri soaring expansively. Otherwise the recorded sound is superb, with brilliance and bite alongside warmth and bloom, both immediate and well balanced. The spoken dialogue is well edited and briskly delivered. Like Kleiber on DG, Previn avoids having a series of party-songs in Act II, whether from visitors or principals, and similarly opts for the *Thunder and lightning polka* instead of the ballet.

Karajan's 1955 version (originally issued on Columbia), was produced by Walter Legge and occupies a very special place in the catalogue. This recording has great freshness and clarity along with the polish which for many will make it a first favourite. Tempi at times are unconventional, both slow and fast, but the precision and point of the playing are magical and the singing is endlessly delightful. Schwarzkopf makes an enchanting Rosalinde, not just in the imagination and sparkle of her singing but also in the snatches of spoken dialogue (never too long) which leaven the entertainment.

Needless to say she makes a gloriously commanding entry in the Party scene, which is in every sense a highspot of Walter Legge's production. As Adèle, Rita Streich (like Schwarzkopf, a pupil of Maria Ivogün) produces her most dazzling coloratura; Gedda and Krebs are beautifully contrasted in their tenor tone, and Erich Kunz gives a vintage performance as Falke. The original mono, crisply focused, has been given a brighter edge but otherwise left unmolested.

Though Boskovsky sometimes fails to lean into the seductive rhythms as much as he might, his is a refreshing account of a magic score. Rothenberger is a sweet, domestic-sounding Rosalinde, relaxed and sparkling if edgy at times, while among an excellent supporting cast the Orlovsky of Brigitte Fassbaender must be singled out as the finest on record, tough and firm, as she is also for Previn. The entertainment has been excellently produced for records, with German dialogue inserted, though the ripe recording sometimes makes the voices jump between singing and speaking. The remastering is admirably vivid.

The Karajan Decca version of 1960 was originally issued – with much blazing of publicity trumpets – as a so-called 'gala performance', with various artists from the Decca roster appearing to do their turn at the 'cabaret' included in the Orlovsky ball sequence. This was a famous tradition of performances of *Die Fledermaus* at the New York Met. in the early years of this century. Now Decca have digitally remastered this original version with remarkable effect.

The sound is sparklingly clear, although the ambience now seems rather less natural and the applause in the Party scene somewhat too vociferous. The party pieces now have a vintage appeal and even Tebaldi's *Viljalied* (rather heavy in style) sets off nostalgia for an earlier era. There is a breathtaking display of coloratura from Joan Sutherland in *Il Bacio*, a Basque folksong sung with delicious simplicity by Teresa Berganza, and Leontyne Price is wonderfully at home in Gershwin's *Summertime*. But the most famous item is Simionato and Bastianini's *Anything you can do, I can do better*, sung with more punch than sophistication, but endearingly memorable, over a quarter of a century after it was recorded.

The performance of the opera itself has all the sparkle one could ask for. If anything, Karajan is even more brilliant than he was on the old Columbia mono issue, and the Decca recording is scintillating in its clarity. Where it does fall short, alas, is in the singing. Hilde Gueden is deliciously vivacious as Rosalinde, a beautifully projected interpretation, but vocally she is not perfect, and even her confidence has a drawback in showing how tentative Erika Köth is as Adèle, with her wavering vibrato. Indeed *Mein Herr Marquis* is well below the standard of the best recorded performances.

Waldemar Kmentt has a tight, German-sounding tenor, and Giuseppe Zampieri as Alfred (a bright idea to have a genuine Italian for the part) is no more than adequate. The rest of the cast are very good, but even these few vocal shortcomings are enough to take some of the gilt off the gingerbread. It all depends on what you ask from *Fledermaus*; if it is gaiety and sparkle above everything, then with Karajan in control this is an excellent recommendation, and it certainly cannot be faulted on grounds of recording.

As a bargain CD *Fledermaus*, Ackermann's 1960 recording is hard to beat, with fine singing from nearly all the principals and with its strong Viennese flavour. The sound has a most attractive ambience and a theatrical perspective of considerable depth, while the voices are very natural and clear. The singing is consistently vivacious. Gerda Scheyrer's Rosalinde brings the only relative disappointment, for the voice is not always steady; but Wilma Lipp is a delicious Adèle and Christa Ludwig's Orlovsky is a delight, second only to Brigitte Fassbaender's assumption of this tricky breeches role.

Karl Terkal's Eisenstein and Anton Dermota's Alfred give much pleasure, and Erich Kunz's inebriated Frosch in the finale comes off even without a translation. Ackermann's direction, lacking something in sparkle and subtlety, is polished, with a real Viennese flavour. The sound has come up vividly – there is a nice combination of atmosphere and clarity. Although this is attractively transferred to CD, this set could also be a splendid tape acquisition for the car (and for home listening, too).

It was not originally intended that Plácido Domingo should sing the role of Alfred as well as conducting for the EMI recording of *Fledermaus*, but the tenor who had been originally engaged cancelled at the last minute, and Domingo agreed to do the double job, singing over accompaniments already recorded. The happiness of the occasion is reflected in a strong and amiable, rather than an idiomatically Viennese, performance. If Domingo's conducting lacks the distinction and individuality of some rivals, it is on the whole more satisfying for not drawing attention to itself in irritating mannerisms.

Lucia Popp makes a delectable and provocative Rosalinde, and Seiffert a strong tenor Eisenstein, with Baltsa a superb, characterful Orlovsky. Eva Lind as Adèle sings girlishly, but the voice is not always steady or well focused. The rest of the cast has no weak link. With ensembles vigorous and urgent, this is a consistently warm and sympathetic account. More dialogue than usual is included – but, distractingly, it is recorded in a different, much less reverberant acoustic.

The glory of the DG set is the singing of the two principal women – Julia Varady and Lucia Popp magnificently characterful and stylish as mistress and servant – but much of the rest is controversial to say the least. Many will be delighted by the incisive style of Carlos Kleiber, deliberately rejecting many older conventions. Though he allows plenty of rhythmic flexibility, he is never easy-going, for in every rubato a first concern is for precision of ensemble; and that does not always allow the fun and sparkle of the score to emerge. In its way the result is certainly refreshing, even electrically compelling, and the recording quality, both clear and atmospheric, is admirable. Hermann Prey makes a forthright Eisenstein, but René Kollo sounds lumberingly heavy as Alfred, and as for the falsetto Orlovsky of Ivan Rebroff, it is grotesque. This is so obtrusive (as is the hearty German dialogue) that for many this set will be unacceptable for repeated listening.

In June 1982, Denon engineers recorded their complete performance of *Fledermaus* on stage at the Sun Palace in Fukuoka during the Vienna Volksoper's visit. It is warm, idiomatic and involving, but there are even more snags than in most live recordings. The slabs of spoken dialogue in German sometimes last for four, five or even six minutes at a time, and hardly one of the principals matches in vocal standard what one expects in studio recordings of operetta. As a Viennese veteran, Waldemar Kmentt gives a vividly characterful portrait of Eisenstein, but the voice is painfully strained for much of the time, sometimes not even able to sustain a steady note.

The other men are capable but often raw of tone, at times producing sing-speech. Mirjana Irosch as Rosalinde suffers from a pronounced vibrato, though the weight of voice is apt. Melanie Holliday is a tinkly Adèle in traditional mould; the voice is not always sweet enough, but she rises well to her big numbers. Dagmar Koller as Prince Orlovsky might be a parody of the traditional mezzo in this role, with Greta Garbo-like tones in her spoken dialogue erupting into a wobbly and fruity singing voice. Binder's brisk conducting is consistently sympathetic.

The *Overture* brings exceptionally vivid orchestral sound but, with the addition of stage microphones for the performance proper, the orchestra recedes. There is a great deal of clumping and banging about on stage, and the audience applauds at every conceivable moment. There is no banding, or even indexing, except at the beginnings of Acts.

(i) *Die Fledermaus* (complete). *New Year's Concert 1951* (includes: *Ägyptischer Marsch; Eljen a Magyar; Geschichter aus dem Wiener Wald; Im Krapfenwald'l; Jockey; Die Libelle; Mein Lebenslauf ist Lieb und Lust; Vergnügungszug*).

(M) ((***)) Decca mono 425 990-2 (2) [id.]. (i) V. State Op. Ch.; VPO, Clemens Krauss.

    Rosalinde (Hilde Gueden), Adèle (Wilma Lipp), Eisenstein (Julius Patzak), Alfred (Anton Dermota), Doctor Falke (Alfred Poell), Orlovsky (Sieglinde Wagner), Frank (Kurt Preger).

In many ways this perfectly cast 1950 set of *Die Fledermaus* is the finest ever recorded. It also has a certain niche in recorded history, as it was one of the very first Decca operatic recordings on LP which was to show what treats the new medium was to bring, and it is surely a gramophone classic by any standards. Hilde Gueden is at her most engaging as Rosalinde, Anton Dermota a free-voiced Alfred, and Patzak gives perhaps the last of his great gramophone performances as Eisenstein. Krauss's warm, relaxed conducting consistently conveys a true Viennese flavour, with all the infectious gaiety one could wish for.

The recording is remarkably kind to the voices, but every subsequent transfer since the set was first issued seems to have made the orchestral strings sound worse. They always sounded thin (something to do with the microphones Decca used in those early days), but the CD remastering makes them seem positively emaciated. If your ear can adapt to this singular drawback, then there are no complaints about the documentation, which includes a translation. The fill-up is the first Krauss New Year's concert (though a studio recording), and the playing of the VPO is again unsurpassed. Here the strings have rather more body, but allowances still have to be made.

Die Fledermaus: highlights.
(M) *** EMI CDM7 69598-2 (from above recording with Rothenberger, Holm, Gedda, Fischer-Dieskau; cond. Boskovsky).
*** Teldec/Warner Dig. 4509 91974-2. Edita Gruberová, Barbara Bonney, Werner Hollweg, Josef Protschka, Netherlands Op. Ch., Concg. O, Harnoncourt.

Although an obvious choice for highlights from this delectable opera would be the excellent EMI selection from the Boskovsky set, Harnoncourt's admirers will surely not be disappointed with the vivacious, brightly recorded set of excerpts from his Teldec recording made with the Concertgebouw Orchestra. With the dialogue omitted and 72 minutes of music, virtually all the key numbers are included, and *Mein Herr Marquis*, for instance, also has an introductory section. With a fresh contribution from the Netherlands Opera Chorus and extremely vivid sound, this is most enjoyable.

A Night in Venice (Eine Nacht in Venedig): complete.
Withdrawn: (M) (***) EMI mono CDH7 69530-2 [id.]. Philh. Ch. & O, Ackermann.
    Annina (Elisabeth Schwarzkopf), Duke of Urbino (Nicolai Gedda), Caramello (Erich Kunz).

A Night in Venice was drastically revised by Erich Korngold many years after Strauss's death, and it is that version, further amended, which appears in this charming 'complete' recording. The basic plot is as follows. Within a general atmosphere of rejoicing, Pappacoda congratulates the crowd for acquiring a real maker of macaroni from Naples – himself! He is now approached by young Enrico Piselli, a nephew of Senator Delacqua. Enrico asks Pappacoda to take a note to the senator's beautiful young wife, Barbara, confirming an assignation for that very night. Pappacoda's own sweetheart, Ciboletta, who is Barbara's maid, now meets him; Annina, a young fish seller, also arrives and Pappacoda teases her about her betrothed, Caramello, who is a barber and general factotum working for the Duke of Urbino. Barbara Delacqua makes her entrance and Pappacoda delivers Enrico's message.

The position of steward is vacant at the residence of the duke and Delacqua hopes to fill it. However, as the duke is a renowned lady-killer, Delacqua thinks it would be wise first to send his wife off by gondola to the island of Murano. Hearing of this plan, Barbara, anxious to meet Enrico, arranges for Annina to take her place in the gondola. The duke now arrives and hears from the suspicious senators that their wives cannot accept his invitations to a proposed ball.

Caramello confides in him that a plot is afoot to keep Barbara out of his clutches but that he, Caramello, will circumvent this. Delacqua, seeking the stewardship, thinks it may be useful to dangle Barbara before the duke, if it can later be arranged for someone else to take her place in his bed. Delacqua now waves goodbye to his 'wife' setting off in the gondola – it is, of course, Annina.

The ballroom in the duke's palace is full of guests and Agricola describes the duke to the ladies present as 'the man of a hundred love affairs'. Nevertheless Annina is delighted when she finds herself in the duke's company disguised as Barbara; the duke is equally delighted with her. Various complications follow. Delacqua now introduces Ciboletta to the duke as his 'wife' and she, instead of seeking the position of steward for Delacqua as was arranged, seeks a position of chief cook for Pappacoda.

The duke takes both Annina and Ciboletta out to supper, and they are waited on most unhappily by Caramello and Pappacoda. But fortunately the ladies are not compromised, for at midnight, by custom, everyone must leave for the Piazza San Marco. Here all the deceptions are unravelled. Delacqua finds that Barbara is not away at Murano; Pappacoda is placated when he discovers that he is to be the duke's chef; the duke is philosophical when he learns that Annina had taken Barbara's place. Barbara convinces her husband that she took the wrong gondola and that Enrico looked after her; Caramello becomes the duke's steward, and no doubt the duke is happy as Annina, in consequence, will never be very far away, for she is to be Caramello's wife!

This single EMI mono CD is a superb example of Walter Legge's Philharmonia productions, honeyed and atmospheric. As a sampler, try the jaunty little waltz duet in Act I between Schwarzkopf as the heroine, Annina, and the baritone Erich Kunz as Caramello, normally a tenor role. Nicolai Gedda as the Duke then appropriates the most famous waltz-song of all, the *Gondola song*; but with such a frothy production purism would be out of place. The digital remastering preserves the balance of the mono original admirably. The three LP sides have been fitted nicely on to a single CD. Like *Die Fledermaus*, this is reissued at mid-price in EMI's 'Champagne operetta' series, and the sobriquet could not be more appropriate.

Wiener Blut (complete).

Withdrawn: (M) (***) EMI mono CDH7 69529-2 [id.]. Philh. Ch. & O, Ackermann.
  Gabriele (Elisabeth Schwarzkopf), Zedlau (Nicolai Gedda), Franzi (Erika Köth), Josef (Erich Kunz), Pepi Pleininger (Emmy Loose), Prime Minister (Karl Dönch).

Withdrawn: (M) **(*) EMI CMS7 69943-2 (2). Cologne Op. Ch., Philh. Hungarica, Boskovsky.
  Gabriele (Anneliese Rothenberger), Zedlau (Nicolai Gedda), Franzi (Renata Holm), Josef (Heinz Zednik), Pepi Pleininger (Gabriele Fuchs), Prime Minister (Klaus Hirte).

*(*) Denon Dig. DC 8105/6 [id.]. V. Volksoper Ch. & O, Bibl.
  Gabriele (Siegrid Martikke), Zedlau (Adolf Dallapozza), Franzi (Elisabeth Kales), Josef (Erich Kuchar), Pepi Pleininger (Helga Papouschek), Prime Minister (Karl Dönch).

Wiener Blut is a piece which – with the composer a bored collaborator – was cobbled together from some of his finest ideas. The result may not be a great operetta, with the plot pretty much of a hotch-potch, but in a recording it makes enchanting listening, with the waltz of the title made into the centrepiece.

The story centres on Count Zedlau, ambassador to Vienna from Reuss-Schleiz-Greiz, a mythical state. Its prime minister, Prince Ypsheim-Gindelbach, is in Vienna for a congress. The count whiles away his hours with his mistress, a dancer, Franziska Caliari, but has just returned from a five-day visit to his wife 'for appearance's sake'. The prime minister has thus mistaken the count's wife for his mistress.

The count tells Josef, his valet, that he wants a rendezvous with an attractive mannequin he has just seen, and Josef must arrange the assignation. Josef suggests that they meet at the fête that evening at Hietzing. The mannequin, Pepi Pleininger, comes in. She is Josef's girl-friend, and he does not realize that she is also the lady to whom he has written the letter of assignation. The prime minister enters and assumes that Franziska (Franzi) is the countess, but the real countess now also arrives, and the prime minister chides the count for bringing his 'mistress' to the villa.

As usual in Viennese operetta, there is a ball (this one at Count Bitowsky's residence) to which they all go. The count and the real countess discuss the failure of their marriage and blame it on their lack of true Viennese spirit (*Wienerblut*). He has, in consequence, become a Viennese Don Juan. He sees Pepi among the guests and slips her the note of assignation (previously written by Josef). Pepi recognizes her lover's handwriting and realizes that the note must therefore have come from the count. The real countess assumes that Pepi is already the count's mistress. There are more misunderstandings to come, but finally the count gallantly vouches for Pepi's innocence, identities are sorted out and the visiting prime minister puts it all down to *Wienerblut*!

To have Schwarzkopf at her most ravishing singing a waltz song based on the tune of *Morning Papers* is enough enticement for the old EMI mono recording. Indeed this superbly stylish performance from the mid-1950s shows Walter Legge's flair as a producer at its most compelling, with Schwarzkopf matched by the regular team of Gedda and Kunz, and with Emmy Loose and Erika Köth in the secondary soprano roles. The original mono recording was beautifully balanced, and the face-lift given here is most tactfully achieved.

The stereo set conducted by Willi Boskovsky makes a delightful entertainment, the performance authentic with a strong singing cast. The recording is atmospherically reverberant, but there is no lack of sparkle. For some there will be too much German dialogue, but that is the only reservation. At present this is withdrawn from the catalogue, but many will rest content with the mono version.

This warmly idiomatic performance by the company of the Vienna Volksoper was recorded live in 1982 in Tokyo. Though the fun of the occasion comes over well, the performance is too flawed to give consistent pleasure, and the extended dialogue will please only fluent German speakers, though it is well acted. Both the principal women soloists are shrill of voice, Elisabeth Kales very edgy as the seductive dancer, Franzi, Siegrid Martikke fluttery as the Countess. Dallapozza as the Count gives the most accomplished performance, though even he overacts. Karl Dönch, veteran bass, also director of the Volksoper, makes a welcome appearance in the character role of the princely Prime Minister. The full text is given, together with translations in minuscule print, but no very relevant information about the operetta itself. There is no banding nor even any index points, except at the beginning of Acts. The recording is dry but realistic enough, not helpful to the singers.

Der Zigeunerbaron (The Gypsy Baron): complete.
Withdrawn: (M) (***) EMI mono CDH7 69526-2 (2) [id.]. Philh. Ch. & O, Ackermann.
   Elisabeth Schwarzkopf, Nicolai Gedda, Hermann Prey, Erich Kunz, Erika Köth.

The Gypsy Baron has had a poor showing in the recording studio, which is particularly surprising because there are relatively few Strauss operettas, and by any standards this is outstanding. The plot (much praised in some quarters) is strangely offbeat. It opens in Hungary.

Ottakar, a young peasant, curses the fact that he cannot find the treasure, supposedly hidden in the old ruined castle outside the village. He loves Arsena, the daughter of a rich pig-farmer, who lives nearby. Czipra, an old gypsy woman, mocks his love as impractical. The castle should, by right, belong to Sandor Barinkay. He is hoping to get it back, helped by Conte Carnero, Commissioner of Morals, who is here with him.

Witnesses are required for the official declaration of ownership. Czipra, when asked, says that she is illiterate, then offers to read the hands of Barinkay and Carnero. She predicts that Barinkay will find happiness and wealth through a faithful wife who will tell him through a dream where he can find treasure. Carnero will also find treasure, a considerable amount of it, which he thought he had lost years ago. Carnero is puzzled, for he cannot recall any such loss.

Zsupan, the pig-farmer, is also asked to be a witness to the deed. He too can neither read nor write; but he makes it plain that, if Barinkay is seeking to become his neighbour, he must not think he will achieve possession of the castle without litigation. Barinkay suggests instead that a liaison with Zsupan's daughter could be the answer to any conflict of interest concerning the real estate.

Zsupan calls his daughter, but her governess, Mirabella, emerges instead. She recognizes Carnero as someone lost to her for 24 years. One of the gypsy's prophecies is thus fulfilled. Arsena now appears, veiled, and flatly refuses Barinkay's offer of marriage: she already has a lover; she desires a noble suitor. Barinkay is angry about his failures but consoles himself by having supper with Czipra and her daughter, Saffi.

Arsena's heart lies with Ottakar (who, we already know, returns her feelings) but Barinkay swears vengeance against her for spurning him. Czipra now reveals that Barinkay is the true owner of the castle; he is in fact the Gypsy Baron. Barinkay tells Zsupan he no longer wishes for the hand of his daughter and will marry Saffi instead. Zsupan is now angry too.

Barinkay, Czipra and Saffi have spent the night in the castle and Czipra says that the whereabouts of the castle treasure has been revealed to her in a dream. Barinkay is sceptical but goes looking nevertheless, and sure enough discovers the treasure where the gypsy indicated. After a gypsy chorus which parodies Verdi's *Il Trovatore*, Zsupan insults the gypsies and they retaliate by robbing him of his valuables.

His cries bring forth Carnero, Ottakar and Arsena, followed by Barinkay and Saffi, who are now married. Ottakar says that he thinks he is on the track of the treasure, as he has found a small hoard, but Barinkay disillusions him by telling him that the main cache has already been discovered. Czipra now discloses that Saffi is not her daughter but a princess descended from the last Pasha of Hungary. She can back up her statement with legal proof. Barinkay now feels inferior to his wife and so he, Ottakar and Zsupan will join the army and all go off to the war.

Finally the story moves to Vienna, where everyone gathers to welcome the victorious army. Barinkay, Ottakar and Zsupan have all returned safely. While Zsupan's exploits have not all been of the military kind, Barinkay and Ottakar are heroes and are rewarded with noble titles. Arsena flies to Ottakar and Saffi greets Barinkay lovingly: they can be happy now, for he feels her social equal.

The musical inspiration of this operetta shows Strauss at his most effervescent, and this superb Philharmonia version from the mid-1950s has never been matched in its rich stylishness and polish. Schwarzkopf as the gypsy princess sings radiantly, not least in the heavenly Bullfinch duet (to the melody made famous by MGM as *One day when we were young*). Gedda, still youthful, sings with heady tone, and Erich Kunz as the rough pig-breeder gives a vintage *echt*-Viennese performance of the irresistible *Ja, das schreiben und das lesen*. The CD transcription from excellent mono originals gives fresh and truthful sound, particularly in the voices.

Strauss, Richard (1864-1949)

Die Ägyptische Helena (complete).
(M) **(*) Decca 430 381-2 (2) [id.]. Detroit SO, Dorati.
  Helena (Gwyneth Jones), Menelaus (Matti Kastu), Hermione / 1st Elf (Dinah Bryant), Aithra
  (Barbara Hendricks), Altair (Willard White).

Last of the six operas in which Strauss collaborated with Hugo von Hofmannsthal, this grand
classical extravaganza was initially designed as a vehicle for the glamorous soprano, Maria
Jeritza (famous above all for her provocative Tosca), and the tenor, Richard Tauber.
Hofmannsthal's device of mingling two Helen legends has an element of jokiness in it, but
Ancient Greece, as so often with Strauss, prompted some heavyweight orchestral writing (echoes
of *Elektra*).

The opera opens with the Trojan War over. In her palace Aithra has a vision of Menelaus and
Helena, the fairest of women, whom her husband is about to kill in revenge for her
unfaithfulness with Paris. Aithra causes a storm to wreck the vessel and soon Menelaus enters,
bearing his golden-haired wife. Aithra intervenes before he can carry out his vow and gives him
a potion of forgetfulness which makes him believe that Helena had been absent and safe from
the touch of man for ten years. The Helen who associated with Paris was a ghostly spirit. Aithra
transports Menelaus and Helena to a distant land where they are lovers once more, with a vision
of happiness.

We are now in a palm grove near the Atlas mountains. Menelaus and Helena waken, refreshed
after their magical journey and their night together. But Menelaus is still confused about the
identity of Helena. Altair, a chieftain, now comes in with his son, Da-Ud, and his followers, and
they bow before Helena. Altair is obviously greatly attracted to Helena. Menelaus is jealous and
again remembers Paris. Helena comforts him and he is invited to join a hunt, led by Da-Ud.

They go off and Aithra returns and tells Helena that the potion she administered to cause
forgetfulness had an antidote with it, so Helena mixes the two potions together for Menelaus.
Meanwhile Altair returns and declares his passion for Helena. The jealous Menelaus and Da-Ud
engage in combat and Da-Ud is slain.

The mixed potion is given to Menelaus; it brings him to his senses, and he stretches out his
arms and embraces Helena. Altair is now the one to be jealous, but Aithra reappears and forbids
him to interfere. Hermione, daughter of Helena and Menelaus, now arrives and is delighted to
see her mother, and the family are all reconciled.

Dorati, using the original Dresden version of the score, draws magnificent sounds from the
Detroit orchestra, richly and forwardly recorded. The vocal sounds are less consistently pleasing.
Gwyneth Jones has her squally moments as Helena, though it is a commanding performance.
Matti Kastu manages as well as any Heldentenor today in the role of Menelaus, strained at times
but with a pleasing and distinctive timbre. The others too are not always helped by the closeness,
but this remains a richly enjoyable as well as a valuable set.

Arabella (complete).
*** Orfeo Dig. C 169882H (2). Bav. State Op. Ch. & O, Sawallisch.
  Arabella (Julia Varady), Zdenka (Helen Donath), Mandryka (Dietrich Fischer-Dieskau),
  Waldner (Walter Berry), Adelaide (Helga Schmidt), Matteo (Adolf Dallapozza).
*** Decca Dig. 417 623-2 (3) [id.]. ROHCG Ch. & O, Tate.
  Arabella (Kiri Te Kanawa), Zdenka (Gabriele Fontana), Mandryka (Franz Grundheber),
  Waldner (Ernst Gutstein), Adelaide (Helga Dernesch), Matteo (Peter Seiffert).
(M) **(*) Decca 430 387-2 (2) [id.]. V. State Op. Ch., VPO, Solti.
  Arabella (Lisa Della Casa), Zdenka (Hilde Gueden), Mandryka (George London), Waldner
  (Otto Edelmann), Adelaide (Ira Malaniuk), Matteo (Anton Dermota).
(M) ** DG 437 700-2 (2) [id.]. Bav. State Op. Ch. & O, Keilberth.
  Arabella (Lisa Della Casa), Zdenka (Anneliese Rothenberger), Mandryka (Dietrich Fischer-
  Dieskau), Waldner (Karl Christian Kohn), Adelaide (Ira Malaniuk), Matteo (Georg Paskuda).

Strauss's highly romantic opera, *Arabella*, with its 'Mr Right' lined up for the heroine, brings
one of his most inspired and charming scores. It takes place in Vienna in the middle of the last
century.

The impoverished aristocratic Waldner family lives in a suite of hotel rooms. Graf Waldner is
a gambler – and not a lucky one. The only hope for the future of the family lies with their
beautiful elder daughter – provided she can find a rich husband. Their younger daughter,

Zdenka, has been brought up as a boy. Her parents wanted a boy, and anyway her mother could not possibly afford to have two daughters 'coming out' at nearly the same time.

Matteo arrives, an army officer who is in love with Arabella. He has received a letter from her (which in fact Zdenka wrote), and asks her whereabouts. She has ignored him until now, and he might well have killed himself. He leaves. Zdenka is upset; she loves him, but he thinks she is a boy!

Arabella and her sister are close, and now they talk together. Arabella has no possible interest in Matteo and tells her sister that she knows that one day the right man will come along. That very afternoon she had briefly met a stranger, and she thinks she has seen him pass by the window, and she wonders if he is her 'Mr Right'. However, she is distracted when Elemer, one of her three official suitors, comes to take her for a sleigh ride. She goes to get ready.

The count has lost more money and is getting desperate. Letters for help have remained unanswered, notably one from an old friend, Mandryka, both rich and eccentric, who he thought would not fail him. There is a knock at the door and a servant announces that a gentleman has called to see Graf Waldner. It is, of course, Mandryka – not the old man, but the nephew, his heir. It seems that he has fallen in love with the photograph of Arabella which her father had sent with his letter, and he wishes to marry her. To finance his journey to Vienna he has sold some forests! He offers Waldner two thousand-gulder notes. Arabella's father can scarcely believe his eyes and ears.

Matteo now confides in Zdenka again. He is desperate to hear from Arabella. Zdenka tells him that she might communicate with him at the Fiakerball that very night (a *Fiaker* is a Viennese two-horse cab). Arabella now leaves for her sleigh-ride dreaming of a romantic stranger.

When Arabella and Mandryka meet that night at the ball, she recognizes him as her stranger and immediately knows he is the 'Mr Right' she has been waiting for. He thinks she is far more beautiful than her picture. They are in love. Mandryka tells her that in his country (Croatia) a glass of water is given by a girl to her betrothed as a token of her commitment to him. Arabella asks Mandryka to give her an hour to herself to adjust to the end of her girlhood.

She never gives Matteo a glance all evening, but Zdenka tries to reassure him, saying that Arabella relies on his love but cannot show her own feelings, then she gives him another letter purporting to come from Arabella, which contains a key. If he comes to Arabella's room in a quarter of an hour, he will receive everything he longs for.

Matteo is astounded – and so is Mandryka, who overhears the arrangement for the assignation. Mandryka flirts with Fiakermilli, a pretty girl, self-consciously glamorous, who had brought Arabella a romantic bouquet, symbolic of her betrothal. Mandryka then receives a genuine note from Arabella, saying she has gone home and that she will be his on the morrow. Wanting to find out the truth, he proceeds back to the hotel with her parents.

The story now continues in the hotel lobby. Matteo is seen descending the stairs, not displeased with himself. Arabella enters and dances happily around, and Matteo is obviously surprised to see her in the hall. He cannot understand her coolness; she cannot appreciate his ardour. Mandryka and her parents enter and Mandryka immediately recognizes Matteo as the man to whom the room-key was given at the ball. He fears the worst, Arabella's protestations of innocence are unheeded, and a duel between the two men is prevented only by the appearance of Zdenka in a negligée, with her hair down, no longer looking a bit like a boy.

She threatens to throw herself in the Danube, and then tells all. The key was to her room, it was pitch-dark and Matteo could not possibly have known that the woman who so warmly gave herself to him was she and not Arabella. All is cleared up, the marriage can go ahead, but Arabella asks for a glass of water and thoughtfully takes it with her as she slowly ascends the staircase. Mandryka is thoroughly ashamed of his suspicions. Then Arabella returns down the stairs, equally deliberately, and holds out the glass of water to him.

This Orfeo set of *Arabella* has an immediate advantage over the Decca version with Kiri Te Kanawa in being on two CDs against the three for the Decca. Both as a performance and in sound-quality it is splendid in every way. The understanding of Sawallisch matches the characterful tenderness of Julia Varady as the heroine and Fischer-Dieskau's fine-detailed characterization of the gruff Mandryka, *der Richtige*, the heroine's 'Mr Right'. Helen Donath too is charming as the younger sister, Zdenka, though the voice might be more sharply contrasted. If there are unappealing elements in an opera which would reach a happy ending far too quickly but for uncongenial twists of plot, this recording clothes them in an authentic Straussian glow of richness and charm. Highly recommended.

Jeffrey Tate's set is most beautifully played and recorded. If with Dame Kiri Te Kanawa in the name-part it might have turned into just another sweetmeat recording for the great soprano, to be classed with her golden discs of Broadway musicals, in fact it brings one of her very finest opera performances on record. She even outshines the most famous of recorded Arabellas, Lisa della Casa, not only in the firm beauty of her voice, but in the word-pointing and detailed characterization.

It is a radiant portrait, languorously beautiful, and it is a pity that so unsuited a soprano as Gabriele Fontana should have been chosen as Zdenka next to her, sounding all the more shrill by contrast. Franz Grundheber makes a firm, virile Mandryka, Peter Seiffert a first-rate Matteo, while Helga Dernesch is outstandingly characterful as Arabella's mother. Though Tate's conducting is richly sympathetic, bringing out the sumptuousness of the score – helped by brilliant Decca recording – his speeds at times are dangerously slow, which might possibly worry established Straussians, if hardly anyone else.

Della Casa soars above the stave with the creamiest, most beautiful sounds and constantly charms one with her swiftly alternating moods of seriousness and gaiety. One moment one thinks of in particular is where in Act I she sees the stranger, *der Richtige* ('Mr Right'), through her window, later to appear as Mandryka. Della Casa conveys wonderfully the pain and disappointment of frustrated young love as the man turns away and passes on. Perhaps Solti does not linger as he might over the waltz rhythms, and it may be Solti too who prevents Edelmann from making his first scene with Mandryka as genuinely humorous as it can be, with the Count's *Teschek, bedien'dich* as he goggles at Mandryka's generosity.

Edelmann otherwise is superb, as fine a Count as he was an Ochs in the Karajan *Rosenkavalier*. Gueden, too, is ideally cast as Zdenka and, if anything, in Act I manages to steal our sympathies from Arabella, as a good Zdenka can. George London is on the ungainly side, but then Mandryka is a boorish fellow anyway. Dermota is a fine Matteo, and Mimi Coertse makes as much sense as anyone could of the ridiculously difficult part of Fiakermilli, the female yodeller. The 1958 recording still sounds amazingly brilliant, though some of the effects could have been more realistic, such as the bells of Elemer's sleigh outside the hotel.

Keilberth's DG set was taken from a live performance celebrating the opening of the Munich Opera House, and inevitably there are the usual noises and distractions that tend to disfigure theatre performances. The sound is certainly no better and probably not as convincing as the earlier, Decca set, made in 1957, and the conducting of Keilberth is considerably less crisp than Solti's then. Moreover Lisa della Casa had in the meantime lost a great deal of the bloom from her voice. Fischer-Dieskau, however, gives a masterly account of the part of Mandryka, far fuller, more mature and beautiful than George London's on Decca. There are a number of minor cuts and the Munich version is used, telescoping Acts II and III together in a way approved by the composer.

(i) *Arabella*: excerpts. (ii) *Capriccio: closing scene. Four Last Songs.*
(M) (***) EMI mono CDH7 61001-2 [id.]. Elisabeth Schwarzkopf, with (i) Anny Felbermayer, Anton Metternich, Nicolai Gedda, Philh. O, Matačić; (ii) Philh. O, Ackermann.

As part of an exceptionally generous collection of classic mono recordings, Schwarzkopf's 1953 version of the closing scene from *Capriccio* comes on the mid-price Références label with both its original coupling, the *Four Last Songs*, also recorded in 1953, and the four major excerpts from *Arabella* (over half an hour of music), which she recorded two years later. This is singing of supreme artistry. Fascinatingly, this separate account of the *Capriccio* scene is even more ravishing than the one in the complete set, also reissued on CD, and the sound is even fuller, astonishing for its period. In the *Arabella* excerpts von Matačić is a richly idiomatic conductor, with Metternich superb as Mandryka, though Anny Felbermeyer is a less distinguished Zdenka. The *Four Last Songs* are here less reflective, less sensuous, than in Schwarzkopf's later version with Szell, but the more flowing speeds and the extra tautness and freshness of voice bring equally illuminating performances. Excellent transfers.

Ariadne auf Naxos (complete).
⊛ (M) (***) EMI mono CMS7 69296-2 (2) [Ang. CDMB 69296]. Philh. O, Karajan.
   Ariadne (Elisabeth Schwarzkopf), Composer (Irmgard Seefried), Zerbinetta (Rita Streich), Bacchus (Rudolf Schock), Music Master (Karl Dönch), Harlequin (Hermann Prey), Dancing Master (Hugues Cuénod), Majordomo (Alfred Neugebauer).
*** Ph. Dig. 422 084-2; *422 084-4* (2) [id.]. Leipzig GO, Masur.
   Ariadne (Jessye Norman), Composer (Julia Varady), Zerbinetta (Edita Gruberová), Bacchus (Paul Frey), Music Master (Dietrich Fischer-Dieskau), Harlequin (Olaf Bär), Dancing Master (Martin Finke), Majordomo (Rudolf Asmus).

(M) **(*) Decca 430 384-2 (2) [id.]. LPO, Solti.

    Ariadne (Leontyne Price), Composer (Tatiana Troyanos), Zerbinetta (Edita Gruberová), Bacchus (René Kollo), Music Master (Walter Berry), Harlequin (Barry McDaniel), Dancing Master (Heinz Zednik), Majordomo (Erich Kunz).

(M) **(*) EMI CMS7 64159-2 (2). Dresden State Op. O, Kempe.

    Primadonna / Ariadne (Gundula Janowitz), Zerbinetta (Sylvia Geszty), Composer (Teresa Zylis-Gara), Tenor / Bacchus (James King), Dancing Master (Peter Schreier), Harlequin (Hermann Prey).

**(*) DG Dig. 419 225-2 (2) [id.]. VPO, Levine.

    Ariadne (Anna Tomowa-Sintow), Composer (Agnes Baltsa), Zerbinetta (Kathleen Battle), Bacchus (Gary Lakes), Music Master (Hermann Prey), Harlequin (Urban Malmberg), Dancing Master (Heinz Zednik), Majordomo (Otto Schenk).

Ariadne auf Naxos was originally planned as a one-Acter to fill a double bill, following after a performance of Molière's play, *Le bourgeois gentilhomme*. When this plan failed to work out, Hofmannsthal, the librettist, in collaboration with the composer, extended the piece with a Prologue, so providing a full evening's entertainment.

The Prologue takes place in a private theatre in a Viennese mansion. Backstage the music master complains to the major-domo that the effect of the serious opera to be performed that evening will be ruined if the planned harlequinade should follow it. The serious opera, *Ariadne*, is a composition by his pupil. The composer is disheartened by the news, even more so when he hears that the two works are to be intermingled. But Zerbinetta persuades him that in the theatre anything and everything is possible and all will be well.

The opera begins on the seashore. Ariadne is asleep and three nymphs are watching over her. When she wakes up, all is melancholy: she loves Theseus but can think only of death. Zerbinetta and her friends try to cheer her up but, when she fails to make any impression, Zerbinetta is philosophical about men and love, drawing on her own unsatisfactory experience. Ariadne retires to her cave, and Harlequin then makes a pass at Zerbinetta and, as he perseveres, finally wins her over to his embrace.

The nymphs gleefully announce the coming of Bacchus; he has escaped from the enchantress, Circe. Hearing him arrive, Ariadne emerges from her cave and welcomes him, thinking he is Hermes, the spirit of death, and she sinks into his arms. Bacchus does not mind this at all, for she is very attractive, and very soon Ariadne's death wish changes to passion which is very much of this world. The trio of nymphs are again apparent, but they are more cheerful now, and Zerbinetta thinks this a capital end to the story.

Karajan's 1954 recording of *Ariadne* brings a performance that even he has rarely matched on record. This classic recording, with a cast never likely to be equalled, is all the more cherishable in this excellent CD transfer on two discs at mid-price. Though the absence of translation in the libretto is a pity, the many index points on CD, cued to the synopsis, can be used almost as easily as a translation alongside the original German words. Elisabeth Schwarzkopf makes a radiant, deeply moving Ariadne, giving as bonus a delicious little portrait of the Prima Donna in the Prologue.

Rita Streich was at her most vivacious in the coloratura of Zerbinetta's aria and, in partnership with the harlequinade characters, sparkles dazzlingly. But it is Irmgard Seefried who gives perhaps the supreme performance of all as the Composer, exceptionally beautiful of tone, conveying a depth and intensity rarely if ever matched. Rudolf Schock is a fine Bacchus, strained less than most, and the team of theatrical characters includes such stars as Hugues Cuénod as the Dancing Master. The fine pacing and delectably pointed ensemble add to the impact of a uniquely perceptive Karajan interpretation. Though in mono and with the orchestral sound a little dry, the voices come out superbly, more vivid than ever they were in the days of LP.

It was with Kurt Masur and the Leipzig Gewandhaus Orchestra that Jessye Norman made one of her most radiant records – of Strauss's *Four Last Songs*. It was an inspired idea for her to return to Leipzig to sing more Strauss, here the title-role in *Ariadne auf Naxos*. Again it is a commanding, noble, deeply felt performance, ranging extraordinarily wide; but Norman does not quite find the same raptness, the inner agony that still makes Elisabeth Schwarzkopf's performance on Karajan's classic mono set unique. Nevertheless Norman provides the perfect focus for a cast as near ideal as anyone could assemble today. Fine as the cast is for Levine's DG set of a year earlier, the Philips one improves on it all the way round. Julia Varady as the

Composer is beautifully cast, bringing out the vulnerability of the character, as well as the ardour, in radiant singing.

The Zerbinetta of Edita Gruberová adds an extra dimension to previous recordings – even to the example of Rita Streich for Karajan – in the way she translates the panache of her stage performance into purely aural terms for recording: at the end of her big aria, the coloratura is thrown off with such defiant swagger you want to stand up and cheer, as indeed in the opera house you would. It is a thrilling performance and, even if the voice is not always ideally sweet, the range of emotions Gruberová conveys, as in her duet with the Composer, is enchanting.

Paul Frey is the sweetest-sounding Bacchus on record yet, lacking just a little in ardour but singing with heady beauty and no sense of strain. Olaf Bär as Harlequin and Dietrich Fischer-Dieskau in the vignette role of the Music Master are typical of the fine team of artists here in the smaller character parts. Masur proves not only a masterly Straussian in the emotional music relating to the tragedy of Ariadne but also in the rhythmic pointing of the harlequinade, regularly preferring speeds on the fast side, but never sounding too taut or breathless. He is helped by the typically warm Leipzig recording, with sound rich and mellow to cocoon the listener, yet finely balanced to allow you to hear the interweaving of the piano as never before, in twentieth-century imitation of a continuo.

Brilliance is the keynote of Solti's set of *Ariadne*. This extraordinary confection has so many elements that within its chosen limits this reading is most powerful and compelling, with very lively playing and recording as well as some strong singing. What the performance is short of is charm and warmth. Everything is so brightly lit that much of the delicacy and tenderness of the writing tends to disappear. Nevertheless the concentration of Solti in Strauss is never in doubt, and though Leontyne Price has given more beautiful performances on record she makes a strong central figure, memorably characterful. Tatiana Troyanos is affecting as the Composer and, as in the Masur set, Edita Gruberová establishes herself as the unrivalled Zerbinetta of her generation, though here she is less delicate than on stage. René Kollo similarly is an impressive Bacchus. The Decca CD transfer is characteristically vivid.

Kempe's relaxed, languishing performance of this most atmospheric of Strauss operas is matched by opulent recording, warmly transferred to CD. Janowitz sings with heavenly tone-colour (marred only when hard-pressed at the climax of the *Lament*), and Zylis-Gara makes an ardent and understanding Composer. Sylvia Geszty's voice is a little heavy for the fantastic coloratura of Zerbinetta's part, but she sings with charm and assurance. James King presents the part of Bacchus with forthright tone and more taste than most tenors. Compared with Karajan's mono set with Schwarzkopf, this is less than ideal, but that has rather dry mono sound and here there is warmth and atmosphere in plenty, and there is a price advantage over the Philips digital stereo set with Jessye Norman.

James Levine conducts a spacious, sumptuously textured reading of *Ariadne* which almost makes you forget that it uses a chamber orchestra. As Ariadne herself, Tomowa-Sintow with her rich, dramatic soprano adds to the sense of grandeur and movingly brings out the vulnerability of the character. But ultimately she fails to create as fully rounded and detailed a character as her finest rivals, and the voice, as recorded, loses its bloom and creaminess under pressure, marring the big climaxes.

Both Agnes Baltsa as the Composer and Kathleen Battle as Zerbinetta are excellent: the one tougher than most rivals with her mezzo-soprano ring, little troubled by the high tessitura, the other delectably vivacious, dazzling in coloratura, but equally finding the unexpected tenderness in the character, the underlying sadness clearly implied in the Prologue duet with the Composer. She brings home just why the boy is so enamoured. The *commedia dell'arte* characters and the attendant theatrical team are strongly taken by stalwarts of the Vienna State Opera, among them Kurt Rydl, Hermann Prey and Heinz Zednik, while the Heldentenor role of Bacchus, always hard to cast, is strongly taken by Gary Lakes, clear-toned and firm, at times pinched but never strained. On tape the voices and orchestra are smooth and natural, but the sound is bass- and middle-orientated, with some lack of definition at the top.

Capriccio (complete).
(***) EMI mono CDS7 49014-8 (2) [Ang. CDCB 49014]. Philh. O, Sawallisch.
  Countess (Elisabeth Schwarzkopf), Count (Eberhard Waechter), Flamand (Nicolai Gedda), Olivier (Dietrich Fischer-Dieskau), La Roche (Hans Hotter), Clairon (Christa Ludwig), Italian soprano (Anna Moffo).
*** DG 419 023-2 (2) [id.]. Bav. R. O, Boehm.
  Countess (Gundula Janowitz), Count (Dietrich Fischer-Dieskau), Flamand (Peter Schreier),

Olivier (Hermann Prey), La Roche (Karl Ridderbusch), Clairon (Tatiana Troyanos), Italian soprano (Arleen Augér).

Who else but Strauss, in this very last of his operas, would have dared so seductively to present a dialogue on the rival demands of words and music in dramatic form? In a salon in a Paris château, where the young widowed Countess Madeleine is celebrating her birthday, a young musician, Flamand, has written the music, Olivier the drama. Flamand and Olivier in their opposing views and interests are also seeking the hand of the countess, while her brother, the count, is preoccupied with a romantic liaison with Clairon. In the end the countess cannot make up her mind between her two artistic suitors.

In the role of the Countess, Elisabeth Schwarzkopf has had no equals. This recording, made in 1957 and 1958, brings a peerless performance from her, full of magical detail both in the pointing of words and in the presentation of the character in all its variety. That is in addition to the sheer beauty of the voice, poised and pure, shaded with immaculate control. For this recording, Schwarzkopf's husband, Walter Legge, as recording manager assembled a cast as starry as could ever be imagined. Not only are the other singers ideal choices in each instance, they form a wonderfully co-ordinated team, beautifully held together by Sawallisch's sensitive conducting.

Even such a vignette role as that of the Italian soprano is taken by Anna Moffo. As a performance this is never likely to be superseded, and it comes as one of the most cherishable of operatic reissues on CD. The pity is that for technical reasons a stereo tape was never completed during the original sessions. The mono sound presents the voices with fine bloom and presence, but the digital transfer makes the orchestra a little dry and relatively backward by comparison.

In this elusive opera it is impossible to avoid comparison with Sawallisch's classic mono version with Schwarzkopf and Fischer-Dieskau. Janowitz is not as characterful and pointful a Countess as one really needs (and no match for Schwarzkopf), but Boehm lovingly directs a most beautiful performance of a radiant score, very consistently cast, beautifully sung and very well recorded for its period (1971). There is full documentation, including translation.

Capriccio: Moonlight music and monologue (closing scene). *Four Last Songs. Die heiligen drei Könige.*
**(*) DG Dig. 419 188-2 [id.]. Anna Tomowa-Sintow, BPO, Karajan.

Before he made this recording of the closing scene from *Capriccio* with Anna Tomowa-Sintow, Karajan, supreme Straussian, had never previously conducted Strauss's last opera. It is a ravishing performance from him and the Berlin Philharmonic, with one of his favourite sopranos responding warmly and sympathetically, if without the final touch of individual imagination that such inspired music cries out for. Similarly in the other late, great masterpiece, the *Four Last Songs*, Tomowa-Sintow's lovely, creamy-toned singing tends – even less aptly – to take second place in the attention. The orchestral version of Strauss's nativity-story song makes an attractive if hardly generous extra item. Warm recording, lacking a little in sense of realism and presence.

Capriccio: closing scene; Daphne: closing scene.
*(*) Chan. Dig. CHAN 8364 [id.]. Carole Farley, RTBF SO, Serebrier.

This couples two of the loveliest soprano passages from Strauss's later operas, potentially a magical coupling, but not when Carole Farley's voice is imperfectly controlled, too edgy and fluttery for this music. She is balanced close to make every word clear; the orchestral sound is vividly caught, though the fruity horn at the start of the *Capriccio* momentarily makes it sound like a brass band playing softly. Texts and translations are given.

Daphne (complete).
Withdrawn: *** EMI Dig. CDS7 49309-2 (2) [Ang. CDCB 49309]. Bav. R. Ch. and SO, Haitink.
Daphne (Lucia Popp), Apollo (Reiner Goldberg), Peneios (Kurt Moll), Leukippos (Peter Schreier), Gaea (Ortrun Wenkel).
*** DG 423 579-2 (2) [id.]. V. State Op. Ch., VPO, Boehm.
Daphne (Hilde Gueden), Apollo (James King), Peneios (Paul Schoeffler), Leukippos (Fritz Wunderlich), Gaea (Vera Little).

Strauss wrote this opera not long before the Second World War, at a time when he was being almost universally accused of simply repeating himself. He turned several times to Greek classical sources, remembering the success of *Ariadne auf Naxos*, but in this delicately beautiful one-Act (100-minute) piece, he gave clear indication of what mastery was to come in his last 'classical' period of *Metamorphosen*, the *Oboe concerto* and the *Four Last Songs*. On record this amiable telling of the story of the nymph Daphne wooed by Apollo and finally turned into a tree makes delightful entertainment.

As the curtain rises we see Peneios' hut within a pastoral setting and shepherds discuss the coming feast day in honour of Dionysus. Daphne now enters, full of love for nature. When a childhood friend, Leukippos, declares his love for her, she rejects him, for her feelings towards him are merely sisterly. She refuses when her mother, Gaea, tries to make her dress up for the festivities. Peneios, Daphne's father, now appears and, pointing to Mount Olympus, says that one day the gods will return among the people.

A stranger appears; it is Apollo, dressed as a shepherd. But he goes unrecognized; rather, they all make fun of him and he is left in Daphne's care. He is attracted to her, calls her 'sister', and says he saw her from his chariot. She does not know who he is but says how she hates to be parted from the sun, laying her head upon his breast. But she is disconcerted when he talks of love.

The feast now commences in praise of Dionysus, and both Daphne and Apollo participate. Suddenly Apollo reveals his identity with a clap of thunder, and at the same time Leukippos declares himself Daphne's suitor. Apollo shoots him with an arrow. Daphne comforts Leukippos, realizing that he is dying, and Apollo is filled with regret at his own impulsive action. He begs Zeus to forgive him for interfering in the affairs of mortals but asks that Daphne be given to him as one of the trees, which she loves so much. Daphne duly changes into a laurel tree and achieves a unique kind of immortality.

Haitink with his fine Bavarian forces takes a rather more restrained and spacious view of the piece than did Karl Boehm, one of whose live performances in Vienna was recorded by DG and has emerged, despite dated sound, with extra freshness and dramatic point on a CD set that for many will be even more involving. However, there are many gains in a studio performance, with beauty of balance so important in this score. The cast is a fine one with Lucia Popp an enchanting, girlish Daphne, Peter Schreier bringing Lieder-like feeling for detail to the role of Leukippos, and Reiner Goldberg producing heroic sounds as Apollo, with little feeling of strain and with no coarseness. Kurt Moll is a fine Peneios. The recording is exceptionally rich yet refined too. The CD transfer brings out the atmospheric beauty of the sound all the more. Sadly, as in other EMI reissues of rare Strauss operas on CD, there is no translation accompanying the libretto.

The DG set is a live recording, made during the 1964 Vienna Festival, and it provides an enticing alternative. It could hardly be better cast, with the tenors James King as Apollo and Fritz Wunderlich as Leukippos both magnificent. Hilde Gueden makes a delectable Daphne and gives one of her finest performances on record, while Karl Boehm, the opera's dedicatee, brings out the work's mellowness without any loss of vitality. The DG documentation is superior to the EMI set, with full translation included.

Elektra (complete).
*** Decca 417 345-2 (2) [id.]. V. State Op. Ch., VPO, Solti.
   Elektra (Birgit Nilsson), Klytemnestra (Regina Resnik), Chrysothemis (Marie Collier), Aegisthus (Gerhard Stolze), Orestes (Tom Krause), Tutor (Tugomir Franc).
**(*) EMI Dig. CDS7 54067-2 (2) [Ang. CDCB 54067]; *EX* 754067-4. Bav. R. Ch. & SO, Sawallisch.
   Elektra (Eva Marton), Klytemnestra (Marjana Lipovšek), Chrysothemis (Cheryl Studer), Aegisthus (Hermann Winkler), Orestes (Bernd Weikl), Tutor (Kurt Moll).
Withdrawn: ** Ph. Dig. 422 574-2; *422 574-4* [id.]. Boston SO, Ozawa.
   Elektra (Hildegard Behrens), Klytemnestra (Christa Ludwig), Chrysothemis (Nadine Secunde), Aegisthus (Ragnar Ulfung), Orestes (Jorma Hynninen), Tutor (Brian Matthews).
(M) ** DG 431 737-2 (2) [id.]. Dresden State Op. Ch. & State O, Boehm.
   Elektra (Inge Borkh), Klytemnestra (Jean Madeira), Chrysothemis (Marianna Schech), Aegisthus (Fritz Uhl), Orestes (Dietrich Fischer-Dieskau), Tutor (Fred Teschler).
* HM Rodolphe RPC 32420/21 [id.]. Fr. R. Ch., Fr. Nat. O, Perick.
   Elektra (Ute Vinzing), Klytemnestra (Maureen Forrester), Chrysothemis (Leonie Rysanek), Aegisthus (Horst Hiestermann), Orestes (Bent Norup), Tutor (Hanna Schaer).

Strauss's *Elektra* is based on a poem by Hugo von Hofmannsthal, and its darkness of atmosphere and the bitterness of the tragedy drew from him one of his most powerful scores. It was first heard in Dresden in 1909.

The curtain rises on an inner court at Mycenae. Elektra, feared and hated by her mother

Klytemnestra and stepfather Aegisthus, lives and eats like a dog. Her father, Agamemnon, was murdered by his wife and her lover, and Elektra anticipates a time when she and her brother, Orestes, will be avenged. Chrysothemis now joins her sister. She is less obsessed about revenge but is fearful for their future. Klytemnestra is a bloated, decaying creature, tormented by dreams.

Elektra tells her that there is a married woman who might be killed with an axe to expiate her sins, then reveals that she means her mother. She asks for her brother to be brought back from exile and warns Klytemnestra that she will be a victim of the gods. Chrysothemis brings news of Orestes' demise, dragged to death by his own horses, and she refuses to help Elektra with any plans for revenge. Elektra is now seen digging frantically in the courtyard for the fatal axe.

A stranger watches her and declares that he and another have brought news of Orestes' death. But when Elektra is obviously heart-broken, he reveals that Orestes is not dead, indeed it is he, and after kissing his sister's hand Orestes now enters the palace and a terrible shriek is heard. Aegisthus follows soon after and is surprised when Elektra offers to light his way into the palace.

He is soon seen and heard crying for help himself, but he cannot avoid his fate at Orestes' hands. Elektra dances ecstatically, like a demon, then suddenly collapses and dies. Chryso-themis bangs on the palace door, crying out her brother's name.

The Decca set of *Elektra* was a *tour de force* of John Culshaw and his engineering team. Not everyone will approve of the superimposed sound-effects, but as in Wagner every one of them has justification in the score, and the end result is a magnificently vivid operatic experience created without the help of vision. Nilsson is almost incomparable in the name-part, with the hard side of Elektra's character brutally dominant. Only when – as in the recognition scene with Orestes – she tries to soften the naturally bright tone does she let out a suspect flat note or two.

As a rule she is searingly accurate in approaching even the most formidable exposed top notes. One might draw a parallel with Solti's direction – sharply focused and brilliant in the savage music which predominates, but lacking the languorous warmth one really needs in the recognition scene, if only for contrast. Those who remember Beecham's old 78-r.p.m. set of the final scene may not be completely won over by Solti, but there is no rival to match this in dramatic power. The brilliance of the 1967 Decca recording is brought out the more in the digital transfer on CD, aptly so in this work. The fullness and clarity are amazing for the period.

Sawallisch may miss the full violence of Strauss's score, which the fierce Solti so brilliantly captures in his vintage Decca version, but, with its warm, wide-ranging sound, the EMI set conveys more light and shade, more mystery. Eva Marton in her characterization of the tormented heroine similarly finds more light and shade than Birgit Nilsson did for Solti, but the voice spreads distressingly under pressure. Notably disappointing is the failure of both singer and conductor to convey the full emotional thrust of Elektra's radiant solo after the great moment of recognition between her and her brother, Orestes (Bernd Weikl in fine, incisive voice). Lipovšek's Klytemnestra is the finest yet on record, and Cheryl Studer as Chrysothemis, well contrasted in bright clarity, has wonderful moments, notably in her solo after the murders. This is the finest of modern digital versions.

Ozawa's version of *Elektra* was recorded at live performances of the opera in Boston in 1988, using the stage cuts. Its great glory is the singing of Hildegard Behrens in the name-part, perhaps finer here than she has ever been on record. Hers is a portrayal that movingly brings out the tenderness and vulnerability in this character, as well as the unbalanced ferocity. She it is – with Christa Ludwig a marvellous foil as Klytemnestra, searingly intense, letting out a spine-chilling off-stage scream at her murder – who provides the performance's dramatic tension, rather than the conductor.

Though this is a live recording, it lacks the very quality which may justify the inevitable flaws in such a project: an underlying emotional thrust. The tension-building passage leading to Elektra's recognition of Orestes is plodding and prosaic and, against radiant singing from Behrens in the carol of joy which follows, the orchestra might as well be playing a Bruckner slow movement, with no emotional underpinning of this supreme moment of fulfilment after pain. The other soloists are disappointing, even Jorma Hynninen who is dry-toned and uningratiating as Orestes. Ragnar Ulfung as Aegistheus is also dry-toned, aptly if unpleasantly so, and Nadine Secunde is far too wobbly as Chrysothemis. Voices are well caught, but the orchestral sound is too dry to bring out the glory of Strauss's orchestration.

The voices in the 1960 DG recording of Boehm, made in the helpful acoustic of the Lukaskirche in Dresden, have warmth and immediacy, underlining the power of Inge Borkh, tough in the title-role with an apt touch of rawness, of Jean Madeira as Klytemnestra, firm and positive, and of Dietrich Fischer-Dieskau, incomparable as Orestes. Their contributions are very vivid; but the distancing of the orchestra, and with it the relative thinness of the strings, means that a vital element in this violent opera is underplayed. The clarity of CD with its full body of sound brings an improvement on the original LPs, but Karl Boehm's masterly timing in this opera deserves to have a more substantial showing. The only weakness to note in the cast is the Chrysothemis of Marianna Schech, thin and unsteady and with touches of shrillness.

The Harmonia Mundi set brings a live recording of a middling performance, well conducted but with too little dramatic bite, when with one exception the singing is undistinguished and sometimes poor, and words are often masked in the cloudy acoustic. The exception is the Klytemnestra of the veteran contralto, Maureen Forrester, not always vocalized perfectly in the stress of the moment, but always projecting superbly a larger-than-life character. All the others, including Ute Vinzing as Elektra and Leonie Rysanek as Chrysothemis (sounding old), suffer from varying degrees of unsteadiness.

(i) *Elektra* (complete); (ii; iii) *Salome* (final scene – 2 versions).
Withdrawn: (M) (***) Standing Room Only mono SRO 833-2 (2). (i) VPO, Boehm; (ii) Leonie Rysanek, Astrid Varnay, Hans Hopf, O, Leitner; (iii) Birgit Nilsson, Bergstrom, Henriksen, O, Ehrling – WAGNER: *Walküre:* excerpts. (**)
(i) Elektra (Birgit Nilsson), Klytemnestra (Leonie Rysanek), Chrysothemis (Regina Resnik), Aegisthus (Wolfgang Windgassen).

The main work on this Standing Room Only set is a live recording of *Elektra* made at the Vienna State Opera in December 1965. It is a superb performance with an almost incomparable cast and with Boehm more intense and electrifying than in his studio recording, reissued by DG. The broadcast sound is limited but very forward and vivid, with voices sounding immediate. The oddity is that Nilsson's vibrato makes her tone warmer than usual, with none of her characteristic 'hoot', suggesting in places that this role may be misattributed. Yet no possible rival is likely to have sung the part with such precision and brilliance. The climactic moment of her solo, following the Recognition scene, brings an ecstatic moment on the word '*Seliger*', with a perfectly controlled crescendo. The first two of the three fill-ups are devoted to live recordings of the closing scene from *Salome*, with Rysanek at her finest with Leitner in 1974, and the young Nilsson already powerful but less detailed in Stockholm with Ehrling in 1953. The briefer Wagner items make up an exceptionally generous coupling.

(i) *Elektra: Soliloquy; Recognition scene; Finale. Salome: Dance of the seven veils; Finale.*
(M) *** BMG/RCA GD 60874 [60874-2-RG]. Inge Borkh, Chicago SO, Fritz Reiner; (i) with Paul Schoeffler, Frances Yeend, Chicago Lyric Theatre Ch.

Inge Borkh never sang *Elektra* at the Met., but this 40-minute group of excerpts, made in 1956, gives a tantalizing indication of what such a performance might have been like. With Borkh singing superbly in the title-role alongside Paul Schoeffler and Frances Yeend, this is a real collectors' piece. Reiner provides a superbly telling accompaniment; the performance of the Recognition scene and final duet are as ripely passionate as Beecham's old 78-r.p.m. excerpts and outstrip the complete versions. By no means does the balance project the singers at the expense of orchestral detail, and the orchestral sound is thrillingly rich, the brass superbly expansive. The CD transfer again confirms the glory of the Chicago acoustics during the Reiner era. For the reissue, Reiner's full-blooded account of *Salome's dance* has been added, and Borkh is comparably memorable in the final scene. Here the 1955 recording is slightly less sumptuous, the voice less flattered on top, but the sound is still characteristically full and vivid. No Straussian should miss this disc.

Die Frau ohne Schatten (complete).
🎗 *** Decca Dig. 436 243-2 (3). VPO, Solti.
Empress (Julia Varady), Emperor (Plácido Domingo), Dyer's Wife (Hildegard Behrens), Barak the dyer (José Van Dam), Nurse (Reinhild Runkel), Spirit-messenger (Albert Dohmen), Voice of the falcon (Sumi Jo), Voice from above (Elzbieta Ardam), Guardian of the threshold (Eva Lind).
*** DG 415 472-2 (3) [id.]. V. State Op. Ch. & O, Boehm.
Empress (Leonie Rysanek), Emperor (James King), Dyer's Wife (Birgit Nilsson), Barak the dyer (Walter Berry), Nurse (Ruth Hesse), Spirit-messenger (Peter Wimberger), Voice of the falcon / Guardian of the threshold (Lotte Rysanek), Voice from above (Gertrud Jahn).
**(*) EMI Dig. CDS7 49074-2 (3) [Ang. CDCC 49074]. Tölz Boys' Ch., Bav. R. Ch. & SO, Sawallisch.
Empress (Cheryl Studer), Emperor (René Kollo), Dyer's Wife (Ute Vinzing), Barak the dyer

(Alfred Muff), Nurse (Hanna Schwarz), Spirit-messenger (Andreas Schmidt), Voice of the falcon (Julie Kaufmann), Voice from above (Marjana Lipovšek), Guardian of the threshold (Cyndia Sieden).

(M) ** Decca 425 981-2 (3) [id.]. V. State Op. Ch., VPO, Boehm.

Empress (Leonie Rysanek), Emperor (Hans Hopf), Dyer's Wife (Christel Goltz), Barak the dyer (Paul Schoeffler), Nurse (Elisabeth Höngen), Spirit-messenger (Kurt Boehme), Voice of the falcon (Judith Hellwig), Voice from above (Hilde Rössl-Majdan), Guardian of the threshold (Emmy Loose).

Die Frau ohne Schatten ('The woman without a shadow') has a curious, if fascinating plot. It is full of symbolism – it has something in common with Mozart's *Die Zauberflöte* – and so far has failed to make its mark on the repertoire. But it remains a masterly score and one which is ideal for exploration with the help of the gramophone. The opera is set in the legendary South Eastern Islands. The emperor is married to the daughter of Keikobad, King of the Spirits. She, too, is a supernatural being who emerged from a white gazelle which the king shot when hunting. They love each other and have been married for twelve moons, but it is a childless marriage. Because she is barren, the empress throws no shadow. To make their union complete, she must bear children and her shadow will be the outward sign of this.

In the darkness the nurse crouches on the roof and a messenger tells her that the empress may stay only three more nights on earth. As she throws no shadow, she must go back to her father, and the emperor will be turned to stone. The emperor now recalls his hunting days and says that he has not seen his favourite falcon since the day he first met his wife. As day dawns, the empress catches sight of the falcon, which warns her of her fate, and she begs the nurse to help her save her husband.

The empress and the nurse now go to call on Barak, the dyer, in his run-down hut; he has three deformed brothers, and his wife nags him. His wife, too, is childless. Barak goes off to market just before the empress and the nurse enter, and the nurse, who has certain magical powers, asks the dyer's wife if she will sell her shadow. The nurse conjures up visions of wealth to tempt her to exchange her own prospect of motherhood in return for gold. The two visitors leave, saying they will return the next day for her answer. The dyer's wife now has a terrible, fiery vision and hears the voices of her unborn children calling to her. But when Barak returns, he finds that his bed is separated from his wife's.

The next day the nurse returns and tempts the dyer's wife with the apparition of a handsome youth, but she does not dare deceive her husband. Meanwhile the emperor finds his falcon, which has returned to the falcon house, while the empress meets Barak and is beginning to have pangs of conscience that he might suffer at her expense.

The nurse now makes a final attempt to get the shadow with her magic arts. Although it is midday, the sky goes dark and Barak's three brothers howl with fright. Barak is now told by his wife that she has sold her shadow, and the brothers light a fire to confirm that she is telling the truth. Barak threatens to kill her and a sword appears in his hand as if by magic.

The empress, who has come to admire Barak, now refuses to accept the shadow at such a price, but his wife now says she had only *wished* to sell her shadow, but had not in fact done so. The empress and nurse depart and suddenly, in a cataclysm, the earth opens and Barak's hut and its contents are engulfed. Barak and his wife are now in a cavern underneath the earth. They are separated by a central wall, and both are unaware of the other's presence. The empress is summoned to her father's judgement hall. Keikobad presides, and her husband is also being judged. The nurse is fearful and decides to return home, and they bid her a final goodbye. The voices of Barak and his wife can be heard calling to each other.

The empress is told to drink the Water of Life then the shadow of the woman will be hers, and she will be human. But she refuses because that would mean that Barak and his wife would pay the penalty. She now sees her husband turned to stone, except for his pleading eyes. Again she is urged to drink. But she is steadfast, and she cries, 'I will not,' and falls to the ground. Immediately the water disappears, light floods the room, and as she rises to her feet she casts a shadow. The emperor is restored to her, the voices of their unborn children are heard and they embrace. They are reunited, and so are Barak and his wife, and the opera ends with the sound of unborn children's voices.

Claimed to be the first single recording project to have cost £1 million, Solti's set of *Die Frau ohne Schatten*, one of his favourite operas, is as much a landmark in his career as his historic first recording of Wagner's *Ring* cycle, still unsurpassed. One reason for the extraordinary expense was that Solti and his Decca colleagues waited patiently until they could assemble what was felt to be the ideal cast. So the Heldentenor role of the Emperor is taken by Plácido Domingo and, as in Solti's recording of Wagner's *Lohengrin*, the superstar tenor gives a performance that is not only beautiful to the ear beyond previous recording but has an extra feeling for expressive detail, deeper than that which was previously recorded.

Similarly, Solti was willing to delay the recording sessions so as to secure Hildegard Behrens as the Dyer's Wife. Vocally that choice is a huge success. What has at times limited her as Brünnhilde in Wagner's *Ring* cycle, her very feminine vulnerability, is here a positive strength, and the voice has rarely sounded so beautiful on record. Julia Varady as the Empress, the woman without a shadow of the opera's title, is even more imaginative than the excellent Cheryl Studer on the rival EMI recording under Sawallisch, with a voice even more beautiful, and José van Dam with his clean, dark voice brings a warmth and depth of expression to the role of Barak, the Dyer, which goes with a satisfyingly firm focus.

Though Reinhild Runkel in the key role of the Nurse is not as firm as Hanna Schwarz on EMI, she is more in character, with her mature, fruity sound. Eva Lind is shrill in the tiny role of the Guardian of the Threshold, but there is compensation in having Sumi Jo as the Voice of the Falcon. With the players of the Vienna Philharmonic, 120-strong, surpassing themselves, and the big choral ensembles both well disciplined and warmly expressive, this superb recording is unlikely to be matched, let alone surpassed, for many years. Solti himself is inspired throughout. For him this opera is the peak of Strauss's genius. He feels deeply that though the symbolism in Hofmannsthal's libretto is dauntingly complex, the basic human relationships are universal and direct, and that is reflected in the warmth of his conducting. Alongside the characteristically high voltage of the whole performance, there is an irresistible emotional thrust and a moving tenderness. This is a recording, with full and vivid sound of demonstration quality, that should at last secure the recognition it has long deserved for Strauss's own favourite among his operas.

Boehm's live DG recording of Strauss's most ambitious, most Wagnerian opera was edited together from two performances at the Vienna State Opera in October 1977 and it provides a magnificent reminder of the conductor at his very finest. Though the Decca set of the mid-1950s – also conducted by Boehm in Vienna but recorded in the studio – still sounds amazingly well, with early stereo very well focused, the new one glows far more warmly. It is a performance to love rather than just to admire, with the opera-house acoustic handled persuasively by the engineers of Austrian Radio to give the solo voices plenty of bloom without losing precision. Inevitably there are stage noises and the balance of the singers varies, but this is outstanding among live recordings. The stage cuts are an irritation, but at least they allow the hour-long Acts to be accommodated each on a single CD. The cast is an excellent one, with Birgit Nilsson making the Dyer's Wife a truly Wagnerian character, richer as well as subtler than her Decca predecessor, Christel Goltz. As before, Leonie Rysanek sings the role of the other heroine, the Empress, musically almost as demanding; amazingly, if anything the voice has grown firmer and rounder between the mid-1950s and 1977. Barak the Dyer is sung by Walter Berry, not always as firmly Sachs-like as Paul Schoeffler was before, but searchingly expressive; and James King in the Heldentenor role of the Emperor is just as remarkable for his finely shaded pianissimo singing as for heroic moments, where he is occasionally strained. On CD the perspectives are impressively caught at all levels of dynamic.

Beautifully recorded in Munich in collaboration with Bavarian Radio, EMI's version of *Die Frau ohne Schatten* with Sawallisch conducting was the first ever to include a really complete text with all the stage cuts restored. Cleverly, EMI jumped in ahead of Decca, the company which has long been planning just such a complete recording with Sir Georg Solti conducting. There is much to enjoy here. Sawallisch is a most persuasive Straussian, relaxed rather than bitingly dramatic, and the Bavarian Radio orchestra plays ravishingly for him, helped by refined digital recording. Cheryl Studer sings radiantly as the Empress, and René Kollo is a powerful Emperor, falling into coarseness only occasionally.

Hanna Schwarz is superb as the Nurse, firmly establishing the magnetism of the performance in her first-scene duet with the Messenger, the excellent young baritone, Andreas Schmidt. Sadly, the whole project is undermined by the casting of the two other major roles. The central figure of the Dyer's Wife brings deeply disappointing singing from Ute Vinzing, no doubt powerful on stage but on record depressingly unsteady, except – paradoxically – when launching out at full cry. Alfred Muff's gritty, unattractive tone as her husband, Barak, is another blot, and his characterization is one-dimensional.

Boehm's 1955 recording is reissued in Decca's Historical series, but it is an example of very early stereo, thanks to a rescue attempt from the original master-tape made by the recording manager, Christopher Raeburn. Since then Karl Boehm has re-recorded the opera live for DG, and that version must take precedence, although it is at full price. Leonie Rysanek is the Empress in both sets; otherwise the singing on the Decca set is variable, with a high proportion of wobblers among the soloists, and Hans Hopf often producing coarse tone as the Emperor. The recording is remarkably good for its period.

Guntram (complete).
Withdrawn: (M) *** Sony Dig. M2K 39737 (2) [id.]. Hungarian Army Ch. & State O, Queler.
  Guntram (Reiner Goldberg), Freihild (Ilona Tokody), The Old Duke (Sándor Sólyom-Nagy), Robert (Istvan Gáti), The Duke's Fool (János Bándi).

Strauss's very first opera suffers from an undramatic libretto written by the composer, a sloppy tale of knights-in-armour chivalry. The setting is medieval Germany. Freihild is married to Duke Robert, a man of tyrannical disposition who does his best to undermine all Freihild's good works. Guntram, an idealistic knight and member of a pacific Christian brotherhood, comes in time to persuade Freihild not to take her own life in despair. He sings of peace and generosity, and Robert attacks him for his pains. In the ensuing struggle, Guntram kills him. He is imprisoned and ponders over his true motives: love of righteousness or of Freihild. His deed is condemned by Freihold, an elder of his brotherhood, as an absolute sin. When Freihild arrives to rescue him, he realizes the truth of his motivation and in expiation decides to leave both the brotherhood and Freihild. He will retire into contemplation and admire his beloved, a benevolent ruler of her estates, from a distance.

Strauss's setting provides a marvellous musical wallow, with the young composer echoing *Don Juan* and other early symphonic poems in sumptuous orchestral writing. Even when he consciously adopts a Wagnerian stance, the music quickly turns sweet, often anticipating the more lyrical side of *Salome*. Heading the cast as the eponymous knight is Reiner Goldberg, open-toned and only occasionally strained. Otherwise the cast is Hungarian, with Ilona Tokody strong and firm, if rarely beautiful, in the taxing role of the heroine, Freihild, originally written with Strauss's wife-to-be, Pauline, in mind. Warmly sympathetic conducting from Eve Queler. The recording acoustic too is attractively rich. The set has been withdrawn as we go to press and we hope it may reappear at mid-price.

Intermezzo (complete).
*** EMI CDS7 49337-2 (2) [Ang. CDCB 49337]. Bav. RSO, Sawallisch.
  Christine (Lucia Popp), Robert Storch (Dietrich Fischer-Dieskau), Anna (Gabriele Fuchs), Baron Lummer (Adolf Dallapozza).

What other composer but Strauss could turn an absurd little incident in his married life into an opera as enchanting as *Intermezzo*? He made no secret of the fact that the central character of Storch, the composer, was himself, and the nagging but loving wife his own Pauline. That is very much the central role – the name Christine the flimsiest of disguises – involving a virtuoso performance which scarcely lets up for an instant. We meet her immediately, at the beginning of the opera which opens in the house of Kapellmeister Storch in Grundlsee.

She and her husband are busy packing for his forthcoming tour and she is not in the best of tempers, scolding him as well as the servants. When he tries to retaliate, she reminds him that she comes from a better family than he, and she then tells her maid that she would admire her husband more if he would stand up to her like a man. Her husband leaves for Vienna, the phone rings and she arranges to go skating with a neighbour.

She runs into a man on skis and, after first abusing him, discovers he is Baron Lummer; she says she is the wife of the composer Storch and that he must come to visit. We next find them dancing at the inn, and later Christine writes a letter to her husband telling of her new escort. In due course the baron suggests he needs financial support for his studies, and later he asks for 1,000 marks. She is beginning to grow impatient with him.

But then a letter arrives, addressing her husband in very affectionate terms, asking for two opera tickets and suggesting an assignation afterwards. It is signed 'Your Mieze Meier'. Who is this woman? Christine packs a bag ready to leave her husband and tells him so in a telegram, yet when she talks to their child in the bedroom she is blamed for her shrewishness.

Now the scene changes to the house of a Viennese councillor, where the guests are gathered to play 'Skat'. Storch arrives late and comments upon his wife's new friend the baron, then the telegram arrives with news of his wife's discovery. Storch leaves quickly; his friends, who hitherto have been blaming his wife's disagreeable temperament, now wonder about Storch himself.

Christine visits a notary to institute proceedings for divorce. But now Stroh, the conductor, seeks Storch out in the Prater in Vienna and during a storm tells him that he thinks the letter demanding the tickets was meant for him. At Storch's request, he goes to visit Christine, who is gathering her things together to leave, and the truth comes out. The baron, who has tried to see the mystery woman, now returns, having bungled the affair. When husband and wife meet again, Christine affects coolness, Storch feigns jealousy of the baron, but reconciliation follows. Even though they quarrel they enjoy each other.

The opera was originally designed for the dominant and enchanting Lotte Lehmann, but even she can hardly have outshone the radiant Lucia Popp. She brings out the charm of the character who, for all his incidental trials, must have consistently captivated Strauss and provoked this strange piece of self-revelation. Inevitably the libretto is very wordy but, with this scintillating and emotionally powerful performance under Sawallisch and with fine recording and an excellent supporting cast, this set is near ideal. The CD transfer is all the more attractive in being issued on only two CDs, but – unforgivably in this of all Strauss operas – no translation is given with the libretto, a very serious omission.

Die Liebe der Danae (complete).
(***) Orfeo mono C 292923 A (3) [id.]. VPO, Clemens Krauss.
 Danae (Anneliese Kupper), Jupiter (Paul Schoeffler), Midas (Joseph Gostic), Xanthe (Anny Felbermayer).

One can very well argue that Strauss reserved for his last years his very greatest music, what with the *Four Last Songs*, *Metamorphosen* and the final opera, *Capriccio*. Yet unfairly the opera immediately preceding *Capriccio*, not given its first performance until long after the composer's death, *Die Liebe der Danae* ('The love of Danaë'), has been more neglected than any. This is the belated first recording, not made in the spectacular stereo that this sumptuous score cries out for but in limited mono sound in an Austrian Radio recording from the very first Salzburg Festival performance in August 1952.

As transferred to CD it has a vivid sense of presence, with the voices full-bodied. Despite the limitations and the intrusive stage noises, *Die Liebe der Danae* here under Clemens Krauss establishes itself as one of Strauss's richest scores. Completed in 1940, it in effect marked the beginning of the last period, warm and mellow like the works which followed, but, unlike them, attempting a scale and complexity that Strauss had left behind in his epic opera, *Die Frau ohne Schatten*, written during the First World War.

Like *Ariadne auf Naxos*, *Daphne* and *Die Aegyptische Helena*, *Die Liebe der Danae* presents Greek myth in light-hearted post-romantic guise. The idea, originally put forward by Hofmannsthal and taken up by Strauss's later librettist, Joseph Gregor, was to superimpose two well-known myths, that of Jupiter appearing to Danaë in a shower of golden rain and that of Midas with his curse of turning everything to gold. They described it as a 'cheerful mythology in three Acts', but that gives no idea of the breadth of treatment.

It is not just lyrical in Strauss's *Daphne* manner, but a genuinely tuneful score, in places harking back to the diatonic Wagner of *Meistersinger* and bringing ensembles that were directly influenced by Strauss's favourite Mozart opera, *Così fan tutte*. Midas is reduced from king to donkey-driver, initially the catspaw for Jupiter in his philandering. In the last of the three Acts Strauss lets himself go expansively in a sequence of duets, first between Danaë and Midas and finally between Danaë and Jupiter who, rather like Hans Sachs in *Meistersinger* (or the Marschallin in *Rosenkavalier*), nobly cedes any rights in the young lover, a situation that plainly touched the aged Strauss.

With the Vienna Philharmonic already restored after the war, Krauss's affectionate reading is backed by some splendid singing, notably from Paul Schoeffler, Sachs-like as Jupiter, and the full-toned heroic tenor, Joseph Gostic as Midas. Anneliese Kupper in the title-role has a few raw moments but she produces pure, creamy tone for the many passages of ravishing cantilena above the stave. With important sequences for Danaë's servant, Xanthe (the resonant Anny Felbermayer), and four mythical queens, Semele, Europa, Alkmene and Leda, the writing for women's voices brings grateful echoes of the *Rosenkavalier* Trio. Sadly the three full-price discs come without a libretto, merely providing a note by Strauss's biographer, Willi Schuh, plus a synopsis in fractured English.

Der Rosenkavalier (complete).
⊛ *** EMI CDS7 49354-8 (3) [Ang. CDCC 49354]. Philh. Ch. & O, Karajan.
 Die Feldmarschallin (Elisabeth Schwarzkopf), Octavian (Christa Ludwig), Baron Ochs (Otto

Edelmann), Sophie (Teresa Stich-Randall), Faninal (Eberhard Waechter), Italian tenor (Nicolai Gedda).

*** EMI Dig. CDS7 54259-2 (3) [Ang. CDCC 54259]. Dresden Op. Ch., Dresden Boys' Ch., Dresden State O, Haitink.

Die Feldmarschallin (Kiri Te Kanawa), Octavian (Anne Sofie Von Otter), Baron Ochs (Kurt Rydl), Sophie (Barbara Hendricks), Faninal (Franz Grundheber), Italian tenor (Richard Leech).

**(*) DG Dig. 423 850-2 (3) [id.]. VPO Ch. & O, Karajan.

Die Feldmarschallin (Anna Tomowa-Sintow), Octavian (Agnes Baltsa), Baron Ochs (Kurt Moll), Sophie (Janet Perry), Faninal (Gottfried Hornik), Italian tenor (Vinson Cole).

** Decca 417 493-2 (3) [id.]. V. State Op. Ch., VPO, Solti.

Die Feldmarschallin (Régine Crespin), Octavian (Yvonne Minton), Baron Ochs (Manfred Jungwirth), Sophie (Helen Donath), Faninal (Otto Wiener), Italian tenor (Luciano Pavarotti).

(M) ****** Sony M3K 42564 (3) [id.]. V. State Op. Ch., VPO, Bernstein.

Die Feldmarschallin (Christa Ludwig), Octavian (Gwyneth Jones), Baron Ochs (Walter Berry), Sophie (Lucia Popp), Faninal (Ernst Gutstein), Italian tenor (Plácido Domingo).

(M) **(**(*))** Decca mono 425 950-2 (3) [id.]. V. State Op. Ch., VPO, Erich Kleiber.

Die Feldmarschallin (Maria Reining), Octavian (Sena Jurinac), Baron Ochs (Ludwig Weber), Sophie (Hilde Gueden), Faninal (Alfred Poell), Italian tenor (Anton Dermota).

Withdrawn: *(*) Denon Dig. C37 7482/4 [id.]. Dresden State Op. Ch., Dresden State O, Vonk.

Die Feldmarschallin (Ana Pusar-Joric), Octavian (Ute Walther), Baron Ochs (Theo Adam), Sophie (Margot Stejskal).

Strauss's greatest opera was a huge success from its very first performance, a success deriving as much from Hofmannsthal's outstanding libretto as from Strauss's glorious music. We have learned too that the Feldmarschallin – its great central character – was less of a key figure when the story was originally plotted out but that she slowly gathered importance (as if she were a real person) until, in the end, she came to dominate the opera.

Before the curtain rises the Feldmarschallin and the young Octavian have been in the throes of a passionate embrace, and we first see him kneeling by the side of her bed. They share breakfast romantically, then Octavian hides as Baron Ochs approaches. Octavian emerges, dressed as a chambermaid, 'Mariandl', and the captivated baron immediately flirts grotesquely. He has come to tell the Feldmarschallin that he plans to marry Sophie, the daughter of the wealthy Herr von Faninal. He asks advice on whom to choose as his 'Rosenkavalier' to bear the ceremonial silver rose to his proposed bride. Octavian's services are duly offered and Ochs leaves the silver rose in the Feldmarschallin's care. Left alone, she muses on the way time passes – too swiftly – for a woman. Octavian returns in his own clothes and she is aware that one day, not too long hence, he will leave her for a younger lover.

Octavian arrives at Sophie's house, elegantly dressed in white and silver, bearing the silver rose. The very good-looking couple are instantly attracted, both displaying all the freshness of youth. Ochs arrives and his coarseness distresses Sophie and angers Octavian. Faninal shows the baron into an anteroom and Sophie now begs Octavian to help her. By now they are very much in love. Valzacchi and Annina come in and, sensing what has happened, immediately call Ochs, who asks Sophie for an explanation. She refuses to answer, but Octavian tells Ochs that Sophie will not marry him and, when he resists, challenges him. Swords are drawn, Ochs receives a scratch on his arm and yells 'Murder!' Faninal enters, apologizes to Ochs, and rages at Sophie and Octavian. He tells Sophie to accept Ochs or enter a convent. Left alone, Ochs recovers his humour, especially when Annina comes in with a letter arranging an assignation with 'Mariandl'.

Octavian has planned to trap Ochs and expose his conduct and, in the scene which follows, arrives in the 'Mariandl' disguise to entice him. They sit on a bed together. Annina rushes in, and the landlord and waiters are scandalized. The police commissioner enters and wishes to know the identity of the girl. Ochs says that she is his fiancée, Sophie von Faninal. Then Faninal himself arrives and furiously denies that the girl in question is his daughter. Sophie enters and Faninal, humiliated, passes out.

Ochs then has the temerity to ask 'Mariandl' if he may escort her home. She refuses and whispers in the police commissioner's ear. Octavian hastily changes his clothes and the landlord announces the Feldmarschallin. Faninal tells Sophie to instruct Ochs never to visit his house again. When the Feldmarschallin hears from Octavian of the prank played on Ochs, she becomes well aware of the love shared by the young couple. Her position creates a scene of great poignancy as she gracefully accepts that she cannot stand in the way of their happiness. She leaves, and Sophie and Octavian fall into each other's arms. The opera ends delightfully as a page-boy picks up a handkerchief Sophie has dropped.

The glory of Karajan's 1956 version, one of the greatest of all opera recordings, shines out the more delectably on CD. Though the transfer in its very clarity exposes some flaws in the original sound, the sense of presence and the overall bloom are if anything more compelling than ever. As to the performance, it is in a class of its own, with the patrician refinement of Karajan's spacious reading combining with an emotional intensity that he has rarely equalled, even in Strauss, of whose music he remains a supreme interpreter. Matching that achievement is the incomparable portrait of the Feldmarschallin from Schwarzkopf, bringing out detail as no one else can, yet equally presenting the breadth and richness of the character, a woman still young and attractive. Christa Ludwig with her firm, clear mezzo tone makes an ideal, ardent Octavian and Teresa Stich-Randall a radiant Sophie, with Otto Edelmann a winningly characterful Ochs, who yet sings every note clearly. Karajan observes some of the stage cuts sanctioned by the composer.

Haitink's EMI set, recorded in Dresden, brings a satisfyingly rich Strauss sound, matching the conductor's beautifully paced reading. Dramatic without a hint of vulgarity, it brings out the nobility of the music. Vocally the biggest triumph is the Octavian of Anne Sofie von Otter, not only beautifully sung but acted with a boyish animation to make most rivals sound very feminine by comparison. The ardent young lover of Act I, the protector of Sophie in Act II, smitten by her beauty, and the larking boy of Act III, who is first embarrassed then is achingly appreciative of the Feldmarschallin's generosity – all these facets of the character are played out with total conviction.

Not that the Rose Knight of the title becomes the centre of the opera, any more than Octavian ever does. If the first great – and predictable – glory of Dame Kiri's assumption of the role of the Feldmarschallin is the sheer beauty of the sound, the portrait she paints is an intense and individual one, totally convincing. Though, not surprisingly, she yields to Schwarzkopf (Karajan) or Crespin (Solti) in detailed inflexion of word-meaning, this is a performance, often animated, which in its clear element of tender, feminine vulnerability brings new lights in each scene. In the great Act III Trio, Dame Kiri's poise makes for a glorious launch of the main melody in pure, creamy tone, and a sense that, with the great renunciation made, the Feldmarschallin is now smiling with vicarious happiness over her former young lover, with her own sadness only hinted at.

The portrait of Sophie from Barbara Hendricks is a warm and moving one, but less completely satisfying, if only because her voice is not quite as pure as one needs for this young, innocent girl. Yet in the presentation of the silver rose the sense of wonder at the start is vividly conveyed, and Hendricks's picture of the prattling girl of the second half of the scene is a delight. Kurt Rydl with his warm and resonant bass makes a splendid Baron Ochs, not always ideally steady but giving the character a magnificent scale and breadth. With a marvellous Viennese accent he gives a rounded characterization, not overdoing the comedy, so that one can register the genuine anger of the Baron in Act II at his bride playing him up – for the moment in no mood for trifling.

Other portraits are just as colourfully presented, notably the sharply detailed Valzacchi of Graham Clark and the Duenna of Julia Faulkner, fruity yet firm. Franz Grundheber makes a convincing toady of Faninal, Richard Leech with golden tone hints at a send-up in the Italian Tenor's aria, and Claire Powell, though not always quite steady, is a formidably characterful Annina. Whatever the detailed reservations over the singing, it is mainly the influence of Bernard Haitink and his long experience conducting this opera at Covent Garden and elsewhere that makes this the most totally convincing and heartwarming recording of *Rosenkavalier* since Karajan's 1956 set. The Staatskapelle are not just brilliant throughout but warmly idiomatic, ever responsive to Haitink's well-chosen speeds, relatively brisk in Act I, broader in the other two Acts. This recording, unlike the Karajan, opens out the small stage cuts sanctioned by the composer.

When Karajan re-recorded this opera in preparation for the 1983 Salzburg Festival with this same DG cast, inevitably he invited comparison with his own classic 1956 recording. The new set brings few positive advantages, not even in recorded sound: for all the extra range of the modern digital recording, the focus is surprisingly vague, with the orchestra balanced too far behind the soloists. One advantage there certainly is: the Vienna Philharmonic, having been brought up with a natural feeling for waltz rhythm, is a degree more idiomatic in providing a genuine Viennese lilt, even if it is also at times less precise. The orchestral balance adds to the impression of relative lightness, and so does the casting.

As successor to Schwarzkopf, Karajan chose one of his favourite sopranos, the Bulgarian Anna Tomowa-Sintow; the refinement and detail in her performance present an intimate view of the Feldmarschallin, often very beautiful indeed, but both the darker and more sensuous sides of the Feldmarschallin are muted. *Da steht der Bub* she sings in the great Act III Trio, and the voice conveys pure maternal joy, hardly any regret for her own loss. The Baron Ochs of Kurt Moll, firm, dark and incisive, is outstanding, and Agnes Baltsa as Octavian makes the lad tough and determined, if not always sympathetic. Janet Perry's Sophie, charming and pretty on stage, is too white and twittery of tone to give much pleasure. For all the flaws, Karajan is once more presented as a supreme Straussian, even more daringly spacious than before (which will not please everyone).

The CD transfer of Solti's version is one of the more disappointing reissues from Decca. The brilliance of the original recording is exaggerated, with some of the compensating body in the sound removed, making the result too aggressive for this gloriously ripe score. Nevertheless it can be tamed and, like other CD versions, this one – which has an absolutely complete text without any statutory cuts – comes on three discs, one per Act. Crespin is here at her finest on record, with tone well focused, convincingly giving a rather maternal maturity to the character. Manfred Jungwirth makes a firm and virile, if not always imaginative Ochs, Yvonne Minton a finely projected Octavian and Helen Donath a sweet-toned Sophie. Solti's direction is fittingly honeyed, with tempi even slower than Karajan's in the climactic moments. The one serious disappointment is that the great concluding *Trio* does not quite lift as it should.

Bernstein's CBS Vienna set commemorates a great theatrical occasion at the beginning of the 1970s when the Viennese were swept off their feet – much to their surprise – by the magic of the American conductor. His direction of this opera at the Vienna State Opera was an almost unparalleled success; his recorded version captures much of the ripeness in the fine, mature Feldmarschallin of Christa Ludwig, which plainly owes much to the example of Schwarzkopf (for whom, on the EMI Karajan set, Ludwig was Octavian). Lucia Popp makes a charming Sophie and Walter Berry a strong, expressive Ochs, less limited in the lower register than one might expect. But Gwyneth Jones's Octavian, despite the occasional half-tone of exquisite beauty, has too many raw passages to be very appealing, a bad blot on the set. Bernstein follows traditional cuts. Surprisingly, when Decca engineers were responsible for the recording itself, the quality is more variable than one would expect, with vulgarly close horn balance.

Decca's mono set with Erich Kleiber was the first ever complete recording of *Rosenkavalier*, and it has long enjoyed cult status. It has many glories, quite apart from the inspired conducting of Kleiber senior. Sena Jurinac is a charming Octavian, strong and sympathetic, and Hilde Gueden a sweetly characterful Sophie, not just a wilting innocent. Ludwig Weber characterizes deliciously in a very Viennese way as Ochs; but the disappointment is the Feldmarschallin of Maria Reining, very plain and lacking intensity, even in the great scene with Octavian at the end of Act I.

She is not helped by Kleiber's refusal to linger; with the singers recorded close, the effect of age on what was once a fine voice is very clear, even in the opening solo of the culminating Trio. And though the Vienna Philharmonic responds in the most idiomatic way to the waltz rhythms, ensemble is not good, with even the Prelude to Act I a muddle. One recalls the notorious castigation of the VPO in rehearsal, when George Szell returned to conduct this opera after the war: 'Gentlemen, you do not seem to know this score!' On that Prelude more than anywhere, the CD transfer brings out a shrillness and lack of body in the orchestral sound, though voices are well caught. On three mid-price CDs, one per Act, this remains a classic set.

In the Denon version, recorded live at the opening of the reconstructed Semper Opera House in Dresden, stage and audience noises are often obtrusive and the orchestra is balanced well behind the solo singers. This can be recommended only to those who want a plain, generally brisk view, with plenty of atmosphere. Vonk's rather metrical manner affects even the waltzes, but the orchestral playing is superb, particularly from the horns. The Yugoslav soprano, Ana Pusar-Joric, has a warm, vibrant voice, and her fresh characterization brings delightful pointing of words; but too often she sits under notes, or slides up to them. Ute Walther is an attractively ardent Octavian and Margot Stejskal a thin-toned Sophie, shrill and fluttery at times. Theo Adam's characterful Ochs is marred by too much gritty, ill-focused tone.

(i) *Der Rosenkavalier* (abridged version); Lieder: (ii) *All' mein Gedanken; Freundliche Vision; Die Heiligen drei Könige; Heimkehr; Ich schwebe; Des Knaben Wunderhorn: Hat gesagt . . .; Morgen; Muttertändelei; Schlechtes Wetter;* *Ständchen* (2 versions); *Traum durch die Dämmerung;* (iii) *Mit deinen blauen Augen; Morgen; Ständchen; Traum durch die Dämmerung.*

(M) (***) EMI mono CHS7 64487-2 (2). (i) V. State Op. Ch., VPO, Robert Heger; (ii) Elisabeth
Schumann; (iii) Lotte Lehmann (with various accompanists).
  Feldmarschallin (Lotte Lehmann), Octavian (Maria Olszewska), Sophie (Elisabeth
Schumann), Baron Ochs (Richard Mayr), Faninal (Victor Madin).

It is good to have a fresh CD transfer, immaculate in quality, of this classic, early, abridged
recording of *Der Rosenkavalier*, containing some 100 minutes of music, made in 1933 in Vienna
by the famous EMI pioneer of opera recording, Fred Gaisberg. Subsequent LP versions have
told us that this is not definitive, as we once may have thought, but Lotte Lehmann as the
Feldmarschallin and Elisabeth Schumann as Sophie remain uniquely characterful, and though
78-r.p.m. side-lengths brought some hastening from Heger, notably in the great Trio of Act III,
the passion of the performance still conveys a sense of new discovery, a rare Straussian magic.
As a bonus, we are offered a glorious Lieder recital featuring both the principal sopranos and
demonstrating Lehmann's darker timbre, with versions of *Traum durch die Dämmerung* and the
soaring *Ständchen*, sung by both artists, and two different Schumann performances of the latter,
one from 1927, the other (with much clearer sound) from 1930. Again excellent CD transfers.

Der Rosenkavalier: highlights.
(M) *** EMI CDM7 63452-2; *EG 763452-4* (from above recording with Schwarzkopf, Ludwig;
  cond. Karajan).
**(*) DG Dig. 415 284-2 [id.] (from above recording with Tomowa-Sintow, Baltsa; cond.
  Karajan).

On EMI we are offered the Feldmarschallin's monologue to the end of Act I (25 minutes); the
Presentation of the silver rose and finale from Act II; and the Duet and closing scene, with the
Trio from Act III, flawlessly and gloriously sung and transferred most beautifully to CD.
  This DG highlights disc, taken from Karajan's re-recording of the complete opera, provides a
generous sample of excerpts, incorporating most of the favourite passages, and including the
tenor aria, lightly sung by Vinson Cole. The richness and beauty of the score are hardly in doubt,
but the flaws noted above are just as apparent.

Salome (complete).
*** DG. Dig. 431 810-2 (2) [id.]. German Opera, Berlin, Ch. & O, Sinopoli.
  Salome (Cheryl Studer), Jokanaan (Bryn Terfel), Herod (Horst Hiestermann), Herodias
  (Leonie Rysanek), Narraboth (Clemens Bieber).
*** Decca 414 414-2 (2) [id.]. VPO, Solti.
  Salome (Birgit Nilsson), Jokanaan (Eberhard Waechter), Herod (Gerhard Stolze), Herodias
  (Grace Hoffman), Narraboth (Waldemar Kmentt).
Withdrawn: *** EMI CDS7 49358-8 (2) [id.]. VPO, Karajan.
  Salome (Hildegard Behrens), Jokanaan (José Van Dam), Herod (Karl-Walter Böhm),
  Herodias (Agnes Baltsa), Narraboth (Wieslaw Ochman).
(M) *** BMG/RCA GD 86644 (2) [6644-2-RG]. LSO, Leinsdorf.
  Salome (Montserrat Caballé), Jokanaan (Sherrill Milnes), Herod (Richard Lewis), Herodias
  (Regina Resnik), Narraboth (James King).
** Sony Dig. S2K 46717; *40-46717* (2) [id.]. BPO, Mehta.
  Salome (Eva Marton), Jokanaan (Bernd Weikl), Herod (Heinz Zednik), Herodias (Brigitte
  Fassbaender), Narraboth (Keith Lewis).

Strauss based his *Salome* on Oscar Wilde's play, using Hedwig Lachmann's translation and
adapting the libretto himself. If not as bleakly malevolent as *Elektra*, its dark, corrupting
sensuality brought forth an extraordinarily imaginative command of orchestral atmosphere, and
the obscenity of the closing scene is among the most powerful (and unpleasant) moments in the
whole world of opera.
  As Wilde and Strauss begin the story, Salome's nubile sensuality is not only exciting Herod's
lascivious gaze but is also stirring the loins of Naraboth, the young Syrian captain of the guard,
who is watching what is going on inside the palace. Meanwhile John the Baptist's voice rises
hollowly from the cistern in the courtyard, where he is imprisoned. Salome suddenly emerges
from the banqueting hall, driven out by her sense of surrounding debauchery yet already
corrupted by it. She is curious to see the prophet when she hears his voice, aware that he has
reviled her mother.
  The soldiers have orders not to let John speak with her, but Naraboth is easily tempted by his
lust for her and, at her wily request, allows the prophet to emerge from his dreadful confining
prison; his appearance is appalling, showing emaciation and suffering, but his will is resolute

and he immediately denounces Herod and Herodias as evil. Salome, at once repelled and fascinated by him, finds desire mounting within her breast. She longs to kiss him on the mouth but he draws back and, when Naraboth fails to restrain her, the Syrian desperately stabs himself with his own sword and falls between them.

John the Baptist tells Salome she is accursed and bids her seek repentance, then he descends into the cistern once more. Herod and Herodias now appear; Herod, in his cups, drunkenly seeks out Salome to the chagrin of his wife. Almost falling over Naraboth's corpse, he orders it to be removed. He then offers Salome food and wine and, finally, even his throne, but she ignores him. Herod's fascination for Salome is equalled by his fear of the prophet, whose voice is heard again.

A dispute now breaks out among a group of Jews, and two Nazarenes talk of the coming of the Messiah. John denounces 'the daughter of Babylon' and Herod is conscious that the very sound of the prophet's voice stimulates Salome's desire. As a distraction, he orders her to dance and promises her anything she desires. She makes this promise into an oath then, with increasing abandon, dances her dance of the seven veils.

As she lies supine and exhausted at its climax, the highly stimulated Herod asks what is her desire, and her response is to demand Jokanaan's head on a silver charger. Herod is aghast but the delighted Herodias takes the ring of death from Herod's finger and gives it to the executioner, who immediately descends into the cistern. Salome leans over the edge to watch, beside herself with impatience. She waits for John's cry, but none is forthcoming; then a huge black arm is held aloft, in its grasp a silver platter on which rests John's head. Salome gloatingly kisses the lips. Now even Herod is repulsed. He orders the soldiers to kill her and they crush her beneath their shields.

The glory of Sinopoli's DG version is the singing of Cheryl Studer as Salome, producing glorious sounds throughout. She builds her interpretation so that the final scene conveys total evil while keeping a semblance of girlishness. Her voice is both rich and finely controlled, with delicately spun pianissimos that chill you the more for their beauty, not least in Salome's attempted seduction of John the Baptist. If this is Studer's finest opera-recording yet, it might also be counted Sinopoli's finest. His reading is often unconventional in its speeds, but it is always positive, thrusting and full of passion, the most opulent account on disc, matched by full, forward recording. As Jokanaan, Bryn Terfel makes a compelling recording début, strong and noble, though the prophet's voice as heard from the cistern sounds far too distant. Among modern sets this makes a clear first choice, though Solti's vintage Decca recording remains the most firmly focused, with the keenest sense of presence.

Solti's recording of *Salome*, originally issued in 1962, was one of the most spectacular of the opera recordings produced by John Culshaw at the Sofiensaal in Vienna. It used what was called the Sonicstage technique – with the sound of Jokanaan's voice in the cistern recorded from another acoustic very precisely – and that sharpness of focus, coupled with opulence of texture, comes out with extraordinary brilliance in the digital transfer on CD. The additional absence of background makes the final scene, where Salome kisses the head of John the Baptist in delighted horror ('I have kissed thy mouth, Jokanaan!'), all the more spine-tingling, with a vivid close-up effect of the voice whispering almost in one's ear.

Nilsson is splendid throughout; she is hard-edged as usual but, on that account, more convincingly wicked: the determination and depravity are latent in the girl's character from the start. Of this score Solti is a master. He has rarely sounded so abandoned in a recorded performance. The emotion swells up naturally even while the calculation of impact is most precise. Waechter makes a clear, young-sounding Jokanaan. Gerhard Stolze portrays the unbalance of Herod with frightening conviction and Grace Hoffman does all she can in the comparatively ungrateful part of Herodias. The CDs show Decca's technology at its most impressive, and the sound is extraordinarily vivid.

Recorded for EMI by Decca engineers in the Sofiensaal in Vienna, Karajan's sumptuously beautiful version faithfully recaptures the flair and splendour of the Salzburg production, which Karajan directed on stage as well as conducted. It was daring of him when preparing both recording and stage productions to choose for the role of heroine a singer then relatively unknown, but Hildegard Behrens is triumphantly successful, a singer who in the early scenes has one actively sympathizing with the girlish princess, and who keeps that sympathy and understanding to a stage where most sopranos have been transformed into raging harpies. The sensuous beauty of tone is ravishingly conveyed, but the recording – less analytical than the Decca set under Solti – is not always fair to her fine projection of sound, occasionally masking the voice.

All the same, the feeling of a live performance has been well captured, and the rest of the cast is of the finest Salzburg standard. In particular José van Dam makes a gloriously noble Jokanaan, and in the early scenes his offstage voice from the cistern at once commands attention, underlining the direct diatonic strength of his music in contrast to the exoticry representing Salome and the court. Karajan – as so often in Strauss – is at his most commanding and sympathetic, with the orchestra, more forward than some will like, playing rapturously. This is a performance which, so far from making one recoil from perverted horrors, has one revelling in sensuousness. The smooth and warm recording for Karajan's version is clarified on CD. If it cannot match the vintage Decca in brilliance or atmospheric precision, it suits Karajan's ripe reading very well.

Montserrat Caballé's formidable account of the role of Salome was recorded in 1968, utterly different from that of Nilsson, much closer to the personification of Behrens on the Karajan set. There are even one or two moments of fantasy, where for an instant one has the girlish skittishness of Salome revealed like an evil inverted picture of Sophie. As for the vocalization, it is superb, with glorious golden tone up to the highest register and never the slightest hesitation in attack. Lewis, Resnik and Milnes make a supporting team that matches the achievement of the Decca rivals, while Leinsdorf is inspired to some of his warmest and most sympathetic conducting on record. The sound has not the pin-point atmosphere of the Decca but is nearer the EMI set in its fullness and vivid projection. The price advantage, too, makes this well worth considering.

Mehta's set brings a supreme performance from Brigitte Fassbaender as Herodias, dominating all her scenes. Otherwise performance and recording are disappointing. Above all the wobbly, ill-focused singing of Eva Marton in the title-role puts the set out of court except for her devotees. In the theatre the sheer volume might make her performance exciting, but on disc the microphone is unforgiving in showing up the unevenness of vocal production. She conveys a compelling lasciviousness in the final scene, but even there Cheryl Studer and Birgit Nilsson are more involving. Bernd Weikl is disappointing too as Jokanaan, sounding too old, and even the glorious sounds of the Berlin Philharmonic are dimmed by the distancing of the recording, blunting the impact of this highly charged work.

Salomé (complete; sung in French).
**(*) Virgin/EMI Dig. VCD7 91477-2 (2) [id.]. Lyon Opera Ch. & O, Kent Nagano.
   Salomé (Karen Huffstodt), Iokanaan (José Van Dam), Hérod (Jean Dupouy), Hérodias (Hélène Jossoud), Narraboth (Jean-Luc Viala).

Nagano's version is unique. Adventurously, he has revived the adaptation of the vocal line which Strauss himself made to accommodate the original Oscar Wilde text in French. It was never used, even in France, but the result is most distinctive, with Nagano drawing finely textured playing from his Lyon Opera Orchestra. Karen Huffstodt is the sensuous soprano who sings Salome, occasionally over-strained. In the final scene the phrase, *Ah! j'ai baisé ta bouche, Jokanaan*, seems all the more dissolute in French. The drawback of the adaptation is that it makes the whole drama seem smaller-scale than in the original German, and that is heightened by the closeness of the voices in the relatively intimate Lyon acoustic.

The transparency and resilience of Nagano's reading of the score also add to that impression, and there is little sense of horror at the tensely pauseful moment of the prophet's execution when Strauss has a solo double-bass play a high harmonic – what should be a chilling effect. Even in the biting drama of the final scene Nagano brings out the lilting dance-rhythms. Yet at the end the big moments of climax are shattering, notably when the head of John the Baptist is held high by the executioner. José van Dam sings with characteristic nobility as Jokanaan, though sounding a little old for the role. Jean Dupouy with rather throttled tenor tone sounds aptly decadent as Herod.

Salome: Dance of the seven veils; Closing scene. Lieder: *Cäcilie; Ich liebe dich; Morgen; Wiegenlied; Zueignung.*
(M) **(*) DG 431 171-2; *431 171-4* [id.]. Montserrat Caballé, Fr. Nat. O, Bernstein – BOITO: *Mefistofele.* **(*)

One of Caballé's earliest and most refreshingly imaginative opera sets was Strauss's *Salome* with Leinsdorf conducting. This version of the final scene, recorded over a decade later with a very different conductor, has much of the same imagination, the sweet and innocent girl still observable next to the bloodthirsty fiend. The remainder of the recital is less recommendable, partly because Caballé underlines the expressiveness of works that remain Lieder even with the orchestral accompaniment. Bernstein too directs an over-weighted account of the *Dance of the seven veils*. The recording is warm and full.

Die schweigsame Frau (complete).
Withdrawn: ** EMI CDS7 49340-2 (3) [Ang. CDCC 49340]. Dresden State Op. Ch., Dresden State O, Janowski.
Morosus (Theo Adam), Aminta (Jeanette Scovotti).

Strauss was already seventy when he tackled this exuberant comic opera, with its libretto by Stefan Zweig based on Ben Jonson's *Epicoene*. It is evidence of Strauss's energy that he revelled in the heavy task of composing and scoring so much fast, brilliant and complex music, the ensembles pointed by touches of neoclassicism.

The opera opens in the London home of Sir Morosus. It is untidy and the bric-à-brac suggests that it belongs to a former seaman. Sir Morosus's housekeeper thinks that it is about time he got married, perhaps to her. However, the barber suggests that he should marry a young and silent wife. Morosus feels himself too old for such an adventure but he is lonely and will consider the suggestion. Henry, his nephew, whom he thought dead, now appears and Sir Morosus disapproves strongly when he finds out that Henry is a member of a theatrical company; moreover he is quite rude to Henry's wife, Aminta, and finally disinherits his nephew. He tells the barber to find him a wife and bring along a priest at the same time. Henry and Aminta are unconcerned, for they are happy in each other's love, and they enjoy their profession. The barber warns the couple that they are throwing away a large fortune, then an idea is born. Why should not Aminta, with Isotta and Carlotta (two other members of the company), all present themselves the following day as candidates for 'the silent wife'?

The housekeeper warns Morosus that some sort of intrigue is afoot, but he pays her no heed and dresses next morning in his finest clothes. The three ladies present themselves one by one. Carlotta is sent packing as a hopeless country bumpkin; Isotta is much too forward when she tries to read his hand. But Aminta (Timida) charms him with her very naturalness. Morosus tells the barber that Aminta is the one for him, but now he has sudden misgivings. Is he not rather a poor bargain at his age? Aminta regrets her deception, but a priest and notary arrive and a mock wedding ceremony is held, with old shipmates joining in the revelry. When alone, Aminta is miserable, but she plays her role as a flighty, bad-tempered shrew. Finally Morosus appeals for Henry's aid and 'Timida' is sent off, hating her part in the whole affair – but it was all for Henry's sake.

Now a gang of workmen redecorate Timida's room (not for the first time) and vigorous banging is heard. Henry and a member of the company, both in disguise, give her a singing lesson. Morosus can stand it no more and is relieved to hear that the Chief Justice of England is coming to consider his case for divorce. There is more confusion in proving that Sir Morosus is not the first man Timida has known, and a disguised Henry admits that his knowledge of her is very intimate indeed. Morosus in despair threatens suicide. So they all tell him he has been hoaxed. Angry at first, he then takes the joke very well – they certainly put on a wonderful show. Perhaps actors are not so bad after all, and anyway, thank goodness for a peaceful life!

You might count it all a lot of fuss over not very much, and this version is not quite as persuasive as it might be, with a church acoustic giving bloom but blurring some detail. Janowski conducts an efficient rather than a magical performance, and Theo Adam's strongly characterized rendering of the central role of Dr Morosus is marred by his unsteadiness. Jeanette Scovotti is agile but shrill as the Silent Woman, Aminta. A valuable set of mixed success. The CD transfer brings the usual advantages but underlines the oddities of the recording. Disappointingly, EMI includes no English translation with the libretto, an omission difficult to forgive in a full-priced set.

Arias from: *Die Ägyptische Helena; Ariadne auf Naxos; Die Frau ohne Schatten; Guntram; Der Rosenkavalier; Salome.*
(M) *** BMG/RCA GD 60398; *GK 60398* [60398-2-RG; *60398-4-RG*]. Leontyne Price, Boston SO or New Philh. O, Leinsdorf; LSO, Cleva.

Leontyne Price gives generous performances of an unusually rich collection of Strauss scenes and solos, strongly accompanied by Leinsdorf (or Cleva in *Ariadne*), always at his finest in Strauss. Recorded between 1965 and 1973, Price was still at her peak, even if occasionally the voice grows raw under stress in Strauss's heavier passages. It is particularly good to have rarities as well as such regular favourites as the Marschallin's monologue from *Rosenkavalier*, the closing scene from *Salome* and Ariadne's lament. Among the luscious items are the solos from

Guntram and *Die Ägyptische Helena* and the Empress's awakening from *Die Frau ohne Schatten*, one of the finest of all the performances here.

Stravinsky, Igor (1882–1971)

Oedipus Rex (opera/oratorio).
*** Sony Dig. SK 48057 [id.]. Patrice Chéreau (narrator), Eric Ericson Chamber Ch., Swedish RSO & Ch., Salonen.
   Oedipus (Vinson Cole), Jocasta (Anne Sofie Von Otter), Creon (Simon Estes), Tiresias (Hans Sotin), Messenger (Nicolai Gedda).
*** EMI Dig. CDC7 54445-2 [id.]. LPO Ch., LPO, Welser-Möst.
   Oedipus (Anthony Rolfe Johnson), Jocasta (Marjana Lipovšek), Creon (John Tomlinson), Tiresias (Alistair Miles), Shepherd (John Mark Ainsley), Messenger (Peter Coleman-Wright).
*** Orfeo Dig. C07 1831A [id.]. Michel Piccoli (narrator), Bav. R. Male Ch. & SO, C. Davis.
   Oedipus (Thomas Moser), Jocasta (Jessye Norman), Creon / Messenger (Siegmund Nimsgern), Tiresias (Roland Bracht).
(M) **(*) Decca 430 001-2 [id.]. Alec McCowen (narrator), John Alldis Ch., LPO, Solti.
   Oedipus (Peter Pears), Jocasta (Kerstin Meyer), Creon (Donald McIntyre), Tiresias (Stafford Dean), Messenger (Benjamin Luxon).

Stravinsky described *Oedipus Rex* as an opera-oratorio. The action is continuous – though divided into two Acts, and again into six tableaux – and the characters are directed each to give the impression of statues. The text is in Latin, and the narrator, speaking in the vernacular, sets the scene. He tells that at the moment of Oedipus' birth a snare was laid for him and that we shall watch the snare closing.

The men of Thebes lament the plague which is killing the townspeople. They beg their king, Oedipus, to help them. Creon (Oedipus' brother-in-law) now returns from Delphi, having consulted the Oracle. It is revealed that the murderer of Laius still lives in Thebes, undetected and unpunished. Oedipus is determined to track down the murderer.

The chorus prays to Minerva, Diana and Phoebus (or Artemis, Athene and Apollo, as they would be in Greek). Oedipus consults Tiresias, who is blind. The narrator describes him as 'the fountain of truth'. Tiresias at first will not answer Oedipus' questions, but when taunted he says that the king's assassin is himself a king. The implication behind these words angers Oedipus and he suggests that Creon and Tiresias are in league to oust him from the throne.

After asking how angry voices can be raised when the city is so stricken, the narrator announces the arrival of Jocasta and continues, 'Oracles often deceive those who consult them. Did they not predict that Laius would die by the hand of his own son? And was Laius not in fact murdered at the crossroads between Daulia and Delphi?' The word 'crossroads' has a terrible effect on Oedipus, for he recalls that on his journey from Corinth to Thebes he himself killed an unidentified stranger at that same crossroads. Jocasta tries to console and reassure him, but Oedipus remains stricken.

A messenger arrives and states that King Polypus is dead and that Oedipus was not his son but was only adopted, having been abandoned by a shepherd on the mountainside. This is confirmed by the shepherd. Jocasta leaves the scene, horror-stricken. Oedipus thinks she despises his lowly birth. The messenger and shepherd both accuse Oedipus of patricide and incest, echoed by the chorus. The truth sinks in, and Oedipus leaves. The narrator now tells of the death of Jocasta, how she hanged herself, and how Oedipus then pierced his eyeballs with a golden pin from her dress. Oedipus is seen in his desperate state and the chorus offers a final lamentation.

Salonen with his Swedish forces and an outstanding cast, more consistent than any previous one, conducts the strongest performance yet on disc of this landmark of modern opera. He offers an ideal combination of rugged power and warmth, delivered expressively but without sentimentality. The pinpoint precision of ensemble of the choruses, substantial but not so big as to impair sharpness of focus, does more than anything else to punch home the impact of this so-called opera-oratorio, with its powerful commentary, Greek-style. The singing of the two principals, Vinson Cole as Oedipus and Anne Sofie von Otter as Jocasta, then conveys the full depth of emotion behind the piece.

Cole's is a lyrical view of the title-role rather than a big heroic one, with the taxing solos strain-free and sung with both precision and depth of feeling. He sings *Invidia fortunam odit* more poignantly than any predecessor, and also Oedipus' final solo, ending on *Lux facta est* ('All is made clear'). Von Otter as Jocasta readily surpasses her predecessors on record with her firm detail and expressive singing. Simon Estes as Creon and Hans Sotin as Tiresias are both firm and resonant, with Nicolai Gedda still strong as the Messenger. With recorded sound both dramatically immediate and warm, and with splendid narration in French from Patrice Chéreau, echoing that of the librettist, Jean Cocteau, this displaces all rivals, even the composer's own American version.

As the years go by, the depth of emotion in Stravinsky's baldly stylized opera-oratorio hits the listener, despite the detached treatment and abrasive idiom. Following that, Franz Welser-Möst and the London Philharmonic take an expressive rather than a severe, neo-classical view. The singing of the men of the London Philharmonic Choir is less incisive than that of the principal rivals but satisfyingly weighty, and the soloists are on balance the most involvingly characterful of any, led by Anthony Rolfe Johnson, magnificent as Oedipus.

Sir Colin Davis's fine Bavarian Radio version for Orfeo was marred by the unsteady Oedipus of Thomas Moser, and Esa-Pekka Salonen's Swedish performance for Sony had an exceptionally light and lyrical Oedipus in Vinson Cole, where Rolfe Johnson is not only weightily heroic but inflects words more meaningfully than any. Marjana Lipovšek brings mature warmth and weight to the role of Jocasta, easily to rival Jessye Norman on Orfeo and Anne Sofie von Otter on Sony, while John Tomlinson as Creon and John Mark Ainsley as the Shepherd are outstanding too. Only the brisk, prosaic French narration of Lambert Wilson sells the listener short.

Recorded live in Munich in 1983, Davis's Orfeo performance is unerringly paced, with rhythms crisply sprung and detail finely touched in. Though the low-level sound is no help, the orchestral playing is first rate. Jessye Norman is a commanding figure as Jocasta, firm and dramatic, making one wish the role was longer. The microphone catches Thomas Moser's voice unevenly, but he is both expressive and cleanly faithful to Stravinsky, even if the culminating moment of *Lux facta est* is understated. Michel Piccoli as narrator uses the original Cocteau text in French with fine dramatic emphasis.

Solti's view of this highly stylized work is less sharp-edged than one would expect, and the dominant factor in the performance is not so much the conductor's direction as the heartfelt singing of Peter Pears in the title-role. It was he who sang the part in the composer's first LP recording, twenty years earlier and, though the voice shows signs of age, the crispness and clarity of his delivery go with an ability to point the key moments of deep emotion with extraordinary intensity. The rest of the vocal team is good, if not outstanding, and the narration (in English) of Alec McCowen is apt and undistracting. The transfer to CD is outstandingly vivid and brilliant.

The Rake's progress (complete).
(M) *** Sony M2K 46299 (2) [id.]. Sadler's Wells Op. Ch., RPO, composer.
  Tom Rakewell (Alexander Young), Anne (Judith Raskin), Nick Shadow (John Reardon), Baba the Turk (Regina Sarfaty), Sellem (Kevin Miller), Mother Goose (Jean Manning).
**(*) Decca Dig. 411 644-2 (2) [id.]. L. Sinf. Ch. & O, Chailly.
  Tom Rakewell (Philip Langridge), Anne (Cathryn Pope), Nick Shadow (Samuel Ramey), Baba the Turk (Sarah Walker), Sellem (John Dobson), Mother Goose (Astrid Varnay).

For *The Rake's progress*, written a quarter of a century after *Oedipus Rex*, Stravinsky and his paired partners, W. H. Auden and Chester Kallman, drew inspiration from the eighteenth-century British painter Hogarth, and his pictures are often used as a source – direct or indirect – for the opera's backcloths. The setting is also eighteenth-century England, and the first scene is set in the gardens of Trulove's house in the country.

Anne, his daughter, and her sweetheart, Tom, sit happily together, rejoicing in their pleasant surroundings which seem made for the love they share together. Trulove has fears about Tom's future but tells him that he has procured for him the offer of a position in the city. Tom declines and Trulove angrily says that his daughter shall not marry a lazy man. But Tom seeks to try his luck with the goddess of fortune rather than waste his time in an office.

He wishes out loud that he had money and, before he has time to draw breath, Nick Shadow appears with good tidings. An unknown uncle has left him a fortune. Tom thanks Nick; Nick smiles benignly on Tom; Anne and Trulove thank God. Nick then interrupts again as Tom and Anne look into each other's eyes. They must go to London at once, as the inheritance involves some business transactions. Trulove has misgivings about Tom's idleness but Nick drags Tom off, agreeing to receive payment for his services a year and a day later.

They are next seen in Mother Goose's brothel among a group of whores and their followers, whose view is that love is too frequently betrayed. Tom spends his first night in London in the arms of the brothel's proprietress. Anne, desolate at having had no word from Tom, decides to go to London to look for him. Very soon it is clear that Tom is disillusioned with his new lifestyle and is longing for Anne and the countryside. He wishes specifically for happiness, and again Nick is at the ready.

Tom is introduced to Baba the Turk, a bearded lady. Conventionality is not the way to happiness, says Nick, and with bravado Tom agrees to marry Baba. Anne has arrived in London and waits apprehensively outside Tom's house. She sees servants and a sedan chair. Tom gets out and tries to get rid of her. London is not the place for virtue; she must forget him. A veiled head peeps out of the sedan chair. It is Baba, and Tom admits she is his wife. Anne leaves and, as Baba enters the house, the veil drops aside to reveal her grotesque beard.

Next we are in Tom and Baba's morning room, cluttered with possessions acquired on their travels. Tom sulks and, when Baba turns lovingly to him, he repulses her; she is sure that he must be in love with the girl she noticed outside. Tom pushes his wig in Baba's face and her misery is complete. Tom dreams of making bread from stones. 'I wish it were true,' says he – and lo! Nick wheels in a large object covered by a dust-sheet. It is a fake, as it is necessary to feed it with both bread and broken china, but Tom believes it will make his fortune. Nick says he should tell his wife; Tom ripostes that she is buried, and indeed she is sitting motionless in the chair, and the room itself shows evidence of decay.

An auction now takes place, for Tom has considerable debts and his possessions are to be sold. Anne comes in. Sellem now auctions off everything until he comes to Baba. When he removes the wig from her face, she is immediately revitalized, like a doll coming to life. She comforts Anne and tells her to 'set him right. He's but a shuttle-headed lad!' With dignity Baba announces that she will return to the stage and resume her career. Tom and Nick are heard below. Anne goes to find Tom. Baba orders her carriage and tells everyone, 'The next time you see Baba you shall pay!'

In a churchyard Nick reveals himself in his true colours. A year and a day have passed and now Nick requires his payment for services rendered: 'your soul which I this night require'. But Nick allows Tom to try to save himself from hell with a game of cards. Tom wins but Nick is furious, and his fate is almost worse than death: insanity. Nick condemns him and sinks out of sight into a grave. Tom sits on a green mound, putting grass in his hair like a child and calling himself Adonis. We are now in Bedlam, a fearful place. Tom is surrounded by madmen. Anne comes in and addresses him as Adonis and he is happy, for his Venus has come to visit. She cradles him and rocks him to sleep with a lullaby. When he wakes up his Venus has left him and he raves, then sinks back on his straw mattress and dies. The curtain falls, and Anne, Baba, Tom, Nick and Trulove point the moral in chorus: 'For idle hands, And hearts and minds, The Devil finds a work to do.'

The Rake of Alexander Young is a marvellous achievement, sweet-toned and accurate and well characterized. In the choice of other principals, too, it is noticeable what store Stravinsky set by vocal precision. Judith Raskin makes an appealing Anne Trulove, sweetly sung if not particularly well projected dramatically. John Reardon too is remarkable more for vocal accuracy than for striking characterization, but Regina Sarfaty's Baba is marvellous on both counts. The Sadler's Wells Chorus sings with even greater drive under the composer than in the theatre, and the Royal Philharmonic play with a warmth and a fittingly Mozartian sense of style to match Stravinsky's surprisingly lyrical approach to his score. The CDs offer excellent sound, with the words remarkably clear and a nice balance between ambient atmosphere and clear projection of the singers.

Riccardo Chailly draws from the London Sinfonietta playing of a clarity and brightness to set the piece aptly on a chamber scale without reducing the power of this elaborately neo-classical piece, so cunningly based on Mozartian models by the librettists, W. H. Auden and Chester Kallman. Philip Langridge is excellent as the Rake himself, very moving when Tom is afflicted with madness. Samuel Ramey as Nick, Stafford Dean as Trulove and Sarah Walker as Baba the Turk are all first rate, but Cathryn Pope's soprano as recorded is too soft-grained for Anne. Charming as the idea is of getting the veteran Astrid Varnay to sing Mother Goose, the result is out of style. The recording is exceptionally full and vivid, but the balances are sometimes odd: the orchestra recedes behind the singers and the chorus sounds congested, with little air round the sound.

Sullivan, Arthur (1842–1900)

(i) *Cox and Box* (libretto by F. C. Burnand) complete; (ii) *Ruddigore* (complete, without dialogue).
(M) *** 417 355-2 (2). (i) New SO of L, Godfrey; or RPO, Nash; (ii) D'Oyly Carte Op. Ch., ROHCG O, Godfrey.
(i) Cox (Alan Styler or Gareth Jones), Box (Joseph Riordan or Geoffrey Shovelton), Bouncer (Donald Adams or Michael Rayner).
(ii) Sir Ruthven Murgatroyd (John Reed), Richard Dauntless (Thomas Round), Sir Despard Murgatroyd (Kenneth Sandford), Adam Goodheart (Stanley Riley), Rose Maybud (Jean Hindmarsh), Mad Margaret (Jean Allister), Dame Hannah (Gillian Knight), Zorah (Mary Sansom), Sir Roderic Murgatroyd (Donald Adams).

Cox and Box, the pre-Gilbertian one-Acter, is based on a play (called *Box and Cox*) with the story of two men sharing the same rooms – one is a hatter, the other works on a newspaper at night – without knowing it, so that Bouncer, the unscrupulous landlord, can collect a double rent. The problems begin when they both share the same day off. The way in which each of the two main characters enters and leaves in turn, interfering with the other's actions, is most ingeniously plotted; as they end up discovering they are long lost brothers, the dénouement satisfies even Bouncer.

The D'Oyly Carte performance is splendid in every way. It is given a recording which, without sacrificing clarity, conveys with perfect balance the stage atmosphere. It was written in 1867 and thus pre-dates the first G&S success, *Trial by Jury*, by eight years. One must notice the lively military song *Rataplan* – splendidly sung by Donald Adams, an ideal Bouncer – which was to set the style for many similar and later pieces with words by Gilbert, and also the captivating *Bacon 'Lullaby'*, so ravishingly sung by Joseph Riordan. Later on, in Box's recitative telling how he 'committed suicide', Sullivan makes one of his first and most impressive parodies of grand opera, which succeeds also in being effective in its own right. However, early copies of this CD issue contained the wrong version of *Cox and Box*, offering, instead of the outstanding 1961 recording under Godfrey, the later and inferior remake conducted by Royston Nash. This is overprojected by a very forward recording which pushes the soloists forward and thus loses much of the feeling of a stage perspective. The effect is vivid and the words are clear, but the result is coarser and none of the performances match their earlier counterparts. Decca tell us that, by the time we are in print, the correct version will have replaced the Nash account on the CDs. Readers who identify their copy as being the later recording can send their discs back to be exchanged (via their dealer).

Ruddigore, too, comes up surprisingly freshly, though it was a pity the dialogue was omitted. The performance includes *The battle's roar is over*, which is (for whatever reason) traditionally omitted. There is much to enjoy here (especially Gillian Knight and Donald Adams, whose *Ghosts' high noon* song is a marvellous highlight). Isidore Godfrey is his inimitable sprightly self and the chorus and orchestra are excellent. A fine traditional D'Oyly Carte set, then, brightly recorded, even if in this instance the Sargent version is generally even finer.

The Gondoliers (complete, with dialogue).
(M) *** Decca 425 177-2 (2). D'Oyly Carte Op. Ch., New SO of L., Godfrey.
Duke of Plaza-Toro (John Reed), Duchess of Plaza-Toro (Gillian Knight), Luiz (Jeffrey Skitch), Marco Palmieri (Thomas Round), Giuseppe Palmieri (Alan Styler), Gianetta (Mary Sansom), Tessa (Joyce Wright), Casilda (Jennifer Toye), Don Alhambra (Kenneth Sandford).

The Gondoliers, attractively set in Venice, gave Sullivan a chance to try his hand at an Italianate musical style, complete with a famous *cachucha*, and if the plot seems rather more contrived, in its final re-identification of mixed-up infants, than either *The Pirates* or *Pinafore*, it still manages a dénouement that satisfactorily resolves the situation for all the major characters.

Marco and Giuseppe Palmieri are two handsome gondolieri who are quite unwilling to choose among the pretty *contadine* (young local girls) who would be happy to be their wives. They leave the choice to fate and happily agree to marry the two girls they catch in a game of blind-man's buff. Thus Marco marries Gianetta and Giuseppe weds Tessa. The Plaza-Toros arrive, duke, duchess and daughter Casilda, betrothed in her infancy to the Prince of Barataria. With them is their drummer, Luiz, with whom Casilda is secretly in love.

The prince in question was spirited away from his homeland by the grand inquisitor when the king began to deviate from a path of religious correctness. Now, with the death of his father in an uprising, the prince is king, and the Plaza-Toros, who have fallen on hard times, are anxious to lay claim to a share of the wealth by virtue of their daughter's position as the betrothed of the new king.

The grand inquisitor is sought out, as it was he who brought the young prince to Venice. Unfortunately, he placed the baby prince with a gondolier who mixed him up with his own son and then died without settling the matter. The two babies were, apparently, Marco and Giuseppe. The only one who knows the truth is an old nursemaid who lives in the mountains. She will be found, but in the meanwhile the two gondolieri must rule Barataria jointly. Casilda keeps hoping that some impediment will prevent her from having to marry either Marco or Giuseppe; the most obvious one seems that both are already married.

The solution arrives with the old nurse, who tells how, long before the grand inquisitor carried out his infant abduction, she had herself spirited away the real prince and left her own baby boy in his place. Thus, one of the gondolieri is the son of Palmieri, one is her own son, and the king is none other than Luiz! Casilda, at least, is overjoyed.

The vintage Decca D'Oyly Carte set remains fully competitive. Isidore Godfrey's conducting is vividly alive and Decca provided a large and excellent orchestra. The solo singing throughout is consistently good. Jeffrey Skitch and Jennifer Toye are a well-matched pair of lovers, and the two Gondoliers and their wives are no less effective. Thomas Round sings *Take a pair of sparkling eyes* very well indeed. The ensemble singing is very well balanced and always both lively and musical. The *Cachucha* is captivating and goes at a sparkling pace. Everywhere one can feel the conductor's guiding hand. The dialogue is for the most part well spoken, and Kenneth Sandford, who is a rather light-voiced Don Alhambra, makes much of his spoken part, as well as singing his songs with fine style. John Reed is a suitably dry Duke of Plaza-Toro: he makes the part his own and is well partnered by Gillian Knight. The recording has recently been remastered for CD and the quality – originally rather edgy – been brought up to Decca's usual high standard.

The Gondoliers (complete, without dialogue).
(M) **(*) EMI CMS7 64394-2 (2) [Ang. CDMB 64394]. Glyndebourne Festival Ch., Pro Arte O, Sargent.
Duke of Plaza-Toro (Geraint Evans), Duchess of Plaza-Toro (Monica Sinclair), Luiz (Alexander Young), Marco Palmieri (Richard Lewis), Giuseppe Palmieri (John Cameron), Gianetta (Elsie Morison), Tessa (Marjorie Thomas), Casilda (Edna Graham), Don Alhambra (Owen Brannigan).

The snag with the Sargent set of *The Gondoliers* is the curiously slow tempo he chooses for the *Cachucha*, while the long opening scene is rather relaxed and leisurely. At the entrance of the Duke of Plaza-Toro, things wake up considerably and, early in the opera, Owen Brannigan as a perfectly cast Don Alhambra sings a masterly *No possible doubt whatever*. From then on and throughout the rest of the opera, there is much to captivate the ear. Edna Graham's Casilda is charmingly small-voiced (by the same token, Elsie Morison is a little heavy in her song, *Kind sir, you cannot have the heart*). But there is a great deal of musical pleasure to be had from this set. It is very well transferred to CD. The age of the 1957 recording shows in the orchestra, but the voices sound fresh, and there is a pleasing overall bloom.

The Gondoliers (complete; without dialogue); *Overture Di Ballo*.
*** That's Entertainment CD-TER2 1187; *ZCTED 1187* (2) [id.]. D'Oyly Carte Opera Ch. & O, John Pryce-Jones.
Duke of Plaza-Toro (Richard Suart), Duchess of Plaza-Toro (Jill Pert), Luiz (Philip Creasy), Marco Palmieri (David Fieldsend), Giuseppe Palmieri (Alan Oke), Gianetta (Lesley Echo Ross), Tessa (Regina Hanley), Casilda (Elizabeth Woollett), Don Alhambra (John Rath).

This splendid new D'Oyly Carte set of *The Gondoliers*, recorded at Abbey Road Studios in 1991, offers the best sound the Savoy operas have ever received on disc and speaks very well for the standards of the resuscitated D'Oyle Carte company. The men are very good indeed, Marco's *Take a pair of sparkling eyes* (David Fieldsend) is fresh and stylish, while Richard Suart's Duke of Plaza-Toro is as dry as you could wish, while the voice itself is resonant, and his duet in Act II with the equally excellent Duchess (Jill Pert), in which they dispense honours to the undeserving, is in the best Gilbertian tradition. The Duchess too shows her metal in *On the day when I was wedded*, taken with brisk aplomb.

Perhaps Gianetta (Lesley Echo Ross) and Casilda (Elizabeth Woollett) are less individually distinctive and slightly less secure vocally than their counterparts on the Godfrey and Sargent versions, but they always sing with charm. The chorus is first class – the men are especially virile at the opening of Act II. The orchestral playing is polished (noticeably elegant in *I am a courtier grave and serious*) and the ensembles are good too: the Luiz/Casilda duet, *There was a time*, is most affecting, while *In a contemplative fashion* has a relaxed charm, though the spurt at the end could have brought more fire.

This apart, John Pryce-Jones conducts with vigour and an impressive sense of theatrical pacing. The finale opens with a burst of energy from the horns and brings an exhilarating closing *Cachucha* to round the opera off nicely. The acoustic of the recording has both warmth and atmosphere, the vocal balance is not too forward, yet words are remarkably clear, a great credit to the company's vocal coach. It was a great pity the dialogue was not included (on CD, providing it is separately cued, the listener who wants just the music can make his or her own choice). However, this particular opera stands up well without it.

(i; ii) *The Grand Duke.* (ii) *Henry VIII: March & Graceful dance.* (iii) *Overture Di Ballo.*
*** Decca 436 813-2 (2) [id.]. (i) D'Oyly Carte Op. Ch.; (ii) RPO, Nash; (iii) Philh. O, Mackerras.
Grand Duke Rudolph (John Reed), Ernest Dummkopf (Meston Reid), Ludwig (Kenneth Sandford), Dr Tannhäuser (Michael Rayner), Prince of Monte Carlo (John Ayldon), Ben Hashbaz (Jon Ellison), Herald (James Conroy-Ward), Princess of Monte Carlo (Barbara Lilley), Baroness von Krakenfeldt (Lyndsie Holland), Julia Jellicoe (Julia Goss), Lisa (Jane Metcalfe).

The Grand Duke was the fourteenth and last of the Savoy operas. In spite of a spectacular production and a brilliant first night on 7 March 1896, the work played for only 123 performances then lapsed into relative oblivion, although it has been revived by amateur societies. The present recording came after a successful concert presentation in 1975, and the recorded performance has both polish and vigour, although the chorus does not display the crispness of articulation of ready familiarity. Yet this represents perhaps the ideal way to sample Sullivan's least-known major score. Less than first-rate Sullivan can still make rewarding listening – even though, compared with the sparkle and melodic inspiration of *HMS Pinafore*, the music of Act II shows a decline. Act I, however, brings a whole stream of lyrically attractive numbers. The quintet, *Strange the views some people hold*, is in the best Sullivan glee tradition, and the inimitable John Reed (as the Grand Duke) has two memorable songs, more melancholy than usual: *A pattern to professors of monarchical autonomy* and the candid *When you find you're a broken-down critter.* In Act II Julia Goss is first rate in her eloquent lament, *So ends my dream . . . Broken ev'ry promise plighted.*

Gilbert's libretto is impossibly complicated, involving a conspiracy in the Grand Duchy of Pfenig-Halbpfenig and a theatrical company performing there. The opera's sub-title, *The Statutory Duel*, refers to the custom of cutting cards instead of firing shots, which leaves certain characters in the story statutorily dead. In true operetta fashion, everything gets sorted out in the end, with the principal couples reunited. If this does not sound very enticing, there are many felicities in the lyrics to reward the dedicated enthusiast.

The recording is characteristically brilliant. The bonuses are well worth having, with Mackerras's account of the *Overture Di Ballo* showing more delicacy of approach than usual, though certainly not lacking sparkle. Here the recording is digital. The other items are somewhat more inconsequential but are vivid enough to give pleasure.

HMS Pinafore (complete, with dialogue).
⊛ (M) *** Decca 414 283-2; *414 283-4.* D'Oyly Carte Op. Ch., New SO of L., Godfrey.
Sir Joseph Porter (John Reed), Captain Corcoran (Jeffrey Skitch), Ralph Rackstraw (Thomas Round), Josephine (Jean Hindmarsh), Dick Deadeye (Donald Adams), Hebe (Joyce Wright), Little Buttercup (Gillian Knight).

HMS Pinafore: highlights.
(B) *** Decca 436 145-2; *436 145-4* (from above D'Oyly Carte Opera recording; cond. Godfrey).

HMS Pinafore was Gilbert and Sullivan's greatest success. It was so popular that at one time pirated versions were running concurrently in America alongside the 'official' version.

Captain Corcoran of the *Pinafore* has arranged an advantageous marriage for his daughter, Josephine, with the First Lord of the Admiralty and, although she has already found the man of her choice in Ralph Rackstraw, a seaman on her father's ship, she prepares herself to do her duty and marry appropriately to her station.

Meanwhile Little Buttercup, a Portsmouth bumboat woman, reveals her warm regard for the captain and she also tells, enigmatically of 'a canker worm which is slowly but surely eating its way into one's very heart'. We learn later that the captain is more than kindly disposed towards Little Buttercup and, were their respective stations in life more equal, he might well consider a permanent liaison with this 'plump and pleasing person'.

The captain also thinks that Josephine's lack of enthusiasm for Sir Joseph's attentions is derived from her too conscious awareness of her social status, and he and Sir Joseph endeavour to persuade her that 'love levels all ranks'. But this only gives her more confidence in her feelings for Ralph. Dick Deadeye, a seaman of singularly ugly countenance and unpleasant disposition, who positively welcomes the hatred of the crew, is now instrumental in revealing that Ralph has declared his love for Josephine and that the young couple are preparing to elope. They are stopped in the act and Ralph is thrown into the ship's dungeon cell.

Fortunately Buttercup is prevailed upon to provide more details of her terrible secret, and it is discovered that the captain and Ralph were mixed up in infancy when babies. They trade places and, when Ralph becomes the captain, the First Lord of the Admiralty no longer feels able to marry Josephine, who is now only the daughter of a common seaman. Thus Captain Ralph and Josephine are happily united, while Corcoran, now reduced to the lower decks, is able to propose to Little Buttercup.

There is a marvellous spontaneity about the invention in *HMS Pinafore* and somehow the music has a genuine briny quality. It would be difficult to imagine a better-recorded performance than the 1960 Decca/D'Oyly Carte set. It is complete with dialogue, and here it is vital in establishing the character of Dick Deadeye, since much of his part is spoken rather than sung. Donald Adams is a totally memorable Deadeye and his larger-than-life personality underpins the whole piece. Among the others, Jeffrey Skitch makes a first-class Captain; Jean Hindmarsh is absolutely convincing as Josephine (it was a pity she stayed with the company for so short a time) and she sings with great charm. Thomas Round is equally good as Ralph Rackstraw.

Little Buttercup could be slightly more colourful, but this is a small blemish; among the minor parts, George Cook is a most personable Bill Bobstay. The choral singing is excellent, the orchestral playing good and Isidore Godfrey conducts with marvellous spirit and lift. The recording has splendid atmosphere and its vintage qualities are very apparent in this remastered form. The sound is bright and open, words are clear and the ambience is splendidly calculated. The highlights are well chosen and quite generous and are offered at bargain price.

HMS Pinafore (complete, without dialogue).
*** That's Entertainment Dig. CDTER2 1150; *ZCTED 1150* [id.]. New Sadler's Wells Ch. & O., Phipps.
    Sir Joseph Porter (Nickolas Grace), Captain Corcoran (Gordon Sandison), Ralph Rackstraw (Christopher Gillett), Josephine (Elizabeth Ritchie), Dick Deadeye (Thomas Lawlor), Hebe (Janine Roebuck), Little Buttercup (Linda Ormiston).

The digital recording of the New Sadler's Wells Opera production has a splendid theatrical atmosphere. It is consistently well cast, with Linda Ormiston a particularly characterful Buttercup and Nickolas Grace making an appropriately aristocratic Sir Joseph Porter. The lovers sing well together and the briny choral numbers of Act I have plenty of zest. Simon Phipps paces the music fluently, if without quite the unerring timing of Godfrey, and this is very enjoyable from first to last.

Alongside the classic Godfrey set, however, the characterization is just that bit less sharp; if you want a fine modern recording, this new one is very entertaining; but the D'Oyly Carte set under Godfrey remains a clear first choice, and the Sargent version a fine alternative. Both offer a surer sense of style and are also considerably more polished. On the Phipps set, three different endings are offered (separately banded so that listeners can make their own choice).

(i) *HMS Pinafore* (complete, without dialogue); (ii) *Trial by Jury*.
(M) *** EMI CMS7 64397-2 (2) [Ang. CDMB 64397]. Glyndebourne Festival Ch., Pro Arte O., Sargent.
    (i) Sir Joseph Porter (George Baker), Captain Corcoran (John Cameron), Ralph Rackstraw (Richard Lewis), Josephine (Elsie Morison), Dick Deadeye (Owen Brannigan), Hebe (Marjorie Thomas), Little Buttercup (Monica Sinclair).
    (ii) Judge (George Baker), Plaintiff (Elsie Morison), Defendant (Richard Lewis), Counsel (John Cameron), Usher (Owen Brannigan).

It is to Owen Brannigan's great credit that, little as he had to do here, without the dialogue he still conveyed the force of Deadeye's personality so strongly. For those who find the dialogue tedious in repetition this is a very happy set, offering some good solo singing and consistently lovely ensemble singing and chorus work. The whole of the final scene is musically quite ravishing, and throughout if Sir Malcolm fails to find quite all the wit in the music he is never less than lively.

George Baker is of course splendid as Sir Joseph, and John Cameron, Richard Lewis and (especially) Monica Sinclair as Buttercup make much of their songs. Elsie Morison is rather disappointing; she spoils the end of her lovely song in Act I by singing sharp. However, she brings plenty of drama to her *Scena* in Act II. The male trio near the end of Act I is outstandingly well sung – full of brio and personality. The coupling with *Trial by Jury* makes this a fine bargain. The recording is bright and lively and does not lack atmosphere.

Iolanthe (complete, with dialogue).
(M) *** Decca 414 145-2; *414 145-4* (2). D'Oyly Carte Op. Ch., Grenadier Guards Band, New SO, Godfrey.
> Lord Chancellor (John Reed), Earl of Mountararat (Donald Adams), Earl Tolloller (Thomas Round), Private Willis (Kenneth Sandford), Strephon (Alan Styler), Queen of the fairies (Gillian Knight), Iolanthe (Yvonne Newman), Phyllis (Mary Sansom), Celia (Jennifer Toye), Lelia (Pauline Wales).

Iolanthe pokes fun with great success at those two most august of British institutions, the House of Commons and the House of Lords. When its hero, Strephon, is forced to confront the machinations of the Lord Chancellor, the fairies threaten to have him elected an MP, and they determine that every bill he promulgates shall become law by magic, including the abolishing of some of the most cherished privileges of the ruling classes. Then a guardsman, Private Willis, states the truism on which British politics was founded, that 'every boy and every gal / That's born into the world alive / Is either a little Liberal / Or else a little Conservative!'

Iolanthe is a fairy who has dared to break fairy regulations and marry a mortal. For this she has been exiled for 25 years, and the fairy community mourns her loss. The Fairy Queen now revokes the banishment, fearing for Iolanthe's well-being, as she has chosen to live in a very damp place. However, Iolanthe reveals to the queen that she has a half-fairy son, Strephon, whom she has wanted to be near. Strephon, now a shepherd, wants very much to wed his sweetheart, a shepherdess named Phyllis, who is a ward of the Lord Chancellor. The Lord Chancellor will not consent, as he has designs on Phyllis himself.

In fact, the Lord Chancellor is Iolanthe's husband, but he believes that she is dead. She must finally reveal her existence in order to safeguard the future of Strephon and Phyllis; but this means breaking her fairy vows, and this time she will face death. All the other fairies come to her rescue and decide to marry all the available peers. If all the fairies are to die, the law will have to be changed. The Lord Chancellor cleverly rewrites the statute to read that all fairies who *don't* marry mortals must die. The day is saved, as even the queen must now find a consort. All fly off to fairyland.

This Decca recording was the first (1960) stereo *Iolanthe*, not the later and generally inferior remake under Nash. Even though Decca's budget had not yet stretched to the Royal Philharmonic Orchestra, the production was given added panache by introducing the Grenadier Guards Band into the *March of the Peers*, with spectacular effect. The only real gain in the later version was that John Reed had refined his portrayal of the Lord Chancellor, but here the characterization is wittily immediate, and the famous *Nightmare song* undoubtedly has greater freshness. (There is still a hint that its virtuosity is not surmounted without considerable concentration.)

Mary Sansom is a convincing Phyllis, and if her singing has not the sense of style Elsie Morison brings to the Sargent EMI set, she is marvellous with the dialogue. Her discourse in Act II with the two Earls – portrayed to perfection by Donald Adams and Thomas Round – is sheer delight. Alan Styler makes a vivid personal identification with the role of Strephon. To create a convincing portrayal of an Arcadian shepherd is no mean feat in itself, but the individuality of Styler's vocal personality and inflexions is curiously appropriate to this role. Iolanthe's final aria (sung by Yvonne Newman) is a shade disappointing: it is a lovely song and it needs a ravishing, melancholy timbre, whereas here the voice does not sound quite secure. But this is a minor lapse in a first-rate achievement.

The chorus is excellent, and the orchestral detail has the usual light Godfrey touch. Indeed, his spirited direction keeps the whole cast on their toes, and the engaging Act I finale (with both composer and librettist at their most inspired) is wonderfully infectious. The remastering is very successful, the sound bright but with an admirable acoustic ambience which allows every word to project clearly.

(i) *Iolanthe* (complete; without dialogue); (ii) *Overture: Di ballo*.
(M) *** EMI CMS7 64400-2 (2). (i) Glyndebourne Festival Ch., Pro Arte O, Sargent; (ii) RLPO, Groves.
> Lord Chancellor (George Baker), Earl of Mountararat (Ian Wallace), Earl Tolloller (Alexander Young), Private Willis (Owen Brannigan), Strephon (John Cameron), Queen of the Fairies (Monica Sinclair), Iolanthe (Marjorie Thomas), Phyllis (Elsie Morison), Celia (April Cantelo), Lelia (Heather Harper).

There is much to praise in this EMI set and they have refurbished the recording very successfully; it suits the studio-based performance and projects the music brightly without loss of inner warmth. The climax of Act I, the scene of the Queen of the Fairies' curse on members of both Houses of Parliament, shows most excitingly what can be achieved with the 'full operatic treatment': this is a dramatic moment indeed. George Baker too is very good as the Lord Chancellor; his voice is fuller and more baritonal than the dry monotone we are used to from John Reed, yet he provides an equally individual characterization.

For some listeners, John Cameron's dark timbre may not readily evoke an Arcadian shepherd, although he sings stylishly. Nevertheless there is much to enjoy. The two Earls and Private Willis are excellent, the famous *Nightmare song* is very well and clearly sung, and all of Act II (except perhaps Iolanthe's recitative and ballad near the end) goes very well. The famous *Trio* with the Lord Chancellor and the two Earls is a joy. The opening scene of Act I is effectively atmospheric, with Monica Sinclair a splendid Fairy Queen. The *Di ballo overture* acts as an attractive encore at the end of the opera.

Iolanthe (complete; without dialogue). *Thespis* (orchestral suite).
**(*) That's Entertainment Dig. CD-TER2 1188; *ZCTED2 1188* (2) [id.]. D'Oyly Carte Opera Ch. & O, John Pryce-Jones.
> Lord Chancellor (Richard Suart), Earl of Mountararat (Lawrence Richard), Earl Tolloller (Philip Creasy), Private Willis (John Rath), Strephon (Philip Blake Jones), Queen of the Fairies (Jill Pert), Iolanthe (Regina Hanley), Phyllis (Elizabeth Woollett).

After the great success of the new D'Oyly Carte *Gondoliers*, this fresh look at *Iolanthe* is something of a disappointment. John Pryce-Jones obviously sees it as a very dramatic opera indeed, and he ensures that the big scenes have plenty of impact (the *March of the Peers*, resplendent with brass, quite upstages the Decca version incorporating a Guards band). But his strong forward pressure means that the music feels almost always fast-paced, and the humour is completely upstaged by the drama, especially in the long Act I finale, which is certainly zestful.

The Lord Chancellor's two patter-songs in Act I, *The law is the true embodiment* and *When I went to the bar*, are very brisk in feeling, and Richard Suart, an excellent Lord Chancellor, is robbed of the necessary relaxed delivery so that the words can be relished for themselves. Jill Pert is certainly a formidable Queen of the Fairies, but elsewhere the lack of charm is a distinct drawback. And the dialogue, particularly between Phyllis and the two Earls, is sadly missed. Clearly Pryce-Jones was seeking a grand-operatic presentation but, if you want that, Sargent is a far better bet, for he does not lose the sense of Gilbertian fun, which emerges only sporadically here, even in the delightful trio, *If you go in*. The sound is splendid and, if that is of paramount importance, this set dwarfs all the previous recordings.

The Mikado (complete, without dialogue).
(M) *** Decca 425 190-2 (2). D'Oyly Carte Op. Ch., RPO, Nash.
> The Mikado (John Ayldon), Nanki-Poo (Colin Wright), Ko-Ko (John Reed), Pooh-Bah (Kenneth Sandford), Yum-Yum (Valerie Masterson), Katisha (Lyndsie Holland).
Withdrawn: (M) **(*) EMI CMS7 64403-2 (2) [Ang. CDMB 64403]. Glyndebourne Festival Ch., Pro Arte O, Sargent.
> The Mikado (Owen Brannigan), Nanki-Poo (Richard Lewis), Ko-Ko (Geraint Evans), Pooh-Bah (Ian Wallace), Yum-Yum (Elsie Morison), Katisha (Monica Sinclair).
(M) **(*) Decca *414 341-4* (2). D'Oyly Carte Op. Ch., New SO, Godfrey.
> The Mikado (Donald Adams), Nanki-Poo (Thomas Round), Ko-Ko (Peter Pratt), Pooh-Bah (Kenneth Sandford), Yum-Yum (Jean Hindmarsh), Katisha (Ann Drummond-Grant).

The humour of Gilbert and Sullivan's enormously successful *Mikado* remains remarkably fresh, and it is difficult to believe that it is just over 100 years old! The opera has even been heard in Japan, where the local audience found it incomprehensible, for its jokes are particularly British and not really concerned with Japanese institutions. Even the Mikado himself, for all his love of executions, is an essentially genial character, nearer Italian *opera buffa* than Japanese Noh plays. But there is nothing Italianate about his moral code, which is inconveniently puritanical.

Before the story begins, he has decreed that flirting shall be a capital crime, with the result that his son, Nanki-Poo, has had to flee the royal court to escape the attentions of the elderly and unprepossessing Katisha, who has accused him of an idle glance. He had to lose either his freedom or his head and now arrives in Titipu as a wandering minstrel and second trombone player in the town band.

The Mikado's decree has also affected Ko-Ko, who was similarly condemned but then was promptly reprieved in order to take up the post of Lord High Executioner, with the curious logic that he can't 'cut off another's head until he's cut his own off'. Pooh-Bah has single-handedly taken over all the other offices of state and the remunerations that go with them.

Nanki-Poo now meets Yum-Yum (one of 'three little maids from school') and falls in love with her. But she can't marry him, for she is already engaged to be married to Ko-Ko – that very afternoon. Something must be done, for the young couple cannot even talk directly of their love, as that too is against the law, outside marriage. Now the news comes of the imminent arrival of the Mikado himself, hoping for an execution – after supper. If Ko-Ko cannot bring himself to cut off his own head he must find a substitute, or the status of Titipu will be lowered to that of a village. The lovelorn Nanki-Poo offers himself as that substitute. He has no wish to live without Yum-Yum (and, looking in her mirror, she can see his point) so, if he can be immediately married to Yum-Yum, he will agree to his four-week honeymoon being terminated by the executioner's axe. The dreaded Katisha now arrives, seeking either a husband or vengeance, but for the moment she gets neither.

Yum-Yum now prepares for her wedding. She should be happy, but it is, after all, a slight drawback that she will be a bride only for a month. Pooh-Bah now enters, rubbing his hands lugubriously. He has discovered a forgotten law decreeing that a condemned man's wife shall be buried alive with him. Yum-Yum has a difficult choice and she is not sure which is worse: death after a month of bliss with Nanki-Poo, or a life-sentence with Ko-Ko.

Now the Mikado and his party arrive with Katisha in tow and Ko-Ko colourfully describes an 'execution' that has already happened in accordance with his majesty's command. All the chief officers of state (Pooh-Bah) were present and can vouch for the efficiency of the beheading. Katisha looks at the execution certificate and whose name does she find on it? Why, that of the Mikado's son, and the punishment for causing the death of the heir apparent is an unpleasant one. Execution, of course. Something lingering – with boiling oil in it.

Ko-Ko is just in time to catch Nanki-Poo and Yum-Yum before they depart on their honeymoon. But Nanki-Poo is not a bit interested in proving that he is alive after all. Katisha would have her own plans ready for him, if he did. The only solution would be for someone else to marry Katisha, and the only possible candidate is Ko-Ko. There is no help for it. She accepts Ko-Ko's proposal, and Nanki-Poo and Yum-Yum can now make their appearance; moreover they will be able to stay married for longer than a month. Katisha is furious, but everyone else is delighted, and the Mikado thinks it a most satisfactory solution.

The 1973 stereo re-recording of *The Mikado* by the D'Oyly Carte company directed by Royston Nash is a complete success in every way and shows the Savoy tradition at its most attractive. The digital remastering for CD adds to the brightness: its effect is like a coat of new paint, so that the G&S masterpiece emerges with a pristine sparkle. Musically this is the finest version the D'Oyly Carte company have ever put on disc. The choral singing is first rate, with much refinement of detail. The glees, *Brightly dawns* and *See how the fates*, are robust in the D'Oyly Carte manner but more polished than usual. The words are exceptionally clear throughout. This applies to an important early song in Act I, *Our great Mikado*, which contains the seeds of the plot and is sometimes delivered in a throaty, indistinct way. Not so here: every word is crystal clear.

Of the principals, John Reed is a splendid Ko-Ko, a refined and individual characterization, and his famous *Little list* song has an enjoyable lightness of touch. Kenneth Sandford gives his customary vintage projection of Pooh-Bah – a pity none of his dialogue has been included. Valerie Masterson is a charming Yum-Yum; *The sun whose rays* has rarely been sung with more feeling and charm, and it is followed by a virtuoso account of *Here's a how-de-do* which one can encore, for each number is cued (there are 37 separate bands on the two CDs).

Colin Wright's vocal production has a slightly nasal quality but one soon adjusts to it and his voice has the proper bright freshness of timbre for Nanki-Poo. John Ayldon's Mikado has not quite the satanic glitter of Donald Adams's classic version, but he provides a laugh of terrifying bravura. Katisha (Lyndsie Holland) is commanding, and her attempts to interrupt the chorus in the finale of Act I are superbly believable and dramatic. On CD the singers are given striking presence, though the bright lighting of the sound has brought more sibilance. As a CD transfer this is less successful than *The Pirates*.

The Sargent set, the first of his series, dates from as early as 1957 and the recording has been given remarkable vividness and presence by the digital remastering. Words are wonderfully crisp and clear. There is much to enjoy. The grand operatic style to the finales of both Acts, the trio about the 'death' of Nanki-Poo and the glee that follows are characteristic of the stylish singing, even if the humour is less readily caught than in the D'Oyly Carte production. Owen Brannigan is a fine Mikado, but the star performance is that of Richard Lewis who sings most engagingly throughout as Nanki-Poo. Elsie Morison is a charming Yum-Yum and Monica Sinclair a generally impressive Katisha, although she could sound more convinced when she sings *These arms shall thus enfold you*.

The earlier (1958) Godfrey set, available only on tape, is enjoyable enough and well cast, but the later Nash recording, on CD only, is preferable in almost all respects. The one exception is Donald Adams's formidable portrayal of the Mikado himself, outstanding in its authority and resonance, which John Ayldon did not match in the later recording. Thomas Round, too, is a very good Nanki-Poo and Peter Pratt an enjoyably lightweight Ko-Ko (though John Reed's portrayal is even more memorable). Jean Hindmarsh is a petite Yum-Yum and Ann Drummond-Grant a compelling Katisha, with both her arias sung movingly. Kenneth Sandford is common to both sets. Isidore Godfrey conducts with characteristic point and sparkle, and the lively tape transfer seldom betrays the age of the original.

The Mikado (complete, but without *Overture* or dialogue).
⊛ *** Telarc Dig. CD 80284 [id.]. WNO Ch. and O, Mackerras.
   The Mikado (Donald Adams), Nanki-Poo (Anthony Rolfe Johnson), Ko-Ko (Richard Suart), Pooh-Bah (Richard Van Allan), Yum-Yum (Marie McLaughlin), Katisha (Felicity Palmer).

It is apt that Sir Charles Mackerras who, forty years ago with his Sullivan-based ballet, *Pineapple Poll*, brought a breath of fresh air into the then copyright-bound world of G&S, should here offer the most scintillating recording of a Gilbert and Sullivan operetta ever put on disc. With the *Overture* omitted (not Sullivan's work) and one of the stanzas in Ko-Ko's 'little list' song (with words unpalatable today), the whole fizzing performance is fitted on to a single, very well-filled disc. The full and immediate sound is a credit to Telarc's American engineers. The cast, with no weak link, is as starry as those in EMI's 'Glyndebourne' series of G&S recordings of thirty years ago; yet, far more than Sir Malcolm Sargent on those earlier recordings, Mackerras is electrically sharp at brisk speeds, sounding totally idiomatic and giving this most popular of the G&S operettas an irresistible freshness at high voltage.

The tingling vigour of Sullivan's invention is constantly brought out, with performances from the WNO Chorus and Orchestra at once powerful and refined. With that sharpness of focus Sullivan's parodies of grand opera become more than just witty imitations. So Katisha's aria at the end of Act II, with Felicity Palmer the delectable soloist, has a Verdian depth of feeling. It is good too to hear the veteran Savoyard, Donald Adams, as firm and resonant as he was in his D'Oyly Carte recording made no less than 33 years earlier. Let us hope that this is to be the first of a series.

The Mikado: highlights.
(B) *** Decca 433 618-2; *433 618-4* [id.] (from above recording; cond. Royston Nash).
**(*) That's Entertainment CDTER 1121 [MCA MCAD 6215]. Richard Angas, Bonaventura Bottone, Eric Idle, Lesley Garrett, Richard Van Allan, Felicity Palmer, ENO Ch. & O, Peter Robinson.

An hour of highlights taken from the above 1973 Decca set and including almost all the key numbers. This bargain issue includes an excellent synopsis of the plot but, strangely, no cast list.

The That's Entertainment selection is quite generous (62 minutes) and includes virtually all the important music; but it will appeal primarily to those wanting a memento of the English National Opera production. As is normal, the performance is dominated by Ko-Ko, and Eric

Idle's characterization will not be to all tastes; moreover the libretto is often considerably altered – most notably in the 'little list' – not always to advantage.

Without the stage action, the performance is less than racy with Peter Robinson generally adopting very relaxed tempi, although there are memorable moments: the *Three little maids from school*, for instance, and indeed the Act I finale with Felicity Palmer a positively malignant Katisha. Here the dramatically wide dynamic range of the recording is very telling. It is naturally balanced, set back in a nice theatrical ambience, and the words are mostly clear (though the choral singing is at times surprisingly slack); but this does not displace either the D'Oyly Carte or the earlier Sadler's Wells recording (not yet issued on CD) and certainly not the Telarc CD mentioned above.

Patience (complete, with dialogue).
(M) *** Decca 425 193-2 (2). D'Oyly Carte Op. Ch. & O, Godfrey.
Patience (Mary Sansom), Bunthorne (John Reed), Grosvenor (Kenneth Sandford), Lady Angela (Yvonne Newman), Lady Ella (Jennifer Toye), Lady Saphir (Beti Lloyd-Jones), Lady Jane (Gillian Knight), Duke of Dunstable (Philip Potter).

In *Patience* Gilbert makes fun of the cult of aesthetics, represented by Bunthorne and his poetry, in contrast with the down-to-earth soldiering of the Dragoons, led by Colonel Calverley, Major Murgatroyd and Lieutenant the Duke of Dunstable. Not so long ago, the twenty lovesick maidens were engaged to be married to these Dragoons Guards, and now they want something altogether more refined. Reginald Bunthorne, the poet, the object of their adoration, is in love with Patience, a dairymaid, who has previously declared that she wants nothing of love at all.

When the Dragoons arrive, they are appalled that Bunthorne, with his hollow poetry, has captured the hearts of the women. Patience is bewildered because she thought that love was something you felt for elderly relatives, and she wonders how she could be expected to feel it for such as Bunthorne. Lady Angela defines love for her as essentially unselfish, and Patience responds to this eagerly, deciding that she will fall in love straight away.

At this opportune moment, Archibald Grosvenor, Patience's childhood friend, enters, but he is so good-looking that she feels she cannot love him because there would be nothing unselfish in such an action. Indeed, all the ladies – except Lady Jane, whose charms are ripe, although a little faded – transfer their affections from Bunthorne to Grosvenor.

The problems are all resolved when the leading Dragoons decide to go in for a change of costume, from crimson to greens and greys, and Bunthorne coerces Grosvenor into cutting his hair, so that the handsome man now looks commonplace. Patience can now love Grosvenor since he no longer looks like a Greek idol, and the Dragoons pair off with the other girls, the Duke of Dunstable choosing Lady Jane, leaving only poor Reginald Bunthorne to lament his continuing bachelorhood.

The D'Oyly Carte *Patience* comes up superbly in its digitally remastered format. The military numbers are splendidly projected and vividly coloured – *When I first put this uniform on* and *The soldiers of our Queen* have an unforgettable vigour and presence, with Donald Adams in glorious voice. Everything seems to be freshened, and the D'Oyly Carte soloists, chorus and orchestra have never sounded better. Mary Sansom takes the lead charmingly and she is especially good in the dialogue. Both Bunthorne and Grosvenor are very well played. The dialogue is at a slightly lower dynamic level than the music, but that only reflects the reality of the theatre. Overall, this is irresistible.

Patience (complete; without dialogue).
(M) *** EMI CMS7 64406-2 (2) [Ang. CDMB 64406]. Glydebourne Festival Ch., Pro Arte O, Sargent (with RLPO, cond. Groves: *Symphony in E (Irish)* ***).
Patience (Elsie Morison), Bunthorne (George Baker), Grosvenor (John Cameron), Lady Angela (Marjorie Thomas), Lady Ella (Heather Harper), Lady Saphir (Elizabeth Harwood), Lady Jane (Monica Sinclair), Duke of Dunstable (Alexander Young).

Patience was another of the great successes of the Sargent series and (like the Decca set) emerges freshly minted in its new transfer. Although there is no dialogue, there is more business than is usual from EMI and a convincing theatrical atmosphere. The recording is vivid, with no lack of warmth, and the singing is consistently good. The chorus is a strong feature throughout and, where the men and women sing different melodic lines, the clarity of each is praiseworthy.

Elsie Morison's Patience, George Baker's Bunthorne and John Cameron's Grosvenor are all admirably characterized, while the military men are excellent too. The many concerted items continually beguile the ear and Sir Malcolm's accompaniments tell splendidly. All in all, this is the sort of production we anticipated when EMI first began their 'Glyndebourne' series, and it can be heartily recommended.

Though it may seem a curious idea to couple *Patience* with Sullivan's *Irish Symphony*, it provides an attractive supplement. It is a pleasing work, lyrical and with echoes of Schumann as much as the more predictable Mendelssohn and Schubert. The jaunty *Allegretto* of the third movement with its 'Irish' tune on the oboe is nothing less than haunting. Groves and the Royal Liverpool Philharmonic give a fresh and affectionate performance, and the CD transfer of the 1968 recording is generally well managed.

The Pirates of Penzance (complete, with dialogue).
(M) *** Decca 425 196-2; *414 286-4*. D'Oyly Carte Op. Ch., RPO, Godfrey.
> Major-General Stanley (John Reed), Pirate King (Donald Adams), Frederic (Philip Potter), Sergeant (Owen Brannigan), Mabel (Valerie Masterson), Edith (Jean Allister), Kate (Pauline Wales), Ruth (Christene Palmer).

The Pirates of Penzance was the second great G&S success and, in appreciating the full horror of Mabel's predicament in the second Act, it is important to realize that the opera first opened in London in 1880.

Frederic has been apprenticed by mistake to a pirate, instead of to a pilot, by his hard-of-hearing nurse, Ruth. The indentured period should end now that Frederic is twenty-one, and he would indeed like to leave the pirate band and adopt a blameless existence. He has been a slave of duty in carrying out his service to them; he will now be duty bound to devote himself to bringing about their demise.

However, before departing he feels he must remind them that they are not very efficient pirates. A captive has only to plead that he is an orphan to be immediately released. Word has got around, and every mariner who falls into their hands now takes advantage of this means of escape. The pirates leave Frederic on shore with Ruth, his nurse, whom he has tentatively agreed to marry, having no experience by which to judge her suitability as a wife.

However, along comes a group of lovely young girls who are quite as much a surprise to Frederic as he is to them. He is a very beautiful young man and when Mabel, the most engagingly forthright of the sisters, arrives, a romance is begun. Frederic remembers too late that they may be in danger from the pirates and, before they can find somewhere to hide, they have been captured. The pirates think this is a prime opportunity to marry, but the girls are saved from this desperate fate by the arrival of their father, Major-General Stanley, who, by claiming to be an orphan, engenders the pirates' pity (for they are known to be tender-hearted where orphans are concerned).

Back at home, General Stanley is most upset about the lie he has told the pirates about being an orphan. Frederic tries to calm the general with the news that tonight he will apprehend the pirates with a band of policemen. However, the pirates have found a loophole through which to reclaim Frederic's loyalty. Frederic, although twenty-one years old, has had only five birthdays, as he was born on 29 February.

As his papers clearly state that his apprenticeship shall last until his twenty-first birthday, his contract with the pirates has not yet expired. Now Frederic is bound to tell the pirates that the general is no orphan, and they quickly plan their revenge. Frederic tearfully tells Mabel of his return to his old calling (he says she must wait for him until 1940!) and, when she is unable to dissuade him, she finds the policemen and tells their sergeant that he will have to take over the capture of the pirates on his own.

In an amazing battle with the reluctant policemen, the pirates emerge victorious and would dispatch their victims, but the police demand of the pirates that they give themselves up in the name of Queen Victoria. This they are unable to refuse. Dropping their swords, they are immediately apprehended, but Ruth lets it be known that these pirates are, in fact, peers of the realm who have been playing at pirating. Each one is pardoned and paired off individually with a Stanley daughter, and all are welcomed back to resume 'their ranks and legislative duties'.

For CD issue, Decca have chosen the second (1968) D'Oyly Carte recording, and Isidore Godfrey is helped by a more uniformly excellent cast than was present on the earlier set. The dialogue is included, theatrical spontaneity is well maintained, and the spoken scenes with the Pirate King are particularly effective. Donald Adams has a great gift for Gilbertian inflexion – some of his lines give as much pleasure as his splendidly characterized singing. Christene Palmer's Ruth is not quite so poised, but her singing is first rate – her opening aria has never been done better.

John Reed's characterization of the part of the Major-General is strong, while Valerie

Masterson is an excellent Mabel; if her voice is not creamy throughout its range, she controls it with great skill. Her duet with Frederic, *Leave me not to pine alone*, is enchanting, sung very gently. Godfrey has prepared us for it in the *Overture*, and it is one of the highlights of the set. Godfrey's conducting is as affectionate as ever, more lyrical here without losing the rhythmic buoyancy; one can hear him revelling in the many touches of colour in the orchestration, which the Royal Philharmonic Orchestra present with great sophistication.

But perhaps the greatest joy of the set is Owen Brannigan's Sergeant of Police, a part this artist was surely born to play. It is a marvellously humorous performance, yet the humour is never clumsy; the famous *Policeman's song* is so fresh that it is almost like hearing it for the first time. The recording is superbly spacious and clear throughout, with a fine sense of atmosphere. The cassettes are also of excellent quality. The CD transfer is remarkable in its added presence. While a slight degree of edge appears on the voices at times, the sense of theatrical feeling is greatly enhanced and the dialogue interchanges have an uncanny realism.

(i–ii) *The Pirates of Penzance* (complete, without dialogue); (ii) *Overtures: Cox and Box; Princess Ida; The Sorcerer;* (iii) *Overture in C (In Memoriam).*

(M) *** EMI CMS7 64409-2 (2) [Ang. CDMB 64409]. (i) Glyndebourne Festival Ch.; (ii) Pro Arte O, Sargent; (iii) RLPO, Groves.
    Major-General Stanley (George Baker), Pirate King (James Milligan), Frederic (Richard Lewis), Sergeant (Owen Brannigan), Mabel (Elsie Morison), Edith (Heather Harper), Kate (Marjorie Thomas), Ruth (Monica Sinclair).

The Pirates was one of the finest of Sir Malcolm Sargent's G&S sets. Besides a performance which is stylish as well as lively, conveying both the fun of the words and the charm of the music, the EMI recording has more atmosphere than usual in this series. Undoubtedly the star of the piece is George Baker; he makes a splendid Major-General. Here is an excellent example of a fresh approach yielding real dividends, and Sargent's slower-than-usual tempo for his famous patter-song means that the singer can relax and add both wit and polish to the words. As in the Decca D'Oyly Carte set, Owen Brannigan gives a rich portrayal of the Sergeant of Police.

The performance takes a little while to warm up: Sargent's accompaniment to the Pirate King's song is altogether too flaccid. Elsie Morison is a less than ideal Mabel: her opening cadenza of *Poor wandering one* is angular and over-dramatic. However, elsewhere she is much more convincing, especially in the famous duet, *Leave me not to pine alone*. The choral contributions (the opening of Act II, for instance) are pleasingly refined, yet have no lack of vigour. *Hail poetry* is resplendent, while the choral finale is managed with poise and a balance which allows the inner parts to emerge pleasingly. The whole performance is in fact more than the sum of its parts.

The recording has transferred with fine presence and realism, and the CDs include some overtures as fillers on the second disc, including *In Memoriam*, a somewhat inflated religious piece written for the 1866 Norwich Festival.

The Pirates of Penzance: highlights.

(B) *** Decca 436 148-2; *436 148-4* [id.]. John Reed, Donald Adams, Owen Brannigan, Valerie Masterson, Peter Potter, Felicity Palmer, D'Oyly Carte Op. Ch., Godfrey.

A 62-minute selection from the vintage 1968 Decca set is self-recommending. Owen Brannigan is an unforgettable Sergeant of Police, Donald Adams a splendid Pirate King, John Reed his inimitable self as the Major-General, and Valerie Masterson a charming Mabel. The CD transfer is bright and lively, to the point of a degree of sibilance on the solo voices, but there is plenty of theatrical atmosphere.

(i) *Princess Ida* (complete; without dialogue); (ii) *Pineapple Poll* (ballet; arr. Mackerras)

(M) *** Decca 436 810-2 (2) [id.]. (i) D'Oyly Carte Op. Ch., RPO, Sir Malcolm Sargent; (ii) Philh. O, Mackerras.
    King Hildebrand (Kenneth Sandford), Hilarion (Philip Potter), Cyril (David Palmer), Florian (Jeffrey Skitch), King Gama (John Reed), Arac (Donald Adams), Guron (Anthony Raffell), Scynthius (George Cook), Princess Ida (Elizabeth Harwood), Lady Blanche (Christene Palmer), Lady Psyche (Ann Hood), Melissa (Valerie Masterson).

Princess Ida has recently been revived in London and, although the Ken Russell production brought a too heavily underlined jokiness, Gilbert's own humour proved to remain fresh, and Sullivan's score itself certainly has no lack of vitality.

Princess Ida and Prince Hilarion were betrothed as babies and have not seen each other since he was two and she was one. The day arrives when Ida should be handed over as a prospective bride to the court of King Hildebrand, but the bad-tempered King Gama and his three warrior-sons arrive without her. Ida has ensconced herself with 100 female pupils in Castle Adamant, where she runs a women's university in which everything relating to males is excluded (here 'hymns' are even called 'hers'). Hilarion will have to devise a way of meeting her.

King Hildebrand is furious and orders the arrest of Gama and his sons, not least because Gama is quite a horrid and offensive person. Hilarion and his friends, Cyril and Florian, are in fact delighted with the adventure of taking on the community of homophobic women and they set out for Castle Adamant the next day.

Hilarion's party have no trouble finding the castle and getting over the wall. Ridiculing the idea of a feminine university, they find some college robes to put on, conveniently disguising their masculinity, and wander about the place, pretending to be prospective pupils. Although their deception is successful with Princess Ida herself when she comes upon them, the ruse is discovered by Lady Psyche, the Professor of Humanities, who happens to be Florian's sister. She is presumed upon to keep their secret. However, Little Melissa has seen the encounter and is more than pleasantly surprised by her first sight of man. Melissa, the daughter of the Professor of Abstract Philosophy, Lady Blanche, now appears and will not for a moment be fooled into thinking that a baritone and two tenors can be girls. Melissa begs her not to expose the men, reminding her that if Ida should marry Hilarion, Lady Blanche, as her deputy, would become head of the university.

Over lunch, Ida makes the visitors welcome and asks them about Hildebrand's court. Hilarion begins, giving an account of himself; but Cyril, a little drunk, sings a very male song, and their disguises are ruined. Ida jumps up in anger but, as she rushes away, she trips and falls into a stream and has to be rescued by Hilarion. This does not cut much ice with the princess, however, and the men are marched off to the castle dungeons.

Hildebrand now arrives at the castle gates, ready to attack, and announcing his intention of executing her brothers if she does not marry Hilarion by the following afternoon. Defiant, the princess prepares her own combat forces.

The women ready themselves for battle, but when the moment arrives, not one is able to fight. King Gama appears at the gates with his sons, and Ida allows them in, although it is against the rules. Her poor father is a broken man; a thoroughly unpleasant creature, he has been so spoiled and cosseted by Hildebrand that now he has nothing left to complain about and so his pleasure in life is gone.

Ida cannot bear his tears and she relents. Her feminist philosophy in ruins, she opens the gates and admits the men outside. Ida's brothers are still willing to defend her and stand up to Hilarion and his friends, but they are no match. Princess Ida finally concedes that she may just have been wrong about men and, as she gives her hand to Hilarion, Melissa turns to Florian, and Psyche to Cyril. This is fake feminism with a vengeance, but it makes for a very entertaining opera.

Sir Malcolm Sargent is completely at home here, and his broadly lyrical approach has much to offer in this 'grandest' of the Savoy operas. Elizabeth Harwood in the name-part sings splendidly, and John Reed's irritably gruff portrayal of the irascible King Gama is memorable; he certainly is a properly 'disagreeable man'. The rest of the cast is no less strong and, with excellent teamwork from the company as a whole and a splendid recording, spacious and immediate, this has much to offer, even if Sullivan's invention is somewhat variable in quality. The CD transfer is outstanding and the 1965 recording has splendid depth and presence. As a bonus we are offered Mackerras's 1982 digital recording of his scintillating ballet score, *Pineapple Poll*. Mackerras conducts with warmth as well as vivacity, and the elegantly polished playing of the Philharmonia Orchestra gives much pleasure. The record was made in the Kingsway Hall with its glowing ambience, and the CD transfer, though brightly vivid, has a pleasing bloom. Indeed the quality is in the demonstration bracket, with particularly natural string textures.

Ruddigore (complete recording of original score, without dialogue).
*** That's Entertainment CDTER2 1128; *ZCTED 1128* [MCA MCAD2 11010]. New Sadler's Wells Op. Ch. & O, Simon Phipps.
   Sir Ruthven Murgatroyd (Gordon Sandison), Richard Dauntless (David Hillman), Sir Despard Murgatroyd (Harold Innocent), Adam Goodheart (John Ayldon), Rose Maybud (Marilyn Hill Smith), Mad Margaret (Linda Ormiston), Dame Hannah (Joan Davies), Zorah (Alexandra Hann), Sir Roderic Murgatroyd (Thomas Lawlor).

Ruddigore was never one of the top favourites among the Savoy operas. The very title, with its unfortunate possible rhyme with 'Bloodygore', possibly offended Victorian sensibilities; that is a pity, for the score contains some of Sullivan's most delightful inspirations. The lyrical writing often echoes Schubert, and the humour is nicely balanced with the melodrama. Sir Despard's duet with the reformed Mad Margaret (*I once was a very abandoned person*) is one of G&S's most delicious inspirations, and the breathless patter-trio in Act II (*My eyes are fully open to my awful situation*) requires much bravura. It is almost (but not quite) unsingable.

The baronets of Ruddigore are subject to a curse which demands that they commit a crime daily or die in considerable agony. This unfortunate situation was brought about by an ancestor who was imprudent enough to burn a witch. The curse causes some trouble in the Cornish village of Rederring as no one wants to marry a Murgatroyd, or be a Murgatroyd. Dame Hannah was once in love with one and was even betrothed, but when she discovered that her lover was an accursed baronet, she gave him up and remained a spinster instead.

Her niece, the pretty Rose Maybud, is quite a challenge to the male community but, having no parents, she has chosen to take her guiding principles from a book of etiquette, and no man so far has reached her high standard. She is secretly much taken with the young farmer, Robin Oakapple, but he's terribly shy, and etiquette won't permit her to speak first.

Anyway, she doesn't know it, but he's a Murgatroyd, who has run away to avoid inheriting the dreaded curse, leaving the title (with its responsibility) to his brother Despard, who believes Robin to be dead. Robin tells his childhood friend, Richard Dauntless, of his secret love for Rose Maybud and, although Richard promises to woo her on Robin's behalf, he soon follows his heart and speaks for himself. She accepts, Robin is cross, and Rose thus has two suitors and no rule of etiquette to follow. She follows her inclination and chooses Robin.

Mad Margaret, who is broody about Sir Despard, comes jealously to pinch Rose Maybud. Poor Mad Margaret is a sad creature, a little like Lucia di Lammermoor, and often succumbing to periods of madness and simmering passion, brought on long ago by the shock of having her betrothed suddenly denied her, just before her wedding, by his unexpected accession to the hated title. Rose tells her of her own impending marriage, which does not help a bit.

Meanwhile Sir Despard is having a very hairy time indeed keeping up with his daily crime, for which he daily atones by an enormous gift to charity. Jilted Richard jealously comes to tell him where he can find his brother, and Sir Despard throws the proposed wedding of Rose and Robin into disarray. Having considered the etiquette of the situation, Rose will marry Despard instead, she thinks. But Sir Despard, an honourable man beneath his imposed badness, remembers that he is still betrothed to Margaret. They can both now reform and become sober teachers in a National School. Every now and then poor Margaret has a momentary relapse into madness, which embarrasses Despard no end: 'Such action is calculated to provoke remark!' They need to find a formula so that he can bring her up sharp when she feels the first pangs of derangement coming on. They decide that he shall use a secret word, 'Basingstoke', as it is 'teeming with hidden meaning'.

Rose is now paired with Richard, and Robin is none too pleased at his new situation, especially at having – as Sir Ruthven – to perform a daily dastardly deed. He refuses, and all the pictures in the family portrait gallery come to life and forcibly impress on him what eternal agony is like. The chief ghost, Sir Roderic, demands that Ruthven (Robin), for a start, might carry off a damsel from the village. Ruthven sends his servant to bring back an unwilling maiden. Old Adam comes back with Dame Hannah, who angrily sets upon Ruthven until he calls for help, and Sir Roderic steps out of his picture-frame again and comes to his aid, only to find himself face to face with Hannah, who was once his betrothed.

Suddenly Ruthven has a brainwave. He reasons that if a baronet of Ruddigore can die only through his failure to commit a crime, then that very failure or refusal is tantamount to suicide. Since suicide is a crime itself, none of the former baronets should have died and passed on the cursed title. Everyone (except the witch-burner) is innocent.

On the first night of the opera in 1887, the logic of that decision was carried right through and *all* the previous baronets were restored to life. But that proved too much for the first-night audience, so it was eventually modified to include just the most recently deceased, Sir Roderick, who now steps out of his portrait to claim the hand of old Hannah. In addition, Robin retrieves his Rose and only Richard is probably dissatisfied with the final turn of events.

What is exciting about the New Sadler's Wells production of *Ruddigore* is that it includes the original finale, created by the logic of Gilbert's plot. In the theatre the original dénouement works admirably, as it does on record. The opera is strongly cast, with Marilyn Hill Smith and

David Hillman in the principal roles and Joan Davies a splendid Dame Hannah, while Harold Innocent as Sir Despard and Linda Ormiston as Mad Margaret almost steal the show. Simon Phipps conducts brightly and keeps everything moving forward, even if his pacing is not always as assured as in the classic Sargent version. The recording is first class, with fine theatrical atmosphere.

Ruddigore (complete; without dialogue).
(M) *** EMI CMS7 64412-2 (2). Glyndebourne Festival Ch., Pro Arte O, Sargent (with CBSO, cond. Sir Vivian Dunn: *The Merchant of Venice* and *The Tempest: incidental music*).
> Sir Ruthven Murgatroyd (George Baker), Richard Dauntless (Richard Lewis), Sir Despard Murgatroyd (Owen Brannigan), Adam Goodheart (Harold Blackburn), Rose Maybud (Elsie Morison), Mad Margaret (Pamela Bowden), Dame Hannah (Monica Sinclair), Zorah (Elizabeth Harwood), Sir Roderic Murgatroyd (Joseph Rouleau).

The EMI set has been most successfully remastered and offers first-class sound, the voices natural and well balanced with the orchestra, and much warmth and bloom on the recording. This matches Sargent's essentially lyrical approach and emphasizes the associations this lovely score so often finds with the music of Schubert. The performance is beautifully sung and the excellence is uniform. Perhaps George Baker sounds a little old in voice for Robin Oakapple, but he does the *Poor little man . . . poor little maid* duet in Act I with great charm and manages his 'character transformation' later in the opera splendidly.

Pamela Bowden is a first-class Mad Margaret, and her short Donizettian' *Scena* is superbly done. Equally Richard Lewis is an admirably bumptious Richard. Perhaps, surprisingly, Owen Brannigan does not make quite as much of the *Ghosts' high noon* song as Donald Adams on the D'Oyly Carte set, but his delicious Act II duet with Mad Margaret has an irresistible gentility (and one can visualize their traditional little dance-movements, so evocatively is this section managed).

The drama of the score is well managed too: Sir Despard's Act I entry has real bravado (the words of the chorus here are wonderfully crisp), and later the scene in the picture gallery (given a touch of added resonance by the recording) is effectively sombre. Even the slightly prissy crowd effects in Act I seem to fall into place, giving an attractive feeling of stylization. Needless to say, this performance contains the traditional ending. A superb reissue just the same, sounding splendid on CD, which brings some interesting bonuses.

The longer orchestral work, the suite of incidental music for *The Tempest*, dates from 1861, when the student composer was only nineteen. Not surprisingly, it made his reputation overnight, for it displays an astonishing flair and orchestral confidence. The *Introduction* may be melodramatic but it is memorably atmospheric too and, although some of the other items are conventional, the *Banquet dance* is charmingly scored and the *Dance of the Nymphs and Shepherds* is already anticipating *Iolanthe*.

The shorter *Merchant of Venice* suite was composed five years later, and almost immediately the writing begins to anticipate the lively style which was so soon to find a happy marriage with Gilbert's words. The performance here is highly infectious, and the sound is first class, bright yet with plenty of depth and a spacious ambience.

(i) *The Sorcerer* (complete, without dialogue); (ii) *The Zoo* (libretto by Bolton Rowe).
*** Decca 436 807-2 (2) [id.]. (ii) nar. Geoffrey Shovelton; (i; ii) D'Oyly Carte Op. Ch., RPO; (i) Godfrey; (ii) Nash.
> (i) Sir Marmaduke Pointdextre (Donald Adams), Alexis (David Palmer), Dr Daly (Alan Styler), John Wellington Wells (John Reed), Lady Sangazure (Christene Palmer), Aline (Valerie Masterson).
> (ii) Aesculapius Carboy (Meston Reid), Thomas Brown (Kenneth Sandford), Mr Grinder (John Ayldon), Laetitia (Julia Goss), Eliza Smith (Jane Metcalfe).

The Sorcerer is the Gilbert and Sullivan equivalent of *L'elisir d'amore*, only here a whole English village is affected, with hilarious results. The scene is Ploverleigh, home of Sir Marmaduke Pointdextre, Bart, whose son, Alexis, is to be betrothed to Aline, daughter of Lady Sangazure. It is a moment of great rejoicing, except for poor Constance Partlet, who is hopelessly in love with Dr Daly, the vicar. Dr Daly seems disinclined to notice her, in spite of her mother's less than subtle attempts to promote a match.

It also appears that, in the days of their youth, Sir Marmaduke and Lady Sangazure shared a mutual passion but were prevented by convention from carrying through with their desires. However, a consuming flame still burns behind their cultivated conversational style. A very old notary supervises the signing of the deed to certify the nuptials of Alexis and Aline, whereupon Alexis expatiates in praise of true love and discloses that he has resolved to make a gift of love to the village in the form of a philtre in their afternoon tea which will make all those who are unmarried and who take it fall rapturously in love with the first person they see. A sorcerer, Mr John Wellington Wells, has come specially from London to produce the potion. Aline is uneasy. The village gathers for the banquet, partakes of the cup and soon falls asleep.

When the villagers begin to wake up, it is obvious that the philtre has worked. Unfortunately, Constance's first sight is the very old notary who is also very deaf and doesn't hear her loving pleas. Sir Marmaduke enters with Mrs Partlet. This was not what Alexis had intended, but he sticks to his resolve that true love is all. John Wellington Wells is now aware of the problems inherent in the mass administration of the philtre. Lady Sangazure comes after him and he finally tells her a lie about a previous betrothal to a maiden from the South Seas.

Aline finally submits to Alexis' wishes and takes the philtre herself. Unfortunately, the first person she spies is Dr Daly. Now Alexis is in despair. He and John Wellington Wells must find a way to counter the effects of the philtre. The sorcerer says that one of them will have to give up his life to the spirit that controls the potion; he would rather it were not himself, as he is expected to do the stocktaking the following week. Alexis agrees, but Aline intervenes with a point of law.

If, when the philtre is reversed, everyone is to be restored to their former love, what will be her fate when Alexis is delivered up? Her logic is flawless and all agree that the victim will have to be John Wellington Wells himself. The sorcerer is gone in a flash of fire, and the mismatches are undone. Alexis and Aline are restored to each other, Constance gets her vicar, Sir Marmaduke and Lady Sangazure are finally able to fall into each other's arms, and Mrs Partlet can have the very old notary.

John Reed's portrayal of the sorcerer himself is one of the finest of all his characterizations, and this is another D'Oyly Carte recording which is especially welcome on CD. The plot drew from Sullivan a great deal of music in his fey, pastoral vein. Returning to this freshly remastered recording, however, one discovers how many good and little-known numbers it contains. By 1966, when the set was made, Decca had stretched the recording budget to embrace the RPO, and the orchestral playing is especially fine, as is the singing of the D'Oyly Carte chorus, at their peak.

The entrance of John Wellington Wells is an arresting moment; John Reed gives a truly virtuoso performance of his famous introductory song, while the spell-casting scene is equally compelling. The final sequence in Act II is also memorable. While the score is undoubtedly uneven in invention, the best numbers are not to be dismissed, especially in so dedicated a performance. The sound is well up to Decca's usual high standard and the CD transfer is first rate, full, atmospheric and with a natural presence for the voices.

The Zoo (with a libretto by Bolton Rowe, a pseudonym of B. C. Stevenson) dates from June 1875, only three months after the success of *Trial by Jury* – which it obviously seeks to imitate, as the music more than once reminds us. The piece was restaged with some initial success in 1879 but, after eighteen performances, was withdrawn. Unpublished, the score lay neglected for nearly a century in the vaults of a London bank. This recorded performance is the first to be associated with the D'Oyly Carte Company. Although the libretto lacks the finesse and whimsicality of Gilbert, it is not without humour, and many of the situations presented by the plot (and indeed the actual combinations of words and music) are typical of the later Savoy Operas.

Thomas Brown (the disguised Duke of Islington) has a charmingly pompous number, *Ladies and gentlemen*, in which he addresses the crowd and requires their good-humoured prompting in the presentation of his speech; and Eliza's song, *I'm a simple little child*, catches the metre and style of the Victorian music-hall. The musical invention itself is often delightful and shows Sullivan's characteristic craftsmanship.

The two couples are given a fetching double-duet, with a romantic melody and a patter-song ingeniously combined. The plot contains reminders of Offenbach's *La Périchole*, which at the time of the first production of *The Zoo* was playing at another theatre in London, in harness with *Trial by Jury*. As the piece has no spoken dialogue it is provided here with a stylized narration, well enough presented by Geoffrey Shovelton. The performance is first class, splendidly sung, fresh as paint and admirably recorded, and it fits very well alongside *The Sorcerer*. The CD transfer is more brightly lit than its companion, and the opera has animal noises to set the scene and close the opera.

Trial by jury (see above and below).

Trial by Jury exists in two excellent, vintage, recorded versions, both of which show their respective casts at their best. Whether you choose George Baker or John Reed as the amiable judge can be dictated solely by coupling, as both recordings are well produced and technically excellent.

A breach of promise case is to be heard in a British court. The jury are presented with a broken-hearted bride and a villainous defendant, but are reminded that they must remain free of bias. The defendant tells his story. He fell in love with the plaintiff, but then fell out of love with her and in love with someone else. The jurymen understand all this, as they were once young and did just the same thing themselves. However, they are now old and respectable, and they decide he is a reprehensible lout.

The judge is greatly taken by the pretty plaintiff and sends her a private note. The defendant, thinking it might help his case, offers to marry the young woman temporarily. This seems highly questionable, and the counsel looks into his law books for a precedent. The defendant tries another tactic, detailing his bad habits of smoking, drinking and perhaps wife-beating when unsober. The judge suggests testing this possibility by getting the defendant drunk, but the plaintiff protests. Exasperated, the judge presents his final solution. He will marry the young lady himself.

(i) *Utopia Ltd* (complete). Overtures: *Macbeth; Marmion. Victoria and Merrie England.*
**(*) Decca 436 816-2 (2) [id.]. (i) D'Oyly Carte Op. Ch.; RPO, Nash.

> (i) King Paramount (Kenneth Sandford), Scaphio (John Reed), Phantis (John Ayldon), Tarara (Jon Ellison), Calynx (Michael Buchan), Lord Dramaleigh (James Conroy-Ward), Captain FitzBattleaxe (Meston Reid), Captain Corcoran (John Broad), Mr Goldbury (Michael Rayner), Sir Bailey Barre (Colin Wright), Mr Blushington (David Porter), Princess Zara (Pamela Field), Princess Nekaya (Julia Goss), Princess Kalyba (Judi Merri), Lady Sophy (Lyndsie Holland), Phylla (Rosalind Griffiths).

Utopia Ltd was first performed in 1893, ran for 245 performances and then remained unheard (except for amateur productions) until it was revived for the D'Oyly Carte centenary London season in 1974, which led to this recording. Its complete neglect is unaccountable; the piece stages well and, if the music is not as consistently fine as the best of the Savoy Operas, it contains much that is memorable.

Moreover Gilbert's libretto shows him at his most wittily ingenious, and the idea of a utopian society *inevitably* modelled on British constitutional practice suggests Victorian self-confidence at its most engaging. Also the score offers a certain nostalgic quality in recalling earlier successes.

Apart from a direct quote from *Pinafore* in the Act I finale, the military number of the First Light Guards has a strong flavour of *Patience*, and elsewhere *Iolanthe* is evoked. *Make way for the Wise Men*, near the opening, immediately wins the listener's attention, and the whole opera is well worth having in such a lively and vigorous account.

Royston Nash shows plenty of skill in the matter of musical characterization, and the solo singing is consistently assured. When Meston Reid as Captain FitzBattleaxe sings 'You see I can't do myself justice' in *Oh, Zara*, he is far from speaking the truth – this is a performance of considerable bravura.

The ensembles are not always as immaculately disciplined as one is used to from the D'Oyly Carte, and *Eagle high* is disappointingly focused: the intonation here is less than secure. However, the sparkle and spontaneity of the performance as a whole are irresistible. The CD transfer shows the 1975 recording as being of Decca's best vintage quality, full, atmospheric and capturing the orchestra splendidly in an admirable balance with the voices. Of the fillers, the *Macbeth overture* is dramatic and brightly coloured but not inspired, and the *Marmion Overture*, too, is not really memorable. The short ballet, *Victoria and Merry England*, includes some pleasing ideas but again is not top-drawer Sullivan. All are vividly played and brightly recorded.

The Yeomen of the Guard (complete, without dialogue).
(M) *** EMI CMS7 64415-2 (2). Glyndebourne Festival Ch., Pro Arte O, Sargent.

> Jack Point (Geraint Evans), Sir Richard Cholmondeley (Denis Dowling), Colonel Fairfax (Richard Lewis), Sergeant Meryll (John Cameron), Shadbolt (Owen Brannigan), Elsie (Elsie Morison), Phoebe (Marjorie Thomas), Dame Carruthers (Monica Sinclair).

(i) *The Yeomen of the Guard* (complete, without dialogue); (ii) *Trial by Jury*.
(M) *** Decca 417 358-2; *417 358-4*. D'Oyly Carte Opera Ch.; (i) RPO, Sargent; (ii) ROHCG O, Godfrey.
(i) Jack Point (John Reed), Sir Richard Cholmondeley (Anthony Raffell), Colonel Fairfax (Philip Potter), Sergeant Meryll (Donald Adams), Shadbolt (Kenneth Sandford), Elsie (Elizabeth Harwood), Phoebe (Ann Hood), Dame Carruthers (Gillian Knight).
(ii) Judge (John Reed), Plaintiff (Ann Hood), Defendant (Thomas Round), Counsel (Kenneth Sandford), Usher (Donald Adams).

The Yeomen of the Guard makes a particularly satisfying compromise between the seriousness of the situation of a wrongly accused prisoner condemned to death in the Tower of London, and the moments of humour inherent in his ingenious rescue. All the characters are finely drawn, and the music, from the *Overture* onwards, shows Sullivan at his most inspired, able at last to write expansively and movingly, as well as light-heartedly as the occasion demands.

As the opera opens, Phoebe, daughter of Sergeant Meryll, serving with the warders of the Tower of London, is spinning, and she immediately rejects the amorous but unrefined advances of Wilfred, the clumsy head-jailer. Wilfred is none too pleased when Phoebe expresses pity for poor Colonel Fairfax who is to be executed this very day, condemned on false charges of witchcraft, brought by a relation who covets his fortune.

There is hope of a last-minute pardon arriving with Sergeant Meryll's son, Leonard, who is expected within the hour, to join the yeomen. Leonard arrives, but no reprieve, so the sergeant plots to disguise Fairfax as his son, while Leonard waits in hiding, thus granting them more time to obtain a pardon.

Meanwhile Fairfax, determined to cheat the scheming relative who is plotting to inherit his estates, begs the lieutenant of the tower to find him someone who will marry him before he is executed. Such a person is found in the form of Elsie, a singer who performs with Jack Point, the jester. She knows the money will help her mother, and it won't be for long. Jack Point swallows his jealousy, and Elsie (blindfolded for the ceremony) is an instant bride. Meanwhile Phoebe manages to steal the key to Fairfax's cell from Wilfred, who is easily distracted because he harbours more than a little passion for Phoebe.

Shortly afterwards, the yeomen welcome their newly arrived but as yet unknown member. However, it is not Leonard Meryll but Fairfax, clean-shaven and now unrecognizable. A hue and cry is raised when the prisoner's escape is discovered, yet in the ensuing days the missing prisoner is not found, and the plot thickens. Elsie falls ill, greatly distressed that she is now married to a man whom she would not even recognize. She is being looked after in Sergeant Meryll's home by Dame Carruthers, the tower housekeeper, who has a soft spot for the sergeant.

Jack Point contrives another trick with Wilfred, who is in disgrace over the escape: they claim to have seen the prisoner in the moat and to have shot him. This appears to free Elsie from her marriage vows, but meanwhile she is being wooed by Fairfax/Meryll, who pretends to show Jack Point how to win a lady's heart but who soon loves Elsie himself.

Phoebe, who has had her eye on the new tower warder for herself, immediately reveals her jealousy. Wilfred catches this slip, as Leonard Meryll is supposed to be her brother. But Phoebe reminds Wilfred that he himself has just shot Fairfax in the moat! Nevertheless, in order to ensure Wilfred's silence, Phoebe promises to marry him.

The real Leonard returns with the pardon, which Fairfax's accuser had tried to delay. Dame Carruthers gets the drift and her price for silence is the hand of the good sergeant (who is well and truly implicated in the plot). Elsie thinks her wedding to Leonard is about to begin when, dramatically, the lieutenant of the tower puts a stop to the affair. Fairfax is alive and Elsie is his wife. Fairfax comes to her.

She is at first horrified, her eyes full of tears, then she looks up and is, of course, delighted to discover she is already married to the man of her choice. But the happiness of the story's dénouement is dimmed by the jester's reaction. Poor Jack Point, heartbroken, sings in a faltering voice his jester's song of a lost lady-love, then falls, senseless, to the ground as the curtain falls.

Sir Malcolm Sargent recorded *The Yeomen of the Guard* in stereo twice very successfully. The later Decca set has marginally the finer recording, but the solo singing in both versions is equally fine. In the Decca version, Sir Malcolm's breadth of approach is at once apparent in the *Overture*, and when the chorus enters (*Tower warders*) the feeling of opera rather than operetta is striking. Indeed, one has seldom heard the choruses expand with such power, nor indeed has the orchestra (especially the brass) produced such a regal sound.

As the work proceeds the essential lyricism of Sargent's reading begins to emerge more and more, and the ensemble singing is especially lovely. There is no lack of drama either, and indeed the only aspect of the work to be played down somewhat is the humorous side. The interjections of Jack and Wilfred in the Act I finale are obviously seen as part of the whole rather than a suggestion of the humour that somehow seems to intrude into the most serious of human situations.

The pathos of the famous Jester's song in Act II is played up, and the only moment to raise a real smile is the duet which follows, *Tell a tale of cock and bull*. But with consistently fine singing throughout from all the principals (and especially from Elizabeth Harwood as Elsie), this *Yeomen* is unreservedly a success with its brilliant and atmospheric Decca recording.

The singing on Sargent's EMI recording (which dates from 1960) is very persuasive. As on his Decca set, the trios and quartets with which this score abounds are most beautifully performed and skilfully balanced, and the ear is continually beguiled. Owen Brannigan's portrayal of Wilfred is splendidly larger than life and Monica Sinclair is a memorable Dame Carruthers. The finales to both Acts have striking breadth, and the delightfully sung trio of Elsie, Phoebe and the Dame in the finale of Act II is a good example of the many individual felicities of this set. *Strange adventure*, too, is most beautifully done. As in the Decca recording, there is very little feeling of humour, but the music triumphs. The sound is excellent, with the CDs bringing greater presence and definition. However, the Decca set also includes Godfrey's immaculately stylish and affectionate *Trial by Jury* with John Reed as the Judge.

COLLECTIONS

'The best of Gilbert & Sullivan': excerpts from: *The Gondoliers; HMS Pinafore; Iolanthe; The Mikado; The Pirates of Penzance.*
(B) *** EMI CDZ7 62531-2; *LZ 762531-4.* Elsie Morison, Edna Graham, Monica Sinclair, Marjorie Thomas, Richard Lewis, Alexander Young, George Baker, John Cameron, Owen Brannigan, Geraint Evans, James Milligan, Ian Wallace, Glyndebourne Festival Ch., Pro Arte O, Sargent.

Sargent's vintage studio recordings of the Savoy Operas were recorded between 1957 and 1963, with a wholly admirable cast. They blew a fresh breeze through the D'Oyly Carte performing tradition (of which Sargent himself had theatrical experience) and set very high musical standards. With very nearly a maximum amount of music included (72 minutes 47 seconds), this makes a fine bargain sampler. The longest selection comes from *The Mikado* (with nine items included), not the strongest of the performances but with many felicities. The slow tempo for the *Cachucha* remains a curious drawback in the excerpts from *The Gondoliers*; but the items from *Iolanthe, The Pirates* and *Pinafore* have plenty of zest, and the lyrical singing is a pleasure throughout, when the cast is so strong. The transfers are fresh and clear, with an abundance of ambience.

'The best of Gilbert and Sullivan': excerpts from: *The Gondoliers; HMS Pinafore; The Mikado; The Pirates of Penzance.*
(B) *** EMI Miles of Music *TC2-MOM 106.* Elsie Morison, Monica Sinclair, Edna Graham, Marjorie Thomas, Richard Lewis, Alexander Young, George Baker, John Cameron, Owen Brannigan, Geraint Evans, James Milligan, Ian Wallace, Glyndebourne Festival Ch., Pro Arte O, Sargent.

'Gilbert and Sullivan favourites': excerpts from: *The Gondoliers; HMS Pinafore; Iolanthe; The Mikado; Patience; The Pirates of Penzance; Ruddigore; The Yeomen of the Guard.*
(B) *** EMI Miles of Music *TC2-MOM 114.* (artists as above, plus) Anthony Raffell, Elizabeth Harwood, Pamela Bowden, Joseph Rouleau; Glyndebourne Festival Ch., Pro Arte O, Sargent.

These two admirable cassette compilations, each offering over 80 minutes of music, should prove stimulating motorway entertainment. The first offers more extensive selections from four favourite operas, while the second ranges more widely; however, as nothing is duplicated, they are complementary. The lollipops are fairly evenly divided: Owen Brannigan's immortal account of the *Policeman's song* from *Pirates* is on *TC2-MOM 114* (which is a marginal first choice), while the longer groups of numbers from that same opera, *Iolanthe* and *Pinafore* on *TC2-MOM 106* contain much that is very engaging indeed. Excellent, fresh transfers with the words coming through clearly.

Highlights from: *The Gondoliers; HMS Pinafore; Iolanthe; The Mikado; The Pirates of Penzance; The Yeomen of the Guard.*
(B) **(*) CfP CD-CFP 4238; *TC-CFP 4238* [id.]. Soloists, Glyndebourne Festival Ch., Pro Arte O, Sargent.

Another attractive selection of highlights offering samples of six of Sargent's vintage EMI recordings. There is some distinguished solo singing and, if the atmosphere is sometimes a little cosy (once again one notices that the *Cachucha* from *The Gondoliers* sounds slower than ever, heard out of context of the complete performance), there is a great deal to enjoy. The recordings have transferred well.

'A Gilbert and Sullivan Gala': Arias, duets and trios from: *The Gondoliers; The Grand Duke; Haddon Hall; HMS Pinafore; Iolanthe; The Mikado; Patience; The Pirates of Penzance; Ruddigore; The Sorcerer; The Yeomen of the Guard.*
Withdrawn: (M) *** EMI CDM7 67802-2 [id.]. Valerie Masterson, Sheila Armstrong, Robert Tear, Benjamin Luxon, Bournemouth Sinf., Alwyn; or N. Sinf., Hickox.

This superb collection combines the best part of two recitals of G&S, the first made by Valerie Masterson and Robert Tear with Kenneth Alwyn in 1982 and recorded at the Guildhall, Southampton, and the second, where the balance is even more realistic, in EMI's No. 1 Studio at Abbey Road, with Sheila Armstrong, Tear and Benjamin Luxon under the direction of Richard Hickox in 1984. The result is one of the most successful (and generous – nearly 73 minutes) anthologies of this repertoire ever put on disc. Quite apart from the excellence of the singing and the sparkling accompaniments, the programme is notable for the clever choice of material, with items from different operas engagingly juxtaposed instead of being just gathered together in sequence. The singing from the first group is particularly fine. Valerie Masterson's upper range is ravishingly fresh and free. It is a pity her *Pinafore* number had to be omitted, but the final cadence of *Leave me not to pine alone (Pirates)* is very touching, and she sings Yum-Yum's famous song from *The Mikado, The sun whose rays*, with a captivating, ingenuous charm. Robert Tear, too, is in excellent form and his *A wandering minstrel* is wonderfully stylish, while *A magnet hung in a hardware shop* has fine sparkle. The *Prithee, pretty maiden* duet (also from *Patience*) is hardly less endearing. In the second recital it is the ensemble items that score, notably the duets from *Ruddigore, The Gondoliers* and the vivacious *Hereupon we're both agreed* from *The Yeomen of the Guard*; the star here is Benjamin Luxon. He is splendid in the principal novelty, *I've heard it said*, from *Haddon Hall*, a vintage Sullivan number even if the words are not by Gilbert, and he is left to end the concert superbly with a bravura account of *My name is John Wellington Wells* from *The Sorcerer*, and a splendidly timed, beguilingly relaxed account of *When you find you're a broken-down critter* from *The Grand Duke*, in which Richard Hickox and the Northern Sinfonia make the very most of Sullivan's witty orchestral comments.

'The world of Gilbert and Sullivan': excerpts from: (i) *The Gondoliers; HMS Pinafore; Iolanthe;* (ii) *The Mikado;* (i) *The Pirates of Penzance;* (iii) *The Yeomen of the Guard.*
(B) *** Decca 430 095-2; *430 095-4* [id.]. Soloists, D'Oyly Carte Op. Ch., New SO or RPO, (i) Godfrey; (ii) Nash; (iii) Sargent.

A quite admirable selection from the vintage series of Decca D'Oyly Carte recordings made between 1959 (*HMS Pinafore* – still the finest of the whole series) and 1973 (Royston Nash's *Mikado*). This was the right choice, as it is much more strongly cast than the earlier, Godfrey set, with John Reed shining brightly as Ko-Ko. His 'little list' song is wonderfully relaxed, and *Tit willow* is charming. He is equally good as Sir Joseph Porter, KCB, in *Pinafore*, where his splendid *I am the monarch of the sea* is preceded by some highly atmospheric stage business. Owen Brannigan's unforgettable portrayal of the Sergeant of Police is demonstrated in the excerpts from *The Pirates of Penzance* (as is Valerie Masterson's charming Mabel), and two of the most delectable items are the Act II trios from *Pinafore* and *Iolanthe*, both liltingly infectious. Sargent's fine *Yeomen of the Guard* is only briefly represented, so we must hope that further selections are to follow. The recording has fine atmosphere and presence throughout; *The Gondoliers*, however, betrays the same slightly degraded treble response of the complete recording. But overall, with 62 minutes of music offered, this is a bargain which will give much delight.

'The world of Gilbert and Sullivan' Vol. 2: excerpts from: (i) *The Gondoliers; HMS Pinafore; Iolanthe;* (ii) *The Mikado;* (i) *Patience; The Pirates of Penzance;* (iii) *Princess Ida;* (i) *Ruddigore; The Sorcerer;* (iii) *The Yeomen of the Guard.*

(B) *** Decca 433 868-2; *433 868-4* [id.]. Soloists, D'Oyly Carte Op. Ch., New SO, RPO, ROHCG O, (i) Godfrey; (ii) Nash; (iii) Sargent.

Volume 2 covers the ten most popular operas and includes ensembles as well as solo items. As ever, John Reed's contribution is outstanding in *Patience, Ruddigore* (where his role is more lyrical) and especially *The Sorcerer* (a virtuoso *My name is John Wellington Wells*) and the delicious *If you give me your attention* from *Princess Ida*. But there is plenty to enjoy here and Donald Adams's *Ghosts' high noon* song from *Ruddigore* is unforgettable. Lively recording with plenty of theatrical atmosphere.

Styne, Jule (born 1905)

Funny girl.
(M) *** EMI ZDM7 64661-2 [id.]. Broadway cast. Ch. & O, Milton Rosenstock.
 Fanny Brice (Barbra Streisand), Nick Arnstein (Sydney Chaplin), Mrs Brice (Kay Medford), Mrs Strakosh (Jean Stapleton), Eddy Ryan (Danny Meehan).

Jule Styne tells how, when they were desperately looking for a suitable lead for this biographical musical, he went night after night for a month to hear a new young singer, Barbra Streisand, go through her act at the Bonsoir in Greenwich Village, and said to himself, 'This has to be Fanny Brice.' He was already committed to Ann Bancroft but, fortunately for everyone concerned, when she heard the show's great songs in draft form, *Don't rain on my parade, The music that makes me dance, Who are you now?* and *People*, Miss Bancroft realized that they were not for her, and so a show-business legend was born and a star created. Streisand made them utterly her own. She was a maverick artistic personality and did not get on with her leading man, Sydney Chaplin. Egos and tempers flared, there were pressures on the plot from the next generation of the Brice family (in real life, Brice's husband went to prison and the marriage broke up). But after five postponements the show finally opened on Broadway in March 1964 and Streisand at one and the same time both became and eclipsed Fanny Brice. In this story of a show-business career more tempestuous than her own, Streisand's vibrant, almost overwhelming vocal personality dwarfs everyone else on this record (as Sydney Chaplin feared), but the sheer adrenalin of her projection of the songs, especially *Don't rain on my parade* with its typically Stynian jagged rhythmic line, and of course the simmering intensity of *People*, is unique. The Capitol/EMI recording has riveting presence and projection so that one has to take a deep breath at the end of the final reprise of *Don't rain on my parade*, after 52 minutes with the electricity sparking at the highest possible voltage.

Szymanowski, Karol (1882–1937)

(i) *King Roger* (opera; complete); (ii) *Harnasie (The Highland Robbers)* (ballet pantomime), *Op. 55.*
*** Olympia OCD 303 A/B [id.]. (i) Polish Pathfinders' Union Children's Ch.; (ii) Bachleda; (i; ii) Warsaw Nat. Op. Ch. & O; (i) Mierzejewski; (ii) Wodiczko.
 Roger II (Andrzej Hiolski), Roxana (Hanna Rumowska), Edrisi (Zdzislaw Nikodem), Shepherd (Kazimierz Pustelak), Archbishop (Marek Dabrowski), Deaconess (Anna Malewicz-Madej).

These two CDs accommodate Szymanowski's masterpiece, the opera *King Roger*, and his last stage-work, the ballet *Harnasie*. Both recordings date from the mid-1960s; they first appeared here, on the Muza label, in very inferior LPs which sounded as if they were made from dog biscuits. The present transfer has made a magnificent job of the originals, which sound strikingly detailed and rich. *King Roger* is the product of Szymanowski's fascination with Eastern mysticism and Arab culture. It is set in twelfth-century Sicily and its opening scene, at Mass in the Cathedral of Palermo, is music of awesome beauty.

The king and his court enter. The archbishop and the abbess urge him to protect the Church, particularly from a new voice who corrupts all who hear. Edrisi, an Arab scholar, explains that they speak of a young shepherd boy. Roxana, the king's wife, begs that the king should at least let the boy speak up in his own defence and the king commands that the boy be brought before him. The crowd call for the boy's death.

Answering the king's questions, the boy shepherd, who has a certain radiance, says that his god is young, beautiful and full of life. Roxana reacts favourably to the boy, which displeases the king. He is tempted to condemn him but finally decides to let him go free. But he must appear at the palace gates that night.

The crowd is displeased, but the boy is satisfied. Later, the king waits for the boy. Edrisi notices that the king is very tense, partly because he is not sure how to react to Roxana's obvious sympathy towards the shepherd. The boy arrives, radiant as ever, almost shining, and his auburn hair flows about his shoulders; four followers are carrying musical instruments. He greets the king in the name of eternal love; he says he comes from Benares, on the banks of the River Ganges. He is the messenger of God: from God he derives his powers.

The horrified king again notices his wife's ardent response. He feels he is hearing blasphemy and silences the boy. The boy's followers now begin an Arabic dance and, when Roxana is again obviously caught up in the shepherd's influence, the king has the boy bound in chains; but they are angrily broken and thrown at the king's feet. The boy then leads off Roxana, and the people follow into 'the kingdom of light'. The king is left alone with Edrisi; then he suddenly throws away his crown, announcing that he too will follow the shepherd, but as a pilgrim, not a king.

The king and Edrisi are now seen in the ruins of a Greek temple and the king calls his wife's name and hears her voice replying in the distance. He calls again, but this time it is the shepherd who answers, Roxana now at his side, and the shepherd calls on him to leave his fears where he left his sword. Roxana suggests that the shepherd's presence fills the world and she encourages the king to throw flowers on the altar. It is now obvious that the shepherd is a personification of the Greek god, Dionysus; his followers are bacchants and maenads, and they whirl into a mad dance in which Roxana ecstatically joins. Then they disappear, and the king is alone again with Edrisi. They greet the rising sun.

It is a strange scenario, but the sense of ecstasy evoked by the music is intoxicating, and the complex textures and unparalleled wealth of colour Szymanowski has at his command are impressive by any standards. The Dionysiac atmosphere will be familiar to those who know *The Song of the night* and the *First Violin concerto*. Andrzej Hiolski is a more than adequate Roger and Hanna Rumowska an excellent Roxana. The whole cast is dedicated and the extensive forces involved, including a children's choir and a large orchestra and chorus, respond to the direction of Mieczyslaw Mierzejewski with fervour.

It is a pity that Rowicki's later account of *Harnasie*, made in the mid-1970s, could not have been chosen in preference to this earlier version, which runs to about 25 minutes, whereas the whole ballet takes about 34. Not that there are any serious inadequacies here, for the playing and singing are totally committed and do justice to its hedonistic nationalism. An indispensable set for all lovers of this composer.

Taneyev, Sergei (1856–1915)

The Oresteia (complete).
**(*) Olympia OCD 195 A/B [id.]. Belorussian State Ch. & O, Kolomizheva.
    Agamemnon (Victor Chernobayev), Clytemnestra (Lidiya Galushkina), Aegisthus (Anatoly Bokov), Orestes (Ivan Dubrovin).

Taneyev regarded *The Oresteia* as his *chef d'oeuvre* and took some seven years over its composition. It was warmly received at its première in 1895 but was never again performed in his lifetime. (Napravnik wanted to cut it and Taneyev refused.) Not surprisingly, considering he was the author of a masterly study on Invertible Counterpoint, he was, as Gerald Abraham put it, 'more interested in Josquin than Chopin', and it hardly seems possible that he should have composed so effective an opera: to compress the whole of the *Oresteia* into the space of 147 minutes and the idiom of a nineteenth-century Russian opera is no mean feat.

The drama proceeds on classical lines – in other words, the action emerges through narratives, monologues and orchestral entr'actes, with no gore on stage. The first scene celebrates Agamemnon's victory in Troy, and Aegisthus' and Clytemnestra's conspiracy to murder him. In the second, Cassandra prophesies Agamemnon's death and her own, which duly occur.

In the second part, Clytemnestra is haunted by Agamemnon's ghost and asks Electra to placate the gods with a sacrifice. Orestes reveals himself to Electra and then, with her assistance, murders Aegisthus and Clytemnestra.

In the third part, Orestes is pursued by the Furies (the Eumenides) and seeks Apollo's forgiveness. Apollo orders him to return to Athens where at the court of Areopagites he is eventually released from guilt, thanks to the intervention of the goddess Athena.

Taneyev's reputation as an academic must be reassessed in light of this piece, for this is not only a finely wrought work; it is full of imaginative touches and effective musical drama. Rimsky-Korsakov spoke of its 'pages of unusual beauty and expressiveness'. This performance, recorded in 1978, was briefly available on DG in a rather smoother transfer than on these Olympia CDs, vivid though they are. There are some splendid singers. There is a tendency for the sound to coarsen on climaxes, though some of the blame for this must be laid at the feet of the orchestra. A most worthwhile issue.

Tavener, John (born 1944)

Mary of Egypt (complete).
*** Collins Dig. 7023-2 (2) [id.]. Ely Cathedral Ch., Britten–Pears Chamber Ch., Aldeburgh Festival Ens., Lionel Friend.
   Mary (Patricia Rozario), Zossima (Stephen Varcoe), Voice of Mother of God (Chloe Goodchild).

Tavener, inspired as he is by his Greek Orthodox faith, says that 'Music is a form of prayer, a mystery', and that applies to this stylized opera. *Mary of Egypt* was recorded live at the Aldeburgh Festival first performances in June 1992 and, characteristically, Tavener compels you to accept his slow pacing and paring down of texture. The idiom brings points in common with the minimalists, but one can hardly miss the dedication behind the writing, giving it something of the magnetic quality which has brought Tavener's concertante cello piece, *The Protecting Veil*, such wide success.

In many ways the disc works better than the live staging when, with the help of the libretto, the developments in the bald, stylized plot can be followed more readily.

The five brief Acts of what Tavener describes as an 'Icon of Music and Dance' tell the story of Mary, the harlot who finds salvation as a hermit in the desert, giving comfort to the pious, ascetic monk, Zossima, teaching him the need for love. The musical landmarks are sharply defined in clear-cut, memorable motifs, with moments of violence set sharply against the predominant mood of meditation.

What is disconcerting is Tavener's use, as a frame for each Act, of a disembodied voice to represent the Mother of God. It sounds like a very raw baritone, but in fact is the voice of Chloe Goodchild, using weird oriental techniques. Her message of salvation, strange though it sounds, comes to be magnetic too.

Under Lionel Friend the performance has a natural concentration, with Patricia Rozario as Mary and the baritone, Stephen Varcoe, as Zossima both outstanding. Their confrontation in Act III brings a radiant duet that acts as a climactic centre-piece to the whole work.

After that, Act IV (a voiceless pageant on Mary's life up to her death) and the equally brief Act V (her burial by Zossima) come almost as epilogue, with the 100 minutes treated as a single span. A synopsis and libretto are provided, but instead of notes there is a 15-minute interview with the composer, informative but disconcertingly overamplified.

Tchaikovsky, Peter (1840–93)

The Snow Maiden (Snegourotchka): complete incidental music.
Withdrawn: **(*) Chant du Monde LDC 278 904 [id.]. Simonova, Martinov, Elnikov, Lomonossov, USSR R, & TV Ch. & O, Provatorov.

This single disc conveniently and generously includes all the 80 minutes of incidental music Tchaikovsky wrote for *The Snow Maiden*, and much of it is vintage material, very delightful, bringing reminders of *Eugene Onegin* in the peasant choruses and some of the folk-based songs, and of the later Tchaikovskian world of *The Nutcracker* in some of the dances. It is true that Tchaikovsky's *Dance of the tumblers* cannot quite match the one from Rimsky-Korsakov's opera in memorability, but, with fine, idiomatic performances, this work is a most cherishable rarity. The soloists are characterfully Slavonic, better caught in the recording than the chorus, which is not helped by backward balance; the bite of their fine singing does not come over fully. Though the digital recording is bright and full-bodied, there is also occasional coarseness in the orchestral sound.

Eugene Onegin (complete).
*** Decca 417 413-2 (2) [id.]. Alldis Ch., ROHCGO, Solti.
  Eugene Onegin (Bernd Weikl), Tatyana (Teresa Kubiak), Lensky (Stuart Burrows), Olga (Júlia Hamari), Prince Gremin (Nicolai Ghiaurov).
**(*) DG Dig. 423 959-2 [id.]. Leipzig R. Ch., Dresden State O, Levine.
  Eugene Onegin (Thomas Allen), Tatyana (Mirella Freni), Lensky (Neil Shicoff), Olga (Anne Sofie Von Otter), Prince Gremin (Paata Burchuladze).
(M) *(*) Olympia OCD 115 A/B [id.]. Bolshoi Theatre Ch. & O, Ermler.
  Eugene Onegin (Yuri Mazurok), Tatyana (Tamara Milashkina), Lensky (Vladimir Atlantov), Olga (Tamara Sinyavskaya), Prince Gremin (Evgeny Nesterenko).
(M) * Sony Dig. MK 45539 [id.]. Sofia Nat. Op. Ch., Sofia Festival O, Emil Tchakarov.
  Eugene Onegin (Yuri Mazurok), Tatyana (Anna Tomowa-Sintow), Lensky (Nicolai Gedda), Olga (Rossitza Troeva-Mircheva), Prince Gremin (Nikola Ghiuselev).

Eugene Onegin, which the composer described as 'lyric scenes', is based on Pushkin. Its characters are intensely Russian, and Tchaikovsky so identified with its heroine, Tatyana, that it affected his approach to his own marriage, making him fear that he himself would be guilty of mirroring the responses of the aloof Onegin.

The first of the lyric scenes takes place in Madame Larina's garden. She and her daughter's nurse, Filipieva, are sitting, making jam. Tatyana and Olga, her daughters, are heard practising a duet which becomes a quartet when the older ladies join them. The reapers are working nearby and soon they present Madame Larina with a decorated sheaf.

Tatyana is a romantic yet serious girl, always reading and dreaming of distant lands; Olga, her sister, is less imaginative and simply loves to dance.

Now Lensky, Olga's fiancé, arrives and soon he and Olga are chatting animatedly together. With him is his friend, Onegin. Tatyana must stay near, perhaps as chaperone, and Onegin takes the opportunity to talk to her. Filipieva speculates about Tatyana's interest in Onegin and, when she reaches her bedroom, tells her about her own life and marriage.

Tatyana hardly listens, then impulsively discloses her own feelings. When the nurse has gone, Tatyana sits down and writes the letter that moved its composer so much. She tells Onegin of her thoughts and fears and longings, and her declaration of love is overwhelming. All this is expressed (and echoed in the orchestra) in one of the great romantic scenas in Russian opera.

In the morning Tatyana hands the letter to Filipieva to deliver. She has poured out her heart in its pages. Later, Onegin comes to her in the garden. He tells her coolly that love and marriage are not for him. He feels for her like a brother, no more. Tatyana is humiliated.

Now a ball is held in honour of Tatyana's birthday. Onegin dances with Tatyana and there is gossip. Because he is bored he dances next with Olga, knowing that this will upset Lensky. The cotillion now becomes a mazurka, and Onegin and Olga continue to dance. The two men quarrel, their feelings run high and a duel is in prospect. The next morning the duel takes place. Lensky thinks of his carefree past and his love of Olga. Then, as honour demands and with reconciliation out of the question, he goes to face his adversary and is shot dead.

Some years have passed; a ball is taking place in St Petersburg in a large, fashionable house, very different from the affair in the country at Madame Larina's. A polonaise commences. Onegin arrives; he has just returned to a social life after years away, travelling, trying to forget the incident which caused the death of his friend Lensky. An Ecossaise begins but changes to a slow waltz on the entrance of Prince Gremin and his wife, Tatyana.

The prince speaks with Onegin and tells him with dignity of the great love he feels for Tatyana and of the happiness she has brought him as his wife for the past two years. Now it is Onegin's turn to write a letter to Tatyana. He tells her that he is passionately in love with her, much as, when she was a girl (it now seems so long ago), she declared her feelings to him.

He enters the living room in Gremin's house and sinks at her feet. She recalls their first meeting (so does Tchaikovsky in the music) and, as they talk together, her old passion flares up to match his. But finally she tells him to remember the path of honour (perhaps she thought also of Lensky) and she finds the strength to walk out of the room.

Solti proves the most sympathetic interpreter, directing one of his warmest performances on disc. Characteristically crisp in attack, he has yet been able to relax with this richly atmospheric score, allowing his singers full rein in rallentando and rubato to a degree one might not have expected of him. The Tatyana of Teresa Kubiak is most moving – rather mature-sounding for the ingénue of Act I, but with her golden, vibrant voice rising to the final confrontation of Act III most impressively. The Onegin of Bernd Weikl may have too little variety of tone, but again this is firm singing that yet has authentic Slavonic tinges. Onegin becomes something like a first-person story-teller.

The rest of the cast is excellent, with Stuart Burrows as Lensky giving one of his finest performances on record. Here for the first time the full range of musical expression in this most atmospheric of operas is superbly caught, with the Decca recording capturing every subtlety – including the wonderful off-stage effects. Though the recording is analogue, not digital, the CD transfer is exceptionally vivid, with full bloom and atmosphere and a fine sense of presence. With Act I complete on the first disc, Acts II and III on the second, this is an opera that fits exceptionally well in CD format.

Eugene Onegin on record has almost always fallen short in the choice of singer for the baritone hero; but the DG version, conducted by Levine and consistently cast from strength, brings a magnificent Onegin in Thomas Allen. As in his vivid characterization of Mozart's Don Giovanni, the voice may be on the noble side for the role, hardly implying caddishness; however, not only the sheer beauty and firmness of sound but also the range of detailed expression, the facial communication implied, make this the most satisfying account of the title-role yet recorded.

It is matched by the Tatyana of Mirella Freni. As in her recording of *Butterfly* with Sinopoli, she is splendid, even at a late stage in her career, at conveying girlish freshness in her voice. The maturing of the character, as in *Butterfly*, is most convincingly conveyed. The other parts are strongly taken, too. The tautened-nerves quality in the character of Lensky comes out vividly in the portrayal by Neil Shicoff, and Anne Sofie von Otter with her firm, clear mezzo believably makes Olga a younger sister, not the usual over-ripe character. Paata Burchuladze is a satisfyingly resonant Gremin and Michel Sénéchal, as on the Solti set, is an incomparable M. Triquet.

What welds all these fine components into a rich and exciting whole is the conducting of James Levine with the Dresden Staatskapelle: passionate, at times even wild in Slavonic excitement, yet giving full expressive rein to Tchaikovskian melody, allowing the singers to breathe. The Leipzig Radio Choir sings superbly as well. The big snag is that, in this most atmospheric of operas, the DG recording is unevocative and studio-bound, with sound close and congested enough to undermine the bloom both on voices and on instruments. There is little feeling of action on stage, with off-stage effects unnaturally distant. In every way the more spacious acoustic in the Solti set is preferable, bringing out far more convincingly the evocative quality of Tchaikovsky's writing.

On two mid-price Olympia discs, the mid-1970s Melodiya recording from the Bolshoi offers a performance including some fine Soviet singers. Though not often imaginative, Yuri Mazurok has a voice exceptionally well suited to the role of Onegin in its range and timbre. Atlantov as Lensky has his ringingly exciting moments and Nesterenko as Gremin sings magnificently. The snag is Milashkina's seriously flawed singing as Tatyana, made to sound shriller and less girlish by the closeness of balance. Only in Act III is her performance acceptable. Mark Ermler is a lively, understanding conductor, but the close balance of all the voices makes this a disappointing set.

After some of Tchakarov's other Russian opera recordings for Sony, this *Eugene Onegin* is a disappointment, despite a rather more starry cast than most in the series. The recording is full and immediate, with the sound brightly caught, but there is little attempt to capture the subtlety of atmosphere, so vital in this work, above all in the haunting off-stage effects, as in the duetting of Tatyana and Olga at the start. They both sound raw and not very steady.

Tomowa-Sintow, who has made so many fine recordings for DG and others, is caught unflatteringly all through, with unevenness in the voice brought out. That is particularly damaging in Act I, including the Letter scene, when there is little that is girlish in the sound. Gedda characterizes splendidly as Lensky, but the voice now sounds too old; and Mazurok, impressive as Onegin, is relatively rough in timbre. Tchakarov takes a literal, rather pedestrian view of the score, failing to convey excitement in the great dance movements. Both the Levine set on DG with Thomas Allen as Onegin and Solti's vintage Decca set in fine analogue sound are preferable, and all in all the Solti remains our prime recommendation.

Eugene Onegin: highlights.

(M) **(*) 427 681-2 [id.] (from above recording with Freni, Allen, Shicoff; cond. Levine).

Even though the Levine set is not our first choice for the complete opera, this 68-minute selection brings out the superb qualities of the singing. It includes the Letter scene (with Freni a freshly charming Tatyana), the Waltz and Polonaise scenes (with the excellent Leipzig Radio

Chorus), other key arias, all strongly characterized, and the entire closing scene (11 minutes). The recording, made in the Dresden Lukaskirche, is too closely balanced and unatmospheric; but as a sampler this is clearly valuable.

Queen of Spades (Pique Dame): complete.

**(*) Sony Dig. S3K 45720 [id.]. Bulgarian Nat. Ch., Sofia Festival O, Tchakarov.

    Herman (Wieslaw Ochman), Lisa (Stefka Evstatieva), Countess (Penka Dilova), Tomsky (Ivan Konsulov), Yeletsky (Yuri Mazurok), Polina (Stefania Toczyska).

** BMG/RCA Dig. 09060 60992-2 (3) [60992-2]. Tanglewood Festival Ch., Boston SO, Seiji Ozawa.

    Herman (Vladimir Atlantov), Lisa (Mirella Freni), Countess (Maureen Forrester), Tomsky (Sergei Leiferkus), Yeletsky (Dmitri Hvorostovsky), Polina (Katherine Ciesinski).

** Ph. 420 375-2 (3) [id.]. Bolshoi Theatre Ch. & O, Ermler.

    Herman (Vladimir Atlantov), Lisa (Tamara Milashkina), Countess (Valentina Levko), Tomsky (Vladimir Valaitis), Yeletsky (Andrei Fedoseyev), Polina (Galina Borisova).

As in *Eugene Onegin*, Tchaikovsky draws on Pushkin for the plot of the *Queen of Spades*. But its atmosphere could hardly be more different, dramatically powerful, rather than lyrical, with the malevolent undertones of the story strongly conveyed, as well as the composer's own preoccupation with fate. For there is a recurring motif to remind us of the countess's sinister secret.

Once again there is a gentle, pastoral opening, but the idyllic mood does not last. We are in the Summer Gardens of St Petersburg in springtime. Two officers, Sourin and Tchekalinsky, are discussing their friend, Herman, and his cautious gambling. He now enters with Count Tomsky; Herman is downcast, for he has fallen in love yet does not know the lady's name. He fears she is above his station and beyond his financial reach.

Tomsky now greets Prince Yeletsky, who has become engaged that morning, and his happiness contrasts with Herman's misery. He indicates his betrothed, Lisa, to Tomsky, and Herman recognizes her as the lady he loves. Lisa, who does not yet know Herman but is conscious of his ardour, is with her grandmother, the countess. They ask Herman's name.

Rumours surround the countess and her past gambling skills, but she no longer plays. Tomsky relates her story. When young, she was ardently admired by Count Saint-Germain (about whom there are hints of diabolic association), but she preferred gambling to love. She was nicknamed 'The Queen of Spades'. One day, however, she lost everything. The count, observing her dismay, offered to reveal his demonic secret of the 'three cards' if she would grant him a single rendezvous.

Indignant at first, she then agreed and, after a night in his embrace, next morning she gambled and had a winning run. It was believed that she passed the secret on to her husband and, years later, to a young admirer. But it seems that she had a warning dream: she would die if a third person, in desperation, tried to take the secret from her. Herman is fascinated by the story. Moreover he decides he will win Lisa away from Prince Yeletsky.

Lisa and her friend, Pauline, sing a duet together in Lisa's room, surrounded by admiring friends. She is gloomy at the prospect of her forthcoming marriage. Herman now appears at her balcony window. She is about to rush away but he begs her to listen to him and ardently declares his love. Lisa is by no means indifferent, but the countess comes in and Herman is forced to hide. He wonders whether she will really perish if someone, 'impelled by despair', demanded to know her secret. She leaves, and Lisa and Herman embrace passionately.

Now a masked ball is in progress. Herman is still obsessed at the thought of the 'three cards' but reads a note which Lisa has sent him. If only he knew the secret, he could be wealthy enough to aspire to Lisa's hand. His two friends whisper, 'Are you then that third man who knows of the three cards?' and he shivers with apprehension. A charming pastoral play is now enacted.

Herman waits for Lisa, who gives him the key to her room, but he must enter through her grandmother, the countess's, room; she will still be playing cards. In due course Herman enters the countess's bedroom but he is forced to hide when she comes in. Suddenly Herman reveals himself and, begging her not to be frightened, he draws a pistol and asks for the secret of the 'three cards'. The old countess dies of shock. Lisa enters and is horrified, even more so when she finds out his reason for being there. She tells him to leave.

Herman is now back at the barracks, miserable at the countess's death. But Lisa has written to say that she forgives him, and she makes a midnight appointment to meet him by the riverbank. Suddenly the door opens, the candle blows out, and the ghost of the countess stands there. She tells Herman to marry Lisa and the secret of the three cards shall be his: 'Three! Seven! Ace!'

Later, Herman and Lisa meet on the bank of the Neva; he suddenly leaves to return to the gambling house. She tries to stop him but, obsessed with winning, he pushes her away and rushes off. Lisa, who has already had experience of her grandmother's obsession, now sees history repeating itself and, in desperation, throws herself over the parapet into the river.

At the gambling house the players are gathering. Tomsky is surprised to see the prince, not a regular; Yeletsky says he has come to take revenge – unlucky in love, lucky at cards. Herman enters and wins twice. He challenges anyone to meet him for the next round and puts all his money on the Ace; the prince accepts his challenge. But the card Herman picks up is not the Ace but the Queen of Spades. With a wild cry Herman once again sees the ghost of the countess. In terror he stabs himself and, as he dies, begs for the prince's forgiveness and mutters Lisa's name as he expires.

Tchakarov in his Sony series of Russian operas conducts a fresh, expressive and alert account of *Queen of Spades*, very well recorded. Wieslaw Ochman makes an impressive Herman, amply powerful and only occasionally rough. Yuri Mazurok is a superb Yeletsky, and the duet of Lisa and her companion, Pauline – one of Tchaikovsky's most magical inspirations – is beautifully done by Stefka Evstatieva and Stefania Toczyska. As the old Countess, Penka Dilova has a characteristically fruity Slavonic mezzo, very much in character, if with a heavy vibrato. The Countess's famous solo is taken very slowly indeed but is superbly sustained. Ensembles and chorus work are excellent, timed with theatrical point. Conveniently, each Act is fitted on a single CD.

Looking at the starry cast-list, you would assume that the RCA version conducted by Ozawa would be a clear winner. Not so when, as a live recording spliced together from performances in Boston and New York, the acoustic is unhelpfully dry, allowing little bloom on the voices, and with the orchestra consigned to the background. The rich contralto of Maureen Forrester fares best in the role of the Countess, and even then the distancing of the voice when she reappears as a ghost adds more bloom. Ozawa moulds the music most persuasively and draws keenly polished playing from the orchestra, but this is not as volatile or naturally dramatic a performance as that on the Sony set from Bulgaria. Both in the conducting and in the singing one registers that this is a concert performance rather than one linked to stage experience. The chorus, for example, sing with knife-edged precision but sound far less idiomatic than their Bulgarian counterparts. Vocally what is disappointing in the set is the contributions of the two principals, Vladimir Atlantov and Mirella Freni, who are no longer young enough to be fully convincing in the roles of Herman and Lisa. Freni in particular sounds strained and unsteady in the big scene with Herman in Act III, and Atlantov, though warmly expressive and still strong and heroic when not under pressure, was fresher in his earlier, Bolshoi recording of 1974, previously available on Philips. The advantage of having star names in the rest of the cast, notably Dmitri Hvorostovsky and Sergei Leiferkus, need not weigh too heavily when their roles are so incidental.

The Bolshoi recording of the *Queen of Spades*, made in 1974, brings a strong if unsubtle reading, atmospherically set against a warmly reverberant acoustic. The sense of presence and atmosphere makes up for shortcomings in the singing, with Vladimir Atlantov as Herman too taut and strained, singing consistently loudly, and with Tamara Milashkina producing curdled tone at the top, not at all girlish. Both those singers, for all their faults, are archetypally Russian, and so – in a much more controlled way – is Valentina Levko, a magnificent Countess, firm and sinister. The CD transfer makes the helpfully vibrant sound the more specific and real-sounding, though a degree of tape-hiss is audible.

Yolanta (complete).
(M) **(*) Erato/Warner Dig. 2292 45973-2 (2) [id.]. Group Vocale de France, O de Paris, Rostropovich.
> Yolanta (Galina Vishnevskaya), Vaudémont (Nicolai Gedda), Robert of Burgundy (Walton Groenroos), Le Roi René (Dimiter Petkov), The Doctor, Ibn Hakia (Tom Krause), Marthe (Viorica Cortez), Brigitte (Tania Gedda), Alméric (James Anderson), Bertrand (Fernand Dumont).

Tchaikovsky's one-Act opera *Yolanta* (*Iolanthe*) is a much later (1892) work than *Eugene Onegin*. It is based on a charming legend which takes place in fifteenth-century France.

King René of Provence has kept from his daughter, Yolanta, the fact that she is blind, and she lives, happily unaware, in the palace, attended by Nurse Marthe and her friends, Brigitte and Laura, who are pledged to maintain the secret. No one else is allowed within her palace quarters.

When the Doctor, Hakia, is summoned, he tells the king that Yolanta will regain her sight only if she recognizes her disability: then her willpower will effect a cure.

The king is reluctant to risk such a revelation, and it is only the arrival of the Duke of Burgundy – to whom Yolanta has been betrothed since birth – with his friend and companion, Vaudémont, that breaks the impasse.

The duke seeks a release from the marriage commitment as he now loves another; meanwhile Vaudémont, finding Yolanta asleep in the garden, wakes her and declares his love for her, which is immediately returned. He discovers the secret when she offers him a white rose as a token of her warm reciprocal feelings, believing it to be red.

When the king finds out what has happened he threatens Vaudémont's execution, so his daughter immediately agrees to putting herself in the hands of the doctor to save the life of her beloved, even though she knows herself obliged to marry the duke. However, the moment she discovers that her marital obligation has been revoked, her great happiness restores her sight. She lifts her eyes to the sky in fervent gratification then joyously turns to behold her father and her lover for the first time.

Tchaikovsky's imagination was obviously touched by the fairytale story and, though the libretto may be flawed, the lyrical invention is a delight. The performance offered here was recorded at a live concert performance in the Salle Pleyel in December 1984, with excellent, spacious sound. Rostropovich's performance has a natural expressive warmth to make one tolerant of vocal shortcomings.

Though Vishnevskaya's voice is not naturally suited to the role of a sweet young princess, she does wonders in softening her hardness of tone, bringing fine detail of characterization. Gedda equally by nature sounds too old for his role, but again the artistry is compelling, and ugly sounds few. More questionable is the casting of Dimiter Petkov as the King, far too wobbly as recorded. However, now reissued on a pair of mid-priced CDs, this is well worth exploring.

Arias from: *The Enchantress; Eugene Onegin; Iolantha; Mazeppa; Queen of Spades.*
*** Ph. Dig. 426 740-2; *426 740-4* [id.]. Dmitri Hvorostovsky, Rotterdam PO, Gergiev –
    VERDI: *Arias.* ***

This Tchaikovsky recital marked the Western recording debut of Hvorostovsky, a golden boy among young baritones. The varied group of arias ideally exhibits both the magnificent dark voice which won him the title of 'Cardiff Singer of the World' and also his way with Russian words. He presents an eager, volatile Onegin, a passionate Yeletsky in *Queen of Spades* and an exuberant Robert in *Iolantha*. One can only hope that he will be guided well, to develop such a glorious instrument naturally, without strain.

Telemann, Georg Philipp (1681–1767)

(i) *Ino* (dramatic cantata); *Ouvertüre in D (suite).*
*** DG Dig. 429 772-2 [id.]. (i) Barbara Schlick, Col. Mus. Ant., Reinhard Goebel.

Both the cantata *Ino* and the delightful seven-movement *Ouvertüre* or *Suite in D* were written in 1765 during what Peter Czornyi's excellent essay calls Telemann's Indian Summer. *Ino* tells the story (taken from Ovid's *Metamorphoses*) of the wife of Athamos who goes mad, kills one of her two sons, and then – with her husband following hot on her heels – throws herself with the other child off the Corinthian cliffs into the sea. There she is welcomed by the Nereids and is made a goddess (Leukothea) while her son is similarly deified as Palemon.

Listening to the effortless flow of remarkable invention, one can almost understand the disappointment of the Leipzig burghers that they could not entice Telemann into their service.

Barbara Schlick is a delightful soloist, just a little lacking in fire and colour, but certainly lacking nothing in charm; and the wind players of the Musica Antiqua, Köln, have a delicacy and virtuosity that are irresistible. The *Réjouissance* in the *Ouvertüre* is – as so often with this ensemble – uncomfortably rushed (the internal-combustion engine had not been invented in the 1760s, let alone Concorde!), but there is so much that is right and thought-provoking about their playing, both here and in this remarkable cantata, that criticism must be muted. The balance captures just the right perspective between soloist and players, and there is a pleasingly warm acoustic.

(i) *Ino* (dramatic cantata); (ii) *Der Tag des Gerichts (The Day of Judgement;* oratorio): complete.
(M) **(*) Teldec/Warner Dig./Analogue 9031 77621-2 (2) [id.]. (i) Roberta Alexander; (ii)

Gertraud Landwehr-Herrmann, Cora Canne-Meijer, Kurt Equiluz, Max Van Egmond, soloists from Vienna Boys' Ch., Hamburg Monteverdi Ch.; (i; ii) VCM, Harnoncourt.

Harnoncourt's alternative version of *Ino* is characteristically full of vitality. As a soloist Roberta Alexander brings rather more dramatic fire and slightly less charm to her soliloquy and, while Harnoncourt's rhythmic emphasis and pacing are not quite as 'uptight' as Goebel's, his direction is certainly not lacking in urgency. The Teldec issue, however, involves two discs and, although these are offered at mid-price, Harnoncourt's coupling, *The Day of Judgement* – the last of Telemann's great oratorios, coming from 1761–2 – is less convincing.

Although there are moments of considerable inspiration in a work subtitled 'a poem for singing in four contemplations', one feels that Telemann was far too urbane a master to measure himself fully against so cosmic a theme. But the work is well worth sampling, particularly as the performers give it so persuasive and musical an advocacy and are, moreover, given the advantage of well-balanced recording. Nevertheless this is not a work that would figure high on the list of priorities for most Telemann admirers. The 1966 sound has been effectively remastered and, although the choral focus is not always completely clean, the overall effect is vivid. It runs to some 84 minutes in length.

Die Tageszeiten.
*** HM/BMG RD 77092 [77092-RC-2]. Mechthild Bach, Mechthild Georg, Hans-Peter Blochwitz, Johannes Mannov, Freiburg Vocal Ens. & Coll. Mus., Schäfer.

Telemann's cantata, *Die Tageszeiten* (1759), is a work of great freshness and inventive resource. Its four sections portray the various times of day (*Morning*, *Midday*, *Evening* and *Night*) and are full of imaginative ideas. Yet, fairly soon after its first appearance on LP in the early 1960s in an excellent performance from Helmut Koch and the Berlin Chamber Orchestra (DG), it returned to obscurity.

This new version, recorded with period instruments and four excellent soloists, makes a different but almost equally strong impression. The strings prompt a fleeting nostalgia for the more robust timbre of modern forces, and the playing under Wolfgang Schäfer could afford to be more full-bodied. But there is some excellent singing, and the recording is clean and well balanced. An enjoyable disc.

Thomas, Ambroise (1811–96)

Hamlet (complete).
(M) *** Decca Dig. 433 857-2 (3) [id.]. WNO Ch. & O, Bonynge.
Hamlet (Sherrill Milnes), Ophélie (Joan Sutherland), Claudius (James Morris), Laërte (Gösta Winbergh), Gertrud (Barbara Conrad), Le Spectre (John Tomlinson).

The weight of Shakespeare is missing in Ambroise Thomas's setting of *Hamlet*, but this is more faithful to the author than Gounod's *Faust* is to Goethe. Moreover Bonynge here provides a far better answer to the problems of Act V. He has devised a composite of Thomas's original happy ending ('*Vive Hamlet, notre roi!*' cries the chorus) and the suicide alternative which Thomas wrote for Covent Garden.

The plot now follows Shakespeare reasonably enough – if with far too many survivors – and the opera is revealed as a surprisingly deft, if inevitably superficial, compression of the play, full of splendid theatrical effects. It has colour, atmosphere, soaring tunes and jolly dances, presented in subtle and often original orchestration, with even a saxophone used to striking effect.

'To be or not to be' ('*Être ou ne pas être*') as a soliloquy may not be as dramatically compelling as the original speech, but Hamlet's swaggering drinking-song greeting the players is most effective, quoted later in mad, Berlioz-like bursts at the climax of the Play scene, when Hamlet's ruse with Claudius has worked. Musically, Ophélie has priority vocally in brilliant and beautiful numbers, with Sutherland taking all the challenges commandingly.

Ophelia's famous Mad scene was one of the finest of her early recordings, and here, 24 years later, she still gives a triumphant display, tender and gentle as well as brilliant in coloratura. The heroine's primacy is reinforced when the role of Hamlet is for baritone, here taken strongly if with some roughness by Sherrill Milnes. Outstanding among the others is Gösta Winbergh as Laërte, heady and clear in the only major tenor role. John Tomlinson as Le Spectre sings the necessary monotones resonantly, James Morris is a gruff Claudius and Barbara Conrad a fruity Gertrude.

The compelling success of the whole performance of a long, complex opera is sealed by Bonynge's vigorous and sympathetic conducting of first-rate Welsh National Opera forces, brilliantly and atmospherically recorded. The layout, with Act I on the first CD and the other four Acts, two apiece, on the other two, is surely ideal, and the documentation is good.

Thomson, Virgil (1896–1989)

Lord Byron (complete).
** Koch Dig. 3-7124-2Y6 (2) [id.]. Monadnock Music, James Bolle.
    Lord Byron (Matthew Lord), Thomas Moore (Richard Zeller), John Hobhouse (Richard Johnson), John Murray (Gregory Mercer), Count Gamba (Thomas Woodman), John Ireland (Stephen Owen), The Hon. Mrs Leigh (Jeanne Ommerlé), Lady Byron (D'Anna Fortunato), Contessa Guiccioli (Adrienne Csengery), Lady Melbourne (Louisa Jonason), Lady Charlotte (Debra Vanderlinde), Lady Jane (Marion Dry).

Lord Byron is the third and last opera of Virgil Thomson, who died in 1989, aged ninety-two. It is a weird piece, set mainly in Poets' Corner in Westminster Abbey after Byron's death, with his heirs and friends in dispute and his ghost periodically commenting. The settings of Byron's own words are fluent but do not avoid blandness, and the lyrical if short-winded invention takes you effectively through the offbeat plot.

The main trouble is that under James Bolle the playing of the Monadnock Festival Orchestra is limp. Soloists are efficient enough. Only periodically does Thomson let you know what he could have done as an opera composer when, Puccini-like, he tellingly points the opening of a big number, as with Byron's solo at the end of Act I or in a splendid duet for Byron and his sister in Act II.

Tippett, Michael (born 1905)

The Ice-break.
*** Virgin/EMI Dig. VC7 91448-2 [id.]. L. Sinf., Atherton.
    Nadia (Heather Harper), Lev (David Wilson-Johnson), Yuri (Sanford Sylvan), Gayle (Carolann Page), Hannah (Cynthia Clarey), Olympian (Thomas Randle).

Produced at Covent Garden in 1976, *The Ice-break* daringly sets the opening Act in an airport-lounge. That and the quickly dated slang in the composer's own libretto suggest a trendiness which originally distracted attention from the universal elements in the story of the black couple, Nadia and Lev.

Nadia waits to greet her husband, just released after twenty years in prison. Yuri, their son, is with her. Her husband's voice is heard over the loudspeaker before he actually appears. Gayle, Yuri's fashionably dressed white girlfriend, is also at the airport with her friend, Hannah. But they are there, with others, to acclaim the returning black sporting champion, Olympian. Gayle quarrels with Yuri, who adopts a racialist position, partly because of Gayle's obsession with Olympian.

Yuri is much less concerned with his mother's problems and makes little attempt to comfort her. At first she thinks the cheering could be for Lev, but she is soon disillusioned. Cheerleader and fans mob Olympian as he passes through and, when everyone has gone, Lev appears, a very drab figure.

Now the older couple are seen in their flat, contemplating their future without much hope. By contrast, all is jollity at Olympian's party. He is a braggart and a womanizer. Gayle makes a play for him, which maddens Yuri. Gayle says she is only trying to make amends for Olympian's years of injustice, but Yuri attacks his rival, who throws him to the ground.

Back at home, Nadia tries to convey to Lev her feelings for their son. But Yuri bursts in on them, dragging Gayle in with him and, facing them angrily, he says, 'What have you come here for?' Later the two couples are together contemplating their different experiences and aspirations. Nadia is hopeful for the future, feeling that light will emerge from darkness; Gayle is very aware of today's reality; Yuri is fearful of the gap between him and his parents.

Later, Yuri and Gayle become part of a masked white chorus. We meet Hannah, a black hospital nurse and Olympian's girlfriend. They have a relationship of sorts, but Hannah wonders if she or anyone can make sense of the violence which surrounds their lives. The dance that follows brings a confrontation between blacks and whites.

Meanwhile Lev and Nadia are unsuccessfully trying to adjust to their new situation as a couple living together, and Lev despairingly rushes out into the night. A scene of mindless violence follows between blacks and whites. Police sirens are heard and there are casualties. Olympian and Gayle are dead, Yuri badly injured. Nadia, too, lies dying.

Lev reads to her. She hears that Yuri might just survive but knows that she will not. Lev is bitter. As she dies, Nadia recalls the sound of sleigh-bells from her youth and she hears the sound of ice breaking on the river.

A psychedelic trip now follows. Astron (described as a psychedelic messenger) denies he is a saviour. Lev watches as Yuri is wheeled into the operating theatre for an operation on his leg which will ensure that he can walk again. The opera ends with the sense that Hannah, Lev and possibly Yuri have separated themselves from their mass culture and become individuals.

This recording, made with similar forces to those used in a highly successful concert performance at the Proms in 1990, presents the piece more as a modern dramatic oratorio than as an opera. Characteristically full of ideas, it is a work for which the listener can readily provide the imaginary settings. The three Acts between them last just under 75 minutes, but that brevity makes the piece feel taut, not short-winded.

The music has the physical impact characteristic of later Tippett, but with less of the wildness that developed in his works of the 1980s. Centrally in Act II comes a lament for one of the principal black characters, the nurse Hannah (beautifully sung by Cynthia Clarey). In its bald simplicity that solo provides a vital, touching moment of repose, warmly emotional, to contrast with the tensions of a plot that centres on violence, racial conflict, with student demonstrations part of the scheme.

David Atherton directs an electrically tense performance, with the American baritone, Sanford Sylvan, singing superbly in the central role of Yuri, a second-generation immigrant, set against Heather Harper as his mother, Nadia, full-voiced and characterful, and David Wilson-Johnson as Lev, the father who in the first scene arrives after 20 years of prison and exile. The single disc comes boxed with libretto and excellent notes by Meirion Bowen.

King Priam (complete).
*** Decca 414 241-2 (2) [id.]. L. Sinf. Ch., L. Sinf., Atherton.
    Priam (Norman Bailey), Hecuba (Heather Harper), Hector (Thomas Allen), Andromache (Felicity Palmer), Paris (Philip Langridge), Helen (Yvonne Minton), Achilles (Robert Tear).

King Priam is yet another attempt by a twentieth-century composer to find something new to express through a plot based on Greek tragedy. It is concerned with choice, or the apparent lack of it, and, like Stravinsky's *Oedipus Rex*, the story moves forward remorselessly to its tragic and seemingly inevitable apotheosis.

Heralds and trumpets introduce the opera, which starts with a discussion of the dream and prophecy by Priam's wife, Hecuba, that her new-born son, Paris, will cause his father's death. Priam and his followers now debate the problems of moral choice and are interrupted as Priam's son, Hector, shows his physical prowess by catching and subduing a wild bull. A young man jumps on its back and rides around.

On his return, Hector offers to teach him the arts of war. Priam will allow this, provided the boy's father agrees and the boy makes his own decision. The boy does, and Priam is startled but pleased when the boy reveals himself to be Paris.

Perhaps the gods have reversed the implications of his own 'choice' of long ago. He reveals fear that Hecuba's dream may indeed come to pass but he accepts the situation.

Guests are now seen leaving the wedding feast of Hector and Andromache. They remark that the hostility between Hector and Paris has caused Paris to leave Troy for Menelaus's court at Sparta. Helen and Paris are passionately involved with each other, and Paris insists on her choice – between himself and Menelaus. Paris soliloquizes about his planned elopement and wonders if humans have any control at all over their affairs.

Hermes now asks Paris to choose among the three graces but warns that, in deciding on one, he may not escape another's wrath. Athene (her part taken by Hecuba) offers courage in battle, Hera (represented by Andromache) satisfaction in marriage; both will curse him when he chooses Aphrodite (Helen); therefore, by eloping with her, he will plunge Greece and Troy into war.

But this is what he does, Troy is besieged, and Hector taunts Paris with running away from a confrontation with Menelaus. Priam tries to patch up the quarrel. Paris now follows Hector into battle.

Achilles is sulking in his tent, his friend Patroclus with him. Achilles longs for peace, and presently they decide that Patroclus shall wear Achilles' armour as he goes off to do battle with the Trojans. Achilles prays that he will return safely.

Paris now arrives to inform Priam that Hector has killed Patroclus and Hector must now wear Achilles' armour to parade before his father. Victory is anticipated and the prospect of destroying the Greek fleet, but it is interrupted by Achilles' vengeful war-cry. Hector is stunned.

Andromache now waits for Hector to return from battle. Hecuba tells her to go to the walls of Troy to call him back. King Priam could end the war if he would send Helen back to Sparta. Hecuba replies that the Greeks mean to take Troy anyway.

Helen enters and there is a general foreboding of death. Priam feels alone and isolated and Paris plucks up courage to tell him that Hector is dead. Paris feels he must in turn kill Achilles. Paris leaves and Priam moans that, had Hector's death been predicted, he would have killed the infant Paris.

Priam now enters Achilles' tent and begs the body of Hector from the Greek who slew him. Priam kisses Achilles' hand – 'the hand of him who killed my son' – and Achilles grants him Hector's body. They anticipate their destiny, Achilles to die at the hand of Paris, Priam to be slain by Achilles' son, Neoptolemus.

Paris offers to fight to defend Priam, who refuses to leave Troy without him. Priam then fails to recognize his own wife, Hecuba; Andromache spurns Paris and his defence of Priam, and Helen takes her place: 'They stand silent together, the beautiful, ill-fated pair.'

Priam sends Paris on his way to a hero's death, leaving Helen to make her peace with her lover's father. Priam comforts her; neither he nor Hector ever reproached her for her part in the events. She leaves.

Priam sinks down before an altar and, after Hermes has appeared before him and departed, Neoptolemus runs his sword through the king and he dies instantly. There is no further choice, if ever there was any at all.

In this superb performance under David Atherton, with an outstanding cast and vivid, immediate recording, the power of Tippett's opera, offbeat as the treatment often is, both musical and dramatic, comes over from first to last. Much more angular in its writing than Tippett's first opera, *The Midsummer Marriage*, it yet contains in its taut sequence of scenes equally memorable and moving moments. Norman Bailey, thanks to his long association with Wagner, sounds agedly noble to perfection. Robert Tear is a shiningly heroic Achilles and Thomas Allen a commanding Hector, vocally immaculate, illuminating every word.

Tubin, Eduard (1905–82)

Barbara von Tisenhusen (complete).
*** Ondine Dig. ODE776-2 (2) [id.]. Estonian Opera Ch. & O, Peeter Lilje.
    Barbara von Tisenhusen (Heili Raamat), Matthais Freisner (Tarmo Sild), Franz Bonnius (Ivo Kuusk), Jürgen von Tisenhusen (Väino Puurabar), Reinhold von Tisenhusen (Ants Kollo).

Tubin left his native Estonia in 1944 and spent the rest of his life in exile in Sweden. He was, however, invited back to Tallinn in the mid-1960s for a production of his ballet, *Kratt* ('The Goblin') and it was during this visit that the Estonian company commissioned this opera.

Although he is largely known for his ten symphonies, all of which are recorded on the BIS label, Tubin served his musical apprenticeship in the 1930s and early '40s in the Vanemuine Theatre in Tallinn, and it is quite clear that he has a real feeling for theatre. His libretto, adapted by Jaan Kross from a short story by the Finnish-born writer, Aino Kallas (her husband was for a time the Estonian Ambassador to Helsinki), concerns illicit passion and is easily summarized: the first scene takes place at a nobleman's wedding in Tallinn in 1551.

Barbara von Tisenhusen, who is one of the guests, attracts attention on account of her extravagant golden dress, and at the end of the scene there are intimations of loose living which horrify her.

In the second scene, set in Rôngu Castle, she is introduced to the new scribe from Brunswick, Franz Bonnius. They fall in love, but marriage between a noblewoman and a commoner is not permitted on pain of death by starvation without the special consent of the family.

Act II opens on the balcony of the castle of her brother, Jürgen, in Rannu, where to Barbara's horror the brothers make wagers on bear-baiting. Barbara and Franz Bonnius elope and make for Lithuania. They are hunted down and she is eventually caught and condemned to death by a family council. The serfs for whom she has shown some sympathy refuse to carry out the sentence, and her brothers eventually dig a hole in an ice-covered lake and drown her.

The opera is not long, consisting of three Acts of roughly 30 minutes each. It has pace, variety of dramatic incident and musical textures, and the main roles in the action are vividly characterized. The musical substance of the opera is largely based on a chaconne-like figure of nine notes, heard at the very outset, yet the theme changes subtly and skilfully to meet the constantly shifting dramatic environment, so that the casual listener will probably not be consciously aware of the musical means Tubin employs. The scene in which a pack of dogs savages the bear for the amusemenet of the brothers comes close to the dark world of the *Eighth Symphony* (the writer Harry Kiirsk calls it 'the cruel scherzo of the opera').

The opening of Act III, in which Barbara is eventually captured, gives an excellent idea of the work's character: it exhibits the strong atmosphere and dramatic skill the score displays. Small wonder, as the notes tell us, that when the opera was first staged in 1968 it played to sold-out houses for no fewer than 50 performances. None of the singers is of star quality but all are dedicated and serve the composer well, and, though the orchestra is not first class, it too plays with spirit and enthusiasm under Peeter Lilje. The recording produces a sound comparable with that of a broadcast relay rather than the opulent sound one can expect from a commercial studio recording. A strong recommendation.

(i) *The Parson of Reigi* (complete). (ii) *Requiem for Fallen Soldiers*.
(*) Ondine Dig. ODE 783-2 (2). Estonian Op. Ch. & O, Paul Mägi; (ii) Urve Tauts, Estonian Nat. Male Ch., Deksnis, Leiten; Tiido, Roos, Eri Klas.
　　(i) Paavali Lampelius (Teo Maiste), Catharina Vycken (Marika Eensalu), Viiu (Annika Tônuri), Jonas Kempe (Ivo Kuusk).

After the success of *Barbara von Tisenhusen* in 1968, the Estonian Opera immediately commissioned Tubin to compose another. The result was *The Parson of Reigi*, which was composed in 1971, between the *Ninth* and *Tenth symphonies*. Like the former, *The Parson of Reigi* is relatively short (82 minutes), and it too turns for its inspiration to Aino Kallas (1878–1956). It also concerns an illicit relationship.

The setting is a remote fishing village, Reigi, in seventeenth-century Estonia, then ruled by Sweden. In the first scene the parson, Paavali Lampelius, splendidly sung by the baritone, Teo Maiste, awaits the arrival from Stockholm of a new deacon. He is warmly welcomed, but his interest in Lampelius's wife and hers in him soon become evident. By the third scene Catharina confides her passion for Kempe to her maid, Viiu, and Lampelius's suspicions are soon aroused. Their love becomes public knowledge and, after an angry confrontation, they elope.

Under Swedish law of the time, adultery was a capital offence; the lovers are recaptured and committed for trial in Tallinn, where they meet their end, to tumultuous bell-tolling.

Tubin's music powerfully evokes the claustrophobic milieu of a small, close-knit fishing community and is particularly successful in conveying atmosphere. The dawn scene where Lampelius blesses the departing fishermen is particularly imaginative, as is the evocation of the white summer nights in the Garden scene, in which Catharina confesses her passion.

As in the case of *Barbara von Tisenhusen*, Tubin's powers of characterization of both the major and supporting roles are striking, and there is a compelling sense of dramatic narrative as well as variety of pace. The performance of the three principal singers is very good and the only let-down is in the quality of the orchestral playing, which is little more than passable. For all its simplicity of plot, *The Parson* makes effective musical theatre and, though the invention is not of quite the same quality as its predecessor, its acquaintance is well worth making.

The *Requiem for Fallen Soldiers* is a highly imaginative piece for mezzo-soprano soloist and male chorus, accompanied, to austere effect, by organ, trumpet, timpani and side-drum. The *Requiem* has a strange history: it was begun in 1950, but Tubin encountered one of those creative blockages that affect many artists and put it on one side after completing the first section. He returned to it only in the late 1970s, almost 30 years later, conducting its first performance in 1981.

This is its second recording, and it is generally to be preferred to the rival account on BIS, coupled with the *Tenth Symphony*. The Estonian singers produced better-focused and darker tone than their Swedish colleagues, though the BIS recording has some amazingly lyrical playing by Håkan Hardenberger. The Estonian player, Urmas Leiten, is very eloquent too. This can be strongly recommended to those interested in the opera.

Vaughan Williams, Ralph (1872–1958)

The Pilgrim's Progress.
(M) *** EMI CMS7 64212-2 (2) [Ang. CDMB 64212]. LPO Ch., LPO, Boult.
  Pilgrim (John Noble), John Bunyan / Lord Hate-Good (Raimund Herincx), Evangelist (John
  Carol Case), Obstinate / Judas Escariot / Pontius Pilate (Christopher Keyte), 1st Shining One
  (Sheila Armstrong), Watchful (John Shirley-Quirk), Branchbearer / Malice (Norma
  Burrowes).
**(*) RNCM PP1/2 (2) [id.]. The Pilgrim (Richard Whitehouse), John Bunyan (Wyn Griffiths)
  & soloists, Ch. & O of Royal N. Coll. of Music, Igor Kennaway.

The appearance on CD of this glowing performance under Boult should effectively ensure that
this inspired opera, one of the composer's culminating life-works, is at last given its due. Though
Vaughan Williams was right in insisting that it is not an oratorio (his description was 'a
morality'), the choral writing frames it, sung with heartfelt warmth by the London Philharmonic
Choir.

In the Prologue, Bunyan is found sitting in Bedford Jail, writing the last words of his Christian
allegory: 'So I awoke, and behold it was a dream.' Then he stands, turns to his listeners and reads
from the beginning. As he reads, there is a vision of the Pilgrim, with a burden on his back. We
see the Pilgrim reading his book. The Evangelist appears and directs him to the Wicket Gate
until he comes 'to the Place of Deliverance'.

Four neighbours, Pliable, Obstinate, Mistrust and Timorous, all try in their different ways to
dissuade him from undertaking so perilous a journey, but the Evangelist encourages him.
Beyond the Wicket Gate is the House Beautiful, and the Pilgrim stumbles through and falls to
his knees in front of the cross.

He hears the voices of the Shining Ones, who take the burden from his back and lay it on the
sepulchre. The Interpreter receives him and he is welcomed into the house. A procession carries
in a white rope and the Shining Ones place it on his shoulders. Now it is night and the Porter
goes his rounds invoking the blessing of sleep.

An open road indicates that it is morning. A herald steps forward. 'This is the king's highway.
It is as straight as a rule can make it,' and he asks, 'Who will go on that way?' The Pilgrim asks
that his name be set down in the book and the scribe does so. Pilgrim is then provided with
armour and we hear the famous words 'Who would true valour see – let him come hither'.

Now the Pilgrim reaches the Valley of Humiliation, a narrow gorge and a bare, grey hill. He
can hear Doleful Creatures howling, but he is instead hailed by Apollyon, who proclaims that he
is king of the region where the Pilgrim was born.

Challenged for his soul, Pilgrim wins the combat but is weak from his wounds. Two Heavenly
Beings bear a branch of the Tree of Life and a cup of the Water of Life, and he is revived.

His next trial is to pass through Vanity Fair, but first he is invested with the Staff of Salvation,
the Roll of the Word and the Key of Promise. Thus protected, he sets off confidently down a
lane with booths on either side. Grotesquely dressed people stand around and 'all that the world
can provide' is for sale.

A procession comes by, led by famous characters who have in the past succumbed to the
temptations of power or gold. They include Demus, Judas Iscariot, Simon Magus, Pontius
Pilate, Worldly Glory. Madame Bubble, Madame Wanton and their promoter, Lord Lechery, all
stand in his way to offer their own particular brand of merchandise, but the Pilgrim waves them
off.

He defies Beelzebub, and Lord Hate-Good condemns him to prison and execution. In his
dungeon the Pilgrim, in despair, asks why God has forsaken him, then he remembers the Key of
Promise and the gates fly open. The Pilgrims' Way lights up before him.

A woodcutter's boy is chopping firewood; the Pilgrim asks how far it is to the Celestial City
and is told it is close by the Delectable Mountains, which he can see in on the horizon. Now the
Pilgrim encounters Mister and Madame By-Ends, talking incessantly, but he leaves them
behind, for he feels much more comfortable with the Shepherds of the Delectable Mountains,
who are kneeling in prayer.

He is tempted to rest with them awhile, but a Celestial Messenger summons him forthwith to
the Celestial City, and his heart is ceremonially pierced with an arrow. He can hear the
Shepherds singing as he passes through the River of Death. Now there is a welcoming chorus
from the City itself and the Pilgrim climbs up to the gates. Angels are there to greet him. The

vision fades and we are back in Reading Jail. Bunyan addresses his listeners: 'O come hither, thy head and thy heart together.'

What comes out in a recorded performance is that, so far from being slow and undramatic, the score is crammed full of delectable ideas one after the other, and the drama of the mind – as in the book – supplements more conventional dramatic incident. John Noble gives a dedicated performance in the central role of Pilgrim, and the large supporting cast is consistently strong. Much of the material of Act I was also used in the *Fifth Symphony* and, like that masterpiece, this opera stands at the heart of the composer's achievement.

Vanity Fair may not sound evil here, but Vaughan Williams's own recoil is vividly expressed, and the jaunty passage of Mr and Mrs By-Ends brings the most delightful light relief. Boult underlines the virility of his performance with a fascinating and revealing half-hour collection of rehearsal excerpts, placed at the end of the second CD. The outstanding quality of the recording, made in Kingsway Hall at the end of 1970 and the beginning of 1971, is confirmed by the CD transfer, which shows few signs of the passing of two decades. The booklet provides the English words, although they emerge clearly anyway.

Enterprisingly, in 1992 the Royal Northern College of Music in Manchester presented a staging which effectively brought out the operatic qualities of a work too often dismissed as an oratorio. Happily, they had sound engineers on hand, and the result is this very vigorous and colourful complete recording. The stage-producer at the College, Joseph Ward, was the tenor who sang the role of Lord Lechery in the earlier recording conducted by Sir Adrian Boult.

Obviously student voices cannot match those of the front-rank singers of the 1970s who appear on the earlier recording, now reissued by EMI. There are some odd balances in the sound too, but the vitality is what matters. Richard Whitehouse as the Pilgrim boldly shoulders the weightiest individual burden, but this is an opera in which good teamwork is more important than individual performances, and under Igor Kennaway the young singers and players perform with a dedication that could hardly be more compelling. The two CDs can be obtained direct from the College and are in the mid-price range.

Verdi, Giuseppe (1813–1901)

Aida (complete).
(M) *** EMI CMS7 69300-2 (3) [Ang. CDMC 69300]. V. State Op. Ch., VPO, Karajan.
  Aida (Mirella Freni), Amneris (Agnes Baltsa), Radames (José Carreras), Amonasro (Piero Cappuccilli), Ramfis (Ruggero Raimondi), King (José Van Dam).
*** Decca 417 416-2 (3) [id.]. Rome Op. Ch. & O, Solti.
  Aida (Leontyne Price), Amneris (Rita Gorr), Radames (Jon Vickers), Amonasro (Robert Merrill), Ramfis (Giorgio Tozzi), King (Plinio Clabassi).
(M) *** Decca 414 087-2 (3). V. Singverein, VPO, Karajan.
  Aida (Renata Tebaldi), Amneris (Giulietta Simionato), Radames (Carlo Bergonzi), Amonasro (Cornell MacNeil), Ramfis (Arnold Van Mill), King (Fernando Corena).
(M) (***) BMG/RCA mono GD 86652 (3) [Victrola 6652-2-RG]. Rome Op. Ch. & O, Perlea.
  Aida (Zinka Milanov), Amneris (Fedora Barbieri), Radames (Jussi Bjoerling), Amonasro (Leonard Warren), Ramfis (Boris Christoff), King (Plinio Clabassi).
(**) EMI mono CDS7 49030-8 (3) [Ang. CDCC 49030]. La Scala, Milan, Ch. & O, Serafin.
  Aida (Maria Callas), Amneris (Fedora Barbieri), Radames (Richard Tucker), Amonasro (Tito Gobbi), Ramfis (Giuseppe Modesti), King (Nicola Zaccaria).
**(*) DG Dig. 410 092-2 (3) [id.]. La Scala, Milan, Ch. & O, Abbado.
  Aida (Katia Ricciarelli), Amneris (Elena Obraztsova), Radames (Plácido Domingo), Amonasro (Leo Nucci), Ramfis (Nicolai Ghiaurov), King (Ruggero Raimondi).
** Sony Dig. S3K 45973 (3) [id.]; 40-45973. Metropolitan Op. Ch. & O, Levine.
  Aida (Aprile Millo), Amneris (Dolora Zajic), Radames (Plácido Domingo), Amonasro (James Morris), Ramfis (Samuel Ramey), King (Terry Cook).
** Decca Dig. 417 439-2 (3). La Scala, Milan, Ch. & O, Maazel.
  Aida (Maria Chiara), Amneris (Ghena Dimitrova), Radames (Luciano Pavarotti), Amonasro (Leo Nucci), Ramfis (Paata Burchuladze), King (Luigi Roni).
** EMI CDS7 47271-8 (3) [Ang. CDCC 47271]. ROHCG Ch., New Philh. O, Muti.
  Aida (Montserrat Caballé), Amneris (Fiorenza Cossotto), Radames (Plácido Domingo), Amonasro (Piero Cappuccilli), Ramfis (Nicolai Ghiaurov), King (Luigi Roni).
** BMG/RCA RD 86198 (3) [6198-2-RC]. Alldis Ch., LSO, Leinsdorf.

Aida (Leontyne Price), Amneris (Grace Bumbry), Radames (Plácido Domingo), Amonasro (Sherrill Milnes), Ramfis (Ruggero Raimondi), King (Hans Sotin).

(M) (**) BMG/RCA mono GD 60300; *GK 60300* (3/2) [60300-RG-2; *60300-RG-4*]. Robert Shaw Ch., NBC SO, Toscanini.

Aida (Herva Nelli), Amneris (Eva Gustavson), Radames (Richard Tucker), Amonasro (Giuseppe Valdengo), Ramfis (Norman Scott), King (Dennis Harbour).

Aida, Verdi's spectacular Egyptian opera, was commissioned by the Khedive to celebrate the completion of the Italian theatre in Cairo. But the theatre had to open without Verdi, for the opera was not finished in time, and it was premièred there two years later, in 1871. Its story, appropriately, draws on Egyptian mythological history.

Ramfis, high priest of Egypt, informs Radames, the captain of the guard, that Ethiopians have invaded Egypt. The goddess Isis will announce who will lead the defending armies. Radames hopes that he will have that honour. He is in love with Aida, slave of Amneris and daughter of Amonasro, the Ethiopian king (although no one is yet aware of her parentage). Amneris sees him elated and, guessing the reason, is jealous for she wants him for herself.

The king enters with Ramfis to say that the capital, Thebes, is threatened and he confirms that Radames has been chosen by Isis to lead the Egyptian armies. Amneris urges him to return victorious, but Aida, although she wants him to be a hero, is torn between her loyalties to her father and her homeland and her love for Radames. In the Temple of Phtha, Radames is presented with consecrated arms, and he goes off to do battle.

The armies do return victorious and a great feast is planned. Amneris is dressed for the celebration, and her Moorish slaves dance for her. She seeks to confirm her suspicions about Aida so she tells her that Radames is dead, and Aida reveals her passion for the army leader. How dare she, a slave, be so presumptuous! The rivalry between the two women now flares up and Aida implores the gods for pity.

As is fitting for a great nation, the spectacle laid on for the return of the triumphal armies has to be seen to be believed. The king places a victor's crown on Radames and tells him that he can demand whatever he wants for himself. Among the Ethiopian captives is Amonasro. Aida sees him and embraces him, but he begs her not to reveal his identity and goes on to declare that the Ethiopian king is dead and asks for mercy for the prisoners. Radames claims the boon granted to him by the king but, instead of Aida, he is given Amneris's hand in marriage.

In a temple of Isis, near the Nile, Ramfis leads Amneris to pray for blessings on her forthcoming marriage. Meanwhile Radames and Aida meet. Things are not going well for them, and in addition she is sadly homesick. To make matters worse, Amonasro demands that his daughter discover the route the Egyptian armies plan to take on their way to attack Ethiopia, then he hides.

Using all her feminine powers of persuasion, Aida convinces Radames that his only possible course of action is to go back with her to her homeland. Cunningly, she asks how they can avoid the army and is told that the army will pass through the Gorge of Napata. Amonasro now steps out from his hiding-place, revealing himself as the Ethiopian king and Aida's father, and Radames realizes he has been betrayed and tricked.

To make matters worse, Amneris and Ramfis have also heard the fatal disclosure. They arrive with soldiers and Amonasro tries to kill Amneris, but Radames steps between them and tells Aida and her father to flee. He then yields himself up to Ramfis.

Amneris sends for Radames and offers to intercede for him with her father, provided he never sees Aida again. He flatly refuses her offer and is subsequently condemned as a traitor, to be buried alive. Amneris curses the sentence. Radames is duly sealed up in the crypt below the Temple of Phtha, but Aida has resourcefully got there first and hidden herself. Thus, while the priests above are praising Isis and Amneris is praying for the man who does not want her, Aida sinks into Radames' arms and the lovers die together to one of Verdi's most glorious, soaring tunes.

Karajan's is a performance of *Aida* that carries splendour and pageantry to the point of exaltation. At the very end of the Triumphal scene, when the march resumes with brass bands, there is a lift, a surge of emotion, such as is captured only rarely on record. Plainly the success of the performance – more urgent if less poised than Karajan's earlier account – owes much to its being conceived in conjunction with a Salzburg Festival production. And for all the power of the pageantry, Karajan's fundamental approach is lyrical, the moulding of phrase warmly expressive from the prelude onwards.

Arias are often taken at a slow speed, taxing the singers more, yet Karajan's controversial choice of soloists is amply justified. On record at least, there can be little question of Freni lacking power in a role normally given to a larger voice, and there is ample gain (as on stage) in the tender beauty of her singing. Carreras makes a fresh, sensitive Radames, Raimondi a darkly intense Ramfis and Van Dam a cleanly focused King, his relative lightness no drawback. Cappuccilli here gives a more detailed performance than he did for Muti on EMI, while Baltsa as Amneris crowns the whole performance with her fine, incisive singing.

Despite some over-brightness on cymbals and trumpet (betraying an analogue original), the Berlin sound for Karajan, as transferred to CD, is richly and involvingly atmospheric, both in the intimate scenes and, most strikingly, in the scenes of pageantry, which have rarely been presented on record with greater splendour. It makes an outstanding choice, the more attractive for being at mid-price.

The Solti version, one of his most inspired readings of Verdi, has Leontyne Price as heroine in the earlier of her two recordings. It was recorded by Decca in Rome and has been refurbished to fine effect. It outshines the later Price version, recorded at Walthamstow ten years later, in sound as in performance. Price is an outstandingly assured Aida, rich, accurate and imaginative, while Solti's direction is superbly dramatic and full of flair, notably in the Nile scene. Merrill is a richly secure Amonasro, Rita Gorr a characterful Amneris, and Jon Vickers is splendidly heroic as Radames. Though the tizzy sound of the cymbals in the digital transfer betrays the age of the recording (1962), making the result fierce at times to match the reading, Solti's version otherwise brings full, spacious sound, finer, more open and with greater sense of presence than most versions since.

There is also a place in the catalogue for Karajan's early stereo version from Decca, which stood unrivalled for many years for its spectacle in this most stereophonic of operas. On Decca, as again on EMI, Karajan was helped by having a Viennese orchestra and chorus, rather than an Italian one that was determined to do things in a 'traditional' manner; but most important of all is the musicianship and musical teamwork of his soloists. Bergonzi in particular emerges here as a model among tenors, with a rare feeling for the shaping of phrases and attention to detail. Cornell MacNeil too is splendid.

Tebaldi's interpretation of the part of Aida is well known and much loved. Her creamy tone-colour rides beautifully over the phrases (what a wonderful vehicle for sheer singing this opera is!) and she too acquires a new depth of imagination. Too dominant a characterization would not have fitted Karajan's total conception, but overall Tebaldi lacks temperament. Vocally there are flaws too; notably at the end of *O patria mia*, where Tebaldi finds the cruelly exposed top notes too taxing.

Among the other soloists Arnold van Mill and Fernando Corena are both superb, and Simionato provides one of the very finest portrayals of Amneris we have ever had in a complete *Aida*. The recording has long been famous for its technical bravura and flair. The control of atmosphere, changing as the scene changes, and some of the off-stage effects are strikingly effective in their microscopic clarity at a distance. Helped by Karajan, the recording team have, at the other end of the dynamic scale, managed to bring an altogether new clarity to the big ensembles. CD enhances that clarity and helps the pianissimos register in a recording with a very wide dynamic range for its period (late 1950s).

Like the EMI set with Callas and Gobbi below, the RCA version in the mid-price Victor Opera series brings a classic performance, more than vital enough to make you forget any limitations of mono sound, particularly when it is transferred with plenty of body. Conducting with great panache and with sure pacing, Perlea's direction is keenly dramatic, and all four principals are at their very finest, notably Milanov, whose poise and control in *O patria mia* are a marvel. Barbieri as Amneris is even finer here than in the Callas set, and it is good to hear the young Christoff resonant as Ramfis.

Though 1950s mono sound in the vintage EMI version from La Scala inevitably falls short in representing the splendours of this opera, Callas's voice and that of Gobbi, two of the most characterful of the century, are vividly caught, to make this a classic, indispensable set. The Nile scene – focus of the central emotional conflict in a masterpiece which is only incidentally a pageant – has never been more powerfully and characterfully performed on record than in this vintage La Scala set. Though Callas is hardly as sweet-toned as some will think essential for an Aida, her detailed imagination is irresistible, and she is matched by Tito Gobbi at the very height of his powers. Tucker gives one of his very finest performances on record, and Barbieri is a commanding Amneris.

Fresh and intelligent, unexaggerated in its pacing, Abbado's version from La Scala is lacking in excitement, partly thanks to relatively dull recording quality. It is stronger on the personal drama than on the ceremonial. Domingo gives a superb performance as Radames, not least in the Nile scene, and the two bass roles are cast from strength in Raimondi and Ghiaurov. Leo Nucci makes a dramatic Amonasro, not always pure of line, while Elena Obraztsova produces too much curdled tone as Amneris, dramatic as she is. In many ways Ricciarelli is an appealing Aida, but the voice grows impure above the stave, and floating legatos are marred. The digital recording – cleaner on CD than in the other formats – fails to expand for the ceremonial, and voices are highlighted, but it is acceptably fresh. The layout is improved on CD, but the increased clarity serves only to emphasize the confined acoustic.

Levine's recording, made with Met. forces in the limited acoustic of the Manhattan Center, has the advantage of using a cast and company already well rehearsed in a stage production, but the result is often heavy-handed. The television relay of this same production, with three of the same principals, was more convincing than this. Plácido Domingo still makes a commanding, imaginative Radames; but, on record and without the help of vision, both Aprile Millo in the title-role and Dolora Zajic as Amneris are disappointing when the recording exaggerates unevenness of vocal production. Millo has lovely moments (as in *O patria mia*) but too much is squally, and Zajic's tangily characterful Amneris is often made to sound very raw. James Morris as Amonasro proves a gruff Verdian, but Samuel Ramey is a formidable Ramfis. In this of all operas you need a more spacious recording than is provided here, to allow for the grandeur of the big crowd-scenes to be fully appreciated.

Based on a production at La Scala, the Decca set conducted by Maazel conveys surprisingly little of the feeling of operatic drama. Its great glory is the singing of Luciano Pavarotti, his first recording of the role of Radames. The voice is magnificent, and the superstar tenor's pointing of word-meaning consistently adds illumination, with the character strongly projected. He dominates the performance. Sadly Maazel, adopting speeds on the slow side, is often disappointingly square and metronomic, lacking Verdian warmth and forward thrust. Nevertheless, with a strong cast there is much to enjoy besides Pavarotti. Maria Chiara uses her lovely soprano with fine feeling for Verdian line, even if the characterization is generalized. Gena Dimitrova is a dull Amneris and Leo Nucci a reliable Amonasro, helping to make the Nile scene the most animated sequence of the whole set. Paata Burchuladze sings with sepulchral darkness but with little feeling for the Italian language. The recording is not ideally spacious in the big ensembles, but it is still full and brilliant in the Decca manner, the best sound accorded to any recent digital set.

Caballé's portrait of the heroine is superb, full of detailed insight into the character and with countless examples of superlative singing. The set is worth having for her alone, and Cossotto makes a fine Amneris. Domingo produces glorious sound, but this is not one of his most imaginative recordings, while the Amonasro of Piero Cappuccilli is prosaic. So is much of Muti's direction – no swagger in the Triumphal scene, unfeeling metrical rhythms in the Death scene – and the CD transfer, though faithful enough, brings out the relatively small scale of the sound, underlining the fierceness of Muti's reading; but solo voices are generally well caught.

There is much to commend in Leontyne Price's 1971 recording of *Aida*, and with a fine cast it is a set that might be worth considering. But it comes inevitably into direct comparison with Price's earlier set, and by that standard it is a little disappointing. Price's voice is not as glowing as it was, and though there are moments where she shows added insight, it is the earlier performance which generates more electricity and has more dramatic urgency. Domingo makes a warm and stylish Radames, Milnes a strong if hardly electrifying Amonasro and Bumbry a superb, imaginative Amneris. It is a pity that the recording, by the most recent standards, does not capture the glamour of the score. Most of the earlier sets are more impressive in sound.

Toscanini's 1949 performance of *Aida* is the least satisfying of his New York opera recordings. Richard Tucker sings well but makes a relatively colourless Radames, and Herva Nelli lacks weight as Aida, neatly though she sings and with some touching moments. Eva Gustavson's Amneris lacks all menace, and Valdengo as Amonasro is the only fully satisfying principal. Yet Toscanini is so electrifying from first to last that his admirers will accept the limited, painfully dry recording.

Aida: highlights (scenes & arias).
(M) *** Decca 417 763-2 [id.] (from above recording with Tebaldi, Simionato, Bergonzi, MacNeil; cond. Karajan).

Aida: highlights.
(M) *** Decca 421 860-2; *421 860-4* [id.] (from above recording with Price, Gorr, Vickers, Merrill; cond. Solti).
(M) (***) BMG/RCA mono GD 60201 [60201-2-RG] (from above recording with Milanov, Barbieri, Bjoerling, Warren; cond. Perlea).
(M) **(*) DG Dig. 435 410-2; *435 410-4* [id.] (from above recording with Ricciarelli, Obraztsova, Domingo, Nucci; cond. Abbado).
(M) *(*) EMI CD-EMX 2174. Rome Op. Ch. & O, Mehta.
    Aida (Birgit Nilsson), Amneris (Grace Bumbry), Radames (Franco Corelli), Amonasro (Mario Sereni), Ramfis (Bonaldo Giaiotti), King (Ferruccio Mazzoli).

While the selection from the Solti recording is fairly generous and represents Leontyne Price as an outstandingly assured Aida, by far the most interesting compilation is the Decca 'Scenes and arias' from John Culshaw's Karajan recording from the early stereo era. With fine singing from the principals and vintage Decca sound-quality, this remastered CD and cassette serves to remind us of an outstanding set, regarded as a yardstick of opera recording in its day.

However, a 65-minute selection from the Abbado set is welcome, with cued synopsis rather than a libretto. It is issued as part of DG's 'Domingo Edition' and the selection – although it includes the Triumphal scene and does not neglect Aida or Amneris – rather concentrates on Domingo's contribution.

The other EMI highlights come from Mehta's very first opera recording, dating from 1967. Nilsson's Aida is undeniably powerful, but her contribution is one of the only points in the performance's favour. Corelli and Bumbry are both below their best form and Sereni is an unimpressive Amonasro. The selection plays for 65 minutes and the CD transfer is bright and vivid, but there are better selections than this for a favourite opera.

Alzira (complete).
*** Orfeo CO 57832 (2) [id.]. Bav. R. Ch., Munich R. O, Gardelli.
    Alvaro (Jan-Hendrik Rootering), Gusmano (Renato Bruson), Ovando (Donald George), Zamoro (Francisco Araiza), Ataliba (Daniel Bonilla), Alzira (Ileana Cotrubas).

Of all the operas that Verdi wrote in his years slaving 'in the galleys' (the composer's own pejorative description of his early period when he was spending countless hours establishing a distinctively personal style of composition) *Alzira*, composed in 1845 to a libretto by Cammarano, was the one he most vigorously rejected. Yet this fine, beautifully sung and superbly paced reading brings out the formidable merits of this very compact piece. It is the shortest of the Verdi operas but its concision is on balance an advantage on record, intensifying the adaptation of Voltaire's story of Inca nobles defying the conformity of Christian conquerors.

The action takes place in and around Lima, Peru. Gusmano, the Spanish governor, is to wed the Inca princess, Alzira. But she in her turn is in love with the Inca warrior, Zamoro, who she believes has died at the hands of the Spaniards.

Zamoro has in fact escaped and returns to claim her. Gusmano would have him arrested and tortured, but his father, Alvaro, whose life Zamoro has saved in the prologue to the opera, intercedes on his behalf. An Inca uprising is announced: Gusmano allows Zamoro to go free, predicting that they will meet on the field of battle.

Once again the Incas are defeated and Zamoro is sentenced to death. In order to save her lover, Alzira agrees to accept Gusmano's proposal of marriage in return for Zamoro's freedom.

During the wedding festivities Zamoro re-enters the palace, disguised as a Spanish soldier, and stabs his rival in the heart. With his dying breath Gusmano forgives Zamoro, orders that he be freed and blesses the couple.

In musical inspiration it is indistinguishable from other typical 'galley' operas, with Verdian melodies less distinctive than they became later, but consistently pleasing. Gardelli is a master with early Verdi, and the cast is strong, helped by warm and well-balanced recording, supervised by Munich Radio engineers.

Aroldo (complete).
(M) ** Sony M2K 79328 (2) [M2K 39506]. NY Oratorio Soc., Westminster Ch. Soc., NY Op. O, Queler.
    Mina (Montserrat Caballé), Aroldo (Gianfranco Cecchele), Briano (Louis Lebherz), Egberto (Juan Pons).

Aroldo is Verdi's radical revision of his earlier unsuccessful opera, *Stiffelio*: he translated the story of a Protestant pastor with an unfaithful wife into this tale of a crusader returning from the Holy Land.

It opens in Egberto's castle. Sounds of rejoicing are heard, but Mina, his daughter, enters and we learn that in the absence of her husband, Aroldo (a Saxon knight), she has been unfaithful. Her lover was Godvino, a guest of her father.

Briano, a holy man, now comes in with Aroldo, who notices his wife's obvious misery. Aroldo, who missed her terribly while he was away, asks for a smile of welcome but she is stricken with remorse. Moreover he notices that a ring, given to her by his mother, is missing from her finger. Mina, very reasonably, feels that the time has come to confess to Aroldo, but her father persuades her against it – the shock might kill him!

Godvino now places a letter for Mina in a large, locked book to which he holds the key. Briano sees his action and tells the others, yet wrongly identifies the culprit as Enrico, Mina's cousin. Aroldo demands that the book be opened. He breaks the lock, the letter falls out, and Egberto swiftly and prudently retrieves it.

Denying it to Aroldo, he destroys it. Aroldo is furious, but Egberto is on his side. He subsequently orders Godvino to meet him for a duel in the graveyard, while Mina prays at her mother's tomb. Godvino tells her he still loves her but she spurns him and asks for the return of her ring, which he refuses. Egberto arrives for the duel.

In all conscience, Godvino holds back – after all, Egberto is Mina's father. Then Aroldo arrives and greets Godvino warmly. Egberto, stung by this familiarity, denounces Godvino as the betrayer of the family honour. Aroldo is furious, but Briano reminds him he is a Christian and should forgive and try and forget. Aroldo, however, collapses, unconscious.

Egberto decides the time has come for vengeance, but he finds that Godvino has left the castle. Egberto considers suicide instead, but Briano once more intervenes. It appears that Godvino has returned. Now everything happens at once. Aroldo confronts Mina, saying that she can have a divorce and he will leave that very night; Mina signs the paper; Egberto rushes in, having killed Godvino; Aroldo goes into the church, while Mina prays for forgiveness.

But the greatest surprise of the opera is still to come, for now we find ourselves on the banks of Loch Lomond! (Imitation bagpipes and a huntsmen's chorus.) Aroldo and Briano have not yet taken the high road but have instead renounced the world and live in a rustic hut. Aroldo consoles himself with the thought that he still loves Mina.

There is a storm on the loch and a boat is driven ashore. Operatic coincidences being what they are, Egberto and Mina wade on to the beach at exactly the right spot and go for shelter to the very hut where the two hermits are languishing. Aroldo tries to send Mina away, but her father assures him that she is repentant and Briano once more comes to the rescue with a quotation from the Bible. Love triumphs.

It is an unconvincing plot, to say the least. But the opera, though less compact than the original, contains some splendid new material such as the superb new aria for the heroine, beautifully sung by Caballé. The final scene too is quite new, for the dénouement is totally different. The storm chorus (with echoes of *Rigoletto*) is most memorable – but so are the rum-ti-tum choruses common to both versions. This recording of a concert performance in New York is lively, though the tenor is depressingly coarse.

Attila (complete).
(M) *** Ph. 426 115-2 (2) [id.], Amb. S., Finchley Children's Music Group, RPO, Gardelli.
    Attila (Ruggero Raimondi), Odabella (Cristina Deutekom), Ezio (Sherrill Milnes), Foresto (Carlo Bergonzi).
** EMI Dig. CDS7 49952-2 [Ang. CDCB 49952]. La Scala, Milan, Ch. & O, Muti.
    Attila (Samuel Ramey), Odabella (Cheryl Studer), Ezio (Giorgio Zancanaro), Foresto (Neil Shicoff).
** Hung. Dig. HCD 12934/5. Hungarian R. & TV Ch., Hungarian State O, Gardelli.
    Attila (Evgeny Nesterenko), Odabella (Sylvia Sass), Ezio (Lajos Miller), Foresto (János B. Nagy).

It is easy to criticize the music Verdi wrote during his 'years in the galleys', but a youthfully urgent work like this makes you marvel not at its musical unevenness but at the way Verdi consistently entertains you. The dramatic anticipations of *Macbeth*, with Attila himself far more than a simple villain, the musical anticipations of *Rigoletto*, and the compression which, on record if not on the stage, becomes a positive merit – all these qualities make for an intensely enjoyable musical experience.

The curtain rises on a piazza in Aquileia. Attila's army has been victorious and general praise and invocations to Wotan take place. Attila is angry to see that some women from among the enemy have been saved. Odabella, daughter of the Lord of Aquileia, leads these Italian women who fought alongside the men. Attila admires her courage and offers her any gift she chooses. She desires a sword. Attila gives her his own. She swears vengeance on her captors.

Ezio, the emissary from Rome, offers Attila control of the world. The Emperor of the East is old, the ruler of the West a youth. Ezio requires only that Italy shall be his.

Attila reacts against this cynical chicanery. How can Italy, whose leader is not a man of honour, manage to defy him? Ezio reminds him that he was defeated at Châlons and warns him that Rome will not submit to his rule. Some of the refugees from Aquileia have built primitive homes among the lagoons. Led by Foresto, this settlement will eventually become Venice. But Foresto is in despair at the loss of Odabella.

In a wood near Attila's camp Odabella mourns her father. Meanwhile Attila tells his servant, Uldino, that he has had a visionary dream in which he was warned against continuing his progress to Rome. Nevertheless he orders his troops to proceed. Then a group of people approaches, children and virgins, led by an old man. It is his dream, come to life.

Ezio receives a letter from the boy-emperor, Valentinian, commanding him to return home. Foresto urges instead that he join forces with him to resist Attila.

Ezio is now entertained at a feast in Attila's camp. A gust of wind extinguishes the burning torches. This gives Foresto his opportunity when Uldino gives Attila a cup for a toast to the assembled guests. Odabella, knowing it is poisoned, warns him not to drink. Foresto proudly claims to have poisoned the drink, but Odabello demands Foresto's safety as the price of her warning. Attila agrees, if Odabella will marry him. She is reproached by the suspicious Foresto.

Attila's camp is separated from Ezio's by a wood. Foresto and Ezio make their plans together; meanwhile Odabella declares that her heart is Foresto's and his alone. So it is that Attila finds his bride-to-be in the arms of Foresto. He reproaches all three: the slave he was to marry, the Roman with whom he has a truce and the criminal whose life he spared. They defy him, and Roman soldiers now appear in force to kill Attila. But Odabella first stabs him through the heart.

Deutekom, not the most sweet-toned of sopranos, has never sung better on record, and the other soloists are outstanding; with the stylish Carlo Bergonzi still at his peak and with Sherrill Milnes and Ruggero Raimondi ideally cast, this all adds up to a remarkably fine performance under Gardelli. The 1973 recording is well balanced and atmospheric, but the remastering for CD has been able to make only a marginal improvement in definition, with the chorus less sharply focused than one would expect on a modern digital set.

Recorded – like the latest Decca sets of *Aida* and *Simon Boccanegra* – in the Studio Abanella, the digital sound on the Muti set is more agreeable than on most of his La Scala recordings; but it has less presence than the much earlier Gardelli analogue recording, and the voices are so spotlit that they lose much of their natural bloom. The team of American principals is a strong one, with Ramey bringing out the nobility of the central character, hardly the barbarian of history. Cheryl Studer makes an outstanding Odabella, consistently imaginative, to have one regretting that the voice is not caught more sweetly. Neil Shicoff sings strongly in the tenor role of Foresto, and so does Giorgio Zancanaro as Ezio, but they cannot match their opposite numbers in the Philips set, Carlo Bergonzi and Sherrill Milnes.

The Hungaroton set, conducted (like the Philips) by the ever-responsive Gardelli, brings the advantage of clean, brilliant digital sound of a quality now expected from Budapest. There is also the magisterial Evgeni Nesterenko in the name-part, and in this bass role a Slavonic rather than an Italianate timbre helps to characterize the invading barbarian. Lajos Miller is a strong Ezio, and Sylvia Sass a characterful Odabella though, like Deutekom on the Philips set, she has her squally moments. The snag is the principal tenor, the strained and unstylish János B. Nagy as Foresto, the knight from Aquileia. He is no match at all for Carlo Bergonzi on the earlier set. Though the role for tenor is less central than in most operas, his singing is a serious blemish.

Un ballo in maschera (complete).
*** Decca Dig. 410 210-2 (2) [id.]. L. Op. Ch., Royal College of Music Junior Dept Ch., Nat. PO, Solti.
  Amelia (Margaret Price), Riccardo (Luciano Pavarotti), Renato (Renato Bruson), Oscar (Kathleen Battle), Ulrica (Christa Ludwig), Sam (Robert Lloyd).
*** DG Dig. 427 635-2 (2) [id.]. V. State Op. Konzertvereinigung, VPO, Karajan.
  Amelia (Josephine Barstow), Riccardo (Plácido Domingo), Renato (Leo Nucci), Oscar (Sumi Jo), Ulrica (Florence Quivar), Sam (Kurt Rydl).
*** DG 415 685-2 (2) [id.]. La Scala, Milan, Ch. & O, Abbado.

Amelia (Katia Ricciarelli), Riccardo (Plácido Domingo), Renato (Renato Bruson), Oscar (Edita Gruberová), Ulrica (Elena Obraztsova), Sam (Ruggero Raimondi).

(M) *** BMG/RCA GD 86645 (2) [6645-2-RG]. RCA Italiana Op. Ch. & O, Leinsdorf.

Amelia (Leontyne Price), Riccardo (Carlo Bergonzi), Renato (Robert Merrill), Oscar (Reri Grist), Ulrica (Shirley Verrett), Sam (Ezio Flagello).

(M) *** EMI CMS7 69576-2 (2) [Ang. CDMB 69576]. ROHCG Ch., New Philh. O, Muti.

Amelia (Martina Arroyo), Riccardo (Plácido Domingo), Renato (Piero Cappuccilli), Oscar (Reri Grist), Ulrica (Fiorenza Cossotto), Sam (Gwynne Howell).

(M) **(*) Ph. 426 560-2 (2) [id.]. ROHCG Ch. & O, Colin Davis.

Amelia (Montserrat Caballé), Riccardo (José Carreras), Renato (Ingvar Wixell), Oscar (Sona Ghazarian), Ulrica (Patricia Payne), Sam (Robert Lloyd).

(***) EMI mono CDS7 47498-8 (2) [Ang. CDCB 47498]. La Scala, Milan, Ch. & O, Serafin.

Amelia (Maria Callas), Riccardo (Giuseppe Di Stefano), Renato (Tito Gobbi), Oscar (Eugenia Ratti), Ulrica (Fedora Barbieri), Sam (Silvio Maionica).

(M) (***) BMG/RCA mono GD 60301 (2) [60301-2-RG]. NBC Ch. & SO, Toscanini.

Amelia (Herva Nelli), Riccardo (Jan Peerce), Renato (Robert Merrill), Oscar (Virginia Haskins), Ulrica (Claramae Turner), Sam (Nicola Moscona).

(M) * Decca 425 655-2 (2). St Cecilia Ac., Rome, Ch. & O, Solti.

Amelia (Birgit Nilsson), Riccardo (Carlo Bergonzi), Renato (Cornell MacNeil), Oscar (Sylvia Stahlman), Ulrica (Giulietta Simionato), Sam (Fernando Corena).

Un ballo in maschera was based on the assassination of King Gustavus III of Sweden, and it had censorship problems. The story was then transferred to Boston, Massachusetts but has more recently been returned to the original, Swedish, eighteenth-century backcloth.

King Gustavus (or Riccardo, Count of Warwick) is about to give an audience in the hall of his palace where Count Ribbing and Count Horn and their followers are conspiring together. Oscar the pageboy brings in Renato Anckarstroem, his secretary, whose wife, Amelia, Gustavus secretly loves.

Anckarstroem tells the king of a plot against him but is not taken seriously; the king is more concerned with preparations for a masked ball, which is to take place shortly. Oscar announces the Minister of Justice, who has come for the king's signature to banish a fortune-teller, Mlle Arvidson (or Ulrica) from the country.

Gustavus' interest is aroused; he will go and see her and test her powers. She receives him in her hut, having previously been seen evoking the powers of darkness. The king enters, dressed as a fisherman. While he is there, Christian, a sailor, enters to have his fortune told, and the prediction is promotion. Gustavus promptly writes out a commission and slips it into the sailor's pocket, whose delight is evident. A servant of Amelia enters, asking for a private session. The crowd is dismissed but the king hides.

Amelia herself now comes in. She tells Mlle Arvidson that she loves Gustavus (he is delighted to hear this) and she wishes to exorcize this guilty passion. The fortune-teller speaks of a magical herb, to be gathered at night from the foot of the gallows. Amelia leaves and Oscar returns with the courtiers and conspirators. Gustavus, still the fisherman, asks that his fortune be told and is told that he will die, killed by someone he knows well and trusts.

All are upset, but Gustavus refuses to take the fortune-teller seriously; she now predicts that his killer will be the next person to shake his hand. The courtiers all decline to do so. Then Anckarstroem enters. The king, now recognized as such, grasps his hand and now is confident that the prophecy is false. But, while there is general acclaim, Mlle Arvidson and Anckarstroem express foreboding about the future.

We now find Amelia seeking the magic herb by the gallows. Gustavus arrives and she tries to send him off – but they obviously love each other. Anckarstroem now comes to warn the king again that conspirators mean to kill him. The two men exchange cloaks and Gustavus makes Anckarstroem swear to escort Amelia (heavily veiled so that she will not be recognized by her husband) back to the city. He must not enquire who she is.

The conspirators meet them and are frustrated that it is Anckarstroem, not the king, with Amelia. They strip away her veil, and Anckarstroem is appalled to discover that it is his own wife. Ribbing and Horn find the whole affair amusing but Anckarstroem declares that he will be revenged and will join the conspiracy the next day; meanwhile he is determined to kill his wife for her unfaithfulness.

But first she begs to see her young son. He agrees then, looking at a portrait of the king, he decides that Gustavus is the guilty party and that his wife shall be spared. Ribbing and Horn arrive and he tells them he will join them. Lots will be drawn to determine who shall assassinate the king. Amelia enters and is compelled to make the draw. From the urn she draws her husband's name. Guessing what is afoot, Amelia plans to warn the king herself.

The scene now changes to the palace. All the invitations have been sent and received, and the masked ball is about to take place. The king first writes out an order appointing Anckarstroem as Governor of Finland. Amelia will go with him, as the king has honourably decided to renounce his love for her.

Oscar brings in an anonymous letter warning of the forthcoming attempt on his life. But the king wants to go to the ball, if only to see Amelia for the last time before she leaves. At the ball itself, Anckarstroem presses the pageboy to tell him which masked figure is the king, saying he has important matters to discuss with him, and so discovers which is the king's costume.

The king now dances with Amelia, who does her best to persuade him to leave at once. He tells her that she will be departing for Finland the next day, so they must make their last farewells. Then Anckarstroem takes his opportunity and shoots (or stabs) the king. He is seized by guards and the assembled company calls for vengeance. But before dying, Gustavus assures Anckarstroem that is wife is guiltless and, as far as he personally is concerned, chaste. Moreover he generously orders that his secretary's life be spared. Anckarstroem repents his action as Gustavus dies.

Shining out from the cast of Solti's most recent recording of *Ballo* is the gloriously sung Amelia of Margaret Price in one of her richest and most commanding performances on record, ravishingly beautiful, flawlessly controlled and full of unforced emotion. The role of Riccardo, pushy and truculent, is well suited to the extrovert Pavarotti, who swaggers through the part, characteristically clear of diction, challenged periodically by Price to produce some of his subtlest tone-colours. Bruson makes a noble Renato, Christa Ludwig an unexpected but intense and perceptive Ulrica, while Kathleen Battle is an Oscar whose coloratura is not just brilliant but sweet too.

Solti is far more relaxed than he often is on record, presenting a warm and understanding view of the score. The recording is extremely vivid within a reverberant acoustic, with orchestra as well as singers given added presence on the pair of CDs with excellent cueing.

Recorded in Vienna early in 1989, *Un ballo in maschera* was Karajan's last opera recording. It was done in conjunction with the new production at that year's Salzburg Festival, which Karajan was scheduled to conduct. He died only days before the first night, while the production was already in rehearsal. The recording makes a fitting memorial, characteristically rich and spacious, with a cast – if not ideal – which still makes a fine team, responding to the conductor's single-minded vision. Karajan's underlining of dynamic contrasts in the final assassination scene, for example, is thrilling, demonstrating his undiminished sense of drama.

Standing out vocally is the Gustavo of Plácido Domingo, strong and imaginative, dominating the whole cast. He may not have the sparkle of Pavarotti in this role, but the singing is richer, more refined and more thoughtful. Karajan's unexpected and controversial choice of Josephine Barstow as Amelia certainly makes for a striking and characterful performance, even if vocally it is flawed, with the tone growing raw under pressure. Nevertheless this is Barstow's finest achievement on record, and dramatically she is most compelling. Leo Nucci, though not as rough in tone as in some of his other recent recordings, is over-emphatic, with poor legato in his great solo, *Eri tu*. Sumi Jo, a Karajan discovery, gives a delicious performance as Oscar the pageboy, coping splendidly with Karajan's slow speed for her Act I solo. Florence Quivar produces satisfyingly rich tone as Ulrica. Though the sound is not as cleanly focused as in the Decca recording for Solti, it is warm and full.

Abbado's powerful reading, admirably paced and with a splendid feeling for the sparkle of the comedy, remains highly recommendable. The cast is very strong, with Ricciarelli at her very finest and Domingo sweeter of tone and more deft of characterization than on the Muti set of five years earlier. Bruson as the wronged husband Renato (a role he again takes for Solti) sings magnificently, and only Obraztsova as Ulrica and Gruberová as Oscar are less consistently convincing. The analogue recording clearly separates the voices and instruments in different acoustics, which is distracting only initially and after that brings the drama closer. Certainly on the CD transfer the overall effect is marvellously vivid, with solo voices firmly placed and the chorus realistically full-bodied and clear.

Leinsdorf's RCA set makes a fine bargain in its CD format at mid-price. All the principals are in splendid voice, and Leinsdorf's direction – too often inflexible in Italian opera – here has resilience as well as brilliance and urgency. Verdi peppers the score with the marking *con eleganza*, and that is exactly what Leinsdorf observes, giving elegance even to the obviously vulgar dance numbers of the final scene. Leontyne Price is a natural for the part of Amelia and, with one notable reservation, hers comes near to being a model interpretation – exact in its observance of Verdi's detailed markings but spontaneous-sounding and full of dramatic temperament.

Only in the two big arias does Price for a moment grow self-conscious, and there are one or two mannered phrases, overloaded with the wrong sort of expressiveness. Robert Merrill, sometimes thought of as an inexpressive singer, here acquired Gobbi-like overtones to add to the flow of firm, satisfying tone. Bergonzi is a model of sensitivity, and the climax of the Act II love-duet is one of the most satisfying moments in the whole opera. Reri Grist makes a light, bright Oscar, and the Ulrica of Shirley Verrett has a range of power, richness and delicacy, coupled with unparalleled firmness, that makes this one of her most memorable recorded performances. Excellent recording, hardly showing its age, in the remastered transfer, with the voices rather forward.

In Muti's EMI set the quintet of principals is also unusually strong, but it is the conductor who takes first honours in a warmly dramatic reading. His rhythmic resilience and consideration for the singers go with keen concentration, holding each Act together in a way he did not quite achieve in his earlier recording for EMI of *Aida*. Arroyo, rich of voice, is not always imaginative in her big solos, and Domingo rarely produces a half-tone, though the recording balance may be partly to blame. The sound is vivid, but no translation is provided for this mid-priced reissue.

Davis's version, based on a Covent Garden production, is particularly good in the way it brings out the ironic humour in Verdi's score. Caballé and Carreras match Davis's lightness, but the dramatic power is diminished. Despite fine recording, this is less satisfying than most of the recordings listed here, lacking the gutsy quality needed.

Serafin's 1957 recording, with voices as ever set rather close but with a fair amount of space round them, is among the best of the sets with Callas from La Scala, and CD focuses its qualities the more sharply. Cast from strength with all the principals – notably Gobbi and Giuseppe di Stefano – on top form, this is indispensable for Callas's admirers.

This was the very last of the complete operas that Toscanini conducted in New York in concert performance. It was given in Carnegie Hall in January 1954, just three months before the maestro finally retired. Though the performance cannot match in exhilaration his unique reading of *Falstaff*, it stands as one of the most cherishable mementoes of his conducting of Verdi. Speeds are often fast and the control characteristically taut, but it is wrong to think of the performance as rigid, when rubato is often so freely expressive. Fascinatingly, in the quintet, *E scherzo od è follia*, Toscanini encourages Jan Peerce to adopt the extra 'ha-has' that had become traditional, defying the idea that he invariably followed the text strictly.

Peerce misses some of the lightness of the role, clear in diction but not very characterful, yet Toscanini's pointing of rhythm regularly brings out the sharp wit of much of the writing. Herva Nelli, one of Toscanini's favourite sopranos in his last years, here gives one of her finest performances, with a beautiful, finely moulded line in her big numbers, including the two arias. Robert Merrill is superb as Renato, singing magnificently in *Eri tu*, while Claramae Turner is firm as a rock as Ulrica. The sound is typically dry, not at all atmospheric, but clean and well detailed with a good sense of presence.

In spite of an impressive list of soloists, with Bergonzi and Simionato ideally cast, Solti's earlier version is disappointing. It has a good opera-house atmosphere but the singing and playing often lack involvement. Birgit Nilsson is a striking but controversial Amelia, singing incisively with her powerful voice but failing to convey the character's gentler side.

Un ballo in maschera: highlights.
*** DG Dig. 429 415-2 [id.] (from above recording with Barstow, Domingo; cond. Karajan).
(M) *** DG 435 411-2; *435 411-4* [id.] (from above recording with Ricciarelli, Domingo; cond. Abbado).

This DG highlights disc is drawn from Karajan's last opera recording, made in 1989, and it is a fitting memorial. Josephine Barstow's contribution may be vocally flawed but her singing is full of charisma; yet it is Domingo who dominates, singing superbly throughout. The selection is generous (71 minutes), following through the opera's narrative with both Acts well represented.

The selection from the Abbado version, which includes the *Prelude* and opens brightly with *S'avanza il conte*, makes a good alternative choice, with a cued narrative for the listener to follow the action. The excerpts are well chosen (as part of the 'Domingo Edition') to represent this artist, but Ricciarelli's splendid contribution is not neglected. The CD transfer faithfully reflects the qualities of the complete set.

La battaglia di Legnano (complete).

(M) *** Ph. 422 435-2 (2) [id.]. Austrian R. Ch. & O, Gardelli.

Lida (Katia Ricciarelli), Arrigo (José Carreras), Rolando (Matteo Manuguerra), Federico (Nikola Ghiuselev).

La battaglia di Legnano is a compact, sharply conceived piece, made the more intense by the subject's obvious relationship with the situation in Verdi's own time. One weakness is that the villainy is not effectively personalized, but the juxtaposition of the individual drama of supposed infidelity against a patriotic theme brings most effective musical contrasts.

Frederick Barbarossa and his army are invading northern Italy and in Milan a defence is being organized, grouping various factions. Rolando leads the Milanese troops, Arrigo the army from Verona. Rolando, Duke of Milan, and Arrigo are old friends and the latter, who was taken prisoner, is delighted to meet Rolando once more.

In a shady place we meet Lida, Rolando's wife, and her ladies in waiting. Marcovaldo, an enemy captive, has fallen in love with Lida, but she repulses him angrily. Arrigo and Rolando now arrive and Marcovaldo concludes that Lida is secretly in love with Arrigo. He is not far wrong. Once alone, Arrigo and Lida declare their mutual feelings and we find that they had once been betrothed. Arrigo reproaches her for marrying Rolando. That she thought him dead at the time is no consolation, and he is bitter.

Arriving in Como, Arrigo and Rolando now try to persuade the local leaders to join forces with them against Barbarossa, but the mayor refuses as he has arranged a treaty with the invader. They beg him to reconsider and argue that Italy's future is at stake. Barbarossa then suddenly makes an entrance. He tells the two envoys to return with news of imminent defeat, for he is camped in force outside the city. In spite of his confidence, the envoys do not lose their conviction that he will be defeated, and the Lombards chorus their spirited decision to fight to the death.

In Milan Cathedral Arrigo is initiated into the ranks of the *Cavalieri della Morte*, a band of warriors who take an oath to rid their country of invaders or die. In Lida's room we see her giving a letter to her maid to deliver to Arrigo; she feels he will die in battle and implores him to visit her before he departs. At the same time Rolando conveys his own premonition of death to Arrigo. He has said goodbye to his family and tells Arrigo that he is now the leader of the 'Death riders'. Arrigo promises that his family will be looked after, should he be mortally wounded.

Marcovaldo intercepts Lida's letter and gives it to Rolando, who now swears vengeance both on his wife and on his friend, who has apparently betrayed him. While Arrigo is writing to his mother, Lida enters and says that they must not meet again. She is puzzled that he has not answered her letter. Rolando is heard at the door, Arrigo conceals Lida on the balcony but Rolando finds her.

He is about to kill Arrigo when trumpets sound a call-to-arms. Rolando knows a far greater punishment for Arrigo would be to prevent him from fighting for his country, so he locks him in his room. However, Arrigo, spurred on by his patriotism, leaps from the balcony crying '*Viva Italia!*'

The people of Milan gather in the cathedral square, Lida with them. News comes that the barbarians from Germany have been routed. Arrigo, mortally wounded, is brought in; he wishes to die in the cathedral. Rolando enters with the group bearing his body. Arrigo swears that he and Lida are innocent, and Rolando accepts his word and forgives his friend. Arrigo kisses the flag and dies, amid general rejoicing.

Gardelli directs a fine performance, helped by a strong cast of principals, with Carreras, Ricciarelli and Manuguerra all at their finest. Excellent recording, with the depth of perspective enhanced on CD.

Il Corsaro (complete).

(M) *** Ph. 426 118-2 (2) [id.]. Amb. S., New Philh. O, Gardelli.

Corrado (José Carreras), Medora (Jessye Norman), Gulnara (Montserrat Caballé), Seid (Gian-Piero Mastromei), Selimo (John Noble).

Verdi did not even bother to attend the first performance of *Il Corsaro* in Trieste in 1848, despite the inclusion in the cast of four of his favourite singers. It seemed as though his 'years in the galleys' had caught up with him in this, the thirteenth of his operas. By the time he had completed the score, Verdi had fallen out of love with his subject, an adaptation of Byron. Only latterly has the composer's own poor view of the piece, predictably parroted through the years, been revised in the light of closer study. One of the first merits of the piece is its compactness, and Piave's treatment of Byron is not nearly as clumsy as has been thought.

The opera opens on the corsairs' island in the Aegean. Corrado, their leader, bewails their lives of exile and crime. A letter warning of military action arrives; Corrado bids his beloved Medora farewell and sets sail.

The next scene takes place in an apartment of the harem of Seid, Pasha of Coron. His favourite slave, Gulnara, hates him. Corrado, disguised as a dervish, now appears and asks Seid for protection from the corsairs.

As sounds of battle are heard, Corrado throws off his disguise and in the course of the fighting he and his corsairs attempt to save the women of the harem. The Act ends with their defeat and his capture.

In the last Act, Seid laments the fact that of all his slaves the one he loves most does not return his feelings. Gulnara has fallen in love with Corrado and pleads for his life.

In the next scene Corrado laments his fate and imprisonment; Gulnara suggests she free him and kill Seid, an offer he at first declines, telling of his love for Medora. A storm arises, but when it abates Gulnara announces Seid's death and together they escape.

The last scene finds Medora near death and without hope of seeing him again. Then the ship arrives carrying Corrado, but the lovers are in each other's arms. Corrado and Gulnara rail against fate; Medora's strength fails. In desperation Corrado throws himself from the cliffs.

Though the characterization is rudimentary, the contrast between the two heroines is effective, with Gulnara, the Pasha's slave, carrying conviction in the *coup de foudre* which has her promptly worshipping the Corsair, an early example of the Rudolf Valentino figure. The rival heroines are splendidly taken here, with Jessye Norman as the faithful wife, Medora, actually upstaging Montserrat Caballé as Gulnara.

Likenesses in many of the numbers to some of the greatest passages in *Rigoletto*, *Trovatore* and *Traviata* give the opera vintage Verdian flavour, and the orchestration is often masterly. Gardelli, as in his other Philips recordings of early Verdi, directs a vivid performance, with fine singing from the hero, portrayed by José Carreras. Gian-Piero Mastromei, not rich in tone, still rises to the challenge of the Pasha's music. On two CDs, with Act III complete on the second, the CD transfer brings a clarification of the excellent, firmly focused and well-balanced Philips sound.

Don Carlos (complete).
(M) *** EMI CMS7 69304-2 (3) [Ang. CDMC 69304]. German Op. Ch., Berlin, BPO, Karajan.
    Don Carlo (José Carreras), Elisabetta (Mirella Freni), Eboli (Agnes Baltsa), Rodrigo (Piero Cappuccilli), Philip II (Nicolai Ghiaurov), Grand Inquisitor (Ruggero Raimondi).
*** EMI CDS7 47701-8 (3) [Ang. CDCC 47701]. Amb. Op. Ch., ROHCG O, Giulini.
    Don Carlo (Plácido Domingo), Elisabetta (Montserrat Caballé), Eboli (Shirley Verrett), Rodrigo (Sherrill Milnes), Philip II (Ruggero Raimondi), Grand Inquisitor (Giovanni Foiani).
**(*) Sony Dig. S3K 52500 (3) [id.]. NY Met. Ch. & O, James Levine.
    Don Carlo (Michael Sylvester), Elisabetta (Aprile Millo), Eboli (Dolora Zajic), Rodrigo (Vladimir Chernov), Philip II (Ferruccio Furlanetto), Grand Inquisitor (Samuel Ramey), Voice from Heaven (Kathleen Battle).
**(*) Decca 421 114-2 (3) [id.]. ROHCG Ch. & O, Solti.
    Don Carlo (Carlo Bergonzi), Elisabetta (Renata Tebaldi), Eboli (Grace Bumbry), Rodrigo (Dietrich Fischer-Dieskau), Philip II (Nicolai Ghiaurov), Grand Inquisitor (Martti Talvela).
**(*) DG Dig. 415 316-2 (4) [id.]. La Scala, Milan, Ch. & O, Abbado.
    Don Carlos (Plácido Domingo), Elisabeth (Katia Ricciarelli), Eboli (Lucia Valentini Terrani), Rodrigue (Leo Nucci), Philippe II (Ruggero Raimondi), Grand Inquisitor (Nicolai Ghiaurov).
(M) (**(*)) EMI mono CMS7 64642-2 (3) [CDMC 64642]. Rome Op. Ch. & O, Santini.
    Don Carlo (Mario Filippeschi), Elisabetta (Antonietta Stella), Eboli (Elena Nicolai), Rodrigo (Tito Gobbi), Philip II (Boris Christoff), Grand Inquisitor (Giulio Neri).
(M) **(*) DG 437 730-2 (3) [id.]. La Scala, Milan, Ch. & O, Santini.
    Don Carlo (Flaviano Labò), Elisabetta (Antonietta Stella), Eboli (Fiorenza Cossotto), Rodrigo (Ettore Bastianini), Philip II (Boris Christoff).

Don Carlos, one of Verdi's finest and most powerful musical spectacles, was written for the Paris Opéra, where the ambitious five-Act version had its first performance in 1867. Later Verdi and Ghislanzoni revised the work and shortened it – notably the first Act – for an Italian version, first heard in 1884. Today a compromise is often made in stage performances, though not in Germany, where the four-Act version is more familiar. Elsewhere, the opening Act containing the Fontainebleau scene is usually left much as it was in the original, and cuts are made at other points.

The Fontainebleau scene, which is a kind of Prologue to the main action, brings the evocative sounds of a hunt in the forest. Princess Elisabeth de Valois, daughter of the King of France, and her page, Thibaut, are seeking their companion riders. Don Carlos, son of King Philip of Spain, makes his entrance as they ride off. He is to marry Elisabeth and is happy at the prospect, even though they have never met.

When she reappears, he tells her he is one of the Spanish envoy's staff. But he then shows her a portrait of Don Carlos and, when she recognizes it, love springs up between them. Yet their hopes of happiness together are to be immediately dashed. Thibaut returns and tells her that King Philip, Carlos's father, intends to marry her. She is to be Queen of Spain.

The action moves to a cloister of the Yuste monastery in Madrid. The tomb of Charles V is nearby and the monks can be heard mourning their late king. Don Carlos enters and a monk tells him that the ghost of Charles V is sometimes seen in the precinct. Rodrigo, Don Carlos's lifelong friend, now arrives from the Spanish province of Flanders, where there are signs of a local rebellion. He senses that his friend is troubled, and Carlos reveals his love for his father's wife, Elisabeth.

Rodrigo suggests he would do better to forget her and go to Flanders to help the oppressed people there. King Philip and his wife now arrive in a stately procession, but neither speaks to Carlos, who becomes even more upset. But the two men reassert their comradeship.

Later the ladies of the court are relaxing in the garden. Thibaut joins them and Princess Eboli sings a Moorish song. The queen enters and Thibaut announces Rodrigo's arrival. He gives the queen a letter from her mother and then surreptitiously slips a second note into her hand. While they talk, Elisabeth reads the clandestine note, which is from Carlos asking to see her. Rodrigo urges her to obey his friend's request.

When they meet, Carlos initially asks her to influence the king to make him Governor of Flanders, but he cannot hold back his feelings and declares his continuing passion for her. She admits she still loves him and they embrace. She swiftly draws away.

The king arrives and is furious to find his wife unattended. The lady-in-waiting who should have been with her is cursorily dismissed. Elisabeth consoles her friend but can do nothing to save her from being banished. She leaves in distress. The king now talks to Rodrigo. He respects his advice and takes him seriously when he speaks of the Spanish religious oppression in Flanders. But he warns Rodrigo to beware of the grand inquisitor. He also mentions in confidence his suspicions of the attachment between the queen and Don Carlos.

Don Carlos now receives an amorous note making an assignation. He thinks it is from the queen and waits in the garden. A veiled figure enters and he welcomes her lovingly before he discovers it is not Elisabeth but the Princess Eboli. She loves him and is furiously jealous as she realizes that his first embrace was intended for Elisabeth. Rodrigo arrives and tries to smooth over her angry disappointment. But Eboli determines on revenge and, when she threatens to reveal the relationship between Carlos and Elisabeth, Rodrigo threatens her life and Carlos has to step in to prevent violence.

Rodrigo now persuades Carlos to pass over to Rodrigo secret papers relating to the leaders of the uprising in Flanders, so that if anything happens he should not be incriminated. One can see why in the following macabre *Auto da fé* scene when, in front of the cathedral, prisoners condemned by the inquisition go to be burned to death at the stake.

Don Carlos now leads in six Flemish deputies, who plead with the king for mercy for their people. He is unrelenting (perhaps he is impotent in front of the grand inquisitor) and he also turns down Carlos's request to be made the ruler of Flanders. The king fears the giving of power which could be turned against himself and, as if to confirm his fears, the impulsive Carlos draws his sword. Philip demands he be disarmed. No one moves to do so until Rodrigo steps in and quietly takes the sword away. As he is taken into custody, Carlos is astonished at his friend's *volte face*.

Philip, alone in his apartment, is joined by the sinister figure of the grand inquisitor. Philip asks how Carlos should be punished. The reply is: by death. The Inquisitor points out that God sacrificed his own son. If Carlos is plotting against the king and, more importantly, the Church, there is no choice. Moreover Rodrigo is equally dangerous. Philip resists but the inquisition is all-powerful.

The queen enters and finds Philip in possession of her stolen jewel-casket. He forcibly opens it; inside is a portrait of Carlos. The king rejects her explanation that she had been previously betrothed to Carlos and accuses her of being unfaithful. It is all too much for her and she faints.

The king is now repentant and calls for Rodrigo and Princess Eboli, who now regrets that she gave Philip the casket. Eboli confides in Elisabeth that she herself loves Carlos (who does not return her feelings) and that she has been seduced by the king. The queen banishes her and Eboli departs, cursing her own allure which has brought her present predicament (*O don fatale*). But, if she has to retire to a convent, first she determines to save Carlos.

Rodrigo, himself in danger, now visits Carlos in prison. Rodrigo is being hunted down by the inquisition because Carlos's papers were found on him. But he accepts his guilt, for he has encouraged a revolt in Flanders. He will go and try to intercede with the king for Carlos's life. At that moment they are rudely interrupted by an assassin who, under orders from the inquisition, shoots Rodrigo down.

As he dies, he urges Carlos to continue the fight for freedom for the people of Flanders. The king now arrives to free Carlos, bringing his sword back to him, but his son denounces him for conspiring to murder Rodrigo. An angry crowd outside, led by Eboli, clamours in support of Carlos. But the ultimate power of the grand inquisitor becomes apparent as he commands the crowd to kneel before their king.

Elisabeth is now in the cloisters at Yuste once more. She kneels before the tomb of Charles V and calls on his spirit to help her. Carlos enters, they re-confirm their mutual love, but on earth they can never possess each other, besides which Carlos has work to do for the cause of Flanders. King Philip enters with the grand inquisitor to arrest him, but they are dumbfounded when the tomb of Charles V opens, a figure in monk's habit emerges, and quietly leads Carlos away.

As in the Salzburg Festival production on which his recording is based, Karajan opts firmly for the later, four-Act version of the opera favoured in Germany, merely opening out the cuts he adopted on stage, notably those in the last Act. The results could hardly be more powerfully dramatic, one of his most involving opera performances, comparable with his vivid EMI *Aida*.

Though a recording can hardly convey the full grandeur of a stage peopled with many hundreds of singers, the *Auto da fé* scene is here superb, while Karajan's characteristic choice of singers for refinement of voice rather than sheer size consistently pays off. Both Carreras and Freni are most moving, even if *Tu che le vanità* has its raw moments. Baltsa is a superlative Eboli and Cappuccilli an affecting Rodrigo, though neither Carreras nor Cappuccilli is at his finest in the famous oath duet. Raimondi and Ghiaurov as the Grand Inquisitor and Philip II provide the most powerful confrontation.

Though many collectors will naturally resist the idea of the four-Act rather than the five-Act version on record, having so vivid a Karajan set at mid-price makes a superb bargain. Though the sound is not as analytically detailed as the earlier EMI version with Giulini, it is both rich and atmospheric, giving great power to Karajan's uniquely taut account of the four-Act version.

Giulini was the conductor who in the Covent Garden production of 1958 demonstrated in the opera house the supreme mastery of Verdi's score. Here he is conducting the same orchestra as Solti directed in the Decca version five years earlier, and predictably, though less bitingly intense, he is more flowing, more affectionate in his phrasing, while conveying the quiet, dramatic intensity which made his direction so irresistible in the opera house. There is extra joy for example in the *Auto da fé* scene as it is pointed by Giulini. Generally the new cast is a little stronger than the old, but each is admirably consistent.

The only major vocal disappointment among the principals lies in Caballé's account of the big aria *Tu che le vanità* in the final Act. Like the Decca set, this one uses the full, five-Act text. The CD transfer of the 1971 analogue recording brings astonishing vividness and realism, a tribute to the original engineering of Christopher Parker. Even in the big ensembles of the *Auto da fé* scene, the focus is very precise yet atmospheric too, not just analytic. The extra bite of realism enhances an already fine version to make it the finest in sound, irrespective of age.

Recorded in the Manhattan Center, New York, James Levine's version with the company of the Metropolitan has full, forward sound, more faithful than most from this source, making it the best digital recommendation for the full, five-Act score. The heavy-handedness of Levine as a Verdian is exaggerated by the sound, but far better that than the tepid results from La Scala in Abbado's recording for DG. With Levine the *Auto da fé* ensemble may lack refinement, taken fast, but it is certainly dramatic, and the whole performance has a thrust and bite that reflect opera-house experience. The cast is very acceptable, if not ideally distinguished.

In the title-role the American tenor, Michael Sylvester, produces fine, clear, heroic tone and, unlike most rivals, he is not afraid to shade his voice down to a pianissimo. Aprile Millo's ripe soprano is very apt for the role of Elisabetta and, though her vibrato tends to become obtrusive, she controls her line well, not least in the perilous phrases of her big Act V aria, *Tu che le vanità*. As Eboli, Dolora Zajic's fruity mezzo is not well caught by the close-up recording, again with unevenness exaggerated, but this is a rich characterization. As King Philip, Ferruccio Furlanetto is not as firm as he usually is, while Vladimir Chernev as Rodrigo is not flattered either, with fluttery timbre exaggerated. He makes little of the character, the key to the whole opera, leaving a disappointing blank where one wants the keenest intensity.

Solti's Decca version, like Giulini's, is of the five-Act score without the additions that Abbado provides. Solti is a purposeful Verdian, but the dramatic temperature fails to rise as it should until the duet between Philip and Rodrigo at the end of Act II (Act I in the four-Act version). Till then Solti tends to be somewhat rigid, but once the right mood is established he does marvellously with his Covent Garden forces, and the result in the *Auto da fé* scene is very fine. Tebaldi too in this most exacting Verdian role warms up well, and gives a magnificent account of *Tu che le vanità* in Act V.

Bumbry and Bergonzi both sing splendidly and, after some rather gritty singing early on, Fischer-Dieskau rises fittingly to Rodrigo's great death scene, sounding almost (but not quite) as moving as Gobbi in the old EMI set (mono). Ghiaurov as Philip takes a strong, direct view, conveying nobility and a sense of stoic pride. The recording is vintage Decca, brilliant and well focused, outstanding for its period; yet the whole performance rather fails to add up to the sum of its parts.

For the dedicated Verdian, Abbado's set brings new authenticity and new revelation. This is the first recording to use the language which Verdi originally set, French; in addition to the full, five-Act text in its composite 1886 form, including the Fontainebleau scene (recorded twice before), there are half a dozen appendices from the original 1867 score, later cut or recomposed. These include a substantial prelude and introduction to Act I, an introduction and chorus to Act III, the Queen's ballet from that same Act (15 minutes long), a duet for the Queen and Eboli in Act IV (even longer), and extra material for the finales of Acts IV and V.

By rights, this should be the definitive recording of the opera, for, as has often been promised, the French text brings an apt darkening of tone compared with the open sounds of Italian, and Abbado is a masterly interpreter of Verdi.

The first disappointment lies in the variable quality of the sound, with odd balances, with voices at times so distant they might be off-stage, and, although the Fontainebleau opening with its echoing horns is arrestingly atmospheric, the *Auto da fé* scene lacks bite, brilliance and clarity. In addition, the very weight of the project, the extra stress on soloists and chorus working on music they know in a language they do not, has tended to prevent the drama from taking flight.

Flair and urgency are missing, yet the cast of soloists is a strong one (even if they are variable in their French), with Plácido Domingo outstanding. Domingo easily outshines his earlier recording with Giulini (in Italian), while Katia Ricciarelli as the Queen gives a tenderly moving performance, if not quite commanding enough in the Act V aria. Ruggero Raimondi is a finely focused Philip II, nicely contrasted with Nicolai Ghiaurov as the Grand Inquisitor in the other black-toned bass role. Lucia Valentini Terrani as Eboli is warm-toned if not very characterful, and Leo Nucci makes a noble Rodrigue.

Whatever the reservations, this makes a fine historic document. The three chrome cassettes represent the highest state of the art, vividly transferred and having no problems with the varying perspectives.

The vintage EMI mono recording offers a seriously cut version of the four-Act score, indifferently conducted by Gabriele Santini, but it is still an indispensable set, with performances from Tito Gobbi as Rodrigo and Boris Christoff as Philip which have never been remotely matched. Gobbi's singing in the Death scene is arguably the finest recorded performance that even this glorious artist ever made, with a wonderful range of tone and feeling for words.

The bitingly dark tone of Christoff as the King also goes with intense feeling for the dramatic situation, making his big monologue one of the peaks of the performance. It may be a sign of declining standards today that the flaws in the other solo singing do not seem as serious as they did when the set was issued in the 1950s. Antonietta Stella, never a very distinctive artist, gives one of her finest recorded performances as Elisabetta, only occasionally squally. As Eboli, Elena Nicolai controls her fruity mezzo well, even if the vibrato becomes obtrusive; and the most serious blot is the singing of the tenor, Mario Filippeschi, and even that is not as coarse or strained as we have often had latterly.

Two of the principal soloists on the analogue DG set – Christoff and Stella – as well as the conductor are the same as in the old HMV mono recording but, quite apart from the advantages of the stereo, this newer set has the advantage of including the Fontainebleau forest scene, whereas the EMI stuck to the heavily cut Paris version. Christoff is again superb. No other bass in the world today comes anywhere near him in this part either in vocal strength, musicianship or power of characterization. The tragic dilemma of the ageing King Philip II has an intense nobility when in Act IV he faces the grim demands of the Inquisitor.

Antonietta Stella is no more successful here than she was on EMI: she still has poor discipline, and in her big aria, *Tu che le vanità*, this makes for some squally sounds. Fiorenza Cossotto proves a warm-voiced Eboli who copes strongly with the difficulties of *O don fatale*. Labò is a surprisingly good Don Carlos. Unlike Filippeschi on the old mono set, he sings expressively and intelligently.

The real loss, of course, in comparing the two versions, is the replacement of Tito Gobbi by Bastianini. Rodrigo's death in the earlier set was vocally one of the high peaks of modern recorded opera. Firm and rich as Bastianini unfailingly is, he does not begin to plumb the character in that way. The DG recording-balance favours the voices, while the orchestra is comparatively distant; but the lively CD transfer makes everything sound more vivid, even if the orchestra is masked in the moments of spectacle. The tingling excitement of the *Auto da fé* scene is inevitably diluted. But this is such a wonderful opera that even these flaws cannot prevent this recording from proving a most moving experience.

Don Carlos: highlights.
(M) *** EMI CDM7 63089-2; *EG 763089-4* (from above recording with Domingo, Caballé, Verrett, Milnes; cond. Giulini).
(M) **(*) DG Dig. 435 412-2; *435 412-4* [id.] (from above recording with Domingo, Ricciarelli, Terrani, Nucci; cond. Abbado).

The disc of highlights from Giulini's 1970 set of *Don Carlos* can be highly recommended. In selecting from such a long opera, serious omissions are inevitable; nothing is included here from Act III to make room for the *Auto da fé* scene from Act IV – some 37 minutes of the disc is given to this Act. With vivid sound, this is most stimulating; the only reservation concerns Caballé's *Tu che le vanità*, which ends the selection disappointingly.

For those with another complete version, the highlights from the Abbado set, sung in French, will be especially worth while, even though there are reservations about the recording. Excerpts from all five Acts are given briefly detailed cues in the synopsis. As it is part of DG's 'Domingo Edition', that artist is generously represented, but he is in excellent form, and Leo Nucci's contribution as Rodrigue is also striking in this 68-minute selection.

I due Foscari (complete).
(M) *** Ph. 422 426-2 (2). Austrian R. Ch. & SO, Gardelli.
    Francesco Foscari (Piero Cappuccilli), Jacopo Foscari (José Carreras), Lucrezia (Katia Ricciarelli), Loredano (Samuel Ramey).
(*) Nuova Era Dig. 6921/2 [id.]. Ch. & O del Teatro Regio di Torino, Maurizio Arena.
    Francesco Foscari (Renato Bruson), Jacopo Foscari (Nicola Martinucci), Lucrezia (Lorenza Canepa), Loredano (Armando Caforio).

I due Foscari brings Verdian high spirits in plenty, erupting in swinging cabalettas and much writing that anticipates operas as late as *Simon Boccanegra* (obvious enough in the Doge's music) and *La forza del destino* (particularly in the orchestral motifs which act as labels for the principal characters). Yet the story itself is tragic, although the Venetian setting again gives Verdi the opportunity for spectacle.

We are in a room in the Doge's palace, where the implacable Council of Ten moves into the council chamber for its deliberations. Jacopo Foscari waits to hear his fate. He is the son of an aged Doge and has been exiled after an accusation of murder. Having illegally returned to his family, he awaits the council's judgement. Lucrezia, Jacopo's wife, rushes in to plead with the Doge, Jacopo's father, for mercy. But her companion, Pisana, tells her that the council have already again condemned Jacopo to exile. Lucrezia rails against the sentence, and privately the old Doge laments that his love for his son is in conflict with his duty as a judge. Lucrezia says she is sure Jacopo is innocent, and his father agrees with her but he is powerless to intercede because of his position.

Jacopo is now cast into the state prison and in delirium he thinks he sees the ghost of another victim of the Council of Ten, failing at first to recognize his wife. They embrace and the Doge, describing himself as a dying man, also arrives to bid farewell to his son. Loredano, a member of the council, now comes to take Jacopo to hear the judgement pronounced. He is the family's enemy, having sworn vengeance on the Foscaris, blaming them for the death of his father and uncle.

In the great hall the council await the arrival of the Doge. Then the judgement is given: Jacopo is to be exiled once more. Lucrezia begs to be allowed to accompany Jacopo, with their children, but is refused. As Jacopo is taken to the state barge, it is carnival time; masked revellers fill the Square of St Mark's. He notices Loredano, who he knows is his enemy, and is filled with despair.

The Doge sits in his private room. Fate has deprived him of three sons, and now a fourth is to leave. Barbarigo, a council member, enters and says that someone else has confessed to the murder for which Jacopo was sentenced. But it is too late. Lucrezia comes in to tell how Jacopo breathed his last as the barge left the lagoon.

The Council of Ten, led by Loredano, demands that the Doge should abdicate on grounds of old age and, when he objects, they threaten him. He defies them at first, but then removes his ring and the cap from his head. As a last edict he orders Loredano from the room. Lucrezia arrives as a great bell is tolling for the election of Malipiero as the new Doge. Old Foscari sinks, exhausted, and dies, a broken old man, his demise watched by the council. Among them Loredano is exultant.

The cast on Philips is first rate, with Ricciarelli giving one of her finest performances in the recording studio to date and with Carreras singing tastefully as well as powerfully. The crispness of discipline among the Austrian Radio forces is admirable, but there is less sense of atmosphere here than in the earlier, London-made recordings in the series; otherwise the Philips sound is impressively present and clear.

Apart from Renato Bruson in the role of the Doge, Francesco Foscari, the Nuova Era set, recorded live in 1984 in Turin with plentiful noise on stage, has little to offer in competition with the fine Philips set under Gardelli. Not even Bruson matches his opposite number, Piero Cappuccilli; and most of the others, including the conductor, fall lamentably short of their Philips rivals. Lorenza Canepa as Lucrezia in particular is a terrible wobbler, not sounding like a young heroine at all. The advantage of digital sound is nil when balances are so faulty, with the chorus dimly caught. Libretto and translation are provided.

Ernani (complete).
(M) **(*) BMG/RCA GD 86503 (2) [6503-2-RG]. RCA Italiana Op. Ch. & O, Schippers.
   Ernani (Carlo Bergonzi), Elvira (Leontyne Price), Don Carlos (Mario Sereni), De Silva (Ezio Flagello).
**(*) EMI Dig. CDS7 47083-8 (3) [Ang. CDC 47082]. Ch. & O of La Scala, Milan, Muti.
   Ernani (Plácido Domingo), Elvira (Mirella Freni), Don Carlos (Renato Bruson), De Silva (Nicolai Ghiaurov).
Withdrawn: ** Hung. Dig. HCD 12259/61 [id.]. Giorgio Lamberti, Sylvia Sass, Kolos Kováts, Lajos Miller, Klára Takács, Hungarian State Op. Ch. and O, Gardelli.

Ernani, the fifth of Verdi's operas, was the first to achieve international success. At this stage in his career Verdi was still allowing himself the occasional imitation of Rossini in a crescendo, or of Bellini in parallel thirds and sixths; but the control of tension is already masterly, the ensembles even more than the arias giving the authentic Verdian flavour. The plot, though convoluted, is peopled with characters of flesh and blood, while the aristocratic grandee, Don Ruy Gomez de Silva, with his Spanish code of honour, is fascinatingly unpredictable in his actions.

The opera's hero, Ernani, previously known as John of Aragon, has become an outlaw. His father, the Duke of Segovia, was slain by order of King Don Carlos's father. Ernani has taken refuge from his pursuers, emissaries of the king, in the mountains of Aragon. There he leads a band of rebel mountaineers. Ernani is in love with Donna Elvira. She, it seems, is about to be united to her relative, the aged Ruy Gomez de Silva, a grandee of Spain. But Donna Elvira is deeply attracted to Ernani.

Don Carlos, King of Castile (afterwards Emperor Charles V), is also violently in love with Elvira. He has discovered that at night a young cavalier (Ernani) goes into her apartments. Carlos imitates the lover's signal, gains admission and declares his own passion. Elvira, not surprisingly, resists and, as Carlos tries to drag her off, a secret panel opens and Ernani confronts him. A violent scene is interrupted by the entrance of Ruy Gomez de Silva. Jealous and angry at finding two rival suitors, the king pretends he has come in disguise to consult about a conspiracy on his life.

Elvira is now led to believe that Ernani is dead, killed by the king's soldiers. She agrees to marry de Silva. On her wedding eve, Ernani seeks refuge in de Silva's castle, disguised as a pilgrim. This makes Ernani de Silva's guest and entitled to protection in the Spanish tradition of honour. Ernani realizes that the wedding is imminent and, tearing off his disguise, he demands to be delivered up to the king; without Elvira he does not want to live. De Silva refuses and goes out. The lovers embrace.

But the king then arrives as Elvira retires. Ernani hides and de Silva refuses to hand him over, putting himself in danger. Elvira intervenes and the king pardons de Silva, but Elvira is a hostage of the king's clemency.

De Silva now seeks to cross swords with Ernani, who declines. He declares his love for her, pointing out that it is unsafe for Elvira to be with the king, who has his own designs on her. He suggests a pact with de Silva to defeat the king's seduction of Elvira and he promises that, once she is safe, he is ready to die and de Silva shall indicate that moment by a call on his hunting horn.

The two men scheme together, and a meeting with other conspirators takes place in the vault of the Cathedral of Aix-la-Chapelle, which contains the tomb of Charlemagne. It is resolved that the king shall be assassinated, and Ernani's name is drawn on the ballot.

But the king had secreted himself in the tomb and he overhears the plot to take his life. A cannon booms outside to announce that he is now head of the Holy Roman Empire. The conspirators imagine that they can see Charlemagne rising up to combat them but the king magnanimously pardons them, restores Ernani to his titles and estates, and unites him with Elvira.

Yet there is not to be a happy ending. De Silva, thwarted in his plan to marry Elvira, waits until the couple appear on the terrace, then places his horn to his lips. Ernani, too chivalrous to avoid his promise, stabs himself in de Silva's presence. Elvira throws herself across his lifeless body.

At mid-price on two CDs in RCA's Victor Opera series, Schippers' set, recorded in Rome in 1967, is an outstanding bargain. Leontyne Price may take the most celebrated aria, *Ernani involami*, rather cautiously, but the voice is gloriously firm and rich, and Bergonzi is comparably strong and vivid, though Mario Sereni, vocally reliable, is dull, and Ezio Flagello gritty-toned. Nevertheless, with Schippers drawing the team powerfully together, it is a highly enjoyable set, with the digital transfer making voices and orchestra sound full and vivid.

The great merit of Muti's set, recorded live at a series of performances at La Scala, is that the ensembles have an electricity rarely achieved in the studio. The results may not always be so precise and stage noises are often obtrusive with a background rustle of stage movement rarely absent for long, but the result is vivid and atmospheric. The singing, generally strong and characterful, is yet flawed. The strain of the role of Elvira for Mirella Freni is plain from the big opening aria, *Ernani involami*, onwards. Even in that aria there are cautious moments.

Bruson is a superb Carlo, Ghiaurov a characterful de Silva, but his voice betrays signs of wear. Ernani himself, Plácido Domingo, gives a commandingly heroic performance, but under pressure there are hints of tight tone such as he rarely produces in the studio. The recording inevitably has odd balances which will disturb some more than others. The CD version gives greater immediacy and presence, but also brings out the inevitable flaws of live recording the more clearly.

Gardelli's conducting is most sympathetic and idiomatic in the Hungarian version and, like Muti's, it is strong on ensembles. Sylvia Sass is a sharply characterful Elvira, Callas-like in places, and Lamberti a bold Ernani, but their vocal flaws prevent this from being a first choice. Capable rather than inspired or idiomatic singing from the rest. The digital recording is bright and well balanced, although the CD transfer brings out how resonant the acoustic is.

Falstaff (complete).

Withdrawn: (M) *** Sony M2K 42535 (2) [id.]. V. State Op. Ch., VPO, Bernstein.

> Falstaff (Dietrich Fischer-Dieskau), Ford (Rolando Panerai), Alice (Ilva Ligabue), Nannetta (Graziella Sciutti), Fenton (Juan Oncina), Mistress Quickly (Regina Resnik), Meg Page (Hilde Rössl-Majdan).

*** DG Dig. 410 503-2 (2) [id.]. LA Master Chorale, LAPO, Giulini.

> Falstaff (Renato Bruson), Ford (Leo Nucci), Alice (Katia Ricciarelli), Nannetta (Barbara Hendricks), Mistress Quickly (Lucia Valentini Terrani), Meg Page (Brenda Boozer), Bardolph (Francis Egerton), Pistol (William Wilderman).

**(*) EMI CDS7 49668-2 (2) [Ang. CDCB 49668]. Philh. Ch. & O, Karajan.

> Falstaff (Tito Gobbi), Ford (Rolando Panerai), Alice (Elisabeth Schwarzkopf), Nannetta

(Anna Moffo), Mistress Quickly (Fedora Barbieri), Meg Page (Nan Merriman), Bardolph (Renato Ercolani), Pistol (Nicola Zaccaria).

Withdrawn: **(*) Ph. Dig. 412 263-2 (2). V. State Op. Ch., VPO, Karajan.

Falstaff (Giuseppe Taddei), Ford (Rolando Panerai), Alice (Raina Kabaivanska), Nannetta (Janet Perry), Fenton (Francisco Araiza), Mistress Quickly (Christa Ludwig), Meg Page (Trudeliese Schmidt), Bardolph (Heinz Zednik), Pistol (Federico Davià).

(M) **(***)** BMG/RCA mono GD 60251; *GK 60251* (2) [60251-RG-2; *60251-RG-4*]. Robert Shaw Ch., NBC SO, Toscanini.

Falstaff (Giuseppe Valdengo), Ford (Frank Guarrera), Alice (Herva Nelli), Nannetta (Teresa Stich-Randall), Mistress Quickly (Cloe Elmo), Meg Page (Nan Merriman), Bardolph (John Carmen Rossi), Pistol (Norman Scott).

** BMG/RCA Dig. 09026 60705-2 (2) [60705-2]. Bav. R. Ch. and RSO, Sir Colin Davis.

Falstaff (Rolando Panerai), Ford (Alan Titus), Alice (Sharon Sweet), Nannetta (Julie Kaufmann), Mistress Quickly (Marilyn Horne), Fenton (Frank Lopardo).

Verdi's *Falstaff* followed six years after *Otello* and was first heard in Milan in 1893. In adapting Shakespeare's *Merry Wives of Windsor* (and drawing also on *Henry IV*), Boito and Verdi accepted the challenge of an entirely new conception. The result, with its often subtle orchestral textures and flowing solo lines, could be seen as a chamber opera, were it not for the ambitious vocal ensembles, remarkably sophisticated in scope and detail. The final effect is masterly and creates a wonderful lightweight entertainment.

We meet Sir John Falstaff immediately, enjoying himself drinking at the Garter Inn and finishing off letters to a pair of the merry wives of Windsor, Mistress Alice Ford and Mistress Meg Page, with whom he hopes to enjoy an amorous relationship. With him are his followers, Bardolph and Pistol; Dr Caius enters, rudely pushing past Bardolph and complaining that Falstaff has broken into his house, beaten his servants and robbed him. But Falstaff is unimpressed, and the Doctor is sent packing. Falstaff cannot pay his bill and he is hoping one or other of his proposed new conquests may be a source of further funds. Bardolph and Pistol, however, decline to deliver the letters, and he scorns their honourable scruples.

Meanwhile the ladies to whom Falstaff's attentions are directed get together in the garden of Ford's house. Mistress Quickly and Nannetta Ford (the daughter) are with them. Falstaff's letters have arrived and they are read out, to general amusement, both women mocking their elderly admirer. They decide he shall be taught a lesson. Ford and Fenton enter, followed by Dr Caius who declares Falstaff a villain. Bardolph and Pistol arrive to tell Ford that Falstaff has designs on his wife. They add their warning concerning Falstaff's financial plight and his hope to refill his coffers at the expense of one or other of the ladies.

Dr Caius, encouraged by Ford, has designs on Nannetta; but her eyes are turned elsewhere, as is only too obvious when she and Fenton come together and enjoy a few stolen kisses. The ladies now send Mistress Quickly with a reply to Falstaff and the men hatch their own plot, which involves Ford visiting the corpulent knight in disguise.

We now return to the Garter Inn. Bardolph and Pistol, having changed allegiances, feign penitence to Falstaff for their earlier behaviour. Mistress Quickly comes in to deliver fond messages from both ladies. Falstaff is told that Alice Ford would welcome a visit between two and three o'clock that afternoon, when her husband will be out.

Bardolph announces a Signor Fontana Brook, who is, of course, Ford. He tells Falstaff of his lack of success in wooing Mistress Ford and offers the knight a purse of gold if he – as an experienced lover – would first assail her virtue, so that Signor Fontana could follow on afterwards. Falstaff is pleased to oblige and he mentions his planned assignation, arranged for that very afternoon (exciting Ford's anger and vengeance); after Falstaff has dressed in his best clothes, the two leave together.

The ladies are gathered in Ford's house and Falstaff is expected at any minute. Nannetta is upset: her father has demanded that she marry, not Fenton, but old Dr Caius. Her friends tell her not to worry, they will arrange something. Meanwhile they have a large laundry basket brought in and all hide, except for Alice, who plays the lute as Falstaff enters. He begins his courtship rather elegantly, but is rudely interrupted by the arrival of Mistress Quickly and is promptly hidden behind a screen. Ford rushes in, with Caius, Fenton, Bardolph and Pistol. Ford is in a very bad temper indeed, and they search high and low for Falstaff, even in the linen basket, but without success.

As they leave to search elsewhere, the frightened Falstaff emerges from hiding and is hidden among the dirtiest laundry. Meanwhile Fenton and Nannetta enter quietly, disappear behind the screen and make good use of their privacy. A kiss is distinctly heard. Ford now returns and looks behind the screen but, instead of encountering Falstaff, finds the young lovers. Fenton is sent packing and Nannetta also rushes off. Alice now summons the servants to throw the basket of dirty linen out through the window and everyone, especially Ford, enjoys the spectacle of Falstaff floating helplessly away on the currents of the River Thames.

Back at the Garter Inn, Falstaff is disconsolate, but still he has not learned his lesson. Mistress Quickly enters with apologies from Alice and finally convinces him that no harm was meant. She now reads out Alice's note suggesting a new meeting place, Herne's Oak in Windsor Forest. Falstaff must come disguised as a 'black huntsman'. (Herne hanged himself from the tree and his ghost is reputed to haunt the area.) The others have been listening to this new arrangement from a safe distance, and they plan to disguise themselves as fairies and immortals, to harry and torment the knight.

Ford instructs Caius to come dressed as a monk, and he shall become Ford's son-in-law. Mistress Quickly, however, overhears this scheme, and the women decide to scuttle Ford's plans. It is Fenton who arrives first at Herne's Oak, but the ladies soon follow and they bring a monk's robes for him to wear too. Falstaff, the 'black huntsman', now enters, followed by Alice, and Falstaff begins amorous advances. Suddenly there is a cry from Mistress Page that witches are coming. Spirits, elves, fairies all appear at once and Falstaff is petrified.

They set upon him in earnest, rolling him over, prodding and pinching him. He begs for mercy then, recognizing Bardolph, realizes he has been tricked. He discovers, too, that Ford and Signor Fontana are one and the same person. Ford now suggests the betrothal between the monk (Dr Caius) and the veiled fairy queen – who turns out to be not Nannetta but Bardolph! Instead, Nannetta is united with her beloved Fenton and Ford is persuaded to accept the match. Even Falstaff takes everything in good part, for geniality is the redeeming side of his nature.

The Sony/CBS set is based on a production at the Vienna State Opera, and the fleetness of execution at hair-raisingly fast speeds suggests that Bernstein was intent on out-Toscanini-ing Toscanini. The allegros may be consistently faster than Toscanini's but they never sound rushed, and always Bernstein conveys a sense of fun; while in relaxed passages, helped by warm Viennese sensitivity, he allows a full rotundity of phrasing, at least as much so as any rival. It does not really matter, any more than it did in the Toscanini set, that the conductor is the hero rather than Falstaff himself. Fischer-Dieskau does wonders in pointing the humour.

In his scene with Mistress Quickly arranging an assignation with Alice, he can inflect a simple *Ebben?* to make it intensely funny, but he finally suffers from having a voice one inevitably associates with baritonal solemnity, whether heroic or villainous. Just how noble Falstaff should seem is a matter for discussion. The others are first rate – Panerai singing superbly as Ford, Ilva Ligabue (also the Alice of the Solti set), Regina Resnik as Mistress Quickly, and Graziella Sciutti and Juan Oncina as the young lovers. Excellent engineering (by a Decca recording team), together with effective remastering have produced a sound-balance which is far fuller and more attractive than the remastered EMI Karajan set.

Recorded at a series of live performances in the Chandler Pavilion in Los Angeles, Giulini's reading combines the tensions and atmosphere of live performance with a precision normally achieved only in the studio. This was Giulini's first essay in live opera-conducting in fourteen years, and he treated the piece with a care for musical values which at times undermined the knockabout comic element. On record that is all to the good, for the clarity and beauty of the playing are superbly caught by the DG engineers, and though the parallel with Toscanini is an obvious one – also recorded at a live performance – Giulini is far more relaxed. Here CD emphasizes the success of the engineers in the matter of balance, besides adding to the refinement of detail and the tangibility of the overall sound-picture. The voices are given fine bloom but in a contrasted stage acoustic.

Bruson, hardly a comic actor, is impressive on record for his fine incisive singing, giving tragic implications to the monologue at the start of Act III after Falstaff's dunking. The Ford of Leo Nucci, impressive in the theatre, is thinly caught, where the heavy-weight quality of Ricciarelli as Alice comes over well, though in places one would wish for a purer sound. Barbara Hendricks is a charmer as Nannetta, but she hardly sounds fairy-like in her Act III aria. The full women's ensemble, though precise, is not always quite steady in tone, though the conviction of the whole performance puts it among the most desirable of modern readings.

Karajan's earlier (1956) recording presents not only the most pointed account orchestrally of Verdi's comic masterpiece (the Philharmonia Orchestra at its very peak) but one of the most sharply characterful casts ever gathered for a recording. If you relish the idea of Tito Gobbi as Falstaff (his many-coloured voice, not quite fat-sounding in humour, presents a sharper character than usual), then this is an outstanding choice, for the rest of the cast is a delight, with Schwarzkopf a tinglingly masterful Mistress Ford, Anna Moffo sweet as Nannetta and Rolando Panerai a formidable Ford.

One reason why the whole performance hangs together so stylishly is the production of Walter Legge: this is a vintage example of his work. Unfortunately the digital remastering has been mismanaged. While the precision and placing of voices on the stereo stage, a model even today, comes out the more clearly on CD, the transfer itself, at a low level and with high hiss, has lost the bloom and warmth of the original analogue master, which was outstanding for its time (indeed, an excerpt from it was included on EMI's first Stereo Demonstration Disc).

Karajan's second recording of Verdi's last opera, made over 20 years after his classic Philharmonia set, has lower standards of precision, yet conveys a relaxed and genial atmosphere. With the exception of Kabaivanska, whose voice is not steady enough for the role of Alice, it is a good cast, with Ludwig fascinating as Mistress Quickly. Most amazing of all is Taddei's performance as Falstaff himself, full and characterful and vocally astonishing from a man in his sixties. The recording is not as beautifully balanced as the Philharmonia set, but the digital sound is faithful and wide-ranging. The CD version captures the bloom of the original, reverberant recording so vividly, one worries less about any oddities of balance, while textures are to a degree clarified.

Toscanini's fizzing account of Verdi's last masterpiece has never been matched on record, the most high-spirited performance ever, beautifully paced for comedy. Even without stereo, and recorded with typical dryness, the clarity and sense of presence in this live concert performance set the story in relief, the finest of Toscanini's New York opera recordings. The cast is excellent, led by the ripe, firm baritone, Giuseppe Valdengo. Such singers as Nan Merriman as Mistress Page, Cloe Elmo as a wonderfully fruity Mistress Quickly and Frank Guarrera as Ford match or outshine any more recent interpreters. Toscanini's favourite soprano in his last years, Herva Nelli, is less characterful as Mistress Ford, rather over-parted but still fresh and reliable.

Where so many digital recordings of opera offer coarse, close-up sound, RCA's set of Verdi's *Falstaff* conducted by Sir Colin Davis suffers from the opposite problem. Soloists and the Bavarian Radio Orchestra are set in a reverberant acoustic which not only confuses detail (with even the semiquaver figure of the opening barely identifiable) but makes it hard for the fun of the piece to come over. Davis, as he has shown many times at Covent Garden, is masterly in his Verdian timing, but the result here fails to sparkle; it is all serious and Germanic. The cast is a good one, including two veterans: Rolando Panerai still strong and resonant in the title-role and Marilyn Horne producing stentorian tones as Mistress Quickly. Sharon Sweet is a forceful Alice, with Julie Kaufmann as Nannetta well matched against Frank Lopardo, stylish in Verdi as he was in Rossini. Yet with such sound it is not a set to recommend with enthusiasm.

La forza del destino (complete).
*** BMG/RCA RD 81864 (3) [RCD3-1864]. Alldis Ch., LSO, Levine.
   Leonora (Leontyne Price), Don Alvaro (Plácido Domingo), Don Carlos (Sherrill Milnes), Padre Guardiano (Bonaldo Giaiotti), Preziosilla (Fiorenza Cossotto), Melitone (Gabriel Bacquier), Marchese (Kurt Moll).
*** DG Dig. 419 203-2 (3) [id.]. Amb. Op. Ch., Philh. O, Sinopoli.
   Leonora (Rosalind Plowright), Don Alvaro (José Carreras), Don Carlos (Renato Bruson), Padre Guardiano (Paata Burchuladze), Preziosilla (Agnes Baltsa), Melitone (Juan Pons), Marchese (John Tomlinson).
(M) *** BMG/RCA GD 87971 (3) [4515-2-RG]. RCA Italian Op. Ch. & O, Schippers.
   Leonora (Leontyne Price), Don Alvaro (Richard Tucker), Don Carlos (Robert Merrill), Padre Guardiano (Giorgio Tozzi), Preziosilla (Shirley Verrett), Melitone (Ezio Flagello), Marchese (Giovanni Foiani).
(M) **(*) EMI CMS7 64646-2 (2) [Ang. CDMC 64646]. Amb. Op. Ch., RPO, Gardelli.
   Leonora (Martina Arroyo), Don Alvaro (Carlo Bergonzi), Don Carlos (Piero Cappuccilli), Padre Guardiano (Ruggero Raimondi), Preziosilla (Biancamaria Casoni), Melitone (Geraint Evans).
**(*) EMI Dig. CDS7 47485-8 (3) [Ang. CDCC 47485]. La Scala, Milan, Ch. & O, Muti.
   Leonora (Mirella Freni), Don Alvaro (Plácido Domingo), Don Carlos (Giorgio Zancanaro), Padre Guardiano (Paul Plishka), Preziosilla (Dolora Zajic), Melitone (Sesto Bruscantini), Marchese (Giorgio Surjan).
(M) ** Decca 421 598-2 (3) [id.]. St Cecilia Academy, Rome, Ch. & O, Molinari-Pradelli.
   Leonora (Renata Tebaldi), Don Alvaro (Mario Del Monaco), Don Carlos (Ettore Bastianini),

Padre Guardiano (Cesare Siepi), Preziosilla (Giulietta Simionato), Melitone (Fernando Corena), Marchese (Silvio Maionica).

La forza del destino followed three years after *Un ballo in maschera* and was premièred in St Petersburg in 1862. Its famous overture was one of the first to act as a chrysalis of the action to follow, containing, as it does, both the 'theme of destiny' with its ascending triplets of semiquavers and Leonora's soaring cantilena from the second Act.

The opera is set in Seville in the mid-eighteenth century. In his castle the Marquis of Calatrava is bidding goodnight to his daughter, Leonora. He has separated her from her suitor, Don Alvaro, regarding him as unworthy of her; however, she is soon discussing with her maid, Curra, plans for an elopement – although upset at having to deceive her father. Alvaro arrives but, just as he and Leonora are about to depart, her father enters and orders Alvaro's arrest. Acceding, Alvaro throws his pistol at the marquis's feet, where it explodes, mortally wounding the marquis, who dies cursing his daughter. She leaves, reluctantly, with Alvaro.

Leonora's brother, Don Carlos, disguised as a student, comes looking for her at an inn in the Spanish village of Hornachuelos, in the mountains. She arrives, wearing male clothing, having become separated from her lover en route. Leonora recognizes Carlos but he does not recognize her.

The gypsy, Preziosilla, telling fortunes, predicts tragedy and declares that Carlos is not really a student. Leonora, who has given up hopes of marital happiness with Alvaro and who is feeling responsible for her father's death, now finds her way to the Monastery of the Madonna degli Angeli. Brother Melitone calls the Father Guardian and, alone with him, Leonora tells her story. He allows her to use a nearby hermit's cave for her future solitary existence.

Alvaro meanwhile is in Valletri, a captain in the Spanish army bearing a false name. He believes Leonora to be dead. Don Carlos arrives and Alvaro rescues him from an attack by robbers. The two men become friends. When alone, Carlos begins to wonder about the identity of his friend and, opening some private papers and letters given to him for safe keeping (as Alvaro has been wounded and fears for his life), finds Leonora's portrait. Both Preziosilla and Father Melitone reappear, the one to entertain, the other to preach.

Carlos now challenges Alvaro to a duel, but Alvaro has no wish to fight his friend and says that it was fate that killed the marquis, not he. Nevertheless, when Carlos reveals that Leonora is alive and that he intends to murder her too, Alvaro is willing for the duel to take place. But it is interrupted by other soldiers, and Alvaro determines that he will find solace in a religious order. He chooses the monastery near which Leonora is already doing penance. Melitone has returned, but the locals prefer the new member of the order, Father Raffaele, who is of course Alvaro. (He does not know that Leonora is near at hand.)

Don Carlos now arrives at the monastery gates, having traced Alvaro, and demands satisfaction. Alvaro gives way, and they fight. Leonora, lonely and emaciated, is praying, but hears the noise of the fight. Alvaro pleads for help from the 'hermit' when Carlos is mortally wounded. Leonora comes out and, recognizing both participants, realizes that the unfortunate Alvaro, having first been instrumental in the death of her father, has now killed her brother too. She rushes to Carlos's side. With his ebbing strength he stabs her and she dies in Alvaro's arms, as the Father Guardian offers her the final sacrament. Alvaro rails against the strange forces that shaped his destiny; Leonora looks forward to a heavenly reunion with her lover and, presumably, with her father and brother too.

James Levine directs a superb performance of an opera which in less purposeful hands can seem too episodic. The results are electrifying, and rarely if ever does Levine cut across the natural expressiveness of an outstanding cast. Leontyne Price recorded the role of Leonora in an earlier RCA version made in Rome in 1956, but the years have hardly touched her voice, and details of the reading have been refined.

The roles of Don Alvaro and Don Carlo are ideally suited to the regular team of Plácido Domingo and Sherrill Milnes, so that their confrontations are the cornerstones of the dramatic structure. Fiorenza Cossotto makes a formidable rather than a jolly Preziosilla, while on the male side the line-up of Bonaldo Giaiotti, Gabriel Bacquier, Kurt Moll and Michel Sénéchal is far stronger than on rival sets. In a good, vivid transfer of the mid-1970s sound, this strong, well-paced version will for many provide a safe middle course between Sinopoli and Muti, with an exceptionally good and consistent cast. Voices come over with fine immediacy, but with plenty of bloom.

Sinopoli's is an exceptionally spacious view of *Forza*, in many ways akin to the similarly distinctive reading of *Il Trovatore*, recorded for DG by Giulini. Like the Giulini performance, this one is refined in its expressive warmth rather than traditionally Italian. Sinopoli draws out phrases lovingly, sustaining pauses to the limit, putting extra strain on the singers. Happily, the whole cast seems to thrive on the challenge, and the spaciousness of the recording acoustic not only makes the dramatic interchanges the more realistic, it brings out the bloom on all the voices, above all the creamy soprano of Rosalind Plowright, here giving a performance to match the one she gave as Verdi's other Leonora, in the Giulini *Trovatore*.

Though José Carreras is sometimes too conventionally histrionic, even strained, it is a strong, involved performance. Renato Bruson is a thoughtful Carlo, while some of the finest singing of all comes from Agnes Baltsa as Preziosilla and Paata Burchuladze as the Padre Guardiano, uniquely resonant. Though the speeds will not please all Verdians, Sinopoli's is a distinctive, deeply felt view that in its breadth conveys the epic nobility of the piece with great authority. Ironically, this fine set was recorded in sessions originally set up for a Philharmonia recording of this same opera with Sinopoli's rival, Muti.

Dating from 1964, the Schippers set, very well cast, makes an outstanding bargain in RCA's Victor Opera series. No soprano of her generation had natural gifts more suited to the role of Leonora in *Forza* than Leontyne Price. Her admirers will cherish this early recording quite as much as her later one with James Levine, also from RCA. The voice in 1964 was fresher and more open; though the clearer, less ambient recording from the Rome studio exposes it in greater detail, on balance this is a more tender and delicate performance than the weightier one she recorded with Levine.

The playing of the Italian orchestra may not be as refined as on the later RCA set, but the reading under Schippers is often more idiomatic, and there is no weak link in the rest of the cast. Richard Tucker as Alvaro is here far less lachrymose and more stylish than he was earlier in the Callas set, producing ample, heroic tone if not with the finesse of a Domingo. Robert Merrill as Carlo also sings with heroic strength, consistently firm and dark of tone; while Shirley Verrett, Giorgio Tozzi and Ezio Flagello stand up well against any rivalry. The sound is remarkably full and vivid for its age, with a fine illusion of presence which quickly makes one forget any analogue hiss.

Gardelli, normally a reliable recording conductor in Italian opera, here gives a disappointing account of a vividly dramatic score. The cast is vocally strong and each member of it lives up to expectations. Moreover the recording – made in 1969 in Watford Town Hall – is first rate, vivid, full and atmospheric. But it is vital in so long and episodic a work that overall dramatic control should be firm. Gardelli's contribution prevents this from being a first choice at mid-price when the Schippers set is available on RCA, although admirers of the individual artists in the EMI cast will find much to enjoy when the sound is so flattering to the voices. The layout places Acts I and II on the first disc, while Acts III and IV are each allotted a CD apiece.

Plácido Domingo is the glory of the Muti set, recorded at La Scala, giving a performance even more commanding and detailed than in the earlier, RCA version with Levine. Mirella Freni is an appealing Leonora, though she is vocally stressed; she is not helped by the recording, which is depressingly boxy and presents the voices unflatteringly in close-up. Though many Verdians will welcome Muti's fast, even hectic speeds, echoing Toscanini, the antithesis of the Sinopoli view, the recorded sound is the factor that puts the set out of court. Giorgio Zancanaro is a powerful Carlo, but Paul Plishka is disappointing as the Padre Guardiano, affected even more than the others by the dry, unhelpful acoustic which removes the bloom from all the voices.

The 1955 Decca set, with Tebaldi on top form, offers formidable competition on three mid-priced CDs, and the recording is outstanding for its time. Tebaldi, as always, makes some lovely sounds, and the *mezza voce* in the soaring theme (first heard in the overture) in *Madre, madre, pietosa Vergine* is exquisite. Mario del Monaco never really matches this. He sings straight through his part – often with the most heroic-sounding noises – with little attention to the finer points of shading that Verdi expects. That the whole performance does not add up to the sum of its parts is largely the fault of the conductor, Molinari-Pradelli. He can be exciting, but his control of ensemble is weak at times. The brilliance and atmosphere of the recording belie its age.

La forza del destino (slightly abridged).
Withdrawn: (***) EMI mono CDS7 47581-8 (3) [Ang. CDCC 47581]. La Scala, Milan, Ch. & O, Serafin.
Leonora (Maria Callas), Don Alvaro (Richard Tucker), Don Carlo (Carlo Tagliabue), Padre Guardiano (Nicola Rossi-Lemeni), Preziosilla (Elena Nicolai), Melitone (Renato Capecchi), Marchese (Plinio Clabassi).

Callas was at her very peak when she took the role of Leonora in the Scala recording. Hers is an electrifying performance, providing a focus for an opera normally regarded as diffuse. Though there are classic examples of Callas's raw tone on top notes, they are insignificant next to the wealth of phrasing which sets a totally new and individual stamp on even the most familiar passages. Apart from his tendency to disturb his phrasing with sobs, Richard Tucker sings superbly; but not even he and certainly none of the others – including the baritone Carlo Tagliabue, well past his prime – begin to rival the dominance of Callas. Serafin's direction is crisp, dramatic and well paced, again drawing the threads together. The 1955 mono sound is less aggressive than many La Scala recordings of this vintage and has been freshened on CD. For those wanting the uniquely intense Callas version and not minding a seriously cut text, this will be strongly recommendable when it is re-released.

La forza del destino: highlights.
(M) ** EMI Dig. CDC7 54326-2 [id.] (from above recording with Freni, Domingo; cond. Muti).

Few are likely to chose Muti's complete set of *La forza del destino* because of the indifferent digital sound, but those wanting to sample Domingo's arresting Don Alvaro might consider this highlights disc. He is included in two excerpts from Act III and three from Act IV. The CD comprises 67 minutes of music and is well documented, but it comes at full price.

Un giorno di regno (complete).
(M) *** Ph. 422 429-2 (2) [id.]. Amb. S., RPO, Gardelli.
    Marchese del Poggio (Fiorenza Cossotto), Giulietta (Jessye Norman), Edoardo (José Carreras), Belfiore (Ingvar Wixell), Gasparo Antonio (Vicente Sardinero), Baron (Wladimiro Ganzarolli).

Un giorno di regno may not be the greatest comic opera of the period, but this scintillating performance under Gardelli clearly reveals the young Verdi as a potent rival even in this field to his immediate predecessors, Rossini and Donizetti. The Rossinian echoes are particularly infectious, though every number reveals that the young Verdi is more than an imitator, and there are striking passages which clearly give a foretaste of such numbers as the duet, *Si vendetta*, from *Rigoletto*.

We are in Baron di Kelbar's castle near Brest; it is the summer of 1733. Preparations are taking place for a double wedding. The baron's daughter, Giulietta, is to marry the rich treasurer to the estates of Brittany, and his niece, the Marchesa del Poggio, a young widow, is to marry Count Ivrea, Commander of Brest. Both women love someone else: Giulietta loves Edoardo de Sanval and the Marchesa, who loves the Cavalier di Belfiore, fears he has jilted her. The baron and the treasurer are honoured that the King of Poland will be a witness at the wedding, and when his arrival is announced we see that in reality this is the Cavalier di Belfiore in disguise.

He is dismayed to find that one of the brides-to-be is the lady he himself loves. She in turn recognizes him and is puzzled by the impersonation. Belfiore now writes to the Polish court, hoping that the real king is now in power so that he may be released from his deception. Meanwhile Giulietta's suitor, Edoardo, despairing of his situation, asks to enlist in the service of the Polish king.

Giulietta reflects that she does not want to marry an old man, but the treasurer, La Rocca, reassures her that she will feel brighter in the morning. Belfiore presents Edoardo as his new squire, and in this role he is able to renew his contact with Giulietta. La Rocca is not blind to their obvious mutual attraction and is angry at having a rival.

Edoardo and Giulietta appeal to the Marchesa for help, which she promises to give. Belfiore now tells the treasurer that, were he not about to get married, because of his respected financial skills he could have a ministry in the Polish government and the hand of a rich Polish princess.

La Rocca accepts this most attractive offer and informs the baron that he is unworthy of Giulietta. The baron is incredulous and draws his sword but, at the noise of the altercation, everyone rushes in and a duel is avoided, although the baron declares that his daughter has been insulted. Giulietta is delighted. The Marchesa now cunningly suggests to the baron that it would humiliate La Rocca if he married his daughter, Giulietta, to Edoardo.

But the baron will not allow the marriage to go ahead because Edoardo is penniless. Belfiore immediately orders the treasurer to endow Edoardo with one of his castles and an income for life. The Marchesa and Belfiore now meet in the garden. She is angry with him for not staying true to her and announces that she will not marry him, but she fails to convince Belfiore. Count Ivrea is announced, to claim the Marchesa as his bride, and she goes off to meet him, vowing to forget her faithless lover. Giulietta is delighted that at last she is to be allowed to marry Edoardo, but Edoardo says he must leave with the king. Belfiore, too, says he must leave on urgent business, and the Marchesa pointedly hopes he will remain for her wedding to Count Ivrea.

News now comes from the Polish court; Belfiore is excited but will not tell anyone the contents of the message until Giulietta is safely betrothed to Edoardo. That done, he announces that Stanislao has been crowned King of Poland, reveals the deception of which he has been part and resumes his true identity as Cavalier di Belfiore. He embraces the delighted Marchesa and the others all accept the inevitable.

Despite the absurd plot, this is as light and frothy an entertainment as anyone could want. Excellent singing from a fine team, with Jessye Norman and José Carreras outstanding, and vivid recorded sound.

I Lombardi (complete).
(M) *** Ph. 422 420-2 (2). Amb. S., RPO, Gardelli.
    Giselda (Cristina Deutekom), Oronte (Plácido Domingo), Pagano (Ruggero Raimondi).
**(*) Hung. Dig. HCD 12498/500 [id.]. Hungarian R. & TV Ch., Hungarian State Op. O, Gardelli.
    Giselda (Sylvia Sass), Oronte (Giorgio Lamberti), Pagano (Kolos Kováts).

If you are looking for sophisticated perfection, *I Lombardi* is not the opera to sample, but the directness of Verdi's inspiration is in no doubt. *Otello* is anticipated in the arias, with Pagano's evil *Credo* and the heroine Giselda's *Salve Maria*. The opera is set at the turn of the tenth century and opens in the Piazza di Sant'Ambrogio in Milan. Rejoicing is heard from the cathedral. We learn that, many years ago, two brothers loved Viclinda, who favoured the elder, Arvino. The younger brother, Pagano, one day struck and wounded Arvino and consequently was banished. Returning from the Holy Land, his offence has been expiated, but the public's view is that he still has the look of evil.

Pagano, Viclinda and her daughter, Giselda, emerge from the cathedral with Arvino. There is a general feeling of foreboding, but Arvino is now declared leader of a crusade. All leave except Pagano and Pirro, his henchman, who are obviously up to no good. Inside the palace, Folco, father of Arvino and Pagano, believes Pagano's repentance is feigned. Pirro leads Pagano towards Arvino's room. A moment later the palace is on fire. Pagano now tries to carry off Viclinda but, hearing Arvino's voice, he realizes he has killed his own father, not his brother. All curse him, and he attempts suicide but fails. He is sent into exile.

The opera now moves to Acciano's palace in Antioch, where the Saracen king receives a group of Muslim ambassadors who call for Allah's vengeance on the invading army of crusaders. They leave and Acciano's son and wife, Oronte and Sofia, enter. Sofia, veiled, is secretly a Christian. Oronte says he loves Giselda, a captive in Antioch. In his view, she is so perfect that her God must be the only true God.

In a mountain-cave overlooking Antioch a hermit (much later revealed as Pagano) prays that he may be able to aid the crusading army to capture Antioch from the Saracens. Pirro, now a converted Muslim, comes to ask for spiritual guidance. Both retreat into the cave when they hear crusaders approaching, led by Armido. The hermit emerges and Arvino does not realize that this is his brother. He asks him to pray for his daughter, Griselda, now a prisoner. The hermit offers comfort, and all declare their hatred for the Saracens.

In the harem Giselda prays to heaven, taunted by her companions. Soldiers pursue the women. Queen Sofia says that her husband and son have both been killed by Arvino, leader of the crusaders. Giselda denounces her father for shedding so much blood, especially that of Oronte, whom she loved. In the Valley of Jehoshaphat, with the Mount of Olives and Jerusalem in the distance, Giselda is found wandering, desolate at her loss of Oronte. Suddenly a man in Lombard clothing is seen; he laments his loss of Giselda which has caused him to adopt a coward's disguise in hopes of seeing her again. It is Oronte, and the lovers embrace. Oronte is determined to adopt Giselda's faith. Meanwhile, in his tent in the Christian lines, Arvino deplores his daughter's flight and, when the news comes of Pagano's presence, his anger turns against his brother.

Oronte has been mortally wounded and lies, dying, in a cave near the River Jordan. Giselda is beside herself with grief and is consoled by a hermit who baptizes Oronte as he dies in her arms. Giselda has a vision of Oronte in her sleep, safely in heaven. The crusaders are preparing for an assault on Jerusalem; Arvino and the hermit arrive to lead them into battle.

Later, in another part of the camp, Arvino and Giselda attend the wounded hermit. In his delirium he reveals his name. Giselda begs Arvino to forgive him as, dying, he begs for one last look at the Holy City as the Christian banners are seen flying over its ramparts.

The opera reaches its apotheosis in the famous *Trio*, well known from the days of 78-r.p.m. recordings. By those standards, Cristina Deutekom is not an ideal Verdi singer: her tone is sometimes hard and her voice is not always perfectly under control, yet there are some glorious moments too, and the phrasing is often impressive. Domingo as Oronte is in superb voice, and the villain, Pagano, is well characterized by Raimondi. Among the supporting cast Stafford Dean and Clifford Grant must be mentioned, and Gardelli conducts dramatically. The recording's atmosphere is well transferred and the action projects vividly.

The Hungaroton set makes a very acceptable alternative to the earlier, Philips set, also conducted by Lamberto Gardelli with warmth and finesse, and it brings the benefit of modern, digital recording. One of the principal glories of the Budapest performance is the brilliant and committed singing of the chorus, turning the Crusaders' Hymn of Act II into a sort of Verdian *Csárdás*. The big ensembles have a warmth and thrust to suggest stage experience and, though the line-up of principals is not quite as strong as on that earlier Philips set, there is no serious weakness; Sylvia Sass, singing with greater evenness and purity than usual, is certainly preferable to the fluttery Deutekom on Philips. Giorgio Lamberti as the hero is no match for Plácido Domingo, heroic of tone but unsubtle; similarly, Kolos Kováts as the Hermit has a glorious natural voice, a really firm bass, but musically is no rival to Raimondi on the earlier set. The sound is excellent, clean and well balanced.

Luisa Miller (complete).
*** Sony Dig. S2K 48073 (2) [id.]. Met. Op. O and Ch., Levine.
   Luisa (Aprile Millo), Rodolfo (Plácido Domingo), Miller (Vladimir Chernov), Walter (Jan-Hendrik Rootering), Federica (Florence Quivar), Wurm (Paul Plishka).
*** Decca 417 420-2 (2) [id.]. L. Op. Ch., Nat. PO, Maag.
   Luisa (Montserrat Caballé), Rodolfo (Luciano Pavarotti), Miller (Sherrill Milnes), Walter (Bonaldo Giaiotti), Federica (Anna Reynolds), Wurm (Richard Van Allan).
*** DG 423 144-2 (2) [id.]. ROHCG Ch. & O, Maazel.
   Luisa (Katia Ricciarelli), Rodolfo (Plácido Domingo), Miller (Renato Bruson), Walter (Gwynne Howell), Federica (Elena Obraztsova), Wurm (Wladimiro Ganzarolli).
(M) *** BMG/RCA GD 86646 (2) [6646-2-RG]. RCA Italiana Op. Ch. & O, Cleva.
   Luisa (Anna Moffo), Rodolfo (Carlo Bergonzi), Miller (Cornell MacNeil), Walter (Giorgio Tozzi), Federica (Shirley Verrett), Wurm (Ezio Flagello).

Levine conducts his forces from the Met. in a red-blooded, exceptionally high-powered reading of this elusive opera, set in the Tyrol in the first half of the eighteenth century. Luisa is the daughter of Miller, an old soldier. She loves Rodolfo, who has concealed his real name from Luisa and her father, and is known to them as Carlo, a peasant.

Old Miller has a premonition that the liaison will not bring happiness to his daughter and this is confirmed when he discovers from Wurm that Carlo is really Rodolfo, the son of his employer, Count Walter. Wurm also has designs on Luisa himself.

Count Walter's niece, the Duchess Federica of Ostheim, arrives at the castle. She had lived there as a child and had cherished a deep affection for Rodolfo but, having married the duke, she had not seen him for some years. Now she returns as a widow, and, at the count's suggestion, as a suitor for his son, although Rodolfo knows nothing of this arranged betrothal.

Wurm tells the count that his son loves Luisa Miller, and the count resolves that the relationship shall be terminated. But Rodolfo, discovering what has happened, tells the duchess that he loves another. He then also discloses his real name to Luisa and her father and reveals his difficult position. (Such candour is rare in opera.)

Needless to say, the count is angry that he cannot induce his son to change his mind, so Luisa and her father are consigned to prison. In his turn, Rodolfo threatens his father that he will reveal that the count, helped by Wurm, assassinated his predecessor, thus obtaining his title and estates.

Luisa's first priority is to save her father's life, so, influenced by Wurm, she writes a letter to say that she encouraged Rodolfo only because she was seduced by his rank and fortune; she also convinces the duchess that her love for Rodolfo was pretence and offers no threat. Then Wurm and the count make sure Rodolfo sees the letter, and Rodolfo now consents to marry the duchess.

Angered by Luisa's supposed treachery, Rodolfo determines to kill both her and himself. When Luisa confirms that the letter was indeed written by her, he pours poison into a cup and they both drink. To be sure of her father's safety, she has sworn to Wurm not to reveal her real feelings for Rodolfo but, as death approaches, she feels a release from her oath, and confesses the truth to her lover. They die together, but Rodolfo first runs his sword through Wurm.

The Sony set of *Luisa Miller* brings the first major recording of the remarkable Russian baritone, Vladimir Chernov. In the role of Miller, the heroine's father, Chernov is even more characterful and musically more individual than his rivals on the other sets, with the power of his singing brought home by the close balance of the voice. That balance is typical of a Sony New York recording which, for all its wide-ranging digital sound, is limited by the acoustic of the Manhattan Center, less spacious than those on the rival Decca and DG recordings, made in the 1970s. Though the sound tends to make Levine's direction seem less subtle than it is, less elegant than Maag on Decca, less refined in texture than Maazel on DG, the impact of the score is brought home formidably.

Consistently the reading benefits from the pacing and control that become natural to players and singers over a series of live performances in the theatre. Maazel's recording was comparably made in conjunction with live performances at Covent Garden, but it does not make the point nearly as strongly as Levine's. It is significant how Plácido Domingo, who takes the role of the hero, Rodolfo, both for Maazel and for Levine, sings with much greater animation in the New York recording. Among the others, Jan-Hendrik Rootering, Florence Quivar and Paul Plishka all sing powerfully, even if all three suffer from occasional unsteadiness.

The snag is the variable quality of Aprile Millo's singing in the title-role. She has the right Verdian timbre, more girlish-sounding than her rivals, but in Act I the coloratura taxes her severely, pushing her into gusty, inelegant moments. From there she markedly improves, so that by the final Act she produces some lovely singing with some beautifully floated high pianissimos. It is in that final Act that the extra dramatic bite of Levine's reading tells most in its impact. Curiously, the final Trio brings rather less close balance for the voices than earlier, but the power is no less intense.

On Decca, Caballé, though not as flawless vocally as one would expect, gives a splendidly dramatic portrait of the heroine, and Pavarotti's performance is full of creative, detailed imagination. Anna Reynolds is first rate as Countess Federica, and Maag's sympathetic reading, by underlining the light and shade, consistently brings out the atmospheric qualities of Verdi's conception. The vivid analogue recording, very well balanced, is the more atmospheric on CD.

Lorin Maazel, making his Covent Garden début in this opera – belatedly in 1978 – went on to record this generally enjoyable set for DG. Though not as affectionate as Peter Maag on the earlier, Decca version, Maazel is unfailingly strong and intense in his treatment of an extraordinary opera in the Verdi canon – predating *Rigoletto* but with flavours of much later: *Don Carlo*, even *Forza*. Though taut in his control, Maazel uses his stage experience of working with these soloists to draw them out to their finest, most sympathetic form.

Ricciarelli gives one of her tenderest and most beautiful performances on record, Domingo is in glorious voice – having just established *Otello* in his central repertory – and Bruson as Luisa's father sings with velvet tone. Gwynne Howell is impressive as the Conte di Walter and Wladimiro Ganzarolli's vocal roughness is apt for the character of Wurm. The snag is the abrasive Countess Federica of Elena Obraztsova.

The RCA set, with a substantial price advantage, provides a performance to compete in many ways with the full-priced versions. It is just as stylish, with Moffo at her very peak, singing superbly, Carlo Bergonzi unfailingly intelligent and stylish, and Verrett nothing less than magnificent in her role as a quasi-Amneris. MacNeil and Tozzi too are satisfyingly resonant, and Fausto Cleva, though not as compelling as Maag or Maazel, tellingly reveals his experience directing the opera at the Met. Good recording, now sounding more vivid and with added presence.

Luisa Miller: highlights.
(M) *** DG 435 413-2; *435 413-4* [id.] (from above recording with Ricciarelli, Domingo; cond. Maazel).

As it opens with the *Overture*, collectors will welcome this, the only current set of highlights from *Luisa Miller*, vividly transferred to CD. The cues are satisfactorily related to the action in the documentation of the 67-minute selection. As this is part of DG's 'Domingo Edition', Rodolfo tends to dominate the chosen excerpts, but Ricciarelli's moving contribution is also strongly featured. Excellent sound.

Macbeth (complete).
(M) *** EMI CMS7 64339-2 (2). Amb. Op. Ch., New Philh. O, Muti.
   Macbeth (Sherrill Milnes), Lady Macbeth (Fiorenza Cossotto), Banquo (Ruggero Raimondi), Macduff (José Carreras).

*** Ph. Dig. 412 133-2 (3) [id.]. German Op. Berlin Ch. & O, Sinopoli.

  Macbeth (Renato Bruson), Lady Macbeth (Mara Zampieri), Banquo (Robert Lloyd),
  Macduff (Neil Shicoff).

*** DG 415 688-2 (3) [id.]. Ch. & O of La Scala, Milan, Abbado.

  Macbeth (Piero Cappuccilli), Lady Macbeth (Shirley Verrett), Banquo (Nicolai Ghiaurov),
  Macduff (Plácido Domingo).

(M) **(*) BMG/RCA GD 84516 (2) [4516-2-RG]. Met. Op. Ch. & O, Leinsdorf.

  Macbeth (Leonard Warren), Lady Macbeth (Leonie Rysanek), Banquo (Jerome Hines),
  Macduff (Carlo Bergonzi).

(M) **(*) Decca 433 039-2 (2) [id.]. St Cecilia Ac., Rome, Ch. & O, Schippers.

  Macbeth (Giuseppe Taddei), Lady Macbeth (Birgit Nilsson), Banquo (Giovanni Foiani),
  Macduff (Bruno Previdi).

** Decca Dig. 417 525-2 (2). Ch. & O of Teatro Communale di Bologna, Chailly.

  Macbeth (Leo Nucci), Lady Macbeth (Shirley Verrett), Banquo (Samuel Ramey), Macduff
  (Veriano Luchetti).

*(*) Hung. HCD 12738/40 [id.]. Hungarian R. & TV Ch., Budapest SO, Gardelli.

  Macbeth (Piero Cappuccilli), Lady Macbeth (Sylvia Sass), Banquo (Kolos Kováts), Macduff
  (Péter Kelen).

Macbeth was the first Verdi opera to be based on a play of Shakespeare. It was premièred in
Florence in 1847 but was not a success, so the composer made considerable revisions for the
Paris revival, eight years later. When Muti's 1976 recording first appeared on CD, it included
(in a three-disc set, as was the original issue) three important appendices: one aria for Lady
Macbeth and two for Macbeth himself, written for the original, 1847 version of the opera.

EMI have now reissued the opera on two mid-priced CDs instead of the original three, though
sadly the unique appendices in the original issue have been left out. The story-line remains the
same in both versions. At the opening we immediately meet the witches, prophesying a grim
future for Macbeth. A messenger then arrives to announce that Macbeth has been granted the
title to the estates of the rebel, Cawdor. Macbeth, who is with Banquo, anticipates a prosperous
future.

Lady Macbeth is now seen reading a letter from her husband, telling her the good news, and
she immediately knows what must be done next. When Macbeth arrives, with Duncan, the
Scottish king, and his son, Malcolm (who are to stay overnight at the castle), the murder is
decided upon with scarcely a word spoken. Macbeth, alone, sees the dagger before him.

The murder accomplished, he staggers away with it still in his grasp. As Lady Macbeth takes it
from him, he is suddenly horrified at the sight of his bloodstained hands. It is she who puts the
murder weapon back into the king's rooms in order to implicate the servants. Banquo and
Macduff enter and discover the murder. When he hears what has happened to his father,
Malcolm prudently departs in haste for England.

Lady Macbeth is enjoying her power as queen but she accuses Macbeth of avoiding her.
Together they decide that Banquo and his son, Fleance, must also die. Later, in a park, assassins
are waiting for them; Banquo is killed but Fleance escapes. A banquet now takes place in the hall
of the castle. Macbeth learns of Banquo's death and that his son is unscathed. Turning to
Banquo's empty seat, he twice sees the ghost of the recently murdered man. Terrified, Macbeth
bursts out with a declaration of his involvement in the murder, and the assembly sense his guilt.
Macduff sets off to join Malcolm in England to plan retribution.

The witches are again seen, sitting round their cauldron. Macbeth appears and demands to
know his fate. A series of apparitions predict his future in vivid detail, and finally the frightened
Macbeth loses consciousness. Lady Macbeth arrives, looking for her husband, and he tells her
that he has been shown the line of kings who will be Banquo's descendants. She rebuts the
meaning of his visions and urges him to regain his confidence. Macbeth leaves in order to kill
MacDuff and his heirs, while his wife is left, desperate in her anxiety that her evil plans will fail.

At Birnam Wood, near the Scottish/English border, the avenging force is gathered. Macduff
receives a letter telling him that his wife and children have been murdered; Malcolm joins him
with forces from south of the border. Back at the castle, Lady Macbeth, already demented, has
been walking in her sleep. Macbeth hears that an army is approaching to attack him, and that his
wife has died. The witches have predicted his immunity from harm caused by 'anyone born of
woman', but Macduff arrives to declare that he was prematurely taken from his mother's womb.
Malcolm enters and is crowned king, and Macbeth acknowledges his defeat.

Muti's 1976 version of *Macbeth*, made at Abbey Road, appeared within weeks of Abbado's, confirming that new standards were being set in this opera on record. This was Muti's first opera set after taking over as principal conductor of the New Philharmonia and, though this is a lucky opera on disc, there is a strong case for putting his dramatic, well-paced and sharply rhythmic reading at the top of the list even though, to get the work on to a pair of CDs, a bad break has been chosen just before the end of Act II. Sherrill Milnes was at his very peak as Macbeth, Fiorenza Cossotto gives one of her very finest performances on disc, firm-toned and abrasive, as Lady Macbeth, while José Carreras and Ruggero Raimondi add to an exceptionally strong team. No rivals on current sets stand above them, with the British chorus outshining Italian rivals. As for the sound, it far outshines in vividness many digital opera-recordings.

A vital element in Sinopoli's conducting of Verdi – perhaps the Toscanini inheritance – is an electrifying fierceness of expression. Here it has one sitting up in surprise over the choruses for witches and murderers, but equally relishing the absence of apology. Even more than his finest rivals, Sinopoli presents this opera as a searing Shakespearean inspiration, scarcely more uneven than much of the work of the Bard himself. In the Banqueting scene, for example, he creates extra dramatic intensity by his concern for detail and by his preference for extreme dynamics, as in the vital stage-whispered phrases from Lady Macbeth to her husband, marked *sotto voce*, which heighten the sense of horror and disintegration over the appearance of the ghost.

Detailed word-meaning is a key factor in this, and Renato Bruson and Mara Zampieri respond vividly. Zampieri's voice may be biting rather than beautiful, occasionally threatening to come off the rails, but, with musical precision as an asset, she matches exactly Verdi's request for the voice of a she-devil. Neil Shicoff as Macduff and Robert Lloyd as Banquo make up the excellent quartet of principals, while the high voltage of the whole performance clearly reflects Sinopoli's experience with the same chorus and orchestra at the Deutsche Oper in Berlin. Some of the unusually slow speeds for the big ensembles make the result all the more tellingly ominous. CD adds vividly to the realism of a recording that is well balanced and focused but atmospheric.

In Abbado's scintillating performance, the diamond precision of ensemble also has one thinking of Toscanini. The conventional rum-ti-tum of witches' and murderers' choruses is transformed and becomes tense and electrifying, helped by the immediacy of sound. At times Abbado's tempi are unconventional, but with slow speeds he springs the rhythm so infectiously that the results are the more compelling. Based on the Giorgio Strehler production at La Scala, the whole performance gains from superb teamwork, for each of the principals is far more meticulous than is common about observing Verdi's detailed markings, above all those for *pianissimo* and *sotto voce*.

Verrett, hardly powerful above the stave, yet makes a virtue out of necessity in floating glorious half-tones, and with so firm and characterful a voice she makes a highly individual, not at all conventional Lady Macbeth. As for Cappuccilli, he has never sung with such fine range of tone and imagination on record as here, and José Carreras makes a real, sensitive character out of the small role of Macduff. Excellent, clean recording, impressively remastered for CD.

On two mid-priced discs in the Victor Opera series, the Leinsdorf version makes a good bargain too, bringing a large-scale performance featuring three favourite principals from the Met. Leonie Rysanek here gives one of her finest performances on record, producing her firmest, creamiest sound for the Sleepwalking scene, even though the coloratura taxes her severely. Leonard Warren, much admired in this part before his untimely death, gives a strong, thoughtful reading, marred by the way the microphone exaggerates his vibrato. Carlo Bergonzi is a stylish, clear-toned Macduff. Good sound for its period.

On Decca, Birgit Nilsson makes a fearsomely impressive Lady Macbeth, sounding like the devil of Verdi's imaginings, but with glorious tone and spot on the note. It is her success and that of Taddei as Macbeth himself that makes it all the more irritating that Schippers was allowed to cut the score (about a quarter of an hour of music is missing). With the variations between the editions, this is always a difficult opera to get right textually, but the solution of whittling down the roles of the witches and the murderers reduces the appeal of this Decca set considerably.

Their rum-ti-tum choruses may not be the greatest Verdi, but without that music the opera loses its balance and the central tragedy is weakened by not being set in relief. Schippers' direction is not as electrifying as that of the best rival versions, but the 1964 Decca recording has transferred vividly to CD and the singing of the two principals is memorable.

Chailly's recording, made for the pretentious French film of the opera, cannot compare with other modern versions. Except for Samuel Ramey as a fine Banquo, none of the principals are at their best, and the ensemble of the Bologna orchestra falls well short of international standards. Shirley Verrett's is a powerful performance as Lady Macbeth, but she was far firmer and just as perceptive ten years earlier in the Abbado version on DG. Leo Nucci gives a generally well-sung, sometimes forced, but undercharacterized portrait of Macbeth himself. Luchetti is not at his freshest either. Good, atmospheric Decca sound hardly sways the balance.

Well conducted and well recorded as it is, the Hungaroton version is not competitive. Both Cappuccilli in the name-part and Sylvia Sass as Lady Macbeth – potentially an exciting combination – are both well past their best and, though there are some fine contributions from the others, the flaws are serious.

Macbeth: highlights.

(M) *** Decca 421 889-2 [id.]. Dietrich Fischer-Dieskau, Elena Suliotis, Nicolai Ghiaurov, Luciano Pavarotti, Ambrosian Op. Ch., LPO, Gardelli.

(M) *** DG 435 414-2; *435 414-4* [id.] (from above recording with Cappuccilli, Verrett, Ghiaurov, Domingo; cond. Abbado).

On Decca a generous selection (75 minutes) from a finely dramatic set, splendidly recorded in the Kingsway Hall in 1971 and flawed only by the variable singing of Suliotis. This is arguably Fischer-Dieskau's finest Verdi performance on record and the cast includes a young Pavarotti as Macduff.

Although the 62-minute set of excerpts from Abbado's *Macbeth* is issued as part of DG's 'Domingo Edition', its compilers recognize that Macduff is only a supporting role, and the principal participants, Cappuccilli and Verrett as Macbeth and Lady Macbeth respectively, are well represented. The witches, too, are not forgotten, and the disc opens with their chorus (*Che faceste?*), and includes the scene of the apparitions from Act III. Splendid sound, vividly atmospheric.

I Masnadieri (complete).

(M) *** Ph. 422 423-2 (2). Amb. S., New Philh. O, Gardelli.

   Massimiliano (Ruggero Raimondi), Carlo (Carlo Bergonzi), Francesco (Piero Cappuccilli), Amalia (Montserrat Caballé).

(M) **(*) Decca Dig. 433 854-2 (2) [id.]. WNO Ch. & O, Bonynge.

   Massimiliano (Samuel Ramey), Carlo (Franco Bonisolli), Francesco (Matteo Manuguerra), Amalia (Joan Sutherland).

As this excellent Philips recording makes plain, the long neglect of *I Masnadieri* ('The Bandits') is totally undeserved, despite a libretto which is a bungled adaptation of a Schiller play. Few will seriously identify with the hero-turned-brigand who stabs his beloved rather than lead her into a life of shame; but, on record, flaws of motivation are of far less moment than on stage.

The story concerns a young man, Carlo, who is disinherited as a result of the scheming of a younger brother, Francesco. He turns into a kind of Robin Hood. As Julian Budden puts it, it is 'no simple tale of a wrong righted' for the hero is 'given to Hamlet-like self-communings and feelings of shame and guilt'.

When Massimiliano, his father, laments that he will die without seeing his favourite son, Francesco enters to tell him the false news of Carlo's death. Massimiliano collapses. Amalia, Carlo's beloved, also believes him dead. She resists Francesco's advances and imagines both Carlo and Massimiliano in heaven; she escapes from the castle but is frightened by the approach of bandits.

Massimiliano was imprisoned after his collapse, and his emaciated appearance prompts Carlo and his fellow-bandits to vow vengeance on Francesco. In the last Act Francesco shows remorse for his misdeeds and meets his end; Carlo complains of his commitment to a life of crime. Amalia, who now finds that Carlo is still alive, offers herself to him, come what may, but, knowing what fate awaits him, Carlo stabs her.

The melodies may only fitfully be out of Verdi's top drawer, but the musical structure and argument often look forward to a much later period with hints of *Forza, Don Carlo* and even *Otello*. With Gardelli as ever an urgently sympathetic Verdian and a team of four excellent principals, splendidly recorded, the Philips set can be warmly welcomed.

I Masnadieri, with four principal roles of equal importance, is not a prima donna's opera, but with Sutherland cast as Amalia it tends to become one. This is a weightier view than Caballé took in the earlier, Philips recording, conveying more light and shade. The cabaletta for her great Act II aria brings a coloratura display with Sutherland still at her very peak.

Though he sings with less refinement than Bergonzi on the rival set, Bonisolli has great flair, as in his extra flourishes in the final ensemble of Act II. Manuguerra also sings strongly; he may not be as refined as his rival, Cappuccilli, but he sounds more darkly villainous. Ramey as

Massimiliano sings with fine clarity, but the voice does not sound old enough for a father. The Welsh National Opera Chorus projects with the lustiness of stage experience, even if the Kingsway Hall acoustic slightly clouds some choral detail. Even so, the digital sound is very impressive in its fullness and depth, and at mid-price this is certainly worth considering, especially by Sutherland fans.

Nabucco (complete).
*** DG Dig. 410 512-2 (2) [id.]. Ch. & O of German Op., Berlin, Sinopoli.
   Nabucco (Piero Cappuccilli), Abigaille (Ghena Dimitrova), Ismaele (Plácido Domingo), Fenena (Lucia Valentini Terrani), Zaccaria (Evgeny Nesterenko).
*** Decca 417 407-2 (2) [id.]. V. State Op. Ch. & O, Gardelli.
   Nabucco (Tito Gobbi), Abigaille (Elena Suliotis), Ismaele (Bruno Previdi), Fenena (Dora Carral), Zaccaria (Carlo Cava).
Withdrawn: **(*) EMI CDS7 47488-8 (2) [Ang. CDCB 47488]. Amb. Op. Ch., Philh. O, Muti.
   Nabucco (Matteo Manuguerra), Abigaille (Renata Scotto), Ismaele (Veriano Luchetti), Fenena (Elena Obraztsova), Zaccaria (Nicolai Ghiaurov).

Nabucco was Verdi's first great success. It was premièred in Milan in 1842. Verdi clearly responded to the plight of the Jews in their Babylonian captivity, for the Act III climax produced the chorus, *Va pensiero*, with its heartfelt call for freedom, which the composer never surpassed in popular esteem, although he wrote similar choruses in later works. As the opera opens, the people and priests in Jerusalem lament their defeat at the hands of Nebuchadnezzar, King of Babylon (Nabucco), and they beg Jehovah to prevent the capture of the Temple. Zaccaria, the High Priest, begs them to have faith in God, but the news that Nabucco is advancing on the Temple causes fresh agitation.

Ismaele, who brought all this ill news, is left alone with Fenena, Nabucco's daughter, a hostage in the hands of the Jews, whom he has loved ever since she rescued him when he was thrown into prison. Abigaille, supposed sister of Fenena, now appears at the head of a band of Babylonian soldiers. She threatens them both with immediate death but tells Ismaele that she loves him and could save him if he returned her love.

Zaccaria now rushes in to announce that Nabucco is approaching the Temple. He threatens to kill Fenena if Nabucco should cross the threshold and desecrate the holy place. Nabucco taunts the defeated Jews, but Ismaele prevents Zaccaria from attacking Fenena. Nabucco then orders the sacking of the Temple.

The Jews are now captive in Babylon. Nabucco, away at war elsewhere, has left Fenena as regent. Abigaille is jealous of her; she looks for and finds a document which proves that Fenena is not Nabucco's daughter but a slave. The High Priest tells Abigaille that Fenena is setting free the Jewish prisoners and urges Abigaille to seize power. He says that a report has been received that Nabucco has been killed in battle. The Jews meanwhile gather in a room in the palace and Zaccaria invokes the guidance of God. The people curse Ismaele but the High Priest reminds them that Fenena, for whose sake Ismaele committed treachery, has now embraced the Jewish faith.

Abdallo, an old officer in Nabucco's service, repeats the rumour of Nabucco's death. Abigaille plans to kill Fenena and she demands her crown. But Nabucco appears, steps betweeen them and places it on his own head. Defying Abigaille to remove it, he proclaims himself God and commands Fenena and Abigaille to bow down before him. There is a mighty clap of thunder, and the crown is torn from him and he is seen to be mad, babbling that not even his own daughter will aid him. Zaccaria proclaims that heaven will punish the blasphemer, and Abigaille snatches the crown.

Abigaille now rules as regent, with the support of the priests. Many Jews are to be sacrificed, among them Fenena. Nabucco is led into Abigaille's presence, furious at seeing her on the throne. She taunts him into sealing the death-sentences on the Jews and, rather than die himself, he grovels in supplication to her. On the banks of the Euphrates the betrayed Jews sing their great chorus, and Zaccaria prophesies the fall of Babylon.

Nabucco, in prison, awakens from a nightmare to hear the crowd crying, 'Death to Fenena!' He prays to Jehovah to pardon his sins and spare her life. Abdallo appears at the head of the guard and frees Nabucco, who rushes out to rescue his daughter. At the place of sacrifice, Fenena is praying, as she and the Jews prepare for death. The arrival of Nabucco and his supporters halts the sacrifice and the false idol is thrown down as if by divine intervention.

All join in a prayer to Jehovah as Abigaille enters. She too is full of remorse and has taken poison. She dies, calling on God for forgiveness. Zaccaria hails the Jewish convert – Nabucco.

This was Sinopoli's first opera recording and it suggests in its freshness, its electricity and its crystal clarification the sort of insight that Toscanini must once have brought. Sinopoli makes Verdi sound less comfortable than traditional conductors, but he never lets the 'grand guitar' accompaniments of early Verdi churn along automatically. One keeps hearing details normally obscured. Even the thrill of the great chorus, *Va, pensiero*, is the greater when the melody first emerges at a hushed pianissimo, as marked, sounding almost off-stage. Strict as he is, Sinopoli encourages his singers to relish the great melodies to the full.

Dimitrova is superb in Abigaille's big Act II aria, noble in her evil, as is Cappuccilli as Nabucco, less intense than Gobbi was on Gardelli's classic set for Decca, but stylistically pure. The rest of the cast is strong too, including Domingo in a relatively small role and Nesterenko superb as the High Priest, Zaccaria. Surprisingly, the bright and forward digital sound is less atmospheric than that of Gardelli's 1965 Decca set with Gobbi and Suliotis, though the CD transfer brings added presence and sharper detail, while emphasizing the dramatic dynamic range.

The vividly real and atmospheric sound in the Decca recording comes up very three-dimensionally on CD, even though tape-hiss is at a higher level than usual. There is more presence than in Sinopoli's DG, but that digital recording copes better with big ensembles. The Viennese choral contribution was less committed than one would ideally like in a work which contains a chorus unique in Verdi's output, *Va, pensiero*; but in every other way this is a masterly performance, with dramatically intense and deeply imaginative contributions from Tito Gobbi as Nabucco and Elena Suliotis as the evil Abigaille.

Gobbi was already nearing the end of his career, but even he rarely recorded a performance so full of sharply dramatic detail, while Suliotis made this the one totally satisfying performance of an all-too-brief recording career, wild in places but no more than is dramatically necessary. Though Carlo Cava as Zaccaria is not ideally rich of tone, it is a strong performance; and Gardelli, as in many other Verdi recordings, shows what a master he is at pointing Verdian inspiration, whether in the individual phrase or over a whole scene, simply and naturally, without ever forcing.

Muti's 1978 set does not match either Sinopoli's DG version or the Gardelli set on Decca. The EMI cast, as impressive as could be assembled at the time, with Manuguerra an imaginative choice as Nabucco, fails nevertheless to equal the three-dimensional characterizations of its competitors. Renata Scotto sings well but is not entirely inside her role; Manuguerra proves strong and reliable but lacks something in flair. Even the recording quality fails to improve on the earlier Decca set, although it is clarified and more vivid than before in its CD format.

Nabucco: highlights.
(M) *** DG Dig. 435 415-2; *435 415-4* [id.] (from above recording with Cappuccilli, Dimitrova, Domingo; cond. Sinopoli).
(M) *** Decca 421 867-2; *421 867-4* [id.] (from above recording with Gobbi, Suliotis, Previdi; cond. Gardelli).
(M) ** EMI CDM7 63092-2; *EG 763092-4* (from above recording with Manuguerra, Scotto, Luchetti; cond. Muti).

A useful collection of highlights from Sinopoli's strong, dramatic and individual complete set, brightly recorded, which, even at full price, is preferable to the highlights from the Muti version.

Suliotis's impressive contribution is well represented on this Decca highlights disc, and there are fine contributions too from Gobbi. Needless to say, the chorus, *Va pensiero*, is given its place of honour (the performance rhythmically a little mannered but eloquent enough), and *Gli arredi festivi* opens the selection, which runs for 58 minutes. The 1965 recording sounds splendid.

Though the EMI disc offers fair measure (nearly 65 minutes) and has an impressive cast-list, it is much less involving, and the 1977/8 recording, made in the Kingsway Hall, loses some of its refinement in the more spectacular moments: the digital clarification of the reverberant original recording has not always brought the crispest focus, although the famous chorus, *Va pensiero*, sounds well enough.

Oberto (complete).
*** Orfeo C 105842 F (3) [id.]. Bav. R. Ch., Munich R. O, Gardelli.
Cuniza (Ruša Baldani), Leonora (Ghena Dimitrova), Imelda (Alison Browner), Riccardo (Carlo Bergonzi), Oberto (Rolando Panerai).

It was left to the enterprising Orfeo label to round off the early Verdi series, with Gardelli conducting, that Philips for so long promoted. *Oberto* (1839) was Verdi's first opera, setting a libretto by Antonio Piazza and Temistocle Solera, and in every way this issue matches the success of those other recordings, despite the change of venue to Munich. Gardelli is a master of pacing and pointing Verdi effortlessly; here he presents a strong case for this earliest of the Verdi canon, revealing in such ensembles as the Trio towards the end of Act I clear forecasts of full mastery to come. Otherwise there is much that reflects the manners and style of Donizetti, as one would expect of a 26-year-old writing in Italy at the time; but the underlying toughness regularly provides a distinctive flavour.

Oberto, Conte di San Bonifacio, has been dispossessed and he returns to his lands to discover that his daughter, Leonora, has been seduced and then abandoned by Riccardo, his usurper. They both present their story to Riccardo's intended bride, Cuniza, and win her sympathy. They then confront Riccardo publicly and Cuniza breaks off her engagement.

Oberto then challenges Riccardo to a duel, in which the latter kills him. Riccardo is remorseful and goes into exile, leaving his property to Leonora; she, desolated by the death of her father, goes into a convent.

Gardelli successfully papers over the less convincing moments, helped by fine playing from the orchestra, an outstanding chorus and first-rate principals. Ghena Dimitrova makes a very positive heroine, powerful in attack in her moment of fury in the Act I finale, but also gently expressive when necessary. Only in cabalettas is she sometimes ungainly. The veterans, Carlo Bergonzi and Rolando Panerai, more than make up in stylishness and technical finesse for any unevenness of voice, and Ruša Baldani is a warm-toned Cuniza, the mezzo role. First-rate recording.

Otello (complete).
*** BMG/RCA GD 82951 (2) [RCD2-2951]. Amb. Op. Ch., Nat. PO, Levine.
    Otello (Plácido Domingo), Desdemona (Renata Scotto), Iago (Sherrill Milnes).
*** Decca Dig. 433 669-2; *433 669-4* (2) [id.]. Chicago SO & Ch., Solti.
    Otello (Luciano Pavarotti), Desdemona (Kiri Te Kanawa), Iago (Leo Nucci).
(M) *** BMG/RCA GD 81969 (2) [1969-2-RG]. Rome Op. Ch. & O, Serafin.
    Otello (Jon Vickers), Desdemona (Leonie Rysanek), Iago (Tito Gobbi).
(M) *** EMI CMS7 69308-2 (2) [Ang. CDMB 69308]. Ch. of German Op., Berlin, BPO, Karajan.
    Otello (Jon Vickers), Desdemona (Mirella Freni), Iago (Peter Glossop).
Withdrawn: **(*) EMI Dig. CDS7 47450-8 (2) [Ang. CD 47450]. La Scala, Milan, Ch. & O, Maazel.
    Otello (Plácido Domingo), Desdemona (Katia Ricciarelli), Iago (Justino Diaz).
**(*) Decca 411 618-2 (2). V. State Op. Ch., VPO, Karajan.
    Otello (Mario Del Monaco), Desdemona (Renata Tebaldi), Iago (Aldo Protti).
(M) (**(*)) BMG/RCA mono GD 60302 (2) [60302-2-RG]. NBC Ch. & SO, Toscanini.
    Otello (Ramon Vinay), Desdemona (Herva Nelli), Iago (Giuseppe Valdengo).

The gap between *Aida* and *Otello* is a long one: 16 years. In between came the *Requiem* and a revision of *Simon Boccanegra*. Then came the great Boito collaboration and, with his help, Verdi re-tells the Shakespearean story very powerfully indeed. The opera contains some of his very finest music, especially during the dreadful closing moments of the tragedy. The opening, too, shows the composer at his most spectacularly evocative in depicting the violent storm at sea, and the waiting crowd, fearful for the safety of Otello's ship.

Finally the weather abates sufficiently for the ship to enter harbour, with Iago and Rodrigo, Montano and Cassio watching from the shore. Otello disembarks and tells the excited crowd that the Turks have been defeated, and he enters the castle.

We now discover the violent passions that animate the principal characters. Rodrigo loves Otello's wife, Desdemona, while Iago, Otello's ensign, hates his master and is jealous of Cassio, promoted over him by Otello.

In the prevalent mood of drinking and celebration, Iago succeeds in getting Cassio drunk and starting a quarrel. Cassio, provoked by Rodrigo, draws his sword and Montano is hurt. Iago sends for Otello, who stops the fighting and, to Iago's satisfaction, demotes Cassio. Finally Otello and Desdemona are left alone, the evening is beautiful, the sea calm, and they blissfully declare their mutual love.

Iago proceeds further with his diabolic plan by pretending to help Cassio regain favour with Otello. He advises Cassio to ask Desdemona to intercede on his behalf. Alone, Iago reveals his creed of evil and his determination to sow suspicion in Otello's heart and mind concerning Desdemona and Cassio. These two meet and, though their conversation is innocent, Iago persuades Otello to watch and invokes his jealousy.

Desdemona is serenaded by Otello's sailors and, for the moment, his suspicions are lulled; but then she asks him to forgive Cassio, and he rejects her request rudely, once again doubting her faithfulness. He complains of a headache, and she tries to place her handkerchief on his forehead to soothe him but he throws it off. Emilia picks it up and Iago demands it from her.

Iago now reports to Otello that he has heard Cassio speaking Desdemona's name in his sleep in the most intimate manner; he then shows Otello the handkerchief, which he says he found in Cassio's possession. Otello is beside himself with anger and swears vengeance.

In the great hall of the castle a herald announces that messengers from Venice will soon arrive. When Desdemona approaches, Iago suggests that Otello be watchful. She again asks him to forgive Cassio, and there is another altercation about the handkerchief, which she cannot produce. Otello's behaviour is violent and he calls her a strumpet. Alone, he is anguished. Iago and Cassio enter together and Otello conceals himself. Iago draws Cassio out on the subject of his amorous conquests but makes sure that Otello only hears remarks that suggest that Desdemona is involved. Iago then produces the handkerchief, and it is made to appear that Cassio had kept it in his room.

Messengers are arriving, led by Lodovico, the Venetian ambassador. Quickly Otello asks Iago to obtain poison for him, but Iago suggests that strangling Desdemona would be more fitting and he offers to kill Cassio. Otello promotes him.

Otello is seething with anger and jealousy and, when Desdemona once more mentions Cassio, he pushes her away. Lodovico has brought a message to say that Otello is recalled to Venice and Cassio is to succeed him as Governor of Cyprus. This is the last straw. Otello completely loses all self-control and throws Desdemona to the floor, scandalizing Lodovico. She pleads with him, to no avail. Left alone with Iago, Otello falls, emotionally exhausted, as Iago looks on triumphantly.

In her bedroom Desdemona talks sadly with Emilia and has a presentiment of tragedy. She prays. Otello enters, looks at her and kisses her three times. She awakens and he coldly accuses her of unfaithfulness with Cassio. She denies this repeatedly, but he tells her that nothing can save her, then stifles her with a pillow. Emilia enters to discover the murder, calls the others and finally exposes Iago. Otello, at last realizing the truth, stabs himself with a dagger and dies alongside Desdemona.

Levine's is the most consistently involving version of *Otello*; on balance, it has the best cast and is superbly conducted, as well as magnificently sung. Levine combines a Toscanini-like thrust with a Karajan-like sensuousness, pointing rhythms to heighten mood, as in the Act II confrontation between hero and heroine over Cassio. Domingo as Otello combines glorious heroic tone with lyrical tenderness. This was recorded soon after he first essayed this most taxing of Italian tenor roles, and if anyone thought he would be overstrained, here is proof to the contrary: he himself has claimed that singing Otello has helped and benefited his voice, and so his subsequent career has proved.

Scotto is not always sweet-toned in the upper register, and the big ensemble at the end of Act III brings obvious strain; nevertheless, it is a deeply felt performance which culminates in a most beautiful account of the all-important Act IV solos, the *Willow song* and *Ave Maria*, most affecting. Milnes too is challenged by the role of Iago. His may not be a voice which readily conveys extremes of evil, but his view is far from conventional: this Iago is a handsome, virile creature beset by the biggest of chips on the shoulder. In the digital transfer for CD of the 1977 analogue original, the voices are vividly and immediately caught, and with ample bloom. The orchestral sound too is fuller and cleaner than in many more recent versions, though there is an occasional hint of roughness in big tuttis.

Solti's Chicago Symphony recording was made in the spring of 1991 from a series of live performances in both Chicago and New York, which marked the close of his long period as music director of the orchestra. With a superstar cast it ran the risk of being merely a media vehicle, but it proves to be a triumph, not quite a first recommendation but a thrilling realization of a supreme masterpiece. Like most of the cast at the time, Solti was recovering from illness, but he has never sounded more warmly communicative in Verdi. The fast speeds never seem too taut or breathless, they simply add to the high voltage of the drama. Leo Nucci, taking the role of Iago for the first time, is sound rather than inspired, warmly Italianate in timbre but lacking in menace. *Era la notte*, fast like much else, becomes a simple narrative, hardly conveying evil.

Dame Kiri Te Kanawa, in a role she has sung many times, produces consistently sumptuous tone, unaffected by the closeness of microphone balance. The *Willow song* is glorious with the last cries of '*Salce!*' reduced to a precisely pitched whisper, before she launches up to a fearless top A-sharp fortissimo. The key element is the singing of Pavarotti as Otello, like Nucci new to his role. Following the pattern of the whole performance, he often adopts faster speeds than usual. He is less meditative, less weighty than his great rival, Domingo, so that such a passage as *Ora e per sempre* makes the hero sound like Radames in *Aida*. He then conveys pure anger rather than irony in his big Act III duet with Desdemona. The cries of '*Sangue!*' before the Oath duet with Iago do not ring out as with Domingo and others, but they are genuinely sung, not shouted.

Whatever the reservations, this is a memorable reading, heightened by Pavarotti's detailed feeling for the words and consistently golden tone. With such close microphone balance, he (like the others) is prevented from achieving genuine pianissimos, but above all he offers a vital, animated Otello, not a replacement for Domingo but a magnificent alternative. The impact of the whole is greatly enhanced by the splendid singing of the Chicago Symphony Chorus, helped by digital sound fuller and more vivid than on any rival set.

The Serafin version in RCA's Victor Opera series makes an outstanding bargain on two mid-priced discs. No conductor is more understanding of Verdian pacing than Serafin and, with sound that hardly begins to show its age (1960), it presents two of the finest solo performances on any *Otello* recording of whatever period: the Iago of Tito Gobbi has never been surpassed for vividness of characterization and tonal subtlety; while the young Jon Vickers, with a voice naturally suited to this role, was in his prime as the Moor. He may lack some of the flair he acquired with experience in this part, but in its fidelity and lack of exaggeration this is preferable to his later recording under Karajan. Leonie Rysanek is a warm and sympathetic Desdemona, not always ideally pure-toned, but tender and touching in one of her very finest recorded performances. The sense of presence in the open, well-balanced recording is the more vivid on CD, thanks to a first-rate transfer.

Karajan directs a big, bold and brilliant account, for the most part splendidly sung, and with all the dramatic contrasts (above all, those in the orchestra) strongly underlined. There are several tiny, but irritating, statutory cuts, but the set, like Serafin's, is offered on two mid-priced CDs and makes an excellent alternative bargain. Freni's Desdemona is delightful, delicate and beautiful, while Vickers and Glossop are both positive and characterful, only occasionally forcing their tone and losing focus. The recording is clarified on CD, with better focus and more bloom than on the much more recent EMI set under Maazel.

Maazel's version, used as soundtrack for the Zeffirelli film but with the text uncut (unlike that of the film), brings a fine performance from Domingo and taut, subtle control from Maazel, particularly good in the spacious, tenderly emotional treatment of the final scene. In many ways Domingo shows how he has developed since he made his earlier recording with Levine; but with a disappointingly negative, unsinister Iago in Justino Diaz, the result often loses in dramatic bite, and Maazel's direction occasionally sags, as in the closing pages of Act II at the end of the Oath duet. Ricciarelli, though not the ideal Desdemona, sings most affectingly, with pianissimos beautifully caught in the *Willow song* and *Ave Maria*. One snag is the sound, which is curiously recessed, with the voices often not quite in focus and little sense of presence.

Karajan's 1961 version, flawed as it is in its casting, yet brings remarkably fine sound to match any version since – a tribute to the artistry of the producer, John Culshaw, and his team of Decca engineers. Culshaw regarded it as an important set and probably could not have imagined that it would become an also-ran in the course of time. This is partly because Aldo Protti offers an undercharacterized Iago. He is always reliable though never imaginative or even sinister – a very obvious drawback in an opera whose plot hinges on Iago's machinations. Del Monaco is hardly a subtle Otello, but his voice is gloriously heroic, and this is one of his finest collaborations with Tebaldi on disc.

Recorded in December 1947 at rehearsals and radio performances in the notorious Studio 8H, Radio City, in New York, Toscanini's historic reading suffers more than usual from dry, limited sound, but in magnetic intensity it is irresistible, bringing home the biting power of Verdi's score as few other recorded performances ever have. Toscanini's speeds are often fast but his feeling for Verdian line is most persuasive, and above all he controls tension to have one experiencing the drama afresh. Ramon Vinay makes a commanding Otello, baritonal in vocal colouring but firm and clear, with a fine feeling for words. Giuseppe Valdengo had few rivals among baritones of the time in this role, strong, animated and clean in attack, though the vocal differentiation between hero and villain is less marked than usual. Herva Nelli is sweet and pure, if a little colourless, as Desdemona. The recording prevents her from achieving a really gentle pianissimo, and Toscanini, for all his flowing lines, fails to allow the full repose needed.

Otello (complete; in English).
Withdrawn: (M) **(*) EMI CMS7 63012-2 (2). Charles Craig, Rosalind Plowright, Neil Howlett, Bonaventura Bottone, ENO Ch. & O, Mark Elder.

Recorded live at the Coliseum in London, the ENO version of *Otello* is inevitably flawed in the sound; but those who seek records of opera in English need not hesitate, for almost every word of Andrew Porter's translation is audible, despite the very variable balances inevitable in recording a live stage production. Less acceptable is the level of stage noise, with the thud and blunder of wandering feet all the more noticeable on CD.

The performance itself is most enjoyable, with dramatic tension building up compellingly. Charles Craig's Otello is most moving, the character's inner pain brought out vividly, though top notes are fallible. Neil Howlett as Iago may not have the most distinctive baritone, but finely controlled vocal colouring adds to a deeply perceptive performance. Rosalind Plowright makes a superb Desdemona, singing with rich, dramatic weight but also with poise and purity. The Death scene reveals her at her finest, radiant of tone, with flawless attack.

Rigoletto (complete).
*** Ph. Dig. 412 592-2 (2) [id.]. St Cecilia Ac., Rome, Ch. & O, Sinopoli.
  Rigoletto (Renato Bruson), Gilda (Edita Gruberová), Duke (Neil Shicoff), Sparafucile (Robert Lloyd), Maddalena (Brigitte Fassbaender).
*** Decca 414 269-2 (2) [id.]. Amb. Op. Ch., LSO, Bonynge.
  Rigoletto (Sherrill Milnes), Gilda (Joan Sutherland), Duke (Luciano Pavarotti), Sparafucile (Martti Talvela), Maddalena (Huguette Tourangeau).
(***) EMI mono CDS7 47469-8 (2) [Ang. CDCB 47469]. La Scala, Milan, Ch. & O, Serafin.
  Rigoletto (Tito Gobbi), Gilda (Maria Callas), Duke (Giuseppe Di Stefano), Sparafucile (Nicola Zaccaria), Maddalena (Adriana Lazzarini).
**(*) DG 415 288-2 (2) [id.]. V. State Op. Ch., VPO, Giulini.
  Rigoletto (Piero Cappuccilli), Gilda (Ileana Cotrubas), Duke (Plácido Domingo), Sparafucile (Nicolai Ghiaurov), Maddalena (Elena Obraztsova).
(M) **(*) BMG/RCA GD 86506 (2) [6506-2-RG]. RCA Italiana Op. Ch. & O, Solti.
  Rigoletto (Robert Merrill), Gilda (Anna Moffo), Duke (Alfredo Kraus), Sparafucile (Ezio Flagello), Maddalena (Rosalind Elias).
(B) ** CfP CD-CFPD 4700; *TC-CFPD 4700* (2). Rome Op. Ch. & O, Molinari-Pradelli.
  Rigoletto (Cornell MacNeil), Gilda (Reri Grist), Duke (Nicolai Gedda), Sparafucile (Agostino Ferrin), Maddalena (Anna Di Stasio).
(M) ** BMG/RCA GD 60172 (2) [60172-2-RG]. Rome Op. Ch. & O, Perlea.
  Rigoletto (Robert Merrill), Gilda (Roberta Peters), Duke (Jussi Bjoerling), Sparafucile (Giorgio Tozzi), Maddalena (Anna Maria Rota).
** Decca Dig. 425 864-2 (2) [id.]. Ch. & O of Teatro Comunale di Bologna, Chailly.
  Rigoletto (Leo Nucci), Gilda (June Anderson), Duke (Luciano Pavarotti), Sparafucile (Nicolai Ghiaurov), Maddalena (Shirley Verrett).
(B) ** Naxos Dig. 8.660013/4 (2) [id.]. Ch. & Slovak RSO (Bratislava), Rahbari.
  Rigoletto (Eduard Tumagian), Gilda (Alida Ferrarini), Duke (Yordi Ramiro), Sparafucile (Jozef Špaček), Maddalena (Ladislav Neshyba).
(M) *(*) DG 437 704-2 (2) [id.]. La Scala, Milan, Ch. & O, Kubelik.
  Rigoletto (Dietrich Fischer-Dieskau), Gilda (Renata Scotto), Duke (Carlo Bergonzi), Sparafucile (Ivo Vinco), Maddalena (Fiorenza Cossotto).
* EMI Dig. CDS7 49605-2 (2) [Ang. CDCB 49605]. La Scala, Milan, Ch. & O, Muti.
  Rigoletto (Giorgio Zancanaro), Gilda (Daniella Dessì), Duke (Vincenzo La Scola), Sparafucile (Paata Burchuladze), Maddalena (Martha Senn).

Rigoletto has always been one of Verdi's greatest popular successes and the very first performance in Venice in 1851 brought an immediately enthusiastic response. Its tragic central character, Rigoletto, the hunchback dwarf with a beautiful daughter, enters fairly soon after the opening.

A party is taking place in the palace of the Duke of Mantua, who immediately displays his devil-may-care attitude towards women (*Questa o quella*). He dances with the attractive young Countess Ceprano. Rigoletto, who is the court jester, mocks Count Ceprano but Marullo, a courtier, suggests that Rigoletto himself keeps a mistress.

Suddenly Count Monterone, a nobleman whose daughter the duke has seduced, pushes his way in. Rigoletto is again cynical in telling the count he is wasting his time but, when Monterone persists, he is arrested and he curses both Rigoletto and the count as he is led off. Revelry continues.

Rigoletto, returning home, is haunted by the curse Monterone has laid on him. Sparafucile, an assassin, offers his services but is refused, and Rigoletto bemoans his own unhappy existence as jester to a duke whom he despises. Gilda – not, as Marullo had suggested, his mistress but his daughter – greets him warmly. She is a kind of prisoner and knows nothing of her father's position at court. He tells her never to leave the house except to go to church and, when he recalls her dead mother, Gilda tries to comfort him in his grief. He warns her attendant, Giovanna, to guard her then leaves.

Meanwhile the duke, having bribed Giovanna, has entered the garden and hidden himself. Thinking herself alone with Giovanna, Gilda remembers a youth she saw in the church who attracted her. It is the duke, who now reveals himself and ardently declares his love for her, telling her he is a student, Gualtier Maldè. The duke leaves after a passionate farewell, and she repeats his name happily (*Caro nome*).

Outside, courtiers are gathering to abduct Rigoletto's 'mistress', and they fool Rigoletto by telling him that Ceprano's wife is the quarry. He offers to help and, blindfolded, he holds a ladder to his own house while Gilda is kidnapped. Too late he rushes into the house to find her gone, and he recalls the curse.

The duke cannot find Gilda and knows nothing of the abduction. The courtiers enter, and the duke realizes that Rigoletto's 'mistress' is in fact his daughter; he goes to console Gilda. Rigoletto enters and furiously denounces the kidnappers – and only then do they, too, realize the truth. He pleads for her to be restored to him. She rushes in and tells him of her feelings for the duke, but Rigoletto's only thought is revenge.

Four weeks pass, and Rigoletto has been waiting for his opportunity. He takes Gilda with him to a decrepit inn which Sparafucile and his sister, Maddalena – who is the decoy – use as a base for murder and robbery. The duke has already arrived and again sings about his view of women (*La donna è mobile*). Rigoletto wants Gilda to see the duke in his true light and – during the famous Quartet – she watches him flirt with Maddalena as her father expresses again his need for revenge.

Rigoletto instructs Gilda to return home, put on boy's clothing and leave immediately for Verona, and she goes off unwillingly. He then arranges the duke's murder with Sparafucile, the body to be placed in a sack. Having made payment for the deed, he says he will return at midnight. Maddalena shows the duke to an upper room for the night, as a storm rises. She then re-enters the lower room and suggests to Sparafucile that he kill Rigoletto, not the 'Apollo' upstairs.

Sparafucile replies that it would be unworthy for an honest assassin to dupe his client, but he will agree to a substitute, should one appear in time. Gilda, having returned in boy's clothing, overhears this conversation and decides to sacrifice herself for the man she loves. The darkness of the storm almost shrouds the violence of the murder.

Rigoletto returns at midnight. He receives the sack from Sparafucile and walks away to throw it in the river. Suddenly he hears the duke's voice (*La donna è mobile*). Appalled, he opens the sack and finds inside the dying Gilda. She begs her father's forgiveness as she expires. With a dreadful cry recalling the curse, Rigoletto prostrates himself on his daughter's body.

Sinopoli conducts a tensely dramatic reading which, in its detailed concentration from first to last, brings out the unity of Verdi's inspiration. Unlike many other conductors who present Verdi freshly at white heat, Sinopoli here has close concern for his singers, with full potential drawn from each in what is on record the most consistent cast yet. Edita Gruberová might have been considered an unexpected choice for Gilda, remarkable for her brilliant coloratura rather than for deeper expression, yet here she makes the heroine a tender, feeling creature, emotionally vulnerable yet vocally immaculate.

As a stickler for the text, Sinopoli eliminates some 'traditional' top notes, as in *Caro nome*. Similarly, Renato Bruson as Rigoletto does far more than produce a stream of velvety tone, detailed and intense, responding to the conductor and combining beauty with dramatic bite. Even more remarkable is the brilliant success of Neil Shicoff as the Duke, more than a match for his most distinguished rivals. Here the Quartet becomes a genuine climax as it rarely has been in complete recordings. Like the others, Shicoff brings out unexpected detail, as does Brigitte Fassbaender as Maddalena, sharply unconventional but vocally most satisfying.

Sinopoli's speeds, too, are at times unconventional, but the fresh look he provides makes this one of the most exciting of recent Verdi operas on disc, helped by full and vivid recording, consistently well balanced and particularly impressive on CD. Cassettes follow the layout of the

LPs, with no attempt to tailor Acts to side-ends. However, the quality is outstandingly vibrant and clear.

Just over ten years after her first recording of this opera, Sutherland appeared in it again – and this set was far more than a dutiful remake. Richard Bonynge from the very start shows his feeling for the resilient rhythms; the result is fresh and dramatic, underlining the revolutionary qualities in the score which we nowadays tend to ignore. Pavarotti is an intensely characterful Duke: an unmistakable rogue but an unmistakable charmer, too. Thanks to him and to Bonynge above all, the Quartet, as on the Sinopoli set, becomes a genuine musical climax.

Sutherland's voice has acquired a hint of a beat, but there is little of the mooning manner which disfigured her earlier assumption, and the result is glowingly beautiful as well as being technically supremely assured. Milnes makes a strong Rigoletto, vocally masterful and with good if hardly searching presentation of character. Urgently enjoyable, the digital transfer on two CDs is exceptionally vivid and atmospheric, underlining the excellence of the original engineering with its finely judged balances, but also enhancing the superimposed crowd noises and the like, which not everyone will welcome.

There has never been a more compelling performance of the title-role in *Rigoletto* than that of Gobbi on his classic Scala set of the 1950s. At every point, in almost every single phrase, Gobbi finds extra meaning in Verdi's vocal lines, with the widest range of tone-colour employed for expressive effect. Callas, though not naturally suited to the role of the wilting Gilda, is compellingly imaginative throughout, and Di Stefano gives one of his finest performances. The digital transfer of the original mono recording (no stereo transcription as in earlier LP reissues) is astonishingly vivid in capturing the voices which are sharply focused, given a fine sense of presence, so that you miss stereo spread remarkably little. With fair bloom on the sound, the highly distinctive timbres of all three principals, notably Gobbi, are superbly caught.

Giulini, ever thoughtful for detail, directs a distinguished performance. Speeds tend to be slow, phrases are beautifully shaped and, with fine playing from the Vienna Philharmonic, the dynamics are subtle rather than dramatic. The conductor seems determined to get away from any conception of *Rigoletto* as melodrama; however, in doing that he misses the red-blooded theatricality of Verdi's concept, the basic essential.

Although it may be consistent with Giulini's view, it further reduces the dramatic impact that Cappuccilli (with his unsinister voice) makes the hunchback a noble figure from first to last, while Domingo, ever intelligent, makes a reflective rather than an extrovert Duke. Cotrubas is a touching Gilda, but the close balance of her voice is not helpful, and the topmost register is not always comfortable. The recording, made in the Musikverein in Vienna, has the voices well to the fore, with much reverberation on the instruments behind. CD focuses the voices even more vividly than before, but that makes the closeness of balance all the more apparent, even if the orchestral sound is cleaner.

Anna Moffo makes a charming Gilda in the Solti set of 1963, well transferred on two mid-priced CDs in the Victor Opera series. Solti at times presses too hard, but this is a strong and dramatic reading, with Robert Merrill producing a glorious flow of dark, firm tone in the name-part. Alfredo Kraus is as stylish as ever as the Duke, and this rare example of his voice at its freshest should not be missed. A good bargain, though there are statutory cuts in the text.

The CfP set is undistinguished, but it is well transferred to both CD and cassette and is inexpensive. Reri Grist's Gilda is lightweight and not strong on charm, but Gedda has some good moments: he gives a strong dramatic lead, and because of this the Quartet is a highlight. MacNeil sings well and, even if he is not a very dominant Rigoletto, the performance is still musically enjoyable. With vivid sound this is fair value.

Jonel Perlea's RCA set is mainly of interest for Jussi Bjoerling's contribution. It opens well, and generally the conductor controls the music effectively. But he is hampered by Robert Merrill's rather hammy Rigoletto and the fact that Roberta Peters, although singing well, does not project the character of Gilda at all. Indeed the whole atmosphere of the set is of a concert performance, and the close of the opera degenerates into melodrama. The 1956 recording is certainly vivid.

Chailly's digital version has the benefit of full and vivid Decca sound, but the performance cannot match the finest existing versions. Pavarotti, recorded very close, undermines the vivacity of his singing by coarse vocal tricks. His earlier recording opposite Sutherland is far preferable. June Anderson makes a strong Gilda but the voice, as recorded, often sounds too heavy; and Leo Nucci, well below form, is far too rough of tone in the title-role, with the voice often unsteady. Chailly's direction is sympathetic but lacks individuality.

Rahbari conducts a neat but rather underpowered account of *Rigoletto*, well played and recorded but lacking full Verdian bite. Though Eduard Tumagian is a young-sounding baritone for the title-role of the hunchback jester, lacking dramatic weight, he sings cleanly and with feeling. The Gilda of Alida Ferrarini is bright and fresh, agile in *Caro nome* with a tight trill at the end. There and elsewhere her singing is slightly marred by an overfondness for under-the-note coloration which, with so precise a voice, often sounds flat. Yordy Ramiro is over-parted as the Duke, with much of his singing crisp and clean, though often strained on top. The Quartet in the final Act is made the more attractive by having four fresh young voices.

Reaction to the DG/Kubelik set will depend very much on response to Fischer-Dieskau's singing of the name-part. There is no denying the care and sensitivity with which he approaches the music, and almost every phrase has the nicety of Lieder-singing, but the end result is oddly unconvincing and mannered.

It is partly that Fischer-Dieskau's voice seems just too young-sounding here for the old jester: you cannot quite believe in him as a grief-stricken father. Bergonzi's Duke is beautifully sung, but the Gilda of Renata Scotto is disappointing. This is yet another example where the engineers seemed to find it impossible to catch the special tangy quality which made her stage appearances so attractive; instead, the sound has the throaty 'little-girl' quality one associates with some pre-electric records of sopranos. Kubelik's conducting is frankly dull and the set can be recommended only to those curious to hear Fischer-Dieskau as Rigoletto. The CD transfer is lively and well balanced.

Muti deliberately chose young singers for the roles of Gilda and the Duke, but both Daniella Dessì and Vincenzo La Scola are pale and disappointing, with the flutter in Dessì's soprano exaggerated by the microphone. They are not helped by Muti holding them to the strict letter of the score, allowing none of the usual moments of individual display in concluding top notes. Muti characteristically is also a stickler for obeying metronome markings, which often seem too fast, making for rigidity, while the recording is strangely muffled, taking the edge off the performance. Giorgio Zancanaro in the title-role has a fine voice, but he uses it squarely and with little imagination; and Paata Burchuladze as Sparafucile is out of style.

(i) *Rigoletto, Act IV* (complete). (ii) *I Lombardi, Act III: Trio.*
(M) (**) BMG/RCA mono GD 60276; *GK 60276* (2); [60276-2-RG; *60276-4-RG*]. (i) Leonard Warren, Zinka Milanov, Jan Peerce, Nicola Moscona, Nan Merriman, All City Highschool Ch. & Glee Clubs; (ii) Vivian Della Chiesa, Jan Peerce, Nicola Moscona; NBC SO, Toscanini – BOITO: *Mefistofele: Prologue.* (***)

These two fascinating Verdi items are wartime recordings, even more limited in sound than most of Toscanini's in his last years. The *I Lombardi Trio* finds the acoustic of the notorious Studio 8H in Radio City at its driest, but the conductor's love for the music still dominates. It is interesting to find a little-known singer, Vivian della Chiesa, emerging strongly alongside Jan Peerce and Nicola Moscona. Equally impressive is the dazzling performance of the NBC Orchestra's concert-master, Mischa Mischakoff, in the virtuoso violin solo of the introduction.

The last Act of *Rigoletto* was given in a wartime fund-raising concert in Madison Square Garden and, though the brittleness of sound is at times almost comic and the tautness of Toscanini's control was unrelenting, the performances of the principals are formidable, with Zinka Milanov at her most radiant. With Toscanini's searing account of the *Mefistofele Prologue*, this makes a generous compilation.

Rigoletto: highlights.
(M) **(*) Ph. Dig. 432 619-2; *432 619-4* [id.] (from above recording with Bruson, Gruberová, Shicoff; cond. Sinopoli).
(M) *** DG 435 416-2; *435 416-4* [id.] (from above recording with Cappuccilli, Cotrubas, Domingo; cond. Giulini).
*** Decca 421 303-2 [id.] (from above recording with Milnes, Sutherland, Pavarotti; cond. Bonynge).

Sinopoli's *Rigoletto* has the most consistent cast on record and, although his tempi are unconventional, this vividly recorded set of highlights is highly recommendable, with Gruberová's brilliantly sung yet tender portrayal of Gilda matched by Neil Shicoff's Duke, and Renato Bruson memorably powerful in the name-part. Unfortunately and disgracefully, the CD offers no notes, synopsis or translation. However, the selection is very generous (71 minutes) and still makes an obvious first choice.

Otherwise there are useful if not quite so generous sets of highlights from both Decca and DG for those who do not want to go to the expense of a complete set. On Decca it was a pity that

Questa o quella had to be given an edited fade. The 61-minute DG collection gets round this problem by including the following number, *Partite? Crudele*. This is now reissued at mid-price as part of the 'Domingo Edition'.

Rigoletto (complete; in English).
Withdrawn: (M) *** EMI Dig. CMS7 69369-2 (2) [id.]. ENO Ch. & O, Elder.
  Rigoletto (John Rawnsley), Gilda (Helen Field), Duke (Arthur Davies), Sparafucile (John Tomlinson), Maddalena (Jean Rigby).

The flair of the original English National Opera production setting *Rigoletto* in the Little Italy area of New York in the 1950s and making the tenor a Mafia boss, the 'Duke', is superbly caught in the EMI version in English. The intensity and fine pacing of the stage performances are splendidly caught in this studio recording, thanks to Mark Elder's keenly rhythmic conducting, making this the most successful of the ENO Verdi sets. Outstanding vocally is the heady-toned Duke of Arthur Davies and, though neither John Rawnsley as Rigoletto nor Helen Field as Gilda has a voice so naturally beautiful, they too sing both powerfully and stylishly. Excellent recording, clean, full and well balanced.

Simon Boccanegra (complete).
⊛ *** DG 415 692-2 (2) [id.]. La Scala, Milan, Ch. & O, Abbado.
  Simon Boccanegra (Piero Cappuccilli), Amelia (Mirella Freni), Gabriele (José Carreras), Fiesco (Nicolai Ghiaurov), Paolo (José Van Dam), Pietro (Giovanni Foiani).
Withdrawn: (M) (***) EMI mono CMS7 63513-2 (2) [Ang. CDMB 63513]. Rome Op. Ch. & O, Santini.
  Simon Boccanegra (Tito Gobbi), Amelia (Victoria De los Angeles), Gabriele (Giuseppe Campora), Fiesco (Boris Christoff), Paolo (Walter Monachesi), Pietro (Paolo Dari).
** Decca Dig. 425 628-2 (2) [id.]. La Scala, Milan, Ch. & O, Solti.
  Simon Boccanegra (Leo Nucci), Amelia (Kiri Te Kanawa), Gabriele (Giacomo Aragall), Fiesco (Paata Burchuladze), Paolo (Paolo Coni), Pietro (Carlo Colombara).
** BMG/RCA RD 70729 (2). RCA Ch. & O, Gavazzeni.
  Simon Boccanegra (Piero Cappuccilli), Amelia (Katia Ricciarelli), Gabriele (Plácido Domingo), Fiesco (Ruggero Raimondi), Paolo (Gian-Piero Mastromei), Pietro (Maurizio Mazzieri).

Simon Boccanegra was not a success at its première in Venice in 1857 and, much later, when he had established his partnership with Arrigo Boito, Verdi made a complete revision. The present version was first heard in Milan in 1881. Even with the revision, its plot-line remains over-complicated, but the opera brings several dramatic confrontations, in the best Verdi style, and a great deal of magnificent music. The opera opens in the church square of San Lorenzo, outside the Fiesco Palace.

Paolo, leader of the Plebeian Party is discussing with Pietro, a goldsmith, the choice of the new Doge. Paolo suggests Simon Boccanegra, who has successfully driven off African pirates from the seas round Venice. Pietro promises popular support in return for a suitable reward. Boccanegra enters and Paolo tempts him with the nomination, saying that as Doge Boccanegra would be given the hand of the woman he loves, Maria Fiesco.

She has already borne him a child but is now imprisoned by her father (the present Doge) in the Fiesco Palace. Boccanegra agrees to accept the nomination. Pietro and Paolo urge the artisans and sailors to support Boccanegra. Jacobi Fiesco emerges from the palace. His daughter, Maria, has just died.

Boccanegra is hoping to be reunited with Maria and instead is bitterly reproached by her father, who will not forgive him for the seduction. But they may be reconciled if Boccanegra will yield up his daughter for her grandfather to see. Boccanegra says the child has vanished from her foster home. Bells ring out to proclaim that Boccanegra is now Doge.

Twenty-five years pass. Boccanegra is still in power but Fiesco, under the name of Andrea, is conspiring against him. In the garden of the Grimaldi Palace, Amelia meets her lover, Gabriele Adorno. She has been brought up by the Grimaldi family (although Count Grimaldi has been banished) and regards Andrea as her guardian.

Pietro now introduces Boccanegra, who wants her to marry Paolo. She asks her lover, Gabriele, to hurry and find Andrea in order to get his consent to their marriage. But Andrea (Fiesco) tells Gabriele that Amelia is not a Grimaldi but of unknown humble stock; she was substituted for the count's dead child in order to save the family fortunes from confiscation by the Doge. Even so, Fiesco gives his permission for Gabriele and Amelia to marry.

The sound of trumpets heralds the arrival of Boccanegra and, alone with Amelia, he hands her a pardon for her 'father', Count Grimaldi. She tells him that she has a lover and does not wish to marry the greedy Paolo, who seeks the Grimaldi fortune. She further explains that she is not a Grimaldi but an orphan, and Boccanegra suddenly realizes that he has found his long-lost daughter, this being confirmed when they compare pictures of her mother. They are mutually delighted and Amelia leaves. Paolo now enters and Boccanegra tells him that he cannot marry Amelia. So Paolo arranges with Pietro to abduct her.

In council, Boccanegra receives an envoy from Tartary seeking peace with Venice. Shouts are now heard from outside the council chamber, and it is obvious that Gabriele is being attacked by the crowd. Paolo is about to leave but the Doge orders the doors to be guarded and sends a herald to proclaim that he awaits the people. More subdued, the crowd enters the chamber, demanding the death of Gabriele.

It transpires that he has killed Pietro, having caught him abducting Amelia. He believes Boccanegra was behind the kidnapping and tries to attack him. Amelia enters and throws herself between the two men, identifying Paolo as the man responsible. Gabriele gives up his sword to Boccanegra, who says he must be imprisoned overnight until the matter is resolved. The Doge vehemently demands that Paolo, as an officer of state, should discover the name of the culprit. Paolo goes off in fear as the demand is taken up by the crowd, who curse the miscreant.

Paolo is put under guard in the Doge's palace. He sends for Andrea and reveals that he is well aware that he is really Fiesco and he offers his support against the Doge, if in return he can marry Amelia. Fiesco refuses. Paolo now pours a slow poison into a glass of wine intended for Boccanegra. Gabriele enters and Paolo convinces him that Amelia is Boccanegra's mistress. Gabriele is insanely jealous.

Amelia is now living with Boccanegra (as his daughter, not his mistress) but she cannot yet tell Gabriele about this new relationship, only assure him that she is faithful to him. Boccanegra now enters, and Gabriele (with murder in his heart) hides. The Doge is upset to hear that his daughter loves Gabriele, for his family, the Adornos, have been plotting against him. As his daughter leaves, he drinks the poisoned wine and wonders whether he can be reconciled with Gabriele.

Gabriele returns, finds him unconscious and is about to kill him when Amelia enters and intervenes. Boccanegra awakens and tells Gabriele to strike the mortal blow, suggesting that by stealing his daughter Gabriele will surely avenge his father's death. Gabriele remorsefully begs Amelia's forgiveness. From outside can be heard the clamour of a crowd seeking to overthrow Boccanegra. Gabriele declares his loyalty to the Doge and says he will try to sway the crowd. Boccanegra is reconciled to the match between Gabriele and his daughter.

The revolt is over. Fiesco is free but Paolo is under sentence of death. He reveals to Fiesco that he has poisoned Boccanegra. The wedding of Gabriele and Amelia is being celebrated. Boccanegra now begins to fail, the poison taking effect. Fiesco steps forward and reveals his true identity and is told by Boccanegra that Amelia is his granddaughter. The two men are reconciled, but Fiesco sadly reveals that Boccanegra is doomed.

Amelia and Gabriele enter, and she too learns of the identity of Fiesco and her true relationship with him. But their joy is marred by the approaching death of Boccanegra. As he dies he decrees that Gabriele shall be his successor and, with Fiesco's support, Gabriele duly becomes the Doge-elect as Boccanegra dies.

Abbado's 1977 recording of *Simon Boccanegra*, directly reflecting the superb production which the La Scala company brought to London at the time, is one of the most beautiful Verdi sets ever made, and the virtual background silence of the CDs enhances the warmth and beauty of the sound, the orchestra fresh and glowing in ambient warmth, the voices vivid and the perspectives always believable. From this one can appreciate not just the vigour of the composer's imagination but the finesse of the colouring, instrumental as well as vocal. Under Abbado the playing of the orchestra is brilliantly incisive as well as refined, so that the drama is underlined by extra sharpness of focus.

The cursing of Paolo after the great Council Chamber scene makes the scalp prickle, with the chorus muttering in horror and the bass clarinet adding a sinister comment, here beautifully moulded. Cappuccilli, always intelligent, gives a far more intense and illuminating performance than the one he recorded for RCA earlier in his career. He may not match Gobbi in range of colour and detail, but he too gives focus to the performance; and Ghiaurov as Fiesco sings beautifully too, though again not as characterfully as Christoff on the deleted EMI set. Freni as Maria Boccanegra sings with freshness and clarity, while Van Dam is an impressive Paolo. With electrically intense choral singing too, this is a set to out-shine even Abbado's superb *Macbeth* with the same company. The libretto is clear, if in small print.

Tito Gobbi's portrait of the tragic Doge of Genoa is one of his greatest on record and emerges all the more impressively, when it is set against equally memorable performances by Boris Christoff as Fiesco and Victoria de los Angeles as Amelia. The Recognition scene between father and daughter has never been done more movingly on record; nor has the great ensemble, which crowns the Council Chamber scene, been so powerfully and movingly presented, and that without the help of stereo recording. Unfortunately there are some minor statutory cuts in the text. The transfer is full and immediate, giving a vivid sense of presence to the voices, though tape-hiss is on the high side.

The glory of Solti's set is the singing of Dame Kiri Te Kanawa as Amelia, a beautiful, touching performance. The freedom and absence of strain in the voice go with an almost Straussian quality in her characterization, with the widest dynamic and expressive range. Giacomo Aragall makes a strong, unforced Gabriele, but the others are less distinguished. As a cast, this line-up hardly matches that of Abbado on the rival DG set. That was also recorded with forces from La Scala, Milan, but in conjunction with a celebrated stage production. Leo Nucci is most disappointing, with the voice showing signs of wear, not nearly steady enough. He sings powerfully, but Boccanegra's solo in the great Council Chamber scene finds the voice spreading.

Burchuladze also is surprisingly less steady than usual, and Paolo Coni as Paolo is capable but undistinguished. What also makes this a less compelling reading compared with the DG is Solti's obsession with observing the metronome markings in the score very precisely, laudable in theory but often questionable in practice; so the great Recognition scene between Boccanegra and his daughter is powerfully dramatic at a speed far faster than usual, but it lacks tenderness and fails to convey the joy of recognition, which Abbado finds so movingly. The sound of the DG analogue version is preferable, though less wide-ranging, with the voices more realistically focused.

Gavazzeni's version cannot compare with the Abbado set on DG whether in conducting, singing or recorded sound. On paper the cast seems very strong but, except for Plácido Domingo, magnificent as Gabriele, they all bring disappointments, with Cappuccilli surprisingly coarse in the name-part, not helped by Gavazzeni's unimaginative, often rushed direction. In the digital transfer the sound is rough, too.

Simon Boccanegra: highlights.
**Withdrawn: ** ** Hung. Dig. HCD 12611 [id.]. Veronika Kincses, János B. Nagy, Lajos Miller, József Gregor, Hungarian State Op. Ch. & O, Patanè.

Though the complete set from which these excerpts are taken (LP only) is a non-starter compared with Abbado's masterly DG version, this makes a useful collection on CD, bringing together some of the finest passages of a still-undervalued masterpiece. Lajos Miller as Boccanegra gives the only performance of real stature, strong and expressive if not always smooth of tone; and the admirable bass, József Gregor, sings Fiesco. Disappointing singing from soprano and tenor, but excellent recording.

Stiffelio (complete).
(M) *** Ph. 422 432-2 (2) [id.]. V. ORF Ch. & SO, Gardelli.
Stiffelio (José Carreras), Lina (Sylvia Sass), Stankar (Matteo Manuguerra), Jorg (Wladimiro Ganzarolli).

Coming just before the great trio of masterpieces, *Rigoletto*, *Il Trovatore* and *La Traviata*, *Stiffelio* was a total failure at its first performance in 1850. The score was in effect destroyed in order to make *Aroldo*, six years later, and only through the discovery of two copyists' scores in the 1960s was a revival made possible.

The plot is set in Austria and concerns Stiffelio, leader of a once-persecuted Protestant sect, who returns to his old parish after a long absence. During this time his wife, Lina, has had an involvement with Raffaele, a young adventurer. Stiffelio's suspicions are soon aroused, as have been those of Lina's father, Stankar.

The latter resolves to shoot himself rather than live in the shameful knowledge of his daughter's infidelity, but Raffaele's arrival and Stiffelio's decision to divorce Lina prompt him to kill his daughter's seducer. The opera ends with Stiffelio publicly forgiving his wife by reading the story of the woman taken in adultery.

Though it lacks some of the beauties of *Aroldo*, *Stiffelio* is still a sharper, more telling work, as the stage production at Covent Garden demonstrated. That is largely because of the originality of the relationships and the superb final scene in which Stiffelio reads from the pulpit the parable of the woman taken in adultery. Gardelli directs a fresh performance, at times less lively than Queler's of *Aroldo* but with more consistent singing, notably from Carreras and Manuguerra. First-rate recording from Philips, typical of this fine series.

La Traviata (complete).
*** Decca Dig. 430 491-2; *430 491-4* (2) [id.]. L. Op. Ch., Nat. PO, Bonynge.
   Violetta (Joan Sutherland), Alfredo (Luciano Pavarotti), Germont (Matteo Manuguerra).
*** Teldec/Warner Dig. 9031 76348-2 (2) [id.]. Amb. S., LSO, Rizzi.
   Violetta (Edita Gruberová), Alfredo (Neil Shicoff), Germont (Giorgio Zancanaro)
**(*) EMI Dig. CDS7 47538-8 (2) [Ang. CDC 47538]. Amb. Op. Ch., Philh. O, Muti.
   Violetta (Renata Scotto), Alfredo (Alfredo Kraus), Germont (Renato Bruson).
(B) **(*) CfP CD-CFP 4450; *TC-CFP 4450* (2). Rome Op. Ch. & O, Serafin.
   Violetta (Victoria De los Angeles), Alfredo (Carlo Del Monte), Germont (Mario Sereni).
**(*) DG 415 132-2 (2) [id.]. Bav. State Op. Ch. & O, Carlos Kleiber.
   Violetta (Ileana Cotrubas), Alfredo (Plácido Domingo), Germont (Sherrill Milnes).
(M) **(*) Decca 411 877-2 (2) [id.]. Ch. & O of Maggio Musicale Fiorentino, Pritchard.
   Violetta (Joan Sutherland), Alfredo (Carlo Bergonzi), Germont (Robert Merrill).
** DG Dig. 435 797-2 (2) [id.]. Met. Op. Ch. & O, Levine.
   Violetta (Cheryl Studer), Alfredo (Luciano Pavarotti), Germont (Juan Pons).
** BMG/RCA RD 86180 (2) [6180-2-RC]. RCA Italiana Op. Ch. & O, Prêtre.
   Violetta (Montserrat Caballé), Alfredo (Carlo Bergonzi), Germont (Sherrill Milnes).
(M) (*(**)) EMI mono CMS7 63628-2 (2) [Ang. CDMB 63628]. La Scala Ch. & O, Giulini.
   Violetta (Maria Callas), Alfredo (Giuseppe Di Stefano), Germont (Ettore Bastianini).
(**) EMI mono CDS7 49187-8 (2) [Ang. CDCD 49187]. Ch. & O of San Carlos Op., Lisbon, Ghione.
   Violetta (Maria Callas), Alfredo (Alfredo Kraus), Germont (Mario Sereni).
(BB) *(*) Naxos 8.660011/2 (2) [id.]. Ch. & Slovak RSO (Bratislava), Rahbari.
   Violetta (Monika Krause), Alfredo (Yordi Ramiro), Germont (Georg Tichy).
(M) * Decca 430 250-2 (2) [id.]. St Celia Ac., Rome, Ch. & O, Molinari-Pradelli.
   Violetta (Renata Tebaldi), Alfredo (Gianni Poggi), Germont (Aldo Protti).

La Traviata, based on the celebrated play, *La Dame aux Camélias*, by Alexandre Dumas *fils*, established Verdi in a contemporary style of music drama. Its plot now seems more 'dated' than any of his other operas, but Verdi's lyrical music more than redeems its sentimentality, so that the doubtful motivation of its male characters, dictated more by the demands of society than by their own deeper feelings, becomes submerged in the opera's powerful atmosphere, and at the close there is a feeling of real tragedy.

The story begins in the house of Violetta Valéry, a courtesan. She welcomes Flora and Baron Douphol, an old admirer. Gastone, another friend, brings in Alfredo Germont, introducing him to her as someone who has admired her for a long time. Dancing begins but Violetta starts to cough; she finds Alfredo by her side, expressing great concern. He tells her that he has loved her for a year. She gives him a camellia, saying that when it withers he may come back to see her once more. The guests leave and Violetta remembers Alfredo with tenderness (*E strano . . . Ah, fors'è lui*) and then realizes she must return to the social whirl (*Sempre libera*).

Alfredo wins her over to an apparently permanent relationship with him, and they are settled in a country villa near Paris. A letter arrives from her friend Flora, inviting her to a party, but she is no longer interested in that kind of frivolity. Violetta's maid tells Alfredo that, on the instructions of her mistress, she has been selling off Violetta's more valuable possessions to maintain their affluent lifestyle. Alfredo sets off for Paris at once to make a personal contribution to their finances.

Giorgio Germont, Alfredo's father, now arrives and denounces Violetta for squandering his son's money, but then he finds he is mistaken. Instead, he asks her to make a sacrifice: his daughter, innocent and in love, faces estrangement from her fiancée because of Alfredo's 'profligate' behaviour. He asks Violetta to leave her lover and to give the impression she no longer cares enough for him to remain faithful. At first Violetta refuses his request but then sadly agrees. Germont is moved by her generosity of spirit.

When he has gone, she writes two letters, one to Flora, accepting the party invitation after all, and one to Alfredo, which she has not quite finished when he returns. He announces that his father is expected. Without mentioning that she has already seen Germont *père* she embraces her lover ardently, then slips away. Alfredo reads her note, which says she is leaving him without giving any explanation. His father now re-enters to take him home (*Di Provenza il mar*). Alfredo immediately suspects that Violetta has returned to Douphol and he resolves to go to Flora's party and take his revenge.

We now move to the ballroom in Flora's house where the party is in full swing. Violetta enters on Baron Douphol's arm. Alfredo goes to the gaming table and wins a considerable sum from the baron. The upset Violetta tries to persuade him to withdraw, but he will agree only if she will accompany him. Her enigmatic refusal mentions a promise to someone whom she cannot name. When asked if she loves this man, poor Violetta is really put on the spot and now has to answer in the affirmative. Alfredo, not realizing she is referring to Germont *père*, insults her and throws his winnings at her feet. All this has been witnessed by Alfredo's father. Violetta declares that her love for Alfredo has dictated her behaviour. Germont senior denounces his son's conduct, and the repentant Alfredo is challenged to a duel by the baron.

Violetta now lives alone with her faithful Annina. She is in the final stages of consumption and there is little money left. The doctor reassures her but tells Annina that Violetta has only a few hours to live. A letter comes from Alfredo's father to gladden her heart: he has told Alfredo of her sacrifice. The duel had produced no ill results, but Alfredo went abroad immediately afterwards. He is now coming to see her. She has a momentary relapse (*Addio del passato*) and revellers are heard in the streets, for it is the time of the carnival.

Alfredo comes in and the lovers embrace. He speaks tenderly of taking her away with him (*Parigi, o cara*) but Violetta's strength is ebbing away. Germont *père*, Annina and the doctor arrive. Violetta gives Alfredo a miniature portrait, asking him to give it to the woman he eventually marries. Suddenly she feels a surge of life, as she relives the first moments of their love together, but her last remaining strength has been used up and she dies in Alfredo's arms.

Sutherland's second recording of the role of Violetta has a breadth and exuberance beyond her achievement in her earlier version of 1963, conducted by John Pritchard. This *Traviata* is dominated by the grand lady that Sutherland makes her. Some of the supremely tender moments of her earlier recording – *Ah dite alla giovine* in the Act II duet with Germont, for example – are more straightforward this time, but the mooning manner is dispelled, the words are clearer, and the richness and command of the singing put this among the very finest of Sutherland's later recordings. Pavarotti too, though he overemphasizes *De' miei bollenti spiriti*, sings with splendid panache as Alfredo. Manuguerra as Germont lacks something in authority, but the firmness and clarity are splendid. Bonynge's conducting is finely sprung, the style direct, the speeds often spacious in lyrical music, generally undistracting. The digital recording is outstandingly vivid and beautifully balanced.

The big success of the Teldec set, consistently refined in its treatment of Verdian rhythms and textures, is the conducting of Carlo Rizzi in his first major opera recording, confirming Welsh National Opera's wisdom in appointing him music director. He draws subtle, refined playing from the LSO, which in turn brings refined singing from a well-matched cast. Giorgio Zancanaro is a characterful Germont, giving depth of feeling to the first scene of Act II up to *Di Provenza il mar*. Though Edita Gruberová's bright soprano acquires an unevenness under pressure, she is freshly expressive and, increasingly through the opera up to the great challenge of the Death scene, produces the most delicate pianissimos, with phrasing and tone exquisitely shaded. She may not match the finest Violettas of the past, and the tenor, Neil Shicoff, sings with markedly less finesse than the other principals, but among the current versions of this opera there is no modern digital version to rival it.

Muti as a Verdi interpreter believes in clearing away performance traditions not sanctioned in the score, so cadential top notes and extra decorations are ruthlessly eliminated; Muti, with no concern for tradition, insists on speeds, generally fast, for which he quotes the score as authority. Thus, at the start of the Act I party music, he is even faster than Toscanini, but the result is dazzling; and when he needs to give sympathetic support to his soloists, above all in the great Act II duet between Violetta and Germont, there is no lack of tenderness. Overall, it is an intensely compelling account, using the complete text (like Bonynge), and it gains from having three Italy-based principals.

Scotto and Kraus have long been among the most sensitive and perceptive interpreters of these roles, and so they are here; with bright digital recording, however, it is obvious that these voices are no longer young, with Scotto's soprano spreading above the stave and Kraus's tenor often sounding thin. Scotto gives a view of Violetta which, even amid the gaiety of Act I, points forward to tragedy, with wonderful expansion in *Ah fors'è lui* on the phrase *Ah quell'amor*. Kraus takes *De' miei bollenti spiriti* slowly, but effectively so, with plenty of extra expression. Bruson makes a fine, forthright Germont, though it does not add to dramatic conviction that his is the youngest voice. Small parts are well taken and the stage picture is vivid. The breadth and range of sound, as well as the firm placing of instruments and voices, are the more present on CD, with the pleasant reverberation clarified.

Even when Victoria de los Angeles made this EMI recording in the late 1950s, the role of Violetta lay rather high for her voice. Nevertheless it drew from her much beautiful singing, not least in the coloratura display at the end of Act I which, though it may lack easily ringing top notes, has delightful sparkle and flexibility. As to the characterization, De los Angeles was a far more sympathetically tender heroine than is common; though neither the tenor nor the baritone begins to match her in artistry, their performances are both sympathetic and feeling, thanks in part to the masterly conducting of Serafin. All the traditional cuts are made, not just the second stanzas. The CD transfer is vivid and clear, with plenty of atmosphere; only the sound of the violins betrays the age of the recording, and that not seriously; the choral focus is remarkably good. Reissued at bargain price, this is worth any collector's money, though only a synopsis is provided.

For many, Cotrubas makes an ideal heroine in this opera; what is disappointing in the DG recording is that the microphone-placing exaggerates technical flaws, so that not only is her breathing too often audible, but her habit of separating coloratura with intrusive aitches is also underlined, and the vibrato becomes too obvious at times. Such is her magic that some will forgive the faults, for her characterization combines strength with vulnerability. But Carlos Kleiber's direction is equally controversial, with more than a hint of Toscanini-like rigidity in the party music, and an occasionally uncomfortable insistence on discipline. The characterful contributions of Domingo and Milnes are both excellent. The recording suggests over-reliance on multi-channel techniques, and the closeness of the microphone-placing, spotlighting not only the soloists but members of the orchestra, is the more apparent on CD, underlining the fierce side of Kleiber's conducting, contrasting strongly with his ripely romantic side.

Opinions on Sutherland's earlier recording of *La Traviata* are sharply divided, and this characteristic performance from her will not win over her determined critics. It is true that her diction is poor, but it is also true that she has rarely sung with such deep feeling on record as in the final scene. The *Addio del passato* (both stanzas included and sung with an unexpected lilt) merely provides a beginning, for the duet with Bergonzi is most winning and the final death scene, *Se una pudica vergine*, is overwhelmingly beautiful. This is not a sparkling Violetta, true, but it is more perfect vocally than almost any other in a complete set. Bergonzi is an attractive Alfredo and Merrill an efficient Germont. Pritchard sometimes tends to hustle things along, with too little regard for shaping Verdian phrases, but the recording quality is outstandingly good in its CD format, which comes at mid-price. However, most collectors will prefer to invest in Sutherland's later, digital set with Pavarotti which in most respects is superior to the 1963 version.

DG, relying on a superstar, Luciano Pavarotti, offers a set recorded in New York, with James Levine conducting a cast based on the Metropolitan Opera production, with Cheryl Studer as Violetta and Juan Pons as Germont. There is much to be said for the beefy energy of Levine in this score, but the recorded sound is relatively coarse, and Pavarotti, for all his detailed feeling for words, does not match his previous recording for Decca opposite Joan Sutherland. Studer too is more exaggerated in expression than she usually is, and Juan Pons is ill-cast as Germont, singing with none of the paternal weight needed.

Caballé too gives a wonderfully posed and pure account of Violetta's music, but this was one of her earlier complete-opera sets, and she still had to learn how to project depth of emotion. Vocally, with such fine technicians as Bergonzi and Milnes as her colleagues, this set is consistently satisfying, but it does not add up as a dramatic experience. One is rarely moved, and that is also partly the fault of the conductor, Georges Prêtre, a degree too detached for Verdi. Good, vivid recording and an absolutely complete text (as also in the Sutherland versions).

Callas's version with Giulini comes into rivalry with another live recording of her in this role, also from EMI but recorded in Lisbon and conducted by Ghione. This La Scala performance was recorded in 1955, three years before the other, when the voice was fresher. In the presence of a great conductor, one who often challenged her with unusually slow speeds, Callas responded with even greater depth of expression. There is no more vividly dramatic a performance on record than this, unmatchable in conveying Violetta's agony; sadly, the sound, always limited, grows crumbly towards the end. It is sad too that Bastianini sings so lumpishly as Germont *père*, even in the great duet of Act II, while Di Stefano also fails to match his partner in the supreme test of the final scene. The transfer is fair, though in places it sounds as though an echo-chamber has been used.

Recorded at a live performance in March 1958, Callas's Lisbon-made version is uniquely valuable in spite of very rough sound. Here, far more than in her earlier, Cetra recording of this opera, one can appreciate the intensity which made this one of her supreme roles, with exquisite detail conveying fleeting emotions even in such an obvious passage as the *Brindisi*. Kraus is a fresh, stylish Alfredo, Sereni a positive Germont, more characterful than in the EMI set with De los Angeles. For Callas admirers – who will not object to the occasional ugliness – it is an essential set. However, the extraneous noises in this live recording – like the prompter's constant groaning – as well as the tape background and the crumbling at climaxes, are made all the clearer on CD; what matters is the vivid sense of presence, with Callas at her most vibrant. A unique historical document.

Like the parallel recording of *Rigoletto*, the Naxos version of *La Traviata* is often underpowered and lacks bite, but it offers an attractive performance from Monika Krause as Violetta. The big test of *Ah dite alla giovine* in her duet with Germont in Act II brings an exquisitely shaded pianissimo, and her *Addio del passato* in Act III is no less touching for being taken at a genuine andante, with less rhythmic freedom than usual. As in *Rigoletto*, Yordy Ramiro sounds over-parted as Alfredo, with a flutter in the voice occasionally becoming intrusive, but he generally sings cleanly. The Germont of Georg Tichy is among the most prosaic on disc, wooden and unresponsive even to Krause's most exquisite singing. The sound, as in other Bratislava recordings, is clear and atmospheric. As in other Naxos operas, copious tracking is linked to a detailed synopsis and full Italian text.

Recorded in 1954, the Tebaldi version of *La Traviata* emerges on CD with the benefit of stereo, a very early example and one which certainly helps to give body to the voices. Though Violetta was not Tebaldi's ideal role – the coloratura of Act I is negotiated accurately rather than with joy – there is much superb singing from her here. The delicacy of her phrasing is a delight, bringing a most tender portrait, though the *Addio del passato* brings a suspicion of intrusive aitches. Her refinement contrasts with the coarseness of Gianni Poggi as Alfredo and the lack of imagination of Aldo Protti as Germont. Yet this is well worth hearing for Tebaldi in her early prime.

La Traviata: highlights.
*** Decca Dig. 400 057-2 [id.] (from above recording with Sutherland, Pavarotti, Manuguerra; cond. Bonynge).
(M) *** EMI CDM7 63088-2; *EG 763088-4* (from above recording with Scotto, Kraus, Bruson; cond. Muti).
(M) **(*) DG 435 417-2; *435 417-4* [id.] (from above recording with Cotrubas, Domingo, Milnes; cond. Carlos Kleiber).

The Decca highlights disc was the first operatic issue on compact disc, and it pointed forward to the extra immediacy possible with the new medium. One item is omitted compared with the LP – Germont's *Di Provenza* – but it still offers just on an hour of music. Pavarotti is less individual than Sutherland but is well placed, and the whole selection brings highly enjoyable performances.

Muti's set is at full price and it isn't a first choice, so many will be glad to have this 61-minute disc or tape of highlights, including both the Act I and Act III *Preludes* and a well-balanced selection from each of the three Acts, with most of the key numbers included.

Carlos Kleiber's set is flawed in several ways – see above – so a highlights disc seems an ideal way to approach it. It comes as part of DG's 'Domingo Edition', and the hour-long selection covers most of the key passages.

La Traviata (complete, in English).
(M) **(*) EMI CMS7 63072-2 (2). ENO Ch. & O, Mackerras.
Violetta (Valerie Masterson), Alfredo (John Brecknock), Germont (Christian Du Plessis).

The latterday economics of the gramophone have allowed few complete opera recordings in English, and this exceptional set, like the *Ring* cycle under Reginald Goodall, was recorded with the help of the Peter Moores Foundation. Unlike the *Ring* cycle, however, it is a studio performance, and it is beautifully balanced and refined in detail. Mackerras directs a vigorous, colourful reading which brings out the drama, and Valerie Masterson is given a belated chance to shine on disc. The voice is beautifully – if not always very characterfully – caught, and John Brecknock makes a fine Alfredo, most effective in the final scene. Christian Du Plessis's baritone is less suitable for recording. The conviction of the whole enterprise is infectious. Clear as most of the words are, it is good that an English libretto is included; but be warned, Verdi in English has a way of sounding on record rather like Gilbert and Sullivan.

Il Trovatore (complete).
⊛ *** BMG/RCA RD 86194 (2) [6194-2-RC]. Amb. Op. Ch., New Philh. O, Mehta.
   Manrico (Plácido Domingo), Leonora (Leontyne Price), Conte di Luna (Sherrill Milnes), Azucena (Fiorenza Cossotto), Ferrando (Bonaldo Giaiotti).
*** DG Dig. 423 858-2 (2) [id.]. Ch. & O of St Cecilia Ac., Rome, Giulini.
   Manrico (Plácido Domingo), Leonora (Rosalind Plowright), Conte di Luna (Giorgio Zancanaro), Azucena (Brigitte Fassbaender), Ferrando (Evgeny Nesterenko).
(M) (***) EMI CDS7 49347-2 (2) [Ang. CDCB 49347]. La Scala, Milan, Ch. & O, Karajan.
   Manrico (Giuseppe Di Stefano), Leonora (Maria Callas), Conte di Luna (Rolando Panerai), Azucena (Fedora Barbieri), Ferrando (Nicola Zaccaria).
(M) (***) BMG/RCA mono GD 86643 (2) [Victrola 6643-2-RG]. Robert Shaw Chorale, RCA Victor O, Cellini.
   Manrico (Jussi Bjoerling), Leonora (Zinka Milanov), Conte di Luna (Leonard Warren), Azucena (Fedora Barbieri), Ferrando (Nicola Moscona).
(M) **(*) EMI CMS7 69311-2 [id.]. German Op., Berlin, Ch., BPO, Karajan.
   Manrico (Franco Bonisolli), Leonora (Leontyne Price), Conte di Luna (Piero Cappuccilli), Azucena (Elena Obraztsova), Ferrando (Ruggero Raimondi).
** Decca 417 137-2 (3) [id.]. L. Op. Ch., Nat. PO, Bonynge.
   Manrico (Luciano Pavarotti), Leonora (Joan Sutherland), Conte di Luna (Ingvar Wixell), Azucena (Marilyn Horne), Ferrando (Nicolai Ghiaurov).
Withdrawn: (M) ** EMI CMS7 63640-2 (2) [Ang. CDMB 63640]. Rome Op. Ch. & O, Schippers.
   Manrico (Franco Corelli), Leonora (Gabriella Tucci), Conte di Luna (Robert Merrill), Azucena (Giulietta Simionato), Ferrando (Ferruccio Mazzoli).
(M) ** Ph. Dig. 426 557-2 (2) [id.]. ROHCG Ch. & O, C. Davis.
   Manrico (José Carreras), Leonora (Katia Ricciarelli), Conte di Luna (Yuri Mazurok), Azucena (Stefania Toczyska), Ferrando (Robert Lloyd).

Il Trovatore ('The troubadour') used to be thought of as Verdi's most popular opera, and it says a good deal for developing public taste that its popularity has been – to a considerable extent – overtaken by some of the later masterpieces. The story, which takes place in fifteenth-century Spain, is complex but exceptionally dramatic, with bold, red-blooded music to match, full of stirring arias, duets and two of the most famous of all operatic choruses. For all its lack of subtlety of characterization, one easily comes under its spell.

As the curtain rises, Ferrando, captain of the guard at Count Luna's castle, cautions his men to keep their eyes open while their master is absent. The count loves Leonora, a lady-in-waiting at the court of Aragon, and is jealously seeking a mysterious troubadour, heard serenading his lady, who is clearly his rival.

Ferrando then tells the retainers the story of the gypsy, Azucena, which underlies the subsequent course of events in the opera. The count's father had two sons. An old gypsy supposedly bewitched the younger of the pair in his cradle, whereupon the old count had her burned to death at the stake. In revenge, the gypsy's daughter, Azucena, abducted the child and apparently threw it into the flames of her mother's pyre, to die beside her.

In the gardens of the Aragon palace, Leonora is listening to her serenader and she confesses to her attendant, Inez, that she loves her unknown troubadour. The count also hears the song and confronts his rival, Manrico. Despite Leonora's protestations, their enmity leads to a duel. Later, Manrico, who won the duel but did not kill his adversary, is seen in the gypsy camp, supposedly the son of Azucena. The gypsies work hard and sing (the *Anvil chorus*). Later Azucena, half crazed with remorse, relates to Manrico the story of the stolen baby.

With horror in her voice, she tells him that she meant to avenge her mother by throwing the abducted infant into the flames but, so distracted was she by her need for vengeance, that by mistake she threw her own child into the fire.

Manrico now questions his own identity and tells her that he spared the count after the duel, because he had a strange feeling that he should not kill him. Azucena tries to retract her confession, then a messenger arrives saying that Leonora, believing Manrico to be dead, is to enter a convent that very evening.

Outside the convent the count, attended by Ferrando, makes clear his love for Leonora (*Il balen*) and we learn of his plans to carry her off before she takes her vows. Manrico and his followers arrive in time to prevent the abduction.

The count and his army (singing their *Soldiers' chorus*) now lay siege to the castle to which Manrico has taken Leonora. Ferrando comes in to tell the count that Azucena has been arrested. She is questioned and is held responsible for the kidnapping of the baby long ago, but she declares herself to be Manrico's mother; and she is condemned to the stake. Inside the castle, Manrico and Leonora are about to be married.

Ruiz enters to report Azucena's capture and Manrico decides to leave Leonora and go to her rescue (*Di quella pira*). But Manrico's brave rescue attempt fails, and now he and his mother are imprisoned together, awaiting execution. Leonora arrives to attempt another rescue and, as she prays off-stage in a *Miserere*, Manrico's voice joins in the supplication. The count enters; Leonora accosts him and eventually offers to be his bride if he will free Manrico. She secretly takes poison but the count accepts her offer exultantly.

In the dungeon the demented Azucena becomes delirious and Manrico tries to bring peace to her tormented mind. They recall the background of his childhood upbringing (*Ai nostri monti*). Leonora enters to tell Manrico he is free but he repels her, guessing the reason for his reprieve. She tells him she has swallowed poison and dies in his arms. The count furiously orders Manrico to be taken outside at once and executed and, at the very moment of his death, Azucena shouts in triumph that the count has just killed his own brother.

Caruso once said of *Il Trovatore* that all it needs is 'the four greatest singers in the world'. Abounding as the opera does in great and memorable tunes, the orchestration does not find Verdi at his most refined, often emerging as a great orchestral guitar. The singers have to create the necessary breadth and beauty of tone, and the proper dramatic projection, making *Il Trovatore* difficult to bring off in the opera house, and even more so on record.

The soaring curve of Leontyne Price's rich vocal line (almost too ample for some ears) is immediately thrilling in her famous Act I aria, and it sets the style of the performance, full-blooded, the tension consistently held at the highest levels. The choral contribution is superb; the famous *Soldiers'* and *Anvil choruses* are marvellously fresh and dramatic. When *Di quella pira* comes, the orchestra opens with tremendous gusto and Domingo sings with a ringing, heroic quality worthy of Caruso himself. There are many dramatic felicities, and Sherrill Milnes is in fine voice throughout; but perhaps the highlight of the set is the opening section of Act III, when Azucena finds her way to Conte di Luna's camp. The ensuing scene with Fiorenza Cossotto is vocally and dramatically quite electrifying. It is vibrantly transferred to CD, to make one of the most thrilling of all Verdi operas on record.

In an intensely revelatory performance, one which is richly red-blooded but which transforms melodrama into a deeper experience, Giulini flouts convention at every point. The opera's white-hot inspiration comes out in the intensity of the playing and singing, but the often slow tempi and refined textures present the whole work in new and deeper detail, product of the conductor's intense study of the work afresh. Even Giulini has rarely matched this achievement among his many fine Verdi records.

More than any previous conductor on record, Giulini brings out the kinship between *Il Trovatore* and *La forza del destino*, above all in the heroine's music, in which inspired casting presents Rosalind Plowright triumphantly in her first international opera recording. Sensuous yet ethereal in *Tacea la notte*, she masterfully brings together the seemingly incompatible qualities demanded, not just sweetness and purity but brilliant coloratura, flexibility and richly dramatic bite and power.

Plácido Domingo sings Manrico as powerfully as he did in the richly satisfying Mehta set on RCA (still a safer choice), but the voice is even more heroic in an Otello-like way, only very occasionally showing strain. Giorgio Zancanaro proves a gloriously firm and rounded Conte di Luna and Evgeny Nesterenko a dark, powerful Ferrando, while Brigitte Fassbaender, singing her first Azucena, finds far greater intensity and detail than the usual roaring mezzo, matching Giulini's freshness. The recording is warm and atmospheric with a pleasant bloom on the voices, naturally balanced and not spotlit. Now on a pair of CDs, it sounds all the firmer and more vivid.

The combination of Karajan and Callas is formidably impressive. There is toughness and dramatic determination in Callas's singing, whether in the coloratura or in the dramatic passages, and this gives the heroine an unsuspected depth of character which culminates in Callas's fine singing of an aria which used often to be cut entirely – *Tu vedrai che amore in terra*, here with its first stanza alone included. Barbieri is a magnificent Azucena, Panerai a strong, incisive Count, and Di Stefano at his finest as Manrico. On CD the 1957 mono sound, though dry and unatmospheric, is one of the more vivid from La Scala at that period, with the voices given bloom as well as immediacy and with Karajan's balancing of the orchestra more clearly defined than in his later, stereo version.

Though dating from 1952, using a cut text as in the Met. production, the Cellini version brings a vivid reminder of that great opera house at a key period. It was recorded, not at the old Met., but in the Manhattan Center and, as transferred, the mono recording has plenty of body, bringing out the beauty of the voices with plenty of presence. Milanov, though at times a little raw in Leonora's coloratura, gives a glorious, commanding performance, never surpassed on record, with the voice at its fullest. Bjoerling and Warren too are in ringing voice, and Barbieri is a superb Azucena, with Cellini – rarely heard on record – proving an outstanding Verdian.

The later Karajan set with Leontyne Price promised much but proved disappointing, largely because of the thickness and strange balances of the recording, the product of multi-channel techniques exploited over-enthusiastically. So the introduction to Manrico's aria, *Di quella pira*, provides full-blooded orchestral sound but then the orchestra fades down for the entry of the tenor, who in any case is in coarse voice. In other places he sings more sensitively, but at no point does this version match that of Mehta on RCA. CD clarifies the sound but makes the flaws in the original recording all the more evident.

Bonynge in most of his opera sets has been unfailingly urgent and rhythmic, but his account of *Il Trovatore* is at an altogether lower level of intensity, with elegance rather than dramatic power the dominant quality. Nor does the role of Leonora prove very apt for Sutherland late in her career; the coloratura passages are splendid, but a hint of unsteadiness is present in too much of the rest. Pavarotti for the most part sings superbly, but he falls short, for example, in the semiquaver groups of *Di quella pira*, and, like Sutherland, Marilyn Horne as Azucena does not produce consistently firm tone. Wixell as the Count sings intelligently, but a richer tone is needed. Most recommendable in the set is the complete ballet music, more brilliantly recorded as well as better played than the rest. On CD the 1977 recording sounds even more vivid and atmospheric than before, with voices very naturally balanced against an open acoustic.

The EMI Rome set of *Il Trovatore* under Schippers is a long way short of the ideal, but Merrill's Conte di Luna is characterful and firmly sung, if sometimes ungainly. Simionato is an excellent Azucena; Tucci, though less assured than her colleagues, sings very beautifully. Corelli is at his powerful best as Manrico, a really heroic, if not always subtle, tenor. His *Di quella pira* displays rather crude histrionics, but its gutsiness is welcome when Schippers' conducting is inclined to be rigid, somewhat preventing the temperature from rising; otherwise Schippers' incisiveness is compelling in an atmospheric recording that is characteristic of the Rome Opera House.

Sir Colin Davis offers a fresh and direct, slightly understated reading. The refinement of the digital recording makes for a wide, clean separation but, with the backward placing of the orchestra, the result does not have the dramatic impact of the Mehta RCA version. The *Anvil chorus* sounds rather clinical and other important numbers lack the necessary swagger. Ricciarelli's Leonora is most moving, conveying an element of vulnerability in the character, but Carreras lacks the full confidence of a natural Manrico. He is less effective in the big, extrovert moments, best in such inward-looking numbers as *Ah si ben mio*. Toczyska's voice is presented rather grittily in the role of Azucena. Mazurok similarly is not flattered by the microphones but, with clean, refined ensemble, this emerges as the opposite of a hackneyed opera.

Il Trovatore: highlights.
(M) *** DG Dig. 435 418-2; *435 418-4* [id.] (from above recording with Domingo, Plowright, Fassbaender; cond. Giulini).
(M) (***) BMG/RCA mono GD 60191 [60191-2-RG] (from above recording with Bjoerling, Milanov, Barbieri; cond. Cellini).
(M) **(*) Decca 421 310-2 [id.] (from above recording with Pavarotti, Sutherland, Horne; cond. Bonynge).

Those who have the earlier RCA set in which Domingo participated should consider these highlights from Giulini's unconventional but highly compelling performance, especially as the CD is offered at mid-price (as part of the DG 'Domingo Edition'). It is generous at 67 minutes, and Domingo is again splendid, as are his excellent supporting cast.

For many, a highlights CD will be the ideal way to approach the outstanding 1952 recording by Cellini, much admired in its day. Two dozen excerpts (68 minutes) span the opera very effectively.

The selection from Bonynge's Decca set is especially valuable as a reminder of Sutherland's

Leonora. Horne is represented by her powerful *Stride la vampa*, Wixell by an undernourished *Il balen*. Excellent recording.

Il Trovatore: highlights (sung in English).
(B) ** CfP CD-CFP 4604; *TC-CFP 4604*. Elizabeth Fretwell, Patricia Johnson, Charles Craig, Peter Glossop, Donald McIntyre, Rita Hunter, Sadler's Wells Op. Ch. & O, Michael Moores.

This potted version of *Il Trovatore* in English dates from 1962. It is vividly recorded, the words are admirably clear and there is plenty of drama in the presentation. However, this is not as successful as the companion selection from Puccini's *Madame Butterfly*. Away from the stage, some of the singing does not stand up too well, although Elizabeth Fretwell (as Leonora) is undoubtedly both strong and stylish, even if *Tacea la notte* is rather shaky. Charles Craig once again is as ringing and well-controlled a tenor as you will find anywhere. Patricia Johnson and Peter Glossop are not quite up to their stage form, but their singing has plenty of conviction and, in scenes like the *Miserere* and the finale to the Convent scene, the presence and depth of the recording are persuasive.

I vespri siciliani (complete).
** BMG/RCA RD 80370 (3) [0370-2-RC]. Alldis Ch., New Philh. O, Levine.
    Elena (Martina Arroyo), Arrigo (Plácido Domingo), Monforte (Sherrill Milnes), Procida (Ruggero Raimondi), Ninetta (Maria Ewing).
** EMI CDS7 54043-2 (3) [Ang. CDCC 54043]; *EX 754043-4*. Ch. & O of La Scala, Milan, Muti.
    Elena (Cheryl Studer), Arrigo (Chris Merritt), Monforte (Giorgio Zancanaro), Procida (Ferruccio Furlanetto), Ninetta (Gloria Banditelli).

I vespri siciliani is a cumbersome, five-Act piece, written for Paris, and, for all the rousing ensembles and elaborate spectacle, not to mention the big half-hour ballet in Act III, it generally lacks the melodic individuality which marks even the lesser-known Verdi operas. Yet it contains many riches over its span of nearly 3½ hours. Epic in scale to please the Parisian audiences, it is a transitional piece, following the firmly confident middle-period Verdi of *Rigoletto*, *Trovatore* and *Traviata*, but not quite achieving the dramatic intensity and musical richness of later operas. The work's great merit is not so much its grandeur as its searching portrayal of the father–son relationship between de Montfort (Monforte), the tyrannical governor of Sicily, and Arrigo, the son he has never known.

As the opera opens, a detachment of French troops is occupying the great square at Palermo. Some are drinking, others are warily watching the Sicilians eyeing them from a distance. The French bemoan their enforced absence from France; the Sicilians express their hatred of the oppressors.

A French officer, de Béthune, discusses with two friends the attitude occupying troops should display towards the women. Elena, the sister of Frederick of Austria, crosses the square. She has been praying for her brother, who was executed for his zealous patriotism, at the orders of Guy de Montfort, the new French Governor of Sicily. A drunken soldier orders her to sing to entertain the French troops.

She obeys, but her voice and words soon become inflammatory, galvanizing the downcast Sicilians. They rush at the French, but the disturbance is quelled by the appearance of the governor, alone and unarmed, at the door of his palace.

The square becomes deserted except for de Montfort and Elena, supported by her attendants. Arrigo rushes in, saying he has been freed from prison. He, too, has openly expressed his patriotic sentiments. De Montfort, feeling a curious sympathy with the young rebel, offers him fame and success in the service of the French but orders him to dissociate himself from Elena. Arrigo spurns his offer and walks into Elena's palace in defiance.

In a valley outside the city. Giovanni da Procida, a banished Sicilian doctor, is stirring up resistance. He salutes his beloved land and calls on the guerrillas to advance with him and deliver Sicily from the French. Elena and Arrigo arrive and he enrols Arrigo as co-leader of the revolt then departs to organize the insurrection. Arrigo now declares his love for Elena and swears to avenge the death of her brother. She demands that he kill the governor as an act of patriotic vengeance. Arrigo is invited to a feast given by the governor. He refuses the invitation, and is arrested.

De Montfort reflects on the injustice he meted out to the mother of his son. She fled from his embrace and brought her child up to hate his father as the oppressor of the Sicilians. From her deathbed she has written to say that the son he has not seen for 18 years is now his sworn enemy. Arrigo is brought in and, confronted by his father, cannot come to terms with the fact that he is related to this man, whom he regards as the enemy of his country. Tearing himself away from the proffered embrace, he escapes.

In the ballroom, a ballet is being performed to entertain de Montfort's guests. Masked figures, with silk ribbons flowing from their cloaks, are in fact Sicilian conspirators, led by Elena and Procida. Arrigo now has a difficult choice: to allow his father to be assassinated, or to betray his friends. He tries to warn de Montfort, but his father refuses to leave the ball. Procida moves forward to kill the governor, but Arrigo steps between the two men and prevents the murder. The conspirators are arrested and the Sicilians denounce Arrigo's treachery.

Arrigo now visits Elena in prison and tells her of his relationship with de Montfort. She understands his situation and admits that her greatest sorrow was the thought that her lover was a traitor. De Montfort orders preparations for a double execution, of Procida and Elena, and Arrigo demands that he die with them.

De Montfort then offers to grant a pardon if Arrigo will address him as father, but Elena and Procida consider that death is preferable to dishonour. The victims are taken to the block and the awaiting headsman's axe. Arrigo believes he has no choice but to accede to his father's dearest wish; the pardon is granted, and the betrothal is announced between Elena and Arrigo.

In the garden of the governor's palace Elena, her wedding about to be celebrated, is joined by Procida, still plotting insurrection. He tells her that the wedding bells will be the signal for the Sicilians to massacre the French.

Elena now astonishes Arrigo by refusing to carry on with the wedding. But de Montfort enters and, knowing nothing of the plot, sweeps aside Elena's objections. The wedding bells chime and the Sicilians rush to the attack. Arrigo tries to defend his father and both are slain. Elena stabs herself; Procida is triumphant.

This opera has been sadly neglected on record; Levine's 1974 RCA set, made in London, remains a first choice, dominated by the partnership of Plácido Domindo and Sherrill Milnes. Their Act II duet, using a melody well known from the *Overture*, is nothing short of magnificent, with both singers at their very peak. Though Martina Arroyo is less responsive than Studer on Muti's EMI alternative version, Domingo, Milnes and the young Ruggero Raimondi are all preferable to the La Scala singers, and the sharpness of focus in both performance and recording exposes the relative fuzziness of Muti's live account. The rest of the singing in the RCA cast is good if rarely inspired, and James Levine's direction is colourful and urgent. Good recording, vividly remastered.

The EMI set offers the most successful of the live recordings made by Muti at La Scala, Milan, an opera house plagued by a difficult acoustic which is dispiritingly dry for the engineers. The atmosphere is well caught and, though Muti can be too tautly urgent a Verdian, his pacing here is well geared to bring out the high drama. Outstanding in the cast is Cheryl Studer as the heroine, Elena, singing radiantly; while the tenor, Chris Merritt, as Arrigo sounds less coarse and strained than he has in the past. Giorgio Zancanaro also responds to the role of Monforte with new sensitivity and, though Ferruccio Furlanetto as Procida lacks the full weight to bring out the beauty of line in the great aria, *O tu Palermo*, his is a warm performance too.

COLLECTIONS

'Pavarotti premières': Aida: overture. Attila: Oh dolore. I due Foscari: Ah sì, chio senta ancora; (ii) *Dal più remoto esilio.* (ii) Ernani: Odi il voto. Simon Boccanegra: Prelude. I vespri siciliani: A toi *que j'ai chérie.* (i) Scene for two tenors and orchestra.
(M) **(*) Sony MK 37228 [id.]. Luciano Pavarotti, La Scala O, Abbado; with (i) Antonio Savastano; (ii) Giuseppe Morresi; Alfredo Giacomotti.

This fascinating collection brings a series of alternative versions and additions generally forgotten, two orchestral, four vocal. The *Overture* to *Aida* and the *Prelude* to *Boccanegra*, later cut, are both worth hearing, but the vocal items, splendidly sung by Pavarotti (with two head-voice top E-flats in the *Due Foscari* item), are even more cherishable. The voice is presented in a different acoustic from that of the orchestra, and the strings sound insubstantial.

Arias: Aida: Se quel guerrier io fossi! . . . Celeste Aida; Pur ti riveggo, mia dolce Aida . . . Tu! Amonasro! Don Carlos: Fontainebleau! Forêt immense et solitaire . . . Je l'ai vue; Ecoute. Les *portes du couvent . . . Dieu, tu seras dans nos âmes.* Nabucco: Che si vuol? Il Trovatore: Quale *d'armi . . . Ah! si, ben mio . . . Di quella pira.*
*** DG Dig. 413 785-2 [id.]. Plácido Domingo with various orchestras & conductors –
PUCCINI: Arias. ***

Domingo's Verdi recital, supplemented by Puccini items from *Manon Lescaut* and *Turandot*, brings an excellent collection of recordings taken from different sources. When working on a complete opera recording, there is no danger of big arias like this simply being churned out without apt characterization. The sound is most vivid throughout.

Arias: *Aida: Celeste Aida. Un ballo in maschera: La rivedrà; Di, tu se fedele; Ma se m'è forza perderti. I due Foscari: Dal più remoto esilio. Luisa Miller: Quando le sere. Macbeth: Ah, la paterna mano. Rigoletto: Questa o quella; Parmi veder; La donna è mobile. La Traviata: De' miei bollenti. Il Trovatore: Di quella pira.*
(M) *** Decca 417 570-2. Luciano Pavarotti (with various orchestras & conductors).

Taken mainly from a recital which Pavarotti recorded early in his career with Edward Downes and the Vienna State Opera Orchestra, this Verdi collection on the mid-priced Opera Gala label can be warmly recommended, a generous collection of favourite items, plus one or two rarer arias.

'Heroines': Aida: Ritorna vincitor! O patria mia. Un ballo in maschera: Ma dall'arido. Ernani: Ernani involami. La forza del destino: Madre, pietosa Vergine; La Vergine; Pace, pace, mio Dio. Macbeth: Sleepwalking scene. Otello: Willow song; Ave Maria. La Traviata: Addio del passato. Il Trovatore: Tacea la notte; D'amor sull'ali rosee.
*** BMG/RCA RD 87016 [RCD1 7016]. Leontyne Price (various orchestras & conductors).

Leontyne Price, peerless in her generation in the more dramatic Verdi roles, is here at her finest in a generous collection of arias, recorded at the peak of her career, with the glorious voice well caught in the transfers.

Arias: *Aida: Ritorna vincitor. Un ballo in maschera: Ecco l'orrido campo. Don Carlos: Tu che le vanità. Ernani: Ernani involami. I Lombardi: O Madre dal cielo. Macbeth: Nel dì della vittoria; La luce langue una macchia. Nabucco: Anch'io dischiuso un giorno. I vespri siciliani: Arrigo! Oh parli.*
*** EMI CDC7 47730-2 [id.]. Maria Callas, Philh. O, Rescigno.

In this first of two Verdi recital records issued to commemorate the tenth anniversary of Callas's death (the second has been withdrawn), the great soprano is at her most commanding, not flawless but thrilling, both in her creative musicianship and in her characterizations, powerfully Shakespearean in the Lady Macbeth arias presented as a sequence, and holding tension masterfully in the long *Don Carlos* scene. Both those performances date from the late 1950s, when the voice was still in fine condition. Though the later items here come from a period when the voice had deteriorated (done in the 1960s but issued only in 1972), Aida's *Ritorna vincitor*, vehemently done, is magnificent for one. Generally good transfers and clean sound.

Arias from: *Un ballo in maschera; La battaglia di Legnano; Il Corsaro; I due Foscari; Ernani; Un giorno di regno;* (i) Duet from *I Lombardi.* Arias from: *Luisa Miller; Rigoletto; Stiffelio; Il Trovatore.*
(M) **(*) Ph. Analogue/Dig. 434 151-2; *434 151-4* [id.]. José Carreras; (i) with Katia Ricciarelli, Ambrosian Op. Ch.; various orchestras and conductors.

Admirers of José Carreras will find him in excellent voice in this series of excerpts from his complete sets recorded between 1973 and 1981. He was miscast as Manrico in *Il Trovatore* and his *Di quella pira* is the only disappointment; however, the somewhat similar *Odio solo, ed odio atroce* from *I due Foscari* is much more successful, and the programme is made the more attractive by all the rare material included here, in which he sounds uncommonly fresh. As it so happens, the highlight is the scena from *I Lombardi* (*Dove sola m'inoltro? . . . Per dirupi e per foreste*) to which Katia Ricciarelli makes a splendid contribution. The one great drawback is the absence of translations or any information about the music: the notes of this 60-minute Insignia collection (as with the rest of this badly produced series) are all biographical. The sound, however, is first rate.

Arias & duets: *Un ballo in maschera: Teco io sto. Il Corsaro: Egli non riede ancora! Don Carlos: Non pianger, mia compagna. Giovanna d'Arco: Qui! Qui! Dove più s'apre libero il cielo; O fatidica foresta. Jérusalem: Ave Maria. I Masnadieri: Dall'infame banchetto io m'involai; Tu del mio; Carlo vive. Otello: Già nella notte densa; Ave Maria. Il Trovatore: Timor di me; D'amor sull'ali rosee; Tu vedrai che amor in terra. I vespri siciliani: Arrigo! Ah, parli a un cor.*

(M) *** BMG/RCA GD 86534 (6534-2-RG]. Katia Ricciarelli, Plácido Domingo, Rome PO or St Cecilia Academy O, Gavazzeni.

At mid-price this collection of Verdi arias and duets from two star singers, both in fresh voice, makes a good bargain. The inclusion of rarities adds to the attractions and, though the sound is not the most modern, it is more than acceptable in the digital transfer. The sound is very bright; although the orchestral sound is a bit thin, both voices are given a good presence.

Arias from: *Un ballo in maschera; I due Foscari; Ernani; La forza del destino; Luisa Miller; Macbeth; Rigoletto; La Traviata; Il Trovatore.*
(M) ** Decca Dig. 421 893-2 [id.]. Leo Nucci, Nat. PO, Armstrong.

This was Leo Nucci's début recital for Decca in 1982. It demonstrates a fine voice and good control of colour and line (as in *Di Provenza il mar* from *Traviata*). But there is nothing here to make the blood tingle, although the digital sound is excellent and Richard Armstrong is a strong and sympathetic accompanist.

Arias: *Don Carlo: Son io, mio Carlo . . . Per me giunto . . . O Carlo, ascolta. Luisa Miller: Sacra la scelta. Macbeth: Perfidi! All'anglo contra me v'unite . . . Pietà, rispetto, amore. La Traviata: Di Provenza il mar. Il Trovatore: Tutto è deserto . . . Il balen.*
*** Ph. Dig. 426 740-2; *426 740-4* [id.]. Dmitri Hvorostovsky, Rotterdam PO, Gergiev – TCHAIKOVSKY: *Arias.* ***

With a glorious voice, dark and characterful, and with natural musical imagination and film-star good looks, Dmitri Hvorostovsky, 'Cardiff Singer of the World' in 1989, on this disc made his recording début in the West not just in Tchaikovsky arias, but here in Verdi, stylishly sung. With a voice of such youthful virility, he hardly sounds like the father-figure of the *Traviata* and *Luisa Miller* items, but the legato in Macbeth's Act IV aria is most beautiful. He also brings the keenest intensity to Posa's death-scene aria from *Don Carlo.*

Arias: *Don Carlos: Tu che le vanità. La Traviata: Ah fors'è lui. Il Trovatore: Timor di me.*
*** Sony Dig. CD 37298 [id.]. Kiri Te Kanawa, LPO, Pritchard – PUCCINI: *Arias.* ***

The Verdi side of Kiri Te Kanawa's Verdi–Puccini recital brings three substantial items less obviously apt for the singer, but in each the singing is felt as well as beautiful. The coloratura of the *Traviata* and *Trovatore* items is admirably clean, and it is a special joy to hear Elisabetta's big aria from *Don Carlos* sung with such truth and precision. Good recording, enhanced on CD.

'Great scenes' from: (i; ii) *Aida;* (i) *Attila;* (ii; iii) *Macbeth;* (iv) *Nabucco; Simon Boccanegra;* (i; ii; v) *Il Trovatore.*
** Decca 436 304-2 [id.]. (i) Joan Sutherland; (ii) Luciano Pavarotti; (iii) Riccardo Casinelli; (iv) Nicolai Ghiaurov; (v) Marilyn Horne; Amb. S., LSO, Abbado.

Easily the best thing here is the final scene from *Aida*, which comes last in the programme: *La fatal pietra . . . O terra addio*, gloriously sung by Sutherland and Pavarotti, striking sparks together. The *Miserere* from *Il Trovatore* (which comes from the same source) is also effective, even if tension is lower. Nothing else here comes up to this level of memorability, although Sutherland is impressive enough in the *Attila* aria (*Santo di patria . . . Allor che i forti corrono*).

Arias & excerpts (recorded 1906 – 16, with Johanna Gadski, Frieda Hempel, Antonio Scotti, Frances Alda, Titta Ruffo, Luisa Tetrazzini, Josephine Jacoby, Pasquale Amato, Alma Gluck, Ernestine Schumann-Heink) from: *Aida; Un ballo in maschera; Don Carlo; La forza del destino; I Lombardi; Macbeth; Otello; Rigoletto; La Traviata; Il Trovatore; Requiem.*
(M) (***) BMG/RCA mono 09026 61242-2.

Like the miscellaneous Caruso collections included in the Recitals section (see below), these recordings were restored by Thomas Stockham using the Soundstream digital process which removes unwanted horn resonances, and the improvement in sound is phenomenal. The voices often sound pristine, and only the heavily scored accompaniments serve to remind the listener of the early recording dates.

There are many famous recordings here and it is good that other singers are featured too, Gadski in *La fatal pietra* from *Aida*, Hempel in *La rivedrà nell'estasi* from *Un ballo in maschera*, Scotti in the excerpts from Act I of *Don Carlo* and Act III of *La forza del destino*, and so on. The version of the Quartet from *Rigoletto* (*Bella figlia*) includes Tetrazzini, Josephine Jacoby and Amato.

The programme is well chosen and the sound revelatory. Sample the superbly stylish *Questa o quella* or *La donna è mobile* (from *Rigoletto*), or the soaring *Ah sì, ben mio* (*Il Trovatore*), all recorded in 1908, which sound amazingly free from the mechanical problems of the early recording process. Surface noise is reduced but still present; yet the ear soon programmes it out.

'Verdi gala': (i) Overture: *La forza del destino*. Arias & choruses from: (ii; iii) *Aida;* (iv; v) *Un ballo in maschera;* (vi) *Don Carlo;* (vii) *Nabucco;* (viii; ii) *Rigoletto;* (ix), (ii; x) *La Traviata;* (vii; xi) *Il Trovatore.*

(M) **(*) Decca Dig. 430 748-3; *430 748-4* [id.]. (i) Nat. PO, Chailly; (ii) Luciano Pavarotti; (iii) Maria Chiara; (iv) Margaret Price; (v) Kathleen Battle; (vi) Paata Burchuladze; (vii) Chicago SO Ch. & O, Solti; (viii) June Anderson; (ix) Leo Nucci; (x) Joan Sutherland; (xi) Susan Dunn.

This collection is well selected and all digitally recorded, but it does not quite match the splendid 'World of Verdi' from the same source (see below), although there is a great deal to enjoy. Chailly gets things off to a good start with a vibrant account of the *Forza del destino Overture*, and Pavarotti's following *Celeste Aida* will disappoint no one. But Maria Chiara's *Ritorna vincitor!* was made after the voice had lost some of its bloom and sounds just a little strained.

By its side, June Anderson's delightfully fresh *Caro nome* (the closing section quite melting) and Susan Dunn's *Tacea la notte* are altogether more beguiling, and the two contrasted excerpts from *Un ballo in maschera* (Margaret Price as Amelia and Kathleen Battle a spirited Oscar), *Morrò, ma prima in grazia* and *Saper vorreste*, are equally enjoyable. Other highlights include Paata Burchuladze's sombrely moving *Ella giammai m'amò* from *Don Carlo* and, of course the magical closing *Traviata* duet from Sutherland and Pavarotti, *Parigi, o cara*, but Leo Nucci's *Di Provenza il mar* has not the same degree of charisma.

'The world of Verdi': (i) Aida: *Celeste Aida;* (ii) *Grand march and ballet.* (iii) *La forza del destino: Pace, pace mio Dio.* (iv) *Luisa Miller: O! Fede negar potessi . . . Quando le sere al placido.* (v) *Nabucco: Va pensiero.* (vi) *Otello: Credo. Rigoletto:* (vii) *Caro nome;* (viii) *La donna è mobile;* (vii; viii; ix) Quartet: *Belle figlia dell'amore.* (x) *La Traviata: Prelude, Act I;* (vii; xi) *Brindisi; Libiamo ne'lieti calici. Il Trovatore:* (xii) *Anvil chorus;* (xiii) *Strida la vampa;* (viii) *Di quella pira. I vespri siciliani:* (xiv) *Mercè, diletti amiche.*

(M) *** Decca 433 221-2; *433 221-4.* (i) Jon Vickers; (ii) Rome Opera Ch. & O, Solti; (iii) Gwyneth Jones; (iv) Carlo Bergonzi; (v) Amb. S., LSO, Abbado; (vi) Geraint Evans; (vii) Joan Sutherland; (viii) Luciano Pavarotti; (ix) Huguette Tourangeau; Sherrill Milnes; (x) Maggio Musicale Fiorentino O, Pritchard; (xi) Carlo Bergonzi; (xii) L. Op. Ch., Bonynge; (xiii) Marilyn Horne; (xiv) Maria Chiara.

Opening with the *Chorus of the Hebrew Slaves* from *Nabucco* and closing with Pavarotti's *Di quella pira* from *Il Trovatore*, this quite outstandingly red-blooded Verdi compilation should surely tempt any novice to explore further into Verdi's world, yet at the same time it provides a superbly arranged 74-minute concert in its own right. The choice of items and performances demonstrates a shrewd knowledge of both popular Verdi and the Decca catalogue, for not a single performance disappoints.

Joan Sutherland's melting 1971 *Caro nome* with its exquisite trills is the first of three splendid excerpts from *Rigoletto*, ending with the famous Quartet, and other highlights include Gwyneth Jones's glorious *Pace, pace, mio Dio* introduced, of course, by the sinisterly scurrying *Forza del destino* motif, Sir Geraint Evans's superb account of Iago's evil *Credo* from *Otello* – here the Decca sound adds to the riveting impact – and Marilyn Horne's dark-timbred *Strida la vampa* from *Trovatore*. Solti, too, is at his most electric in the great March scene from *Aida*. The stereo throughout is splendidly vivid and this bargain collection is worth every penny of its modest cost.

Choruses: Aida: *Triumphal march and ballet music. Attila: Urli, rapine. La Battaglia di Legnano: Giuriam d'Italia. I Lombardi: O Signore, del tetto natio. Nabucco: Gli arredi festivi; Va pensiero. Otello: Fuoco di gioia. Il Trovatore: Vedi! le fosche; Squilli, echeggi.*

(M) ** Decca 417 721-2 [id.]. Ch. & O of St Cecilia Ac., Rome, Carlo Franci.

This collection was first issued in 1965 and with the remastered reissue the impression remains that the upper range of chorus and orchestra has an unnatural brightness. In all other respects the quality is very good, inner detail is sharp and the big climaxes open up well. The performances are vivid, with a willingness to sing softly and, indeed, sometimes a degree of refinement in the approach surprising in an Italian chorus. The *I Lombardi* excerpts are especially appealing, but all the little-known items come up freshly. The trumpets in the *Aida* Triumphal scene get the full stereo treatment.

Choruses from: *Aida; Un ballo in maschera; Don Carlo; I Lombardi; Macbeth; I Masnadieri; Nabucco; Otello; Rigoletto; La Traviata; Il Trovatore. Requiem Mass: Sanctus.*
*** Decca Dig. 430 226-2; *430 226-4* [id.]. Chicago Symphony Ch. & SO, Solti.

Choruses from: *Aida; La battaglia di Legnano; Don Carlo; Ernani; La forza del destino; Macbeth; Nabucco; Otello; La Traviata; Il Trovatore.*
(BB) *** Naxos Dig. 8.550241 [id.]. Slovak Philharmonic Ch. & RSO, Oliver Dohnányi.

The Solti collection is not drawn from the maestro's previous complete opera sets but is a first-class studio production, recorded in Orchestra Hall, Chicago, with Decca's most resplendent digital sound. The choral balance is forward, but there is plenty of depth too, and the wide dynamic range emphasizes, for instance, the dramatic contrast at the repeated cries of 'Gerusalem!' from *I Lombardi* (a thrilling moment), while the gentle opening of *Va pensiero* from *Nabucco* (which was sung spontaneously by the crowds in the streets of Milan as Verdi's funeral cortège passed by) is beautifully focused.

Solti is on top form. Besides the many exciting histrionic moments there are many refined touches too, notably in the stylish *La Traviata* excerpt, with soloists from the chorus, and the flashing fantasy of *Fuoco di gioia* from *Otello*. The Brigands in *I Masnadieri* sing of 'plunder, rape and arson' with great good humour, and the concert closes with the joyous *Sanctus* from the *Requiem* which, like the rest of the 70-minute programme, demonstrates the refined excellence of the Chicago Chorus, so splendidly prepared by their founder and director, Margaret Hillis. Full translations are included.

Although the super-bargain Naxos collection by the excellent Slovak Philharmonic Choir, trained by Marian Vach, is not as spectacularly recorded as the Decca Solti disc, the sound is very realistic, and in some ways the slightly recessed choral balance in the Bratislava Radio Concert Hall is more natural: it certainly does not lack impact and, in the *Fire chorus* from *Otello*, detail registers admirably.

Under Oliver Dohnányi's lively direction the chorus sings with admirable fervour. *Patria oppressa* from *Macbeth* is particularly stirring, and *Va pensiero*, with a well-shaped line, is movingly projected. The *Soldiers' chorus* from *Il Trovatore* has a jaunty rhythmic feeling that is, if anything, more attractive than Solti's bolder approach. The two novelties from *La battaglia di Legnano* were well worth including, and the second, *Giuramento*, includes four impressive male soloists.

The collection ends resplendently with the Triumphal scene from *Aida*, omitting the ballet, (which Solti includes) but with the fanfare trumpets blazing out on either side most tellingly. With a playing time of 56 minutes this is excellent value in every respect.

Choruses: *Aida: Gloria all'Egitto. Don Carlos: Spuntato ecco il dì. I Lombardi: Gerusalem!; O Signore, del tetto natio. Macbeth: Patria oppressa! Nabucco: Va pensiero; Gli arredi festivi. Otello: Fuoco di gioia! Il Trovatore: Vedi! le fosche; Or co' dadi . . . Squilli, echeggi.*
**(*) Ph. Dig. 412 235-2 [id.]. Dresden State Op. Ch. & State O, Varviso.

Varviso's collection of choruses brings polished but soft-grained performances, beautifully supported by the magnificent Dresden orchestra. Gentler choruses are excellent, but the dramatic ones lack something in bite. One of the highlights is the *Fire chorus* from *Otello* in which the choral and woodwind detail suggests the flickering flames of bonfires burning in Otello's honour. The recording is warmly atmospheric, with CD adding a degree more presence and definition.

Choruses: *Attila: Urli, rapine, gemiti, sangue; Viva il re dalle mille foreste; Del ciel l'immensa volta; Chi dona luce al cor?. Ernani: Un patto! un giuramento! Si redesti il Leon di Castiglia. La forza del destino: La Vergine degli angeli. Compagni, sostiamo; Nella Guerra; Rataplan. I Lombardi: Gerusalem!; O Signore, dal tetto natio. Macbeth: Patria oppressa!. Nabucco: Gli arresti festivi; Va pensiero. Rigoletto: Zitti, zitti. Il Trovatore: Vedi! le fosche (Anvil chorus). Requiem: Sanctus.*
*** EMI Dig. CDC7 54484-2. La Scala, Milan, Ch. & O, Muti.

Deriving from various sets made between 1987 and 1992, these vividly sung and brilliantly recorded choruses cover the full Verdian range, from the deeply eloquent *Va pensiero* and powerful *Patria oppressa* to the jollier items, including the appalling celebration of rape and pillage from *Attila: Urli, rapine!* There are good notes and translations and the digital sound is first class but, with 54 minutes of music offered, this would have been even more tempting at mid-price.

Villa-Lobos, Heitor (1887–1959)

Magdalena.
*** Sony Dig. SK 44945 [id.]. Judy Kaye, George Rose, Faith Esham, Kevin Gray, Jerry Hadley, New England O, Evans Haile.

Until this disc appeared, not many remembered that Villa-Lobos had written a Broadway musical. The promoters of *Song of Norway*, the musical based on Grieg's music, wanted to follow it up with a comparable one on South America, as being 'as far from the fjords of Norway as an author could possibly get'. They thought to use the music of Villa-Lobos, but the composer, much to everyone's surprise, took control of the project, to make it his own, rather than anyone else's, score.

In the South American jungle, Padre José leaves the mission on a journey to other missions further down the Magdalena river. He leaves Maria, his most loyal convert, in charge during his absence. Maria promises to guard the chapel and the Madonna. Maria loves Pedro, a young man who scoffs at religion and resists all efforts on Maria's part to reform him. Major Blanco, the aide who manages General Carabaña's estates, comes to Maria: all the Muzos have stopped work in the general's emerald mines. Maria is unable to help, and the major departs for Paris to warn the general.

In Paris, General Carabaña is a *bon vivant*, rather fat and sinister, who spends much time at Madame Teresa's Little Black Mouse Café. Major Blanco brings news of the strike in the emerald mines. The general begs Teresa to return to Colombia with him and promises to give her the Carabaña emerald necklace. She agrees to go.

Back in Colombia, the Muzos give a fiesta to welcome General Carabaña, and Pedro comes along with some drunken Indians of the pagan Chivor tribe, who create general havoc. Pedro comes later to Maria, quite contrite. Maria accepts his apologies and Pedro is able to sweep her away in a flood of passion, whereupon the Chivors sneak into the chapel and steal the Madonna.

Although Pedro announces his intention of marrying her on Padre José's return, when word comes that the Madonna is missing, Maria realizes she has been deceived. Meanwhile, Teresa learns that the general has agreed to settle his strike by marrying Maria, and he has even offered her the Carabaña emerald necklace she, Teresa, had been promised. In revenge, she prepares a non-stop parade of food, and the *bon vivant* dies at the table of a heart attack. Teresa exits with her emeralds.

Pedro appears but is unrepentant. Maria bids him goodbye and Pedro goes off into the jungle, defeated by Maria's faith. With the next sunrise comes the sound of the Muzos singing. Gift-bearers approach the empty shrine. Pedro appears, carrying the Madonna, which is safely reinstalled in the shrine. Maria is reunited with Pedro. With Padre José back with his flock, all is well.

It is a colourful, vigorous piece, alas lacking the big tunes you really need in a musical, but full of delightful ideas. It tells the sort of story that Lehár might have chosen, only translated to South America. Sadly, in spite of an enthusiastic response from everyone, it closed on Broadway in 1948 after only eleven weeks. The present recording was prompted by a concert performance to celebrate the Villa-Lobos centenary, a splendid, well-sung account of what is aptly described as 'a musical adventure'.

Vivaldi, Antonio (1675–1741)

L'Incoronazione di Dario (opera; complete).
Withdrawn: **(*) HM Dig. HMC 901235/7 [id.]. John Elwes, Gérard Lesne, Michèle Ledroit, Michel Verschaeve, Isabelle Poulenard, Agnès Mellon, Dominique Visse, Nice Bar. Ens., Bezzina.

Set in the fifth century BC at the Persian court, this Vivaldi opera involves the conflict which followed the death of King Cyrus and the succession of Darius. Written in 1717, it is one of Vivaldi's earlier operas, in places reflecting the great oratorio he had written the year before, *Juditha triumphans*, reworking three numbers. The opera here receives a lively performance, generally well sung. John Elwes as Darius himself, though stylish, does not sound as involved as some of the others, notably the male alto, Dominique Visse, who is superb both vocally and dramatically as the female confidante, Flora. Reliable singing from the whole cast, and first-rate recording. The full libretto is provided only in Italian, with translated summaries of the plot in English, French and German.

Juditha triumphans (oratorio) complete.
(M) *** Ph. 426 955-2 (2) [id.]. Birgit Finnila, Ingeborg Springer, Júlia Hamari, Elly Ameling, Annelies Burmeister, Berlin Radio Soloists Ch. & CO, Negri.

Described as a 'military' oratorio, *Juditha triumphans* demonstrates its martial bravado at the very start, as exhilarating a passage as you will find in the whole of Vivaldi. The vigorous choruses stand as cornerstones of commentary in a structure which, following convention, comes close to operatic form, with recitatives providing the narrative between formal *da capo* arias.

Though Vivaldi fell into routine invention at times, the wonder is that so much of this music is so vividly alive, telling the story from the Apocrypha of Judith cutting off the head of the enemy general, Holofernes (we have recounted this in greater detail elsewhere). As the cast-list will suggest, this Philips version rightly gives the castrato roles to women, with a generally stylish line-up of singers. It is a pity that the role of Judith is taken by one of the less interesting singers, Birgit Finnila, and that Elly Ameling takes only a servant's role, though it is one which demands more brilliant technique than any. Overall, however, this is a considerable success. The excellent 1974 recording re-emerges vividly in its CD format.

Montezuma (arr. Malgoire).
** Astree/Audivis E 8501 (2) [id.]. Vocal Ens., Grande Écurie et la Chambre du Roy, Jean-Claude Malgoire.
Montezuma (Dominique Visse), Mitrena (Danielle Borst), Teutile (Isabelle Poulenard), Fernando Cortes (Nicolas Rivenq), Ramiro (Brigitte Balleys), Asprano (Luis Masson).

Vivaldi did write an opera called *Montezuma* but the music has not survived. However, the libretto by Girolamo Giusti was saved, and Jean-Claude Malgoire has culled together some music the composer wrote for other occasions (operatic and otherwise) to fit this story of the famous Mexican historical figure.

As the opera opens, he has been beaten in battle and takes refuge with his wife, Mitrena. He gives her a dagger to use on herself and their daughter, Teutile, if they are taken prisoner by the Spanish. Teutile loves Ramiro (Cortes' younger brother) and wants to use it prematurely when her lover lets her down. Fernando Cortes now arrives; Montezuma's arrow, intended for his family, wounds him. Ramiro, alone with Teutile, tries to convince her that the Spanish invasion is honourable. Montezuma returns in disguise, still planning to kill his family; Ramiro intervenes and hides them both, then seeks a truce.

Eventually the Mexican emperor is put in chains. Mitrena laments but Asprano, the leader of the Mexican troops, arrives to offer hope. The dialogue between the principal participants and their conflicting interests and loyalties is impossible to resolve, and the soldiers on both sides prepare to fight. But first there is to be a sacrifice to the Mexican god, Uccilibos. Teutile agrees to submit, but her mother declares that Fernando (who has been captured and imprisoned in a tower) should be sacrificed alongside her. Ramiro helps his brother to escape and the tower is burned down without him. Ramiro then comes back to save Teutile.

Finally Montezuma and his wife attempt unsuccessfully to kill Fernando and Ramiro. Fernando pardons them, Ramiro is given permission to marry Teutile, and Montezuma accepts the situation.

The work cobbled together by Malgoire is quite successful in its own right, and it is a pity that the recording is not more flattering; it is very dry and lustreless and the orchestra has virtually no supporting resonance. The voices and words are clear and truthfully caught but, as the recording was made 'live', so are various other stage-noises, though this is not an insuperable drawback. The singing is generally enjoyable, particularly that of Dominique Visse in the title-role, though Isabelle Poulenard is also an appealingly nimble Teutile, and Nicolas Rivenq is a strong Cortes. Mitrena's part demands a very wide range, and this is encompassed impressively by Danielle Borst. Her shamed call to the gods at the end of Act I shows her at her finest. Malgoire paces convincingly, though the effect is not red-bloodedly dramatic because of the thin orchestral textures. The restricted acoustic effect means that this is not strongly recommendable to the average collector, but it is by no means to be written off. The documentation, with full libretto, is more than adequate though the print (as so often with CDs) is too small for comfort.

L'Olimpiade: highlights.

Withdrawn: (B) **(*) Hung. White Label HRC 078 [id.]. Kolos Kováts, Klára Takács, Mária Zempléni, Lajos Miller, László Horváth, Budapest Madrigal Ch., Hungarian State O., Szekeres.

In the very inexpensive White Label series of Hungaroton recordings, a generous collection of highlights from Vivaldi's opera, *L'Olimpiade*, is well worth investigating. Though currently withdrawn, it is due to be restored to the catalogue shortly, as the Hungaroton White Label series is to be manufactured in the UK. An early delight in this selection is the work's most attention-grabbing number, a choral version of what we know as *Spring* from *The Four Seasons*. Ferenc Szekeres' conducting of the Hungarian State Orchestra is too heavy by today's standards, now that we are attuned to period performance, but the singing of soloists and choir is good, and the recording is brightly focused, with clean directional effects.

Orlando Furioso (complete).

*** Erato/Warner 2292 45147-2 (3) [id.]. Sol. Ven., Scimone.

Orlando (Marilyn Horne), Angelica (Victoria De los Angeles), Alcina (Lucia Valentini Terrani), Bradamante (Carmen Gonzales), Medoro (Lajos Kozma), Ruggiero (Sesto Bruscantini), Astolfo (Nicola Zaccaria).

Though the greater part of this opera consists of recitative – with only 15 arias included on the three discs, plus one for Orlando borrowed from a chamber cantata – it presents a fascinating insight into this neglected area of Vivaldi's work. Scimone has heavily rearranged the order of items as well as cutting many, but, with stylish playing and excellent recording, it is a set well worth a Vivaldi enthusiast's attention.

The scene is the enchanted island of the sorceress Alcina, who has stolen it from her sister, Logistilla, symbol of truth and reason. Through her magic, Alcina conceals her true appearance and appears to be so beautiful that she is able to bewitch all those who stumble into her realm.

Orlando is an enthusiastic knight who is in love with Angelica, but Angelica is mourning the loss of her beloved Medoro. As she looks at the sea, she sees a tiny boat about to founder on the shore. It is Medoro, near death. Angelica calls for help, and Alcina appears and heals Medoro with her magic. Suddenly Orlando appears.

Enraged with jealousy, he would kill Medoro, but Alcina intervenes again by convincing Orlando that Medoro is Angelica's brother. Orlando begs forgiveness for his jealousy, and Angelica professes her love for him, making Medoro jealous.

Alcina is alone when Ruggiero, another knight, arrives on a winged steed and is very much taken by the beauty of the place. Alcina is enchanted by Ruggiero and soon bewitches him with water from two magic springs. Bradamante, his wife, arrives and is frantic when she finds him in the arms of Alcina; nor does he recognize her. When later she finds him alone, she is able to break the spell by touching her beloved with the gold ring he once gave her as a token of his love; having managed this trick, however, she scorns him and leaves.

Orlando comes along and tries to console Ruggiero with the reminder that peace always follows a storm. A third knight, Astolfo, arrives and, bewitched by Alcina, tries to win her love but she laughs at him, saying that one man is not enough for her. Bradamante and Ruggiero find each other again and are reconciled.

Angelica has a plan to get rid of Orlando. She leads him into a trap by sending him up a mountain which is under the spell of Alcina. She pretends that the source of eternal youth is held in the mountain, guarded by a fierce monster.

Orlando bravely goes but, once inside the mountain, it seals itself and he is the prisoner of Alcina. In his anger he is able to break through the rock. Meanwhile Angelica and Medoro have been married in a wooded grove and have carved their inscriptions on two trees. Coming upon this incontrovertible evidence, Orlando explodes with rage and is driven insane.

Ruggiero and Astolfo mourn the fate of Orlando, whom they believe to be dead, and enlist the help of the good sorceress, Melissa, to help them take revenge on Alcina. The two knights wait in front of the temple of the infernal Hecate to attack Alcina. Alcina calls to the gods to help her find Ruggiero, but Bradamante, disguised as a man named Aldarico, puts the sorceress off by attracting her interest. Orlando reappears in a state of madness, inspiring much compassion in Ruggiero and Bradamante. Angelica arrives too and Orlando rebukes her in an incoherent manner. The others charge Angelica with treachery which has brought on this sad state and she weeps in repentance.

Alone and deranged, Orlando attempts to embrace what he takes to be Angelica, but it is a

statue of the wizard, Merlin, which Alcina has placed in the temple as the repository of her
magic powers. The statue is defended by the invincible guard, Arontes, and in a furious battle
Orlando kills him. He then pulls down the statue, embraces it and falls asleep, not knowing that
he has broken the spell.

The magic of the sorceress and her realm is at an end. Alcina appears and is accused by
Ruggiero and Bradamante. Angelica realizes that they have all allied themselves with Alcina,
and they are suitably chagrined. But Orlando, who wakes up and returns to his senses, forgives
them and wishes them happiness.

Outstanding in a surprisingly star-studded cast is Marilyn Horne in the title-role, rich and
firm of tone, articulating superbly in divisions, notably in the hero's two fiery arias. In the role
of Angelica, Victoria de los Angeles has many sweetly lyrical moments and, though Lucia
Valentini Terrani is less strong as Alcina, she gives an aptly clean, precise performance. The
remastering has somewhat freshened a recording which was not outstanding in its analogue LP
form, and a good booklet with translation is provided with the CD set.

Wagner, Richard (1813–83)

Die Feen (complete).
*** Orfeo Dig. C062833 (3) [id.]. Bav. R. Ch. & SO, Sawallisch.
  Ada (Linda Esther Gray), Farzana (Kari Lövaas), Semina (Krisztina Laki), Arindal (John
  Alexander), Lora (June Anderson), Morald (Roland Hermann), Fairy King (Kurt Moll),
  Gernot (Jan-Hendrik Rootering), Drolla (Cheryl Studer), Groma (Roland Bracht).

Wagner was barely twenty when he wrote *Die Feen*, his first opera, the story of a fairy who
marries a mortal and is threatened with separation from him. Ada is in fact half-mortal, half-
supernatural, and she agrees to marry Arindal, King of Tramond, provided he does not ask her
identity. He cannot restrain his curiosity, and Ada and her magic kingdom disappear.

Arindal is returned to his court but Ada, wanting to rejoin him, can do so only if he is tested
with various tribulations. These he fails and curses her, only to learn that as a result she will now
be turned to stone for 100 years.

His despair leads him to follow her into the underworld and he finally brings her back to life
by singing and playing the lyre. He renounces his earthly kingdom and they live happily together
in fairyland.

It is amazing how confident the writing is, regularly echoing Weber but stylistically more
consistent than Wagner's next two operas, *Das Liebesverbot* and *Rienzi*. The piece is through-
composed in what had become the new, advanced manner and, even when he bows to
convention and has a *buffo* duet between the second pair of principals, the result is distinctive
and fresh, delightfully sung here by Cheryl Studer and Jan-Hendrik Rootering.

This first complete recording was edited together from live performances given in Munich in
1983 and has few of the usual snags of live performance but plenty of its advantages. Sawallisch
gives a strong and dramatic performance, finely paced; central to the total success is the singing
of Linda Esther Gray as Ada, the fairy-heroine, powerful and firmly controlled.

John Alexander as the tenor hero, King Arindal – finally granted immortality to bring a happy
ending – sings cleanly and capably; the impressive cast-list boasts such excellent singers as Kurt
Moll, Kari Lövaas and Krisztina Laki in small but vital roles. Ensembles and choruses – with
the Bavarian Radio Chorus finely disciplined – are particularly impressive, and the recording is
generally first rate. On CD the realism is enhanced, with the sound more vivid and sharply
focused.

Der fliegende Holländer (complete).
(M) *** Ph. Dig. 434 599-2 (2) [id.]. (1985) Bayreuth Festival Ch. & O, Nelsson.
  Holländer (Simon Estes), Senta (Lisbeth Balslev), Daland (Matti Salminen), Erik (Robert
  Schunk), Mary (Anny Schlemm), Steuermann (Graham Clark).
(M) *** EMI Dig. CMS7 64650-2 (2) [id.]. V. State Op. Ch., BPO, Karajan.
  Holländer (José Van Dam), Senta (Dunja Vejzovic), Daland (Kurt Moll), Erik (Peter
  Hofmann), Mary (Kaja Borris), Steuermann (Thomas Moser).
**(*) Decca 414 551-2 (3) [id.]. Chicago SO Ch. & O, Solti.
  Holländer (Norman Bailey), Senta (Janis Martin), Daland (Martti Talvela), Erik (René
  Kollo), Mary (Isola Jones), Steuermann (Werner Krenn).
(M) **(*) Decca 417 319-2 (2) [id.]. ROHCG Ch. & O, Dorati.

Holländer (George London), Senta (Leonie Rysanek), Daland (Giorgio Tozzi), Erik (Karl Liebl), Mary (Rosalind Elias), Steuermann (Richard Lewis).

(M) ** EMI CMS7 63344-2 (3) [Ang. CDMC 63344]. BBC Ch., New Philh. O, Klemperer.

Holländer (Theo Adam), Senta (Anja Silja), Daland (Martti Talvela), Erik (Ernst Kozub), Mary (Annelies Burmeister), Steuermann (Gerhard Unger).

(M) ** DG 437 710-2 (2) [id.]. (1971) Bayreuth Festival Ch. & O, Karl Boehm.

Holländer (Thomas Stewart), Senta (Gwyneth Jones), Daland (Karl Ridderbusch), Erik (Hermin Esser), Mary (Sieglinde Wagner), Steuermann (Harald Ek).

Der fliegende Holländer, which followed closely after *Rienzi*, marked a big leap forward in Wagner's search for an operatic style of his own. The *Overture* immediately sets the scene for this powerful opera, with stormy orchestral passages conjuring up the might and ferocity of the sea, contrasted with the gentler mood of Senta's *Ballad*, which relates the legend on which the story is based. The curtain then rises on a Norwegian ship, anchored in a cove off the Norwegian coast.

Captain Daland goes below as the storm abates, leaving the steersman in charge. Eventually he falls asleep. Now a ghostly vision of another ship slowly moves alongside, the spectral crew furl the sails, and the legendary Dutchman approaches the shore. We learn of the curse from which he suffers: once he tried to round the Cape of Good Hope in the teeth of a roaring gale and swore that, if he had to keep on sailing for ever, he would accomplish it. His oath was heard by the devil and now he is condemned to sail the sea until Judgement Day, without escape, unless he should find a woman who will be faithful until death; once every seven years he may go ashore in search of her.

The most recent span has passed and now he seeks his feminine salvation (*Die Frist is um*). Daland speaks to the Dutchman, who tells of ill-luck and disaster at sea. The Dutchman seeks his hospitality and shows that he has treasure aboard his ship. When he hears that Daland has a marriageable daughter, his hopes rise. Both ships set sail for Daland's home port.

In Daland's house, Senta, his daughter, her old nurse, Mary, and her friends sing as they sit and spin. But Senta only has eyes for the portrait on the wall of the famous Flying Dutchman. Her friends tease her about her obsession, especially when Erik, the huntsman, is seeking her hand. Senta now recalls the curse and the hoped-for redemption, and she suddenly becomes conscious of her destiny to save the Dutchman.

Erik hears her passionate declaration as he enters and is perplexed by her behaviour. He reports the arrival of her father's ship, and the women depart to prepare a homecoming for their menfolk. Erik and Senta are left alone and he begs her to be faithful to him. She now tells him of her compassion for the wanderer and, very perturbed, he relates a dream in which he saw her father leading the pale stranger to her embrace. She interrupts him, sensing that her destiny is at hand. Erik goes off, fearing that she is no longer his.

Left alone, Senta again dreamily recalls the story on which her hopes rest. Her father now appears, and the Dutchman stands beside him. Senta is transfixed and she does not run to embrace her father as usual. As he asks for her warmth and hospitality towards his guest, she has already given her heart to the sepulchral Dutchman and, when her father asks her to consider him as a future husband, not a word need be spoken between them. The two stand in a daze, scarcely comprehending the fulfilment of their mutual dream. She vows eternal faithfulness. Their betrothal will be announced at a forthcoming feast-day.

The two ships can be seen in the bay, lying at anchor together. Whereas on the Norwegian ship the sailors are singing and dancing, the Dutch vessel is eerily still. The Norwegian women take food and drink to both but get no response from the Dutch crew. Suddenly the sea begins to surge and a curious blue light haloes the Dutch ship; the ghostly crew sing a wild chorus, striking fear into the hearts of the Norwegian sailors, who make the sign of the cross and leave in haste. Strange, disembodied laughter is heard from the Dutch crew.

Senta and Erik now emerge from the house, Erik reminding her of her commitment to him. The Dutchman steps forward and Erik recognizes the man from his dream. The Dutchman has heard Erik's words and chides Senta for her seeming infidelity, then he gives orders for the ship to set sail. He tells Senta that he only wants to save her from eternal damnation, the lot of all those women who have not kept their vows to him.

But Senta answers that she already knows his situation and will steadfastly save him from the curse. He takes no notice, and the Dutch ship puts to sea. Erik tries in vain to restrain Senta but she rushes to a great rocky promontory, cries out to her lover, then plunges into the angry sea. At that very moment the Dutchman's ship is sucked down in a whirlpool and, as the sun sets, the forms of Senta and the Dutchman are seen rising to heaven together. The Dutchman's torment is ended.

The biting intensity of a Bayreuth performance has rarely been more thrillingly caught than in the fine Philips recording from the 1985 season. Woldemar Nelsson, with the team he had worked with intensively, conducts a performance even more glowing and responsively paced than those of his starrier rivals. The cast, also less starry than some, is yet more consistent than any, with Lisbeth Balslev as Senta firmer, sweeter and more secure than any current rival, raw only occasionally, and Simon Estes a strong, ringing Dutchman, clear and noble of tone. Matti Salminen is a dark and equally secure Daland and Robert Schunk an ardent, idiomatic Erik. The veteran, Anny Schlemm, as Mary, though vocally overstressed, adds pointful character, and the chorus is superb, wonderfully drilled and passionate with it. Though inevitably stage noises are obtrusive at times, the recording is exceptionally vivid and atmospheric. On two mid-priced discs in the Philips Bayreuth series, it makes an admirable first choice as well as being an outstanding bargain.

The extreme range of dynamics in EMI's recording for Karajan, not ideally clear but rich, matches the larger-than-life quality of the conductor's reading. He firmly and convincingly relates this early work not so much to such seminal earlier works as Weber's *Der Freischütz* as to later Wagner, *Tristan* above all. His choice of José van Dam as the Dutchman, thoughtful, finely detailed and lyrical, strong but not at all blustering, goes well with this. The Dutchman's Act I monologue is turned into a prayer as well as a protest in its extra range of expression. Van Dam is superbly matched and contrasted with the finest Daland on record, Kurt Moll, gloriously biting and dark in tone, yet detailed in his characterization.

Neither the Erik of Peter Hofmann, nor – more seriously – the Senta of Dunja Vejzovic matches such a standard, for Hofmann has his strained and gritty moments and Vejzovic her shrill ones. They were both better cast in Karajan's *Parsifal* recording. Nevertheless, for all her variability Vejzovic is wonderfully intense in *Senta's Ballad* and she matches even Van Dam's fine legato in the Act II duet. The CD transfer underlines the heavyweight quality of the recording, with the *Sailors' chorus* for example made massive, but effectively so, when Karajan conducts it with such fine spring. The banding is not generous, making the issue less convenient to use than most Wagner CD sets, and the break between the two CDs is not ideally placed.

Solti's first Wagner opera recording in Chicago marked a change from the long series he made in Vienna. The playing is superb, the singing cast is generally impressive, and the recording is vividly immediate to the point of aggressiveness. What will disappoint some who admire Solti's earlier Wagner sets is that this most atmospheric of the Wagner operas is presented with no Culshaw-style production whatever. Characters halloo to one another when evidently standing elbow to elbow, and even the Dutchman's ghostly chorus sounds very close and earthbound.

But with Norman Bailey a deeply impressive Dutchman, Janis Martin a generally sweet-toned Senta, Martti Talvela a splendid Daland, and René Kollo, for all his occasional coarseness, an illuminating Erik, it remains well worth hearing. The brilliance of the recording is all the more striking on CD, but the precise placing so characteristic of the new medium reinforces the clear impression of a concert performance, not an atmospheric re-creation.

Dorati, with rhythms well sprung, draws strong and alert playing and singing from his Covent Garden forces in a consistently purposeful performance, helped by Culshaw-style sound-effects. The well-spread recording is full and atmospheric and, like the Philips set, the reissue is offered on two mid-price CDs. George London's Dutchman brings one of his most powerful performances on disc, occasionally rough-toned but positive. Leonie Rysanek may sound too mature for Senta, but as a great Wagnerian she brings a commanding presence and the most persuasive sense of line. There is no weak link in the rest of the cast, well set up at the start by the characterful Richard Lewis as the Steersman.

Predictably, Klemperer's reading is spacious in its tempi – involving a third disc in its CD reissue – and the drama hardly grips you by the throat. But the underlying intensity is irresistible. This could hardly be recommended as a first choice, but any committed admirer of the conductor should try to hear it. It is a pity that Anja Silja was chosen as Senta, even though she is not as squally in tone here as she can be. Otherwise a strong vocal cast, much beautiful playing (particularly from the wind soloists) and a lively if not particularly atmospheric recording, made to sound drier still in its CD format.

The fact that Boehm's 1971 Bayreuth recording is from a live performance in this instance reduces its appeal, for the chorus, poorly disciplined in their singing, are noisy on stage, and this is distracting. Gwyneth Jones sings beautifully in pianissimo passages but develops a wobble which worsens as she puts pressure on the voice. Thomas Stewart is better focused in tone than he sometimes is. Boehm's searching interpretation is well worth hearing, but on balance this is a disappointing set. No complaints about the CD transfer, which is vividly atmospheric.

Götterdämmerung and the three other *Ring* operas (Part I, *Das Rheingold;* Part II, *Die Walküre;* Part III, *Siegfried;* Part IV, *Götterdämmerung*).

Götterdämmerung is here placed in alphabetical sequence, as has been our normal practice throughout this *Guide*. This takes it out of its time-frame within the Nibelungen saga for which it becomes the apotheosis. Readers concerned with tracing the narrative should therefore begin with *Das Rheingold* (see below) and move on through Parts II and III before reading the final Part below.

Götterdämmerung (complete).
*** Decca 414 115-2 (4) [id.]. V. State Op. Ch., VPO, Solti.
   Brünnhilde (Birgit Nilsson), Siegfried (Wolfgang Windgassen), Hagen (Gottlob Frick), Alberich (Gustav Neidlinger), Gunther (Dietrich Fischer-Dieskau), Gutrune (Claire Watson), Waltraute (Christa Ludwig).
*** DG 415 155-2 (4) [id.]. German Op. Ch., BPO, Karajan.
   Brünnhilde (Helga Dernesch), Siegfried (Helge Brilioth), Hagen (Karl Ridderbusch), Alberich (Zoltan Kélémen), Gunther (Thomas Stewart), Gutrune (Gundula Janowitz), Waltraute (Christa Ludwig).
*** Ph. 412 488-2 (4) [id.]. (1967) Bayreuth Festival Ch. & O, Boehm.
   Brünnhilde (Birgit Nilsson), Siegfried (Wolfgang Windgassen), Hagen (Josef Greindl), Alberich (Gustav Neidlinger), Gunther (Thomas Stewart), Gutrune (Ludmila Dvořáková), Waltraute (Martha Mödl).
*** EMI Dig. CD7 54485-2 (4) [Ang. CDCD 54485]. Bav. R. Ch., RSO, Haitink.
   Brünnhilde (Eva Marton), Siegfried (Siegfried Jerusalem), Hagen (John Tomlinson), Alberich (Theo Adam), Gunther (Thomas Hampson), Gutrune (Eva-Maria Bundschuh), Waltraute (Marjana Lipovšek).
(M) *** Ph. 434 424-2 (4) [id.]. (1979) Bayreuth Festival Ch. & O, Pierre Boulez.
   Brünnhilde (Gwyneth Jones), Siegfried (Manfred Jung), Hagen (Fritz Hübner), Alberich (Hermann Becht), Gunther (Franz Mazura), Gutrune (Jeannine Altmeyer), Waltraute (Gwendoline Killebrew).
(M) **(*) RCA/Eurodisc Dig. GD 69007 (4) [69007-2-RG]. Leipzig R. Ch., Berlin R. Ch., Dresden State Op. Ch., Dresden State O, Janowski.
   Brünnhilde (Jeannine Altmeyer), Siegfried (René Kollo), Hagen (Matti Salminen), Alberich (Siegmund Nimsgern), Gunther (Hans Günter Nocker), Gutrune (Norma Sharp), Waltraute (Ortrun Wenkel).

The fourth and final part of Wagner's *Ring* cycle follows on directly after Part III (*Siegfried*), telling the story of Siegfried and his meeting with Brünnhilde. In the Prologue to *Götterdämmerung*, the three Norns are seen weaving the Rope of Fate, near the rock where Brünnhilde lay awaiting her lover for so long. They tell of Wotan's power crumbling, and the thread breaks. The Norns descend for ever into the subterranean darkness of the earth. Brünnhilde and Siegfried are celebrating their love, after the joy of reciprocated human passion. But now Siegfried must seek adventure. He gives Brünnhilde the Ring as a token of his love, and she gives him Grane, her horse. She watches, still protected by Loge's circle of fire, as he leaves, and Siegfried sets off on his journey down the Rhine.

On its banks, in the Gibichungs' castle, Hagen, Alberich's son, Gunther (Lord of the Gibichungs), and his sister, Gutrune, discuss how they might enhance the family's fame and fortunes. Hagen wishes that Gunther would marry Brünnhilde and that Siegfried should be joined with Gutrune.

Only Siegfried can penetrate the flame barrier that guards Brünnhilde, so Hagen cunningly plans to use a potion to make Siegfried lose his memory of her and instead fall in love with Gutrune. Siegfried's horn signals his arrival at the castle.

Hagen, Gunther and Siegfried now discuss the hoard of gold of the Nibelungs and the Tarnhelm which Siegfried holds, but Siegfried tells them he has already given the Ring to a woman.

Gutrune gives Siegfried the potion in a drinking horn and it takes immediate effect. He feels passion for Gutrune and, when Brünnhilde's name is mentioned, he partially recalls her but then she is lost to his memory.

In exchange for Gutrune's hand Siegfried promises to help Gunther procure Brünnhilde.

Solemnly Siegfried and Gunther swear eternal brotherhood. They go off in a boat to bring back Brünnhilde, while Gutrune is delighted at the prospect of Siegfried as a husband. Hagen, Alberich's offspring, thinks only of the Ring, his natural heritage.

Waltraute (one of the Valkyries) visits Brünnhilde on the rocky mountain. She emphasizes that things are not going well for the gods and that Wotan has lost his confidence in the future. If Brünnhilde returned the Ring to the Rhinemaidens, perhaps the curse would be lifted. But Brünnhilde flatly refuses; she will never abandon her human love.

Siegfried's horn-call is heard again and Brünnhilde goes out to meet him, but this is Siegfried in Gunther's form, wearing the Tarnhelm. He tells her he is a Gibichung named Gunther and that she must follow him. She invokes the protection of the Ring but he snatches it from her finger. Her spirit is broken and they spend the night in the cave with the sword between them.

Alberich now visits Hagen in the Gibichungs' Hall to spur him on to get the Ring from Siegfried so that the gods can be overthrown. He leaves at dawn. Siegfried returns successfully, and Hagen summons the Gibich vassals, who arrive in force for the wedding party. Gunther and Brünnhilde arrive by boat.

Siegfried and Gutrune walk together in front of Brünnhilde and she is devastated, unable to believe that he does not recognize her. She is angry to see the Ring, which she thought Gunther had taken from her, on his hand and she accuses Siegfried of betrayal.

Siegfried assures Gunther that his sword separated him from Brünnhilde during the night. Now the furious Brünnhilde is ready to agree with Hagen's plan to kill Siegfried and she tells Hagen that Siegfried's only vulnerable spot is his back.

Hagen impresses on Gunther that only the death of Siegfried will enable them to obtain the Ring, and all agree that Siegfried must die. The wedding procession with the ill-matched couples, Gutrune and Siegfried, Gunther and Brünnhilde, now forms up.

Next morning Siegfried and his party are out hunting and the three Rhinemaidens are swimming in the river, still mourning for their lost gold. They tease Siegfried, who has become separated from the hunt, and ask him for the Ring. At first he refuses, but then he offers it. They tell him that its curse will soon affect him and, out of bravado, he changes his mind and retains the Ring, and they swim away.

The huntsmen, with Hagen and Gunther, arrive and a meal is prepared. They all drink and Hagen asks how Siegfried understands bird-song; Siegfried tells his story: of his sword, the death of Fafner, and so on. Hagen now squeezes some juice into Siegfried's drinking horn; this acts as an antidote to the other potion and revives his memory. He remembers the last part of his adventure and his passage through the fire to awaken Brünnhilde. Gunther now understands that Siegfried and Brünnhilde are truly lovers.

Ravens, portents of death, are flying overhead. Hagen draws Siegfried's attention to the birds then plunges his spear into Siegfried's back. As he dies, Siegfried remembers his passage through the flames and his first discovery of Brünnhilde, and their subsequent rapture together. Gunther orders the vassals to carry Siegfried's body back to the castle, and the procession moves off slowly in the moonlight.

Back at the Hall of the Gibichungs, Gutrune waits for Siegfried. Hagen enters and tells her Siegfried has been killed by a boar. She is devastated and falls upon the body, then blames her brother. Gunther admits that Hagen killed Siegfried, but Hagen claims justification and demands the Ring. Gunther refuses and is killed in the fight which follows. Hagen now steps forward to remove the Ring from Siegfried's finger – but, without warning, the hand rises menacingly in the air.

Brünnhilde now enters. She has spoken to the Rhinemaidens and everything is clear to her. She demands vengeance as Siegfried's rightful wife. Gutrune blames her but she will have none of it. She orders a great funeral pyre to be built for Siegfried, and his body is laid at its peak. She draws the Ring from his finger and places it on her own. It will be purified by the flames.

Now holding a firebrand, she sends messengers – two ravens – to Wotan to invite him and Loge to the burning of Valhalla. Brünnhilde lights the pyre and when it is blazing rides her horse Grane into the conflagration to join her lover. The flames burn higher and higher, the Rhine overflows and everything is engulfed.

The three Rhinemaidens swim in the waves. Hagen, still intent on possessing the Ring, throws himself into the flood and two of the maidens draw him down; the third holds the Ring aloft. The waters subside, but in the glowing sky Valhalla is consumed in the fiery furnace.

In Decca's formidable task of recording the whole *Ring* cycle under Solti, *Götterdämmerung* provided the most daunting challenge of all; characteristically, Solti and the Vienna Philharmonic and the Decca recording team under John Culshaw were inspired to heights even beyond earlier achievements. Even the trifling objections raised on earlier issues have been eliminated here. The balance between voices and orchestra has by some magic been made perfect, with voices clear but the orchestra still rich and near-sounding.

On CD, the weight of sound in this 1964 recording comes out with satisfying power in its digital transfer, so giving the brilliance of the upper range its proper support. The big ensembles come over particularly well, and Culshaw's carefully planned, highly atmospheric sound staging is the more sharply focused, exhilaratingly so in the fall of the Gibichung Hall at the end. Access to the set is first class, with rather more generous cueing than in rival versions.

Solti's reading had matured before the recording was made. He presses on still, but no longer is there any feeling of over-driving, and even the *Funeral march*, which in his early Covent Garden performances was brutal in its power, is made into a natural, not a forced, climax. There is not a single weak link in the cast.

Nilsson surpasses herself in the magnificence of her singing: even Flagstad in her prime would not have been more masterful as Brünnhilde. As in *Siegfried*, Windgassen is in superb voice; Frick is a vivid Hagen, and Fischer-Dieskau achieves the near impossible in making Gunther an interesting and even sympathetic character. As for the recording quality, it surpasses even Decca's earlier achievement. This is a landmark in the history of recording, and Decca have also surpassed themselves in the excellence of the tape transfer, with remarkably little background noise.

Recorded last in Karajan's *Ring* series, *Götterdämmerung* has the finest, fullest sound, less brilliant than Solti's on Decca but with glowing purity in the CD transfer to match the relatively lyrical approach of the conductor, with Helga Dernesch's voice in the Immolation scene given satisfying richness and warmth. Karajan's singing cast is marginally even finer than Solti's, and his performance conveys the steady flow of recording sessions prepared in relation to live performances.

But ultimately he falls short of Solti's achievement in the orgasmic quality of the music, that quality which finds an emotional completion in such moments as the end of Brünnhilde's and Siegfried's love scene, the climax of the *Funeral march* and the culmination of the Immolation. At each of these points Karajan is a degree less committed, beautifully as the players respond, and warm as his overall approach is.

Dernesch's Brünnhilde is warmer than Nilsson's, with a glorious range of tone. Brilioth as Siegfried is fresh and young-sounding, while the Gutrune of Gundula Janowitz is far preferable to that of Claire Watson on Decca. The matching is otherwise very even. The balance of voices in the recording may for some dictate a choice: DG brings the singers closer, gives less brilliance to the orchestral texture. Nevertheless, next to Solti's Decca set, such scenes as the summoning of the vassals in Act II lack weight.

Boehm's urgently involving reading of *Götterdämmerung*, very well cast, is crowned by an incandescent performance of the final Immolation scene from Birgit Nilsson as Brünnhilde. Small wonder that she herself has always preferred this version to the fine one she recorded three years earlier for Solti in the studio. It is an astonishing achievement that she could sing with such biting power and accuracy in a live performance, coming to it at the very end of a long evening.

The excitement of that is matched by much else in the performance, so that incidental stage-noises and the occasional inaccuracy, almost inevitable in live music-making, matter hardly at all. This recording, which appeared on LP in the early 1970s, has been transformed in its CD version. The voices are well forward of the orchestra, but the result gives a magnetically real impression of hearing the opera in the Festspielhaus, with the stage movements adding to that sense of reality. Balances are inevitably variable, and at times Windgassen as Siegfried is less well treated by the microphones than Nilsson. Generally his performance for Solti is fresher – but there are points of advantage, too.

Josef Greindl is rather unpleasantly nasal in tone as Hagen, and Martha Mödl as Waltraute is unsteady; but both are dramatically involving. Thomas Stewart is a gruff but convincing Gunther and Dvořáková, as Gutrune, strong if not ideally pure-toned. Neidlinger as ever is a superb Alberich. Anyone preferring a live recording of the *Ring* will find Boehm's final instalment the most satisfying culmination.

The obvious reservation to make over Haitink's studio recording, made in Munich, is with the singing of Eva Marton as Brünnhilde. This very big voice has never recorded well, when the unevenness of vocal production is exaggerated by the microphone in a way that at times comes close to pitchless yelping. Her contributions seriously mar Haitink's *Walküre* and *Siegfried* recordings, but in *Götterdämmerung* the damage is even more clearly outweighed by the set's positive qualities. Marton may sing with a heavy vibrato but there is no problem, as there often has been, over identifying which notes she is aiming at. And here, more than usual, the scale of her dramatic soprano is impressively caught, an archetypal Brünnhilde voice in timbre if not in firmness.

Haitink's reading is magnificent. In its strength, nobility and thrustfulness it crowns all his previous Wagner, culminating in a forceful and warmly expressive account of the final Immolation scene. Siegfried Jerusalem here clearly establishes himself as the finest latterday Siegfried, both heroic and sweet of tone. Thomas Hampson is a sensitive and virile Gunther, John Tomlinson a sinister but human Hagen, Marjana Lipovšek a warmly intense Waltraute and Eva-Maria Bundschuh a rich, rather fruity Gutrune. Among modern digital versions this is a good first choice, even if it hardly replaces such vintage versions as Solti's and Boehm's.

Recorded in analogue sound in 1979, a year before the rest of his Bayreuth cycle, Boulez's version is warm and urgent. The passion of the performance is established in the Dawn music before the second scene of the Prologue and, with a strong, if not ideal cast, it has a clear place as a first-rate mid-price recommendation, far more involving than Janowski's studio recording. Jeannine Altmeyer, the Brünnhilde in that, sings Gutrune here, sweet but not always ideally clean of attack. Fritz Hübner is a weighty Hagen, even if the voice is not sufficiently distinct from that of Franz Mazura, the powerful Gunther.

Gwendoline Killebrew is a rich, firm Waltraute. Manfred Jung as Siegfried gives a fresh, clean-cut performance, and Dame Gwyneth Jones as Brünnhilde, always very variable, has some splendid moments. Despite some painfully unsteady notes in the Immolation scene, she concludes with a splendidly strong account of her final phrase. The analogue sound is aptly atmospheric but lacks something in weight in the brass, making the *Funeral march* less powerful than it should be, though there is no lack of excitement at the end of Act II as Hagen, Gunther and Brünnhilde swear to kill Siegfried.

With sharply focused digital sound, Janowski's studio recording hits refreshingly hard, at least as much so as in the earlier *Ring* operas. Speeds rarely linger but, with some excellent casting – consistent with the earlier operas – the result is rarely lightweight. Jeannine Altmeyer as Brünnhilde rises to the challenges not so much in strength as in feeling and intensity, ecstatic in Act I, bitter in Act II, dedicated in the Immolation scene. Kollo is a fine, heroic Siegfried, only occasionally raw-toned, and Salminen is a magnificent Hagen, with Nimsgern again an incisive Alberich on his brief appearances. Despite an indifferent Gunther and Gutrune and a wobbly if characterful Waltraute, the impression is of clean vocalization matched by finely disciplined and dedicated playing, all recorded in faithful studio sound with no sonic tricks. Now reissued on four CDs at mid-price, this is certainly worth considering, for the background silence adds to the dramatic presence and overall clarity, which is strikingly enhanced.

The Twilight of the Gods (*Götterdämmerung:* complete; in English).
(M) *** EMI CMS7 64244-2 (5) [id.]. ENO Ch. & O, Goodall.
   Brünnhilde (Rita Hunter), Siegfried (Alberto Remedios), Hagen (Aage Haugland), Alberich
   (Derek Hammond-Stroud), Gunther (Norman Welsby), Gutrune (Margaret Curphey),
   Waltraute (Katherine Pring).

Goodall's account of the culminating opera in Wagner's tetralogy may not be the most powerful ever recorded, and certainly it is not the most polished, but it is one which, paradoxically, by intensifying human as opposed to superhuman emotions, heightens the epic scale. The very opening may sound a little tentative (like the rest of the Goodall English *Ring*, this was recorded live at the London Coliseum), but it takes no more than a few seconds to register the body and richness of the sound. The few slight imprecisions and the occasional rawness of wind-tone actually seem to enhance the earthiness of Goodall's view, with more of the primeval saga about it than the magnificent, polished, studio-made *Ring* cycles.

Both Rita Hunter and Alberto Remedios give performances which are magnificent in every way. In particular the golden beauty of Remedios' tenor is consistently superb, with no Heldentenor barking at all, while Aage Haugland's Hagen is giant-sounding to focus the evil, with Gunther and Gutrune mere pawns. The voices on stage are in a different, drier acoustic from that for the orchestra but, considering the problems, the sound is impressive. As for Goodall, with his consistently expansive tempi he carries total concentration – except, curiously, in the scene with the Rhinemaidens, whose music (as in Goodall's *Rhinegold* too) lumbers along heavily.

The Twilight of the Gods (Götterdämmerung): Act III: excerpts in English.
(M) *** Chan. CHAN 6593 [id.]. Rita Hunter, Alberto Remedios, Norman Bailey, Clifford Grant, Margaret Curphey, Sadler's Wells Op. Ch. & O, Goodall.

Originally recorded by Unicorn in the early 1970s, even before the Sadler's Wells company had changed its name to the English National Opera, the single Chandos CD brings an invaluable reminder of Reginald Goodall's performance of the *Ring* cycle when it was in its first flush of success. The two-LP set is here transferred on to a single CD, lasting 66 minutes and covering the closing two scenes. In many ways it possesses an advantage over even the complete live recording of the opera, made at the Coliseum five years later, when Rita Hunter and Alberto Remedios are here obviously fresher and less stressed than at the end of a full evening's performance. It is good too to have this sample, however brief, of Clifford Grant's Hagen and Norman Bailey's Gunther, fine performances both. Fresh, clear recording, not as full as it might be. But at mid-price this CD is well worth investigating.

Lohengrin (complete).
⊛ *** Decca Dig. 421 053-2 (4) [id.]. V. State Op. Concert Ch., VPO, Solti.
Lohengrin (Plácido Domingo), Elsa of Brabant (Jessye Norman), Ortrud (Eva Randová), Telramund (Siegmund Nimsgern), King Henry (Hans Sotin), Herald (Dietrich Fischer-Dieskau).
*** EMI CDS7 49017-8 (3) [Ang. CDCC 49017]. V. State Op. Ch., VPO, Kempe.
Lohengrin (Jess Thomas), Elsa of Brabant (Elisabeth Grümmer), Ortrud (Christa Ludwig), Telramund (Dietrich Fischer-Dieskau), King Henry (Gottlob Frick), Herald (Otto Wiener).
(M) **(*) Ph. Dig. 434 602-2 (4) [id.]. (1990) Bayreuth Festival Ch. & O, Peter Schneider.
Lohengrin (Paul Frey), Elsa of Brabant (Cheryl Studer), Ortrud (Gabriele Schnaut), Telramund (Ekkehard Wlaschiha), King Henry (Manfred Schenk), Herald (Eike Wilm Schulte).
Withdrawn: (M) **(*) EMI CMS7 69314-2 (4) [Ang. CDMD 69314]. German Op. Ch., Berlin, BPO, Karajan.
Lohengrin (René Kollo), Elsa of Brabant (Anna Tomowa-Sintow), Ortrud (Dunja Vejzovic), Telramund (Siegmund Nimsgern), King Henry (Karl Ridderbusch), Herald (Robert Kerns).

Solti rounded off his complete cycle of the Wagner operas in the Bayreuth canon (the first conductor to do so) with this incandescent performance of *Lohengrin*, in which Wagner combined the myth of the Holy Grail and the legend of the Swan Knight. The Prelude, with its haunting ethereal beauty evoking the sanctity of the Grail, rises to an overwhelming climax then sinks back into quiet serenity. The curtain then rises on a pastoral scene, set on the banks of the River Scheldt, near Antwerp.

The people of Brabant, called to arms by a herald, gather before the king, who exhorts them to join together to repel the Hungarian barbarians from Germany; however, there is local friction which needs to be resolved first. Many oppose the claim of Count Friedrich von Telramund to the ducal succession of Brabant, and the king calls on Telramund, who is present with his wife, Ortrud, to give an account of the dispute.

Telramund relates that he was left in charge of the late duke's children when the duke died. The duke's son, Gottfried, disappeared after he and his sister, Elsa, went into the forest, and Telramund accuses Elsa of her brother's murder in order to claim the dukedom for herself. Elsa is sent for but seems unable to answer the accusations. She tells of a dream in which a champion appeared to her, dressed in shining armour (*Einsam in trüben Tagen*). Telramund, encouraged by his wife, repeats the accusation of Elsa's complicity, and the king decrees that the dispute shall be settled by a combat between Telramund and any man who will champion Elsa.

The herald calls twice for someone to step forward but there is no answer. Elsa prays fervently, then the crowd is astonished to see, on the river, a swan drawing along a boat in which stands the knight in shining armour. Telramund and Ortrud are transfixed with awe, but Elsa gazes confidently at heaven. The knight, Lohengrin, steps ashore and, confirming Elsa's innocence, offers himself as her champion and husband.

He imposes one condition: she must never ask his origin or name. She promises and they pledge their love for each other. In spite of the intimidating arrival of the knight, Telramund faces him bravely but is felled with a powerful blow. Yet Lohengrin knows that it is Ortrud – who practises the black magic of Odin – who is the evil influence over Telramund, and he spares his life.

On the cathedral steps Telramund and Ortrud consider the implications of the fight.

Telramund blames his disgrace on his wife (for his lands have been forfeit) but she tells him that the knight's power could be vanquished if Elsa could be made to demand to know his name and origin. Ortrud and Elsa now meet; Elsa says she will try to have Telramund restored to favour, but Ortrud determines to undermine Elsa's belief in her knight.

At dawn Telramund is banished, and it is also decreed that the knight, having married Elsa, shall become Guardian of Brabant and lead the assault on the Hungarian invaders. But Telramund defies the edict and is hidden by friends.

Elsa's wedding is about to be celebrated but, just as she is ready to enter the cathedral, Ortrud stands before her and taunts her for her ignorance of her husband-to-be. Elsa says she trusts him implicitly, but Ortrud names him as a traitor. Lohengrin now arrives with the king and shields Elsa from Ortrud. Telramund stands before them and demands that Lohengrin declare his origins. Lohengrin maintains his silence, but Elsa now is beginning to wonder about him. They all enter the cathedral.

The famous *Wedding march* accompanies Elsa's procession into the bridal chamber where she is joined by Lohengrin and, when alone, they declare their mutual love. Though he calls her Elsa, she cannot speak his name and she implores him to reveal it to her. The door bursts open and Telramund stands before them with four of his nobles; Lohengrin kills him with a single blow, and the nobles kneel before him. He tells Elsa he must go to the king and disclose his identity; their chance of happiness has gone.

The king and his nobles are gathered on the riverbank, preparing for war. Telramund's body is carried in and Elsa, saddened, follows the cortège. To everyone's dismay Lohengrin says he cannot now lead the army, for Elsa has broken her vow and has demanded to know his identity. He is Lohengrin, a Knight of the Holy Grail and the son of Parsifal; now that his secret is revealed, his power is gone and he must leave them.

Elsa desperately begs him not to leave her, but the swan approaches, drawing an empty boat. Lohengrin embraces Elsa for the last time and gives her his sword, horn and ring for her brother, should he return. He predicts a victory for the king in the coming battle. Ortrud triumphantly reveals that she turned Gottfried, Elsa's brother, into a swan, which now serves Lohengrin. Had Lohengrin been able to remain, it would have been possible to restore Gottfried to human form, but this is now impossible.

Lohengrin sinks to his knees and prays, and a white dove appears over the boat. The swan sinks and Gottfried appears in its place and is acclaimed as the new Brabantian ruler. Ortrud is enraged but impotent. The boat bearing Lohengrin is now drawn away by the dove and, as Elsa watches him depart, she falls dead in her brother's arms.

Solti's recording was the last made by the Decca engineers in their favourite Vienna venue, the Sofiensaal, where most of Solti's earlier Wagner sets, including the *Ring* cycle, had been recorded. With its massive ensembles, *Lohengrin* presents special problems, and the engineers here excel themselves in well-aerated sound that still has plenty of body. Solti presents those ensemble moments with rare power and panache, but he also appreciates the chamber-like delicacy of much of the writing, relaxing far more than he might have done earlier in his career, bringing out the endless lyricism warmly and naturally. It was bold to choose for the principal roles two of today's superstar singers.

It is Plácido Domingo's achievement singing Lohengrin that the lyrical element blossoms so consistently, with no hint of Heldentenor barking; at whatever dynamic level, Domingo's voice is firm and unstrained. In the Act III aria, *In fernem Land*, for example, he uses the widest, most beautiful range of tonal colouring, with ringing heroic tone dramatically contrasted against a whisper of head voice, finely controlled.

Jessye Norman, not naturally suited to the role of Elsa, yet gives a warm, commanding performance, always intense, full of detailed insights into words and character. Eva Randová's grainy mezzo does not take so readily to recording, but as Ortrud she provides a pointful contrast, even if she never matches the firm, biting malevolence of Christa Ludwig on the Kempe set. Siegmund Nimsgern, Telramund for Solti as for Karajan, equally falls short of his rival on the Kempe set, Fischer-Dieskau; but it is still a strong, cleanly focused performance. Fischer-Dieskau here sings the small but vital role of the Herald, while Hans Sotin makes a comparably distinctive King Henry. Radiant playing from the Vienna Philharmonic, and committed chorus work too. This is one of the crowning glories of Solti's long recording career.

Kempe's is a rapt account of *Lohengrin*, just as compelling as Solti's on the Decca set. It remains one of his finest memorials on disc. Kempe looked at Wagner very much from the spiritual side, giving *Lohengrin* deeper perspectives than usual. The link with early Wagner is less obvious; instead one sees the opera as the natural pair with *Parsifal*, linked no doubt in

Wagner's mind too, since in mythology Parsifal was the father of Lohengrin. The intensity of Kempe's conducting lies even in its very restraint, and throughout this glowing performance one senses a gentle but sure control, with the strings of the Vienna Philharmonic playing radiantly.

The singers too seem uplifted, Jess Thomas singing more clearly and richly than usual, Elisabeth Grümmer unrivalled as Elsa in her delicacy and sweetness, Gottlob Frick gloriously resonant as the King. But it is the partnership of Christa Ludwig and Fischer-Dieskau as Ortrud and Telramund that sets the seal on this superb performance, giving the darkest intensity to their machinations in Act II, their evil heightening the beauty and serenity of so much in this opera.

Though the digital transfer on CD reveals roughness (even occasional distortion) in the original recording, the glow and intensity of Kempe's reading comes out all the more involvingly in the new format. The set is also very economically contained on three CDs instead of the four for all rivals, though inevitably breaks between discs come in the middle of Acts.

In his live recording from the 1990 Bayreuth Festival Peter Schneider conducts a strong, well-paced reading, avoiding the exaggerations that mar the Wagner interpretations of some more celebrated conductors. Yet he is neither stiff nor lacking in imagination, and the great Act II duet between Elsa and Ortrud culminates in a warmly volatile reading of the glorious concluding melody, always a key passage, with Cheryl Studer as Elsa shading her phrases most tenderly. Sadly, Gabriele Schnaut is a squally Ortrud, hardly a match for her.

Elsa was one of the roles which first won Studer international fame, not least at Bayreuth, bright and girlish at the start in *Elsa's dream* and bringing out the equivocal development of the character. The Canadian, Paul Frey, is a strong, noble Lohengrin, sweeter-toned than most latterday Heldentenors, though with a slow vibrato occasionally obtruding. Ekkehard Wlaschiha, best known for singing Alberich in the *Ring*, is a dark, sinister Telramund, and Manfred Schenk makes a powerful King Heinrich.

The digital sound is atmospheric, with plenty of detail, even though the chorus is placed rather backwardly. Schneider may not convey the visionary intensity that Kempe so movingly achieves on his classic set but, at mid-price on four CDs, with the outer Acts each complete on a single disc, it makes an excellent recommendation for anyone wanting a digital recording at less than full price.

Karajan, whose DG recording of *Parsifal* is so naturally intense, fails in this earlier but related opera to capture comparable spiritual depth. So some of the big melodies sound a degree over-inflected; and the result, though warm and expressive and dramatically powerful, with wide-ranging recording, misses an important dimension. Nor is much of the singing as pure-toned as it might be, with René Kollo too often straining and Tomowa-Sintow not always able to scale down in the necessary purity her big, dramatic voice.

Even so, with strong and beautiful playing from the Berlin Philharmonic, it remains a powerful performance, and it makes a fair bargain version on four mid-priced CDs – but remember that the Kempe version, on one disc fewer, is comparable in price. The CD booklet offers the libretto without an English translation, but a synopsis instead.

Die Meistersinger von Nürnberg (complete).
*** DG 415 278-2 (4) [id.]. German Op., Berlin, Ch. & O, Jochum.
   Hans Sachs (Dietrich Fischer-Dieskau), Walther (Plácido Domingo), Eva (Catarina Ligendza), Pogner (Peter Lagger), Beckmesser (Roland Hermann), David (Horst Laubenthal), Magdalene (Christa Ludwig).
**(*) Decca 417 497-2 (4) [id.]. Gumpolds-kirchner Spätzen, V. State Op. Ch., VPO, Solti.
   Hans Sachs (Norman Bailey), Walther (René Kollo), Eva (Hannelore Bode), Pogner (Kurt Moll), Beckmesser (Bernd Weikl), David (Adolf Dallapozza), Magdalene (Júlia Hamari).
(M) **(*) Ph. 434 611-2 (4) [id.]. (1974) Bayreuth Festival Ch. & O, Varviso.
   Hans Sachs (Karl Ridderbusch), Walther (Jean Cox), Eva (Hannelore Bode), Pogner (Hans Sotin), Beckmesser (Klaus Hirte), David (Frieder Stricker), Magdalene (Anna Reynolds).
(M) (***) EMI mono CHS7 63500-2 (4) [Ang. CDHD 63500]. (1951) Bayreuth Festival Ch. & O, Karajan.
   Hans Sachs (Otto Edelmann), Walther (Hans Hopf), Eva (Elisabeth Schwarzkopf), Pogner (Friedrich Dalberg), Beckmesser (Erich Kunz), David (Gerhard Unger), Magdalene (Ira Malaniuk).
(M) (***) EMI mono CMS7 64154-2 (4) [Ang. CDMD 64154]. St Hedwig's Cathedral Ch., German Op., Berlin, Ch., Berlin State Op. Ch., BPO, Kempe.
   Hans Sachs (Ferdinand Frantz), Walther (Rudolf Schock), Eva (Elisabeth Grümmer), Pogner

(Gottlob Frick), Beckmesser (Benno Kusche), David (Gerhard Unger), Magdalene (Marga Höffgen).

**(*) EMI CDS7 49683-2 (4) [Ang. CDCD 49683]. Leipzig R. Ch., Dresden State Op. Ch. & State O, Karajan.

Hans Sachs (Theo Adam), Walther (René Kollo), Eva (Helen Donath), Pogner (Karl Ridderbusch), Beckmesser (Geraint Evans), David (Peter Schreier), Magdalene (Ruth Hesse).

(M) ** BMG/RCA GD 69008 (4) [Eurodisc 69002-2-RG]. Bav. State Op. Ch., Bav. State O, Keilberth.

Hans Sachs (Otto Wiener), Walther (Jess Thomas), Eva (Claire Watson), Pogner (Hans Hotter), Beckmesser (Benno Kusche), David (Friedrich Lenz), Magdalene (Lilian Benningsen).

The mastersingers flourished in the main cities of Germany during the fourteenth, fifteenth and sixteenth centuries among the artisans and emerging middle classes. Musical competitions were judged by a strict code of rules and 32 faults were enumerated to be avoided. Scriptural or devotional subjects were usual and in Nuremberg there were four judges, the first making a comparison with the Bible text chosen, the second criticizing the prose, the third the rhymes, and the fourth the tune. The winner was the performer with the fewest marks set against him. Hans Sachs, the most famous of the mastersingers, was born in 1494 and died in 1576; he is credited as being the author of 6,000 poems.

As Wagner's opera opens, a young knight, Walther von Stolzing, a visitor to the church of St Catherine, is watching Eva, the daughter of Pogner, the goldsmith. At once attracted to her, he discovers from her maid, Magdalene, that Eva's hand is to be the prize in the mastersingers' contest the next day, although Eva can refuse the winner if she wishes. If she does so, however, she must remain single. Walther decides to compete.

An apprentice, David, betrothed to Magdalene, arrives to prepare for the preliminary song trial and he gives Walther the details of the challenge. Pogner now enters with Beckmesser, the town clerk, who desires Eva for himself. Pogner welcomes Walther then makes the official announcement about the contest and the prize. Walther is allowed to show what he can do, with Beckmesser as 'marker'.

He sings a song of spring and love, and at the finish Beckmesser's slate is covered with markings; he is anxious to discredit Walther because of his own interest in Eva. The other masters observe critically that the song broke the strict rules but the great mastersinger, Hans Sachs, shoemaker-poet, speaks up for him. (Here Wagner is undoubtedly mirroring his experience of trying to establish his own genius against a hidebound musical establishment.) Walther's contribution is unacceptable – he is not qualified to enter the contest.

It is now evening and the apprentices are looking forward to the following day as they close the shutters of their premises. David tells Magdalene that Walther has failed the preliminary trial and this news is passed on to Eva, who is very attracted to her young suitor. David is working late in Sachs' shop, and Walther's song haunts his memory. Eva arrives, and Sachs, who is very fond of her, realizes that she loves Walther but perhaps feels she is being too impulsive.

Beckmesser now comes to serenade Eva, but Magdalene takes her place at the window so that Eva can meet Walther again. They openly declare their love and she is willing to elope with him, but Sachs steps in to prevent them going off. As Beckmesser begins his serenade, Sachs counters with a noisy cobbler's song and thoroughly irritates him. However, they finally agree that Sachs will listen and act as marker for the serenade, banging his hammer on the shoe on which he is working for each fault. Beckmesser's effort is far from perfect and is punctuated by regular taps from Sachs' hammer. Meanwhile David arrives and, realizing that it is Magdalene sitting in the window, jealously sets on the unwitting serenader. Walther and Eva make one more attempt to elope, but Sachs again intervenes and takes Walther back into the house. Beckmesser retires, disconsolate, to repair his damaged lute, and the nightwatchman's horn can be heard in the distance.

The next morning Sachs is in his workshop and David enters apologetically after the events of the previous evening. But Sachs is in a good mood. It is St John's Day and Sachs ponders the folly of humanity in his *Wahnmonolog*. Walther enters and is gently instructed by Sachs in the intricacies of the song contest, but the inspired Walther is able to dictate a song that came to him in a dream – all but the last verse. Sachs is impressed and writes down the words of the song. Beckmesser, seeing the written poem, puts it in his pocket, assuming Sachs was the author and planning to compete himself. Sachs assures him that he can use the song himself if he wishes and saying that the authorship will not be revealed. Beckmesser leaves, overjoyed.

Eva now enters, prettily dressed up and making the excuse of a shoe that needs attention. Walther's joy at seeing his beloved inspires the last verse of the song, which Sachs praises. Eva, enjoying the warmth of her feelings, tells Sachs that, had she not fallen in love with Walther, she would have chosen Sachs as her husband. But old Sachs knows the legend of 'Tristram and Isolde' and has no ambition to be the King Mark of the situation. The new song is given its name in a quintet in which David and Magdalene join (*Selig, wie die Sonne*).

It is the day of the great contest, and banners are flying to decorate the festive meadow. Brightly dressed apprentices guide people to their seats and Pogner leads in Eva, Magdalene with her. Then comes the majestic procession of the mastersingers, heralded by trumpets. There is dancing, and one of Sachs' own songs is heard. It is he who announces the rules of the contest.

Secretly Beckmesser has been trying to memorize the words of the new song and arranging a suitable tune. He steps forth, looking somewhat ridiculous, and stumbles up to the rostrum. The crowd is amused. He plays a few chords on his lute but mixes up the words so much that they lose all meaning. Angry at being ridiculed, he turns on Sachs, proclaiming him the author of the poem.

All, including the masters, are surprised at this revelation, but Sachs denies authorship, saying that he could not possibly have conceived as great a song as this. Walther steps forward, bows to the masters and, to the enthusiastic acclaim of everyone present, sings the glorious Prize song.

Though not a member of the guild, he is plainly the winner, and Eva crowns him with the victor's wreath then both kneel before Pogner, who blesses the couple. Pogner is about to invest Walther as a master, but Walther feels this honour is too great and declines. Sachs steps forward and proudly invokes the glory of German art. Eva takes the wreath from Walther and places it on Sachs, while the latter endorses Walther's election to the guild by placing the Masters' chain round his neck.

Jochum's is a performance which, more than any, captures the light and shade of Wagner's most warmly approachable score, its humour and tenderness as well as its strength. The recording was made at the same time as live opera-house performances in Berlin, and the sense of a comedy being enacted is irresistible. With Jochum, the processions at the start of the final *Festwiese* have sparkling high spirits, not just German solemnity, while the poetry of the score is radiantly brought out, whether in the incandescence of the Act III *Prelude* (positively Brucknerian in hushed concentration) or the youthful magic of the love music for Walther and Eva.

Above all, Jochum is unerring in building long, Wagnerian climaxes and resolving them – more so than his recorded rivals. The cast is the most consistent yet assembled on record. Though Catarina Ligendza's big soprano is ungainly at times for Eva, it is an appealing performance, and the choice of Domingo for Walther is inspired, bringing out the lyrical element. The keystone is the searching and highly individual Sachs of Fischer-Dieskau, a performance long awaited. Obviously controversial (you can never imagine this sharp Sachs sucking on his boring old pipe), Fischer-Dieskau with detailed word-pointing and sharply focused tone gives new illumination in every scene.

The Masters – with not one woolly-toned member – make a superb team, and Horst Laubenthal's finely tuned David matches this Sachs in applying Lieder style. The recording-balance favours the voices, but on CD they are made to sound just slightly ahead of the orchestra. There is a lovely bloom on the whole sound and, with a recording which is basically wide-ranging and refined, the ambience brings an attractively natural projection of the singers.

The great glory of Solti's set is not the searing brilliance of the conductor but rather the mature and involving portrayal of Sachs by Norman Bailey. For his superb singing the set is well worth investigating, and there is much else to enjoy, not least the bright and detailed sound which the Decca engineers have, as so often in the past, obtained with the Vienna Philharmonic, recording Wagner in the Sofiensaal. Kurt Moll as Pogner, Bernd Weikl as Beckmesser (really singing the part) and Júlia Hamari as Magdalene (refreshingly young-sounding) are all excellent, but the shortcomings are comparably serious.

Both Hannelore Bode and René Kollo fall short of their (far from perfect) contributions to earlier sets and Solti, for all his energy, is rhythmically heavy at times in this most appealing of Wagner scores, exaggerating the four-square rhythms with even stressing, pointing his expressive lines too heavily and failing to convey real spontaneity. It remains an impressive achievement, and those who must at all costs hear Bailey's marvellous Sachs should not be deterred, for the Decca sound comes up very vividly on CD. Yet that merit is hardly enough to compensate for the vocal shortcomings.

Die Meistersinger is an opera which presents serious problems for an engineer intent on recording it at a live performance. Not only do the big crowd scenes, with their plentiful movement, bring obtrusive stage-noises; the sheer length of the work means that, by Act III, even the most stalwart singer is flagging. It follows that the Bayreuth performance, recorded during the Festival of 1974, is flawed; but the Swiss conductor, Silvio Varviso, still proves the most persuasive Wagnerian, one who inspires the authentic ebb and flow of tension, who builds up Wagner's scenes concentratedly over the longest span, and who revels in the lyricism and textural beauty of the score.

It is not a lightweight reading and, with one exception, the singing is very enjoyable indeed, with Karl Ridderbusch a firmly resonant Sachs and the other Masters, headed by Klaus Hirte as Beckmesser and Hans Sotin as Pogner, really singing their parts. Jean Cox is a strenuous Walther, understandably falling short towards the end; Hannelore Bode as Eva brings the one serious disappointment, but she is firmer here than on Solti's later set. For all the variability, the recording, retaining its atmosphere in the CD transfer, gives enjoyment, even if the stage noises are the more noticeable.

Recorded live at the 1951 Bayreuth Festival, Karajan's earlier EMI version has never quite been matched since for its involving intensity. The mono sound may be thin and the stage noises often distracting, but, with clean CD transfers, the voices come over very well, and the sense of being present at a great event is irresistible. The great emotional moments – both between Eva and Walther and, even more strikingly, between Eva and Sachs – bring a gulp to the throat more predictably than in any other set.

The young Elisabeth Schwarzkopf makes the most radiant Eva, singing her Act III solo, *O Sachs, mein Freund!*, with touching ardour before beginning the Quintet with flawless legato. Hans Hopf is here less gritty than in his other recordings, an attractive hero; while Otto Edelmann makes a superb Sachs, firm and virile, the more moving for not sounding old. There are inconsistencies among the others but, in a performance of such electricity, generated by the conductor in his early prime, they are of minimal importance.

The four mid-priced CDs are generously indexed and come with a libretto but no translation. EMI should have indicated the index points not just in the libretto, but in the English synopsis as well.

Though Kempe's classic EMI set is in mono only, one misses stereo surprisingly little when, with closely balanced voices, there is such clarity and sharpness of focus. The orchestra rather loses out, sounding relatively thin, but with such an incandescent performance – not quite as intense as Karajan's live Bayreuth version of 1951 but consistently inspired – one quickly adjusts. The cast has no weak link. Elisabeth Grümmer is a meltingly beautiful Eva, pure and girlish, not least in the great Act III Quintet, and Rudolf Schock gives the finest of all his recorded performances as Walther, with his distinctive timbre between lyric and heroic well suited to the role. Ferdinand Frantz is a weighty, dark-toned Sachs, Gottlob Frick a commanding Pogner, Benno Kusche a clear-toned Beckmesser and Gerhard Unger an aptly light David.

EMI, in setting up their star-studded later stereo version, fell down badly in the choice of Sachs. Theo Adam, promising in many ways, has quite the wrong voice for the part, in one way too young-sounding, in another too grating, not focused enough. After that keen disappointment there is much to enjoy, for in a modestly reverberant acoustic (a smallish church was used) Karajan draws from the Dresden players and chorus a rich performance which retains a degree of bourgeois intimacy. Anyone wanting an expansive sound may be disappointed, but Karajan's thoughtful approach and sure command of phrasing are most enjoyable.

Donath is a touching, sweet-toned Eva, Kollo here is as true and ringing a Walther as one could find today, Geraint Evans an incomparably vivid Beckmesser, and Ridderbusch a glorious-toned Pogner. The extra clarity of CD gives new realism and sense of presence to a recording not specially impressive on LP. With the finest Eva on any current set, it is a good choice for those who are not upset by Adam's ungenial Sachs.

The Keilberth set was recorded at the very first performance given in the rebuilt Opera House in Munich in November 1963. That brings inevitable flaws, but the voices are generally bright and forward and the atmosphere is of a great occasion. The team of Masters includes such distinguished singers as Hans Hotter as Pogner and Josef Metternich as Kottner; but Otto Wiener in the central role of Hans Sachs is too unsteady to be acceptable on record. Jess Thomas makes a ringing and accurate if hardly subtle Walther, and Claire Watson a fresh-toned but uncharacterful Eva. Keilberth paces well but tends to bring out the rhythmic squareness. Like Karajan's inspired Bayreuth recording of 1951, this comes on four mid-priced CDs, but has the advantage of stereo sound.

Die Meistersinger: excerpts.
(M) *** DG 435 406-2; *435 406-4* [id.] (from above recording with Fischer-Dieskau, Ligendza, Domingo; cond. Jochum) – WEBER: *Oberon* excerpts. ***

Instead of a normal set of highlights for this reissue in the 'Domingo Edition', DG have sensibly concentrated on the items featuring Domingo as Walther. The selection runs for nearly 40 minutes and, while some of the excerpts involve fades, sometimes at both ends, the effect is not too distracting. The sound is first rate and the coupling with excerpts from Weber's *Oberon* an equally happy choice.

Parsifal (complete).
⊛ *** DG Dig. 413 347-2 (4) [id.]. German Op. Ch., BPO, Karajan.
    Parsifal (Peter Hofmann), Amfortas (José Van Dam), Gurnemanz (Kurt Moll), Kundry (Dunja Vejzovic), Klingsor (Siegmund Nimsgern), Titurel (Victor Von Halem).
*** Decca 417 143-2 (4) [id.]. V. Boys' Ch., V. State Op. Ch., VPO, Solti.
    Parsifal (René Kollo), Amfortas (Dietrich Fischer-Dieskau), Gurnemanz (Gottlob Frick), Kundry (Christa Ludwig), Klingsor (Zoltan Kélémen), Titurel (Hans Hotter).
(M) (***) Teldec/Warner mono 9031 76047-2 (4) [id.]. (1951) Bayreuth Festival Ch. & O, Knappertsbusch.
    Parsifal (Wolfgang Windgassen), Amfortas (George London), Gurnemanz (Ludwig Weber), Kundry (Martha Mödl), Klingsor (Hermann Uhde), Titurel (Arnold Van Mill).
(M) **(*) DG 435 718-2 (3) [id.]. (1970) Bayreuth Festival Ch. & O, Boulez.
    Parsifal (James King), Amfortas (Thomas Stewart), Gurnemanz (Franz Crass), Kundry (Gwyneth Jones), Klingsor (Donald McIntyre), Titurel (Karl Ridderbusch).
(M) **(*) Ph. Dig. 434 616-2 (4) [id.]. (1985) Bayreuth Festival Ch. & O, Levine.
    Parsifal (Peter Hofmann), Amfortas (Simon Estes), Gurnemanz (Hans Sotin), Kundry (Waltraud Meier), Klingsor (Franz Mazura), Titurel (Matti Salminen).
(M) **(*) Erato/Warner Dig. 2292 45662-2 (4) [id.]. Prague Philharmonic Ch., Monte Carlo PO, Jordan.
    Parsifal (Reiner Goldberg), Amfortas (Wolfgang Schöne), Gurnemanz (Robert Lloyd), Kundry (Yvonne Minton), Klingsor (Aage Haugland), Titurel (Hans Tschammer).
**(*) Ph. 416 390-2 (4). (1962) Bayreuth Festival Ch. & O, Knappertsbusch.
    Parsifal (Jess Thomas), Amfortas (George London), Gurnemanz (Hans Hotter), Kundry (Irene Dalis), Klingsor (Gustav Neidlinger), Titurel (Martti Talvela).
Withdrawn: **(*) EMI Dig. CDS7 49182-8 (5) [id.]. WNO Ch. & O, Goodall.
    Parsifal (Warren Ellsworth), Amfortas (Phillip Joll), Gurnemanz (Donald McIntyre), Kundry (Waltraud Meier), Klingsor (David Gwynne), Titurel (Nicholas Folwell).

The legend of Parsifal – originally Spanish – dates from the thirteenth century; Montsalvat was the Spanish name for the stronghold of the Knights of the Holy Grail. Wagner places the site of the castle of Klingsor – the knights' antagonist – in that part of Spain, then under Arab rule. The grail is the cup in which the blood of the crucified Christ was kept, and the spear with which he was wounded was also preserved by the order.

In a forest in the domain of the Holy Grail an aged knight, Gurnemanz, calls for prayer. They must make preparation for the arrival of Amfortas, king of the knights, who will bathe in the nearby lake, as he suffers greatly from a wound which refuses to heal. Suddenly a strange woman, Kundry, reputed to be a sorceress, enters and rushes to Gurnemanz; she gives him a small crystal flask and cries that it is balsam for the king. She throws herself on the ground to rest and watches as Amfortas is carried in.

Amfortas talks to a knight and speaks of 'a guileless fool made wise by pity' who will bring him relief from his suffering. Kundry hands him the crystal flask and, when he thanks her, she laughs mockingly. When Gurnemanz asks her where the flask came from she tells him, 'From farther away than your thought can travel.' Amfortas leaves and Gurnemanz now tells how the Grail and Spear were delivered to Titurel, father of Amfortas.

He had founded a company of knights to guard these precious relics and later handed them on to his son. Klingsor was a knight who had transgressed and so was banned from membership of the brotherhood. He then created a garden near the knights' domain, full of seductive women to tempt them.

Kundry was the woman who scorned Christ on the way to Calvary. While she tries to expiate her guilt, she is an ambivalent character, often used as a tool of evil by Klingsor. She was responsible for the event which caused the suffering of Amfortas. He was seduced by her, and

Klingsor was able to take the Holy Spear and cause the wound which will not heal. The Spear must be recovered if he is to be cured.

Animal life is sacred in the domain of the Grail, so when a wounded swan flies over the lake everyone is horrified. The young man who shot the swan is Parsifal. When questioned, however, he seems unable to give his name or declare his origin. He first boasts of his marksmanship, knowing nothing of the sacred nature of living beings; but gradually he awakens to a sense of his wrong-doing and displays a touching, child-like grief. Kundry, still present, states that the youth's father was slain in battle and that he was reared by his mother, now dead.

Gurnemanz takes Parsifal to the great hall of the knights, where they assemble for holy communion. The aged Titurel tells his son to uncover the Grail, but Amfortas' great pain seems heightened by the ceremony. When uncovered the Grail glows in the darkness and it is consecrated. Parsifal watches without comprehending what he has seen (for he is the 'guileless fool'); Gurnemanz finds his attitude unacceptable and sends him away.

Klingsor anticipates that Parsifal will soon appear in his domain and hopes to trap him with the help of Kundry, who is in his power. He orders her to seduce him, and she has no choice but to obey. Parsifal is taken to the magic garden and the beautiful maidens do their best to entice him. Yet it is only Kundry who makes any impression on him. But when, after recalling his mother, she tries to kiss him, he remembers Amfortas' painful wound and recalls the sight of the Grail, and he backs away.

Now Kundry believes he can help her atone for her sin but he says it will not be in the way she wishes. Finally Parsifal rejects her advances; he feels that, by being strong against such temptations, he may also help Amfortas. As he repulses her, she curses him and says he will never again find the Castle of the Grail.

She calls to Klingsor, who aims the Sacred Spear at Parsifal. But his throw is interfered with by a mysterious force, and the Spear remains suspended over Parsifal's head. He picks it up and with it makes the sign of the cross. In a moment the garden disintegrates and becomes an arid desert. Parsifal goes off with the Spear and calls to Kundry so that she knows he has gone.

Some years pass. The aged Gurnemanz finds Kundry outside his hermit's hut. She is half dead from exposure and is plainly dressed, almost as if a penitent. No longer wild, she offers to serve him. It is Good Friday, and he takes her inside the hut as Parsifal appears, dressed in black armour. He is refused entry because of his dress, so he removes his armour and Gurnemanz sees him as the foolish youth who long ago killed the swan. Parsifal tells him that, because of Kundry's curse, through all his long travels he could not find his way back, but now he brings the Holy Spear.

Gurnemanz is greatly relieved, for the knights have declined to a sorry state: Amfortas has consistently refused to uncover the Grail since it brings him such suffering, and Titurel is dead. There has been nothing but despair in the Castle of the Grail. But now the day of rejoicing has come, Parsifal is to be the new King of the Grail. Both Kundry and Gurnemanz bathe his feet and sprinkle water on his brow.

The knights again gather in the great hall of the Grail. The bells ring out. Two processions take place, one with Amfortas and the Grail, the other with Titurel's coffin. The knights mourn before the altar and ask Amfortas to uncover the Grail so that they may all receive its life force. He refuses, begging that they kill him. Parsifal now enters. He places the Spear on Amfortas' wound and it heals instantly. Amfortas is absolved, but it is Parsifal who is now consecrated as king. He commands finally that the Grail be revealed, and it glows and radiates with light. Amfortas and the knights kneel in homage and Kundry, whose curse has been lifted, sinks into the sleep of death.

Communion, musical and spiritual, is what the intensely beautiful Karajan set provides, with pianissimos shaded in magical clarity and the ritual of bells and offstage choruses heard as in ideal imagination. If, after the Solti recording for Decca, it seemed doubtful whether a studio recording could ever match in spiritual intensity earlier ones made on stage at Bayreuth, Karajan proves otherwise, his meditation the more intense because the digital sound allows total silences.

The playing of the Berlin orchestra – preparing for performance at the Salzburg Easter Festival of 1980 – is consistently beautiful; but the clarity and refinement of sound prevent this from emerging as a lengthy serving of Karajan soup. He has rarely sounded so spontaneously involved in opera on record. Kurt Moll as Gurnemanz is the singer who, more than any other, anchors the work vocally, projecting his voice with firmness and subtlety. José van Dam as Amfortas is also splendid: the *Lament* is one of the glories of the set, enormously wide in dynamic and expressive range. The Klingsor of Siegmund Nimsgern could be more sinister, but the singing is admirable. Dunja Vejzovic makes a vibrant, sensuous Kundry who rises superbly to the moment in Act II where she bemoans her laughter in the face of Christ.

Only Peter Hofmann as Parsifal leaves any disappointment; at times he develops a gritty edge on the voice, but his natural tone is admirably suited to the part – no one can match him today – and he is never less than dramatically effective. He is not helped by the relative closeness of the solo voices, but otherwise the recording is near the atmospheric ideal, a superb achievement. The four CDs, generously full and offering an improved layout, are among DG's finest so far, with the background silence adding enormously to the concentration of the performance.

It was natural that, after Solti's other magnificent Wagner recordings for Decca, he should want to go on to this last of the operas. In almost every way it is just as powerful an achievement as any of his previous Wagner recordings in Vienna, with the Decca engineers surpassing themselves in vividness of sound and the Vienna Philharmonic in radiant form. The singing cast could hardly be stronger, every one of them pointing words with fine, illuminating care for detail.

The complex balances of sound, not least in the *Good Friday music*, are beautifully caught; throughout, Solti shows his sustained intensity in Wagner. There remains just one doubt, but that rather serious: the lack of that spiritual quality which makes Knappertsbusch's live version so involving. However, the clear advantage of a studio recording is the absence of intrusive audience noises which, in an opera such as this with its long solos and dialogues, can be very distracting. The remastering for CD, as with Solti's other Wagner recordings, opens up the sound, and the choral climaxes are superb. On CD, the break between the second and third discs could have been better placed.

Hans Knappertsbusch was the inspired choice of conductor made by Wagner's grandsons for the first revivals of *Parsifal* after the war. The Teldec historic reissue is taken from the first season in 1951 and makes a striking contrast with the later Knappertsbusch recording, made in stereo for Philips 11 years later. The 1951 performance is no less than 20 minutes longer overall, with Knappertsbusch, always expansive, even more dedicated than in his later reading. The cast is even finer, with Wolfgang Windgassen making other Heldentenors seem rough by comparison, singing with warmth as well as power. Ludwig Weber is magnificently dark-toned as Gurnemanz, much more an understanding human being than his successor, Hans Hotter, less of a conventionally noble figure. Martha Mödl is both wild and abrasive in her first scenes and sensuously seductive in the long Act II duet with Parsifal, and Hermann Uhde is bitingly firm as Klingsor. Though the limited mono sound is not nearly as immediate or atmospheric as the later stereo, with much thinner orchestral texture, the voices come over well, and the chorus is well caught.

Boulez's recording, made live at Bayreuth in 1970, was only the third version ever issued, yet it has remained the most radical of all. The speeds are so consistently fast that in the age of CD it has brought an obvious benefit in being fitted – easily – on three discs instead of four, yet Boulez's approach, with the line beautifully controlled, conveys a dramatic urgency rarely found in this opera, and never sounds breathless. Traditional Wagnerians may well resist, and certainly Boulez misses the spiritual intensity of a Karajan or a Knappertsbusch, but those listeners less committed will find the results refreshing, with textures clarified in a way characteristic of Boulez.

Even the flower-maidens sing like young apprentices in *Meistersinger* rather than seductive beauties. James King is a firm, strong, rather baritonal hero, Thomas Stewart a fine, tense Amfortas, and Gwyneth Jones as Kundry is in strong voice, only occasionally shrill, though Franz Crass is disappointingly unsteady as Gurnemanz. The live Bayreuth recording is most impressively transferred to CD, economically reissued at mid-price.

James Levine's conducting of *Parsifal* at Bayreuth brought a landmark in an already distinguished career. With this spacious, dedicated performance he completely shook off any earlier associations as an American whizzkid conductor which, even after many years at the Met., still clung to him.

Of all the Wagner operas this is the one that gains most and loses least from being recorded live at Bayreuth, and the dedication of the reading, the intensity as in an act of devotion, comes over consistently, if not with quite the glow that so marks Karajan's inspired studio performance.

Unfortunately the singing is flawed. Peter Hofmann, in far poorer voice than for Karajan, is often ill-focused, and even Hans Sotin as Gurnemanz is vocally less reliable than usual. The rest are excellent, with Franz Mazura as Klingsor, Simon Estes as Amfortas and Matti Salminen as Titurel all giving resonant, finely projected performances, well contrasted with each other. Waltraud Meier is an outstanding Kundry here, as in Goodall's studio performance, singing at Bayreuth with more dramatic thrust, for Goodall with more security.

The recording, though not the clearest from this source, captures the Bayreuth atmosphere well. The reissue at mid-price in the Philips Bayreuth series makes it the more attractive.

Jordan's 1981 recording with Monte Carlo forces, clean and fresh but lacking in weight and spiritual depth, was used for the controversial film of the opera. Its great merit is the singing of Reiner Goldberg in the name-part, one of his least flawed recordings. Though the voice is not always well focused, Robert Lloyd's Gurnemanz brings fine singing too, making the character more youthful-sounding than usual. Aage Haugland's Klingsor has nothing sinister in it, but rather masculine nobility, and Yvonne Minton makes a fine, vehement Kundry.

This digital, mid-priced set offers full, natural sound, vivid yet warmly atmospheric in its CD format, and is certainly recommendable to those who liked the film. However, it comes on four CDs against Boulez's three. The documentation is good, with a clear libretto, but the cues are relatively ungenerous.

Knappertsbusch's expansive and dedicated reading is superbly caught in the Philips set, one of the finest live recordings made in the Festspielhaus at Bayreuth, with outstanding singing from Jess Thomas as Parsifal and Hans Hotter as Gurnemanz. Though Knappertsbusch chooses consistently slow tempi, there is no sense of excessive squareness or length, so intense is the concentration of the performance, its spiritual quality, and the sound has undoubtedly been further enhanced in the remastering for CD.

The snag is that the stage noises and coughs are also emphasized and the bronchial afflictions are particularly disturbing in the *Prelude*. However, the recording itself is most impressive, with the choral perspectives particularly convincing and the overall sound warmly atmospheric. Even so, this set seems too highly priced.

It is sad that EMI opted to spread the Goodall version on to five CDs, when the rivals take only four, even the Levine which is barely less spacious in its speeds. However, as the set has just been withdrawn, EMI are probably planning a more economically laid-out, mid-priced reissue. Certainly the vividness of the sound and the absence of background add to the immediacy and dedication. Goodall in his plain, unvarnished, patiently expansive reading characteristically finds deep intensity in a strong, rough-hewn way. He may lack the ethereal beauties of Karajan, for here *Parsifal* is brought down to earth, thanks not just to Goodall but to the cast which with one exception stands up well to international competition.

It was plainly a help that these same singers had appeared together under Goodall on stage in the Welsh National Opera production. Donald McIntyre gives one of his very finest performances as Gurnemanz, with more bloom than usual. Waltraud Meier's powerful, penetrating voice suits the role of Kundry well, while the American, Warren Ellsworth, has power and precision, if little beauty, as Parsifal. Only the ill-focused Amfortas of Phillip Joll is disappointing, too gritty of tone, though he too makes the drama compelling.

Das Rheingold (complete).
*** Decca 414 101-2 (3). VPO, Solti.
  Wotan (George London), Fricka (Kirsten Flagstad), Loge (Set Svanholm), Mime (Paul Kuen), Alberich (Gustav Neidlinger).
(M) *** Ph. 434 421-2 (2) [id.]. (1980) Bayreuth Festival O, Boulez.
  Wotan (Donald McIntyre), Fricka (Hanna Schwarz), Loge (Heinz Zednik), Mime (Helmut Pampuch), Alberich (Hermann Becht).
**(*) DG 415 141-2 (3) [id.]. BPO, Karajan.
  Wotan (Dietrich Fischer-Dieskau), Fricka (Josephine Veasey), Loge (Gerhard Stolze), Mime (Erwin Wohlfahrt), Alberich (Zoltan Kélémen).
**(*) Ph. 412 475-2 (2) [id.]. (1967) Bayreuth Festival O, Boehm.
  Wotan (Theo Adam), Fricka (Annelies Burmeister), Loge (Wolfgang Windgassen), Mime (Erwin Wohlfahrt), Alberich (Gustav Neidlinger).
(M) **(*) RCA/Eurodisc Dig. GD 69004 (2) [69004-2-RG]. Dresden State O, Janowski.
  Wotan (Theo Adam), Fricka (Yvonne Minton), Loge (Peter Schreier), Mime (Christian Vogel), Alberich (Siegmund Nimsgern).
** EMI Dig. CDS7 49853-2 (2) [Ang. CDCB 49853]. Bav. RSO, Haitink.
  Wotan (James Morris), Fricka (Marjana Lipovšek), Loge (Heinz Zednik), Mime (Pater Haage), Alberich (Theo Adam).
** DG Dig. 427 607-2 (3). Met. Op. O, Levine.
  Wotan (James Morris), Fricka (Christa Ludwig), Loge (Siegfried Jerusalem), Mime (Heinz Zednik), Alberich (Ekkehard Wlaschiha).

As *Das Rheingold* – the first opera in the *Ring* saga – opens, three Rhinemaidens (Woglinde,

Wellgunde and Flosshilde) guard the river's treasure, the Rhinegold. As they swim and play they are watched by a misshapen dwarf, Alberich. He longs to possess just one of the maidens; but they are not for him, and they enjoy teasing him unmercifully. As he pursues them hopelessly, the glint of the Rhinegold catches his attention. He is told about the magic power of the gold. If a man fashions a ring from it and renounces love in favour of power, he will rule the world.

The frustrated Alberich takes his opportunity, snatches part of the gleaming gold and utters the required renunciation. The rocks and water disappear and in their place a magnificent castle materializes high on a mountain – the new home of the gods. The Rhine can be seen flowing far below.

Wotan, their leader, and Fricka (his wife) have been asleep; but now Wotan awakens, admiring the new castle, while Fricka reminds him that he unrealistically promised the builders (two giants: Fasolt and Fafner) that they should have her sister, Freia, Goddess of Love, Spring and Youth, as their reward. Freia enters, craving protection from these two terrifying creatures. Loge, God of Fire, is crafty enough to help Wotan avoid having to keep his promise, and Wotan relies on his assistance.

The giants now demand their reward and Wotan vacillates. Freia calls for help, and Froh and Donner, two other gods, enter. Froh embraces Freia while Donner threatens the giants with his hammer. Loge now enters and tells Wotan that he cannot help him with his promise, but – knowing that the giants are listening – he relates how Alberich has stolen the gold.

The giants now decide that this gold would be a better bargain than Freia, but Wotan refuses them; he wants the gold for himself. Freia is taken off by the giants as a hostage while Wotan makes up his mind. Loge returns to the others who are now looking old and faded, since Freia, who represents youth, has left them.

Wotan decides to accompany Loge to Nibelheim, the land of the Nibelungs. They descend deep into the earth and a cacophony of anvils is heard from an underground cavern. Alberich has already made his slaves fashion a ring from the stolen gold. Moreover his brother, Mime, has forged a magic helmet, which he calls the Tarnhelm, from the same metal. The helmet gives its wearer the power to become invisible or to assume any shape desired.

The treacherous Alberich puts it on and is at once invisible. He beats his brother and goes off in triumph. Wotan and Loge try in vain to placate Mime, then Alberich returns with more treasure. Alberich boasts of his powers and predicts the downfall of the gods. Loge throws doubt on his claims and taunts Alberich (who, besides being ugly, is not very bright) to prove his words by turning first into a dragon then into a toad. In this latter form he is easily captured and Loge grabs the Tarnhelm.

Wotan and Loge now demand the Rhinegold as Alberich's ransom for freedom. He grudgingly agrees, but then they take further advantage of their situation by demanding also the Tarnhelm for Loge and the Ring for Wotan. Alberich furiously curses the Ring: anyone who wears it will die (*Verflucht sei dieser Ring!*). Wotan and Loge return to the domain of the gods where Froh and Fricka enter with Donner, and the giants come back, accompanied by Freia. They will hand her over when the ransom of gold is paid. Fasolt insists that the mountain of gold should be high enough to hide Freia; Wotan agrees, and Loge and Froh pile high the hoard of gold blocks. The Tarnhelm is added to conceal her hair; when only her eyes are visible the two giants also demand the Ring. Wotan has no choice but to accede, but Erda, Goddess of Earth, Wisdom and Destiny, warns him not to part with the Ring. Alberich's curse immediately begins to work, however.

The two giants quarrel over the gold, Fafner demanding the larger share. They fight and Fasolt is killed. Fafner leaves. Loge (cynically) congratulates Wotan for parting with the Ring. Wotan and Fricka are about to enter their castle together, but first Wotan wishes to consult Erda. Donner swings his hammer and the mighty blow sets off a spectacular thunderstorm.

The clouds slowly disperse and a dazzling rainbow bridge appears. Wotan names the castle of the gods Valhalla, and he leads Fricka across the bridge, followed by Froh, Freia and Donner. Loge watches from the side, and the Rhinemaidens can be heard again singing sadly of the loss of the gold. But Valhalla and all it stands for is in danger from the threat of the cursed golden Ring.

Das Rheingold was appropriately the first of Solti's cycle. Recorded in 1958, it remains in terms of engineering the most spectacular, an ideal candidate for transfer to CD with its extra clarity and range. Noises and movements in the lowest bass register, virtually inaudible on LP, become clearly identifiable on CD; but the immediacy and precise placing of sound are thrilling, while the sound-effects of the final scenes, including Donner's hammer-blow and the rainbow bridge, have never been matched since. The sound remains of demonstration quality, to have one cherishing all the more this historic recording with its unique vignette of Flagstad as Fricka.

Solti gives a magnificent reading of the score, crisp, dramatic and direct. He somehow brings a freshness to the music without ever overdriving or losing an underlying sympathy. Vocally, the set is held together by the unforgettable singing of Neidlinger as Alberich. Too often the part – admittedly ungrateful on the voice – is spoken rather than sung, but Neidlinger vocalizes with wonderful precision and makes the character of the dwarf develop from the comic creature of the opening scene to the demented monster of the last.

Flagstad learnt the part of Fricka specially for this recording, and her singing makes one regret that she never took the role on the stage; but regret is small when a singer of the greatness of Flagstad found the opportunity during so-called retirement to extend her reputation with performances such as this. Only the slightest trace of hardness in the upper register occasionally betrays her, and the golden power and richness of her singing are for the rest unimpaired – enhanced even, when recorded quality is as true as this.

As Wotan, George London is sometimes a little rough – a less brilliant recording might not betray him – but this is a dramatic portrayal of the young Wotan. Svanholm could be more characterful as Loge, but again it is a relief to hear the part really sung. Much has been written on the quality of the recording, and without a shadow of a doubt it deserves the highest star rating. Decca went to special trouble to produce the recording as for a stage performance and to follow Wagner's intentions as closely as possible. They certainly succeeded. An outstanding achievement.

Like the Boehm set, also recorded live by Philips at Bayreuth, the Boulez version, taken from the 1980 Festival, the last year of the Patrice Chéreau production, comes on only two discs and has the advantage of a more modest medium price. The early digital sound has plenty of air round it, giving a fine impression of a performance in the Festspielhaus with all its excitement, though voices are not caught as immediately as on the Boehm set.

Sir Donald McIntyre, seriously neglected by the record companies, here gives a memorable and noble performance, far firmer than his rival for Boehm, Theo Adam. Heinz Zednik is splendid as Loge and Hanna Schwarz is a powerful Fricka, while Siegfried Jerusalem brings beauty of tone as well as distinction to the small role of Froh. Hermann Becht is a weighty rather than incisive Alberich, and the only weak link is Martin Egel's unsteady Donner. Though not as bitingly intense as Boehm, Boulez, with speeds almost as fast, shatters the old idea of him as a chilly conductor.

Karajan's account is more reflective than Solti's; the very measured pace of the *Prelude* indicates this at the start and there is often an extra bloom on the Berlin Philharmonic playing. But Karajan's very reflectiveness has its less welcome side, for the tension rarely varies. One finds such incidents as Alberich's stealing of the gold or Donner's hammer-blow passing by without one's pulse quickening as it should. Unexpectedly, Karajan is not as subtle as Solti in shaping phrases and rhythms.

There is also no doubt that the DG recording managers were not as painstaking as John Culshaw's Decca team, and that too makes the end result less compellingly dramatic. On the credit side, however, the singing cast has hardly any flaw at all, and Fischer-Dieskau's Wotan is a brilliant and memorable creation, virile and expressive. Among the others, Veasey is excellent, though she cannot efface memories of Flagstad; Gerhard Stolze with his flickering, almost *Sprechstimme* as Loge gives an intensely vivid if, for some, controversial interpretation. The 1968 sound has been clarified in the digital transfer but, while the compact discs bring out the beauty of Fischer-Dieskau's singing as the young Wotan the more vividly, generally the lack of bass brings some thinness.

The transfer to CD of Boehm's 1967 live recording made at Bayreuth is outstandingly successful. His preference for fast speeds (consistently through the whole cycle) here brings the benefit that, as with Boulez, the whole of the *Vorabend* is contained on two CDs, a considerable financial advantage. The pity is that the performance is marred by the casting of Theo Adam as Wotan, keenly intelligent but rarely agreeable on the ear, at times here far too wobbly. On the other hand, Gustav Neidlinger as Alberich is superb, even more involving here than he is for Solti, with the curse made spine-chilling. It is good too to have Loge cast from strength in Wolfgang Windgassen, cleanly vocalized; among the others, Anja Silja makes an attractively urgent Freia. Though a stage production brings nothing like the sound-effects which make Solti's set so involving, the atmosphere of the theatre in its way is just as potent.

The Eurodisc set of *Das Rheingold*, also part of a complete cycle, comes from what used to be East Germany, with Marek Janowski a direct, alert conductor of the Dresden State Orchestra, and more recently of the Royal Liverpool Philharmonic. This performance is treated to a digital recording totally different from Solti's. The studio sound has the voices close and vivid, with the orchestra rather in the background. Some Wagnerians prefer that kind of balance, but the result here rather lacks the atmospheric qualities which make the Solti *Rheingold* still the most compelling in sound, thanks to the detailed production of the late John Culshaw.

With Solti, Donner's hammer-blow is overwhelming; but the Eurodisc set comes up with only a very ordinary 'ping' on an anvil, and the grandeur of the moment is missing. Theo Adam as Wotan has his grittiness of tone exaggerated here, but otherwise it is a fine set, consistently well cast, including Peter Schreier, Matti Salminen, Yvonne Minton and Lucia Popp, as well as East German singers of high calibre. The CDs sharpen the focus even further, with clarity rather than atmosphere the keynote.

Haitink's version of *Rheingold*, the second instalment in his EMI *Ring* cycle made in conjunction with Bavarian Radio, follows the same broad pattern as the first to be issued, *Die Walküre*, strong and expansive rather than dramatic, with tension often not quite keen enough. Vocally too the performance has its flaws. Marjana Lipovšek makes a superb Fricka, rich and well projected, but James Morris – also the Wotan in the rival Levine cycle for DG – sounds grittier than before; the fascinating choice of a noted Wotan of the past for the role of Alberich, Theo Adam, proves a mixed blessing. The often unconventional characterization is magnetic, but Adam can no longer sustain a steady note. Unlike the Solti, Karajan and Levine versions, the EMI set requires only two CDs instead of the more usual three. The recording is warm and full rather than brilliant or well focused.

Recorded in conjunction with the latest production of *The Ring* at the Met. in New York, the Levine version brings a strong cast, and it will appeal mainly to those who have had experience of the opera-house performances. Yet neither in sound nor in pacing does the performance capture the sense of live experience very vividly. Though the quality is acceptable, there is too little sense of presence, and the voices lose some of their bloom. James Morris as Wotan, for example, sounds rougher than he does for Haitink; but Ekkehard Wlaschiha is a far firmer Alberich than Theo Adam, and Christa Ludwig makes a characterful Fricka, if not as rich as Lipovšek. Zednik translates very effectively from Loge in the EMI set to Mime at the Met., with Siegfried Jerusalem a powerful if undercharacterized Loge. The balance of advantage lies with the Haitink version, and Levine's slow speeds mean that, unlike the EMI, the DG takes three discs. Levine paces Donner's hammer-blow more dramatically – but neither can compare with the vintage Solti set; for Levine, the sword theme on the trumpet is disappointingly obscured.

The Rheingold (complete, in English).
(M) **(*) EMI CMS7 64110-2 (3). ENO O, Goodall.
  Wotan (Norman Bailey), Fricka (Katherine Pring), Loge (Emile Belcourt), Mime (Gregory Dempsey), Alberich (Derek Hammond-Stroud).

Goodall's slow tempi in *Rheingold* bring an opening section where the temperature is low, reflecting hardly at all the tensions of a live performance, even though this was taken from a series of Coliseum presentations. The recording too, admirably clean and refined, is less atmospheric than *Siegfried*, the first of the series to be recorded. Nevertheless the momentum of Wagner gradually builds up so that, by the final scenes, both the overall teamwork and the individual contributions of such singers as Norman Bailey, Derek Hammond-Stroud and Clifford Grant come together impressively. Hammond-Stroud's powerful representation of Alberich culminates in a superb account of the curse. The spectacular orchestral effects (with the horns sounding glorious) are vividly caught by the engineers and impressively transferred to CD, even if balances (inevitably) are sometimes less than ideal.

Rienzi (complete).
(M) ** EMI CMS7 63980-2 (3) [id.]. Leipzig R. Ch., Dresden State Op. Ch., Dresden State O, Hollreiser.
  Rienzi (René Kollo), Irene (Siv Wennberg), Steffano Colonna (Nikolaus Hillebrand), Adriano Colonna (Janis Martin), Paolo Orsini (Theo Adam), Raimondo (Siegfried Vogel), Baroncelli (Peter Schreier).

It is sad that the flaws in this ambitious opera prevent the unwieldy piece from having its full dramatic impact, although it was Wagner's first success, when produced at Dresden in 1841. Its setting is fourteenth-century Rome.

As the opera begins, the pope has fled and violence erupts between two noble houses, Orsini and Colonna. Orsini tries to abduct Rienzi's sister, Irene, and Adriano Colonna saves her. Cardinal Raimondo desperately tries to quell the rioting until the Tribune, Cola Rienzi, appears, together with two of his henchmen, Cecco del Veccio and Baroncelli, and manages to restore some sort of order. Rienzi orders the city gates be shut as unrest flares up outside the city. The cardinal says that the church will support all attempts to break the power of the nobles, and Rienzi calls on the people to be ready as soon as they hear the trumpets sound the alarm.

Irene now tells her brother that it was Adriano who saved her from Paolo Orsini. Though himself a noble, Adriano detests the present lawlessness, but it is difficult for him to act against his own family. However, eventually he agrees to help restore the rule of law. Rienzi will protect Irene, and Adriano and she are lovers. A long trumpet-call sounds and Rienzi is proclaimed king, promising freedom for the people from the oppression of the noble families.

At last the Capitol enjoys peace, if only temporarily, and the major families offer Rienzi their support. But Colonna and Orsini are quietly plotting against Rienzi while publicly acknowledging his leadership. Adriano overhears a murder being planned, but Rienzi refuses to take his warning seriously. Rienzi asserts Rome's refusal to be part of the Holy Roman Empire and takes over the emperor's powers in the name of the people.

At the celebrations the nobles attempt to assassinate him but the chain mail beneath his robes protects him and they fail. The conspirators, including Adriano's father, are condemned to immediate execution but Adriano and Irene both persuade Rienzi to spare the lives of the usurpers, provided they swear an oath of loyalty.

Yet another insurrection follows, and this time Rienzi shows no mercy to the nobles. Adriano once more is faced with a dilemma: where does his greatest loyalty lie – to Irene's brother or to his father? He prays for reconciliation between them. In the battle, Colonna and Orsino die, but the people are again victorious and a great battle-hymn is heard. Adriano mourns for his father, swearing revenge against Rienzi, who understands his feelings.

Such heavy casualties have been endured that faith in Rienzi is shaken; plotting begins yet again, led by Baroncelli and Cecco. Adriano now resolves to kill Rienzi. A procession arrives at the church. Irene is with Rienzi, who addresses the crowd. But the church excommunicates him, and everyone deserts him except Irene, despite Adriano's pleas.

Rienzi now finally faces disaster. Irene maintains her loyalty and Adriano cannot undermine it. She stands with Rienzi, as Baroncelli and Cecco, having swayed the populace in their favour, set the Capitol on fire, and the tower in which Rienzi and Irene are trapped, collapses, also burying Adriano.

This recording is far from complete, but the cuts in the enormous score are unimportant and most of the set numbers make plain the youthful, uncritical exuberance of the ambitious composer. The accompanied recitatives are less inspired, and no one could count the Paris-stye ballet music consistent with the rest, delightful and sparkling though it is.

Except in the recitative, Heinrich Hollreiser's direction is strong and purposeful, but much of the singing is disappointing. René Kollo at least sounds heroic, but the two women principals are poor. Janis Martin in the breeches role of Adriano produces tone that does not record very sweetly, while Siv Wennberg as the heroine, Rienzi's sister, slides most unpleasantly between notes in the florid passages. Despite good recording, this can only be regarded as a stop-gap.

Der Ring des Nibelungen (complete).

⊛ (M) *** Decca 414 100-2 (15) [id.]. Birgit Nilsson, Kirsten Flagstad, Wolfgang Windgassen, Dietrich Fischer-Dieskau, Hans Hotter, George London, Christa Ludwig, Gustav Neidlinger, Gottlob Frick, Set Svanholm, Gerhard Stolze, Kurt Boehme, Marga Höffgen, Joan Sutherland, Régine Crespin, James King, Claire Watson, VPO, Solti.

(M) *** Ph. 420 325-2 (14) [id.]. Birgit Nilsson, Wolfgang Windgassen, Gustav Neidlinger, Theo Adam, Leonie Rysanek, James King, Gerd Nienstedt, Hermin Esser, Martti Talvela, Kurt Boehme, Anja Silja, Helga Dernesch, Thomas Stewart, Marga Höffgen, (1967) Bayreuth Festival Ch. & O, Boehm.

(M) *** DG 435 211-2 (15) [id.]. Josephine Veasey, Dietrich Fischer-Dieskau, Gerhard Stolze, Zoltan Kélémen, Helga Dernesch, Oralia Dominguez, Jess Thomas, Thomas Stewart, Régine Crespin, Gundula Janowitz, Jon Vickers, Martti Talvela, Helge Brilioth, Christa Ludwig, Karl Ridderbusch, BPO, Karajan.

(M) *** Ph. Dig./Analogue 434 421/4-2 (12); *Videos:* 070 401/4-3 (all available separately). Gwyneth Jones, Donald McIntyre, Manfred Jung, Hermann Becht, Heinz Zednik, Helmut Pampuch, Ortrun Wenkel, Peter Hofmann, Jeannine Altmeyer, Matti Salminen, Fritz Hübner, Franz Mazura, (1979/80) Bayreuth Festival Ch. & O, Pierre Boulez.

(M) **(*) BMG/RCA Dig. GD 69003 (14) [69003-2-RG]. Jeannine Altmeyer, René Kollo, Theo Adam, Peter Schreier, Siegmund Nimsgern, Siegfried Vogel, Yvonne Minton, Ortrun

Wenkel, Matti Salminen, Lucia Popp, Siegfried Jerusalem, Jessye Norman, Kurt Moll, Cheryl Studer, Leipzig R. Ch., Dresden State Op. Ch. & O, Janowski.

(M) (***) EMI mono CZS7 67123-2 (13) [Ang. CDZM 67123]. Ludwig Suthaus, Martha Mödl, Ferdinand Frantz, Julius Patzak, Gustav Neidlinger, Wolfgang Windgassen, Hilde Konetzni, Rita Streich, Sena Jurinac, Gottlob Frick, RAI Ch., Rome SO, Furtwängler.

The story of Wagner's great *Ring* saga is told under each of the four separate operas which make up the Nibelungen sequence: *Das Rheingold*, *Die Walküre*, *Siegfried* and finally *Götterdämmerung*. Having himself completed the text, Wagner began work on the music for his mighty project in November 1853, and *Götterdämmerung* was finally completed 21 years later, in the autumn of 1874.

The Decca set – one of the great achievements of the gramophone – is reissued on CD in a special edition of 15 discs at medium price, a bargain of bargains for those who have not already invested in the separate issues. Solti's was the first recorded *Ring* cycle to be issued, and it has never been surpassed. Whether in performance or in vividness of sound, it continues to set standards three decades after Decca's great project was completed.

That project was the brainchild of the Decca recording producer of the time, John Culshaw, whose concept was to portray in sound as vividly as possible the full impact of Wagner's stage directions, whether they related to what was possible in the theatre or not. To that degree, sound recording was made to transcend the opera house.

First recorded was *Rheingold*, which caused a sensation when it was issued, not least because of the closing scenes with Donner's great hammer-blow and the rainbow bridge, which remain demonstration passages even now, superbly transferred to CD. As for the casting, that too has never been surpassed, certainly not by latterday studio recordings. Even the role of the Woodbird in *Siegfried* is uniquely cast, with the young Joan Sutherland outshining all rivals.

Nilsson and Windgassen as Brünnhilde and Siegfried may not be as spontaneous-sounding in this studio performance as in their live, Bayreuth recording for Boehm, but the freshness and power are even greater.

Solti's remains the most electrifying account of the tetralogy on disc, sharply focused if not always as warmly expressive as some. Solti himself developed in the process of making the recording, and *Götterdämmerung* represents a peak of achievement for him, commanding and magnificent. Though CD occasionally reveals bumps and bangs inaudible on the original LPs, this is a historic set that remains as central today as when it first appeared.

Anyone who prefers the idea of a live recording of the *Ring* cycle can be warmly recommended to Boehm's fine set, more immediately involving than any. Recorded at the 1967 Bayreuth Festival, it captures the unique atmosphere and acoustic of the Festspielhaus very vividly. Birgit Nilsson as Brünnhilde and Wolfgang Windgassen as Siegfried are both a degree more volatile and passionate than they were in the Solti cycle, recorded earlier for Decca, with Nilsson at her most incandescent in the final Immolation scene, triumphant at the end of her long performance.

Gustav Neidlinger as Alberich is also superb, as he was too in the Solti set; and the only major reservation concerns the Wotan of Theo Adam, in a performance searchingly intense and finely detailed but often unsteady of tone even at that period. Boehm's preference for urgent speeds, never letting the music sag, makes this an exciting experience, and in *Rheingold* it brings the practical advantage that the *Vorabend* comes on only two CDs instead of three, bringing the total for the set to 14 instead of 15 discs. The sound, only occasionally constricted, has been vividly transferred.

Karajan's recording of the *Ring* followed close on the heels of Solti's for Decca, providing a good alternative studio version which equally stands the test of time. The manner is smoother, the speeds generally broader, yet the tension and concentration of the performances are maintained more consistently than in most modern studio recordings. Though the recordings were linked with stage productions in Salzburg and at the Met. in New York, they preceded the stagings and bring a broadly contemplative rather than a searingly dramatic view of Wagner. Casting is generally good, with few failures, again generally better than in modern studio recordings.

Casting is not quite consistent between the operas, with Régine Crespin as Brünnhilde in *Walküre*, but Helga Dernesch at her very peak in the last two operas. The casting of Siegfried is changed between *Siegfried* and *Götterdämmerung*, from Jess Thomas, clear and reliable, to Helge Brilioth, just as strong but sweeter of tone. The original CD transfers are used without change for this mid-price compilation. The recording, pleasantly reverberant, is not as immediate or involving as Solti's Decca, with fewer dramatic sound-effects.

On Philips comes the *Ring* cycle conducted by Pierre Boulez that first had non-opera-goers glued to their TV sets, especially when it was shown an Act at a time (with sur-titles), so that the drama could be fully relished without longueurs. The cycle is available on both VHS video cassettes and laser discs, but for those who prefer to have the music without Patrice Chéreau's controversially eccentric production values, the CDs are offered at mid-price, and each opera is available separately and as such is discussed above and below.

It may come as a surprise to those who think of Boulez as a cold conductor that his is, alongside Boehm's, the most passionate *Ring* available. Speeds are fast, putting the complete cycle on fewer CDs than usual (12 against the more usual 14 or 15). Gwyneth Jones, handsome as Brünnhilde on stage, lurches between thrilling, incisive accuracy and fearsome yowls. Opposite her as Siegfried, Manfred Jung is, by Heldentenor standards, commendably precise and clean, but at times he sounds puny, not helped by microphone balances. But none of these obvious drawbacks can hide the fact that the recording – digital in the first three operas, analogue in *Götterdämmerung* – gives a thrilling idea of what it feels like to hear *The Ring* at Bayreuth. Boulez's concentration falters hardly at all.

The fast speeds convey conviction, making one ever eager to hear more rather than to contemplate. The 1979/80 cast was better than average. Donald McIntyre as Wotan has rarely if ever sounded so well on record, while Peter Hofmann as Siegmund is more agreeable here than he has been on other Wagner records, such as the Karajan *Parsifal*.

Dedication and consistency are the mark of the Eurodisc *Ring*, a studio recording made with German thoroughness by the then East German record company. Originally packaged cumbersomely by Eurodisc on 18 CDs, RCA here reissue it on 14 mid-priced discs, to make it much more attractive. Voices tend to be balanced well forward of the orchestra, but the digital sound is full and clear to have one concentrating on the words, helped by Janowski's direct approach to the score. Overall this is a good deal more rewarding than many of the individual sets that have been issued at full price over the last five years.

When in 1972 EMI first transferred the Italian Radio tapes of Furtwängler's studio performances of 1953, the sound was disagreeably harsh, making sustained listening unpleasant. In this digital transfer, the boxiness of the studio sound and the closeness of the voices still take away some of the unique Furtwängler glow in Wagner, but the sound is acceptable and actually benefits in some ways from extra clarity.

Each Act was performed on a separate day, giving the advantage of continuous performance but with closer preparation than would otherwise have been possible. Furtwängler gives each opera a commanding sense of unity, musically and dramatically, with hand-picked casts including Martha Mödl as a formidable Brünnhilde, Ferdinand Frantz a firm-voiced Wotan and Ludwig Suthaus (Tristan in Furtwängler's recording) a reliable Siegfried. In smaller roles you have stars like Wolfgang Windgassen, Julius Patzak, Rita Streich, Sena Jurinac and Gottlob Frick.

The Ring 'Great scenes': Das Rheingold: Entry of the Gods into Valhalla. Die Walküre: Ride of the Valkyries; Magic fire music. Siegfried: Forging scene; Forest murmurs. Götterdämmerung: Siegfried's funeral march; Brünnhilde's immolation scene.
(M) *** Decca 421 313-2. Birgit Nilsson, Wolfgang Windgassen, Hans Hotter, Gerhard Stolze, VPO, Solti.

These excerpts are often quite extended – the *Entry of the Gods into Valhalla* offers some ten minutes of music, and the *Forest murmurs* from *Siegfried* starts well before the orchestral interlude. Only *Siegfried's funeral march* is in any sense a 'bleeding chunk' which has to be faded at the end; and the disc closes with twenty minutes of Brünnhilde's Immolation scene.

Der Ring: excerpts: Das Rheingold: Zur Burg führt die Brucke (scene iv). Die Walküre: Ein Schwert verhiess mir der Vater; Ride of the Valkyries; Wotan's farewell and Magic fire music. Siegfried: Notung!; Brünnhilde's awakening. Götterdämmerung: Brünnhilde, heilige Braut! Siegfried's death and Funeral music.
(B) *** DG 429 168-2; *429 168-4* (from complete recording; cond. Karajan).

The task of selecting highlights to fit on a single disc, taken from the whole of the *Ring* cycle, is an impossible one. But the DG producer of this record has managed to assemble 70 minutes of key items, mostly nicely tailored, with quick fades. The one miscalculation was to end with *Siegfried's funeral march* from *Götterdämmerung*, which leaves the listener suspended; it would have been a simple matter to add the brief orchestral postlude which ends the opera. Nevertheless there is much to enjoy, and this makes a genuine sampler of Karajan's approach to the *Ring* – even the *Ride of the Valkyries* is comparatively refined. The late-1960s sound is excellent.

Siegfried (complete).
*** Decca 414 110-2 (4). VPO, Solti.
    Siegfried (Wolfgang Windgassen), Brünnhilde (Birgit Nilsson), Wanderer (Hans Hotter), Mime (Gerhard Stolze), Alberich (Gustav Neidlinger), Erda (Marga Höffgen), Fafner (Kurt Boehme), Woodbird (Joan Sutherland).
*** Ph. 412 483-2 (4) [id.]. (1967) Bayreuth Festival O, Boehm.
    Siegfried (Wolfgang Windgassen), Brünnhilde (Birgit Nilsson), Wanderer (Theo Adam), Mime (Erwin Wohlfahrt), Alberich (Gustav Neidlinger), Erda (Vera Soukupová), Fafner (Kurt Boehme), Woodbird (Erika Köth).
(M) *** Ph. Dig. 434 423-2 (3). (1980) Bayreuth Festival O, Boulez.
    Siegfried (Manfred Jung), Brünnhilde (Gwyneth Jones), Wanderer (Donald McIntyre), Mime (Heinz Zednik), Alberich (Hermann Becht), Erda (Ortrun Wenkel), Fafner (Fritz Hübner), Woodbird (Norma Sharp).
**(*) EMI Dig. CDS7 54290-2 (4) [Ang. CDCD 54290]. Bav. RSO, Haitink.
    Siegfried (Siegfried Jerusalem), Brünnhilde (Eva Marton), Wanderer (James Morris), Mime (Pater Haage), Alberich (Theo Adam), Erda (Jadwiga Rappé), Fafner (Kurt Rydl), Woodbird (Kiri Te Kanawa).
(M) **(*) RCA/Eurodisc Dig. GD 69006 (4) [69006-2-RG]. Dresden State O, Janowski.
    Siegfried (René Kollo), Brünnhilde (Jeannine Altmeyer), Wanderer (Theo Adam), Mime (Peter Schreier), Alberich (Siegmund Nimsgern), Erda (Ortrun Wenkel), Fafner (Matti Salminen), Woodbird (Norma Sharp).
** DG 415 150-2 (4) [id.]. BPO, Karajan.
    Siegfried (Jess Thomas), Brünnhilde (Helga Dernesch), Wanderer (Thomas Stewart), Mime (Gerhard Stolze), Alberich (Zoltan Kélémen), Erda (Oralia Dominguez), Fafner (Karl Ridderbusch), Woodbird (Catherine Gayer).
** DG Dig. 429 407-2 (4) [id.]. NY Met. O, Levine.
    Siegfried (Reiner Goldberg), Brünnhilde (Hildegard Behrens), Wanderer (James Morris), Mime (Heinz Zednik), Alberich (Ekkehard Wlaschiha), Erda (Brigitta Svendén), Fafner (Kurt Moll), Woodbird (Kathleen Battle).

Before *Siegfried* begins there is a lapse of time after the conclusion of the events related in *Die Walküre*, Part II of the *Ring* cycle. As predicted by Brünnhilde, Sieglinde has given birth to Siegfried. The cunning dwarf, Mime, has reared the boy, knowing that one day Siegfried will be able to kill Fafner, who has possession of both the Rhinegold and the Ring and, in guarding it, has assumed the form of a dragon. Mime plans to murder Siegfried afterwards and thus obtain the Ring and the treasure for himself.

We first see Mime working in his cavern, trying to forge a sword from the fragments which Siegfried's dying mother left behind. Siegfried enters, driving before him a bear which frightens Mime; but he hands Siegfried his newest sword and Siegfried breaks it straight away, scorning Mime's work. Siegfried loathes him and he asks who his real parents were. Mime says that he is both mother and father to him but, on threat of strangulation, tells him about Sieglinde and shows him the fragments of Nothung. Siegfried orders Mime to repair the sword so that he can take it and leave, never to return. But Mime fails again to forge the new sword from the old.

A wanderer (Wotan) now appears, and Mime characteristically refuses him hospitality. The Wanderer asks Mime to test his (the Wanderer's) wits with three questions and says he will forfeit his head if he cannot answer them. His answers – about the Nibelungs, the giants, and the gods – are correct. Now it is Mime's turn, and he fears the questions but answers the first two correctly. The third – who will repair the sword? – he cannot answer, and the Wanderer states that it can be mended only by someone who has never known fear. The Wanderer goes off without claiming Mime's life, as he had feared. Siegfried returns and Mime hides but, when he tells Siegfried what the Wanderer said, Siegfried does not understand: he cannot comprehend fear. He decides therefore to remake the sword himself.

Siegfried hammers away and he sings his forging song, *Nothung, Nothung!* Finally the weapon is finished, and with one blow he splits the anvil in two. Mime is terror-stricken but plans to guide Siegfried to Fafner and, when the dragon is slain, he will poison Siegfried and take the Ring.

Outside Fafner's lair, Alberich keeps watch. The Wanderer arrives and Alberich recognizes that it is Wotan. Alberich foolishly boasts that one day, when Fafner dies, he himself will conquer Valhalla. The Wanderer ignores him and announces that a young hero will soon arrive and kill Fafner, who is duly warned of his fate. Wotan leaves and Alberich resumes his vigil.

As morning dawns, Mime and Siegfried appear. Mime is still trying to show Siegfried the experience of fear, but Siegfried is unimpressed by the thought of the dragon and listens instead to the sounds of the forest. He lifts his silver horn and its call arouses Fafner, who knows what to expect.

Siegfried is victorious, but before expiring Fafner warns him against Mime. Siegfried removes his sword from the dragon's body and in so doing is burned by its blood, which gives him the magic power to understand the songs of the birds. The woodbird tells him of the treasure, the Ring and the Tarnhelm inside the cave. Siegfried enters the cave.

Mime and Alberich quarrel but they hide as he emerges. Again the woodbird sings a warning of Mime's treachery. Mime tries to trap Siegfried but the dragon's blood enables him to hear what Mime is thinking and ignore what he says so that, when he proffers the poison, Siegfried kills him.

Siegfried rests after all these exertions, then is spurred on as the woodbird tells of a bride, Brünnhilde, who, encircled by fire, awaits a hero to awaken her. In answer to further questioning the bird says that Brünnhilde can be awakened only by a man who knows no fear. Siegfried realizes that he is that man, and the bird leads him to the sleeping Brünnhilde, Siegfried prudently takes the Ring and the Tarnhelm with him.

In a wild, rocky place the Wanderer summons his past lover, the Earth Goddess Erda (the mother of Brünnhilde and her sisters). She rises from a deep chasm and suggests that he consult the Norns (Fates) but he persists in asking her whether destiny can be averted. He is thinking of the predicted demise of the gods. Erda speaks of their daughter, Brünnhilde, and Wotan recalls her punishment for disobedience. (She tried to help defend Siegmund, father of Siegfried, but his destiny was death at the hands of Hunding.)

Erda is weary and wishes only to sleep, but Wotan insists on her listening to him. He says that he has bequeathed the world to Siegfried who, without greed, should be immune from the curse of the Ring; Siegfried and Brünnhilde together will redeem the world. He then dismisses Erda after she will not confirm whether or not this will all come to pass. She returns to her chasm.

Siegfried approaches, led by the woodbird, and the Wanderer questions him about Mime, Fafner, his sword and his knowledge of the woman encircled by fire. But anger and animosity grow between them, Siegfried becoming insolent. Wotan, insulted, bars his way forward, but Siegfried presses on, shattering the god's spear. Wotan gathers up the fragments and he leaves. Siegfried wends his way upwards towards the circle of fire and passes unscathed through the flames. Brünnhilde lies there, awaiting him, and he is astonished to find her wearing armour, with weapons beside her.

He thinks at first she is a man, then feels emotions within him he has never experienced before. He decides that perhaps this is the fear that Mime has spoken of. He bends over and kisses her, and Brünnhilde wakes up, sensing great joy but also regret that she is no longer a Valkyrie. She experiences love for Siegfried, anger at her awareness of her womanhood, no longer to stay a maiden. She asks Siegfried to leave her alone and untouched; but she cannot deny her humanity, and soon the intensity of his passion arouses her and they embrace ardently.

Culshaw tackled this second recording in Solti's *Ring* series after a gap of four years following *Das Rheingold*. By then he was using what he called the 'Sonicstage' technique, which on compact disc makes the sepulchral voice of Fafner as Dragon all the more chilling. On CD, this 1962 recording comes out very well, with full brilliance and weight as well as extra clarity. The gimmicks may be made the more obvious, but they are good ones.

Siegfried has too long been thought of as the grimmest of the *Ring* cycle, with dark colours predominating. It is true that the preponderance of male voices till the very end, and Wagner's deliberate matching of this in his orchestration, gives a special colour to the opera, but a performance as buoyant as Solti's reveals that, more than in most Wagner, the message is one of optimism.

Each of the three Acts ends with a scene of triumphant optimism – the first Act in Siegfried's forging song, the second with him in hot pursuit of the woodbird, and the third with the most opulent of love duets.

Solti's array of singers could hardly be bettered. Windgassen is at the very peak of his form, lyrical as well as heroic. Hotter has never been more impressive on records, his Wotan at last captured adequately. Stolze, Neidlinger and Böhme are all exemplary and, predictably, Joan

Sutherland makes the most seductive of woodbirds. Only the conducting of Solti leaves a tiny margin of doubt.

In the dramatic moments he could hardly be more impressive, but that very woodbird scene shows up the shortcomings: the bird's melismatic carolling is plainly intended to have a degree of freedom, whereas Solti allows little or no lilt in the music at all. But it is a minute flaw in a supreme achievement. With singing finer than any opera house could normally provide, with masterly playing from the Vienna Philharmonic and Decca's most opulent recording, this is a set likely to stand comparison with anything the rest of the century may provide.

The natural-sounding quality of Boehm's live recording from Bayreuth, coupled with his determination not to let the music lag, makes his account of *Siegfried* as satisfying as the rest of his cycle, vividly capturing the atmosphere of the Festspielhaus, with voices well ahead of the orchestra. Windgassen is at his peak here, if anything more poetic in Acts II and III than he is in Solti's studio recording, and just as fine vocally. Nilsson, as in *Götterdämmerung*, gains over her studio recording from the extra flow of adrenalin in a live performance; and Gustav Neidlinger is unmatchable as Alberich. Erika Köth is disappointing as the woodbird, not sweet enough, and Soukupová is a positive, characterful Erda. Theo Adam is at his finest as the Wanderer, less wobbly than usual, clean and incisive.

Like the first two music-dramas in his Bayreuth *Ring* cycle, Boulez's version takes a disc less than usual and comes at mid-price in the Philips Bayreuth series. Here the advantage is even greater when each Act is complete on a single disc; it encourages one to appreciate all the more the sweep and concentration of the interpretation. It was recorded in 1980, the last year of the controversial Patrice Chéreau production, when, after teething troubles, Boulez had won the warm regard of the orchestra.

If anything, Boulez is even more warmly expressive than in *Rheingold* or *Walküre*, directing a most poetic account of the *Forest murmurs* episode and leading in each Act to thrillingly intense conclusions. Unfortunately in Act I the Philips engineers have cut off the sound too quickly after the final chord, presumably to avoid applause. Manfred Jung is an underrated Siegfried, forthright and, by latterday standards, unusually clean-focused, and Heinz Zednik is a characterful Mime.

As in the rest of the cycle, Sir Donald McIntyre is a noble Wotan, though Hermann Becht's weighty Alberich is not as strongly contrasted as it might be. Norma Sharp as the Woodbird enunciates her words with exceptional clarity and, though Gwyneth Jones as Brünnhilde has a few squally moments, she sings with honeyed beauty when the Idyll theme emerges, towards the end of the love duet, rounding the performance off with a magnificent, firm top C. The digital sound is full and atmospheric, though it is a pity that the brass is not caught as weightily as it might be.

It is sad that both the modern digital recordings made by Haitink and Levine should be seriously flawed. In *Siegfried*, as much as in the other *Ring* operas, Haitink has the advantage. His speeds are generally a degree faster, with a sharper dramatic sense, and the choice of Siegfried Jerusalem in the title-role of Siegfried is far preferable to that of the seriously flawed Reiner Goldberg. Jerusalem more than any Heldentenor since Wolfgang Windgassen sings the notes with a beauty and clarity of focus that allow the lyrical strength as well as the detailed meaning of Wagner's words to come across.

James Morris is the Wanderer in both recordings, rather sweeter on the ear in the EMI set. Neither Eva Marton for Haitink nor Hildegard Behrens for Levine sings steadily as Brünnhilde; Behrens is better focused, but she seems just as overstressed as the loud and gusty Eva Marton on EMI. The weighty Theo Adam makes an unsteady Alberich, vocally far less impressive than Wlaschiha for Levine, but the long-experienced Adam conveys far more of the dramatic bite.

Overall Levine is markedly less successful than Haitink at conveying the feeling of a live dramatic performance – which is surprising, when his version was directly based on the stage production at the Met. in New York. Neither recording is as firmly focused as those in the pioneering Solti set on Decca, but Haitink's EMI has more atmosphere, with a keener sense of presence.

Dedication and consistency are the mark of the Eurodisc *Ring*, recorded with German thoroughness in collaboration with the East German state record company. The result – with Janowski, direct and straight in his approach, securing superb playing from the Dresdeners – lacks a degree of dramatic tension, but he does not always build the climaxes cumulatively, so there is no compensation for any loss of immediate excitement.

So the final scene of Act II just scurries to a close, with Siegfried in pursuit of a rather shrill woodbird in Norma Sharp. The singing is generally first rate, with Kollo a fine Siegfried, less strained than he has sometimes been, and Peter Schreier a superb Mime, using Lieder-like qualities in detailed characterization. Siegmund Nimsgern is a less characterful Alberich, but the voice is excellent; and Theo Adam concludes his portrayal of Wotan/Wanderer with his finest performance of the series.

The relative lightness of Jeannine Altmeyer's Brünnhilde comes out in the final love-duet more strikingly than in *Walküre*. She may be reduced from goddess to human, but the musical demands are greater. Nevertheless, the tenderness and femininity are most affecting as at the entry of the idyll motif, where Janowski in his dedicated simplicity is also at his most compelling.

Clear, beautifully balanced digital sound, with voices and instruments firmly placed. On CD, the opera's dark colouring is given an even sharper focus against the totally silent background.

When Siegfried is outsung by Mime, it is time to complain and, though the Karajan/DG set has many fine qualities – not least the Brünnhilde of Helga Dernesch – it hardly rivals the Solti or Boehm versions. Windgassen on Decca gave a classic performance, and any comparison highlights the serious shortcomings of Jess Thomas. Even when voices are balanced forward – a point the more apparent on CD – the digital transfer helps little to make Thomas's singing as Siegfried any more acceptable. Otherwise, the vocal cast is strong, and Karajan provides the seamless playing which characterizes his cycle. Recommended only to those irrevocably committed to the Karajan cycle.

Siegfried: highlights.
*(*) DG Dig. 437 548-2 [id.] (from above recording with Goldberg, Behrens; cond. Levine).

The DG issue offers a generous selection of highlights – over 77 minutes – but the set from which it is drawn is relatively undistinguished (see above), and at full price this disc is difficult to recommend.

Siegfried (complete, in English).
(M) *** EMI CMS7 63595-2 (4). Sadler's Wells Op. O, Goodall.
   Siegfried (Alberto Remedios), Brünnhilde (Rita Hunter), Wanderer (Norman Bailey), Mime (Gregory Dempsey), Alberich (Derek Hammond-Stroud), Erda (Anne Collins), Fafner (Clifford Grant), Woodbird (Maurine London).

Compounded from three live performances at the London Coliseum, this magnificent set gives a superb sense of dramatic realism. More tellingly than in almost any other Wagner opera recording, Goodall's spacious direction here conveys the genuine dramatic crunch that gives the experience of hearing Wagner in the opera house its unique power, its overwhelming force. In the *Prelude* there are intrusive audience noises, and towards the end the Sadler's Wells violins have one or two shaky moments, but this is unmistakably a great interpretation caught on the wing.

Remedios, more than any rival on record, conveys not only heroic strength but clear-ringing youthfulness, caressing the ear as well as exciting it. Norman Bailey makes a magnificently noble Wanderer, steady of tone, and Gregory Dempsey is a characterful Mime, even if his deliberate whining tone is not well caught on record. The sound is superbly realistic, even making no allowances for the conditions. Lovers of opera in English should grasp the opportunity of hearing this unique set.

The transfer is remarkably vivid and detailed, kind to the voices and with a natural presence, so that the words are clear yet there is no edge or exaggeration of consonants. This was the first of Goodall's *Ring* cycle to be transferred to CD and the orchestral recording is drier than in the others of the series: the brass sound brassier, less rounded than in *The Twilight of the Gods* for instance, but not less effective. The strings, however, have plenty of body and bloom.

Tannhäuser (Paris version; complete).
*** DG. Dig. 427 625-2 (3) [id.]. Ch. & Philh. O, Sinopoli.
   Tannhäuser (Plácido Domingo), Elisabeth (Cheryl Studer), Wolfram (Andreas Schmidt), Venus (Agnes Baltsa), Hermann (Matti Salminen), Walther (William Pell).
*** Decca 414 581-2 (3) [id.]. V. State Op. Ch., VPO, Solti.
   Tannhäuser (René Kollo), Elisabeth (Helga Dernesch), Wolfram (Victor Braun), Venus (Christa Ludwig), Hermann (Hans Sotin), Walther (Werner Hollweg).

Both Solti and Sinopoli prefer the later, Paris version of the score. The differences lie mainly – though not entirely – in Act I in the scene between Tannhäuser and Venus. Wagner rewrote most of the scene at a time when his style had developed enormously. The love music here is closer to *Walküre* and *Tristan* than to the rest of *Tannhäuser*. The hero's harp song enters each time in its straight diatonic style with a jolt; but this is only apt, and the richness of inspiration, the musical intensification – beautifully conveyed here – transform the opera.

As the opera opens, Tannhäuser is in the Venusberg obviously enjoying the attentions of Venus, with his head virtually in her lap. But he has become weary of his abandoned existence and wants to go back to Earth. Venus pleads with him to stay and, when he obviously means to leave, she tells him angrily that he can have no hope of salvation. He replies that his hope rests with the Virgin.

At the sound of her name, Venus and her kingdom immediately disappear and we move to a valley near Wartburg. A shepherd boy plays his pipe while pilgrims are chanting as they pass by. Tannhäuser falls to his knees and prays. Now huntsmen are heard and the Landgrave of Thuringia arrives with his minstrel knights. Walther and Biterolf fail to recognize Tannhäuser. A third knight, Wolfram, realizes who he is.

Tannhäuser is then welcomed; others, including the Landgrave, beg him to return to their company. But Tannhäuser is conscious of his transgressions and resists their overtures. Then Wolfram mentions the Landgrave's niece, Elisabeth, telling Tannhäuser that she loves him (which is unselfish of Wolfram, for he himself loves Elisabeth). Tannhäuser now changes his mind and agrees to join them.

In the Minstrels' Hall in Wartburg, Elisabeth, delighted that Tannhäuser has returned, sings her greeting (*Dich teure Halle*). She is disturbed that when she asks about his long absence he gives evasive replies. But they are now both very much in love, and Wolfram feels his own love for Elisabeth is hopeless. The two men leave her as the Landgrave enters to tell her that he approves her choice and that a contest among the minstrel knights is about to be promulgated. The great march scene brings the grand entrance of the participants. The theme of the contest is to be songs of love.

Elisabeth draws a slip of paper bearing Wolfram's name: he is the first contestant. With harp accompaniment he sings of the purity of love and implies that his source of inspiration is Elisabeth. Walther, the second contestant, also sings of love's simplicity. But Tannhäuser's song is of sensual love, amazing his audience. Scandalized, Biterolf challenges him to fight, amid general approval, but the Landgrave and Wolfram quieten the audience and Tannhäuser sings again, this time a song of praise to Venus, obviously recalling his earlier experiences. The ladies rush away and the knights and nobles draw their swords. But Elisabeth stands in front of Tannhäuser to protect him and asks them to allow him a chance of salvation. They are sure he is accursed but accede to her ardent plea. Tannhäuser prays to God for forgiveness. The Landgrave states that Tannhäuser's only hope of salvation is for him to join a party of pilgrims about to depart for Rome, where he must seek personal absolution from the pope. Threatened with death if he does not go, Tannhäuser rushes to join the pilgrims.

Wolfram observes Elisabeth as she prays for Tannhäuser. Then they watch as the pilgrims pass by on their return from Rome; Tannhäuser is not with them. Elisabeth goes away alone and Wolfram plays his harp, comparing his beloved to the evening star (*O du mein holder Abendstern*). He finishes his song as a ragged pilgrim enters.

Tannhäuser is looking for the way back to the Venusberg. He tells Wolfram that he has suffered many tribulations on his pilgrimage to Rome and that the pope refused to absolve him, saying that on the papal staff a leaf shall never grow, so Tannhäuser can never know salvation.

There is nothing left for him but to return to the arms of Venus. He calls on her, and visions of her realm are seen and her voice is heard. Wolfram valiantly tries to hold on to Tannhäuser, and in desperation evokes Elisabeth's name. Tannhäuser repeats the name as in a dream. The vision of Venus disappears.

Dawn comes, voices are heard, and a funeral cortège approaches. Elisabeth is dead and the Landgrave party escorts her bier. Because she interceded for him, Tannhäuser is absolved. He falls across her body and dies. A second group of younger pilgrims now comes in with strange news. The pope's staff has miraculously burst into bloom, signifying Tannhäuser's salvation.

Following up his fine Lohengrin with Solti for Decca, Plácido Domingo here makes another Wagnerian sortie, bringing balm to ears wounded by the general run of German heroic tenors. Pressured as he is by the jet-set life of a superstar, it is amazing that he can produce sounds of such power as well as such beauty. In the narration of Act III, it is a joy to hear such a range of tone, dynamic and expression, even if he cannot match his rival, René Kollo, on Solti's Decca set in the agony of the culminating word, '*verdammt*', 'damned'.

Continuing on after his experience conducting this opera at Bayreuth (though that was the Dresden, not the Paris, version) Giuseppe Sinopoli here makes his most passionately committed opera recording yet, warmer and more flexible than Solti's Decca version, always individual, with fine detail brought out, always persuasively, and never wilful.

Recorded not with Bayreuth forces but in the studio with his own Philharmonia Orchestra, the extra range and beauty of the sound bring ample compensation for a recording that does not attempt to create the sound-stage of Solti's version. Agnes Baltsa is not ideally opulent of tone as Venus, but she is the complete seductress. Cheryl Studer – who sang the role of Elisabeth for Sinopoli at Bayreuth – gives a most sensitive performance, not always ideally even of tone but creating a movingly intense portrait of the heroine, vulnerable and very feminine. Matti Salminen in one of his last recordings makes a superb Landgrave and Andreas Schmidt a noble Wolfram, even though the legato could be smoother in *O star of Eve*.

Solti provides an electrifying experience, demonstrating beyond a shadow of doubt how much more effective the Paris revision of *Tannhäuser* is, compared with the usual Dresden version. Quite apart from that, however, Solti gives one of his very finest Wagner performances to date, helped by superb playing from the Vienna Philharmonic and an outstanding cast, superlatively recorded. Dernesch as Elisabeth and Ludwig as Venus outshine all rivalry; and Kollo, though not ideal, makes as fine a Heldentenor as we are currently likely to hear.

The CD transfer reinforces the brilliance and richness of the performance. The sound is outstanding for its period (1971), and Ray Minshull's production adds to the atmospheric quality, with the orchestra given full weight and with the placing and movement of the voices finely judged.

Tannhäuser (Dresden version; complete).
(M) **(*) Ph. 434 607-2 (3) [id.]. (1962) Bayreuth Festival Ch. & O, Sawallisch.
     Tannhäuser (Wolfgang Windgassen), Elisabeth (Anja Silja), Wolfram (Eberhard Waechter), Venus (Grace Bumbry), Hermann (Josef Greindl), Walther (Gerhard Stolze).
** EMI Dig. CDS7 47296-8 (3) [Ang. CDC 47295]. Bav. R. Ch., RSO, Haitink.
     Tannhäuser (Klaus König), Elisabeth (Lucia Popp), Wolfram (Bernd Weikl), Venus (Waltraud Meier), Hermann (Kurt Moll), Walther (Siegfried Jerusalem).

Sawallisch's version, recorded at the 1962 Bayreuth Festival, comes up very freshly on CD. Though the new medium brings out all the more clearly the thuds, creaks and audience noises of a live performance (most distracting at the very start), the dedication of the reading is very persuasive, notably in the Venusberg scene where Grace Bumbry is a superb, sensuous Venus and Windgassen – not quite in his sweetest voice, often balanced rather close – is a fine, heroic Tannhäuser.

Anja Silja controls the abrasiveness of her soprano well, to make this her finest performance on record, not ideally sweet but very sympathetic. Voices are set well forward of the orchestra, in which strings have far more bloom than brass; but the atmosphere of the Festspielhaus is vivid and compelling throughout. Now reissued at mid-price in the Philips Bayreuth/Wagner Edition, this makes a good choice for those wanting the Dresden version of the opera.

Haitink's unexpected pursuit of lightness and refinement, almost as though this is music by Mendelssohn, makes for a reading which, for all its beauties, lacks an essential dramatic bite. Consistently he refines the piece, until you can hardly believe that this is an opera which deeply shocked early Victorians with its noisy vulgarity. Haitink's performance tends to sound like a studio run-through, carefully done and with much intelligence, but largely uninvolved.

It is not helped by a strained hero in Klaus König and a shrewish-sounding Venus in Waltraud Meier. The serious disappointment of the first Act then tends to colour one's response to the rest too, though Lucia Popp, stretched to the limit in a role on the heavy side for her, produces some characteristically beautiful singing as Elisabeth. Bernd Weikl is an intelligent but uningratiating Wolfram. Finely balanced sound, the more impressive on CD, beautifully atmospheric in the processional scenes. Banding is sparse, with limited index points added.

Tannhäuser (Paris version): highlights.
(M) *** DG Dig. 435 405-2; *435 405-4* [id.] (from above complete recording, with Domingo, Studer, Baltsa; cond. Sinopoli).

As this 'Domingo Edition' CD readily demonstrates, Tannhäuser was the Spanish tenor's finest Wagnerian role. These highlights also give a bird's-eye picture of Sinopoli's overall achievement and, by using groups of sequential excerpts, edited fades are minimal. The Grand March scene could have been cut off after its final cadence, but it was probably better to use also the following brass link. However, the last item, *Dahin zog's mich, wo ich der Wonn' und Lust*, lacks any kind of finality.

Tannhäuser: Overture and highlights.
**(*) Teldec/Warner Dig. 4509 91973-2 [id.]. Tannhäuser (René Kollo), Elisabeth (Kiri Te Kanawa), Wolfram (Håkan Hagegård), Venus (Waltraud Meier), Amb. S., Philh. O, Janowski.

After a very fine account of the *Overture* (wonderful cascades from the Philharmonia violins at the close), Sony provide an enjoyable hour-long selection with the Ambrosian Singers, very well recorded, contributing impressively in the March scene and *Pilgrims' chorus.* Kiri Te Kanawa's warm portrayal of Elisabeth is a little soft-centred, and René Kollo's Tannhäuser is also a romantic view. Wolfram's *O du mein holder Abendstern* ('O star of eve') is sung simply and affectingly. Throughout, the experienced Wagnerian, Marek Janowski, directs without too much pressure, but the closing scene comes off very dramatically. The recording is vividly natural and well balanced.

Tristan und Isolde (complete).
(M) *** EMI CMS7 69319-2 (4) [Ang. CDMD 69319]. German Op. Ch., Berlin, BPO, Karajan.
    Tristan (Jon Vickers), Isolde (Helga Dernesch), Brangäne (Christa Ludwig), King Marke (Karl Ridderbusch), Kurwenal (Walter Berry).
*** Ph. 434 425-2 (3) [id.]. (1966) Bayreuth Festival Ch. & O, Boehm.
    Tristan (Wolfgang Windgassen), Isolde (Birgit Nilsson), Brangäne (Christa Ludwig), King Marke (Martti Talvela), Kurwenal (Eberhard Waechter).
(M) *** Decca 430 234-2 (4) [id.]. V. Singverein, VPO, Solti.
    Tristan (Fritz Uhl), Isolde (Birgit Nilsson), Brangäne (Regina Resnik), King Marke (Arnold Van Mill), Kurwenal (Tom Krause).
*** Ph. Dig. 410 447-2 (5) [id.]. Bav. R. Ch., RSO, Bernstein.
    Tristan (Peter Hofmann), Isolde (Hildegard Behrens), Brangäne (Yvonne Minton), King Marke (Hans Sotin), Kurwenal (Bernd Weikl).
(***) EMI mono CDS7 47322-8 (4) [Ang. CDC 47321]. ROHCG Ch., Philh. O, Furtwängler.
    Tristan (Ludwig Suthaus), Isolde (Kirsten Flagstad), Brangäne (Blanche Thebom), King Marke (Josef Greindl), Kurwenal (Dietrich Fischer-Dieskau).
**(*) DG Dig. 413 315-2 (4) [id.]. Leipzig R. Ch., Dresden State O, Carlos Kleiber.
    Tristan (René Kollo), Isolde (Margaret Price), Brangäne (Brigitte Fassbaender), King Marke (Kurt Moll), Kurwenal (Dietrich Fischer-Dieskau).

Fired by the great love-story (and by the experience of his own unavailing devotion for Mathilde Wesendonck, wife of his Zürich friend and supporter), Wagner's chromatic realization of human passion reached its zenith in *Tristan und Isolde,* an extraordinary combination of the poetic expression of the human condition and unrestrained, sensuous, lyrical ardour. After it was written, nothing in music would ever be the same again.

As the story opens, Isolde, attended by Brangäne, is sailing from Ireland (lately conquered) to Cornwall, to be the bride of the ageing King Mark. The singing of a young sailor awakens her and she talks to Brangäne and rails at her fate. Seeking a breath of fresh air for her mistress, Brangäne draws back the curtains. Tristan, a Cornish knight and the king's nephew, has been instructed to bring Isolde back from Ireland, and he now stands in full view with his squire, Kurwenal, and the sailors.

Isolde's gaze towards Tristan is scornful, then she imperiously orders Brangäne to bring him to her; but Kurwenal makes excuses on his master's behalf, for Tristan has his pride. Angry at being slighted, Isolde relates to Brangäne how Tristan had killed her betrothed, Morold, saying his name was Tantris. She had stifled her feelings of revenge and helped him to recover and regain his strength after the fight. She now has the indignity of being taken by this same man across the sea to be the wife of the old king. She curses Tristan and seeks death for herself.

Brangäne, who has not yet realized that her mistress loves Tristan in spite of herself, suggests that the magic potions of Isolde's mother would ensure the love of King Mark. But Isolde is not thinking of a love-potion, but of poison for herself and Tristan. Now nearing land, Kurwenal comes to tell the women to prepare to disembark but Isolde says she will not leave until Tristan comes to apologize for his diffident behaviour. Kurwenal disappears to tell him, and Isolde instructs her servant to prepare poisoned drinks for them both. Brangäne is appalled at this.

Tristan now enters and Isolde reminds him that she succoured him when he was near death's door and, moreover, that he killed the man she wished to marry. Tristan offers his sword, but she says they should drink together; realizing her intention, and perhaps because he loves her, he drinks. But it is not poison. Brangäne has substituted a love-potion which takes immediate effect and they fall into each other's arms in an embrace of the greatest ardour. The ship reaches shore, King Mark steps on board and then Brangäne reveals the truth to Isolde . . . and she faints.

Isolde waits for Tristan in the garden outside King Mark's castle. The king has departed on a hunt and Isolde is about to signal to her lover when Brangäne stops her: Melot, a courtier and (supposedly) Tristan's friend who organized the hunting party, is suspicious of Isolde. But Isolde sends Brangäne to keep watch and extinguishes a torch, the signal to Tristan. He comes and the lovers are caught up in feelings of great ecstasy and passion (*O sink'hernieder, Nacht der Liebe*).

Brangäne's warning sounds, indicating to the lovers that dawn is approaching. Kurwenal enters, telling Tristan to save himself. Simultaneously Melot and the king arrive. Melot asks the king whether his warnings were not justified, and Mark is full of sorrow that his nephew should betray him so cruelly. Tristan looks at Isolde questioningly and, knowing what he means, Isolde declares that she will accompany Tristan wherever he must go. Melot draws his sword and Tristan throws himself on the traitor's weapon. Gravely wounded, he sinks into Kurwenal's arms.

Kurwenal journeys back to Tristan's castle in Brittany, taking the wounded knight with him. Tristan awakens and longs for Isolde. Kurwenal promises he shall see her. Tristan, in delirium, re-enacts his passionate experiences with Isolde. But time goes by, he sinks into a state of despair and a death-wish overtakes him. Outside a shepherd plays his pipe merrily, which is a sign, and Kurwenal says that Isolde's ship is near.

They watch it approach, then Tristan in a frenzy tears the bandage from his wound. Isolde enters and he falls into her arms and dies. Kurwenal says that a second ship is approaching. They are ready to defend the castle and, when Melot enters, Kurwenal kills him. Brangäne scales a wall to look for Isolde and is thankful to find her still alive.

In fact Mark has come without any violent intentions; Brangäne has told him of the love-potion and he is saddened by the death of Tristan. But the great human love Tristan and Isolde shared needed no potion, springing from the depths of their very beings. Isolde no longer wants to live, and she finally sinks into Brangäne's arms and dies over the body of Tristan. Mark, overawed, silently invokes a benediction over the dead lovers.

Karajan's is a sensual performance of Wagner's masterpiece, caressingly beautiful and with superbly refined playing from the Berlin Philharmonic. At the climactic points of each Act Karajan is a tantalizing deceiver, leading you to expect that the moment of resolution will not be fully achieved, but then punching home with a final crescendo of supreme force. He is helped by a recording (variably balanced, but warmly atmospheric) which copes with an enormous dynamic range.

Dernesch as Isolde is seductively feminine, not as noble as Flagstad, not as tough and unflinching as Nilsson, but the human quality makes this account if anything more moving still, helped by glorious tone-colour through every range. Jon Vickers matches her, in what is arguably his finest performance on record, allowing himself true pianissimo shading.

The rest of the cast is excellent too. Though CD brings out more clearly the occasional oddities of balance – the distancing of the chorus at the end of Act I, and of the lovers themselves during the gentler parts of the love-duet – the 1972 sound has plenty of body, making this (on four mid-priced CDs) an excellent first choice, with inspired conducting and the most satisfying cast of all.

Boehm's Bayreuth performance, recorded at the 1966 Festival, has a cast that for consistency has seldom been bettered on disc. Now on only three CDs, one disc per Act, the benefit is enormous in presenting one of the big Wagner operas for the first time on disc without any breaks at all, with each Act uninterrupted.

The performance is a fine one. Boehm is on the urgent side in this opera (one explanation for the economical layout) and the orchestral ensemble is not always immaculate; but the performance glows with intensity from beginning to end, carried through in the longest spans.

Birgit Nilsson is in astonishingly rich and powerful voice. She sings the *Liebestod* at the end of the long evening as though she was starting out afresh, radiant and with not a hint of tiredness, rising to an orgasmic climax and bringing a heavenly pianissimo on the final rising octave to F-sharp.

Opposite Nilsson is Wolfgang Windgassen, the most mellifluous of Heldentenoren; though the microphone balance sometimes puts him at a disadvantage to his Isolde, the realism and sense of presence of the whole set has you bathing in the authentic atmosphere of Bayreuth. The darkness of the opening of Act III on lower strings has never sounded more sepulchrally threatening. Making up an almost unmatchable cast are Christa Ludwig as Brangäne, Eberhard

Waechter as Kurwenal and Martti Talvela as King Mark, with the young Peter Schreier as the Young Sailor.

Solti's performance is less flexible and sensuous than Karajan's, but he shows himself ready to relax in Wagner's more expansive periods. On the other hand, the end of Act I and the opening of the Love duet have a knife-edged dramatic tension. Birgit Nilsson responds superbly to Solti's direction. There are moments when the great intensity that Flagstad brought to the part is not equalled but, more often than not, Nilsson is masterly in her conviction and – it cannot be emphasized too strongly – she never attacks below the note as Flagstad did, so that miraculously, at the end of the Love duet the impossibly difficult top Cs come out and hit the listener crisply and cleanly, dead on the note; and the *Liebestod* is all the more moving for having no soupy swerves at the climax.

Fritz Uhl is a really musical Heldentenor. Only during one passage of the Love duet (*O sink' hernieder*) does he sound tired, and for the most part this is a well-focused voice. Dramatically he leaves the centre of the stage to Isolde, but his long solo passages in Act III are superb and make that sometimes tedious Act into something genuinely gripping. The Kurwenal of Tom Krause and the King Mark of Arnold van Mill are both excellent and it is only Regina Resnik as Brangäne who gives any disappointment. The production has the usual Decca/Culshaw imaginative touch, and the recording matches brilliance and clarity with satisfying co-ordination and richness.

Bernstein's was the first *Tristan* on CD; worthily so, but originally it was not only expensive but cumbersome in five separate 'jewel-boxes'. Now it has been reissued on four CDs, although the side-breaks between the discs are now not ideal, coming not just in mid-Act but also in mid-scene in each instance. Nevertheless the fine quality of the recording is ravishing in the transfer, the sound rich, full and well detailed, a tribute to the Bavarian engineers working in the Herkulessaal in Munich. 'For the first time someone dares to perform this music as Wagner wrote it,' was Karl Boehm's comment when he visited Bernstein during rehearsals for this *Tristan* recording, made live at three separate concert performances.

The surprise is that Bernstein, over-emotional in some music, here exercises restraint to produce the most spacious reading ever put on disc, more expansive even than Furtwängler's. Bernstein's rhythmic sharpness goes with warmly expressive but unexaggerated phrasing, to give unflagging concentration and deep commitment.

The love-duet has rarely if ever sounded so sensuous, with supremely powerful climaxes – as at the peak of *O sink'hernieder*. Nor in the *Liebestod* is there any question of Bernstein rushing ahead, for the culmination comes naturally and fully at a taxingly slow speed. Behrens makes a fine Isolde, less purely beautiful than her finest rivals but with reserves of power giving dramatic bite. The contrast of tone with Yvonne Minton's Brangäne (good, except for flatness in the warning solo) is not as great as usual, and there is likeness too between Peter Hofmann's Tristan, often baritonal, and Bernd Weikl's Kurwenal, lighter than usual. The King Mark of Hans Sotin is superb.

It was one of the supreme triumphs of the recording producer, Walter Legge, when in 1952 with his recently formed Philharmonia Orchestra he teamed the incomparable Wagnerian, Wilhelm Furtwängler, with Kirsten Flagstad as the heroine in *Tristan und Isolde*. It was no easy matter, when Furtwängler was resentful of Legge at the time for sponsoring his rival, Karajan, and he agreed to the arrangement only because Flagstad insisted. The result has an incandescent intensity, typical of the conductor at his finest, and caught all too rarely in his studio recordings.

The concept is spacious from the opening *Prelude* onwards, but equally the bite and colour of the drama are vividly conveyed, matching the nobility of Flagstad's portrait of Isolde. Some of the sensuousness of the character is missing, but the richly commanding power of her singing and her always distinctive timbre make it a uniquely compelling performance. Suthaus is not of the same calibre as Heldentenor, but he avoids ugliness and strain, which is rare in Tristan.

Among the others, the remarkable performance is from Fischer-Dieskau as Kurwenal, young for the role in 1953 but keenly imaginative. One endearing oddity is that – on Flagstad's insistence – the top Cs at the opening of the love duet were sung by Mrs Walter Legge (Elisabeth Schwarzkopf). The Kingsway Hall recording was admirably balanced, catching the beauty of the Philharmonia Orchestra at its peak.

The CDs have opened up the original mono sound, and it is remarkable how little constriction there is in the biggest climaxes, mostly shown in the *fortissimo* violins above the stave. The voices ride triumphantly over the orchestra (the balance is superbly judged) and at *mezzo forte* and *piano* levels there is striking atmosphere and bloom, with the vocal timbres firm and realistically focused. CD cueing is not generous (24 bands over the four discs) and the libretto typeface, though clear, is minuscule.

Kleiber directs a compellingly impulsive reading, crowned by the glorious Isolde, the most purely beautiful of any complete interpretation on record, of Margaret Price. Next to more spacious readings, his at times sounds excitable, almost hysterical. Fast speeds tend to get faster, for all his hypnotic concentration. But the lyricism of Dame Margaret, feminine and vulnerable, is well contrasted against the heroic Tristan of Kollo, at his finest in Act III. Kurt Moll makes a dark, leonine King Mark, but Fischer-Dieskau is at times gritty as Kurwenal and Brigitte Fassbaender is a clear but rather cold Brangäne. On CD the oddities and inconsistencies of sound (including odd bumps) are the more apparent; but with voices set well back in a spacious acoustic, the sound is still sensuously beautiful.

Tristan und Isolde (slightly abridged).
(M) (***) EMI mono CHS7 64037-2 (3) [Ang. CDHC 64037]. ROHCG Ch., LPO, Beecham/Reiner.
Tristan (Lauritz Melchior), Isolde (Kirsten Flagstad), Brangäne (Margarete Klose / Sabine Kalter), King Marke (Sven Nilsson / Emanuel List), Kurwenal (Herbert Janssen).

What was originally promised as a complete recording of Beecham conducting *Tristan* at Covent Garden in the Coronation season of 1937 proved to be a mixture of recordings made, not only then, but in the previous year as well. In both recordings Melchior and Flagstad take the title-roles, with Herbert Janssen as Kurwenal, three legendary singers in those roles, but the parts of King Mark and Brangäne were sung by different singers in each year – and, above all, Fritz Reiner was the conductor in the 1936 recordings.

It says much that the end-result, a jig-saw of pieces lovingly put together by Keith Hardwick, is so consistent. It is astonishing to find that the warmly expansive account of Act I is the work of Reiner, while it is Beecham who is responsible for the urgent view of Act II with its great love duet – part of it cut, following the manner of the day. Act III is divided between Beecham in the first part, Reiner in the second.

Whatever the inconsistencies, the result is a thrilling experience, with Flagstad fresher and even more incisive than in her studio recording with Furtwängler of 15 years later, and with Melchior a passionate vocal actor, not just the possessor of the most freely ringing of all Heldentenor voices. Though the orchestral sound is mostly dim and distant, the voices come over vividly and it is easy to forget the limitations. Each Act – with cuts in Act III as well as in Act II – is fitted conveniently and economically on a single disc.

Die Walküre (complete).
*** Ph. 412 478-2 (4) [id.]. (1967) Bayreuth Festival O, Boehm.
Siegmund (James King), Sieglinde (Leonie Rysanek), Brünnhilde (Birgit Nilsson), Wotan (Theo Adam), Fricka / Siegrune (Annelies Burmeister), Hunding (Gerd Nienstedt).
*** Decca 414 105-2 (4) [id.]. VPO, Solti.
Siegmund (James King), Sieglinde (Régine Crespin), Brünnhilde (Birgit Nilsson), Wotan (Hans Hotter), Fricka (Christa Ludwig), Hunding (Gottlob Frick).
(M) (***) EMI mono CHS7 63045-2 (3). VPO, Furtwängler.
Siegmund (Ludwig Suthaus), Sieglinde (Leonie Rysanek), Brünnhilde (Martha Mödl), Wotan (Ferdinand Frantz), Fricka (Margarete Klose), Hunding (Gottlob Frick).
(M) *** Ph. 434 422-2 (3) [id.]. (1980) Bayreuth Festival O, Boulez.
Siegmund (Peter Hofmann), Sieglinde (Jeannine Altmeyer), Brünnhilde (Gwyneth Jones), Wotan (Donald McIntyre), Fricka (Hanna Schwarz), Hunding (Matti Salminen).
(M) *** RCA/Eurodisc Dig. GD 69005 (4) [69005-2-RG]. Dresden State O, Janowski.
Siegmund (Siegfried Jerusalem), Sieglinde (Jessye Norman), Brünnhilde (Jeannine Altmeyer), Wotan (Theo Adam), Fricka (Yvonne Minton), Hunding (Kurt Moll).
**(*) EMI Dig. CDS7 49534-2 (4) [Ang. CDCD 49534]. Bav. RSO, Haitink.
Siegmund (Reiner Goldberg), Sieglinde (Cheryl Studer), Brünnhilde (Eva Marton), Wotan (James Morris), Fricka (Waltraud Meier), Hunding (Matti Salminen).
**(*) DG 415 145-2 (4) [id.]. BPO, Karajan.
Siegmund (Jon Vickers), Sieglinde (Gundula Janowitz), Brünnhilde (Régine Crespin), Wotan (Thomas Stewart), Fricka (Josephine Veasey), Hunding (Martti Talvela).
** DG Dig. 423 389-2 (4) [id.]. NY Met. Op. O, Levine.
Siegmund (Gary Lakes), Sieglinde (Jessye Norman), Brünnhilde (Hildegard Behrens), Wotan (James Morris), Fricka (Christa Ludwig), Hunding (Kurt Moll).

(M) ** Decca 430 391-2 (3) [id.]. LSO, Leinsdorf.
   Siegmund (Jon Vickers), Sieglinde (Gré Brouwenstijn), Brünnhilde (Birgit Nilsson), Wotan
   (George London), Fricka (Rita Gorr), Hunding (David Ward).

Die Walküre, Part II of the *Ring* cycle, takes place a long time after the events related in *Das Rheingold*. Wotan (with Erda, the Goddess of Earth and Wisdom) has fathered nine warrior-maidens, known as the Valkyries. They have formed an army to defend the gods, by bringing fallen heroes to Valhalla. Brünnhilde is Wotan's favourite daughter. But Wotan's fecundity knows no bounds. Calling himself Wälse and adopting the form of a mortal, he has two more children, Siegmund and Sieglinde, known as the Wälsungs; their mother was human. He hopes that, being half-gods, they will help him in the struggle to repossess the Ring.

As the curtain rises we see a forest hut, in the centre of which is a huge ash tree. Hunding and his wife, Sieglinde, are the owners of the hut. A storm occurs. Siegmund is fleeing from his enemies, the Neidings; exhausted, he staggers in and craves permission to rest. Sieglinde gives him water and the two are very attracted to each other (not surprisingly, when they are brother and sister).

Hunding now returns and, noticing Siegmund's likeness to his wife, questions him. He says his name is Wehwalt, son of Wolfe; he has lost his mother, who was killed, and his sister, who was abducted while his father and he were defending themselves from enemies. More recently he had tried to save an unknown woman from a forced marriage but had been defeated.

Hunding realizes this stranger is his enemy, but he tells Siegmund he may remain overnight, but on the following day they must fight. Weaponless, Siegmund wonders how he will defend himself but, before Sieglinde leaves, she indicates the ash tree with significant emphasis. Conscious of his growing love for Sieglinde, Siegmund now inspects the tree. His father had promised to provide him with a sword when he needed one, and a shaft of light beams on to the place in the tree to which Sieglinde had drawn his attention.

She now returns in night attire, having drugged her husband. She recalls her wedding and how, while the guests celebrated, an old man plunged a sword into the ash tree. Strong men have since tried, unsuccessfully, to withdraw it; and they both know it is intended for Siegmund. They embrace and slowly their love turns to passion.

He tells her his father's name, Wälse, and that he is a Wälsung. They are now aware that they are brother and sister. She tells him his true Christian name, Siegmund (Victory). Forthwith, he pulls the sword out of the tree and calls it Nothung. Then, as moonlight floods the room, their mutual ardour overcomes them and they join together in passionate physical union.

Hunding is now pursuing Sieglinde, who left with Siegmund. In a wild place in the mountains, Wotan summons Brünnhilde to protect his son, and she sounds her mighty war-cry. Then she prudently warns Wotan that his wife, Fricka, is near and she leaves.

Fricka's chariot is drawn by two rams; as Goddess of Marriage, she demands that Siegmund be punished: Hunding must kill him. Wotan (hardly a paragon of marital fidelity himself) finally consents. Brünnhilde's war-cry is heard and Fricka leaves.

Brünnhilde is upset to see her father so unhappy. He retells the story of Alberich and the Ring, of Erda's certainty of the coming downfall of the gods, and of their struggle to survive with the help of the Valkyries and their army of heroes. But now, to satisfy Fricka, his son Siegmund must die. Brünnhilde, agonized, begs that Siegmund be allowed the victory over Hunding. Wotan angrily demands that she ensure that Siegmund is beaten.

Siegmund and Sieglinde now enter. Sieglinde suffers remorse; she fears for her brother, vividly imagining the pursuing Hunding with his hounds. She faints. Brünnhilde enters and tells Siegmund that he must accompany her to Valhalla. He refuses, for Sieglinde will be unable to go with him. Brünnhilde offers to protect Sieglinde and their unborn child after his death. Siegmund says he will kill the sleeping Sieglinde rather than leave her defenceless.

Greatly moved by his concern, Brünnhilde prevents him using his sword and promises to ensure his victory against Hunding. She leaves and Siegmund bids his farewell to Sieglinde while she is still asleep.

As he goes to do battle with Hunding, a thunderstorm breaks out. Brünnhilde protects Siegmund with her shield. There is a red glow and Wotan reappears. Siegmund's sword shatters on Wotan's spear. Hunding kills Siegmund and Wotan, looking sadly at the body of his son, waves his hand and Hunding falls dead. Wotan now vows to punish Brünnhilde for her disobedience.

The Valkyries ride past in splendour to the most famous of all Wagner's orchestral descriptions, carrying the bodies of heroes slain in battle. They assemble on a mountain-top.

Brünnhilde arrives, supporting Sieglinde. Because she defied Wotan, her sisters will not help her hide Sieglinde from him.

Sieglinde at first has no wish to live but changes her mind when told she will bear Siegmund's child. Brünnhilde sends her eastwards to the forests where Fafner, in the form of a dragon, guards both the Rhine's treasure and the Ring. Before Sieglinde departs, Brünnhilde gives her the broken pieces of Siegmund's sword and foretells that her (as yet unborn) son will become a hero, to be called Siegfried. He must re-forge the sword and it will assure his victory.

The Valkyries shield Brünnhilde when the angry Wotan arrives but she steps forward and faces him. He tells her that, because of her disobedience, she will no longer be a Valkyrie but will become an ordinary mortal. She will rest in a magic sleep until awakened by a human being. She must marry the first man who finds her.

Her sisters beg Wotan for mercy, but he is adamant and only partially relents when Brünnhilde asks that only a hero be permitted to awaken her. Then, moved by her determination and courage, he calls upon Loge to encircle her with a ring of fire. Wotan proclaims that anyone fearing his spear should penetrate that fire at his peril. Sorrowfully he gazes on the recumbent figure of his daughter as the flames spring up round her.

Anyone wondering whether to invest in the Boehm *Ring* cycle, recorded live at Bayreuth in 1967, should sample the end of Act I of this account of *Die Walküre*, where the white heat of the occasion makes the scalp prickle. When Siegmund pulls the sword, Nothung, from the tree – James King in heroic voice – Sieglinde (Leonie Rysanek) utters a shriek of joy to delight even the least susceptible Wagnerian, matching the urgency of the whole performance as conducted by Boehm.

Rarely if ever does his preference for fast speeds undermine the music; on the contrary, it adds to the involvement of the performance, which never loses its concentration. Theo Adam is in firmer voice here as Wotan than he is in *Rheingold*, hardly sweet of tone but always singing with keen intelligence. As ever, Nilsson is in superb voice as Brünnhilde. Though the inevitable roughnesses of a live performance occasionally intrude, this presents a more involving experience than any rival complete recording. The CD transfer transforms what on LP seemed a rough recording, even if passages of heavy orchestration still bring some constriction of sound.

Recorded last in Solti's series, *Die Walküre* in some ways had the most refined sound, to make the CD version particularly impressive, amazingly fine for 1965, with voices and orchestral detail all the more precisely placed. Solti's conception is more lyrical than one would have expected from his recordings of the other three *Ring* operas. He sees Act II as the kernel of the work, perhaps even of the whole cycle.

Acts I and III have their supremely attractive set-pieces which must inevitably make them more popular as entertainment, but here one appreciates that in Act II the conflict of wills between Wotan and Fricka makes for one of Wagner's most deeply searching scenes. That is the more apparent when the greatest Wotan of his day, Hans Hotter, takes the role, and Christa Ludwig sings with searing dramatic sense as his wife. Before that, Act I seems a little underplayed.

This is partly because of Solti's deliberate lyricism – apt enough when love and spring greetings are in the air – but also (on the debit side) because James King fails to project the character of Siegmund, underplaying the word-meaning. Crespin has never sung more beautifully on record, but even that cannot cancel out the shortcoming. As for Nilsson's Brünnhilde, it has grown mellower, the emotions are clearer, and under-the-note attack is almost eliminated. Some may hesitate in the face of Hotter's obvious vocal trials; but the unsteadiness is, if anything, less marked than in his EMI recordings of items done many years earlier

Furtwängler's 1954 recording of *Die Walküre*, made in Vienna only months before the conductor's death, was – astonishingly to us today – the first integral one ever to be issued on commercial disc. Bruno Walter had earlier recorded all three Acts complete, but at widely different venues and periods. In this superb reissue on three mid-priced CDs – complete with notes, libretto and translation – it stands as the keenest possible competitor to the latest digitally recorded versions – in most ways outshining them.

Except for those totally allergic to mono sound, even as well balanced as this, the EMI Références set could well be the answer as a first choice, when not only Furtwängler but an excellent cast and the Vienna Philharmonic in radiant form match any of their successors. As in his *Tristan* recording, Furtwängler proves a spacious Wagnerian who yet carries you along with such intensity and feeling for line that there is no sensation of slowness, only of surging momentum.

Even more than in *Tristan*, Ludwig Suthaus proves a satisfyingly clear-toned Heldentenor, never strained, with the lyricism of *Winterstürme* superbly sustained. Neither Leonie Rysanek as Sieglinde nor Martha Mödl as Brünnhilde is ideally steady, but the intensity and involvement of each is irresistible, classic performances both, with detail finely touched in and well contrasted with each other. Similarly, the mezzo of Margarete Klose as Fricka may not be very beautiful, but the projection of words and the fire-eating character match the conductor's intensity.

Rather in contrast with the women soloists, both bass and baritone are satisfyingly firm and beautiful. Gottlob Frick is as near an ideal Hunding as one will find, sinister but with the right streak of arrogant sexuality; while the Wotan of Ferdinand Frantz may not be as deeply perceptive as some – his death-dealing to Hunding at the end of Act II misses the necessary heart-stopping quality – but to hear the sweep of Wagner's melodic lines so gloriously sung is a rare joy.

The 1954 sound is amazingly full and vivid, with voices cleanly balanced against the inspired orchestra. Far more than Furtwängler's live recording of the *Ring* from Rome, this *Walküre* (the first of a *Ring* project which sadly went no further) is a superb memorial to his Wagnerian mastery. The only snag of the set is that, to fit the whole piece on to only three CDs, breaks between discs come in mid-Act, both in Act II: after the *Ho-jo-to-hos* have died away and before the Wotan–Fricka duet starts, and before the final Siegmund–Sieglinde duet.

The major advantage of the Boulez Bayreuth version of 1980 is that it comes at mid-price on only three discs, with atmospheric digital sound and a strong, if flawed, cast. It brings the aesthetic advantage that the only break between discs within an Act comes early in Act II. By 1980 Peter Hofmann's tenor had already grown rather gritty for Siegmund; the long Act I duet with Sieglinde is not as mellifluous as it should be, with even the *Winterstürme* solo not sweet enough.

Jeannine Altmeyer, who later graduated to Brünnhilde in the Janowski studio recording, is generally reliable and Donald McIntyre makes a commanding Wotan, Hanna Schwarz a firm, biting Fricka and Gwyneth Jones, always an uneven singer on disc, is at her least abrasive, producing beautiful, gentle tone in lyrical passages. Boulez's fervour will surprise many, even if he does not quite match Boehm's passionate urgency in this second instalment of the tetralogy.

The Eurodisc *Ring* cycle is one for Wagnerians who want to concentrate on the score, undistracted by stereo staging or even by strongly characterful conducting. Janowski's direct approach matches the relative dryness of the acoustic, with voices fixed well forward of the orchestra – but not aggressively so. That balance allows full presence for the singing from a satisfyingly consistent cast.

Jessye Norman might not seem an obvious choice for Sieglinde, but the sound is glorious, the expression intense and detailed, making her a superb match for the fine, if rather less imaginative Siegmund of Siegfried Jerusalem. The one snag with so commanding a Sieglinde is that she overtops the Brünnhilde of Jeannine Altmeyer who, more than usual, conveys a measure of feminine vulnerability in the leading Valkyrie, even in her godhead days.

Miss Altmeyer, born in Los Angeles of a German father and an Italian mother, may be slightly over-parted, but the beauty and frequent sensuousness of her singing are the more telling, next to the gritty Wotan of Theo Adam. With its slow vibrato under pressure, his is rarely a pleasing voice, but the clarity of the recording makes it a specific, never a woolly sound, so that the illumination of the narrative is consistent and intense. Kurt Moll is a gloriously firm Hunding, and Yvonne Minton a searingly effective Fricka. On CD, the drama and urgency of the recording have even greater bite; moreover its mid-priced reissue on four instead of five discs makes it marginally more competitive.

Haitink recorded this first instalment of a complete *Ring* cycle before he had conducted the piece in the opera house. His is a broad view, strong and thoughtful yet conveying monumental power. That goes with searching concentration and a consistent feeling for the detailed beauty of Wagner's writing, glowingly brought out in the warm and spacious recording, made in the Herkulessaal in Munich.

The outstanding performance comes from Cheryl Studer as Sieglinde, very convincingly cast, giving a tenderly affecting performance to bring out the character's vulnerability in a very human way. At *Du bist der Lenz* her radiant singing brings an eagerly personal revelation, the response of a lover.

Despite some strained moments, Reiner Goldberg makes a heroic Siegmund, far finer than most today; and Eva Marton is a noble, powerful Brünnhilde, less uneven of production than she has often been on record. Waltraud Meier makes a convincingly waspish and biting Fricka and Matti Salminen a resonant Hunding.

James Morris is a fine, perceptive Wotan, and the voice, not an easy one to record, is better focused here than in Levine's rival DG version of this opera from the Met. If a modern digital recording of *Walküre* is essential, this is the best choice, but both the original Solti recording on Decca – sounding amazingly fresh and better focused than any – and Boehm's live Bayreuth recording on Philips remain on balance preferable.

The great merits of Karajan's version in competition with those of Solti are the refinement of the orchestral playing and the heroic strength of Jon Vickers as Siegmund. With that underlined, one cannot help but note that the vocal shortcomings here are generally more marked, and the total result does not add up to quite so compelling a dramatic experience: one is less involved.

Thomas Stewart may have a younger, firmer voice than Hotter, but the character of Wotan emerges only partially; it is not just that he misses some of the word-meaning, but that on occasion – as in the kissing away of Brünnhilde's godhead – he underlines too crudely. A fine performance, none the less; and Josephine Veasey as Fricka matches her rival, Ludwig, in conveying the biting intensity of the part.

Gundula Janowitz's Sieglinde is above all beautiful, while Crespin's Brünnhilde is impressive but nothing like as satisfying as her study of Sieglinde on the Solti Decca set. The voice is at times strained into unsteadiness, which the microphone seems to exaggerate. The DG recording is good, but not quite in the same class as the Decca – its slightly recessed quality is the more apparent in the CD transfer. The bass is relatively light, but an agreeable bloom is given to the voices, set in an atmospheric acoustic, all made the more realistic on CD.

Levine's version is based on the stage production at the Metropolitan, but was recorded in a New York studio, the first instalment of DG's newest *Ring* cycle. Though Levine's speeds are often very slow, his conducting consistently reflects the timing of a stage performance, and the playing of the Met. orchestra is brilliant. Unfortunately, the sound, though wide-ranging in frequency and dynamic and with spectacular brass and timpani, has little bloom on it, lacking depth of focus from front to back. The impact is still powerful, but it is partly the fault of the recording that some of the solo singing sounds less agreeable than it might.

Though Hildegard Behrens makes a fascinating and distinctive Brünnhilde, bringing out an element of vulnerability, the unevenness in the voice under pressure is often exaggerated. Gary Lakes makes a throaty, limited Siegmund and his weaknesses are underlined by the power of the Sieglinde of Jessye Norman, magnetically compelling in every phrase but, in contrast to Behrens, conveying little vulnerability and not quite fitting the role, however intense and powerful the expression. When she tells Siegmund that he represents the spring, *Du bist der Lenz*, she gives it all the emphasis of an earth-mother.

The DG recording brings out the lack of sweetness in James Morris's voice as Wotan, but it is a noble, highly intelligent reading, while Kurt Moll is a magnificent Hunding; Christa Ludwig as Fricka sings with just as much heartfelt intensity here as she did 30 years earlier, taking the same role in the Decca *Ring* cycle with Solti. Compared with that classic version, with its vivid production by John Culshaw for stereo, the new one – for all the glories of wide-ranging digital sound – is shallow and even coarse.

The 1961 Decca set of *Die Walküre* hardly matches what Solti was later to achieve, despite recording of outstanding quality for its period. The LSO playing is first class, Leinsdorf is vigorous and thrustful, and the result is always exciting, but it lacks repose where necessary, and this affects the singers. Vickers is too strenuous in the spring greeting, but most of his performance is superbly rich and heroic. Gré Brouwenstijn is even finer as Sieglinde; her vibrant voice is radiant. David Ward is a resonant Hunding, Rita Gorr a strong Fricka.

Nilsson is excellent as Brünnhilde, if not as commanding as in her later recordings. The Wotan of George London too often has a rough edge and the recording brings out the unevenness of vocal production as well as a throaty timbre, but by latterday standards this is still a powerful performance. On only three mid-priced CDs this makes a good alternative to the Furtwängler mono set for those who insist on full, atmospheric stereo.

The Valkyries (complete; in English).
(M) *** EMI CMS7 63918-2 (4). ENO O, Goodall.
   Siegmund (Alberto Remedios), Sieglinde (Margaret Curphey), Brünnhilde (Rita Hunter), Wotan (Norman Bailey), Fricka (Ann Howard), Hunding (Clifford Grant).

Like *Siegfried*, this was recorded live at the Coliseum and, with minor reservations, it fills the bill splendidly for those who want to enjoy the *Ring* cycle in English. With the voices balanced a little more closely than in *Siegfried*, the words of Andrew Porter's translation are a degree clearer but the atmosphere is less vivid. The glory of the performance lies not just in Goodall's spacious direction but in the magnificent Wotan of Norman Bailey, noble in the broadest span but very human in his illumination of detail.

Rita Hunter sings nobly too, and though she is not as commanding as Nilsson in the Solti cycle she is often more lyrically tender. Alberto Remedios as Siegmund is more taxed than he was as Siegfried in the later opera (lower tessituras are not quite so comfortable for him) but his sweetly ringing top register is superb. If others, such as Ann Howard as Fricka, are not always treated kindly by the microphone, the total dramatic compulsion is irresistible. The CD transfer increases the sense of presence and at the same time confirms the relative lack of sumptuousness.

Die Walküre, Act I (complete).
(M) (***) EMI mono CDH7 61020-2 [id.]. Lotte Lehmann, Lauritz Melchior, Emanuel List, VPO, Bruno Walter.
(M) **(*) Decca 425 963-2 [id.]. Kirsten Flagstad, Set Svanholm, Arnold Van Mill, VPO, Knappertsbusch.

Bruno Walter's 1935 recording of Act I of *Walküre* has been transferred to CD with astonishing vividness in this EMI Références issue. Though in the days of 78-r.p.m. discs the music had to be recorded in short takes of under five minutes, one is consistently gripped by the continuity and sustained lines of Walter's reading, and by the intensity and beauty of the playing of the Vienna Philharmonic. Lotte Lehmann's portrait of Sieglinde, arguably her finest role, has a depth and beauty never surpassed since, and Lauritz Melchior's heroic Siegmund brings singing of a scale and variety – not to mention beauty – that no Heldentenor today begins to match. Emanuel List as Hunding is satisfactory enough, but his achievement at least has latterly been surpassed.

Flagstad may not have been ideally cast as Sieglinde, but the command of her singing with its unfailing richness, even after her official retirement, crowns a strong and dramatic performance, with Svanholm and Van Mill singing cleanly. The early stereo still sounds vivid.

Die Walküre: excerpts: Act II: *Kehrte der Vater nur Heim!;* Act III: *Schützt mich und helft in höchster Not.*
(M) (**) Standing Room Only SRO 833-2. Birgit Nilsson, Leonie Rysanek, James King, (1965) Bayreuth Festival O, Boehm – R. STRAUSS: *Elektra* etc. (***)

These *Walküre* excerpts were recorded live at the 1965 Bayreuth Festival, not as refined in sound or as performances as on the complete Boehm Philips recording. With such a cast they make a valuable fill-up for the exceptionally generous Strauss coupling from Standing Room Only.

Die Walküre: Act III (complete).
Withdrawn: (M) *** Decca 425 986-2 [id.]. Kirsten Flagstad, Otto Edelmann, Marianna Schech, VPO, Solti.
(M) (***) EMI mono CDH7 64704-2 [id.]. Astrid Varnay, Sigurd Bjoerling, Leonie Rysanek, (1951) Bayreuth Festival O, Karajan.

This Decca recording was made in 1957. Flagstad came out of retirement to make it, and Decca put us eternally in their debt for urging her to do so. She sings radiantly. This great artist seemed to have acquired an extra wisdom and an extra maturity in interpretation in her period away from the stage. The meticulousness needed in the recording studio obviously brought out all her finest qualities, and there is no more than a touch of hardness on some of the top notes to show that the voice was no longer as young as it had been. Edelmann is not the ideal Wotan but he has a particularly well focused voice, and when he sings straight, without sliding up or sitting under the note, the result is superb and he is never wobbly.

But it is Solti's conducting that prevents any slight blemishes from mattering. His rethinking of the score means that time and time again, at particularly dramatic points, one finds that the increased excitement engendered is merely the result of a literal following of all Wagner's markings. Not surprisingly, the recording too is remarkably vivid, anticipating the excellence of the great *Ring* project which was to follow.

Recorded in 1951, the first season after the war, Karajan's Bayreuth version of Act III shows the still-young conductor working at white heat. Speeds are far faster than in his DG studio recording, and very close to those in his live recording made at the Met. in 1969 (Nuova Era). Ensemble inevitably is not as taut as it was in the studio performance, but the electricity is far keener, and his cast is a characterful one.

Astrid Varnay is an abrasive Brünnhilde, presenting the Valkyrie as a forceful figure, even in penitence prepared to stand up against her father. Leonie Rysanek is a warm Sieglinde, powerful rather than pure, with a rather obtrusive vibrato even at that date. Sigurd Bjoerling by contrast, the least-known of the principals, proves a magnificently virile Wotan, steady as a rock in the *Farewell*, but colouring the voice with a near-shout at the command, '*Loge, hier!*' The mono sound is transferred with bright immediacy, with some harshness on top but plenty of weight in the bass. This makes a splendid supplement to Karajan's superb Bayreuth *Meistersinger*, also recorded live in 1951.

Die Walküre: highlights.
(M) *** Decca 421 887-2 [id.] (from above recording with King, Crespin, Nilsson, Hotter; cond. Solti).
*** EMI Dig. CDC7 54328-2 [id.] (from above recording with Goldberg, Studer, Marton, Morris; cond. Haitink).

The mid-priced Solti highlights disc is not as generous as some (54 minutes) but is spectacularly well recorded. The items chosen, opening with Siegmund's (James King) *Winterstürme wichen dem Wonnemond*, ravishingly lyrical, and including the *Ride of the Valkyries*, make a particularly satisfying reminder of some of the finest moments in the set. Recommendable to those who cannot stretch to the full opera.

Those who have chosen another complete set will surely want a reminder of Haitink's glowingly spacious EMI set. The selection here is generous – 76 minutes – and it includes Cheryl Studer's *Du bist der Lenz* within the 21 minutes from Act I, while the excerpts from Act III include the *Ride of the Valkyries*, and it ends with the *Magic fire music* sequence at the end of the opera. Splendidly rich recording.

VOCAL COLLECTIONS

'*Wagner singing on record':* Excerpts from: (i) *Der fliegende Holländer;* (ii) *Götterdämmerung;* (iii) *Lohengrin;* (iv) *Die Meistersinger von Nürnberg;* (v) *Parsifal;* (vi) *Das Rheingold;* (vii) *Siegfried;* (viii) *Tannhäuser;* (ix) *Tristan und Isolde;* (x) *Die Walküre.*
(M) EMI mono/stereo CMS7 64008-2 (4) [id.]. (i) Hans Hermann Nissen, Arthur Endrèze, Marta Fuchs, Friedel Beckmann, Elisabeth Rethberg, Birgit Nilsson, Hans Hotter; (ii) Florence Austral, Walter Widdop, Emanuel List, Ludwig Weber, Herbert Janssen, Marjorie Lawrence; (iii) Rethberg, Aureliano Pertile, Martial Singher, Lawrence, Hina Spani, Lotte Lehmann, Margarete Klose, Marcel Wittrisch, Helge Roswaenge; (iv) Friedrich Schorr, Georges Thill, Germaine Martinelli, Rudolf Bockelmann, Lauritz Melchior, Elisabeth Schumann, Gladys Parr, Ben Williams, Torsten Ralf, Tiana Lemnitz; (v) Frida Leider, Alexander Kipnis, Fritz Wolff; (vi) Schorr; (vii) Nissen, Maria Olczewska, Emil Schipper, Leider, Rudolf Laubenthal, Germaine Lubin; (viii) Maria Müller, Max Lorenz, Maria Reining, Herbert Janssen, Gerhard Hüsch, Kirsten Flagstad; (ix) Leider, Nanny Larsen-Todsen, Anny Helm, Melchior, Meta Seinemeyer, Lorenz; (x) Lawrence, Marcel Journet, Rudolf Bockelmann.

This collection, compiled in Paris as '*Les Introuvables du Chant Wagnerien*', contains an amazing array of recordings made in the later years of 78-r.p.m. recording, mostly between 1927 and 1940. In 49 items, many of them substantial, the collection consistently demonstrates the reliability of Wagner singing at that period, the ability of singers in every register to produce firm, well-focused tone of a kind too rare today. Some of the most interesting items are those in translation from French sources, with Germaine Lubin as Isolde and Brünnhilde and with Marcel Journet as Wotan, both lyrical and clean-cut. The ill-starred Marjorie Lawrence, a great favourite in France, is also represented by recordings in French, including Brünnhilde's Immolation scene from *Götterdämmerung*.

Not only are such celebrated Wagnerians as Lauritz Melchior, Friedrich Schorr, Frida Leider, Lotte Lehmann and Max Lorenz very well represented, but also singers one might not expect, including the Lieder specialist, Gerhard Husch, as Wolfram in *Tannhäuser* and Aureliano Pertile singing in Italian as Lohengrin. Significantly, Meta Seinemeyer, an enchanting soprano who died tragically young, here gives lyric sweetness to the dramatic roles of Brünnhilde and Isolde; and among the baritones and basses there is none of the roughness or ill-focus that marks so much latterday Wagner singing.

It is a pity that British-based singers are poorly represented, but the Prologue duet from *Götterdämmerung* brings one of the most impressive items, sung by Florence Austral and Walter Widdop. First-rate transfers and good documentation.

Der fliegende Holländer: Senta's ballad. Götterdämmerung: Immolation scene. Tannhäuser: Elisabeth's greeting; Elisabeth's prayer. Tristan und Isolde: Prelude and Liebestod.
*** EMI Dig. CDC7 49759-2 [id.]. Jessye Norman, Amb. Op. Ch., LPO, Tennstedt.

Der fliegende Holländer: Senta's ballad. Götterdämmerung: Brünnhilde's immolation. Tannhäuser: Dich teure Halle. Tristan und Isolde: Prelude and Liebestod.
*(*) Sony CD 37294. Montserrat Caballé, NYPO, Mehta.

As a Wagnerian, Tennstedt tends to take a rugged view, and it is a measure of his characterful, noble conducting that his contribution is just as striking as that of the great soprano who is the soloist in these items which, unlike most, have little feeling of being 'bleeding chunks', instead making up a satisfying whole. After a poised and measured account of *Isolde's Liebestod*, Norman is at her most commanding as Elisabeth, both in the outburst of the *Greeting* and in the hushed, poised legato of the *Prayer*. *Senta's ballad* is also superb, and Brünnhilde's Immolation scene brings thrilling singing over a daringly wide range of tone and dynamic, conveying feminine warmth, vulnerability and passion, as well as nobility.

There are moments of tender intensity in Caballé's recital, illuminatingly perceptive of detail; but the singing is too often flawed, when the voice is not well suited to the heavier roles, and Caballé disguises her weakness in mannerism. The recording is only fair; and this is a collection for Caballé admirers, rather than for the general collector.

Choruses from: *Der fliegende Holländer; Lohengrin; Die Meistersinger; Parsifal; Tannhäuser.*
(M) *** Decca 421 865-2 (from complete sets, cond. Solti).

Solti's choral collection is superb, with an added sophistication in both performance and recording – especially in the subtle use of ambience and perspectives – to set it apart from the DG Bayreuth disc, good though that is. The collection opens with a blazing account of the *Lohengrin* Act III *Prelude*, since of course the *Bridal chorus* grows naturally out of it. But the *Pilgrims' chorus*, which comes next, creates an electrifying pianissimo and expands gloriously, while the excerpts from *Die Meistersinger* and *Parsifal* show Solti's characteristic intensity at its most potent.

Arias from: *Götterdämmerung; Lohengrin; Die Meistersinger; Rienzi; Siegfried; Tannhäuser; Tristan; Die Walküre.*
Withdrawn: (M) (***) EMI mono CDH7 69789-2. Lauritz Melchior, LSO, Barbirolli; or Berlin State Op. O, Leo Blech.

No Heldentenor on record has outshone Lauritz Melchior in this Wagner repertory. This collection in the Références series brings together 15 items recorded in his first full maturity between 1928 and 1931, when the magnificent voice was at its freshest. Not that the *Walküre* excerpts here improve on his incomparable performance as Siegfried in Bruno Walter's complete Act I of 1936 (also on Références CD – see above); but, fascinatingly, Barbirolli in the second of the three excerpts, *Winterstürme*, relaxes him more than Leo Blech did on the other two. The selection ends with Melchior's glorious singing of Walther's two arias from *Meistersinger*, noble and shining. Excellent transfers, with the voice given astonishing presence.

Arias: *Götterdämmerung:* (i) *Zu neuen Taten; Starke Scheite schichter. Lohengrin: Euch Lüften mein Klagen. Parsifal:* (i) *Ich sah' das Kind. Tristan: Mild und leise. Die Walküre: Du bist der Lenz; Ho-jo-ho!.*
(M) (***) BMG/RCA mono GD 87915 [87915-2-RG]. Kirsten Flagstad, (i) with Lauritz Melchior, San Francisco Op. O or Victor SO (both cond. Edwin McArthur); Phd. O, Ormandy.

Recorded for RCA in America between 1935 and 1940, this first generation of Wagner recordings by Flagstad reveals the voice at its noblest and freshest, the more exposed in consistently close balance on the 78s of the period. It is a pity that only two of the shortest items – from *Lohengrin* and *Walküre* – have Ormandy conducting. Most of the rest are conducted by Flagstad's protégé, Edwin McArthur, including the two longest, the big duet for Parsifal and Kundry and Brünnhilde's Immolation scene. Yet the grandeur of Flagstad's singing is never in doubt, the commanding sureness, and, though the orchestral sound is unflatteringly dry, the voice is gloriously caught in clean transfers.

'Wagner gala': Lohengrin: Prelude to Act III. Rienzi: Overture. Excerpts from: Der fliegende Holländer; Lohengrin; Die Meistersinger; Rienzi; Tannhäuser; Tristan und Isolde; Die Walküre.

(M) **(*) Decca 421 877-2. George London; Gwyneth Jones; James King; Kirsten Flagstad; Tom Krause; Birgit Nilsson; VPO, Solti or Stein.

A generous and vivid concert (74 minutes) but hardly a gala occasion. It was a happy idea to open the programme with James King's appealing account of Rienzi's *Prayer*, based on the gorgeous lyrical tune which makes us all remember the *Overture*. He also sings Walther's *Prize song* from *Die Meistersinger* nobly. Other highlights include Kirsten Flagstad in *Die Männer Sippe* from *Die Walküre* and *Elsa's dream* from *Lohengrin*, and Birgit Nilsson's comparatively restrained, early-1960s account of the *Tristan Liebestod*, spaciously recorded with Knappertsbusch, before she undertook the complete set.

OTHER COLLECTIONS

Siegfried idyll. Lohengrin: Prelude to Acts I & III. Die Meistersinger: Overture. Die Walküre: Ride of the Valkyries; (i) *Wotan's farewell and Magic fire music.*
*** ASV Dig. CDDCA 666; *ZCDCA 666* [id.]. Philh. O, Francesco d'Avalos, (i) with John Tomlinson.

Francesco d'Avalos may not be a Furtwängler, but his pacing of this attractively assembled Wagner concert is most convincing. The opening *Siegfried idyll* has all the requisite serenity and atmosphere; here, as elsewhere, the Philharmonia play most beautifully. The boldly sumptuous recording brings a thrilling resonance and amplitude to the brass, especially trombones and tuba, and in the expansive *Meistersinger overture*, and again in *Wotan's farewell* the brass entries bring a physical frisson. John Tomlinson's noble assumption of the role of Wotan, as he bids a loving farewell to his errant daughter, is very moving here, and the response of the Philharmonia strings matches the depth of feeling he conveys. With the Valkyries also given a splendid sense of spectacle, this collection should have a wide appeal.

Siegfried idyll; Tannhäuser: overture; (i) *Tristan: Prelude and Liebestod.*
*** DG Dig. 423 613-2 [id.]. (i) Jessye Norman; VPO, Karajan.

This superb Wagner record was taken live from a unique concert conducted by Karajan at the Salzburg Festival in August 1987. These three items, lasting little more than 50 minutes, were rehearsed for 13 hours. The result, both at the concert and here on record, has the feeling of a microcosm of Wagner, between them summing up the early period, the *Ring* cycle and the supreme achievement of *Tristan*.

The *Tannhäuser overture* has never sounded so noble and the *Siegfried idyll* has rarely seemed so intense and dedicated behind its sweet lyricism; while the *Prelude and Liebestod*, with Jessye Norman as soloist, bring the richest culmination, sensuous and passionate, but remarkable as much for the hushed, inward moments as for the ineluctable building of climaxes. The recording gives little or no idea of a live occasion, thanks to rather close balance, but the glow of the Vienna Philharmonic at its peak is beautifully captured.

Siegfried idyll. Tristan und Isolde: Prelude and Liebestod. Die Walküre: (i) *Act I, scene iii; Act II: Ride of the Valkyries.*
(***) BMG/RCA mono RD 84751 [RCA 5751-2-RC]. (i) Helen Traubel, Lauritz Melchior; NBC SO, Toscanini.

It is sad that Toscanini never recorded a Wagner opera complete. Despite harsh, limited, mono recording, this CD makes it clear just how incandescent were the Toscanini performances of Wagner and how, with his ear for balance, he brought brightness and transparency to the scores.

Götterdämmerung: Dawn and Siegfried's Rhine journey; Siegfried's death and funeral march; (i) *Brünnhilde's immolation. Siegfried: Forest murmurs. Die Walküre: Ride of the Valkyries.*
*** Erato/Warner Dig. 2292 45786-2 [id.]. (i) Deborah Polaski; Chicago SO, Barenboim.

Here Barenboim dons his Furtwänglerian mantle to splendidly spacious effect. Even with tempi measured, he secures playing of great concentration and excitement from the Chicago orchestra, and the recording is one of the finest made in Chicago's Orchestra Hall for many years. With resplendently sonorous brass – yet with plenty of bite in the hammered chords of despair of the powerful funeral sequence – and rich, expansive violins, this is very compelling indeed.

Without artificial brilliance but with plenty of weight, the *Ride of the Valkyries* opens the programme vigorously; then *Forest murmurs* brings glowing atmospheric magic. Deborah

Polaski makes a bold, passionate Brünnhilde, and if her voice is not flattered by the microphones, and under pressure her vibrato widens and there is a loss of focus at the climax of the *Immolation scene*, this is still histrionically thrilling, and Barenboim and the orchestra provide an overwhelming final apotheosis.

Walton, William (1902–83)

Troilus and Cressida: Scenes: Act I: (i) *Is Cressida a slave?; Slowly it all comes back;* Act II: *How can I sleep if one last doubt remain;* (ii) *Is anyone there?;* (i) *If one last doubt; Now close your arms; Interlude; From isle to isle chill waters;* Act III: *All's well!; Diomede! Father!.*
(M) *** mono/stereo EMI CDM7 64199-2. (i) Philh. O; (ii) ROHCG O; composer.
  (i) Troilus (Richard Lewis), Cressida (Elisabeth Schwarzkopf), Evadne (Monica Sinclair).
  (ii) Cressida (Marie Collier), Pandarus (Peter Pears).

Walton wrote this superbly lyrical and atmospheric opera with Schwarzkopf in mind to play the heroine. She never sang the part on stage, but these highlights are more than enough to show what we missed. The melodies may not be as immediately striking as Puccini's but they grow more haunting on repetition, and it would be hard to find a more directly appealing, modern romantic opera.

The selections are well chosen, and for the reissue a reminder of Sir Peter Pears's Pandarus is now included. As a Decca artist he was not included in the original EMI recording, but now his brief duet with Marie Collier (the Cressida of the 1963 Covent Garden revival) can happily be included. It was recorded in stereo in 1968, again using the Kingsway Hall – the venue for the original sessions 13 years earlier. With Walter Legge then producing, it is not surprising that the mono quality is almost as impressive as the later stereo, particularly the scene in Act III (*All's well*) with Cressida, Evadne and the Watchman, which has a magical sense of perspective. A most valuable and rewarding reissue.

Weber, Carl Maria von (1786–1826)

Euryanthe (complete).
Withdrawn: (M) *** EMI CMS7 63509-2 (3) [Ang. CDMC 63509]. Leipzig R. Ch., Dresden State O, Janowski.
  Euryanthe (Jessye Norman), Eglantine (Rita Hunter), Adolar (Nicolai Gedda), Lysiart (Tom Krause).

Much has been written about the absurdity of the plot of *Euryanthe*, as unlikely a tale of chivalry and troubadours as you will find; as this fine recording bears out, however, the opera is far more than just a historic curiosity and we hope the records will be restored to the EMI catalogue before too long.

The opera takes place at the royal court of Prémery. War against rebellious barons is over, the kingdom of Louis VI is peaceful, and the graceful court conventions are noticeably evident. Count Adolar is, however, miserable. To remedy this, the king invites Euryanthe to court. But Adolar has a rival in Lysiart, Count of Nevers, who casts suspicion on the virtue of Euryanthe. The two noblemen pledge each other their domains on a trial of her fidelity.

At the castle in Nevers the sweet-natured Euryanthe longs for Adolar's return. Her friend, Eglantine of Paiset, is with her. Eglantine (whose family were outlawed because of the rebellion) had also loved Adolar at one time and her feelings are still strong; she hints that Euryanthe's trust in him may be betrayed. But Euryanthe hotly defends him and she talks in confidence of a secret she shares with him.

Weber provides ghostly music as she relates how Adolar's late sister, Emma, had appeared to them as a spirit and had related how she had taken poison from her ring after her lover had died in battle. Her soul can find peace only when the tears of an innocent girl have been wept over her ring.

Eglantine and Euryanthe pledge to keep faith with each other in this matter, but Eglantine soon reveals her jealousy of Euryanthe, and it is obvious that she will not keep her word. Instead, she plans to ransack Emma's tomb, where she hopes to find evidence of Euryanthe's duplicity which may be used to convince Adolar that she is not as innocent as she seems. Trumpets now herald the arrival of Lysiart, who is to escort Euryanthe back to the king's court. Euryanthe greets him warmly.

Later, at the Nevers castle, Lysiart, uncertain of gaining any success over Euryanthe's trial of fidelity, finds himself falling in love with her. He has mixed-up feelings: frustrated longing, jealousy of Adolar and a thirst for vengeance. Hearing Eglantine's admission that she has stolen Emma's ring from her tomb and means to use it as a means of harming Euryanthe, Lysiart promises Eglantine that, if she will give him the ring, he will use it against Euryanthe and furthermore he will marry Eglantine. If he is successful, Adolar's lands will belong to them both.

Now back in Prémery, Adolar and Euryanthe are reunited and declare their great love for each other. But the king and his courtiers enter with Lysiart, who announces that he has won the wager. Adolar is angry, while Euryanthe cannot comprehend what it is all about, until Lysiart produces the ring, implying that she gave it to him, and she realizes that the family secret is betrayed. Adolar believes that in addition she has been unfaithful.

Adolar renounces his possessions in Lysiart's favour and, wearing black armour, leads Euryanthe from the court. He takes her into the wilderness where she protests her innocence but begs his forgiveness for revealing the family secret; but he plans to kill her. A serpent slides between them, and she bravely stands between him and the monster, so he kills it.

After this episode he decides (because of her courageous willingness to die for him) not to murder her, but simply to abandon her. She prays that he will visit her grave and that nature and the flowers will proclaim her innocence. However, the royal hunting party is now approaching, and the king is speedily convinced of Euryanthe's innocence and Eglantine's guilty machinations. But all this has been too much for poor Euryanthe, who collapses.

Lysiart is now lord of Adolar's estates and his coming wedding to Eglantine is celebrated. But soon it is clear that she is suffering from ghostly visions of Emma. Adolar appears and challenges Lysiart, but the king prevents the two from fighting a duel. He also announces that Euryanthe is dead. Eglantine now confesses her complicity in the plot against Euryanthe, and Lysiart stabs her.

The king orders his arrest, but Adolar says his own behaviour has been even more reprehensible. Euryanthe is brought in by the hunters, not dead, but merely exhausted. She revives and is restored to Adolar. As she cries, her tears fall on to Emma's ring which Adolar is wearing on his finger. So Emma's troubled spirit is at last at rest.

For all the faults of the plot, the juxtaposition of two sopranos, representing good and evil, is formidably effective, particularly when the challenge is taken by singers of the stature of Jessye Norman and Rita Hunter. Hunter may not be the most convincing villainess, but the cutting edge of the voice is marvellous; and as for Jessye Norman, she sings radiantly, whether in her first delicate cavatina or in the big aria of Act III. Tom Krause as the villain, Lysiart, has rarely sung better and Nicolai Gedda, as ever, is the most intelligent of tenors. Good atmospheric recording (as important in this opera as in *Freischütz*) and vivid remastering, while the direction from Marek Janowski makes light of any longueurs.

Der Freischütz (complete).
(M) *** EMI CMS7 69342-2 (2). German Op. Ch., Berlin, BPO, Keilberth.
  Agathe (Elisabeth Grümmer), Max (Rudolf Schock), Aennchen (Lisa Otto), Kaspar (Karl Christian Kohn), Ottokar (Hermann Prey), Hermit (Gottlob Frick), Kuno (Ernst Wiemann).
*** DG 415 432-2 (2) [id.]. Leipzig R. Ch., Dresden State O, Carlos Kleiber.
  Agathe (Gundula Janowitz), Max (Peter Schreier), Aennchen (Edith Mathis), Kaspar (Theo Adam), Ottokar (Bernd Weikl), Hermit (Franz Crass), Kuno (Siegfried Vogel).
Withdrawn: **(*) Decca 417 119-2 (2) [id.]. Bav. R. Ch. & SO, Kubelik.
  Agathe (Hildegard Behrens), Max (René Kollo), Aennchen (Helen Donath).
** Ph. Dig. 426 319-2 (2) [id.]. Dresden Op. Ch. & State O, Sir Colin Davis.
  Agathe (Karita Mattila), Max (Francisco Araiza), Aennchen (Eva Lind), Kaspar (Ekkehard Wlaschiha), Hermit (Kurt Moll).
Withdrawn: ** Denon Dig. C37 6433/5 [id.]. Dresden State Op. Ch. & O, Hauschild.
  Agathe (Jana Smitková), Max (Reiner Goldberg), Aennchen (Andrea Ihle), Kaspar (Ekkehard Wlaschiha), Ottokar (Hans-Joachim Ketelsen), Hermit (Theo Adam), Kuno (Gunther Emmerlich).

Weber's *Der Freischütz* ('The Marksman') was an enormous success in its day (1821). It seemed the very epitome of German romanticism, and few operas have an overture which creates the work's ambience so surely. If, in the opera house, the principal characters seem made of cardboard, the powerful atmosphere is another matter, and the music is full of memorable ideas and dramatically original orchestral effects.

The story takes place in Bohemia in the middle of the seventeenth century. We first meet

Max, its hero, just after he has been defeated in a shooting contest by Kilian, a wealthy peasant. Cuno, the hereditary forester, is worried that for some time Max has made a poor showing at his skills with firearms. Max hopes to marry Cuno's daughter, Agathe, and eventually take over Cuno's position. To accomplish this, he must win the honours in a shooting tournament the very next day. Max is totally downcast.

The orchestral mood becomes more sinister and we are aware of Samiel, a wild huntsman, hovering, unseen by Max, in the background. Kaspar, Max's colleague, now appears. He is of forbidding appearance – no doubt because he has already made a contract with Samiel by which he will lose his soul unless he can find a replacement. He hands Max his gun, telling him to shoot at an eagle overhead. The bird dies at his feet.

Kaspar now explains that the gun contained a magic bullet which never misses its target. Kaspar invites Max to meet him in the Wolf's Glen at midnight. There the magic bullets are moulded and, if Max uses one of these on the morrow, he will be sure to win Agathe and the hereditary title of forester. Max is greatly tempted and, longing for victory, finally agrees to meet Kaspar as suggested. Kaspar is sinisterly triumphant.

Agathe sits with her cousin, Aennchen, the more frivolous of the two. Agathe feels foreboding yet declares her love for Max in one of Weber's most ravishing arias (*Leise, leise, fromme Weise*) but, when he arrives, he tells them that he cannot stay because he shot a deer in the Wolf's Glen and must retrieve it. The girls try to stop him from going, for they know it is a place haunted by evil spirits. But Max goes anyway, and in the glen the spirit of Samiel awaits him.

So does Kaspar and together they mould seven magic bullets. Six of these will find their mark, the seventh will go wherever Samiel directs. Max is warned by the ghost of his mother and by a vision in which Agathe appears, but he is determined to go on with his macabre task. The visions become wilder and wilder and finally Max collapses as the village clock indicates that the midnight hour has passed.

We return to the radiant Agathe, in her bridal dress, but now she is praying, still sensing that evil is round her. The bridesmaids gaily enter, but she finds in the box they are carrying a wreath instead of a garland. However, Aennchen makes her a new one out of white roses. A spirited hunting chorus announces the beginning of the shooting contest. During the hunt the six magic bullets have been used but not the seventh.

Kaspar climbs a tree to watch the proceedings from a distance; he is sure Max will be Samiel's victim. Prince Ottokar, Max's employer, and the whole village are there to watch. The prince points to a flying dove; at the same moment Agathe appears, accompanied by a hermit from whom came the white roses in her garland. She calls out to Max not to shoot, for she knows that the dove represents herself.

But she is too late, Max has pulled the trigger. Agathe falls, but she has only fainted. The bullet has found its mark in Kaspar, who falls from the tree, fatally wounded. Samiel had no real power over Max, for he had not come to the Wolf's Glen of his own free will, but only because Kaspar had tempted him. Consternation reigns.

Max confesses and is banished by the prince. But the hermit intervenes and asks the prince to forgive Max. Moved by the old man's plea, the prince puts Max on a year's trial. If he is worthy, he will be pardoned and can marry Agathe.

Keilberth's is a warm, exciting account of Weber's masterpiece which makes all the dated conventions of the work seem fresh and new. In particular the Wolf's Glen scene in atmospheric stereo of a quality remarkable for 1958 acquires something of the genuine terror that must have struck the earliest audiences.

The casting of the magic bullets with each one numbered in turn, at first in eerie quiet then in crescendo amid the howling of demons, is superbly conveyed. The bite of the orchestra and the proper balance of the voices in relation to it, with the effect of space and distance, also helps to create the illusion.

Elisabeth Grümmer sings sweetly and sensitively, with Agathe's prayer exquisitely done. Lisa Otto characterizes well with genuine coquettishness. Rudolf Schock as Max is a Heldentenor who can sustain a legato line better than most. The Kaspar of Karl Kohn is generally well focused and the playing of the Berlin Philharmonic is finely polished. With such atmospheric sound this is an exceptionally enjoyable set.

The DG set marked Carlos Kleiber's first major recording venture. The young conductor, son of a famous father, had already won himself a reputation for inspiration and unpredictability, and this fine, incisive account of Weber's atmospheric and adventurous score fulfilled all expectations. With the help of an outstanding cast, excellent work by the recording producer, and electrically clear recording, this is a most compelling version of an opera which transfers well to recording.

Gundula Janowitz sings with ravishing purity as Agathe, well contrasted with the Aennchen of Edith Mathis, while Peter Schreier is a sensitive Max. Only occasionally does Kleiber in meticulous treatment of detail betray a fractional lack of warmth, but the full drama of the work is splendidly projected in the enhanced CD format. Not only is there added presence for the voices, but Weber's inspired orchestral colouring is the more vivid, while the famous Wolf's Glen scene is made superbly atmospheric.

Kubelik takes a direct view of Weber's high romanticism. The result has freshness but lacks something in dramatic bite and atmosphere. There is far less tension than in the finest earlier versions, not least in the Wolf's Glen scene which, in spite of full-ranging, brilliant recording, seems rather tame, even with the added projection of CD. The singing is generally good – René Kollo as Max giving one of his best performances on record – but Hildegard Behrens, superbly dramatic in later German operas, here seems clumsy as Agathe in music that often requires a pure lyrical line. The 1981 recording has been vividly remastered on to a pair of CDs.

After his years of experience at Covent Garden, Sir Colin Davis paces this magic score very well indeed, and the Dresden forces respond with some fine playing and singing. To add to the drama there are plenty of production sounds, even including the barking of hounds, with shots that have you jumping out of your seat. Even so, this is a set that fails to convey the full drama of this high-romantic horror story, most strikingly of all in the Wolf's Glen scene, where the casting of the magic bullets sounds tame, not frightening at all.

The singing is flawed too. Karita Mattila's warm, vibrant soprano is apt enough for Agathe, and she controls the soaring lines of her two big arias very beautifully, but *Und ob die Wolke* brings under-the-note coloration which may distress some ears. As Max, Francisco Araiza is seriously stressed, with the basically beautiful voice sounding throaty, and Eva Lind is unpleasantly fluttery and shallow as Aennchen. Ekkehard Wlaschiha, best known as Alberich in the *Ring*, is darkly sinister as Kaspar, and it is good too to have Kurt Moll as the Hermit. The impact of the performance is blunted by the heavy reverberation, more than usual in recordings from the Lukaskirche in Dresden.

On 13 February 1985 the Semper opera house in Dresden was re-opened, lovingly rebuilt and restored after wartime destruction 40 years earlier. Japanese engineers from Denon worked with East German colleagues to record this first performance in the theatre, capturing the atmosphere very vividly. Those who like live recordings of opera will not mind the occasional odd balance and the bouts of coughing from the audience, but the conducting of Wolf-Dieter Hauschild is not always electrifying enough to compensate. The Wolf's Glen scene, when the magic bullets are cast, lacks the full tingle of horror, though Ekkehard Wlaschiha, as Kaspar, and Reiner Goldberg are both first rate. Jana Smitková makes a tender and vulnerable Agathe, though she is not always steady of tone. Much of the rest of the singing is indifferent, though the chorus work is lively. Moreover the set is uneconomically laid out on three CDs.

Oberon (complete).
(M) *** DG 419 038-2 (2) [id.]. Bav. R. Ch. & SO, Kubelik.
    Oberon (Donald Grobe), Rezia (Birgit Nilsson), Hüon (Plácido Domingo), Scherasmin (Hermann Prey), Fatima (Júlia Hamari), Puck (Marga Schiml), Mermaid (Arleen Augér).
*(*) EMI Dig. CDS7 54739-2 (2) [id.]. Cologne Concert Soc., Conlon.
    Oberon (Gary Lakes), Rezia (Deborah Voigt), Hüon (Ben Heppner), Scherasmin (Dwayne Croft), Fatima (Delores Ziegler), Puck (Victoria Livengood), Mermaid (Machiko Obata).

Rarely has operatic inspiration been squandered so cruelly on impossible material as in Weber's *Oberon*. We owe it to Covent Garden's strange ideas in the mid-1820s as to what English opera should be that Weber's delicately conceived score is a sequence of illogical arias, scenas and ensembles, strung together by an absurd pantomime plot. Though, even on record, the result is slacker because of that loose construction, one can appreciate the contribution of Weber in a performance as stylish and refined as this. The original issue included dialogue and a narrative spoken by one of Oberon's fairy characters. In the reissue this is omitted, cutting the number of discs from three to two, yet leaving the music untouched.

The curtain rises to reveal Oberon's bower. Fairies sing round the sleeping king. Puck enters and explains that Oberon has quarrelled with Titania; he will not be reconciled with her until he can find two lovers constant through all perils and temptations. Puck has already roamed the whole world to find the unattainable.

Oberon next hears the story of Sir Hüon of Bordeaux, a young knight who, in response to an insult, has killed the son of Charlemagne in single combat. For this he has been condemned by the emperor to proceed to Baghdad and slay him who sits at the caliph's right hand, and also to claim the caliph's daughter as his bride.

Oberon decides that this unlikely pair shall be the instrument of his reunion with Titania. He conjures up Hüon and Scherasmin (his squire) and they remain asleep in front of him. Then he shows the caliph's daughter, Rezia, to the knight in a vision.

She is introduced by the famous horn-call from the *Overture* and she calls for help. Oberon awakens Hüon with fairy music and he promises to carry out his mission. He is given a magic horn to protect him. With a wave of his wand Oberon transports Hüon and Scherasmin to Baghdad.

On their journey Hüon and his squire rescue a Saracen prince, Babekan, from a lion. As it happens, he is betrothed to Rezia and, thoroughly evil, he unsuccessfully attacks his rescuers. Next they encounter an old woman who tells them that Rezia is to be wed the next day, but the princess too is influenced by a vision and resolves to be Hüon's alone; she believes he will shield her from Babekan.

At the palace of Haroun el Rashid, Rezia tells Fatima that she will marry the knight alone; Fatima assures her that her deliverance is at hand. Now the caliph is seen with Babekan, weary of waiting for his bride and seated at the caliph's right hand.

Rezia is sent for, a clash of swords is heard and Rezia is seen in the arms of her knight, who next vanquishes Babekan. Then, after a blast on the magic horn, the guards are frozen like statues, and he and Scherasmin carry off Rezia and Fatima, the latter falling in love with Scherasmin.

All four board a ship and Puck, using his spirits, causes the ship to founder. Hüon is the hero: he saves the wreck's survivors, including Rezia, who shows her appreciation of his formidable resources by singing of the power of the sea in her famous *Ocean, thou mighty monster*.

She spies a ship, but it is a pirate ship and she is abducted, while Hüon, saved by Oberon's command, finds himself left senseless on the beach. Both Puck and Oberon return and there is a masque-like tableau involving Neptune and his mermaids.

Fatima and Scherasmin are now slaves in Tunis. Puck transports in Hüon. Fatima thinks Rezia is also in Tunis. So she is, a captive in the palace of the emir who takes a fancy to her for his harem, but he respects her honour. Meanwhile Hüon receives a message from Rezia and finds his way to the palace, where instead he meets the emir's wife, Roshana, who falls for him; she is angry with her husband for preferring his beautiful captive and says that if Hüon will help her to dispatch her husband, he can have the throne of Tunis.

But he refuses to be seduced, either by her or by the wealthy prize. As he rushes off, he is seized by the emir's guards and Roshana tries to kill her husband. The emir arranges a large funeral pyre to burn up Hüon – and Rezia, too, when she declares she is his wife.

Fortunately the magic horn is miraculously restored to Scherasmin, and once more its call is effective, though this time everyone wants to dance. Hüon and Scherasmin feel it is reasonable now to call on Oberon to get them all out of the mess and, sure enough, they are all transported to the court of Charlemagne. Hüon tells the emperor that his commands have been fulfilled and Rezia is with him to prove it. He claims his pardon, and Oberon and Titania, too, are reconciled by the efforts of two such staunch and faithful lovers.

With Birgit Nilsson commanding in *Ocean, thou mighty monster*, and excellent singing from the other principals, helped by Kubelik's ethereally light handling of the orchestra, the set can be recommended without reservation, for the recording remains of excellent quality.

Conlon's EMI version presents the Mahler edition of this ragbag of a work, re-ordering the items and presenting them in German translation with a linking narration, often as melodrama, over orchestral links drawn from material in the *Overture*. Sadly, the performance is not only indifferently cast, Conlon's direction is prosaic, lacking the fairytale fantasy which this often magical score requires.

Ben Heppner has an attractive tenor, with both lyric and heroic qualities apt for the role of Hüon, but he is strained by the impossibly high tessitura. Gary Lakes' heroic tenor is far rougher in the surprisingly less prominent role of Oberon, and Deborah Voigt, though fresh of tone, is rather over-parted as Rezia, particularly in face of the formidable demands of *Ocean, thou mighty monster*. Delores Ziegler as Fatima is more aptly cast, though even she grows unsteady under pressure. The low-level sound with edgy violins and over-close dialogue undermines the magic still further.

Oberon: excerpts.
(M) *** DG 435 406-2; *435 406-4* [id.] (from above recording with Grobe, Nilsson, Domingo; cond. Kubelik) – WAGNER: *Meistersinger excerpts.* ***

As with the coupled excerpts from Wagner's *Meistersinger*, the present selection – part of DG's 'Domingo Edition' – sensibly concentrates on the items featuring Domingo as Hüon. Even so (apart from the stirring introduction to *Von Jugend auf in dem Kampfgefild*) room is found to demonstrate Weber's penchant for brass writing in the Act III *March*, using themes familiar in the *Overture* (which is not included).

Weill, Kurt (1900–1950)

Der Dreigroschenoper (The Threepenny Opera): complete.
*** Decca Dig. 430 075-2; *430 075-4* [id.]. Berlin RIAS Chamber Ch. & Sinf., Mauceri.
Macheath (René Kollo), Polly Peachum (Ute Lemper), Jenny Smith (Milva), Peachum (Mario Adorf), Frau Peachum (Helga Dernesch), Brown (Wolfgang Reichmann), Street Singer (Rolf Boysen).
(M) *** Sony MK 42637 [id.]. Ch. & Dance O of Radio Free Berlin, Brückner-Rüggeberg.
Jenny (Lotte Lenya), Macheath (Erich Schellow), Mr Peachum (Willy Trenk-Trebisch), Mrs Peachum (Trude Hesterburg), Polly Peachum (Johanna Von Kóczián), Tiger Brown (Wolfgang Grunert), Street Singer (Wolfgang Neuss).
Withdrawn: (M) ** Ph. 426 668-2; *426 668-4* [id.]. Frankfurt Op. Ch. & O, Wolfgang Rennert.
Jenny (Edith Teichmann), Macheath (Hans Korte), Mr Peachum (Franz Kutschera), Mrs Peachum (Anita Mey), Polly Peachum (Karin Huebner), Tiger Brown (Albert Hoermann), Street Singer (Dieter Brammer).

By cutting the dialogue down to brief spoken links between numbers and omitting instrumental interludes which merely repeat songs already heard, Decca's all-star production is fitted on to a single, generously filled CD. The aim has been to return to the work, a modern *Beggar's opera*, as conceived before Brecht exaggerated its propagandist political overtones. As recorded, with John Mauceri drawing incisive playing from the RIAS Sinfonietta and with bright, full, close-up sound, its saltiness and bite are enhanced, together with its musical freshness.

The opening is not promising, with the Ballad- singer's singing voice – as opposed to his tangy spoken narration – sounding very old and tremulous. There are obvious discrepancies too between the opera-singers, René Kollo and Helga Dernesch, and those in the cabaret tradition, notably the vibrant and provocative Ute Lemper (Polly Peachum) and the gloriously dark-voiced and characterful Milva (Jenny). That entails downward modulation in various numbers, as it did with Lotte Lenya, but the changes from the original are far less extreme.

Kollo is good – but even more compelling is Dernesch, whose *Ballad of sexual obsession* in Act II is the high-spot of the whole entertainment. A pity the third verse had to be omitted for reasons of space, though it was also cut before the first (1928) stage performance.

The co-ordination of music and presentation makes for a vividly enjoyable experience, even if committed Weill enthusiasts will inevitably disagree with some of the controversial textual and interpretative decisions.

The CBS alternative offers a vividly authentic recording of *The Threepenny Opera*, Weill's most famous score, darkly incisive and atmospheric, with Lotte Lenya giving an incomparable performance as Jenny. All the wrong associations, built up round the music from indifferent performances. melt away in the face of a reading as sharp and intense as this. Bright, immediate, real stereo recording, made the more vivid on CD.

On two mid-priced discs the Philips version of *The Threepenny Opera* is welcome but is rather less of a bargain than the full-priced Decca single disc. The 1966 performance here has plenty of bite, even if some of the women's voices have little of the snarling character that one really wants in this 'black' music.

However, for anyone except the most fluent German-speaker, a full text is essential; instead, here one has only an essay on how the Weill work relates to *The Beggar's Opera*, plus a very compressed synopsis of the story. The numbers are all cued separately, with the titles translated; but one sometimes needs to do a detective job to discover which characters are singing what. Without the right information, a work which relies far more than most operas on its words (by

Brecht) can be only partially appreciated, even though the recording is lively, with the voices given a vivid presence.

Happy End (play by Brecht with songs); *Die sieben Todsünden (The Seven Deadly Sins).*
(M) *** Sony mono/stereo MPK 45886 [id.]. Lotte Lenya, male quartet & O, Ch. & O, Brückner-Rüggeberg.

Originally recorded in mono in the mid-1950s, the CBS performance of *The Seven Deadly Sins*, with the composer's widow as principal singer, underlines the status of this distinctive mixture of ballet and song-cycle as one of Weill's most concentrated inspirations. The rhythmic verve is irresistible and, though Lenya had to have the music transposed down, her understanding of the idiom is unique. The recording is forward and slightly harsh, though Lenya's voice is not hardened, and the effect is undoubtedly vivid. *Happy End* was made in Hamburg-Harburg in 1960. Lenya turned the songs into a kind of cycle (following a hint from her husband), again transposing where necessary, and her renderings in her individual brand of vocalizing are so compelling they make the scalp tingle. Many of these numbers are among the finest that Weill ever wrote. The excellent notes by David Drew are preserved with the CD, but the texts are printed out in German without any translations. The sound is again forwardly balanced, but the CD transfer still provides a backing ambience.

The Rise and Fall of Mahagonny (complete).
(M) **(*) Sony M2K 77341 (2) [M2K 37874]. NW German R. Ch. and O, Brückner-Rüggeberg.
Jenny (Lotte Lenya), Jim Mahoney (Heinz Sauerbaum), Trinity Moses (Horst Günter), Leokadja Begbick (Gisela Litz), Fatty (Peter Markwort), Jake Schmidt / Toby Higgins (Fritz Göllnitz), Alaska Wolf Joe (Sigmund Roth), Pennybank Bill (Georg Mund).

Mahagonny, with its curiously potent mixture of allegory, fantasy-drama, disillusion and cynical philosophy, is Weill's most celebrated piece, alongside his modern setting of *The Beggar's Opera.*

Mahagonny is situated in a desolate part of America and, as the story begins, three strangely assorted people get out of a battered old truck, Mrs Leokadja Begbick, Trinity Moses and Fatty the bookkeeper. All are on the run from the police. They reason among themselves: if they cannot proceed further, why not stop here and found a new city, where no one has to work and where there are prize-fights every third day.

Mrs Begbick decides all this in an extended soliloquy. The city is to be 'like a net which is put out to catch edible birds'. And so it came to pass that the City of Mahagonny was founded and 'the first sharks moved in'. Jenny now enters, a mulatto from Cuba, together with six other girls. They sit on their suitcases and introduce themselves in the famous *Alabama Song.*

The news of the founding of a city of pleasure soon reaches all the major metropolises. While Fatty and Moses sing the praises of Mahagonny, its inhabitants themselves hymn their own special brand of misery. Very soon all the malcontents of the continent move in. Outstanding among the newest arrivals are four lumberjacks who, anticipating the pleasures to come, paraphrase the *Bridesmaids' song* from Weber's *Der Freischütz.*

Jim Mahoney is the hero and Mrs Begbick makes him and the others welcome. Trinity Moses now offers a choice from the pictures of the available girls and Jake offers $30 for Jenny. She protests at her low market value, and Jim says perhaps he will take her instead. When the others leave, he and Jenny sadly list all the mundane things that make up their existence, but their final comment is that perhaps everything loses its excitement in the end.

People are beginning to leave town and Fatty says that the police are about to catch up with Mrs Begbick. Jake and two of his friends espouse the pleasures of unlimited freedom, but Jim is depressed at the lack of any thought or purpose in life; the local inn is called Nothing Barred.

A hurricane now takes place in which the police pursuing Mrs Begbick are killed; Jim asks, what sort of horror is a hurricane compared with mankind, and he sings 'As you make your bed, you must lie in it.'

The sins to be celebrated in the Nothing Barred are enumerated. First is gluttony; Jake sits down to dine, eats three whole calves, and dies. The second is love; in a back room a man and a girl are sitting, with Mrs Begbick as the procurer seen between them. *The Mandalay song* is heard. The third favoured occupation is fighting; Joe is knocked out and pronounced dead; the fourth sin is booze; and the ultimate capitalist crime is not to be able to pay for it.

A court scene ensues as Jim is put on trial. Widow Begbick sits as judge, Fatty is the defence counsel and Moses prosecutes. Jim is accused of seducing Jenny, singing cheerfully during the typhoon, corrupting the entire city, sending his friend to his death in a prize-fight, and not paying for the whiskey he drank. Each time the question is asked: 'Who is the injured party?' The verdict is death, for failing to pay for the whiskey.

After a tender farewell between Jenny and Jim, he consigns her to his best friend and walks to his execution. Jim has no regrets. Life is meant to be drained in gigantic draughts. Strapped to the electric chair, he asks if they do not know there is a God.

During the execution the others act out the coming of God to Mahagonny. Loudspeakers herald the high cost of living and this inevitably leads to the end of the city of nets. In the finale, dominated by *As you make your bed* and the *Alabama song*, a procession enters carrying banners and the opera ends with the thought that 'We can't help ourselves, or you, or anyone.'

Though Lotte Lenya, with her metallic rasping voice, was more a characterful *diseuse* than a singer, and this bitterly inspired score had to be adapted to suit her limited range, it remains a most memorable performance. This began a whole series of Weill recordings and, like the later ones, this lacks atmosphere, with voices (Lenya's in particular) close-balanced. Even now one can understand how this cynical piece caused public outrage when it was first performed in Leipzig in 1930.

Der Silbersee (Silverlake): complete.
*** Capriccio Dig. 60 011-2 (2) [id.]. Cologne Pro Musica Ch., Cologne RSO, Latham-König.
    Severin (Wolfgang Schmidt), Fennimore (Hildegard Heichele), Olim (Hans Korte), Frau von Luber (Eva Tamassy), Baron Laur (Udo Holdorf), Lottery Agent (Frederic Mayer).

Till now *Der Silbersee*, containing some of Weill's most inspired theatre music and many memorable tunes, has been known on record through the 'recomposed' version in English which was prepared for the New York City Opera in 1980, incorporating material from other Weill sources. This restoration of the original, written just before Weill left Nazi Germany, aims to cope with the basic problem presented by having his music as adjunct, not to a regular music-theatre piece, but to a full-length play by Georg Kaiser. Between Weill's numbers a smattering of the original dialogue is here included to provide a dramatic thread, and the speed of delivery adds to the effectiveness.

Led by Hildegard Heichele, bright and full-toned as the central character, Fennimore, the cast is an outstanding one, with each voice satisfyingly clean-focused, while the 1989 recording is rather better- balanced and kinder to the instrumental accompaniment than some from this source, with the voices exceptionally vivid. Particularly telling is the finale with its haunting slow waltz bearing a timely 'green' message. The Overture and Act I are complete on the first disc, Acts II and III on the second. Libretto, notes and background material are first rate, as in the rest of Capriccio's Weill series.

Street scene: complete.
*** TER Dig. CDTER2 1185 (2) [id.]. ENO Ch. and O, Carl Davis.
    Anna (Kristine Ciesinski), Frank (Richard Van Allan), Rose (Janis Kelly), Sam (Bonaventura Bottone), 1st Nursemaid (Fiametta Doria), 2nd Nursemaid (Judith Douglas), Jenny (Charles Daniels).
** Decca Dig. 433 371-2 (2) [id.]. Scottish Op. Ch. & O, Mauceri.
    Anna (Josephine Barstow), Frank (Samuel Ramey), Rose (Angelina Réaux), Sam (Jerry Hadley), 1st Nursemaid (Arleen Augér), 2nd Nursemaid (Della Jones), Jenny (Barbara Bonney).

Street scene was Kurt Weill's attempt, late in his Broadway career, to write an American opera as distinct from a musical. It has few if any of the easy, catchy tunes of most musicals or earlier Weill and, though it presents the events over 24 hours in a Manhattan tenement house with brilliant control of timing and tension, the piece falls far short of *Porgy and Bess* as an American opera.

The TER set was made with the cast of the ENO production at the Coliseum, and the idiomatic feeling and sense of flow consistently reflect that. Some of the solo singing in the large cast is flawed, but never seriously, and the principals are all very well cast – Kristine Ciesinski as the much-put-upon Anna Maurrant, Richard van Allan as her sorehead husband, Janis Kelly sweet and tender as the vulnerable daughter, and Bonaventura Bottone as the diffident young Jewish neighbour who loves her.

Those are only a few of the sharply drawn characters, and the performance on the discs, with dialogue briskly paced, reflects the speed of the original ENO production. Warm, slightly distanced sound.

Though the starry Decca version, issued simultaneously with the TER, has a cast with many more international names and the recording has a firmness and sharpness of focus beyond the TER, it cannot match its rival in flow and idiomatic feeling for Weill's score. Too often the performance sounds too literal, failing to flow, with speeds occasionally dragging. Samuel Ramey is too noble-voiced to sound fully convincing as the crusty Frank Maurrant, and others too are less characterful than their rivals, though Josephine Barstow brings telling weight to the role of the mother, Anna.

Der Zar lässt sich photographieren (complete).
**(*) Capriccio Dig. 10 147 [id.]. Cologne R. O, Latham-König.
   Tsar (Barry McDaniel), Angèle (Carla Pohl), False Angèle (Marita Napier).

This curious one-Act *opera buffa*, first heard in 1928, is Weill's first comic opera, but his last theatre-piece that is through-composed. With the playwright Georg Kaiser, his collaborator on several previous pieces, he produced a wry little parable about assassins planning to kill the Tsar when he has his photograph taken. Angèle, the photographer, is replaced by the false Angèle, but the Tsar proves to be a young man who simply wants friendship, and the would-be assassin, instead of killing him, plays a tango on the gramophone, before •he Tsar's official duties summon him again. Jan Latham-König in this 1984 recording directs a strong performance, though the dryly recorded orchestra is consigned to the background. The voices fare better, though Barry McDaniel is not ideally steady as the Tsar.

COLLECTIONS

American and Berlin theatre songs: *Aufstieg und Fall der Stadt Mahagonny: Havanna song; Alabama song; Wie man sich bettet. Die Dreigroschenoper: Die Moritat von Mackie Messer; Der Song vom nein und ja* (Barbara-song); *Die Seeräuber-Jenny. The Firebrand of Florence: Sing me not a ballad. Happy End: Bilbao song; Surabaya-Johnny. Knickerbocker Holiday: September song; It never was you. Lady in the Dark: Saga of Jenny. Lost in the Stars: Stay well; Trouble time; Lost in the stars. Love Life: Green-up time. One Touch of Venus: Foolish heart; Speak low. Street Scene: Lonely house; A boy like you.*
(M) (***) Sony mono MK 42658 [id.]. Lotte Lenya, Ch. & O, Maurice Levine or Roger Bean.

This collection combines American and German theatre songs, recorded by Lotte Lenya in the 1950s; her vocal range may be limited but her timbre is unique in repertoire she uniquely understood. The recording is bright, clean and clear.

Theatre songs: *Aufstieg und Fall der Stadt Mahagonny: Alabama song; Wie man sich bettet. Das Berliner Requiem: Zu Potsdam unter den Eichen. Die Dreigroschenoper: Die Moritat von Mackie Messer; Salomon song; Die Ballade von der sexuellen Hörigkeit. One Touch of Venus: I'm a stranger here myself. Der Silbersee: Ich bin eine arme Verwandte; Rom war eine Stadt; Lied des Lotterieagenten. Songs: Je ne t'aime pas; Nannas-Lied; Speak low; Westwind.*
*** Decca Dig. 425 204-2; *425 204-4* [id.]. Ute Lemper, Berlin R. Ens., John Mauceri.

Ute Lemper is nothing if not a charismatic singer, bringing a powerful combination of qualities to Weill: an ability to put over numbers with cabaret-style punch as toughly and characterfully as Lotte Lenya herself, as well as a technical security that rarely lets her down. The choice of items is both attractive and imaginative, bringing together popular favourites and relative rarities like the brilliant *Lied des Lotterieagenten* from *Der Silbersee*.

Lemper is not the least troubled with singing in English as well as in German, and the recording vividly captures the distinctive timbre of her voice in both media. Decca is right to be promoting this artist strongly. Many will find her singing more seductive than that of Lotte Lenya, and the accompaniments are a pleasure in themselves, most atmospherically recorded in both media.

Theatre songs, Vol. II: *Happy End: Bilbao-song; Surabaya Johnny; Was die Herren Matrosen sagen; Der Song von Mandelay; Das Lied vom Branntweinhändler; Youkali. Lady in the Dark: One life to live; Saga of Jenny; My ship. Marie Galante: Les filles de Bordeaux; Le train du Ciel; Le grand Lustucru; Le Roi d'Aquitaine; J'attends un navire.*
*** Decca Dig. 436 417-2 [id.]. Ute Lemper, London Voices, Berlin RIAS Sinf., John Mauceri; Jeff Cohen (piano).

In her second collection of Weill's theatre songs, Ute Lemper's darkly abrasive style is as effective as ever in famous numbers like the *Bilbao-Song, Surabaya-Johnny* and *Der Song von Mandelay. A saga of Jenny* (with the London Voices) is particularly enticing, while *My ship*, with its introductory inconsequential humming, shows the singer demonstrating her own brand of unsentimental nostalgia.

The surprise highlight of the disc is the collection of indelible excerpts from *Marie Galante*, sung in French with all the magnetism of a French *chanteuse*. The piece was written for Paris in 1934 and its bitter-sweet romanticism is hauntingly French: every one of these five numbers is a potential hit. *J'attends un navire* was adapted from a song in *Happy End* and became very popular in France during the Second World War, being associated with the Resistance, as the French people waited for the allied invasion.

Weinberger, Jaromir (1896–1967)

Schwanda the Bagpiper: complete.
Withdrawn: (M) *** Sony M2K 79344 (2) [M2K 36926]. Bav. R. Ch., Munich R. O, Wallberg.
	Schwanda (Hermann Prey), Dorotka (Lucia Popp), Babinsky (Siegfried Jerusalem), Queen (Gwendoline Killebrew), Magician (Alexander Malta), Devil (Siegmund Nimsgern).

The famous polka set the seal on the immediate international success of this colourful updating of the *Bartered Bride* formula. Weinberger wrote it when he was thirty, but he never wrote another work that had anything like the same success. He went to America, where in disillusion he committed suicide in 1967. None of that sadness comes out in the frothy mixture of *Schwanda*, a folk-tale involving a robber charmer who woos beautiful young Dorotka, wife of Schwanda. The supernatural is lightly invoked in a trip to hell (Schwanda the charmer there) with the devil introduced.

As the story begins, Babinsky, a robber, is hiding from the foresters at the house of Schwanda and his wife, Dorotka. Schwanda agrees to accompany him into the wide world, visit the court of an unhappy queen and make his fortune.

The queen is in the power of a wicked sorcerer, but when Schwanda arrives and plays the celebrated polka on his bagpipes her spirits rise and she falls in love with him. She proposes marriage and Schwanda, forgetting Dorotka, accepts and kisses her.

The sorcerer and Dorotka confront the queen, who is enraged and orders Schwanda's trial. While awaiting execution he asks for his bagpipes but they cannot be found anywhere. Babinsky turns the executioner's axe into a broom, returns the bagpipes and unlocks the gate. Dorotka asks if he ever kissed the queen. He replies that, if he has, he will go to hell – which is where the next Act takes place.

The devil orders Schwanda to play but he refuses, whereupon the devil plays them himself. He tricks Schwanda into signing away his soul, but Babinsky comes smartly to the rescue and regains it by beating the devil in a game of cards. Schwanda returns to Earth: Babinsky, who covets Dorotka for himself, tells him that she is now an old woman. When she eventually appears, the truth emerges and they are happily reunited.

Prey (as Schwanda), Popp (as his wife) and Jerusalem (as Babinsky, the charmer) make a first-rate team of principals, lending musical flair as well as vocal glamour. Ensemble work is first rate too, most important in this opera, with the polka taken rather slowly and bouncily. Now on two CDs instead of the original three LPs, the recording has enhanced presence and realism.

Willson, Meredith (1902–84)

The Music Man.
⊛ (M) *** EMI ZDM7 64663-2 [id.]. Original Broadway cast. Ch. & O, Herbert Green.
	Harold Hill (Robert Preston), Marian Paroo (Barbara Cook), Mrs Paroo (Pert Kelton), Winthrop Paroo (Eddie Hodges), Marcellus Washburn (Iggie Wolfington), The Buffalo Bills: Ewart Dunlop (Al Shea), Oliver Hix (Wayne Ward), Jacey Squires (Vern Reedbills), Olin Britt (Bill Spangenberg).

Meredith Willson's *The Music Man* (which arrived in 1957) was perhaps the last of the series of guileless, folksy musicals, genuine small-town Americana, spawned by Rodgers and Hammerstein's *Oklahoma!*. Brooks Atkinson of *The New York Times* described it as 'American as apple pie and a Fourth of July peroration'.

The tale of the visiting salesman whose scam is to purvey musical instruments and uniforms for a boys' band plus a nebulous 'think' system of tuition – but who knows not a note of music himself – is based on its composer/writer's memories of boyhood life in Mason City, Iowa.

It makes a charming and exhilarating concoction and has a splendid score, with a style derived not only from the Broadway show tradition but also from the barber's shop, barn dance and cake-walk rhythms (the exuberant *Shipoopi*), with even a whiff of revivalist church chorales. The vigorous recitative of *Ya got trouble* is brilliantly original.

But it is the tunes that count in a musical, and what sweeping, rumbustious, pictorial splendour there is in *Seventy-six trombones*, out-Sousa-ing Sousa. How good too are the simpler *Wells Fargo wagon*, the sentimental *Good-night my someone*, *My white knight* and the delightful *Till there was you* (the only Broadway show tune adopted by the Beatles).

The lead was offered to Ray Bolger, Phil Harris, Danny Kaye and Gene Kelly, among others (the film version to Cary Grant!) but Robert Preston finally took it . . . and made it is his own. It turned him into a star. His crisp delivery of Harold Hill's glib sales pitch is mesmerizing, as indeed is the bravura choral-talk of the opening number, *Rock Island*, without any music at all, built round the rhythms of the railway track. Indeed Robert Preston's style of rhythmic patter-singing is worthy to be compared with that of the great Gilbertians, including Martyn Green and John Reed.

Another great plus point of the original Broadway cast is the young Barbara Cook as Marian the librarian, who succumbs to Harold's charms but who soon discovers that he is a fraud. At the time she was fresh from Bernstein's abortive first production of *Candide* and she sings her lyrical numbers with great charm and naturalness, so that one can really believe the dénouement of the story when the unscrupulous con-man finally loses his heart to her and has the courage to stay and present his 'band' to the townsfolk.

As usual with the finest original-cast recordings, there is a special and refreshing communicated awareness among the participants that they have helped to bring to life something new and special. No complaints about the barber's shop quartet, the Buffalo Bills, who are especially good in the luscious combination of *Lida Rose* and *Will I ever tell you*.

Herbert Green directs the orchestra with great spirit and spontaneity, but in the end this is Robert Preston's triumph: just sample his delivery of the catchy *Marian the librarian* to be won over. The early Capitol stereo is amazingly good and the documentation leaves nothing to be desired, judged by the usual standards of CD presentation.

The Unsinkable Molly Brown.
(m) **(*) EMI ZDM7 64761-2 [id.]. Original Broadway cast. Ch. & O, Herbert Greene.
  Molly Tobin Brown (Tammy Grimes), J. J. 'Leadville Johnny' Brown (Harve Presnel), Prince Delong (Mitchell Gregg).

The Unsinkable Molly Brown offers the same musical formula as *The Music Man*, only with the principal character a female, and a score whose inspiration is noticeably diluted compared with the piece that made the composer's reputation. The show's heroine was a Colorado frontier woman who began her life as a poor Missouri white and ended up marrying a miner who struck it rich. Unsuccessful as a society lady in Denver, she then travelled abroad as a loner and survived the *Titanic* on one of the lifeboats.

For all the show's musical disappointments, Tammy Grimes *is* Molly Brown, and her patter-dialogue (as in *I ain't down yet*) is comparable with the projection of her predecessor in *The Music Man*, Robert Preston. As before, the show draws on America's folksy musical tradition (*Belly up to the bar* suitably boisterous), while *I'll never say no*, her husband's courting song, unconsciously quotes a tune from the Brahms *Horn trio*.

The choral writing is always attractive, and *The Denver Police* even brings in an Irish jig. The snag is that when the plot takes Molly to Europe, the music goes with her. The catchy *Keep-a-hoppin'* arrives when Johnny returns home without her.

Harve Presnel is a sympathetic (if rather cultured) Johnny, and the original cast zestfully make the very most of their opportunities. The recording was adequately funded, so that Don Walker's opulent orchestrations sound really good. Plenty of information is provided about the show, and the music, if never memorable, is always pleasing.

Wolf-Ferrari, Ermanno (1876–1948)

Il segreto di Susanna (complete).
Withdrawn: (m) *** Sony MK 36733 [id.]. Renata Scotto, Renato Bruson, Philh. O, Pritchard.

Susanna's secret is that she smokes (against Edwardian convention in a woman), and she sings a rare aria describing the bliss of the tobacco addict: 'Oh what joy to follow with half-closed eyes the fine cloud that rises in blue spirals, more delicately than a veil.' But her husband's detection of the unmistakable fumes persuades him that he has a rival for his wife's favours. Of course all is resolved at the end in a moonlit scene, as the reconciled partners go up in smoke together.

Considering the fragile plot, the music itself is surprisingly dramatic, though pleasingly lyrical too, even if nothing else is quite as memorable as the scintillating overture. Scotto and Bruson make the very most of their opportunities and Sir John Pritchard and the Philharmonia keep everything sparkling. The recording, from 1981, is first rate and has fine liveliness and presence in its CD format. There are, however, only four access cues for the whole opera.

Wright, Robert (born 1914) and Forrest, George (born 1915)

(i) *Kismet* (Borodin, orch. Arthur Kay). (ii) *Timbuktu!:* excerpts.
*** That's Entertainment Dig. CDTER2 1170 (2) [id.]. (ii) Rosemary Ashe, Valerie Masterson, Bruce Hubbard, Simon Green, Edmund Barham, Bonaventura Bottone; Ambrosian Ch., Philh. O, John Owen Edwards.
(i) Imam / Bangleman / Chief of Police (Bonaventura Bottone), Hajj (Donald Maxwell), Marsinah (Valerie Masterson), Lalume (Judy Kaye), Caliph (David Rendall), Wazir (Richard Van Allan), Ayah (Rosemary Ashe).

When Robert Wright and George Forrest were looking for a classical composer (out of copyright) to provide a score for a pseudo-Arabian Nights entertainment, they first thought of Rimsky-Korsakov. The choice of Borodin was made by a Russian musician, Vladimir Dukelsky, a colleague of Edwin Lester who commissioned a show that was to be one of the most successful of all musicals not written by Rodgers, Loewe or Lloyd Webber!

The tale centres on Hajj's protective love for his daughter, Marsinah, who in turn loves the Caliph, with the villain, Wazir (here well taken by Richard van Allan), not to be taken too seriously. After the ebullient *Overture*, the piece opens with *Sands of time*, set to the glorious music of Borodin's *In the Steppes of Central Asia*, and the ear is surprised at what an effective vocal line is provided by its sinuous oriental melody, especially when sung so richly by Bonaventura Bottone as the Imam.

Indeed, although the spoken dialogue is not an asset, the vocal arrangements throughout have great vitality, and the clever interpolation of theme after theme from unexpected Borodin sources constantly tickles the ear.

The most famous numbers, *And this is my beloved*, *Baubles, bangles and beads* and, of course, *Stranger in paradise* (with David Rendall and Valerie Masterson admirably cast as the Caliph and Marsinah) have a fine romantic sweep; while purists should stand back, there is little sense of Borodin being vulgarized.

Donald Maxwell makes an authoritative and resonant Hajj (the role originally made famous by Alfred Drake), the Ambrosian Chorus sing with obvious relish, and the show consistently sparkles in the hands of John Owen Edwards.

The Abbey Road recording is both spacious and brilliant and has all the necessary opulence. As an appendix, we are offered an additional number, *Bored*, added for the 1956 MGM film and sung here by Judy Kaye, plus a brief selection from *Timbuktu!*, a companion piece. It was originally a vehicle for Eartha Kitt, with a comparably exotic plot and an original score not unlike a pastiche of *Kismet*, if less memorable.

Song of Norway (Grieg, orch. & arr. Arthur Kay).
** That's Entertainment Dig. CDTER2 1173 (2) [id.]. Yin Kin Sieow (piano), Amb. Ch., Philh. O, John Owen Edwards.
Rikaard Nordraak (David Rendall), Nina Hagerup (Valerie Masterson), Edvard Grieg (Donald Maxwell), Louisa Giovanni (Diana Montague), Mother Grieg (Elizabeth Bainbridge), Father Grieg (Richard Van Allan).

This coach-party hokum about Grieg's relationship with fellow Norwegian composer, Rikaard Nordraak, is managed very professionally but, unlike *Kismet* where the music is not robbed of its essential vitality, here Grieg loses his innocent charm. There are exceptions. *Midsummer's eve* makes an agreeably luscious waltz, *I love you* (with new words) comes off well enough, although Valerie Masterson fails to make it memorable, and *Rikaard's farewell* is touching. *Strange music* (ingeniously but very loosely based on *Wedding day in Troldhaugen*) understandably became a pop hit.

But when we hear the orchestra play the introduction to Act II and later three numbers from the incidental music to *Peer Gynt*, it is only too obvious that Grieg is best left alone. No complaints about the singing and playing, although the dialogue would have been better omitted. The Ambrosians sing very professionally and John Owen Edwards directs with enthusiam. But those who love Grieg's music unadulterated should stay clear.

Zandonai, Riccardo (1883–1944)

Francesca da Rimini: excerpts from Acts II, III & IV.
(M) **(*) Decca 433 033-2 (2) [id.]. Magda Olivero, Mario Del Monaco, Monte Carlo Op. O, Rescigno - GIORDANO: *Fedora*. **(*)

Magda Olivero is a fine artist who has not been represented nearly enough on record, and this rare Zandonai selection, like the coupled set of Giordano's *Fedora*, does her some belated justice. It would have been preferable to have a complete version of this ambitious opera – the publisher Tito Ricordi tended to think more highly of it than of the contemporary operas of his other, more famous, client, Puccini – but these selections give a fair flavour.

The love story it dramatizes also inspired Tchaikovsky's symphonic poem, only the nightmare whirlwinds of Dante's Inferno are not included in Zandonai's opera, which centres on the passionate love between Francesca and Paolo. He is the youngest brother of Giovanni, the deformed hunchback she is forced to marry.

Decca opted to have three substantial scenes recorded rather than snippets, and in the first scene the young lovers meet at the top of a tower soon after the forced marriage. Then in Act II they read together the story of King Arthur's Guinevere and her lover, Lancelot, and find an affinity with the legendary pair.

Giovanni's other brother, Malatestino, also desires Francesca but she scornfully rejects his advances, and in jealousy he tells Giovanni of the relationship between Francesca and Paolo. Subsequently Giovanni surprises the lovers and in the altercation which follows Francesca receives the fatal sword-thrust intended for her lover. Giovanni then kills Paolo too, and the lovers die in the eternal embrace which condemned them in the eyes of the church.

Although Mario del Monaco as Paolo is predictably coarse in style, his tone is rich and strong and he does not detract from the achievement, unfailingly perceptive and musicianly, of Olivero as Francesca herself. Excellent, vintage 1969, Decca sound.

Francesca da Rimini: Act III: *No, Smaragdi, no!... Inghirlandata di violette*.
(M) **(*) Decca 436 301-2 [id.]. Francesca (Renata Tebaldi), Paolo (Franco Corelli), Lehman Ch., SRO, Anton Guadagno - *Recital of Duets and arias*. **

It is good to have this 19-minute scene from Act III of Zandonai's opera to supplement the more substantial set of excerpts from Magda Olivero and Mario del Monaco (see above). Tebaldi's performance, though dating from 1972 at the very end of her recording career, makes one wish Decca had encouraged her to record the opera complete. Corelli is not the most subtle partner but obviously responds to the beauty of her singing at the music's emotional climax. The recording is only fair by Decca standards, but the quality of Tebaldi's contribution more than compensates.

Zemlinsky, Alexander von (1871–1942)

Eine florentinische Tragödie (opera; complete).
Withdrawn: *** Schwann Dig. CD 11625 [id.]. Doris Soffel, Kenneth Riegel, Guillermo Sarabia, Berlin RSO, Albrecht.

A Florentine Tragedy is the more pretentious and less effective of the two Wilde-based one-Act pieces which have been turned into a highly successful Zemlinsky double-bill. Dramatically it is pure hokum. It presents a simple love-triangle: a Florentine merchant returns home to find his sluttish wife with the local prince. Zemlinsky in 1917 may have been seeking to repeat the shock tactics of Richard Strauss in *Salome* (another Wilde story) a decade earlier; but the musical syrup which flows over all the characters makes them far more repulsive, with motives only dimly defined. The score itself is most accomplished; it is here compellingly performed, more effective on disc than it is in the opera house. First-rate sound.

Der Gerburtstag der Infantin (opera; complete).
*** Schwann Dig. 314013 [id]. Berlin RSO, Albrecht.
   Donna Clara (Inge Nielsen), Dwarf (Kenneth Riegel), Ghita (Béatrice Haldas), Major-domo
(Dieter Weller).

   The Birthday of the Infanta, like its companion one-Acter, was inspired by a story of Oscar
Wilde, *The Dwarf*. Analysed coldly, it is the repellent story of a hideous dwarf caught in the
forest and given to the infanta as a birthday present. Even after recognizing his own
hideousness, he declares his love to the princess and is casually rejected. He dies of a broken
heart, with the infanta untroubled – 'Oh dear, my present already broken.'
   Zemlinsky, dwarfish himself, gave his heart to the piece, reproducing his own rejection at the
hands of Alma Mahler. In this performance, based on a much-praised stage production, Kenneth
Riegel gives a heart-rendingly passionate performance as the dwarf declaring his love. His
genuine passion is intensified by being set against lightweight, courtly music to represent the
infanta and her attendants. With the conductor and others in the cast also experienced in the
stage production, the result is a deeply involving performance, beautifully recorded.

Vocal Recitals and Choral Collections

Licia Albanese (soprano)

Arias from: PUCCINI: *Madama Butterfly; La Bohème; Manon Lescaut; Tosca; Turandot; La Rondine; Suor Angelica.* VERDI: *La Traviata.* MOZART: *Le nozze di Figaro.* CILEA: *Adriana Lecouvreur.* CHARPENTIER: *Louise.* TCHAIKOVSKY: *Eugene Onegin.*
(M) (***) BMG/RCA mono GD 60384 [60394-2-RG].

With the distinction of having sung the role of Mimì in two historic recordings, opposite Gigli in 1938 and with Toscanini conducting in New York in 1946, Licia Albanese was a favourite singer at the Met. in the immediate post-war period. As the range of these recordings indicates, she was not limited to the Puccini repertory, though that was always at the centre, above all *Butterfly*. Her bright, clear voice might have seemed ideal for recording, but sadly a trick of vibrato often marred the sweetness and purity and made it sound older than it was, particularly under pressure.

These recordings, mostly made between 1945 and 1950, present her at her peak, and consistently the charm and power of characterization make each item compelling. Fascinatingly, the last and longest of the items, of Tatiana's letter scene from Tchaikovsky's *Eugene Onegin*, was from a role she never sang on stage. Here Stokowski conducting his own orchestra adds to the natural warmth and expressiveness. Good bright transfers.

Ambrosian Chorus, Soloists, L. Sinf., John McGlinn

'Broadway showstoppers' (with (i) Kim Criswell; (ii) Brent Barrett; (iii) Rebecca Luker; (iv) George Dvorsky; (v) Davis Gaines; (vi) Judy Kaye; (vii) Cris Groenendaal; (viii) Jeanne Lehman; (ix) Linda Richardson, Tracey Miller; (x) Kevin Colson): GERSHWIN: *Demi-Tasse Revue:* (i) *Swanee;* (ii) *Come to the moon.* YOUMANS: *No, no, Nanette:* (iii; iv) *Tea for two.* SCHWARTZ: *The Band Wagon:* (v) *Dancing in the dark. Between the Devil:* (i; iv; vi) *Triplets.* KERN: *Sunny:* (ii; iii) *Who? Sweet Adeline:* (iii; vi) *Here am I;* (vi) *Why was I born?;* (ii; iv; vi; vii) *Some girl on your mind;* (v; vi) *Don't ever leave me. Oh, Lady! Lady!!:* (viii) *Bill. Very warm for May:* (iii; iv; vii; viii) *All the things you are.* BERNSTEIN: *1600 Pennsylvania Avenue:* (v; ix) *The President Jefferson luncheon party march;* (v; vi; x) *Duet for one.* WEILL: *Knickerbocker Holiday:* (x) *September song.*
*** EMI Dig. CDC7 54586-2 [id.].

A marvellous collection of Broadway numbers, all with show-stopping potential, many of which are virtually unknown today. Sometimes, as with the P. G. Wodehouse / Jerome Kern *Bill*, the song was withdrawn from the original show and resurfaced later. *Bill* eventually became famous in *Show Boat*, with slightly revised lyrics by Oscar Hammerstein II, who initially received the credit for its romantic imagery. But later he made handsome amends, sending Wodehouse $5,000 in back-royalties and ensuring in the theatre programme for the 1946 revival that the public was told the name of the original author. Here it is freshly sung, not by the husky-voiced Magnolia but by a charming soubrette soprano, Jeanne Lehman, and we are given the original words.

Tea for two, one of the most endearing of all musical-comedy duets, is most winningly done by Rebecca Luker and George Dvorsky (who also gives us a vibrant *Dancing in the dark*), and Kevin Colson is wonderfully suave in Kurt Weill's *September song*. The two ballads from Kern's *Sweet Adeline* (*Why was I born?* and the duet, *Here am I*) are delightfully shared by Judy Kaye and Rebecca Luker, and the ensemble, *Some girl on your mind*, has an inescapably dated but very infectious rhythmic flavour: it was written at a time when 'moon' and 'spoon' made a very convenient rhyme.

But it is the sparkle of the lively numbers that stays in the memory, including the unexpectedly catchy *Come to the moon* which, like Gershwin's better-known *Swanee*, comes from a forgotten review of 1919. Most vibrant of all are the excerpts from *1600 Pennsylvania Avenue* ('A musical about the problems of housekeeping'), featuring the rare combination of Alan Jay Lerner and Leonard Bernstein.

The exuberant and wittily orchestrated *Sunday luncheon party* (choral) *march* is readily matched by the intoxicating bravura of *Duet for one*, with Judy Kaye playing both the outgoing and ingoing Presidents' ladies in alternation. The concert ends with Jerome Kern's *All the things you are*, presented as a ravishing ensemble, with chorus. The recording is splendid: it has presence and plenty of theatrical atmosphere, and the documentation (including all the lyrics) could hardly be bettered.

Victoria De los Angeles (soprano)

Opera arias from: VERDI: *Ernani; Otello.* PUCCINI: *La Bohème.* BOITO: *Mefistofele.* ROSSINI: *La Cenerentola.* MASCAGNI: *Cavalleria Rusticana.* CATALANI: *La Wally.* MOZART: *Le nozze di Figaro.* WAGNER: *Tannhäuser; Lohengrin.* MASSENET: *Manon.* GOUNOD: *Faust.*
(M) (***) EMI mono CDH7 63495-2 [id.].

Most of the items here are taken from an early LP recital by De los Angeles that has rarely been matched in its glowing beauty and range of expression. The *Willow song* and *Ave Maria* from *Otello* have never been sung with more aching intensity than here, and the same goes for the Mascagni and Catalani arias. The final cabaletta from *Cenerentola* sparkles deliciously with De los Angeles, as so often, conveying the purest of smiles in the voice. The CD reissue is augmented by the valuable Mozart, Massenet, Gounod and Wagner items, all recorded in the days of 78s.

Francisco Araiza (tenor)

'The romantic tenor' (with Munich R. O, Weikert): LEHÁR: *Das Land des Lächelns: Dein ist mein ganzes Herz. Giuditta: Freunde, das Leben ist lebenswert. Der Zarewitsch Wolgalied.* ROSSINI: *La danza.* BERNSTEIN: *West Side Story: Maria.* GREVER: *Jurame.* CHOPIN: *In mir klingt ein Lied.* PONCE: *Estrellita.* LEONCAVALLO: *Mattinata.* LENNON/MCCARTNEY: *Yesterday.* DI CAPUA: *O sole mio.* TAUBER: *Der Singende Traum: Du bist die Welt für mich.* LARA: *Granada.* MARTINI: *Plaisir d'amour.* DI CURTIS: *Non ti scordar di me.*
** BMG/RCA Dig. 09026 61163-2.

A perfectly acceptable recital, demonstrating a pleasant voice and a genuine sense of operatic style. But there is nothing here to set the world on fire, and this is a recital aimed specifically at Araiza's admirers.

Agnes Baltsa (soprano)

'Great voice': Arias and excerpts (with various other artists) from: MOZART: *Don Giovanni.* BIZET: *Carmen.* VERDI: *La forza del destino.* WAGNER: *Tannhäuser.* R. STRAUSS: *Der Rosenkavalier.*
(B) **(*) DG Dig. 431 101-2 [id.].

This was the first of eight recitals assembled by DG featuring their leading contracted vocal artists under the generic title 'Grosse Stimmen'. The content here is fairly generous (64 minutes), but the recital (like the rest of the series) is issued without documentation of any kind, except for a list of contents: titles, artists and recording dates. The excerpts here come from various complete sets, and Baltsa's vibrant personality is at its most compelling in three excerpts from *Carmen*, supported by Carreras, with Karajan at the helm.

She is a strong Donna Elvira in *Don Giovanni* (although the microphones do not always flatter her) and impressively brilliant as Preziosilla in the *Rataplan* number from *Forza del destino*, although charm is not her strong suit. She has plenty of character as Octavian in *Der Rosenkavalier*, blending well with Janet Perry's Sophie in the Silver Rose presentation scene, But in her seduction of Domingo's noble Tannhäuser her tone is rather unyielding. It is a fair portrait, nevertheless, if not exactly an endearing one, for her stage personality comes over as rather hard, although the programme is undoubtedly aptly chosen and this is fair value at bargain price.

Baritones and Basses

'Ten Top Baritones and Basses': ((i) Leo Nucci; (ii) Samuel Ramey; (iii) Martti Talvela; (iv) Fernando Corena; (v) Tito Gobbi; (v) Dietrich Fischer-Dieskau; (vii) Paata Burchuladze; (viii) Ettore Bastianini; (ix) Sherrill Milnes; (x) Nicolai Ghiaurov): Arias from: ROSSINI: (i) *Il barbiere di Siviglia.* MOZART: (ii) *Nozze di Figaro;* (iii) *Die Zauberflöte.* DONIZETTI: (iv) *L'elisir d'amore.* VERDI: (v) *Nabucco;* (vi) *La Traviata;* (vii) *Don Carlo;* (viii) *La forza del destino;* (ix) *Otello.* MUSSORGSKY: (x) *Boris Godunov.*
(M) *** Decca Dig./Analogue 436 464-2 [id.].

This is one of four highly stimulating Decca collections, each devoted to a different operatic vocal genre. If not all the performances here have the interpretative depth of Tito Gobbi's magnificent scena from *Nabucco (Son pur queste mie membra! . . . Dio di Giuda! . . . Cadran, cadranno i perfidi)*, or the gripping drama of Sherrill Milnes' *Credo* from *Otello*, there are plenty of vocal thrills, not least Paata Burchuladze's *Ella giammai m'amò* from *Don Carlo* and Nicolai Ghiaurov's powerful *Death of Boris* (with the Sofia Radio Chorus), which closes the concert. There is plenty of musical variety.

The programme opens with Leo Nucci's fizzing *Largo al factotum* from *Il Barbiere* and this is followed by Samuel Ramey's sparkling *Non più andrai* from Solti's complete set of *Figaro*, and here the conductor's drive is as striking as the vocalism. Martti Talvela's gloriously resonant *O Isis und Osiris* from *Die Zauberflöte* follows on to make a satisfying contrast. Vintage, characteristically vivid Decca recording throughout and a playing time of 73 minutes.

Mattia Battistini (baritone)

'Prima voce': Arias from: TCHAIKOVSKY: *Eugene Onegin.* VERDI: *Un ballo in maschera; Ernani; La Traviata; Macbeth; Don Carlos.* FLOTOW: *Marta.* DONIZETTI: *La Favorita; Don Sebastiano; Linda di Chamounix.* HÉROLD: *Zampa.* BERLIOZ: *Damnation de Faust.* MASSENET: *Werther.* THOMAS: *Hamlet.* NOUGUÈS: *Quo Vadis?.*
(M) (***) Nimbus mono NI 7831; *NC 7831* [id.].

As with other Nimbus issues, the transfers are remarkably kind to the voice and are probably nearer to how Battistini sounded 'live'. It is a remarkable voice, with a fine, clear upper range. The programme is well chosen and the recordings date from between 1902 and 1922. While obviously the Verdi excerpts are essential to show the calibre of any baritone, it is good to have the rare *Pourquoi tremblez-vous?* from *Zampa*.

Teresa Berganza (mezzo-soprano)

Operatic arias (with ROHCG O or LSO, Gibson) from: GLUCK: *Orfeo ed Euridice; Alceste; Elena e Paride.* PERGOLESI: *La serva padrona.* CHERUBINI: *Medea.* PAISIELLO: *Nina pazza per amore.* ROSSINI: *Il Barbiere di Siviglia; L'Italiana in Algeri; Semiramide; La Cenerentola; Stabat Mater.*
(M) *** Decca 421 327-2 [id.].

This wide selection from Berganza's repertory comes mainly from recordings of the 1960s, when the voice was at its most beautiful, although the *Cenerentola* excerpt is from 1959. The musical intensity combines formidably with an amazing technique (shown throughout the Rossini excerpts), and only occasionally in the classical arias does one sense a lack of warmth. First-rate recording, vividly transferred.

'Great voice': Excerpts from: BIZET: *Carmen.* ROSSINI: *Il barbiere di Siviglia; La Cenerentola; Stabat Mater.* MOZART: *La clemenza di Tito.* FALLA: *El amor brujo.*
(B) **(*) DG 431 102-2 [id.].

Berganza's fresh-voiced mezzo, agile and secure and not without charm, is attractively bright-eyed in Rossini and crisply stylish in Mozart, but her Carmen is a little lacking in red-blooded projection. The darker side of the voice and its ready Spanish inflexion come over splendidly in the four excerpts from Falla's *El amor brujo*, although the flamenco style has a cultured veneer: it is strong without being earthily uninhibited. The voice records well and this is overall an enjoyable 63 minutes. But there is no documentation, except for a list of titles and recording dates.

Carlo Bergonzi (tenor)

Operatic arias from: VERDI: *Aida; Luisa Miller; La forza del destino; Il Trovatore; Un ballo in maschera; Don Carlo.* MEYERBEER: *L'Africaine.* GIORDANO: *Andrea Chénier.* CILEA: *Adriana Lecouvreur.* PUCCINI: *Tosca; Manon Lescaut; La Bohème.*
(M) *** Decca 421 318-2 [id.].

This recital of his early stereo recordings shows Bergonzi on peak form. He does not attempt the rare pianissimo at the end of *Celeste Aida*; but here among Italian tenors is a thinking musical artist who never resorts to vulgarity. The recording (of whatever vintage) has transferred well and retains the bloom on the voice. This is essentially a programme of favourites, but everything sounds fresh.

Carlo Bergonzi; Giuseppe Di Stefano; Bruno Previdi (tenors)

'Nessun dorma (Famous tenor arias)' from VERDI: *Aida; Luisa Miller; Un ballo in maschera; La forza del destino.* MEYERBEER: *L'Africaine.* MASSENET: *Werther.* BIZET: *Carmen.* GOUNOD: *Faust.* PUCCINI: *Tosca; La Fanciulla del West; Turandot.* GIORDANO: *Andrea Chénier; Fedora.* MASCAGNI: *Cavalleria Rusticana.*
(B) **(*) Decca 433 623-2; *433 623-4.*

Bergonzi sings stylishly, ardently and intelligently in arias from Verdi and Meyerbeer. Giuseppe di Stefano shows his feeling for the French repertoire and ends with exciting accounts of the two famous tenor arias from *Tosca*. Then Bruno Previdi takes over, a less charismatic artist but with an appealing voice and a finely spun line in excerpts like *Amor ti vieta* from *Fedora*. His *Nessun dorma* is potent too, though less individual than with Pavarotti. He is very well recorded, while the Bergonzi and Di Stefano items are much earlier (the late 1950s) and the orchestral sound is less ample. Fair value (64 minutes).

Berlin German Opera Chorus and Orchestra, Sinopoli

Opera choruses: MOZART: *Die Zauberflöte: O Isis und Osiris.* BEETHOVEN: *Fidelio: O welche Lust.* WEBER: *Der Freischütz: Huntsmen's chorus; Viktoria! Viktoria!* WAGNER: *Tannhäuser: Grand march.* VERDI: *Nabucco: Va, pensiero. I Lombardi: O Signore, dal tetto natio. Macbeth: Patria oppressa. Il Trovatore: Anvil chorus. Aida: Gloria all'Egitto . . . Vieni, o guerriero vindice.*
*** DG Dig. 415 283-2 [id.].

A splendid collection of choruses, full of character, the atmosphere of each opera distinctive. The pianissimo at the beginning of the famous *Fidelio Prisoners' chorus* has striking intensity, while the exuberant *Hunting chorus* from *Freischütz* is irresistible in its buoyancy. On the other hand, Sinopoli's broadening of the sustained tune in the short *Aida* excerpt may for some seem too deliberate. Needless to say, the orchestral playing is first class; the balance, with the orchestra placed vividly forward and the chorus set back within a warmly resonant acoustic, is most convincing, although words are not always sharply clear. A well-balanced and rewarding compilation in all other respects, extremely vivid in its compact disc format.

Jussi Bjoerling (tenor)

Opera arias from: DONIZETTI: *L'Elisir d'amore.* VERDI: *Il Trovatore; Un Ballo in maschera; Aida.* LEONCAVALLO: *I Pagliacci.* PUCCINI: *La Bohème; Tosca; La Fanciulla del West; Turandot.* GIORDANO: *Fedora.* CILEA: *L'Arlesiana.* MEYERBEER: *L'Africana.* GOUNOD: *Faust.* MASSENET: *Manon.* FLOTOW: *Martha.* ROSSINI: *Stabat Mater.*
(M) (***) EMI mono CDH7 61053-2.

The EMI collection on the Références label brings excellent transfers of material recorded between 1936 and 1947 on the tenor's home-ground in Stockholm. The voice was then at its very peak, well caught in those final years of 78 r.p.m. discs, with artistry totally assured over this wide range of repertory.

Operatic recital: PONCHIELLI: *La Gioconda: Cielo e mar.* PUCCINI: *La Fanciulla del West: Ch'ella mi creda. Manon Lescaut: Tra voi belle.* GIORDANO: *Fedora: Amor ti vieta.* CILEA:

L'Arlesiana: Lamento di Federico. VERDI: *Un ballo in maschera: Di' tu se fedele. Requiem: Ingemisco.* MASCAGNI: *Cavalleria Rusticana: Tu qui, Santuzza?* (with Renata Tebaldi); *Intanto, amici . . . Brindisi; Mamma, quel vino.* LEHÁR: *Das Land des Lächelns: Dein ist mein ganzes Herz.*
(M) *** Decca 421 316-2; *421 316-4.*

John Culshaw's autobiography revealed what an unhappy man Jussi Bjoerling was at the very end of his career, when all these recordings were made by Decca engineers for RCA. You would hardly guess that there were problems from the flow of headily beautiful, finely focused tenor tone. These may not be the most characterful renderings of each aria, but they are all among the most compellingly musical. The recordings are excellent for their period (1959 – 60). The Lehár was the last solo recording he made before he died in 1960. The transfers to CD are admirably lively and present.

Arias and excerpts from: VERDI: *Rigoletto* (with Hjördis Schymberg); *Requiem.* BIZET: *Les pêcheurs de perles; Carmen.* OFFENBACH: *La belle Hélène.* GOUNOD: *Roméo et Juliette.* MASSENET: *Manon.* PONCHIELLI: *La Gioconda.* MASCAGNI: *Cavalleria rusticana.* BORODIN: *Prince Igor.* PUCCINI: *Manon Lescaut; La Bohème* (with Anna-Lisa Bjoerling). GIORDANO: *Andrea Chénier.* Songs: RACHMANINOV: *In the silence of the night; Lilacs.* LEONCAVALLO: *Mattinata.* TOSTI: *Ideale.* BEETHOVEN: *Adelaïde.* R. STRAUSS: *Morgen.*
(M) (**(*)) EMI mono CDH7 64707-2 [id.].

The second Références collection – particularly generous, with a 77-minute programme – is if anything even more attractive than the first, offering recordings over the full range of the great tenor's 78-r.p.m. recording career with EMI, from 1933 (*Vladimir's Cavatina* from *Prince Igor*) to 1949 (*O soave fanciulla* from *La Bohème*, with Anna-Lisa Bjoerling). Again the voice is in peak form, ringing out with that penetrating yet glowing vocal production that was the hallmark of Bjoerling's timbre, while the singing itself has that innate sense of style which made him such a satisfying artist.

It is a pity that the CD transfers are so very bright and edgy, affecting the orchestra as well as the voice. This is particularly annoying in the delicate *Manon* excerpt (*Instant charmant . . . En fermant les yeux*) from 1938, where the violins are particularly tiresome; but the overall tendency to shrillness tends to tire the ear before the recital is half-way through. One wonders why this effect cannot be mitigated – the voice does not lack either vividness or presence without artificial enhancement.

(i) Stuart Burrows (tenor), (ii) Joan Sutherland (soprano)

'*The world of operetta*' (with Amb. Light Op. Ch., New Philh. O, Bonynge; Nat. PO, Robin Stapleton or Bonynge): LEHÁR: *Land of Smiles:* (i) *You are my heart's delight. Paganini: Girls were made to love and kiss;* (ii) *Love live forever. The Merry Widow:* (ii) *Vilja;* (ii) *Love unspoken* (Waltz duet; with Werner Krenn). *Frasquita:* (i) *Farewell my love. Fredericka: Maiden, o maiden.* ROMBERG: *The Student Prince:* (ii) *Students' chorus; Deep in my heart, dear;* (i) *Serenade. The Desert Song:* (ii) *Desert song.* FRIML: *Rose Marie: Indian love call.* GERMAN: *Tom Jones: Waltz song.* SIECZYNSKI: (i) *Vienna, city of my dreams.* O. STRAUS: *The Chocolate Soldier:* (ii) *My hero.* MILLÖCKER: *The Dubarry: The Dubarry.*
(B) *** Decca 433 223-2; *433 223-4* [id.].

It was a brilliant idea for Decca to centre a bargain collection of operetta excerpts in English on Stuart Burrows and Joan Sutherland. These recordings come from two quite different sources, but they match up admirably. Stuart Burrows is stirring in *You are my heart's delight*, charmingly vivacious in *Girls were made to love and kiss* and wonderfully heady in the *Serenade* from *Frasquita*, while Joan Sutherland is at her most ravishing in the *Indian love call* from *Rose Marie* and in *Vilja*. Sutherland combines with Werner Krenn in the most delightful operetta number of all, the Waltz duet, *Love unspoken*, from *The Merry Widow*. The whole programme is vivacious and vividly recorded, and it makes a perfect counterpart to Decca's bargain Viennese anthology, sung in German, '*Golden operetta*' – see below.

Montserrat Caballé (soprano)

'Rossini, Donizetti and Verdi rarities' (with RCA Italiana Ch. & O, (i) Cillario; (ii) Guadagno; (iii) Amb. Op. Ch., LSO Cillario): Arias & excerpts from: (i) ROSSINI: *La Donna del Lago; Otello; Stabat Mater; Armida; Tancredi; L'assedio di Corinto.* (ii) DONIZETTI: *Belisario; Parisina d'este* (with Margreta Elkins, Tom McDonnell). *Torquato Tasso; Gemma di Vergy.* (iii) VERDI: *Un giorno di regno; I Lombardi; I due Foscari* (with Maja Sunara); *Alzira; Attila; Il Corsaro; Aroldo* (with Lajos Kozma).
(M) *** BMG/RCA GD 60941 (2).

Between 1968 and 1970 Montserrat Caballé made three separate LP collections of rare arias by Rossini, Donizetti and Verdi and, although not everything included is as rare today, novelties still remain, especially in the Donizetti section. This was the last to be recorded and here Caballé's conviction as well as her technical assurance make for highly dramatic results in scenas that not so many years ago would have been laughed out of court. The placing of the voice in the *Belisario* item is superbly assured from the very start, and the control of tone is immaculate, with never a hint of forcing even in the most exposed fortissimo. It makes these rarities more attractively convincing that the arias are presented with surrounding detail from a group of well-chosen supporting artists.

The Rossini selection is no less rewarding, though the aria from the *Stabat Mater* hardly qualifies as a rarity. The Verdi arias, taken from operas of the early years when the composer was working 'in the galleys', make a further commandingly brilliant recital when sung with such assurance. Caballé is again at her finest, challenged by the technical difficulties as well as by the need to convey the drama. She makes one forget that between the big memorable tunes there are often less-than-inspired passages. Fine accompaniments throughout, and splendidly smooth and vivid CD transfers ensure the success of these two discs, between them offering 144 minutes of music.

Operatic excerpts (with Luciano Pavarotti, Sherrill Milnes, Agnes Baltsa) from VERDI: *Luisa Miller.* BELLINI: *Norma.* BOITO: *Mefistofele.* PUCCINI: *Turandot.* GIORDANO: *Andrea Chénier.* PONCHIELLI: *La Gioconda.*
(M) *** Decca 421 892-2 [id.].

This is another of those outstanding Decca anthologies which adds up to more than the sum of its parts. There are 76 minutes of vibrant and often beautiful singing. Although the disc centres on Caballé and is described as 'Operatic arias', there are in fact plenty of duets, and ensembles too. All the excerpts come from highly recommended complete sets, and Pavarotti figures often and strongly. In Bellini, Giordano or Boito, and especially as Liù in *Turandot*, Caballé is often vocally ravishing, and she finds plenty of drama and power for Verdi and Ponchielli. There are at least two and sometimes three or four items from each opera, admirably chosen to make a consistently involving entertainment. Alas, the back-up notes are inadequate, concentrating on Caballé's association with each of the operas included. Nevertheless this rewarding collection can be recommended to novices as well as to experienced collectors.

'Great voice': excerpts from: GOUNOD: *Faust; Roméo et Juliette.* MEYERBEER: *Les Huguenots.* CHARPENTIER: *Louise.* BIZET: *Carmen.* PUCCINI: *Manon Lescaut* (with Plácido Domingo). R. STRAUSS: *Salome* (Closing scene).
(B) ** DG 431 103-2 [id.].

Most of the content of Caballé's contribution to DG's *'Grosse Stimmen'* series is drawn from a 1971 recital of French arias. Although the quality of the voice is in no doubt, this was not in fact one of this artist's more distinctive recitals. The vocal line is sometimes not perfectly judged (her earlier, RCA recording of Charpentier's *Depuis le jour* was finer; here the aria's key moments are managed confidently, but the performance as a whole is simply less beautiful). In the Gounod numbers the style is not fined down enough: the voice seems a trifle unwieldy. The Meyerbeer item is the most convincing.

DG's recording is warm with a resonant acoustic, kind to both the voice and the superb orchestral playing from the New Philharmonia under Reynald Giovaninetti. The duet from *Manon Lescaut* (*Tu, tu amore?*) with Domingo is vibrantly exciting but the recording, made at a live performance, is somewhat less flattering. (It is included also on Domingo's recital in this series.) The highlight here is the final scene from *Salome*, recorded with Leonard Bernstein in 1978, although the orchestral sound could ideally be more sumptuous. But the performance is imaginatively full of contrasts, the sweet, innocent girl still observable next to the bloodthirsty fiend. The disc is poorly presented, with nothing about music or artist, only titles and recording dates.

Montserrat Caballé (soprano), Shirley Verrett (mezzo soprano)

'Great operatic duets' (with Amb. Op. Ch., New Philh. O,, Guadagno) from: ROSSINI: Semiramide. DONIZETTI: Anna Bolena. BELLINI: Norma. OFFENBACH: Contes d'Hoffmann. VERDI: Aida. PUCCINI: Madama Butterfly. PONCHIELLI: La Gioconda.
(M) ** BMG/RCA GD 60818.

One might have thought that the vibrancy of Shirley Verrett's personality would have sparked off some real excitement here; in fact, however, it is the lyrical moments of the recital – obviously rehearsed with great care – that provide the highlight of this otherwise slightly disappointing collection. Both the Rossini and Donizetti scenes are slightly dull, but Mira, o Norma is gorgeously done, and the singers make equally ravishing sounds in the Flower duet from Madama Butterfly, by far the most memorable item in the second half of the recital. Vivid sound.

Maria Callas (soprano)

Operatic recital: CILEA: Adriana Lecouvreur: Ecco, respiro appena . . . Io son l'umile; Poveri fiori. GIORDANO: Andrea Chénier: La mamma morta. CATALANI: La Wally: Ebben? Ne andro lontana. BOITO: Mefistofele: L'altra notte. ROSSINI: Il barbiere di Siviglia: Una voce poco fa. MEYERBEER: Dinorah: Shadow song. DELIBES: Lakmé: Bell song. VERDI: I vespri siciliani: Boléro. CHERUBINI: Medea: Dei tuoi figli. SPONTINI: La Vestale: Tu che invoco; O Nume tutelar; Caro oggetto.
⊛ (***) EMI mono CDC7 47282-2 [id.].

This fine recital disc is a conflation of two of Callas's most successful earlier LPs. The Medea and Vestale items were originally coupled with extracts from complete opera sets and might otherwise have been left in limbo. These are recordings from the 1950s, when the voice was still in fine condition and the artistry at its most magnetic. Callas's portrait of Rosina in Una voce was never more sparklingly viperish than here, and she never surpassed the heart-felt intensity of such numbers as La mamma morta and Poveri fiori. Some items may reveal strain – the Bell song from Lakmé, for example – but this has many claims to be the finest single Callas recital on CD, very well transferred.

'Mad scenes and Bel canto arias' (with Philh. O, Rescigno): DONIZETTI: Anna Bolena: Piangete voi; Al dolce guidami. La figlia del reggimento: Convien partir. Lucrezia Borgia: Tranquillo ei possa . . . Come è bello. L'Elisir d'amore: Prendi, per me sei libero. THOMAS: Hamlet: A vos jeux; Partagez-vous mes fleurs; Et maintenant écoutez ma chanson. BELLINI: Il Pirata: Oh! s'io potessi . . . Col sorriso d'innocenza; Sorgete, Lo sognai ferito esangue.
*** EMI CDC7 47283-2 [id.].

If, as ever, the rawness of exposed top-notes mars the sheer beauty of Callas's singing, few recital records ever made can match, let alone outshine, her collection of mad scenes in vocal and dramatic imagination. This is Callas at her very peak; Desmond Shawe-Taylor suggested this as the collection which, more than any other, summed up the essence of Callas's genius. For the CD reissue further arias have been added, notably excerpts from Donizetti's La figlia del reggimento, L'Elisir d'amore and Lucrezia Borgia (from the mid-1960s), a fair example of the latter-day Callas, never very sweet-toned, yet displaying the usual Callas fire. However, the singing here is less imaginative and there are few phrases that stick in the memory by their sheer individuality. Nevertheless, the main part of the recital is indispensable; the digital remastering has enhanced the originally excellent recordings and given the voice striking presence.

'Callas à Paris' (with Fr. Nat. R. O, Prêtre): GLUCK: Orphée et Eurydice: J'ai perdu mon Eurydice. Alceste: Divinités du Styx. BIZET: Carmen: Habañera; Séguedilla. SAINT-SAËNS: Samson et Dalila: Printemps qui commence; Amour! Viens aider; Mon coeur s'ouvre à ta voix. MASSENET: Manon: Adieu, notre petite table; Je marche sur tous les chemins. Le Cid: Pleurez, mes yeux. GOUNOD: Roméo et Juliette: Je veux vivre. THOMAS: Mignon: Je suis Titania. CHARPENTIER: Louise: Depuis le jour.

*** EMI CDC7 49059-2.

The original LP collection, 'Callas à Paris', dating from 1961 with the singer at her most commanding and characterful, is here augmented with five items from the sequel disc of two years later, when the voice was in decline. The vocal contrast is clear enough, and the need at the time to patch and re-patch the takes in the later sessions makes the results sound less spontaneous and natural. But the earlier portraits of Carmen, Alceste, Dalila and Juliette find Callas still supreme. Her mastery of the French repertory provides a fascinating slant on her artistry.

'The unknown recordings': WAGNER: Tristan: Liebestod. VERDI: Don Carlos: Tu che le vanità. I Lombardi: Te vergin santa. I vespri siciliani: Arrigo! Ah, parli a un core, Attila: Liberamente or piangi. BELLINI: Il Pirata: Col sorriso d'innocenza. ROSSINI: Cenerentola: Non più mesta. Guglielmo Tell: Selva opaca. Semiramide: Bel raggio lusingher.
*** EMI CDC7 49428-2 [id.].

The collection brings together unpublished material from several sources, mainly alternative recordings of arias which appeared earlier in other versions, but also live recordings made in Athens and Amsterdam. The alternative readings all bring us fresh illumination of a supreme artist who was both deeply thoughtful and spontaneous in that she never merely repeated herself. These items of early Verdi, Rossini and Bellini are all most cherishable, but just as fascinating is her very early Athens account of Isolde's Liebestod in Italian and her 1959 Holland Festival performances of passages from Bellini's Il Pirata and Verdi's Don Carlos. Variable recording, helped by skilled and refined EMI transfers.

Arias: ROSSINI: Il barbiere di Siviglia: Una voce poco fa. VERDI: Macbeth: La luce langue. Don Carlos: Tu che le vanità. PUCCINI: Tosca: Vissi d'arte. GLUCK: Alceste: Divinités du Styx. BIZET: Carmen: Habañera; Séguedilla (with Nicolai Gedda). SAINT-SAËNS: Samson et Dalila: Printemps qui commence. MASSENET: Manon: Je ne suis faiblesse (Adieu, notre petite table). CHARPENTIER: Louise: Depuis le jour.
(M) ***** EMI CD-EMX 2123; TC-EMX 2123.**

This compilation on the EMI Eminence label brings together at bargain price some of Callas's most cherishable performances, mostly taken from recital material. An excellent sampler, well recorded and satisfactorily transferred.

'The incomparable Callas' (Arias from): BELLINI: Norma. DONIZETTI: Lucia. VERDI: Ernani; Aida. PONCHIELLI: La Gioconda. PUCCINI: Tosca. GLUCK: Orphée et Eurydice. GOUNOD: Roméo et Juliette. THOMAS: Mignon. MASSENET: Le Cid. BIZET: Carmen. SAINT-SAËNS: Samson et Dalila.
(M) ***** EMI CDM7 63182-2 [id.].**

One might quibble whether the title 'The incomparable Callas' is apt when applied to these particular items, mostly taken from complete operas and recitals recorded in the 1960s. Her later sets of Lucia and Norma are both well represented here, but even finer is the Suicidio! from her second version of Ponchielli's La Gioconda, among her finest achievements. The Carmen items taken from the complete set are more questionable in their fierceness but are totally individual – as indeed, flawed or not, is the last-recorded item here, Aida's Ritorna vincitor, made in 1972. The transfers capture the voice well.

José Carreras (tenor)

Arias from: PUCCINI: Manon Lescaut; Turandot. LEONCAVALLO: Zaza; I Pagliacci; La Bohème; I Zingara. GIORDANO: Andrea Chénier. PONCHIELLI: La Gioconda; Il Figliuol Prodigo. MASCAGNI: L'amico Fritz. GOMES: Fosca. CILEA: L'Arlesiana. MERCADANTE: Il Giuramento. BELLINI: Adelson e Salvini.
(M) ****(*) Ph. 426 643-2; 426 643-4.**

Including some attractive rarities, this is an impressive recital. Carreras is never less than a conscientious artist, and though one or two items stretch the lovely voice to its limits, there is none of the coarseness that most tenors of the Italian school would indulge in. Excellent sound and vivid transfers.

'The essential José Carreras': Arias from: PUCCINI: La Bohème; Manon Lescaut; Turandot; Tosca. LEONCAVALLO: I Pagliacci. DONIZETTI: L'elisir d'amore; Lucia di Lammermoor.

VERDI: *Il Trovatore; Luisa Miller*. BERNSTEIN: *West Side Story*. Neapolitan songs. FRANCK: *Panis angelicus*.
*** Ph. 432 692-2; *432 692-4* [id.].

José Carreras has a less flamboyant personality than Pavarotti and less vocal presence than Domingo – but he is a very pleasing singer in his own right and his style is entirely without vulgarity. In the famous Puccini warhorses some might prefer more robust fervour, but one can believe in Mimì being attracted to a Rodolfo who sings as winningly as this, and the Donizetti arias also suit the voice well. If *Di quella pira* from *Trovatore* was a less suitable choice, Carreras makes up for it in the Neapolitan songs, which are sung with a refined lyrical fervour that is refreshing, even if sometimes listeners may seek a more gutsy, peasant style. Accompaniments are always sympathetic, the sound is first class, and the recital plays for 70 minutes; even so, this should have been offered at mid-price.

(i) José Carreras, (ii) Plácido Domingo and (iii) Luciano Pavarotti
(tenors)

'In concert at the Baths of Caracalla, Rome, 7 July 1990' (with Maggio Musicale Fiorentino O & Rome Op. O, Mehta): Arias from: (i) CILEA: *L'Arlesiana*. (ii) MEYERBEER: *L'Africaine*. (iii; ii) PUCCINI: *Tosca*; (ii) *Turandot*. (iii) LEHÁR: *Das Land des Lächelns*. (i) GIORDANO: *Andrea Chénier*. (i–iii) Songs by DE CRESCENDO; CARDILLO; DE CURTIS; LARA; SOROZÁBAL. Medley including excerpts from BERNSTEIN: *West Side Story*. LLOYD WEBBER: *Memory. La vie en rose; Mattinata; 'O sole mio; Amapola*. Encores.
*** Decca 430 433-2; *430 433-4* [id.].

Planned years in advance to coincide with the football World Cup in Rome in 1990, this unmatchable extravaganza relied on the devotion of all three great tenors to that game. The success of the resulting record with the wider musical public means that our comments are of no real consequence. A series of purple patches – even the orchestra goes over the top – vividly recorded and with the voices close-miked inevitably brings a feeling of coarseness, although there are undoubted physical thrills if you enjoy loud, straining, tenor *fortissimos*.

There are a few, rarer moments of quiet singing. José Carreras was not in his best voice, yet he is still impressive in *L'Improvviso* from *Andrea Chénier*, as is Domingo in the Lehár and the excerpt from the Spanish zarzuela. Pavarotti's Puccini makes the usual strong impact but can be heard with more finesse on his studio recordings. However, there is certainly a sense of occasion here, with the rivalry between the three superstars in the culminating trio a special delight: a far cry from the animosity that comparable tenors of the past often showed towards one another.

Enrico Caruso (tenor)

'Opera arias and songs': Arias from: VERDI: *Rigoletto; Aida*. MASSENET: *Manon*. DONIZETTI: *L'Elisir d'amore*. BOITO: *Mefistofele*. PUCCINI: *Tosca*. MASCAGNI: *Iris; Cavalleria Rusticana*. GIORDANO: *Fedora*. PONCHIELLI: *La Gioconda*. LEONCAVALLO: *I Pagliacci*. CILEA: *Adriana Lecouvreur*. BIZET: *Les pêcheurs de perles*. MEYERBEER: *Les Huguenots*. Songs.
(M) (***) EMI mono CDH7 61046-2 [id.].

The EMI collection on the Références label brings together Caruso's earliest recordings, made in 1902 and 1904 in Milan with misty piano accompaniment. The very first were done impromptu in Caruso's hotel, and the roughness of presentation reflects that; but the voice is glorious in its youth, amazingly well caught for that period. It was that sound of these very recordings which, more than anything else, first convinced a wide public that the gramophone was more than a toy.

'Prima voce': Arias from: DONIZETTI: *L'Elisir d'amore; Don Sebastiano; Il duca d'Alba*. GOLDMARK: *La regina di Saba*. GOMEZ: *Lo schiavo*. HALÉVY: *La juive*. LEONCAVALLO: *I Pagliacci*. MASSENET: *Manon*. MEYERBEER: *L'Africana*. PUCCINI: *Tosca; Manon Lescaut*. VERDI: *Aida; Un ballo in maschera; La forza del destino; Rigoletto; Il Trovatore*.
(M) (***) Nimbus mono NI 7803 [id.].

The Nimbus method of transfer to CD, reproducing ancient 78s on a big acoustic horn gramophone of the 1930s, tends to work best with acoustic recordings, when the accompaniments then emerge as more consistent with the voice. There is an inevitable loss of part of the recording range at both ends of the spectrum, but the ear can often be convinced. This Caruso collection, very well chosen to show the development of his voice, ranges from early (1904) recordings of Massenet, Puccini and Donizetti with piano accompaniment to the recording that the great tenor made in 1920, not long before he died, of his very last role, as Eleazar in Halévy's *La juive*, wonderfully characterized.

'*Verismo arias (1906– 1916)*' from PUCCINI: *La Bohème* (with Nellie Melba, Geraldine Farrar, Antonio Scotti); *Tosca; Madama Butterfly* (with Farrar, Scotti). PONCHIELLI: *La Gioconda.* MASCAGNI: *Cavalleria rusticana.* LEONCAVALLO: *La Bohéme; Pagliacci.* FRANCETTI: *Germania.* GIORDANO: *Andrea Chénier.* PUCCINI: *Manon Lescaut.*
(M) *** BMG/RCA 09026 61243-2.

French opera (1906– 1916): Highlights from GOUNOD: *Faust* (with Geraldine Farrar, Antonio Scotti, Marcel Journet). Arias from: MASSENET: *Le Cid; Manon.* BIZET: *Carmen.* SAINT-SAËNS: *Samson et Dalila.* BIZET: *Les pêcheurs de perles.* HALÉVY: *La juive.*
(M) *** BMG/RCA 09026 61244-2.

These two discs, alongside a Verdi collection (see under the composer), are phenomenally well transferred with the aid of special digital techniques that seek to eliminate the unwanted resonances of the acoustic horn used in the original recording process. This restoration was achieved in the early 1980s using a Soundstream programme, master-minded by Thomas Stockham. The results are uncannily successful: the voice emerges with remarkable freshness and purity (sample the *Flower song* from *Carmen*) and only the accompaniments, heavily laden with wind and brass, give the game away; otherwise one might think the recordings much more modern. The two selections include many famous records, covering the decade of 1906–16, and it is good to hear such singers as Melba, who joins Caruso in the duet, *O soave fanciulla*, and Farrar, Viafora and Scotti in the Act III *Bohème Quartet.* Farrar, Journet and Scotti are also present in the seven items from *Faust* included on the French recital. There are obviously more issues to come, and they will be most welcome.

Feodor Chaliapin (bass)

Russian opera arias: MUSSORGSKY: *Boris Godunov: Coronation scene; Clock scene; Farewell and Death of Boris.* GLINKA: *Life for the Tsar: They guess the truth. Russlan and Ludmilla: Farlaf's Rondo; Field O field.* DARGOMINSKY: *Russalka: You young girls are all alike; Mad scene and death of the miller.* RUBINSTEIN: *The Demon; Do not weep, child.* BORODIN: *Prince Igor: Khan Konchak's aria.* RIMSKY-KORSAKOV: *Sadko: Song of the Viking guest.* RACHMANINOV: *Aleko: The moon is high.*
✧ (M) (***) EMI mono CDH7 61009-2 [id.].

Not only the glory of the voice, amazingly rich and consistent as recorded here between 1908 (aged 35) and 1931, but also the electrifying personality is vividly caught in this superb Références CD. The range of expression is astonishing. If posterity tends to think of this megastar among basses in the role of Mussorgsky's *Boris* (represented here in versions previously unissued), he is just as memorable in such an astonishing item as *Farlaf's Rondo* from *Russlan and Ludmilla*, with its tongue-twisting chatter made thrilling at such speed and with such power. The presence of the singer is unwaveringly vivid in model transfers, whether the original recording was acoustic or electric.

Boris Christoff (bass)

'*The early recordings (1949– 52)*': excerpts from: MUSSORGSKY: *Boris Godunov; Khovanshchina.* BORODIN: *Prince Igor.* RIMSKY-KORSAKOV: *Sadko; The Legend of the invisible city of Kitezh.* TCHAIKOVSKY: *Eugene Onegin.* MUSSORGSKY: *Songs. Russian folksongs.*
(M) (***) EMI CDH7 64252-2 [id.].

The magnetic quality of Christoff's singing is never in doubt here, and the compulsion of the singer's artistry as well as the vivid individuality of his bass timbres make this a real portrait, not just a collection of items. These were his first recordings of the *Boris Godunov* excerpts (in which he assumes three different characters), and in musical terms he probably never surpassed them.

But his characterization here is just as impressive as the singing itself, full of variety. The EMI transfers are bold and brightly focused, less mellow than the effect Nimbus usually achieve, but with the most vivid projection.

(The) Comden and Green Songbook

'The Comden and Green Songbook': (with (i) John Reardon; (ii) Adolph Green; (iii) Cris Alexander; (iv) Betty Comden; (v) Nancy Walker; (vi) Rosalind Russell; (vii) Jacquelyn McKeever; (viii) Sydney Chaplin; (ix) Jordan Bentley; (x) Judy Holliday; (xi) Eddie Lawrence; (xii) Leslie Uggams; (xiii) Robert Hooks; (xiv) Allen Case; (xv) Clifford Allen, Garrett Morris; (xvi) John Cullum; (xvii) Madeline Kahn; (xviii) Imogene Coca; (xix) George Coe, Dean Dittman): BERNSTEIN: On the Town: (i; ii; iii) New York, New York; (ii; iv) Carried away; (v) I can cook too; (i) Lucky to be me; (ii; iii; iv; v) Some other time. Wonderful Town: (vi; vii) Ohio; (vi) One hundred easy ways to lose a man; (viii) A quiet girl; (ix) Pass that football. STYNE: Bells are Ringing: (x) It's a perfect relationship; (viii; x) Long before I knew you; (xi) It's a simple little system; (x) Drop that name; (viii; x) Just in time. Hallelujah, Baby!: (xii) My own morning; (xii; xiii; xiv) Talking to yourself; (xii; xiii; xv) The slice; (xii) Being good. COLEMAN: On the Twentieth Century: (xvi; xvii) Our private world; (xviii) Repent; (xvi; xviii; xix); Five zeros; (xvi) The legacy.
*** Sony SK 48202 [id.].

This is an estimable collection, indispensable for anyone who enjoys the racy vitality of the American musical theatre. The names of Betty Comden and Adolph Green have deservedly become legendary in the field of lyric writing – their credits here speak for themselves – and it is good that Adolph Green's visual/vocal personality has been captured on the video of the Barbican concert performance of Bernstein's Candide. Comden and Green were both born in the same year, 1915, and they formed a unique writing partnership over half a century, during a time when the Broadway musical was at its peak. They must have considered themselves lucky to have collaborated on several of the finest musical scores in the history of the genre, among which the two Bernstein shows can certainly be counted.

Bells are Ringing and On the Twentieth Century (neither of them fashionable at the moment) are sleepers, and both are surely due for revival. Indeed the only reason this CD was not allotted one of I. M.'s Rosettes is because the selection from the latter show is ill-conceived. Certainly the four songs here are well done. Imogene Coca's Repent is a collector's item, John Cullum is especially good in Our private world, and Five zeros is a fizzing ensemble. But where is She's a nut, and why are none of the marvellously rhythmic train evocations included?

But for the rest, the selection and performances combine spontaneously and exhilaratingly, often to make the hairs on the nape of the neck tingle. John Reardon's resonant New York, New York (such a superb opener for On the Town that it almost dwarfs the rest of the show), Nancy Walker's I can cook too and Rosalind Russell's canny advice on One hundred ways to lose a man are highlights of the Bernstein oeuvre (and some marvellous things happen in the orchestra, too).

Jule Styne's Bells are Ringing is a most engaging piece, and Judy Holliday's It's a perfect relationship readily demonstrates the score's quality, while Eddie Lawrence captivates in the Sullivanesque patter song, It's a simple little system, with its string of names of famous classical composers. The four excerpts from Hallelujah, Baby! also show Styne very nearly at his best, and throughout the performances are of the highest calibre. Excellent sound, too, while the documentation cannot be faulted. There is 77 minutes of splendid music here.

Giuseppe De Luca (baritone)

'Prima voce': Arias from: VERDI: Don Carlos, Ernani, Il Trovatore, La Traviata, Rigoletto. ROSSINI: Il Barbiere di Siviglia. DONIZETTI: L'elisir d'amore. BELLINI: I Puritani. DIAZ: Benvenuto Cellini. PUCCINI: La Bohème. PONCHIELLI: La Gioconda. WOLF-FERRARI: I gioielli della madonna. Songs: DE LEVA: Pastorale. ROMILLI: Marietta.
(M) (***) Nimbus mono NI 7815 [id.].

There has never been a more involving account on record of the Act IV Marcello–Rodolfo duet than the one here with De Luca and Gigli, a model of characterization and vocal art. The baritone's mastery emerges vividly in item after item, whether in the power and wit of his pre-electric version of Largo al factotum (1917) or the five superb items (including the Bohème duet and the *Rigoletto* numbers, flawlessly controlled) which were recorded in the vintage year of 1927. Warm Nimbus transfers.

Emmy Destinn (soprano)

Arias from: THOMAS: *Mignon*. PUCCINI: *Madama Butterfly; Tosca*. VERDI: *Aida; Il trovatore* (with Giovanni Martinelli); *Un ballo in maschera*. PONCHIELLI: *La gioconda*. WAGNER: *Tannhäuser*. GOMES: *Il guarany* (with Enrico Caruso). MOZART: *Die Zauberflöte*. DVOŘÁK: *Rusalka*. KOVAROVICH: *Nazarene*. TCHAIKOVSKY: *The Queen of Spades* (with Maria Duchêne). SMETANA: *Hubicka*. Songs by SCHUBERT, BACH/GOUNOD (with Bourdon, Lapitino), MOZART, GOUNOD, STANGE, LISZT, JINDRICH, DESTINN, HESS, STEPHAN, DVOŘÁK. Folksongs (with Gilly).
(M) (**(*)) Romophone mono 81002-2 (2) [id.].

Emmy Destinn was the leading dramatic soprano of her day, the choice of Strauss for the role of Salome and of Puccini for Minnie, the Girl of the Golden West. Yet, as this wide-ranging collection makes clear, the poise of her singing, its perfect control, was at least as remarkable as the power.

The finest examples here, all of them flawlessly controlled, include Aida's *O patria mia* and Tosca's *Vissi d'arte*. Pamina's *Ach ich fühl's* is similarly poised, with a superb trill at the end. The 37 items offer Destinn's complete Victor recordings made between 1914 and 1921, but the choice of the opening item is unfortunate, when the aria from Thomas's *Mignon* (in German, not French) has Destinn singing with an ugly yodelling tone, using excessive portamento. As a Czech, she includes a number of Czech folksongs, but then sings the *Rusalka* aria in German, not Czech. The transfers capture the voice vividly, but surface hiss tends to be high.

Divas

'Prima voce': Divas 1906–35 (Luisa Tetrazzini; Nellie Melba; Adelina Patti; Frieda Hempel; Amelita Galli-Curci; Rosa Ponselle; Lotte Lehmann; Eva Turner; Nina Koshetz; Eidé Norena; Maria Nemeth; Claudia Muzio): Arias from: VERDI: *Un ballo in maschera; Rigoletto; Aida; Il Trovatore*. THOMAS: *Mignon*. MOZART: *Die Zauberflöte*. ROSSINI: *Il barbiere di Siviglia*. MASSENET: *Manon*. PUCCINI: *Madama Butterfly*. BEETHOVEN: *Fidelio*. RIMSKY-KORSAKOV: *Sadko*. BORODIN: *Prince Igor*. GOUNOD: *Roméo et Juliette*. BOITO: *Mefistofele*. Songs: YRADIER: *La calesera*. DENAUDY: *O del mio amato ben*.
(M) (***) Nimbus mono NI 7802 [id.].

The six supreme prima donnas on this compilation are all very well represented. The soprano voice benefits more than most from the Nimbus process, so that with extra bloom Tetrazzini's vocal 'gear-change' down to the chest register is no longer obtrusive. She is represented by three recordings of 1911, including Gilda's *Caro nome* from *Rigoletto*; and Galli-Curci has three items too, including Rosina's *Una voce poco fa* from *Il barbiere di Siviglia*. The tragically short-lived Claudia Muzio and the Russian, Nina Koshetz, have two each, while the others are each represented by a single, well-chosen item. They include Melba in *Mimi's farewell*, the 60-year-old Patti irresistibly vivacious in a Spanish folksong, *La calesera*, and Frieda Hempel in what is probably the most dazzling of all recordings of the Queen of the Night's second aria from *Zauberflöte*.

'Prima voce': Divas Volume 2, 1909–40 (Frieda Hempel, Amelita Galli-Curci, Geraldine Farrar, Selma Kurz, Mabel Garrison, Alma Gluck, Maria Ivogün, Sigrid Onegin, Lotte Schöne, Eidé Norena, Rosa Ponselle, Frida Leider, Ninon Vallin, Maggie Teyte, Nina Koshetz, Kirsten Flagstad, Mafalda Favero): Arias from: BELLINI: *I Puritani*. MOZART: *Le nozze di Figaro; Die Entführung aus dem Serail*. PUCCINI: *Tosca*. VERDI: *Rigoletto; La forza del destino*. OFFENBACH: *Les contes d'Hoffmann; La Périchole*. GODARD: *Jocelyn*. BIZET: *Carmen*. J. STRAUSS JR: *Die Fledermaus*. THOMAS: *Hamlet*. WAGNER: *Tristan und Isolde; Die Walküre*. MASSENET: *Werther*. PONCE: *Estrellita*. MASCAGNI: *Lodoletta*.
(M) (***) Nimbus mono NI 7818 [id.].

As in the previous *Divas* volume, the choice of items will delight any lover of fine singing, a most discriminating choice. Maria Ivogün, the teacher of Schwarzkopf, contributes a wonderfully pure and incisive *Martern aller Arten* (*Entführung*) dating from 1923, and Lotte

Schöne is unusually and characterfully represented by Adele's *Mein Herr Marquis* from *Fledermaus*. Frida Leider's *Liebestod* is nobly sung but is surprisingly fast by latterday standards. Maggie Teyte sings delectably in an aria from *La Périchole*; and though some of the pre-electric items in Nimbus's resonant transfers suggest an echo-chamber, the voices are warm and full.

Plácido Domingo (tenor)

'Bravissimo, Domingo': VERDI: *Il Trovatore: Di quella pira. Un Ballo in maschera: Teco io sto* (with Leontyne Price). *Rigoletto: La donna è mobile. Otello: Ah! Mille vite; Sì, pel ciel marmoreo giuro! Don Carlos: Dio, che nell'alma infondere* (both with Sherrill Milnes). *Aida: Se quel guerrier io fossi ... Celeste Aida. La Traviata: Lunge da lei ... De'miei bollenti spiriti.* PUCCINI: *Tosca: E lucevan le stelle. Manon Lescaut: Oh, sarò la più bella!; Tu, tu, amore tu?* (with Leontyne Price). *Turandot: Non piangere Liù.* LEONCAVALLO: *Pagliacci: Recitar! Mentre preso ... Vesti la giubba.* CILEA: *Adriana Lecouvreur: L'anima ho stanco.* GOUNOD: *Roméo et Juliette: L'amour! L'amour! Ah! Lève-toi, soleil. Faust: Quel trouble inconnu; Salut! Demeure chaste et pure.* GIORDANO: *Andrea Chènier: Un dì all'azzurro spazio.* MASCAGNI: *Cavalleria Rusticana: Mamma; mamma! Quel vino è generoso.* BIZET: *Carmen: Flower song.*
*** BMG/RCA RD 87020 [RCD1 7020].

This selection of recordings ranges wide over Domingo's recording career. The opening items come from complete sets and *Di quella pira* immediately establishes the ringing vocal authority. The excerpts from *Cav.* and *Pag.* are equally memorable, as are the duets with Sherrill Milnes. With over 72 minutes offered, this is generous enough; although the remastered recordings sometimes show their age in the orchestra, the voice always remains fresh.

'Bravissimo Domingo!', Volume 2: VERDI: *Rigoletto: Questa o quella; Ella mi fu rapita!; Parmi veder le lagrime. I vespri siciliani: Giorno di pianto, di fier dolore. Il Trovatore: Ah, sì ben mio. Luisa Miller: Oh! fede negar potessi; Quando le sere al placido. La forza del destino: Oh, te che in seno agli angeli.* PUCCINI: *Tosca: Dammi i colori; Recondita armonia. La Bohème: Che gelida manina.* BELLINI: *Norma: Meco all'altar de Venere* (with Amb. Op. Ch.). MASCAGNI: *Brindisi; Viva il vino spumeggiante* (with John Alldis Ch.). WAGNER: *Lohengrin: In fernem Land.* MASSENET: *Werther: Pourquoi me réveiller?* DONIZETTI: *L'Elisir d'amore: Una furtiva lagrima.* TCHAIKOVSKY: *Eugene Onegin: Lensky's aria.* FLOTOW: *Martha: M'apparì, tutt'amor.* GIORDANO: *Andrea Chénier: Come un bel dì di maggio.*
*** BMG/RCA RD 86211 [RCA-6211-2-RC].

Opening stylishly with *Questa o quella*, and always establishing his sense of Verdian line, this second RCA collection is if anything even more attractive than the first. There is not a single below-par performance, and Domingo seems as at home in Tchaikovsky's and Wagner's lyricism as he is in the Italian repertoire. *Che gelida manina* is noble as well as eloquent, and the Donizetti and Flotow arias show the warm timbre of this remarkably consistent artist. Excellent remastering throughout the 72 minutes of music offered. However, the two-disc set (GD 60866 – see below) duplicates much of this repertoire and is even better value at mid-price.

'Great love scenes' (with Renata Scotto, Kiri Te Kanawa, Ileana Cotrubas): PUCCINI: *Madama Butterfly: Love Duet. La rondine: Tu madre!* CILEA: *Adriana Lecouvreur: La dolcissima effigie.* MASSENET: *Manon: Toi!* GOUNOD: *Roméo et Juliette: Va, je t'ai pardonné.* CHARPENTIER: *Louise: Vois la ville qui s'eclaire.*
(M) *** Sony MK 39030 [id.].

This compilation from various CBS opera sets brings an attractively varied group of love duets, with Domingo matched against three splendid heroines. Scotto is the principal partner, better as Adriana than as Butterfly, Juliette or Manon, but still warmly individual, responding to the glory of Domingo's singing which is unfailingly beautiful and warmly committed. The wonder is that his exceptional consistency never falls into routine; these are all performances to have one wanting to go back to the complete operas. Good recording.

'The Plácido Domingo album': Arias from: MOZART: *Don Giovanni.* FLOTOW: *Martha.* GOUNOD: *Faust; Roméo et Juliette.* BIZET: *Carmen.* WAGNER: *Lohengrin.* DONIZETTI: *L'elisir d'amore.* PUCCINI: *La Bohème; Tosca* (with Paul Plishka); *Turandot.* LEONCAVALLO: *Pagliacci.* GIORDANO: *Andrea Chénier.* MASCAGNI: *Cavalleria rusticana.* TCHAIKOVSKY: *Eugene Onegin.* VERDI: *Il Trovatore* (with Leontyne Price); *La Traviata; Rigoletto; Luisa Miller; Simon*

Boccanegra; Un ballo in maschera; I vespri siciliani; Aida; Don Carlo (with Sherrill Milnes); *Otello* (with Katia Ricciarelli and Milnes); *La forza del destino.*
(M) *** BMG/RCA GD 60866 (2) [60866-2].

With 31 items included, on a pair of mid-priced CDs playing for some 137 minutes, this is as attractive a Domingo collection as the current catalogue offers, particularly as the selection, while ranging widely over popular repertoire, devotes the second CD entirely to Verdi, roles which suit the strength of his personality and show the voice at its most vibrant, especially the thrilling *Di quella pira* from *Il Trovatore.* The selection ranges over Domingo's RCA recording career, covering a decade of excellence from 1969 to 1978.

Most of the items come from his complete sets, but the opening *Il mio tesoro* derives from an early recital and very fine it is, quite different from John McCormack's famous version, but showing almost comparable breath control. Domingo is equally at home in Tchaikovsky's and Wagner's lyricism and brings an extra dimension to Italian repertoire. *Che gelida manina* (after an engaging little gasp from Mimì – Caballé, though she is uncredited) is noble as well as eloquent. The Donizetti and Flotow arias show the warm timbre of this remarkably consistent artist, just as Bizet's *Flower song* shows his eloquence and ardour, and Verdi's *Questa o quella* his crisp rhythmic style. Excellent remastering throughout: the voice is brightly and cleanly caught: the RCA engineers were not afraid to have him sing directly into their microphones.

'Gala opera concert' (with LAPO, Giulini): DONIZETTI: *L'Elisir d'amore: Una furtiva lagrima. Lucia di Lammermoor: Tombe degl'avi miei . . . Fra poco.* VERDI: *Ernani: Mercé, diletti amici . . . Come rugiada; Dell'esilio nel dolore . . . O tu che l'alma adora. Il Trovatore: Ah si, ben mio; Di quella pira. Aida: Se quel guerrier io fossi . . . Celeste Aida.* HALÉVY: *La Juive: Rachel, quand du Seigneur.* MEYERBEER: *L'Africaine: Pays merveilleux . . . O Paradis.* BIZET: *Les Pêcheurs de perles: Je crois entendre encore. Carmen: La fleur que tu m'avais jetée* (with R. Wagner Chorale).
*** DG Dig. 400 030-2 [id.].

Recorded in 1980 in connection with a gala in San Francisco, this is as noble and resplendent a tenor recital as you will find. Domingo improves in detail even on the fine versions of some of these arias he had recorded earlier, and the finesse of the whole gains greatly from the sensitive direction of Giulini, though the orchestra is a little backward. Otherwise excellent recording, with tingling digital brass in the *Aida* excerpt; on the compact disc the honeyed beauty of the voice is given the greatest immediacy. The orchestra too gains resonance in the bass and this added weight improves the balance.

'The best of Domingo': VERDI: *Aida: Se quel guerrier . . . Celeste Aida. Rigoletto: La donna è mobile. Luisa Miller: Oh! fede negar . . . Quando le sere. Un ballo in maschera: Forse la soglia . . . Ma se m'è forza perderti; Di tu se fedele. La Traviata: Lunge de lei . . . De' miei bollenti spiriti.* BIZET: *Carmen: Flower song.* FLOTOW: *Martha: Ach so fromm.* DONIZETTI: *L'Elisir d'amore: Una furtiva lagrima.* OFFENBACH: *Contes d'Hoffmann: Legend of Kleinzach.*
*** DG 415 366-2 [id.].

A popular recital showing Domingo in consistent form, the voice and style vibrant and telling, as the opening *Celeste Aida* readily shows, followed by an agreeably relaxed *La donna è mobile.* In the lyric arias, the *Flower song* and the excerpts from *Martha* and *L'Elisir d'amore* there is not the honeyed sweetness of a Gigli, but in the closing *Hoffmann* scena the sheer style of the singing gives special pleasure. The sound is vivid throughout and the CD brings the usual enhancement, though marginally. However, much of this repertory is included in the 'Domingo Edition' at mid-price – see below.

Arias from: VERDI: *Rigoletto; Aida; Il Trovatore; La Traviata; Ernani; Macbeth.* DONIZETTI: *L'Elisir d'amore; Lucia di Lammermoor.* BIZET: *Carmen; Les Pêcheurs de perles.* MEYERBEER: *L'Africaine.* PUCCINI: *La Fanciulla del West.* LEHÁR: *Land des Lächelns.* Songs: LEONCAVALLO: *Mattinata.* LARA: *Granada.* CURTIS: *Non ti scorda.* GREVER: *Mucho.* CARDILLO: *Catari, catari.*
(B) *** DG *419 091-4* [id.].

A self-recommending tape offering nearly an hour and a half of Domingo on excellent operatic form. The programme includes obvious favourites but some less-expected items too, and the songs are welcome in showing the great tenor in lighter mood. A bargain, very useful for the car.

'The Domingo Edition': Highlights from: BIZET: *Carmen* (435 401-2; *435 401-4*). PUCCINI: *La Fanciulla del West* (435 407-2; *435 407-4*); *Manon Lescaut* (435 408-2; *435 408-4*); *Turandot*

(435 409-2; *435 409-4*). VERDI: *Aida* (435 410-2; *435 410-4*); *Un ballo in maschera* (435 411-2; *435 411-4*); *Don Carlos* (453 412-2; *435 412-4*); *Luisa Miller* (435 413-2; *435 413-4*); *Macbeth* (435 414-2; *435 414-4*); *Nabucco* (435 415-2; *435 415-4*); *Rigoletto* (435 426-2; *435 416-4*); *La Traviata* (435 417-2; *435 417-4*); *Il Trovatore* (435 418-2; *435 418-4*). WAGNER: *Tannhäuser* (435 405-2; *435 405-4*); *Die Meistersinger*; WEBER: *Oberon* (435 406-2; *435 406-4*). *French opera*: excerpts from: MEYERBEER: *L'Africaine*. GOUNOD: *Roméo et Juliette*. BERLIOZ: *Requiem; Damnation de Faust*. HALÉVY: *La Juive*. DE LISLE: *La Marseillaise* (arr. Berlioz) (with Ch. & O de Paris, Barenboim: 435 403-2; *435 403-4*). *French opera*, Vol. 2, excerpts from: BERLIOZ: *Béatrice et Bénédict*. MASSENET: *Werther*. BIZET: *Les pêcheurs de perles*. SAINT-SAËNS: *Samson et Dalila* (435 404-2; *435 404-4*). Arias and excerpts from: DONIZETTI: *Lucia di Lammermoor; L'elisir d'amore*. MASCAGNI: *Cavalleria rusticana*. MOZART: *Don Giovanni*. VERDI: *Ernani*. PUCCINI: *Tosca* (435 419-2; *435 419-4*). Songs & tangos: *Amapola; Volver; Mañequita linda; Maria; Ay, ay, ay; Non ti scordar di me; Uno; Alma de bohemio; Granada; Mi Buenos Aires querido; Siboney; Júrame*. LEONCAVALLO: *Mattinata*. LEHÁR: *Dein ist mein ganzes Herz* (435 420-2; *435 4204-4*).
(M) **(*) DG Analogue/Dig. 435 400-2; *435 400-4* (20).

DG's '*Domingo Edition*', 20 discs at mid-price, aims to be a comprehensive tribute to a unique tenor, concentrating on representing him in his complete opera recordings. Domingo himself in his note on the series promises that 'it contains many of the recordings I count among my best', and he is 'especially pleased that this Edition is not just a collection of tenor arias', but instead a mixture of long and short items that give an impression of each opera. No fewer than 16 of the 20 discs are operatic highlights issues, all of which have separate listings in the composer index, with three more devoted to what are broadly described as arias, but which range far wider than that in their selection from the Domingo discography on DG. The last disc is devoted to middle-of-the road material, *Songs and Tangos* collecting items from 1976 and 1981, rather disappointing, when the arrangements are so souped-up and the voice aggressively over-amplified. Only one of the recordings here was made before 1976, but then they followed thick and fast, representing him in a wide range of his finest roles, yet this collection tends to underline the problems the DG engineers often seem to have had over recording so large a voice. Instead of having it firmly focused, it has regularly been given a halo of reverberation at a slight distance. Nonetheless, no one could miss its glorious bloom.

The highlights discs generally offer between 65 and 70 minutes of music, with none lasting under an hour (and several are the only available selections of excerpts from that particular opera), but the discs of separate arias and ensembles are much less generous at around 50 minutes. They are partly drawn from complete sets of various kinds – including Daniel Barenboim's Paris recordings of Berlioz's *Requiem, Damnation of Faust* and *Béatrice et Bénédict* – and partly from two 'Gala' recordings, made live, the 1984 recital from Los Angeles conducted by Giulini and Domingo's visit to the Met. in New York in 1988, conducted by James Levine with Kathleen Battle as his partner in duets. It is a charming rarity to have Domingo here in a baritone role, singing Don Giovanni to Battle's Zerlina in *La ci darem la mano*. That comes from the third of the discs of separate items, devoted to the Italian repertory and ranging from Mozart to Mascagni and Puccini by way of Donizetti (items from *Lucia* and *L'elisir d'amore*) and Verdi. All these CDs and tape equivalents are available separately, and it is sensible to pick and choose according to taste. Overall this represents a formidable achievement.

Operatic scenes from: OFFENBACH: *Contes d'Hoffmann* (with Joan Sutherland, Huguette Tourangeau). BIZET: *Carmen* (with Tatiana Troyanos, Kiri Te Kanawa). WAGNER: *Lohengrin* (with Eva Randová, Jessye Norman, Hans Sotin).
(M) *** Decca 421 890-2 [id.].

Here are extended excerpts from three of Domingo's most rewarding Decca opera sets, 21 minutes and five arias from his first, most successful *Tales of Hoffmann*, nearly half an hour from *Carmen*, and two key arias from his superb *Lohengrin* with Solti – the line and colour of *In fernem Land* make this performance truly memorable. But this is essentially for Domingo admirers who prefer recitals to complete sets, or even highlights.

'*Great voice*': Excerpts from: BIZET: *Carmen* (with Teresa Berganza). PUCCINI: *Manon Lescaut* (with Montserrat Caballé); *Fanciulla del West*. VERDI: *La Traviata* (with Ileana Cotrubas); *Macbeth*. WAGNER: *Tannhäuser*. Songs: CATARI: *Core 'ngrato*. LARA: *Granada*. LEONCAVALLO: *Mattinata*. FREIRE: *Ay, ay, ay*. CURTIS: *Non ti scordar di me*.
(B) **(*) DG 431 104-2 [id.].

Certainly the collection assembled for DG's '*Grosse Stimmen*' series shows Domingo in his best light. Opening with the *Flower song* from *Carmen* (noble in line rather than melting), it includes also the vibrant 'live' *Manon Lescaut* duet which is also featured on the companion Caballé recital (only this time, curiously, the applause is cut off the end). Stylish in Verdi and warmly moving in Walther's *Prize song* from *Die Meistersinger*, with resonant choral backing, the disc ends with a few top Italian pops, over-recorded but certainly making an impact. But the selection (59 minutes) is not as generous as other CDs in this series, and as usual there is no documentation other than titles. At bargain price, however, many will be tempted.

'*Domingo sings Caruso*': Arias from LEONCAVALLO: *La Bohème; Pagliacci.* DONIZETTI: *L'Elisir d'amore.* MASSENET: *Manon; Le Cid.* CILEA: *L'arlesiana.* FLOTOW: *Martha.* PUCCINI: *La Fanciulla del West; La Bohème.* VERDI: *Rigoletto; Aida.* MEYERBEER: *L'Africana.* GOUNOD: *Faust.* HALÉVY: *La juive.* MASCAGNI: *Cavalleria rusticana.*
(M) **(*) BMG/RCA 09026 61356-2 [id.].

This rather perversely named reissue is based on the contents of an LP originally called, more pertinently, 'The art of Plácido Domingo', recorded in 1971 with the LSO under Santi. Four more items have been added, but all are from the same period and, like the others, show the strong, resonant voice and the scope of Domingo's artistry at that stage in his career. With clear, direct sound, the heroic stage presence comes over well, the ringing tone able to impress in a lyrical phrase, even though more fining-down of the tone and a willingness to sing really softly more often would enhance the listener's pleasure. But in the theatre this is obviously a voice to thrill, and the engineers have captured it directly and realistically, from the sobbing verismo of *Pagliacci* to the crisp aristocracy in *Rigoletto*. The selection is an interesting one – the opening aria from Leoncavallo's *Bohème* suggests that this opera is worth reviving.

Plácido Domingo, José Carreras (tenors), Montserrat Caballé (soprano)

'*Barcelona Olympic Games ceremony*' (with Juan Pons, Teresa Berganza, Giacomo Aragall, Barcelona SO, Garcia Navarro): *Barcelona Games medley* (arr. Parera). Arias from: MASSENET: *Le Cid.* DONIZETTI: *La Favorita* (Domingo). BELLINI: *Norma.* MASSENET: *Hérodiade* (Caballé). VERDI: *Macbeth; Un ballo in maschera* (Pons). LEONCAVALLO: *Pagliacci.* VERDI: *Otello* (Carreras). ROSSINI: *L'Italiana in Algeri.* THOMAS: *Mignon* (Berganza). PONCHIELLI: *La Gioconda* (Aragall). OFFENBACH: *Contes d'Hoffmann: Barcarolle* (Caballé & Berganza).
**(*) BMG/RCA Dig. 09026 61204-2 [61204-2; *61204-4*].

This CD was, very sensibly, recorded in the studio six months before the Barcelona Olympics opening ceremony. The 13-minute 51-second pot-pourri which opens it, cleverly arranged by Tony Parera, uses snippets from a dozen favourite operas, ingeniously assembled into what used to be called a 'musical switch'. The singers enter into the spirit of the thing, and the result is a teeming cascade of memorable ideas. Then each of the six singers has a chance to shine in at least one complete aria. Not surprisingly, Domingo steals the show. Caballé's *Casta diva* is finely conceived but squally on top. Berganza is good in Rossini but at her most charming in the tuneful *Connais-tu le pays?* from *Mignon*. Carreras is better in Leoncavallo than in Verdi's *Otello*, but at this stage in his career perhaps not really suited to either role; but Caballé and Berganza join together for a seductive *Barcarolle*, which is an undoubted highlight. Most of the other items are less distinctive.

Emma Eames (soprano)

Arias from: GOUNOD: *Faust; Roméo et Juliette.* PUCCINI: *Tosca.* MOZART: *Don Giovanni; Die Zauberflöte* (with Emilio De Gogorza). *Le nozze di Figaro* (with Marcella Sembrich). VERDI: *Otello.* BIZET: *Carmen.* MASCAGNI: *Cavalleria rusticana.* MASSENET: *Chérubin.* DELIBES: *Lakmé.* WAGNER: *Lohengrin.* MESSAGER: *Véronique.* Songs by BOHM, BACH/GOUNOD, HAHN, BEACH, TOSTI, MASSENET, SCHUBERT, ARNOLD, EMMETT, HOLLMAN, FAURÉ (with de Gogorza), PARKER, NEVIN, KOECHLIN, HENSCHEL, BEMBERG (with remarks by Emma Eames).
(M) (***) Romophone mono 81001-2 (2) [id.].

Most of these recordings of the American soprano, Emma Eames, date from 1905 and 1906, the earlier ones involving piano accompaniment, even in operatic items. The voice in these transfers is variably caught, sometimes rather faint, behind heavy surface hiss. Yet the flexibility of the voice, as well as its purity and projection, come out splendidly in such items as the two versions of the *Jewel song* from *Faust* and duplicate versions of the *Ave Maria* from Verdi's *Otello*, as well as a rapt account of Tosca's *Vissi d'arte*. Some of the most attractive excerpts are the duets with the superb baritone, Emilio de Gogorza.

Dietrich Fischer-Dieskau (baritone)

'Great voice': Arias from: MOZART: *Die Zauberflöte; Don Giovanni; Le nozze di Figaro.* WAGNER: *Die Meistersinger.* Lieder: MAHLER: *Lieder eines fahrenden Gesellen: Ging heut' morgen übers Feld. Ich atmet' einen linden Duft.* BEETHOVEN: *Zärtliche Liebe; Es war einmal ein König.* BRAHMS: *Heimweh II.* SCHUBERT: *Die schöne Müllerin: Das Wandern. Winterreise: Der Lindenbaum. Der Musensohn.* SCHUMANN: *Dichterliebe, Op. 48: Im wunderschönen Monat Mai. Liederkreis, Op. 39: Mondnacht.* WOLF: *Der Feuerreiter.* R. STRAUSS: *Heimliche Aufforderung.*
(B) *** DG 431 105-2 [id.].

This is one of the most enjoyable and rewarding of DG's '*Grosse Stimmen*' series, although the lack of translations is particularly serious in the case of the Lieder. Fischer-Dieskau is always a joy in Mozart and particularly so as Papageno in *Die Zauberflöte*, a role he never assumed on stage. As Hans Sachs in *Meistersinger* he is wonderfully warm in the *Fliedermonolog* and, after the second, more spectacular choral excerpt from Wagner's opera (*Ehrt eure deutschen Meister*), the Mahler songs which follow make a tender contrast. Indeed Fischer-Dieskau's Lieder singing can stand any amount of aural scrutiny and the rest of the programme is delightfully chosen, especially the lovely Schumann songs, followed by the lively Wolf *Der Feuerreiter*. The recordings range over three decades of his recording career from 1958 (an engaging account of Beethoven's *Es war einmal ein König*) to 1984 and the final song, Richard Strauss's *Heimliche Aufforderung*, which has much subtlety of word-colouring.

Mirella Freni (soprano)

'Verismo arias' (with O del Teatro La Fenice, Robert Abbado): from: CILEA: *L'Arlesiana; Adriana Lecouvreur.* GIORDANO: *Andrea Chénier.* CATALANI: *La Wally; Loreley.* ALFANO: *Risurrezione.* MASCAGNI: *Cavalleria Rusticana; Lodoletta; Iris.* ZANDONAI: *Francesca da Rimini.* PUCCINI: *Gianni Schicchi.*
(M) ** Decca Dig. 433 316-2 [id.].

An interesting and enterprising programme, recorded in 1990. But Freni should have tackled this very demanding programme earlier in her long career. This is singing which would readily pass muster in the opera house and which is potentially beautiful and always characterful. But even with the very experienced Christopher Raeburn producing the sessions, the voice is not flattered by the microphones and, too often under stress, the singing is strained and approaching squalliness. Otherwise the recording is first class, and the accompaniments are very sympathetic.

Mirella Freni and Renata Scotto (sopranos)

Duets and Arias (with Nat. PO, Leone Magiera): MERCADANTE: *Le due illustri rivali: Leggo già nel vostro cor.* BELLINI: *Bianca e Fernando: Ove son? che m'avvene? Sorgi, o padre. Norma: Dormono entrambi . . . Mira o Norma . . . Sì, fino all'ore.* MOZART: *Le nozze di Figaro: Cosa mi narri? . . . Sull'aria.* ROSSINI: *Guglielmo Tell: S'allontanano alfine! . . . Selva opaca, deserta brughiera* (cond. Riccardo Chailly).
(M) **(*) Decca 436 302-2 [id.].

Although it does not lack charm, the Mozart duet here will win no awards for style, but otherwise this is a fascinating (1978) celebration of the vocal skill of two singers who might have been thought too alike to make good duettists – though her vibrato readily identifies Scotto. By her latterday standards she is in excellent voice, with the top more perfectly under control if occasionally squally – the more noticeable by the side of Freni's smooth legato. This account of the big *Norma* scene, including *Mira, o Norma*, is more relaxed and delicate than the one to which Scotto contributed in the complete Sony/CBS set of the opera. The other Bellini item is also most welcome, with its dreamy melody in compound time, and so is the even rarer

Mercadante duet with its traditional chain of thirds. Matilde's lovely Act II soliloquy from *William Tell*, meltingly sung by Freni, is added as a bonus for the CD issue. Excellent sound and fairly good documentation.

Amelita Galli-Curci (soprano)

'*Prima voce*': Arias from: AUBER: *Manon Lescaut*. BELLINI: *I Puritani; La Sonnambula*. DONIZETTI: *Don Pasquale; Linda di Chamounix; Lucia di Lammermoor*. GOUNOD: *Roméo et Juliette*. MEYERBEER: *Dinorah*. ROSSINI: *Il Barbiere di Siviglia*. THOMAS: *Mignon*. VERDI: *Rigoletto; La Traviata*.
(M) (***) Nimbus mono NI 7806 [id.].

'Like a nightingale half-asleep,' said Philip Hope-Wallace in a memorable description of Galli-Curci's voice, but this vivid Nimbus transfer makes it much more like a nightingale very wide-awake. More than in most of these transfers made via an acoustic horn gramophone, the resonance of the horn itself can be detected, and the results are full and forward. Galli-Curci's perfection in these pre-electric recordings, made between 1917 and 1924, is a thing of wonder, almost too accurate for comfort, but tenderness is there too, as in the Act II duet from *La Traviata* (with Giuseppe de Luca) and the *Addio del passato*, complete with introductory recitative, but with only a single stanza. Yet brilliant coloratura is what lies at the root of Galli-Curci's magic, and that comes in abundance.

Miriam Gauci (soprano)

'*Soprano arias from Italian operas*' (with Brussels R. & TV O, Alexander Rahbari) from: VERDI: *Don Carlo; Otello; Forza del destino*. CATALANI: *La Wally*. PUCCINI: *Manon Lescaut; Tosca; Suor Angelica; Gianni Schicchi; Turandot; Le Villi; La Bohème*.
(BB) **(*) Naxos Dig. 8.550606 [id.].

Miriam Gauci is a fresh young soprano from Malta who has already recorded *Madama Butterfly* for Naxos. Here she sings a baker's dozen of popular lyrical and dramatic arias, mostly by Puccini, and shows her warmth and purity of line and an agreeable freshness. Individual characterization of the different characters is as yet unformed but, whether in the *Willow song* and *Ave Maria* from Verdi's *Otello* or Liù's arias from *Turandot*, this singing gives genuine pleasure. She is sympathetically if not vibrantly accompanied and the Naxos recording is well balanced and kind to the voice. A promising début and, with 69 minutes of music, quite a bargain.

Beniamino Gigli (tenor)

Opera arias from: GOUNOD: *Faust*. BIZET: *Carmen; Les Pêcheurs de perles*. MASSENET: *Manon*. HANDEL: *Serse*. DONIZETTI: *Lucia di Lammermoor; L'Elisir d'amore*. VERDI: *Rigoletto; Aida*. LEONCAVALLO: *I Pagliacci*. MASCAGNI: *Cavalleria Rusticana*. PUCCINI: *La Bohème; Tosca*. GIORDANO: *Andrea Chénier*. PIETRI: *Maristella*.
⊛ (M) (***) EMI mono CDH7 61051-2 [id.].

No Italian tenor has sung with more honeyed beauty than Beniamino Gigli. His status in the inter-war period as a singing superstar at a time when the media were less keenly organized is vividly reflected in this Références collection of eighteen items, the cream of his recordings made between 1927 and 1937. It is specially welcome to have two historic ensemble recordings, made in New York in 1927 and originally coupled on a short-playing 78 r.p.m. disc – the *Quartet* from *Rigoletto* and the *Sextet* from *Lucia di Lammermoor*. In an astonishing line-up Gigli is joined by Galli-Curci, Pinza, De Luca and Louise Homer. Excellent transfers.

'*Prima voce*': Volume 1 (1918–24): Arias from: BOITO: *Mefistofele*. CATALANI: *Loreley*. DONIZETTI: *La Favorita*. FLOTOW: *Martha*. GIORDANO: *Andrea Chénier*. GOUNOD: *Faust*. LALO: *Le roi d'Ys*. LEONCAVALLO: *Pagliacci*. MASCAGNI: *Iris*. MEYERBEER: *L'Africana*. PONCHIELLI: *La Gioconda*. PUCCINI: *Tosca*. Songs.
(M) (***) Nimbus mono NI 7807 [id.].

Gigli's career went on so long, right through the electrical 78-r.p.m. era, that his pre-electric recordings have tended to get forgotten. This collection of 22 items recorded between 1918 and 1924 shows the voice at its most honeyed, even lighter and more lyrical than it became later, with the singer indulging in fewer of the mannerisms that came to decorate his ever-mellifluous singing. In aria after aria he spins a flawless legato line. Few tenor voices have ever matched Gigli's in rounded, golden beauty, and the Nimbus transfers capture its bloom in a way that makes one forget pre-electric limitations. In the one item sung in French, by Lalo, he sounds less at home, a little too heavy; but the ease of manner in even the most taxing arias elsewhere is remarkable, and such a number as the *Serenade* from Mascagni's *Iris* is irresistible in its sparkle, as are the Neapolitan songs, notably the galloping *Povero Pulcinella* by Buzzi-Peccia. One oddity is a tenor arrangement of Saint-Saëns's *The Swan*.

'Prima voce': Volume 2 (1925–40). Arias from: DONIZETTI: *L'elisir d'amore; Lucia di Lammermoor*. PUCCINI: *Manon Lescaut; La Bohème; Tosca*. VERDI: *La forza del destino; La Traviata; Rigoletto*. THOMAS: *Mignon*. BIZET: *I pescatori di perle*. PONCHIELLI: *La Gioconda*. MASSENET: *Manon*. GOUNOD: *Faust*. RIMSKY-KORSAKOV: *Sadko*. GLUCK: *Paride ed Elena*. CILEA: *L'Arlesiana*. CACCINI: Song: *Amarilli*.
(M) (***) Nimbus mono NI 7817 [id.].

Issued to celebrate the Gigli centenary in 1990, the Nimbus selection concentrates on recordings he made in the very early years of electrical recording up to 1931, when his voice was at its very peak, the most golden instrument, ideally suited to recording. The items are very well chosen and are by no means the obvious choices, though it is good to have such favourites as the *Pearlfishers duet* with de Luca and the 1931 version of Rodolfo's *Che gelida manina*. The Nimbus transfers are at their best, with relatively little reverberation.

Arias and excerpts from: GIORDANO: *Andrea Chénier*. DONIZETTI: *La Favorita; L'elisir d'amore; Lucia di Lammermoor*. GOUNOD: *Faust; Roméo et Juliette*. LALO: *Le roi d'Ys*. PUCCINI: *Tosca*. PONCHIELLI: *La Gioconda*. BIZET: *Les pêcheurs de perles*. VERDI: *Attila; I Lombardi*. GOMES: *Lo schiavo; Il Guarany*.
(M) (***) BMG/RCA mono GD 87811 [7811-2-RG].

This RCA compilation with its bright, forward CD transfers of the original 78s underlines the astonishing consistency of Gigli's golden tenor over the whole of his long recording career, whether in heroic outbursts or in gentle *bel canto*. The selection ranges wide, from pre-electrics like Chénier's big aria, always a favourite with him, to ten items from the early electric period – 1925–30 – and with two little songs by Gomes from 1951 as a postscript. Specially notable from these American recordings are the duets and trios with his great contemporaries at the Met. in New York, Ezio Pinza, Titta Ruffo and Elisabeth Rethberg. The voice is consistently close and immediate, with an astonishing sense of presence, yet with none of the histrionic harshness one can expect from other tenors.

Great Singers

'Prima voce': Great singers 1909–38 (Luisa Tetrazzini; Enrico Caruso; Ernestine Schumann-Heink; John McCormack; Amelita Galli-Curci; Riccardo Stracciari; Rosa Ponselle; Giacomo Lauri-Volpi; Eva Turner; Lawrence Tibbett; Conchita Supervia; Beniamino Gigli; Marian Anderson; Tito Schipa; Claudia Muzio; Richard Tauber): Arias from: BELLINI: *La Sonnambula; I Puritani; Norma*. LEONCAVALLO: *Pagliacci*. MOZART: *Don Giovanni; Die Zauberflöte*. ROSSINI: *Il Barbiere di Siviglia*. PUCCINI: *Turandot*. VERDI: *Un ballo in maschera*. BIZET: *Carmen*. PUCCINI: *La Bohème*. SAINT-SAËNS: *Samson et Dalila*. MASCAGNI: *L'amico Fritz*. Song: REFICE: *Ombra di Nube*.
(M) (***) Nimbus mono NI 7801 [id.].

This was the first of Nimbus's series of archive recordings, taking a radical new view of the problem of transferring ancient 78-r.p.m. vocal recordings to CD. The best possible copies of shellac originals have been played on an acoustic machine with an enormous horn, one of the hand-made Rolls-Royces among non-electric gramophones of the 1930s, with thorn needles reducing still further the need to filter the sound electronically. The results have been recorded in a small hall, and the sound reproduced removes any feeling of boxy closeness. Those who have resisted the bottled or tinny sound of many historic recordings will find the Nimbus transfers more friendly and sympathetic, even if technically there is an inevitable loss of recorded information at both ends of the spectrum because of the absolute limitations of the possible frequency range on this kind of reproducer.

This compilation makes a good starting point, even if the method still does not provide the ideal answer. The Tetrazzini item with which the selection opens, *Ah non giunge* from Bellini's *La Sonnambula*, is one of the supreme demonstrations of coloratura on record, and the programme goes on to a magnificent Caruso of 1910 and an unforgettable performance of the coloratura drinking-song from Donizetti's *Lucrezia Borgia* by the most formidable of contraltos, Ernestine Schumann-Heink.

Then follows John McCormack's famous account of *Il mio tesoro* from Mozart's *Don Giovanni*, with the central passage-work amazingly done in a single breath. Other vintage items include Galli-Curci's dazzling account of *Son vergin vezzosa* from Bellini's *I Puritani*, Eva Turner in her incomparable 1928 account of Turandot's aria, Gigli amiably golden-toned in *Che gelida manina* from *La Bohème*, and a delectable performance of the *Cherry duet* from Mascagni's *L'amico Fritz* by Tito Schipa and Mafalda Favero, riches indeed!

Thomas Harper (tenor)

'Famous tenor arias' (with Slovak R. Ch. & R. O (Bratislava), Michael Halász) from: LEONCAVALLO: *Pagliacci*. VERDI: *Un ballo in maschera; Aida; Don Carlos; Rigoletto; Macbeth; Il Trovatore*. PUCCINI: *Tosca; La Fanciulla del West; La Bohème; Manon Lescaut; Turandot*. GIORDANO: *Andrea Chénier*. PONCHIELLI: *La Gioconda*.
(BB) **(*) Naxos Dig. 8.550497 [id.].

The American, Thomas Harper, born in Oklahoma is revealed in his début recital for Naxos as a fine, intelligent, lyric tenor singing with consistent vocal bloom. He is especially sympathetic in Puccini, not going over the top, but with the vocal timbre often quite heady (*Che gelida manina* has a splendid climax) while the purple patches from *Tosca* and *Turandot* will disappoint no one. In Verdi the line is impressively moulded (witness *Celeste Aida*), but sometimes lacking that last degree of temperament which can curdle the blood. *Come, un bel dì* from Andrea Chénier opens most sympathetically, and is convincingly built to a thrilling climax, the voice resonant and full and Michael Halász accompanies impressively. There is plenty of promise here and the excellent Naxos recording certainly provides a good showcase.

Frieda Hempel (soprano)

Arias from: VERDI: *Rigoletto; La traviata; Ernani; Un ballo in maschera*. DONIZETTI: *Lucia di Lammermoor*. ROSSINI: *Il barbiere di Siviglia*. MOZART: *Le nozze di Figaro; Die Zauberflöte*. MEYERBEER: *Les Huguenots; Robert le Diable*. GOUNOD: *Mireille*. OFFENBACH: *Les contes d'Hoffmann*. LORTZING: *Der Wildschütz*. Song: MANGOLD: *Zweigesang*.
(M) (***) Nimbus mono NI 7849; NC 7849 [id.].

This is one of the very finest of all the Nimbus 'Prima voce' series. The 78-r.p.m. sources are immaculate, background noise is steady and no problem. The recordings are nearly all early, mostly made between 1910 and 1913, the rest in the following four years, except for the final song which was much later (1935). It is an extraordinary voice, with an almost unbelievably free upper tessitura. The divisions in the Adam *Variations* (on 'Twinkle, twinkle little star') make you want to laugh, they are so outrageous, taking off into the vocal stratosphere like a series of shooting stars. *Caro nome*, too, which opens the programme arrestingly, is wonderfully free and open, and the final cadence is taken up. Even more than the *Lucia* Mad scene, Rossini's *Una voce poco fa*, with its added decorations, shows how a soprano voice can sparkle when the intonation is spot-on. Both are sung in German.

Frieda Hempel's Mozart is less stylish; the famous *Der Hölle Rache* almost runs away before the end. But the ravishing vocal line in *Ah fors' è lui*, with a deliberate tenuto on the cadence, is followed by a wonderfully frivolous cabaletta. The recording quality is astonishingly consistent and the vocal richness comes across with uncanny realism, while the decorations in Strauss's *Wine, women and song* make one's hair stand on end. Not to be missed.

Barbara Hendricks (soprano)

Operetta arias (with Philh. O, Lawrence Foster): LEHÁR: *Giuditta: Meine Lippen sie küssen so heiss. Die lustige Witwe: Vilja. Friederike: Warum hast du mich wach geküsst?*. STOLZ: *Der Favorite: Du sollst der Kaiser meiner Seele sein*. ZELLER: *Der Vogelhändler: Schenkt man sich Rosen in Tyrol*. J. STRAUSS JR: *Die Fledermaus: Klänge der Heimat*. MESSAGER: *Madame Chrysanthème: Le jour sous le soleil béni. L'amour masqué: J'ai deux amants*. OFFENBACH: *La vie parisienne: Autrefois plus d'un amant. Le voyage dans la lune: Monde charmant que l'on ignore*. SULLIVAN: *The Pirates of Penzance: Poor wand'ring one. The Mikado: The sun whose rays are all ablaze*. ROMBERG: *New Moon: One kiss; Lover come back to me*. HERBERT: *Naughty Marietta: Ah! sweet mystery of life; Italian street song: Ah! my heart is back in Napoli.*
**(*) EMI Dig. CDC7 54626-2 [id.].

This is a valuable collection, for so many operettas are remembered by a single number, and some of them are here. The selection is generous (71 minutes), and the documentation is adequate, although, extraordinarily, the lyrics are offered in French and German only, except where the original language is English, and then the German versions are omitted! But there are musical snags, too. Although Barbara Hendricks makes some gloriously rich sounds, the recording, made at EMI's Studio No. 1 at Abbey Road, is given too much resonance, and the brightness, so essential in this repertory, is blunted. The style of the singing, too, is essentially languorous, which especially suits the lovely *Le jour sous le soleil béni*.

Messager's *Madame Chrysanthème* is the French equivalent of Puccini's *Madama Butterfly*, and this romantic aria ravishingly expresses the Japanese heroine's heartbreak when her French lieutenant returns to his ship. But the earlier numbers by Lehár, Stolz and Zeller fail to effervesce, although again there is an exception with *Warum hast du mich wach geküsst?* ('Why have you kissed my heart awake?') from *Friederike*, where Hendricks' warmly sensuous, melancholy style is appropriate in a lament from another abandoned lover.

But Offenbach's *La vie parisienne* needs more of an uninhibited feeling of champagne corks popping and, although the waltz song for *Le voyage dans la lune* has charm, Lawrence Foster's rubato here (as elsewhere) is unconvincingly mannered, and one feels that he was not the right choice of accompanist for this programme. More surprisingly, the coloratura in *Poor wand'ring one* from *The Pirates of Penzance* lacks sparkle.

Yum-yum's lyrical aria from *The Mikado* brings rich timbre and an eloquent line, and it is good to hear the Philharmonia Orchestra glowing in the charmingly scored accompaniments, both here and in *I could have danced all night* from *My Fair Lady* (delicious sounds from the woodwind), which has an agreeable lyrical flow. The playing is even more memorable in the comparatively restrained *Lover come back to me*, with its nostalgic orchestral introduction sounding quite gorgeous.

Then at the very close of the recital, after a delectable *Ah! sweet mystery of life* is built to a fine climax, the music-making suddenly sparks into vivacity in the *Italian street song*, from the same Victor Herbert operetta (*Naughty Marietta*) – a delicious performance, complete with chorus, to bring the house down. If only everything had had this kind of exuberance, the recital would have been a winner.

Marilyn Hill Smith (soprano), Peter Morrison (baritone)

'Treasures of operetta' (with Concert O, Barry): ZIER: *Der Schatzmeister; Do re mi fa sol la si*. J. STRAUSS JR: *Casanova: O Queen of my delight*. KÁLMÁN: *Gypsy Princess: Let me dance and let me sing*. STRAUS: *Chocolate Soldier: My hero*. TAUBER: *Old Chelsea: My heart and I*. MESSAGER: *Veronique: Trot here and there*. HERBERT: *Naughty Marietta: Tramp! tramp! tramp! tramp!*. LEHÁR: *The Merry Widow: Love unspoken; I'm off to Chez Maxim. Giuditta: On my lips every kiss is like wine*. ZELLER: *Der Obersteiger: Don't be cross*. MONCKTON: *The Arcadians: Charming weather.*
**(*) Chan. Dig. CHAN 8362 [id.].

One has to make an initial adjustment to a style of performance which is very English, evoking memories of the Palm Court tradition of Anne Ziegler and Webster Booth. Marilyn Hill Smith sings freshly and often very sweetly, and she is genially partnered by the warm, easy-going baritone of Peter Morrison. Moreover, the orchestral accompaniments have plenty of flexibility and lilt, and the resonantly rich recording is exactly right for the music. With almost every number a 'hit', this is very attractive of its kind.

'*Treasures of operetta*' Vol. 2 (with Amb. S., Concert O, Barry): JACOBI: *Sybil: The Colonel of the Crimson Hussars.* POSFORD: *Balalaika: At the Balalaika.* MONCKTON: *The Quaker Girl: A bad boy and a good girl.* MILLOCKER: *Der arme Jonathan: The doleful primadonna.* ZIER: *Der Schatzmeister: O let me hold your tiny little hand. Der Fremdenführer: Military life.* GERMAN: *Merrie England: The yeomen of England.* LEHÁR: *The Merry widow: Vilja. Paganini: Girls were made to love and kiss.* STOLZ/BENATSKY: *White Horse Inn: My song of love.* MESSAGER: *Monsieur Beaucaire: Lightly, lightly.* J. STRAUSS JR: *Casanova: Nuns' chorus.*
**(*) Chan. Dig. CHAN 8561 [id.].

If anything, this is more successful than the first collection, with many novelties among the more familiar items, and the charming duet from *The Quaker Girl* an obvious highlight. Extra support is given by the excellent Ambrosian Singers, and the presentation and recording are both of a high standard.

Marilyn Horne (mezzo-soprano)

Arias from: ROSSINI: *Il barbiere di Siviglia; Semiramide; L'italiana in Algeri; La Cenerentola.* BELLINI: *I Capuleti ed i Montecchi.* DONIZETTI: *Lucrezia Borgia; La figlia del reggimento.* (M) *** Decca 421 891-2 [id.].

Apart from Orsini's vivacious *Il segreto per esser felice* – a winner if ever there was one – which comes from the 1963 complete set of *Lucrezia Borgia*, all these items are drawn from two recitals which Marilyn Horne made for Decca in 1964/65, conducted by her husband, Henry Lewis. It is the Rossini items for which she is rightly famous, but in the excerpt from *La figlia del reggimento* she is in equally striking form and her singing continually delights and astonishes with its remarkable range – virtuosity exploited with red-blooded fervour. Excellent recording, with the voice sounding very fresh.

Italian Opera: 'Favourite Italian opera'

'Favourite Italian opera' (sung by: (i) Amb. S., LSO, Abbado; (ii) Carlo Bergonzi; (iii) Luciano Pavarotti; (iv) Giuseppe Di Stefano (v) Fiorenza Cossotto; (vi) Renata Tebaldi; (vii) Franco Corelli; (viii) St Cecilia Ch. & O, Rome, Serafin; (ix) Mirella Freni; (x) Anita Cerquetti; (xi) Ettore Bastianini; (xii) Giulietta Simionato; (xiii) Bruno Previdi; (xiv) Mario Del Monaco; (xv) Maria Chiara): excerpts from: VERDI: (i) *Nabucco;* (ii) *Aida;* (iii) *Rigoletto.* DONIZETTI: (iv) *L'elisir d'amore;* (v) *La Favorita.* PUCCINI: (vi) *Gianni Schicchi; La Rondine;* (vii) *Tosca;* (viii) *Madama Butterfly;* (ix; iii) *La Bohème;* (iii) *Turandot.* BELLINI: (x) *Norma.* ROSSINI: (xi) *Il barbiere di Siviglia;* (xii) *La Cenerentola.* (xiii) GIORDANO: *Fedora.* LEONCAVALLO: *Pagliacci.* CATALANI: *La Wally.*
(M) ** Decca 421 895-2.

A perfectly good but not distinctive collection, generous in playing time (75 minutes) and offering consistently vivid (if occasionally slightly dated) sound. Highlights include Pavarotti in *La donna è mobile* from *Rigoletto* and *Nessun dorma* from *Turandot* (which ends the recital), and he is joined by Freni for *Sì, mi chiamano Mimì* from *Bohème*. Di Stefano, Tebaldi, Bergonzi and Simionato all make sterling contributions, but other performances, though rousing, are more routine.

Maria Ivogün (soprano)

'*Prima voce*': Arias from: HANDEL: *L'allegro, il penseroso ed il moderato.* DONIZETTI: *Don Pasquale; Lucia di Lammermoor.* ROSSINI: *Il barbiere di Siviglia.* VERDI: *La Traviata.* MEYERBEER: *Les Huguenots.* NICOLAI: *Die lustigen Weiber von Windsor.* J. STRAUSS: *Die Fledermaus;* also Waltzes: *An der schönen blauen Donau, Geschichten aus dem Wienerwald* and *Frühlingsstimmen.* Songs: SCHUBERT: *Horch, horch, die Lerche; Winterreise: Die Post;* KREISLER: *Liebesfreud;* CHOPIN: *Nocturne in E flat, Op. 9/2.* 2 Folksongs arr. Gund: *O du liabs ängeli; Z'Lauterbach hab' i'mein Strumpf velor'n.*

(M) (***) Nimbus mono NI 7832; *NC 7832* [id.].

Maria Ivogün is a less familiar name today than in the 1920s when she took Covent Garden by storm. Hers was a small voice but enchantingly focused; in that, she has much in common with a more familiar recent name, Rita Streich. She sang with both charm and sparkle, and the present Nimbus transfers show just what a delightful artist she was. Whether in Donizetti or Meyerbeer or, indeed, in the Strauss waltzes (*Frühlingsstimmen, G'schichten aus dem Wiener Wald* and the *Blue Danube*) this is singing to give great refreshment. The recordings were for the most part made between 1917 and 1925, and these respond especially well to the Nimbus transferring system, but the folksongs were electrical, and her very last records, made in 1932.

Sena Jurinac (soprano)

Opera arias from: MOZART: *Così fan tutte; Idomeneo.* SMETANA: *The Bartered Bride; The Kiss.* TCHAIKOVSKY: *Joan of Arc; Queen of Spades.* R. STRAUSS: *Four Last Songs (Vier letzte Lieder).*
(M) (***) EMI mono CDH7 63199-2 [id.].

This EMI Références issue, very well transferred, celebrates a magical, under-recorded singer. It brings together all of Jurinac's recordings for EMI outside the complete operas, and adds a live radio recording from Sweden – with Fritz Busch conducting the Stockholm Philharmonic Orchestra – of Strauss's *Four Last songs*, most beautifully done, if with rather generalized expression. Busch was also the conductor for the Glyndebourne recordings of excerpts from *Così fan tutte* and *Idomeneo.*

London Symphony Chorus, LSO, Richard Hickox

Opera choruses: BIZET: *Carmen: Toreador chorus.* VERDI: *Il Trovatore: Anvil chorus. Nabucco: Gli arredi festivi; Va pensiero. Macbeth: Che faceste?. Aida: Grand march.* GOUNOD: *Faust: Soldiers' chorus.* BORODIN: *Prince Igor: Polovtsian dances.*
(B) *** Pickwick Dig. PCD 908; *CIMPC 908.*

Most collections of opera choruses are taken from sets, but this is a freshly minted digital collection of favourites, sung with fine fervour and discipline. The opening *Toreador chorus* from *Carmen* is zestfully infectious and the *Soldiers' chorus* from *Faust* equally buoyant. The noble line of Verdi's *Va pensiero* is beautifully shaped by Hickox, with the balance between voices and orchestra particularly good. In *Gli arredi festivi* from *Nabucco* and the famous Triumphal scene from *Aida* the orchestral brass sound resonantly sonorous, even if the fanfare trumpets could have been more widely separated in the latter piece. The concert ends with Borodin's *Polovtsian dances* most excitingly done. The recording, made at the EMI Abbey Road studio, has the atmosphere of an idealized opera house, and the result is in the demonstration bracket, with a projection and presence fully worthy of this polished but uninhibited singing.

Giovanni Martinelli (tenor)

'Prima voce': Arias from: GIORDANO: *Andrea Chénier; Fedora.* LEONCAVALLO: *Pagliacci.* MASCAGNI: *Cavalleria Rusticana; Iris.* TCHAIKOVSKY: *Eugene Onegin.* VERDI: *Aida; Ernani; La forza del destino; La Traviata.*
(M) (***) Nimbus mono NI 7804 [id.].

This collection of 17 fine examples of Martinelli's very distinctive and characterful singing covers his vintage period from 1915 to 1928, with one 1927 recording from Verdi's *La forza del destino* so clear that you can hear a dog barking outside the studio. The other two items from *Forza* are just as memorable, with Martinelli joined by Giuseppe de Luca in the Act IV duet, and by Rosa Ponselle and the bass, Ezio Pinza, for the final duet, with the voices astonishingly vivid and immediate.

'Prima voce, Volume 2': Arias from: PUCCINI: *La Bohème; Tosca; Madama Butterfly* (with Frances Alda). PONCHIELLI: *La Gioconda.* VERDI: *Aida; Un ballo in maschera; Rigoletto; Don Carlos; Il Trovatore.* LEONCAVALLO: *Pagliacci.* MEYERBEER: *L'Africana.* BIZET: *Carmen.* ROSSINI: *Guillaume Tell.* MASSENET: *Werther.*
(M) (***) Nimbus mono NI 7826 [id.].

Martinelli's second collection is hardly less distinctive than the first, and admirers of this great tenor should not be disappointed with the transfers, which are well up to the convincingly natural standard now being achieved by the Nimbus process.

John McCormack (tenor)

'Prima voce': Arias and excerpts from: DONIZETTI: Lucia di Lammermoor; L'elisir d'amore; La figlia del reggimento. VERDI: La Traviata; Rigoletto. PUCCINI: La Bohème. BIZET: Carmen; I pescatori di perle. DELIBES: Lakmé. GOUNOD: Faust. PONCHIELLI: La gioconda. BOITO: Mefistofele. MASSENET: Manon. MOZART: Don Giovanni. WAGNER: Die Meistersinger. HERBERT: Natomah. HANDEL: Semele; Atalanta.
(M) (***) Nimbus mono NI 7820 [id.].

With the operas represented ranging from Handel's Atalanta and Semele to Natomah, by Victor Herbert, the heady beauty of McCormack's voice, his ease of production and perfect control are amply illustrated in these 21 items. His now legendary 1916 account of Il mio tesoro from Don Giovanni, with its astonishing breath control, is an essential item; but there are many others less celebrated which help to explain his special niche, even in a generation that included Caruso and Schipa. Characteristic Nimbus transfers.

Lauritz Melchior (tenor)

'Prima voce': Arias from: WAGNER: Siegfried; Tannhäuser; Tristan und Isolde; Die Walküre; Die Meistersinger; Götterdämmerung. LEONCAVALLO: Pagliacci. MEYERBEER: L'Africana. VERDI: Otello.
(M) (***) Nimbus mono NI 7816 [id.].

The Nimbus disc of Melchior, issued to celebrate his centenary in 1990, demonstrates above all the total consistency of the voice between the pre-electric recordings of Siegfried and Tannhäuser, made for Polydor in 1924, and the Meistersinger and Götterdämmerung extracts, recorded in 1939. Of those, the Siegfried–Brünnhilde duet from the Prologue of Götterdämmerung is particularly valuable. It is fascinating too to hear the four recordings that Melchior made with Barbirolli and the LSO in 1930–31: arias by Verdi, Leoncavallo and Meyerbeer translated into German. As a character, Otello is made to sound far more prickly. Characteristic Nimbus transfers.

Mezzos

Mezzos: 'Ten Top Mezzos' ((i) Cecilia Bartoli; (ii) Marilyn Horne; (iii) Frederica Von Stade; (iv) Agnes Baltsa; (v) Regina Resnik; (vi) Janet Baker; (vii) Christa Ludwig; (viii) Fiorenza Cossotto; (ix) Grace Bumbry; (x) Teresa Berganza): Arias from: ROSSINI: (i) Il Barbiere di Siviglia; (ii) La Cenerentola. MOZART: (iii) Nozze di Figaro. (iv) Idomeneo. SAINT-SAËNS: (v) Samson et Dalila. PURCELL: (vi) Dido and Aeneas. WAGNER: (vii) Götterdämmerung. DONIZETTI: (viii) La Favorita. VERDI: (ix) Don Carlo. GLUCK: (x) Paride ed Elena.
(M) *** Decca Dig./Analogue 436 462-2 [id.].

Not surprisingly, Decca open this well-ordered recital with their current top star who scintillatingly shows her paces in Rosina's Una voce poco fa. Then Frederica von Stade follows with an equally winning Voi che sapete, extracted from Solti's Figaro. Other highlights include Dame Janet's justly famous and very touching Dido's lament, and Christa Ludwig's hardly less moving account of Waltraute's narration from Götterdämmerung, with glorious brass sounds from the VPO and Solti making his presence felt – just as he does in Le nozze di Figaro. The final two items bring, first, a ravishing stream of pure mezzo tone from Teresa Berganza in the lovely O del mio dolce ardor from Gluck's Paride ed Elena, then the vibrant Marilyn Horne in top sparkling form in her famous version of Non più mesta from La Cenerentola. Splendidly vivid recording throughout, although the microphones are not entirely kind to Fiorenza Cossotto in the excerpt from La Favorita (which, incidentally, opens with some gorgeous horn playing).

Claudia Muzio (soprano)

Arias from: BELLINI: *La Sonnambula; Norma.* VERDI: *Il Trovatore; La Forza del destino.* BOITO: *Mefistofele.* MASCAGNI: *Cavalleria Rusticana.* PUCCINI: *La Bohème; Tosca.* CILEA: *L'Arlesiana; Adriana Lecouvreur.* GIORDANO: *Andrea Chénier. Songs.*
Withdrawn: (M) (***) EMI mono CDH7 69790-2.

This is a superb celebration of one of the greatest Italian sopranos of the century, one who died tragically young and whose recording career failed to encompass the very period when she was, by all accounts, at her very greatest. All twenty items on this Références CD come from her last years, 1934 and 1935 (she died of a heart complaint in 1936). Already her advancing illness can be detected in the limitation she set herself on lyrical flights in the upper register. *Casta diva* here would have expanded more generously a few years earlier; but, once that is said, every single item brings magical communication, highly individual in expression and timbre, with the voice shaded and varied in tone and dynamic so that one is mesmerized by phrase after phrase.

There are few accounts of Mimi's arias from *La Bohème* to match these – with the close of the *Farewell* wonderfully veiled in tone; while the Cilea, Giordano and Boito items have a depth of expression never surpassed. The beauty of legato line in the Bellini items and the tonal variety in the Verdi arias, conveying tragic intensity, remain models for all time. Keith Hardwick's superb transfers bring the voice to us wonderfully refreshed and clarified, almost as though Muzio were still in our presence.

'Prima voce': Arias from: MASCAGNI: *Cavalleria Rusticana.* VERDI: *La forza del destino; Otello; Il Trovatore; La Traviata.* PUCCINI: *Tosca; La Bohème.* GIORDANO: *Andrea Chénier.* BOITO: *Mefistofele.* CILEA: *Adriana Lecouvreur; L'Arlesiana.* BELLINI: *La Sonnambula.* Songs by BUZZI-PECCIA; PERGOLESI; REGER; DELIBES; REFICE.
(M) (***) Nimbus mono NI 7814 [id.].

This Nimbus collection of recordings by the sadly short-lived Claudia Muzio duplicates much that is contained on the EMI Références CD of her. The main addition here is the Act III duet from *Otello* with Francesco Merli, but some cherishable items are omitted. The Nimbus acoustic transfer process sets the voice more distantly as well as more reverberantly than the EMI, with its distinctive tang less sharply conveyed.

Birgit Nilsson (soprano)

'Great voice': Arias from MOZART: *Don Giovannni.* WEBER: *Oberon.* WAGNER: *Tannhäuser; Tristan und Isolde.* R. STRAUSS: *Salome.* BEETHOVEN: *Ah! Perfido, Op. 65.*
(B) **(*) DG 431 107-2 [id.].

Birgit Nilsson's representation in DG's *'Grosse Stimmen'* series certainly demonstrates the forcefulness of her vocal personality. She is a formidable Donna Anna breathing fire in *Or sai chi l'onore* (though her coloratura in *Non mi dir* is uncomfortably strained) and equally arresting in Rezia's famous *Ozean du Ungeheuer* from Weber's *Oberon.* She can be tender, too, as Elisabeth in *Tannhäuser* but, although the key scene from Strauss's *Salome* (recorded live in 1972) shows her full vocal power, it is – not surprisingly – Isolde's *Liebestod*, taken from the 1966 Bayreuth recording and passionately conducted by Karl Boehm, which shows her at her peak, radiant of tone and completely in control to the last note. Alas, like the other CDs in this series, there is no information provided about either singer or music, except for titles and recording dates. But at bargain price it is otherwise well worth considering.

Opera Arias

'Opera arias' (sung by: (i) Plácido Domingo; (ii) Renata Scotto; (iii) Ileana Cotrubas; (iv) Kiri Te Kanawa) from: DONIZETTI: (i) *L'elisir d'amore.* BELLINI: (ii) *Norma.* VERDI: *Otello;* (iii) *Rigoletto.* PUCCINI: (i; ii) *Madama Butterfly;* (iii); (iv) *La Bohème;* (iv) *Gianni Schicchi; Tosca.* MOZART: (iii) *Nozze di Figaro;* (iv) *Don Giovanni.*
**(*) Sony SBK 46548 [id.].

A generally well-selected 68-minute programme. It opens impressively with Domingo's *Una furtiva lagrima* and, apart from Renata Scotto's *Casta diva* from *Norma*, where the voice sounds unwieldy, all the performances are distinctive. Scotto is much more at home as Madama

Butterfly in her big aria and in the Love duet with Domingo. Ileana Cotrubas provides an attractive *Deh vieni* from *Nozze di Figaro*. Whether in Puccini or Mozart's *Don Giovanni*, Kiri Te Kanawa gives of her creamy best and the sound is very good throughout.

Opera arias: 'Great opera arias'

'Great opera arias' (sung by: (i) Giacomo Aragall; (ii) Kiri Te Kanawa; (iii) José Carreras; (iv) Luciano Pavarotti; (v) Frederica Von Stade; (vi) Leo Nucci; (vii) Susan Dunn; (viii) Joan Sutherland; (ix) Hildegard Behrens; (x) Nicolai Ghiaurov; (xi) Mirella Freni; (xii) Montserrat Caballé; (xiii) Marilyn Horne) from: PUCCINI: (i) *Tosca;* (ii; iii) *Manon Lescaut;* (iv) *La Bohème.* MOZART: (v) *Le nozze di Figaro.* ROSSINI: (vi) *Il Barbiere di Siviglia.* VERDI: (vii) *Ernani;* (viii) *I Masnadieri.* MASSENET: (iv) *Werther.* BEETHOVEN: (ix) *Fidelio.* BOITO: (x; xi) *Mefistofele.* GIORDANO: (xii) *Andrea Chénier.* ROSSINI: (xiii) *La donna del lago.*
(M) **(*) Decca 436 472-2 [id.].

These are all undoubtedly key arias, performances are of a high standard, and the recording is consistently vivid. But as an anthology this does not add up, as do some Decca collections (such as their 'Top Ten' series). The two *Mefistofele* excerpts, and the items from Kiri Te Kanawa, Leo Nucci, Frederica von Stade and Pavarotti, are obviously highlights, though it is disconcerting to have applause suddenly bursting in at the end of the two arias recorded live in New York.

Opera Choruses

'Great opera choruses' from: VERDI: *Nabucco* (Mormon Tabernacle Ch., Rudel); *Macbeth* (Teatro Comunale di Bologna, Chailly); *Aida* (La Scala, Milan, Maazel). BELLINI: *Norma* (WNO Ch., Bonynge). BEETHOVEN: *Fidelio* (Chicago Symphony Ch., Solti). WAGNER: *Lohengrin* (VPO, Solti). BOITO: *Mefistofele: Prologue* (London Op. Ch., Trinity Boys' Ch., Fabritiis).
(M) **(*) Decca 430 742-2; *430 742-4* [id.].

The highlight of this digital collection of choruses is the complete *Prologue* from Chailly's vibrant recording of Boito's *Mefistofele*, where the Devil (Nicolai Ghiaurov at his most commandingly resonant) sets up a wager with heaven, promising to tempt Faust away from his philosophizing, to enjoy more hedonistic pleasures. The many layered texture of choral and brass sounds is splendidly captured by the Decca engineers, and the result is both dramatic and highly atmospheric.

The disc, however, opens with the Mormon Tabernacle Choir, without the benefit of the flattering Tabernacle resonance, giving an eloquent but not very histrionic account of Verdi's *Va pensiero*, which ends with a self-conscious sustaining of the final choral note in a long diminuendo. This ensures that the drama of Chailly's *Patria oppressa* is the more striking, followed by a comparably vividly recorded, but not especially excitingly sung *March scene* from *Aida*.

The Welsh National Opera Chorus then come on stage to demonstrate lustily just how it should be done, in a Bellini purple patch, heralded by some engulfingly spectacular crashes on the tam tam. Solti takes over for a movingly contoured account of the *Prisoners' chorus* from *Fidelio*, then his brilliant Act III *Lohengrin Prelude* really wakes things up and the *Bridal chorus* – again given sophisticated choral sound – makes a telling contrast.

'Famous Opera choruses' (various artists) from: VERDI: *Nabucco; Il Trovatore; Aida; Macbeth.* LEONCAVALLO: *Pagliacci.* PUCCINI: *Madama Butterfly.* GOUNOD: *Faust.* WAGNER: *Tannhäuser.* TCHAIKOVSKY: *Eugene Onegin.* MUSSORGSKY: *Boris Godunov.*
(B) ** Decca 433 601-2; *433 601-4*.

A generally rewarding bargain collection, given characteristically vivid Decca sound. Many favourites are here, with the *Aida* triumphal scene taken from Karajan's spectacular, early, Vienna set. The Waltz scene from *Eugene Onegin* comes from another early set, made in Belgrade, and includes the Introduction to Act II. The scene from *Boris Godunov* is a studio recording, with the Covent Garden Opera Chorus ably conducted by Edward Downes and with Joseph Rouleau as Boris. The inclusion of items (the Wagner and Leoncavallo excerpts) contributed by the perfectly adequate Kingsway Chorus under Camerata is the only curious choice.

Opera: 'Favourite Opera'

'Favourite opera' (with (i) Robert Massard; (ii) Elena Obraztsova; (iii) Nicolai Gedda; (iv) Ernest Blanc; (v) Joan Sutherland; (vi) Roger Soyer and Helen Donath; (vii) Walter Berry; (viii) Plácido Domingo; (ix) Maria Callas; (x) Mirella Freni; (xi) Rome Op. Ch., Santini; (xii) Charles Craig; (xiii) Carlo Del Monte and Victoria De los Angeles; (xiv) La Scala, Milan, Ch., Von Matačić; (xv) Luciano Pavarotti; (xvi) Elisabeth Schwarzkopf and Jeannine Collard; (xvii) Tito Gobbi; (xvii) Paris Op. Ch., Prêtre): Arias, duets and choruses from: (i; ii) BIZET: *Carmen;* (iii; iv) *Les pêcheurs de perles.* MOZART: (v; vi) *Don Giovanni;* (vii) *Die Zauberflöte.* PUCCINI: (viii) *Manon Lescaut;* (ix) *Tosca;* (x; iii) *La Bohème;* (iii) *Turandot.* VERDI: (xi) *Nabucco;* (xii) *Rigoletto;* (xiii) *La Traviata;* (xiv) *Il Trovatore.* (xv) MASCAGNI: *L'amico Fritz.* (xvi) OFFENBACH: *Contes d'Hoffmann.* (ix; xvii) ROSSINI: *Il barbiere di Siviglia.* (xvii) GOUNOD: *Faust.*
(B) ** CfP CD-CFP 4602; *TC-CFP 4602.*

A curiously planned recital, with some operatic plums, let down by some under-par performances. Neither the opening *Toreador song* from *Carmen* nor the famous duet which follows, *Au fond du temple saint* from Bizet's *Pearl fishers,* is a performance to really grab the listener. Of course there are very good things here, both predictable (Joan Sutherland's recording of *Non mi dir* from *Don Giovanni,* Maria Callas's *Vissi d'arte* from *Tosca* and Pavarotti's attractive excerpt from Mascagni's *L'amico Fritz*) and perhaps less obviously so (Charles Craig's freshly stylish *La donna è mobile* from *Rigoletto*); but the recorded sound varies noticeably with the sources, and the closing *Soldiers' chorus* from *Faust* is disappointingly lacking in brilliance.

Operatic Duets: 'Duets from famous operas'

Duets sung by: (i) Nicolai Gedda; (ii) Ernest Blanc; (iii) Jussi Bjoerling and Victoria De los Angeles; (iv) Carlo Bergonzi; (v) Maria Callas; (vi) Mirella Freni; (vii) Eberhard Waechter and Graziella Sciutti; (viii) Tito Gobbi; (ix) Gabriella Tucci; (x) Franco Corelli; (xi) Evelyn Lear and D. Ouzounov; (xii) Antonietta Stella; (i; ii) BIZET: *Les Pêcheurs de perles: Au fond du temple saint.* (iii) PUCCINI: *Madama Butterfly: Bimba dagli occhi.* (iv; v) *Tosca: O dolci mani.* (i; vi) *La Bohème: O soave fanciulla.* (vii) MOZART: *Don Giovanni: Là ci darem la mano.* (v; viii) ROSSINI: *Il barbiere di Siviglia: Dunque io son'.* (ix; x) VERDI: *Il Trovatore: Miserere d'un'alma già vicina.* (xi) MUSSORGSKY: *Boris Godunov: O Tsarevich I beg you.* (x; xii) GIORDANO: *Andrea Chénier: Vicini a te.*
(B) **(*) CfP CD-CFP 9013; *TC-CFP 4498.*

There are not many operas that hold their reputation in the public memory by means of a male duet, but *The pearl fishers* is one, and a sturdy performance of *Au fond du temple saint* makes a suitable centre-point of this collection of purple duos. The CD, however, opens with the genial lyricism of *Là ci darem la mano,* from the 1961 Giulini set of *Don Giovanni* with Eberhard Waechter and Graziella Sciutti singing most winningly. The star quality of the artists is noticeable through most of these extracts. Highlights include this beautifully relaxed *Là ci darem,* the short Rossini item, and the *La Bohème* duet (which seldom fails). There is also a blaze of melodrama from *Andrea Chénier.*

As a programme, the effect of a series of such full-blooded passionate vocal embraces is perhaps a little wearing. But otherwise, with generally lively recording, few will be disappointed. The cassette is smoothly transferred, if without quite the range of the CD. This has been admirably remastered to make the most of the different recording sources – the vocal timbres are particularly smooth and natural, without loss of projection.

Operatic Duets: 'Great love duets'

'Great love duets' (sung by Joan Sutherland, Mirella Freni, Luciano Pavarotti, Renata Tebaldi, Franco Corelli, Margaret Price, Carlo Cossutta): PUCCINI: *Madama Butterfly; La Bohème; Tosca; Manon Lescaut.* VERDI: *Otello; La Traviata.*
(M) *** Decca 421 308-2.

This collection is both generous and well chosen, starting and ending with duets from two of Karajan's outstanding Puccini recordings for Decca, *Madama Butterfly* and *La Bohème,* both with Freni and Pavarotti. The *Bohème* item includes not only the duet *O soave fanciulla* but the two favourite arias which precede it, *Che gelida manina* and *Si, mi chiamano Mimì*. Sutherland is represented by *La Traviata*, Tebaldi by *Manon Lescaut* and Margaret Price by *Otello*, all very well transferred.

Operatic Duets: 'Great operatic duets'

'Great operatic duets' (sung by Joan Sutherland, Luciano Pavarotti, Mirella Freni, Christa Ludwig, Marilyn Horne, Carlo Bergonzi, Dietrich Fischer-Dieskau, Mario Del Monaco, Ettore Bastianini): from DELIBES: *Lakmé*. PUCCINI: *Madama Butterfly*. BELLINI: *Norma*. VERDI: *La Forza del destino; Don Carlo*. OFFENBACH: *Contes d'Hoffmann*.
(M) *** Decca 421 314-2.

Again at mid-price, Decca provides a further excellent collection of duets, ranging rather more widely, from some of the company's finest recordings of the 1960s and '70s. The choice is imaginative and the transfers excellent, to bring out the fine quality of the original analogue sound.

'Great operatic duets' (sung by: (i) Joan Sutherland / Luciano Pavarotti; (ii) Margaret Price / Pavarotti; (iii) Kiri Te Kanawa / Giacomo Aragall; (iv) Te Kanawa / José Carreras; (v) Montserrat Caballé / Agnes Baltsa / Pavarotti / Sherrill Milnes; (vi) Sutherland / Caballé) from VERDI: (i) *La Traviata; Otello*; (ii) *Un ballo in maschera*. PUCCINI: (iii) *Tosca;* (iv) *Manon Lescaut*. PONCHIELLI: (v) *La Gioconda*. BELLINI: (vi) *Norma*.
(M) *** Decca 430 724-2; *430 724-4* [id.].

A splendid collection, with every item full of vibrant star-quality and offered in typically vivid Decca sound. Pavarotti and Sutherland are well matched in *La Traviata*, and later he makes an equally charismatic partnership with Margaret Price in *Teco io sto* from Verdi's *Un ballo in maschera*, while Sutherland duets equally impressively with Caballé in the *Norma* excerpt. Kiri Te Kanawa, in glorious voice, and Carreras pair thrillingly in *Manon Lescaut*, and the 67-minute recital ends with a foretaste of Pavarotti's Love duet from *Otello*, but with Sutherland sounding not quite at her best, in a 1988 version recorded in New York with Bonynge.

Operetta: 'Golden operetta'

'Golden operetta': J. STRAUSS JR: *Die Fledermaus: Mein Herr Marquis* (Hilde Gueden); *Csardas* (Gundula Janowitz). *Eine Nacht in Venedig: Lagunen waltz* (Werner Krenn). *Wiener Blut: Wiener Blut* (Gueden). *Der Zigeunerbaron: O habet acht* (Pilar Lorengar). *Casanova: Nuns' chorus* (Joan Sutherland, Amb. S.). ZELLER: *Der Obersteiger: Sei nicht bös'* (Gueden). LEHÁR: *Das Land des Lächelns: Dein ist mein ganzes Herz* (Jussi Bjoerling). *Die lustige Witwe: Vilja-Lied* (Sutherland); *Lippen schweigen* (Renata Holm, Krenn). *Schön ist die Welt* (Krenn). *Der Graf von Luxemburg: Lieber Freund . . . Bist du's, Lachendes Gluck* (Holm, Krenn). *Giuditta: Du bist meine Sonne* (Waldemar Kmentt). LECOCQ: *Le Coeur et la main: Bonsoir Perez le capitaine* (Sutherland). OFFENBACH: *La Périchole: Letter song. La Grande Duchesse de Gérolstein: J'aime les militaires* (Régine Crespin).
(M) *** Decca 421 319-2.

A valuable and generous anthology, not just for the obvious highlights: Joan Sutherland's *Vilja* and the delightful contributions from Hilde Gueden – notably a delicious *Sei nicht bös'* – recorded in 1961 when the voice was at its freshest; but also Régine Crespin at her finest in Offenbach – the duchess reviewing her troops, and the charming *Letter song* from *La Périchole*. In their winningly nostalgic account of the *Merry Widow waltz* Renate Holm and Werner Krenn hum the melody, having sung the words, giving the impression of dancing together. The recording throughout is very good.

Luba Orgonasova (soprano)

'Favourite soprano arias' (with Slovak RSO (Bratislava), Will Humburg): BELLINI: *I Puritani: Qui la voce sua soave. I Capuleti ed i Montecchi: Oh, quante volte, oh quante! La Sonnambula: Come per me sereno*. PUCCINI: *Turandot: Signore, ascolta. Gianni Schicchi: O mio babbino caro*.

La Rondine: Chi'l bel sogno di Doretta. DONIZETTI: *Linda di Chamounix: O luce di quest'anima. Lucia di Lammermoor: Mad scene.*
(BB) *** Naxos Dig. 8.550605 [id.].

For I.M., Luba Orgonasova, the young soprano from Bratislava, is the vocal discovery of the year, indeed of the last several years. It is extraordinary that such a mature artist with a ravishing vocal line and musicianship to match, should be launched by a super-bargain label, and one cannot help but make the comparison with that exquisitely famous early recital of Joan Sutherland for Decca which also included the same aria from *Linda di Chamounix* and the famous *Lucia* Mad scene. It is no exaggeration to say that the charm and precision of Luba Orgonasova's performance of the latter showpiece can be spoken of almost in the same breath as Sutherland's remarkable Decca début LP. Indeed Orgonasova's style at times seems to be modelled somewhat on her famous predecessor, although her vocal personality is all her own, whether as an engaging Liù in *Turandot*, or confidently taking on Bellini's two most famous heroines, Elvira in *I Puritani*, or Amina in *La Sonnambula*. She is a natural for Puccinian legato, even if she overdoes the tenuto in *O mio babbino caro*. The sparkle of the cabalettas both in Bellini and in the aria from Donizetti's *Linda di Chamounix* is a delight in itself, and throughout this recital she is greatly helped by the support of Will Humburg and the Slovak Radio Symphony Orchestra who follow her so flexibly and sympathetically. At super-bargain price this is a record not to be missed.

Adelina Patti (soprano)

'The Era of Adelina Patti' ((i) Adelina Patti; (ii) Victor Maurel; (iii) Pol Plançon; (iv) Mattia Battistini; (v) Mario Ancona; (vi) Lucien Fugère; (vii) Francisco Vignas; (viii) Emma Calvé; (ix) Maurice Renaud; (x) Fernando De Lucia; (xi) Francesco Tamagno; (xii) Nellie Melba; (xiii) Félia Litvinne; (xiv) Wilhelm Hesch; (xv) Lillian Nordica; (xvi) Mario Ancona; (xvii) Edouard De Reszke; (xviii) Marcella Sembrich; (xix) Francesco Marconi; (xx) Mattia Battistini; (xxi) Lilli Lehmann; (xxii) Sir Charles Santley) Arias from: VERDI: (ii) *Falstaff;* (i, iii,) *Don Carlos;* (iv, xx) *Ernani;* (v, xiv) *Otello.* ADAM: (iii) *Le Chalet.* GLUCK: (vi) *Les Pèlerins de la Mecque.* MOZART: (i, ii, xx) *Don Giovanni;* (i, vii, xxi) *Le nozze di Figaro.* MEYERBEER: (vii) *Le Prophète.* BIZET: (viii) *Carmen.* MASSENET: (ix, xi) *Hérodiade;* (x) *Manon.* THOMAS: (xii) *Hamlet.* WAGNER: (xiii) *Lohengrin;* (xiv) *Die Meistersinger von Nürnberg.* ERKEL: (xv) *Hunyadi László.* DONIZETTI: (xvi) *La favorita;* (xix) *Lucrezia Borgia;* (xii) *Lucia.* BELLINI: (i) *La Sonnambula;* (xviii) *I Puritani.* FLOTOW: (xvii) *Marta.* ROSSINI: (x) *Il barbiere di Siviglia.* GOMES: (xx) *Il Guarany.* Songs by TOSTI; (vi) RAMEAU; (i, vi) YRADIER; (i) HOOK; (i) BISHOP; (ix) GOUNOD; (xv) R. STRAUSS; (xxii) HATTON.
(M) (***) Nimbus mono NI 7840/41 [id.].

The very first item on this wide-ranging collection of historic recordings has one sitting up at once. The voice ringing out from the loudspeakers prompts cheering from the singer's little audience. The clear-toned baritone is singing *Quand'ero paggio* from Verdi's *Falstaff* and, encouraged, he repeats it. More cheering and a third performance, this time in French, to cap the occasion. The singer is Victor Maurel, the baritone whom Verdi chose as his first Falstaff in 1893 and, before that, his first Iago in *Otello*. The recording dates from 1907, and many lovers of historic vocal issues will remember it well. Yet hearing it on the Nimbus transfer to CD brings a sense of presence as never before.

That company's controversial technique of playing an ancient 78 disc with a thorn needle on the best possible acoustic horn gramophone is at its most effective here, with exceptionally vivid results on these acoustic recordings. They not only convey astonishing presence but also a sense of how beautiful the voices were, getting behind the tinny and squawky sounds often heard on old 78s. This is an ideal set for anyone not already committed to historic vocals who simply wants to investigate how great singing could be 90 years ago, providing such an unexpected mix of well-known items and rarities, to delight specialists and newcomers alike.

The first of the two discs offers recordings that Nimbus regards as technically the finest of their day, including Patti in 1906, not just singing but shouting enthusiastically in a Spanish folksong, *La Calesera*, *'Vivan los españoles!'* Recorded much later in 1928 comes the French baritone, Lucien Fugère, eighty at the time but singing with a firm focus that you might not find today in a baritone in his twenties.

The second of the two discs has just as fascinating a mixture, but the recordings 'have not survived the decades so well'. Even so, it is thrilling to hear Sir Charles Santley, born in 1834, the year after Brahms, singing *Simon the Cellarer* with tremendous flair at the age of seventy-nine, and the coloratura, Marcella Sembrich, sounding even sweeter in Bellini than on previous transfers.

Luciano Pavarotti (tenor)

'The world's favourite arias' from: LEONCAVALLO: *I Pagliacci.* FLOTOW: *Martha.* BIZET: *Carmen.* PUCCINI: *La Bohème; Tosca; Turandot.* VERDI: *Rigoletto; Aida; Il Trovatore.* GOUNOD: *Faust.*
**(*) Decca 400 053-2 [id.].

As one would expect from Pavarotti, there is much to enjoy in his ripe and resonant singing of these favourite arias, but it is noticeable that the finest performances are those which come from complete sets, conducted by Karajan (*Bohème*), Mehta (*Turandot*) and Bonynge (*Rigoletto*), where with character in mind Pavarotti's singing is more intense and imaginative. The rest remains very impressive, though at under 40 minutes the measure is short. The transfer to compact disc has resulted in slight limitation of the upper range to take out background noise; however, the vividness of the voice is enhanced in the process. Nevertheless collectors would do far better to invest in one of the more generous recitals listed below. The best buy among Pavarotti recitals is undoubtedly '*Tutto Pavarotti*' – see below – offering two well-filled discs at mid-price, even if there are no accompanying translations.

'Pavarotti's greatest hits': PUCCINI: *Turandot: Nessun dorma. Tosca: Recondita armonia; E lucevan le stelle. La Bohème: Che gelida manina.* DONIZETTI: *La fille du régiment: O mes amis . . . Pour mon âme. La Favorita: Spirito gentil. L'Elisir d'amore: Una furtiva lagrima.* R. STRAUSS: *Der Rosenkavalier: Di rigori armato.* LEONCAVALLO: *Mattinata.* ROSSINI: *La danza.* DE CURTIS: *Torna a Surriento.* BIZET: *Carmen: Flower song.* BELLINI: *I Puritani: A te o cara. Vanne, O rose fortunata.* VERDI: *Il Trovatore: Di qual tetra . . . Ah, si ben mio; Di quella pira. Rigoletto: La donna è mobile; Questa o quella. Requiem: Ingemisco. Aida: Celeste Aida.* FRANCK: *Panis angelicus.* GOUNOD: *Faust: Salut! Demeure.* SCHUBERT: *Ave Maria.* LEONCAVALLO: *I Pagliacci: Vesti la giubba.* PONCHIELLI: *La Gioconda: Cielo e mar.* DENZA: *Funiculi, funicula.*
*** Decca 417 011-2; *417 011-4* (2) [id.].

This collection of 'greatest hits' can safely be recommended to all who have admired the golden beauty of Pavarotti's voice. Including as it does a fair proportion of earlier recordings, the two discs demonstrate the splendid consistency of his singing. Songs are included as well as excerpts from opera, including *Torna a Surriento, Funiculi, funicula,* Leoncavallo's *Mattinata* and Rossini's *La Danza.* The sound is especially vibrant on CD, but sometimes a little fierce on cassette.

'Anniversary': PUCCINI: *La Bohème: Che gelida manina. Tosca: Recondita armonia; E lucevan le stelle.* GIORDANO: *Andrea Chénier: Colpito qui m'avete . . . Un dì, all'azzuro spazio; Sì, fui soldato; Come un bel dì di maggio.* BELLINI: *La Sonnambula: Ah! perchè non posso odiarti.* PONCHIELLI: *La Gioconda: Cielo e mar.* VERDI: *La Traviata: Lunge da lei . . . De' miei bollenti spiriti. Un ballo in maschera: Di' tu se fedele; Forse la soglia attinse . . . Ma se m'è forza perderti.* LEONCAVALLO: *Pagliacci: Vesti la giubba.* BOITO: *Mefistofele: Dai campi; Giunto sul passo estremo.* ROSSINI: *Guglielmo Tell: Non mi . . . Oh muto asil.* MASCAGNI: *Cavalleria Rusticana: Addio.*
**(*) Decca 417 362-2; *417 362-4* [id.].

Pavarotti's recital celebrated the 25th anniversary of his operatic début. It is a good compilation of mixed items from complete opera sets, some of them relatively rare and mostly imaginatively done, though the *Andrea Chénier* items could be subtler. Good, bright recording of various vintages.

Donizetti and Verdi arias (with Vienna Op. O, Downes): DONIZETTI: *Dom Sébastien, roi de Portugal: Deserto in terra. Il Duca d'Alba: Inosservato, penetrava . . . Angelo casto e bel. La Favorita: Spirito gentil. Lucia di Lammermoor: Tombe degli avi miei . . . Fra poce a me.* VERDI: *Un Ballo in maschera: Forse la soglia . . . Ma se m'è forza perderti. I due Foscari: Ah si, ch'io sento ancora . . . Dal più remoto esiglio. Luisa Miller: Oh! fede negar potessi . . . Quando le sere al placido. Macbeth: O figli . . . Ah, la paterna mano.*

(M) *** Decca 421 304-2.

Pavarotti's 'Opera Gala' issue of Verdi and Donizetti represents the tenor in impressive performances of mainly rare arias, recorded early in his career in 1968, with the voice fresh and golden. Good, full recording.

'King of the high Cs': Arias from: DONIZETTI: La fille du régiment; La Favorita. VERDI: Il Trovatore. R. STRAUSS: Der Rosenkavalier. ROSSINI: Guglielmo Tell. BELLINI: I Puritani. PUCCINI: La Bohème.
(M) *** Decca 421 326-2; 421 326-4.

The punning title may not be to everyone's taste, but this is another attractively varied Pavarotti collection, now offered at mid-price, a superb display of his vocal command as well as his projection of personality. Though the selections come from various sources, the recording quality is remarkably consistent, the voice vibrant and clear; the accompanying detail and the contributions of the chorus are also well managed. The Donizetti and Puccini items are particularly attractive.

'Tutto Pavarotti': VERDI: Aida: Celeste Aida. Luisa Miller: Quando le sere al placido. La Traviata: De' miei bollenti spiriti. Il Trovatore: Ah si ben mio; Di quella pira. Rigoletto: La donna è mobile. Un ballo in maschera: La rivedrà nell'estasi. DONIZETTI: L'elisir d'amore: Una furtiva lagrima. Don Pasquale: Com'è gentil. PONCHIELLI: La Gioconda: Cielo e mar. FLOTOW: Martha: M'appari. BIZET: Carmen: Flower song. MASSENET: Werther: Pourquoi me réveiller. MEYERBEER: L'Africana: O paradiso. BOITO: Mefistofele: Dai campi dai prati. LEONCAVALLO: Pagliacci: Vesti la giubba. MASCAGNI: Cavalleria Rusticana: Addio alla madre. GIORDANO: Fedora: Amor ti vieta. PUCCINI: La Fanciulla del West: Ch'ella mi creda. Tosca: E lucevan le stelle. Manon Lescaut: Donna non vidi mai. La Bohème: Che gelida manina. Turandot: Nessun dorma. ROSSINI: Stabat Mater: Cuius animam. BIZET: Agnus Dei. ADAM: O holy night. DI PAPUA: O sole mio. TOSTI: A vucchella. CARDILLO: Core 'ngrato. TAGLIAFERRI: Passione. CHERUBINI: Mamma. DALLA: Caruso.
(M) *** Decca 425 681-2; 425 681-4 (2) [id.].

Opening with Dalla's Caruso, a popular song in the Neapolitan tradition, certainly effective, and no more vulgar than many earlier examples of the genre, this selection goes on through favourites like O sole mio and Core 'ngrato and one or two religious items, notably Adam's Cantique de Noël, to the hard core of operatic repertoire. Beginning with Celeste Aida, recorded in 1972, the selection of some twenty-two arias from complete sets covers Pavarotti's distinguished recording career with Decca from 1969 (Cielo e mar and the Il Trovatore excerpts) to 1985, although the opening song was, of course, recorded digitally in 1988. The rest is a mixture of brilliantly transferred analogue originals and a smaller number of digital masters, all or nearly all showing the great tenor in sparkling form. The records and equivalent tapes are at mid-price, but there are no translations or musical notes.

'The essential Pavarotti': Arias from VERDI: Rigoletto; Il Trovatore. PUCCINI: La Bohème; Tosca; Turandot. DONIZETTI: L'Elisir d'amore. FLOTOW: Martha. BIZET: Carmen. LEONCAVALLO: I Pagliacci. Songs by TOSTI; LEONCAVALLO; DENZA; DI CURTIS and others.
(M) *** Decca 430 210-2; 430 210-4 [id.].

This recital, compiled from Decca's back catalogue, was launched with considerable accompanying hype – posters even appeared on the London Underground – and in consequence the disc managed to enter the charts alongside Nigel Kennedy's recording of Vivaldi's Four Seasons. Many of the recordings offered here are also included in the mid-priced two-disc set, 'Tutto Pavarotti', which offers far more music for only a little more outlay, and thus is more representative of Pavarotti's 'essential' repertoire. However, the present programme, vividly transferred to CD, certainly shows the great tenor in good form, not only in the most popular of popular arias but also in the songs like O sole mio, Torna a Surriento! and a sparkling version of Rossini's La Danza.

'Gala concert at the Royal Albert Hall' (with RPO, Kurt Adler): Arias from: PUCCINI: Tosca; Turandot. VERDI: Macbeth; I Lombardi; Luisa Miller. Un giorno di regno: Overture. DONIZETTI: Lucia di Lammermoor. CILEA: L'Arlesiana. DE CURTIS: Song: Torna a Surriento. BERLIOZ: Les Troyens: Royal hunt and storm.
(M) **(*) Decca 430 716-2; 430 716-4.

This disc celebrates a much-hyped appearance by Pavarotti at the Royal Albert Hall in 1982, in the days when one tenor alone was enough! It would be unfair to expect much subtlety before such an eager audience, but the live recording conveys the fever well. There are bold accounts of the two most famous arias from *Tosca*, and the celebrated *Nessun dorma* from *Turandot*, and even simple recitatives as intimate as Macduff's in *Macbeth* are proclaimed grandly. The bright digital recording shows up some unevenness in the voice, but no one will miss the genuine excitement, with the electricity of the occasion conveyed equally effectively on disc or tape.

Luciano Pavarotti (tenor) and Mirella Freni (soprano)

Arias and duets from: PUCCINI: *Tosca; La Bohème.* ROSSINI: *Guglielmo Tell.* BOITO: *Mefistofele.*
(M) *** Decca 421 878-2; *421 878-4.*

Both artists come from the same small town in Italy, Modena, where they were born in 1935; less surprisingly, they studied under the same singing teacher. Their artistic partnership on record has always been a happy one, and perhaps reached its zenith in their 1972 *Bohème* with Karajan (unexpectedly, recorded in the Jesus-Christus Kirche, Berlin). Their great introductory love-duet as Mimì and Rodolfo, perhaps the most ravishing in all opera (from *Che gelida manina*, through *Sì, mi chiamano Mimì* to the soaring *O soave fanciulla*) is an obvious highlight here, but the much less familiar *Lontano, lontano* from *Mefistofele* shows no less memorably that the voices were made for each other. It was a very good idea to include a substantial selection from their 1978–9 *Tosca* (recorded in the Kingsway Hall), not a first choice as a complete set, but with some marvellous singing in Act III, of which some 17 minutes is offered (including *E lucevan le stelle* and the dramatic finale of the opera). The recital opens very spontaneously with 13 minutes from Act I (*Mario! Mario!*), the engagingly temperamental interplay between the lovers, in the Church of Sant'Andrea della Valle. The only slight disappointment is Freni's *Vissi d'arte*; otherwise this is 70 minutes of vintage material, given Decca's top drawer sound.

Ezio Pinza (bass)

Opera arias from: ROSSINI: *Mosè in Egitto.* BELLINI: *Norma; I Puritani.* DONIZETTI: *Lucia di Lammermoor; La Favorita.* HALÉVY: *La Juive.* GOUNOD: *Faust.* THOMAS: *Mignon.* VERDI: *Il Trovatore; La forza del destino; Simon Boccanegra; I vespri siciliani; Requiem.* BOITO: *Mefistofele.* MEYERBEER: *Robert le Diable.*
(M) (***) EMI mono CDH7 64253-2 [id.].

One of the greatest of all basses, Ezio Pinza immediately shows his calibre here in the very opening excerpt from Rossini's *Mosè in Egitto*, singing of great beauty and enormous control. He is hardly less impressive in Verdi, and this well-chosen programme demonstrates not only a magnetic vocal projection but a natural feeling for line. He was a singers' singer, yet he projected his characters on stage very powerfully too. Nearly all these recordings were made when the voice was at its peak, and the transfers are bright and clear in the way of this EMI Référence series.

Rosa Ponselle (soprano)

'Prima voce': Arias from: BELLINI: *Norma.* PONCHIELLI: *La Gioconda.* SPONTINI: *La vestale.* VERDI: *Aida; Ernani; La forza del destino; Otello.* Songs by: ARENSKY; RIMSKY-KORSAKOV; DE CURTIS; DI CAPUA; JACOBS-BOND.
(M) (***) Nimbus mono NI 7805.

One of the most exciting American sopranos ever, Rosa Ponselle tantalizingly cut short her career when she was still at her peak. Only the Arensky and Rimsky songs represent her after her official retirement, and the rest make a superb collection, including her classic accounts of *Casta diva* from Bellini's *Norma* and the duet, *Mira o Norma*, with Marion Telva. The six Verdi items include her earlier version of *Ernani involami*, not quite so commanding as her classic 1928 recording, but fascinating for its rarity. Equally cherishable is her duet from *La forza del destino* with Ezio Pinza.

Arias from: VERDI: *Ernani; Otello; La forza del destino; Aida.* MEYERBEER: *L'Africana.*
SPONTINI: *La Vestale.* PONCHIELLI: *La Gioconda.* BELLINI: *Norma.* BACH-GOUNOD: *Ave
Maria.* RIMSKY-KORSAKOV: *The nightingale and the rose* & Songs.
(M) (***) BMG/RCA mono GD 87810 [7810-2-RG].

The clarity and immediacy of the RCA transfers make a complete contrast with the warmly
atmospheric Nimbus transfers of the same singer. Though the voice is exposed more, with less
bloom on it, the character and technical command are, if anything, even more impressively
presented. To sample the greatness of Ponselle, try her dazzling 1928 account of *Ernani
involami* or her poised *Casta diva.* Notable too is the final trio from *La forza del destino* with
Martinelli and Pinza, even more immediate than on Nimbus's Martinelli disc.

Leontyne Price (soprano)

'The Prima Donna Collection': Disc 1 (with RCA Italiana Op. O, Molinari-Pradelli; New Philh.
O, Santi; LSO, Downes; Philh. O, Henry Lewis): Arias from: PURCELL: *Dido and Aeneas.*
MOZART: *Le nozze di Figaro.* VERDI: *La Traviata; Otello* (with Corinna Vozza). MEYERBEER:
L'Africaine. MASSENET: *Manon.* CILEA: *Adriana Lecouvreur.* G. CHARPENTIER: *Louise.* (with
New Philh. O, Santi): PUCCINI: *Turandot* (with Daniele Barioni & Amb. Op. Ch.). KORNGOLD:
Die tote Stadt. BARBER: *Vanessa.*

Disc 2: HANDEL: *Atalanta.* MOZART: *Don Giovanni.* WEBER: *Der Freischütz.* WAGNER:
Tannhäuser. VERDI: *Macbeth* (with Corinna Vozza, Robert El Hage). BOITO: *Mefistofele.*
DVOŘÁK: *Rusalka.* DEBUSSY: *L'enfant prodigue.* GIORDANO: *Andrea Chénier.* ZANDONAI:
Francesca da Rimini. PUCCINI: *Suor Angelica.* MENOTTI: *Amelia goes to the ball.*

Disc 3: GLUCK: *Alceste.* MOZART: *Don Giovanni.* VERDI: *I Lombardi; Simon Boccanegra.*
FLOTOW: *Martha.* OFFENBACH: *La Périchole.* WAGNER: *Die Walküre.* J. STRAUSS JR: *Die
Fledermaus.* BIZET: *Carmen.* MASCAGNI: *Cavalleria rusticana.* MASSENET: *Thaïs.* PUCCINI:
Gianni Schicchi. POULENC: *Les dialogues des Carmélites.*

Disc 4: HANDEL: *Semele.* MOZART: *Idomeneo.* BERLIOZ: *La Damnation de Faust.* WEBER:
Oberon. BELLINI: *Norma* (with Boris Martinovich, Amb. Op. Ch.). VERDI: *Rigoletto.* WAGNER:
Tristan und Isolde. LEONCAVALLO: *Pagliacci.* CILEA: *Adriana Lecouvreur.* BRITTEN: *Gloriana.*
(M) *** BMG/RCA 09026 61236-2 (4).

This remarkable anthology is drawn from a series of recitals which Leontyne Price recorded
for RCA in London and Rome between 1965 and 1979, including many items made when she
was at the very peak of her form. It is irritating that the individual recording dates are not given,
but the programme appears to be laid out generally in the order they were recorded, although
there are a few exceptions. Some of the very finest performances come on Disc 1.

The famous *Lament* from Purcell's *Dido and Aeneas* makes a moving opener, the voice
wonderfully fresh, and the following performances are all gloriously sung – clearly these early
sessions with Molinari-Pradelli in Rome were highly productive.

But there are many fine things elsewhere. The *Sleep-walking scene* from Verdi's *Macbeth* on
Disc 2 is a disappointment (Lady Macbeth is plainly not one of her best parts), but her *Come in
quest' ora bruna* from *Simon Boccanegra* is very fine, and she finds unusual expressive depth in
Offenbach's Act III Prison aria from *La Périchole.* She is, not unexpectedly, superb in *Voi lo
sapete* from *Cavalleria rusticana* (disc 3) and a highlight from the final disc is the passionately
felt *D'amour l'ardente flamme* from Berlioz's *Damnation de Faust.*

The languorously played cor anglais solo here is characteristic of the consistent excellence of
the accompaniments and, like the voice, they are beautifully recorded. Care has been taken with
detail, so that in the long scene from Act I of *Norma* (with *Casta diva* at its centre) there is
support from the Ambrosian Chorus, recorded in fine perspective. As she has already recorded a
complete *Carmen,* it is good to hear the great diva singing richly in the subsidiary role of
Micaela, and the programme includes a fair sprinkling of novelties, not least a rare excerpt from
Britten's *Gloriana.* In a programme as long as this (approaching five hours of music) there are
bound to be minor vocal flaws, but they are suprisingly few, and vocally the performances are
amazingly consistent. A feast of opera, very well ordered – each disc makes a satisfying solo
recital.

(The) Record of Singing, Volume IV

'The Record of Singing', Volume 4, Disc 1. Arias from: BIZET: *La jolie fille de Perth* (Gwen Catley); *Carmen* (Jennie Tourel). PUCCINI: *La rondine* (Dorothy Kirsten). HANDEL: *Atalanta* (Florence Quartararo). CHARPENTIER: *Louise* (Eleanor Steber). MOZART: *Die Zauberflöte* (Dorothy Maynor). KORNGOLD: *Die tote Stadt* (Joan Hammond). WAGNER: *Tannhäuser* (Astrid Varnay); *Lohengrin* (Helen Traubel). GLUCK: *Alceste* (Rose Bampton). SAINT-SAËNS: *Samson et Dalila* (Blanche Thebom). BACH: *Mass in B min.* (Kathleen Ferrier). ELGAR: *Sea pictures* (excerpt) (Gladys Ripley). Songs by: HOOK (Margaret Ritchie); VILLA-LOBOS (Elsie Houston); HAHN (Maggie Teyte); WOLF (Flora Nielsen); MONRO (David Lloyd).

Disc 2. Arias from: BOUGHTON: *The immortal hour* (Webster Booth). HERBERT: *Naughty Marietta* (Jan Peerce). MOZART: *Don Giovanni* (Walter Midgley). VAUGHAN WILLIAMS: *Hugh the Drover* (James Johnston). PONCHIELLI: *La Gioconda* (Richard Tauber). PURCELL: *King Richard II* (Alfred Deller). LEONCAVALLO: *Pagliacci* (Leonard Warren). MASSENET: *Hérodiade* (Robert Merrill). HANDEL: *Judas Maccabaeus* (Norman Walker); *Scipio* (Oscar Natzke). MUSSORGSKY: *Boris Godunov* (George London). Songs arr. BRITTEN (Peter Pears) and by: PEEL (Robert Irwin); VILLA-LOBOS (Frederick Fuller); NIN (Igor Gorin); WOLF (Mack Harrell); DELL'ACQUA (Mado Robin); DE SÉVERAC (Martha Angelici); MOZART (Irène Joachim); HAHN (Géori Boué); FAURÉ (Ginette Guillamat); RIMSKY-KORSAKOV (Renée Doria).

Disc 3. Arias from: LALO: *Le Roi d'Ys* (Suzanne Juyol). GODARD: *La vivandière* (Solange Michel). SAINT-SAËNS: *Samson et Dalila* (Hélène Bouvier). BERLIOZ: *Les Troyens* (Rita Gorr). MASSENET: *Werther* (Raoul Jobin). MOZART: *Die Zauberflöte* (Erika Köth). BEETHOVEN: *Fidelio* (Elisabeth Schwarzkopf). LEHÁR: *Eva* (Maria Reining). TCHAIKOVSKY: *Queen of Spades* (Sena Jurinac). VERDI: *Aida* (Ljuba Welitsch). BRAHMS: *Liebeslieder waltzes* (excerpt). WOLF: *Elfenlied* (Irmgard Seefried). Songs by: RESPIGHI (Victoria De los Angeles); ANON. (Suzanne Danco); RAVEL (Irma Kolassi); LIPATTI: *4 Songs* (Hugues Cuénod); DUPARC (Pierre Bernac); GOUNOD (Camille Maurane); BASSANI (Gérard Souzay); SCHUBERT: *2 Songs* (Elisabeth Schumann); MOZART (Maria Stader); REGER (Elisabeth Grümmer).

Disc 4. Arias from: PUCCINI: *Tosca* (Gré Brouwenstijn). R. STRAUSS: *Arabella* (Leonie Rysanek); *Capriccio* (Anton Dermota). MENOTTI: *The Consul* (Inge Borkh). MOZART: *Don Giovanni* (Hugo Meyer-Welfing); *Die Zauberflöte* (Walther Ludwig and Erich Kunz); *Così fan tutte* (Marko Rothmüller). WAGNER: *Tannhäuser* (Ludwig Weber). WEBER: *Der Freischütz* (Peter Anders and Josef Hermann). LORTZING: *Undine* (Rudolf Schock). BEETHOVEN: *Fidelio* (Paul Schoeffler). Lieder from SCHUBERT: *Die schöne Müllerin* (Julius Patzak); SCHUMANN: *Liederkreis* (Dietrich Fischer-Dieskau); and by: PFITZNER (Friedel Beckmann); R. STRAUSS (Hilde Konetzni); WOLF (Elisabeth Höngen); SCHUBERT (Karl Schmitt-Walter); BRAHMS (Hans Hotter).

Disc 5. Arias from: MOZART: *Die Zauberflöte* (Gottlob Frick). PURCELL: *Dido and Aeneas* (Kirsten Flagstad). CILEA: *Adriana Lecouvreur* (Stefan Islandi). BIZET: *Les pêcheurs de perles* (Nicolai Gedda). GOUNOD: *Roméo et Juliette* (Jussi Bjoerling); *Judex* (Kim Borg). OFFENBACH: *Contes d'Hoffmann* (Hugo Hasslo). WAGNER: *Tannhäuser* (Joel Berglund). MUSSORGSKY: *Khovanshchina* (Zara Dolukhanova); *Sorochintsy Fair* (Georgi Vinogradov). OFFENBACH: *La Périchole* (Claudia Novikova). RIMSKY-KORSAKOV: *The Snow Maiden* (Ivan Zhadan). VERSTOVSKY: *Askold's tomb* (Georgi Nelepp). SMETANA: *Dalibor* (Beno Blachut). Songs by: SCHUBERT (Theo Herrmann); SIBELIUS (Lorri Lail); DEBUSSY (Gjurgja Leppée); DOWLAND (Askel Schiotz); WOLF (Bernhard Sönnerstedt); MUSSORGSKY (Mascia Predit); TCHAIKOVSKY (Nadezhda Obukhova).

Disc 6. Arias from: NAPRAVNIK: *Dubrovsky* (Ivan Kozlovsky). RIMSKY-KORSAKOV: *Sadko* (Pavel Lisitsian). TCHAIKOVSKY: *Mazeppa* (Andrei Ivanov). VERDI: *Nabucco* (Boris Christoff); *Il Trovatore* (Beniamino Gigli); *Otello* (Mario Del Monaco); *Don Carlos* (Gino Bechi). DONIZETTI: *L'elisir d'amore* (Ferruccio Tagliavini); *La Favorita* (Paolo Silveri). THOMAS: *Mignon* (Giuseppe Di Stefano). BOITO: *Mefistofele* (Giovanni Malipiero). MASSENET: *Werther* (Giacinto Prandelli). GIORDANO: *Andrea Chénier* (Tito Gobbi). PUCCINI: *Tosca* (Giampiero Valdengo). Songs by: BORODIN (Boris Christoff); TCHAIKOVSKY (Mark Reisen); RUBINSTEIN (Boris Gmyrya); KODÁLY (Endre Koréh); FALVO (Luigi Infantino); TOSTI (Giuseppe Valdengo).

Disc 7. Arias from: BELLINI: *La Sonnambula* (Raffaele Arié); *I Capuleti ed i Montecchi* (Margherita Carosio). GLINKA: *A Life for the Tsar* (Nicola Rossi-Lemeni). MUSSORGSKY: *Boris Godunov* (Tancredi Pasero). MASSENET: *Werther* (Giulietta Simionato). VERDI: *Il Trovatore* (Fedora Barbieri); *Don Carlos* (Margherita Grandi); *Il Trovatore* (Zinka Milanov). DONIZETTI: *La Favorita* (Ebe Stignani). BIZET: *Les pêcheurs de perles* (Alda Noni). PUCCINI: *Turandot* (Elena Arizmendi); *Manon Lescaut* (Renata Tebaldi); *La Bohème* (Sara Scuderi). ROSSINI: *Armida* (Maria Callas). Songs by: A. SCARLATTI (Magda László); RESPIGHI (Ala Anzellotti); BELLINI (Gabriella Gatti).
*** (M) EMI mono CHS7 69741-2 (7) [id.].

This is the culminating volume of a massive survey of vocal recording in the 78-r.p.m. era, master-minded by Keith Hardwick, who both chose the items and made the immaculate transfers. The project, covering recordings from the 1890s onwards, took 15 years to complete, and this is the only volume to be issued on CD so far, covering the very last years of the short-playing 78, from the beginning of the Second World War until roughly 1955. This brings in such singers as Dietrich Fischer-Dieskau, Elisabeth Schwarzkopf, Victoria de los Angeles and Tito Gobbi, whose recording was mainly done in the LP era.

Well known as they are, Hardwick's choice of items for them is endlessly illuminating – Schwarzkopf in Marzelline's aria from Beethoven's *Fidelio*, for example, or an early account of 'Nemico della patria' from Giordano's *Andrea Chénier*, with Gobbi at his most thrilling.

There are also the singers from earlier eras represented whose extended careers closed in this period, such as Elisabeth Schumann and Beniamino Gigli, again represented by unexpected and rare recordings. As in previous volumes, items are grouped in national schools, and it is endlessly fascinating to have well-known stars put side by side with those whose recording careers faded relatively early – as for example Gobbi set against his fellow Italian baritones, Paolo Silveri and Giampiero Malaspina. The latter's account of Scarpia's *Te Deum* from Puccini's *Tosca* has a tiny contribution from the Spoleta of the occasion, none other than Keith Hardwick himself.

Many items were published for the very first time in the LP version of this volume, having been shelved for a generation, and for the CD set Hardwick has taken the opportunity of adding extra singers to the list, including the formidable French soprano, Suzanne Juyol, and the sensitive German mezzo, Friedel Beckmann. And how good to hear Maria Reining in her prime, when on record she has always been best known for her Marschallin in Decca's pioneering *Rosenkavalier*, recorded when the voice was far less secure.

The selection aptly ends with Maria Callas, a superstar here observed in a live recording of a rare virtuoso variation-solo from Rossini's *Armida*, brilliantly done. Enjoyment is enormously enhanced by the highly informative biographical notes provided by John T. Hughes, giving information otherwise often hard to come by, particularly with the lesser-known singers. One hopes that the earlier volumes will soon also be issued on CD.

Regina Resnik (mezzo-soprano)

'Golden Jubilee': Arias from BIZET: *Carmen*. TCHAIKOVSKY: *Jeanne d'Arc*. SAINT-SAËNS: *Samson et Dalila*. WAGNER: *Die Walküre*. VERDI: *Il trovatore; Don Carlo* (all with ROHCG O, Edward Downes); *Falstaff; Un ballo in maschera*. R. STRAUSS: *Elektra* (with Birgit Nilsson). J. STRAUSS JR: *Die Fledermaus*. LEHÁR: *Merry Widow*. BORODIN (arr. Wright/Forrest): *Kismet*.
(M) ******* Decca 421 897-2 [id.].

This collection is issued to celebrate the artistry and range of Regina Resnik who made her stage début in 1942. Most of the programme derives from a 1961 recital to which excerpts from complete sets in which she was featured have been added. The *Carmen* and *Delilah* items are magnificent. She is in top form here, and where in the complete *Tristan und Isolde* her Brangaene was decidedly unsteady, she is firmer on this occasion, with the vibrato under better control. The sense of line, too, is commanding, and there is an urgency about the different characterizations. The *Joan of Arc* aria is sung in Russian, and in the *Walküre* excerpts Resnik sounds appropriately fierce as the scolding Fricka. She is even more impressive as Clytemnestra in *Elektra* in her scene with Birgit Nilsson (*Ich will nichts hören . . . Ich habe keine güten Nächte*) and makes a memorably saturnine Orlovsky in *Die Fledermaus*. The Offenbach *Can can*, too, is as racy as anyone could ask. A very well-selected programme (75 minutes) and vivid recording.

Katia Ricciarelli (soprano), José Carreras (tenor)

'Duetti d'amore' from PUCCINI: *Madama Butterfly*. VERDI: *I Lombardi*. DONIZETTI: *Poliuto; Roberto Devereux*.
(M) *** Ph. 426 644-2; *426 644-4*.

The two Donizetti duets are among the finest he ever wrote, especially the one from *Poliuto*, in which the hero persuades his wife to join him in martyrdom. This has a depth unexpected in Donizetti. Both these items receive beautiful performances here; the Puccini love duet is made to sound fresh and unhackneyed, and the *Lombardi* excerpt is given with equal tenderness. Stylish conducting and refined recording.

Royal Opera House, Covent Garden

Royal Opera House, Covent Garden (An early history on record). Singers included are: Nellie Melba, Enrico Caruso, Luisa Tetrazzini, John McCormack, Emmy Destinn, Johanna Gadski, Friedrich Schorr, Eva Turner, Renato Zanelli, Lotte Lehmann, Elisabeth Schumann, Maria Olczewska, Feodor Chaliapin, Beniamino Gigli, Conchita Supervia, Lawrence Tibbett, Richard Tauber, Kirsten Flagstad, Lauritz Melchior. Arias from: GOUNOD: *Faust*. VERDI: *Rigoletto; Otello*. DONIZETTI: *Lucia di Lammermoor*. VERDI: *La Traviata*. PUCCINI: *Madama Butterfly; Tosca*. WAGNER: *Götterdämmerung; Die Meistersinger; Tristan und Isolde*. R. STRAUSS: *Der Rosenkavalier*. MUSSORGSKY: *Boris Godunov*. GIORDANO: *Andrea Chénier*. BIZET: *Carmen*. MOZART: *Don Giovanni*.
(M) (***) Nimbus mono NI 7819 [id.].

Nimbus's survey of great singers at Covent Garden ranges from Caruso's 1904 recording of *Questa o quella* from *Rigoletto* to the recording of the second half of the *Tristan* love duet, which Kirsten Flagstad and Lauritz Melchior made in San Francisco in November 1939, a magnificent recording never issued in Britain and little known which repeated the partnership initiated during the 1937 Coronation season at Covent Garden. The Vienna recording of the *Rosenkavalier* trio with Lehmann, Schumann and Olczewska similarly reproduces a classic partnership at Covent Garden, while Chaliapin's 1928 recording of the *Prayer* and *Death of Boris* was actually recorded live at Covent Garden, with the transfer giving an amazingly vivid sense of presence. Those who like Nimbus's acoustic method of transfer will enjoy the whole disc, though the reverberation round some of the early offerings – like the very first, Melba's *Jewel song* from *Faust* – is cavernous. Particularly interesting is the 1909 recording of part of Brünnhilde's immolation scene, with Johanna Gadski commandingly strong.

Tito Schipa (tenor)

Arias from: MASSENET: *Werther; Manon*. CILEA: *L'Arlesiana*. ROSSINI: *Il Barbiere di Siviglia*. DONIZETTI: *L'Elisir d'amore; Lucia di Lammermoor*. LEONCAVALLO: *Pagliacci*. VERDI: *Rigoletto; La Traviata*. MOZART: *Don Giovanni*. HANDEL: *Xerxes*. BELLINI: *La Sonnambula*. Songs by TOSTI and others.
(M) (***) BMG/RCA mono GD 87969 [7969-2-RG].

RCA provides vivid, very immediate transfers of a sparkling collection of Neapolitan songs as well as arias. Few tenors have matched Schipa for the point and personality of his singing within his carefully chosen limits. It is like being face to face with the singer.

'Prima voce': Arias from: MASCAGNI: *Cavalleria rusticana; L'amico Fritz*. VERDI: *Rigoletto; Luisa Miller*. DONIZETTI: *Lucia di Lammermoor; Don Pasquale; L'elisir d'amore*. LEONCAVALLO: *Pagliacci*. MASSENET: *Manon; Werther*. ROSSINI: *Il barbiere di Siviglia*. THOMAS: *Mignon*. FLOTOW: *Martha*. CILEA: *L'Arlesiana*.
(M) (***) Nimbus mono NI 7813 [id.].

The first nine items on this well-chosen selection of Schipa's recordings date from the pre-electric era. The voice is totally consistent, heady and light and perfectly controlled, between the *Siciliana* from Mascagni's *Cavalleria*, recorded with piano in 1913, to the incomparable account of more Mascagni, the *Cherry duet* from *L'amico Fritz*, made with Mafalda Favero in 1937. It says much for his art that Schipa's career continued at full strength for decades after that. The

Nimbus transfers put the voice at a slight distance, with the electrical recordings made to sound the more natural.

Peter Schreier (tenor)

'Great voice': Arias from: MOZART: Così fan tutte; Die Entführung aus dem Serail; Don Giovanni. WEBER: Der Freischütz. TAUBER: Der Singende Traum. KÁLMÁN: Gräfin Mariza. RAYMOND: Maske in Blau. Lieder: SCHUBERT: Schwanengesang: Ständchen. Die schöne Müllerin: Ungeduld. Am Brunnen vor dem Tore. SCHUMANN: Im wunderschönen Monat Mai. Dichterliebe: Schöne Wiege meiner Leiden. TOSELLI: Serenade. CHOPIN, arr. Melichar: In mir klingt ein Lied. SILCHER: Ännchen von Tharau; Wenn alle Brünnlein fliessen. TRAD.: Du, du liegst mir am Herzen.
(B) **(*) DG 431 109-2 [id.].

Peter Schreier is a very personable lyric tenor, and it is always a pleasure to have a tenor recital without straining histrionics. He is pleasingly stylish in Mozart and even better in Max's recitative and aria (Durch die Wälder) from Der Freischütz, which is spirited as well as polished. The operetta excerpts perhaps could unleash more sheer passion, but it is good to have the excerpt from Raymond's Blue Mask, a semi-musical from the beginning of the 1930s with a curious stylistic mix, which continues to survive in the German repertoire. Schreier's easy Lieder style in famous songs of Schubert and Schumann is not without depth of feeling, and he is captivating in the lollipops, notably the Melichar arrangement of a very famous Chopin melody and Silcher's delightful Ännchen von Tharau. As usual in DG's 'Grosse Stimmen' series, there is no proper back-up documentation.

Ernestine Schumann-Heink (contralto)

'Prima voce': Arias from: DONIZETTI: Lucrezia Borgia. MEYERBEER: Le Prophète. WAGNER: Das Rheingold; Rienzi; Götterdämmerung. HANDEL: Rinaldo. Songs by: ARDITTI; BECKER; SCHUBERT; WAGNER; REIMANN; MOLLOY; BRAHMS; BOEHM & TRAD.
(M) (***) Nimbus mono NI 7811 [id.].

Ernestine Schumann-Heink was a formidable personality in the musical life of her time, notably in New York, as well as a great singer. 'I am looking for my successor,' she is reported as saying well before she retired, adding, 'She must be the contralto.' Schumann-Heink combines to an astonishing degree a full contralto weight and richness with the most delicate flexibility, as in the Brindisi from Donizetti's Lucrezia Borgia. This wide-ranging collection, resonantly transferred by the Nimbus acoustic method, presents a vivid portrait of a very great singer.

Elisabeth Schwarzkopf (soprano)

'Elisabeth Schwarzkopf sings operetta' (with Philh. Ch. and O, Ackermann): HEUBERGER: Der Opernball: Im chambre séparée. ZELLER: Der Vogelhändler: Ich bin die Christel; Schenkt man sich Rosen. Der Obersteiger; Sei nicht bös. LEHÁR: Der Zarewitsch: Einer wird kommen. Der Graf von Luxembourg: Hoch Evoë, Heut noch werd ich Ehefrau. Giuditta: Meine Lippen. J. STRAUSS JR: Casanova: Nuns' chorus; Laura's song. MILLÖCKER: Die Dubarry: Ich schenk mein Herz; Was ich im Leben beginne. SUPPÉ: Boccaccio: Hab ich nur deine Liebe. SIECZYŃSKY: Wien, du Stadt meiner Träume (Vienna, city of my dreams; song).
⊛ *** EMI CDC7 47284-2 [id.].

This is one of the most delectable recordings of operetta arias ever made, and it is here presented with excellent sound. Schwarzkopf's 'whoopsing' manner (as Philip Hope-Wallace called it) is irresistible, authentically catching the Viennese style, languor and sparkle combined. Try for sample the exquisite Im chambre séparée or Sei nicht bös; but the whole programme is performed with supreme artistic command and ravishing tonal beauty. This outstanding example of the art of Elisabeth Schwarzkopf at its most enchanting is a disc which ought to be in every collection. The compact disc transfer enhances the superbly balanced recording even further, manages to cut out nearly all the background, give the voice a natural presence, and retain the orchestral bloom.

Opera arias: MOZART: *Le nozze di Figaro; Così fan tutte; Don Giovanni.* HUMPERDINCK: *Hänsel und Gretel.* LEHÁR: *Die lustige Witwe*; J. STRAUSS JR: *Die Fledermaus.* PUCCINI: *Turandot.* R. STRAUSS: *Ariadne auf Naxos; Der Rosenkavalier; Capriccio.* VERDI: *Messa da requiem.*

(M) (***) EMI stereo/mono CDM7 63657-2.

This fine collection of arias is taken from various sets Schwarzkopf contributed to in the 1950s. They range from Mozart operas, conducted by Karajan and Furtwängler, to the glories of her supreme recordings of Strauss operas, Ariadne's lament, the Marschallin's final solo in Act I of *Rosenkavalier* and the Countess's final aria in *Capriccio.* Also featured is the *Recordare* from de Sabata's early recording of the Verdi *Requiem.*

Irmgard Seefried (soprano)

Scenes and arias from: MOZART: *Il rè pastore; Così fan tutte; Le nozze di Figaro.* BIZET: *Carmen.* HANDEL: *Giulio Cesare.* WEBER: *Der Freischütz.* THOMAS: *Mignon.* LORTZING: *Der Wildschütz.* R. STRAUSS: *Der Rosenkavalier.* RESPIGHI: *Il tramonto.*

(M) *** DG mono/stereo 437 677-2 (2) [id.].

Admirers of Irmgard Seefried will find little to disappoint here and much to cherish. The two CDs span her operatic recording career from the *Il rè pastore* aria (*L'amerò sarò, costante* – a delightfully fresh opener) of 1952, to her *Der Wildschütz* aria and duet of 1965. Here she is joined by the splendid Christoph Stepp, and these two excerpts from an opera little-known outside Germany are among the highlights. If *Deh vieni* from *Nozze di Figaro* is impeded by Fricsay's lazy tempo, the aria from *Fidelio* with the same conductor (Marzelline's *O wär ich schon mit dir vereint*) is captivating, while Agathe's two big scenas from *Der Freischütz*, with Jochum (1959) are most appealing. So, too, are the *Mignon* excerpts, sung in German, which in *Dort bei ihm ist sie jetzt* (*Elle est là, près de lui!*) alters the character of the music, not necessarily detrimentally when the voice is so creamy, to offset the German consonants. Here the accompaniments by the Lamoureux Orchestra of Paris under Jean Fournet are authentic. As Fiordiligi in *Così fan tutte*, we hear Seefried first in 1953, where her *Come scoglio* is stylish, but lacking in vehemence, but her *Per pietà* infinitely touching; later (1962) she is heard in duet with Nan Merriman (*Sorella, cosa dici? . . . Prenderò quel brunettino*). Other highlights are Cleopatra's arias from Acts I and III of *Giulio Cesare*, and, again with Karl Boehm conducting, her assumption of the role of Octavian in an early 1958 complete set of *Der Rosenkavalier.* With Rita Streich as Sophie, the 'Presentation of the silver rose' is memorably lovely. Even if Marianne Schech, as the Marschallin, is decidedly below the level set by her colleagues, these four excerpts (forty minutes of music) are well worth having. Irmgard Seefried retired from the operatic stage in the mid-1960s and went on to concentrate on Lieder, and of course, a teaching role. So it is good that this set also includes her 1959 recording of Respighi's *Il tramonto* (The sunset), a setting of verses by Shelley, which in its radiant pictorialism is a kind of symphonic poem for voice and orchestra. Her lovely performance brings out fully Respighi's glowing Italianate colouring. The CD transfers are immaculate, the quality of the earlier mono recordings remarkably truthful and free from either vocal or orchestral edginess. Good documentation, but no translations.

Sopranos

'Great sopranos of our time' ((i) Renata Scotto; (ii) Elisabeth Schwarzkopf; (iii) Joan Sutherland; (iv) Birgit Nilsson; (v) Victoria De los Angeles; (vi) Mirella Freni; (vii) Maria Callas; (viii) Ileana Cotrubas; (ix) Montserrat Caballé): (i) PUCCINI: *Madama Butterfly: Un bel dì;* (vi) *La Bohème: Sì, mi chiamano Mimì.* (ii) MOZART: *Così fan tutte: Come scoglio.* (iii) *Don Giovanni: Troppo mi spiace . . . Non mi dir.* (iv) WEBER: *Oberon: Ozean du Ungeheuer.* (v) ROSSINI: *Il Barbiere di Siviglia: Una voce poco fa.* (vii) DONIZETTI: *Lucia di Lammermoor: Sparsa è di rose . . . Il dolce suono . . . Spargi d'amaro.* (viii) BIZET: *Les Pêcheurs de perles: Comme autrefois.* (ix) VERDI: *Aida: Qui Radames . . . O patria mia.*

(M) *** EMI CD-EMX 9519; TC-EMX 2099.

An impressive collection drawn from a wide variety of sources. It is good to have Schwarzkopf's commanding account of *Come scoglio* and Nilsson's early recording of the

Weber, not to mention the formidable contributions of Callas and the early Sutherland reading of *Non mi dir*, taken from Giulini's complete set of *Giovanni*. The CD transfers are bright and vivid, and this makes a fascinating mid-priced anthology.

Soprano arias: 'Famous soprano arias' (sung by: (i) Régine Crespin; (ii) Renata Tebaldi; (iii) Maria Chiara; (iv) Joan Sutherland; (v) Gwyneth Jones; (vi) Felicia Weathers; (vii) Elena Suliotis) from: PUCCINI: (i) *Madama Butterfly;* (ii) *Gianni Schicchi;* (iii) *La Bohème;* (ii) *Tosca.* CATALANI: (iii) *La Wally.* VERDI: (iv) *Rigoletto;* (iii) *I vespri siciliani;* (v) *Aida;* (i) *Otello.* GOUNOD: (iv) *Faust.* PONCHIELLI: (viii) *La Gioconda.*
🏵 (B) *** Decca 433 624-2; *433 624-4.*

The compiler of this 67-minute programme is to be congratulated for remarkable vocal discernment and awareness of the potential in the Decca back-catalogue. It would be difficult to conceive a more winning recital of miscellaneous popular arias derived from this source, opening with the most famous soprano aria of all, *Un bel dì*, excitingly and tenderly sung by Régine Crespin. It is gratifying to see the art of Maria Chiara acknowledged: she is enchanting in the *Boléro* from Verdi's *I vespri siciliani* and makes a ravishing Mimì. Felicia Weathers is both captivating and individual in her long scena from *Otello*, while Tebaldi's *O mio babbino caro* has great vocal charm. She ends the recital with a characteristically melting account of *Vissi d'arte*, made in 1960. Sutherland's two contributions were also recorded in that same year: her lyrical coloratura in *Caro nome* is quite delicious. Dame Gwyneth Jones is in glorious voice in the two major arias from *Aida* (1968), while Elena Suliotis, sometimes an uneven singer, is at her strongest and most commanding in her searingly powerful *Suicidio* from *La Gioconda*, vocally as well as dramatically thrilling.

Sopranos: 'Ten Top Sopranos' ((i) Mirella Freni; (ii) Régine Crespin; (iii) Kiri Te Kanawa; (iv) Kathleen Battle; (v) Leontyne Price; (vi) Jessye Norman; (vii) Birgit Nilsson; (viii) Renata Tebaldi; (ix) Montserrat Caballé; (x) Joan Sutherland): Arias from: PUCCINI: (i) *La Bohème;* (ii) *Madama Butterfly.* MOZART: (iii) *Le nozze di Figaro.* VERDI: (iv) *Un ballo in maschera;* (v) *Aida.* WAGNER: (vi) *Lohengrin.* R. STRAUSS: (vii) *Elektra.* CATALANI: (viii) *La Wally.* PONCHIELLI: (ix) *La Gioconda.* DONIZETTI: (x) *Lucia di Lammermoor.*
(M) *** Decca Analogue/Dig. 436 461-2 [id.].

Like the others in this well-planned Decca series, this selection, arranged with skill, shows the enormous strength of this company's back-catalogue. Many of the excerpts here are among the the finest performances of their generation. Mirella Freni's Mimì (well matched by Pavarotti's Rodolfo) opens the programme enticingly, and it ends with Dame Joan Sutherland's miraculous early recording of the Mad scene from *Lucia di Lammermoor*, very much in a class of its own among recent recorded performances. In between come Dame Kiri's Countess (taken from the complete *Figaro*), Jessye Norman, a warmly intense Elsa (in *Lohengrin*), Birgit Nilsson's electrifying Elektra (*Allein! Weh, ganz allein*), and Leontyne Price's thrilling *Ritorna vincitor!* from *Aida*. (All these sets readily show how Solti could galvanize an opera recording.) And one must not forget (for she is unforgettable) Tebaldi's contribution (*Ebben? . . . Ne andrò lontana*, from *La Wally*), Caballé's *Suicidio!* from *La Gioconda*, or indeed Régine Crespin's *Un bel dì*, which comes from a studio recital but sounds like the real thing. As usual in this series, the sound is consistently vivid, but the documentation concentrates on the artists.

Frederica Von Stade (mezzo-soprano)

Opera arias: ROSSINI: *Otello: Quanto son fieri i palpiti; Che smania. Ohimè! che affanno! Assisa a piè d'un salice; Deh calma, o Ciel.* HAYDN: *La fedeltà premiata: Per te m'accesse amore; Vanne . . . fuggi . . . traditore! Barbaro conte . . . Dell'amor mio fedele. Il mondo della luna: Una donna come me; Se lo commando ci veniro.* MOZART: *La clemenza di Tito: Torna di Tito a lato; Tu tosti tradito.*
*** Ph. 420 084-2 [id.].

Von Stade's Philips recital is a splendid compilation of some of her finest performances from complete sets of rare operas. It is sad that the Philips Haydn series did not achieve wider circulation, when it included such delectable items as those here; it is also valuable to have reminders of her contribution to the Rossini *Otello* set and to Colin Davis's recording of Mozart's *Clemenza di Tito*. Good original sound, well transferred.

Rita Streich (soprano)

'Arias and waltzes' (with Berlin RIAS Ch. & O, Kurt Gaebel or Richard Kraus; German Op., Berlin, Ch. & O, Reinhard Peters): Arias from: MOZART: *Le nozze di Figaro.* RIMSKY-KORSAKOV: *Le coq d'or; Sadko.* DONIZETTI: *Lucia di Lammermoor; Linda di Chamounix.* DVOŘÁK: *Rusalka.* NICOLAI: *Die lustigen Weiber von Windsor.* PUCCINI: *Gianni Schicchi; Turandot.* SUPPÉ: *Boccaccio.* J. STRAUSS JR: *Die Fledermaus* (also Waltzes: *Geschichten aus dem Wienerwald; Frühlingsstimmen*). BELLINI: *I Capuleti ed i Montecchi.* MEYERBEER: *Dinorah.* VERDI: *Falstaff* (also *Lo spazzacamino* 'The chimney sweep'). BIZET: *Les pêcheurs de perles.* MASSENET: *Manon.* OFFENBACH: *Contes d'Hoffmann.* DELIBES: *Lakmé.* Songs: SAINT-SAËNS: *Le rossignol et la rose.* ARDITI: *Parla waltz.* GODARD: *Berceuse de Jocelyn.*
⊛ (M) *** DG mono 435 748-2 (2) [id.].

DG have created an enchanting two-disc anthology from their archive of recordings of Rita Streich, whose exquisite art is unknown to many of the younger generation. The prettiest coloratura soprano voice of the second half of the twentieth century (and she was hardly less attractive to look at!), she measured up well to all the competition from the 'Golden Age'. It was a small voice but perfectly formed, and it recorded marvellously well. Her upper tessitura glittered like a diamond necklace in famous display arias like Delibes's *Bell song* from *Lakmé*, and she was the perfect temperamental Doll in Offenbach's *Tales of Hoffmann*. She was also a delightful Mozartian. Her Queen of the Night's arias from *Die Zauberflöte* – see our main composer index – have never been surpassed, and she opens this programme with a quite lovely account of Susanna's *Deh vieni* from *Le nozze di Figaro*. But, alongside the flute-like coloratura she brought to Bellini and Donizetti, she could also ravish the ear with gentle lyricism in the simplest way. She scintillated in the waltzes of Johann Strauss (especially *Voices of spring* and the *Waltz song (Mein Herr Marquis)* from *Die Fledermaus*) and was at her most winning in slighter lollipops. Many of the most memorable pieces included here come from a recital she recorded in 1958 with the Berlin RIAS Choir and Radio Orchestra under Kurt Gaebel, in the Jesus Christus Kirche. Included were the Strauss waltzes and *Die Fledermaus* excerpts, Dvořák's *Invocation to the moon*, the charming *Hab'ich nur deine Liebe* from *Boccacio* and the equally delightful *Shadow song* from *Dinorah*. Godard's highly romantic *Berceuse* is the most famous item, but it is in the deliciously fragile Saint-Saëns vocalise, *Le rossignol et la rose*, and in Verdi's captivating song of the chimney sweep (*Lo spazzacamino*) that her magic sends a shiver of special pleasure to the nape of the neck. She chose the former to represent her art on the BBC's 'Desert Island Discs' programme.

Conchita Supervia (mezzo-soprano)

'In opera and song': BIZET: *Carmen*: excerpts (with Gaston Micheletti, Andrée Vavon, Andrée Bernadet). Arias from: ROSSINI: *L'Italiana in Algeri; Il barbiere di Siviglia; La Cenerentola.* GOUNOD: *Faust.* THOMAS: *Mignon.* SAINT-SAËNS: *Samson et Dalila.* SERRANO: *La Alegría del Batallón; El mal de amores.* Songs: FALLA: *7 Canciones populares españolas.* BALDOMIR: *Meus amores.* YRADIER: *La Paloma.* VALVERDE: *Clavelitos.*
(M) (***) Nimbus mono NI 7836/7 (2); NC 7836/7 [id.].

Readers who remember the 78s of Conchita Supervia, especially in Rossini – and in particular her dark, brittle mezzo with its wide vibrato ('like the rattle of shaken dice', as one critic described it) sparkling in the divisions of *Una voce poco fa* – may be astonished to discover the degree of vocal charm in other roles. Her reputation for dazzling the ear in Rossini was surely deserved (and she helped to restore *La Cenerentola* and *L'Italiana in Algeri* to the repertoire). Her Carmen, too, is unforgettable, as is her Delilah – but, more unexpectedly, her Mignon is also a highlight here, as is the brief Delibes item. As usual, the Nimbus transfers are kind to the voice (there is no suggestion of the 'death rattle' of one unkind description) and almost certainly more truthful than the edgier, brighter quality we have had from some other sources. The recordings date from between 1927 and 1935.

Joan Sutherland (soprano)

'Greatest hits': HANDEL: *Samson: Let the bright Seraphim.* ARDITI: *Il bacio.* LEHÁR: *Merry widow: Vilja.* J. STRAUSS JR: *Casanova: Nuns' chorus.* DONIZETTI: *Fille du régiment: Salut à la*

France! DELIBES: *Lakmé: Bell song.* BELLINI: *Norma: Casta diva.* GOUNOD: *Faust: Jewel song.*
DONIZETTI: *Lucia di Lammermoor: Mad scene.*
(M) *** Decca 417 780-2; *417 780-4* [id.].

A collection like this, well chosen to entertain, is self-recommending at mid-price. The recordings all come from the period when the voice was at its freshest: *Let the bright seraphim*, the *Bell song* from *Lakmé*, and the vivacious *Jewel song* from *Faust* in 1961, while the luscious version of *Vilja* (with chorus) was made in 1963. The lively excerpt from *La fille du régiment* comes from the complete set, as does the Mad scene from *Lucia di Lammermoor* – the 1961 first recording, under Pritchard. The sound is consistently vivid, and there is a first-class tape. A bargain.

'Opera gala': BELLINI: *Norma: Sediziosa voce . . . Casta diva . . . Ah! bello a me ritorna.*
DONIZETTI: *Lucia di Lammermoor: Ancor non giunse . . . Regnava nel silenzio. Il dolce suono mi colpi di sua voce! . . . Ardon gl'incensi. Linda di Chamounix: Ah! tardai troppo . . . O luce di quest'anima.* VERDI: *Ernani: Surta è la notte . . . Ernani involami. I vespri siciliani: Merce, dilette.*
🏵 (M) *** Decca 421 305-2 [id.].

Sutherland's 'Opera Gala' disc is one of the most cherishable of all operatic recital records, bringing together the glorious, exuberant items from her very first recital disc, made within weeks of her first Covent Garden success in 1959 and – as a valuable supplement – the poised account of *Casta diva* she recorded the following year as part of the *'Art of the Prima Donna'*. It was this 1959 recital which at once put Sutherland firmly on the map among the great recording artists of all time. Even she has never surpassed the freshness of these versions of the two big arias from *Lucia di Lammermoor*, sparkling in immaculate coloratura, while the lightness and point of the jaunty *Linda di Chamounix* aria and the *Boléro* from *I vespri siciliani* are just as winning. The sound is exceptionally vivid and immediate, though the accompaniments under Nello Santi are sometimes rough in ensemble.

'Romantic French arias' (with SRO, Bonynge) from: OFFENBACH: *Robinson Crusoé; La Grande-Duchesse de Gérolstein.* MEYERBEER: *Dinorah; Robert le Diable.* CHARPENTIER: *Louise.*
AUBER: *Manon Lescaut; Fra Diavolo.* BIZET: *Les pêcheurs de perles; Vasco da Gama.*
MASSENET: *Cendrillon.* MASSÉ: *Les noces de Jeannette.* GOUNOD: *Mireille; Le Tribut de Zamora; Faust.* LECOCQ: *Le coeur et la main.*
(M) *** Decca 421 879-2; *421 879-4* [id.].

This 73-minute recital encompasses much of the cream of a two-LP album, recorded in September 1969; for those new to the selection it will come as a delightful surprise to discover that Offenbach's *Robinson Crusoé* includes an irresistible waltz-song for the heroine as she steps ashore on Crusoe's island and is met by cannibals (*Take me to the man I adore*). Sutherland opens with that and sings here and in all the other brilliant numbers with great flair and abandon, relishing her virtuosity. The romantic side is represented by such enchanting items as Massenet's sad little Cinderella aria, Dinorah's sweet lullaby for her pet goat, a nightingale aria from Victor Massé's *Les noces de Jeannette* and a ravishing account of *Depuis le jour* from *Louise* to make most modern rivals sound pale and thin. Bizet's rare *Chanson bohème* from *Vasco da Gama* is most engaging, and the aria from his *Pearlfishers* is the only relative disappointment. The sound-balance in the Victoria Hall, Geneva, is quite well managed, but the CD transfer makes the voice sound brighter than usual.

'Operetta gala' (with New Philh. O, Bonynge): Arias from: OFFENBACH: *La Grande-Duchesse; La Périchole.* ZELLER: *Der Vogelhändler.* MILLOCKER: *Die Dubarry.* FALL: *Medley.* LEHÁR: *Eva; Paganini; Die lustige Witwe (The merry widow); Paganini.* O. STRAUS: *Ein Walzertraum; The Chocolate soldier.* HEUBERGER: *Der Opernball.* J. STRAUSS JR: *Casanova.* KREISLER: *The King steps out.* POSFORD: *Balalaika.*
(M) *** Decca 421 880-2; *421 880-4* [id.].

Opening with the vivacious military song from *La Grande-Duchesse de Gérolstein* (which derives from her French compilation), Sutherland goes on to charm us with the *Letter song* from *La Périchole* and then offers a substantial selection from her 1966 (two-disc) lilting, whooping operetta compilation, originally entitled rather cosily *'Love, live forever'*. This covers very much the same ground as Schwarzkopf's (full-priced) operetta collection. Sutherland may not always match Schwarzkopf in the haunting Viennese quality which inhabits such an enchanting number as *Im chambre séparée* (although her sensuous charm is disarming); but she is splendid in a fizzing number like *The Dubarry*, with the Ambrosians providing enthusiastic support, and the Leo Fall potpourri has comparable élan. What is immediately obvious is Sutherland's own delight in singing this music, and the accompaniments have matching infectious qualities, with Bonynge obviously entirely at home, providing the necessary light touch and idiomatic feeling for rubato. The sumptuous recording catches the glory of Sutherland's voice to perfection against a sparklingly rich orchestral and vocal backing. The chorus are splendid throughout.

'The age of Bel canto' (with Marilyn Horne, Richard Conrad, LSO or LPO, Bonynge): Arias & excerpts from: PICCINI: *La buona figliuola.* HANDEL: *Samson.* BONONCINI: *Astarto; Griselda.* SHIELD: *Rosina.* MOZART: *Die Zauberflöte.* BOIELDIEU: *Angela.* ROSSINI: *Semiramide.* WEBER: *Der Freischütz.* DONIZETTI: *Don Pasquale.* VERDI: *Attila.* BELLINI: *La straniera.* GRAUN: *Montezuma.*

(M) *** Decca 421 881-2; *421 881-4* [id.].

The original (1963) two-LP recital *'The age of Bel canto'*, from which virtually the whole of this mid-price reissue is taken, included arias for mezzo-soprano and tenor, as well as ensembles. It was understandable that Sutherland's contributions to the whole, not just solos but ensembles too, should one day be hived off like this; and a very impressive disc it makes. It is good to be reminded what a fine Mozartian Sutherland is, in the Queen of the Night's *O zittre nicht*, and the delightful point of Shield's *Light as thistledown* is irresistible. As for her duet, *Serbami ognor* from *Semiramide*, it brings a performance of equal mastery. Added to the items from the original set, to make up a total timing of nearly 72 minutes, comes a generous addition – two charming arias from the Sutherland/Bonynge 1966 records of *Griselda* and *Montezuma*. Here the balance is brighter, the voice more forward: in the main recital there is a more natural, concert-hall effect, very realistically transferred to CD.

'Command performance' (with LSO or New Philh. O, Bonynge): Arias from: WEBER: *Oberon.* MASSENET: *Le Cid.* MEYERBEER: *Dinorah; Les Huguenots.* LEONCAVALLO: *Pagliacci.* VERDI: *I Masnadieri; Luisa Miller.* ROSSINI: *La cambiale di matrimonio.* BELLINI: *Beatrice di Tenda.*

(M) *** Decca 421 882-2; *421 882-4* [id.].

The idea behind this 1963 'Command performance' recital was that Queen Victoria would have asked for just such a concert, had she been able to invite Joan Sutherland to Windsor. The LP issue was a presentation set of two records, provided with a lavishly illustrated booklet and notes by Andrew Porter. The reissue includes the contents of the first of the two LPs (thus omitting the frothier items) and, to make the concert more generous, her scena *O beau pays de la Touraine* from *Les Huguenots* (the opera with which she made her stage farewell in Sydney) is added as an appendix, ravishingly sung, taken from her (1969) complete set. There are now new, more succinct notes from Alan Blyth. As to Sutherland's singing, there was still too much of the 'mooning' style which had overtaken her in the early 1960s, words disappearing in the quest for ever more cooingly beautiful tone; but the coloratura is ecstatically beautiful, enlivening what would otherwise be too consistently languid an experience. The rare Verdi and Bellini arias are especially welcome. The recording is of Decca's best vintage, especially rich in the *Les Huguenots* excerpt.

'Tribute to Jenny Lind' (with various orchestras, Pritchard or Bonynge): Arias from BELLINI: *Beatrice di Tenda; I Puritani; La sonnambula.* DONIZETTI: *Rosamonda d'Inghilterra; La fille du régiment.* MOZART: *Le nozze di Figaro.* MEYERBEER: *L'étoile du nord.* ROSSINI: *Semiramide.* VERDI: *I Masnadieri.* Songs: ARDITI: *Il bacio.* BENEDICT: *The gypsy and the bird.* BISHOP: *Lo! here the gentle lark.*

(M) *** Decca 421 883-2; *421 883-4* [id.].

This recorded tribute from one great singer to another encompasses virtually the whole of Joan Sutherland's career onwards from her delectably fresh (1961) recording of Rosamonda's aria (Donizetti), complete with flute obbligato, and three frothier items from the original second LP of 'Command performance' (1962) with Benedict's *The gypsy and the bird*, a piece of Victorian nonsense of course, but providing with its trills and roulades a glorious opportunity for display – one of her most inspired pieces of singing on record. The 1968 *Fille du régiment* is justly celebrated, while the Meyerbeer excerpts come from her (1969) two-LP set of French repertoire, the bulk of which is available on the CD listed above. It is good to have the Mozart arias, to experience her ravishing phrasing in this repertoire. The three Bellini scenas demonstrate her varying vocal production between 1966 and 1980, when the *La sonnambula* excerpt, astonishingly agile, yet displayed a slight beat in the voice in the lyrical line. The careers of the two sopranos linked in the title were comparably successful, and their remarkable coloratura, impressive breath control and felicitous ornamentation had a good deal in common, but Sutherland almost certainly had the greater emotional range. Excellent sound throughout: all in all, a fascinating 74-minute collection.

'The art of the prima donna': ARNE: *Artaxerxes: The soldier tir'd.* HANDEL: *Samson: Let the bright seraphim.* BELLINI: *Norma: Casta diva.* I Puritani: *Son vergin vezzosa; Qui la voce. La Sonnambula: Come per me sereno.* ROSSINI: *Semiramide: Bel raggio lusinghier.* GOUNOD: *Faust: Jewel song. Roméo et Juliette: Waltz song.* VERDI: *Otello: Willow song. Rigoletto: Caro nome. La Traviata: Ah fors' è lui; Sempre libera.* MOZART: *Die Entführung aus dem Serail: Marten aller Arten.* THOMAS: *Hamlet: Mad scene.* DELIBES: *Lakmé: Bell song.* MEYERBEER: *Les Huguenots: O beau pays.*
⊛ (M) *** Decca 425 493-2 (2) [id.].

This ambitious early two-disc recital (from 1960) remains one of Joan Sutherland's outstanding gramophone achievements, and it is a matter of speculation whether even Melba or Tetrazzini in their heyday managed to provide sixteen consecutive recordings quite as dazzling as these performances. Indeed, it is the Golden Age that one naturally turns to rather than to current singers when making any comparisons. Sutherland herself by electing to sing each one of these fabulously difficult arias in tribute to a particular soprano of the past, from Mrs Billington in the eighteenth century, through Grisi, Malibran, Pasta and Jenny Lind in the nineteenth century, to Lilli Lehmann, Melba, Tetrazzini and Galli-Curci in this, is asking to be judged by the standards of the Golden Age. On the basis of recorded reminders she comes out with flying colours, showing a greater consistency and certainly a wider range of sympathy than even the greatest Golden Agers possessed. The sparkle and delicacy of the *Puritani Polonaise*, the freshness and lightness of the mad scene from Thomas's *Hamlet*, the commanding power of the *Entführung* aria and the breathtaking brilliance of the Queen's aria from *Les Huguenots* are all among the high spots here, while the arias which Sutherland later recorded in her complete opera sets regularly bring performances just as fine – and often finer – than the later versions. The freshness of the voice is caught superbly in the recording, which on CD is amazingly full, firm and realistic, far more believable than many new digital recordings.

'Prima donna assoluta': Arias from OFFENBACH: *Contes d'Hoffmann.* DONIZETTI: *Fille du régiment; Lucia di Lammermoor.* GOUNOD: *Faust.* BELLINI: *I Puritani.* VERDI: *La Traviata.*
(B) *** Decca 425 605-2.

Issued on Decca's cheapest label, this captivating recital concentrates on excerpts from Sutherland's complete sets. However, the closing *Lucia di Lammermoor* Mad scene derives from her famous 1959 Decca début record, conducted by Nello Santi, representing one of the most magical and thrilling displays of coloratura ever recorded: the luminous freshness of the voice is unforgettable. The other recordings come from between 1960 and 1972, and this disc is in every way a bargain. The documentation, however, is entirely biographical.

Joan Sutherland (soprano), Marilyn Horne (mezzo-soprano) and Luciano Pavarotti (tenor)

'Duets and trios from the Lincoln Center' (with NY City Op. O, Bonynge): excerpts from VERDI: *Ernani; Otello; Il Trovatore.* BELLINI: *Norma.* PONCHIELLI: *La Gioconda.*
**(*) Decca Dig. 417 587-2 [id.].

Not all gala concerts make good records, but this is an exception; almost every item here puts an important gloss on the achievements of the three principal stars in the concerted numbers. These have been extracted from the original two-LP set to make a single CD playing for 72 minutes. It is good to have a sample not only of Sutherland's Desdemona but of Pavarotti's Otello in their account of the Act I duet. The final scene from *Il Trovatore* is more compelling here than in the complete set made by the same soloists five years earlier. The microphone catches a beat in the voices of both Sutherland and Horne, but not as obtrusively as on some studio discs. Lively accompaniment under Bonynge; bright, vivid digital recording, but over-loud applause.

Joan Sutherland and Luciano Pavarotti (tenor)

Operatic duets (with Nat. PO, Bonynge) from: VERDI: *La Traviata; Otello; Aida* (with chorus). BELLINI: *La Sonnambula.* DONIZETTI: *Linda di Chamounix.*
*** Decca 400 058-2 [id.].

This collection offers a rare sample of Sutherland as Aida (*La fatale pietra . . . O terra, addio* from Act IV), a role she sang only once on stage, well before her international career began; and with this and her sensitive impersonations of Desdemona, Violetta and the Bellini and Donizetti heroines, Sutherland might have been expected to steal first honours here. In fact these are mainly duets to show off the tenor, and it is Pavarotti who runs away with the main glory, though both artists were plainly challenged to their finest and the result, with excellent accompaniment, is among the most attractive and characterful duet recitals. The recording is admirably clear and well focused, and the sophistication of orchestral detail is striking in the *Otello* and *Aida* scenes which close the recital; and this is especially striking on the compact disc which, though a remastered analogue recording, gives the artists remarkable presence. The cassette too is extremely well managed.

Operatic duets from: DONIZETTI: *Lucia di Lammermoor; L'elisir d'amore; Maria Stuarda; La fille du régiment.* VERDI: *Rigoletto.* BELLINI: *I Puritani.*
(M) *** Decca 421 894-2 [id.].

Taken from the complete opera recordings they made together from the late 1960s onwards, this collection of duets finds both superstars in glowing form, with Decca recordings of the finest vintage for the period very well transferred to CD. However, this is a straight reissue of a full-priced CD and now the measure (55 minutes 39 seconds) is not particularly generous.

Richard Tauber (tenor)

'Opera arias and duos' (with (i) Elisabeth Rethberg; (ii) Lotte Lehmann) from: MOZART: *Don Giovanni.* MÉHUL: *Joseph.* OFFENBACH: *Les Contes d'Hoffmann.* THOMAS: *Mignon.* TCHAIKOVSKY: *Eugene Onegin.* SMETANA: (i) *The Bartered Bride.* WAGNER: *Die Meistersinger.* PUCCINI: *Turandot;* (i) *Madama Butterfly.* KORNGOLD: (ii) *Die tote Stadt.*
(M) (***) EMI mono CDH7 640292 [id.].

Tauber's voice was one of the most distinctive of the century, and it was sad that, towards the end of his career, the light repertory of operetta so dominated in the public view of him. This selection from the inter-war years (1919–29) includes many of his most famous recordings, notably the excerpts from *Eugene Onegin, Tales of Hoffmann* and *The Bartered Bride*. In the duets from the latter and from *Madama Butterfly* he is joined by Rethberg and in *Die tote Stadt* by Lotte Lehmann. As usual in the EMI Références series, the transfers seek above all to give the voice a vivid presence, and this also means that the effect is sometimess less smooth and there are elements of distortion or interference. For the most part, however, the voice is vividly compelling.

'Prima voce': Arias from: R. STRAUSS: *Der Rosenkavalier.* WAGNER: *Die Walküre; Die Meistersinger.* KIENZL: *Der Evangelimann.* PUCCINI: *Tosca; La Bohème; Madama Butterfly; Turandot.* VERDI: *Il Trovatore.* MOZART: *Don Giovanni; Die Zauberflöte.* TCHAIKOVSKY: *Eugene Onegin.* BIZET: *Carmen.* KORNGOLD: *Die tote Stadt.* LORTZING: *Undine.* OFFENBACH: *Les contes d'Hoffmann.*
(M) (***) Nimbus mono NI 7830; *NC 7830* [id.].

The Nimbus transfers come from the same decade, between 1919 and 1929, and, although there is some duplication of repertoire, Tauber admirers will probably want both CDs. The effect of Nimbus transfers is always most impressive in the pre-electric recordings, which predominate here, but the voice is always naturally focused, even in the 1929 excerpt from Offenbach's *Tales of Hoffmann*. The effect is mellower, more rounded than in the EMI transfers.

Richard Tauber (tenor) and Lotte Schöne (soprano)

'Prima voce; Operetta arias' from LEHÁR: *Paganini. Zigeunerliebe. Der Land des Lächelns. Die lustige Witwe.* SUPPÉ: *Die schöne Galatea.* SCHUBERT/BERTÉ: *Das Dreimäderlhaus (Lilac time).*

J. STRAUSS JR: *Die Fledermaus; Der lustige Krieg; Indigo und die vierzig Räuber; Cagliosto in Wien.* KÁLMÁN: *Gräfin Mariza. Die Zirkusprinzessin.* MILLÖCKER: *Der arme Jonathan.* ZELLER: *Der Vogelhändler; Der Obersteiger.* NESSLER: *Der Trompeter von Säckingen.*
(M) (***) Nimbus mono NI 7833; *NC 7833* [id.].

These imaginatively chosen operetta excerpts, recorded over the same period (1919–29) as the operatic collections above, explain Tauber's phenomenal popularity over so many years. The collection is the more tempting for its inclusion of the contributions of Lotte Schöne, a delightful artist. Moreover there is much here that is very rare, and it is a pity that no duets were available – these are all solo items. The transfers are most successful.

Renata Tebaldi (soprano)

'The Early Recordings': VERDI: *Aida: Act I, Ritorna vincitor!; Act III* (complete; with Ebe Stignani, Dario Caselli, Aldo Protti, Mario Del Monaco, Ac. di Santa Cecilia Ch. & O, Erede); *Il Trovatore: Tacea la notte placida.* Arias from: GOUNOD: *Faust.* PUCCINI: *Madama Butterfly; Manon Lescaut; Tosca; La Bohéme.*
(M) (***) Decca mono 425 989-2 [id.].

This fascinating collection includes the very first records Tebaldi made for Decca in November 1949, in effect the start of a new era in operatic recording. More recital recordings were made in 1951. (I. M. remembers the great impact her initial mono LP made on him at the time, with the ravishing bloom of her lyrical line bringing a frisson of excitement and sentient pleasure which he has never forgotten.) This led to her early version of *Aida* of 1952, here represented by Act III, opposite two of her regular partners, neither showing anything like her finesse: the coarse Mario del Monaco and the colourless Aldo Protti, firmer here than he was to become. Though her later recordings are more refined in expressive detail, the freshness of these performances is a delight and, with the reservations noted concerning the mixed blessings of the *Aida* cast, our Rosette for her two-disc set, below, could be extended to cover many of the earlier items included here. Good transfers.

'La Tebaldi': (arias recorded 1955–68): PUCCINI: *Madama Butterfly; La Bohème; Tosca; Gianni Schicchi; Suor Angelica; Turandot; La rondine.* BOITO: *Mefistofele.* VERDI: *Aida; Otello; Il Trovatore; La forza del destino; Don Carlo; Un ballo in maschera; Giovanna d'Arco.* ROSSINI: *Guglielmo Tell.* CILEA: *Adriana Lecouvreur; L'arlesiana.* GIORDANO: *Andrea Chénier.* CATALANI: *La Wally.* PONCHIELLI: *La Gioconda.* MASCAGNI: *Cavalleria rusticana.* REFICE: *Cecilia.*
🏵 (B) *** Decca 430 481-2 (2) [id.].

This two-disc collection superbly celebrates one of the sopranos with a special place in the history of recording, the prima donna who in the early days of LP most clearly reflected a great period of operatic expansion. Unlike her great rival, Callas, thrilling, dynamic, unpredictable, often edgy and uneven on record, Tebaldi was above all reliable, with her creamy-toned voice, exceptionally even from top to bottom, and with its natural warmth ideally suited to recording. The 24 items here, entirely devoted to the Italian opera, cover the full range of her repertory from her justly famous assumption of the role of Butterfly to her personification of Leonora in *La forza del destino*, while she was an unforgettably moving Mimì in *La Bohème*. Many of the items are taken from the complete sets she recorded for Decca, generally more freely expressive than those originally issued on recital discs. The actual interpretations are totally consistent, though over the years the detail grew ever more refined. Excellent transfers. An indispensable set for all those who respond to this lovely voice, bringing a magical feeling of vulnerability to her personifications, when she creates a gentle, glowing pianissimo.

Renata Tebaldi (soprano) and Franco Corelli (tenor)

Arias and duets (with SRO & Ch., Anton Guadagno) from: PUCCINI: *Manon Lescaut; La Bohème; Tosca.* CILEA: *Adriana Lecouvreur.* PONCHIELLI: *La Gioconda.* VERDI: *Aida.* ZANDONAI: *Francesca da Rimini.*
(M) ** Decca 436 301-2 [id.].

These recordings were made towards the end of Tebaldi's singing career. Franco Corelli was often her partner at the Met. and he, more noticeably than she, demonstrates a fair degree of wear and tear on the voice. The recording of the five duets which are the kernel of this recital dates from 1972, and the two-dimensional stereo is unflattering to both artists. Their chosen style is the epitome of the Italian verismo tradition in vibrant but somewhat coarse-sounding excerpts from *Manon Lescaut, Adriana Lecouvreur, Aida,* and *La Gioconda* – Tebaldi's last stage role, and one of the more successful items (*Ma chi vien? . . . Oh! la sinistra voce!*). By far the most impressive excerpt is the nineteen-minute scene which offers the Act 3 love duet between Francesca and Paolo in Zandonai's *Francesca da Rimini,* and even includes a chorus. At its emotional climax Tebaldi sings with ravishing tenderness. Corelli is obviously moved by his partner, and responds accordingly. Among the solos, it is good to hear Tebaldi change roles to sing *Musetta's waltz song* from La *Bohème,* and the result is agreeably, tonally rich, like a natural Countess taking over Susanna's role in *Nozze di Figaro.* In 1969 Tebaldi could still sing *Ritorna vincitor* ripely and movingly, even if there is a hint that she is not quite secure vocally. Corelli contributes lusty versions of the two famous tenor arias, *Recondita armonia* and *E lucevan le stelle* from *Tosca.*

Tenors

'Great tenors of our time' (with (i) Carlo Bergonzi; (ii) Franco Corelli; (iii) Plácido Domingo; (iv) Nicolai Gedda; (v) James McCracken; (vi) Luciano Pavarotti; (vii) Jon Vickers): (ii) VERDI: *Aida: Se quel guerrier . . . Celeste Aida.* (v) *Otello: Niun mi tema.* (i) *La forza del destino: O tu che in seno.* (iv) BIZET: *Les Pêcheurs de perles: Je crois entendre.* (vii) *Carmen: Flower song.* (i) PUCCINI: *Tosca: E lucevan le stelle.* (ii) *Turandot: Nessun dorma.* (iii) *Manon Lescaut: Donna non vidi mai.* (ii) GIORDANO: *Andrea Chénier: Come un bel dì.* (vi) MASCAGNI: *L'Amico Fritz: Ed anche . . . oh amore.* (iv) GOUNOD: *Faust: Salut! Demeure.* (viii) SAINT-SAËNS: *Samson et Dalila: Arrêtez, o mes frères.*
(M) **(*) EMI CD-EMX 2114; *TC-EMX 2114.*

EMI compiled this anthology ingeniously from many sources; for example, Luciano Pavarotti, an exclusive Decca artist from early in his international career, had earlier still taken part in EMI's complete set of *L'Amico Fritz,* so providing the excerpt which completes this constellation of great tenors. Not that each is necessarily represented in the most appropriate items, and the compilation does have one wishing (for example) that Vickers rather than McCracken was singing *Otello,* though that excerpt is valuable for preserving a sample of Barbirolli's complete set of that opera. And although Vickers does not make an ideal Don José, it is useful to have his *Flower song,* since the set from which it comes is one of the less recommendable versions. The transfers are clear and fresh, the voices given immediacy, the orchestral backing suitably atmospheric. Considering the variety of the sources (dating from 1959 – Plácido Domingo's fine *Salut! Demeure* – to 1974 – the same artist's stirring *Celeste Aida,* which opens the programme), the recording is remarkably consistent.

Tenors: 'Ten Top tenors' ((i) Luciano Pavarotti; (ii) Franco Corelli; (iii) José Carreras; (iv) Giuseppe Di Stefano; (v) Giacomo Aragall; (vi) Jon Vickers; (vii) Carlo Bergonzi; (viii) Mario Del Monaco; (ix) Jussi Bjoerling; (x) Plácido Domingo): Arias from: PUCCINI: (i) *La Bohème;* (ii) *Tosca;* (iii) *Manon Lescaut;* (iv) *Turandot.* VERDI: (v) *Simon Boccanegra;* (vi) *Aida;* (vii) *Luisa Miller.* MEYERBEER: *L'Africaine.* (vi) WAGNER: *Die Walküre.* GIORDANO: (viii) *Fedora.* LEONCAVALLO: *Pagliacci.* PONCHIELLI: (ix) *La Gioconda.* CILEA: *L'Arlesiana.* MASSENET: (iv) *Werther.* BIZET: (x) *Carmen.* OFFENBACH: *Les Contes d'Hoffmann.*
(M) *** Decca 436 463-2 [id.].

For most opera lovers this collection (which is most elegantly described in French as '*Dix tenors exceptionnels*') will make an easy first choice among the four Decca anthologies celebrating the different genres of operatic vocalism. Certainly no one could complain about the star-quality of the cast-list here, and the selection is equally apt. The other fascinating discovery that emerges from this CD is that tenor arias are usually shorter than those for sopranos, mezzos, basses and baritones. The operatic characters normally assumed by these latter voices tend to soliloquize more, whereas the characteristic tenor number is a potent burst of passion. So there is room on this 75-minute CD for *two* items from each artist, and that means most of the top favourite arias are here. Pavarotti opens up ravishingly with his luscious *Che gelida manina,* and Domingo closes with one of the longer and jollier items, *The Legend of Kleinzach.* In between, Corelli is in glorious voice in the two most famous *Tosca* arias, and his other colleagues all show their ability to thrill or make one catch a breath. Even Mario del Monaco, the belter, is at home in *Vesti la giubba*. A splendid programme, vividly sung and recorded, and just about adequately documented.

Tenor arias: 'Great tenor arias'

'Great tenor arias' (sung by: (i) Luciano Pavarotti; (ii) Jussi Bjoerling; (iii) Mario Del Monaco; (iv) Carlo Bergonzi; (v) James McCracken; (vi) Bruno Previdi; (vii) Giuseppe Di Stefano). Arias from: (i) FLOTOW: *Martha.* (ii) CILEA: *L'Arlesiana;* (iv) *Adriana Lecouvreur.* GIORDANO: (ii) *Fedora;* (iii; vi) *Andrea Chénier.* (iv) MEYERBEER: *L'Africaine.* VERDI: (iii) *Un ballo in maschera;* (v) *La forza del destino;* (vi) *Il Trovatore.* (vii) MASSENET: *Manon; Werther.* (i) DONIZETTI: *La Favorita.* (v) LEONCAVALLO: *Pagliacci.*
(M) ** Decca 421 869-2.

It is always illuminating to hear the voices of different tenors juxtaposed. Pavarotti with his warm, lyrical line, heard at its most beguiling in the opening *M'apparì* from *Martha*, the heady upper range of Carlo Bergonzi in Meyerbeer's *O paradiso*, and the fine, stylish – indeed melting – line of Giuseppe di Stefano in Massenet. Previdi is more robust in a traditional way, but he is thrilling in *Un dì all'azzurro spazio* from *Andrea Chénier*, while James McCracken's histrionics in *Vesti la giubba* are hardly less compelling. Mario del Monaco must have been very impressive in the opera house, but on record he is often and consistently too loud, as in his contribution from *Un ballo in maschera*. There are other good things here, but overall this is not an indispensable collection.

Luisa Tetrazzini (soprano)

'Prima voce': Arias from: BELLINI: *La Sonnambula.* DONIZETTI: *Lucia di Lammermoor.* ROSSINI: *Il Barbiere di Siviglia.* THOMAS: *Mignon.* VERACINI: *Rosalinda.* VERDI: *Un ballo in maschera; Rigoletto; La Traviata; Il Trovatore; I vespri siciliani.* Songs.
(M) (***) Nimbus mono NI 7808 [id.].

Tetrazzini was astonishing among coloratura sopranos not just for her phenomenal agility but for the golden warmth that went with tonal purity. The Nimbus transfers add a bloom to the sound, with the singer slightly distanced. Though some EMI transfers make her voice more vividly immediate, one quickly adjusts. Such display arias as *Ah non giunge* from *La Sonnambula* or the *Bolero* from *I vespri siciliani* are incomparably dazzling, but it is worth noting too what tenderness is conveyed through Tetrazzini's simple phrasing and pure tone in such a tragic aria as Violetta's *Addio del passato*, with both verses included. Lieder devotees may gasp in horror, but one of the delightful oddities here is Tetrazzini's bright-eyed performance, with ragged orchestral accompaniment, of what is described as *La serenata inutile* by Brahms – in fact *Vergebliches Ständchen*, sung with a triumphant if highly inauthentic top A at the end, implying no closure of the lady's window!

Georges Thill (tenor)

French opera arias (with orchestras conducted by Bigot; Heurteur; Gaubert; Szyfer; Frigara): BERLIOZ: *La Damnation de Faust: Nature immense, impénétrable et fière. Les Troyens à Carthage: Inutiles regrets.* BIZET: *Carmen: La fleur que tu m'avais jetée.* GLUCK: *Alceste: Bannis la crainte et les alarmes.* GOUNOD: *Faust: Quel trouble inconnu me pénètre. Roméo et Juliette: L'amour, l'amour* (with Germaine Feraldy). MASSENET: *Le Cid: O noble lame étincelante; O souverain! O Juge! O père. Werther: Invocation à la nature; Un autre est son époux!.* ROSSINI: *Guillaume Tell: Asile héréditaire.* SAINT-SAËNS: *Samson et Dalila: Air de la meule.*
Withdrawn: (M) (***) EMI mono CDM7 69548-2.

Georges Thill left an enormous discography, and this selection of 78 r.p.m. discs made between 1927 and 1936 will come as a revelation to younger collectors unacquainted with his work. He made his début at the Paris Opéra in 1924 and soon established himself as the greatest French tenor of his day. The tone is splendidly full and round and the phrasing masterly. In an age when one is lucky to make out what language is being sung, let alone the actual words, his diction is an object-lesson. Every word resonates, and yet it is the musical line which remains paramount. At 74 minutes, this is a generous sampling of his recorded legacy, very well transferred and absolutely indispensable to anyone who cares about singing.

Lawrence Tibbett (baritone)

Arias from: LEONCAVALLO: *Pagliacci*. ROSSINI: *Il Barbiere di Siviglia*. VERDI: *Un ballo in maschera; Simon Boccanegra; Falstaff*. PUCCINI: *Tosca*. BIZET: *Carmen*. GOUNOD: *Faust*. WAGNER: *Die Walküre*. GRUENBERG: *Emperor Jones*. HANSON: *Merry Mount*. GERSHWIN: *Porgy and Bess*.
(M) (***) BMG/RCA mono GD 87808 [7808-2-RG].

The glorious, characterful timbre of Tibbett's baritone is superbly caught in RCA's clear, immediate transfers, with the vibrato never obtrusive as it can be on some records. It is sad that so commanding a singer was heard relatively little outside America; but this is a superb memorial, not just for the classic arias but for such an item as the excerpt from Louis Gruenberg's *Emperor Jones*, a role he created.

'Tibbett in opera': excerpts from: LEONCAVALLO: *Pagliacci*. BIZET: *Carmen*. PUCCINI: *Tosca*. VERDI: *Un ballo in maschera; Simon Boccanegra; Rigoletto; Otello*. ROSSINI: *Il barbiere di Siviglia*. GOUNOD: *Faust*. WAGNER: *Tannhäuser; Die Walküre*.
(M) (***) Nimbus mono NI 7825 [id.].

The scale and resonance of Lawrence Tibbett's voice come over vividly in this fine selection of his recordings made between 1926 and 1939. The Nimbus process allows the rapid vibrato in his voice to emerge naturally, giving the sound a thrilling richness in all these varied items. Particularly interesting is the longest, the whole of *Wotan's farewell*, with Stokowski conducting the Philadelphia Orchestra in 1934. It is an over-the-top performance that carries total conviction, even if the sheer volume produces some clangorous resonances in the Nimbus transfer. Also memorable is the celebrated *Boccanegra* Council chamber sequence, recorded in 1939 with Martinelli and Rose Bampton in the ensemble.

Eva Turner (soprano)

Opera arias and songs: Arias from VERDI: *Il Trovatore; Aida*. PONCHIELLI: *La Gioconda*. PUCCINI: *Tosca; Madama Butterfly; Turandot*. MASCAGNI: *Cavalleria Rusticana*. WAGNER: *Lohengrin; Tannhäuser*. Songs: GRIEG: *I love thee*. TOSTI: *Goodbye*. RONALD: *O lovely night*. DEL RIEGO: *Homing*. D'HARDELOT: *Because; Sometime in my dreams*.
(M) (***) EMI mono CDH7 69791-2.

The art of Eva Turner is superbly celebrated in this generous selection of recordings made between 1928 and 1933. They include not only her celebrated 1928 recording of Turandot's *In questa reggia* but also magnificent samples of her portrayals as Aida, Leonora in *Trovatore* and La Gioconda, as well as half a dozen songs and ballads. Most fascinating of all are her two Wagner recordings, of *Elsa's dream* from *Lohengrin* and *Elisabeth's greeting* from *Tannhäuser*, sung in English. These were never issued, and Dame Eva's copy of the latter, the only one surviving, was broken into three pieces. It was lovingly reassembled so that it could be played, if with persistent clicks. The CEDAR process (Computer Enhanced Digital Audio Restoration) was then used to eliminate the clicks, automatically filling in each microscopic gap with surrounding material in a way impossible if the process is to be done laboriously by hand. The finished result is among the most thrilling of all the recordings ever made by Dame Eva, rich and intense. (It is a delight also to have Dame Eva's spoken introduction, recorded in June 1988 when she was in her ninety-eighth year, lustily emphatic in the most characterful way. Walter Legge used to say that her top Cs projected right through the back wall of Covent Garden and out into Bow Street, and her speaking voice, even in her late nineties, makes you believe it.) Keith Hardwick's transfers, quite apart from the help from CEDAR, are models of their kind, with the voice astonishingly vivid.

Fritz Wunderlich (tenor)

'Great voice': Arias and excerpts from: MOZART: *Die Zauberflöte; Die Entführung aus dem Serail.* VERDI: *La Traviata* (with Hilde Gueden); *Rigoletto* (with Erika Köth); *Don Carlos* (with Hermann Prey). TCHAIKOVSKY: *Eugene Onegin.* LORTZING: *Zar und Zimmermann; Der Waffenschmied.* ROSSINI: *Der Barbier von Sevilla.* PUCCINI: *La Bohème* (with Prey); *Tosca.* Lieder: SCHUBERT: *Heidenröslein.* BEETHOVEN: *Ich liebe dich.* TRAD.: *Funiculi-funicula; Ein Lied geht um die Welt* (with R. Lamy Ch.).
(B) *** DG 431 110-2 [id.].

Of the eight collections in DG's *'Grosse Stimmen'* series, this is easily the most attractive – 70 minutes of gloriously heady tenor singing from one of the golden voices of the 1960s. Mozart's *Dies Bildnis* makes a ravishing opener, and *Hier soll ich dich denn sehen* from *Die Entführung* is equally beautiful. Then come two sparkling excerpts from *La Traviata* with Hilde Gueden and some memorable Tchaikovsky, like all the Italian repertoire, sung in German. The Rossini excerpt is wonderfully crisp and stylish. Wunderlich is joined by the charming Erika Köth in *Rigoletto* and by Hermann Prey for the rousing *Don Carlos* duet (*Sie ist verloren . . . Er ist's! Carlos!*) and the excerpt from *Bohème*. Last in the operatic group comes the most famous *Tosca* aria, *Und es blitzen die Sterne* (not too difficult to identify in Italian) sung without excess histrionics. The Schubert and Beethoven Lieder are lovely, and, if the two final popular songs (with chorus) bring more fervour than they deserve, one can revel in everything else. Excellent recording throughout. It is a pity there are no translations or notes, but with singing like this one can manage without them. A splendid bargain.

And Finally . . .

. . . 'Karaoke Opera'

'Karaoke Opera' (with Susan McCulloch, Anne-Marie Owens, John Oakman, Steven Page, Prague Philharmonic Ch., Czech PO, Julian Bigg): Arias & duets from: BIZET: *Carmen; Les pêcheurs de perles.* SAINT-SAËNS: *Samson et Dalila.* OFFENBACH: *Les Contes d'Hoffmann.* PUCCINI: *Madama Butterfly; La Bohème; Gianni Schicchi; Turandot.* ROSSINI: *Il barbiere di Siviglia.* VERDI: *La Traviata; Rigoletto.* MOZART: *Don Giovanni.* LEONCAVALLO: *Pagliacci.* (M) **(*) Pickwick Dig. DPCD 1015 (2) [id.].

Here are two famous duets and 14 favourite arias enjoyably sung by four excellent young British singers, admirably accompanied by the Czech Philharmonic Orchestra with chorus under Julian Bigg. Having used these performances as a model, you can then try to measure up to their standards, if not Pavarotti's! If you can find a fellow baritone/tenor, you are all set for the *Pearlfishers'* *Au fond du temple saint*, which is offered in three different permutations (with tenor, with baritone, or orchestra alone). The *Barcarolle* from *The Tales of Hoffmann* is offered twice, with the mezzo part provided or with the orchestra alone. In all the solo arias there is just the orchestra, and you will need to use earphones, for the dynamic range of the recording is wide and if you sing out lustily you will probably not be able to hear the quieter moments of the accompaniments.

A bright idea, not let down by poor documentation – all the texts are here, both in the original language and in English, and there are helpful hints about pronunciation. So, if you have always wanted to be seductive in Carmen's *Seguidilla* or take the roof off with Puccini's *Nessun dorma*, here is your chance!

Index of Singers

Whenever a singer's name occurs more than once on the same page of this book (either because that singer appears in the listing of more than one version of a work or because his or her name appears in more than one work on the same page) we have indicated this fact by repeating the relevant page number in this Index. We hope that this will prove helpful to readers.

Ackland, Joss, 393
Adam, Noelle, 344
Adam, Theo, 6, 6, 210, 225, 243, 258, 258, 258, 418, 424, 520, 522, 529, 535, 535, 535, 538, 539, 539, 542, 542, 542, 551, 551, 561, 561
Adams, Donald, 428, 428, 430, 432, 433, 435, 437, 438, 438, 441, 444, 444
Adani, Mariella, 297
Adler, Bruce, 96
Adorf, Mario, 565
Adrian, Max, 21
Agache, Alexandru, 79
Ahlin, Cvetka, 257
Ahmad, Irfan, 4
Ahnsjö, Claes Hakon, 79, 150, 150, 151, 152, 155, 155, 254, 255
Ainsley, John Mark, 33, 122, 136, 143, 189, 220, 425
Aitken, Maria, 393
Alagna, Roberto, 74
Alaimo, Simone, 82, 232, 356, 361, 372
Alan, Hervey, 243, 332
Alarie, Pierrette, 30
Albanese, Licia, 297, 297, 309, 322, 391, 575
Alberghetti, Anna Maria, 287
Albert, Donnie Ray, 98
Albert, Laurence, 89
Alda, Frances, 513, 597
Aldredge, Tom, 392
Aler, John, 3, 20, 30, 89, 107, 108, 144, 226, 272, 358
Alexander, Carlos, 280
Alexander, Cris, 585
Alexander, Jace, 390
Alexander, Jason, 96
Alexander, John, 10, 12, 519
Alexander, Roberta, 99, 134, 148, 233, 243, 454
Alexashkin, Sergei, 294
Alexeev, Valery, 267
Allegri, Maria Garcia, 196
Allen, Betty, 170
Allen, Clifford, 585
Allen, Thomas, 18, 44, 44, 108, 113, 165, 184, 207, 226, 232, 232, 247, 248, 257, 327, 353, 450, 457
Alliot-Lugaz, Colette, 49, 53, 56, 65, 212, 272, 273
Allister, Jean, 428, 437
Alperyn, Graciela, 25
Altmeyer, Jeannine, 6, 522, 522, 539, 539, 542, 551, 551
Alva, Luigi, 125, 151, 153, 154, 217, 227, 232, 233, 353, 353, 353, 357, 364

Amara, Lucine, 184, 296
Amato, Pasquale, 513
Ameling, Elly, 155, 517
Ancona, Mario, 603, 603
Anderberg, Viveka, 32
Anders, Peter, 608
Anderson, James, 453
Anderson, June, 3, 22, 29, 120, 201, 257, 366, 366, 496, 514, 519
Anderson, Marian, 593
Andersson, Anders, 93
Andreas, Christine, 349
Andreoli, Florindo, 184
Andrews, George Lee, 395
Andrews, Julie, 345, 346, 348
Angas, Richard, 278, 435
Angelici, Martha, 608
Anthony, Trevor, 40, 42, 332
Anzellotti, Ala, 609
Aragall, Giacomo, 81, 113, 196, 204, 314, 326, 500, 590, 600, 602, 620
Araiza, Francisco, 20, 50, 82, 113, 226, 227, 232, 243, 257, 257, 274, 353, 356, 357, 364, 373, 465, 479, 561, 576
Ardam, Elzbieta, 413
Argenta, Nancy, 33, 108, 109, 126, 141, 145, 146, 152, 220, 258, 330, 332
Arié, Raffaele, 79, 609
Arizmendi, Elena, 609
Arkhipova, Irina, 264, 267
Armstrong, Karan, 157
Armstrong, Sheila, 446, 460
Arroyo, Martina, 214, 232, 233, 468, 481, 510
Arthur, Maurice, 83
Arvidson, Jerker, 32
Ashe, Rosemary, 4, 65, 350, 571
Asmus, Rudolf, 408
Atlantov, Vladimir, 267, 450, 452, 452
Augér, Arleen, 25, 62, 124, 130, 138, 149, 154, 155, 207, 218, 223, 224, 232, 238, 245, 246, 248, 254, 340, 410, 563, 567
Ausensi, Manuel, 353
Austral, Florence, 557
Auvinen, Ritva, 174
Avdeyeva, Larissa, 293
Ayars, Ann, 111
Ayldon, John, 430, 433, 439, 441, 443

Baccaloni, Salvatore, 232, 297
Bach, Mechthild, 455

Bacquier, Gabriel, 18, 29, 53, 55, 68, 77, 84, 89, 203, 214, 227, 233, 248, 264, 272, 274, 274, 279, 290, 341, 363, 481
Badioli, Carlo, 297
Baiano, Valeria, 356
Bailey, Norman, 41, 72, 257, 350, 457, 519, 526, 528, 538, 545, 555
Bailey, Pearl, 31
Bainbridge, Elizabeth, 10, 44, 158, 318, 327, 571
Baird, Julianne, 220
Baker, George, 431, 431, 433, 436, 438, 441, 445, 445
Baker, Gregg, 97
Baker, Janet, 18, 43, 46, 50, 83, 86, 86, 109, 112, 134, 143, 225, 227, 326, 598
Baker, Marilyn, 40
Baker-Genovesi, Margaret, 221
Baldani, Ruša, 492
Baldin, Aldo, 151, 152, 248, 257
Ball, Michael, 24
Ballard, Kaye, 288, 346
Balleys, Brigitte, 210, 517
Balslev, Lisbeth, 519
Balthrop, Carmen, 170
Baltsa, Agnes, 9, 25, 73, 82, 109, 196, 224, 227, 232, 242, 246, 248, 257, 285, 353, 356, 364, 376, 398, 408, 418, 421, 461, 472, 481, 545, 576, 580, 598, 602
Bamber, Peter, 334
Bampton, Rose, 6, 608
Bándi, János, 128, 416
Banditelli, Gloria, 51, 106, 123, 510
Baniewicz, Wiera, 196
Bannatyne-Scott, Brian, 332
Bär, Olaf, 257, 258, 398, 407
Barabas, Sari, 358
Barbacini, Paolo, 353
Barbaux, Christine, 25, 207
Barber, Lynn, 171
Barbieri, Fedora, 196, 318, 461, 461, 468, 479, 507, 507, 609
Barclay, Yvonne, 71
Barham, Edmund, 571
Barioni, Daniele, 311, 607
Barlay, Zsuzsa, 312
Baronti, Dullio, 297
Barová, Anna, 167
Barrett, Brent, 97, 189, 575
Barstow, Josephine, 4, 39, 288, 467, 567
Bartfai-Barta, Eva, 128
Bartholomew, Ian, 392
Bartlett, Michael, 391
Bartoli, Cecilia, 227, 245, 248, 353, 375, 375, 598

Bartolini, Lando, 343
Barton, Steve, 187
Basiola, Mario, 184, 305
Bastian, Gert, 271
Bastianini, Ettore, 101, 196, 285, 296, 472, 481, 503, 577, 596, 602
Bastin, Jules, 18, 18, 20, 200, 216, 227, 248, 278, 290, 340
Batten, Tom, 63
Battistini, Mattia, 577, 603
Battle, Kathleen, 74, 144, 227, 232, 238, 248, 353, 408, 467, 472, 514, 542, 613
Batty, Christine, 397
Bayo, Maria, 368
Bazsinka, Zsuzsanna, 200
Beaton, Morag, 158
Beavers, Dick, 349
Bechi, Gino, 101, 196, 608
Becht, Hermann, 383, 522, 535, 539, 542
Becker, Josef, 396
Beckerbauer, Stefan, 109
Beckmann, Friedel, 557, 608
Bednáf, Václav, 193
Begányi, Ferenc, 367
Begg, Heather, 21
Begley, Kim, 10
Behrens, Hildegard, 6, 16, 191, 411, 413, 421, 542, 548, 551, 561, 600
Beilke, Irma, 257
Belarsky, Sidor, 6
Belcourt, Emile, 272, 278, 288, 538
Bell, Donaldson, 158
Bello, Vincenzo, 184
Beňačková, Gabriela, 85, 167, 388, 389
Benelli, Ugo, 184, 184, 213, 248, 353, 357, 360
Benningsen, Lilian, 248, 529
Benoit, Jean-Christoph, 207
Benson, Jodi, 96
Bentley, Jordan, 585
Berberian, Cathy, 218, 220
Berbié, Jane, 55, 68, 200, 227, 247, 248, 277, 340, 340, 341, 372, 376
Berganza, Teresa, 25, 90, 125, 225, 225, 227, 232, 248, 248, 264, 279, 305, 353, 353, 357, 364, 577, 589, 590, 598
Berger, Erna, 232, 257
Berglund, Joel, 608
Berglund, Rut, 258
Bergonzi, Carlo, 60, 79, 184, 196, 296, 305, 305, 314, 325, 461, 466, 468, 468, 472, 477, 481, 486, 488, 490, 492, 496, 503, 503, 514, 514, 578, 578, 596, 601, 602, 620, 620, 621
Bergquist, Eleanor, 202
Bergström, Lasse, 93
Berman, Karel, 167, 193
Bernac, Pierre, 608
Bernadet, Andrée, 614
Bernheimer, Julia, 257
Berry, Walter, 4, 6, 16, 162, 175, 226, 232, 232, 232, 232, 257, 258, 258, 398, 398, 398, 405, 408, 413, 418, 548, 601
Bertin, Pascal, 127

Bertocchi, Sergio, 71
Best, Jonathan, 380
Beudert, Mark, 22
Bevan, Maurice, 330, 331, 333
Bevan, Nigel, 333
Bexton, David, 393
Bianco, René, 30
Bickley, Susan, 327
Bieber, Clemens, 421
Bierbaum, Andrea, 52
Bieshu, M., 10
Bikel, Theodore, 345, 348
Bindi, Jean-Louis, 57
Bisatt, Susan, 71
Bischoff, Romain, 382
Bise, Juliette, 340
Bisson, Yves, 3
Bjoerling, Anna-Lisa, 579
Bjoerling, Jussi, 196, 196, 296, 305, 309, 314, 325, 461, 496, 507, 578, 601, 602, 608, 620, 621
Bjoerling, Sigurd, 556
Bjørkøy, Kåre, 117, 119
Blachut, Beno, 168, 608
Blackburn, Harold, 38, 441
Blackwell, Harolyn, 97
Blake, Rockwell, 71
Blake Jones, Philip, 433
Blanc, Ernest, 25, 30, 113, 277, 377, 601, 601
Blankenheim, Toni, 14
Blanzat, Anne-Marie, 84
Blasi, Angela Maria, 254, 297
Blazer, Judy, 96
Blegen, Judith, 248, 256, 297
Blessed, Brian, 187
Blochwitz, Hans-Peter, 6, 148, 210, 227, 233, 242, 258, 455
Blom, Inger, 93
Blyden, Larry, 348, 394, 395
Boatwright, McHenry, 98, 99
Bobbie, Walter, 188
Bockelmann, Rudolf, 557, 557
Bode, Hannelore, 528, 528
Boehme, Kurt, 232, 258, 414, 539, 539, 542, 542
Boesch, Christian, 263
Bogart, John Paul, 320
Böhm, Karl-Walter, 421
Bokov, Anatoly, 448
Boky, Colette, 25
Boldin, Leonid, 170
Bona, Jacques, 57
Bonazzi, Elaine, 369
Bonilla, Daniel, 465
Bonisolli, Franco, 108, 490, 507
Bonner, Tessa, 33, 220, 327
Bonney, Barbara, 24, 74, 116, 117, 162, 232, 233, 248, 258, 384, 402, 567
Booth, Webster, 608
Boozer, Brenda, 478
Borg, Kim, 86, 257, 280, 608
Borgioli, Armando, 314
Borisova, Galina, 293, 452
Borkh, Inge, 280, 320, 411, 413, 608
Bormida, Ida, 196
Borodina, Olga, 267, 294
Borowska, Joanna, 227, 267

Borriello, Mario, 305, 309
Borris, Kaja, 519
Borst, Danielle, 214, 218, 517
Borthayre, Jean, 205
Boschkowá, Nelly, 305
Bostock, Angela, 83
Bott, Catherine, 220, 397
Bottone, Bonaventura, 22, 278, 350, 435, 496, 567, 571
Boué, Géori, 608
Boulin, Sophie, 57, 107, 125
Bouvier, Hélène, 608
Bowden, Pamela, 158, 441, 445
Bowen, Kenneth, 38
Bowman, James, 38, 41, 50, 129, 130, 134, 136, 138, 139, 218, 330, 334
Boyer, Marie, 48
Boysen, Rolf, 565
Bracht, Roland, 257, 425, 519
Bradshaw, Sally, 69, 123
Brammer, Dieter, 565
Brandstetter, John, 23
Brannigan, Owen, 36, 41, 42, 44, 122, 330, 429, 431, 432, 433, 433, 437, 438, 438, 441, 443, 445, 445
Braun, Victor, 545
Brecknock, John, 183, 506
Brendel, Wolfgang, 257, 398, 398
Brett, Charles, 135, 149
Brightman, Sarah, 187, 187
Brilioth, Helge, 522, 539
Broad, John, 443
Brodersen, Edith, 271
Bronhill, June, 95, 182, 278
Brouwenstijn, Gré, 1, 552, 608
Brown, Donna, 126, 143, 179
Brown, Wilfred, 332, 332
Browner, Alison, 492
Browning, Susan, 394, 395, 395
Brownlee, John, 227, 232
Brua, Claire, 57
Bruce, Carol, 171
Bruna Rasa, Lina, 196
Bruscantini, Sesto, 73, 76, 226, 247, 353, 356, 357, 481, 518
Bruson, Renato, 79, 153, 196, 309, 314, 325, 376, 465, 467, 468, 476, 477, 478, 481, 486, 488, 496, 503, 570
Bryant, Dinah, 274, 405
Bryant, Jim, 24
Bryne, Barbara, 394
Brynner, Yul, 345
Bryson, Peabo, 345
Bryson, Roger, 380
Bubbles, John, 99
Buchan, Michael, 443
Buchanan, Isobel, 13, 142, 207
Büchner, Eberhard, 242
Bulman, Michael, 393
Bumbry, Grace, 25, 202, 462, 465, 472, 547, 598
Bundschuh, Eva-Maria, 522
Burbridge, Tessa, 392
Burchuladze, Paata, 232, 267, 353, 376, 450, 461, 481, 496, 500, 514, 577
Burles, Charles, 68, 272, 277, 277, 376

Burmeister, Annelies, 248, 258, 517, 520, 535, 551
Burnett, Carol, 391
Burns, Karla, 171, 288
Burrowes, Norma, 25, 122, 135, 143, 144, 150, 160, 162, 238, 330, 460
Burrows, Stuart, 19, 225, 232, 233, 238, 258, 264, 450, 579
Burt, Michael, 157
Busch, David, 224
Buttrey, John, 330
Byers, Alan, 334

Caballé, Montserrat, 10, 10, 12, 13, 14, 33, 33, 79, 81, 101, 113, 184, 196, 227, 285, 297, 309, 314, 320, 322, 324, 325, 325, 325, 360, 363, 372, 421, 423, 461, 465, 468, 471, 472, 486, 490, 503, 558, 580, 581, 589, 590, 600, 602, 612, 613
Cable, Margaret, 123, 138
Cachemaille, Gilles, 18, 65, 112, 212, 214, 227, 232, 358
Caddy, Ian, 93
Cadelo, Cettina, 52
Caforio, Armando, 476
Cahill, Teresa, 44
Calabrese, Franco, 247, 372
Caley, Ian, 81
Callas, Maria, 10, 10, 13, 13, 25, 59, 78, 78, 79, 184, 196, 285, 297, 305, 309, 314, 314, 320, 353, 372, 461, 468, 483, 496, 503, 503, 507, 512, 581, 601, 601, 609, 612
Callaway, Liz, 391
Calm, Birgit, 318
Calvé, Emma, 603
Cameron, John, 86, 332, 429, 431, 431, 433, 436, 443, 445, 445
Caminada, Anita, 13
Campora, Giuseppe, 324, 500
Canali, Anna Maria, 79, 196, 305
Canepa, Lorenza, 476
Caniglia, Maria, 101, 314
Canne-Meijer, Cora, 358, 455
Canonici, Luca, 371
Cantelo, April, 36, 40, 332, 433
Cantor, Philippe, 56, 57, 327
Capecchi, Renato, 74, 74, 184, 248, 357, 483
Cappuccilli, Piero, 12, 12, 25, 50, 78, 196, 232, 285, 461, 461, 468, 472, 476, 481, 488, 488, 490, 491, 496, 500, 500, 507
Carelli, Gabor, 155
Cariou, Len, 395
Carlin, Mario, 320
Carlsen, Toril, 117
Carlyle, Joan, 184
Carol Case, John, 460
Caroli, Paolo, 10
Carosio, Margherita, 609
Carpenter, John, 188
Carral, Dora, 357, 491

Carreras, José, 24, 25, 74, 79, 83, 90, 101, 102, 120, 184, 196, 207, 279, 297, 297, 305, 309, 314, 314, 314, 320, 322, 324, 326, 326, 360, 368, 369, 376, 388, 461, 468, 471, 471, 472, 476, 481, 484, 488, 500, 502, 507, 512, 582, 583, 590, 600, 602, 610, 620
Carroli, Silvano, 314
Carroll, David, 96
Carroll, Diahann, 344
Carson, Danielle, 349
Carter, Clive, 392
Caruso, Enrico, 583, 586, 593, 610
Case, Allen, 585
Caselli, Dario, 619
Casinelli, Riccardo, 513
Casoni, Biancamaria, 73, 481
Cass, Cathy, 33, 100
Cass, Lee, 346
Cassidy, Jack, 348, 395
Cassidy, Patrick, 390
Castaing, Danièle, 277
Castets, Maryse, 358
Castle, Joyce, 22
Casula, Maria, 225, 247
Catania, Claudia, 188
Catellani, Aurora, 13
Catley, Gwen, 608
Cava, Carlo, 353, 491
Cavallari, Rina, 10
Cavalli, Floriana, 324
Cazzaniga, Renato, 13
Cecchele, Gianfranco, 465
Cerquetti, Anita, 285, 596
Cesari, Renato, 305
Chakaris, George, 24
Chaliapin, Feodor, 584, 610
Chamonin, Jocelyne, 84
Chance, Michael, 51, 109, 136, 144, 146
Chaplin, Sydney, 447, 585
Chappell, Jacquey, 393
Chard, Geoffrey, 208
Chastain, Don, 97, 344
Chekerliski, Constantin, 35
Chernikh, L., 269
Chernobayev, Victor, 448
Chernov, Vladimir, 472, 486
Chiara, Maria, 325, 325, 461, 514, 514, 596, 613
Chiesa, Vivian Della, 499
Childs, Lucinda, 103
Chingari, Mario, 301
Christ, Rudolf, 281, 281, 398
Christiansen, Blanche, 161
Christiansen, Christian, 156
Christoff, Boris, 35, 113, 267, 461, 472, 472, 500, 584, 608, 608
Ciesinski, Katherine, 32, 84, 294, 452
Ciesinski, Kristine, 567
Cioni, Renato, 78
Ciurca, Cleopatra, 60
Clabassi, Plinio, 461, 461, 483
Clarey, Cynthia, 97, 456
Clark, Graham, 81, 248, 519
Clark, Joan, 105
Clark, Patricia, 135, 326
Clarke, Adrian, 49

Clarke, Christina, 330
Clarkson, Julian, 135
Clary, Wilton, 346
Clayton, Jan, 171
Clement, Maris, 22
Clemmons, François, 98
Clinton, Gordon, 70
Coates, Edith, 78
Coburn, Pamela, 6, 253, 258
Coca, Imogene, 63, 585
Cochran, William, 47
Coe, George, 63, 585
Cold, Ulrik, 178, 397
Cole, Vinson, 224, 418
Coleman-Wright, Peter, 425
Coles, Priti, 227
Collard, Jeannine, 161, 340, 601
Collier, Marie, 309, 411, 560
Collins, Anne, 95, 257, 545
Collins, Dorothy, 391, 394, 395
Collins, Kenneth, 10
Colombara, Carlo, 297, 500
Colson, Kevin, 575
Comden, Betty, 391, 585
Comeaux, Elizabeth, 64
Comencini, Maurizio, 356
Command, Michèle, 84, 161
Companeez, Irene, 285
Comte, Adrienne, 192
Condò, Nucci, 368
Coni, Paolo, 71, 184, 309, 500
Connell, Elizabeth, 383
Conrad, Barbara, 455
Conrad, Richard, 125, 616
Conried, Hans, 287
Conroy-Ward, James, 430, 443
Conwell, Judy, 241
Cook, Barbara, 21, 345, 348, 391, 569
Cook, George, 438
Cook, Terry, 461
Cookson, Peter, 287
Corbelli, Alessandro, 58, 369
Cordes, Marcel, 281
Cordier, David, 142
Corelli, Franco, 10, 25, 25, 113, 184, 196, 320, 324, 325, 325, 465, 507, 572, 596, 601, 601, 619, 620, 620
Corena, Fernando, 61, 73, 74, 232, 238, 247, 296, 297, 319, 320, 353, 353, 364, 461, 468, 482, 577
Cornwell, Joseph, 33, 100
Corréas, Jérôme, 330, 350
Corsi, Rina, 196
Cortez, Viorica, 453
Cortis, Marcello, 364
Cossa, Dominic, 74, 134, 214
Cossotto, Fiorenza, 10, 13, 14, 77, 101, 196, 247, 285, 305, 325, 461, 468, 472, 481, 484, 487, 496, 507, 596, 598
Cossutta, Carlo, 90, 601
Costa, Mary, 297
Cotrubas, Ileana, 25, 30, 50, 55, 74, 77, 151, 162, 205, 227, 241, 246, 248, 254, 256, 263, 318, 318, 325, 465, 496, 503, 587, 589, 599, 612
Courtis, Jean-Philippe, 89, 178, 376

Covey-Crump, Rogers, 33, 122, 329, 334
Cox, Jean, 528
Craig, Charles, 309, 324, 496, 510, 601
Crass, Franz, 6, 232, 257, 257, 532, 561
Crawford, Michael, 187
Creasy, Philip, 429, 433
Creffield, Rosanna, 360
Crespin, Régine, 203, 278, 280, 418, 539, 539, 551, 551, 602, 613, 613
Criswell, Kim, 17, 287, 288, 575
Croft, Dwayne, 563
Crook, Howard, 57, 179
Crosby, Kim, 392
Cross, Joan, 46
Cross, Richard, 10
Csengery, Adrienne, 456
Csurja, Tamás, 379
Cuberli, Lella, 227, 248, 371, 373
Cuénod, Hugues, 50, 247, 340, 407, 608
Cullis, Rita, 193
Cullum, John, 63, 585
Cummings, Claudia, 104
Cupido, Alberto, 20, 60
Curphey, Margaret, 525, 526, 555
Curry, Diane, 99
Cypher, Jon, 348
Czerwenka, Oskar, 1

D'Angelo, Gianna, 277, 296
D'Artegna, Francesco Ellero, 50, 82, 297
D'Intino, Luciana, 361
D'Orazi, Attilio, 60
D'Orsay, Fifi, 391
Dabrowski, Marek, 447
Dal Monte, Toti, 305
Dalberg, Friedrich, 528
Dale, Clamma, 98
Dale, Laurence, 222, 366, 376
Dalis, Irene, 532
Dallapozza, Adolf, 6, 164, 243, 398, 403, 405, 416, 528
Damonte, Magali, 53
Danco, Suzanne, 19, 66, 162, 232, 247, 340, 340, 340, 608
Dani, Lucia, 196
Danieli, Lucia, 305, 318
Daniels, Barbara, 297
Daniels, Charles, 33, 93, 330, 567
Dankworth, Jacqueline, 392
Dara, Enzo, 73, 74, 353, 353, 357, 364, 364, 372, 373
Dari, Paolo, 500
Darian, Anita, 345
Davià, Federico, 297, 479
David, Antoine, 53, 56
Davies, Arthur, 63, 70, 86, 86, 193, 209, 500
Davies, Eirian, 380
Davies, Joan, 81, 439
Davies, Maldwyn, 36, 124, 127, 144
Davies, Ryland, 62, 78, 204, 227, 243
Davies, Tudor, 171
Davrath, Netania, 161, 162

Dawson, Anne, 36, 93
Dawson, Lynne, 33, 107, 112, 136, 143, 220, 238, 327, 329, 330
De Carlo, Yvonne, 391
De Carolis, Natale, 232, 364, 368, 369, 371
De Gabarain, Marina, 356
De Gogorza, Emilio, 590
De Gutzman, Josie, 188
De Haan, John David, 176
De Kanel, Vladimir, 294
De Luca, Giuseppe, 585
De Lucia, Fernando, 603
De Mey, Guy, 51, 52, 52, 106, 112, 125, 141, 190, 258, 337, 381
De Montmollin, Marie Luise, 192
De Montmollin, Marie-Luise, 162, 340, 340
De Narké, Victor, 90
De Nyzankowskyi, Oleg, 192
De Palma, Piero, 10, 13, 184, 311, 320
De Reszke, Edouard, 603
De Reyghere, Greta, 338
De Simone, Bruno, 356
De la Mora, Fernando, 78
De los Angeles, Victoria, 19, 25, 90, 113, 196, 205, 207, 277, 296, 305, 305, 318, 318, 325, 353, 500, 503, 518, 576, 601, 601, 608, 612
Dean, Donna, 327
Dean, Michael, 123, 139
Dean, Stafford, 37, 70, 94, 217, 425
Del Ferro, Leonardo, 79
Del Monaco, Mario, 25, 50, 60, 101, 102, 184, 196, 285, 301, 309, 314, 318, 320, 481, 493, 572, 596, 602, 608, 619, 620, 621
Del Monte, Carlo, 318, 503, 601
Delétré, Bernard, 48, 51, 56, 337, 350
Della Casa, Lisa, 227, 232, 247, 405, 405
Deller, Alfred, 41, 330, 331, 333, 608
Deller, Mark, 330, 331, 333
Dempsey, Gregory, 538, 545
Dempsey, Richard, 392
Dene, Jószef, 34
Dénes, Zsuzsanna, 89
Denize, Nadine, 191
Denley, Catherine, 135, 139, 258
Dens, Michel, 205
Děpoltová, Eva, 91, 192
Derenne, Paul, 340
Dermota, Anton, 227, 232, 232, 257, 398, 401, 405, 418, 608
Dernesch, Helga, 6, 405, 522, 539, 539, 542, 545, 548, 565
Desailly, Jean, 161
Desderi, Claudio, 226, 247
Dessì, Daniella, 71, 184, 297, 496
Destinn, Emmy, 586, 610
Deutekom, Cristina, 258, 264, 466, 485
Devia, Mariella, 58, 74
Devlin, Michael, 151, 152
Di Cesare, Ezio, 241
Di Mauro, Anna, 196

Di Nissa, Bernadette Manca, 361, 371
Di Stasio, Anna, 196, 305, 319, 496
Di Stefano, Giuseppe, 13, 74, 78, 79, 184, 196, 297, 305, 309, 314, 314, 325, 325, 468, 496, 503, 507, 578, 596, 608, 620, 621
Diakoff, Vera, 192
Diakov, Anton, 267, 377
Diaz, Justino, 50, 274, 352, 369, 493
Dickie, John, 227
Dickie, Murray, 247
Dilova, Penka, 452
Dimchewska, Martya, 267
Dimitrova, Ghena, 325, 461, 491, 492
Dittman, Dean, 63, 585
Dives, Tasmin, 208
Dobrianowa, Nadejda, 267
Dobson, John, 44, 211, 426
Dohmen, Albert, 413
Doležal, Vladimir, 192
Dolton, Geoffrey, 76
Dolukhanova, Zara, 608
Domgraf-Fassbaender, Willi, 227
Domingo, Plácido, 10, 25, 25, 25, 33, 33, 55, 60, 74, 78, 100, 113, 184, 184, 195, 196, 196, 199, 202, 207, 264, 274, 274, 297, 301, 301, 305, 309, 309, 311, 313, 314, 314, 318, 318, 320, 323, 325, 326, 353, 376, 376, 398, 413, 418, 461, 461, 461, 462, 467, 468, 468, 472, 472, 477, 481, 481, 485, 486, 486, 488, 491, 493, 493, 496, 500, 503, 507, 507, 510, 511, 513, 526, 528, 545, 563, 580, 583, 587, 590, 599, 601, 620, 620
Dominguez, Oralia, 539, 542
Donat, Zdislawa, 263
Donath, Helen, 6, 25, 109, 155, 164, 180, 181, 210, 218, 233, 241, 245, 248, 258, 284, 303, 318, 327, 405, 418, 529, 561, 601
Dönch, Karl, 16, 398, 403, 403, 407
Donovan, Aloysius, 288
Doria, Fiametta, 567
Doria, Renée, 608
Douglas, Craig, 392
Douglas, Judith, 567
Douglas, Nigel, 43
Dowdy, Helen, 171
Dowling, Denis, 70, 443
Drake, Alfred, 288
Drake, Bryan, 37, 38, 45
Dran, Thierry, 212, 273
Dressen, Dan, 43, 64
Drobková, Drahomira, 85
Drummond-Grant, Ann, 434
Dry, Marion, 456
Du Plessis, Christian, 72, 81, 84, 506
Dua, Octave, 322
Dubosc, Catherine, 49, 51, 112, 265, 289, 290
Dubroff, Alexis, 288
Dubrovin, Ivan, 448
Duchêne, Maria, 586
Dudziak, Francis, 112, 212

Duesing, Dale, 226, 232, 382
Dumont, Fernand, 453
Dunn, Susan, 383, 514, 600
Dupouy, Jean, 20, 216, 423
Dupuy, Martine, 289
Duradev, Georgy, 170
Dussaut, Catherine, 56
Duval, Pierre, 79
Dvofáková, Ludmila, 522
Dvorsky, George, 288, 575
Dvorsky, Miroslav, 184
Dvorský, Peter, 74, 167, 168, 305, 309, 388
Dyer, Lorely, 70
Dyer, Olive, 46

Eames, Emma, 590
Earle, Roderick, 81, 333
Eda-Pierre, Christiane, 18, 161, 162, 238
Eddie, Robert, 209
Eddy, Nelson, 346, 348
Edelmann, Otto, 6, 232, 405, 418, 528, 556
Eder, Claudia, 274
Edgar-Wilson, Richard, 397
Eensalu, Marika, 459
Egerton, Francis, 183, 478
Eisen, Artur, 264
Eisinger, Irene, 227
Eisler, David, 22
Ek, Harald, 520
Eklöf, Marianne, 117
El Hage, Robert, 607
Elenkov, Stefan, 13
Elgar, Anne, 369
Elias, Rosalind, 3, 305, 305, 496, 520
Eliasson, Sven Olaf, 221
Elkins, Margreta, 78, 82, 125, 580
Elliott, Paul, 123, 131, 135, 329, 331, 332, 333, 334
Ellison, Jon, 430, 443
Ellsworth, Warren, 532
Elming, Poul, 156
Elmo, Cloe, 479
Elmore, Steve, 394
Elvira, Pablo, 195
Elwes, John, 52, 130, 331, 333, 338, 338, 516
Emili, Romano, 183
Emmerlich, Gunther, 561
Endrèze, Arthur, 557
Engen, Kieth, 6, 270, 282
Equiluz, Kurt, 181, 222, 242, 455
Ercolani, Renato, 247, 320, 479
Erkkilä, Eero, 191, 380
Ernster, Deszö, 232
Escourrou, Pierre-Marie, 161
Esham, Faith, 25, 248, 516
Esser, Hermin, 520, 539
Esswood, Paul, 56, 103, 134, 135, 140, 143, 218, 222
Estes, Simon, 20, 25, 99, 242, 376, 519, 532
Etcheverry, Henri-Bertrand, 66
Evangelatos, Daphne, 49
Evans, Damon, 97, 288

Evans, Geraint, 44, 74, 227, 233, 248, 248, 429, 433, 443, 445, 445, 481, 514, 529
Evans, Harvey, 391, 394, 395
Evans, Wynford, 330
Evstatieva, Stefka, 35, 196, 452
Ewer, Graeme, 183
Ewing, Maria, 65, 100, 232, 510

Facini, Francesco, 356
Fagotto, Gianpaolo, 51, 131
Fairhurst, Robin, 40
Falewicz, Magdalena, 109
Farkas, Katalin, 128, 140, 283
Farley, Carole, 289, 410
Farrar, Geraldine, 584, 584, 586
Fassbaender, Brigitte, 14, 89, 92, 162, 225, 227, 241, 264, 284, 383, 398, 398, 421, 496, 507, 548
Fauché, François, 52
Favat, Dominique, 350
Favero, Mafalda, 322, 586
Fedoseyev, Andrei, 452
Felbermayer, Anny, 162, 407, 417
Feldman, Jill, 52, 52, 55, 56, 57, 57, 146, 327, 336
Felle, Amelia, 364
Feller, Carlos, 227, 248
Felty, Janice, 1
Feraldy, Germaine, 621
Ferland, Danielle, 392
Fernandi, Eugenio, 320
Ferrarini, Alida, 496
Ferraro, Pier Miranda, 285
Ferrier, Kathleen, 111, 608
Ferrin, Agostino, 13, 496
Ferro, Daniel, 345
Field, Helen, 63, 70, 169, 193, 500
Field, Pamela, 443
Fieldsend, David, 429
Filippeschi, Mario, 10, 472
Findlay, Jane, 146
Fink, Bernarda, 127, 131, 133, 221, 374
Finke, Martin, 407
Finley, Gerald, 332
Finnie, Linda, 209, 340
Finnila, Birgit, 248, 517
Fioravanti, Giulio, 60, 309
Fischer, Gillian, 332
Fischer-Dieskau, Dietrich, 4, 6, 6, 15, 15, 47, 62, 108, 143, 158, 210, 232, 232, 247, 248, 248, 253, 257, 257, 258, 284, 386, 396, 398, 405, 405, 407, 409, 409, 411, 416, 472, 478, 490, 496, 522, 526, 526, 528, 532, 535, 539, 539, 548, 577, 591, 602, 608
Fish, Matthew Adam, 265
Fisher, Gillian, 128, 149, 329, 331
Fisher, Sylvia, 36, 43
Fisichella, Salvatore, 366, 368
Fissore, Enrico, 353, 372
Flagello, Ezio, 79, 81, 125, 227, 233, 468, 477, 481, 486, 496
Flagstad, Kirsten, 105, 327, 535, 539, 548, 551, 556, 556, 557, 558, 559, 586, 608, 610
Flannery, Susan, 393
Flechter, Guy, 112

Fliegner, Christian, 109
Flohr, Mária, 140
Flynn, Eric, 393
Focile, Nuccia, 72
Foiani, Giovanni, 472, 481, 488, 500
Foldi, Andrew, 369
Folwell, Nicholas, 532
Fondary, Alain, 301, 376
Fontana, Gabriele, 405
Ford, Bruce, 213, 351
Forrester, Maureen, 134, 148, 411, 452
Forsyth, Julian, 4
Forti, Carlo, 13
Fortunato, D'Anna, 456
Fortune, George, 396
Fouchécourt, Jean-Paul, 48, 56, 57, 217, 350
Fournier, Brigitte, 109, 289
Fowler, Beth, 97
Franc, Tugomir, 225, 411
Franck, Joseph, 264
Franklin, David, 232
Frantz, Ferdinand, 528, 540, 551
Franz, Joy, 392
Fredericks, Charles, 171
Frellesvig, Anne, 178
Freni, Mirella, 25, 25, 25, 33, 73, 74, 113, 125, 184, 195, 232, 232, 247, 296, 297, 305, 305, 309, 314, 314, 322, 324, 325, 325, 325, 326, 362, 450, 452, 461, 472, 477, 481, 493, 500, 591, 591, 596, 600, 601, 601, 601, 602, 606, 612, 613
Fretwell, Elizabeth, 510
Frey, Paul, 383, 407, 526
Frick, Gottlob, 6, 6, 6, 232, 239, 257, 270, 281, 281, 389, 522, 526, 529, 532, 539, 540, 551, 551, 561, 608
Friedman, Maria, 393
Friedmann, Gérard, 278
Friedrich, Heinz, 281
Froman, Jane, 349
Fryatt, John, 183, 248
Fuchs, Gabriele, 403, 416
Fuchs, Marta, 557
Fugère, Lucien, 603
Fuller, Frederick, 608
Fuller, Lorenzo, 288
Fullerton, Fiona, 288
Furlanetto, Ferruccio, 120, 227, 227, 232, 248, 248, 351, 362, 472, 510
Fyson, Leslie, 371

Gadjev, Zdravko, 267
Gadski, Johanna, 513, 610
Gahmlich, Wilfried, 238, 238
Gaifa, Carlo, 73
Gaines, Davis, 575
Gal, Zehava, 366
Gale, Elizabeth, 109, 144, 232
Gall, Axelle, 196
Gall, Jeffrey, 52, 131, 147
Gallacher, Andrew, 173
Gallagher, Helen, 349, 349
Gallagher, Peter, 188

Galli-Curci, Amelita, 586, 586, 592, 593
Galliard, Peter, 107
Galliver, David, 122, 332
Gallo, Lucio, 353
Galushkina, Lidiya, 448
Galusin, Vladimir, 267
Gambill, Robert, 385, 386
Ganzarolli, Wladimiro, 155, 227, 232, 247, 364, 484, 486, 502
Garber, Victor, 390
Garcisanz, Isabel, 54
Gard, Robert, 209
Gardeil, Jean-François, 56, 57, 190
Gardino, Jolanda, 372
Gardner, Jake, 202
Garino, Gérard, 62, 187
Garrett, Lesley, 435
Garrison, David, 17, 97, 171
Garrison, Mabel, 586
Gasdia, Cecilia, 141, 351, 361, 373, 374
Gáti, Istvan, 89, 283, 379, 416
Gatta, Dora, 247
Gatti, Gabriella, 609
Gauci, Miriam, 184, 305, 309, 592
Gaudel, Christiane, 55
Gautier, Georges, 53, 290
Gavanelli, Paolo, 297
Gavazzi, Ernesto, 184
Gayer, Catherine, 542
Gaynor, Mitzi, 347
Gedda, Nicolai, 3, 18, 22, 25, 25, 30, 74, 86, 89, 92, 105, 113, 176, 180, 181, 181, 200, 207, 227, 232, 243, 257, 265, 277, 284, 294, 297, 305, 324, 325, 363, 372, 376, 386, 398, 398, 402, 403, 403, 404, 407, 409, 418, 450, 453, 496, 560, 582, 601, 601, 608, 620
Gedda, Tania, 453
Gémes, Katalin, 381
Gens, Véronique, 337
Georg, Mechthild, 455
George, Donald, 465
George, Michael, 122, 126, 136, 139, 329, 334
Gerelo, Vassily, 294
Gergalov, Alexandr, 294
Germann, Greg, 390
Geszty, Sylvia, 258, 408
Ghazarian, Sona, 6, 468
Ghiaurov, Nicolai, 13, 13, 33, 34, 35, 77, 78, 113, 113, 203, 206, 232, 264, 264, 267, 267, 285, 296, 320, 353, 362, 450, 461, 461, 472, 472, 472, 477, 488, 490, 491, 496, 496, 500, 507, 513, 577, 600
Ghiuselev, Nikola, 35, 214, 214, 264, 267, 277, 294, 335, 450, 471
Giacomini, Giuseppe, 196
Giacomotti, Alfredo, 59, 511
Giaiotti, Bonaldo, 199, 320, 465, 481, 486, 507
Gibin, João, 301
Gielgud, John, 190
Gigli, Beniamino, 101, 184, 196, 297, 305, 314, 592, 593, 608, 610
Gilford, Jack, 97
Gillett, Christopher, 208, 431

Gilma, Sylvaine, 340
Gimenez, Edoardo, 248, 373
Giménez, Raúl, 372, 378
Gingold, Hermione, 393, 395
Ginn, Michael, 127
Giraudeau, Jean, 341
Gjevang, Anne, 117, 271, 386
Glanville, Mark, 72
Gleason, Joanna, 392
Glossop, Peter, 21, 37, 95, 493, 510
Gluboky, Piotr, 344
Gluck, Alma, 513, 586
Glynne, Howell, 95
Gmyrya, Boris, 608
Gobbi, Tito, 79, 102, 184, 184, 305, 314, 314, 318, 318, 318, 323, 353, 461, 468, 472, 478, 491, 493, 496, 500, 577, 601, 601, 608
Gøbel, Bodil, 178
Goeke, Leo, 184
Goff, Charles, 97
Goldberg, Reiner, 6, 410, 416, 532, 542, 551, 561
Golden, Annie, 390
Göllnitz, Fritz, 566
Goltz, Christel, 414
Gomez, Jill, 2, 41, 337
Gonda, Anna, 16
Gondek, Juliana, 139
Gonzales, Carmen, 196, 297, 518
Gonzalez, Dalmacio, 120, 359
Goodchild, Chloe, 449
Gooding, Julia, 147, 220, 332
Gorin, Igor, 608
Gorr, Rita, 289, 377, 461, 552, 608
Gorshin, Frank, 96
Gorzyńska, Halina, 106
Goss, Julia, 430, 441, 443
Gostic, Joseph, 417
Gottlieb, Peter, 50
Graae, Jason, 17, 97
Grace, Nickolas, 4, 22, 431
Graham, Edna, 429, 445, 445
Graham, Susan, 18
Grahame, Gloria, 346
Graml, Helmut, 281
Gramm, Donald, 19
Grandi, Margherita, 609
Grant, Clifford, 204, 209, 247, 255, 256, 526, 545, 555
Gray, Kevin, 516
Gray, Linda Esther, 519
Green, Adolph, 22, 391, 585
Green, Simon, 571
Greenawald, Sheri, 32
Greenberg, Sylvia, 382
Greene, Leon, 29
Greenwood, Charlotte, 346
Gregg, Mitchell, 344, 570
Gregor, József, 34, 59, 61, 62, 113, 128, 140, 283, 283, 367, 378, 502
Gregoriam, Gegam, 294
Gregory, André, 391
Greindl, Josef, 257, 281, 522, 547
Griffiths, Gwyn, 309
Griffiths, Rosalind, 443
Griffiths, Wyn, 460
Grigoryan, G., 10
Grimes, Tammy, 570

Grist, Reri, 227, 233, 238, 248, 254, 468, 468, 496
Grobe, Donald, 15, 158, 181, 563
Groenendaal, Cris, 287, 575
Groener, Harold, 96
Groenroos, Walton, 108, 282, 383, 453
Grossmann, Walter, 257
Gruber, Ferry, 281
Gruberová, Edita, 9, 79, 79, 82, 109, 162, 224, 233, 238, 242, 245, 246, 255, 255, 257, 258, 274, 398, 402, 407, 408, 468, 496, 503
Grümmer, Elisabeth, 162, 232, 526, 528, 561, 608
Grundheber, Franz, 16, 207, 405, 418
Grunert, Wolfgang, 565
Guardino, Harry, 395
Guarrera, Frank, 479
Gueden, Hilde, 74, 232, 247, 258, 398, 401, 405, 410, 418, 602, 623
Guelfi, Giangiacomo, 196
Guglielmi, Margherita, 357
Guillamat, Ginette, 608
Guiot, Andréa, 25
Guittard, Laurence, 395
Gulyás, Dénes, 89, 283, 304, 378
Günter, Horst, 566
Gustavson, Eva, 462
Gutorovich, Nilokai, 170
Gutstein, Ernst, 270, 405, 418
Gwynne, David, 380, 532

Haage, Pater, 383, 385, 535, 542
Hacquard, Mario, 202
Hadary, Jonathan, 390
Hadjieva, Ludmila, 265
Hadley, Jerry, 22, 72, 171, 190, 254, 257, 297, 516, 567
Haefliger, Ernst, 6, 232, 257, 280
Hagegard, Erland, 387
Hagegård, Håkan, 116, 117, 232, 248, 548
Hägganser, Mari Anne, 118, 387
Haldas, Béatrice, 573
Hall, Carol, 333
Hall, George, 287
Hall, John, 49
Hall, John Graham, 41
Hall, Juanita, 347, 347
Hall, Pamela, 395
Hallstein, Ingeborg, 6
Hamari, Júlia, 13, 20, 62, 162, 187, 196, 367, 450, 517, 528, 563
Hamel, Michel, 162, 277, 340
Hammond, Joan, 608
Hammond-Stroud, Derek, 525, 538, 545
Hammons, Thomas, 1
Hampshire, Susan, 393
Hampson, Thomas, 17, 70, 113, 210, 227, 227, 233, 248, 258, 288, 297, 385, 522
Hanley, Regina, 429, 433
Hann, Alexandra, 439
Hannan, Eilene, 69
Hannula, Kaisa, 17
Hannula, Tero, 103
Hansen, Ib, 271

Hansen, Kai, 221
Hansli, Asbjørn, 117
Hansmann, Rotraud, 220, 221
Hanson, Tripp, 96
Hanssen, Vessa, 117
Hanzalíková, Ludmilla, 193
Harbour, Dennis, 462
Hardy, Rosemary, 173, 331, 333, 333
Harju, Marianne, 17
Harper, Heather, 41, 43, 44, 46, 135, 137, 148, 217, 233, 248, 332, 433, 436, 438, 456, 457
Harper, James, 282
Harrell, Mack, 608
Harrhy, Eiddwen, 72, 83, 124, 127, 330
Harries, Kathryn, 169, 202
Harris, Diana, 331
Harris, Dinah, 393
Harris, Holly, 348
Harvey, Peter, 327
Harwood, Elizabeth, 41, 181, 296, 325, 325, 386, 436, 438, 441, 444, 445
Haskin, Howard, 382
Haskins, Virginia, 346, 348, 468
Hasslo, Hugo, 608
Haugan, Björn, 32, 93
Haugland, Aage, 16, 156, 267, 271, 271, 384, 525, 532
Hauptmann, Cornelius, 89, 225, 238, 242, 258
Hayden, Sophie, 188
Hayes, Marvin, 31
Haymon, Cynthia, 97
Haywood, Lorna, 211
Healy, David, 17
Hearn, George, 391
Hedegaard, Ole, 156
Heichele, Hildegard, 567
Heilmann, Uwe, 6, 238, 243, 255, 258
Hellekant, Charlotte, 17
Helletsgruber, Luise, 227, 232
Hellman, Claudia, 280
Hellwig, Judith, 258, 414
Helm, Anny, 557
Hemmings, David, 40, 46
Hempel, Frieda, 513, 586, 586, 594
Hemsley, Thomas, 41, 105, 327
Henderson, Roy, 232
Hendricks, Barbara, 30, 54, 89, 97, 109, 118, 146, 152, 162, 178, 242, 243, 248, 257, 297, 320, 405, 418, 478, 595
Henry, Didier, 65, 202
Henry, Suzanne, 392
Heppner, Ben, 563
Herford, Henry, 41
Herincx, Raimund, 29, 326, 460
Herman, Sylvia, 386
Hermann, Josef, 608
Hermann, Roland, 519, 528
Herrmann, Theo, 608
Herzog, Colette, 340
Hesch, Wilhelm, 603
Hesse, Ruth, 175, 413, 529
Hesterburg, Trude, 565
Hetherington, Hugh, 173

Hibberd, Linda, 380
Hiestermann, Horst, 411, 421
Higueras, Ana Maria, 90
Hill, Annabelle, 288
Hill, Martyn, 40, 122, 127, 135, 140, 330, 331, 334, 397
Hill, Wendy, 123
Hill Smith, Marilyn, 22, 171, 180, 350, 439, 595
Hillebrand, Nikolaus, 538
Hillebrecht, Hildegard, 47, 257
Hillman, David, 439
Hillner, John, 96
Hindmarsh, Jean, 428, 430, 433
Hines, Jerome, 216, 488
Hiolski, Andrzej, 447
Hirst, Linda, 218
Hirsti, Marianne, 238
Hirte, Klaus, 403, 528
Hoch, Beverley, 258
Hodge, Patricia, 288
Hodges, Eddie, 569
Hodgson, Alfreda, 86, 285
Hoel, Lena, 32
Hoermann, Albert, 565
Hoff, Renate, 258
Höffgen, Marga, 257, 529, 539, 539, 542
Hoffman, Grace, 421
Hoffstedt, Gertrud, 107
Hofmann, Peter, 6, 519, 532, 532, 539, 548, 551
Högman, Christina, 107, 131, 221
Holden, Poppy, 33, 100
Holdorf, Udo, 567
Holgate, Ron, 394
Holl, Robert, 233, 256, 382, 385
Holland, Lyndsie, 430, 433, 443
Hölle, Matthias, 395
Holliday, Judy, 585
Holliday, Melanie, 398
Hollweg, Ilse, 118, 239
Hollweg, Werner, 181, 210, 241, 242, 243, 246, 248, 256, 256, 402, 545
Holm, Renata, 258, 398, 403, 602
Holmgren, Carl GustafGustaf, 117
Höngen, Elisabeth, 248, 414, 608
Hood, Ann, 438, 444, 444
Hooks, Robert, 585
Hopf, Hans, 1, 413, 414, 528
Hoppe, Carl, 270
Hordern, Michael, 94
Horne, Marilyn, 10, 12, 24, 25, 31, 81, 109, 125, 141, 144, 149, 216, 318, 345, 353, 364, 370, 371, 371, 375, 376, 479, 507, 513, 514, 518, 596, 598, 600, 602, 616, 617
Hornik, Gottfried, 257, 257, 418
Hoskins, Bob, 93
Hotter, Hans, 257, 281, 383, 409, 529, 532, 532, 539, 541, 542, 551, 557, 608
Houston, Elsie, 608
Howard, Ann, 22, 318, 392, 555
Howard, Christopher, 24
Howard, Jason, 350, 393
Howarth, Judith, 86
Howell, Gwynne, 6, 9, 86, 301, 352, 468, 486

Howells, Anne, 21, 217
Howland, Beth, 394
Howlett, Neil, 496
Hubbard, Bruce, 97, 171, 571
Hübner, Fritz, 522, 539, 542
Huebner, Karin, 565
Huemer, K., 181
Huffstodt, Karen, 423
Hughes, Janet, 50
Hunt, Lorraine, 146, 221
Hunter, Rita, 29, 510, 525, 526, 545, 555, 560
Hüsch, Gerhard, 257, 557
Hutcherson, LeVern, 31
Huttenlocher, Philippe, 56, 66, 90, 114, 217, 227, 340, 397
Hvorostovsky, Dmitri, 196, 452, 454, 513
Hynninen, Jorma, 191, 248, 379, 387, 411

Idle, Eric, 435
Ignatowicz, Ewa, 106
Ihle, Andrea, 561
Ihloff, Jutta-Renate, 241
Infantino, Luigi, 608
Ingram, Michael, 40
Iñigo, Paloma Perez, 90
Innocent, Harold, 439
Irons, Jeremy, 190
Irosch, Mirjana, 181, 398
Irving, George S., 349
Irwin, Robert, 608
Isakova, Nina, 170
Isherwood, Nicholas, 123
Islandi, Stefan, 608
Ivanov, Andrei, 608
Ivanova, E., 293
Ivey, Dana, 394
Ivogün, Maria, 586, 596

Jackson, Richard, 93
Jacobs, René, 48, 52, 52, 56, 109, 125, 140, 191, 397
Jacoby, Josephine, 513
Jahn, Gertrud, 16, 413
Jakobsson, Anna-Lisa, 17, 379
James, David, 52
James, Eirian, 147, 258
James, Olga, 31
Janowitz, Gundula, 6, 210, 227, 247, 257, 408, 409, 522, 539, 551, 561, 602
Jansen, Jacques, 66
Janssen, Herbert, 6, 551, 557, 557
Jaresch, August, 258
Jedenáctík, Vladimir, 193
Jedlička, Dalibor, 165, 166
Jeffes, Peter, 54
Jellison, John, 390
Jenkins, Neil, 180, 330, 350, 360
Jenkins, Timothy, 242
Jerusalem, Siegfried, 6, 92, 113, 175, 180, 181, 257, 383, 522, 535, 540, 542, 547, 551, 569
Jindrák, Jinfich, 193
Jo, Sumi, 258, 358, 372, 413, 467
Joachim, Irène, 66, 608
Jobin, Raoul, 105, 608
Johansen, Ronnie, 156

Johansson, Eva, 156
Johns, Glynis, 395
Johnson, David, 253
Johnson, Douglas, 242
Johnson, Justine, 391, 394
Johnson, Patricia, 15, 29, 247, 510
Johnson, Richard, 456
Johnson, Samuel, 103
Johnson, Susan, 188
Johnston, James, 608
Joll, Phillip, 193, 532
Jonason, Louisa, 456
Jonášová, Jana, 388
Jonelli, Hans, 192
Jones, Aled, 129
Jones, Della, 2, 13, 22, 39, 41, 72, 81, 83, 124, 134, 144, 147, 151, 213, 218, 232, 248, 327, 567
Jones, Gordon, 33
Jones, Gwyneth, 405, 418, 514, 520, 522, 532, 539, 542, 551, 559, 613
Jones, Isola, 195, 519
Jones, Shirley, 345, 346
Jossoud, Hélène, 423
Journet, Marcel, 557, 584
Jung, Manfred, 522, 539, 542
Jungmann, Dorothea, 191
Jungwirth, Manfred, 6, 255, 418
Juranek, Lidia, 106
Jurinac, Sena, 6, 232, 243, 247, 248, 257, 418, 540, 597, 608
Juyol, Suzanne, 608

Kabaivanska, Raina, 60, 479
Kahn, Madeline, 63, 585
Kale, Stuart, 4, 278
Kales, Elisabeth, 263, 403
Kállay, Gábor, 140
Kallisch, Cornelia, 248
Kálmándi, Mihály, 200
Kalmár, Magda, 59, 113, 304, 367
Kalter, Sabine, 551
Kaludov, Kaludi, 35, 267, 309
Kanunnikova, Ludmilla, 294
Kapp, Miroslav, 192
Karczykowski, Ryszard, 181
Karnobatlova, Blagovesta, 335
Karousatos, Nickolas, 335
Karpíšek, Milan, 192
Kasrashvili, M., 293
Kastu, Matti, 405
Katanosaka, Eiko, 220
Kaufmann, Julie, 50, 109, 414, 479
Kavrakos, Dimitri, 232, 378
Kaye, Judy, 189, 516, 571, 575
Kayevchenko, Valentina, 170
Kazaras, Peter, 23
Kélémen, Zoltan, 6, 181, 267, 522, 532, 535, 539, 542
Kelen, Péter, 200, 342, 488
Keller, Marthe, 161
Keller, Peter, 258
Kelly, David, 158
Kelly, Janis, 393, 567
Kelly, Megan, 4
Kelton, Pert, 569
Kennedy, Roderick, 36, 81
Kenny, Yvonne, 25, 76, 83, 95, 213, 238, 245, 257

Kent, Larry, 288
Kern, Patricia, 20, 95, 327, 327
Kernan, David, 393, 394
Kerns, Robert, 305, 526
Kerr, Deborah, 345
Kerr, John, 347
Kert, Larry, 97, 394, 395
Ketelsen, Hans-Joachim, 561
Keyte, Christopher, 135, 332, 334, 460
Kiberg, Tina, 178, 271
Kiley, Richard, 344
Killebrew, Gwendoline, 155, 522, 569
Kimbrough, Charles, 394
Kincses, Veronika, 62, 113, 305, 343, 502
King, Andrew, 33, 100
King, Dennis, 287
King, James, 408, 410, 413, 421, 532, 539, 539, 551, 551, 556, 559
King, Malcolm, 18, 232
King, Mary, 173
Kingsley, Ben, 345
Kipnis, Alexander, 557
Kirchstein, Leonore, 158
Kirk, Lisa, 288, 288
Kirkby, Emma, 33, 100, 121, 123, 127, 129, 131, 136, 138, 138, 141, 149, 220, 327, 334
Kirsten, Dorothy, 608
Kit, Mikhail, 294
Kitchen, Linda, 213
Kitchiner, John, 158
Klán, Josef, 91
Klein, Peter, 257
Klemperer, Werner, 383
Klenov, O., 269
Klietmann, Martin, 62
Kline, Kevin, 63
Klose, Margarete, 257, 551, 551, 557
Kmentt, Waldemar, 1, 320, 398, 398, 421, 602
Knapp, Josef, 181
Knibbs, Jean, 135, 330, 333
Knight, Andrew, 71
Knight, Gillian, 305, 324, 428, 428, 430, 432, 436, 444
Kniplová, Naděžda, 167
Kogel, Richard, 281, 281
Köhler, Axel, 218
Kohn, Karl Christian, 15, 47, 158, 232, 282, 405, 561
Kolassi, Irma, 608
Koller, Dagmar, 181, 398
Kollo, Ants, 458
Kollo, René, 6, 174, 181, 398, 408, 413, 519, 522, 526, 528, 529, 532, 538, 539, 542, 545, 548, 548, 561, 565
Konetzni, Hilde, 540, 608
König, Klaus, 547
Konsulov, Ivan, 452
Kopp, Miroslav, 388
Koptanova, N., 293
Korbich, Eddie, 96, 390
Koréh, Endre, 608
Korn, Artur, 248
Korolev, D., 293

Koroleva, Glafira, 264
Korte, Hans, 565, 567
Koshetz, Nina, 586, 586
Kostia, Raili, 212
Köstlinger, Josef, 327
Köth, Erika, 398, 403, 404, 542, 608, 623
Kotscherga, Anatolij, 267
Kourchoumov, Pavel, 335
Kováts, Kolos, 4, 59, 363, 477, 485, 488
Kowalski, Jochen, 109, 148
Kozlovsky, Ivan, 608
Kozma, Lajos, 220, 518, 580
Kozub, Ernst, 520
Kraft, Jean, 196
Kraus, Alfredo, 3, 13, 29, 79, 81, 116, 205, 207, 226, 297, 496, 503, 503
Kraus, Michael, 177, 258
Kraus, Otakar, 181
Krause, Monika, 503
Krause, Tom, 6, 20, 25, 25, 73, 105, 227, 227, 248, 264, 282, 398, 411, 453, 548, 559, 560
Krebs, Helmut, 398
Krejčík, Vladimir, 165, 167
Krenn, Werner, 181, 182, 225, 245, 264, 387, 519, 579, 602
Kreppel, Walter, 232
Krivtchenia, Alexei, 267
Krumm, Hendrik, 212
Kruse, Heinz, 177, 257
Kruse, Tone, 387
Kubiak, Teresa, 450
Kuchar, Erich, 403
Kudriavchenko, Ekaterina, 344
Kuebler, David, 6, 246
Kuen, Paul, 248, 281, 535
Kuettenbaum, Annette, 258
Kuhlmann, Kathleen, 101, 124
Kuhse, Hanne-Lore, 258
Kunz, Erich, 181, 227, 248, 257, 398, 402, 403, 404, 408, 528, 608
Kupper, Anneliese, 417
Kurz, Selma, 586
Kusche, Benno, 181, 281, 281, 398, 529, 529
Kusnjer, Iván, 192
Kutschera, Franz, 565
Kuusk, Ivo, 458, 459
Kuusoja, Maiju, 212
Kweksilber, Marjanne, 48, 109, 397
Kwella, Patrizia, 123, 124, 127, 128, 131, 138, 141, 144, 160, 218, 220, 222

La Scola, Vincenzo, 496
Labò, Flaviano, 472
Laciura, Anthony, 248
Laderoute, Joseph, 6
Ladysz, Bernard, 78
Lafayette, Lenora, 323
Lafont, Jean-Philippe, 19, 54, 112, 272, 277
Lagger, Peter, 233, 247, 281, 528
Laghezza, Rosa, 196
Lagrange, Michèl, 290
Lail, Lorri, 608
Lakes, Gary, 191, 408, 551, 563

Laki, Krisztina, 140, 283, 519
Lallouette, Olivier, 133
Lambert, Juliet, 97
Lambert, Mark, 395
Lamberti, Giorgio, 25, 313, 314, 318, 477, 485
Landwehr-Herrmann, Gertraud, 455
Landy, Tonny, 150, 271
Lane, Betty, 98
Lane, Elizabeth, 334
Lane, Nathan, 188
Lang, Harold, 288
Lang, Rosemarie, 210
Langdon, Michael, 37, 160, 248
Langridge, Philip, 16, 20, 39, 95, 143, 160, 169, 327, 340, 384, 426, 457
Langston, John, 22
Langton, Diane, 393
Lansbury, Angela, 94, 394, 395
Laplénie, Michel, 327, 336
Larmore, Jennifer, 78, 133, 218
Larsen, Liz, 188
Larsen-Todsen, Nanny, 557
Lasser, Ingeborg, 16
László, Magda, 609
Laubenthal, Hansgeorg, 239
Laubenthal, Horst, 6, 16, 175, 528
Laubenthal, Rudolf, 557
Laurens, Guillemette, 55, 56, 57, 141, 190, 218, 327, 337
Lauri-Volpi, Giacomo, 593
Lavin, Linda, 395
Lawless, James, 43
Lawlor, Thomas, 431, 440
Lawrence, Eddie, 585
Lawrence, Marjorie, 557
Lawrenson, John, 148
Lawson, Denis, 349
Lax, Eva, 128
Lazzari, Agostino, 319
Lazzarini, Adriana, 196, 496
Le Coz, Claudine, 112
Le Maigat, Pierre-Yves, 49
Le Texier, Vincent, 18, 337
LeRoux, François, 49, 53, 65, 273
Leanderson, Rolf, 336
Lear, Evelyn, 15, 15, 257, 267, 601
Lebherz, Louis, 465
Lecouvreur, Aimée, 55
Ledroit, Michèle, 516
Leech, Richard, 113, 214, 398, 418
Leeming, Peter, 37, 38
Legay, Henri, 30, 205
Leggate, Robin, 150, 382
Lehane, Maurene, 148
Lehman, Jeanne, 575
Lehmann, Lilli, 603
Lehmann, Lotte, 421, 556, 557, 586, 610, 618
Lehtinen, Matti, 174, 212
Leider, Frida, 557, 586
Leiferkus, Sergei, 289, 452
Leitner, Lotte, 258
Lemariová, Marcela, 119, 193
Lemnitz, Tiana, 257, 557
Lemper, Ute, 565, 568, 568
Lenya, Lotte, 565, 566, 566, 568
Lenz, Friedrich, 6, 257, 529

Leonard, Sarah, 272
Leppée, Gjurgja, 608
Lerer, Norma, 153, 221, 336
Lesne, Gérard, 56, 397, 516
Levko, Valentina, 452
Lewis, Keith, 232, 421
Lewis, Richard, 86, 86, 243, 323, 421, 429, 431, 431, 433, 438, 441, 443, 445, 445, 520, 560
Lieb, Günther, 258
Liebeck, Ann, 25
Liebermann, Melinda, 103
Liebl, Karl, 520
Ligabue, Ilva, 478
Ligendza, Catarina, 528
Lilley, Barbara, 430
Lilo, 287
Lima, Luis, 206
Limarilli, Gastone, 301
Lincoln, Mary, 392
Lind, Eva, 162, 242, 257, 274, 398, 413, 561
Lindholm, Berit, 21
Lindner, Brigette, 257
Lindroos, Peter, 17, 271, 282
Lindsley, Celina, 157, 192
Linval, Monique, 25
Lipovšek, Marjana, 89, 109, 134, 162, 209, 258, 267, 318, 395, 411, 414, 425, 522, 535
Lipp, Wilma, 257, 258, 398, 401
Lisitsian, Pavel, 608
Liss, Rhonda, 104
List, Emanuel, 551, 556, 557
Little, Vera, 410
Litvinne, Félia, 603
Litz, Gisela, 270, 566
Livengood, Victoria, 563
Livingstone, Laureen, 171
Lloyd, David, 327, 608
Lloyd, Robert, 18, 79, 86, 95, 144, 204, 207, 225, 232, 239, 248, 257, 297, 334, 352, 353, 376, 467, 468, 488, 496, 507, 532
Lloyd-Jones, Beti, 436
Lokka, Maija, 191
Lombardo, Bernard, 58, 79
London, George, 248, 257, 277, 314, 405, 520, 532, 532, 535, 539, 552, 559, 608
London, Maurine, 545
Long, Shorty, 188
Loonen, Bernard, 330
Loose, Emmy, 181, 227, 257, 258, 403, 414
Lootens, Lena, 131, 152
Lopardo, Frank, 232, 353, 364, 479
Lord, Matthew, 456
Lorengar, Pilar, 108, 109, 158, 227, 258, 264, 389, 602
Lorenz, Max, 557
Lorenz, Siegfried, 242, 291
Losch, Liselotte, 257
Lott, Felicity, 44, 143, 248
Lövaas, Kari, 151, 155, 519
Lovano, Lucien, 340
Lowe, Marion, 105
Lubin, Germaine, 557
Lublin, Eliane, 25
Luccardi, Giancarlo, 13

Luchetti, Veriano, 59, 488, 491
Ludgin, Chester, 23
Ludwig, Christa, 4, 6, 10, 22, 162, 226, 227, 232, 257, 258, 281, 305, 398, 409, 411, 417, 418, 467, 479, 522, 522, 526, 528, 532, 535, 539, 539, 545, 548, 548, 551, 551, 598, 602
Ludwig, Walther, 608
Luft, Lorna, 96
Luker, Rebecca, 17, 97, 189, 575
Lukin, Márta, 140
Lund, Art, 188
Luperi, Mario, 58
Luxon, Benjamin, 2, 42, 46, 86, 143, 151, 155, 174, 425, 446
Lyons, Colette, 171
Lyons, Jeff, 97
Lytting, Katia, 371

MacDougall, Jamie, 332
MacNeil, Cornell, 184, 196, 301, 461, 468, 486, 496
MacRae, Gordon, 345, 346
Macdonald, Kenneth, 78
Mackie, Neil, 144
Macurdy, John, 232
Maddalena, James, 1
Madeira, Jean, 411
Madin, Victor, 421
Maero, Philip, 305
Magnant, Philippe, 18
Maionica, Silvio, 468, 482
Maiste, Teo, 459
Majkut, Erich, 248
Maksimenko, Eugene, 170
Malagnini, Mario, 183
Malaniuk, Ira, 405, 405, 528
Malas, Spiro, 74, 78, 134, 370
Malewicz-Madej, Anna, 447
Malfitano, Catherine, 116
Malipiero, Giovanni, 608
Maliponte, Adriana, 25
Mallory, Victoria, 394
Malmberg, Urban, 117, 118, 408
Malone, Carol, 356
Malta, Alexander, 16, 232, 569
Mandikian, Arda, 46, 327
Mann, Paul, 103
Mann, Terence, 390
Manning, Jean, 426
Mannov, Johannes, 455
Manuguerra, Matteo, 13, 196, 207, 471, 490, 491, 502, 503
Marc, Alessandra, 177
Marconi, Francesco, 603
Marcucci, Maria, 196
Margiono, Charlotte, 227
Margita, Štefan, 192
Marherr-Wagner, Elfriede, 257
Marimpietri, Lydia, 50
Marin-Degor, Sophie, 112
Mariotti, Alfredo, 233
Marks, Alfred, 17, 94
Markwort, Peter, 566
Marshall, Larry, 98
Marshall, Lois, 239
Marshall, Margaret, 109, 151, 227, 378
Marti, Bernabé, 12, 324

Martikke, Siegrid, 403
Martin, Andrea, 71, 227
Martin, Janis, 519, 538
Martin, Mary, 17, 347, 348
Martin, Millicent, 394
Martin, Mireille, 162
Martinelli, Germaine, 557
Martinelli, Giovanni, 322, 586, 597
Martino, Adriane, 196
Martinovich, Boris, 35, 104, 214, 265, 607
Martinpelto, Hillevi, 242
Martinucci, Nicola, 184, 476
Marton, Eva, 4, 33, 50, 101, 102, 175, 301, 314, 320, 324, 325, 326, 343, 411, 421, 522, 542, 551
Martynov, A., 293
Marusin, Yuri, 294
Mas, Margaret, 318
Maslennikov, Alexei, 267, 267, 293
Mason, Anne, 76, 248
Massa, Fulvio, 368, 369, 371
Massard, Robert, 25, 113, 601
Massell, Deborah, 107
Massi, Bernice, 344
Massis, René, 58, 108
Masson, Luis, 280, 517
Masterson, Valerie, 65, 134, 183, 360, 433, 437, 438, 438, 441, 446, 506, 571, 571
Mastromei, Gian-Piero, 471, 500
Mathis, Edith, 19, 152, 154, 223, 224, 225, 232, 242, 245, 247, 255, 256, 257, 270, 561
Matorin, Vladimir, 264, 269
Matteuzzi, William, 351, 353, 361, 361, 374
Matthews, Brian, 411
Mattila, Karita, 226, 232, 385, 561
Maurane, Camille, 66, 340, 608
Maurel, Victor, 603
Maurette, Jean-Luc, 202
Maxwell, Donald, 41, 42, 65, 211, 350, 571, 571
Mayer, Frederic, 567
Maynor, Dorothy, 608
Mayor, Andrew, 71
Mayr, Richard, 421
Mazura, Franz, 14, 384, 522, 532, 539
Mazurok, Yuri, 264, 450, 450, 452, 507
Mazzaria, Lucia, 183
Mazzieri, Maurizio, 151, 155, 500
Mazzoli, Ferruccio, 297, 465, 507
McAlpine, William, 95, 182, 243
McArdle, Andrea, 288
McCarthy, Mary, 391, 394
McCormack, John, 593, 598, 610
McCoy, Seth, 335
McCracken, James, 25, 216, 325, 383, 620, 621
McCue, William, 248
McCulloch, Susan, 625
McDaniel, Barry, 184, 241, 408, 568
McDonall, Lois, 81
McDonnell, Tom, 580
McFadden, Claron, 122, 139, 150
McFarland, Robert, 104

McGillan, Howard, 391
McGovern, Maureen, 97, 288
McIntyre, Donald, 19, 66, 425, 510, 532, 532, 535, 539, 542, 551
McKechnie, Donna, 394, 394
McKeever, Jacquelyn, 585
McKenna, Virginia, 288
McKenzie, Julia, 392, 394
McKnight, Anne, 297
McLaughlin, Marie, 127, 227, 232, 258, 327, 435
McMartin, John, 391, 394
McNair, Sylvia, 18, 65, 144, 225, 242, 254
Medford, Kay, 447
Meehan, Danny, 447
Meier, Waltraud, 376, 532, 532, 547, 548, 551
Melba, Nellie, 584, 586, 603, 610
Melbye, Mikael, 258
Melchert, Helmut, 15
Melchior, Lauritz, 551, 556, 557, 558, 558, 559, 598, 610
Melis, György, 304
Mellon, Agnès, 51, 52, 55, 56, 57, 179, 190, 336, 338, 350, 516
Melville, Chris, 393
Menotti, Tatiana, 297
Mentzer, Susanne, 72, 196, 232, 243, 372
Mercer, Gregory, 456
Mercuriali, Angelo, 13, 320
Merman, Ethel, 395
Merri, Judi, 443
Merrill, Dina, 349
Merrill, Robert, 25, 78, 196, 296, 297, 309, 318, 353, 461, 468, 468, 481, 496, 496, 503, 507, 608
Merriman, Nan, 226, 479, 479, 499
Merritt, Chris, 76, 104, 351, 361, 362, 374, 510
Mertens, Klaus, 141
Mesguich, Daniel, 162
Mesplé, Mady, 3, 68, 207, 277, 277, 280
Messthaler, Ulrich, 131
Metcalfe, Jane, 430, 441
Metternich, Anton, 407
Metternich, Josef, 162
Meven, Peter, 6
Mey, Anita, 565
Meyer, Kerstin, 425
Meyer-Welfing, Hugo, 608
Michalková, Alzbeta, 196
Micheau, Janine, 25, 30, 30, 66
Michel, Solange, 608
Micheletti, Gaston, 614
Michenkin, Arkadi, 344
Middlemass, Frank, 189
Midgley, Walter, 608
Migenes, Julia, 25
Migliette, Adrienne, 340
Mikuláš, Peter, 227
Milanov, Zinka, 196, 314, 461, 499, 507, 609
Milas, Spiro, 188
Milashkina, Tamara, 450, 452
Milcheva, Alexandrina, 35, 60, 267
Mildmay, Audrey, 232
Miles, Alistair, 79, 86, 143, 425

Milhaud, Madeleine, 162
Miljakovic, Olivera, 267
Miller, Kevin, 426
Miller, Lajos, 34, 113, 294, 305, 466, 477, 502
Miller, Tracey, 575
Millet, Danielle, 68
Milligan, James, 243, 438, 445, 445
Millo, Aprile, 461, 472, 486
Mills, Bronwen, 71, 76, 93
Mills, Erie, 22
Milnes, Sherrill, 25, 60, 78, 100, 184, 206, 227, 232, 285, 297, 297, 301, 313, 314, 325, 335, 362, 421, 455, 462, 466, 472, 481, 486, 487, 493, 496, 503, 503, 507, 510, 514, 577, 580, 587, 588, 602
Milva, 565
Mineo, Sal, 287
Mineva, Stefka, 264
Minich, Peter, 181
Minjelkiev, Bulat, 267
Minter, Drew, 123, 139, 146, 381
Minton, Yvonne, 10, 14, 20, 86, 225, 227, 247, 258, 418, 457, 532, 535, 539, 548, 551
Miricioiu, Nelly, 314
Mishchevski, Anatole, 170, 269
Mishutin, Anatoli, 264
Mitchell, Cameron, 345
Mitchell, Leona, 97, 325
Mitchell, Warren, 94, 190
Mitchinson, John, 2, 69, 86, 193, 326
Mixová, Ivana, 193
Modesti, Giuseppe, 59, 461
Mödl, Martha, 6, 522, 532, 540, 551
Moffo, Anna, 25, 79, 109, 247, 297, 297, 305, 311, 409, 479, 486, 496
Mola, Cinzia, 183
Moll, Kurt, 6, 207, 233, 238, 247, 254, 258, 258, 258, 291, 410, 411, 418, 481, 519, 519, 528, 532, 540, 542, 547, 548, 551, 552, 561
Mollet, Pierre, 66, 340
Molnár, András, 89
Monachesi, Walter, 500
Mongelli, Andrea, 301
Monk, Debra, 390
Monoyios, Ann, 217
Montague, Diana, 10, 79, 108, 165, 213, 350, 358, 571
Montarsolo, Paolo, 232, 353, 357, 357
Monteil, Denise, 25
Montevecchi, Liliane, 288, 391
Montgomery, Brian, 301
Monti, Nicola, 13, 184
Moore, John J., 393
Mora, Barry, 70
Morath, Hélène, 192
Moreno, Rita, 345
Morgan, Beverly, 23
Morison, Elsie, 332, 429, 431, 431, 433, 433, 436, 438, 441, 443, 445, 445
Morison, Patricia, 288
Morozov, Alexandr, 294
Morresi, Giuseppe, 13, 511

Morris, Garrett, 585
Morris, James, 20, 82, 94, 206, 227, 274, 455, 461, 535, 535, 542, 542, 551, 551
Morris, Richard, 208
Morrison, Ann, 96
Morrison, Jackie, 189
Morrison, Peter, 595
Moscona, Nicola, 6, 34, 297, 468, 499, 499, 507
Moser, Edda, 181, 232, 243, 258
Moser, Thomas, 58, 241, 255, 256, 382, 425, 519
Moses, Geoffrey, 193
Moyle, Julian, 29, 171
Muff, Alfred, 414
Mühle, Anne-Marie, 222
Müller, Maria, 557
Müller, Rufus, 33
Müller-Molinari, Helga, 52, 140
Mund, Georg, 566
Munsel, Patrice, 288
Murcell, Raymond, 369
Murgatroyd, Andrew, 327
Murray, Ann, 65, 79, 94, 95, 134, 227, 242, 248, 258, 274, 327
Murray, William, 157
Muzio, Claudia, 586, 593, 599
Myers, Michael, 19
Myers, Pamela, 394, 394
Myrlak, Kazimierz, 106

Nadler, Sheila, 1
Nafé, Alicia, 90, 142, 227, 248
Nagy, János, 34
Nagy, János B., 466, 502
Nalepka, Brian, 96
Nam, L., 10
Napier, Marita, 568
Napoli, Catherine, 147, 217
Nash, Heddle, 227
Natali, Valiano, 79
Natzke, Oscar, 608
Neblett, Carol, 174, 297, 301
Neidlinger, Gustav, 522, 522, 532, 535, 535, 539, 539, 540, 542, 542
Nelepp, Georgi, 608
Nelli, Herva, 462, 468, 479, 493
Nelson, Elisabeth Comeaux, 43
Nelson, Gene, 346, 391
Nelson, Judith, 52, 123, 128, 138, 327, 330, 334, 397
Nelson, Martin, 393
Nelson, Portia, 346, 348, 348
Nemeth, Maria, 586
Neri, Giulio, 472
Neshyba, Ladislav, 496
Nessi, Giuseppe, 184, 320
Nesterenko, Evgeny, 4, 74, 113, 450, 466, 491, 507
Netchipailo, Victor, 267
Neugebauer, Alfred, 407
Neukirch, Harald, 238, 258
Neuss, Wolfgang, 565
Neway, Patricia, 348
Newman, Phyllis, 391
Newman, Yvonne, 432, 436
Nicholas, Paul, 187
Nichols, Mary, 100
Nicolai, Claudio, 257, 281

Nicolai, Elena, 472, 483
Nicolesco, Mariana, 248, 311
Nicoll, Harry, 180
Nielsen, Flora, 608
Nielsen, Inge, 156, 253, 573
Nienstedt, Gerd, 539, 551
Niessner, Anton, 181
Nigl, Georg, 224
Nikodem, Zdzislaw, 447
Nilon, Paul, 72
Nilsson, Birgit, 232, 238, 301, 320, 325, 411, 413, 413, 413, 421, 465, 468, 488, 522, 522, 539, 539, 541, 542, 542, 548, 548, 551, 551, 552, 556, 557, 559, 563, 599, 609, 612, 613
Nilsson, Raymond, 44
Nilsson, Sven, 551
Nimsgern, Siegmund, 6, 92, 105, 162, 191, 248, 313, 318, 367, 425, 522, 526, 526, 532, 535, 539, 542, 569
Nirouët, Jean, 52, 125
Nissen, Hans Hermann, 557
Nixon, Leigh, 333
Nixon, Marni, 24, 345
Nizienko, Nikolai, 344
Noble, John, 36, 460, 471
Nocker, Hans Günter, 522
Noguera, Louis, 30
Noni, Alda, 357, 609
Noorman, Jantina, 327
Nordica, Lillian, 603
Norena, Eidé, 586, 586
Norman, Jessye, 6, 20, 25, 90, 105, 150, 150, 155, 196, 241, 247, 272, 274, 274, 327, 382, 383, 407, 425, 471, 484, 526, 540, 551, 551, 558, 559, 560, 589, 613
Northrop, Pat, 349
Norup, Bent, 156, 411
Nossek, Carola, 6
Novák, Richard, 85, 192, 388
Novikova, Claudia, 608
Nowicka, Barbara, 106
Nucci, Leo, 60, 73, 74, 74, 101, 242, 311, 314, 323, 353, 353, 373, 461, 461, 467, 472, 478, 488, 493, 496, 500, 513, 514, 577, 600
Nurmela, Kari, 184

O'Hara, Paige, 97, 171
O'Neill, Dennis, 13, 301
Oakman, John, 625
Obata, Machiko, 563
Obraztsova, Elena, 5, 60, 196, 207, 376, 461, 468, 486, 491, 496, 507, 601
Obukhova, Nadezhda, 608
Ochman, Wieslaw, 85, 167, 242, 294, 421, 452
Oelke, Alice, 15
Ogéas, Françoise, 340
Ognivtsiev, Alexander, 267, 293
Ohotnikov, Nikolai, 267, 294
Oke, Alan, 429
Olczewska, Maria, 557, 610
Oliver, Alexander, 143
Olivero, Magda, 102, 301, 572
Ollendorff, Fritz, 353

Ollmann, Kurt, 22, 24
Olmeda, Martine, 202
Olsen, Derrik, 192
Olsen, Stanford, 238
Olson, Marcus, 390
Olsson, Catharina, 93
Olszewska, Maria, 421
Ommerlé, Jeanne, 456
Oncina, Juan, 73, 356, 358, 478
Onegin, Sigrid, 586
Opie, Alan, 83
Opthof, Cornelius, 9
Orciani, Patrizia, 371
Orgonasova, Luba, 238, 297
Orieschnig, Dominik, 224
Orliac, Jean-Claude, 3, 337
Ormiston, Linda, 42, 431, 439
Osterwald, Bibi, 348
Otava, Adenék, 193
Otelli, Claudio, 232
Ott, Karin, 257
Otto, Lisa, 226, 257, 257, 561
Ouzounov, D., 601
Owen, Stephen, 456
Owen, Thelma, 40
Owens, Anne-Marie, 625

Pacetti, Iva, 184
Paci, Leone, 184
Padmore, Mark, 71
Page, Carolann, 456
Page, Elaine, 187
Page, Stephen, 350
Page, Steven, 625
Page, Veronica, 393
Pagliuca, Silvano, 183
Painter, Christopher, 211
Palacio, Ernesto, 141, 361, 364, 366, 366, 371, 372
Palade, Doina, 25
Palmer, Christene, 437, 438, 441
Palmer, David, 438, 441
Palmer, Felicity, 86, 160, 242, 248, 256, 327, 386, 435, 438, 457
Palombini, Vittoria, 305
Pampuch, Helmut, 535, 539
Pancella, Phyllis, 248
Pánczél, Eva, 379
Panerai, Rolando, 13, 74, 78, 184, 184, 196, 226, 227, 296, 297, 303, 305, 318, 326, 364, 478, 478, 479, 479, 492, 507
Pape, René, 176
Papouschek, Helga, 403
Parr, Gladys, 557
Parry, William, 390, 390, 390
Partridge, Ian, 21, 126, 131, 141, 149, 330, 332
Pasco, Richard, 42
Pasero, Tancredi, 609
Paskalis, Kostas, 25
Paskuda, Georg, 405
Pastine, Gianfranco, 368
Patinkin, Mandy, 391, 394
Patti, Adelina, 586, 603
Patzak, Julius, 401, 540, 608
Paul, Thomas, 19
Paulee, Mona, 188
Paunov, Milen, 267
Paunova, Mariana, 84, 294

Paut, Françoise, 55
Pavarotti, Luciano, 9, 10, 12, 13, 33, 74, 74, 77, 78, 78, 82, 84, 101, 184, 184, 195, 196, 242, 285, 296, 305, 314, 320, 325, 325, 326, 362, 418, 461, 467, 486, 490, 493, 496, 496, 503, 503, 507, 511, 512, 513, 514, 514, 580, 583, 596, 600, 601, 601, 602, 602, 604, 606, 617, 618, 620, 620, 621
Pawk, Michele, 96
Payne, Patricia, 318, 468
Pears, Peter, 36, 37, 37, 38, 38, 40, 41, 43, 44, 45, 46, 46, 86, 122, 320, 330, 386, 425, 560, 608
Pease, James, 44
Pedaci, Francesca, 58
Peerce, Jan, 6, 297, 468, 499, 499, 608
Peeters, Harry, 243
Pell, William, 545
Pendachanska, Alexandrina, 104
Penkova, Reni, 35
Penrose, Timothy, 144, 330
Peper, Uwe, 238
Perillo, Linda, 332
Pernet, André, 55
Perry, Douglas, 104
Perry, Janet, 257, 418, 479
Pert, Jill, 429, 433
Pertile, Aureliano, 557
Petel, Bernard, 161
Peters, Bernadette, 392, 394
Peters, Roberta, 257, 353, 496
Peterson, Kurt, 391
Petkov, Angel, 265, 267
Petkov, Dimiter, 264, 294, 335, 387, 453
Petri, Mario, 364
Petzoid, Martin, 176
Pezzino, Leonard, 277
Phillips, Norman, 192
Phillips, Sian, 349, 393
Piau, Sandrine, 48, 350
Piavko, Vladislav, 264, 267
Picchi, Mirto, 59
Pieczonka, Adrianne, 258
Pierard, Catherine, 258
Pierotti, Raquel, 358
Pilarczyk, Helga, 16
Pinza, Ezio, 347, 348, 606
Pirazzini, Miriam, 59, 305
Pisani, Bernard, 273
Pistone, Charles, 188
Pizzarelli, John, 96
Plançon, Pol, 603
Platt, Ian, 72, 213
Platt, Norman, 330
Playten, Alice, 395
Plesner, Gurli, 178, 271
Plishka, Paul, 113, 202, 248, 265, 297, 297, 322, 481, 486, 587
Plowright, Rosalind, 83, 209, 274, 481, 496, 507
Plümacher, Hetty, 258, 280
Plummer, Christopher, 346
Pluzhnikov, Konstantin, 267
Poell, Alfred, 6, 247, 401, 418
Poggi, Gianni, 503
Pohl, Carla, 568

Póka, Eszter, 312
Polaski, Deborah, 559
Poleri, David, 19
Polgár, László, 83, 113, 128, 200, 224, 233, 385
Poli, Afro, 297
Políková, Jana, 119
Pollet, Françoise, 161, 214
Polozov, Vyacheslav, 265
Polster, Hermann Christian, 210
Pons, Juan, 78, 83, 90, 184, 184, 196, 199, 301, 305, 314, 465, 481, 503, 590
Ponselle, Rosa, 586, 586, 593, 606
Pope, Cathryn, 278, 426
Popken, Ralf, 123, 139
Popov, Mincho, 265
Popov, Stoyan, 267
Popov, Vladimir, 267
Popova, Maria Petrova, 267
Popp, Lucia, 6, 74, 92, 109, 162, 165, 167, 209, 225, 225, 227, 233, 242, 247, 248, 255, 257, 257, 264, 281, 318, 388, 398, 398, 410, 416, 418, 540, 547, 569
Porter, David, 443
Poschner-Klebel, Brigitte, 267
Posselt, Marita, 177
Potter, Peter, 438
Potter, Philip, 436, 437, 438, 444
Poulenard, Isabelle, 52, 52, 57, 106, 125, 516, 517
Power, Patrick, 327
Prager, Stanley, 348
Prandelli, Giacinto, 608
Prandelli, Giancinto, 318
Praticò, Bruno, 74, 183, 356, 371
Pratt, Peter, 433
Predit, Mascia, 608
Prégardien, Christoph, 142, 150, 152, 221, 386
Preger, Kurt, 401
Prescott, Jonathan, 152
Presnel, Harve, 570
Preston, Jean, 162
Preston, Robert, 569
Previati, Fabio, 297, 364, 368
Previdi, Bruno, 325, 488, 491, 578, 596, 621
Prey, Hermann, 92, 164, 174, 181, 227, 241, 247, 258, 284, 353, 398, 404, 407, 408, 408, 410, 561, 563, 569, 623
Pfibyl, Vilém, 91, 167
Price, Janet, 83
Price, Leontyne, 25, 99, 227, 238, 305, 313, 314, 324, 408, 424, 461, 462, 468, 477, 481, 481, 507, 507, 512, 587, 587, 587, 607, 613
Price, Margaret, 227, 233, 248, 258, 467, 514, 548, 601, 602
Priday, Elizabeth, 332
Prikopa, Herbert, 181
Prince, Daisy, 391
Prince, Faith, 188
Pring, Katherine, 525, 538
Pringle, John, 209
Procházková, Jaroslava, 193
Prokina, Jelena, 267, 294

Protschka, Josef, 6, 385, 385, 395, 402
Protti, Aldo, 493, 503, 619
Provvisionato, Francesca, 368, 369
Puglisi, Lino, 301
Pusar-Joric, Ana, 418
Pustelak, Kazimierz, 447
Putnam, Ashley, 297
Pütz, Ruth-Margret, 257, 270
Puurabar, Väino, 458

Quartararo, Florence, 608
Quilico, Gino, 29, 30, 54, 58, 89, 205, 297, 309, 358
Quilico, Louis, 204
Quivar, Florence, 20, 98, 467, 486

Raamat, Heili, 458
Raffalli, Tibere, 162, 273
Raffanti, Dano, 9, 359
Raffeiner, Walter, 16
Raffell, Anthony, 21, 438, 444, 445
Ragin, Derek Lee, 131, 133, 143, 146, 147
Ragon, Gilles, 57, 57, 337
Raimondi, Ruggero, 10, 12, 25, 232, 248, 265, 297, 314, 320, 353, 356, 364, 366, 373, 461, 461, 462, 466, 468, 472, 472, 472, 481, 485, 487, 490, 500, 507, 510
Rainbird, James, 211
Raitt, John, 17
Raitzin, Misha, 265
Ralf, Torsten, 557
Ralston, Terri, 394, 395
Ramey, Samuel, 4, 10, 32, 33, 72, 78, 79, 142, 144, 150, 201, 232, 232, 247, 257, 274, 314, 353, 359, 361, 364, 366, 368, 372, 373, 426, 461, 466, 472, 476, 488, 490, 567, 577
Ramirez, Alejandro, 248
Ramiro, Yordi, 305, 496, 503
Randle, Thomas, 456
Randová, Eva, 91, 165, 167, 526, 589
Raphanel, Ghyslaine, 25, 53, 214, 273
Rappé, Jadwiga, 542
Raskin, Judith, 109, 227, 426
Rath, John, 429, 433
Ratti, Eugenia, 13, 238, 468
Rautio, Nina, 309
Ravaglia, Emilia, 357
Rawnsley, John, 95, 232, 500
Rayam, Curtis, 142, 170
Rayner, Michael, 430, 443
Rayner Cook, Brian, 69
Reardon, John, 369, 426, 585
Réaux, Angelina, 32, 297, 567
Rebroff, Ivan, 398
Reed, John, 428, 428, 430, 430, 432, 433, 436, 437, 438, 438, 441, 443, 444, 444
Reedbills, Vern, 569
Reeve, Scott, 22, 104
Rehfuss, Heinz, 66, 192, 340, 340
Reichmann, Wolfgang, 565
Reid, Meston, 430, 441, 443
Reinhart, Gregory, 49, 52, 56, 338

Reining, Maria, 418, 557, 608
Reisen, Mark, 608
Remedios, Alberto, 525, 526, 545, 555
Remedios, Ramon, 171
Remick, Lee, 391, 395
Renaud, Maurice, 603
Rendall, David, 83, 227, 311, 350, 571, 571
Resick, Georgine, 227
Resnik, Regina, 3, 25, 94, 182, 398, 411, 413, 421, 478, 548, 598, 609
Retchitzka, Basia, 192
Rethberg, Elisabeth, 557, 618
Rex, Sheila, 42
Reynolds, Anna, 486, 528
Rhodes, Jane, 277
Rhys-Williams, Stephen, 173
Ricciardi, Franco, 13
Ricciarelli, Katia, 25, 74, 83, 297, 314, 320, 320, 325, 359, 361, 373, 461, 468, 471, 472, 476, 478, 486, 493, 500, 507, 512, 513, 588, 610
Richard, Lawrence, 180, 433
Richardson, Linda, 575
Richardson, Marilyn, 208, 257
Richardson, Stephen, 173
Ridderbusch, Karl, 6, 92, 164, 284, 410, 520, 522, 526, 528, 529, 532, 539, 542, 548
Riegel, Kenneth, 14, 18, 157, 232, 265, 572, 573
Riegler, Friedl, 257
Rigby, Jean, 500
Riley, Stanley, 428
Rime, Noémi, 57, 190
Rinaldi, Alberto, 62, 184, 233
Rinaldi, Margherita, 243
Ringholz, Teresa, 369, 382
Riordan, Joseph, 428
Ripley, Gladys, 608
Rippon, Michael, 135, 158, 160
Ritchard, Cyril, 287
Ritchie, Elizabeth, 431
Ritchie, Margaret, 608
Rivadeneyra, Ines, 90
Rivas, Carlos, 345
Rivenq, Nicolas, 517
Rivera, Chita, 394, 395
Robbin, Catherine, 18, 130, 138, 225
Roberts, Joy, 334
Roberts, Stephen, 86
Robertson, Liz, 393
Robin, Mado, 608
Robinson, Faye, 44
Robson, Ann, 309
Robson, Christopher, 49
Robson, Elizabeth, 29
Robson, Nigel, 126, 136, 146, 242
Rocca, Patrick, 212
Rocco, James, 97
Rodde, Anne-Marie, 337
Rodgers, Joan, 227, 248
Roebuck, Janine, 431
Rogan, John, 392
Rogers, Nigel, 218, 220, 327
Roggero, Margaret, 196
Rolandi, Gianna, 247

Rolfe Johnson, Anthony, 44, 94, 122, 130, 131, 135, 143, 144, 150, 154, 155, 220, 222, 223, 225, 242, 254, 256, 258, 425, 435
Rolph, Marti, 391, 394
Romero, Angelo, 73
Roni, Luigi, 461, 461
Rootering, Jan-Hendrik, 232, 465, 486, 519
Rørholm, Marianne, 133
Rose, George, 516
Ross, Gill, 332
Ross, Lesley Echo, 429
Ross, Philip Arthur, 349
Rossi, Alessandra, 356
Rossi, John Carmen, 479
Rossi-Lemeni, Nicola, 10, 13, 372, 483, 609
Rössl-Majdan, Hilde, 247, 258, 414, 478
Roswaenge, Helge, 257, 557
Rota, Anna Maria, 496
Roth, Sigmund, 566
Rothenberger, Anneliese, 92, 243, 258, 398, 403, 405
Rothmüller, Marko, 608
Rouleau, Joseph, 370, 441, 445
Round, Thomas, 182, 428, 428, 430, 432, 433, 444
Rounseville, Robert, 21, 345
Roux, Michel, 30, 66, 358
Rowles, Polly, 344
Rozario, Patricia, 49, 449
Rubin, Arthur, 391
Ruffo, Titta, 513
Ruick, Barbara, 345
Rule, Charles, 63
Rumowska, Hanna, 447
Rumyantsev, V., 293
Runkel, Reinhild, 176, 413
Ruohonen, Seppo, 174
Rus, Marjan, 248
Russell, Rosalind, 585
Ruzicka, Kurt, 181
Rydl, Kurt, 6, 248, 382, 398, 418, 467, 542
Rysanek, Leonie, 6, 411, 413, 413, 413, 414, 421, 488, 493, 520, 539, 551, 551, 556, 556, 608
Rysanek, Lotte, 413

Saarman, Risto, 178
Sabbatini, Giuseppe, 297
Sacchi, Franca, 285
Saccomani, Lorenzo, 184
Saedén, Erik, 32, 93
Saffer, Lisa, 123, 139
Salminen, Matti, 238, 258, 379, 380, 519, 522, 532, 539, 540, 542, 545, 551, 551
Salomaa, Petteri, 17, 248
Salonga, Lea, 345
Salzmann, Jean-Marc, 350
Sandford, Kenneth, 428, 428, 430, 432, 433, 433, 436, 438, 441, 443, 444, 444
Sandifer, Virginia, 391, 395
Sandish, Dale, 97
Sandison, Gordon, 431, 439
Sandtnerová, Marta, 119

Sandve, Kjell Magnus, 117
Sansom, Mary, 428, 428, 432, 436
Sánta, Jolán, 200
Santell, Marie, 288
Santley, Charles, 603
Sarabia, Guillermo, 30, 572
Sardi, Ivan, 232, 248
Sardinero, Vicente, 79, 195, 309, 484
Sarfaty, Regina, 426
Sarti, Gastone, 52
Sass, Sylvia, 4, 59, 89, 233, 466, 477, 485, 488, 502
Satre, Ana Raquel, 78, 196
Sauerbaum, Heinz, 566
Saunders, Terry, 345
Sautereau, Nadine, 25
Savastano, Antonio, 511
Savidge, Peter, 135
Savignol, Pierre, 30
Savory, Catherine, 193
Scarabelli, Adelina, 297
Scattola, Carlo, 297
Schaer, Hanna, 84, 411
Schäfer, Markus, 152, 210
Scharinger, Anton, 148, 233, 253, 258, 327
Schech, Marianna, 257, 411, 556
Scheele, Märta, 336
Schellenberger-Ernst, Dagmar, 109
Schellow, Erich, 565
Schenk, Manfred, 526
Schenk, Otto, 408
Scheppan, Hilde, 257
Scheyrer, Gerda, 398
Schiml, Marga, 225, 318, 563
Schiotz, Askel, 608
Schipa, Tito, 593, 610
Schipper, Emil, 557
Schirrer, René, 19, 146, 336
Schlemm, Anny, 162, 519
Schlick, Barbara, 133, 141, 142, 454
Schmid, Edith, 258
Schmidinger, Josef, 181
Schmidt, Andreas, 6, 113, 157, 162, 242, 248, 258, 258, 274, 414, 545
Schmidt, Helga, 405
Schmidt, Manfred, 281
Schmidt, Trudeliese, 242, 327, 479
Schmidt, Wolfgang, 567
Schmidt Johansen, Mogens, 178, 271
Schmiege, Marilyn, 150, 248
Schmitt-Walter, Karl, 281, 608
Schnaut, Gabriele, 6, 385, 526
Schnitzer, Petra Maria, 257
Schock, Rudolf, 6, 407, 528, 561, 608
Schoeffler, Paul, 1, 227, 258, 410, 413, 414, 417, 608
Schöne, Lotte, 586, 618
Schöne, Wolfgang, 14, 256, 532
Schopper, Michael, 51
Schorr, Friedrich, 557, 610
Schortemeier, Dirk, 191

Schreier, Peter, 224, 225, 227, 232, 233, 238, 238, 242, 243, 245, 245, 253, 254, 255, 256, 258, 258, 258, 281, 382, 408, 409, 410, 529, 535, 538, 539, 542, 561, 611
Schröter, Gisela, 258
Schubert, Claudia, 142
Schulte, Eike Wilm, 526
Schuman, Patricia, 371
Schumann, Elisabeth, 421, 557, 608, 610
Schumann-Heink, Ernestine, 513, 593, 611
Schunk, Robert, 519
Schürhoff, Else, 162, 257
Schwarz, Gotthold, 142, 150
Schwarz, Hanna, 14, 162, 164, 210, 223, 257, 258, 414, 535, 551
Schwarzkopf, Elisabeth, 162, 180, 181, 181, 226, 226, 232, 232, 247, 248, 257, 277, 281, 320, 327, 398, 402, 403, 404, 407, 407, 409, 417, 478, 528, 560, 601, 608, 611, 612
Schymberg, Hjördis, 579
Sciutti, Graziella, 73, 125, 232, 247, 311, 478, 601
Scott, Norman, 462, 479
Scotti, Antonio, 513, 584, 584
Scotto, Renata, 59, 60, 100, 184, 195, 216, 297, 305, 305, 314, 318, 318, 320, 323, 324, 324, 325, 325, 491, 493, 496, 503, 570, 587, 591, 599, 612
Scovotti, Jeanette, 336, 345, 424
Scuderi, Sara, 609
Secunde, Nadine, 291, 411
Seefried, Irmgard, 6, 232, 248, 248, 257, 407, 608
Seiffert, Peter, 303, 318, 398, 405
Seinemeyer, Meta, 557
Seleznev, G., 10
Sembrich, Marcella, 590, 603
Semellaz, François, 190
Sénéchal, Michel, 30, 55, 277, 279, 280, 296, 322, 340, 341
Senn, Martha, 162, 183, 196, 496
Serbo, Rico, 72
Sereni, Mario, 74, 79, 196, 297, 305, 311, 465, 477, 503, 503
Serge, John, 370
Serra, Luciana, 258, 274
Serraiocco, Danilo, 364
Sgourda, Antigone, 233
Shakesnider, Wilma, 98
Shane, Hal, 96
Shankley, Jeff, 187
Sharp, Frederick, 70
Sharp, Norma, 522, 539, 542, 542
Shaver, Bob, 348
Shaw, Geoffrey, 334
Shea, Al, 569
Sheppard, Honor, 330, 331, 333
Shew, Timothy, 188
Shicoff, Neil, 25, 79, 274, 450, 466, 488, 496, 503
Shilling, Eric, 278
Shimell, William, 58, 232
Shirai, Mitsuko, 395
Shirley, George, 66, 155, 227, 243

Shirley-Quirk, John, 20, 37, 37, 38, 38, 41, 42, 45, 46, 86, 137, 143, 327, 330, 386, 460
Shkolnikova, Elena, 264
Shuard, Amy, 324
Shulman, Michael, 390
Shutta, Ethel, 391, 394
Sieden, Cyndia, 238, 414
Siepi, Cesare, 78, 232, 232, 238, 247, 285, 296, 482
Sigmundsson, Kristin, 232
Sild, Tarmo, 458
Silja, Anja, 16, 382, 520, 539, 547
Sills, Beverly, 134, 352
Silvasti, Jorma, 379
Silveri, Paolo, 608
Sima, Gabriele, 257
Simionato, Giulietta, 60, 101, 196, 196, 285, 318, 357, 364, 461, 468, 482, 507, 596, 609
Simmons, Jean, 393
Simoneau, Léopold, 30, 226, 239, 243, 258
Sinclair, Jeannette, 358
Sinclair, Monica, 78, 95, 125, 247, 326, 358, 429, 431, 433, 433, 436, 438, 441, 444, 445, 445, 560
Singher, Martial, 19, 162, 557
Sinyavskaya, Tamara, 289, 450
Skinner, John York, 140
Skitch, Jeffrey, 428, 430, 438
Skovhus, Boje, 184
Sleep, Wayne, 187
Slowakiewicz, Alicia, 106
Smalls, Alexander B., 98
Smith, Alexis, 288, 391, 394
Smith, Alma Jean, 108
Smith, Andrew, 98
Smith, Carol, 19, 196
Smith, Donald, 29
Smith, Jennifer, 127, 127, 130, 135, 139, 217, 220, 330, 331, 332, 333, 337
Smith, Malcolm, 294
Smith, Martin, 65
Smitková, Jana, 561
Smythe, Russell, 72
Snashall, Mark, 158
Soames, René, 70
Söderström, Elisabeth, 66, 162, 167, 168, 218, 248
Soffel, Doris, 92, 257, 572
Sokolov, Andrei, 264
Sólyom-Nagy, Sándor, 89, 113, 283, 342, 368, 416
Sönnerstedt, Bernhard, 608
Sordello, Enzo, 305
Sørensen, Christian, 271
Sorensen, Marvin, 162
Soskin, Gabrielle, 40
Sotin, Hans, 6, 6, 227, 462, 526, 528, 532, 545, 548, 589
Souez, Ina, 227, 232
Soukupová, Vera, 85, 193, 542
South, Richard, 4
Souzay, Gérard, 336, 608
Soyer, Roger, 21, 56, 68, 82, 207, 233, 601
Spacagna, Maria, 200
Špaček, Jozef, 496

Spagnoli, Pietro, 74, 183, 371
Spanellys, Georgette, 25
Spangenberg, Bill, 569
Spani, Hina, 557
Speiser, Elisabeth, 109
Spence, Patricia, 139
Spencer, Kenneth, 171
Spiess, Ludovic, 267
Spina, Mario, 184
Spisar, Oldřich, 119
Springer, Ingeborg, 517
Squires, Shelagh, 278
Sramek, Alfred, 233
St Hill, Krister, 177
Stader, Maria, 232, 248, 257, 608
Stafford, Ashley, 126, 330, 331, 332
Stahlman, Sylvia, 468
Stamm, Harald, 385
Stapleton, Jean, 447
Staunton, Imelda, 392
Steber, Eleanor, 3, 6, 608
Steblianko, Alexei, 267
Steffe, Edwin, 391
Steffek, Hanny, 181, 226
Steiger, Anna, 227
Steiger, Rod, 346
Steinsky, Ulrike, 257
Stejskal, Margot, 418
Stella, Antonietta, 324, 472, 472, 601
Stene, Randi, 117
Stevens, Risë, 247
Stevens, Tony, 394
Stewart, Thomas, 281, 520, 522, 522, 532, 539, 539, 542, 551
Stich-Randall, Teresa, 418, 479
Stier, Gothart, 210
Stignani, Ebe, 10, 609, 619
Stilwell, Richard, 66, 247, 327
Stoddart, John, 29
Stoklassa, Gertraut, 175
Stolze, Gerhard, 15, 258, 280, 282, 411, 421, 535, 539, 539, 541, 542, 542, 547
Storojev, Nikita, 242, 265
Stracciari, Riccardo, 593
Straka, Peter, 14
Stratas, Teresa, 14, 171, 181, 184, 227
Strauss, Isabel, 16
Streeton, Jane, 71
Streich, Rita, 257, 398, 407, 540, 614
Streiff, Danielle, 202
Streisand, Barbra, 447
Streit, Kurt, 107, 227
Stricker, Frieder, 528
Strienz, Wilhelm, 257
Stringer, Marcie, 391
Stritch, Elaine, 349, 391, 395
Strobhauer, Hans, 181
Studer, Cheryl, 78, 113, 232, 257, 274, 362, 385, 411, 413, 421, 466, 503, 510, 519, 526, 540, 545, 551
Studholme, Marion, 44
Stutzmann, Nathalie, 65, 127, 149, 161
Styler, Alan, 428, 428, 432, 441
Suart, Richard, 429, 433, 435
Sukis, Lilian, 224, 241

Suliotis, Elena, 490, 491, 613
Sullivan, Jo, 188
Summers, Jonathan, 39, 44, 183, 376
Sunara, Maja, 580
Supervia, Conchita, 593, 610, 614
Surjan, Giorgio, 362, 481
Susca, Vito, 301
Süss, Reiner, 256
Suthaus, Ludwig, 540, 548, 551
Sutherland, Joan, 9, 10, 10, 12, 12, 13, 25, 60, 68, 72, 74, 78, 78, 78, 81, 82, 94, 113, 122, 125, 125, 129, 142, 182, 204, 206, 214, 231, 274, 320, 325, 325, 326, 370, 371, 455, 490, 496, 503, 503, 507, 513, 514, 514, 539, 542, 579, 589, 600, 601, 601, 602, 602, 602, 612, 613, 613, 614, 617, 618
Sutton, Sheryl, 103
Suzuki, Pat, 348
Svanholm, Set, 535, 539, 556
Švehla, Zdeněk, 193
Svendén, Brigitta, 542
Svetlev, Mikhail, 264
Svorc, Antonín, 389
Sweet, Sharon, 232, 479
Sylvan, Sanford, 1, 456
Sylvester, Michael, 472
Székely, Mihály, 5
Szilágyi, Béla, 123
Szilágyi, Károly, 200
Szmytka, Elzbieta, 226
Szönyi, Olga, 5
Szücs, Márta, 62

Tabbert, William, 347, 348
Tabiadon, Adelisa, 71
Taddei, Giuseppe, 184, 226, 232, 247, 314, 479, 488
Tagliabue, Carlo, 483
Tagliavini, Ferruccio, 78, 396, 608
Taillon, Jocelyne, 89, 90, 340
Takács, Klára, 34, 59, 101, 113, 342, 477
Takács, Tamara, 305, 312
Talvela, Martti, 174, 233, 238, 258, 263, 267, 472, 496, 519, 520, 532, 539, 539, 548, 551, 577
Tamagno, Francesco, 603
Tamassy, Eva, 567
Tamblyn, Russ, 24
Tanner, Susan Jane, 187
Tappy, Eric, 66, 161, 192, 263
Tate, Stephen, 187
Tauber, Richard, 593, 608, 610, 618, 618
Tauberová, Maria, 193
Tauts, Urve, 459
Te Kanawa, Kiri, 24, 25, 94, 113, 162, 172, 190, 227, 227, 232, 232, 247, 248, 255, 257, 264, 309, 311, 314, 324, 324, 325, 326, 398, 405, 418, 493, 500, 513, 542, 548, 587, 589, 599, 600, 602, 613
Tear, Robert, 14, 18, 20, 37, 45, 86, 143, 157, 160, 165, 238, 242, 243, 247, 247, 256, 258, 332, 387, 446, 457

Tebaldi, Renata, 50, 60, 101, 196, 296, 301, 305, 309, 314, 318, 318, 319, 320, 325, 325, 461, 472, 481, 493, 503, 572, 579, 596, 601, 609, 613, 613, 619, 619
Teeter, Lara, 96
Teichmann, Edith, 565
Tellefsen, Rut, 116
Temichev, V., 269
Terentieva, Nina, 344
Terfel, Bryn, 63, 232, 421
Terkal, Karl, 398
Terrani, Lucia Valentini, 150, 154, 357, 359, 364, 373, 472, 478, 491, 518
Tesarowicz, Romuald, 265
Teschler, Fred, 411
Tessmer, Heinrich, 257
Tetrazzini, Luisa, 513, 586, 593, 610, 621
Teyte, Maggie, 586, 608
Thau, Pierre, 376
Thayer, Rosemary, 105
Thebom, Blanche, 548, 608
Theyard, Harry, 352
Thill, Georges, 55, 557, 621
Thomas, David, 100, 121, 123, 128, 131, 138, 138, 141, 144, 218, 221, 327, 330, 331, 333, 334
Thomas, Jess, 526, 529, 532, 539, 542
Thomas, Kelvin, 208
Thomas, Marjorie, 86, 429, 431, 433, 436, 438, 443, 445, 445
Thomas, Mary, 332
Thomas, Nancy, 40
Thompson, Adrian, 93
Thompson, Arthur, 98
Thomson, Paul, 208
Thorsteinsson, Jon, 335
Tibbett, Lawrence, 593, 610, 622
Tichy, Georg, 305, 503
Ticozzi, Ebe, 196
Tierney, Vivien, 180
Tiilikainen, Sauli, 17
Tinkler, Mark, 22, 392
Tinsley, Pauline, 243
Titus, Alan, 25, 50, 151, 248, 479
Toczyska, Stefania, 104, 294, 396, 452, 507
Todorov, Todor, 35
Tokody, Ilona, 34, 199, 312, 313, 318, 342, 416
Tomei, Giulio, 322
Tomlinson, Gregory, 209
Tomlinson, John, 9, 13, 83, 124, 134, 135, 193, 227, 248, 425, 455, 481, 500, 522, 559
Tomowa-Sintow, Anna, 176, 232, 232, 248, 257, 264, 408, 410, 418, 450, 526
Tônuri, Annika, 459
Töpper, Hertha, 248
Törnqvist, Pirkko, 282
Touraine, Geneviève, 340
Tourangeau, Huguette, 78, 82, 142, 204, 206, 214, 274, 496, 514, 589
Tourel, Jennie, 608
Toye, Jennifer, 428, 432, 436

Tozzi, Giorgio, 3, 296, 297, 301, 347, 353, 461, 481, 486, 496, 520
Trama, Ugo, 50
Traubel, Helen, 559, 608
Treigle, Norman, 33, 134
Treleaven, John, 72
Trempont, Michel, 212, 273, 277, 277, 279, 280
Trenk-Trebisch, Willy, 565
Trigeau, Jacques, 279
Trimarchi, Domenico, 74, 151, 154, 155, 155, 353, 357, 364
Troeva-Mircheva, Rossitza, 265, 450
Troyanos, Tatiana, 24, 25, 207, 227, 241, 247, 248, 327, 383, 408, 410, 589
Truhitte, Dan, 346
Tschammer, Hans, 532
Tselovalnik, Evgenia, 267
Tubb, Evelyn, 33, 100
Tucci, Gabriella, 184, 507, 601
Tucker, Mark, 221, 332
Tucker, Richard, 297, 305, 461, 462, 481, 483
Tumagian, Eduard, 184, 196, 294, 496
Turner, Claramae, 345, 468
Turner, Eva, 322, 586, 593, 610, 622
Tuscher, Nata, 192
Tysklind, Stig, 93

Udovick, Lucille, 243
Uggams, Leslie, 585
Uhde, Hermann, 532
Uhl, Fritz, 16, 280, 411, 548
Ulbrich, Andrea, 200
Ulfung, Ragnar, 411
Unger, Gerhard, 6, 164, 239, 241, 257, 520, 528, 529
Upshaw, Dawn, 201, 245, 248, 258
Urbanová, Vlasta, 119
Urbas, Ivan, 297

Valaitis, Vladimir, 452
Valdengo, Giampiero, 608
Valdengo, Giuseppe, 462, 479, 493, 609
Vale, Ludek, 192
Valentino, Frank, 297
Valère, Simone, 161
Valjakka, Taru, 212, 380
Välkki, Anita, 380
Valletti, Cesare, 238, 305, 353, 364
Vallin, Ninon, 55, 586
Vámossy, Éva, 379
Van Allan, Richard, 4, 18, 227, 232, 435, 435, 486, 567, 571, 571
Van Bork, Hanneke, 258
Van Dam, José, 6, 18, 20, 25, 25, 29, 65, 66, 89, 90, 107, 113, 191, 205, 226, 227, 232, 248, 248, 257, 257, 263, 274, 289, 341, 376, 413, 421, 423, 461, 500, 519, 532
Van Egmond, Max, 220, 222, 455
Van Evera, Emily, 33
Van Kesteren, John, 281
Van Mill, Arnold, 461, 532, 548, 556

Van Nes, Jard, 148, 258, 383
Van Vrooman, Richard, 16
Van der Kamp, Harry, 51
Van der Meel, Nico, 232
Van der Sluis, Mieke, 338, 338
Van der Walt, Deon, 227
Vanaud, Marcel, 89, 178
Vanderlinde, Debra, 456
Vandersteene, Zeger, 336
Vaness, Carol, 226, 232, 232
Vanhecke, François, 338
Vantin, Martin, 257
Vanzo, Alain, 30, 68, 90, 278
Varady, Julia, 4, 62, 120, 143, 196, 225, 225, 242, 245, 248, 396, 398, 405, 407, 413
Varcoe, Stephen, 33, 125, 126, 127, 135, 136, 140, 149, 152, 160, 327, 329, 330, 331, 332, 333, 449
Vargas, Milagr, 103
Vargas, Ramón, 369
Varnay, Astrid, 196, 282, 413, 426, 556, 608
Vasiliev, N., 10
Vaughan, Vyn, 40
Vavon, Andrée, 614
Veasey, Josephine, 9, 18, 21, 41, 327, 535, 539, 551
Vedernikov, Alexander, 264
Vejzovic, Dunja, 519, 526, 532
Vele, Ludek, 192
Vento, Marc, 376
Ventris, Christopher, 380
Venuti, Maria, 258
Verdon, Gwen, 287
Vermillion, Iris, 82, 254, 257
Verrett, Shirley, 81, 109, 352, 468, 472, 481, 486, 488, 488, 496, 581
Verschaeve, Michel, 57, 337, 516
Vessières, André, 192, 340
Veverka, Jaroslav, 193
Viala, Jean-Luc, 18, 112, 273, 289, 290, 423
Vickers, Jon, 6, 6, 21, 25, 44, 377, 461, 493, 493, 514, 539, 548, 551, 552, 620, 620
Vignas, Francisco, 603
Vihavainen, Satu, 379
Villa, Eduardo, 178
Villa, Luisa, 78
Villisech, Jacques, 220, 337
Vinay, Ramon, 493
Vincenzi, Edda, 10
Vinco, Ivo, 247, 285, 496
Vinogradov, Georgi, 608
Vinzing, Ute, 411, 413
Vishnevskaya, Galina, 42, 265, 267, 294, 386, 453
Visse, Dominique, 49, 51, 52, 55, 56, 56, 57, 133, 139, 221, 327, 336, 516, 517
Vita, Michael, 349
Vlachopoulos, Zoë, 111
Vodička, Leo Marian, 389
Vogel, Christian, 535
Vogel, Siegfried, 242, 258, 538, 539, 561
Vogel, Volker, 383
Voigt, Deborah, 563
Voinarovski, V., 269

Volkova, Svetlana, 294
Von Halem, Victor, 532
Von Ilosvay, Maria, 162
Von Kannen, Günther, 238, 248
Von Kóczián, Johanna, 565
Von Otter, Anne Sofie, 19, 20, 93, 106, 107, 109, 136, 162, 220, 225, 226, 242, 248, 274, 327, 418, 450
Von Pataky, Koloman, 232
Von Stade, Frederica, 18, 66, 151, 154, 162, 171, 200, 201, 207, 225, 227, 247, 248, 287, 368, 598, 600, 613
Vozza, Corinna, 79, 196, 607, 607
Vrenios, Anastasios, 214
Vyvyan, Jennifer, 40, 43, 46, 330, 386

Waara, Scott, 188
Waechter, Eberhard, 1, 16, 181, 231, 247, 398, 398, 409, 418, 421, 547, 548, 601
Wagner, Chuck, 392
Wagner, Sieglinde, 257, 401, 520
Wahlgren, Per-Arne, 93
Wakefield, John, 217
Wales, Pauline, 432, 437
Walker, Blythe, 335
Walker, Nancy, 394, 585
Walker, Norman, 608
Walker, Penelope, 41
Walker, Sarah, 93, 134, 135, 209, 426
Wallace, Ian, 247, 353, 356, 358, 433, 433, 445, 445
Wallén, Martti, 17, 380
Wallis, Delia, 209
Walters, Nigel, 222
Walther, Ute, 418
Walton, Jim, 391
Wand, Betty, 24
Ward, David, 552
Ward, Joseph, 9, 10, 158
Ward, Wayne, 569
Warfield, William, 99
Waring, Derek, 288
Warren, Leonard, 314, 461, 488, 499, 507, 608
Watkinson, Carolyn, 121, 126, 141, 145, 218, 382
Watson, Claire, 44, 232, 522, 529, 539
Watson, Curtis, 211
Watson, Jean, 44
Watson, Lilian, 25, 41, 165, 209, 217, 226, 238, 278
Watts, Helen, 18, 41, 86, 137, 143
Waugh, Nancy, 340
Weathers, Felicia, 613
Webb, Barbara, 38
Weber, Ludwig, 257, 418, 532, 557, 608
Weber, Peter, 263
Weede, Robert, 188
Weidinger, Christine, 141, 246
Weikenmeier, Albert, 16
Weikl, Bernd, 74, 74, 105, 233, 284, 398, 411, 421, 450, 528, 547, 548, 561
Welch, Charles, 391

Welch, Elisabeth, 288, 393
Welch, Jonathan, 297
Welitsch, Ljuba, 608
Welker, Hartmut, 6, 176
Weller, Dieter, 92, 573
Wells, Mary, 330
Welsby, Norman, 525
Welting, Ruth, 162, 200, 254
Wend, Flore, 340
Wenkel, Ortrun, 157, 257, 410, 522, 539, 540, 542, 542
Wennberg, Siv, 538
Wessel, Kai, 142
West, Kevin, 71, 71
Westcott, Frederick, 272
Westenberg, Robert, 392
Western, Hilary, 393
Westi, Kurt, 156, 271
White, Jeremy, 33
White, Wendy, 23
White, Willard, 97, 97, 122, 170, 209, 405
Whitehouse, Richard, 460
Whitmore, James, 346
Whitworth, John, 332
Widdop, Walter, 557
Wiemann, Ernst, 561
Wiener, Julia, 35
Wiener, Otto, 418, 526, 529
Wiens, Edith, 209, 253, 386
Wieter, Georg, 281
Wilderman, William, 478
Wildhaber, Helmut, 257
Wilkof, Lee, 390
Williams, Ben, 557
Williams, La Verne, 24
Wilson, Georges, 161
Wilson-Johnson, David, 36, 86, 456
Wimberger, Peter, 413
Winbergh, Gösta, 58, 73, 74, 227, 232, 238, 455
Windgassen, Wolfgang, 6, 413, 522, 522, 532, 535, 539, 539, 540, 541, 542, 542, 547, 548
Winkler, Hermann, 16, 242, 411
Winslade, Glenn, 242
Winslow, Pamela, 392
Wise, Patricia, 14
Wistreich, Richard, 33, 52, 100
Wittrisch, Marcel, 557
Wixell, Ingvar, 74, 81, 184, 232, 247, 256, 297, 305, 314, 318, 324, 468, 484, 507
Wlaschiha, Ekkehard, 6, 526, 535, 542, 561, 561
Wohlers, Rüdiger, 6
Wohlfahrt, Erwin, 247, 535, 535, 542
Wolff, Beverly, 134, 369
Wolff, Fritz, 557
Wolfington, Iggie, 569
Wood, Peggy, 346
Woodman, Thomas, 456
Woodrow, Alan, 222
Woods, Sheryl, 104
Woollett, Elizabeth, 429, 433
Workman, Charles H., 351
Wright, Ben, 392
Wright, Colin, 433, 443

Wright, Joyce, 428, 430
Wulkopf, Cornelia, 223
Wunderlich, Fritz, 15, 257, 270, 389, 410, 623
Wyatt, Walker, 222
Wyner, Susan Davenny, 340

Yachmi, Rohangiz, 227
Yakar, Rachel, 48, 66, 179, 210, 227, 242, 263, 289, 327, 338
Yakovenko, S., 293
Yeend, Frances, 413
Young, Alexander, 105, 135, 137, 148, 426, 429, 433, 436, 445, 445
Yurchenko, L., 10

Zaccaria, Nicola, 10, 13, 78, 297, 301, 320, 320, 353, 371, 461, 479, 496, 507, 518

Zádori, Mária, 381
Zahradníček, Jíří, 166
Zajic, Dolora, 289, 461, 472, 481
Zakharenko, L., 269
Zampieri, Giuseppe, 78, 398
Zampieri, Mara, 301, 488
Zanasi, Furio, 133
Zanasi, Mario, 184
Zancanaro, Giorgio, 101, 362, 466, 481, 496, 503, 507, 510
Zanelli, Renato, 610
Zanetti, Monique, 48, 56, 57, 350
Zeani, Virginia, 325
Zednik, Heinz, 16, 16, 238, 248, 248, 257, 258, 267, 403, 408, 408, 421, 479, 535, 535, 535, 539, 542, 542
Zeller, Richard, 456
Zempléni, Mária, 378

Zennaro, Iorio, 364, 368
Zhadan, Ivan, 608
Žídek, Ivo, 166, 193
Ziegler, Delores, 178, 226, 227, 258, 563
Zien, Chip, 392
Ziesak, Ruth, 6, 258
Zimmermann, Margarita, 29, 361, 366
Zimnenko, Leonid, 382
Zítek, Václav, 91, 166, 389
Zlesák, Antonín, 193, 193
Zoghby, Linda, 151, 153
Zylis-Gara, Teresa, 58, 232, 408